The Complete Book of Roses

Gerd Krüssmann

Translated by Gerd Krüssmann and Nigel Raban

Timber Press
in cooperation with
The American Horticultural Society

©Timber Press, Portland, Oregon
1981

Library of Congress Cataloging in Publication Data

Krüssmann, Gerd.
   The complete book of roses.

   "Revised and updated from the German edition:
Rosen, Rosen, Rosen, 1974."
   Bibliography: p.
   Includes indexes.
   1. Roses. 2. Rose culture. I. Title.
SB411.K7813 1981   635.9'33372   81-16611
ISBN 0-917304-64-0   AACR2

Translated by:
Gerd Krüssmann and
Nigel Raban

1981
Timber Press
Portland, Oregon

*In the list of roses at the end of this book, certain
existing details of plant protection have been omitted;
this does not imply that such cultivars are unprotected
by breeders rights.*

Dedicated in sincerest friendship
to the outstanding rose hybridizer of our time,
the late Wilhelm Kordes of Sparrieshoop
whom I was privileged to know as "Uncle Willy"

Publisher's Preface

This English language edition of Dr. Gerd Krüssmann's *Rosen, Rosen, Rosen* was undertaken to give rose growers and lovers in the English-speaking world access to this monumental work.

Dr. Krüssmann translated the last half while Nigel Raban translated the first. In the course of translation the book was thoroughly revised and updated, notably the section on genetics and the dictionary of rose cultivars.

Just as the principal work was being completed a great misfortune befell the world of horticulture with Dr. Krüssmann's passing.

Numerous people offered their assistance in helping on the remaining details of revision. The publisher wishes to acknowledge their help not only in the acknowledgements section, but here as well.

It is the publisher's hope that this edition will not serve only its initial purpose of giving English language readers access to this definitive work, but also serve as a small tribute to its author, one of the giants of horticulture.

Preface to the German Edition

Let no man who writes a book presume to say when he will have finished. When he imagines that he is drawing near his journey's end, Alps rise on Alps and he continually finds something to add and something to correct. (Gibbon)

Just a hundred years ago, the publishing firm of Paul Parey in Berlin brought out a book on roses by Th. Nietner which dealt comprehensively with the whole question of the rose and gave a short description of some 5,000 different rose varieties. Today, this work is very difficult to find and only a few good copies still exist; consequently the publishers expressed a desire to bring out a new and comprehensive book on roses which would bring the story of our knowledge of that flower completely up to date and at the same time would encompass a list of the most important old and modern varieties. This book is now presented to the public after four years of work.

Although the book is broadly based, as was intended by the publishers, nevertheless all the knowledge about the rose which has been accumulated in the last hundred years has had, inevitably, to be somewhat compressed. During my research new facts and records kept turning up, reminding us acutely of Goethe's words that "a work was never truly complete; it could only be described as finished when everything possible had been done in the course of time and circumstances".

This work relies heavily upon other books on roses which have been published in the past. It is a recital of world-wide and critical appraisals. The motto for this preface should be carefully noted: that much, which from generation to generation has been repeated without careful thought, shows itself as untrustworthy if one goes back to the original sources, not only to all the precedents in an historical context, but also to the origins of a rose or to its genetics. As these are very humerous, such sources can only be briefly indicated. References in each chapter give information on the material that has been used. Roughly one hundred different American and English rose annuals have been thoroughly studied, as well as books on genetics and works on antiquity and archaeology. The classifications of the wild roses have been made a matter of careful study. All the known species, and their different forms, which are to be found in today's gardens are covered; of the hundreds of forms of the genus *Rosa* which have been recorded, it seems unnecessary to deal with those which are not in cultivation.

The list of varieties of garden roses contains, for the most part, those cultivars which appear in the five great German rose gardens of Dortmund, Insel Mainau, Uetersen, Weihenstephan and Zweibrücken; the exact locations are indicated by code letter in each case. The important historical varieties are also recorded as are those novelties which have come on the market in the last year or two. The "garden value" of many roses is given and also, most importantly, the results of the American Rose Trials which go under the delightful name of "Proof of the Pudding".

A great many specialists have given willingly of their time in order to clear up certain difficult questions. The reader cannot possibly imagine what vast, international correspondence was conducted in order to write just the few pages devoted to the word "rose" itself as it appears in no less that 105 different languages, or of the lists of important rosarians and rose societies which have had to be collected and organized.

This foreword would undoubtedly be incomplete without my expression of gratitude to the publishing house of Paul Parey and, in particular, to Dr. Friedrick Georgi, who has always been so ready to meet any request of mine and who took such care and trouble to ensure that the book finally appeared in its present form.

Dortmund (German National Rosarium)
Spring, 1974   Gerd Krüssmann

Acknowledgements

Dr. Gerd Krüssmann

It is quite impossible to thank all those who have given me so unstintingly of their help. At the forefront, however, must stand Wilhelm Kordes (since unhappily deceased), and his son, Reimer, who read the whole manuscript and made most useful and important comments on it; indeed, Wilhelm Kordes went so far as to make a personal trip to Crete in order to see for himself the oldest existing pictures of the rose. Both of them, assisted by my dear wife, have overseen all the corrections. To them all, and also to Dr. Reiner Deppe, who has read the entire manuscript and who has made many useful suggestions, I extend my warmest and most heartfelt thanks. Professor Dr. H.D. Wulff of Saarbrücken has checked the section on genetics and cytology and has given much useful advice and many references. To both these gentlemen, my heartiest thanks.

Space permits me to record only briefly the great help given by numerous other distinguished individuals. In particular I must mention Professor Dr. Th. Eckart of Berlin (the literature of antiquarian botany); Mrs. Rona Hurst of England (archaeological and genetics material); Dr. Kilpper of Essen and Professor Dr. F. Kirchheimer of Freiburg i. Br (both for problems connected with paleobotany); Professor Dr. H. Kruse of Tokyo (for reading and extending the section on the comparison of nomenclature in various languages); Dr. Lapin of Moscow (Russian terminology); André Leroy of Niort in France (advice and help with many historical problems); Dr. P.B. Pal of India (translation from Hindi); and last, but not least, Len Turner M.B.E., the Secretary of the Royal National Rose Society of England. To all these people for their help I say a sincere "thank you". I am also extremely grateful for all the advice and additional material and contribution which I have received from rose growers around the world.

Mr. Nigel Raban

Most sincere thanks to Dr. A. Roberts of the North-East London Polytechnic for his careful and detailed revision of the section on genetics and color chemistry and to W.A. Warriner and Dr. Charlene Harwood for all the time and help they gave to amending the chapter on pests and diseases to make it conform with current American practice.

English Language Edition Publisher

Many thanks to the following: Stuart Mechlin, formerly Curator of the Portland International Rose Test Gardens, for continuing technical advice and encouragement in the process of bringing the manuscript to a state suitable for publication; to W.A. Warriner for assistance in a number of technical details in the preparation of this edition; Reuben C. Newcomb for technical help and a leading role in the final update on the Rose Dictionary; Fred Edmunds, Jr. and Allan Harrington for their contributions in assisting in updating the cultivars section; and to George Rose for continuing support and advice.

I further wish to acknowledge the help of the Consul of the Federal Republic of Germany in Seattle for much help. The assistance of Inter Nationies in facilitating the translation is gratefully acknowledged.

Contents

CONTENTS

X

CONTENTS

Roses in the Pre-historic Era

When did the rose first evolve? That is inevitably a question which all rose lovers ask themselves at some time. Certainly it can be assumed that it was long before the evolution of Man and that, therefore, roses existed over 12 - 15 million years ago.

Paleobotanists and geologists have found plant remains in stones, in coal seams and other geologic formations from which they have been successful in obtaining evidence which can be compared with plant life as it exists today. Often this fossilized material is so well preserved that it is possible to correlate it with certainty, or at least with a high degree of probability, with the living material of modern times. This is especially true with conifers and many varieties of ferns. For instance, *Metasequoia*, already known in fossilized form from both Japan and Spitzbergen, was found to be alive and well in China in 1945. Comparison and reliable classification of the fossilized remains of conifers *(Ginkgo, Taxodium, Sequoia, Pinus,* etc.) make us realize that such plants were already well established before most others had emerged or were still in the course of development.

In the case of roses, and here we must look at the complete genus, it is difficult to find concrete evidence from pre-historic times; plant remains from the Tertiary period in Eastern Asia, North America and Europe have been found which the paleontologists have been prepared to ascribe to the genus *Rosa*. These fossils can be seen in Figs. 4-6. However, well known rosarians, among them Robert Keller (in *Syn. Ros. spont. Eur. Med.,* p. 47) regard these discoveries, upon which the proposition of the existence of the genus *Rosa* in the Middle Tertiary period is' founded, as insufficient. Keller adopts the position that such analogies and conclusions of a geographical plant relationship with roses of the present day "can only be adjudged to have a more or less likely probability". Unfortunately, on this assumption we cannot know with any certainty just where or when the genus *Rosa* originated.

While it is a basic requirement that every botanist have at his disposal an exact definition of every part of a plant in order to identify it, thus far, for roses, only a few leaves, a few short pieces of stem prickles (thorns) and one or two other bits have been found. Some of these can be identified as being, in all probability, roses, but unfortunately no example of a bloom has ever been found; it is uncertain if the plant material illustrated in Fig. 6 is indeed a flower bud or the residue of a hip.

Despite this, some of the finds have been attributed to the genus *Rosa* by the paleobotanists (see Table on p. 5).

A short description of the most important fossils in the order in which they were found is best taken from the work of F. Kirchheimer (1950).

The date given after the author's name is the year in which his description was published and not the year in which the fossil was actually found; in many cases, of course, both dates are the same.

Rosa penelopes Unger (1848). Found in Parschlug, Steiermark, Austria; A rose prickle with a piece of stem (Fig. 4).

R. nausicaa Wessell & Weber (1856). Found in Rott near Siegburg, and also in Orsberg near Ling (Rhineland); small leaves and two hooked (uncinate) prickles (Fig. 4).

R. basaltica Ludwig (1857). Found in Homberg near Cassel. Ostensibly a pinnate leaf; it was ascribed in 1907 by Schindehütte to the genus *Hedycaria* of the family *Monimiaceae.*

R. angustifolia Ludwig (1860). Found in Münzenberg near Butzbach, Hesse. First believed to be a pinnate rose leaf it was ascribed to the genus *Rhus (Rhus muenzenbergensis)* in 1868.

R. lignitum Heer (1869). Found in Rixhöft near Putzig; later found in 1882 at Kundratitz near Leitmeritz, Bohemia; in 1904 in Himmelsberg, Fulda and in 1906 at Zschipkau near Senftenberg, Lausitz. Pinnate leaves (Fig. 4).

R. bohemica Engelhardt (1882). Found in Kundratitz, Bohemia. The leaves are virtually identical to those of the contemporary *R. pimpinellifolia* (Fig. 4).

R. hilliae Lesquereux (1883). Found in Florissant, Colorado, 1927 and in 1933 at Post and Harney County, Oregon; in 1936 in Modec County, California; in

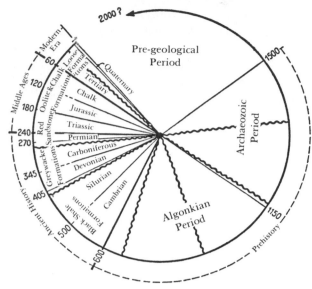

Figure 1. The breakdown of the various historical eras of the earth in millions of years; the waved lines indicate the major periods of earth movements. (from v. Bülow, *Geology for All*)

1938 in Contra Cost, California. The 1883 discovery was of a group of three leaves on one stem, in 1927 just one leaf was found; they bear a strong resemblance to contemporary roses; the remains of a stem in another fossil found nearby was probably unrelated to this. (Fig. 6)

R. chareyrei Boulay (1887). Found in Rochessauve near Privas in the Department of Ardèche, France. Pinnate leaves reminiscent of *R. canina*; some pieces of stem with prickles were also discovered.

R. ruskiniana Cockerell (1908). Found in Florissant, Colorado. This fossil looked like a young rosebud with feathery, glandular sepals, but has not been identified conclusively. (Fig. 6).

R. wilmattae Cockerell (1908). Found in Florissant, Colorado. The remains of a leaf with five pinnae; not very different from other finds in Florissant (*R. scudderi*).

R. glangeaudii Marty (1912). Found in Varennes, Puy-des-Domes, France. Leaflets.

R. inquirenda Knowlton (1916). Found in Florissant, Colorado. A five-pointed, star-shaped remnant similar to the flattened calyx of a rose hip. Uncertainty as to whether this does in fact belong to the genus *Rosa*. (Fig. 6).

R. scudderi Knowlton (1916). Found in Florissant, Colorado. A leaf fossil with seven pinnae, the end of the leaf much elongated, with the lower leaves much shorter than the upper (Fig. 6).

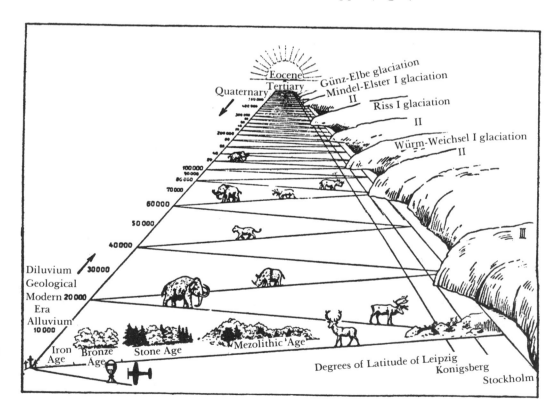

Figure 2. Diagram of historical and pre-historical eras showing development from the Ice Age on. Each section represents 10,000 years (see v. Bülow, *Geology for All*)

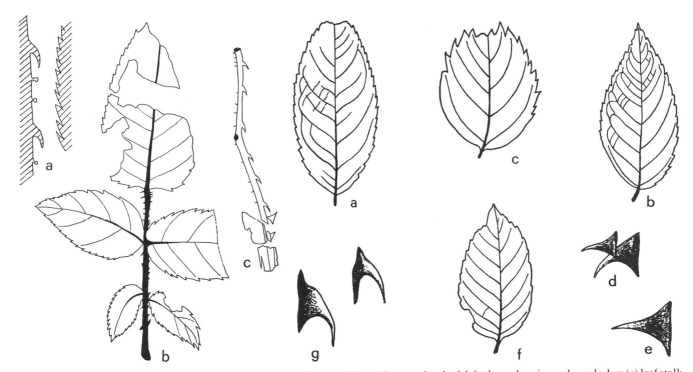

Figure 3. (left) *Rosa* spec. Weyland (1934). (a) Peduncular glands and prickles; (b) complete leaf; left above showing enlarged edge; (c) leaf stalk with side leaves (from D.K. Ferguson, found in Kreuzau near Düren)

Figure 4. (right) Rose fossils, European Tertiary period. (a) *Rose bohemica* (1885, leaf); (b) *R. lignitum* Heer (leaf according to Engelhardt, 1885); (c-d) *R. nausicaes* Wessel & Weber (1856, leaf and two prickles); (e) *R. penelopes* Unger (1869, prickles); (f) *Rosa* spec. (leaf according to Stefanoff and Jordanoff 1934); (g) *Rosa* spec. (prickles according to Szafer 1938)

R. aff. *gallica* L. (1929). Found in Kurilo near Sofia, Bulgaria. Leaf remains similar to those of *R. gallica*, nevertheless it is quite possible that this might be from some variety of *Prunus*.

R. aff. *dumetorum* Thuill (1929). Found in Kurilo near Sofia, Bulgaria. Not positively identified, but the leaves are very similar to *R. dumetorum*.

R. *hoerneri* Chaeney (1935). Found in Tieh-chiang-kon, Kanshu, China. The leaves are very similar to those of *R. acicularis*.

R. *cetera* Hollick (1936). Found in the Matanuska Cook Inlet, Alaska. Lateral leaf 3.8 cm./1.5 in. long by 1.6 cm./0.6 in. wide, probably from the same area as *R. confirmata* and very similar to *R. bohemica* and *R. lignitum*. (Fig. 6).

R. *confirmata* Hollic (1936). Found in the Matanuska Cook Inlet, Alaska. Terminal leaf 3.2 cm./1.25 in. long by 1.3 cm./0.5 in. wide; the side leaves might be the same as *R. cetera* (Fig. 6).

R. *multiflora* Thunberg (1937). Found in Akashi near Kobe, Japan. These fossils were interpreted as the remains of a stem of *R. polyantha* (= *R. multiflora* Thunb.); this is thought to be reliable. (Fig. 5).

R. *akashiensis* Miki (1937). Found in Akashi near Kobe, Japan and in Katada near Kyoto. This fossil appears very similar to the modern *R. roxburghii*; the impression of the leaves, the stems with prickles and the hips all seem to belong to the same species. (Fig. 5).

R. *chanwangensis* Chaney (1938). Found in Chanwang, Shantung, China. Leaf fossils which resemble our *Rosa rugosa*.

Rosa spec. Weyland (1934; 1971). Found in Kreuzau near Düren. Leaves and various remains of side foliage and prickles. Probably belongs to the genus *Rosa*. Unnamed as yet. (Fig. 3).

Rosa spec. Knobloch (1961). Found in Priskenberg, N. Bohemia. Leaves and the remains of a small leaf at the end of the left stem. An exact description and the name of this discovery are still awaited.

Rosa bohemica Engelhardt — 1968 C. Bucek published the results of his research on the impressions of about 40 leaves and hips, which had been found in Bechlej-

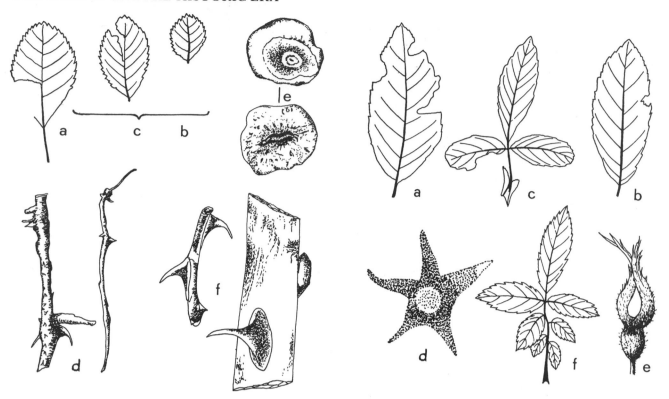

Figure 5. (left). Rose fossils from the Tertiary Period in Asia. (a-e) *R. akashiensis* Miki 1937. (a) Terminal leaf; (b-c) side leaves; (d) piece of stem with prickles; (f) *R. polyantha* S & Z., fossil (prickly stem, according to Miki 1937).

Figure 6. (right). Rose fossils from the Tertiary Period in N. America. (a) *R. cetera* Hollick 1936 (side leaves); (b) *R. confirmata* Hollick 1936 (terminal leaf); (c) *R. hilliae* Lesquereux 1883 (leaf); (d) *R. inquirienda* Knowlton 1967 (calyx); (e) *R. ruskiniana* Cockerell 1908 (bud); (f) *R. scudderi* Knowlton 1916 (leaf).

ovice together with individual prickles on their pieces. He came to the conclusion that *R. lignitum* and *R. bohemica* Engelhardt are one and the same species.

R. usyuensis Tanai (1955). Found in Yoshioka and Abusa, Japan. Impressions of leaves which, due to the serration and veining, have been ascribed to *Rosa;* very similar to *R. chanwangensis* from China.

C.E. Resser (1942) has given an explanation for this dearth of rose fossils. He believes that the early roses had the same soil and location requirements as do those today, for the fossil discoveries of the Tertiary period were often associated with other twig and branch specimens such as one would expect to encounter. Roses do not like wet or marshy ground or areas where there is a danger of flooding, i.e., conditions under which fossilization occurs easily. Under the drier conditions which they prefer, the possibility of fossilization becomes very

remote. This could probably only have happened through strong volcanic eruption releasing a cloud of dust which would cover everything; ensuing rains would form a protective mud in which plants and animals would be encapsulated from the air and therefore protected from bacterial destruction and thus would eventually be found intact by paleontologists. Although thus far comparatively few roses have been found, this certainly does not mean that we shall not have better luck in the future and it may well be that such fossils are already hiding unrecognized in some museum.

Finally, a short note on Florissant, so highly esteemed by paleontologists. This is a small town 30 miles west of Colorado Springs at about 2,438 m./8,000 ft. above sea level. The fossils found there had been preserved in a form of red sediment composed of mud and volcanic ash. The finds made in the area between 1883 and 1916, were, unfortunately, dispersed to a number of museums and private collections.

Tabulated List of known Rose discoveries from the Prehistoric Era, according to their age.

Evolutionary Structure		Age in millions of years	Fossilized Roses			Found in			Date of Discovery
Period	Division		Flora	*Rosa*	Modern Comparison	Europe	North America	Asia	
Quaternary	Alluvial (Present Time)		Contemporary Flora	—	—	—	—	—	—
	Diluvial	0.3							
Tertiary Late Tertiary	Pliocene			akashiensis!	roxburghii	—	—	Japan	1937
				multiflora!	multiflora	—	—	Japan	1937
				hoerneri +	acicularis	—	—	China	1935
				bohemica +	pimpinellifolia	Bohemia	—	—	1882
			Dryas-Flora	glangeaudii +		France	—	—	1912
				aff. dumetorum ?	dumetorum	Bulgaria	—	—	1929
			Magnoliaceae	chareyrei +	canina	France	—	—	1887
				aff. gallica ?	gallica	Bulgaria	—	—	1929
	Miocene			angustifolia ?		Germany	—	—	1860
				hilliae !		—	U.S.A., Col, Cal, & Oregon	—	1883
			Myricaceae	ruskiniana +		—	U.S.A., Col, Cal & Oregon	—	1908
				scudderi +		—	U.S.A., Col, Cal & Oregon	—	1916
			Lauraceae	wilmattae +		—	U.S.A., Col, Cal & Oregon	—	1908
				lignitum +		Germany	—	—	1869
			Palmae	penelopes ?		Austria	—	—	1848
				chanwangensis +	rugosa	—	—	Japan	1938
				usyuensis +	taiwanensis	—	—	Japan	1955
				nausicaes ?	indica	Germany	—	—	1856
				basaltica ?		Germany	—	—	1857
Early Tertiary	Oligocene			inquirenda ?		—	U.S.A., Colorado	—	1916
		25							
	Eocene			cetera +		—	U.S.A., Alaska	—	1936
				confirmata +		—	U.S.A., Alaska	—	1936
	Paleogene	60							
Cretaceous		95	No finds to date			—	—	—	—

Explanation of symbols: — ! = positive identification; + = probable; ? = doubtful

BIBLIOGRAPHY

BORCHARD, R. Of very Ancient Roses. Rose Annual 1966, pp. 31-33.

BUZEK, C. Tertiary Flora from the Northern Part of the Petipsy Area (North-Bohemian Basin). Ustr. Ustav. Geolog. 1971: pp. 61-62 & Plate 24. Prague 1971.

FERGUSON, D.K. The Miocene Flora of Kreuzau, Western Germany. I. The Leaf-remains. Verh. Kon. Ned. Ak. Wetensch., Nat.2.Ser., 60(15): Ill.30. Amsterdam 1971.

GOTHAN, W. Über die Vorgeschichte der Rosengewächse. Ros.Z. 1923: pp. 19-20.

KIRCHHEIMER, F. Die geologische Geschichte der Rosengewächse. Mitt. Labor. Freitag zu Bodman, 1941; pp. 120-124. Die Rose in der geologischen Vergangenheit. Rosenjahrbuch 1950: pp. 5-23 (with 4 illustrations).

KNOBLOCH, E. Die oberoligozäne Flora des Pirskenberges bei Sluknov in Nord-Böhmen. Sbornik Ustr. Ustav. Geolog. 24: 278. Prague 1961.

RESSER, C.E. Very Ancient Roses. Amer. Rose Ann. 1942. pp. 11-15.

TANAI, T. and SUZUKI, N. Miocene Floras of Southwestern Hokkaido, Japan. Tertiary Floras of Japan I: pp. 9-149 (1963).

The "Rose" in the Language of the World

The first authority to make a short collection of the different names and symbols for the rose in various languages was J. D. Schleiden in 1873. He maintained that all the various names used were in fact one and the same word which, being subjected to various dialectic alternatives in the individual languages, produced differing sounds.

In his view it originated with the Aryan root-word *vrod* (or perhaps better, *vrdh*), but doubt was cast on this by H. Kruse (Tokyo). His theory on the matter focused on the great spread of Semitic languages, which were under very little Aryan influence, and the meaning of the word itself. If *vrod* (*vrdh*) meant something like 'growth' in general, then it is an unacceptable theory that this encompassed the rose alone. Kruse believes it is more reasonable to assume that our word rose comes from the word *ward* of a pre-Aryan language, originating in the Caucasus, which developed from the Semitic languages; there are many similar words in Armenian.

If this theory is accepted, then the following can be developed:

ward → *warda* → *wareda* → *waridi* → *wered* → *urt*
└ *vrad* → *wrodon* → *brodon* → *rhodon* → *rhodia*
rhodia → *rosa* → *rose* → *rozsa* → *ruze* → *ruusu* → etc

How, out of the word *ward*, one gets *gul* → *kul* → *gol* I frankly have no idea.

gul → *gül* → *kul* → *golab* → *gulab* → *gulap* → *gulabi* → *kulab*

The Celtic word *rodd* or *rhudd* (= 'red') is believed by some authorities to be similar in sound and therefore a possible origin for the word "rose". However, this proposition is somewhat unsatisfactory since the Aryan word for 'red' — *erythros* is unrelated to the rose, according to a brief footnote by Kruse.

A short review on hedge roses produced by Zander and Teschner will be referred to later.

The following summary is, unfortunately, incomplete but generally in the different European languages the corresponding words for "rose" tend to be dissimilar while in all Semitic languages the word for the rose is either the same or very similar.

The languages which do not use the Latin alphabet have been transcribed in the accompanying table in their own form and also as they would appear if written in Roman lettering. This survey has been checked against the system worked out by F. Bodmer.

LANGUAGES WITH KNOWN COMMON CONNECTIONS.

I. Aryan Languages
  a. German

rose, rose	(Danish, English, German, Norwegian)
ros	(Swedish)
rós	(Icelandic)
roos	(Afrikaans, Dutch, Flemish)
reuse	(Burgundian)

  b. Celtic

rós	(Gaelic)
rhos	(Celtic; according to Hegi, *roschaill*)
reus	(Breton)

  c. Roman

rosa	(Italian, Latin, Portuguese, Spanish)
rose	(French)
roser	(Provençal)
rozé, roz	(Wallon)
trandafir	(Rumanian; also the same in Moldavian but in Cyrillic characters)

  d. Slavonic

růže	(Czech, Slovakian)
róza	(Polish)
rože	(Slovenian)
ruže	(Serbo-Croat)
Ruža	(Byelorussian)
Trojanda	(Ukrainian)
Roza	(Bulgarian, Russian)

Figure 7. The word *ward* in ornamental Arabic lettering, drawn by Sami Krui, S. J., Beirut.

Ancient Egyptian
ouert (uncertain)

Aeolic
wrodon

Tibetan
se-ba

Avestic (Zend)
vareda

Greek
rhodon

Punjabi
gulāb

Kanarese
gulabi

Hindi; Marathi
gulāb

Modern Greek
trianta-phylla

Mongolian
sarnai čečeg

Burmese
hninzi

Korean
dschang-mi

Sanskrit
japā

Thai (Siamese)
kulap

Malayalam
panineer

Tamil
roja

Oriya
gulāb

Bengali, Assam
golāp

Singhalese
rosa

Chinese
chiang-wei

Chinese
mei-kuei

Aramaic
wardâ

Malaysian
mawar

Gujarati
gulāb

Figure 8. Table 1 (Continued in Fig. 9)

كُلاب	Urdu *gulab*	Троянда	Ukrainian *Trojanda*
شيلان	Kurdish *sîlan*	Ружа	Byelorussian *Ruza*
وَرْدَة	Arabic *ward*	Վարդ	Armenian *Vard*
గులాబి	Telegu *gulabi*	ვარდი	Georgian *Vardy*
וֶרֶד	Hebrew *wered*	Трандафир	Moldavian *Trandafir*
		Кул	Azerbaijanian *Kul*
گل	Modern Persian *gul*	Атиргул	Usbek *Atirgul*
		Кулгіи	Kazakh *Kulgin*
		Кызыл гул	Kirghiz *Kyzyl gul*
		Гул	Tajik *Gul*
ばら	Japanese *bara*	бэгул гул	Turkoman *Begul gul*
		Гөлчэчэк	Tartar *goechechek*
		Кызыл гөл	Bashkir *Kyzyl gol*
		Лежнöг рöд бьдмöг	Komi *Lezneg Röd Bydmeg*
RÓS	Gaelic (Erse) *ros*	Оошк цецг	Kalmuck *Oshk tsetsk*
		Сарнай цэцэг	Mongolian *Sarnaj tsetseg*
ОҮРТ	Coptic *ourt*	Розо [сэсэг]	Bureyat *Roza (seseg)*

Figure 9. Table 2. The left half of the column shows the word "rose" in the vernacular script, and on the right the name of the language; in italics below the approximate transcription in Roman characters is given. (Original)

e. Baltic languages
  roze   (Lettish)
  roze   (Lithuanian)

f. Greek
  wrodon   (Aeolian; about the time of Sappho)
  brodon   (Aeolian; of a later date)
  rhodon   (Classical Greek)
  triantaphylla (Modern Greek)

g. Albanian
  trĕndafil

h. Armenian
  vard

i. Persian (Ancient)
  vareda   +Ancient Persian *ca.* 6 - 400 B.C.; in
  — ? —   cuneiform.
                    ++Avestic (Zend) *ca.* 600 B.C. in
                      Aramaic characters.

8

(Middle Period Persian)

varta	Pehlevi (= middle Persian) in Aramaic characters
unidentified	Parthian; also in Aramaic Sogh; in its own writing, 8-900 A.D. Chwarezmic; in Arabic up to 1400 A.D. Sakai; in Indian writing

Modern Persian (Iranian)

gul	Farsi
gul	Pushto
gul	Tajik
šîlan	Kurdish

k. Modern Indian languages

golāp	(Assam, Bengali)
gulāp	(Oriya)
gulāb	(Hindi, Punjabi, Gujerati, Marathi, Urdu)

Sanskrit
japā

II. Finno-Ugrian languages

ruusu	(Finnish)
Roos	(Estonian)
rósza	(Hungarian)

III. Semitic languages

kasìŠAR	(Assyrian cuneiform
SILA ŠAR	acc. Thompson)
wered	(Hebrew)
wardâ (wrād)	(Aramaic)
ward(a)	(Arabic)
urt	(Coptic; of the late Egyptian period 712-332 B.C., and written in Greek)

Semitic dialects of Ethiopia and Eritrea

caga, gaga } *gaka, kaga* }	Amharic Tigris
kalokhim, } *koloschim* }	Tigris

IV. Hamitic languages

ourt	(Ancient Egyptian; written in hieroglyphics in the time of the Old Kingdom, 2660-2160 B.C.)

Kushic dialects

dayero	(North) Somalia
ga-aga	Galla (Arussi)

V. Indo-Chinese languages

ch'iang-wei } *mei-kuei* }	(Chinese)
rgya-bse	(Tibetan; pronounced kwa-se)
hninzi	(Burmese)
kulab	(Bangkok-Thai)

VI. Malaysian and Javanese languages

mawar	(Malaysian, Indonesian)

VII. Altaic languages

gül	(Turkish)
Kul	(Azerbaijan)
Kizil gul	(Kirghiz)
Atirgul	(Usbek)
Goechechek	(Tartar)
Kizil gol	(Bashkir)

VIII. Dravidian languages

rojapu	(Tamil)
gulabi	(Telegu, Kanarese)
panineer	(Malayalam)

IX. Bantu dialects

waridi	(Swahili)

LANGUAGES WITH NO CLEAR FAMILY CONNECTIONS

X. Mongolian languages

Sarnai čečeg	(Mongolian)
Ošk ceceg	(Kalmuck)
Begul gul	(Turkoman)
Ležneg Röd Bidmeg	(Komi = Syriac)
Rozo seseg	(Bureyan)

XI. Other languages

bara	(Japanese)
dschang-mi	(Korean)
hoa h'ông	(Vietnamese)
rosa	(Singhalese; possibly taken from the Portuguese)
vardi	(Georgian)

F. Seiler (Vol. I, p. 46) is of the opinion, as was Schleiden, that the word "rose" probably originated from one of the Aryan dialects in the Middle East, but this is only half the story. Seiler, noting the word root *vardhos* (= 'thornbush'), speculates that this later assumed the special meaning 'rose'. This word could well have become *vard* (Armenian) and *vareda* (Avestic or Zend) and from there easily passed into Persian and the various Semitic dialects, but retaining the original meaning of 'thornbush'. Still later it appeared in the Greek of Sappho's day (*ca.* 600 B.C.) as *wrodon*, then *brodon*, and finally *rhodon*. After this the rose bush itself was known in Greece as *batos* (= 'bush') or *kynosbatos* (= 'hawthorn'), and it was only the flowers themselves which were called *rhodon*, which came to be used for almost any large flower, while any plant with small flowers was referred to as *ion*.

However, this word, in turn, came to have the accepted meaning of violet (Zander and Teschner).

The Romans, who obtained the rose as a garden plant from the Greeks, called it *rosa* (taken from *rhodon* or, Kruse believes, from the plural *rhodia*). They also called it *flos roseus*; a term applied particularly to the flowers because the bush itself was called *rubus*.

Just when the word *rose* appeared in German has never been satisfactorily determined, but it was probably with the arrival of the first garden roses *ca.* 800 A.D.

At this time, no great distinction was made between the various 'thorn bushes'; the earliest German word for these is *brama*, Old High German used *hiufo*. From *brama* came the German word *brombeere*, 'bramble' in English, which was used to describe not only brambles (*Rubus*), but also *Rosa canina*.

The German word *hagebutte* ('hip') appears in a number of dialects: *hiufo* (Old High German) became *hiefe* in Middle German; *hiepo* in Old Saxon and *heopa* in Anglo-Saxon and ended up as 'hip' or 'hep' in modern English, as *hyben* in Danish, as *nype* in Norwegian and *nypon* in Swedish.

The German word *Heckenrose* ('Dog Rose') was *hâeg Dorn* in early English; in modern Danish it is *hyben-torn*; *nypetorn* in both Norwegian and Swedish and also appears in a number of Swiss dialects as *Haglidorn*.

In early German, according to Fischer, wild roses were usually not referred to as 'Rose', but as 'Hawthorn', 'Sweetbriar', *Burzeldorn* and *Weithagen*.

The word terminal *-butte* in *hagebutte* ('hip') carries the same meaning as *butzen* = *klumpen* = 'ball' (according to Hegi). He writes (Vol. IV, pp. 976-977) that there are many other German usages for the word *Heckenrose* ('Dog Rose').

The original words in use for the wild roses continued in Germany well into the Middle Ages and they were already different from the terminology used for garden roses, as the following examples show:

In *Physica* by the Blessed Hildegard (1098-1179), the word *hyffa* was used for the Dog Rose and *rose* for the garden rose.

In *Buch der Natur* by Konrad von Megenberg (1309-1374) *rosendorn* or *veltdorn* implied the Dog Rose, whereas *rosarius* or *rosenpaum* was the garden rose; in *De Hortis Germaniae* by Konrad Gesner (1561) he says that "*Rosa sylvestris*, the little rose of May, is known in Germany as Hanrose, Haberrose and Feldtrose . . . "

In this connection it should also be said that the exact meaning of the word *Rosengarten* ('rose garden') as used in the Middle Ages remains a controversy. Zander and Teschner state that there is evidence to show that garden roses first arrived in Germany about the year 800 A.D. and that before that time rose gardens as such only contained the wild or species roses. Therefore we must understand that the "rose garden" of that period was an open place with hedges of wild roses where festivals and gatherings were held. The *Hortus Rosarum* is supported by a document of 1325 to this effect.

The word *Rosarium* was certainly in use in ancient Rome where it meant a rose garden, preserved for the use and enjoyment of its owner, while the *rosetum* was a commercial undertaking, i.e., a rose nursery somewhat similar to modern nurseries for growing cut flowers, however the distinctions between these terms do not appear to have been rigidly maintained. *Rosarius* probably meant a rose bush, as stated above (Megenberg).

In the Middle Ages, the word *Rosarium* was much used in literature in the way that today we use the words catalog or collection. For example, the titles of *Rosarium* and *Rosarius* used by Arnaldus von Villanova, who died in 1310, are means of describing himself as the Collector (Compilator) or Gatherer of Roses *(Rosarius)* because they are a collection of extracts from the writings of philosophers.

Guido de Baysio entitled his work on church law, which appeared in the year 1300, *Rosarium*.

Thomas á Kempis produced a "Mystical Rosarium" (*Rosarium mysticum animae fidelis*, 1553) and we also find amongst his works one entitled *Hortulus Rosarum* ("The Little Rose Garden") (according to Beissel, pp. 248, *et seq.*).

For the compilation and collection of words from more than 100 different languages which I have been most kindly given by a number of Institutions, I extend my deepest thanks. I received particular help from Professor Dr. H. Kruse, Tokyo, who read the manuscript and made some important corrections; from Dr. P. Lapin, Assistant Director of the Central Botanic Gardens in Moscow, who has given me the details of the various words for "rose" in the 20 official languages of the Soviet Union and the autonomous Republics of the U.S.S.R.; to Dr. B.P. Pal, Director, Indian Agricultural Research Institute, New Delhi, for 11 Indian words, and finally to Dr. Pichi Sermolli, Perugia, for five of the Ethiopian dialects.

BIBLIOGRAPHY

BEISSEL, St.   Geschichte der Verehrung Marias im Mittelalter Freiburg, 1909.

BODMER, F.   Die Sprachen der Welt (German trans. of The Loom of Language). Cologne 1955.

BROCKHAUS.   Encyclopaedia, 20 vols; 17 completely revised in the Grossen Brockhaus edition; Vols. 1-18 consulted. Wiesbaden 1966-1973.

FISCHER, H.   Mittelalterliche Pflanzenkunde. New Edition. Hildesheim 1967.

HEGI, G.   Flora von Mitteleuropa, Vol IV. Munich 1924.

SCHLEIDEN, M.J.   Die Rose; Geschichte und Symbolik Leipzig 1873.

SILER, F.   Entwicklung der deutschen Kultur im Spiegel des deutschen Lehnwortes. Vol I.

TÄCKHOLM, V.   Faraos Blomster. Stockholm 1969.

THOMPSON, R.C.   A Dictionary of Assyrian Botany. London 1949.

ZANDER, R. and TESCHNER, C.   Der Rosengarten; eme geschichtliche. Studie durch 2 Jahrtausende. Frankfurt (Order) 1939.

The Geographical Distribution of Modern Roses

The natural geographic spread of modern roses lies in the Northern Hemisphere between 20 and 70 degrees latitude; there are no indigenous roses in the Southern Hemisphere. Because of the practical possibilities of planting roses in almost all climates, they have been brought to every country in the world, but this is unrelated to their natural distribution. In spite of this, we must not forget that today in South America, Australia and, above all, New Zealand numerous roses grow and flourish.

How this original geographical distribution arose is unknown, although a theory relating geography to the the chromosome count has been developed (see p. 17).

The area covered by the genus, in the light of present knowledge, includes all of Europe and Asia with the exception of some Arctic and tropical regions and some areas of Central Asia (see Map, Fig. 10). In central and south western Asia lies the center of the genus *Rosa* as it is known today. In Africa, we find wild roses only in the extreme north-west, i.e., Algiers, Morocco, Tunis and Ethiopia. In North America many rose species are to be found in the U.S.A. and Canada, whereas in Mexico only one species, *R. montezumae* has been discovered.

R. clinophylla, the rose of the tropics, comes from N. India and East Bengal and, due to the climatic conditions which it demands, is very rarely found in cultivation in Europe.

Most of the species roses have been cultivated in the last 150 years, thanks to botanical expeditions, particularly by the English, Americans and French, and today may be seen in botanic gardens and specialist rose gardens throughout Europe and North America. It should be particularly noted that the European and North American roses only bloom once a year, whereas in Asia, there are species which are recurrent (flower twice or more annually). The only true yellow roses and almost all the natural climbers also come from this area.

A single species, *R. acicularis*, is to be found in the polar regions of Europe, Asia and North America. In northern Norway, however, many of our modern roses are cultivated, particularly the frost-hardy *R. rugosa* and its garden forms.

THE ROSES OF EUROPE

The size of this book would have to be vastly increased in order to give details of the thousands of known rose forms in Central and Northern Europe; for that purpose, the student will have to turn to the specialist literature: Ascherson & Graebner, Schwertschlager, Christ, Keller, Crépin, etc., and to the *Flora Europaea*, Vol. 2 (1968). H. Christ (1873) gives a good

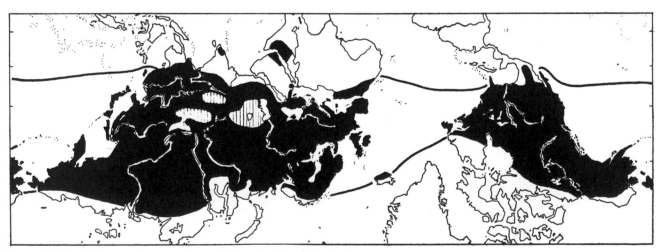

Figure 10. Map of the complete natural area of the genus *Rosa* (Original, corrections by Dr. Jäger)

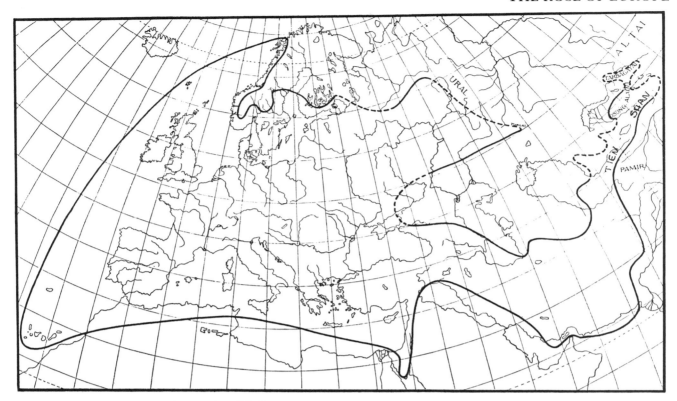

Figure 11. Distribution of the Section *Caninae* (Täckholm).

description from the geographical point of view of the roses of Switzerland with additional information on the surrounding areas of Central and Southern Europe. Some general comments from his work are worth quoting here:

> If we look first at the Swiss Jura from Salève to Schaffausen then we can, with reason, say that this mountain range is the most privileged rose garden of Europe. No other area can produce such a wide variety of forms, such a wealth of types and cultivars.

> Roses are plants for the hills and mountainsides and they need the proximity of trees and rich moist soil in which to grow. Consequently most of the species start their lives in hilly areas, they love to be in complete isolation but without the problem of quick drying soil. The true mountain roses *(R. pendulina, reuteri, coriifolia, montana, glauca)* are almost always to be found within the tree-line without making much attempt to rise higher. Those observed at greater altitudes include *R. pomifera* (6,000 feet) *R. reversa* (6,250 feet) *R. pendulina* and *R. cinnamomea* (6,500 feet).

The following table of the European species roses is based upon the data given in the *Flora Europaea*, Vol. 2, but varieties which have not been found in cultivation have been omitted. Examples marked (**X**) indicate that they are species from outside Europe which have naturalized themselves by one means or another within Europe.

Distribution of the European Species Roses.

Species Section	Scandinavia	Western Europe	Central Europe	Southern Europe	Eastern Europe	S. Eastern Europe
canina	X	X	X	X	X	X
pimpinellifolia	X	X	X	X	X	X
rubiginosa	X	X	X	X	X	X
tomentosa	X	X	X	X	X	X
sherardii	X	X	X	—	—	—
rugosa	(X)	(X)	(X)	—	—	—
mollis	X	X	—	—	—	—
majalis	X	—	X	—	—	—
acicularis	X (NE)	—	—	—	—	—
micrantha	—	X	X	X	—	—
glauca	—	X	X	X	—	—
arvensis	—	X	X	X	—	—
agrestis	—	X	X	X	—	—
stylosa	—	X	X	—	—	X
elliptica	—	X	X	—	—	—
villosa	—	—	X	X	—	—
pendulina	—	—	X	X	—	—
gallica	—	X	X	X	—	—
foetida	—	—	(X)	(X)	—	—
jundzillii (marginata)	—	—	X	—	X	—
blanda	—	—	(X)	—	—	—

13

Species Section	Scandinavia	Western Europe	Central Europe	Southern Europe	Eastern Europe	S. Eastern Europe
sempervirens	—	—	—	X	—	—
serafinii	—	—	—	X	—	X
glutinosa	—	—	—	X	—	X
sicula	—	—	—	X	—	—
montana	—	—	—	X	—	—
orientalis	—	—	—	—	—	X
phoenicia	—	—	—	—	—	X

A list of the species roses growing in the Soviet Union has been produced by Sokolov and Swjasewa, *Geographical Situation of Trees in the U.S.S.R.* (Vol. 7 of the series "Derewja i Kustarniki"), Moscow 1965; published in Russian with information on the distribution of the roses by area, but lacking maps.

DETAILS OF THE ASIATIC ROSE SPECIES.

It is only possible to list here the species which are of garden importance and in cultivation.

a. The Middle East

Rosa	*corymbifera*	*hemisphaerica*	*marginata*
	heckeliana	*horrida*	*mollis*

b. More than one area

	Middle East	Persia	Central Asia	Himalayas	China
iberica	X	X	—	—	—
canina	X	X	X	—	—
orientalis	X	X	—	—	—
xanthina	—	—	X	—	X
laxa	—	—	X	—	X
sericea	—	—	—	X	X
moschata	—	X	—	X	—
glutinosa	X	X	X	—	—
persica	—	X	X	—	—
foetida	X	X	X	—	—

c. Central Asia

Rosa	*beggeriana*	*fedtschenkoana*	*primula*	*ecae*

d. Himalayas

Rosa	*gigantea*	*moschata*	*webbiana*	*macrophylla*	*sericea*

e. China, including Korea. (X) = also found in Japan

Rosa	*banksiae*	*forrestiana*	*roxburghii*
	banksiopsis	*fortuniana*	*rugosa* (X)
	bracteata	*giraldii*	*sericea*
	caudata	*helenae*	*sertata*
	cerasocarpa	*hemsleyana*	*setipoda*
	chinensis	*laevigata*	*sinowilsonii*
	cymosa	*laxa*	*soulieana*
	davidii	*luciae* (X)	*sweginzowii*
	elegantula	*moyesii*	*wichuraiana* (X)
	ernestii	*multibracteata*	*willmottiae*
	farreri	*odorata*	*xanthina*
	filipes	*prattii*	

f. Japan

Rosa	*acicularis*	*luciae*	*roxburghii*
	davurica	*multiflora*	*sambucina*
	iwara	*rugosa*	*wichuraiana*

Asia, the Original Home of the Rose   About 60% (possibly more) of all our garden flowers fruits and vegetables originated in Asia. In one valley alone the French missionary and botanist, Abbé David, found more than 200 different cultivars of *Rhododendron*! Today it is regarded as the world's focal point for that genus. Wilson found, in a moist area near the river Min, which is a tributary of the Yangtse, thousands upon thousands of *Lilium regale* all of them self-sown.

Generally, roses come from the lowlands, but are nevertheless found at higher elevations, some right up to the snow-line while others extend down to the sand dunes at the sea's edge.

In China, in the river deltas and higher up on the plains, and even in the shadows of the mountains themselves, natural plant growth has long since been supplanted by human cultivation and by pasture land. Nature, undisturbed by human interference, with all its great multiplicity of plant material, is now only found in the eastern parts of the Himalyas and in Northern China at altitudes of 1,517-2,958 m./5,000-9,750 ft. above sea level. These areas are, for the most part, rugged and almost inaccessible so that in the deep valleys and on the steep hillsides, settlements and farming are scarcely possible, while the natural plant life is, in many ways, most favorably encouraged through protection from wind, a rich, moist soil, and a moderate climate.

Ernest H. Wilson, (*A Naturalist in Western China*, Vol. I, p. 18) gives a vivid description of the wild roses as follows:

> "Rose bushes abound everywhere, and in April perhaps afford the greatest show of any one kind of flower. *Rosa laevigata* and *R. microcarpa* are more common in fully exposed places. *Rosa multiflora*, *R. moschata* and *R. banksiae* are particularly abundant on the cliffs and crags of the glens and gorges, though by no means confined thereto. The Musk and Banksian Roses often scale tall trees, and a tree thus festooned with their branches laden with flowers is a sight to be remembered. To walk through a glen in the early morning or after a slight shower, when the air is laden with the soft delicious perfume from myriads of Rose flowers, is truly to walk through an earthly paradise."

Rosa bracteata, unfortunately not completely winter-hardy, but in its consummate flower form is a particularly beautiful Chinese species rose; the famous cultivar 'Mermaid' is a descendent of it.

Rosa gigantea, the largest-flowered rose in the world also comes from China where, according to Kingdon Ward, it was to be seen growing up to 30 m./100 ft. in height and was able to climb to the very top of fairly tall trees.

Rosa chinensis minima, the forefather of our miniature roses, also comes, as its name implies, from China.

Robert Fortune brought the first Tea Rose and the first yellow rose to Europe.

Apart from the beauty of the flowers, the Asiatic roses are endowed with large, handsome shiny leaves, big prickles, scented foliage and reddish bark.

Rosa foetida bicolor (syn. 'Austrian Copper'), of which the interior is reddish-scarlet and the exterior golden yellow, was originally found somewhere in S.W. Asia and is such an exceptional parent that with it our modern hybridizers have been able to attain the wonderful colors seen in many of our roses today.

Rosa multiflora has, admittedly, quite small white flowers, but the trusses are large and there are numerous red hips in winter. Today it is widely used as an understock and also as a hedge rose.

Rosa rugosa comes from the rocky coast of Japan.

In conclusion, some information should be given regarding the climate, particularly the amount of rainfall. For the most part, the continent of Asia is well supplied with water, but there are substantial regional differences as the following examples show (the figures given are the average yearly rainfall):

In the rain forests of the central massif of the Himalayas, 450-750 cm./180-300 in. A similar amount falls in Bhutan, Nepal and Tibet.

Malaysia and Burma, 250 cm./100 in.
Cambodia, Laos and Thailand, 150-250 cm./60-100 in.
Japan, 150-200 cm./60-80 in.
China, 100-150 cm./40-60 in.
Korea and Siberia, 75-100 cm./30-40 in.
Afghanistan and Pakistan, 25-50 cm./10-20 in.
Iran, 12.5-25 cm./5-10 in.
Iraq, roughly 20 cm./8 in.

The Gobi desert in Mongolia is one of the most arid parts of the world.

ROSES IN NORTH AFRICA

Very few roses originated in N. Africa. *Rosa canina*, *Rosa corymbifera* (= *R. dumetorum*) and *Rosa sempervirens* come from Morocco, Algeria and Tunis and *R. sicula*, *R. agrestis* (= *R. arabica* Crépin) from Egypt; *R. richardii* (= *R. sancta*) and *R. moschata* var. *abyssinica* (= *R. abyssinica* Lindl.) from Ethiopia, or Abyssinia as it used to be called, though the latter varieties really originated in the Red Sea area and the Yemen. Of the latter two there are some specific examples:

R. moschata var *abyssinica* (=*R. abyssinica* Lindl.) is the only wild rose of its country; it is distinguished from *R. moschata* proper by its much weaker growth and the fact that it is much more prickly. The descriptions in various reference books are decidedly contradictory. G. S. Thomas tells us that the rose originated in Syria (where it is, however, unknown today) in the 4th century. It is exceptionally winter-hardy and can be successfully established in hilly areas up to and above 2,275 m./7,500 ft.; it is of a climbing habit, mostly rambling through large bushes or the smaller trees; the flowers are white, 7-10 cm./2.75-4 in. across, recurrent, flowering in April-May and again in September-October. In Ethiopian nurseries this rose has been used successfully as an understock.

The second rose, *R. richardii* (=*R. sancta*) is believed to have been an Ethiopian form of *R. gallica* and may also have originated in the Middle East. In Ethiopia, it grows chiefly in the mountains in the northern part of the country. It was named "sancta" because it was this flower which was placed in graves from the 1st to the 5th century A.D. It still plays a part in religious rites. Due to this it is often found growing in the vicinity of churches.

15

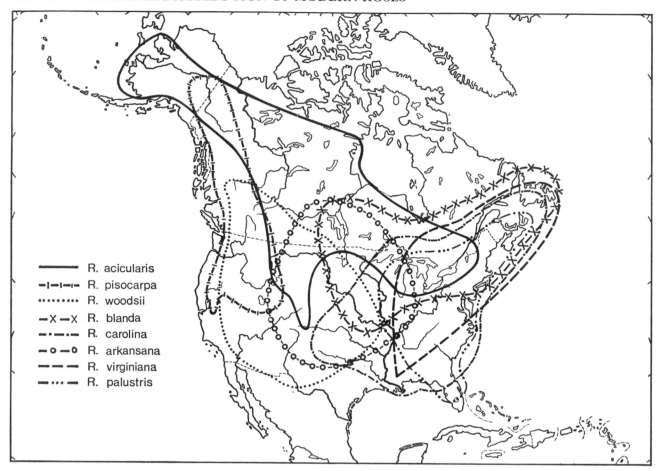

Figure 12. Map showing the distribution of the most important N. American roses. (Original)

DISTRIBUTION OF THE ROSE IN N. AMERICA

Th. M. Little (1942) has given us a rather superficial account of the species roses of N. America in addition to a number of maps which have served as the basis for the map in Fig. 12. Just as in Europe, so here the number of species which have been described is very large, totaling about 170. The number was originally placed at 127 by von Rydberg, while Erlanson believed that there were only 20 species worthy of identification. In effect, Rehder has accepted the nomenclature put forward by Erlanson, although he has left some varieties within the class of individual species (*R. suffulta* Greene; *R. macounii* Greene). The American roses belong to the *Cinnamomeae* section with four exceptions. These are *R. setigera* which comes from the *Synstylae,* as its only representative, and the section *Minutifoliae* which today has been generally accepted as a sub-genus *Hes-*

perhodos (including the varieties *R. stellata* and *R. mirifica*).

The roses with the greatest area of natural habitat in N. America are *R. acicularis* in the Far North, *R. blanda* in the North-East, *R. carolina, R. palustris* and *R. virginiana* in the East, *R. arkansana* in the Mid-West and finally *R. woodsii* in the Middle and Far West. The remaining species inhabit smaller but nevertheless quite extensive areas. These species are the following:

R. nutkana, R. gymnocarpa and *R. pisocarpa* in the North-West as well as a small area of *R. rugosa* on the south coast of Alaska which obviously arrived there from the Far East. In the West, we find *R. californica* in California, *R. spithamea* in the Sierra Nevada; *R. drummondii* in both California and Oregon. *R. engelmannii* is found in the Rocky Mountains and *R. foliolosa* in the South (Texas, Oklahoma and Arkansas). Finally, *R. nitida* has been described as being indigenous to the North-East.

CHROMOSOME-GEOGRAPHY IN THE GENUS *ROSA*

Although there will be a much more detailed description of the chromosomes in roses on page 183, it is necessary to discuss it here in connection with the geographical distribution of the genus.

THE INFLUENCE OF GEOGRAPHY ON THE CHROMOSOMES OF THE GENUS *ROSA*

The cytologists and geneticists (O. Rosenberg, 1903, 1909; G. Täckholm, 1920, 1922; K. Blackburn and J.W.H. Harrison, 1921; C.C. Hurst, 1925, 1927, 1929, 1931) were all able to make a careful comparison of a mass of information regarding the cytological relationships of the genus *Rosa*. They established that the rose's gametic cells have seven chromosomes and that the somatic cells has $2 \times 7 = 14$ chromosomes.

7 is the haploid number, the basic or single number of the genus and is usually indicated by the use of the letter n or x (i.e., $n = 7$ or $x = 7$).

14 is the diploid number which appears in the somatic cells and is usually written as $2n$ or $2x = 14$.

Now, there are cases in the genus *Rosa*, as in other genera, in which $2x = 21, 28, 35, 42$ and even 56 chromosomes which show up in the somatic cells; all these numbers are, as will be observed, multiples of 7. This represents a polyploid progression, as is the case in most cultivated plants, and in many wild plant species. The various stages of this progression are designated as follows:

haploid   (single, basic) $x = 7$

diploid   (double) $2x = 14$
triploid   (triple) $2x = 21$
tetraploid   (fourfold) $2x = 28$
pentaploid   (fivefold) $2x = 35$
hexaploid   (sixfold) $2x = 42$
octoploid   (eightfold) $2x = 56$

However, the behavior of the rose, particularly in the case of the section *Caninae*, is not as simple as that. "Here is a group of forms with quite individual behavior in opposition to that which usually takes place in plants in which the seed of the male and female parents are throughout different even though they always show a chromosome number which is divisible by 7. We find therefore forms with 35 and also some with 28 and 42 chromosomes. The chromosome number in the somatic hep of *R. vulgaris* is for example 35; the pollen hep however is only 7 whilst the female hep has 28 chromosomes. *R. britzensis* is also 35 but here the division is 14 for the pollen hep and 21 for the seed hep. The total of the chromosomes in the male and female heps always comprises the total numbers of the chromosomes." (Rathlef, 1937). For more information on this turn to page 183.

The cytologists have found that within a given genus the species with the smallest number of chromosomes are the oldest historically. From this they were able to establish that, for a particular species, stocks with quite widely differing chromosome counts could be encountered; such varieties demonstrate the process of evolution.

The following table gives the chromosome count of the five most important sections of the genus as given by Glasau:

Diploid Chromosome number(s) occurring in the species $2n =$	*Cinnamomeae* (51 spec.)		*Caninae* (26 spec.)		*Synstylae* (19 spec.)		*Pimpinellifolia* (9 spec.)		*Carolinae* (7 spec.)	
	with $2n$	% of Total	with $2n$	% of Total	with $2n$	% of Total	with $2n$	% of Total	with $2n$	% of Total
14	20	39.22	—	—	18	94.7	5	55.55	2	28.57
14, 21	2	3.92	—	—	—	—	—	—	—	—
14, 21, 28	1	1.96	—	—	—	—	—	—	—	—
14, 28	6	11.86	—	—	1	5.3	4	44.45	3	42.86
14, 28, 42, 56	1	1.96	—	—	—	—	—	—	—	—
28	12	23.73	5	19.23	—	—	—	—	2	28.57
28, 34, 35, 42	—	—	1	3.85	—	—	—	—	—	—
28, 42	1	1.96	—	—	—	—	—	—	—	—
35	—	—	10	38.46	—	—	—	—	—	—
35, 42	—	—	6	23.08	—	—	—	—	—	—
34, 35, 42	—	—	1	3.85	—	—	—	—	—	—
42	8	15.69	3	11.54	—	—	—	—	—	—

For the individual plant species, the polyploid condition, i.e. the multiform situation of the chromosomes, has a very practical aspect because such species are much more likely than others in similar sites to extend their area of habitation; settling in regions with different soil and climatic conditions much more easily.

In the Far East, the true home of the genus, there is, according to Flory, a small incidence of polyploidy; with the genus' removal to both the west and north, as far as N. America, this incidence increases until it finally reaches the octoploid stage in the most northerly areas of *R. acicularis*. This is the highest number of chromosomes in the entire genus. The experts have concluded from this that the octoploid state of *R. acicularis* sufficiently enhanced its fitness to enable it to survive in an Arctic climate.

In this connection we can go briefly into the "septet" theory put forward by C.C. Hurst in 1925. He speaks of a hypothetical decaploid ($2x = 70$) in the development of the genus which lost "septets" through mutation until the diploid state was finally reached. It should be noted that Heribert-Nilsson (1953, pp. 287, 295) did not consider Hurst's theory tenable; for further information see p. 189.

BIBLIOGRAPHY.

BRETSCHNEIDER, E.   History of European Botanical Discoveries, 2 Vols. Reprint of the original edition 1898. Leipzig 1962.

COWAN, J.M.   The Journeys and Plant Introductions of GEORGE FORREST London 1952.

DAY, V.F.P.   Roses in the Arctic. Rose Annual 1967: pp. 121-122.

KEAYS, F.L.   Old China and the Rose. ARA 1942: pp. 7-10.

LEWIS, W.H.   Species Roses in the United States and their relation to modern Roses. ARA 1970: pp. 78-85 (with maps).

LI, H.L.   The Garden Flowers of China; containing a section on 'The Roses of China'. Philadelphia 1959.

LIMPRICHT, W.   Botanische Reisen in den Hochgebirgen Chinas und Ost-Tibets. Repert. spec. nov. Beih. 22; 1-515 (1922).

LITTLE, T.M.   The distribution of North American Rose species. ARA 1942: pp. 37-49 (with 9 maps).

SOKOLOV, S.J.A. and SWJASEWA, O.A.   Geography of Trees in the USSR (Vol. 7 of Derewja i Kustarniki). Moscow 1965 (in Russian).

STOUT, W.   Asia's Part is Rose History. ARA 1950: pp. 109-114.

—   Asia, Land of Flowers. ARA 1959: pp. 150-155.

The Rose in Myth and Legend

There are countless myths and legends in which the rose appears and in almost every country in the Northern Hemisphere we find examples of it on coins, coats of arms, flags, banners, seals, paintings and *objets d'art*.

Legends concerning the rose are entwined with Gods, Kings, Princes of the Church and Saints as well as with Brahma, Buddha, Mohammed, Vishnu, Confucius, Zoroaster, several Popes, the Crusaders, Nero, Cleopatra, Alexander the Great, St. Francis of Assisi, Elizabeth of Hungary, Mary Queen of Scots, St. Vincent, Venus, Cupid, Zephyrus, Aphrodite and many more. Some of the more delightful of these legends may be briefly told as follows.

Asia   In the oldest religious and spiritual works in Zend (Avestan), in the teachings of ancient Persia and in Sanskrit, the superb literature of ancient India, the rose always plays a symbolic role in the creation of the world and of mankind. Vishnu, the supreme God of India, formed his bride, Lakshmi, from 108 large and 1,008 small rose petals. Thus, the rose early became a symbol of beauty.

While the Greeks and Romans dedicated the rose to the Gods, the Persians, in their poems and paintings, associated it with the nightingale. Once the flowers complained in Heaven that their Queen, the Lotus blossom, slept by night. In order to bring about a reconciliation, Allah named the white rose Queen of Flowers. The nightingale was so enamored of the beauty of the rose that she flew down to embrace it, and thereby pierced her breast with its sharp thorns. From the drops of her blood falling upon the earth grew new roses and from that day there were red roses in Persia.

According to one Moslem legend, the rose sprang from the beads of sweat of the Prophet Mohammed. In another they came not from the Prophet, but from the perspiration of a lady named Joun whose appearance was white at dawn but rosy at midday.

It has often been said that, in the beginning, roses were without thorns and that these only appeared through the wickedness of mankind, after the Fall and the expulsion of Adam and Eve from the Garden of Eden.

A young maiden was to be burned at the stake in Bethlehem. As the flames reached up around her, she prayed for God's help and at once the flames were extinguished. From the embers sprang red roses and from the unfired sticks, white roses.

While no myth or legend mentions any specific variety of rose, the moss rose has been connected with the Blood of Christ, in the belief that His wounds dripped onto moss while He hung upon the cross.

Greece   The oldest evidence of the rose comes from legends and poetry which give us proof of the existence of the rose and its cultivation in Ancient Greece.

Here Aphrodite, the Goddess of Love, was seen as the creator of the rose. In one tale Adonis, her lover, was mortally wounded, when hunting, by a wild boar. She hastened to his side and from the mixture of his blood and her tears grew a superb, fragrant, blood-red rose. In another version, Adonis was more superficially wounded and Aphrodite, while running to him, scratched herself on the thorns of a rose bush. Her blood started to flow at once and the white flowers on the bush turned to red. Finally, there is a story which tells us of the origin of the white rose: Aphrodite was born of sea-foam and from this foam, wherever it fell to the ground, grew white rose bushes.

Aphrodite is credited with having invented the rose wreath with which the Greeks and Romans decorated their guests at banquets and revels. However, the wreath of roses was also a symbol of Dionysus (Bacchus), and he had to look after all drunken revelry, as Pindar tells us. Later, Eros was always represented by both sculptors and painters, adorned with garlands of roses, as were the Muses and the Graces.

Eos, the "rosy-fingered" Goddess of the morning was of surpassing beauty. According to one legend, the rose has remained upon earth as the symbol and evidence of her first appearance, the first dawn.

Rhodanthe (= 'Rose bloom'), the delectable young Queen of Corinth had many admirers who always followed her around.

When, one day, three of them were too importunate, she fled into the Temple of Diana and called loudly for help in keeping them from her. Passers-by were so overcome by the beauty of the young Queen that they started to show her the honor and reverence which they had formerly given to Diana. Apollo, Diana's brother, was so enraged by this that he immediately transformed Rhodanthe into a rose bush, and the three suitors into a worm, a fly and a butterfly.

Rome The pattern of the Greek legends is closely followed by those which developed in Rome. In one Venus was loved by Adonis, but also desired by Mars, the God of War. Mars decided to have Adonis killed, but, at the last moment, he was hurriedly warned by Venus. In her haste, she let her foot slip in a rose bed, from the blood which flowed from the scratches onto the ground sprang up red roses.

Flora, the Goddess of Spring and of Flowers, one day found the dead body of her dearest and most beautiful nymph; inconsolable, she begged all the Gods to come to her aid to change the dead body of her loved one into the most beautiful flower which would be recognized as Queen of all Flowers. Apollo, God of the Arts, gave her the breath of life, Bacchus bathed her in nectar, Vertumnus gave her fragrance, Pomona fruit, and Flora herself finally gave a diadem of petals, and thus the rose was born.

Cupid, one of the Gods of Love, knocked over, with his wing, a bowl of wine standing on a table beside Bacchus; from this pool of wine on the ground came a rose bush. The rose was also consecrated to Venus as the symbol of beauty.

There is one particularly delightful story which is as follows:

The God Zephyrus loved Flora so much that he changed himself into a rose because the Goddess had no interest other than flowers. When Flora saw the rose, she kissed it and thus fulfilled Zephyrus' wish.

Once Bacchus followed a young and very pretty nymph into the forest where she became entangled in a thorn bush. When Bacchus reached her, in order to thank the bush for its unexpected but timely help, he touched it with his staff and ordered it immediately covered with red roses.

Yet another story is told of Roselia, a young maiden who was dedicated from her birth to the cult of Diana. However, when she had grown up, her mother wanted her to marry a young man by the name of Cymedor. After the marriage, as the young couple was leaving the Temple, they were discovered by Diana who was violently enraged at their action. Her arrow pierced Roselia's heart and she sank to the ground, dead. When Diana saw Cymedor kneeling beside his dead bride, she repented of her dreadful deed and changed the girl's lifeless body into a beautiful bush of roses.

Venus was wont to sleep in a bed the pillows of which were daily filled with fresh rose petals. Ceres, the Goddess of the Harvest, was in the habit of decorating her basket of fruit with roses and anemones.

And it is said that the very word "rose" originated when Flora, the Goddess of Flowers, in pain upon being struck by Cupid's arrow, was unable to properly pronounce the word Eros but made it sound like "ros". From this the word "rose" becomes a synonym for Eros; both in Rome and in Greece it is the symbol of youth, of vitality, love, beauty and the fruitfulness of nature.

Bibliography, see page 39.

PLATE 1

Roman mosaic with a rose design from the 2nd century A.D. Found 1903/4 in the ruins of a luxurious Roman Villa in El-Djem in the east of Tunisia (formerly known as Thysdrus). (Now in the Museum at Aloui, from *Rosenzeitung*, 1913)

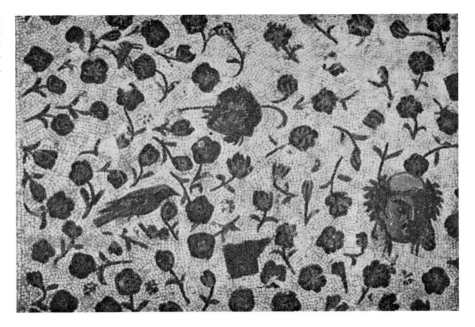

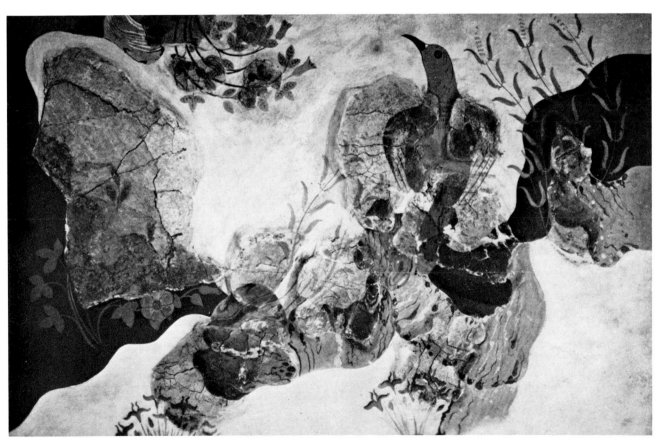

The famous fresco of the "Blue Bird" in the Palace of Knossos, Herakleion Museum, Crete. It was painted in the 16th century B.C. (See p. 28).

PLATE 2

Silver drachma coins from Rhodes; obverse, the head of Apollo; reverse, rose with grapes. (408-395 B.C.) (See p. 228)

Two drachma piece from Rhodes; obverse, the head of the Sun God; reverse, rose and buds, on the left a bunch of grapes and the letter "E". (See p. 228)

Bulgarian 10 stotinki coin of 1913, bearing a wreath of roses, laurel and ears of corn. (See p. 228)

Three and a half drachma piece from Rhodes; obverse, the head of the Sun God with rays; reverse, rose bloom with buds. (88-43 B.C.)

A drachma from Rhodes; the reverse shows a fully opened rose surrounded by seeds. (See p. 228)

The Order of the Rose of Lippe, W. Germany, given for services in the Arts and Sciences, First Class (obverse).

The Order of the Rose instituted by the Emperor Pedro of Brazil in 1829 to honor his wife, Amalia.

The Rose in the Classical Period up to 500 A.D.

1. Historical inscriptions on stone
2. Commemorative inscriptions and wall paintings
3. The Bible and other religious texts
4. Classical authors
5. Coins
6. Discoveries in tombs

Something must be said here about the "coins" of the Tsudes (or Tschudes)[1], an Aryan people, studied by Schleiden, whose graves date from about 3000 B.C.

This information comes from an anonymous article (probably by a college professor named Müller) in Johann Joseph Haigold's book *Beylagen zum Neuveränderten Russland* (Riga and Leipzig, 1770). In his article entitled "Old graves found in Siberia", he tells us about excavations or "prospecting" in the districts around Kolywana-Wosksenskoj-Zaweb in Siberia as follows:

Much that has been written on the early history of the rose, particularly that period which leads up to the birth of Christ, has proven to be contradictory. Sadly, it must be said that many of the authors in their works did not pay sufficient attention to, or perhaps did not know of, the work accomplished by men like C. C. Hurst, A. Wylie, E. T. Bechtel and others in this area. In addition to these works numerous archaeological and historical texts have been consulted for the information in this survey (see the bibliography at the end of the chapter).

Some of what is known about this period, has now been proven conclusively. Our knowledge of the particulars of the rose in the classical period comes from the following sources:

---

1 Tsudes or Tschudes is a comprehensive name for the Finnish-Hungarian peoples Ingerns, Livonians, Wespens and Wotens. "Burrowing" is the name that has been given to the information gleaned about these people, in workings which have extended up to 60 feet deep into pre-historic and early graves and underground passages where, in fact, prospecting was being carried out in both the Urals and Altai mountains for various metals.
BIBLIOGRAPHY: A.M. Tallgren in *Reallexicon der Vorgeschichte;* published by M. Erbert, 1925.

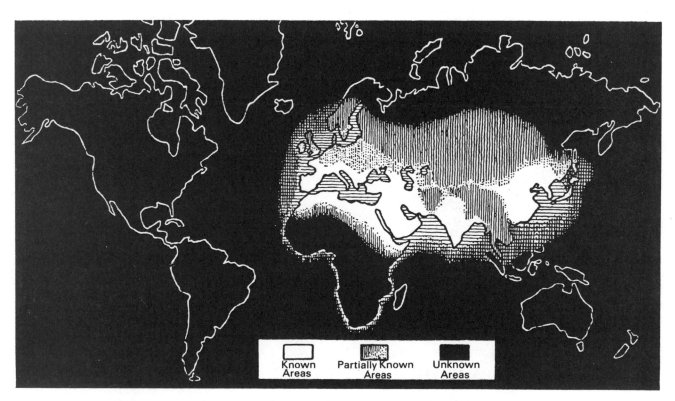

Known Areas   Partially Known Areas   Unknown Areas

Figure 13. Map of the World *ca.* 250 B.C. (according to Buschick, *Die Eroberung der Erde:* Hannover, 1930).

Figure 14. The world as known to Homer, 900 B.C. (according to R. Buschick, *Die Eroberung der Erde;* Hannover, 1930)

"There were also found a number of silver coins which carried no inscriptions. At the very least they are older than the introduction of the Mohammedan religion by the Tartars."

Schleiden also states that these "coins" might have "borne some impression of a full-blown rose". Unfortunately, we are not told where these "coins" are now preserved and positively identifiable coins are only known to exist from about 500 B.C. The oldest coins with impressions of roses upon them came from Rhodes between 400 B.C. and 80 B.C., while in N. Asia the earliest are of a much later date. With this knowledge the examples given by Schleiden must be suspect.

China It was probably in this country, with its ancient culture, that man first grew roses as garden plants. It is believed that it was during the reign of the legendary Chin-Nun (2737-2697 B.C.) that Chinese garden cultivation really began. Confucius (551-479 B.C.), the teacher and philosopher, wrote that a large number of roses had been planted in the Imperial gardens in Peking. Also there has come down to us, in the Imperial library, an extensive catalog of roses; elsewhere one reads of 600 works concerning the rose alone. It is therefore understood that what they are speaking of are general works on the subject of flowers, for the rose never played in China the great and important role of either the peony or *chrysanthemum.* A similar situation existed in Japan where the cherry tree was much more important than the rose.

During the Han dynasty (206 B.C.-8 A.D.) the number of Chinese pleasure gardens became so great that the agricultural production of the flat farmlands was seriously threatened. The Government was forced to close, or at least to reduce in size, many large gardens and parks in order to assure the population of a reasonable supply of food.

It is impossible to say just when the China and Tea roses were developed, but they must have been grown in China for at least 2,000 years. During that time, either through selection or hybridization, certain particularly beautiful varieties arose which, at the beginning of the 19th century, found their way to Europe. Many roses had been in cultivation in Chinese gardens for centuries before they became known in the West.

Persia. We know relatively little about the roses grown in the time of the Medes and Persians. We can be sure that the Persians had learned the art of obtaining rose water and Attar of Roses and they must, therefore, have been quite accustomed to rose cultivation. Joret (*op. cit.,* p. 14) says that N.E. Iran, particularly the area around Masenderan, was a veritable rose paradise where highly fragrant roses were extensively cultivated. This area could well have been the cradle of the European garden roses which, from here, traveled through the Middle East to Greece and to Mesopotamia, Syria and Palestine.

In many books on roses the rose is also referred to as the symbol of the power of the state in Persia. This use seems to have been introduced by Cyrus, King of the Persians, about the time of the overthrow of Babylon in 538 B.C.; it was his personal symbol of office. Staves or maces with silver roses, apples, lilies, eagles, etc. were used as tangible symbols of authority. In archaeological literature nothing has been said about this; all that one can see today of the various artifacts and memorial inscriptions which have come down to us are rosettes, not roses. These rosettes represent either lotus blooms or the flowers of the omnipresent *Chrysanthemum coronarium,* or they might even be purely geometric designs (see Figs. 16 & 17).

Assyria, Babylon and Mesopotamia The monuments, artifacts and wall paintings from Mesopotamia provide us with no evidence to support the belief that roses were

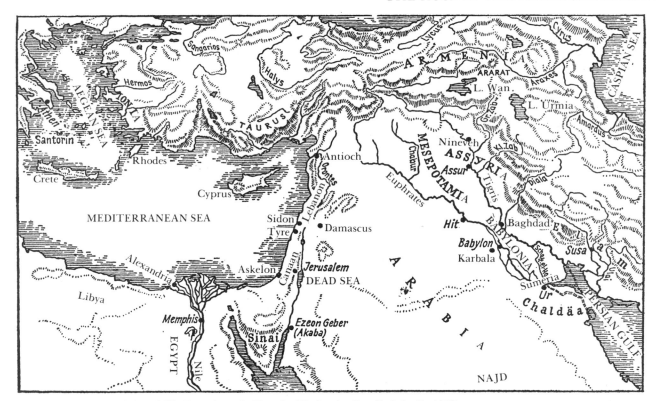

Figure 15. General Map of the Middle East. (from R. Hennig, *Wo lag das Paradies?;* Berlin 1950)

growing in this area at a very early date; they played no part as decorative or cultural items. Various examples from archaeological literature give a better impression of the history of that time and are complemented by various dates from other areas which do not have any direct bearing on roses.

Ca. 3500 B.C. The Sumerians moved from Central Asia to Mesopotamia.

Ca. 3000 B.C. The first Sumerian city states of Ur, Uruk, Kisch, Eridu and Nippur were formed, ruled either by Kings or Princely Priests; in Mesopotamia both barley and emmer wheat *(Triticum dicoccum)* were cultivated.

2800 to 2400 B.C. The first dynasty of Ur; the funeral sites of the Princes; the "Mosaic Symbol" of Ur has been found; royal headdress with plant motifs in gold.

2350-2170 B.C. The Akkadian Dynasty (Semitic); Sargon I (2350-2295), the supreme Overlord, traveled through the Middle East and the Mediterranean. During his invasion over the Taurus mountains (today part of Turkey), he took as booty from the Hittites, an ancient Aryan people of the Middle East,

two varieties of fig, vines and other plants which were brought back to his palace at Akkad. Also mentioned at this time were the pear tree and pistachio nuts. According to Weidener (1922) there is no mention of roses; the opposite is often cited in garden literature.

2250 B.C. The zenith of the Sumerian-Akkadian culture; discovery of the cuneiform writing of the Sumerians in Assyrian dialect which was the diplomatic language of the Near East at that time; it was also used in Syria, in most of the Middle East and in Egypt right up to the time of the birth of Christ, when already, ca. 1000 B.C., it had replaced Aramaic as the colloquial language. In cuneiform writing the first appearance of the rose is recorded for us by the English archaeologist Sir Leonard Woolley who, during his excavations of the Royal tombs at Ur in Chaldea, found clay tablets bearing inscriptions. The rose was apparently always known as *SILA-ŜAR* or *kasi ŜAR*. Nevertheless it is still only a "likely probability" that the rose is intended; the word appears only in connection with rosewater and Attar of Roses (R.C. Thompson 1949; pp. 194-199).

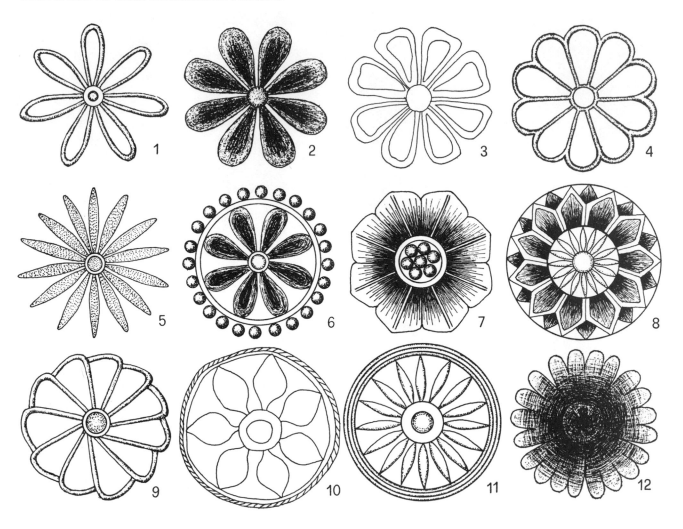

Figure 16. Use of the Rosette in Classical Art (1). (Original)

1 Rosette (Lotus bloom) on a proto-Attic vase of *ca.* the 8th-9th century B.C. (Louvre).
2 Rosette from the headband of a Hittite ruler (Lotus bloom); the petals are spoon-shaped, the center in the form of a button.
3 Rosette on a Hittite stone basin from Elbistan (Lotus ?); flat with incised lines.
4 Rosette on an Assyrian vase from Babylon, Temple of Nineveh (Lotus bloom ?); *ca.* 1000 B.C.; petals flat and bright blue, the center yellow with raised outline.
5 Rosette (Lotus bloom) on an amphora from Melos, Greece; 650 B.C. (National Museum, Athens).
6 Rosette on a stucco wall, the border of a representation of a Sassanid king hunting wild boar; 3rd to 7th century A.D., from the vicinity of Valamin near Teheran.
7 Rosette of a Lotus bloom from the same wall as No. 8.
8 Double rosette on a wall in Bodh Gaya, N. India; about the time of the Birth of Christ.
9 Rosette on a Hittite gold disk, probably the symbol of the Sun God; petals flat with raised edges; *ca.* 2000 B.C.
10 Rosette on an Etruscan vase of the 7th century B.C.; flat with only the edges incised.
11 Rosette from an Etruscan headstone of the 6th century B.C.; both the petals and the center are embossed, also the three rings on the perimeter.
12 Rosette from Hadrian's Arch in Antalya (Turkey); *ca.* 130 A.D.; cup-shaped, the petals with three deep incisions, the center button-shaped with five hollowed-out cavities.

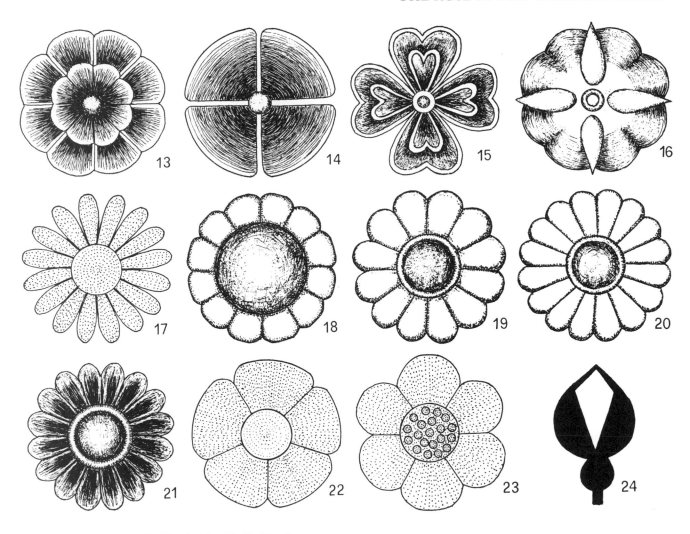

Figure 17. Use of the Rosette in Classical Art (2). (Original)

13 Rosette from a fragment of the Temple of Demeter at Eleusis near Athens (double poppies); 700 B.C.

14 Rosette in the fresco in the Villa of Boscoreale, Pompeii (destroyed 63 A.D.); from L. Curtius, *Die Wandmalerei Pompejis*. (Is this not more likely to be a poppy?)

15 Double cruciform rosette from a stucco wall (see also No. 6) 3rd to 7th century A.D.

16 Rosette from a golden bowl of the period of the Persian King, Khusrau II (590 - 628 A.D.); the decoration consists of three rings with 18 rosettes.

17 Rosette on a set of decorative wall tiles in the Palace of Nebuchadnezzar II, at Ischtar-Tor in Babylon; *ca.* 600 B.C. All the rosettes are white with yellow centers on a blue ground (therefore probably *Chrysanthemum coronarium*).

18 Rosette on a bronze door in Balawat, later Assyrian Kingdom, *ca.* 860 B.C.; petals in relief, the center button-shaped (probably *Chrysanthemum coronarium*).

19 Rosette from a ceremonial pedestal of King Tukultiminurtas I of Asshur (1235 - 1198 B.C.); the petals curved, the center circle in relief, the center itself in button form; middle period Assyrian. This rosette, with its 12 petals and central disk, is to be seen, in very similar form, in a relief on the canopy over the throne in the Room of a Hundred Pillars at Persepolis (550 - 351 B.C.), also in the Palace of Darius in Persepolis in a relief on the staircase in the Hall of Xerxes ("Lion attacking a Bull") and, finally, in the same building on the outside staircase ("The Payment of Tribute by the Syrians and Bactrians") (probably *Chrysanthemum*).

20 Rosette from the relief on the floor of the Palace of Assurbanipal in Nineveh; *ca.* 650 B.C. (probably *Chrysanthemum coronarium*).

21 Persian rosette from Susa, capital of the Achmenides; the petals concave and spoon-shaped, the center in button form with a raised ring; similar rosettes (probably *Chrysanthemum*) with 12 petals, but otherwise identical form, have been found at Persepolis. See No. 20.

22 Minoan rose with 5 petals in the Fresco of the Blue Bird in the Palace of Knossos, Crete; 1500 B.C.

23 Another rose from the same fresco at Knossos, but this time with 6 petals; 1500 B.C.

24 Rosebud on the lid of a Chaldaean crater; *ca.* 530-525 B.C. (in Würzburg).

Chaldaea is the Greek name for Babylon, that fruitful valley between the Lower Euphrates and the Tigris, close to the Persian Gulf, which today is the lowland region of Iraq.

2000 B.C. Babylon was founded on the Euphrates, about 80 km./50 mi. south of Baghdad, close to the modern town of Hillah, at the beginning of the century. It was destroyed by the Assyrians in the 7th century B.C. and then rebuilt around 605 B.C. with the so-called Tower of Babel which was some 90 m./294 ft. high.

1830-1530 B.C. First Babylonian dynasty; Hammurabi (1728-1686 B.C.) ruled all of Babylon, Assyria and Mesopotamia.

1700 B.C. (or perhaps earlier). The founding of Nineveh, the capital of Assyria on the east bank of the Tigris opposite what is now the modern town of Mosul; rosettes were sculpted in stone on the cornices and mouldings of the banquet halls; Delaporte draws our attention to a model in the Louvre of the ancient city of Nineveh which shows these "roses" and also a floor decoration with a design of six-petaled "roses", the border of which is decorated with lotus buds and flowers. In the year 602 B.C., Nineveh was destroyed by the Medes; it was never rebuilt.

1200 B.C. The Medes and Persians often used the rose on staves and maces as religious symbols; according to C.C. Hurst this could well have been a form of R.

gallica which probably had already appeared in a wild form in this area. (No illustration of any such item has ever been seen).

809-806 B.C. The country was ruled by Sammuramat, the mother of the Assyrian King Adadnirari, for just three years; she came from Babylon and is better known by her Greek name of Semiramis. Her Hanging Gardens are ascribed even today to Nebuchadnezzar II.

605-562 B.C. Nebuchadnezzar II of Babylonia. His reign marked the period of the greatest expansion of the Chaldean dynasty; he brought Babylon to its greatest architectural flowering through his enormous building program. His palace had four separate courtyards of which the third and largest was surrounded by yellow pillars which bore on an azure ground a wide band decorated with white "roses" with yellow centers, and blue lozenges set in yellow (according to Delaporte it seems absolutely certain that these were flowers of *Chrysanthemum coronarium* and not roses). At this time, it was the chrysanthemum flower and not the rose which was the most important floral motif in both art and architecture.

In the southern part of the city of Babylon were found what have become known all over the world as the famous Hanging Gardens of Semiramis; these wonders of the ancient world were buildings of arched construction covered with plants and featuring water courses.

Figure 18. The Mediterranean Area in the Classical Period. (Original)

"The Hanging Gardens have been for hundreds of years, maybe thousands, one of the greatest wonders of the world. Through legend they have always been connected with the name of Semiramis and they were allowed to fall into disrepair by Didor. The use of the word 'hanging' has greatly helped to enhance the fame of the building, although the expression 'cremastos' (= hanging) and 'pensilis' (= suspended, i.e. hanging from piers) was certainly not so much a wonder for the old technicians as it is for us. 'Pensilia' meant to the Romans 'balconies' and there was certainly nothing very astonishing about that in their case. What put the Hanging Gardens in the Seven Wonders of the World was the creation of a garden on the roof of a building itself in everyday use". (R. Koldewey, p. 100).

587 B.C. Jerusalem is completely destroyed; the Jewish upper classes were carried off into captivity in Babylon by Nebuchadnezzar.

539 B.C. Cyrus II, King of Persia, founder of the Persian Empire, overthrew Babylon and various Phoenician towns which he then incorporated into his own kingdom. He permitted part of the exiled Jewish community to return to Jerusalem. It was at this time that the "Hanging Gardens" were allowed to fall into decay.

The "rose" was made the symbol of office by Herod's decree (no representation of this symbol has ever been found in archaeological literature, Author).

331 B.C. The conquest of Babylonia by Alexander the Great.

Palestine Whether the Jews at the time of Solomon, who lived in the 10th century B.C. and was responsible for the building of the Temple between 962 and 955, actually knew about roses is still a controversy. Several extracts and references on this subject are given on page 56.

During the time of the Roman occupation of the Holy Land, however, roses were in great use for embellishment and decoration at festivals, particularly by the Romans themselves. These roses came either from nurseries at Rome or from Egypt.

Crete The oldest known representation of a rose was found by the British archaeologist, Sir Arthur Evans, during his excavations at Knossos.

Figure 19. The Island of Crete with the principal sites of excavation and citadels. 1. Knossos; 2. Phaistos; 3. Hag Triada; 4. Mallia; 5. Gurnia; 6. Tylissos; 7. Asomatos; 8. Gortyn; 9. Lyktos; 10. Lato; 11. Aptara; 12. Diktynnaion; 13. Mochlos. (according to Kirsten and Kraiker)

Knossos lies on the northern side of the island, directly south-east of Heraklion and was, at the time of King Minos, an important town although today nothing but ruins remain. The famous palace measuring just over 140 sq. m./1,495 sq. ft. was built between 2000 and 1700 B.C. and decorated with beautiful frescoes, some of which still exist. About 1450 B.C. the palace was destroyed by an exceptionally violent earthquake, but was soon rebuilt, then burned down and, towards the end of the 15th century B.C., was completely destroyed. The pinnacle of the Minoan culture, much evidence of which remains today, lasted from 1700 to 1400 B.C. The complete decay of the cultural sites in Crete began in about 1150 B.C. Excavations and partial restoration were carried out between 1898 and 1936.

In the House of Frescoes is found the famous "Fresco with Blue Bird" showing various flowers. About this fresco, Sir Arthur Evans writes (in *The Palace of Minos*, Vol. 2):

From the rocks grow wild peas or vetches — the pods shown simultaneously with the spiky flowers —clumps of what seem to be dwarf Cretan Irises, blue fringed with orange and, for variety's sake, pink-edged with deep purplish green. To the left, for the first time in Ancient Art, appears a wild rose bush, partly against a deep red, and partly against a white background, and other coiling sprays of the same plant hang down from a rockwork arch above. The flowers are of a golden rose colour dotted with deep red. The artist has given the flowers six petals instead of five, and has reduced the leaves to groups of three like those of the strawberry.

Much has been written about this picture of the rose from the 17th century B.C. by archaeologists and botanists and it has been proved to be a real puzzle. The yellow flowers and the bluish-green leaves look like *Rosa persica*, but the number of petals and leaflets are incomplete. Other botanists are of the view that it was a form of *Rosa gallica*, artistically altered and simplified. Möbius (1933), who revised Evans' interpretations of

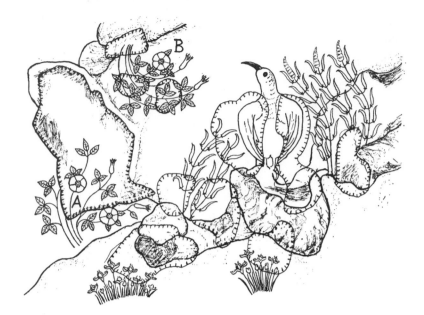

Figure 20. The famous "Fresco with Blue Bird" is in fact a reconstruction of various fragments which have been put together according to the whim of the restorer. No one knows whether the original really looked like this or whether the fragments even belonged in the positions in which they have been re-assembled. (Original)

the Minoan paintings, is convinced that the habit, the flowers, the buds with the somewhat protruding red tips of the petals, the many yellow anthers in the center as well as the clearly visible prickles are characteristic of a rose, but he thought it was probably a rose growing wild in Crete, perhaps *Rosa canina* or *R. dumetorum.*

Rona Hurst is more critical about the frescoes at Knossos (1967) and, as an expert in archaeology as well as botany, she points out that the great earthquake, *ca.* 1450 B.C., shattered the frescoes, the pieces of which were then restored in a way which combined little knowledge with much imagination. The empty places between the restored remnants of the frescoes were painted by someone who was certainly no expert. The new figures were much more stylized than the originals and the new colors are generally more brilliant than the rather faded 3,500-year-old originals; interestingly, frescoes from Egyptian tombs, which are even older, have not faded.

Rona Hurst, at the time of her visit to Crete in 1964, observed that the roses in the fresco were neither light brown nor yellow, but were clearly pink. Her husband, C.C. Hurst, had earlier identified these roses, when he saw them in England with Evans, as *Rosa sancta* (= *R. richardii*) the "Holy Rose" of Abyssinia and Egypt.

There is only one original rose in the fresco, (see Fig. 20), all the others were painted during the restoration. However, this original flower is pale pink, has five petals and looks like any other rose. When Evans (*op. cit.*) says that the blooms are of a beautiful golden rose color he did not mean the golden yellow which we know today but undoubtedly intended to imply that the newly painted roses had been given a golden sheen. Also, the Blue Bird has lost its original head which was also restored from the imagination.

To sum up, we can say, in agreement with Rona Hurst, that this fresco certainly represents a rose and that it is the oldest known picture of a rose. In the original, it was a light pink with five petals and three leaflets; possibly *Rosa richardii* (= *R. sancta*) or a form of *Rosa gallica.* That the remnants of the fresco were restored in the correct positions is very dubious. All that has been said by the botanists, including Möbius, refers to the roses which were later additions, not to the original fragment.

In Knossos Evans found pieces of pottery similar to the handles of cups, painted on the outside with a pattern of leaves and on the inside with a decoration in relief which ran down from the handle into the bowl of the cup. The stems represented bore five or seven leaflets, so they were described as roses by both Evans and Möbius, although both flowers and thorns were lacking (cf. Fig. 21).

Figure 21. Pottery flower vases in cup form; found in a stone cache in Knossos. The decorated branch painted on them has often been identified as representing a rose stem.

Finally, a find at Monastiraki in northern Crete produced a stone cover or lid from an early bronze age settlement. This cover of bright green steatite (soapstone) (Buchholz and Kragheorghis, No. 1,120) shows a five-pointed star deeply incised between the points, in the middle is a large knob which serves as a handle. This sample, although cracked, is strongly reminiscent of a single rose flower turned face down. (Fig. 22)

Greece The Mycenaeans who lived in what is now Greece at about 1400 B.C., were of different origins than the Greeks of a more ancient period. Their culture did not achieve the high standard of the Minoans in Crete. Theseus said that they were a subject people and had to pay tribute to the Greeks. Both Greeks and Mycenaeans could certainly write but they used their calligraphy only as a form of "bookkeeping". In Crete, which was overrun and conquered by the Mycenaeans in the 14th century B.C. a number of small tablets were found which modern scholars have been able to decipher. A very important find from the point of view of the rose dating *ca.* 1200 B.C., was found in the Palace of Nestor at Pylos in the Peloponnese. On one of these small tablets (a form of receipt or delivery note) notations were made concerning "rose-scented oil". On tablet No. 1,223 we read

To Ti-No, oil scented with sage for anointment . . . . LM 2
also rose-scented for anointment . . . . . LM 2
"LM" is, according to Young, a unit of measure; the

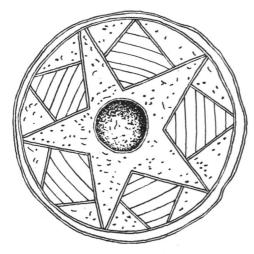

Figure 22. Cover in green soapstone (steatite) of the early Bronze Age from N. Crete. The star design is reminiscent of a rose bloom seen from beneath, showing calyx and petals; the center forms a knob to lift the lid. 15th century B.C. (Original)

exact quantity it represents is unknown, but it was probably about 11 l./3 gal. When the Palace of Nestor was destroyed by fire, in the 12th century B.C., these "delivery notes" were fused together in the great heat and thus preserved.

After the decline of Crete, there is no further information about roses for a long time. Homer, the legendary blind poet who lived in the 9th century B.C. and to whom we owe the *Iliad* and the *Odyssey,* was the first to cite the rose in Greek literature. He tells us that Hector, who was killed by Achilles during the siege of Troy (1206 B.C.), was rubbed with oil of roses after his death and then embalmed by Aphrodite in the Greek camp during the night. He goes on to say that Achilles' shield was decorated with roses. From this, we can conclude that the rose had been part of the general culture for some time and was probably already being widely grown in Greece.

Sappho, the famous Greek poetess, who lived on the island of Lesbos in the 8th century B.C. was the first to celebrate the rose in poetry. She called it the "Queen of Flowers" and so it has remained. From this point, many other poets have sung the praises of the rose.

Archilochus (719-663 B.C.), a poet from Asia Minor, paid special homage to the rose in his lyrics. Whether he knew the rose from seeing it growing in Greece or had seen it elsewhere on his travels is uncertain. In one poem he writes:

She held a spray of myrtle lightly in her hand
and with it the finest flowers of the rose

The poet Stesichorus (604-555 B.C.) who lived in Himera, the Greek colony on the north coast of Sicily, which was completely destroyed by the Carthaginians in 408, was the instigator of the heroic ballads and said that a wreath of roses should crown revellers' temples. We learn from Solon (640-560 B.C.), the Greek lawyer and administrator, that girls who had lost their virtue and were considered to be "fallen women" were forbidden to wear the rose wreath. Stesichorus also speaks of a "common woman" as follows:

dead must you lie and be forgotten, for in life
you were not decorated with the Roses of the Muses

By the year 500 B.C., rose cultivation in Greece must have been on a very large scale, for Pindar (520-447 B.C.), the musician and poet of Athens, described the city as follows:

The sweet scent of violets pervades the whole with
delight and roses crown the brow

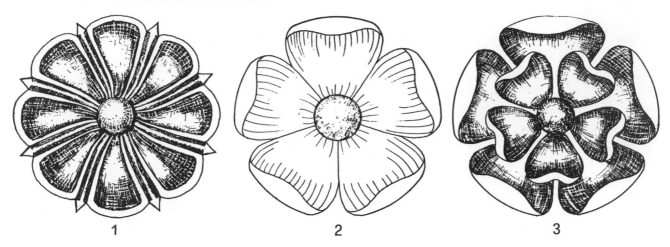

Figure 23. 1. Rosette from a capital on the Artemision (Temple of Diana) at Ephesus; 6th century B.C. (Br. Museum, London); 2. Rose (certainly not a rosette) from the hem of the garment on the great statue of Artemis before the Basilica at Ephesus; 4th century B.C. (?); 3. A form of double rose from the sarcophagus of Celsus Polemaeanus; in the Celsus library; *ca.* 135 A.D., founded by Celsus' son in memory of his father who lived to see its completion; also in Ephesus[1]. (Original)

No precise descriptions of roses have been found so we can only speculate on their appearance and which varieties were in cultivation.

We must spend more time considering the work of Anacreon (580-490 B.C.), the Greek lyric poet at the Court of Polycrates on Samos. He spoke of love and of wine and told the story of the mythical origins of the rose; how the sea foam which covered the Goddess Aphrodite (or Venus, as the Romans called her) as she rose from the waves, turned into white roses to cover her nakedness. Many authors of rose books call attention to the fact that Anacreon in his "Ode 51" produced the first poem dedicated to the rose. Translations of this are rare so it is printed here in its entirety:

> The Spring comes garland bearing,
> And wreath and blossom wearing;
> And we will aye be singing
> The Roses she is bringing,
> Come! Comrades! songs are ringing
> To Summer's Rose! Sweet Summer's Rose.
>
> Like Breath from heaven's own portals
> Come Roses bright to mortals;
> The Graces sound their praises:
> The Loves in flow'ry mazes,
> Each one, his voice upraises,
> To sing with joy Cithera's toy.

Plant pleasing to the Muses,
With love all song infuses;
The fragrance from its treasure
It pours with equal measure
On him, whose touch is pleasure,
Or him who strays in thorny ways.

The wise delight and revel
In Roses' bright apparel;
When purple wine is flowing,
When banquets loud are growing
The Rose from colours glowing,
Gives crimson leaves for wine-god's wreaths.

The Dawn is Rosy-fingered;
O'er nymphs have Rose tints lingered;
Love's colour, blooms yet clearer,
On Rosy-hued Cithéra!
What theme, to poets dearer
Than soft Rose light on Goddess bright.

This flower takes off diseases,
In sickness gently pleases;
Its old age cannot sever
The scent it loses never;
And dead, we keep for ever
The perfumed air of Roses fair.

Come! Hear! its birth I'm telling
When Pontus, from his dwelling
Brought forth Cithéra tender;
The blue seas did surrender
Love's Queen, who rose in splendour,
From laughing foam with Gods to roam.

When Zeus his Goddess shewing.
Who, from his brain was growing;
No longer he retained her,
But Queen of War! proclaimed her;

---

1 Ephesus, the original Ionian colony in Asia Minor, had already been settled by 1200 B.C.; it later became the most important city in Asia Minor of the ancient world. The Temple of Artemis (Diana) which was founded in the 6th century B.C. has always been regarded as one of the Seven Wonders of the World.

Athéne! Great! he named her;
And forth she came, War-Queen to reign.

The Earth her bloom unfolded,
And sprays of blossom moulded;
Her glowing Roses forming
With colours from the morning,
Made flowers for Gods adorning —
Thus Earth did bear the Rose Gods wear.

(Trans. Mrs. Herbert Hills, 1884)

Now we come to Herodotus (490-*ca.*420 B.C.), regarded as the "Father of Historians". He described the famous "Rose with 60 petals" of King Midas of Phrygia, a country in Asia Minor which was under Lydian and Persian rule during the 6th century B.C. King Midas went into exile in Macedonia, but managed to take his roses with him. Herodotus, a native of Halicarnassus in Caria, also in Asia Minor, must have been accustomed to roses from his youth on. He tells us of the beautiful garden belonging to Midas in Macedonia; the 60-petaled roses were more strongly scented than any which he had previously encountered.

Originally it was thought that this was probably *Rosa centifolia*, but today there is general agreement that it was a fully-petaled form of *Rosa gallica* or a very double *Rosa alba* which were both in existence at that time.

Alexander the Great (356-323 B.C.) undoubtedly brought back with him from the East, after his various military expeditions and conquests, both seeds and plants, amongst which there must have been some roses.

The next important source of information is Theophrastus (372-287 B.C.), known as the "Father of Botany". He makes a clear distinction between the two types of rose, namely *rhodon*, roses with double flowers (see the quotation from his work at the end of this section) and *kynosbaton*, the dog or wild rose, *Rosa canina,* and its various forms. Furthermore, he says that the inhabitants of the Christian community of Philippi (known today as Felab), founded in 356 B.C. by Philip II of Macedonia, collected the roses growing wild in the area on the slopes of Mount Pangaeus and planted them in their gardens. It is also likely that it was here or nearby that King Midas' rose garden was situated. The roses themselves were likely to have been some form of *Rosa gallica,* or double forms of it. When Theophrastus, and later Pliny, wrote of the "hundred-petaled rose" *(Rosa centifolia* or *rhóda hekatontóphylla)* we are incorrect in supposing these roses to be the same as our *Rosa centifolia* as has so often been erroneously stated. *Rosa centifolia* is a child of our time, a complex hybrid, which was bred in the 16th century in Holland and propagated and disseminated from that country.

There are other points from Theophrastus which need clarification: in his description of the methods of cultivation of roses in his time, he compares the method of propagation from seed with the new practice of division. It is stated in old text books that the Greeks were in the habit of lifting their roses yearly and replanting them, what this undoubtedly meant is this division of the plants, since at that time the method of budding was not known. Perhaps the plants themselves were of such strong growth that it was possible to take layers or runners from them yearly. It is also incorrect that the Greeks "burned off" their roses each year, had they done so they would not have had any crop of bloom. This is either a case of misunderstanding or bad translation; in an old French book Pliny reports Theophrastus as saying that "the roses were pruned back each year and consigned to the bonfire", just as we do today with our prunings. From this however, we can see that the rose was quite important in Greece at that time.

Theophrastus also discussed roses in Egypt which came into bloom some two months earlier than in Europe. Thirty years later Callixenes of Rhodes gives similar information. From these dates we can conclude that roses must have been introduced into Egypt about the year 300 B.C.; from where is unknown, although it may have been from Greece.

In Athens, Epicurus (341-271 B.C.) had his own rose garden created, within the city, in order to have a constant supply of fresh blooms. This was undoubtedly the most important private rose garden of that time.

The Island of Rhodes was also so rich in rose cultivation that, by the 4th century B.C., coins were being struck there which bore pictures of a rose (Plate 2).

Theocritus of Syracuse (*ca.* 305-270 B.C.). the founder of the school of Greek pastoral poetry, sang the praises and beauties of the garden roses.

Dioscurides (1st century A.D.) wrote an important work (*Materia Medica* or "The Basic Description of the Medicinal Drugs, in 6 Books") which appeared in a German translation in 1546 and, at that time, was completely up to date; in this book numerous methods of using roses, both for healing and for beauty treatment, are detailed.

Finally, we turn to our last Greek author, Plutarch (46-120 A.D.), the Greek historian who observed that garlic was customarily planted near rose bushes because it was believed that this increased their fragrance!

We know a little more of the relationship between the ancient Greeks and the rose. As an artistic people they appreciated roses with their noble, perfect flowers. There was very little room for private rose gardens in their cities. The streets were narrow so the richer citizens built the back of their houses on to the streets and the living rooms looked out on to the gardens at the rear where there were borders with lilies, violets, roses and other flowers. It was generally believed, at the time, that the scent of the flowers helped to keep the household healthy. The private garden was the preserve of the lady of the house. However, there were other gardens where small rose bushes with exceptionally fine blooms were cultivated; these were known as "Gardens of Adonis". Such rose bushes were often planted in silver pots and in this way container culture of roses began, as Theophrastus tells us. Later, even roof gardens came into fashion.

Theophrastus was a very acute observer. He writes of roses in his time as follows:

"The roses differ in the number of their petals; some have five, others twelve or twenty, a few even have as many as a hundred. But they differ also in their beauty, in their color and in the sweetness of their scent. Some are coarse and in the case of the large-flowered fragrant roses the calyx below the bloom is rough. The sweetest scented roses come from Cyrene."

In another passage, he writes that the roses have red, pink and white flowers. Regarding the highly scented roses, this could be a form of *Rosa damascena*, but what he means by the "roses of Cyrene" is still unclear. Cyrene was a Greek colony founded in the 7th century B.C. in N. Africa; it was later known as Cyrenaica, the district around the modern town of Benghazi.

Rome Information about the rose in ancient Rome is so extensive that the material must be broken down into sections in order to put it into perspective. Therefore, what follows is a chronological account of the rose taken from ancient Roman literature from the 3rd century B.C. to the fall of the Empire. An entire section will be devoted to Pliny because he wrote so much about roses. Finally, there is a section on the rose in daily life, on rose cultivation and the rose garden in

Figure 24. *Rosa foetida;* taken from a drawing in Dioscurides' *Materia Medica* dated 512 A.D.

Rome.

a. *Chronological details from Roman literature.*

The rose was well known early on in Rome. It was introduced by the Greek settlers who also formed colonies in N. Africa, Sicily and Spain.

It is likely that the rose also reached both Gaul (France) and England through the services of Greek travelers.

Marcus Porcius Cato (234-149 B.C.), the Senator and Roman statesman, tried to halt the general moral decay which was occurring in Rome. One of his complaints was that roses were awarded for all, even the most trivial, military triumphs, and that this cheapened its value as a symbol of high honor. Nevertheless, he encouraged the planting and cultivation of roses in every private garden, in order to satisfy the enormous demand for blooms for wreaths and garlands.

The wearing of rose chaplets was forbidden in time of war. When, during the second Punic War (218-201 B.C.), Lucius Flavius, a money-lender, was seen at the window of his shop in broad daylight wearing a garland of roses on his head, the Senate had him thrown into prison immediately.

Marcus Tullius Cicero (106-43 B.C.), the famous Roman orator and politician, accused the disloyal Governor of Sicily, Caius Cornelius, of an excessively luxurious way of life and of extorting enormous sums of money from the Sicilian people, but particularly condemned him for his habit during his travels in the countryside, of sitting on a cushion stuffed with rose petals and wearing a wreath of roses on his head. To make matters worse he also held a small smelling-bag of rose petals under his nose!

Varro (117-28 B.C.) tells us in his book, *Res Rustica*, the contemporary method of rose propagation. Virgil (70-19 B.C.), whose full name was Publius Vergilius Maro, the Roman poet, wrote many poems on the general subject of agriculture; more will be said about him and his work shortly (p. 35).

Horace, Quintus Horatius Flaccus (65-8 B.C.), also a Roman poet, observed how the ever-increasing cultivation of the rose was taking place at the cost of reducing the corn harvest (*Odes* II 15, 5). In spite of these protests, it was blithely continued.

The period from 43 B.C. to 14 A.D. is called the Golden Age of Ancient Rome. Ovid, Publius Ovidius Naso (43 B.C.-18 A.D.), the Roman poet, mentions the "Rose of Enna" in Sicily.

At the time of Gaius Octavianus Augustus (63 B.C.-14 A.D.), the first Roman Emperor, roses were still regarded as something of a luxury but they quickly became a necessity in the course of daily life. It was customary to create private rose gardens in order to enjoy their fragrance and to have a ready supply of fresh-cut blooms. It even became fashionable to take a holiday in Paestum at the time that the roses were in bloom. Everywhere in the house and at the table roses were in daily use. They were used at funerals and the Romans went so far as to institute a special rose festival in honor of the dead.

Lucius Annaeus Seneca (3 B.C.-65 A.D.), Roman philosopher and the teacher of Nero, who committed suicide on Nero's orders, wrote a very important work entitled "An Enquiry into the Natural Sciences" which remained the general text book on physics into the Middle Ages. He also described a method of forcing roses with warm water and of their cultivation in "forcing houses". From him, we have some information regarding the Sybarites (the inhabitants of the city of Sybaris, today Sibari, on the river of the same name in Lucania in Southern Italy, which, in 510 B.C., was destroyed by the Greeks) who were noted for their gluttony and lasciviousness. It was said of them that when a Sybarite saw a slave at work, he "broke out into a sweat". One, Sminirides, complained that he could not sleep at night, because in his bedroom strewn with rose petals, he had lain on a single folded petal which had been so uncomfortable that it had kept him awake.

Regarding Pliny, who lived from 23-79 A.D., more will be said shortly. Here it is sufficient to note that he describes Albion (Britain) as the "Island of White Roses" and believed that the name had been given because of the white roses growing there. The consensus of opinion today, however, is that the name Albion is an older, perhaps pre-Celtic, name for Britain (excluding Ireland) and that it probably comes from the white cliffs of Dover. "Albion" had already been written about by the Roman poet Avienus in the 6th-5th centuries B.C. It must be said here, however, that some authorities deny that Albion and Britain are one and the same.

Now we come to Lucius Domitius Ahenobarbus Nero (37-68 A.D.), the cruel and spendthrift Roman Emperor who, at a single famous banquet, spent no less than 4,000,000 sesterces (about $400,000) on the supply of roses. On another occasion he gave instructions that the beach at the city of Baiae should be strewn with countless roses; this probably cost him in the region of $225,000.

He especially liked, and in this was imitated by later Emperors, to produce at his banquets and orgies a rain of roses falling from the ceiling upon his guests and, on occasion, in such vast quantities that some of the guests were stifled under the weight of petals. In order to supply this immense quantity of flowers, extensive nurseries were needed and the majority of these were situated in the area around Paestum.

Martial, Marcus Valerius Martialis (41-100 A.D.), a Roman poet born in Spain, tells us to what extent the cultivation had grown in his time in the following couplet:

O Nile, the Roman Roses are now much finer than thine!
Your Roses we need no longer; but send us your corn.

33

In spite of this, roses were still imported from Egypt. Martial tells us of a ship which carried rose blooms together with other gifts from Memphis in the Nile delta to the Emperor Domitian and how disconcerted the Egyptians were to find roses blooming everywhere in Rome! It was undoubtedly this incident that moved Martial to write the verse quoted above.

In the time of Domitian, Titus Flavus Domitianus (51-96 A.D.), Emperor of Rome 81-96 A.D., Rome was a fragrant sea of roses, as we are told by some of its inhabitants.

Tacitus (55-115 A.D.), the Roman author, tells us that after the battle of Bedriacus, between Cremona and Verona, the Emperor Vitellius, who was notorious for his debauchery and indolence in state affairs, visited the battlefield. Tacitus was filled with righteous anger for, as the Emperor walked through the unburied piles of soldiers' corpses, his way was strewn with laurels and with roses and the roses were thereby dishonored and degraded.

Lucius Junius Moderator Columella *ca.* 60 A.D., a Roman real estate owner, was the author of 12 books on the subject of agriculture. In these he provides information on the cultivation of the roses which came into flower late in season. This method of cultivation differs from that used by the Greeks. He states, as Varro had done a hundred years before, that the bushes should be pruned every year before the beginning of March and he adds that with good cultivation the plants will last for many years. From this we can conclude that the rose bushes were always carefully pruned, but were never cut down to ground level.

Pliny the Younger (61-113 A.D.) describes in his letters his two properties at Tusci and Laurentinum; in Tusci he had a rose garden and he had selected the sunniest spot for planting the bushes.

Lucianus (120-180), a Greek author and itinerant teacher in Italy and Gaul, criticized with heavy irony the foibles of his time and how the Romans thought nothing of their roses in summer and then immediately longed for them in winter.

As has been said above, it was customary at the more ostentatious feasts for the guests to be showered with rose petals from the ceiling. When Heliogabalus (204-222),who came from Emasa in Syria and was the High Priest of the Sun God, became Roman Emperor at the age of 14, he wanted his reign to begin with a special and outstanding feast. He arranged for three showers of rose petals to fall so thickly and speedily that many of his guests suffocated; the Emperor had earlier ordered that all the doors be bolted and barred so that no one was able to escape.

Our last author must be Palladius, Rutilius Taurus Aemilianus. A landed proprietor of the 4th century A.D., he tells us much about roses in his 14 books on agriculture and horticulture; he maintained that they should be planted in February or March, either as cuttings or sown directly from seed. The soil around established plants should be well hoed and any weak or bad stems should be cut away. Elsewhere, he says that the cuttings can also be set out in the ground in November. Early flowers can be obtained by sprinkling the plants with warm water; the soil should be a light, moist loam, though he continues that the flowers would be especially fragrant if grown under dry conditions. It was very important to choose a sunny position and apply plenty of manure.

These directions for cultivation must have been heeded for after the complete collapse of the Roman Empire, 476 A.D., there were still a great many roses grown. They probably continued to be cultivated mostly in the monasteries and then not only for the sake of the flowers, but for the many medicinal attributes which were claimed for both the flowers and the hips.

b. *Pliny the Elder and the Roses of his Day*

This author produced a Natural History in 37 volumes; he lived to see only the first 10 completed, the remaining 27 appeared after his death. He died in 79 A.D., the year of the great eruption of Vesuvius when Herculaneum and Pompeii were destroyed. At this point, it is necessary to go into some detail and to quote directly from Pliny's text; some critical comment is also called for. The rose is dealt with in Volume 21, Chapter 10 and therein he writes as follows:

> Our countrymen know among garden plants very few kinds of chaplet flowers, practically violets only and roses. The rose grows on what is not so much a shrub as a thorn, appearing also on a bramble (i.e. a wild rose, Ed.); there too it has a pleasant, if faint, perfume.

> The most famous kinds of roses recognised by our countrymen are those of Praeneste and those of Campania. Some have added the Milesian rose, because of its brilliant fiery color, though it never has more than 12 petals.

> Next after it is esteemed the Trachinian, of a less brilliant red, and then the Alabandian, less highly prized, with whitish petals; the least prized, having very many, but very small petals, is called the prickly rose.

Those with the fewest petals have five, but in other roses they are more numerous, since there is one kind called the hundred-petalled rose. In Italy this grows in Campania, but also in Greece around Philippi, which however, is not its native soil.

Mount Pangaeus in the neighbourhood grows a rose with many but small petals. The natives transplant it, improving the variety by mere change of of place.

(Trans. W.H.S. Jones Litt. D., F.B.A. Cambridge, Mass. 1951)

Many botanists have tried to identify the roses mentioned by Pliny. Today we believe that this has been achieved and that they are the following:

The Rose of Praeneste; this was the most highly prized of all and the last to come into flower (= *Rosa gallica*).

The Rose of Campania, also very highly thought of, with bright green or bluish foliage and white, scented flowers (= *Rosa alba*).

The Rose of Trachys (from the town of Heraclea Trachys). It bore pink flowers (probably *R. damascena*).

The Rose of Miletus; the flowers were a bright red with no more than 10 petals, late flowering (= *R. gallica*).

The Rose of Cyrene; in general the most fragrant, it gave ointment of outstanding quality (= *R. moschata* ?).

The Rose of Pangaeus; a wild species originating in the area of Mount Pangaeus near Philippi, was dug up by the local inhabitants and planted in their gardens (= *R. gallica*).

Alabandica (from Alabana in Caria); carrying many whitish flowers, not so generally popular (probably *R. alba* or a form of it).

Coroniola. The "Autumn Rose", medium-sized blooms, identification uncertain, probably *Rosa sempervirens*; the flowers were extensively used for small chaplets.

Spineola. The "Thorny Rose". Only very briefly described; authorities think that it may well have been *R. pimpinellifolia* var. *myriacantha* which formerly was widespread in both Northern Italy and Southern France.

The "Hundred-petaled Rose". This was to be found not only in Campania, but also in Greece at Philippi and is very often "identified" without a moment's hesitation as *Rosa centifolia*. However, the modern *centifolia* is quite different; the old "hundred-petaled" rose is really *Rosa damascena*. Apparently, it was never used for making wreaths or garlands."

Graecula. The little Greek rose; probably *R. canina*.

Graeca. *Lychnis* in Greek. This was not a rose but was *Agrostemma coronaria*.

Macetum. "Its stems resemble that of the mallow and the leaves remind us of the olive". Some botanists believe that this was *Rosa moschata* while others think that it was, in fact, a mallow, *Alcea rosea*.

c. *The "Rose of Paestum"*

Much that has been written about the "Rose of Paestum" is now known to be false; N. Young (*q.v.*) has detailed all the mis-information for us:

Probably the oldest and best-established of these ghost roses is the Rose of Paestum, that perpetual flowering rose which, we are so often told, flourished in classical times, and was mentioned by Vergil. It was not mentioned by Vergil. The sole justification for this claim lies in three words, in which the poet makes a passing reference to biferi rosaria Paesti — 'the rose-gardens of twice-bearing Paestum'. The epithet "twice-bearing' (which is not attached to any particular rose, be it noted, nor even to the rose-gardens, but to the City of Paestum) is obviously ambiguous; it might mean twice in time or twice in quantity. But some five hundred years later, an obscure scholar named Servius, who took it upon himself to edit the works of Vergil, set against this passage the gloss: 'Paestum, a City of Calabria where roses blow twice in a year'. From this point the myth-makers have never looked back.

Not only did Vergil make no mention of the Rose of Paestum; what is much more important is that Pliny, the great Natural Historian, who listed all the roses known to the Roman world of his day, made no mention of it either. Pliny was born some forty years after the death of Vergil, and must have been perfectly familiar with the reference to the roses of Paestum to be found in his works, and those of Horace, Ovid and many lesser writers. Paestum was a famous and flourishing centre of the rose trade, and the 'roses of Paestum' meant no more then than we should mean today by the 'cabbages of Covent Garden'. Paestum was the best-known source of roses, but it produced no special variety of its own, perpetual or once-flowering. In describing the town as 'twice-bearing' Vergil probably meant no more than 'fruitful' or 'prolific'. Nevertheless, it is always possible that his 'twice' was meant to refer to time rather than quantity, and that his commentator Servius spoke nothing but the truth. The Romans — as we also learn from Pliny — were familiar with methods of forcing roses by heat, and in an important entrepot like Paestum there would have been two rose harvests, one forced and one natural. It would therefore have been quite correct to say that in Paestum 'roses blow twice in a year' — only it was not the same roses which flowered both early and late.

Today, most authorities believe that the "Rose of Paestum" was a form of *Rosa damascena*.

d. *The Rose and Its Use in Ancient Rome.*

So much is known in this field that it could fill a long chapter without any difficulty; in order to avoid repetition only that which does not appear elsewhere in this book will be said here.

Rose Culture and The Rose Trade. The center of rose

growing in the Ancient World was Paestum about 60 miles south of Naples in Lucania on the Gulf of Salerno. Paestum was founded *ca.* 600 B.C. by the Greeks as their city of Poseidonia. About the year 270 B.C., the city was taken over by the Romans who found the famous rose gardens. We are told by the Latin poets that the sale of roses was often left to the prettiest girls in the district. It was customary among the upper classes to go to Paestum when the roses were in bloom. The cultivation of roses for profit was called *roseta* which must be carefully distinguished from *rosaria* which were the rose gardens serving purely decorative purposes.

When we visit Paestum today to see the splendid ruins of the old temples, we find a marshy stretch of land which no longer bears any resemblance to the exceptionally fertile coastal strip of former days. The reason for this is that the river Silarus (now the Sele) became choked with mud during the fall of the Roman Empire and turned into a swamp, which put an end to large-scale rose cultivation.

Visitors to the Temples find it hard to understand why the Italian authorities planted modern roses on this historic site. After many protests, this anachronism is now to be rectified and the beds will be replanted with *Rosa damascena*.

Almost as well known as Paestum for rose growing was the small town of Praeneste, today called Palestrina, about 13 km./20 mi. south-east of Rome, where mostly the late-flowering *Rosa gallica* was cultivated. The fields themselves must have stretched right up to the city boundary. Yet a third center lay in the vicinity of Leporia from which the roses of Campania came. This area extended from the highway between Cumae and Puteoli up to Capua, about 20 km./30 mi. north of Naples.

Of all the private rose gardens, those of Lucullus (117-57 B.C.), the Roman General, at Baiae on the sea coast near Naples, where he owned a luxurious villa, are worthy of special mention. Equally famous were the gardens of Tarquinius Superbus in Rome.

Here it will be helpful to quote from Friedländer (1934) concerning the gardens in Rome.

> Everywhere the great mass of buildings was broken up and bordered with the green of the gardens and parks. At all times of the year the brightness of green foliage was to be seen on every side. The Esquiline was covered with the gardens of Maecenas, Epaphroditus, Torquatus and others and also by an extensive park; the gardens of Acilier, Lucullus and Sallust covered the whole of the lower slopes of Monte Pincio and the surrounding valleys so that from the modern Porto del Popolo to the Santa Croce in Gerusalemme there seemed to be a single colossal park, broken only by the Baths of Diocletian. Also, the outer precincts of the palaces had extensive gardens with fine old trees, alive with the song of birds; the Lotus trees (i.e. *Celtis*) were especially popular on account of the shade which they gave to these town gardens. Six of these trees, in the garden of the orator Crassus on the Palatine Hill, (in 92 B.C.) were considered to be as fine as the Palace itself, which was destroyed 150 years later in Nero's fire. Even from the roofs and from the balconies, flowers and sweet smelling bushes distributed their fragrance. Particularly on the right bank of the Tiber and the surrounding hills, stretched out marvellous gardens, some of which were Imperial property. Such places were much visited by the public.

The rose gardens in Ancient Rome were, so we are told by the antiquarian authorities, composed of hedges and divided up into beds in which individual rose bushes were planted.

In order to obtain rose blooms in winter, the practice of forcing in special houses had already commenced. This involved treating roses grown under glass with warm water to bring on the blooms. This was such a wonder that it was highly praised by the poets Virgil, Ovid and Horace. In roses grown in the open, the blooms were brought on early by digging trenches between the rows of plants, or around them; these trenches were then filled with warm water twice daily.

Even with these methods, however, supply could not approach the public demand for roses. It must be remembered that this ancient method of cultivation should not be compared with our modern means of cut flower production and also that the production was probably, in fact, quite small by our standards.

There remained nothing else for them to do but to import cut roses to fulfill their requirements. This was possible from areas with warmer climates, of which the most important was the Nile delta in Egypt and, secondarily, Carthage. Whole shiploads came directly to Rome from Egypt; this journey took six days. How the blooms were kept fresh over this relatively long period of time is unknown today. Nero was supreme in his demand for roses in winter. However, in the winter of 89-90 A.D. so many roses were brought from Paestum to Rome, that the streets were literally red with rose wreaths and Egypt, which usually exported roses in winter, could have imported them on this particular occasion from Paestum, according to Martial.

Egypt Of roses in the time of the Pharoahs, nothing is known with any real certainty.

At the time when the famous frescoes in the Palace of

PLATE 3

'Blush China' from a painting on silk with a deer; Huan Ch'uan, 965 (detail)

Turkish-Cypriot plate with rose decoration; early 15th century (Victoria & Albert Museum, London)

Rose. Detail of a painting by Chan Ching-Feng, on silk; 16th century, Ming Dynasty (from H.L.Li.)

Rosa rugosa, from a Chinese painting ("New Year's Day") Chao Ch'ang (*ca.* 1000)

PLATE 4

Chinese Rose Garden

Two Lovers in a Rose Arbor from the *Roman de la Rose*

(These two illustrations are taken from *History of Garden Art* by M.L. Gothein)

The "Rose Garden" in the Dolomites, Gruppos del Catinaccio with the Torri del Vajolet, 2,926 m./9,600 ft.

Minos in Crete were first completed, Egypt was ruled by Queen Hatshepsut (1490-1496 B.C.). She sent her fleet out to the land of Punt, on the African coast of Somalia, in order to collect plants for her palace garden, and myrrh, a gum resin. Paintings which represent this expedition can still be seen in Hatshepsut's palace on the west bank of the Nile opposite Luxor, but there are no roses in the drawings.

King Tuthmosis III, the stepson and successor of Hatshepsut, undertook a campaign against Syria, *ca.* 1450 B.C., at the end of which he returned with much booty, including at least 275 different varieties of plants. The King was so delighted about this that he had all these plants sculpted in relief at Karnak, a town in Upper Egypt on the right bank of the Nile near both Luxor and Thebes, with details of them recorded in hieroglyphics. They may now be seen in the "Botanical Room", a side room of Tuthmosis' feasting chamber at the east end of the great Temple of Ammon at Karnak. Although the King was determined that these reliefs should be as life-like as possible, modern botanists are not convinced that they are completely correct. G. Schweinfurth attempted an interpretation of all these sculptures (1919); V. Täckholm has also written about them. Had there been roses in the collection, they would certainly have been depicted. In light of this, it seems quite unlikely that roses were known in Egypt at that time.

Woenig (1897) who studied the plants of Ancient Egypt, asserts that roses were unknown until the year 631 B.C. for there is no mention of them in the papyrus scrolls. Therefore the Coptic word *ouert, ourt, or werd* put forward by Schleiden which appears in the old hieroglyphic writings of the 14th century B.C. may well not be correctly interpreted; it is shown here in Fig. 8. Woenig (*op. cit.,* 18) believes that roses were not grown in Egypt before the time of Ptolemy, in the 4th century B.C., and then only in the Nile valley.

Alexander the Great (356-323 B.C.), King of Macedonia, came to Egypt, more as liberator than as conqueror, in 332 B.C. He installed his favorite, Ptolemaeus, who founded the Lagidian dynasty which lasted for some 300 years, and instituted a form of Greek government. The Greeks must have brought with them the roses which they had long cultivated and which were so beloved and highly praised.

For a long time nothing is heard about roses in Egypt, except that they were exported to Rome in large quantities. Whether the ruling classes followed the prevailing fashion of the "Rose Cult" is unknown. There is only one recorded fact in this connection: when Cleopatra VII (69-30 B.C.) went to meet her lover, Marcus Antonius, in 42 B.C., she gave a state banquet in his honor; the floor of the hall was covered to a depth of two feet in roses. According to other sources, it was the throne room rather than the banquet hall which was filled with flowers, for which Cleopatra paid out the equivalent of $750 in gold. Whether this "knee-deep rose carpet" originated in Egypt, where roses were plentiful, and was then adopted by the Romans, is unclear.

Both then and later, the rose was represented in all official ceremonies in Egypt just as it was in Greece and in Rome; almost all wreaths and garlands were made of roses, while the Lotus flower, which until then had been used almost exclusively for such purposes, was eclipsed and soon forgotten.

The exact regions in which roses were grown in Egypt during the period of the Roman Empire is unknown. However, Dr. Girardi, leader of the scientific mission which followed Napoleon's invasion of Egypt in 1800, said then that there was still an important area of rose cultivation some 500-750 acres in size in the vicinity of Medin-el-Faiyum and that there were also about 30 ovens for the distillation of rosewater for the wealthy members of the local population. By degrees, however, rose growing diminished and was supplanted by cotton production.

Pliny reported that the ancient Egyptians were capable of producing artificial flowers, including roses. The flower petals were cut out of very thin woodshavings, then colored and scented with rose balm. Later such artificial flowers were also made from paper and other materials and exported to Greece and Italy.

Finally, something must be said about the "Holy Roses" that have existed in Egypt for at least 2,000 years.

When, in 1888, archaeologists were excavating an old Egyptian tomb, dating from about the time of the Birth of Christ, at Hawar in the district of Faiyum, they found a wreath of roses which had remained in good condition. They sent this material for identification to Kew, London, and also to one of the most knowledgeable rose experts of the day, F. Crépin, in Brussels. He identified it as *Rosa sancta* (= *R. richardii* Rehd.) a close relative of *Rosa gallica* with single, pale pink blooms which undoubtedly is not indigenous to Egypt but must have been brought there from Asia Minor.

THE ROSE IN THE CLASSICAL PERIOD

The German Professor, G. Schweinfurth, who spent nearly his entire life in Egypt, found such roses in graves in Middle Egypt and even representations of roses on frescoes and on fabric, but they were generally single blooms with just five petals. Therefore it is certain that the Egyptians grew the same varieties as the Greeks and that in addition to the native roses they also had *R. gallica, R. damascena* and the "hundred-petaled rose".

The "Holy Rose" (*R. richardii*) of the Egyptian graves, still grows today, although not as abundantly as it did a hundred years ago. In 1920 a monk stated that the "Holy Rose" was to be found at Mau-Tsada, a mountain village at 2,427 m./8,000 ft. in Northern Ethiopia. Formerly, this rose grew wherever there was a church, but today virtually the only remaining plants are those few in Mau-Tsada. Those flowers not eaten by the local goats are collected by the priests and mixed with incense.

THE ROSE IN DAILY LIFE

The rose gardens, the sacred grove of roses, the legendary rose gardens of Venus, etc. were the chief means whereby roses were produced for the decorations at festivals of both rooms and guests, for important ceremonial presentations, for the needs of personal cleanliness, for the decoration of tombs and, finally, for religious sacrifices and funeral services. Never before or since has the world known a time in which the rose played so great and important a role as it did during the period of the Roman Empire.

During festivals, not only were homes decorated with roses, but the streets were strewn with blooms, monuments and statues of the Gods were crowned with garlands and wreaths. At such times, people wore wreaths and chaplets of roses, even the slaves and the street musicians; these wreaths were made, not only of complete flowers, but also of individual petals and were considered a particularly dignified form of adornment. The custom of using crowns of roses had been adopted by the Romans from the Greeks, but it was also customary among the ancient Hebrews. The theory that the Babylonians also wore similar rose wreaths must be questioned because they had no known source of roses.

Those who were wealthy enough dined reclining indolently on rose petals, according to Cicero who sharply criticized this practice. Even mattresses were stuffed with rose petals.

The Roman "playboy" called his girlfriend *mea rosa* ('my rose') and customarily presented her with the first spring roses.

When soldiers went on active duty they adorned themselves and their chariots with roses, and did the same when they returned home in triumph. The Emperor permitted Generals to bear a rose on their shields, a custom which persisted long after the fall of the Empire. This may be the reason that so many old European familial coats of arms incorporate the rose.

Roses were not forgotten at the great drinking sessions. Many of the revellers wore chaplets of roses on their heads, believing that this would help keep their heads cool and themselves sober. Also, the scent of roses helped overcome the unpleasant stale smell of wine in their hair. Later, according to many authorities, it became customary to float rose petals in the wine.

Rosewater was in common use and at special feasts it flowed freely from the public fountains. In Roman kitchens rose petals were used in the preparation of desserts, jellies, rose honey and rose wine.

The rose was dedicated to the Goddess of Love and to the God of Wine by both the Romans and the Greeks. Wine, women and roses were naturally associated in the minds of both these peoples. The early Christian church did not approve of this association and it was some centuries before the Virgin Mary came to be called the Rose of Heaven.

To the Romans, the rose also became the symbol of secrecy because the petals close over the stamens as the lips do over the mouth. If a rose was painted or sculpted on the ceiling of any room it always signified that talk and discussion held there was confidential. The expression *sub rosa* was virtually synonymous with "secret". This custom is said to have originated when the Greeks were defeated by the Persian King Xerxes in 479 B.C. The Greek Generals assembled in a grove of roses near the Temple of Minerva and discussed a surprise counter-attack on Xerxes' troops by sea; this led to a famous victory. This secret battle plan drawn up "under the roses" symbolized for the Greeks, and later in Germany, France and England into the Middle Ages, the fact that any agreement made *sub rosa* was always confidential and the partners to it obliged to secrecy. In England there was a saying about the white rose as follows: "Death to him, who under my secrecy betrays his oath."

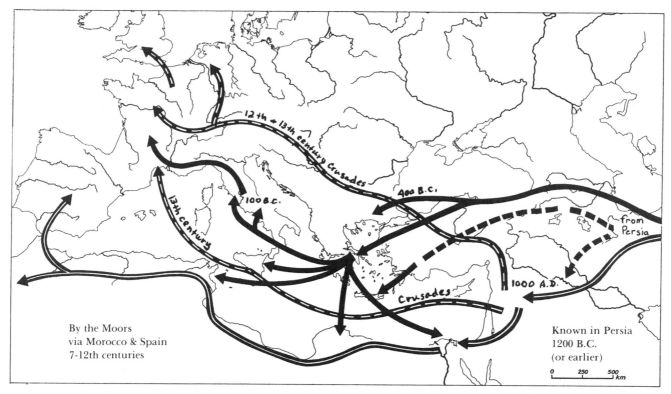

Figure 25. The probable dissemination of garden roses in the Ancient World and the Middle Ages. From Persia (already known from 12th century B.C. ▓▓▓▓ first going to Asia Minor (- - - -) then in 5th century B.C. to Macedonia and Greece (▬▬▬). From there it goes on to Rome, Egypt, Sicily and S. France (▬▬▬). From 7th-12th centuries, through the spread of Islam from Asia Minor to Egypt — N. Africa and Spain (▓▓▓▓) and finally, during the Crusades in the 12th and 13th centuries from the Holy Land to France, Germany and England (▬■▬■). (Original)

Until quite recently many people in Europe wore roses behind the ear to signify that they heard everything but said nothing.

Finally, the rose was the flower of death for both the Greeks and the Egyptians. Roses were often planted, as they are today, on graves. May 11th was the Festival of the Dead in Rome, called *dies rosarius* or *dies rosae*; later, in the Christian era, this became the *Domenica de rosa* or *pasqua rosa* (= Whitsunday) in Italy.

BIBLIOGRAPHY

ANSON, L.   Numismata Graeca; Greek coin types, classified for immediate identification. Part III Agriculture; Plants, Trees, Fruits, Flowers. London 1910.

ARIAS, PAOLO ENRICO & MAX HIRMER.   Tausend Jahre griechische Vasenkunst 109 pp. Plate 240. Munich 1960.

(A.S.).   Les Roses de Paestum. Les Amis des Roses, No. 316, 18-26 (1973). 10 color plates of modern Paestum, but none of roses and only a short text.

BALIS, J.   Roses d'antan. Rosa Belgica 1964: 6-10.

BECHTEL, E.T.   Ancient cultivated Roses. Amer. Rose Annual 1950: 13-23.

BEISSEL, S.T.   Geschichte der Verehrung Marias im Miltelalter. Freiburg 1909.

BERNHARD, O.   Pflanzenbilder auf griechischen und römischen Münzen. Veröff. schweiz. Ges. f. Gescg. d. Med. u. Naturw. 3. Zurich 1925.

BERTSCH, K. & F.   Geschichte unserer Kulturpflanzen; mit umfangreichen Literaturverzeichnis. Stuttgart 1947. (no examples of roses)

BOETTICHER, C.   Der Baumkult der Hellenen. Berlin 1856.

BORCHARD, RUTH.   The Garden Roses of Antiquity. The Rose 10: 195-200 (1962).

—   The Rose in Ancient Greece. The Rose 12:46-50 (1963).

BRETZL, H.   Botanische Forschungen des Alexanderzuges. Strasburg 1902.

BUCHHOLZ, H.G. & V. KRAGHEORGHIS.   Altägäis und Altkypros. Tübingen 1971.

BUNYARD, E.A.   The earliest illustration of the Rose in Europe. RA 1937.

BUSCHAN, G.   Vorgeschichtliche Botanik der Cultur- und Nutzpflanzen der Alten Welt auf Grund prähistorische Funde. 280 pp. 1895.

CURTIUS, LUDWIG.   Die Wandmalerei Pompejis. 472 pp. Darmstadt 1960.

DELAPORTE, L.   Die Babylonier. Freiburg 1933.

FELLNER, S.   Die homerische Flora. Vienna 1897.

FISCHER, KLAUS.   Schöpfungen indischer Kunst. Von den frühesten

Bauten und Bildern bis zum mittelalterlichen Tempel. Cologne 1959. (275 Ill.)

FLETCHER, H.L.G.   The Rose Anthology. London 1963.

FRIEDELL, E.   Kulturgeschichte Ägyptens und des alten Orients. 3rd Edn. Munich 1951.

FRIEDLÄNDER, L.   Sittengeschichte Roms; ungekürzte Textausgabe. Berlin and Vienna 1934.

FRYE, R.   (Kindlers Kulturgeschichte). 575 pp. Zurich 1962 (Translated from English).

GOFF, B.L.   Symbols of prehistoric Mesopotamia. New Haven-/London 1963.

GRIMAL, P.   Römische Kulturgeschichte. Munich 1961.

HAIGOLD, J.J.   Beylagen zum Neuveränderten Russland 2: 208. Riga and Leipzig 1770. Contains details of the Tsuden graves with the ''alleged'' oldest coins with rose designs.

HEHN, V.   Kulturpflanzen und Haustiere in ihrem Übergange von Asien nach Europa. 8th Edn. Berlin 1911.

HURST, C.C.   Notes on the origin and evolution of the Rose. Jour. R.H.S. 66: 73-82, 242-250, 282-289 (1941).

HURST, RONA.   The Minoan Rose. Rose Ann. 1967: 59-64.

IMHOOF-BLUMER and KELLER.   Tier- und Pflanzenbilder auf Münzen und Gemmen des klassischen Altertums. Leipzig 1889.

JESSEN, K.F.W.   Botanik der Gegenwart und Vorzeit. Leipzig 1864.

JORET, C.   La Rose dans l'Antiquité et au moyen âge. Paris 1892.

KEIMER, L.   Die Gartenpflanzen im alten Ägypten. Vol. 1 (incomplete). 187 pp. Berlin 1924.

KIRSTEN, E. and W. KRAIKER.   Griechenlandkunde, ein Führer zu den klassischen Stätten. 472 pp. 102 Ill, 9 Plates. Heidelberg 1955.

KOCH, K.   Die Bäume und Sträucher des alten Griechenlands. 2nd Edn. 270 pp. Berlin 1884.

KOLDEWEY, R.   Das wiedererstehende Babylon. 328 pp. 255 Ill. Leipzig 1913.

KORDES, W.   Unsere Ur-Gartenrosen. Rosen-Jb. 26: 118-130 (1962).

KRÜSSMANN, G.   Als Gärtner im alten Babylon. Deutsche Baumschule 25: 35-38 (1973).

KÜMMEL, O.   Ägyptische und mykenische Pflanzenornamentik. Diss. Freiburg 1901.

LANGKAVEL, B.   Botanik der späteren Griechen, vom 3-13 Jahrhundert. Berlin 1866. (Reprinted Amsterdam 1964).

LENZ, H.O.   Botanik der alten Griechen und Römer. 776 pp. Gotha 1859.

MATZ, F.   Kreta und frühes Griechenland. 1964.

MEISSNER, B.   Babylonien und Assyrien. 2 Vols. Heidelberg 1920-1925. (Comprehensive study with many illustrations).

MÖBIUS, M.   Pflanzenbilder der minoischen Kunst in botanischer Betrachtung. Jahrb.d.dtsch.archäol.Inst. 48: 1-39 (1933).

—   Geschicht der Botanik. Von den ersten Anfängen bis zur Gegenwart. Jena 1937.

MURR, J.   Die Pflanzenwelt der griechischen Mythologie. Innsbruck 1890.

NYBERG, S.   Religion des alten Iran. Osnabrück 1966.

OSTEN, H.H.v.d.   Die Welt der Perser. Stuttgart 1956. (Mainly illustrations of monuments).

OTTE, H.   Handbuch der kirchlichen Kunstarchäologie. 1859.

PARS, H.   Göttlich aber war Kreta. Freiburg 1957.

(PLINY.   English translation with commentary on Roses). ROSTOCK, J. and H.T. RILEY.   The Rose; twelve varieties of it. Amer. Rose Ann. 1951.

REINERS, R.   Die Pflanze als Symbol und Schmuck im Heiligtum.

RIEMSCHNEIDER, M.   Die Welt der Hethiter. Stuttgart 1954. (Mainly illustrations of monuments, sculpture and implements).

SALIS, A. von.   Die Kunst der Griechen. Zurich 1953.

SARRE, FRIEDRICH.   Die Kunst des alten Persien. 152 Ill. Berlin 1925.

SCHACHERMEYR, F.   Die ältesten Kulturen Griechenlands, 300 pp., 77 drawings, 11 maps and 16 plates. Stuttgart 1955. (Deals with the period 5000-2000 B.C. in Greece and Crete).

SCHLEIDEN, M.J.   Die Rose. Geschichte und Symbolik in etnographischer und kulturhistorischer Beziehung. 322 pp. Leipzig 1873.

SCHWEINFURTH, G.   Über Pflanzenreste aus altägyptischen Gräbern. In: Ber. Dtsch. Bot. Ges. 1184: 351-370.

—   Ägyptens auswärtige Beziehungen hinsichtlich der Culturgewächse. In: Verh. Berliner Anthropol. Ges. 1891: 649-669.

—   Pflanzenbilder im Tempel von Karnak. (Theben). Bot. Jahrb. 55: 464-480 (1919).

SEWARD, B.   The symbolic Rose. New York 1960.

STRENG, G.   Das Rosettenmotiv in der Kunst- und Kulturgeschichte. 1918.

STROMMENGER, E. und HIRMER.   5000 Jahre Mesopotamien. Munich 1962.

TÄCKHOLM, VIVI.   Faraohs Blomster. 308 pp. (Many illustrations and an excellent bibliographical reference). Stockholm 1969.

TARN, W. and G.T. GRIFFITH.   The Hellenistic Civilization. 448 pp., 3 plans. Darmstadt 1966.

VACANO, O.W. von.   Die Etrusker. Stuttgart 1955.

—   Die Etrusker in der Welt der Antike. RoRoRo-volume. Hamburg 1957.

WEIDNER, E.   Der Zug Sargons von Akkad nach Kleinasien. Boghazköi- Studien, 6th part, 57-99. Leipzig 1922.

WENDLAND, P.   Die hellenistisch-römische Kultur in ihren Beziehungen zum Judentum und Christentum. Tübingen 1912. (No details on plants).

WENIGER, L.   Altgriechischer Baumkultus. Leipzig 1919.

WILPERT, J.   Die Malerei in den Katakomben Roms. 1903.

WOENIG, Franz.   Die Pflanzen im alten Aegypten, 2nd Edn. 429 pp. Leipzig 1807.

WOLF, W.   Die Welt der Agypter. Stuttgart 1954.

WYLIE, A.P.   The History of Garden Roses. Parts I-III. Jour. R.H.S. 79: 555-571 (1954); 80: 8-24, 77-87 (1955).

YOUNG, N.   Ghosts of the Rose World. The Rose 15: 110-114.

ZANDER, R. and C. TESCHNER.   Der Rosengarten; eine geschichtliche Studie durch 2 Jahrtausende. Frankfurt (Oder) 1939.

The Rose in the Middle Ages ca. 500-1500 A.D.

ROSES IN FRANCE AND GERMANY

The fall of Rome, and the decay of its culture, brought the love of roses to an end, cultivation of them stopped completely and for several centuries there is little reference to the rose. Of course, it continued to exist, but this flower which, in earlier days, had been a symbol of love, beauty and the joy of life, served now almost entirely as a remedy for a variety of illnesses. Only from France is there any information on the rose in this period. This, although somewhat controversial, may nevertheless be accurate.

King Hildebert I (511-558), the son of Clovis I, according to a report given at the time by the poet, Fortunatus Venantius, laid out a rose garden at his palace in Paris for his wife, Ulthrogotho. This garden, like the palace itself, was situated between the Seine and the Abbey of St. Germain-des-Prés.

The only other piece of information is of Medardus, Bishop of Noyon (475-545) who initiated a rose festival. Every year at this feast he gave a wreath of roses and 20 gold crowns to the most virtuous maiden in his diocese in order to provide her with a suitable dowry. Apparently, in those days, competition for "virtue" was very great. Wreaths of roses or chaplets could only be worn in France at that time by ladies of rank, and young men in Paris; simple country girls were only allowed to wear them at weddings or at special rose festivals organized by the Church.

Except for a few monastery gardens which continued to grow them, there were almost no garden roses in private cultivation as there had been during the Roman period. It was not until the time of Charlemagne (742-814) that the rose began to appear in certain official areas; this means that their planting was by official order and took place as the result of the *Capitulare de villis* (i.e. an imperial order to landowners) which was an agricultural regulation introduced by Charlemagne for the Crown lands which are today believed to have been founded in 794. Paragraph 70 of his order gives details of all the plants which were to be put into such gardens. The paragraph begins:

> Volumes quod in horto omnes herbas habeant ide est 1) lilium 2) rosas . . .
> ("It is our wish that you shall have every form of plant in the garden particularly 1) lilies 2) roses . . .")

Lilies and roses therefore head this list which altogether covers about 100 different plants. Unfortunately, due to the absence of contemporary evidence, we do not know which varieties of roses were concerned. However, it is probable that it was only *Rosa gallica* with the occasional *Rosa alba* which might have been brought into the area by Roman legionnaires. Apart from these two, there can only have been the wild roses like *Rosa canina*, among others. Roses at this time were highly valued for medicinal purposes and *Rosa canina* provided the drugs *Fructus Cynosbati* and *Semen Cynosbati* (Dog rose hips and Dog Rose seed) while *Rosa gallica* gave *Flores Rosae* (Flowers of Roses).

Apart from the monastery gardens and the Crown properties, the ladies of the manors had small herb or medicinal gardens for their own use in which they grew a few roses, initially for their herbal properties, but later for their beauty and decorative qualities. Garden roses were still very expensive to buy and were the special pride of their owners. At that time the rose was so wrapped in mystery that it is not surprising that references to it are so sparse. We have chiefly the Benedictine monasteries to thank for the old roses that were propagated and thereby remained in circulation. In each monastic establishment of the Middle Ages, there was at least one monk who specialized in the medical properties of the rose, among other plants.

The design of a monastery garden has come down to us in the famous architectural plans of the monastery at St. Gallen of the year 820 (or 830). Among the plants which were recommended, and for which there was to be a bed of each, is the rose.

The next authority is Wilfred Strabo (Walafridus Strabus) (809-849) who was Abbot of the monastery at Reichenau on Lake Constance. He left a poem of 444 hexameters in which he praises no less than 23 garden plants, amongst them the rose, although he gives no specifics.

Then we come to the Blessed Hildegarde, Abbess of the Convent of St. Ruprechtsberg near Bingen, 1098-1179, who was an exceptionally cultured, progressive and gifted woman, associated with many of the important people of her time. She was the author of two works on medical botany for maintaining health and curing disease. In these books, she deals with some 300 different varieties of plants, mostly indigenous, 40 of which are trees. Her list also includes the rose as a plant with healing properties.

By the year 1200, it seems that the rose had become much more wide-spread and appreciated, from the evidence of many of the contemporary poets, and as can be seen in the illustrations in the *Roman de la Rose*. In these, roses are seen growing on fences or planted as hedges, the latter seem to have been mostly *Rosa rubiginosa* (from the scented foliage) or forms of *Rosa canina*.

Albert the Great (1193-1280), more commonly known as Count Albert of Bollstädt, Bishop of Regensburg, a Dominican monk, was also well versed in botany and wrote some very interesting descriptions of the rose in his time. He uses what was probably an Arabic word *bedegar* for *Rosa rubiginosa*; described the hedge rose, *Rosa canina* and *Rosa arvensis*, and, of the garden roses, gives details of a double white rose, undoubtedly *Rosa alba*, and a similar pink rose.

At the time of Louis XI (1226-1270) everyone who had the right to cultivate roses had to present three rose chaplets each year to the mayor of their town on January 6th (the Feast of the Epiphany) and give a basket of roses for the preparation of rosewater on Ascension Day.

In 1236 a book entitled *Roman de la Rose* appeared in France; it is basically an allegorical poem by Guilleaume de Lorris. Although incomplete, the first part runs to more than 4,000 verses in which the Lover, in a dream, seeks to win the object of his affections embodied in the form of a rose. The poem also has a strongly didactic aspect which was borrowed from the *Ars Amandi* ("The Art of Love") by Ovid. About 1275, the second *Roman de la Rose* appeared with the same format and principal characters, but with another 18,000 verses by Jean de Meung. In this second version the love poem was secondary to the compilation of the philosophical beliefs of the time and a satire on the scholastic and court beliefs of the day. Until Rabelais (*ca.* 1490-1533) no book in French was more widely known and read and there are numerous copies of it, many of which are illustrated with very beautiful miniatures.

Thibault IV (The Minstrel) (1201-1253), King of Navarre, Count of Champagne and Brie, on returning from the Seventh Crusade in the year 1250, brought from the Holy Land a double form of *Rosa gallica* which he started to propagate extensively at his chateau in Provins. Over the years this rose produced the variety which is known today as *Rosa gallica officinalis*.

Rosa damascena was also probably brought to France from Syria at the time of the Crusades; it flourished in its new surroundings. According to Gravereaux, it had originally been introduced from S. Italy by the Phoenicians as the "Rose of Paestum" but Avicenna states that it was also in cultivation, and being improved, in Syria.

At the Synod of Nîmes in 1284, all Jews were ordered to wear a rose on the breast to distinguish them from the Christians and "not receive the same consideration". From this we can conclude that roses were being widely grown and were easily obtainable. What was done in the months that the roses were not in bloom remains a mystery.

By 1300, rose cultivation in France was already on a considerable scale and use of them for decoration in the home, on banquet tables and for personal adornment was rapidly increasing. A number of cities enjoyed special privileges for rose growing, particularly Rouen in France and Florence in Italy.

The Italian author, Crescentius, mentions both red and white roses in his book *Agricultura* (1307); these were probably the roses known today as *R. gallica* and *R. alba*.

Contemporary paintings and building decorations make it clear that rose growing in the Renaissance, from about 1340 to the end of the 16th century, had become a major activity. Many of the old roses of the day appear in the works of the great masters, Raphael, Leonardo da Vinci, Michelangelo, Botticelli and Jan Breughel the Elder, and most of them can be easily identified.

From the end of the 14th century roses were regularly distributed in the French Court of Justice, a specially appointed *Roserier de la Cour* delivered the necessary blooms. He procured them from Fontenay-aux-Roses just outside Paris, where the locals specialized in rose growing.

In 1350, Konrad von Megenberg (1309-1374), Canon of Regensburg and former Rector of Vienna, produced the first German book on natural history, entitled *Buch der Natur.* It does not contain much on roses and indeed his botanical knowledge is not, on the whole, very impressive; he even reverts to using the word *bedegar* for roses.

THE WARS OF THE ROSES IN ENGLAND
(1455-1485)

Just when roses first came to England is unknown. Other than the white rose, *R. alba*, which had probably been introduced by the Romans, and possibly *R. gallica*, English literature tells us that the first garden roses were probably brought by returning crusaders, therefore some time in the 12th century, or later. The varieties introduced must have been *R. canina* and the double form of *R. gallica*. It is noteworthy that in the ancient cathedrals, Canterbury for example, only single roses, probably the indigenous roses *R. canina* or *R. rubiginosa*, are represented.

We must now look at the Wars of the Roses in England. These were not fought over the rose itself, but are so named because the two antagonists took a white and red rose respectively as their badges. There is hardly a book on the subject which has not gone into some detail on the history of these two heraldic roses and, as a rule, quite incorrectly. N. Young (*The Rose*, 15) maintains that the usual identification of these two badges with *R. gallica* and *R. alba* is very unreliable since there is no supporting contemporary evidence.

The first source we must examine comes from the French author Opoix who, about a century ago, wrote a history of his native town of Provins. He states correctly that Edmund, first Earl of Lancaster (also known as Edmund Langley and "Crouchback", the second son of Henry III of England) went to Provins in 1279 in order to revenge the murder of the English Governor, Wil-

liam Pentecost, and suppress a rebellion. Opoix adds, without any reliable justification, that Edmund, on his return to England, took the red rose of Provins as his coat of arms and that the rival House of York chose a white rose. However, the House of York was not to come into existence for another hundred years. Therefore there could have been no rivalry between the two families at that time. They were both offshoots of the House of Plantagenet and it was later that they were in contest for the throne.

Both family lines died out by the year 1500. In 1279 Edmund Lancaster was 34 years old and it is certain that he must have chosen his coat of arms long before this, probably when his elder brother, King Edward I, took a golden rose as his badge. As their mother also displayed a rose, the color of which has not been recorded, in her arms, this very likely influenced them.

N. Young sums up by saying that all these heraldic roses were patterned after the roses of the hedgerow and in no way represented cultivated garden roses. That heraldic roses were in azure or any of the other heraldic colors adds emphasis to this theory.

Figure 26. The "Badge of England". (Original)

In 1455, the War of Succession, in which the two families came close to annihilating one another, broke out. The first battle took place on May 22nd at St.

Figure 27. Coins bearing representations of roses on either the obverse or reverse. Left: rose-noble of the time of Edward IV (1465); the ship with the single rose in its hull represents the birth of English sea-power. The coin on the right dates from the time of Henry VII and was struck to commemorate the union of the Houses of York and Lancaster.

Albans and was very cruelly fought. After thirty blood-stained years, the Wars of the Roses ended in 1485 at the Battle of Bosworth Field. In 1486 Henry Tudor, who was related to the house of Lancaster, married Elizabeth of York and thus united, as Henry VII (1485-1509), these two powerful families. At the same time, he merged the two heraldic badges into the "Tudor Rose", placing the small white rose upon the red. The Tudor Rose is still the badge of the ruling House of England and is known as the "Royal Badge" (Fig. 26). Just when the rose became the national emblem is unknown, but it is thought to have been in the year 1486. Elsewhere there is a reference to the fact that Edward I (1272-1307) was the first English King to take the rose as his symbol, but this was a golden rose (see above), not the Tudor Rose.

In 1465, Edward IV had a very beautiful gold coin struck which showed a small rose on both sides. This coin goes under the name of "rose-noble" and is much sought after by collectors (Fig. 27).

Now a third rose, called the "York and Lancaster" the proper name of which is *Rosa damascena versicolor*, must be discussed. There are numerous legends and stories about this rose which attempt to relate it to the end of the Wars of the Roses and with the bi-color Tudor Rose. The story goes that this rose was first seen in 1486 at the time of the wedding of Henry Tudor and Elizabeth of York. Many people have assumed that there is a connection between this rose and the badges of the two embittered families. In fact, these legends are without historical foundation, having been first described by Monardus in 1551, 70 years after the Wars of the Roses. It is a sport of *R. damascena*, semi-double, sometimes white, sometimes a variable pink and sometimes flecked with both pink and white. It is often confused with *R. gallica versicolor* (= "Rosa Mundi") which is probably much older, possibly going back to the 12th century, although it was only first described by de l'Obel in 1581.

PERSIAN, ARABIAN AND MOORISH ROSES IN THE MIDDLE AGES

As has been said before, most experts today maintain that Western roses must have originated in Persia where they have long been loved and where the production of Attar of Roses had its earliest beginnings. Between the 9th and 14th centuries, Persian poets, notably Omar Khayyam, continually sang the praises of their country and the sweet perfume of its roses. The whole nation seems to have been a rose garden, especially the cities of Shiraz and Isfahan.

A. Mazaheri (1957) wrote of Moslem life in about the 9th century, and how the Orientals tended their gardens with great devotion. The inner courtyard of the home was a garden, often laid out as if it was a series of rooms, always symmetrical, with a fountain as the central feature; when guests were expected the servants threw rose petals on the water. The rich plantings of flowers, especially the many roses, moved the poets of the day to ever-new paeans of praise. The gardeners were clever, imaginative men who patiently experimented with their material and undoubtedly found and introduced many "novelties". We can be sure that they would have sought roses with velvety, dark red petals; others had bright colors or even showed a mixture of white and red in a single bloom.

During the period of Islamic expansion, between the 8th and 10th centuries, from India to Spain, the rose underwent a new wave of popularity with the arrival in Spain of the Moors (Arabs) from N. Africa. Joret, a French scholar who specialized in roses, says that in the 9th century the Moors of Morocco were already growing both red and white roses. Ibn Tamin, a poet of the 13th century, knew of a yellow rose, although admittedly only by hearsay, and even claimed that there were reports of a black rose growing in Persia.

Joret goes on to tell us of an 11th century botanist who mentioned a white "camphor rose" with a hundred petals. In the opinion of Gravereaux this was a double white form of *R. moschata*; its perfume was reminiscent of camphor, according to the Arabian author, Ibn-el-Facel. This rose later became widespread in S. Europe and was also grown in Persia.

When Saladin (1138-1193), Sultan of Egypt and Syria, fought and defeated the great army of the Crusaders at Hittin, north-west of Tiberias, and occupied Jerusalem, he would not enter the Mosque of Omar, which had been converted into a church by the Christians, until the whole building, from floor to ceiling, had been washed and purified with rosewater. Five hundred camel loads were needed for this and they must have been brought from Damascus.

In the 12th century, an Arab reference is found relating to the roses grown in Morocco. Called "mountain roses", they had only five petals. This same reference also mentions a red rose and a white rose, both of which were double. The most highly prized, however, was a rose which apparently did not open fully and had between 40 and 50 petals.

The "blue rose" haunted the Moorish mind. Joret reports that they had a rose which was red on the outside and blue within; but this is somewhat unreliable. There are modern moss roses and varieties of *gallica* which are a deep violet or purple in color. Our old *Veilchenblau* ('Violet Blue') has buds which are a deep purple opening to violet with a white eye. The Moors certainly never had any roses of a pure blue.

The hips of the dog rose were used extensively for medicinal purposes. The Moors liked their rose gardens to be as colorful as possible, they planted the more vigorous roses in large pots and put these in groups of six or eight on marble steps, one above the other, which gave the impression of a whole tree in flower, in different colors.

The poet Saadi describes in his book on roses (1258) the popularity which the rose enjoyed in Persia.

About 1300, the Arabian historian and traveler, Abu-el-Feda, gave an account of the "sweetest white rose of Nisibin" (today Nusaybin in the Turkish province of Mardin); a town in existence since 1000 B.C.

Also in the 13th century, a book written by the Arabic author Ibn-el-Awam gave details of the roses in cultivation in the East at that time, in addition to all the knowledge that they had acquired from the Greeks and Romans.

The "Rose of the Magicians and Fire-Worshippers" in Persia is none other than *R. gallica*, dating back to 1200 B.C., according to Ibn-el-Awam. As one can learn from the Avesta (Zoroastrian Holy Scriptures) it was entrusted to the care of an angel; it is also the poet Shelaladdin- Rumi's "rose of Djour".

Jamain, a French hybridizer, whose book appeared in 1870, says that very old, tough bushes of roses were to be found in the palaces of Valencia, Cordoba and Granada. The Moors sowed rose seeds in the fall, and propagated them during the winter as well by means of both cuttings and plant-division. They also propagated by taking strong shoots from old bushes.

The "Yellow Rose of Asia" (*Rosa foetida*) is mentioned by Arabic writers from the 12th century; botanically it is first described in 1586 by Dalechamp. In Arabic lists of rose varieties, *R. foetida bicolor* is also described and it seems that this rose was cultivated in Tripoli while the normal yellow rose was to be found near Alexandria. There is even a "Rose of China" described, but this is certainly an error; it might have been a mallow, or a translation error might have been made by writing *Rose de Chine* instead of *Rose de Chien* ('Dog Rose').

In the 14th century, the poet Mohammed Schemsaddin, better known as Hafiz, praised the rose in many poems and songs. The rose was also the flower of the cult of Ormuz (the Persian name for Ahura-Mazdah, the living God or Great Creator of the Persian religion).

Mahommed II, who captured Constantinople in 1453, refused to enter the Church of Sophia until it had been completely purified with rosewater; then, and only then, could it again function as a mosque.

In the 15th century, the enormous wealth of rose production in Peshawar, according to contemporary sources, must have been greater than that of such popular rose-growing areas as Teheran, Azerbaijan, and generally the rest of the Orient. In the previous century, Persia was a veritable bower of roses and today the town of Shiraz in the Fars Province is still the rose-growing center for the Attar of Roses industry.

THE ROSE AND THE MOGULS

According to Q.L. Matthews, Tamerlane (1336-1405), the founder of the second Mongol Empire and a descendant of Genghis Khan (1155-1227), conquered much territory during his drive towards the West; he rebuilt the city of Samarkand and laid out gardens in the northern part of the city. When Tamerlane's descendents came to Persia, Afghanistan and India, an interest in flowers and gardens was awakened in them: the natives were passionately in love with the rose; from time immemorial they had planted and cultivated roses which played an essential part in their religion, their poetry, their art and even their daily life. When Babur (1483-1530; great-grandson of Tamerlane), founder of the great Mogul dynasty, first became overlord of Turkestan and then later of Hindustan, he brought with him, during his military campaigns to the West, plants which he had found blooming in the East; trees which he found in the north of his territories, he had planted in the south and vice versa. From every part of his domains he brought seeds and flowering plants and had them sown when he returned home. He was the creator of the great and justly famous Indian gardens, and, although his country was arid, flat and infertile, he nevertheless managed to produce superb gardens and was followed in this practice by his chief nobles. It is said of him that he planted a garden in every corner of his kingdom, and roses everywhere. His grandson, Akbar, also took great interest in gardening, but it was Jehangier Khan, Akbar's son, who inherited the real passion for gardening from Baber and who created the most beautiful gardens of all; for his wife, Nur Jehan, he made the "Garden of Delight" (Nishit Bagh) in Agra and Shalimar in the Kashmir valley. These Moguls with their love of gardening and, by the number of seeds they planted, were able to select and thus improve the rose in a way which had never been done before. Matthews is of the opinion that, in the gardens of Kashmir and Persia at this time, the recurrent rose appeared as a result of continuous re-selection. The "Hundred-petaled Rose" (Goul sad Berk) became famous throughout the Orient from the gardens in Kashmir. Towards the end of the eighteenth century, *Rosa chinensis* and its red-flowered form, *semperflorens*, came from India, being then known as the Bengal rose. These two roses, along with the yellow and the Tea Rose, revolutionized cultivation of the genus, for these cultivars bore the wonderful gift of recurrency. It is certain that they originated in China, but when and from where they came is unknown.

The Rose in China Roses have been grown in China for a very long time. Among the Chinese paintings of the 10th century A.D. there are botanical drawings of Tea Roses, but it seems more than likely that they had been known long before that. There are also pictures of *Rosa rugosa* (Mei kuei).

Rosa laevigata, known in the United States as the 'Cherokee Rose', deserves a special mention. It is illustrated by Ch'iu Huang Peng Ts'ao in his "Famine Herbal" of 1406 (Fig. 28) and it was very well established in the wild. There it was known as Chin Ying Tzu ("Golden Cherry," due to its reddish hips). According to H. L. Li it was introduced into Europe in the 16th century[1] by the East India Company. It first appears in European literature in the *Amaltheum Botanicum* by Leonard Plukenet, London (1705: p.

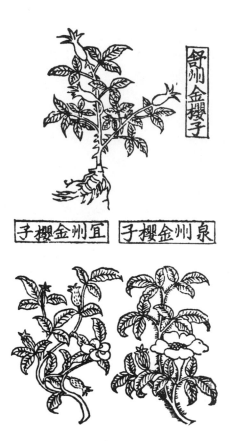

Figure 28. *Rosa laevigata*, in various stages. From the "Famine Herbal" (after H.L. Li)

185) under the name of *Rosa alba cheusanensis foliorum marginatis et rhacchi medio spinosis*. It was soon taken to America where it easily established itself in the wild in the southern states.

It was described in 1803 by Michaux as *Rosa variegata* from material collected by Pursh in Georgia. Both believed that they were dealing with a true American rose species. R.E. Shepherd (1954, p. 91) finds it hard to believe that this rose could have been brought from Europe to America. He notes the legend that Chinese missionaries discovered America in the 5th century and could have brought the rose with them, but admits that this seems unlikely. H. L. Li (1959) states that it might have been the famous and legendary Buddhist, Fa Hsien, who discovered America, but this story is strongly disputed by many authors.

Rosa rubus (in Chinese T'u Mi) was already being grown in many Chinese gardens at the time of the Sung Dynasty (960-1279). Due to its very late flowering, it was said by poets that "when T'u Mi blooms, the season of flowers is over".

---

1 This is hardly possible, for the English East India Company was not founded until the year 1600; the correct date is probably 1698.

Despite the Chinese preference for the peony, the Emperor Chin Ming (Ming Dynasty, 1368-1644) had many roses in his gardens. Only the Emperor, his family and the very high court officials were permitted to use these gardens and the rosewater and Attar of Roses produced from them. People of lower social standing who illegally produced and used rosewater could be sentenced to death.

Figure 29. *Rosa multiflora.* From the "Famine Herbal" (after H.L. Li)

In China, the home of so many species roses of great decorative value, there were also many other roses in cultivation very early. As is true today, one of the most common then was *R. multiflora.* Many of its garden forms were in cultivation, for example:

var. *thunbergiana,* with small white flowers;
var. *cathayensis* (Fen T'uan Ch'iang Wei or 'Powderpuff Rose') with large, pink, flat flowers in flat trusses; 'Platyphylla' (Chi Chi Mei or 'Seven Sisters Rose'), deep pink to red, large-flowered, from which came 'Crimson Rambler'; 'Carnea' (Ho Hua Chi'ang Wei or 'Lotus Rose'); bright pink, double.

R. chinensis (Yueh Chi or Yueh Yueh Hung) was extremely popular because it bloomed throughout the summer. It is found today growing wild in the hills and on the lower slopes in Central China. Cultivated in China for centuries, it exists in both bush and climbing form. The flowers vary through carmine to pink and white and even to yellow; they are slightly fragrant. Until the end of the 19th century, this was the only recurrent rose.

Rosa banksiae (Mu Hsiang or 'Grove of Fragrance') from south and south-west China has been grown in Chinese gardens at least as long. There are a number of forms, all of which originated in China; all are fragrant except the double yellow variety.

Rosa odorata, the Tea Rose (Hsiang Shu Yueh Chi or 'Scented Monthly Rose') also came from China.

The last important Chinese garden rose was *R. xan-thina* (Huang Tz'u Mei); both the double and semi-double forms, which flower only once in the season, still grow in the foothills of northern China. Most of these notes about the old Chinese roses are taken from examples given by H.L.Li.

The Rose in Japan The first literary mention of roses is in the famous *Manyoshu* or "Collection of a Thousand Leaves", a group of poems from the 8th century which will be quoted later.

One of the most important early works in which the rose is mentioned is the *Story of Genji* which was written in the Heian period (794-1192) by Murasaki Shikibu. This poetess says of the rose, which was very dear to her: "The most beautiful rose is a half-opened bud at the foot of a bridge."

In the Edo period, books on the subject of rose growing were often published, but the care of roses was, as in Europe, the special preserve of the upper classes. Only in 1868, after the restoration of the Meiji, did rose growing become open to all.

Eight species are indigenous to Japan, of which four were particularly singled out by the poets: *R. multiflora, R. wichuraiana, R. rugosa* and *R. laevigata.*

R. multiflora (No ibara or Nihon-no-Bara) was the most prized and also the most widely grown in Japan; it inhabited three-quarters of the country. As in China, various forms appeared in Japan:

'Crimson Rambler', dark red.
'Seven Sisters', a double form.
'Watsoniana' (Sho-no-suk-ibara).
'Platyphylla' (Sakura-bara or 'Cherry Blossom Rose') with flowers 3.2 cm./1.25 in. in diameter.

There is a large collection of *multiflora* hybrids in the Hirakata Park, near Osaka.

var. *adenochaeta* (Tsukuschi ibara), S. Japan, flowers pink, leaves longer than the type, very smooth and glandular; found from the Ryuku Islands as far as Taiwan and the Philippines.

R. wichuraiana (Teri-ha-no-ibara). Named after Wichura, 1680, brought to Europe in 1873; has a fragrance of clover and a creeping habit. It is found mostly in the coastal areas of Honshu, Shikoku, Kyushu extending to the Ryuku, Taiwan, Korea and China. Wild variants have not been found to date, except a form with brighter, shinier leaves.

R. rugosa (Hama-nasu) has the largest hips of any rose; these reach their full size about two months after the flowers have faded. It generally inhabits the coastal strip in northern Japan. It likes cool conditions, from the sandy coast of Hokkaido and Honshu south to Kanto on the Pacific coast and to the San'n district (on the west side of Honshu); it is also found in the northern parts of the Far East and in the Kuriles. Very popular as a garden rose in Japan; in the wild it is found in both large- and small-flowered varieties, both single and double. Brought to Europe in 1845 by Thunberg where it later naturalized itself.

R. laevigata (Naniwa-ibara). Has certainly been grown from very early times, although a native of China; brought to Europe in 1698 by the East India Company. Today, often planted in S. Japan as a hedge due to its vigorous growth pattern in this climate. The flowers are white, borne out to a stem, flat, 6-9 cm./2.5-3.5 in. in diameter; scent reminiscent of gardenia. In Japan there is also a red form (*rosea*) known as Hayota. Attempts to hybridize from this variety have not been successful.

ROSES AND THE EARLY BOTANISTS

Although information is somewhat scanty, enough is known to determine which plants were cultivated in the gardens of the "Fathers of Botany". It must be emphasized, however, that in many cases it is difficult to identify the rose varieties as they were described by different authors and that it is easy to arrive at the wrong conclusions. It must also be remembered that many of these authors of the Middle Ages were apothecaries. The roses which they obtained from every part of Germany were often nameless, so they themselves named them for the first time. The drawings in the books are often very beautiful, but many resemble each other closely; perhaps they were taken by one draftsman from the work of another. The following descriptions of roses from the most important botanical books published between 1485 and 1666 will develop a clearer picture of the garden roses of the period.

In *Hortus Sanitatis Germanice* ("The Garden of Health") by Johann Wonnecke, the doctor in the town of Kaub from 1484 to 1503, there is only one illustration of roses (see Fig. 30). The text deals with the rose purely from a medicinal point of view.

Otto Brunfels (1488-1534) wrote the *Contrafayt Kreuterbuch* (1532, and frequently reprinted thereafter) which contains very fine illustrations. Plate 146, in

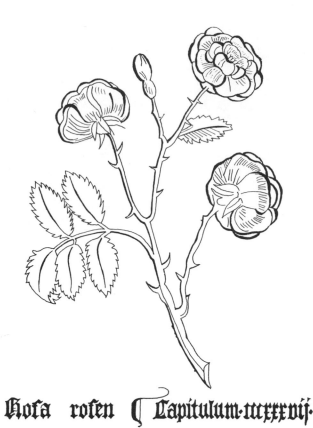

Figure 30. Rose from the *Hortus Sanitatis Germanice* ("Garden of Good Health", German: Mainz 1485).

particular, shows a beautiful rose which may well have been *Rosa damascena*.

Of the 40 books which Leonard Fuchs (1501-1566) produced, only the *New Kreuterbuch* (1543) is known and read today. It is one of the most important works of early botanical literature. Fuchs says that the "Rose has double origins, that is to say from seed and from plants growing in the wild. The seeds produce in the garden, roses which are red or white, single or double. Roses from seed grow exclusively in the gardens where they are sown. The wild ones may be found anywhere on moorland or in hedges. Roses are the last flowers to come into bloom in the Spring." To illustrate this, there is a delightful plate which shows a rose with two single and a number of double flowers; in both cases the stipules carry five leaflets.

Hieronymus Bock (1498-1554), or Tragus in Latin, is usually very clear and precise in his descriptions of plants, however that part of his text which deals with roses is not. Of the 465 woodcuts in the 1577 edition of his *New Kreutterbuch*. Only one is of a rose which is, again, half wild and half cultivated. He writes about it as follows:

Figure 31. Rose, wild (r) and cultivated (l); from Hieronymus Bock's *Kreutterbuch*, 1551 Edition. (redrawn)

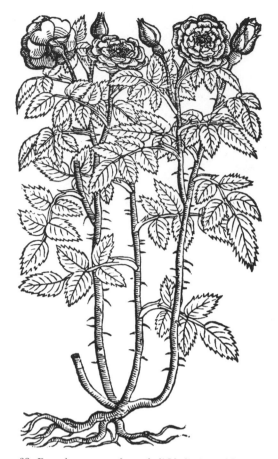

Figure 32. *Rosa damascena*; from de l'Obel's *Kruydtboeck*. (1581)

Everyone loves his roses / the ones that please me most are the so-called health or field roses (i.e. *R. canina, R. rubiginosa* and *R. arvensis*) / then the single red rose / and thirdly the double red and the pink rose / and lastly the double white rose. It should be known / that when they are still fresh / the scent is better from afar / than nearto. The opposite is true of dried roses.

Konrad Gessner (Gesner) (1516-1565) of Zürich, wrote two very important works, the *Horti Germaniae* of 1561, and the *Catalogus Plantarum* in which he described ten varieties as follows:

There are double white roses in our gardens in great abundance . . . Single red roses are also common with us in the towns . . . Just this day I saw in a friend's garden a rose which was half white and half purple.
Lemon colored or golden roses.
Sweet smelling yellow moss roses. In Augsburg many people grown fine yellow roses in their gardens, though, I am told, these are scentless.
hedgeroses . . .
Alexandrian, Persian or Damascene, mostly flesh pink, were formerly quite rare with us but now we have them in quantity in these pink tones. These roses were often brought to us by Italians, French, German and other people and they were called 'Damasks' as they came from Damascus . . . In our case it is now about thirty years since we became aware of them. Large Indian roses, golden yellow.

A hedge rose, blooming in May and usually called by us 'The Little Rose of May' is also much grown in our gardens. Another smaller hedge rose which grown on open, dry hillsides and of which the whole shrub is sweet-smelling like wine and consequently is known as the Wine Rose.
Moss or Damascene roses, small, white and single . . . believed that they have come from the hedge rose and they are generally called flesh-coloured or thirty-petalled on account of their thirty petals or sometimes named either white or centifolia. Moss rose (different from the foregoing) both single and double.

Jakob Theodor of Bergzabern (1520-1590), who called himself Tabernaemontanus, was a pupil of H. Bock; in his *Kräuterbuch*, he deals with 3,000 plant varieties of which he illustrates 2,400. On pp. 1493-1496, there are drawings of 11 roses, each occupying a quarter page and very beautifully executed. They are as follows, the modern equivalents are in parentheses:[1]

Rosa alba (*R. alba semiplena*)
R. rubra (*R. gallica*)
R. Provincialis Major (*R. centifolia*)

[1] The original method of writing the names in the various botanical books has been kept both here and on the following pages.

Figure 33. *Rosa holosericea* (i.e. a form of *R. gallica*) from del'Obel's *Kruydtboeck* II.

R. provincialis minor (R. centifolia)

R. sine spinis (R. francofurtana?)

R. muscata alba (R. moschata?? white and single)

R. muscata alba multiplex (R. centifolia muscosa alba)

R. lutea (R. foetida)

R. eglenteria (R. pimpinellifolia)

R. sylvestris (R. canina)

R. arvina (R. arvenis)

In 1731, the same author published his "Completely New *Kräuter-buch*", in which eleven roses are again illustrated and these are undoubtedly *Rosa alba, R. gallica* (called *R. rubra*), *R. provincialis (major), R. provincialis minor* (i.e. *R. gallica parvifolia?*), *R. sine spinis (R. francofurtana?), R. moschata (alba* and *alba multiplex), R. lutea, R. rubiginosa* ('Englenteria'), *R. canina* (called *R. sylvestris*) and *R. spinosissima* (called *R. arvina*).

Charles de l'Ecluse (Clusius) (1525-1609), of Arras, then a part of Flanders, wrote in 1583 that *Rosa batavica* (which is the same as *centifolia*) was being grown in Holland. He traveled through Hungary up to the Turkish border and from there brought back to Holland both *Rosa foetida* and *Rosa hemisphaerica*. He also wrote that in Hans Fugger's garden in 1580 there were no less than 775 rose bushes and that Georg von Fugger grew the first Moss Rose, possibly obtained from Clusius, who had journeyed through Holland, France and the Mediterranean countries, in 1565.

Adam Lonitzer (Lonicerus) (1528-1586) of Marburg, produced many botanical works; his *Kreuterbuch* went through 20 editions between 1557 and 1783. The illustrations were mostly copied from Bock and Fuchs. Regarding roses, he wrote little that we did not already know from Albertus Magnus 300 years earlier. Here is his text on roses:

> the wild roses are called by the Greeks cynorrhodos, which is the canina rose, what we call field roses, hedge roses, Ladies' rose, sweetbrier, corn cockle, harvest roses, heath roses, and wild roses. Regarding the domestic hybrids or cultivated garden roses: they have, before anything else in the garden, a most delicious fragrance, their foliage is green with dark markings and with many soft hooked thorns, the leaves are blackish and deeply etched. Both types have marked distinctions, for some have white, some red or pink, some purple, some yellow for color; some are double and some single.

Matthias de l'Obel (1538-1619), from Flanders, was court botanist to James I of England and had a garden in Hackney. He published his work *Plantarum seu*

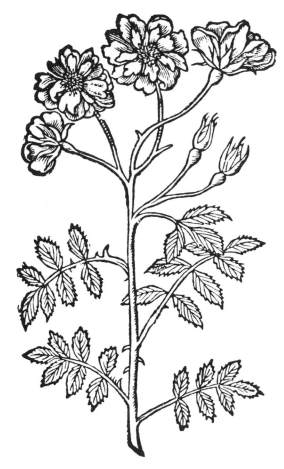

Figure 34. "Double Musk Rose" (*Rosa moschata*); from de l'Obel's *Kruydtboeck* II.

Stirpium Icones in 1576, containing 2,173 woodcuts of various plants; for details of these he relied heavily on Fuchs. He describes and illustrates *Rosa centifolia, R. gallica, R. canina, R. cinnamomea, R. eglanteria, R. spinosissima, R. foetida* and three forms of *R. moschata*. Where he learned about roses is unknown; for instance, why should he omit the already well-known *R. alba* and *R. damascena*? The illustrations of the three varieties of *moschata* are not sufficiently precise to identify them absolutely and there is the possibility that he confused *R. moschata* with *R. arvensis*, which was also known at that time as the "European Musk Rose".

Caspar Bauhin (1560-1624) of Basel, also a famous botanist, described about 600 plants in his work *Pinax theatri botanici* (Basel, 1623). Among the 19 wild and 17 "cultivated" roses known to him, were *R. centifolia* and *R. damascena*; he is also the first to mention *R. arvensis*.

Figure 35. *Rosa Hollandica siue Batue* (= *R. centifolia*); from Gerard's *Herball.* (1597)

Figure 36. *Rosa Prouincialis siue Damascena;* from Gerard's *Herball.* (1597)

John Gerard (1545-1612), surgeon of Holborn, grew nine varieites of roses in his garden in 1596 and produced his famous *Herball* in 1597. At that time it was accepted as the standard reference work, but soon lost much of its importance after the appearance of Parkinson's *Paradisus terrestris*. A year earlier, he had brought out a *Catalogus Plantarum* in which 16 varieties of roses are described with 14 illustrations.

It was John Parkinson (1569-1629), Apothecary of London, who, in his work *Paradisus terrestris* ("The Earthly Paradise"), first provides real information on the multiplicity of rose varieties in the English gardens of his day. He describes no less than 24 in detail and in the chronological order of their introduction; 14 were also illustrated. This list is the most important rose resumé of the later Middle Ages and it is therefore reproduced here:

R. *Anglica alba*

R. *Incarnata* (*R. Belgica siue Vitrea*)

R. *Anglica rubra* (*R. rubra* according to Gerard)

R. *Damascena* (*R. prouincialis* according to Gerard)

R. *Prouincialis* siue *Hollandica Damascena* (*R. Damascena flore multiplici* according to Gerard)

R. *Prouincialis rubra* (*R. rubra flore maximo* according to Gerard)

R. *Prouincialis alba* (Witte Prouensche Roose according to de l'Obel)

R. *versicolor* (*R. Praenestina variegata plena* in Hort. Eystett.) i.e. *R. gallica versicolor*.

R. *Chrystallina;* similar to the preceding according to Parkinson, though showing more red in the stripes.

R. *rubra humilis* siue *pumilis*

PLATE 5

"Hie stritet sifort und der berner"
("Here Siegfried and Dietrich von Bern are fighting.")

"Also munch ylsan ein kussen wart von der jungfrowen."
("And so the monk Ilsan got a kiss from the maiden.")

These two illustrations come from the only illuminated manuscript on roses, written in Strasburg *ca.* 1420. ("The Lay of the Nibelungen.") (Heidelberg University — Bibl. Cod. pal. germ. 359 Fol. 22v, 49r and 61r)

The "1,000 year old Rose Tree" on Hildesheim Cathedral (1972) (Photo: J. Breloer)

PLATE 6

The Rose-Screen in the Cistercian Monastery at Stams, Tyrol. Made between 1709/16 by the metalworker Bernhard Bachnitzer; right, enlarged detail.

The "Ave Maria" by Veit Stoss at the East end of the Choir in St. Lawrence Church at Nuremburg showing a beautiful carved wreath of roses (1517-1518).

"The Virgin with Rose Hedge" Painting by Martin Schongauer in St. Martin's Cathedral at Colmar, Alsace. The roses in the background have been identified as *R. gallica officinalis* (1473).

R. Francofurtensis (*R. sine Spinis* according to Gerard)

R. Hungarica

R. Holosericea simplex & *multiplex* (*R. holosericea* according to Gerard)

R. sine spinis simplex & *multiplex* (Thornless Rose, single and double)

R. Cinnamomea simplex & *multiplex*

R. lutea simplex (our modern *R. foetida*)

R. lutea multiplex siue *flore pleno* (i.e. *R. hemisphaerica*)

R. Moschata simplex & *multiplex*

R. Moschata multiplex altera (probably a *moschata* hybrid)

R. Hispanica Moschata simplex (*R. moschata Hispanica* according to Gerard)

R. Pomifera maior (i.e. *R. pomifera*)

R. siluestris odora siue *Eglenteria simplex* (i.e. *R. Rubiginosa*)

R. siluestris odora siue *Eglenteria flore duplici* (double form of *R. rubiginosa*)

R. semper virens

Any attempt to interpret the relation between the roses described and illustrated by the individual authors is better left undone as it is only too easy to err. The writers often named the roses quite arbitrarily and the drawings themselves are unreliable. Wilde made an attempt to compare the roses described by Gessner (1561), Wirsing (1582) and Tabernaemontanus (1588), but with considerable reservations.

Basilius Besler (1581-1629), an apothecary, wrote the *Hortus Eystettensis*, commissioned by Johann Conrads von Gemmingen, Bishop of Eichstätt. The book contained 1,100 beautiful illustrations of plants with exemplary fidelity to nature. These included six full page plates of the following roses:

Rosa Damascena flore pleno

Rosa lutea maxima flore pleno

R. provincialis flore incarnato plena

R. centifolia rubra

R. praenestina variegata (*R. gallica versicolor*)

R. provincialis flore albo

R. Milesia flore rubro pleno (a form of *R. gallica*)

R. albo flore simplici (*R. alba*)

R. flore albo pleno (*R. alba plena*)

R. damascena flore simplici

R. rubicunda (The Tidbit Rose; semi-double *gallica*)

R. lacteola Camerarii

Figure 37. Medieval Garden, surrounded by a hedge, *ca.* 1600.

R. ex rubro nigricans flore pleno; semi-double

R. praecox spinosa alba (*R. pimpinellifolia*)

R. rubra praecox flore simplici (*R. majalis*)

R. cinnamomea (double red cinnamon rose)

R. lutea flore simplici (*R. lutea*)

R. eglenteria (*R. rubiginosa*)

R. Milesia rubra flore simplici

R. sylvestris flore rubro (*R. canina*)

R. sylvestris odorata incarnato flore

J.S. Elsholz in his book *Neuangelegter Gartenbau oder Unterricht in der Gärtnerei* (1666) describes how it was possible to make roses bloom "out of season".

The Italian Count Octavius Brembatus lib. I. Protei Legati plants stocks in various receptacles in every month throughout the year; first he deprives them of water and nourishment for a time, then gives them a lot of water so that they are forced rapidly into growth and by carrying out these changes every month he manages to maintain a rose garden in perpetual bloom.

The last book to be mentioned is *Phytanthozaiconographia* by J.W. Weinmann (1683-1741) which appeared between 1737 and 1741, in four fine folio volumes with some 1,000 illustrations. Weinmann was an apothecary in Regensburg and he includes in the drawings a number of roses, but none of them bore any similarity to the modern *Rosa centifolia*. From this we can conclude that it was unkown to him, and that it had

Figure 38. Garden showing a rose arbor *ca.* 1600.

not managed to reach him, by that time, from Holland.

It is often not understood that roses in the Middle Ages played a secondary role. This is shown when the wealth of detail given in the Herbals to the various garden plants is examined below:

In Sweertius' (Emmanuel Sweert) *Florilegium*, which was published in 1612 in Frankfurt, there are descriptions of 32 tulips, 39 anemones, 44 hyacinths, 60 daffodils, but only 9 roses.

In France the disparity was even more striking. Jean de la Quintinie (1620-1701), Head Gardener to Louis XIV at Versailles, wrote, in his book *Instructions pour les jardin fruitiers et potagers* (Paris, 1690), details on 77 anemones, 225 carnations, 437 tulips and only 14 roses.

Apart from the beginning of the development of *R. centifolia* in Holland, the position of the rose remained unchanged until the recurrent Chinese roses were introduced; this produced a dramatic upsurge in interest and production. Around 1800, Guillemeau could still write in *Histoire Naturelle de la Rose*, p. 15, that at the time only about 100 varieties were known, many of which only had single flowers. Propagation consisted mostly of root division, layering or cuttings. The process of budding was known, but seldom used, similarly sowing seed was not done much because, as Theophrastus had already said, it was too tedious a process. This opinion was continually repeated by later authors until it became accepted as fact, with the result that almost no new varieties became available. It was only when sowing seed was recognized as not being too "boring" that the position was altered, with the following results:

In 1815 there were about 250 varieties in existence

In 1828 there were about 2,500

In 1845 there were about 5,000

In 1912 just in the Roseraie de l'Hay in Paris there were no less than 8,000!

Further development will be fully dealt with in the chapter "History and Development of the Modern Garden Rose" which begins on page 67.

ANOTHER LOOK AT PERSIA

On page 22, the rose in Persia was examined; as might be expected, development took place there as well. The country was at that time a veritable rose paradise; the rose was the emblem of the Godhead, the holy plant of Islam. Therefore the rose was highly prized and extensively grown by Moslems.

The Persians, had a special place in their rose gardens (*gulistan* = 'rose garden' or 'rose ground') for the Spring Festival, where roses bloomed and nightingales sang.

The gardens of Kashmir, Peshawar and Shiraz must truly have been like Paradise. Their special rose was *Rosa damascena*, the rose of the Persians. John Chardin, according to Loudon, reported in 1686 that he had found no parterres, mazes or any of the other usual features of European gardens, but instead gardens full of lilies, peach trees and roses. Many English authors from 1650 to 1800, affirm Loudon's claim, indicating that where gardens were concerned, there was no country in the world where the rose was grown to such perfection as in Persia.

The rose gardens of Shiraz and Teheran were especially highly esteemed; apparently they were laid out in the form of a series of terraces.

Isfahan, the Persian City of Roses was, at the end of the 16th and beginning of the 17th centuries, the capital city of the Safavid dynasty. At that time, when the country was ruled by Shah Abass the Great, the city was noted for its numerous mosques, bridges and monuments, all built on the ruins of prehistoric Iranian cultures. The favored flower was the rose.

The modern main street in Isfahan, the Chaharbagh ('Four Gardens') is named for the four gardens which flank it, stretching a mile along the street.

Even today there are many roses in the public parks and private gardens. There is also a scientifically managed rose nursery and a trial ground of about 2.8 ha./7 acres. Rose shows are held annually. The best time to visit the gardens is the last two weeks of May when the plants are usually in full bloom.

Figure 39. Persian embroidery of the early 17th century from Isfahan, representing (left) *R. foetida* and (right) 'Persian Yellow' with nightingales and a deer (from a Persian exhibition; redrawn)

THE ROSE IN GERMAN POETRY

While the rose does not appear in the rather sparse poetry of Old High German, the religious poetry took its models from the Classics, it is used in many songs of the Middle Ages. Here it is the flower of Spring, of the pastures, the heath and the garden. Individual parts of the body such as mouth, cheek and chin were associated with the rose and women were compared to it, especially the Blessed Virgin Mary.

The rose gardens of the Middle Ages, for instance the rose garden of Kriemhild of Worms which was "a mile long and half a mile wide", are not to be equated with modern gardens. Such a garden was generally a pasture or meadow on which knights held their tournaments and jousts. The area was not enclosed with roses, but with "a fine border" (of what is unknown).

However, in time, rose gardens of the modern type did develop. As can be seen from numerous paintings and illustrations in contemporary books, many gathering places were surrounded with hedges of wild roses, probably *R. rubiginosa* or *R. canina*. In the center of these rose gardens there may also have been some individual rose bushes.

The second famous rose garden celebrated in the "Song of the Little Rose Garden" of the 13th century, belonged, according to a Tyrolean folk tale, to the King of the Dwarfs, Laurin. The garden was surrounded by a silken thread; whoever damaged it in any way lost his right hand and left foot to Laurin. It must have looked like a real battlefield, and the roses must have had a hard time of it. Laurin had another piece of property called the "Meadow of the Hollow Hill", but this was a more typical pleasure garden or meeting place where festivities could take place, with an old lime tree and flowers; there is no mention of any roses.

It would be possible to cite other instances from early German poetry, but for this it is best to refer to the extensive work done by Fehrle whose study of the subject is so vast as to be almost cumbersome. The work of Zander and Teschner gives a good general impression of the rose garden as it appeared in the Middle Ages.

THE ROSE IN THE BIBLE

References to the rose in the Bible are not only poor but also, due to errors in translation or in explanation,

Figure 40. From the *Heldenbuch* ("Book of Heroes") "Here fought Dietlieb von Steyer and Walther von Wachsenstein. And each of them wore a chaplet of roses." (*ca.* 1500)

often untrustworthy. The rose is only mentioned seven times in the Bible: twice in the Old Testament, in the Song of Solomon and Isaiah, and five times in the Apocrypha, in the Wisdom of Solomon and Ecclesiasticus. There is also a reference in the Third Book of Maccabees which is not included in our Bible.

The relevant quotations are as follows:

The Song of Solomon, chap. 2, verses 1-2 and 16:
I am the rose of Sharon and the lily of the valleys. As the lily among the thorns, so is my love among the daughters. My beloved is mine and I am his; he feedeth among the lilies.

Isaiah, chap. 35, verse 1:
The wilderness and the solitary place shall be glad for them; and the desert shall rejoice and blossom as the rose.

The Wisdom of Solomon, chap. 2, verse 8:
Let us have costly wines and perfumes to our heart's content, and let no flower of spring escape us. Let us crown ourselves with rosebuds before they can wither.

2 Esdras, chap. 2, verse 19:
seven great mountains covered with roses and lilies.

Ecclesiasticus, chap. 24, verse 14:
There I grew like a cedar of Lebanon . . . like roses at Jericho.

Ecclesiasticus, chap. 39, verse 13:
Listen to me, my devout sons, and blossom like a rose planted by a stream.

Ecclesiasticus, chap. 50, verse 8:
as the flower of roses at the dawning of the day.

The quotation from 3 Maccabees 7, 17 describes the City of Ptolemy as "rose-bedecked according to the custom of the place". According to Wehrhahn this is not the town in Cyrenaica, but one at Bachr Jusuf in Egypt, west of Medinet-el Fayyoum, now known as el-Lahum. The book was written in Greek about the time of the Birth of Christ.

These references, and the interpretations of them by botanists and biblical commentators merit a closer look.

In the Song of Solomon and in Isaiah, the latter written about 750 B.C., the "Rose of Sharon" and the "lily" appear in the English Authorized Version, but in the Hebrew text the same word is used in both places. The Greek text speaks first of *anthos* ('flower') and in Isaiah *krinon* ('lily'). Some botanists feel that a narcissus was intended, or perhaps either *Colchicum autumnale* or *Anemone fulgens*. The two references in the Old Testament remain unclear, but there is little doubt that they do not refer to roses, however sad this may be about a much-loved passage.

In the Apocrypha the rose is first mentioned in the Wisdom of Solomon. This book was copied into Greek between the years 100 and 50 B.C., probably by a Jewish scholar, well versed in Greek, who lived in Alexandria. He writes of rose chaplets worn by the guests at banquets which was very much in the contemporary Greek fashion. We already know that this was a custom in that country, as it was later in Rome. When we recall that roses were exported to Rome from Egypt then we can be sure that here the author really does mean the rose and we may well consider it to have been *Rosa gallica*.

The Book of Ecclesiasticus was transcribed in Palestine between 190 and 170 B.C., originally in Hebrew, and then about 130 B.C. into Greek by the author's grandson. The word *rhodon* ('rose') appears in two different places, i.e. 24, 14 and 39, 13. In a third passage (50, 8), however, the original Hebrew test has been retained and the word *shoshanna* has been translated as 'rose'. Although this has usually been translated as 'lily' it is generally considered, as both P. Ascherson and H. Christ tell us, to have been an *Iris*. This could also apply to 39, 13 where the plants are described as growing beside a stream. It should be said here that the New English Bible, in 50, 8 reverts to the use of 'rose': "like a rose in spring or lilies by a fountain of water".

Therefore the Bible does not provide conclusive evidence that there were roses in Palestine before the Birth of Christ.

English and American experts do not hold the view that where the word 'rose' is used in the Bible, a rose is indeed meant, for this translation from the Hebrew probably relates to a bulb of some sort, possibly a *Crocus*, but the whole uncertainty turns upon the possibility of faulty translation. It is uncertain just what the "Rose of Sharon" was, the "Ebony Flower" or "Ebony Saffron". In any case the "Rose of Sharon" had nothing to do with *Hibiscus syriacus* from "Syria" (actually from China) which is known as the "Rose

of Sharon" in England today. Furthermore, oleander, *Nerium oleander*, and tulips, *T. montana* and *T. sharonensis*, must not be ignored.

Were there any wild roses in Palestine? The answer must be "yes," just as there are roses growing there today, and *Rosa phoenicia*, with its fleeting white pannicles of sweetly scented bloom, must have been amongst them. It is found today in Turkey, Syria, and Lebanon as well as Palestine.

The "Rose of Jericho" was not a rose at all but was associated with the "Plants of the Resurrection". Three plants are described here and illustrated in Plate 9.

Asteriscus pygmaeus (Coss. & Dur.) or *Osteospermum pygmaeum* (Benth. & Hook.), the "Rose of Jericho of the Crusaders" is a small (approx. 10 cm./4 in.

Figure 41. From the *Heldenbuch* ("Book of Heroes"); the frontispiece to the Song of the Rose Garden ("Here follows the Rose Garden at Worms with a fair company"); *ca.* 1500.

high), member of the *Compositae* with quite short radiate flowers in little heads surrounded by star-shaped bracts. The grey leaves are tomentose and quickly dry up and fall off. The flower heads close up in hot dry weather to prevent a dispersal of seed, but open up quickly as soon as there is any moisture. It is to be found in the Jordan valley, particularly near Jericho, and also in the deserts of N. Africa and S.W. Asia.

Anastatica hierochuntica L., the "true Rose of Jericho" belongs to the *Cruciferae*; this is an annual, about 10 cm./4 in. high, of upright growth, having an umbelliferous appearance; the leaves are small, greyish-green, star-shaped and hairy, later falling off; the flowers are small and white; after setting the seed the plant dries up and dies, becoming claw-shaped and curling in upon itself. The plants are not uprooted by the wind and blown hither and thither over the plains as has often been said, but remain in their original position. In times of drought the stems remain curled up, but when the rains come they open out and disseminate their seed. Like *Asteriscus*, it is to be found in the same areas, although not in the immediate vicinity of Jericho. In the Middle Ages, it was known as *Rosa sanctae Maria*, 'Mary's Rose' or the 'Plant of the Resurrection'.

The third "false Rose of Jericho" is *Selaginella lepidophylla*, a member of the *Selaginellaceae* (club-moss) from the dry areas of Mexico and Central America. It grows in small, flat rosettes, which roll up into a ball about the size of a tennis ball in drought conditions. As a result of a high content of a greasy oil which protects the protoplasm from drying out, the plants can remain alive throughout the year and are revived when the rainy season comes. However, even a dead plant will open up when put into water and close again when dry. This *Selaginella* is more common today than the other two.

BIBLIOGRAPHY

Early Botanical Works (Herbals, etc.)

ALBERTUS MAGNUS. Naturalia. Strasburg 1548.

BAUHIN, CASPAR. Pinax theatri botanici. 522 pp. Basel 1623.

BESLER, BASILIUS. Hortus Eystettensis. 367 plates with text. Nürnberg 1613, reprinted Münich 1964.

BOCK, HIERONYMUS. New Kreutterbuch. 530 woodcuts. Strasburg 1577. New Edition Münich 1964.

BRUNFELS, OTTO. Contrafayt Kreüterbuch. 332 pp. 170 Ill. Strasburg 1532. New Edition Münich 1964.

CAMERARIUS, JOACHIM. Hortus medius et philosophicus. With appendix, Frankfurt 1588.

CLUSIUS, CAROLUS (Charles de l'Ecluse). Rariorum aliquot stirpium per Pannoniam Austriam et vicinitatis Historia. Antwerp 1583.

ELSHOLZ, JOHANN SIEGESMUND. Neuangelegter Gartenbau oder Unterricht von der Gärtnerei. Colln a.d. Spree 1666.

FUCHS, LEONHART. New Kreüterbuch. 680 pp. 518 Ill. Basel 1543. New Edition Münich 1964.

GERARD, JOHN. The Herball. 1,392 pp. 1,800 Ill. London 1597.

GESSNER, CONRAD. Catalogus Plantarum. 162 pp. Frankfurt 1543.

— De Hortis Germaniae. Strasburg 1561.

HILDEGARDIS DE PINGUIA. Physica S. Hildegardis. 121 pp. Strasburg 1533.

LOBELIUS, MATTIAS (de l'Obel). Plantarum seu stirpium icones. 2 vols., 1,442 pp. 1,742 Ill. Antwerp 1576.

LONITZER, ADAM. Kreuterbuch, neu zugericht. 342 sheets, 708 Ill. Frankfurt 1557.

MEGENBERG, KONRAD VON. Buch der Natur. 292 pp. Augsburg 1475.

PARKINSON, JOHN. Paradisi in sole Paradisus terrestris. 2 editions. 612 pp. 110 Ill. London 1656.

— Theatrum Botanicum, or a herball of a large extent. 1,775 pp. 2,716 Ill. London 1640.

QUINTINIE, JEAN DE LA. Instructions pour les Jardins fruitiers et potagers. Paris 1690.

STRABO, WALAFRID. Hortulus. Translated by R. PAYNE. Pittsburgh 1966.

SWEERT, EMANUEL. Florilegium. In 2 parts with 560 Ill. Frankfurt 1612.

TABERNAEMONTANUS, JAKOB THEODOR. Neuw Kreuterbuch. 818 pp. 558 Ill. Frankfurt 1588.

— Eicones planatarum seu stirpium, arborum, fruticum, herbarum, lignorum, radicum omnis generis. 1,128 pp. 2,400 Ill. Frankfurt 1590.

WEINMANN, JOHANN WILHELM. Phytanthoza Iconographia. 4 vols. with over 4,000 Ill. Regensburg 1737-1741.

WONNECKE, JOHANN. Ortus sanitatis auff teutsch Ein Garten der Gesundheit. Mainz 1485. New Edition Münich 1966.

Additional Works of Reference

BAUMANN, H. Zur Geschichte und Gestalt des Rosengartens. German Rose Annual 22: 106-145 (1961)

CRISP, F. Mediaeval Gardens. London 1924.

FEHRLE, ERNST. Rose und Rosengarten im deutschen Mittelalter. Heidelberg 1922.

FISCHER-BENZON, R. VON. Altdeutsche Gartenflora. Kiel 1894.

GRIMM, W. Der Rosengarten. Göttingen 1836.

HASHAGEN, J. Kulturgeschichte des Mittelalters. Hamburg 1950.

HERRING, P. Studier i Rosens Kulturhistorie. 191 pp. Copenhagen 1928.

KAUFMANN, A. Der Gartenbau im Mittelalter und wahrend der Renaissance. 5 Lectures. Berlin 1892.

LAUENSTEIN, D. Der deutsche Garden des Mittelalters bis in das Jahr 1400. Gottingen 1900.

LORRIS, G. DE, & G.J. DE MEUNG. Le Roman de la Rose. Edited by M. Gorce. Paris 1933.

MATTHEWS, Q.L. The Rose with the Moguls. A.R.A. 1945.

MAZAHÉRI, ALY. So lebten die Muselmanen im Mittelalter. Stuttgart 1957.

OPOIX. Histoire et description de Provins. *Ca.* 1807. (see Rose Annual 1954, p. 141.)

RICE, D.T. Die Kunst des Islam. Münich 1965.

THE ROSE IN THE BIBLE

SA'DI, MUSLIHEDDIN. Der Rosengarten. Translated by K.H. GRAF, 1846. New Edition Münich 1923.

SPRINGER, A. Paris im 13. Jahrhundert. 1856.

STEINVORTH, H. Die fränkischen Kaisergärten, die Bauerngärten in Niedersachsen und die Fensterflora derselben. From the Year Book of the Nat. Hist. Soc. of the Principality of Lüneburg 11: 33-66 (1890).

UHLAND, L. Zum Rosengarten von Worms. Edited by PFEIFFER, Vol. 6. 1861.

WEIN, K. Deutschlands Kulturpflanzen um die Mitte des 16 Jahr. Beih. Bot. C. Bl. 1914.

WILDE, J. Kulturgeschichte der Sträucher und Stauden. 303 pp. Speyer 1947.

YOUNG, N. Ghosts of the Rose World. The Rose 15: 110-114.

Biblical References

BORCHARD, R. Did Abraham know the Rose? The Rose 11: 128-131 (1962).

The Bible as translated into German by Martin Luther. 1,435 pp. Stettin (undated).

GRÄSMUCK, H. Die Rosen von Jericho. Deutsch. Baumsch. 25: 126-128 (1973).

JEANS, G.E. The Rose of the Bible. Rose Annual 1946: 78-80.

MOLDENKE, H. Plants of the Bible. 1952.

WALKER, W. All the Plants of the Bible. London 1958.

WEHRHAHN, H.R. Biblische Rosenstudien. German Rose Annual 1936: 74-76.

The Rose of the Modern Era From *CA.* 1500 to the Beginning of Modern Hybridization

This chapter, which commences in the Middle Ages and continues through to the beginning of our own century, cannot really be associated with a particular era of civilization, nor can everything be said regarding all the different facets of the development of the modern garden rose. It is intended as an orderly and chronological extract of all the various factors concerned. Of particular importance is the section on the introduction of the rose from Asia, particularly from China.

Germany The rose was quite commonly cultivated from the 16th century on, although not in any great quantity, as can be seen from the old "herbals", from numerous paintings and from the popular ballads of the day.

1539 *Rosa damascena* in cultivation; according to H. Bock.

1561 *Rosa moschata* in cultivation (Gessner), also recorded by Tabernaemontanus, (1588).

Koelreuter's theory of plant hybridization, which gave the clearest proof of the sexual processes and fertilization of plants and the research for which was carried out in a thoroughly scientific manner, received little recognition from his contemporaries. He described the functions of the individual parts of the flower and the role of insects in the process of pollination. As Koelreuter finally became garden superintendent of the royal park in Karlsruhe from 1761-1766, it is almost incomprehensible that other gardeners took so little interest in his experiments. Many of his contemporaries continued to use the old method of simply sowing seed and then just waiting to see what would come up.

It was probably between 1790 and 1800 that budding was first practiced on *R. canina* collected from the wild for standards and half-standards. Gradually, during the 19th century, the practice of budding for the propagation of bush roses increased. It is uncertain where this first started, although it was probably in France which, at that time, was the leading rose-growing country.

One of the best informants from the end of the 18th century, is Dr. C.G. Rössig of Leipzig. Extracts of his work published in 1799 follow:

> The propagation of roses is done by root division cuttings, layering or budding and this latter either by growing or dormant eyes; from those varieties which produce ripe and viable seedpods, by sowing the seed.
>
> Propagation by root division or by cuttings is the quickest and easiest method; most varieties send up each year a lot of new shoots from the base which in their first summer reach 1-2 feet high. These are taken off in the fall or in favourable weather conditions in winter or even the following spring with a piece of root attached and are then planted out, the weaker in a nursery bed, the stronger in their permanent position where under normal conditions they will bloom in the following summer.
>
> Also in the case of plants which have thrown a good number of suckers of good-sized stems, propagation can be carried out by a division of the plant. In this case the whole bush is dug up and separated into pieces and immediately replanted in its required position; this is best done in the fall but can also be done in winter and the spring.
>
> Layering should be done to young shoots. If much propagation in this manner is proposed, Mr. Leuder suggests a special layering bed[1]. For this purpose, a number of stems are needed and after a year or two these are pruned back hard to the ground and in the following summer many new shoots springing from the base, can either be cut or bent in the next fall or winter so that the bark is broken and pegged down; they will then put out roots which in the following fall can be planted out in the nursery bed. Propagation by layering has been found most successful, so far, with the Monthy, Damask and Sweet Briars. Some varieties root more slowly in the fall which is particularly the case with the large dog-rose, *Rosa villosa*, the musk rose, *Rosa moschata*, the moss rose, *Rosa muscosa*, all of which often take two years to root well.
>
> In the case of roses which do not throw many side shoots, and this is often so with the finest varieties, propagation must be carried out by budding, alternatively this method can be used to obtain taller bushes or to have more than one variety growing on a single stock. For this purpose the tallest and strongest shoots of the so-called 'Frankfurt' rose or others which throw long sturdy shoots from the base, are most often selected.

We get the impression that budding as a means of propagation was only used in case of special need before it became a general practice. This is borne out in Wilhelm Keller's *Catalogue* (1828). He was a market gardener in Duisburg and issued a voluminous list of his roses, including all the French varieties, the names of which he had translated into German. He certainly had no qualms about what he charged for his roses for which he usually got between 1 and 3 Guilders (each about 16 Groschen); the plants were undoubtedly of a quality which would not be acceptable today. He advertised that, generally, the roses he offered for sale "would be grown on their own roots but that if such a variety

---

[1] i.e. Beds for the parent plants.

were not so available, then a budded one would be supplied in its place''.

1800 *Rosa chinensis* (pink) and the carmine variety of *semperflorens* were to be found in all of the most important European rose gardens.
1820 King Frederick William III of Prussia had a rose garden laid out on the Island of Pfau near Potsdam; this is dealt with in greater detail on p. 142.

Other important rose collections of the first half of the 19th century were to be found in Düsseldorf (Arnz; van Baerle), and in Berlin-Witzleben (Deppe). In these gardens the roses were planted purely for display.

Around 1820, James Booth was the proprietor of an important nursery at Klein-Flottbeck near Altona where he also raised roses. In 1816, he put out one of his own novelties 'Königin von Dänemark' (probably *R. alba* × *R. damascena*) which is still grown today. This prompted a violent quarrel with Prof. Lehmann, the Director of the Botanic Gardens in Hamburg, who maintained that this variety had long been known in France. Both parties wrote furious letters in which they strenuously attacked each other. Lehmann failed to produce proof and the 'Königin von Dänemark' was credited to Booth.

Let us now look at how breeding new varieties began in Germany. The first man to name a rose which he himself had introduced was Schwarzkopf, the Head Gardener to the Landgraf Frederick II of Hesse, of the Schloss Weissenstein near Cassel (see p. 000.) His rose was called 'Pearl of Weissenstein'. Schwarzkopf had been Head Gardener since 1769 and had created this

rose garden which was probably the first of its kind in Germany.

Ernst Herger, a hybridizer in Köstritz, had about 2,000 varieties in cultivation in 1857, the largest collection in Germany at that time. The plants, of course, were for sale.

Doctor Freidrich Ruschpler, of Dresden, an amateur hybridizer, put out a variety 'Dr. Ruschpler' in 1856. His son Paul produced four other cultivars between 1877 and 1878.

About 1870, Paul, who owned a nursery in Dresden, began breeding and selecting standards from seed. The young seedlings were carefully selected and gave first class standards, which made the collection of wild stems from the woods and hedgerows unnecessary. Prior to this, there were firms in Germany who specialized in supplying wild standards, mostly in Thuringia and Hesse. How these stems looked before and after cutting, can be seen in Fig. 42.

Modern field cultivation by budding was developed by W. Kordes in Holstein (1953) from the work of E. L. Meyn (1880) who planted *canina* understocks in rows for the first time, and also improved them. In the course of the next ten years this practice was adopted by the nurseries of Gustav Frahm, Elmshorn; J.F. Müller, Rellingen; J. Timm & Co., Elmshorn; Conrad Maass, Rellingen; Wilhelm Kordes, Elmshorn; Matthias Tantau, Uetersen; etc.

The Rev. Droegemüller of Neuhaus-Elbe introduced 11 new varieties between 1886 and 1895.

Peter Lambert began hybridizing about 1885. His 'Kaiserin Auguste Viktoria' appeared in 1891; by 1906 he had brought out six of his own seedlings. All the

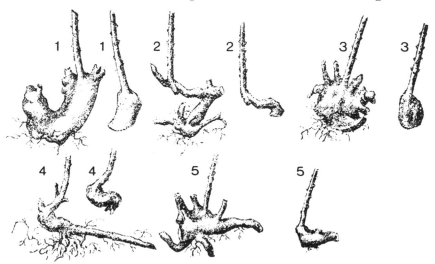

Figure 42. This is what the ''wild stocks'', which were originally used for standards before the introduction of the modern seedling stems, looked like. The illustration shows five bare-root stocks, on the right in each case the stock has been prepared for planting. (from *Rosen-Zeitung*)

other German hybridizers, and there are about 150 altogether, started after 1900. The more important of them are included in the section on hybridizers and their work (p. 152), the remainder were amateurs who introduced at most one or two cultivars.

In 1893, the German Rose Society (Verein Deutscher Rosenfreunde) was founded.

Holland   In 1601, Clusius obtained the double yellow rose *Rosa hemisphaerica,* from Friedrich Maier of Strasburg.

In the 17th century, the apothecary in the city of Leyden bought 26,000 *aertrosen* ('wild roses') and 8,459 *provisyroosen* ('conservatory roses') from a rose nurseryman in Noordwijk for medicinal purposes. At this time there was a *roosenoly-stokerij* (attar of roses distillery) in Spaarndam.

In Noordwijk, in 1809, there were two big market gardens which also grew roses. The blooms were collected, the petals shredded and pickled in casks and sent to the East Indies for the production of Attar, which was then shipped back to Holland for sale (according to Geldof). Many reference books state that in the 17th and 18th centuries in Holland, the *centifolia*[1], the 'Rose of Batavia' and later the 'Rose des Peintres' were developed. In time there came to be about 2,000 varieties, or at least varietal names, including moss roses.

In the second half of the 19th century, the van Eeden nursery in Haarlem was the principal rose grower, but no hybrids introduced by them are known and no reference list of roses cites this firm as the originator of any variety.

Luxembourg   By 1853, there were twelve rose nurseries which were dealing in some 3,000 varieties, mostly budded on *R. manettii* understocks. The most important firm was Soupert & Notting which became well known for its own introductions, some 60 in number, of which 'Eugene Fürst', 'Tour de Malakoff' and 'Violacée' are still extant.

Italy   In the previous section it was shown that, in addition to Rouen in France, Florence was already famous for its roses by the 15th century. Everything that was known about roses at that time could be studied there. Due to this, the rose, which had suffered a decline after the Fall of Rome, regained its position as a cultivated plant.

1551   *Rosa lutea* was in the Aldovrandi herbarium in Padua; in cultivated form, it was brought from Persia in 1836 by a British diplomat, Sir Henry Willock.

Looking ahead in time: by the end of the 19th century the farmers on the Italian Riviera were begining to cut down their olive orchards and restrict their corn crops in order to increase rose growing for the cut flower trade. What a parallel to ancient times!

England   By the year 1800, there were already rose nurseries of considerable size in or near London (Hammersmith, Chelsea, Islington and Hackney). William Paul's nursery at Cheshunt was started about 1820 and soon achieved pre-eminence.

At the beginning of the 19th century, the Ayrshire Roses originated in Scotland from a cross between *R. arvensis* and the *Pimpinellifoliae* (known in England as Scotch or Burnet roses).

1815   Brown of Slough, England obtained a seedling from 'Hume's Blush' crossed with a *gallica* which he called 'Brown's Superb Blush'. At first it was considered a *chinensis* hybrid but was later regarded as a Hybrid Tea and thus the first of its kind, preceding the Bourbons, the Noisettes, and the Hybrid Perpetuals which have always been regarded as the forerunners of the Hybrid Teas.

1827   Sweet published the *Hortus Britannicus* in which he described 107 species and 1,059 cultivars, most o the latter coming from *R. gallica*.

1880   Henry Bennett of Shepperton, England brought

---

[1] *Rosa centifolia*. There are four theories as to its origin:
  1. Bieberstein suggests that it came from the Caucasus and that it grew wild there; this opinion is not accepted by Russian botanists.
  2. It may have existed in Ancient Rome; although this has been advanced in many books on roses, it is not a view shared by botanists.

3. It may have been gradually developed in Holland between 1580 and 1710, possibly from a double form of *gallica;* this theory has been generally accepted by both botanists and gardeners.

4. Finally, according to N. Young (1971), there is no conclusive information regarding its origin.

out a dark red Hybrid Tea called 'William Francis Bennett' and which, when he exhibited it in 1884, he was able to sell for $5,000.

Although most of the old Hybrid Perpetuals were raised in France, England became their true home. Nowhere were they better grown, and even the climate seemed to suit them better since they appreciated the continual variation from warm to cool. Admittedly some of the blooms were affected by "balling", but it had long been observed in England that when cool days followed hot ones, many of the blooms opened to perfection. Consequently, the opinion was held in both England and Ireland that no more perfect Hybrid Perpetuals were grown anywhere in the world than in these two countries (Foster-Melliar).

North America Henry William, Baron von Stiegel, glass manufacturer, was probably the first to form a collection of roses here. By 1773, he had already accumulated many varieties.

One of the oldest nurseries in N. America was the Prince nursery, founded in 1737 by Robert Prince at Flushing, Long Island. He was well established in the international market and was responsibe for the distribution of many plants throughout the country. In 1846, his grandson, William Robert Prince, issued a rose catalog which included more than 700 varieties.

1811   *Rosa chinensis* ('Old Blush') had by this time reached America. In the rice fields of John Champney of Charleston, South Carolina, a new rose was born, called 'Champney's Pink Cluster' (*R. chinensis × R. moschata*) which was to be the forerunner of the Noisette roses.

When the development of American interest in rose eeding, and how well it has done in the last 50 years, is considered then its earliest beginnings must be recorded:

1815   John Champney of Charleston, South Carolina produced the Noisette rose.
1836   Samuel and John Feast produced *setigera* hybrids in Baltimore, Maryland.

France France is dealt with last because early French rose breeding was so dependent on the Empress Joséphine, who has been given a special section (p. 100). Presented now are only a few facts which do not appear there.

1815   Comte Lelieur, in charge of the Royal Gardens, discovered a seedling of a chance across which had the bright red color of the Portland Rose and the recurrency of *R. chinensis*. He named it 'Rose Lelieur', but this did not please the King who wanted it to be called 'Rose du Roi', and so was introduced under this name by Souchet in 1816.

1817   The French botanist Bréon discovered, as a result of his visit to the Ile de Bourbon (now Réunion Island), a natural cross between *R. chinensis* and *R. damascena*, the seeds of which he sent to Jacques, then head gardener to the Duc d'Orléans at Neuilly. The result was four or five seedlings of which the best was named *Rosa canina borbonica*. From this came the Bourbon roses of which there were finally 428 varieties.

The two nurserymen Desportes and Prévost issued their catalogs in 1829; Desportes offered 2,000 varieties for sale.

By 1860 France was exporting about 800,000 cultivated roses and 100,000 wild stocks. At the Paris flower market 4,000,000 francs worth of roses alone were sold annually, and 150,000 francs spent on forced roses of which there were only 25 varieties.

By 1870, the number of varieties in cultivation had risen to 6,000.

THE INTRODUCTION OF THE ROSE FROM ASIA

The descriptions of Marco Polo (1254-1324), and later, other travelers, soldiers and sailors, upon their return from the Orient, awakened the interest, first of the botanists, and then of the gardeners in Europe. However, some centuries were to pass before there was a general understanding of the plant kingdom of Asia. Indeed we cannot yet lay claim to more than a good general knowledge of the plants of that region, much remains still to be uncovered. The discovery of the *Metasequoia* in 1944 was certainly not the end of the story.

Many Asiatic countries, particularly those where communication is still difficult, have closed their borders to botanical expeditions. The great technical problems of an earlier time (difficult travel, long marches on foot, inadequate means of preserving living plant material and transporting it quickly) would be easily overcome today by helicopter use and by packing the plants in plastic and sending them by air, if only the countries concerned would co-operate and provide the necessary facilities.

Of the many distinguished plant collectors of the 19th and 20th centuries there is only space here to mention the most important and those who sent various roses home.

Aitchison, J.E.P. (1836-1898), English; Afghanistan (1880, *Rosa ecae*).

Booth, J.J., English; Bhutan, *ca.* 1850.

David, Abbé Armand (1826-1900); French missionary, W. China.

Delavay, Abbé J.M. (1834-1895); French missionary, Yunnan, China.

Falconer, Hugh (1808-1865), English; India.

Farrer, Reginald (1880-1920), English; Tibet, Burma, China.

Forrest, George (1873-1932), English; China.

Fortune, Robert (1812-1880), English; China and Japan.

Henry, Augustine (1857-1930), Irish; China.

Hooker, J. Dalton (1817-1911), English; the Himalayas.

Kerr, William, English; in China from 1804-1813.

Meyer, F.N., American (born in Holland); Turkestan and E. Asia. (1911, *Rosa primula*).

Purdo, W. (1880-1921), English; Kan-su, China.

Rock, Joseph (1884-1962), Austrian; China and Tibet.

Siebold, Philip Franz von (1796-1866), German; Japan.

Soulie, J.A., Père (1858-1905); French Missionary, China.

Wallich, Nathanael (1786-1854), born Danish, a naturalized Briton; India.

Ward, Francis Kingdon (1885-1958), English; W. China, N. Burma.

Wichura, Max Ernst (1818-1866), German; Japan.

Wilson, Ernest H. (1876-1930), English; China, Japan, Korea.

The Asian roses provided the antecedents for both the modern garden roses and the climbing roses. As Shepherd has pointed out, the Asiatic species are, in part, recurrent. In addition, Asia is the only source of yellow-flowered and climbing roses.

The eight most important ancestors of the garden roses are all Asian:

Rosa chinensis	*Rosa moschata*	*Rosa multiflora*
Rosa wichuraiana	*Rosa damascena*	*Rosa foetida*
Rosa odorata		*Rosa rugosa*

China, the "Mother of the Garden" In the 16th century, shortly after the arrival of the Portuguese, Canton was the only Chinese city open to international trade. The Portuguese were soon followed by the Dutch and, in 1684, by the English who established a branch of what would later become the East India Company. Countless new plants reached England through their efforts. The Fa Tee nursery (or Fa Ti, i.e. 'Flowerland') was about 4 km./3 mi. outside the city of Canton, standing on the south bank of the Chu Chiang river. It was still in existence in the middle of the 19th century and was by then certainly 200 or more years old. Robert Fortune described this nursery. For 150 years, English plant collectors could only obtain plants which were delivered by this nursery or which were to be found in the immediate vicinity of Canton. The most important dates regarding Chinese roses are as followed:

1733   A China Rose appeared in the Herbarium of the Dutch botanist, Gronovius. Its origin is unknown, nor has the rose itself been identified. It may have reached Holland in a dried state.

1752   *Rosa chinensis* (also known as *Rosa indica*) reached Sweden from Canton in both living and dried form; the latter is now in the Linnean Collection in London.

1759   *Rosa chinensis* with pink flowers arrived in England; it was also known as 'Parson's Pink China' and 'Old Blush'. The date is somewhat uncertain.

1792   The Chinese were still refusing to allow Europeans to travel in their country. When the English appeared in the ports to trade they were very strictly controlled by the Imperial authorities. In order to resolve these persistent difficulties, a British mission under Lord Macartney went to Peking. This was an opportunity for George Staunton, the mission's secretary, and a number of others to make a collection of plants from the Shantung and Kian Provinces, among them being *Rosa bracteata* which became known as the 'Macartney Rose'.

1792   A captain in the Honorable East India Company (also known as John Company) brought a dark red rose from the Botanic Gardens, Calcutta to Gilbert Slater, one of the Company's directors who lived in Knots Green, England. This was sold under the name of 'Slater's Crimson China' which was later changed to the name we use today, *Rosa chinensis* var. *semperflorens*.

1804   Thomas Evans sent the first *multiflora* rose from China (*R. multiflora* var. *carnea* Thory); the ordinary *R. multiflora* came to France from Japan in 1862; it was sent to England in 1875.

1807   William Kerr, who was sent out by The Royal Horticultural Society brought back the double white *Rosa banksiae*, named after Lady Banks, the wife of Joseph Banks, President of the Society.

1809   Sir Abraham Hume imported the first Tea Rose which was given the name of 'Hume's Blush Tea-scented China'. It is no longer in existence.

1810   *Rosa lawranceana*, a dwarf form of *R. chinensis* var. *semperflorens*, was introduced from Mauritius by Sweet; it must have originated in China and been taken to Mauritius by the French.

1816   Abraham Hume sent *Rosa multiflora platyphylla*, or 'Seven Sisters Rose' from China to England.

1823   When it was learned in England that there also existed a double yellow form of *Rosa banksiae*, the Royal Horticultural Society immediately sent John D. Parks to China to seek it out. Parks traveled to Canton and not only obtained this rose but also the yellow Tea rose, *R. odorata ochroleuca*, which until then had only been known in Europe from Chinese paintings. It was put out under the name of 'Park's Yellow Tea-scented China'. It no longer exists, but all Tea roses come from it and 'Hume's Blush'.

1825   *Rosa roxburghii* (the cultivated form) was brought by Roxburgh from the Botanic Gardens, Calcutta and from Canton to England; the wild form arrived between 1860 and 1870 from Japan.

1844   Robert Fortune, the famous English plant collector, made four journeys to China. The first, to 1850   for the Royal Horticultural Society, started in

the Fa-Tee nursery in Canton. Although he only had permission to go to the nurseries, temple gardens and private gardens of Canton, Fortune was not to be put off so easily. He had his head shaved, donned a pigtail, and, dressed as a Chinese, was able to travel freely and fulfill his mission. He brought back three roses: *Rosa anemoneflora* (i.e. *R. laevigata* × *R. multiflora*) which he found in a garden in Shanghai and sent back to England in 1844. The next year he discovered, in a Mandarin's garden in Ningpo, the rose which was to become known in England as 'Fortune's Double Yellow' and which is still in cultivation. The third rose, *R. fortuniana*, he found in gardens in Shanghai and Ningpo and sent to England in 1850.

1881   Bretschneider sent *Rosa przewalskii* (or *R. bella* Rehd & Wils.) from the hills around Peking to the Botanic Gardens in Petersburg and to the Arnold Arboretum.

1888   General Collett found *Rosa gigantea* in the Shan Hills of Upper Burma.

1890   From seeds sent him by the French missionaries Delavay, Farges and Soulie, Vilmorin produced the following roses: *R. sericea pteracantha*, *R. moyesii*, *R. setipoda*, *R. sertata* and *R. souliea-na*.

1897   Guiseppe Giraldi, an Italian missionary, sent *Rosa caudata* to Europe.

1899   Hugh Scallon (Father Hugo) sent seeds of *Rosa hugonis* to Kew Gardens from W. China.

It was Ernest H. Wilson, known as "Chinese Wilson", who brought back the most roses from his numerous expeditions, originally undertaken on behalf of Kew Gardens and later for the Arnold Arboretum. The varieties were:

1901   *Rosa omeiensis*;

1903   *R. prattii* and *R. sweginzowii*;

1904   *R. murielae* and *R. willmottiae*;

1907   *R. banksiopsis*, *R. gentiliana*, *R. giraldii* with var. *venulosa*, *R. helenae*, *R. multiflora var. cathayensis*, *R. rubus*, *R. saturata*;

1908   *R. corymbulosa*, *R. davidii* with var. *elongata*, *R. filipes*, *R. glomerata*, *R. moyesii* var. *rosea*, *R. roxburghii* var. *normalis*;

1910   *R. multibracteata*;

1917   *R. koreana* (from Korea)

1905   John G. Jack brought *R. jackii* from China.

1907   Frank N. Meyer sent the double yellow *R. xan-thina* from Peking to the U.S.A. and two years later sent the single form var. *spontanea* from Lushang in Shantung province.

Bibliography

BRETSCHNEIDER, E.   History of Botanical Discoveries. 2 vols. St. Petersburg (1898). — Reprinted Leipzig (1962).
COX, E.H.M.   Plant Hunting in China. London (1945).
GELDOF. W.   Boomkwekerij in vroegere eeuwen (9). De Boomkwekerij, s'Hertogenbosch (1958).

KÖLREUTER, JOS. GOTTLIEB.   Historie der Versuche, welche von dem Jahre 1691 bis auf das Jahr 1752 über das Geschlecht der Pflanzen angestellt worden sind. Münich (1771).
—   Vorläufige Nachricht von einigen das Geschlecht der Pflanzen betreffenden Versuchen und Beobachtungen. Leipzig (1761-1766).
KORDES, W.   Das Rosenanbaugebiet Holstein. Rosenjahrb. 7: 27-35 (1953).
LEMMON, K.   The Golden Age of Plant Hunters. London (1968).
SARGENT, C.S.   Plantae Wilsonianae Vols. 1-3. Cambridge, Mass. (1916-1917).
WARD, F. KINGDON.   The Romance of Plant Hunting. London (1924).
YOUNG, N. and WYATT, L.A.   The Complete Rosarian. London (1971).

The History and Development of the Modern Garden Rose from 1750 to the Present Day

For the sake of clarity the individual rose divisions in this chapter will follow the classification of the American Rose Society. This will certainly be easier for the reader and by beginning once again with the earliest roses will show how crossing one group with another will produce a third.

Historical details of the first roses can be found in the chapter dealing with the Classical Period; similarly the roses of the Middle Ages were dealt with in their chapter. In addition, the chapter on the hybridizers and their work contains many details which will complete the picture.

SHRUB ROSES

Formerly, this was a comprehensive group for any rose which it was difficult to accommodate elsewhere. Since 1965, with the issue of *Modern Roses VI*, an attempt has been made to put each shrub rose under its original species. The following species with their garden forms or hybrids will be described here:

1. *R. acicularis*	4. *R. canina*	8. *R. moyesii*
2. *R. blanda*	5. *R. glauca*	9. *R. rugosa*
3. *R. pendulina*	6. *R. pimpinellifolia*	10. *R. rubiginosa*
	7. *R. roxburghii*	

Rosa acicularis Lindl.   From this species, which is almost polar in its habitat, has come one hybrid known as 'Pike's Peak', raised by Gunter and sent out by Bobbink & Atkins in 1940. F.L. Skinner of Dropmore, Canada has experimented with it and produced some frost-hardy varieties, but these have not received much attention in Europe.

Rosa blanda Ait.   A vigorous N. American species with prickles only at the base of the shoots. It is very frost-resistant and so could be useful for breeding in N. America and Canada.

F.L. Skinner, Dropmore, Canada crossed *R. blanda* with a Hybrid Perpetual and in 1925 obtained 'Betty Bland'. It is deep pink, semi-double and the best known of its type.

N.E. Hansen, Brooking, S. Dakota obtained a number of varieties, all virtually without prickles, notably 'Pax Iola' which is similar to 'Tausendschön' except that the stems are redder.

P.H. Wright, Saskatoon, Canada crossed *R. blanda* with 'Betty Bland' and produced 'Helen Bland', 1950.

Rosa pendulina L.   The attribution of *R. l'heritiera-nea*, the 'Boursault Rose', to a cross between *R. chinensis* and *R. pendulina* is very unlikely according to the chromosome count made by G.D. Rowley (comp. Thomas, *Climbing Roses*, p. 123). No cultivated varieties have come from it and only a few relatively unimportant natural hybrids.

Rosa canina L.   For the great number of *canina* under-stocks, see p. 111. Hermann Kiese crossed 'Général Jacqueminot' with *R. canina*, and obtained the rigorous shrub rose 'Kiese'. This was put out in 1910 and is still available. Stems have many prickles; single red flowers.

Rosa glauca Pourr.   (= *R. rubrifolia* Vill.) Miss Isabella Preston of Ottawa, Canada crossed this species with *R. rugosa*; one of the resultant offspring, called 'Carmenetta' (1923), is still in commerce. The botanical designation of the hybrids from *R. glauca* × *R. rugosa* of *R. rubrosa* Preston was made by her in 1926. These hybrids were known prior to 1903. P.H. Wright crossed 'Hansa'' with *R. glauca* and got 'Hansette' (1938).

Rosa pimpinellifolia L.   (= *R. spinosissima*). In the literature on the subject, garden forms derived from this are known as *spinosissima* hybrids, often called 'Scotch Roses' in England. The older cultivars were also known as 'Burnet Roses' ("burnet" being the English word for *Pimpinella*). It is believed that this rose was in existence in Europe prior to 1600 since it is referred to in the Herbals of Dodonaeus and Gerard. The area in which it grows covers a large part of Europe and Central Asia (see Map, Fig. 119).

In 1793, two Scotsmen, Robert Brown and his brother began to cultivate *R. pimpinellifolia* plants which had

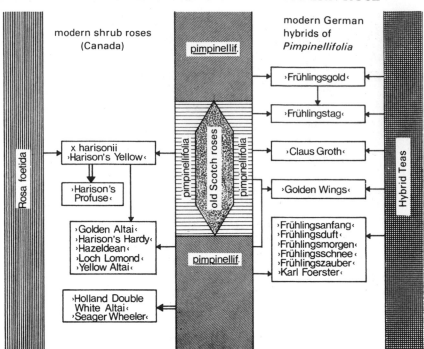

Figure 43. *Rosa pimpinellifolia* and its most important descendents (after Rowley, with alterations) cover a large part of Europe and Central Asia (see Map, Fig. 119).

been collected from the wild, sowing seeds and making selections from the resultant offspring. Rowley says that eight varieties were chosen and named. Shortly thereafter, other growers adopted this idea: Austin in Glasgow, Malcolm in Kensington, Lee in Hammersmith and others in Europe and N. America. These roses achieved such popularity that the hybridizers named each and every one. Thus G. Don in 1832 could catalog 25 double and 149 single cultivars and 14 botanical varieties. The arrival of the recurrent Bengal Roses (*R. chinensis*) doomed these and all other summer-flowering varieties. Just a few remain and these are rare, for example, 'Albo-plena', double white; 'Lutea Plena', lemon-yellow, dwarf; 'Old Yellow Scotch', sulphur-yellow, cup-shaped; 'Staffa' pale pink fading to creamy white with pinkish tones; 'King William III', deep purple; 'Painted Lady', silvery-white with deep purple center, double. Of the single varieties 'Maxima Lutea', yellow; 'Miss Anne's Rose', light purple, and 'Mrs. Colville', carmine with a white eye, are worthy of mention.

G.F. Harison, in New York, produced a delightful semi-double yellow rose, called *Rosa harisonii;* it was probably a cross of *R. pimpinellifolia* and 'Persian Yellow' and was soon grown all over N. America. It achieved such popularity in Texas that the internation-

ally famous song "The Yellow Rose of Texas" was written about it (see also p. 220).

'Stanwell Perpetual', the only recurrent variety, is not a *spinosissima* according to today's interpretation, but was bred in 1838 by Lee from *R. damascena* var. *semperflorens* × *R. pimpinellifolia*.

Some breeding work continued until the early 1920s when F.L. Skinner and P.H. Wright, both of Canada, produced a number of new varieties, none of which are now available commercially.

About 1930, almost exactly 100 years after Don's catalog, William Kordes took up this line again, using the two strong-growing forms, *R. pimpinellifolia* var. *altaica* and *R. pimpinellifolia* var. *hispida*, both of which grow to 1.8 m./6 ft. These were crossed with the Hybrid Tea 'Joanna Hill', among other varieties, and from this he obtained the 'Frühlings' group which, although summer-flowering, is only covered with a mass of bloom in its season (see Fig. 43). Most are semi-double, but 'Maigold' and 'Maiwunder' are double. From *R. pimpinellifolia* var. *altaica* × 'Frau Karl Druschki' came 'Karl Foerster' in 1931. M. Tantau bred 'Claus Groth' from 'R.M.S. Queen Mary' × *R. pimpinellifolia* and in the U.S.A. Shepherd brought out 'Golden Wings', also a shrub rose, in 1956, from 'Soeur Thérèse' × (*R. pimpinellifolia* var. *altaica* × 'Ormiston Roy').

PLATE 7

Notre Dame, Paris, South Transept Rose Window (13th century).

Detail of the carved roses in the Rose Window, Notre Dame.

PLATE 8

Arch of Roses springing from the capitals; west facade, central door, the Cathedral, Basel (14th century).

Carved double roses; west door, Church of St. Elizabeth, Marburg (13th century).

'Ormiston Roy' came from S.G.A. Doorenbos in The Hague; its parentage was *R. pimpinellifolia* × *R. xanthina*, 1953. Since then no further hybrids from *R. pimpinellifolia* have appeared on the market.

Rosa roxburghii Tratt. (= *R. microphylla* Roxburgh). The double form was found by Dr. Roxburgh in 1814 in Canton, China and sent to the Botanic Gardens, Calcutta; from there it went to England where it flowered for the first time in 1824. The single form was not discovered until nearly 100 years later, again in China, in 1908 and it is only this form which is now in cultivation. It can grow up to 3.6 m./12 ft. tall and it must be possible to obtain some very strong-growing seedlings from it. Little work has been done in this direction as the following particulars show:

1905   Henkel bred *R. micrugosa* from *R. roxburghii* × *R. rugosa*.

1901   'Jardin de la Croix' originated at Roseraie de l'Hay, Paris, from *R. roxburghii* × ?; pink, semi-double.

1939   Dr. Hurst, in Cambridge, England, produced *R. coryana* from *R. roxburghii* × ? *R. macrophylla*.

?   'Roxana' = *R. roxburghii* × *R. sinowilsonii* from Sir Frederick Stern.

1945   'Tantau's Triumph' from Tantau, 'Baby Chateau' × *R. roxburghii*; this cultivar has many descendants.

Rosa moyesii Hemsl. & Wils.   Introduced from China in 1894 and 1903, it is one of the most beautiful of the species roses. It is a dark red with dark stamens. There is also a pink form, *R. moyesii* var. *rosea*. Van Fleet (U.S.A.) made some early crosses and other hybridizers later followed suit with these results:

1919   'Heart of Gold' (*R. wichuraiana* × *R. setigera*) × *R. moyesii*. Strong-growing shrub, blooms deep carmine with white center, anthers dark brown.

1920   *R. pruhoniciana* Schneid. (= *R. hillieri*). Introduced by Hillier. *R. moyesii* × ?. Single, deep red.

1925   *R. highdownensis*. *Moyesii* seedling from Sir Frederick Stern of Highdown, Goring-by-Sea, Sussex, England.

1927   'Nevada', bred by Pedro Dot of Spain from 'La Giralda' × *R. moyesii*. The parents of 'La Giralda' are tetraploid while *R. moyesii* is hexaploid. 'Nevada' therefore ought to be pentaploid with 14 chromosomes from 'La Giralda' and 21 from *R. moyesii* yet it is only tetraploid, as Wylie established in 1954. Consequently it is improbable that the male parent was a typical form of *moyesii* but was more likely a tetraploid from the *Cinnamomeae* group.

1928   *R. wintonensis* = *R. moyesii* × *R. setipoda*; from Hillier.

1938   'Geranium'. A selected seedling from Wisley; compact growth, few prickles, flowers a glowing red.

1938   'Sealing Wax'. Also from Wisley, but the flowers a bright pink, from *R. moyesii* var. *rosea*.

1950   'Eos'. *R. moyesii* × 'Magnifica', from Ruys in Dedemsvaart.

1951   'Fred Streeter'. A chance seedling from *R. moyesii* found by Jackman of Woking, England.

1956   'Eddie's Crimson', from Eddie, Canada. 'Donald Prior' × *moyesii* hybrid.

1959   'Marguerite Hilling'; sport of 'Nevada', pink, introduced by Hilling, England.

1962   'Eddie's Jewel'. 'Donald Prior' × *R. moyesii*, the same as 'Eddie's Crimson'.

Kordes also crossed *R. moyesii* with van Rossem's selected form 'Superba' and obtained some winter-hardy Hybrid Polyantha; 'Independence' × *R. moyesii* 'Superba' (pentaploid); 'Planten un Blomen' × *R. moyesii superba* (tetraploid).

Rosa rugosa Thunb.   While only introduced to Europe from Japan in 1796, it very quickly established itself and is now one of the most wide-spread species in Europe. In books it is first mentioned in 1784. The typical wild form only grows to about 0.9 m./3 ft. tall and spreads by means of numerous suckers; the length of the stems is covered with bristly prickles. The foliage is dark green and, due to the deeply etched veins, appear very wrinkled (*ruga* = 'wrinkle' in Latin). The flowers are of a fair size, both purplish-pink and white, and are single. The hips are very large, rather flat and globose, but exceptionally fine and containing a great deal of pulp. Extremely hardy.

The following details of the history of this species are known:

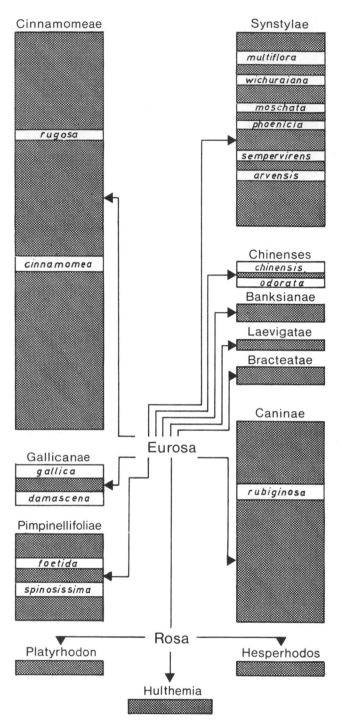

Figure 44. The wild ancestors of our garden roses. The size of each rectangle indicates the number of species in that section. The species used in hybridizing are named in their appropriate squares. (after Wylie, with alterations)

About 1000 A.D. this rose was already being accurately depicted in Chinese paintings of the period (according to Bunyard).

1784   European travelers reported its existence.

1796   Introduced into Europe from Japan, but remained confined to botanic gardens for some time.

1845   Introduced into the U.S.A.

1887   Breeding with this species began in France, later on in Germany and after that in the U.S.A.

The *rugosa* hybrids can be divided into 9 groups according to their parentage (Hamblin, 1965), as follows:

1. *Rugosa* distinguished by foliage and fruit. Flowers very large and usually fully double, flat, color generally reddish-purple, fragrant.

1892   'Blanc Double de Coubert' (Cochet-Cochet), white.

1894   'Belle Poitevine' (Bruant), white.

1894   'Souvenir de Christophe Cochet' (Cochet-Cochet), pink.

1895   'Souvenir de Pierre Leperdrieux' (Cochet-Cochet), red.

1898   'Delicata' (Cooling, England), light lilac-pink.

1899   'Atropurpurea' (William Paul), R. rugosa × R. damascena, purple-red.

1899   'Souvenir de Philémon Cochet' (Cochet-Cochet), white and pink.

1901   'Rose à Parfum de l'Hay' and about ten other varieties from Jules Gravereaux; deep purple-red.

1905   'Hansa' (Schaum & van Tol, Holland), reddish-purple.

1914   'Frau Dagmar Hartopp' (Hastrup), clear pink seedling.

1939   (?) 'Scabrosa' (int. Harkness), mauve-pink.

2. *Rugosa* — recurrent, of the Hybrid Perpetual type. Strong-growing, more vigorous than the ordinary Hybrid Perpetuals; *rugosa* origins not noticeable except for the larger prickles, leaves and flowers. For example:

1893   'Arnold' (Jackson Dawson, U.S.A.) = R. rugosa × 'Général Jacqueminot'.

1925   'Bergers Erfolg' (V. Berger), rugosa seedling × 'Richmond'.

1899   'Conrad Ferdinand Meyer' (F. Muller) = rugosa hybrid × 'Glorie de Dijon'; must be included in this group; clear pink.

1907 'Nova Zembla' (Mees, 1907). White sport of 'Conrad Ferdinand Meyer'.

3. *Rugosa* of *gallica* type.
Very little similarity to *R. rugosa*, very hardy, but of little decorative value. For example:

1898 'Agnes Emily Carman' (E.S. Carman, U.S.A.) = *R. rugosa* × *R. harisonii*.

1901 'Alice Aldrich' (J.T. Lovett, U.S.A.) = *R. rugosa* × 'Caroline de Sansal'.

4. *Rugosa* of *chinensis* type.
Like *R. rugosa*, tall-growing, foliage slightly wrinkled, flowers in trusses, recurrent and very hardy; like large Floribunda, but only of value in cold climates.

1887 'Mme. Georges Bruant' (Bruant), waxy white.

1900 'New Century' (Van Fleet), flesh pink.

5. *R. rugosa* × *R. foetida*.
There are only two known varieties.

1900 'Agnes' (Saunders, U.S.A.), *R. rugosa* × 'Persian Yellow'. Amber-yellow, double, not a strong grower, many prickles; was formerly very popular.

1923 'Grace' (Saunders), *R. rugosa* × *R. harisonii*, apricot-yellow, double; did not appear commercially.

6. *Rugosa* of the Floribunda type.
Mostly 0.9-1.2 m./3.4 ft. tall, bushy and very hardy; blooms mostly small (as in the case of the 'Dianthiflora') or like normal Floribundas.
   a) The so-called 'Dianthiflora' with fimbriated petals; all, unfortunately, without scent.

1918 'F.J. Grootendorst' (de Goey/Grootendorst, Holland), bright red.

1923 'Pink Grootendorst'; a pink sport.

1936 'Grootendorst Supreme'; dark red sport.

1962 'White Grootendorst' (Eddy, U.S.A.); white sport.

? 'Weisse Nelkenrose' (= 'White Grootendorst' ?), white.
   b) Floribunda with *rugosa* origins.

1890 'Clothilde Soupert' (Soupert & Notting), white and pink.

1912 'Schneezwerg' (Lambert), white.

1931 'Heidekind' (V. Berger), brilliant pink.

1938 'Erna Grootendorst' (Grootendorst), dark crimson.

7. *Rugosa* of Hybrid Tea type.
These can be omitted; they are unimportant and practically unknown; in any case, they are valueless in comparison with the true Hybrid Teas.

8. *Rugosa* of climbing habit.
Some are full climbers, some pillar roses; also useful for ground cover; very prickly and hardy; mostly single. For example:

1900 'Lady Duncan' (Jackson Dawson, U.S.A.) = *R. wichuraiana* × *R. rugosa*.

1919 'Max Graf' (Bowditch, U.S.A.), *R. rugosa* × *R. wichuraiana*. For details of *R. kordesii*, which is related, see p. 97.

9. *Rugosa* × Climbing Hybrid Teas.
Very vigorous and bushy, blooms of Hybrid Tea type; not recommended for very cold areas as they will not withstand temperatures below -18° C/0° F.

1931 'Dr. Eckener' (Berger), 'Golden Emblem' × *rugosa* seedling.

1935 'Golden King' (Beckwith), sport of 'Dr. Eckener'.

Rosa rubiginosa L. (= *R. eglanteria* L.). The Apple Rose, Sweet Briar, or Eglantine. Native to Europe and W. Asia. In cultivation from very early times. Grows 1.8-2.7 m./6-9 ft. tall; stems covered with hooked prickles; foliage scented like ripe apples, particularly after rain; blooms bright pink, 2 or 3 together, slightly fragrant; hips ovoid.

1551 Known to have been in cultivation at this date.

1890 Lord Penzance began breeding with the species in England; he made crosses with the most diverse roses; his seedlings first appeared in 1894 and a number of them are still grown. They are all pink to carmine in color, single or semidouble and all have the scented foliage. The following 10 varieties were bred by him:

1894 'Amy Robsart', deep pink.

1894 'Anne of Geierstein', deep carmine.

1894 'Brenda', peach-pink.

1894 'Lady Penzance' (= *R. penzanceana* Rehd.); = *R. rubiginosa* × *R. foetida bicolor*, pink with yellow center.

1894 'Lord Penzance', *R. rubiginosa* × *R. harisonii*, pink tinted with yellow.

1894 'Lucy Ashton', *R. rubiginosa* × unknown Hybrid Perpetual, white edged with pink.

1894 'Meg Merrilees', carmine-pink.

1895 'Greenmantle', bright pink with white eye.

1895 'Julia Mannering', pearl-pink.

1895 'Lucy Bertram', deep carmine with white eye.

1916 'Magnifica' (Herm. A. Hesse), 'Lucy Ashton' × 'Lucy Ashton', purplish-red.

1928 'Rosenwunder', (Kordes), 'Magnifica' × 'W.E. Chaplin', rose-red.

1940 'Fritz Nobis' (Kordes), 'Magnifica' × 'Joanna Hill', white.

1940 'Josef Rothmund' (Kordes), 'Magnifica' × 'Joanna Hill', orange-red.

1949 'Rosendorf Ufhoven' (Kordes), 'Magnifica' × 'General MacArthur', carmine.

1950 'Till Uhlenspiegel' (Kordes), 'Magnifica' × 'Holstein', red with a white eye.

1950 'Obergärtner Wiebicke' (Kordes), 'Magnifica' ×

'Johannes Boettner', pink.

1950 'Eos' (Ruys), 'Magnifica' × *R. moyesii*, pink and white.

Kordes made further crosses with 'Obergärtner Wiebicke', and using 'Baby Château' as the pollen parent came up with 'Florence Mary Morse' and 'Gertrud Westphal' in 1951, and by using 'Independence' ('Kordes Sondermeldung'), produced 'Ama' in 1955.

Finally, details must be given of five varieties, all of which are descendents of *rubiginosa*:

1955 'Aschermittwoch' (Kordes), silvery-gray to white; climber.

1955 'Flammentanz' (Kordes), a glowing crimson; non-recurrent.

1953 'Sparrieshoop' (Kordes), light pink; large-flowered shrub.

1956 'Alchymist' (Kordes), golden-yellow; climber.

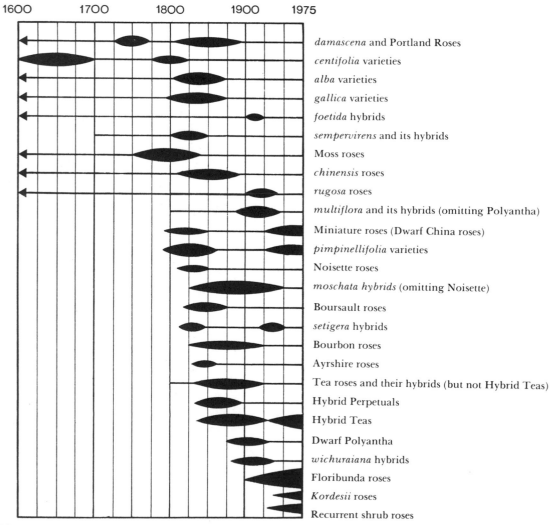

Figure 45. The distribution of the individual groups of garden roses in the last 375 years. (from R. E. Shepherd, altered and enlarged)

1967 'Rote Flamme' (Kordes), dark crimson; climber.

THE OLD GARDEN ROSES

The "old" roses remain and, although they are mostly grown in specialist rose gardens and by dedicated amateurs, they must be included here.

"A rose is an 'old' rose if it belongs to a group which existed before 1867". This was the definition proposed by the Classification Committee and the Old Garden Rose Committee of the American Rose Society (ARS), and approved by that Society in 1966.

The year 1867 was chosen because this was when the "first" Hybrid Tea, 'La France' was introduced. All classes which were in existence before that date became known as "old garden roses" even if individual varieties appeared at a later date (e.g. 'Maman Cochet', 1893); the only criterion is that the characteristic features of the class should be clearly identifiable (see table on p. 72).

Old roses within this class are: Moss roses, *R. alba* (prior to 1800), China (prior to 1819), Noisette (1819), Bourbon and Portland (1817), Tea roses (1833), Boursault (1892), *foetida* hybrids (1837), Hybrid Perpetuals (1837), *R. pimpinellifolia* (= *spinosissima*) including the Kordes hybrids (1932) and the species roses.

Those NOT in the list of old roses are:
Hybrid Teas (since 1867)
Floribunda
Grandiflora
Polyantha
Hybrid musks
rubiginosa hybrids (1894)
rugosa hybrids
multiflora hybrids
wichuraiana hybrids
Kordesii varieties
Shrub roses

At the beginning of the 19th century there were only three main groups of roses in W. Europe: *gallica*, *centifolia* and *damascena*. There was, however, confusion between the groups, as they were all quite similar to one another.

Rosa gallica L. This is the French Rose or Rose of Provins. It originated in W. Asia, possibly in the Caucasus and was certainly known to the Medes and Persians by the 12th century B.C. It has been frequently mentioned in many books and has been used as a religious symbol, appearing frequently in sculpture and on buildings. Surprisingly, it is not referred to in archaeological literature. In contrast, the use of rosettes, which have been interpreted as roses in various art forms, were in fact Lotus flowers or the flowers of *Chrysanthemum coronarium* which was very common in Asia Minor (Fig. 16).

Very probably, *R. gallica* was very early established throughout most of Europe (see Map, Fig. 122) and has long been used to obtain the raw materials for perfume. The typical form grows about 0.9 m./3 ft. tall with rather coarse, darkish green leaves and carries its flowers upright on fairly thick stalks; the stems have only a few small prickles. The flowers are usually red, but there were always varieties which were pink. It spreads freely by means of suckers; this was formerly important as a method of propagation, but today is regarded as a defect. It is modern opinion (Shepherd) that the red rose described by Pliny in his "Natural History" in 79 A.D., can have been none other than *R. gallica* since the

Rosa præneſtina variegata

Figure 46. *Rosa gallica versicolor*. (from Besler's *Hortus Eystettensis* where it is called *Rosa praenestina variegata*)

description does not fit any other rose of that time. All this has been dealt with fully in the chapters "The Rose in the Classical Period" and "The Rose in the Middle Ages".

From the 13th to the 18th centuries, it was extensively grown at Provins, a small town south of Paris; cultivation reached its peak in the 17th century. This was the type known as *R. gallica officinalis*, the 'Apothecary's Rose', with single red flowers from which essential oil was obtained; this is confirmed in a document of 1310. It is also identical to the 'Red Rose of Lancaster'. In 1600, the numerous Apothecarys' shops of Provins were all engaged in the production and sale of rose oil.

1583 'Rosa Mundi' (= *R. gallica variegata* or *R. gallica versicolor*); illustrated by Besler (Fig. 46).

1596 Gerard described in his *Herball* a "velvet rose"; in all probability this was what is known today as 'Tuscany'.

R. gallica conditorum, the 'Tidbit' or Hungarian rose was first grown in Germany in 1900 (Dr. Dieck), although it had long been in cultivation in Hungary.

1670 The growing of *gallica* roses was taken up in Holland; propagation was by means of seed and, as a result of chance pollination by insects, many new varieties appeared.

1811 The Empress Joséphine had at least 167 different *gallica* varieties in her collection. It was at this time that Descemet became the first French hybridizer to produce new varieties by making controlled crosses.

1827 'Duc d'Angoulême' (= 'Duchesse d'Angoulême'), pink.

1831 'Camaieux', rosy purple streaked with white.

1837 'Anaïs Ségalas' (Vibert). Often called a *centifolia* but is better placed in this group. Carmine, edged with rosy lilac.

1840 'Cardinal de Richelieu'. One of the oldest Dutch roses and originally called 'Rose Van Sian' by its grower; Laffay rechristened it when he introduced it into France. Violet-purple.

1841 'Oeillet Parfait' (Foulard), bright pink with darker stripes.

1842 'Cosimo Ridolfi' (Vibert), striped lilac-pink.

1845 'La Rubanée' (= 'Perles des Panachées' and 'Village Maid') (Vibert) striped rose-purple and white.

1845 'Belle Isis' (Parmentier), flesh pink.

1846 'Tricolore de Flandre' (Van Houtte), bright pink with darker stripes.

1848 William Paul describes in his book 471 varieties and 52 hybrids of *R. gallica*, but actually at that time there were about 2,000 varieties available in France of which at least 500 had been raised by Vibert.

1853 'Georges Vibert' (Robert) purple-red streaked with white.

1853 'Vivid' (A. Paul, England), magenta.

1872 'Belle des Jardins' (Guillot), a seedling from 'La Rubanée', violet-red striped with white.

1876 'Violacée' (= 'La Belle Sultane') (Soupert & Notting) purple shaded with violet.

1947 'Rose des Maures' re-introduced under the name of 'Sissinghurst Castle'; purplish-violet.

1952 'Scharlachglut' (= 'Scarlet Fire') (Kordes) = *R. gallica* × 'Poinsettia', scarlet.

Of the other varieties of *gallica* neither the grower nor the year of introduction are known; they have therefore been disregarded.

Rosa damascena Mill. (= *R. gallica* var. *damascena* Voss; *R. calendarum* Borkh.)
The Damask Rose. Contemporary opinion is that this is probably a natural seedling from *R. gallica* × *R. phoenicia* to which the summer flowering (i.e. non-recurrent) varieties can be ascribed, while the recurrent varieties probably came from *R. gallica* × *R. moschata*, however this theory has not yet been proven.

The origins of this rose are uncertain. Most authorities believe that it came from Damascus, in Syria, but Graham Thomas (1964) is almost certain that the 'Damask Rose' was not related to Damascus but to damask, the highly-prized fabric. The intention may have been to indicate that these roses were exceptional in some way, possibly the scent, which today is not regarded as being particularly special.

S.F. Hamblin (1965) thinks that *R. damascena* came first from Persia and then from Damascus and was brought to Europe between 1254 and 1270 by the Crusader Robert de Brie from whose castle in Champagne it was gradually dispersed throughout France.

The species *R. damascena* grows to 1.5-2.4 m./5-8 ft. tall, the stems are curved and arching giving the effect of climbing, and are covered with both large and small hooked prickles; the leaves are similar to those of *centifolia* but soft and hairy; the flowers are nodding, whereas those of *R. gallica* are held stiffly upright, usually of one shade of clear pink, the inner petals being shorter than the outer, blooming usually in corymbs; the scent at first is slight and increases in intensity as the flower matures. The hips are long and slender (they are much rounder in *R. gallica*). Extremely hardy. Whether it is still in cultivation is uncertain.

Before "breeding" with *R. damascena* began, the two-toned red and white *R. damascena versicolor* was well known and often called the 'York and Lancaster Rose' because it appeared after the English Wars of the Roses (1455-1485). It was first described by Monardes in 1551, and in its flowers the colors of the two embattled Houses of York (the white rose) and Lancaster (the red rose) were joined. The blooms are variable, some white, some pink and some with both colors at once, in contrast to *R. gallica versicolor*, with which it is often confused and of which the petals are always pink and white striped.

Graham Thomas believes that 'York and Lancaster' is a sport from *R. damascena trigintipetala* and therefore concludes that the latter, which is so important commercially for the production of rose oil, must have been in cultivation for a very long time, not just for the last 200 years in Bulgaria.

The Damask Roses, which are classified today as summer-flowering, are generally only in the white or soft pink color range; the purple and brownish-red tones of *R. gallica* are absent; all are summer-flowering only. The following are some dates of historical interest with notes on the most important varieties:

1520 Dr. Linacre, court surgeon to Henry VII and Henry VIII of England, brought the Damask Rose from Italy to his country.

1544 Matthiolus wrote that the Damask rose had been known in Italy for a number of years.

1551 Monardes (Spain) says it had been grown in his country for the past 30 years, but for much longer than that in Italy, France and Germany.

1580 Montaigne found *R. damascena* (or was it *R. chinensis?*) in a monastery in Ferrara (Italy) which stayed in bloom until November (see also p. 80).

1689 The Bulgarian Attar rose, *R. damascena trigintipetala* was mentioned for the first time.

1750 'Celsiana' was already growing in France; pale pink.

1813 'Marie Louise' was established in Malmaison;

deep pink.

1817 'Petite Lisette', rich rose.

1830 'Madame Zoetmans' (Maret), almost white with a hint of flesh pink.

1827 'Leda' ("The Painted Damask"), originated in England, pink, with carmine tinge.

1832 'Mme. Hardy', best known of all the Damasks; pure white.

? 'Blush Damask'. Place and date of introduction unknown; soft pink.

Before Isfahan' (= "Rose d'Isfahan"). Believed to have
1832 been used in Turkey for the production of Attar of Roses, but this has not been confirmed. Rose-red.

Circa This was the peak where Damask Roses are con-
1850 cerned, and at least 300 varieties were introduced. However, the Hybrid Perpetuals and the Hybrid Teas came along and superseded the Damasks, the popularity of which quickly declined.

1890 'Omar Khayyam' was found in Persia; light pink.

1849 'La Ville de Bruxelles' (Vibert), pink.

1912 'Hebe's Lip' (W. Paul). Very short flowering season. White tipped with red.

1938 'Gloire de Guilan'. Used in Persia for the production of Attar. Introduced into England in 1949 by Hilling under this name. Pink.

1939 'Oratam' (Jacobus), Hybrid *damascena* × 'Souvenir de Claudius Pernet'; coppery-pink.

"Autumn-Flowering" (recurrent) Damasks

As was said above, in addition to the "summer-flowering" or non-recurrent Damasks, there are also the "autumn-flowering" or recurrent varieties. This was emphasized by Virgil about 50 B.C. when he wrote of a rose having "a double Spring". However, he might have meant the "Rose of Paestum" (= Rose of Pompeii), botanically *Rosa bifera*. About 125 years later, Pliny wrote of the twice-bearing rose of Cyrene, which was more fragrant than any other rose, and of the rose of Carthage, which bloomed in both spring and fall.

It can be assumed that these two Italian roses were not really recurrent and that the blooms from Carthage and Cyrene were imported, for both places had a much warmer climate than Italy. Thus, the roses in N. Africa rested in January-February and July-August and it was possible to arrange these phases so that the Damask roses came into bloom in the following months although other types of rose, under the same conditions, would not react in this way. One thing, however, is certain and that is that the property of recurrency in the Damasks is recessive and noticeable in certain individual cultivars, for prior to 1781 there were in both Europe and N. Africa no other recurrent roses and the recurrent Damasks had long been extensively grown and widely acclaimed.

By 1785 there were four varieties of the *Rose des Quatre Saisons*, as it was known, growing in France; possibly it had been brought back by Montaigne from Italy; the so-called "red" variety was, in fact, a deep pink.

1795 André Dupont of the Luxemburg Gardens, Paris, brought a pink *R. damascena* from Florence; it proved to be identical to the "red" variety already available.

1812 The first recurrent Damask was found in the gardens of the Palace at St. Cloud; its antecedents are unknown, but were possibly *R. damascena × R. chinensis*.

1848 William Paul listed more than 100 recurrent Damasks (*Quatre Saisons*) in his catalog.

The "autumn-blooming" Damasks were crossed with other roses and produced much more recurrent varieties which went under the name of "Portland Roses". For details see p. 82.

Rosa alba L. The White Rose. Not a wild species but a hybrid with somewhat controversial origins, being either *R. gallica × R. corymbifera* or *R. damascena × R. canina*. The latter combination is not improbable because the chromosome ratio in *R. alba* is irregular, as it is in *R. canina*. *Rosa alba* and its varieties grow 1.8-2.7 m./6-9 ft. high and are dense, almost impenetrable shrubs with large drooping bluish-green leaves; the flowers are milky white, tinged with pink in some varieties, loose and in most cases semi-double, very fragrant; the numerous scarlet hips are long and smooth.

It is still unknown when this rose, of which there are about 200 different varieties, first appeared as a garden rose; it may have been the Roman white rose which was being grown at least 2,000 years ago.

It certainly reached England very early on, and was possibly taken there by the Romans.

The white rose was well know and widely grown in the Middle Ages and the form *semiplena* can be identified in many paintings of the period. The following historical details are of interest:

13th century. Albertus Magnus gave an account of the "White Rose".

1307 Crescentius, the Italian agricultural writer recommended it for hedging purposes.

1455 to 1485 In the English Wars of the Roses, the badge of the House of York was a white rose, that of the opposing House of Lancaster, a red rose. Although there are any number of references to the "White Rose of York" being either *R. alba* or a garden hybrid of it, Norman Lambert (*Rose Annual*, 1931) has refuted this theory and suggests that, in all probability, it was *R. arvensis* (compare p. 98 re: *R. arvensis*).

1473 Martin Schongauer's painting "The Virgin of the Rose Hedge" in Colmar shows two kinds of roses; the semi-double white is *R. alba semiplena* and the red is probably *R. gallica officinalis* (Plate 6).

15th century. White roses which can be identified as *R. alba maxima* and 'Maiden's Blush' often appear in Italian paintings.

1506 A picture by Lucas Cranach[1] shows a young man with a basket of roses which he is offering to St. Dorothea; they are the same roses seen in Schongauer's painting. The roses which shower down upon the goddess in Botticelli's "Birth of Venus" are *R. alba semiplena*. In many paintings of the Renaissance this rose is easily identified by its flower form and the color of its foliage.

1750 The first recorded use of a white rose for the production of Attar in company with the much more important pink *R. damascena trigintipetala* (Kazanlik); in Bulgaria.

The dates of introduction and the names of the growers of very few of the *alba* varieties are known.

1816 'Königin von Dänemark', (J. Booth, Hamburg), flesh pink.

1818 'Jeanne d'Arc', flesh pink.

1835 'Mme. Plantier' (= *alba × R. moschata*) (Plantier), white.

1836 'Félicité Parmentier' (Parmentier). In growth and foliage more like *R. damascena*; flesh pink.

1848 'Mme. Legras de St. Germain', white.

1876 'Pompon Blanc Parfait', white.

Rosa centifolia L.　Called Centifolia, Cabbage Rose or Provence Rose. There are many differing opinions regarding the historical development of this rose. C. C. Hurst (1941), one of the most reliable authorities in this field, considers it to be the youngest of all the "old" roses. It was established in Europe about the end of the 15th century and its total development, from beginning to end, occurred in Holland from 1580 to 1710. In that time about 200 varieties of *centifolia* were introduced; by the year 1800 about 100 were still being grown.

For many years it was believed, even by Hurst & Breeze, (1922), that *R. centifolia* was the old rose of which Theophrastus gave so detailed an account (*ca.* 300 B.C.) and which both Herodotus and Pliny called the "Hundred-petaled" rose. This view has now been abandoned because an examination of the chromosomes shows that this is not a true species; the statement that *R. centifolia* is to be found growing wild in woodlands in the Caucasus has been positively denied by Russian botanists. It has been discovered that it is a complex hybrid of four species, namely *R. gallica, R. phoenicia, R. moschata* and *R. canina* which probably came together in garden cultivation. This combination can have come about naturally in various ways, but just how it did in this case is uncertain. The most likely way, according to Hurst, would be a cross between *R. bifera* (= *R. gallica* × *R. moschata*) × *R. alba*) = *R. canina* × *R. damascena*), but experience in rose-breeding has shown that it is rarely as simple as that. At least we can be clear about one thing, that the *centifolia* was developed in Holland (compare with the notes on p. 62). The relevant dates are:

1596　First mention in Gerard's Catalog where it is named *Rosa damascena flore multiplici,* "the Great Holland Rose", commonly called "Province Rose".

1597　Gerard, *Herball: Rosa Hollandica sive Batava,* "The Great Holland Rose" or "Great Province".

1581　L'Obel calls the Centifolia *Rosa damascena maxima.*

1601　Clusius describes it as *Rosa centifolia batavica.*

1629　In Parkinson, it is Red Province.

1733　Miller (for the first time?) changes "Province" into "Provence" and also gives it the Latin name of *Rosa provincialis.*

1753　Linnaeus gave it the name *Rosa centifolia* which has been retained.

1768　Miller describes the "Cabbage Rose" under the name of *Rosa provincialis* or Provence Rose since he regarded Linnaeus' diagnosis (1753 & 1762) as unsatisfactory; his designation was accepted by a number of contemporary authorities.

1820　Lindley cleared up Miller's mistake and from this point on the "Cabbage Rose" has been classified as *Rosa centifolia*, in accordance with Linnaeus.

As the *centifolia* have very double blooms, they do not set many seeds; the garden varieties are all the result of mutation. The dates of introduction for some of them are as follows:

1664　'Parvifolia' (= 'Pompon de Bourgogne')

17 . .　'Rose des Peintres'. This is the rose portrayed so often in Dutch paintings of the 18th century, particularly in van Huysum's work. G.S. Thomas thought that this was the ordinary *centifolia*, but it seems to have been a separate variety.

1775　'Unique Blanche', white.

1789　'De Meaux' (Sweet), bright pink.

17 . .　'Petite de Hollande', rosy red.

1801　'Bullata', pink.

1805　'Spong', rosy-red.

1820　'Cristata' (= 'Chapeau de Napoléon'), found in Switzerland, pink.

1823　'Ombrée Parfaite' (Vibert), light pink shading to purple.

18 . .　'Duc de Fitzjames', deep carmine.

18 . .　'Fantin Latour', blush pink.

18 . .　'Robert le Diable', scarlet-pink fading to purple.

18 . .　'The Bishop', cerise-magenta fading to bluish-purple.

1845　'Paul Ricault' (Portemer), rosy red.

1847　'Juno' (Laffay), flesh pink.

1856　'Tour de Malakoff' (Soupert & Notting), mauve-pink shaded with purple.

1856　'La Noblesse' (Soupert), light pink.

1845　*centifolia variegata* (= 'Unique Panachée'), large globose blooms, white, striped with pink and lilac; if overfed, or if the soil is too rich, the flowers tend to be pure white. Introduced by Vibert of Angers. Often confused with 'La Rubanée' (= 'Panachée Double', 'Perle des Panachées', or 'Village Maid'), which is a *gallica* also brought out by Vibert in 1845, large, double, rose-purple and white striped.

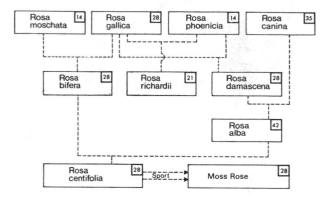

Figure 47. The development of *Rosa centifolia* and the Moss Roses (from Rowley and Hurst, with alterations)

Moss Roses These can be placed genetically in the same group as the *cristata* varieties of cactus, in other words abnormal forms which are interesting horticulturally, but which have little chance of surviving in the wild.

For the rose itself this habit of forming moss is not a step forward, but is an affliction brought about by various circumstances. And, as will be discussed later, it seems to be accompanied by sterility.

The origin of the Moss Roses has been the subject of much argument, but it is now generally agreed that they are mutations (sports) of *R. centifolia*. Thus there are:
1. *R. centifolia muscosa*, in existence prior to 1750 (other forms before 1696);
2. *R. centifolia cristata*, 1820.

The "moss" varies from variety to variety, according to the growth habit, the time of year and even to the individual plant. The arrangement of the sepals is always the same; moving clockwise the first two are mossed, then a smooth one, then one mossed and the last smooth (see Fig. 48). In the bud the two smooth sepals are covered by the three mossed ones but even the former show little mossy streaks; this applies to all Moss Roses.

The habit of forming "moss", or small glandular growths on the sepals, is always present to some extent (see *ARA* 1968: p. 54; Fig. 3), and certainly on all varieties of Hybrid Tea, Floribunda, Grandiflora, Polyantha and Miniature. With changes in the leaf structure come changes in the prickles and in the oil glands. Therefore, they are mutations which do not arise from the devel-

opment of new genes but through the obstruction or partial obstruction of specific characteristics.

Miniature Moss Roses raised by Moore have been described in detail by the hybridizer in *ARA* 1968 pp. 49-60 with 4 illustrations.

The development of the Moss Rose is marked by the following dates:

1696 Moss Roses recorded as growing in Carcassonne, S. France (compare the date 1746 below).
1720 Established in the Botanic Gardens, Leyden (according to Boerhave).
1727 Miller brought plants from Leyden to London.
1735 'White Moss' introduced in England; white.
1746 Ducastel was apparently growing Moss Roses in Northern France (according to Paquet, 1845; Jamain & Forney, 1873) in the Cotentin, Massin and La Manche and says that he had brought them from Carcassonne where they had already been growing for half a century.
1788 'Shailer's White Moss' (= *muscosa alba*) introduced in England.
1801 'Mossy Rose de Meaux' introduced in England and exported to France.
1807 *R. centifolia andrewsii*, single, pink.
1810 'White Bath' (= 'Clifton Moss Rose'), introduced in England; a better and purer white than *muscosa alba* (1788), but probably not a truly different variety.
1820 'Crested Moss' — see under *R. centifolia*.
1820 A number of single Moss Roses appeared; later these were crossed with Hybrid Teas which produced recurrent Moss Roses. These, however, no longer exist. Formerly there were no yellow Moss Roses despite the fact that there was a great demand for them; 'Golden Moss' did not make its appearance until 1930, and it is not very exciting.
1843 'Comtesse de Murinais', (Vibert), white.
1845 'Laneii' (Laffay), carmine.
1845 'Nuits de Young', violet.
1850 By this time there were about 50 named varieties of Moss Rose; the number would later reach 200.
1852 'Gloire des Mousseux' (Laffay), carmine-pink.
1854 'Salet' (Lacharme), rosy red.
1872 'Mme. Moreau' (Moreau-Robert), pink edged with white.
1873 'Soupert & Notting' (Pernet), deep pink.
1880 'Blanche Moreau' (Moreau-Robert), white.

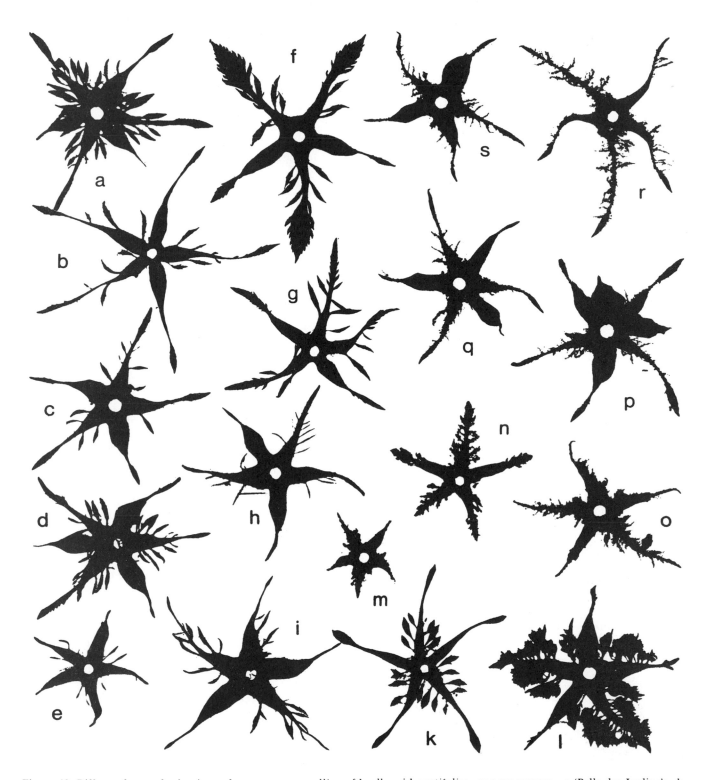

Figure 48. Different forms of calyx in garden roses. a-e *gallica;* f-h *alba;* i-l *centifolia;* m-s moss roses. a 'Belle des Jardins'; b 'Scharlachglut'; c 'Président Dutailly'; d 'Belle de Crecy'; e 'Cardinal de Richelieu'; f 'Maiden's Blush'; g *alba carnea;* h 'Königin von Dänemark'; i *centifolia major;* k 'Reine des Centfeuilles'; l *centifolia cristata;* m 'Nuits de Young'; n 'Mme. Moreau'; o 'Blanche Moreau'; p 'William Lobb'; q 'Reine des Mousseux'; r 'Malvina'; s 'Laneii'. (Original, ¾ life size)

1890 'Striped Moss' (= 'Oeillet Panachée') in England.

1890 'Crimson Globe', carmine-red.

1898 'Mme. Louis Lévêque' (Lévêque), salmon pink.

1911 'Goethe' (Lambert), magenta.

1930 'Golden Moss' (Dot), yellow.

1956 'Parkzauber' (Kordes), dark crimson.

1958 'Black Boy' (Kordes), very dark red.

1958 'Blue Boy' (Kordes), reddish-violet.

The China Rose. *Rosa chinensis* (also known as the Bengal Rose). A rose of the greatest importance in breeding because its has two properties lacked by other roses: it is recurrent and there is a true red in the color of the flowers. The historical dates surrounding this rose are somewhat controversial even among reputable authors. The following data are taken in part from research done by C.C. Hurst.

10th century. In Chinese paintings of the time, roses are shown which are probably identical to the 'Blush Tea-scented China' which was sent to England in 1809.

1529 Probably the first picture of *R. chinensis* by a European painter (Angelo Bronzino of Florence; National Gallery, London No. 651; "Venus and Cupid"; Cupid is holding the pink *R. chinensis* in both hands). Hurst says these are identical to 'Pink China' and concludes that this rose must have been growing in Italy in the 16th century.

1580 The French philosopher Montaigne on a visit to the Jesuit monastery at Ferrara in November of that year, saw roses still in bloom and was told that they flowered throughout the year. These are probably the same roses as those of 1529 (or *R. damascena*; see p. 75).

1733 Gronovius, the Dutch botanist, received a dried specimen of a red China Rose which he called Chineesche Eglantier Roosen in his herbarium; this was not 'Blush China' as has often been suggested. It was this rose on which Jacquin based his illustration in 1768 of a red China Rose. The date on the sheet in the Herbarium is 1733 and therefore the more commonly given date of 1704 must be incorrect.

1750 Peter Osbeck, plant collector and pupil of Linnaeus, sailed for China and the East Indies. He returned in 1752 and wrote a book on his travels in which he says that on October 29, 1751 he found *Rosa indica* in the Custom House garden in Canton. Perhaps it is this rose which appears in Linnaeus' Herbarium on sheet 38 as a "Blush Tea China".

1781 The pink form of *R. chinensis* was brought to Holland by the Netherlands East India Company and was planted in the Botanic Gardens at Leyden and at Haarlem; from there it found its way to England.

1789 The captain of a British East Indiaman found a red recurrent rose in a garden in Calcutta, brought it to England and gave it to Gilbert Slater, a director of the Company. Slater was a keen gardener and propagated the rose which he passed on to his friends as the 'Bengal Rose'. It was illustrated in Curtis' Botanical Magazine in 1794 as *Rosa semperflorens*. By 1798 it was being grown in Paris by Cels and Thory.

1789 Sir Joseph Banks, Director of Kew Gardens, brought a pink China back with him from a visit to Holland; it was put into commerce as 'Parson's Pink China' (= 'Old Blush'). Early voyagers had brought this rose to Holland from the old Fa Tee nursery in Canton which had bred many, including this one, which were being widely grown in local gardens. Moreover, it had been in cultivation since 1700 in the Botanic Gardens of Calcutta and Singapore. The variety reached Charleston, South Carolina in 1800 where it is believed to have played a part in the origins of the climbing Noisette.

1802 *Rosa indica* var. *alba* was found as a sport in an English garden.

1805 A miniature form was produced in England from 'Parson's Pink China'. This was sent to Lyon and was later involved in the production of the first Polyantha Roses.

1809 *Rosa odorata*, apparently a hybrid of *R. chinensis* × *R. gigantea*, was introduced by Sir Abraham Hume from the East Indies. It was illustrated in 1810 by Andrews as *R. indica odorata;* later it was called *R. indica fragrans* Thory, *R. thea* Savi, and 'Hume's Blush Tea-scented China'.

1810 A chance cross between 'Parson's Pink China' and an autumn-flowering Damask on the Island of Réunion, then known as the Ile de Bourbon, produced a new group of roses which were given the name of Bourbon Roses.

1815   The first hybrids between 'Hume's Blush Tea-scented China' and *R. gallica* appeared in England, among them 'Brown's Superb Blush'; most of them must have been triploid and therefore sterile, but about 1830 there were some fertile tetraploids such as 'Malton' and 'Athalin'. Although these latter two have long since disappeared and been forgotten they did play a part in the creation of our modern roses. Although in other respects they resembled the China Roses, they were not recurrent.

1824   The first Tea Rose was imported by Parks from China for The Royal Horticultural Society; it was a large-flowered fragrant yellow rose which was put into commerce as 'Park's Yellow Tea-scented China'. It was sent to Hardy in Paris in 1825 and he used it for breeding. It is now believed to be a cross of *R. chinensis* × *R. gigantea* and has the official name of *R. odorata ochroleuca*. It was probably diploid, and disappeared about 1882. When painted by Redouté, it was called *R. indica sulphurea*.

Of the early hybrids which are still grown today, the following are worthy of notice:

1825   'Gloire des Rosomanes' (Vibert), glowing crimson.

1832   'Cramoisi Supérieur' (Coquereau), syn. 'Agrippina'; crimson-red.

1840   'Hermosa' (Marcheseau), very similar to the modern Floribunda; pale pink.

1897   'Gruss an Teplitz' (Geschwind/Lambert), bears close resemblance to the Hybrid Teas but lacks their high-pointed buds and has no fragrance; crimson.

For the dwarf Bengal or China Roses, see Miniature Roses p. 90.

The Bourbon Roses   As a result of crossing the China Roses with other varieties several new groups appeared, including the Bourbons. Their origin and further development took place on the Ile de Bourbon (now Reunion Island), one of a group of islands about 800 km./500 mi. east of Madagascar in the Indian Ocean. The French settlers were in the habit of surrounding their fields with rose hedges, usually of 'Parson's Pink China' and *R. damascena bifera* (= *Rose des Quatre Saisons*).

1817   Monsieur Bréon, Director of the island's Botanic Garden, found, in a hedge on the property of a M. Périchon, a rose which seemed to him different from the two types normally growing there. He dug it up and removed it to the Botanic Garden for further study, eventually coming to the conclusion that it was a new variety coming from a natural cross between the China and the Damask. However, L. Chaix (1851) says that this rose had been known for many years on the island where it was widely grown under the name of 'Rose Edwards'.

1819   Bréon sent seeds of his new rose to his friend, Jacques, Head Gardener to the Duc d'Orléans at Neuilly, Paris. Jacques and M. Loiseleur-Deslongchamps were certain that here was a completely new rose and it was given the name of the 'Bourbon Rose'.

1822   Redouté painted it as *Rosa canina burboniana*.

1823   'Rose Edwards' was imported from the Ile de Bourbon to Paris both as seedlings and as grown bushes according to M. Pirolle (Ref. L. Chaix). Perhaps there were two different roses and there is a possibility that 'Rose Edwards' was a hybrid of *R. chinensis*, *R. damascena* and *R. centifolia*. Shepherd (p. 77) casts doubt on the story of its origin in Réunion as he says that there was a rose called 'Rose Edwards' which had been growing for many years in the Botanic Gardens, Calcutta. So whether it came from Calcutta or from Réunion remains something of a mystery. Although it is generally believed that 'Rose Edwards' no longer exists, Nancy Steen (1967, p. 99) writes that she was sent the rose by P.B. Pal from New Delhi.

1828   Desportes named it *Rosa burboniana*.

Of the countless Bourbon varieties of the time, only a small number remain:

1823   'Rosier de l'Ile de Bourbon' (Jacques), deep pink.

1834   'Queen of Bourbons' (Mauget), fawn and rose.

1840   'Coupe d'Hébé' (Laffay), deep pink.

1843   'Souvenir de la Malmaison' (Béluze), flesh pink.

1851   'Louise Odier' (Margottin), rosy red.

1867   'Boule de Neige' (Lacharme), pure white.

1868   'Zéphirine Drouhin' (Bizot), pink with white base.

1872   'Reine Victoria' (J. Schwartz), pink.

1874 'Commandant Beaurepaire' (Moreau-Robert), rose-pink streaked with violet and white.

1878 'Mme. Pierre Oger' (Oger), sport of 'Reine Victoria', pale pink.

1880 'Mme. Isaac Pereire' (Garcon), deep pink.

1909 'Variegata di Bologna' (Bonfiglioli), white with purple stripes.

1920 'Adam Messerich' (Lambert), rose-red.

The Noisette Roses (*Rosa chinensis* × *Rosa moschata*). These cluster-flowered roses appeared in America and are either of tall-growing climbing habit or bushy, resembling the Tea roses. All are recurrent and the flowers are white, pink or yellow.

1802 John Champney, a rice grower in Charleston, South Carolina, crossed *R. moschata* with 'Parson's Pink China', which he had recently received from his neighbor, Philippe Noisette, whose brother Louis in Paris had sent it to him. The resultant seedling was named *Rosa moschata hybrida*.

1811 In the intervening nine years the rose became well-known and was being sold under the name of 'Champney's Pink Cluster'. Champney himself was not commercially interested in it and had handed it over to Philippe Noisette, who looked after its propagation and began to make his own crossings with it. In 1817 he sent both seeds and plants to his brother in Paris.

1818 Louis Noisette named the best of his seedlings 'Rosier de Philippe Noisette' while the others were just called Noisette Roses.

1818 John Fraisier, also of Charleston, produced a seedling which was very similar to 'Champney's Pink Cluster' and which was put on the market as 'Fraisier's Pink Musk'.

1821 Redouté painted *Rosa noisettiana*, which by this time had become widely distributed.

1825 About this time the French rose-breeders started to try to obtain yellow Noisette Roses and to this end they crossed 'Blush Noisette' with 'Park's Yellow China'. The resultant seedlings gave not only strong-growing Noisettes, but also quite normal Tea roses and some climbing Teas. Those worthy of mention are:

1828 'Aimée Vibert' (Vibert), 'Champney's Pink Cluster' × double *R. sempervirens*. White.

1842 'Céline Forestier' (Trouillard), climbing Tea.

1843 'Chromatella' (Coquereau), climbing Tea, yellow.

1843 'Solfatare' (Boyeau), climbing Tea, yellow.

1837 Dr. Manetti of the Botanic Garden, Monza, Milan, raised the semi-double *Rosa manettii* which has had varying popularity as an understock and is supposed to be susceptible to black spot.

The Portland Roses The history of the first rose of this group is, according to Graham Thomas (1967, p. 109), probably a legend which arose in Italy. In that country there was a collection of old roses, including *R. chinensis* which, in that favorable climate, is winter hardy. In the vicinity of Paestum, south of Naples, a light red rose was found in about 1800, which, according to Hurst, was a descendant of 'Slater's Crimson China' but was more likely to have been a cross between *R. damascena* and *R. chinensis semperflorens*. The Duchess of Portland, a keen rose grower, was in Italy at the time, heard of this rose and arranged to take it back to England with her. There it was called 'Duchess of Portland' and accepted as the first rose of a new group.

It is likely that a plant of this new variety was sent to Paris where it played a part in the development of 'Rose du Roi'. The French eagerly began to breed from them and before long there were 150 varieties of Portland on the market. All bore similarities to the Bourbons, but the blooms were usually on short stalks and did not stand clear of the foliage. By 1850 most of the varieties had disappeared. The actual breeding of many was unknown, but they made, within the Damasks, a separate sub-group with the stronger colors of the *gallicas* and more petals, though the flowers were relatively small; they were often non-recurrent. It is small wonder that, with the arrival of the Hybrid Perpetuals, they very quickly disappeared. In old rose books they are often described as *Rosa bifera* because they occasionally produced a second crop of flowers. Here is a short list of the most important varieties:

ca. 1800 'Duchess of Portland', bright scarlet.

1812 'Rose Lelieur' (1815 re-named 'Rose du Roi' and 1819 in England, 'Lee's Crimson Perpetual'), bright red and violet.

'Bernard' and 'Mogador' were two sports of 'Rose du Roi'.

1849 'Coeline Dubos' (Dubos), bright pink.

1844 'Palmyre' (Laffay), bright pink.

1845 'Blanc de Vibert' (Vibert), white.

1860 'Pergolèse' (Moreau-Robert), purplish-crimson.

1883 'Rembrandt' (Moreau-Robert), the last of the Portlands; scarlet-red.

The Tea Roses These roses, close relatives of the Chinas, are similar to them but the flowers are larger, more fragrant and semi- to fully double; the colors are yellow to apricot, white and pink to bright red; only deep yellow and dark red are missing. The sepals are undivided. Unhappily, their hardiness in Central and Western Europe is unreliable and they generally have to be grown under glass in these areas. However, they do very well where the summer is long, for example in Southern Europe. (See the Tea Rose in China, p. 81).

1808 The first Tea Rose was sent to England by the East India Company, from the Fa Tee nurseries in Canton, to Sir Abraham Hume who received it in 1810. He called it 'Hume's Blush'. It was semi-evergreen and the flowers were pink.

1824 The second Tea Rose, sent to Europe by John Damper Parks who collected plants for the Royal Horticultural Society in China and Java. It had bright yellow double blooms and became known as 'Park's Yellow Tea-scented China' (= *R. odorata ochroleuca* Lindl.).

1821 Between this date and 1830, the French hybridizers put out 27 Tea Roses according to Desportes' catalog. It is interesting to compare this with the list giving details of breeder and year of introduction by E. E. Robinson in his *A Short History of the Tea Rose*.

1830 About this time the development of the tea Rose began in earnest in Europe; it did not end until the arrival of the Hybrid Teas. The first varieties came from France and were bushy in habit; soon climbing cultivars appeared; these can be subdivided into three groups:

1. This is the largest group, and is comprised of climbing sports of the normal Teas which they resemble in every other way.

2. Hybrids from a bush Tea with the vigorous Bourbon 'Gloire de Dijon'. They have large, shiny foliage and are somewhat more winter hardy.

3. Crosses between the Teas and the Noisettes often combining the best characteristics of both parents, and consequently a difficult group to place; the first varieties attributed to this group, 'Chromatella' and 'Larmarque', are now regarded as Noisettes!

From 1821 to 1940, no fewer than 1,382 Tea Roses were raised and commercially introduced by 274 hybridizers. Most of them were French, and among the most successful was the family of Nabonnand who raised 188 varieties on the Golfe Juan between 1877 and 1914.

The most important varieties were:

1833 'Adam' (Adam, Rheims), deep lilac-pink. The first Tea Rose with known parentage.

1838 'Devoniensis', found by a Mr. Foster in his garden in Plymouth, Devon, England and introduced in 1841 by Lucombe; white with tints of cream and blush. The first English Tea Rose.

1839 'Safrano' (Beauregard), saffron yellow and apricot.

1843 'Niphetos' (Bougère), white.

1843 'Solfaterre' (= 'Solfatare') (Boyeau), saffron yellow.

1845 'Fortune's Double Yellow', introduced by Robert Fortune. He wrote to the firm of Standish & Noble:

"I found this rose in the garden of a wealthy Mandarin in Ningpo where it had completely covered a wall and was a mass of bloom. The Chinese call it Wang-jang-ve or 'yellow rose'. I sent it to the R.H.S. in 1845."

Initially, the English had only disappointments with this much-praised variety, for it was not understood for some time that the plants must not be cut back hard because they only flower on the previous year's wood.

1848 'Mme. Bravy' (Guillot), creamy white and pink.

1851 'Sombreuil' (Moreau-Robert), creamy white and pink.

1853 'Gloire de Dijon' (Jacotot), salmon pink shaded yellow.

1857 'Duchesse de Brabant' (Bernede), soft pink.

1864 'Maréchal Niel' (Pradel), sulphur yellow.

1869 'Cathérine Mermet' (Guillot fils), flesh pink tinted lilac.

1871 'Marie van Houtte' (Ducher), creamy yellow.

1872 'Anna Olivier' (Ducher), pink.

1878 'Mme. Lambard' (Lacharme), salmon pink shaded yellow.

1882 'Papa Gontier' (Nabonnand), coppery-pink.

1888 'G. Nabonnand' (Nabonnand), pink shaded yellow.

1893 'Maman Cochet' (P. Cochet), pink.

1897 'Générale Schablikine' (Nabonnand), bright coppery red.

1905 'Freiherr von Schilling' (Jacobs), pink and yellow.

1905 'Charlotte Klemm' (Türke), red and orange.

1906 'Penelope' (J. Williams), dark red with white center.

1908 'William R. Smith' (Smith/Henderson), white shaded pink.

1910 'Lady Hillingdon' (Lowe & Shawyer), deep apricot-yellow.

The important periods of Tea Rose development are shown in the following table compiled by E. E. Robinson.

Dates	Varieties grouped according to color			
	Red	Yellow	White	Various
1821-1830	16	1	6	23
1831-1840	27	6	8	41
1841-1850	16	5	15	36
1851-1860	48	20	18	86
1861-1870	24	28	12	64
1871-1880	71	53	34	158
1881-1890	153	72	37	262
1891-1900	209	118	75	402
1901-1910	135	64	54	253
1911-1920	15	12	8	35
1921-1930	6	5	3	14
1931-1940	1	3	1	5
	721	387	271	1,379

The Hybrid Perpetuals This group can really be called the link between the old and modern roses. Their career began in 1837 and ended in 1900. In that span of time no less than 4,000 varieties were introduced, almost all in France, with a few in England and Germany. The origin of the Hybrid Perpetuals is difficult to pin down because almost all the important groups of garden roses played a part in their development. The breeding lines of the older varieties are not reliably authenticated because the details of the parent varieties are often not known with any certainty; the seedlings produced were the result of chance crosses by insects. The best of such seedlings

were then selected and, since they were so numerous, many were named.

Until 1847 the breeding of this type of rose was really confined to France; it was Laffay who had the most success in obtaining varieties with larger flowers. Vibert is another who deserves recognition. The climber 'Gloire des Rosomanes' (1825) and also the 'Rose du Roi' were among the parents of the first of the new group.

Most of the Hybrid Perpetuals have inherited the strong growth of their predecessors, but they also have numerous prickles, and large, fully double, long-lasting blooms, although there were a few single varieties, and strong scent. The range of color extends from pink to carmine to a rich, dark crimson. Yellow is totally absent even though a great many crosses were made after 1914 between 'Frau Karl Druschki' and various yellow Hybrid Teas by S. F. Hamblin (1942).

In Europe it was customary to refer to this group as the Remontant [recurrent] Roses but in both America and England they became known as Hybrid Perpetuals and sometimes as "continuous flowering roses"; an overstatement since their flower production does not begin to compare with that of the modern roses. Of the 4,000 varieties mentioned above, only about 100 remain today. Of these the most important are:

1837 'Princesse Hélène' (Laffay), purple. The earliest cultivar.

1837 'Prince Albert' (Laffay), carmine.

1838-1842 about 30 varieties appeared in France.

1840 'Mme. Verdier' (Verdier), white.

1842 'Eliza Balcombe' (Laffay), white.

1842 'La Reine' (Laffay), rose pink, cupped. Very important parent of later varieties.

1842 'Baronne Prévost' (Desprez), bright pink.

1846 'Géant des Batailles' (Mérard), scarlet.

1853 'General Jacqueminot' (Roussel), rich rosy red. Important parent of later introductions.

1853 'Jules Margottin' (Margottin), carmine-pink, little fragrance.

1860 'Reine des Violettes' (Mille-Mallet), violet-red fading to violet.

1861 'Prince Camille de Rohan' (E. Verdier), deep crimson, very double.

1865 'Fisher & Holmes' (Verdier), velvety scarlet.

1869 'Paul Neyron' (Levet), deep pink, enormous blooms.

1872-1879 Verdier alone named about 350 Hybrid Perpetuals.

1875 'Eugène Fürst' (Soupert & Notting), deep carmine, very fragrant.

1882 'Ulrich Brunner fils' (Levet), bright carmine, fragrant.

1884 The catalog of William Paul & Sons lists over 800 Hybrid Perpetuals, but only 9 Hybrid Teas.

1886 'Erinnerung an Brod' (Geschwind), cherry red, scented.

1887 'Mrs. John Laing' (Bennett), pink with lilac tinge, fragrant.

1890 'Roger Lambelin' (Schwartz), deep velvety crimson with white edge.

1897 'Baron Girod de l'Ain' (Reverchon), carmine edged with white; a sport of 'Eugène Fürst'.

1901 'Frau Karl Druschki' (Lambert), white, no fragrance. According to current opinion, and on the basis of its parentage, this should be a Hybrid Tea, but in appearance it has all the characteristics of a Hybrid Perpetual.

1905 'Hugh Dickson' (Dickson), scarlet-crimson.

1907 'Gloire de Chédane Guinoisseau' (Chédane & Pajotin), bright crimson, fragrant.

1910 'Georg Arends' (Hinner), crimson, fragrant; almost entirely lacking prickles.

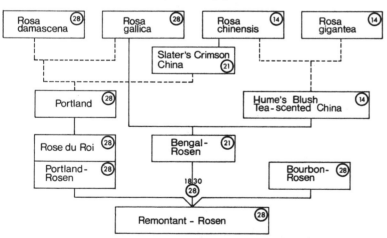

Figure 49. The development of the Hybrid Perpetual; the chromosome count is shown in circles. (after Wylie, with alterations)

THE HYBRID TEAS

The history of the oldest among the groups of modern roses has been inaccurately reported in the books on the subject, according to N. Young (1960), who writes:

It has been said, unkindly but with some truth, that the literature of the rose consists of 75 per cent folklore, 24 per cent uninformed personal prejudice and 1 per cent fact.

His first example to support this contention is the "myth" of 'La France' (Guillot, 1867), which was considered the first of the hybrid teas. In the 19th century, as the modern classification developed, it was the practice to place each new variety in the same group as its female parent; if it deviated too much, then the word "hybrid" was put in front of the group name. Thus a "hybrid tea" was a rose produced from the seed of a Tea which had been pollinated by a rose of another group. The pollen parent was not taken into account because it was frequently unidentified, and it was then generally believed that the pollen parent played only a secondary role in the production of the new hybrid. (There was very little planning in the crosses made before 1860). Today, it is recognized that this belief was mistaken and that every rose inherits its particular qualities quite impartially from either the pollen and/or the seed parent.

Although 'Hume's Blush Tea-scented China' was apparently incapable of self-pollination, nevertheless "one day she gave birth to a little daughter" of which the pollen parent was probably a *gallica*. This "little daughter" was brought out in England in 1815 as 'Brown's Superb Blush', the first true Hybrid Tea. However, it was non-recurrent and was probably triploid and sterile.

The Hybrid Teas which were developed after this were:

1825 'Duc de Choiseul' (Vibert).

1826 'Jaune Desprez' (Desprez), yellow.

1830 'Lamarque' (Maréchal), white with yellow center. (In the two preceding varieties, 'Park's Yellow Tea-scented China' was the pollen parent and the original Noisette Rose the seed parent; they should really go into the Noisette group, but the Noisette roses were self-sterile and produced no true-to-type descendants. Therefore these two varieties are incorrectly called 'Noisette' and the "ancestors of the Noisette line". In fact, both they and their descendants, 'Charomotella', 'Maréchal Niel', 'William Allen Richardson', 'Alister Stella Gray' and others are all Hybrid Teas! That 'Park's Yellow China' was the pollen and not the seed parent is unimportant because the descendants would have been the same even if the cross had been the other way around; cf. N. Young.)

1833 'Smith's Yellow'.

1853 'Gloire de Dijon' (Jacotot), the result of a cross between an unknown Tea and 'Souvenir de la Malmaison', also strictly a Hybrid Tea.

1859 'Victor Verdier' (Lacharme), from 'Jules Màrgottin' × 'Safrano'. It is amusing to note that the English hybridizer, Pemberton, believed that this must have had more Tea Rose "blood" than the other Hybrid Perpetuals because it was always so badly attacked by rabbits. It may be inferred that the rabbits knew more about breeding than the hybridizers of the day!

1867 'La France' (Guillot fils). The record which says that the parents were 'Mme. Victor Verdier' and 'Mme. Bravy' is a clear invention. What is much more likely is what Guillot himself is quoted as saying, namely that he found the plant in a bed of chance seedlings from Teas; consequently he could know nothing of the parentage. Guillot was not a true hybridizer for, in the next twelve years, he only introduced another two varieties, also chance seedlings.

1873 'Captain Christy' (Lacharme); immediately designated a Hybrid Tea.

1872 'Cheshunt Hybrid' (George Paul).

1883 'Lady Mary Fitzwilliam' (Bennett), from 'Devoniensis' × 'Victor Verdier'.

1888 'Souvenir of Wootton' (John Cook); the first American hybrid tea; dark red; from 'Bon Silène' × 'Louis van Houtte'.

1890 'Mme. Caroline Testout' (Pernet-Duchet), from 'Mme. de Tartas' × 'Lady Mary Fitzwilliam'. It is from this date that the classification of 'Hybrid Tea' came into general use.

This was the time that rose breeding, particularly of the Hybrid Teas, really gained momentum, and in the intervening period to the present day more than 6,000 Hybrid Teas have been named and registered, making this the largest group of all. Many of the early cultivars were strong growing and hardy, but many more were delicate due to their ancestry of the frost-tender Tea Roses. Over time, with progressive crossing, in-breeding and the pursuit of fixed breeding patterns, the Hybrid Teas degenerated considerably. The results of crossing with *R. foetida*, producing the Pernetiana roses, were even worse. Admittedly, this broadened the color range but it markedly weakened the plant's capacity to withstand disease, particularly Black Spot and Rust; and also hampered their strength of growth.

The following breeders, to name but a few, were active at that time:

In England, Wm. Paul, Dickson and Cook.

In Germany, Peter Lambert, Nicola Welter, Droegemüller, et al.

In France, Pernet-Ducher.

In Holland, Verschuren.

In the U.S.A., E.G. Hill.

The so-called "Pernetiana Roses" must be discussed here. They have now been completely absorbed by the Hybrid Teas, although they were initially regarded as a separate group. But first it is necessary to go back a little.

The Hybrid Teas produced predominantly pink, red or white flowers and all the tones within that range, but, if the descendants of 'Park's Yellow Tea-scented China' are excluded, a true yellow was missing. A golden yellow, comparatively large-flowered, species, *R. foetida* (= *R. lutea*) was brought by Clusius to Europe from Asia Minor in 1542. It was established in Austria, from where it was eventually widely distributed.

1596 Gerard, in England, already knew of this rose and called it 'Austrian Yellow' and its sport 'Austrian Copper' which is identical to *R. foetida bicolor*, this last being a rose with a wonderful color combination of golden yellow on the outside and coppery red inside. It was undoubtedly much more beautiful than the indigenous yellow heath rose, *R. pimpinellifolia*. Both, however, have a fault in that they lack a pleasant scent; indeed they have been accused of smelling like the leaf maggot which is found in soft fruit. In addition, the foliage was very susceptible to Black Spot; finally, and decisively, the flowers were sterile.

1836 Sir Henry Willock found a large-flowered, double, golden yellow form of *R. foetida* in Persia, which was given the name of 'Persian Yellow'. It had the same faults of the former pair, but it was fertile.

1900 Pernet-Ducher finally succeeded in making a breakthrough. In nearly all rose books the details of this cross are incorrectly reported. In reality, he crossed the violet-red Hybrid Perpetual 'Antoine Ducher' with 'Persian Yellow'.

Most of the seedlings were without merit, so all were discarded with the exception of one which was particularly vigorous. When, one day, he found a beautiful scented yellow flower in his seed bed, he saw to his excitement that it was a rather frail, self-sown seedling; he named it 'Soleil d'Or' and it became of immense importance in the breeding of Pernetiana Roses. Pernet-Ducher made further crosses with his yellow roses and obtained, among others, 'Souvenir de Claudius Pernet' in 1920. Soon all the hybridizers were making crosses with the yellow roses and from these came the full color range found in present day roses. Nevertheless, it must not be forgotten that by 1940 the Hybrid Teas had reached the summit of their perfection and were already starting to show the first signs of degeneration.

1945   The Hybrid Tea 'Peace' (= 'Mme. A. Meilland', 'Gloria Dei') was introduced by F. Meilland and this was the great turning point. This extraordinarily vigorous rose was not only very healthy and fertile, but bore large, noble blooms with all the characteristics that could be desired. This began new period of active hybridization which has continued to the present day. There are only a very few roses like 'Peace' which can claim to be truly international.

To conclude this section, there follows a short list of the most important hybrid teas since 1912:

1912 'Ophelia' (W. Paul), flesh pink.
1914 'Hadley' (Montgomery Co.), red.
1926 'Briarcliff' (Pearson), deep pink.
1926 'Mrs. Pierre S. du Pont' (Mallerin), golden yellow.
1926 'Rapture' (Traendly & Schenk), deep pink.
1935 'Crimson Glory' (Kordes), crimson.
1935 'Texas Centennial' (Watkins), red with gold flush.
1945 'Peace' (Meilland), yellow edged with rose pink.
1947 'Virgo' (Mallerin), white.
1949 'Rouge Meilland' (Meilland), red.
1950 'Karl Herbst' (Kordes), dark scarlet.
1950 'Spek's Yellow' (Verschuren), yellow.
1950 'Sutter's Gold' (Swim), yellow.
1954 'Baccara' (Meilland), red.
1957 'Kordes' Perfecta' (Kordes), cream tipped with crimson.

1960 'Super Star' (= 'Tropicana') (Tantau), coral-orange.

THE GRANDIFLORA ROSES

In 1946, W.E. Lammerts, U.S.A., crossed the Hybrid Tea 'Charlotte Armstrong' with the Floribunda 'Floradora'. From the 81 seedlings produced, one was selected in 1948 which showed exceptionally strong growth with blooms up to 10 cm./4 in. across. It was introduced commercially in 1954 as 'Queen Elizabeth' (= 'The Queen Elizabeth Rose'). Looking back at its parentage, it can be seen that it represents a mid-point between the Hybrid Tea and the Floribunda. Upon introduction in the United States and later in Europe, this rose received the highest awards at competitive trials. The All America Rose Selection (AARS) considered that it was necessary to institute a new classification for this rose. They coined the name "Grandiflora" for it. When this decision was made known, there was very strong criticism in England and the United States, for the name *Rosa grandiflora* was already in use, although as a synonym:

Rosa grandiflora Salisbury (1797) = **Rosa gallica** L.
Rosa grandiflora Lindley (1825) = **Rosa spinosissima**
    var. **altaica** (Willd) Bean.

The use of this name for a rose group contradicted the international rules of nomenclature which applied throughout horticulture. In the U.S.A. there was not too much concern with these rules, since Grandiflora is undoubtedly a name which would promote sales of the rose. As a result, American catalogs and even the American Rose Society officially accepted the group name of Grandiflora. It cannot be expected that American commercial nurseries will abandon such a useful term.

In England another name was chosen: Floribunda-Hybrid Tea type, which is certainly botanically correct but cumbersome. In Germany and other European countries the U.S. practice of using Grandiflora, or sometimes Floribunda Grandiflora has been adopted. Probably, in time, all rose nurseries will adopt the standard as it is set out in *Modern Roses*.

Of these roses the following are noteworthy:

1950 'Carrousel' (Duehrsen), dark red.
1951 'Independence' (= 'Kordes Sondermeldung') (Kordes), pure scarlet.
1954 'Queen Elizabeth' (Lammerts), pink.
1955 'Montezuma' (Swim), orange-red.

1955 'Miss France' (Gaujard), scarlet.
1956 'Queen of Bermuda' (Bowie), orange-vermilion.
1956 'Coup de Foudre' (Hémeray), fiery red.
1956 'Burning Love' (Tantau), scarlet.
1962 'Diamant' (Kordes), orange-scarlet.
1965 'Apricot Nectar' (Boerner), pinkish-apricot.
1966 'Lucky Lady' (Armstrong & Swim), bright pink.

(In the *Handbook for Selecting Roses 1973*, published by the ARS, about 40 varieties of Grandiflora are named which before that date had been called either Hybrid Tea or Floribunda.)

In appearance these roses are very similar to the Hybrid Teas having, for the most part, long buds and large, rather loose, double flowers coming either singly or in small trusses.

THE POLYANTHA ROSES

The origins of this group are not as complicated as they have been made to seem. Some of the conclusions developed by L. Levy (1931) and R. Shepherd (1954) must be accepted as a basis for its early history. The sequence of events were roughly as follows:

About 1865, Robert Fortune, who had been an active plant collector in China and Japan for a number of years, sent a low-growing, non-recurrent form of *Rosa multiflora* home to England. The flowers were pink, semi-double and came in trusses. In 1870 the Mayor of Lyon in France received a plant of it which was put into the local park. One way or another it was soon widely distributed and came into the hands of Jean Sisley, also of Lyon, who obtained a number of interesting seedlings from it. It is very likely that he sent one of these seedlings to his friend, the nurseryman Guillot in Lyon, and that the latter propagated it and put it into commerce under the name of 'Ma Pâquerette' in 1875.

There is another piece of information about the origin of the name *R. polyantha*. By 1784, the Swedish botanist, Thunberg, had named the modern *R. multiflora*; in 1834, the two German botanists, Siebold and Zuccarini gave the name *R. polyantha* to the same rose without realizing that Thunberg had done this. Finally, in 1876, the French gardener, Carrière, gave Guillot's prototype the name of *R. polyantha*, also without knowing that this name was already in existence. Rehder (1902) called the same rose *R. multiflora* × *R. chinensis* without further specification. In French horticulture, however, the name *R. polyantha* was retained and has continued to be accepted as the group name.

At this point other hybridizers, at first the French, then Bennett and G. Paul in England, Soupert & Notting in Luxembourg, Peter Lambert and Nicola Welter of Trier, Germany, began to take an interest in the Polyanthas.

Most of the varieties are low-growing, very bushy and floriferous; the blooms are generally quite small, 2.5-3.8 cm./1-1.5 in. across, either single or double, excellent for mass bedding, but also recommended as cut flowers. Most cultivars come from European breeders and there have been a great many sports. The foliage is very reminiscent of *R. multiflora*; many of the later introductions are descendants of *R. wichuraiana*, like 'Ellen Poulsen', or, more obviously, 'The Fairy', a sport of 'Lady Godiva'. Levavasseur made crossings with 'Crimson Rambler' and Poulsen with 'Dorothy Perkins', as did Tantau ('Johanna Tantau').

The most important varieties in the development of this group are listed below; for a complete list of those which had appeared by 1930, see L. Levy (1931).

1880 'Cécile Brunner' (Ducher), pink on yellow ground. (The parent of 'Gabrielle Privat', 'Bo-Peep', etc.)
1881 'Mignonette' (Guillot), pink and white, very free-flowering and hardy.
1883 'Perle d'Or' (Dubreuil), yellow.
1887 'Gloire des Polyantha' (Guillot), pink on white ground.
1889 'Clothilde Soupert' (Soupert & Notting), soft pink with white center.
1889 'Eugénie Lamesch' (P. Lambert), ochre-yellow with pink edge.
1889 'Léonie Lamesch' (P. Lambert), coppery red, center yellow.
1901 'Katharina Zeimet' (P. Lambert), pure white.
1903 'Mme. Norbert Levavasseur' (Levavasseur), carmine.
1906 'Aennchen Müller' (J.C. Schmidt), bright pink.
1909 'Orléans Rose' (Levavasseur), vivid red.
1910 'Yvonne Rabier' (Turbat), white, cream center.
1914 'Echo' (P. Lambert), deep pink shading to white.
1915 'Greta Kluis' (Kluis & Koning), carmine.
1918 'Eblouissant' (Turbat), dark red.
1925 'Superba' (de Ruiter), carmine.
1928 'Johanna Tantau' (Tantau), white with pinkish-yellow center.

1929 'Gloria Mundi' (de Ruiter), orange-scarlet.

1930 'Paul Crampel' (Kersbergen), orange-scarlet.

1931 'Flamboyant' (Turbat), bright scarlet.

1932 'The Fairy' (Bentall), pink.

1937 'Orange Triumph' (Kordes), orange-scarlet.

In concluding these notes on the Polyantha Roses, something must be said about the so-called "Compacta Roses" which were developed by de Ruiter using the Polyanthas. They have a very crowded habit of growth with stiff stems, terminating in cone-shaped trusses of bloom some 15-23 cm./6-9 in. across. The plants are about 30-46 cm./12-18 in. tall and 30 cm./12 in. broad. Longer shoots should be trimmed back. The parentage of some varieties is known. They were put out in England and Germany under the name of the 'Seven Dwarfs'.

1954 'Happy' (= 'Alberich'), 'Robin Hood' × 'Katharina Zeimet'. Bright red, semi-double, very small blooms.

1954 'Doc' (= 'Degenhard'). 'Robin Hood' × Polyantha seedling. Pink, semi-double.

1954 'Dopey' (= 'Eberwein'). 'Robin Hood' × Polyantha seedling. Crimson, semi-double.

1954 'Sleepy' (= 'Balduin'). ('Orange Triumph' × 'Geheimrat Duisberg') × Polyantha seedling. Deep pink, double, very small flowers.

1955 'Sneezy' (= 'Bertram'), pink, single.

1955 'Bashful' (= 'Giesebrecht'), reddish-pink with white eye, single.

1956 'Grumpy' (= 'Burkhardt'). Pink, single.

The parentage of the last three varieties is unknown.

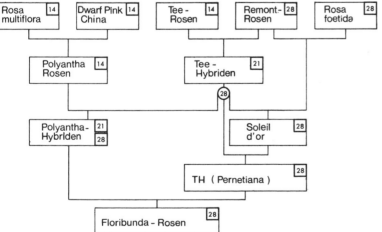

Figure 50. Development of the Floribunda Roses. Circled figures show the chromosome count. (from Wylie, with alterations)

The Hybrid Polyantha Happily this somewhat unfortunate name is being abandoned and the varieties which were formerly grouped under this heading have now been transferred to the Floribunda group where they best belong. There is no clear dividing line between Hybrid Polyantha and Floribunda. There is, however, one objection to the nomenclature: the Polyantha Roses are hybrids and it is incorrect to furnish hybrids of hybrids with another group name. The American decision to unite both in the one group is not only meaningful but of great practical advantage to the ordinary gardener.

THE FLORIBUNDA ROSES

The name was originated by Dr. J.H. Nicholas, U.S.A., and has been used since 1930 for crosses made between the Hybrid Teas and the Polyanthas. From this point of view, the first Floribunda arrived in 1908 in Germany; it was the variety 'Gruss an Aachen' (Geduldig).

The characteristics of the Floribundas are a strong, vigorous plant, of short to medium height. The blooms are mostly in large or fairly large trusses and the individual flowers are flat or cup-shaped, often double like the Tea Roses and of medium to large size. With a few exceptions, they are scentless.

The yellow Floribundas tend to show weaker growth than the other colors and their foliage is usually a brighter green.

The group covers the whole color range, from white to deepest crimson, from pale yellow to gold, orange and copper and includes lilac ('Lavender Pinocchio') to the purple of 'News'. Logically, there are many bicolors in yellow and red, pink and red, red and white, lilac and brown and other combinations.

Svend Poulsen of Denmark began the development of this group for he was particularly interested in breeding roses which would withstand the cold Scandinavian winters and yet produce the maximum number of blooms in its short summers. His first introduction was 'Rödhätte' (1911), followed by 'Else Poulsen' (1924) and 'Kirsten Poulsen' (1925). (All three of these varieties were formerly called Hybrid Polyantha.)

After the appearance of 'Else Poulsen' and 'Kirsten Poulsen', rose breeders all over the world began to take an interest in this new group and their efforts have been unabated ever since. The number of new roses introduced each year has become vast. Among the most active of the hybridizers, the following should be mentioned: M. Tantau, Wilhelm and Reimer Kordes, Svend and Niels Poulsen, Prior, Le Grice, Harkness, Meilland, de Ruiter, S. McGredy, Alex and Pat Dickson and, among the Americans, Boerner, Swim, Lindquist, Howard, Lammerts. The outstanding varieties which have been produced can be found in the section on the hybridizers and their work (see p. 152 *et seq.*).

From the almost endless list of cultivars, those which had a special influence on further hybridization should be given here. (For a detailed description see the Selected List of Varieties p. 303 *et seq.*)

1908 'Gruss an Aachen' (Geduldig), soft salmon pink.
1911 'Rödhätte' (Poulsen), cherry red.
1912 'Ellen Poulsen' (Poulsen), cherry red.
1919 'Natalie Nypels' (Leenders), rose pink.
1921 'Coral Cluster' (Murrell), coral pink.
1921 'Joseph Guy' (A. Nonin), cherry red.
1924 'Else Poulsen' (Poulsen), rose pink.
1925 'Kirsten Poulsen' (Poulsen), scarlet.
1930 'Frau Astrid Späth' (Späth), pink.
1931 'Heidekind' (V. Berger), rose pink.
1932 'D.T. Poulsen' (Poulsen), blood red.
1933 'Fortschritt' (Kordes), yellowish-pink.
1934 'Betty Prior' (Prior), dark carmine.
1934 'Donald Prior' (Prior), dark red.
1935 'Anne Poulsen' (Poulsen), carmine.
1936 'Dagmar Späth' (Späth), white.
1936 'Rosenelfe' (Kordes), pink.
1936 'Baby Château' (Kordes), crimson.
1938 'Poulsen's Yellow' (Poulsen), yellow.
1938 'Holstein' (Kordes), dark crimson.
1939 'World's Fair' (Kordes), deep crimson.
1940 'Pinocchio' (Kordes), salmon pink.
1942 'Käthe Duvigneau' (Tantau), glowing red.
1946 'Alain' (Meilland), crimson.
1946 'Fanal' (Tantau), red.
1947 'Garnette' (Tantau), red.
1947 'Fashion' (Boerner/Jackson & Perkins), deep peach.
1948 'Lavender Pinocchio' (Boerner), lavender-pink.
1949 'Masquerade' (Boerner), red and yellow.
1950 'Independence' (Kordes), pure scarlet.
1952 'Red Favorite' (Tantau), velvety crimson.
1952 'Moulin Rouge' (Meilland), deep red.
1956 'Circus' (Swim), yellow and red.
1957 'Sarabande' (Meilland), orange-red.
1958 'Allgold' (Le Grice), yellow.

1958 'Dickson's Flame' (Dickson), scarlet-flame.
1959 'Lilli Marlene' (Kordes), velvety crimson.
1964 'Marlena' (Kordes), crimson-scarlet.
1963 'Europeana' (de Ruiter), dark crimson.
1968 'News' (Le Grice), rich claret.
1971 'Picasso' (McGredy), red and white.
1971 'Prominent' (Kordes), orange-vermilion.

THE MINIATURE ROSES (= Dwarf China Roses)

These are low-growing roses which, generally, do not exceed 30 cm./12 in. in height, in exceptional cases 6/cm./24 in. if the other characteristics conform: the shoots are thin and wiry with short internodes; the leaves are small in groups of 3 or 5 and generally only 1.9 cm./0.75 in. long and 1.3 cm./0.5 in. across or even less; the blooms may be either single or double coming in trusses of not more than 10 florets. Very winter hardy. Their origins are undoubtedly in China.

The facts of their introduction into Europe are unclear and the literary versions of it are frequently contradictory. However, most authorities are of the opinion that this rose was found in the Botanic Garden on the island of Mauritius in the Indian Ocean by Robert Sweet and taken, by him, to England. This is the version given by Lindley (*Rosarum Monographia*, 1820) and by Sydenham Edwards (*Botanical Register*, 1822).

1815 Described by Sims as *Rosa semperflorens minima* in the *Botanical Magazine*, Plate 1762; it was also called 'Miss Lawrence's Rose'. It is possible that there were already a number of roses of this type, for Sims says that these plants were mostly advertised as "freshly imported from China" but he could well mean that they were mostly seeds not plants. Sims was unclear as to their true botanical classification, and this was first examined in detail by Voss in 1894.

1817 Described by Thory and painted by Redouté as *R. indica pumila* (Redouté, *Les Roses*, Plate 115).

1818 Described by Sweet as *R. lawrenceana* (in *Hort. Suburb. Lond.*) with the statement that it had come from Mauritius in 1810, but with no indication that he was responsible for its introduction. It is possible that A.P. de Candolle of Geneva, before the arrival of the plant in England, had received a plant from Mauritius himself and had grown and propagated it in his own garden. For when it was found again by Roulet in 1920, growing in the Swiss Jura, he was told that for at least 100 years it had been a popular windowbox plant with the country people in the region; these must have been descendants of the plants grown by de Candolle.

Just when the breeding of miniature roses began is uncertain, but the following dates are important:

1823 Parisian gardeners were cultivating a dwarf rose both for forcing and also as a container plant; it was marketed under the name of 'Pompon de Paris'.

1850 The same rose was being grown in many German gardens, but thereafter gradually slipped into obscurity.

1848 At this time William Paul, England, had about 15 miniature varieties for sale.

1906 The catalog of Simon & Cochet lists 59 miniatures.

1917 Colonel (or Doctor) Roulet found a miniature rose in a pot on the window-sill of a farmhouse in Mauborget in the Swiss Jura, at 1,367 m./3,750 ft. He sent the plant to Henri Correvon, at Chêne-Bourg near Geneva, who at once set about trying to find more plants. Unfortunately, Mauborget had suffered a major fire which had destroyed nearly everything, but he found the same rose growing in the vicinity of Onnen and took cuttings from it.

1920 Correvon released the rose under the name of *Rosa roulettii* (was the double "T" a slip of the pen?); later both P. Lambert and Kordes came to the conclusion that it was identical to 'Pompon de Paris'. It was promoted commercially as "the smallest rose in the world".

1929 The rose was sent to England from Germany by Georg Arends of Wuppertal, who had been the first to propagate it extensively.

In the meantime, hybridizers had been working with this variety; among them were: Jan de Vink, Holland (11 varieties between 1935-1958); Pedro Dot, Spain (15 varieties, 1939-1961); W. Kordes (4 varieties); M. Tantau (1 variety); Meilland (2 varieties after 1961); Ralph S. Moore of the United States has introduced more than 50 varieties and is still producing.

These are some of the more important miniatures:

1936 'Oakington Ruby' (C.R. Bloom, Cambridge), dark red sport of 'Pompon de Paris'.

1936 'Tom Thumb' (= 'Peon') (J. de Vink), crimson with a white eye.

1940 'Baby Gold Star' (Dot), yellow.

1940 'Midget' (J. de Vink), carmine-red.

1940 'Pixie' (J. de Vink), white.

1942 'Rosina' (Dot), yellow.

1944 'Perla de Alcanada' (Dot), carmine.

1945 'Perla de Montserrat' (Dot), pink edged with pearl.

1945 'Perla Rosa' (Dot), bright pink.

1946 'Sweet Fairy' (J. de Vink), apple-blossom pink.

1946 'Para Ti' (= 'Pour Toi') (Dot), white tinted with yellow.

1947 'Granate' (Dot), dark red.

1947 'Mon Petit' (Dot), light red.

1948 'Presumida' (Dot), yellow.

1949 'Anny' (Dot), pink fading to white.

1950 'Bo-Peep' (J. de Vink), rose pink.

1950 'Cineraria' (Dot), red and white.

1950 'Rosada' (Dot), pink.

1950 'Red Imp' (J. de Vink), crimson.

1951 'Red Elf' (J. de Vink), crimson.

1952 'Cinderella' (J. de Vink), white.

1954 'DwarfKing' (Kordes), carmine.

1954 'Queen of the Dwarfs' (Kordes), deep pink.

1956 'Baby Masquerade' (Tantau), lemon to rose red.

1956 'Coralin' (Dot), red.

1957 'Little Buckaroo' (Moore), red with white eye.

1960 'Eleanor' (Moore), coral pink.

1960 'Easter Morning' (Moore), white.

1961 'Scarlet Gem' (Meilland), orange-scarlet.

1962 'New Penny' (Moore), orange-red to coral-pink.

1963 'Bit O'Sunshine' (Moore), deep yellow.

1964 'Baby Darling' (Moore), orange.

1965 'Rosmarin' (Kordes), white with pink center.

1965 'Starina' (Meilland), orange-scarlet.

1967 'Little Sunset' (Kordes), salmon pink to white.

There are also some climbing sports of the varieties listed above.

THE CLIMBING ROSES

The following is a general botanical survey based on an extract from the work of G.D. Rowley and taken from G.S. Thomas (1965).

The section *Synstylae* of the genus *Rosa* is easily

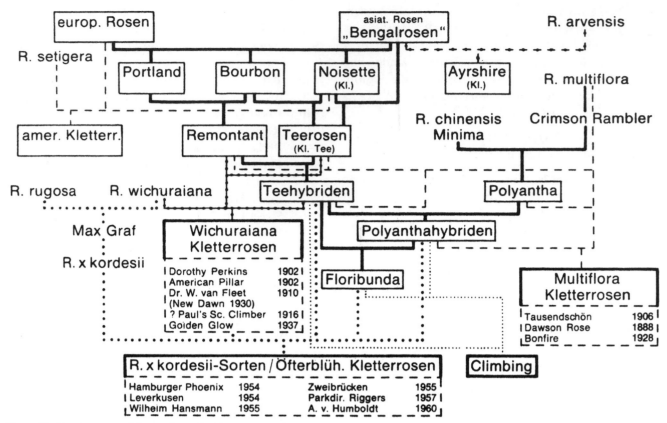

Figure 51. Development of the modern climbing roses. (J. Sieber)

recognized from the other sections, because the forms which belong to it have a tendency to climbing growth; this habit is also possessed by 4 other smaller sections viz. *Indicae, Banksianae, Laevigatae* and *Bracteatae*. All are diploid, with 14 chromosomes, as are their garden descendants. Most of the species in this section come from S.E. Asia and are stretched out along the southern border of the genus through India and Arabia to N. Africa and Europe; as usual, there is one exception to the rule and this is *R. setigera* which is a native of N. America.

In addition to their climbing habit, there are other features which are common to the *Synstylae*: differing length of the stems, small, mostly white blooms in large flat or cone-shaped pannicles, and the styles which protrude from the flower, joined together in a single column, which often remain on the small, red hips. The botanists' opinion is that the sub-division of this section embraces from 2 to 12 different species, although Hurst maintains that they all belong to a single species. Hurst's viewpoint is based upon the *R. moschata* group which appears to have an uninterrupted pattern of hab-

itation from Europe through N.W. Africa and Arabia (*R. abyssinica*), India (*R. brunonii*), Manchuria (*R. maximowicziana*) to the summit of its diversity in Central China with *R. sinowilsonii*, the leaves of which are up to 30 cm./12 in. long.

It is also worth noting that with this rose, the change from bush to climbing form in the wild also showed a preference for a different habitat, that is to say the bush forms predominated in open countryside while the climbers preferred wooded areas where their long trailing stems had something to cling to; as young plants they experienced shaded conditions and later unfolded their blossoms above the undergrowth.

Natural hybrids between the bush and climbing forms are rare but in the case of the forerunners of the garden hybrids such crosses were often made, and produced intermediate forms. However, there were often climbing sports of the bush roses and vice versa, and through propagation these sports could be "fixed", as happened on numerous occasions.

C.C. Hurst maintained that the length of the blooming period in roses was determined by a strain of low-growing plants which were sports of a climbing variety, and produced only short, flowering shoots instead of the long trailing stems. This theory is impossible. Today there are many tall, long-blooming garden roses; recurrent blooming is not connected with the descendants of the climbing roses.

The problem of this group's composition was satisfactorily resolved by both the Americans and the English in two different ways.

The Americans divide them into two groups:

1. Ramblers.
   Plants with very whippy stems which need support; small flowers; majority descended from *R. wichuraiana* and both recurrent and non-recurrent.
2. Large-Flowered Climbers.
   Plants with long, stiff stems; the flowers are larger and held in loose clusters, mostly recurrent. These include the climbing sports of the bush roses.

The English system is as follows:

I. Climbing Species
   a) single-flowered species
   b) double-flowered forms of the species
II. Climbing Varieties prior to 1970
   a) Varieties with whippy, pliant growths
   b) Varieties with stiff growths; sub-divided into
      1. The climbing Bourbons
      2. The climbing Noisettes
      3. The climbing Teas
      4. The climbing Hybrid Teas
      5. The Kordesii climbers
III. Climbing varieties after 1970
   a) Upright Climbers (Pillar Roses) not exceeding 2.4 m./8 ft. in height
   b) Climbing varieties exceeding 2.4 m./8 ft.

The most important species used in the development of today's climbing roses are *R. multiflora, wichuraiana, moschata, sempervirens* and *arvensis*. Brief details on these follow.

Rosa multiflora This species, from East Asia, was first introduced in 1860. It grew up to 3 m./10 ft. tall and had numerous strong shoots which were often almost entirely lacking prickles. In the U.S.A., some years ago, Dr. Lyle of Texas made a careful selection of various clones which were of special interest for areas with a mild climate. The small white blooms appear in very large trusses in June. Certain forms of *R. multiflora*, early arrivals from China, are useful in breeding programs.

1804 *R. multiflora carnea* was taken to England by Thomas Evans of the East India Company; it became the basic seed parent of the *multiflora* climbers; the flowers are pale pink, small and double.

1817 Charles Greville, in London, received the 'Seven Sisters Rose' (*R. multiflora platyphylla*) from China; it is similar to *carnea* but the leaves are bigger and wrinkled; it is probably *R. multiflora carnea × R. rugosa*; lilac-pink to crimson, variable in size and in the number of petals; very strong-growing in the fall with a resultant tendency not to ripen and so suffer frost damage.

1844 *R. multiflora alba* introduced from Japan. Very double, opening pale pink then fading to white.

1862 Coignet, a French engineer in the employ of the Japanese government, sent seeds of *R. multiflora* to the Mayor of Lyon who passed them on to Guillot.

1893 Introduction of 'Crimson Rambler'. The engineer, Robert Smith, Professor at the University of Tokyo, found this rose in a local garden where it was known as Sakura-Ibara or 'Cherry Rose'; in China it was called Shi-tz-mei (= 'Ten Sisters'). Smith sent it home to a friend in Scotland, Thomas Jenner, who christened it 'The Engineer' and passed it on to J. Gilbert in Lincoln. He increased his number of plants and it was shown for the first time at the Royal Horticultural Society in 1890. Turner, a nurseryman in Slough, bought the sole rights to the rose, started to build up stocks and finally put it on the market in 1893, creating quite a sensation. The parentage is unknown; it could be either a hybrid or a mutation from *R. multiflora cathayensis*.

Today the *multiflora* descendants, where the climbing varieties are concerned, have been superceded by similar, but improved, recurrent varieties. A few of them are still noteworthy:

1895 'Thalia' (Schmitt/Lambert), white.
1896 'Aglaia' (Schmitt/Lambert), straw yellow.
1903 'Blush Rambler' (Cant), blush pink.
1904 'Hiawatha' (Walsh), crimson.
1906 'Tausendschön' (J.C. Schmidt), pink, without prickles.
1907 var. *cathayensis* was brought to Europe.
1909 'Veilchenblau' (J.C. Schmidt), violet.
1913 'Gruss an Freundorf' (Praskac), dark crimson.
1921 'Violette' (Turbat), deep violet, somewhat darker than 'Veilchenblau'.

1923 'Phyllis Bide' (Bide), yellow shaded with pink.

1939 'Chevy Chase' (Hansen), was considered to be an improved 'Crimson Rambler' although not related.

1952 'Coral Dawn' (Boerner), rose pink, recurrent.

1956 'Solo' (Tantau), fiery red, recurrent.

Rosa wichuraiana, (including R. luciae) and their descendants. It must be disturbing for the reader to learn that varieties were formerly ascribed to *R. wichuraiana*, come, in part, from another similar species, *R. luciae*. G.S. Thomas described this in detail in 1965, but apparently he has been ignored, so this position must now be explained.

Rosa luciae Franchet & Rochebrune ex Crépin (1871) was found in China in 1844 by Callery and sent to Europe in 1870. It is very similar to the better-known *R. wichuraiana*, although more upright in its growth; it has mostly 7 leaves, smaller and thinner, long and pointed, the upper side shiny; the flowers are 1.9-3.8 cm./0.75-1.5 in. wide, white and appear in May-June. It is native to Eastern China, Japan and Korea. It is less hardy than *R. wichuraiana*. Pictured in the *Botanical Magazine*, plate 7421.

Rosa wichuraiana Crépin (1886) = *R. luciae wichuraiana* Koidz. (1913). Discovered in 1861 by Dr. Max Wichura; exported from Japan in 1817. Prostrate growth; evergreen, leaves about 7.6 cm./3 in. long, rounded or ovoid and robust, terminal leaves similar in size; flowers about 3.8 cm./1.5 in. across, June-July. Indigenous to Japan, Korea, Taiwan, and Eastern China. Very hardy.

If the two species are compared, the correct botanical description of *R. luciae* must be given first priority. Yet this has not been the case even though the Americans regard the two species as one. It is only known for sure that Barbier used *R. luciae* in his breeding program. The development in hybridization took the following course:

1861 Dr. Max Ernst Wichura sent *R. wichuraiana* from Japan to Germany, but the plants died.

1880 He sent a second batch of plants to the Botanic Gardens in Munich and Brussels; Crépin saw them in Brussels and named them after Dr. Wichura.

1883 Horvath began to cross them, using 'Cramoisi Supérieur' and 'Pâquerette' as pollen parents, and produced four large-flowered, winter-hardy, climbing roses which were put on the market in 1898 and 1899 by Pitcher & Mandar of South Orange, N.J. under the names of 'Pink Roamer', 'South Orange Perfection', 'Manda's Triumph' and 'Universal Favorite'. In addition, using 'Maréchal Niel', he obtained 'Evergreen Gem'.

1890 The nursery of L. Späth, Berlin, had started cultivating this species, and sent plants to the Arnold Arboretum in the United States where it was propagated and distributed to other American gardens and nurseries, most importantly to Michael H. Horvath of the Newport Nursery, Rhode Island.

1899 Manda obtained two hybrids 'Gardenia' and 'May Queen', both of which are still grown in England.

1900 Barbier of Orléans, France visited Horvath in the U.S.A. and also started hybridizing, using *R. luciae* as the seed parent and obtaining, among others, 'Alberic Barbier' and 'Paul Transon' which were made available commercially.

In the United States at this time there were a number of hybridizers, all of whom were using *R. wichuraiana*, including: Jackson Dawson (of the Arnold Arboretum), Dr. W. van Fleet (in Glenn Dale, Maryland), James A. Farrell (of the nursery of Hoopes Bro. & Thomas Co., West Chester, Penn.), Jackson & Perkins (Newark, N.Y.), and M.H. Walsh of Woods Hole, Mass., who alone brought out 40 new varieties between 1901 and 1920.

Apart from those already mentioned, the following are some of the most important of the *wichuraiana* hybrids:

1900 'Lady Duncan' (Dawson) = **R. jacksonii** Willm. (*R. rugosa* × *R. wichuraiana*), pink.

1901 'Dorothy Perkins' (Jackson & Perkins), pink.

1901 'René André' (Barbier), saffron yellow turning pink and carmine.

1902 'Debutante' (Walsh), rose pink.

1903 'Léontine Gervais' (Barbier), salmon orange and yellow.

1904 'Gerbe Rose' (Fauque), pale pink.

1904 'La Perle' (Fauque), pale yellow to white.

1905 'American Pillar' (van Fleet), carmine with white eye.

1905 'Lady Gay' (Walsh), rich, rose pink.

1905 'Minnehaha' (Walsh), pink fading to white.

1909 'Alexandre Girault' (Barbier), carmine.

1909 'Excelsa' (Walsh), deep pink to crimson.

1909 'Fräulein Octavia Hesse' (Herme A. Hesse), yellowish-white.

1910 'Dr. W. van Fleet' (van Fleet), flesh pink fading to white.

1911 'Wichmoss' (Barbier), blush pink fading to white.

1915 'Dr. Huey' (Thomas), deep crimson.

1918 'Auguste Gervais' (Barbier), coppery-salmon.

1921 'Albertine' (Barbier), coppery-salmon.

1924 'Mary Wallace' (van Fleet), rose pink.

1926 'Breeze Hill' (van Fleet), flesh pink tinted with apricot.

1927 'Thelma' (Easlea), coral pink.

1930 'New Dawn' (Somerset Nurseries), a perpetual-flowering sport of 'Dr. W. van Fleet'. Still widely grown today. It received the American Plant Patent No. 1. Blush Pink.

1932 'Blaze' (Kallay), scarlet.

1945 'City of York' (Tantau), creamy white.

In conclusion, mention must be made of de Ruiter's 'Compacta' roses which also had R. wichuraiana among their ancestors (see p. 89).

For details of *Rosa kordesii*, see p. 97.

Rosa moschata The Musk Rose. The history of this rose, in contrast to the usual information given in books on roses, is very unclear. G.S. Thomas (1965: pp. 48-57) has made a particular effort to clear up the numerous uncertainties which surround this rose. The following statement draws together that which was previously known with some certainty and Graham Thomas' own opinions and discoveries.

Rosa moschata and *Rosa brunonii* are often linked today, although the latter is viewed as the Asiatic form and deviates from the type in its strength of growth (9.1-10.6 m./30-35 ft. in height), the greater hairiness of the foot-stalks, leaves and calyx; the leaves are somewhat smaller as are the flowers although these are in larger corymbs; it usually blooms only once in the season (see also note on the year 1824).

The true, typical *R. moschata* is very old; it is believed to have come to southern Europe, North Africa and Madeira from either India or southern China. The rose which today is recognized as the true form grows only 3-4.5 m./10-15 ft. tall and blooms in late summer or at the beginning of the fall; its leaves are more elliptical in shape. It is still grown, but is seen very rarely.

What is generally regarded as *R. moschata* in present-day gardens, a plant growing some 9.1-10.6 m./30-35 ft. tall and described by Ray (1688) as *R. moschata major*, is either a form of *R. moschata nepalensis* or a hybrid of it.

1521 The (true) *R. moschata* was brought to England from Spain, according to John Amble, an inhabitant of a monastery in southern England (Shepherd).

1540 and 1560 are also given as the dates of introduction into England.

1565 A German gardener, Solomon Gessner, found the Musk Rose growing at a monastery in Augsburg; he propagated it and distributed it throughout Germany.

1590 By this time, it seems to have been in general cultivation.

1596 Weston reported *R. moschata plena* as being in cultivation.

1596 The "Musk Rose" of Shakespeare's *Midsummer Night's Dream* and the work of the English poets Bacon and Keats. Authorities now concur that this was *Rosa arvensis*. This bloomed in July, had some fragrance and is native to England. Shakespeare, although a lover of nature, was no botanist and his terminology is often unreliable.

1597 Gerard, in his *Herball*, stated that the Musk Rose bloomed in the autumn.

1629 Parkinson described both single and double Musk Roses. He observed that the scent of the rose came from the stamens, a fact which Graham Thomas not only confirms (1964), but which he maintains applies to the whole *Synstylae* section.

1688 John Ray mentioned a *R. moschata minor*, 2.7-3 in./9-10 ft. tall and a *R. moschata major* which bloomed in June. Of the latter, he said that it could not have been the true *R. moschata* because that did not bloom until the end of the summer or early in the fall.

1762 *R. moschata* described by Herrmann as being autumn-blooming.

1768 The same comment made by Miller.

1802 The first Noisette Rose appeared from the cross *R. moschata* × *R. chinensis*. See p. 82.

1807 *R. moschata abyssinica* (Lindl.) Rehd. was

brought from Ethiopia although it was probably originally from China; has more prickles and is less hardy. Used for breeding purposes by the Rev. G. Schoener in California but with disappointing results.

1820 Lindley described *R. brunonii*; the name is a Latin form commemorating Robert Brown.

1824 Lindley changed his mind about *R. brunonii* and rechristened it *R. moschata nepalensis*.

1829 Nine hybrids which had been introduced since the beginning of the 19th century by Desportes, Prévost, Vibert and Wells are listed in Desportes' catalog. Presumably they are all descendants of *R. moschata*, for the first Noisette Roses did not reach Paris until 1825 and were not widely distributed. These early hybrids were of little importance.

1835 'The Garland' (Wells), *R. moschata* × *R. multiflora*, is looked upon as being the oldest variety from *R. moschata*.

1866 Bernaix introduced *R. moschata grandiflora*.

1879 Introduction of *R. moschata nastarana*, the Persian Musk Rose (= *R. pissardii* Carr.); possibly a hybrid of *R. chinensis* × *R. moschata*. Flowers white tinged with pink, semi-double, 5 cm./2 in. across, fragrant, recurrent and vigorous. Therefore, flowers on new growth are sure to bloom even if severely frosted during the winter. Believed to have been long cultivated in Persia to the present day.

Next come the *moschata* hybrids. This name is not really correct, for the *moschata* ancestors lie several generations back, but since this is the terminology which has been adopted it is best to retain it for the sake of clarity.

1904 'Trier' (Peter Lambert), the first recurrent shrub rose. It encouraged the hybridizers to attempt to breed more roses of this type. Until 1919, there were only a few of these recurrent shrubs, and they were given the general name of 'Lambertiana Roses'. Details of the most important follow, although today, since they have been superceded by the modern recurrent shrub roses and by the hybrids from *R. kordesii*, they are usually only found in specialist rose collections.

1909 'Excellenz von Schubert' (P. Lambert), deep pink.

1913 'Arndt' (P. Lambert), flesh pink.

1914 'Lessing' (P. Lambert), rose pink streaked with white.

1916 'Von Liliencron' (P. Lambert), yellowish-pink.

1917 'Hoffmann von Fallersleben' (P. Lambert), salmon red.

1919 'Heinrich Conrad Söth' (P. Lambert), rose pink with a white eye.

1922 'Chamisso' (P. Lambert), pink with a yellow center.

In addition, the breeding of *moschata* hybrids was begun in England at about this time.

1912 The Rev. J.H. Pemberton, of Havering-atte-Bower, Essex, produced not less than 23 individual varieties, some of which were low-growing some tall and some climbers. The majority were summer-flowering only, but others gave their best crop in the fall on wood made in that season. The colors vary from white through yellow to carmine and they are fragrant, some very much so. The most important of his varieties are:

1913 'Moonlight' (Pemberton), lemon-white.

1923 'Penelope' (Pemberton), shell pink.

1930 After Pemberton's death, his work was taken over by J.A. Bentall, a nurseryman, who introduced a number of Pemberton's seedlings.

It was at this point that Kordes started work on the breeding of recurrent shrub roses, making use of either the *moschata* hybrids or the so-called 'Lambertiana Roses'. He crossed varieties of *moschata* ancestry with Hybrid Teas and other roses. The following varieties produced are still available:

1933 'Eva' ('Robin Hood' × 'J.C. Thornton'), carmine.

1934 'Skyrocket' ('Robin Hood' × 'J.C. Thornton'), crimson.

1934 'Nymphenburg' ('Sangerhausen' × 'Sunmist'), salmon pink shaded with orange.

1935 'Hamburg' ('Eva' × 'Daily Mail Scented Rose'), crimson.

1949 'Berlin' ('Eva' × 'Peace'), orange-scarlet.

1949 'Bonn' ('Hamburg' × 'Independence'), orange-scarlet.

1950 'Elmshorn' (Hamburg' × 'Verdun'), deep pink.

1951 'Grandmaster' ('Sangerhausen' × 'Sunmist'), apricot.

1956 'Ilse Haberland', pink and yellow.

1964 'Bischofsstadt Paderborn', cinnabar-scarlet.

1966 'Lichtkönigin Luise', golden yellow.

1969 'Westerland', orange and red.

M. Tantau also experimented with breeding recurrent shrub roses and produced the following:

1955 'Lichterloh' cinnabar red.

1956 'Dirigent' blood red.

1962 'Feuerwerk' bright orange.

1970 'Fountain' deep, velvety red. This was the first shrub rose to win the RNRS President's International Trophy.

Rosa kordesii and other recurrent climbing roses Within the ever-increasing number of recurrent climbers, the *kordesii* hybrids form a separate group due to their origins. They are by no means all climbing roses as their upright habit of growth and freedom of bloom also makes them suitable shrub roses; in the following list those within the latter category are marked (+). This new race has greater garden value and, since its arrival, the varieties which were summer-flowering only have begun to disappear and indeed have become, for practical purposes, unsaleable; for the hybridizers there is the opportunity of entirely new combinations in cross breeding. In the development of *Rosa kordesii*, the following are the salient facts:

1919 In the nursery of J.H. Bowditch of Connecticut, U.S.A., a chance seedling from *R. rugosa* × *R. wichuraiana* was found and introduced as 'Max Graf'. It displayed a vigorous trailing growth, very healthy foliage and great winter hardiness, and it soon gained considerable popularity in the United States for ground-cover purposes. The pinkish blooms were sterile for all practical purposes.

circa 1925 W. Kordes obtained a plant of 'Max Graf'; in spite of every effort they only managed to get it to set seed on three occasions.

1940 Kordes obtained two seedlings from a 'Max Graf' self-cross; one of these was reminiscent of *R. rugosa* both in its foliage and in its upright growth habit; the other was more like *R. wichuraiana* with long trailing stems.

1942 The *rugosa*-type seedling and its progeny were destroyed by the winter frosts, but the other, although given no protection, came through unscathed and flowered in the following year with loose, double, red blooms, followed by bottle-shaped hips. More than 75% of the seeds germinated. This event, where an almost completely sterile hybrid produced highly fertile offspring, was explained in 1951 by H.D. Wulff after research into amphidiploids (= a doubling of each genome in the zygote).

1951 The seedling was named *Rosa kordesii* by H.D. Wulff and described by him in *Der Züchter* 21: pp. 123-132, in which it was shown conclusively that the new variety had indeed come from its authentic seed parents. Kordes immediately started to cross with this new rose, using it both as seed and pollen parent and raised thousands of seedlings from it. Among these was a group of recurrent plants of climbing habit and with exceptional resistance to winter frosts. The best were gradually put on the market and are listed here:

1954 'Hamburger Phoenix' (Kordes), = *R. kordesii* × unknown seedling, orange-red.

1954 'Leverkusen' (Kordes), = *R. kordesii* × 'Golden Glow', light yellow.

1955 'Wilhelm Hansmann' (Kordes), *R. kordesii* × ('Baby Chateau' × 'Else Poulsen'), deep crimson (+).

1955 'Dortmund' (Kordes), = *R. kordesii* × unknown seedling, red with a white eye.

1955 'Zweibrücken' (Kordes), = *R. kordesii* × 'Independence', deep crimson, (+).

1956 'Aurora' (Kordes), *R. kordesii* hybrid, orange-yellow.

1956 'Köln am Rhein' (Kordes), = *R. kordesii* × 'Golden Glow', salmon pink.

1956 'Bengt M. Schalin' (Kordes), = *R. kordesii* × 'Eos', non-recurrent, rose red, (+).

1957 'Ilse Krohn' (Kordes), = *R. kordesii* × 'Golden Glow', white.

1957 'Karlsruhe' (Kordes), = *R. kordesii* × 'Golden Glow, deep pink, (+).

1957 'Parkdirektor Riggers' (Kordes), = *R. kordesii* × 'Our Princess', red.

1958 'Bad Neuenahr' (Kordes), = *R. kordesii* seedling, scarlet.

1959 'Heidelberg' (Kordes), = *R. kordesii* × ?, crimson, (+).

1959 'Ritter von Barmstede' (Kordes), = *R. kordesii* × ?, deep pink.

1960 'Raymond Chenault' (Kordes), = *R. kordesii* × 'Montezuma', bright red.

1960 'Alexander von Humboldt' (Kordes), = *R. kordesii* × 'Cleopatra', scarlet, (+).

1961 'Illusion' (Kordes), = *R. kordesii* × 'Montezuma', blood red to cinnabar.

1962 'Morgengruss' (Kordes), = *R. kordesii* × 'Cleopatra', pink and orange.

1963 'Gruss an Koblenz' (Kordes), = *R. kordesii* × ?, bright scarlet, (+).

1964 'Ilse Krohn Superior' (Kordes), sport of 'Ilse Krohn', pure white.

1964 'Sympathie' (Kordes), = 'Wilhelm Hansmann' × 'Don Juan', dark red.

1966 'Goldstern' (Tantau), one of the best climbing yellow roses available at the time, (+).

     (+ can also be grown as a free-standing shrub)

In addition to the *kordesii* varieties, a number of other recurrent climbing roses were introduced about the same time; some were sports of Hybrid Teas, others came from different groups. The outstanding varieties were:

1950 'Climbing Sutter's Gold' (Armstrong), orange-yellow.

1952 'Solo' (Tantau), dark red.

1958 'Royal Gold' (Jackson & Perkins), yellow.

1958 'Golden Showers' (Germain's), yellow.

1960 'Climbing Queen Elizabeth' (Wheatcroft), salmon pink.

1962 'Climbing Ballet' (Kordes), pink.

1963 'Casino' (McGredy), soft yellow.

1965 'Climbing Tropicana' (Heitmann), coral orange.

1967 'Bantry Bay' (McGredy), pink.

1968 'Swanlake' (McGredy), white tinged with pink.

1970 'Cordon Rouge' (Vilmorin), red.

Rosa arvensis and its descendants This ancient rose once grew wild over the greater part of Europe, but it has played a very undistinguished role in the breeding of new roses, and it enjoyed considerably more respect in the past than it does at present.

Norman Lambert in the *Rose Annual* of 1931 expressed his strong conviction that it was not *Rosa alba* which was the 'White Rose of York' but *Rosa arvensis*. He had made frequent visits to Yorkshire and to Towton, the battlefield where the forces of the House of York overcame the Lancastrians, in particular. Many wild white roses still grow there, as they have done for centuries. There are also impenetrable rose thickets. It is very possible that the rose selected to symbolize the House of York was a native of the country and one found in great abundance, and that could only have been *Rosa arvensis*. Despite the fact that many authorities maintain that it was *Rosa alba*, there is, as N. Lambert says, certainly room for doubt.

1596 Shakespeare speaks, in the *Midsummer Night's Dream*, of the scent of the "Musk Rose". The rose experts now seem to generally agree that he was actually speaking of *R. arvensis* which blooms in summer and has some scent, while the true Musk Rose, which was rare in Shakespeare's time, does not flower until much later.

1623 Caspar Bauhin of Basel, describes a *Rosa candida* which must really have been *R. arvensis*.

1762 Well established in various Botanic Gardens; Hudson, in his *Flora Anglica*, gives it the name of *R. arvensis*.

1767 The Edinburgh Botanic Gardens sent a man to North America to collect new and unknown plants. He brought back a strong, vigorous rose which soon attracted the attention of gardeners in Ayrshire. At first it was called the 'Orangefield Rose' but this was later changed to the 'Ayrshire Rose'. This rose was unrelated to the true Ayrshires, which came later, for, in spite of conflicting reports, it seems clear that this was a hybrid of *Rosa setigera*.

circa 1830 Scottish gardeners like Brown of Perth, Martin of Dundee, and Robert Austin of Glasgow began hybridizing with these roses which were given the collective name of 'Ayrshire Roses'. There were about 60 varieties in all, and all were crosses between *R. arvensis* and other contemporary roses, although some were just chance seedlings; not much is known about them today since very few of them still exist. They were mostly white to pink, double, with little or no scent, but the growth was strong and hardy and they were used as the climbers of their day. 'Venusta Pendula' is an old *arvensis* hybrid of unknown parentage which was rediscovered by W. Kordes in the Ohlsdorf Cemetery in Hamburg and re-established commercially by him.

1931 'Dusterlohe' (Kordes), probably the only modern

hybrid of *arvensis* ('Venusta Pendula' × 'Miss E.C. van Rossem'), rose red.

Rosa sempervirens These evergreen roses from the Mediterranean area occupy, geographically speaking, a middle ground. To the east they border the area of *R. moschata*, and to the west and north the territory of *R. arvensis*; in their appearance, too, they are intermediate to these two species.

1623 Was first described as *Rosa moschata sempervirens*.

1629 (or earlier). Was introduced into England and was therefore the earliest form of climbing rose in cultivation.

1824-1832 Used by Jacques, Head Gardener to the Duc d'Orléans at the Château de Neuilly, for cross-breeding; in those years he produced about 40 varieties, but of these only two remain today:

1826 'Adélaide d'Orléans' (Jacques), pale rose.

1827 'Félicité et Perpétue' (Jacques), double, white tinted with cream, fragrant. Named in memory of the two martyrs, St. Felicitas and St. Perpetua who were thrown to the lions in Carthage in 203 A.D.

Rosa setigera The Prairie Rose. A native of the U.S.A. where its habitat stretches from the Atlantic to the Rocky Mountains, which means that it inhabits virtually every state in the East and Middle West; it blooms in June-July.

1803 Was named by Michaux.

1810 First grown in Europe. Was used for breeding. Shepherd (1954, p. 43) made the important observation that it could segregate into male and female forms and that the plants bearing fertile seeds often had sterile pollen while in poor seed bearers, the pollen was very fertile. In its natural habitat it is common to find large bushes which completely lack hips next to other plants which are covered with them.

1825 William Prince in Flushing, N.Y. began hybridizing with this rose but none of his seedlings ('Seraphine' 1840 and 'Gracilis' 1841) became know in Europe nor do they still exist.

The next hybridizers to use this rose were the brothers John and Samuel Feast of Baltimore; they produced a number of varieties which are occasionally still to be found in England:

1843 'Baltimore Belle', pale pink, very double.

1843 'King of the Prairies', bright red.

1843 'Queen of the Prairies', bright pink striped with white. This was the Feasts' best variety.

The hybrids produced by the Americans Prince and Pierce between 1840 and 1850 seem to have disappeared from the records.

1886 Geschwind of Hungary produced 'Souvenir de Brod', cerise, very double, fragrant.

1925-1942 A number of hybrids, most of which were crosses between *R. setigera* and various Hybrid Teas, came from M.H. Horvath of Mentor, Ohio. The most important still in cultivation are:

1934 'Captain Kidd', blood red, double, fragrant and very hardy.

1934 'Doubloons', golden yellow, large and double.

1934 'Jean Lafitte', deep pink, very double.

1934 'Long John Silver', silvery-white, double and very vigorous.

1942 'Meda', shrimp pink, double; a very pretty rose.

BIBLIOGRAPHY

ALLEN, E.F. *Rosa kordesii* and its Hybrids. The Rose 17, 203-205 (1969).

B.P. (PARK). Grandiflora! RA 1959: 119-120.

CARABIN, J.R. The admirable old Roses. ARA 1951: 194-201.

CHAIX, L. Histoire du Rosier du Bourbon; in Flore des Serres et des Jardins de l'Europe 7: 77-80 (1851) — There is a very good English translation of this important work by MOREY (1953).

CHANDLER, A. Outlines of Rose History. ARA 1953: 123-128.

COGGIATI, S. Storia breve dell'ibridazione delle rose in Italia. Ann. della Rose 1972: 31-45. With details of all the Italian hybridizers.

GIBSON, M. Shrub Roses for every Garden. London 1973. 195 col. Plates.

GREGORY, C.W. The Compacta Roses. The Rose 10: 35-37 (1961).

HAMBLIN, S.F. The Centennial of the Hybrid Perpetuals. ARA 1942: 17-26.

— History of the Modern Rose. American Rose Magazine; February-November 1965. French translation in 'Rosa Belgica'.

HURST, C.C. Notes on the origin and evolution of our garden Roses. Jour. RHS 1941: 73-82; 242-250; 282-289.

HURST and BREEZE. Notes on the origin of the Moss Rose. Jour. RHS 1922: 26-42.

JANICKE, W. Rosen der 'Bügerkönigszeit' (bis 1840). Rosen-Jb. 32: 97-99 (1966).

KORDES, W. *Rosa chinensis* Jacq. und *Rosa chinensis semperflorens* Koehne. Rosenjahrbuch 1953: 89-93.

— Der Rosenstreit (betr. 'Königin von Dänemark'). R.Jb. 1961: 214-215.

— The History of *Rosa kordesii* Wulff. RA 1965: 99-102.

LEROY, A. Histoire des Roses. Paris 1954.

— Les Rosiers. 4th Edition, 200 pp. 58 Ill. Paris 1970.

LEVY, L. The Advance of the Hybrid Polyantha. RA 1938: 162-165.

— The History and Evolution of the dwarf Polyantha. RA 1931: 75-85.

MERRELL, J.   The Bourbon Roses. The Rose 13: 249-254 (1965).

MOREY, D.H.   The Bourbon Rose. ARA 1953: 163-167.

PERNET-DUCHER, J.   Die Entstehungsgeschichte der *Rosa Pernetiana* 'Soleil d'Or'. German translation reprinted from Möll. Dtsch. Gärt. Z. 1900, in Rosen-Jb 1956: 117-118.

RATHLEF, H. VON.   Vererbungsstudien an der Edelrose. Z. f. Pflanzenzücht. 1928: 9-47.

RIES, W.   Züchtung der Zwergrosen. Rosenjahrbuch 1953: 82-89.

ROBINSON, E.E.   A Short History of the Tea Rose. The Rose 17: 178-183 (1969).

ROBINSON, R.   Check List of Red Tea Roses. The Rose 13: 62-67 (1965).

——   The early Hybrid Perpetuals. The Rose 13: 195-202 (1965).

Rosenzeitung. Gravereaux's geschichtlich geordnete Tabelle alter Rosenarten.

ROWLEY, G.   The Scotch Rose and its Garden Descendants. Jour. RHS: 433-438 (1960?).

SAAKOV, S.G.   The Origin of Garden Roses and the Direction of their Breeding. 26 pp. 1 plate. Leningrad 1965; in Russian but with a complete summary in English.

SCHMID, G.   Rosensorten zur Goethezeit in Weimar. Rosen-Jb. 1939: 107-114.

SHEPHERD, R.   Origin of Rose Types. ARA 1950: 33-37.

——   History of the Rose. 264 pp. 26 Ill. New York 1954.

SIEBER, J.   Entwicklungsgeschichte der Rosen. Rosenjahrbuch 1968: 5-37.

STEMMLER, D. and N. ITO.   Roses of Yesterday. Kansas City 1967.

THOMAS, G.S.   Damask Roses. RA 1964: 37-41.

——   Bourbon Roses. The Rose 11: 159-169; 229-237 (1963).

——   *Rosa rugosa* RA 1967: 27-32.

WILDING, J.H.   The Romance of the Floribundas. RA 1959: 152-156.

WINTON-LEWIS, B.A.P.   Rugosa roses. The Rose 13: 136-140 (1965).

WULFF, H.D.   *Rosa kordesii*, eine neue amphidiploide Rose. Der Züchter 21: 123-132 (1951).

WYLIE, ANN P.   The History of Garden Roses. Jour. RHS 1954: 555-571; 1955: 8-24; 77-87.

YOUNG, N.   The History of the Hybrid Teas. The Rose 1960: 159-166 and a correction on p. 266.

THE EMPRESS JOSÉPHINE, MALMAISON,[1] THE EARLY FRENCH HYBRIDIZERS AND REDOUTÉ

Nobody, before or since, has had so great an influence on rose growing as the French Empress Joséphine. She is integral to the great period of the early French hybridizers. But first let us look at some of the important dates in her career.

Joséphine was a Creole born on June 23, 1763 and baptized Marie-Josephe Rose Tascher de la Pagerie, the daughter of an impoverished nobleman who held the post of Harbor Superintendent in Martinique. At the age of 16, she went to Paris and, shortly after her arrival, married the Vicomte de Beauharnais, to whom she bore two children. Her son, Eugène, became a soldier under his future step-father, Napoleon Bonaparte, while her daughter married Napoleon's brother, Louis and became Queen of Holland. In 1794, de Beauharnais was arrested and executed during the Reign of Terror. His wife was also arrested and might have suffered his fate, but the events of the 9th Thermidor led to her freedom and the restoration of her husband's confiscated property. Soon thereafter she was introduced to Napoleon at a Ball in the Palais Luxemburg and they were married in 1796. Napoleon disliked her name of Marie-Josephe Rose and called her Joséphine.

In 1798, he bought the Chateau Malmaison for her and spent much of his time there, until he became First Consul in 1802. It was there that Joséphine began to assemble her famous collection of paintings, sculpture and jewelry. She soon became intensively involved in creating her garden; she sent her gardener to England and also employed English gardeners, among them the great Scottish garden designer, Thomas Blaikie (1750-1838).

She organized, with great energy, the collecting of rare plants from all over the world for her garden; helped not only by scientists but also by diplomats and soldiers. During the Napoleonic Wars all ships captured were thoroughly searched for plants and seeds that they might be carrying. One of her gardeners, the Irishman John Kennedy, was given a passport which enabled him to pass freely through the British and French lines in order to buy plants and return with them to France.

However, roses particularly captivated Joséphine; she had a rose garden laid out at Malmaison by André Dupont which soon became the largest and most beautiful of its time and on which no expense was spared. She attempted to collect every known rose variety and was in constant communication with rose gardeners and nurserymen in England, Belgium, Holland and Germany while the French rosarians came and went at her bidding. The greatest botanists of the day were hers to command and the position of Head Gardener or Garden Superintendent to the Empress, who had acquired the influence and importance of a Minister of State, was coveted. The first Head Gardener was Brisseau de Mirbel, 1803-1806; he was followed by Goujaud, who was known as "Bonpland" for his talent with

---

[1] "Malmaison" and "La Malmaison" are used interchangeably in the literature of the period, including French, but it seems that the official name as it appears in documents of Napoleon's time was always "Malmaison".

PLATE 9

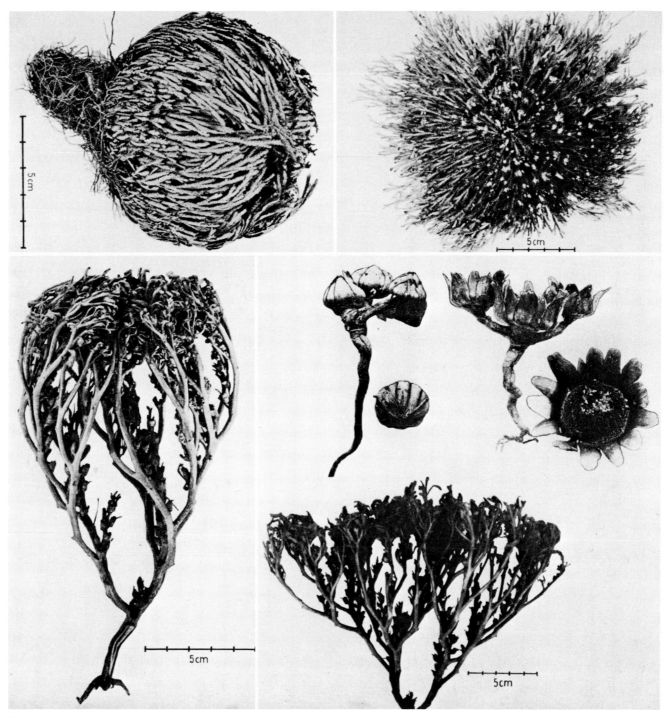

The "Roses of Jericho"
Above *Selaginella lepidophylla*, right open, left closed; *Anastatica hierochuntica*, lower left closed, lower right open; *Asteriscus pygmaeus*, center right open, center left closed. (Photo: Grasmück)

PLATE 10

The Empress Joséphine at Malmaison.
(from a painting by Prud'hon, Louvre)

Pierre-Joseph Redouté (1759-1840)
the "Raphael of the Rose".

The Chateau Malmaison (from a painting by Auguste Garneray, Musée Nationale, Malmaison), showing a cavalcade moving off across the
Park of the Chateau.

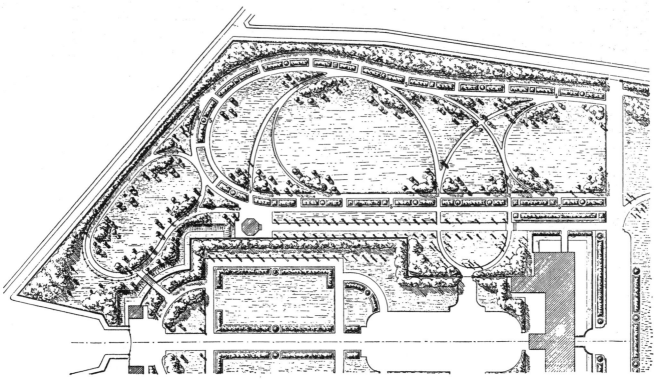

Figure 52. The Empress Joséphine's Rose Garden at Malmaison. The roses were situated on the main axis in long rectangular beds. (from a plan by E. Touret.)

plants. He had been associated with Humboldt in the collection of plants and numerous seeds, in Central America, which had been brought back to France. In addition, the two botanists, E.P. Ventenat and Delahaye worked on her behalf. In the garden, she had over 300 varieties of Erica and many Cacti, dahlias and peonies. In the years 1803 and 1804 not less than 200 plants new to Europe bloomed for the first time at Malmaison.

Pierre Joseph Redouté must now be examined. This legendary painter of roses has often been represented incorrectly, but if the information given by André Leroy, undoubtedly one of the most reliable authorities, is followed, repetition of the errors of the past can be avoided. Pierre Joseph Redouté, often referred to as the "Raphael of the Rose", was born in the Ardennes in Belgium, in 1759 and early showed considerable promise as a painter. Two of his brothers had settled in Paris as professional artists so Pierre Joseph followed them and joined one brother who was employed in the theater as a scene painter. It was inevitable that other artists would recognize his talent and he was noticed by the Court painter Gerard van Spaendonck, in charge of painting flowers for the Jardin des Plantes, but who preferred commissions from wealthy clients. Spaen-

donck, therefore, was in need of a young man to whom he could entrust the work of making these botanical drawings and found him in Pierre Joseph Redouté.

He worked first as an illustrator for various botanists, doing 500 plates for L'Heritier, then for Desfontaine on the *Flora Atlantica*, followed by de Candolle's *Histoire des Plantes Grasses*, Michaux's *Histoire des Chênes d'Amérique* and finally the *Nouveau Duhamel* by Loiseleur-Deslongchamps. At this point he had not yet painted any roses. Next, he received the appointment of drawing-master to Queen Marie Antoinette and later to the Empress Joséphine, and this included what today we would call the job of "decorator." As a result of this connection he became acquainted with Ventenat who, on Joséphine's suggestion, advised him to do his plant drawings in color. Between 1802 and 1816 he produced his great work *Les Liliacées* in 8 volumes with 486 color plates. This was dedicated to his patroness, the Empress, who, having died in 1814, did not live to see the completion of the work.

Three years after her death, the first volume of *Les Roses* came out and seven years later (1824) the whole work in three volumes of 30 parts and 167 color plates was completed. The price was set at 750 francs; today its

101

value is about $30,000. There followed an octavo edition of 160 plates in three volumes, published between 1824 and 1826, which sold for 140 francs. Last in 1828 to 1830 another octavo edition appeared in which the number of plates was increased to 181. The text throughout was written by Thory.

It is noteworthy that, contrary to modern belief, the work was neither commissioned by Joséphine nor is there any account of Malmaison in it. Both Redouté and Thory emphasize that the original roses for the work were carefully gathered from gardens in Paris, Sèvres, Versailles and various nurseries. For the success of their work they had to thank men like Thouin, Bosc, Le Lieur, Dupont, Cels, Vilmorin, Noisette, Descemet and Biquelin, all of whose rose treasures were freely placed at their disposal. Only a very few roses came from the greenhouses of Boursault, but from de Candolle and other naturalists both in France and beyond, came varieties which would not flower in the Parisian climate. Humboldt and Bonpland provided a new rose which they had found in Mexico. In short, many scientists and hybridizers gave great help to make this major work a reality.

It is clear that Redouté was not simply trying to represent the Empress Joséphine's roses, but rather to present an original idea. He usually painted in watercolor, a very new method in France, which he may have discovered through Bartolozzi during a visit to London in the 1780s. Previously, French drawings of this type had been in gouache, a mixture of water color and Chinese white.

In this work he painted three distinct groups of roses: those of antiquity, those of the Middle Ages and the modern roses of his time.

The first group included *R. canina*, *R. pimpinellifolia*, *R. sempervirens*, Provins Roses, Centifolia Roses, Damask Roses, *R. alba*, *R. muscosa*; all straightforward roses which, for the most part, had come from spontaneous mutations and from which, in the course of centuries further mutations had arisen. Obviously the *gallica* varieties also belong here.

Of the group of roses from the Middle Ages, the most important were *R. foetida*, from which Pernet-Ducher ultimately produced his Pernetiana Roses, its "bicolor" form, and *R. hemisphaerica*.

To the third group belong the roses which came to Europe from the Far East, such as the Tea Rose, the Chinas and also such roses as *R. rugosa*, *R. bracteata*,

the American species with the first Noisette 'Champney's Pink Cluster', the Bourbons and the Boursaults, which Thory called *R. reclinata*.

Finally, a little must be said of Redouté's last years. He was penniless and had to continue painting in order to survive. He produced his least impressive work, *Choix des Roses*, during this period. On June 19, 1840, while painting a lily which a young pupil had brought him, he suffered a sudden heart attack. His head fell forward on his work and his eyes closed for the last time.

But to return to the Empress Joséphine and her roses. Quite early, she came to know André Dupont, the foremost rosarian of his time in France. His nursery in the Rue Fontaine-au-Roi was purchased by the State in 1813 and the collection of roses had been planted in the gardens of the Palais Luxembourg near the Orangerie. Hardy, the superintendent of the Luxembourg, was in charge of the garden, and about 1830 made numerous crossings with various roses of which the best known hybrid is *R. hardii*.

An equally well-known contemporary, Descemet, had his nursery in St. Denis and was also the local Mayor. Many varieties are attributed to him and by 1815, it is believed that he had amassed no less than 15,000 seedlings. These he sold to Vibert who grew them on at Chenevières-sur-Marne.

Another hybridizer of the time was Cels, considered to have the finest nursery in Europe, and who created a very famous garden at Montrouge.

M. de Vilmorin had a collection of roses of considerable importance before Dupont became prominent. Guerrapain had an establishment at Troyes. Parmentier was Mayor of Enghien near Brussels. Godefroy lived in Ville d'Avry. Le Lieur was the superintendent of the Imperial Gardens at Ville-sur-Arc. Ledru was Mayor of Fontenay-aux-Roses, the home of the rose collection of Ledru-Rollin.

From all these different gardeners came the roses which were planted at Malmaison. In addition, even more were brought from England, where the Empress had found an indefatigable collaborator in John Kennedy. Further, the Dutch nurseries of van Eeden provided her with a number of rose seedlings.

The efforts to build up the rose collection at Malmaison, which was open for all French gardeners to visit, led to great competition among gardeners. Outstanding among them were the rose nurserymen Laffay, Desprez, Vibert, Prévost and Noisette.

While in the 18th century most cultivated roses originated in Holland with a few English "hybrids" in existence, the Empress' continuing efforts made the rose an essentially French flower and this it remained until well into the 20th century when competition in the field of hybridization became fierce in both Germany and N. America.

At the beginning of the 19th century, as can be seen from old catalogs, there were already a considerable number of varieties, but there were still more names than there were varieties. Guillemeau and Vibert (1829) say that many plants had 10 to 15 different names. This came about because most roses started their career in Holland, often unnamed and from unknown sources, so the French rosarians christened them as they pleased. Even the Empress herself took part in the game of naming a rose to which she took a particular liking. Some examples of her handiwork are:

'L'Empereur' after the husband whom she idolized.
'Roxelande' after the river in the vicinity of her birthplace.
'Belle Aurore', 'Calypso', 'Cuisse de Nymphe Emue', 'Grand Monarque', 'Noire Couronné', 'Majestueuse', 'Euphrosyne', 'Le Feu Amoureux', 'Le Rosier des Dames' and 'Pallas'.

The Empress Joséphine's rose garden which ultimately contained about 250 varieties, was started in 1804 and worked on until her death on May 29, 1814. Napoleon had divorced her in 1809 because she had not been able to bear him a child. Of the 250 varieties, there were 167 *gallica*, 27 *centifolia*, 3 Moss Roses, 9 Damasks, 22 Chinas, 4 *pimpinellifolia*, 8 *alba*, 3 *foetida* and the species *R. moschata, alpina, banksiae, laevigata, rubrifolia, rugosa, sempervirens* and *setigera*.

Let us compare these figures with the numbers available from the trade: Fillassier in his catalog of 1791 offered 25 varieties; Desportes, one of the biggest nurserymen, listed in 1829, 2,562 of which 1,213 were *gallica*, 120 *centifolia*, 112 *alba*, and 18 Moss Roses, although many of these designations are dubious. This tremendous expansion of new varieties must undoubtedly be credited to the encouragement which the professional gardeners received from the Empress to continue experimenting with new crosses. It is now generally agreed that it was André Dupont who first made carefully planned crosses by means of hand-pollination.

In 1814 the now lonely woman was still living in Malmaison when the Czar Alexander I of Russia visited her and promised assistance in her difficulties. On his departure, she took a rose from a vase and gave it to him saying it was a "Souvenir of Malmaison". It was not, of course, the rose known today by this name; ours is a Bourbon rose which was put out by Béluze of Lyon in 1843. After the death of Joséphine, her son, Eugéne, inherited Malmaison. He died in 1824 and five years later it was sold by his heirs to the Swedish banker, Hagermann. In succeeding years, it changed hands several times and during the Franco-Prussian war of 1870/1 it was severely damaged. On October 21, 1870 the battle, which was part of the siege of Paris, raged around the chateau and was renewed on January 18-20, 1871 when the house was sacked and the gardens destroyed. The State, which had owned the property since 1870, seemed to have very little interest in it, for they sold it off. In 1896 it was acquired by a wealthy gentleman, André Osiris-Iffla, who began to restore it, but who finally handed it over to the French Government in 1904.

It appears that from then on nothing was done. Jean Ajalbert, who was Curator from 1907 to 1917, stated in 1910 that the condition of the garden was chaotic, full of nothing but weeds and rubbish except for a vegetable patch worked by one of the laborers. It was in this year that final restoration of the garden, although in a completely different style, was started, due mainly to the efforts of Jean Ajalbert, Jules Gravereaux and Mme. Philippe de Vilmorin.

Between the years 1900 and 1905 Jules Gravereaux, one of the most important French rosarians, started to collect in his own garden of L'Hay all the varieties which the Empress had grown. He was helped in this task by M. Thuilleaux, another rosarian from La Celle, St. Cloud. With the help of the Redouté plates, these two managed to find 197 of the varieties. The Malmaison catalog of 1912 details these in full and they are given at the end of this chapter for they represent a list of great historical interest.

Gravereaux gave all these roses to Malmaison in 1912, because, at long last, the Service d'Architecture des Palais Nationaux had to decided to proceed with the restoration of the park from plans drawn up by Eugène Touret.

In 1907 Gravereaux had provided a collection of old roses for the formation of the Rose Garden at Bagatelle in Paris.

The Chateau of Malmaison is now a museum and the

superb collection of *objects d'art* assembled by the Empress is housed in a number of rooms open to the public. The Park is also in good condition and contains a number of roses which are, however, only modern roses.

The following is the list of roses which Gravereaux had rediscovered by 1910, planted in the Roseraie de l'Hay and designated "The Roses of the Empress Joséphine". They are planted in the following sequence, bearing the numbers 1 to 197, beginning with A. Those which are planted in the turf outside the beds do not belong to the original collection. They have been given the numbers 201-420 and appear in the official catalog on pages 103-106.

I. The Empress Joséphine's Collection of Roses

1.	'Agathe carnée'	Provins
2.	'Beauté Insurmontable'	Prov.
3.	'Rose du Sérail'	Prov.
4.	'Mousseuse Couleur de Chair'	Centifolia
5.	'Aigle Brun'	Prov.
6.	'Bouquet de Vénus'	Prov.
7.	'Belle Junon'	Cent.
8.	'La Maculée'	Prov.
9.	'La Louise'	Cent.
10.	'Incomparable'	Prov.
11.	'La Belle Lauré'	Spinosissima
12.	'Admirable'	Prov.
13.	'Oeillet'	Cent.
14.	'Rosier de Francfort' (= *R. turbinata*)	
15.	*centifolia*	Cent.
16.	'Grandeur Royale'	Prov.
17.	'Aimable Pourpre'	Prov.
18.	'Aimable Amie'	Prov.
19.	'Rosier d'Amour'	Prov.
20.	'Rouge Superbe Actif'	Prov.
21.	'Adèle'	Prov.
22.	'Perle de l'Orient'	Cent.
23.	'Aglaia'	Prov.
24.	'Rosier de Quatre Saisons'	Damask
25.	'Bengale d'Automne'	Bengal
26.	'Bengale Bichonne'	Beng.
27.	'Don Pedro'	Dam.
28.	'Beauté Tendre' (= 'Elisa')	Alba
29.	'Unique Rose'	Cent.
30.	'Belle Hébé'	Prov.
31.	'Rosier des Dames'	Cent.
32.	'Velours Pourpre'	Prov.
33.	'Unique Admirable'	Cent.
34.	'Nymphe'	Cent.
35.	'Belle Aimable'	Prov.
36.	'Rosier Mousseux'	Cent.
37.	'Le Rosier Evêque'	Prov.
38.	'Ornement de Parade'	Cent.
39.	'La Tendresse'	Prov.
40.	'La Pucelle'	Cent.
41.	'Nouveau Petit Serment'	Cent.
42.	'Belle Sultane'	Prov.
43.	'Cuisse de Nymphe'	Alba

44.	'Alector Cramoisi'	Prov.
45.	'Van Huysum'	Dam.
46.	'Bacchante'	Prov.
47.	'Rose du Roi' ('Rose Le Lieur')	Dam
48.	'Achille'	Prov.
49.	'André du Pont'	Prov.
50.	'Pimprenelle de Marienbourg'	Spin.
51.	'Rosier Vilmorin'	Cent.
52.	'Belle Biblis'	Prov.
53.	'Unique Blanche'	Prov.
54.	'Grand Napoléon'	Cent.
55.	'Agathe Fatime'	Prov.
56.	'Nouveau Intelligible'	Prov.
57.	'La Virginale'	Alba
58.	'Cocarde Pale'	Prov.
59.	'Bengale à odeur de Thé'	Beng
60.	'Bengale Cerise'	Beng.
61.	'Beauté Touchante'	Prov.
62.	'Capucine Rouge' (= *foetida bicolor*)	Foetida
63.	'Cuisse de Nymphe émue'	Alba
64.	'Jaune à Fleurs doubles'	Foet.
64(a).	'Rosier de la Chine'	China
65.	'Feu Amoureux'	Cent.
66.	'Sans Pareille'	Prov.
67.	'La Quatre Saisons Continue'	Dam.
68.	'York and Lancaster'	Prov.
69.	'Mousseuse de la Flèche'	Cent.
70.	'Rosier Musqué'	Moschata
71.	'Victorine la Couronné'	Prov.
72.	'La Bien-Aimée'	Prov.
73.	'Triomphe de Flore'	Prov.
74.	'Thalie la Gentille'	Prov.
75.	'Temple d'Apollon'	Prov.
76.	'Superbe en Brun'	Prov.
77.	'Sultane Double'	Prov.
78.	'Soleil Brillant'	Prov.
79.	'Provins Renoncule'	Prov.
80.	'Rosemonde'	Prov.
81.	'Rosier van de Eeden'	Prov.
82.	'Rose Pluton'	Prov.
83.	'Rosier des Parfumeurs'	Prov.
84.	'Provins Marbré'	Prov.
85.	'Pourpre Charmant'	Prov.
86.	'Grande et Belle'	Prov.
87.	*Rosa setigera*	
88.	*Rosa arvensis*	
89.	*Rosa ferruginea* (= *R. glauca*)	
90.	*Rosa banksiae*	
91.	*Rosa carolina*	
92.	*Rosa sempervirens*	
93.	*Rosa centifolia bullata*	Cent.
94.	'Bengale Angévine'	Beng.
95.	'Bengale Blanc'	Beng.
96.	'Mousseuse Rouge'	Cent.
97.	*Rosa laevigata*	
98.	'Rose Bengale à fleurs simples'	Beng.
99.	'Bengale Aimée'	Beng.
100.	'Bengale à Bouquets'	Beng.
101.	'Bengale Cramoisi'	Beng.
102.	'Bengale Sanguine'	Beng.
103.	'Bengale Guenille'	Beng.
104.	'Miss Lawrance Rose'	Beng.

105. 'Rosier des Indes'	Beng.
106. 'Miss Lawrance Rouge'	Beng.
107. 'Bengale Commun'	Beng.
108. 'Bengale de Cels'	Beng.
109. 'Fleur de Vénus'	Beng.
110. 'Bengale Pompon'	Beng.
111. 'Rose du Bengale'	Beng.
112. 'Bengale Cent Feuilles'	Beng.
113. *Rosa clinophylla*	
114. 'Belle Mathilde'	Spin.
115. 'Isabelle'	Prov.
116. 'Grosse Cerise'	Prov.
117. 'Illustre'	Prov.
118. 'Hector'	Prov.
119. 'Henriette'	Prov.
120. 'Belle Hélène'	Prov.
121. 'Grand Sultan'	Prov.
122. 'Grand Monarque'	Prov.
123. 'Pourpre Ardoisé'	Prov.
124. 'Feu non rouge'	Prov.
125. 'La Félicité'	Dam.
126. 'Euphrosine l'Elégante'	Prov.
127. 'Estelle'	Prov.
128. 'Duc de Guiche'	Prov.
129. 'Belle Parade'	Prov.
130. 'Cramoisi Triomphant'	Prov.
131. 'Pimprenelle à fleurs roses'	Spin.
132. *Rosa alpina*	
133. 'Junon'	Prov.
134. 'Nouveau Monde'	Prov.
135. 'Clio'	Prov.
136. 'Chloris'	Prov.
137. 'Bizarre Triomphant'	Prov.
138. 'Bouquet Charmant'	Prov.
139. 'Carmin Brillant'	Prov.
140. *Rosa foetida*	
141. 'Nouvelle Gagnée'	Prov.
142. 'Noire Couronnée'	Prov.
143. 'Minerve'	Prov.
144. 'Manteau Pourpre'	Prov.
145. 'Lustre d'Eglise'	Prov.
146. 'Majestueuse'	Prov.
147. 'Le Rire Niais'	Cent.
148. *Rosa cinnamomea*	
149. *Rosa rugosa*	
150. 'Calypso'	Prov.
151. 'Rose of York'	Alba
152. 'La Roxelane'	Prov.
153. 'Rosée du Matin'	Alba
154. 'L'Empereur'	Prov.
155. 'Beauté Virginale'	Alba
156. 'Ombre Panachée'	Prov.
157. 'Nouveau Rouge'	Prov.
158. 'Ombre Superbe'	Prov.

159. 'Belle Aurore'	Alba
160. 'Ornement de la Nature'	Prov.
161. 'Pallas'	Prov.
162. 'Jeune Henri'	Prov.
163. 'Passe-Princesse'	Prov.
164. *Rosa rugosa*	
165. 'Passe Velours'	Prov.
166. 'Rose Chou'	Cent.
167. 'Pompon Mignon'	Cent.
168. 'Rose des Peintres'	Cent.
169. 'Panachée Superbe'	Prov.
170. 'L'Amitié'	Dam.
171. 'Agathe de la Malmaison'	Prov.
172. 'Beauté Renommée'	Prov.
173. 'Cerisette la Jolie'	Prov.
174. 'Héloise'	Prov.
175. 'Agathe Royale'	Prov.
176. 'Assemblage des Beautés'	Prov.
177. 'Beauté Superbe'	Prov.
178. 'Aimable Rouge'	Prov.
179. 'Belle sans Flatterie'	Prov.
180. 'Josephina'	Prov.
181. 'La Précieuse'	Prov.
182. 'Beauté Suprenante'	Prov.
183. 'La Pintade'	Prov.
184. 'Belle Olymphe'	Prov.
185. 'Belle Brune'	Prov.
186. 'Capricornus'	Cent.
187. 'L'Enfant de France'	Prov.
188. 'Mousseuse Blanche'	Cent.
189. 'Centfeuille de Descemet'	Cent.
190. 'Parure des Vierges'	Cent.
191. 'Quatre Saisons d'Italie'	Dam.
192. 'Céleste'	Alba
193. 'Belle Flore'	Prov.
194. 'Belle Galathée'	Prov.
195. 'Mousseuse Blanche Nouvelle'	Cent.
196. 'Belle Pourpre'	Prov.
197. 'Cramoisi Eblouissant'	Prov.

The numbers 201 to 420 were to be found in Malmaison in 1912; they were all roses of the turn of the century.

BIBLIOGRAPHY

BOUVIER, R., and E. MAYNIAL.   Der Botaniker von Malmaison, Aimé Bonpland. Berlin 1948.

GRAVEREAUX, J.   La Malmaison; les roses de l'Impératrice Joséphine. pp. 106. Paris 1912.

___ La Rose dans les Sciences, dans les Lettres et dans les Arts. pp. 144. Paris 1906.

___. Les Roses cultivées à l'Hay, en 1902. pp. 232. Paris 1902.

GLOTIN, R. Joséphine de Beauharnais Impératrice; special edition for Jardins de France; pp. 19. Undated (1972?).

Garden Cultivation and Propagation of Roses

(REIMER KORDES AND GERD KRÜSSMANN)

For reasons of clarity, this chapter has been laid out in tabulated form. The details correspond to the working methods of an average nursery, with experienced personnel, and therefore are not directly applicable to small establishments or amateur gardeners.

CULTIVATION IN THE OPEN

Propagation by budding.

Bush Roses.

Work Program	Time	Details
Planting of the understocks	**1st Year** early Spring	Size of the understocks varies considerably: in the case of *canina* the best sizes are 6-8/0.24-0.31 and 8-12 mm./.31-0.5 in.; in the case of *multiflora* 3-4/0.1-0.15, 4-6/0.15-0.24 or 6-8 mm./0.24-0.3 in; 8-12 mm./0.3-0.5 in. would be too thick. The size is calculated on the thickness of the neck of the stock just below the surface growth. Planting distance: 16×70/6.3 ×28 or 16×75 cm./6.3×30 in. gives a plantation of 80,000 per 1 ha./2.5 acres after allowing for the maneuvering of machines.

Planting is done by machine, cutting four rows at a time. The normal rate by this method is one ha./2.5 acres every three hours, though this will of course take longer if a single or double furrow machine is used.

Early planting is important in order to ensure that the stocks are property developed at budding time. |
| Care of the understocks | | Immediately after planting the soil should be drawn up around the plants and "Gesatop" (Simazin) should be applied to the ground when it is moist. |

Work Program	Time	Details
Budding	From the first week in June to the first week in September	The understocks will be cleaned and exposed mechanically (in the case of small quantities this will be done by hand) and the necks of the stocks will be cleaned with a rag. The operating team is made up as follows:

One Cleaner
Two Budders
One Tier, using rubber budding ties, one man for each pair of budders
One man whose job is to dethorn and prepare the budding sticks for each four budders.

Daily output for budding: Preparation of the eyes 120-125 per hour.

Insertion of bud into stocks up to 300 per hour.

Tying from 300-600 per hour.

Budding with refrigerated eyes is only practiced in the U.S.A. and France; the sticks are usually cut in October-November and kept under refrigeration at approx. 0° C/32° F, which keeps them in good condition until budding time.

Two weeks after budding it can be seen if the eyes have "taken". |
| Hoeing up | 2 weeks after budding | This stops the eyes from growing out and loosens the soil in the rows; if the budding is late, this hoeing up is often omitted. |
| Control of growth | | Particularly vigorous varieties with good ripe eyes will have a "take" of up to 95%; best results are always obtained under warm conditions; failures come with wet weather and falling temperatures.

Poor results are also attributed to stock and cultivar, e.g. 'Garnette' and 'Florida von Scharbeutz' on 'Heinsohn's Record; or 'Europeana' on 'Laxa', etc. |
| Heading back | **2nd Year** February-March. | The understock is cut back horizontally at the top of the "T" cut. In large businesses this will be done in January-February with a cutting machine which removes the top growth, while the final cut is done by hand with a power tool. The prunings are then burned. |

Work program	Time	Details
		In small establishments, heading back takes place a little later and the top growths are then rolled up, carried away and burned.
Plant protection	March	Immediately after heading back and burning the tops, the fields are sprayed with Simazin applied as directed.
Pinching out	Every 10 days from May until June	When the maiden growth is 4-6 cm./1.5-2.4 in. high they should be pinched back to two leaves to make the plants branch out; at the same time any suckers must be removed.
Plant protection	May to September	For details against mildew, blackspot, rust, greenfly and other insects, see p. 121.
Lifting	Beginning of October	Lifting begins when the plants have been ripened off sufficiently by nature; if this has not gone normally the following actions can be taken:
Defoliation		a) The shoots can be shortened by machine which will encourage defoliation;
		b) a defoliating machine, which can handle 150,000 stocks per day, can be driven through the rows;
		c) with most of the foliage off, the remaining leaves can be taken off in the packing shed by machine.
		Lifting is done with an undercutting machine drawn behind a tractor.
		Time element: 1 ha./2.5 acres every 6-8 hours, depending on the weather and state of the soil. In bad ground it will be slower and in very wet conditions slower still as there will have to be double undercutting.
Sorting & Packing		Generally done in the packing shed after grading according to the Government regulations (see p. 108).
Storage		In a refrigeration unit at 0°-1° C/32°-34° F and 98% humidity, with special protection to prevent drying-out; should withstand being stored to the end of May.
Plant Protection	Every 2 weeks	Protection against fungus diseases by gassing or spraying with "Benomyl".
Heeling in	Immediately after lifting	In establishments without refrigeration and also in exceptional cases in

Work Program	Time	Details
		other firms, in order to improve the ripening process.
Dispatch	From October	Generally this is now done in paper cartons or in pallets, loose; must be packed in accordance with the regulations (see p. 108).

Standard roses

Work Program	Time	Details
Planting of the understocks	**1st year** early Spring	The same as for the bush roses but strong understocks must be used, 6-8 mm./0.24-0.31 in. and 8-12 mm./0.3-0.5 in. Great care is necessary for the protection of the plants, particularly from the shoot-boring sawfly.
Lifting	November	After lifting, the stocks are sorted into categories according to the regulations, and heeled in. Unsuitable stocks are re-used for bush roses.
Preparation	Winter	Growth is restricted to the best and straightest stems.
Planting out	**2nd year** in the Spring	Planting area approx. 25 × 90 cm./10 × 35 in. (not more than 4-5 plants to the square meter/square yard according to the regulations); after planting must be staked and tied twice and the ground cleaned.
Budding	June to September	2 or even 3 eyes to each stock except in the case of bush roses.
Heading Back	November	Top growth of the stock should be cut back hard, the retaining wires released, the stocks laid down and covered over to protect them during the winter.
Re-raising Pruning	**3rd year** March	The stems should be brought upright and the heads pruned back to the topmost eye. The stems are then staked and tied.
Stopping	From May on	As in the case of the bush roses, in order to obtain as many breaks from the eyes as possible to comply with Government regulations.
Additional cultivation	Summer	As for the bush roses. Protection and spraying are very important.
Lifting	End of October	Undercut and lifted by machine, sorted, bundled and labelled in accordance with the orders.

GARDEN CULTIVATION AND PROPAGATION OF ROSES

Climbing Roses

Work Program	Time	Details
		Cultivation as for the bush roses but the long growths must be staked and tied, particularly the climbing sports which are very liable to be blown out.

Listing by grades of budded stocks

Between 65-80% of the newly-dug bushes are sorted out into the grades laid down by the German Nurserymen's Association (BdB). Of this number 80-85% go into Grade A, 10-15% into Grade B and up to 5% are rejected.

Précis of the rules for grading laid
down by the BdB in
effect from April 1972

(III) ROSES

1. *Bush roses*

Grade A:

This is a newly-dug plant, budded during the summer months, with at least three normally developed, well-ripened stems, at least two of which must have come from the original bud, while the third shoot may have started into growth up to 5 cm./2 in. above. The plants are then sorted and packed in bundles of 10.

Grade B:

In this case smaller plants are acceptable but they, none-theless, must be well-developed, strong bushes with at least two good shoots 30 cm./12 in. long, well-ripened and coming from the original bud. The plants will be sorted into bundles of 10 as before.

2. *Standard roses*

Stocks for standards should be the best quality *canina* understocks. Other understocks must be clearly named.

Grade A:

The standard stem must be strong and fully grown with good fibrous root growth. It must not have sizeable scars or signs of damage. The crown must have at least three strong, well-developed shoots coming from two of the original buds. The stem must measure at least 9 cm./3.5 in. diameter immediately below the budding point.

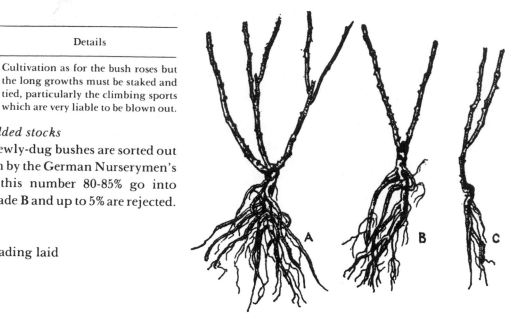

Figure 53. Examples of the Grades A & B for bush roses (C would be unacceptable). (Original)

The lengths of the standard stems must be as follows:

Ordinary standard	*ca.* 90 cm./35 in.
Half standard	*ca.* 60 cm./24 in.
Standards (weeping)	*ca.* 140 cm./55 in.

Grade B:

The conditions for stem and root growth are the same as for Grade A. The shoots from the head may come from just one bud, but this must have thrown at least two normally developed shoots.

THE AMERICAN GRADING SYSTEM

This system is based upon the number of canes and their size, and places a plant in one of three grades: 1, 1½ (commonly called "halfs"), or 2.

Grade Number 1:

At least three strong canes 2 or more of which are at least 45 cm./18 in. long in Hybrid Teas and Grandifloras. Floribunda canes need to be 38 cm./15 in. long, while Climbers must be 60 cm./24 in. Polyanthas must have a minimum of 4 canes at least 30 cm./12 in. long, and are not graded below this.

Grade Number 1½:

Two canes 38 cm./15 in. long for Hybrid Teas and

Grandifloras, 35 cm./14 in. for Floribundas, 45 cm./18 in. for Climbers.

Grade Number 2:

Two canes of 30 cm./12 in. for Hybrid Teas, Gradifloras and Climbers. No others are in this grade.

Late propagation of dormant eyes   Just like normal budding, but budding can take place in the autumn and the stocks can be lifted after six months. This is a form of economy which is only applicable to the culture of cut roses grown under glass.

Propagation by cuttings   (mainly for container-grown miniature roses; process takes six months)

Work program	Time	Details
Parent plants are forced.	March–April.	Cuttings are taken when sufficiently grown and put into propagating beds.
Potting up	After 4 weeks	7 cm./3 in. pot is sufficient; the plants will come into bloom in this and can be sold in it.
Stopping	As required	

Propagation by cuttings in the case of other roses is technically possible, but they do not grow as quickly or evenly on their own roots, and do not produce such satisfactory results as budding within the same period of time.

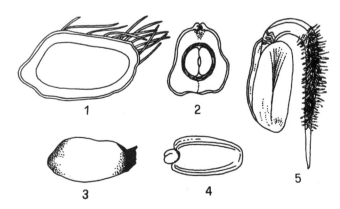

Figure 54. 1. Achene (seed) of *R. canina* cut longitudinally, showing the thick rind and the bristles; 2. cross-section of 1; 3. The seed with husk removed; 4. as 3 but with the seed skin removed, showing the embryo and the two large cotyledons; 5. The embryo. (Enlarged 7 ×; after Rowley, 1956, with alterations)

Use of cuttings as understocks   This method is used in warm areas like S. Africa, New Zealand, and California, where the understocks are mostly from *R. multiflora* whose cuttings root very easily. Two months after planting in the open the cutting is strong enough to be budded. In our case the use of cuttings as understocks is certainly possible but too uncertain, since severe frost during the early stages can bring about very heavy losses.

In Holland cuttings of *Rosa rugosa hollandica* are often used for standards and are produced primarily for the English market.

The Production of Understocks (Species)

Work program	Time	Details
Harvesting the hips	September–October	The well-ripened hips should be left in little heaps for a few days, they are then passed through a coarse mill such as a potato mill; after the flesh has rotted off, they are washed clean.
Stratification	November	The clean seeds are put in layers in damp sand to stratify. *canina* seeds must remain like this for at least a year.
Sowing the seed	Spring	*multiflora* seed may be sown in the spring following its harvest, but *canina* must wait for the second year when the seeds begin to show signs of sprouting. Sowing is usually done in beds 1 m./3 ft. wide in 5 rows with 40 cm./16 in. between each seed.
		According to tests conducted by Rowley, only about 33% of *canina* seeds germinate. Taking 1 kg./2.2 lb. of seed as a criterion, one can expect to achieve about 6,000 plants from 'Inermis', 4,000 from 'Pfanders' and between 8,000 and 10,000 from *R. multiflora*.
Plant protection	Every two weeks during the growing period	Treatment to protect against the usual pests and diseases by normal methods; healthy stocks are indispensable for high quality rating and market grading. Points are lost for any defective stocks.
Lifting	November	With under-cutting and lifting machine.
Sorting & Packing	After lifting	6,000–8,000 stocks can be handled per day.

Work Program	Time	Details
Storage	After sorting and packing	Under refrigeration; but must be kept ready for early delivery.

Extract of the Quality Regulations of the BdB as established April 1972

3. *Understocks for bush and standard roses (seedling briars)*

These briars are seedlings of *Rosa canina* and its varieties, the so-called selected *canina*, as well as other wild species, for example *R. rubiginosa, R. multiflora*. They must be one year old and are grouped under the heading "seedlings" and designated (S).

Rose understocks Grade A must have a straight, smooth neck at least 25 mm./1 in. in length. The plant growth above the neck shall not be trimmed back less than 15 cm./6 in. Mildew is commonplace despite this designated length, and occurs in up to 10% of the briars. However, some mildewing of shoots produced in late autumn would not reduce their grade, provided the wood of the shoots is sound and well-ripened.

Crooked understocks can be used to produce standard stems if trained appropriately.

4. *Standard stems*

Standard stems are generally three-year-old selected shoots, although occasionally they may be two years old, from *R. canina* and its varieties, the so-called high class *canina* of which the shoots have been reduced to a single stem for the budding of the standard. *Rosa rugosa* (*R. rugosa hollandica*) and wild stems cut from hedgerows can also be used for this purpose.

Grade A:

The stems must be one year old, upright and well-ripened. Any slight bend is permissble only in the lowest part of the stem immediately above the root formation.

(The stems must be healthy, i.e. free from scars, damage and rust; they must not show any damage arising from the cutting of the tap root.)

(The roots must be well spaced, and at least three in number and 10 cm. in length from the point where they grow away from the stock. The stems are either delivered after careful trimming of the tap root or with the smaller roots cut back to 5-10 cm. It is also permissable for the stems to go out without the small side roots being trimmed back. The type and quality of the stems must be stated on both the order and the invoice. The incidence of prickles is dependent upon the variety of the stock and is therefore not taken into account in assessing the grading.)

Sorting and packing of standard stocks

Height in cm./in.	Diameter	Quantity in Pack	Packing

1. Standard stems

80-100/32-40	At least 5 mm./0.2 in.	10	2 or 3
100-120/40-47	at the point of		ties around
120-140/47-55	budding, but only		the bundle
140-160/55-63	4 mm./0.16 in. in		
160-200/63-80	the case of		
(Measured to the	'Pollmeriana'		
point of budding			

2. Yearling Understocks

No prescribed height	3-4, 4-6 mm./0.1-0.16, 0.16-0.24 in.	100	1 or 2 ties
	6-8 mm./0.24-0.3 in.	50	
	8-12 mm./0.3-0.5 in.	25	

Rose understocks for propagation

The idea that a budded plant will generally be of lesser value than one grown on its own roots is not borne out in reality; on the contrary, a variety budded on the correct understock is considered to be superior to anything else. Various facts in this connection should be taken into consideration:

1. No single stock is the best one for every area. Therefore, the stock must be selected which will grow best in the particular area in which it is to be planted.

2. The modern selected *canina* from which the seed has been harvested from prepared seed beds gives uniformly good results. This also applies to *R. multiflora* and the other species, some propagated asexually, used in other parts of the world.

3. It is the results, the health and quality of the plants themselves which must be the deciding factor; to arrive at a final conclusion is in itself the work of a lifetime.

European nurserymen use the following understocks,

Less important are: 'Brogs' and 'Pollmeriana'.

Of little importance: 'Heinsohnn's Rekord', 'Kokulinsky' and 'Senffs'.

The most important types being: *R. canina inermis*, 'Pfanders', 'Laxa'; *multiflora* and "thornless multiflora".

For shrub roses: *R. rubiginosa*.

For glasshouse roses: 'Manettii' (*R. indica major* is now only used in warm southern areas).

The characteristics of the most popular understocks (Tabulated in order of importance)

Designation	Good Qualities	Bad Qualities
R. canina *inermis* (from Gamon of Lyon, *ca.* 1905)	Almost without prickles, very strong growth with long shoots, growth continuing well into winter; can be budded from June to December; almost all hybrids grow well on it, even under glass; good root formation and minimal foliage disease; is the best *canina* stock available today, especially for Hybrid Teas. Floribundas and Climbers; unsuitable for standards as the young growth is too thin; very good near the sea; root formation excellent.	Does not take kindly to drought when it defoliates. Seed germination tends to be difficult; European conditions require that it be budded early as dry weather soon stops the growth.
'Pfänders' (from Jakob Pfänder of Beuren, Württemberg, 1945)	Good for standards; very strong-growing; healthy; also good for bush roses; frost hardy; much used today; seeds germinate well. Very suitable for all roses including Hybrid Teas Floribundas and Climbers.	Roots rather long and thin; prickles few but very sharp; subject to mildew.
'Laxa' correct name of which is *R. coriifolia froebelii* Rehd.) Distributed by Froebel, Zurich 1890. Not widely used, mostly found in S. England and the Rhineland.	Almost without prickles and of upright growth; has an ideal neck for budding and throws no suckers; all dark red Hybrid Teas grow very well on it and have a fine luminous color; very suitable for difficult chalky soils; has the strongest root formation of all understocks.	Budding must be completed before the end of July, as growth stops then; it is not compatible with some of the Tea roses; needs a lot of potash and lime and, if this balance is not met, is susceptible to severe attacks of rust.
R. multiflora Thunb. (Native of Japan & Korea)	Strong growth; takes the eyes well; seed germinates very well in the first spring after harvesting. Can also be increased by cuttings; growth can be three times as big as *canina*. Excellent for roses in containers and also good for Floribundas and Climbers.	Stems are very whippy with many prickles; sometimes difficult to bud because of the growth of small fibrous roots around the neck of the stock.
'Thornless multiflora" (Various types are available commercially)	Without prickles and therefore very easy to handle when budding; very strong growing and almost mildew free; takes all varieties well. An ideal understock.	As with *multiflora* proper, has to be prepared some time before budding on account of the growth of hairy roots around the neck.
R. 'Dr. Huey'	Used by growers in Southern California and Arizona. Best rootstock for alkaline soils. Grown as a cutting.	Does not do well in acid soils.
R. multiflora 'Burr'	Most widely used rootstock in U.S. Best rootstock for acid soils. Should be used for roses grown in northeast, southern, midwest, and northwest regions of U.S.	Does not do well in alkaline soils.
R. multiflora fortuniana	Used by growers in Florida to deal with the unique soils of Florida.	

111

GARDEN CULTIVATION AND PROPAGATION OF ROSES

Designation	Good Qualities	Bad Qualities
R. canina	Used by Canadian growers. Plants on this rootstock do well in all of North America. Rootstock plants grown as seedlings.	When plants are young this rootstock tends to keep plants small. However, in time, the plants grow to the same size as plants on other rootstocks.
R. laxa	The principal rootstock used in North America for tree roses. It provides long, strong canes for the high graft used on tree roses.	
'Brög's Thornless' (Introduced commercially by Robert Brög of Rickenbach bei Uberlingen, 1902)	Nearly without prickles, very vigorous; takes most hybrids well; no diseases on the foliage; suitable for heavy clay soils; the sap runs well into the autumn and therefore gives a long budding period; the neck is thin; now mostly used for greenhouse-grown cut flower roses.	The roots are very long and thin, and comparatively few in number. In a hard winter can be susceptible to frost and, as a standard, is susceptible to both rust and canker, not particularly hardy; many varieties make only short stems; the wood is pithy and easily broken in storage.
'Pollmeriana' (Selected by Pollmer, Grossenhain, 1904; is connected with *R. coriifolia*, and is not *R. setigera* × *R. canina*, as often stated)	Tall and upright growth; takes most hybrids well; also useful for standards; particularly popular in the Dresden area and very successful there; also good in the Rhineland; has a strong vigorous root growth; good for greenhouse-grown roses.	Only moderately vigorous, and stops growth early so budding has to be completed quickly; unsuitable for areas near the sea; subject to mildew.
'Heinsohn's Rekord' (From Heinsohn Bros., Wedel, introduced 1935)	Very strong and vigorous; also useful for standards; Hybrid Teas take well on this stock.	Susceptible to rust; growth tends to be crooked making cultivation difficult; many prickles and very prone to mildew. All Polyantha roses and *multiflora* descendants, after making a good start, tend to slow down and this also applies to *foetida* and related species.
'Kokulinsky' (From Kokulinsky Nurseries, Berlin-Lichtenrade, prior to 1927)	Nearly without prickles, very vigorous; takes all hybrids well, especially white varieties and the Tea roses; good root formation and useful for standards; grows equally well under all soil conditions. Plants grown on this stock are long-lived and have good color quality, especially the Hybrid Teas. On soils with high potash content, where it seldom contracts rust, this is one of today's best understocks.	Very subject to rust and therefore always a cultivation problem; has a tendency to bark damage when young; does not germinate easily.
'Senffs' (From Senff, Zerbst, 1919)	Nearly without prickles, shiny foliage, very good for Hybrid Teas (should not be budded when the sap is running very freely). Has a vigorous root growth.	Very subject to bark diseases and somewhat prone to Black Spot; not advisable for standards as is too pithy. Strong tendency to sucker.
R. rubiginosa (= 'Sweet Briar'; chiefly used for shrub roses)	Suited to hot dry soils and must be budded low down; stimulates recurrency in the hybrid and is considered to intensify the color, although this is dubious; the best stock for *foetida* hybrids.	Many prickles; budding in the first season after planting often produces weak plants; does not transplant well.
R. manettii Crivelli Used in S. France and Algiers for roses grown under glass, 1834.	Very tolerant of varying soil conditions; the best stock for American greenhouse roses for budding under glass in the winter.	Is useless for the open ground as it will only withstand temperatures down up -15° C/5° F; is only propagated by cuttings; is difficult to bud and therefore is often better grafted; both Tea and *foetida* hybrids take badly.

112

Designation	Good Qualities	Bad Qualities
R. indica major	What is mostly known in Europe as *odorata* is almost always none other than *indica major*; on the Riviera it is a very useful understock but in more northern areas its lack of winter hardiness reduces its usefulness.	
R. odorata (From China) Only used in the U.S.A. as the stock for some cut flower roses.	Especially suitable for forcing roses in winter; superior for Tea and *foetida* hybrids; can be used for both budding and grafting.	Only fair winter hardiness; cannot be considered for growing in the open.
R. rugosa hollandica (= *R. rugosa* × *manettii;* 'Boskoop's Rugosa') Various selected forms are to be found in Holland, e.g. 'Spek's Improved'.	Very hardy, growth stiff and upright; gives large flowers in good quantity; widely used in Holland (and formerly in Germany) for standards, as it is only this variety that really thrives in the moist soil at Boskoop, where both *canina* and *multiflora* fail; a good stock for container roses.	Very prone to suckering; the budded plants are not long-lived; standards are not viable on this stock because they are very hard and easily broken; needs a light, sandy soil and a lot of moisture; only propagated by cuttings.

CULTIVATION UNDER GLASS

Propagation in Winter (Whole process under glass)

Work program	Timing	Details
Bring the stocks gently into growth	January	Bring up to the optimum size of 8-12 mm./0.3-0.5 in. then clean off.
Propagation		Graft behind the bark.
		Choose sticks from well-ripened stems from greenhouse-grown plants. (Sticks from open ground tend to fail.) From February take half ripe sticks with one leaf from the green house.
		Bind in position with a self-adhesive tie which will rot away. Where maiden growth is weak, pinch it back gently. Tie with three twists of cotton thread which will rot away easily and quickly.
		Productivity very variable depending on the method; One man working alone and not having to clean the stocks or tie, should do 50-60 per hour. With a team, a higher rate is possible but is dependent on the sticks, whether they are dry or half-ripe, with many or with few prickles; teams are made up as follows:
		Eight budders, four tying, two cleaning the stocks, one cutting the sticks and one covering up.
Packing		Immediately after propagation, put in boxes of soil or wrap in balls of peat; deliver to client when the shoots are 15-20 cm./6-8 in. long.

(For further details of cultivation in greenhouses up to the point of cutting the blooms see as follows.)

Rose cultivation under glass

Soil Requirements. The soil should be sandy loam, well drained and rich in humus and manure; the humus content should be 7-8%; the pH 5.5-6.5 in soil with adequate trace elements, but 5.5 in peaty ground or there will be danger of chlorosis.

Planting Distance. Beds should be 1.2 m./4 ft. wide with four rows 30 cm./12 in. between rows and about 35 cm./14 in. between plants in the rows, however, it is quite common in Germany, France and Holland to have two or three rows with 55 cm./22 in. gaps and 20 cm./8 in. between the plants, which is 6 to 6.5 plants to the square meter/square yard.

Fertilizing (von Hentig's Culture Chart). Moderately accommodating to mineral salts; the concentration should be 0.15% in light soil and up to 0.25% in heavy; in no cases should this be exceeded. Inorganic fertilizers can be made to the following formula: Nitrogen (N) 10-30%, Superphosphate (P_2O_5) 60-80%, Sulphate of Potash (K_2O) 85-100%, CaO 150 mg. per 100 g./0.005 oz. per 3.5 oz. for really dry soil (for sub-soil rich in humus a larger amount may be used), Kieserite (MgO) 20-25 mg./0.0007-0.0009 oz. and traces of Magnesium Sulphate, Sulphate of Iron and Boron. Application to established beds should be 250-350 g./8.8-12.3 oz. per sq. m./sq. yd. applied yearly. If there is an excess of superphosphate of lime (P_2O_5) then a later application of 18-6-12 should be given. There is, thus far, no general agreement on the value of CO_2.

Watering. Mist sprayers should be installed just above the ground; overhead watering is also very useful for applying foliar feeds and preventative sprays, though it will also encourage the development of both mildew and Black Spot. The moisture content of the soil must be carefully controlled. The water requirement is about 1 cu. m./1 cu. yd. to the sq. m./sq. yd. per year.

Forcing Methods.
1. Partial Forcing: forcing starts in February, with a winter rest from September to October; produces 4-5 crops of bloom.

2. Full Forcing: a short rest period during the summer, forcing starts in September and continues through the winter.

3. Cold House: resting period throughout the winter followed by natural growth under glass producing flowers at the end of April to May.

Temperatures. In the case of newly planted bushes, start at 5-6° C/41-43° F, as the buds swell, gradually increase the heat first to 8°/46° and then to 12° C/54° F; when the first leaves are showing raise the temperature to 15° C/59° F; this can later be increased to 20° C/68° F.

In the case of older, established plants, after pruning, start at 8-10° C/46-50° F and gradually increase to 18-21° C/64-70° F until the flower buds are showing, then stabilize at 16-20° C/61-68° F.

Production of Bloom. Under normal conditions 5 crops ought to be obtained; cultivation will not begin before the middle to end of January; there will be a period of not less than 60 days to the first flowers and further crops should come along every 40-50 days, increasing in autumn to 60-70 days; a halt is made in the flowering cycle by the so-called "summer rest period". In July-August nothing should be cut for about 4-5 weeks and the plants allowed to bloom themselves out, then prune back to 3-4 eyes and recommence the entire process.

Productivity. Research by Professor Dr. Böhnert on the productivity of roses forced under glass, over the first four years of growth, has yielded the following information:

Variety	Yield per Plant	Yield per sq. m./ sq. yd.	Length of Stem in %			
			10-20 cm./ 4-8 in.	20-40 cm./ 8-16 in.	40-60 cm./ 16-24 in.	60-90 cm./ 24-35 in.
Happiness	9.3	109	1	31	51	17
Karl Herbst	11.5	131	10	74	16	—
New Yorker	13.5	154	3	52	40	5
Gretel Greul	15.4	176	7	49	41	5
Peace	13.0	148	2	41	47	10
Golden Scepter	14.3	163	—	25	57	18
Golden Rapture	18.6	212	2	54	41	3

Vogelmann (see Storck, 1969) gives the yield of four of the more recent varieties:

Variety	Date of Planting	Plants per sq. m./ sq. yd.	Plant life in years	Yield per year		
				in Germany		in Holland
				per plant	per sq. m./ sq. yd.	per sq. m./ sq. yd.
Roses *under glass*	Autumn/ Spring	10-13 av. 12	5-8	10-20	H.T. 100-200 Flor. up to 300	177
'Baccara' Heating from 1-A II				9.5	115	*ca.* 115
'Super Star' Cut flower III-XII				10	125	—
'Golden Rapture'				16	200	*ca.* 180
'Garnette'				25	300	*ca.* 300
Open Ground	Autumn	2.5-3	6-7	10-20	30-60	—

Quality Specification. In general: blooms, stems and foliage must all be fresh, healthy and free from damage of any kind. The flowers must be ready for cutting and the color must be representative of the variety. The stem must be firm and straight and the blooms held upright. The length of the stem must be in proportion to the size of the flower.

Packing. 20 stems to the bunch. The roses must be wrapped in approved paper and sorted into individual varieties.

Grading:
Quality I A: Stem at least 60 cm./24 in. long. Must be above average in form and color. The flowers must be even in size.
Quality I: Stem at least 50 cm./20 in.

Quality II: Stem at least 38 cm./15 in.
Quality III: Stem at least 28 cm./11 in.
Quality IV: Stem at least 20 cm./8 in. This grade includes roses with weaker or slightly bent stems.

Grade for wreaths: all other roses, including those grown in the open, of any stem length, provided the blooms are fresh and undamaged.

Roses grown in the open. Any weather damage must be recorded in the delivery book.

Packing: 20 stems of one variety to the bunch.
Grading: Long: at least 45 cm./18 in. in length
Medium: at least 30 cm./12 in. in length.
Short: at least 18 cm./7 in. in length.
Wreaths. Any roses which do not comply with the above specifications.

Time and Motion Study of the Cultivation of Roses under Glass

Production Method I for Hybrid Teas.
(Rothenburger 1970)

Area of glasshouse: 1,000 sq. m./1,200 sq. yd.
Planting: III-IV (Winter propagation).
Crop: 1st year, 2.5 flowers per plant, 50 per sq. m./sq. yd.
2nd year, 4.5 flowers per plant, 100 per sq. m./ sq. yd.
from 3rd year, 5 flowers per plant, 110 per sq. m./sq. yd.
Plants removed: 8th year.

Work program	Plants / Flowers	Space Allocation to each operation	Productivity per hour for each operation	Time factor for each 1,000 sq. m./ 1,200 sq. yd. per hour
First Year.				
1. Preparation of the soil, incorporation of manure and planting.	8,000	1,000 sq.m./ 1200 sq. yd.	5 sq.m./ 6 sq. yd.	200
2. Watering and applying inorganic fertilizers (100 times)	—	1,000 sq.m./ 1200 sq. yd.	1500 sq.m./ 1800 sq. yd.	70

Work Program	Plants / Flowers	Space Allocation to each operation	Productivity per hour of each operation	Time factor for each 1,000 sq.m./ 1,200 sq. yd. in hours
3. Staking and tying. Pinching out and cutting back[1] (1 and 3 times)	—	750 sq.m./ 900 sq. yd.	18 sq.m./ 22 sq. yd.	126
4. Disbudding[2] (3 times)	—	750 sq.m./ 900 sq. yd.	150 sq.m./ 180 sq. yd.	15
5. Spraying against pests and diseases. (15 times)	—	1,000 sq.m./ 1200 sq. yd.	700 sq.m./ 840 sq. yd.	21
6. Hoeing & Weeding[3] (Twice)	—	750 sq.m./ 900 sq. yd.	30 sq. m./ 36 sq. yd.	50
7. Harvesting (100 times in season). Cutting, sorting & packing by machine, wrapping the bunches in paper	50,000	10 roses per bunch	110 bunches	455

Hours of work involved in the first year for 50,000 saleable roses including planting (approx.) 950

Second Year.

	Plants / Flowers	Space Allocation	Productivity	Time factor
1. Watering and application of inorganic fertilizers (150 times)	—	1,000 sq. m./ 1,200 sq. yd.	1,500 sq. m./ 1,800 sq. yd.	105
2. Pinching out and cutting back[4] (6 times)	—	750 sq. m./ 900 sq. yd.	18 sq. m./ 22 sq. yd.	250
3. Disbudding (5 times)	—	750 sq. m./ 900 sq. yd.	150 sq. m./ 180 sq. yd.	25
4. Spraying against pests and diseases (25 times)	—	1,000 sq. m./ 1,200 sq. yd.	700 sq. m./ 840 sq. yd.	35
5. Hoeing and weeding[3] (4 times)	—	750 sq. m./ 900 sq. yd.	30 sq. m. 36 sq. yd.	100

Notes.
1. "Stopping" is pinching back of the first shoots; this has to be done twice so this operation has to be doubled, i.e. adding 10 working hours. "Cutting back" is necessary pruning and cleaning up after each crop of flower.
2. This is based on the average of a process learned by experience. It can often be of greater consideration in case of the smaller-flowered Floribundas than with some of the Hybrid Teas.
3. This operation can be minimized by the soil condition (peat, etc.). The working time must be seen as a compromise between the addition of peat, or peat and manure, after pruning and, if the need arises, the clearing up of weeds, fallen leaves and prunings.
4. This comprises cutting back, either as a means of stopping or of holding back the flower and also the after-bloom pruning.

115

Work Program	Plants / Flowers	Space Allocation to each operation	Productivity per hour of each operation	Time factor for each 1,000 sq.m./1,200 sq. yd. in hours
6. Harvesting (150 times) as in the first year	100,000	10 roses per bunch	120 bunches	833
Hours of work involved in the second year for 100,000 saleable roses (approx.)				1,350
From third year on 1 to 7 times as for the second year plus additionally about 10% for cutting 5 crops instead of 4.5 crops				550
2. Crop. Twice the size of the first year	110,000	10 Roses per bunch	120 bunches	917
Hours of work involved from the third year to produce 110,000 saleable roses per year (approx.)				1,475

Production Method IIa

For small-flowered Floribundas. (Rothenburger 1970)
Work program for the crop.
The various operations throughout are the same as for work program I
Crop. 1st year, 100 blooms to the sq. m./sq. yd.; from the 2nd year onwards, 200 to the sq. m./sq. yd.

Work program	Number of blooms	Number in each package	Productivity per hour for each operation	Time factor for each 1,000 sq. m./1,200 sq. yd. per hour
First year of cultivation. Cropping, cutting, sorting, bundling by machine (100 times), and packing the bunches in paper	100,000	10 roses per bunch	130 bunches	769
From the second year of cultivation on: Cut flower				
Crop as above, but doubled	200,000	10 roses per bunch	145 bunches	1,380
Hours of work involved for the second year on to produce 200,000 salesable roses. (approx.)				1,900
Hours of work needed to produce 1,000 saleable roses not including planting and any removals				9.5

Production Method IIb
for small-flowered Floribundas

Working time for the crop which is NOT finally packed in paper
All the other work is similar to Production Method I

Work program	Number of Blooms	Number in each package	Productivity per hour for each operation	Time factor for each 1,000 sq. m./1,200 sq. yd. per hour
From the second year of cultivation on: Cropping (200 times) cutting, sorting and packing by machine	200,000	10 roses per bunch	180 bunches	1,111
Working time for the second year on for 200,000 saleable roses (approx.)				1,630

Total time factor involved for various rose varieties
(official figures for West Germany 1968/69)

Variety	Crop of blooms for each full year of production and per 1,000 sq. m./1,200 sq. yd.	Total time factor in hours for each 1,000 sq. m./1,200 sq. yd.
'Baccara'	7,000	900-1,200
'Dr. A.J. Verhage'	8,500	1,000-1,200 (1,600)*
'Super Star'	12,000	1,300-1,400
'Golden Rapture'	13,000	1,400-1,600
Small-flowered Floribundas	20,000	1,600-1,800

*One report puts the figure as high as 1,600 hours

Other cultural methods

Hydroponics. As far as is known this has not been extensively tested but has been widely practiced in the U.S.A. for the past 20 years. The quality of the cut flowers appears to be very good.

Cultivation in Sand. Used in France by Meilland for his seedlings; also practised in the United States.

Cultivation in Perlite or Similar Substances. Used experimentally in both the United States and Norway.

Cultivation in Peat. Under trial in Finland but still highly controversial; similar culture is in use for the production of understocks from cuttings.

PLATE 11

1

2

3

4

Rose Pests and Diseases

1. Bud droop caused by either *Botytis cinerea* or something of a non-parasitic nature.
2. Red Spider mite. *Tetranychus urticae*, greatly enlarged.
3. Stem canker on rose stems caused by *Septoria rosae*.
4. Downy mildew (*Peronospora sparsa*) on foliage.
5. Damage to foliage caused by the Leaf-Rolling Rose Sawfly (*Blennocarpa pusilla*).
6. Fallen leaves caused by Rose Leaf-Hopper (*Typhlocyba rosae*).

  L. Light colored patches on the upper side of the leaves;
  R. Larvae and young on the underside of the leaves.

(All illustrations courtesy of Pape)

5

6

What does the grower look for in a first class cut rose?

1. High output and yield.
2. Good longevity as a cut flower and ability to withstand a certain amount of rough handling as it has to be handled a number of times; i.e. in cutting, sorting, packing, unpacking, dethorning, being put in vases, and finally, selling.
3. Good, healthy, disease-resistant foliage.
4. Good form and color with a long stem.

Varieties of Greenhouse Roses 1965-1973

(The dates as given by Noack/Kallauch/von Hentig, 1972)

Variety	Type	Color	Appraisal	Commercial Introduction
Color Group red				
'Garnette'	Floribunda	garnet red	++	1947
'Baccara'	Hybrid Tea	geranium red	+++	1954
'Velvet Times'	H.T.	rose red	+	1960
'Furore'	H.T.	orange-red	+ (Holland)	1965
'Lovita'	H.T.	deep red	+	1966
'Nordia'	Flor.	bright red	+	1968
'Diorette'	Flor.	salmon pink	+	1969
'Pimlico'	Flor.	geranium red	+	1970
'Prominent'	Flor.	orange-red	+	1971
'Ilona'	H.T.	red	? (new)	1973
'Magic Moment'	H.T.	bright red	? (new)	1972
Color Group orange				
'Super Star'	H.T.	coral orange	+	1960
'Zorina'	Flor.	grenadine red	++	1965
'Königin der Rosen'	H.T.	nasturtium red, exterior buttercup yellow	++	1966
'Belinda'	Flor.	bronzy-gold	+++	1971
'Mercedes'	Flor.	grenadine red	? (new)	1974
Color Group pink				
'Carol Amling'	Flor.	rose pink	++	1953
'Kordes' Perfecta'	H.T.	cream flushed with pink & crimson	+ (France only)	1957
'Carina'	H.T.	rhodamine pink	++	1963
'Marimba'	Flor.	coral pink	++	1964
'America's Junior Miss'	Flor.	soft coral pink	+	1965
'Pink Puff'	Flor.	bright pink	++	1967
'Bridal Pink'	Flor.	deep pink	+	1969
'Sonia'	Flor.	china pink	+++	1969

Variety	Type	Color	Appraisal	Commercial Introduction
'Interflora'	H.T.	rich salmon pink	+	1970
'Lara'	H.T.	salmon pink	++ (France)	1970
'Forsyte'	H.T.	deep salmon	(Holland only)	1971
'Fabergé'	Flor.	yellowish-salmon	?	1970
'Rosali'	Flor.	salmon	+	—
'Mambo'	Flor.	salmon	?	1970
'La Minuette'	Flor.	white and bright pink	?	1973
Color Group yellow				
'Golden Rapture'	H.T.	yellow	+	1933
'Arlene Francis'	H.T.	golden-yellow	+	1958
'Dr. A.J. Verhage'	H.T.	buttercup yellow	++	1961
'Samba'	Flor.	golden-yellow	+	1964
'Spanish Sun'	Flor.	pale yellow	+	1968
'Peer Gynt'	H.T.	golden-yellow	++	1968
'Minigold'	Flor.	golden-yellow	++	1970
'Evergold'	Flor.	golden-yellow	++	1970
'Mabella'	H.T.	bright yellow	++	1971
'Precilla'	H.T.	golden-yellow	++	1973
'Yellow Belinda'	Flor.	golden-yellow	++	1973
'Bellona'	Flor.	golden-yellow	? (new)	1974
Color Group white				
'White Knight'	H.T.	white with greenish tinge	+	1957
'Tiara'	Flor.	white	+	1960
'Jack Frost'	Flor.	creamy white	++	1962
'Pascali'	H.T.	white	++	1963
'Akito'	Flor.	white	? (new)	1971
Various colors				
'Lady X'	H.T.	lilac	—	1964
'Mainzer Fastnacht'	H.T.	lilac	—	1964
'Shocking Blue'	Flor.	lilac	—	1974
'Sonora'	Flor.	buff yellow & pink	-	1965
'Esther Ofarim'	Flor.	orange & yellow	++	1971
'Anabell'	Flor.	salmon pink	++	1973

+++ Outstanding varieties 1972/73
 ++ Good to satisfactory
 + Not entirely reliable
 ? Experience of these varieties insufficient for appraisal.

Leading varieties for greenhouse work 1945-1965
(from Noack/Kallauch/von Hentig altered and expanded)

Variety	Type	Color according to catalog	Introducer	Introduced
Red.				
'Better Times'	H.T.	cerise-red	J.H. Hill	1934
'Red Better Times'	H.T.	clear red	Asmus	1937

Variety	Type	Color according to catalog	Introducer	Introduced
'Poinsettia'	H.T.	bright scarlet	Howard & Smith	1938
'Perle van Aalsmeer'+ (Holland)	H.T.	deep red	Verschuren	1941
'Garnette'+	Flor.	garnet red	M. Tantau	1941
'New Yorker'	H.T.	bright scarlet	Jackson & Perkins	1948
'Happiness'	H.T.	crimson-carmine	Meilland	1949
'Karl Herbst'	H.T.	dark scarlet	Kordes	1950
'Independence'	H.T.	pure scarlet	Kordes	1950
'Spartan'	Flor.	orange-red	Boerner-Jackson & Perkins	1955
'Montezuma'	H.T.	orange-red	Armstrong Nurseries	1956
'Tradition'	H.T.	scarlet-crimson	Kordes	1966
Orange.				
'Katherine Pechtold'	H.T.	coppery-orange	Verschuren-Pechtold	1934
'Anthéor'	H.T.	reddish-apricot	Meilland	1947
'Souvenir de 'Jacques Verschuren'	H.T.	apricot-salmon	Verschuren-Pechtold	1950
'Super Star'+	H.T.	coral-orange	M. Tantau	1960
Pink.				
'Gretel Greul'	H.T.	carmine	Greul	1939
'Printemps'	H.T.	old rose	Mallerin	1948
'Chic'	Flor.	geranium pink	Jackson & Perkins	1953
'Kordes Perfecta'	H.T.	cream & salmon pink	Kordes	1957
'Ballet'	H.T.	deep pink	Kordes	1958
'Elysium'	Flor.	light salmon	Kordes	1961
Yellow.				
'Roselandia'+ (Holland)	H.T.	light yellow	Stuart Low & Co.	1924
'Golden Rapture'+	H.T.	golden-yellow	Kordes	1933
'Peace'	H.T.	golden-yellow edged with rose pink	Meilland	1945
'Golden Scepter'	H.T.	deep yellow	J. Spek	1947
'Golden Masterpiece'	H.T.	golden-yellow	Boerner-Jackson & Perkins	1953
White.				
'Mme. Jules Bouché'	H.T.	white	Croibier	1911
'Virgo'	H.T.	white with blush	Mallerin	1947
'White Knight'+	H.T.	white with greenish tinge	Meilland	1957

+Still in cultivation today.

Selection of roses suitable for container-culture, 1973
(from Noack/Kallauch/von Hentig with alterations)

Variety	Type	Color	Introducer	Introduced
Red.				
'Dick Koster' fulgens	Poly-antha	light red	D.A. Koster	1940
'Rote Gabrielle Privat'	Poly.	red	Kordes	1941
'Garnette'	Flor.	garnet red	M. Tantau	1947
'Mothersday'+	Poly.	deep red	F.J. Grootendorst de Ruiter	1950
'Happy'	Poly.	currant red		1954
'Dwarfking'	Miniature	carmine	Kordes	1954
'Coralin'	Min	red	P. Dot	1956
'Little Buckaroo'	Min.	bright red with white eye	R.S. Moore	1957
'Vatertag'+	Poly.	salmon-orange	M. Tantau	1959
'Scarlet Gem'	Min.	orange-scarlet	Meilland	1961
'Starina'	Min.	orange-scarlet	Meilland	1968
'Maywonder'+	Poly.	orange-scarlet	Grootendorst	1968
Pink.				
'Gabrielle Privat'	Poly.	carmine-pink	B. Privat	1931
'Carol Amling'	Flor.	deep rose pink	Amling	1953
'Queen of the Dwarfs'	Min.	dull carmine	Kordes	1955
'Marimba'	Flor.	coral pink	G. Verbeek	1964
'Rosmarin'	Min.	silvery-pink	Kordes	1965
'Little Sunset'	Min.	salmon pink with yellow background	Kordes	1967
Yellow.				
'Baby Masquerade'	Min.	lemon-yellow to rose red	M. Tantau	1955
'Colibri'	Min.	orange-yellow	Meilland	1958
'Bit o'Sunshine'	Min.	buttercup yellow	R.S. Moore	1963
White.				
'Sneprinsesse'	Poly.	white	F.J. Grootendorst	1946

+Varieties which are still rewarding to grow.

Varieties for growing in the open 1973

Variety	Type	Color	Introducer	Introduced
Red.				
'Ena Harkness'+	H.T.	crimson-scarlet	Norman/ Harkness	1946
'Roter Stern'+++	H.T.	orange-red	? Meilland	1954
'Baccara'+	H.T.	geranium red	Meilland	1954
'Montezuma'+	H.T.	orange-red	Armstrong	1956

Variety	Type	Color	Introducer	Introduced

Orange.

Variety	Type	Color	Introducer	Introduced
'Souvenir de Jacques Verschuren'	H.T.	apricot-salmon	Verschuren-Pechtold	1950
'Super Star'+++	H.T.	coral-orange	M. Tantau	1960
'Prominent'+++	Flor.	orange-red	Kordes	1971

Pink.

Variety	Type	Color	Introducer	Introduced
'Gretel Greul'+	H.T.	carmine-pink	Greul	1939
'Queen Elizabeth'+++	Flor.	clear pink	Lammerts	1955
'Elysium'+	Flor.	light salmon	Kordes	1961
'Carina'+++	H.T.	clear pink	Meilland	1963

Yellow.

Variety	Type	Color	Introducer	Introduced
'Peace'++	H.T.	yellow with pink edge	Meilland	1945
'Golden Scepter'+	H.T.	deep yellow	Jan Spek	1947
'Sutter's Gold'++	H.T.	golden-orange	Swim-Armstrong	1950
'Eclipse'+	H.T.	golden-yellow	Jackson & Perkins	1955
'Rumba'+	Flor.	center yellow, outer petals red	D.T. Poulsen	1960
'Gold Crown'+	H.T.	golden-yellow	Kordes	1962
'King's Ransom'++	H.T.	clear yellow	Jackson & Perkins	1960

White.

Variety	Type	Color	Introducer	Introduced
'Pascali'++	H.T.	creamy white	L. Lens	1963
'Youki San'+	H.T.	white	Meilland	1965

+++ Still among the leading roses for growing in the open.
 ++ Good to satisfactory for growing in the open.
  + Of waning interest or insufficient evidence to be classified.

BIBLIOGRAPHY

BÖHNERT, E., and E. MÜHLENDYK. Sortenbeobachtungen an Treibrosen. Gartenbauwiss. 21: 208-227 (1956).

HENTIG, W.-U. VON. Vergleich von Rosensorten unter Glas. Gartenwelt 63: 362-364 (1963).

KRÜSSMANN, G. Die Baumschule. 3rd Edition. Berlin. 1964.

LEEMANS, J.A. Rootstocks for Roses. Boskoop 1964.

MOE, R. Kulturen von Topfrosen nach neuen Erkenntnissen. Gartenwelt 71: 295-300 (1971).

___. Neue Methode für die Anzucht von Rosen auf einiger Wurzel. Gartenwelt 73: 191-194 (1973). — Behandelt Versuche mit der Hausrose 'Garnette' in Norwegen.

MÖHRING, H.-K., & O. LAMBRECHT. Kulturtechnisches Taschenbuch des Betriebsleiters im Blumen- und Zierpflanzenbau. 2nd Edition Berlin 1972.

NOACK, E., W. KALLAUCH & W.-U. VON HENTIG. Rosenkultur unter Glas und im Freiland. 3rd Edition Berlin 1972.

PENNINGSFELD, F. Boden und Nährstoffansprüche von Schnittrosen. Südd. Erwerbsgärtner 21: 87-91 (1967).

ROTHENBURGER, W. Arbeitsbedarfrosen; bei Storck (1969).

ROWLEY, G.D. Germination in *Rosa canina*. ARA 1956: 70-73.

RÜNGER, W. Licht und Ertrag von Hausrosen. Gartenwelt 67: 5-6 (1967).

RUPPRECHT, H. Rosen unter Glas. Melsungen 1970.

STEFFEN, L. Rosen unter Glas und Treibgehölze. Stuttgart (1969). Die richtigen Unterlagen wählen. Gartenwelt 72: 405-407 (1972).

STORCK, H. Gartenbau, Betriebsführung, Produktion. Stuttgart 1969.

TAYLOR, G.M. The root system of our garden Roses; a historical record of the art of budding. RA 1944: 15-19.

TINCKER, M.A.H. Rose seeds; their after-ripening and germination. Jour. RHS 60: 399-417 (1935) Report of trials.

VOGELMANN (see STORCK 1969)

WENNEMUTH, G. Ergebnisse zur Unterlagenfrage. R.Jb. 1969: 64-74.

ZIMMER, K. Erträge einiger Hausrosen-Sorten im ersten Standjahr. Gartenwelt 68: 196 & 242 (1968).

___. Untersuchungen an Freilandrosen I und II; ein Beispiel für die Auswertung von Sortenvergleichen. Gartenwelt 70: 427-428 and 473-474 (1970).

Rose Plant Production In California

(by William A. Warriner, of Jackson & Perkins Co., Medford, Oregon)

In the United States, rose plants are produced mostly in two areas; one around Tyler in east Texas and the other in Kern County, California. There are also production areas in Arizona, Oregon and Pennsylvania.

Understock varieties are Dr. Huey, selected strains of *Rose multiflora*, *Rose multiflora* seedlings and, for greenhouse varieties, *Manetti*. Most understocks are planted as hardwood, unrooted cuttings, except in Pennsylvania, where seedlings are used.

Nine-inch-long cuttings are made from previous season's growth in a stool block or from a production field. The season for planting is early November through December. Lower eyes are removed from the cuttings to reduce suckering.

Before planting, the fields are very carefully prepared to insure a flat, evenly sloped surface for efficient irrigation. The soil is usually fumigated with a Methyol bromide/chloropicrin gas to kill weeds, and most diseases. An herbicide is also applied before planting.

Cuttings are hand planted in pre-marked rows, 15 cm./6 in. apart in rows spaced 107 cm./42 in. apart. Irrigation immediately follows planting and then occurs every five or six days, until rooted.

Budding begins, in California, in late April and should be finished by mid-June to insure a good take. Hot weather in mid-summer causes a severe loss in bud take. Buds are wrapped with a specially formulated rubber band that will disintegrate soon after the graft has healed. The budding patch used in Europe usually deteriorates too rapidly in the hot California sun.

Plants grown in the long, hot season in central California produce hard canes with a small pith and large wood portion. This kind of wood keeps very well in cold storage. This fact allows growers to collect bud sticks in December and store them lightly frozen in polyethylene bags until the budding season. Fresh wood is not readily available in the best budding season.

When the plants are to be grown in one season, usually for delivery to greenhouses, the understock is "broken over" by cutting half-way through, above the bud, and bending the top over. Early in the season this is done about three weeks after budding, but later in the budding period only a ten day wait is necessary.

After the budded eye has grown out to a bloom stage, the understock top is removed. At this time, additional fertilizer is applied to the field and the plants are grown on to maturity until the end of December.

Plants are mowed, after budwood is collected for the next year's budding, down to about 30 cm./12 in. and then dug. Storage is facilitated by using polyethylene liners in corrugated boxes and kept at just under freezing, about -1° C/30° F.

The understock of plants intended for garden use is left intact until January for the year following budding. The fields are mowed with equipment that chops the brush to eliminate the need for hauling it away. When the bulk of the tops have been removed, the understocks are then cut, with hand shears, just above the bud union.

In the second year, the young plants are fertilized early in the season and, of course, irrigated frequently. In the Texas area, irrigation is less common because the area receives much rainfall. California growers often mow the tops of rose bushes about three times during the summer, to encourage branching and to reduce the bulk and facilitate care.

Digging of garden plants begins after the collection of next season's budwood, as with greenhouse plants. Storage of the plants is also the same. These plants grown in a hot summer climate, hardened off with cool autumn weather, and stored frozen in polyethylene containers, can stay viable until mid-summer, if necessary. The planting season in the United States extends from December in the South to April in the North.

Protection from Pests and Diseases (Dr. Martin Hemer, revised by W.A. Warriner and Dr. Charlene Harwood)

The rose, in all its many forms, is normally a long-lived plant. Even under glass it will last from five to seven years while, if grown in the open, its life-span can be quite unlimited, but to achieve this highly desirable result good husbandry is most important.

What is understood as "good husbandry" in its broadest sense are the measures taken to ensure that the plant will give up to its fullest potential. This starts with the correct choice of variety for the position and the soil in which it is to grow. First, roses must have light and air and second, they need a suitable soil for their nourishment. This soil should be deep, without too much lime and in a good state of cultivation.

After planting, manure and much care is needed because many pests and diseases can be encouraged, even produced, by lack of precautionary measures (overfeeding, drying out, becoming waterlogged, severe alterations in temperature, etc.).

Experienced gardeners have found that the best-tended plants, as a rule, display the best resistance to pests and diseases.

In a narrower sense, plant protection, as described in this section, is concerned with the prevention and protection against disease, damage by insects, viral invasions, physiological disorders and removal of weeds.

Roses grow as well under glass as they do in the open, but there are, inevitably, certain differences in treatment which will help with protection against pests and diseases. For instance, rust, which can be so devastating to roses grown in the open, can be almost completely controlled in the greenhouse. On the other hand, spider mites can prove to be a most serious pest to all kinds of roses under glass although their attacks in the open are heaviest in areas with a low summer rainfall.

These examples show why it is necessary to study the biological nature of the most important pests and diseases. Only by doing this is it possible to understand what measures can be taken to avoid putting an undue burden upon the cultivation and environment of the plants.

In compliance with the laws for the use of pesticides, only officially approved substances may be used in nurseries producing garden plants. This has the advantage that the various chemicals used have all been tested over a number of years by official research services; it is also important to know that most of the preparations have been tested for their effectiveness. Due to their lack of commercial prospects, not all preparations are introduced (in the case of dimethoate there are at least 22 variations) and, therefore, the choice is limited to those preparations which have proved to be the most satisfactory either under trial or under practical application.

It goes without saying that compatibility and freedom from scorching or marking the plants is an important feature. Further information on the proper use of the preparation has to be given by the manufacturer under the terms of the official registration and it is vital that these be studied by the purchaser before use. This will save much disappointment and possible losses.

FUNGUS DISEASES.

Mildew. Symptoms: White or greyish spots on the leaves, calyxes and shoots, particularly on the young growth; fallen leaves are often wrinkled and of a reddish tinge. Severe infection results in malformation of both leaves and flowers.

Source: Fungus *Sphaerotheca pannosa* var. *rosae* Lév.
The mycelium over-winters in the leaf-buds and will then quickly spread in the spring to the young shoots, infecting the plants in their most susceptible period of growth. Mildew on roses seems to be encouraged by humid conditions, moderate temperatures of 21-27° C/70-80° F, drafts and lush, tender growth caused by over-application of nitrogen. It is unfortunate that conditions which are optimal for rose production are also close to being optimal for mildew.

Protection: Prevention. Choice of resistant varieties.
For cultivation under glass, continuous spraying with fungicides is often necessary. As protection has to be carried out during the flowering period, it is obviously advisable to choose a remedy which will cure the disease but leave no unsightly marks on blooms and foliage. Of the approved preparations which fulfill these conditions, the following can be recommended: *Dodemorph* (Milban anti-mildew component 0.25%

w/w) or *Triforine* (Funginex 0.075%). For roses grown in the open the following are suitable: *Benomyl* (Dupont Benlate 0.1%), *Thiophanate* (Topsin — M 0.1%), *Cycloheximide* (Acti-dione PM .01%), etc. The possibility of a little residue on the plants must be taken into account when purchasing any of these preparations.

Under glass, the use of a normal concentration in bright sunlight may product some slight discoloration at the edges of the leaves; varieties which are susceptible to this include 'Zorina', 'Sonia' and 'Baccara' (always refer to the instructions given by the supplier).

In the case of a severe attack either in open ground or under glass, it is advisable to spray once a week and certainly not less than once every 8-14 days. A regular change in the type of spray used has proved beneficial in both trials and general practice.

Downy or Black Mildew. Symptoms: the upper surface of the leaves shows irregular brown or brownish-purple spots and a tendency to shrivel. On the underside, a magnifying glass will show small, whitish-grey fungal tufts. In severe attacks, the leaves curl up and fall off at the slightest touch.

Source: Fungus *Peronospora sparsa* Berk.

Humidity, splashing water and moderate temperatures (about 21° C/70° F.) encourage an outbreak which is most likely in moist, humid summers either under glass or in protected areas if the plants are being grown in the open. It has been found that individual varieties tend to react differently to this disease.

Protection: Preventive spraying with *Mancozeb* (Dithane M-45 0.2%). When spraying it is very important to ensure that the undersides of the leaves are wetted. At critical periods, spraying should be repeated every 7-10 days during periods of rainy weather.

Black Spot. Symptoms: the disease will appear during the summer, on the upper side of the leaves, in the form of black or dark brown spots, up to 1 cm./0.4 in. in width and with ragged edges; on some varieties which throw soft growth, the spots may also appear on the green bark. The leaves turn yellow and fall off and the soil around the plant may become covered with them. The defoliated plants will strive to throw out new shoots and will generally become weakened in growth and more susceptible to frost damage in the winter.

Source: Fungus *Diplocarpon rosae* Wolf.

There appear to be a number of different strains, and individual rose cultivars behave very differently in their susceptibility. With years of observation, it has been found that only certain climbing and shrub roses have a genuine resistance to the disease. The following varieties appear to be particularly susceptible: 'Tip Top', 'Dreamland', 'Valeta', 'Michèle Meilland', 'Cologne Carnival' and 'Gretel Greul'.

Protection: Prevention. Ample feeding with manure, clearing away all infected leaves. It is advisable not to plant in shady areas and to avoid splashing infected plants with water as this will spread the spores. Thorough and repeated spraying with *Triforine* (Funginex 0.075%), *Mancozeb* (Dithane M — 45 0.2%) or *Chlorothalonil* (Daconil 2787 0.1%).

Rose Rust. Symptoms: on new growth, in the spring and early summer, orange-red pustules form on the undersides of the leaves, mostly on roses grown in the open or in the wild. These pustules contain a large number of spores. As the summer advances, these spots spread all over the leaves producing urediniospores. From August on, the black teliospores, which are capable of overwintering, are produced. The leaves turn yellow and fall off; the shoots grow deformed and are easily snapped off.

Source: Fungus *Phragmidium mucronatum*.

It will overwinter either as mycelium on the stems or as spores on the foliage which has fallen to the ground. The dormant urediniospores on such leaves may be carried around by the wind or by insects and are therefore capable of infinite renewal. The teliospores are also able to withstand the winter and, indeed, seem to need freezing before they will germinate, which they do on new foliage. The fungus itself exists in a number of different strains, each differing in its ability to transmit infection. Some rose understocks seem to be more susceptible than others, and for a long time *R. laxa* was incorrectly thought to be the worst; this was refuted in research carried out at Bath University by Dr. John Howden. *R. multiflora* is considered relatively immune.

Protection: Collect all fallen leaves, burn prunings, bury or burn leaves and prune all affected parts, apply plenty of manure and be careful not to overdo the amount of nitrogen and potash.

Preventive measures during growth include spraying with *Mancozeb* (Dithane M — 45 0.2%), *Triforine* (Funginex 0.075%) and other similar materials.

The systemic spray *Oxycarboxin* (Plantvax) used at 0.1% is also effective in stopping an outbreak of the disease after it has started. Re-spraying may be necessary in suitable weather conditions.

"Grey Mold" on rose stems. Symptoms: a greyish, powdery mildew appears on the young growth and foot-stalks. Spotting of the blooms will also occur. The fungus prefers cool, moist weather (35° C/60° F.), but can also infect at higher temperatures. After pruning, the disease tends to run down the stem so that more and more has to be cut away. The worst effects are often experienced if the plants are under cover or growing in unheated greenhouses.

Source: Fungus *Botrytis cinerea* Pers. Not on the whole a very persistent parasite, and one which only appears if the plants are growing under unsuitable conditions such as lack of light and air, too much humidity, incorrect feeding, etc.

Protection: humidity control, not allowing the deposit to build up by maintaining a free passage of air around the plant. Spray with *Benomyl* (Dupont Benlate 0.1%), *Anilazin* (Dyrene 0.3%) or *Dichoran* (Botran 0.1%). Any treatment will have to be repeated at regular intervals.

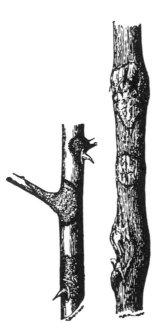

Figure 55. Brand Canker on Roses, (*Coniothyrium wernsdorfiae*). (Pape)

Brand Canker. Symptoms: the green bark of the previous year's stems develops reddish-brown or purple oval shaped spots. These later turn brown, and spread as the disease develops. In severe cases the stem will collapse and die.

Source: Fungus *Coniothyrium wernsdorfiae* Laubert. Most common in spring and late summer and resulting from damage to stem from either wounds or frost. Heavy applications of wet manure late in the season may also contribute to infection. Some varieties are more susceptible than others.

Protecton: Careful pruning followed by spraying with *Captan* (Orthocide 0.1%), *Folpet* (Ortho-Phaltan 0.1%) or *Mancozeb* (Dithane M — 45 0.2%).

Stem Canker. Symptoms: Similar to *Coniothyrium*. Source: Fungus *Leptosphaeria coniothyrium*.

Protection: As for *Coniothyrium*.

Various other Cankers. *Sphaceloma rosarum* (Anthracnose or purple-spotting). Small, dark red spots appear on the leaves and stems. These spots often grow together and form larger spots.

Septoria rosae. (Leaf scorch). Irregular blackish spots with reddish or purple edges, 3-12 mm./0.1-0.5 in. in size develop on the leaves.

Gnomonia rubi. Large brown spots with purple edges. Yellowing and die-back of the stems. Infection in spring on frost-damaged buds. It is possibly transferred from blackberries to roses.

Diplodia rosarum. Dark spots on stems and foot-stalks.

Protection: in all cases of canker, see *Coniothyrium*.

Cylindrocladium or Crown Canker. Symptoms: Plants are usually attacked at the budding point, the first indication being discoloration of the bark which spreads, slowly to very rapidly, to encircle the whole stem. The plants weaken, throw poor stems and blooms and finally die. The disease appears worse in plants which have been winter-budded, and in Europe has been found in roses imported from the U.S.A.

PROTECTION FROM PESTS AND DISEASES

Source: Fungus *Cylindrocladium scoparium* Morgan. The fungus is a relatively weak parasite which attacks in unfavorable growing conditions such as very wet soil, deep planting, etc.

Protection: Prevention; avoid infected ground, ensure that the plants are healthy and well-ripened, avoid wet or water-logged soil. When planting, ensure that the union of scion and stock is at ground level. Control may be attempted by spraying with *Benomyl* (Dupont Benlate 0.05%) at the rate of 4 liters/4.2 qts. to the sq. m./sq. yd.

Verticillium Wilt.   Symptoms: Wilting and leaf fall in summer. Under glass there is a tendency for the buds to droop when being forced in February. The varieties 'Belinda' and 'Sonia' appear to be particularly susceptible.

Source: Fungus *Verticillium* sp.

Protection: Treatment of the soil by watering with *Benomyl* (Dupont Benlate 0.1%) at 10 liters/11 qts. to the sq. m./sq. yd.

INSECTS AND RELATED PESTS

Spider mites.   (*Tetranychus urticae* Koch, et al.)
The most serious pest in greenhouses. First, small, honey-colored eggs appear on the leaves, particularly along the veins, followed by fine webs; the foliage turns yellow and falls off. The ovoid, eight-legged mites are 0.5 mm./0.02 in. long and, after feeding, change in color from greenish-white to reddish-brown. In the greenhouse they are usually found in the vicinity of doors and ventilators where there is a current of dry air. In the open they are usually only a problem during very dry summers, when they can cause considerable damage.

Protection: prevention; providing and maintaining the optimum growing conditions for the plants. Avoid drafts and dry air, particularly when using artificial heating. Careful control of the humidity, which should not fall below 70%, by the use of a hygrometer. Balanced feeding.

Thanks to the new preparations now available, control, which was formerly difficult, has now become easier. However, it is still uncertain due to the resistance which has been built up towards some preparations,

and to the degree of compatibility of the acaricides with the rose; this varies from one cultivar to another.

Within this context, the following preparations and treatments have been found effective:
Spraying with *Mevinphos* (Phosdrin 0.05%), *Propargitz* (Omite 0.04%) or *Fenabutin-oxide* (Vendex).

To hinder the development of resistance, spray with *Penatc* (Pentac 0.08-0.1%), *Omethoate* (Folimat 0.1%), *Tricyclohexyl-Zinnhydroxide* (Plictran 0.1%), or with *Dicofol* (Kelthane MF 0.1%).

For roses grown in the open, particularly in amateurs' gardens, the insecticides containing phosphoric acid such as Metasystox 0.1% or Dimethoate 0.1% should be used, as these are also effective against greenfly and other insects. When spraying, a fine jet and high pressure is required to ensure that the plant is thoroughly wetted. In order to avoid unnecessary marking of the plants, do not exceed the recommended concentrations. Spraying should be repeated at weekly intervals to kill off any further mites which may have hatched in the meantime. A form of biological control has been attempted but does not presently seem to be practical.

Rose Aphid (Green Fly)   (*Macrosiphum rosae* and other aphid spp.)
Large colonies of these will develop on shoots and flower buds. They are sucking insects which, by their depredations, stunt and cause the young shoots to wither.

Protection: at first appearance, apply *Demeton* (Metasystox) or *Dimethoate* 0.1%, either by spray or sprinkler. In the case of resistant strains, either in newly planted greenhouses or in the open, dust with *Aldicarb* (Temik 10G) at 5 g./0.18 oz. to the sq. m./sq. yd. of soil surface.

Rose Leaf Hopper.   (*Typhlocyba rosae* L.)
Their presence is indicated by pale, mottled areas on the leaves. On the underside of the leaf will be found greenish-yellow, broad-headed insects, similar to greenfly; these make small jumping movements. In the open they are often found in quantity from May to July and from the end of August into September. A severe infestation will inhibit the growth of the rose.

Protection: spraying with *Dimethoate* or *Parathion* preparations 0.1%, *Mevinphos* (Phosdrin 0.05%), being careful to wet the undersides of the leaves and the ground under the plant. Since the eggs are laid in the bark of the young shoots, an intensive spray of an oil-based *parathion-ethyl* compound (Folidol or Eftol oil 0.5%) is advisable.

Capsid Bug. (*Lygus pratensis* L., *L. pabulinus* L., etc.)

The young leaves and flower buds show numerous tiny holes where the insect has extracted the sap. In very severe attacks, which are likely to occur in hot, dry seasons, the foliage has a vesicular appearance, the shoots are weakened and the flowers misshapen. The insects themselves, which may be grey-green or brownish in color, have usually disappeared by the time the damage becomes visible.

Protection: Good methods of cultivation at the time of starting into growth. In the case of a severe infestation, which is likely to be most apparent in very sheltered positions or in the early morning, the plants should be treated with *Parathion* (E 605 f 0.035% or E 605 powder), or with one of the available phosphorus insecticides.

Thrips. (*Thrips* spp.)

These insects are about 1 mm./0.04 in. in length, very small and dark brown in color with fringed wing tips. Damage is caused when they attack the plant tissue and suck out the sap. There is a preference for buds which are on the verge of opening. The petals take on a crumpled effect and have brown marks and stains around the edges.

Protection: control of temperature and humidity, as both heat and dryness encourages the development of thrips. Special chemical preparations are needed to control these insects for, unfortunately, they are, on the whole, impervious to the insecticides which deal successfully with other pests. *Acephate* (Orthene) is useful.

Leaf-Rolling Sawflies (Various sawfly genera)

The individual leaves are rolled up into tubular form. Within these tubes, about the end of July, the larvae are to be found. The leaves turn yellow and fall off. Climbing roses appear particularly susceptible.

Protection: In individual cases, remove the damaged leaves and, at the first sign of infestation, spray with

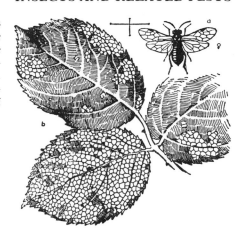

Figure 56. Leaves skeletonized by the larvae of the Rose Slug Sawfly (*Caliroa aethiops*). Above, an enlarged drawing of the Sawfly. (Pape)

Parathion, Malathion or *Dimethoate* according to the manufacturer's instructions. Be sure that the undersides of the leaves are thoroughly wetted.

Oher Sawflies. Rose Slug Sawfly (*Caliroa aethiops*) is about 6-10 mm./0.2-0.4 in. in length and bright green on top, the slug-like larvae skeletonize the foliage mostly from the upper side so that it turns brown and develops a sieve-like appearance. Severe infestations occur in some seasons.

Rose Boring Sawfly. (*Arge rosae* L.). The leaves are eaten from the outer edge towards the mid-rib. The larvae are about 2 cm./0.8 in. long, bluish-green with yellow and black spots. Their bodies are usually curled in the shape of the letter S.

Figure 57. Rose Sawfly (*Arge rosae*) a Sawfly, b Head of the male (3×), c Larvae feeding, d Egg-laying on the stem, e Cross-section of the stem showing eggs after insertion (3×). (Pape)

125

PROTECTION FROM PESTS AND DISEASES

The Banded Rose Sawfly. (*Emphytus cintus* L.). The larvae eat out small circular areas without breaking through to the upper epidermis, later they start at the edge of the leaves and eat through to the mid-rib. Protection against all forms of sawflies is similar to that given for the Leaf Rolling Sawfly.

Rose Maggots and Caterpillars.. Shoots and foliage are eaten and the leaves are often rolled up. Occasionally the buds are attacked. The culprits cover a wide range of genera.

Brown Rose Maggot (*Cacoecia rosana* L.), Golden Rose Maggot (*Tortrix bergmanniana* L.), Garden Rose Maggot (*Teras forskaleana*), Brown Bud Maggot (*Argyroploce ochroleucana* Hb.); the latter is particularly partial to the buds of roses grown under glass.

On occasion the caterpillars of some butterflies can cause extensive damage, particularly in greenhouses. Some examples are: Gipsy Moth (*Lymantria dispar* L.), Brown-tail Moth (*Enproctis chrysorrhea* L.), Lackey Moth (*Malacosoma neustria* L.), Lambda Moth (*Phytometra gama* L.) and the Winter Moth (*Cheimatobia brumata* L.).

Protection: as soon as an attack is observed, apply either *Azinphosmethyl* (Guthion H 0.2%), *Mevinphos* (Phosdrin 5 0.05%) or *Methomyl* (Lannate).

Budding Maggots. (*Clinodiplosis oculiperda* Rübs.) These gall mites, 1.5 to 2 mm./0.06-0.08 in. in length, lay their eggs in the budding point, and the larvae, with their voracious appetites, hamper the development of the eye. The fully grown larvae over-winter in the soil and pupate in the spring. Nothing can be seen of their depredations for several months and then in the early part of the year severe damage can be observed throughout a nursery plantation.

Protection: soil must be carefully drawn up around the budded stocks to hinder the laying of eggs. Since DDT was banned, chemical protection is more difficult than it once was. As a substitute, *Lindane* (Nexit 0.1%) will give some, although limited, control.

Scale Insects. Plants with weak growth are susceptible to attack by various scales. Some examples are: Scurfy Scale (*Aulacaspis rosae* Bché.), round, white in color and 2-2.5 mm./0.08-0.1 in. in size;

Comma Scale (*Lepidosaphes ulmi* L.), curved shell, dark brown, very numerous; Brown Scale (*Eulecanium corni* Bché.), oval shaped, light brown. Their active feeding, by sucking the sap, leads to weakened growth and their viscous deposits disfigure the plants.

Protection: spray the plants before growth starts with an oil-based *Parathion-ethyl* (Folidol or Eftol Oil 0.5%). Later, when juveniles are active, apply *Malathion* (Malathion-Merck, etc. 0.2%). Spraying should be repeated at weekly intervals.

Cane Borers. When attacked by these, the tips of the shoots will suddenly wilt and dry up; damage can be severe. When a shoot is split open, a cavity will be found containing a grub about 1.5 cm./0.6 in. long and yellowish-white in color. Another kind of borer lays eggs on pruning wounds. The larvae hatch and bore down into the canes.

Protection: prune back and burn the damaged shoots before the larvae hatch (August at the latest). Spray with a persistent-contact insecticide such as *Lindane* (Strong Nexit 0.1%) or *Azinphos* (Guthion H 0.2%) to kill off all active flies or larvae emerging from the eggs. Paint pruning wounds with tree paint.

Weevils. (*Otiorrhynchus sulcatus* K. and other spp.) These are about 10 mm./0.4 in. in length, black in color with yellowish hairs. They gnaw at stems, buds and budded understocks above ground level. Their larvae are grub-like, 10-12 mm./0.4-0.5 in. long, and they seem to be on the increase in greenhouses and in nurseries.

Protection: careful observation and, on attack, immediate use of *Azinphos* (Guthion H 0.2%), *mevinphos* (Phosdrin 5 0.05%) or *Lindane* (Strong Nexit 0.1%). Control of the larvae is not easy, but watering with Aldrin or the application of a suitable powder should give good results. As an alternative, Lindane, in either liquid or powder form, may be tried.

Nematodes. These suck and damage the fine, hair-look roots of the plant. Their presence in the soil manifests itself in soil sickness, lack of fertility, poor root growth and, sometimes, chlorosis in the plants. There are various types, all of which are injurious:

Root Knot Nematode. (*Meloidogyne* spp.) This

causes knobbly swellings of the roots, while the undersides become coated with a woolly substance. If diagnosis is uncertain, recourse should be had to the local farm advisor.

Protection: in the open, take preventive action by weeding frequently. Nematodes can be reduced by planting one of the *Tagetes* groups. For attacks in the greenhouse, the soil must be pasteurized by steaming for 15-20 minutes at 90-95° C/194-203° F, or by the use of a chemical fumigant such as *Dazomet* (Mylone, 40-50 per sq. m./1.4-1.8 oz. per sq. yd.). *Methlbromide* (Brom-o-bas 50 g. per sq. m./1.8 oz. per sq. yd.) or *Methyliso-cyanate* + DD (Vorlex, 50 ml. per sq. m./0.05 qt. per sq. yd.).

Other Eelworms. (*Pratylenchus* spp.) These cause the rotting and dying off of small rootlets. The commonest form is *Pratylenchus (pratensis) crenatus*.

Protection: in the open, by crop rotation with turnips, potatoes and rape, but avoid the use of the *leguminae*. In small areas of cultivation *Tagetes* may be used to assist control. For direct protection, see directions for soil pasteurization and fumigation. A build-up can easily be avoided by these means but the manufacturer's instructions must be strictly followed. In existing rose plantations *Aldicarb* (Temik 10G 5 g. per sq. m./0.18 oz. per sq. yd.) may be applied.

VIRUS DISEASES

Rose Mosaic   (*Rose Virus* 1)

First described in 1928, it is now to be found in almost all rose establishments. The symptoms vary greatly depending upon variety and circumstance, but are most apparent in a temperature range of 15-20° C/59-68° F. A typical effect is the appearance of chlorotic spots which usually start at the center and spread outward, and may invade the whole leaf. They may also show up as bright yellow rings or wavy lines. The results are often stunted growth, short flower stems and pallid blooms. Infection occurs followng budding or grafting. It has not been proved that insects are the carriers. Experimental heat treatment for 5 minutes at 52° C/126° F has proven a possible remedy. It does, however, appear that the source of the trouble occurs in the actual propagation.

Yellow Mosaic   (*Rose Virus* 2).

Very similar in appearance to Rosa Mosaic, but the chlorotic patches are a brighter yellow and thus easier to diagnose. A wide variety of symptoms indicates the existence of a number of different strains of the virus. Infection occurs after budding or grafting. Protection is only possible by using completely healthy material when propagating.

Rose Wilt   (*Rose Virus* 3).

This disease tends to come in periodic epidemics. Bad years are followed by seasons when the disease is practically non-existent. Typical symptoms are a peculiar bending of the foliage on the young growth. At the same time, elliptical necrotic patches appear on the leaves, which fall off. As the disease spreads, the young shoots take on a yellowish color and the base of the pedicel is often blackened. Infected plants may appear to recover, but his does not last. Infection follows budding or grafting and also occurs through a carrier, which in this case is probably the rose aphid (*Macrosiphum rosae* L.).

Immediate burning of infected plants and protection against aphids will help prevent any further outbreak.

Rose Streak   (*Rose Virus* 4).

Has only appeared, to the best of our knowledge, in America, but it could spread to Europe and other continents. The characteristics of the disease are reddish-brown rings on the leaves and young growth. Infected leaves usually fall off. The symptoms spread from the leaf to the pedicel. Infection follows budding or grafting. The carrier is unknown.

As it is very difficult, if not impossible, for the average grower to identify the individual viruses, it is advisable to employ the services of a plant pathologist in all cases of a severe outbreak. The use of budding material from suspected plants should be avoided. When budding, all tools must be kept scrupulously clean.

NON-PARASITIC DISEASES

Chlorosis or   Caused by lack of iron. The young
"Green Sickness"   foliage turns yellow at the edges
and the leaf stalk shows similar patches. The source of the trouble is usualy iron defi-

ciency, too much lime, an excess of phosphoric acid or manganese, excessive moisture or damage to the root system.

Protection: soil analysis, plentiful use of peat and acidic manures, spraying with an iron compound such as Fetrilon, Sequestrene 138 Fe or some other chelate of iron. Application of foliar feed will help improve growth.

Lack of manganese produces yellowing of the older leaves, starting in the center of the plant and moving towards the edges.

Protection: after soil analysis, apply sulphate of manganese, either to the soil or to the foliage, at the rate of 0.5%.

Defoliation. There is always a danger of defoliation in greenhouse roses during the spring and fall, since they require a very narrow temperature range and carefully controlled humidity. Falling temperatures combined with rising humidity hinder the growth of the plant through transpiration. A critical point is reached if the plants are given too much water by hosing. The drops of water lie on the leaves like morning dew and make the plant perspire; this is the moment of greatest danger for, with addition of heat and ventilation, the water deposit damages the plants and causes various physiological disturbances leading, in a few days, to complete defoliation followed by damage to the whole structure of the plant. This in turn means that a whole crop of bloom may be lost.

Varieties which seem to be especially susceptible are 'Baccara', 'New Yorker' and 'Zorina'.

The correct diagnosis of the cause of plant disease or damage is by no means easy, since varying symptoms are displayed by individual varieties growing under a number of differing conditions. If in doubt, the grower is always well-advised to consult the local plant pathologist or agricultural institute in order to obtain a correct analysis.

Notes on the Use of various Chemical Agents available for Plant Protection.

Product	Comments
A. Fungicides.	
Milban	Not to be used under glass at high temperatures. Can be used freely in the open without causing any spray damage.
Funginex	No limitations and no spray damage.
Benlate	Highly compatible and consistent; unfortunately leaves noticeable spray marks.
B. Insecticides & Acaricides	
Metasystox	At high temperatures, the leaves of 'Baccara' are affected. No trouble when used in the open.
Pentac	Compatible and reliable; slight spray damage.
Kelthane MF	Not reliable in greenhouses; varieties susceptible to foliage damage include: 'Baccara', 'Zorina', 'Nordia', 'Golden Garnette' and 'Carina'. No limitations in the open.
Folimat	This should not be used at times of high temperature nor in very bright sunlight; varieties susceptible to foliage damage include: 'Junior Miss', 'Baccara' and 'Garnette'.
Dimethoate	Useful preparation in the open. If used under glass at high temperatures there may be damage to young shoots.

BIBLIOGRAPHY.

Aglukon-Beratungsservice. Kulturanleitung Gartenbau — Treibrosen (1972).
HEDDERGOTT, H. Taschenbuch der Pflanzenarztes. Münster Landwirtschaftsverlag Hiltrup (1972).
HEMER, M. Bekämpfung von Mehltau und Schwarzfleckenkrankheit an Rosen. Deutsche Baumschule 1971: 77-79.
HOWDEN, J.C.W. Report on the Rust Work at Bath. R.A. 1973 113-119.
KLINKOWSKI, M. Virosen der Rose. Pflanzliche Virologie, Vol II 242-245. Berlin (1958).
NOACK, E., W. KALLAUCH and W.-U. VON HENTIG. Rosenkultur unter Glas und im Freiland. 3rd Edn. Berlin (1972).
PAETZOLD, M. Kulturbedingungen entscheiden über Rosenkrankheiten. Gartenwelt 72: 414-418 (1972).
PAPE, H. Krankheiten und Schädlinge der Zierpflanzen und ihre Bekämpfung. 5th Edn. Berlin (1964).
SCHINDLMAYER, B. Schädlinge und Krankheiten der Rose. Minden (1954).
STAHL, M. and H. UMGELTER. Pflanzenschutz im Blumen- und Zierpflanzenbau. Stuttgart (1959).
—, and —. Aktuelle Pflanzenschutzprobleme bei Rosen. Der Erwerbsgärtner 27: 1447-1452.
WOESSNER, D. Probleme mit Rosen. Dielsdorf (1973).

Rose Gardens —
Rose Trials —
Rose Societies

ROSE GARDENS — ROSE TRIALS

Since the rose garden is the showplace for flower display, as well as the testing ground for new seedlings, it is best if both are dealt with together. The lists which follow are compiled alphabetically both as regards the countries and the places within those countries in which the gardens are situated.[1]

Some no longer exist, but gardens of historical importance are described; the names of these gardens have been printed in **capitals** to distinguish them from the gardens which are still in existence.

The international rose trials are, incontestably, an outstanding piece of publicity for the town or city concerned, and are often a communal event, although opportunity for publicity for the rose itself must never be neglected. Apparently, only a few of the trials are completely neutral. The very severe tests applied by The Royal National Rose Society in England place it in the forefront. Likewise, the All-German Rose Trials, which unfortunately appear to be little known abroad and therefore fail, often, to receive the consideration and regard which is their due. The two American trials of the All-America Rose Selection and the Proof of the Pudding, as well as other trials, will be dealt with in detail at the end of this chapter.

Austria. Baden near Vienna. *The Austrian Rosarium* Established by the City of Baden and the Austrian Horticultural Trade, who run the Rosarium. Laid out in 1967 under the direction of W. Writzmann; size 9 ha./22.25 acres, containing about 50,000 roses of 800 varieties. The Rosarium also maintains the Austrian Trial Grounds which, at its international trials judged by nurserymen, awards the Arms of the City of Baden struck in Gold, Silver and Bronze together with

[1] All details have been assembled from data available in 1973. Only gardens in Europe have been included.

Certificates of Merit. The annual number of visitors approaches one million; a printed guide is available. Dr. Ernst Matula, Alfred Grumer, Albert Stöckl and Joseph Stöckl were all instrumental in creating the garden.

Linz. *Rosarium in the Botanic Gardens.* Administered by the City of Linz. 6,000 sq. m./7,200 sq. yds. in size, laid out by the Horticultural Director Sigurd Lock, there are about 1,000 roses of 300 varieties with a preponderance of the old and historically important cultivars.

Vienna. *Donaupark W.I.G. 1964.* Administered by the City of Vienna (Horticultural Dept.). The garden covers 2 ha./5 acres and has 20,000 roses of 195 varieties; the annual number of visitors is between 600,000 and 800,000.

Belgium. Genk, Limburg Province, *District of Bokrijk*; Rozentuin Koningin Astridpark. Laid out in 1950, reorganized in 1968. Size is approximately 1 ha./2.5 acres, of which about half is planted with roses, some 15,000 plants of 150 varieties.

Gent. Although there are a number of individual rose displays, there is no rosarium as such.

Kalmthout. *Arboretum de Belder.* A private collection of roses enclosed within the Arboretum, comprising chiefly the species and shrub roses together with some of the older varieties. Visiting by arrangement.

Courtrai. Province of West Flanders. *Internationale Rozentuin voor de Noordzeelanden,* Chateau t'Hooghe, Doornickse Steenweg 281. Administered by the Provincial authorities Burg 4, Bruges. In addition to the display garden, there is a trial ground for new roses. Special awards are: the "Golden Rose", Gold and Silver medals and a special prize for fragrance.

Melle. *Rosarium de Rijksstation voor Sierplantenteelt.* Founded in 1962, it is administered by the Ministry of Agriculture. The garden extends to 3 ha./7.5 acres and contains 14,000 roses of about 150 varieties. There is a library with 250 books; a descriptive list is also available.

Roeulx (about 9.6 km./6 mi. north-east of Mons). A *Rosarium* in the Hospice des Veillards, administered by the Provincial authorities of Hainaut. Annual Rose Trials are held here with awards of Gold and Silver

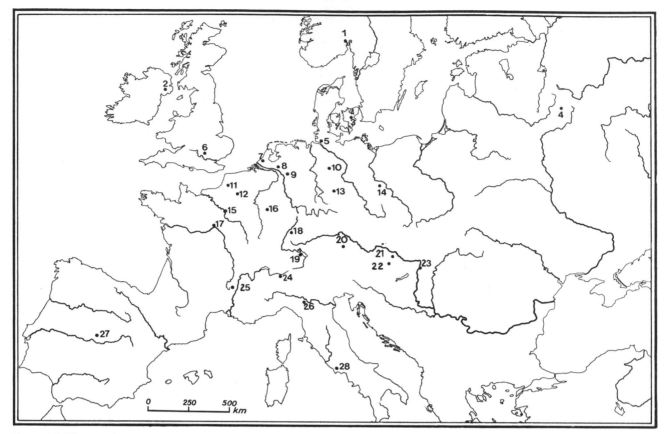

Figure. 58. The most important Rose Gardens and Trial Grounds in Europe (Original)

1. Vollebeek	8. Wageningen	15. Paris L'Hay	22. Baden near Vienna
2. Belfast	9. Dortmund	16. Zweibrücken	23. Gudateteny
3. Copenhagen	10. Rethmar	17. Orléans	24. Geneva
4. Moscow	11. Courtrai	18. Baden-Baden	25. Lyon
5. Hamburg, Uetersen	12. Roeulx	19. Insel Mainau	26. Monza
6. London, St. Albans, Hitchin	13. Sangerhausen	20. Weihenstephan	27. Madrid
7. The Hague	14. Forst	21. Vienna	28. Rome

medals, certificates and a special award for the rose with the best scent.

Tervuren. Various displays of roses, but no specialist Rosarium.

Czechoslovakia. Brno. *Rosarium in the Arboretum of the Forestry School*, Zemedelska 1, Brno. Laid out in 1966 on 0.7 ha./1.75 acres with 4,000 roses of 150 varieties. Not presently open to the public, this garden was founded at the instigation of the Czech. Rose Society.

Lidice. *The Rose Garden of Peace and Friendship.* Administered by the District of Lidice. Laid out in 1952 by Streitova, an engineer; covers 2 ha./5 acres with 5,000 roses of 250 varieties; the roses were given by growers from all over the world. The late Harry Wheatcroft of England was actively involved with this garden. The number of visitors annually is about 70,000 to 80,000.

Olomouc. *Flora Olomouc.* Within the format of the "Flora" (Flower Festival) of 1972, a special rose garden was laid out, by Engineer M. Otepka, on about 2.6 ha./6.5 acres and planted with 5,600 roses of 270 varieties. There are 100,000 visitors a year, and it is planned to increase the garden still further.

Pruhonice near Prague. *Rosarium in the Botanical Garden of the Czechoslovak Academy of Science.* Founded in 1963. Size 2.2 ha./5.5 acres, with 12,000 roses of 1,270 varieties. Mainly used for scientific purposes, but open to the public. The collection is arranged in accordance with the various classes of roses.

Figure 59. The Rose Garden in Valby Park, Copenhagen. (1972)

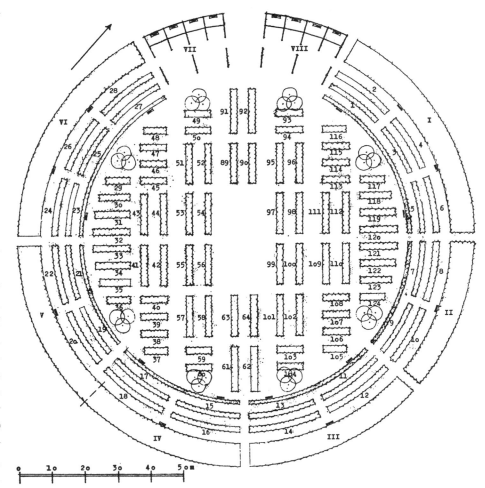

Zvolen. Rosarium in the Arboretum in the Forestry School. Founded in 1965 by Prof. Svoboda, 2.5 ha./6 acres in size, with 14,000 roses of about 1,000 varieties. From 1954 to 1955 under the direction of Prof. Svoboda who was succeeded by Engineer V. Visnovska. The annual number of visitors is between 40,000 and 50,000. Many of the older varieties brought from Yalta, Budapest, Lvov, Moscow, etc. are on display.

Denmark. Copenhagen. *Rose Garden in Valby Park.*
Administered by the City of Copenhagen, it is about 1.5 ha./3.75 acres in size. It was laid out in 1964 by the Head Gardener to the City, J. Bergmann, who continued as its superintendent until 1969 when his place was taken by H. Degnbol. There are about 12,000 roses of 275 varieties as well as a trial ground for new seedlings which is not open to the public. These trials are judged by members of the trade four times yearly for a two year period; there is also an "unofficial trial" in the Rosarium itself conducted by votes from the visitors and organized by the Horticultural Department of the city. Dr. Svend Poulsen was closely involved in the creation of this garden. (See Fig. 59).

There are other smaller Danish rose gardens which deserve mention:

Castle of Egeskov, Fünen. Count Ahlefeldt-Laurvig has created a very beautiful rose garden here.

Kolding. *The Geographical Garden.* This botanic garden, created in 1965 by Axel Olsen, contains a fine collection of roses.

Kvistgard. *The Rose Nurseries of the Poulsen Firm.* This contains about 4,000 roses of 100 varieties, most are of their own hybridizing.

Castle of Lerchenborg, Seeland. The Rose Garden of Count Lerche-Lerchenborg. Chiefly composed of the Meilland varieties, there are a few from other hybridizers.

Löve, Seeland. The Petersen Rose Collection is well worth a visit for the numerous old roses which are the owner's specialty.

East Germany. Forst (Lausitz). *The Forst Rose Garden.* Originally laid out in 1913 by the garden superintendent Alfred Boese; it is about 15

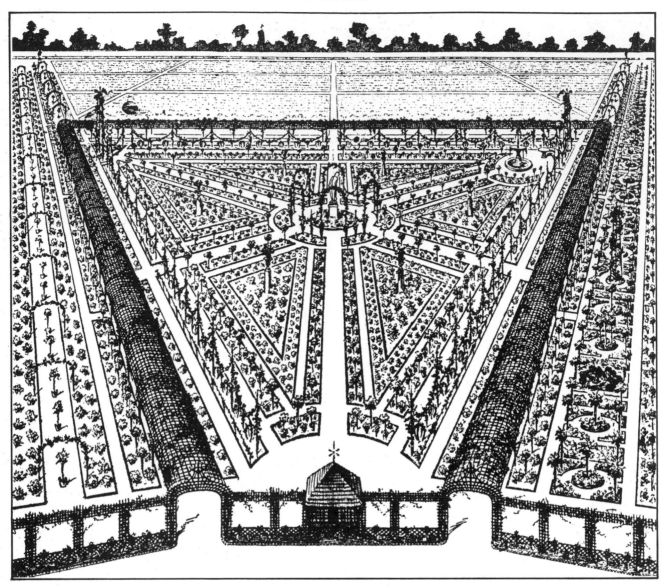

Figure 60. The "Roseraie de l'Hay". (from a plan by Edouard André)

ha./37 acres in size with some 40,000 roses of 400 varieties. The annual number of visitors is approximately 100,000; printed guidebooks are available.

Under the control of the civic authorities.

Sangerhausen. *The Sangerhausen Rosarium.* Founded in 1903 by the German Rose Society (VDR) with Albert Hoffman playing a leading part, it is now under the control of the civic authorities. The garden is 12.5 ha./30 acres in size and contains between 50,000 and 60,000 roses of 6,000 varieties with an extremely wide range covering all classes (Bourbon, Centifolia, Multiflora, Noisette, Polyantha, Portland, Gallica, Hybrid Perpetuals, Rugosa, Tea, Hybrid Teas and Species); catalog and guide are available, but there is no library. Those closely associated with the garden include Peter Lambert of Trier, from 1897; Albert Hoffmann, from 1898; Professor Ewald Gnau, from 1898 to 1934; Richard Vogel, from 1902; Max Vogel from 1926 to 1949 and Professor H. von Rathlef, responsible for instituting the Rose Research Center in the Rosarium, from 1935 to 1944. The annual number of visitors is approximately 130,000.

Other rose gardens of appreciable size are to be found in:

PLATE 12

Wilhelm Kordes(†), Germany

O.L. Weeks, U.S.A.

Alex Cocker, Scotland

Reimer Kordes, Germany

Niels Dines Poulsen, Denmark

Matthias Tantau, Germany

Sam McGredy, New Zealand

Patrick Dickson, N. Ireland

Jack Harkness, England

PLATE 13

G. de Ruiter, Holland

Edward LeGrice, England

Ralph S. Moore, U.S.A.

Graham S. Thomas, England

Dr. C.C. Hurst (†), England

Robert Jelly, U.S.A.

Dr. Gunnar Täckholm (†), Sweden

Dr. François Crépin (†), Belgium

Dr. G.A. Boulenger (†), Belgium

Berlin-Treptow. Rose garden in the Treptow Park.

Dresden. Rose garden at Neustädter Elbufer.

Erfurt. The International Garden Exhibition "IGA".

Eisenhüttenstadt. Rose Display on the Diehloer Höhe.

Torgau. The Castle Rose gardens.

Wörlitz bei Dessau. Rose Island in the Wörlitzer Park.

France. In many towns and cities throughout the country there are noteworthy rose gardens which do not fall into the category of "Rosarium"; some of these are: Angers, Doué-la-Fontaine, Belle-garde-du-Loiret, and Marseille.

L'Hay-les-Roses (Val de Marne) *La Roseraie.* This world-famous rose garden, laid out in 1895 by Jules Gravereaux, is of particular interest for its collection of the old roses, especially those grown in the early days of French hybridization. About 11 ha./27 acres in size it contains 25,000 roses of 6,000 varieties. In the group known as the "Roses of Malmaison" there are about 40 varieties from the time of the Empress Joséphine. (See Fig. 60).

Lyon. *Parc de la Tête d'Or.* Contains three rose gardens covering 7 ha./17.25 acres with 100,000 roses, and arranged as follows:

1. La Roseraie Paysagère Nouvelle which must be the most beautiful rose garden in all of France.
2. The collection of roses in the Botanical Garden.
3. The small Rosarium in which the national rose trials of the City of Lyon and the French Rose Society are held. These are only open to French roses. The jury meets once yearly and awards, in addition to silver-gilt medals and certificates, a Gold Medal for the best French rose.

Orléans. *La Roseraie du Parc Floréal.* A large rose garden in which the international trials for new varieties already in commerce take place. The jury, composed of both amateurs and nurserymen, meets annually and makes the following awards: the "Golden Rose of Orléans", Gold medals, certificates and other special awards.

Paris. *Parc de Bagatelle,* situated in the Bois de Boulogne in the north-western part of the city. The park was purchased by the City of Paris in 1904 with the intention of making it into a permanent memorial to the art of garden cultivation with particular emphasis on the 18th century. The planning was under the control of J.C.N. Forestier, then Director of Parks in Paris. For the initial planting, Jules Gravereaux gave 1,200 rose varieties. Shortly thereafter it became the practice to exhibit roses regularly and to make awards. Since 1907 international trials have been instituted by the City of Paris with a jury of amateurs and nurserymen to award the Bagatelle Gold Medal, which was only omitted in 1910 and 1912. The first such award to a German rose went to Kordes' 'Independence' in 1943. The trial itself tends to be a friendly and convivial occasion and, thereby, may be said to lose something of its professional importance. The garden contains about 7,000 roses with 150 beds of novelties which undergo a three year trial. The awards consist of the Gold Medal and certificates.

St. André at Cannet des Maures. This is the private trial ground of the Meilland Nurseries.

Historic Rose Gardens

In the first half of the 19th century, the most famous collection of roses in Paris was in the LUXEMBOURG GARDENS, originally designed by Dupont and carried on by Hardy, who increased its holdings by means of his own seedlings and purchases of others. He separated it into three sections which were not open to the public, but the gardens were easily viewed from the public right-of-way and presented a fine spectacle. This collection contained some 1,800 to 2,000 varieties.

MALMAISON, on the western outskirts of Paris, was formerly famous for the roses and collections of other plants brought there by the Empress Joséphine (see p. 100); at present only a few modern roses grow here.

ST. CLOUD. The Comte Lelieur established a rose garden here in 1812.

ST. DENIS. Descemet, one of the first important rose hybridizers, created a Rosarium here in 1800 in which he planted all 300 of the then-known roses. It is thought to have been destroyed by British troops in 1815, but it is often asserted that, in order to save them, most of the roses had been previously removed and added to the collection formed by Vibert, in whose hands the collection grew to some 10,000 plants (Jamain).

Saverne in Alsace. In the local Rose Garden, before the turn of the century, French nurserymen and amateurs had established a trial ground for new seedlings with co-operation from abroad. The awards included gold and Silver Medals and Certificates.

Great Britain Bayfordbury, Herts. The National Rose
a. *England.*   Species Collection in the John Innes Horticultural Institution, formed by Gordon D. Rowley in 1948, contained about 800 plants and was the most authentic and comprehensive collection of the species roses in the world. Unfortunately, after Professor Rowley's departure, the collection was broken up. However, a considerable portion was preserved and replanted by the Royal National Rose Society at their garden in St. Albans.

Hitchin, Herts. The private gardens of the firm of R. Harkness & Co. About 5 ha./12 acres in size, these contain 30,000 roses of some 750 varieties, including many of the old roses, grouped in 350 beds.

London. *Regent's Park, Queen Mary's Garden.* Undoubtedly one of the most important displays of roses in England, it was founded in 1932 as the "National Rose Garden". It became, with the approval of King George V, "Queen Mary's Garden" in 1935. Containing about 40,000 roses of every kind, some planted in beds of one variety, some in mixed beds, its development was largely the work of S. Miller Gault, MBE, VMH, DHM, who was Superintendent from 1955 to 1969.

Mottisfont Abbey, near Romsey, Hants. The property of The National Trust, this is about 1 ha./2.5 acres of walled garden. The formation of both garden and collection was supervised by Graham S. Thomas, Garden Consultant to The National Trust. There are about 500 varieties of the old garden roses as well as species and climbing forms.

Richmond. Kew Gardens. In front of the great Palm House about 550 roses of both old and modern varieties are planted; there are also: a collection of species, pergolas carrying the climbers and a hedge of the Hybrid Musk 'Penelope'. A particularly interesting item is a bed of the 90-year-old 'Mme. Caroline Testout' growing on its own roots and still in healthy condition.

St. Albans, Herts. *Bone Hill, the Gardens of The Royal National Rose Society.* Covering 5 ha./12 acres, this garden displays nearly 1,000 species and varieties, in addition to which there is the New Seedling Trial Ground which has, at any one time, 6 plants of each of 500-600 new varieties under trial. The gardens are open to the public as well as to Society members from the middle of June to the end of September. The Royal National Rose Society Rose Festival is held here annually at the beginning of July.

The Royal National Rose Society has made arrangements with various Parks Authorities to have new roses, which have received awards, to be planted in their local display gardens so that members living at a distance from St. Albans can have the opportunity to study the new varieties. These selected gardens are situated as follows:

Cardiff, S. Wales.	Roath Park.
Edinburgh, Scotland.	Saughton Park.
Glasgow, Scotland.	Pollok Park.
Harrogate, Yorks.	Harlow Car.
Norwich, Norfolk.	Heigham Park.
Nottingham, Notts.	The Arboretum.
Southport, Lancs.	Rotten Row.
Taunton, Somerset.	Vivary Park.
Tees-side (Redcar).	Borough Park.

The English trials are held at St. Albans, and each variety is on trial for 3 years. The 21 judges must make at least three visits annually, marking all seedlings in their second and third years. The rules are very strict: no award is made to a rose in its first year, and in the second it can only receive a Trial Ground Certificate; not until the third year, if its marks are high enough, can it be given a Gold Medal. The supreme award for the best rose of the year is the "President's International Trophy" which is not restricted to any particular class; to merit this trophy, a rose must also have won a Gold Medal. Since 1966, a special award called the "Edland Memorial Medal" is given to the most fragrant rose which has received at least a Trial Ground Certificate. While the Gold Medal is only given to one or two roses a year, the awards of Certificate of Merit and Trial Ground Certificate are unlimited.

The following is a list of the winners of the "President's International Trophy" and Gold Medal since 1952:

1952 'Moulin Rouge' (Meilland)
1953 'Concerto' (Meilland)
1954 'Spartan' (Boerner)
1955 'Queen Elizabeth' (Lammerts)

1956 'Faust' (Kordes)
1957 'Kordes Perfecta' (Kordes)
1958 'Dickson's Flame' (A. Dickson)
1959 'Wendy Cussons' (Gregory)
1960 'Super Star' (Tantau)
1961 'Mischief' (McGredy)
1962 No award
1963 'Elizabeth of Glamis' (McGredy)
1964 'Fragrant Cloud' (Tantau)
1965 'Grandpa Dickson' (A. Dickson)
1966 No award
1967 'City of Belfast' (McGredy)
1968 'Molly McGredy' (McGredy)
1969 'Red Planet' (A. Dickson)
1970 'Alec's Red' (Cocker)
1971 'Fountain' (Tantau)
1972 'Topsi' (Tantau)
1973 No award
1974 'Matangi' (McGredy)
1975 No award
1976 'Priscilla Burton' (McGredy)
1977 'Silver Jubilee' (Cocker)
1978 No award

b. *N. Ireland.* Belfast. International Trials are held in the Sir Thomas and Lady Dixon Park, Upper Malone; the whole park covers 60 ha./150 acres, of which about 3 ha/7.5 acres are planted with 20,000 roses of some 500 different varieties. The Park is controlled by the Parks Department of the City of Belfast; the planning of the Rose Garden was carried out in 1964 by Reginald Wesley. Each year a great international competition is held at which the following awards are given: Gold Medal and City of Belfast Award for the best Hybrid Tea, the "Golden Thorn" by the Ministry of Agriculture for N. Ireland, for the best Floribunda, and the Uladh Award for Fragrance by the Chamber of Commerce. In addition, up to six Certificates of Merit may be given annually.

Derriaghy near Belfast. This private rose garden, which formerly belonged to the firm of S. McGredy, is no longer in existence.

Holland. Amsterdam. *Rosarium in Amstel Park.* Laid out in 1970 for the "Floriade" by the Horticultural Department of the City of Amsterdam. The original adviser was the landscape architect, E. Mos, of the Horticultural Dept. of Amsterdam-East.

The size of the garden is 1 ha. 2.5 acres, and it contains about 10,000 roses of some 230 varieties. The garden is open daily from 9 a.m. to 9 p.m. Entry is free.

The Hague. *The Rosarium at Westbroekpark.* Administered by the city of The Hague, Horticultural Department. Laid out in 1960 by J. Rijnveld. At present it contains about 20,000 plants of 350 varieties. International Trials are held here for three different classes:

Competition A. Varieties not yet marketed, judged only by nurserymen; a running evaluation through the season is kept by the Parks Department.

Competition B. Varieties which are already available commercially, judged by amateurs and nurserymen; again a running evaluation is kept by the Parks Department.

Competition C. Roses which are particularly suitable for growing in parks and private gardens, judged by nurserymen.

Awards: the best rose of the year is designated "The Golden Rose of The Hague" and each of the individual winners receives a Gold Medal; there are also Certificates of Merit. The most fragrant rose in Sections A and B receives the "Crystal Award for Scent", selected by a panel of female judges. (See Fig. 61)

Wageningen. *The Rose Collection of the Instituut voor de Veredeling van Tuinbouwgewassen* (Section for Classification and Registration). This collection may only be visited with official permission. It belongs to the Agricultural College, and was laid out in 1947. It is about 0.5 ha./1.25 acres in size and contains 4,000 roses of 780 varieties. The library has a wide range of magazines and periodicals concerning roses. The superintendent from 1947 to 1965 was Dr. B.K. Boom who was succeeded by Mr. F. Schneider.

Hungary. Budatétény. *The Rosarium of the Horticultural Research Institute.* This contains about 3,000 varieties of which 100 are of the Institute's own hybridizing program.

Italy. Monza (Milan Province). *Rosarium Villa Reale.* Headquarters of the Italian Rose Society. Founded in 1963, it is about 1 ha./2.5 acres, planted with 5,000 roses of 1,000 varieties with 440 sq. m./530 sq. yds. of greenhouses. Designed by V. Faglia of Monza, it has many thousands of visitors each year. The

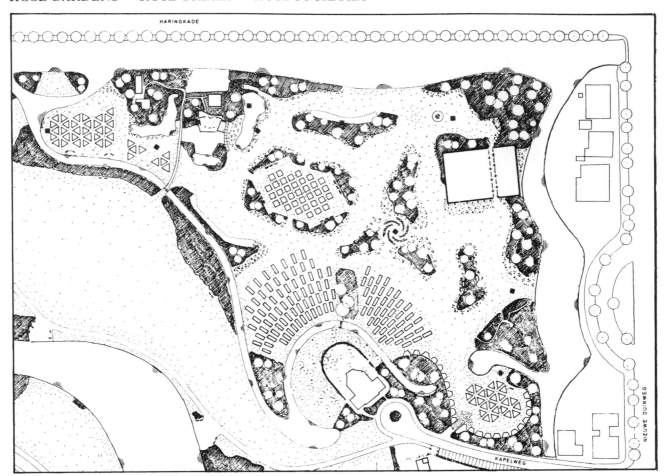

Figure 61. The Rosarium in Westbroekpark, The Hague.

Society's official trials are held here and are as follows:

International Competition for the best scented rose with no class restriction; the prize is the "Gold Crown of Queen Theudelinde".

International competition for the "Rose of the Year"; the awards are a Gold medal for the best Hybrid Tea and another for the best in any other class. National competition for the "Most Beautiful Rose of Italy", open only to Italian hybridizers; a Gold Medal is awarded.

Rome. *Roseto di Roma.* The civic rose garden on Monte Aventino, started in 1928. The beds are laid out in semi-circular fashion giving the appearance of an amphitheater; there are about 1,000 varieties with five plants of each, as well as species and climbers. There is also a trial ground for an annual competition held under the auspices of the City of Rome. The jury is made up of both amateurs and nurserymen, and awards of Gold Medals and Certificates of Merit are made.

Luxembourg. Bad Mondorf. *The Rose Garden.* Controlled by the civic authorities. Laid out in 1958, it covers 1.5 ha./3.5 acres. The official adviser from 1957 to 1960 was Oscar Scheerer of Zweibrücken. The annual number of visitors is about 150,000.

Norway. Vollebekk. *The Rosarium of the Agricultural College* (Noregs Landbrukshøgskole Aas). Property of the State. 3.6 ha./9 acres in size with 2,800 roses of 370 varieties, including many of their own seedlings and a large number of the old roses. Professor Olav Aspesaeter was very involved in the formation of the garden from 1957 to 1964; there is also a library.

Rumania. Timisoara. *The Rose Garden.* The original construction by Arpad Mühle

136

took place before the First World War, and the garden then contained about 600 varieties; during the Second World War it was completely destroyed. At the present time the authorities in Timisoara are planning to create a new rose garden of 9 ha./22 acres, in which 1,500 rose varieties will be planted with 25 bushes of each variety. Planned completion for 1975. It should be the most important rose garden in southeast Europe.

Spain. Madrid. *Rosaleda del Parque del Oeste.* Laid out and maintained by the City of Madrid. About 2 ha./5 acres in size, there are 30,000 roses in 300 beds of 100 plants each. International trials are held under the auspices of the City authorities and the jury meets once a year to choose the best rose which is given the "Prize of the City of Madrid"; also given are Gold medals and Certificates of Merit. It was the opinion of the late Wilhelm Kordes that nowhere in the world was it possible to see larger and finer quality blooms than in this garden.

Sweden. Nörrkoping. *Rosariet vid Statens Trädgardsskola* (The Rosarium of the National Horticultural College). Laid out between 1965 and 1970 by the Rector of the College, Helmer Hellgren, who is still in charge; there are about 275 varieties, mostly only one plant of each, with special emphasis on those which are very winter-hardy and the older roses (*rugosa* hybrids, etc.). A printed guide with detailed descriptions of the varieties is available.

Switzerland. Berne. *The Berne Rose Garden* (formerly the Cemetery Rose Garden; the cemetery was closed in 1913, although the last burial had taken place in 1818!). In 1918 it was converted to a specialist rose garden 2.3 ha./5.5 acres in size, 1.5 ha./3.75 acres of which are planted with 12,500 roses of 190 varieties; the work was carried out by Emil Albrecht who was the Garden Superintendent to the City. In 1957 it was completely reorganized by his successor Mr. Liechti. The administration and control is the responsibility of the city authorities. With its collection of mature trees and its views of the Alps and the old part of the city, the garden is one of the most beautiful and popular walks in Berne.

Braunwald, Glarus. Administered by the District Council and created by them in co-operation with the Swiss Rose Society; there are altogether six gardens at altitudes ranging from 1,200-1,900 m./4.000-6,200 ft.; each garden is about 100-200 sq. m./120-240 sq. yds. in size and is planted with 150 varieties, 10 to 20 bushes of each. The trials of these Alpine roses last for five years. Dietrich Woessner is closely associated with this garden.

Dottikon, Aargau. *Rothenbühl Display Garden.* This is the private display garden of the nursery firm of Richard Huber; laid out in 1949, it is 1.2 ha./3 acres in size and contains about 15,000 roses of 700 varieties. It has about 10,000 visitors annually; catalogues are available.

Frauenfeld, Thurgau. The private rose garden of Max Stutz, garden designer; it was laid out in 1957 and is about 1,000 sq. m./1,200 sq. yds.; it contains an outstanding collection of some 280 old and 200 modern varieties. Visitors are permitted. A detailed plan and list of varieties was published in *Rosenblatt* 15 (1971).

Geneva. *Parc de la Grange.* Administered by the City authorities. The Rosarium in the park was created in 1941 by Eric Bois and Armand Auberson. It contains about 12,000 roses of 180 varieties. There are annual rose trials for varieties not yet in commerce. The judging is done by the Park authorities and the jury meets only once. The awards consist of the Special Award of the City of Geneva with Gold and Silver medals, Certificates of Merit and a cup for the most fragrant rose. (See Fig. 61)

Neuheusen am Rheinfall, Schaffhausen. *Charlottenfels.* Administered by the Canton of Schaffhausen, this is the Park of the Agricultural College of Charlottenfels, comprising about 6 ha./15 acres of which a little more than 0.25 ha./0.5 acres is devoted to roses; there are about 14,000 bushes of 700 varieties. It was developed into a proper rosarium in 1938 by Dietrich Woessner who was associated with it until 1971. This is one of the loveliest rose gardens in Switzerland.

Rapperswill, St. Gallen. *The Public Rose Garden.* 1,050 sq. m./1,260 sq. yds. in size, laid out in 1965 by the Chamber of Commerce of Rapperswil-Jona, proposed by Councillor Hans Rathgeb and brought into existence by Dietrich Woessner; there are about 4,500 roses of 110 varieties; there are 30,000 visitors annually. Another garden with emphasis on the old roses is under construction.

Schloss Heidegg, Lucerne. *The Castle Rose Garden.*

Figure 62. The Rosarium in the Parc de la Grange, Geneva.

Administered by the Canton of Lucerne, it was laid out in 1951 by Professor G. Boesch, as the result of a suggestion made by Chancellor Adenauer on the occasion of his state visit in 1951. 1,550 sq. m./1,855 sq. yds. in size with 520 varieties. *Litt. Rosenblatt* 3 (1961).

Zürich. *"Muraltengut"*, 203 Seestrasse. Laid out in 1961 by the Horticultural Department of the City of Zürich, it contains 2,000 roses of 65 varieties. There are about 10,000 visitors annually.

West Germany. Baden-Baden. In this city there are two rose gardens and also the *Gönner Park* in the Kurgarten on the Lichtentaler Allee which was laid out between 1908 and 1910 by Professor Länger of the Technical High School, Karlsruhe, and named after a former mayor of the city; it contains about 25,000 roses of 150 different varieties.

The *Trial Ground* for new roses *Auf dem Beutig* is especially well known for, since 1952, it has been an internationally established trial with a permanent jury of professional rose-growers who judge the seedlings on several occasions each year, and who are enlarged into a major jury once the roses are in season. The founder of the trials was W. Rieger (1952-1971) who was succeeded

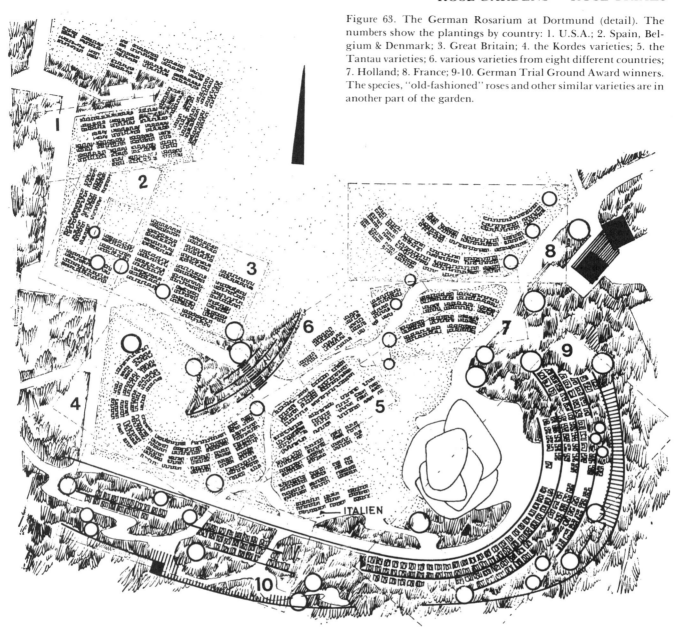

Figure 63. The German Rosarium at Dortmund (detail). The numbers show the plantings by country: 1. U.S.A.; 2. Spain, Belgium & Denmark; 3. Great Britain; 4. the Kordes varieties; 5. the Tantau varieties; 6. various varieties from eight different countries; 7. Holland; 8. France; 9-10. German Trial Ground Award winners. The species, "old-fashioned" roses and other similar varieties are in another part of the garden.

by B. Weigel in 1972 as the overall superintendent of the trials. Gold, Silver and Bronze Medals and, occasionally, special awards are given.

Dortmund. The Rosarium of the German Rose Society; Am Kaiserhain 25. Founded in 1969 by the German Rose Society (VDR); sponsored by the City of Dortmund; Ministerial patron, D. Deneke. Covers approximately 10 ha./25 acres, but still has ample room for expansion. Contains about 40,000 plants of 2,500 different varieties. These are arranged according to their country of origin and each country has its own hybrid-izers grouped together; there is an extensive collection of the species, and a library containing 350 volumes and general archives. Every alternate year a convention is held by the VDR; in the off-years seminars are given. Guidebooks to the gardens and a list of the varieties are available. The gardens have some 2 million visitors each year. W. Rieger founded the Rosarium when President of the VDR. The planning and construction was carried out by the horticultural department of the City of Dortmund. (see Fig. 63)

The work of the Rosarium is associated with the German Rose Registry where all varieties known to be marketed in Germany are recorded; these numbered about 1,500 by 1974. (see p. 199)

Frankfurt-am-Main. *Rose garden in the Palm Garden.* This was originally laid out in 1884 with about 10,000 plants; today its 800 sq. m./960 sq. yds. contain about 6,000 roses. The founder was the former director A. Siebert. There is also a library. Each year a Rose Show is held with awards of Gold, Silver and Bronze medals presented by the garden's "Society of Friends". There are about 1.3 million visitors each year. A reorganization of the garden took place in 1962 under the direction of O. Derreth.

Hamburg. *International Horticultural Exhibition 1973.* At this exhibition, an area of approximately 1 ha./2.5 acres was laid out with 15,000 rose bushes of 25 different varieties; in addition, there was a competition for new varieties with 20 plants of each. Also displayed was a collection of old roses which were no longer available commercially.

Insel Mainau. *Rose Garden on the Island of Mainau in Lake Constance.* Owned by Count Lennart Bernadotte. In 1871, the Grand Duke Frederick of Baden had this laid out as an "Italian Garden"; it was extended in 1946 and today covers 8.5 ha./20 acres planted with about 30,000 roses of 1,000 different varieties, of which the collection of shrub roses forms a most important part. A list giving details of the varieties is available. Roughly 1.5 million people visit each year. Karl Raff,

from 1941 to 1961 and Josef Raff (since 1956) have both been very involved with the development of the garden.

Karlsruhe. *The Rose Garden.* Sponsored by the City of Karlsruhe. About 0.9 ha./2.25 acres in size with 10,000 rose bushes of 140 varieties. Started in 1917 by then Garden Superintendent Ries and reorganized in 1967 by J. Klahn. Both Professor Dr. Richard Hansen and Professor Ludwig Roemer have been closely associated with the garden since 1967.

Mainz. *The City Rose Garden.* Laid out in 1925 by the City of Mainz under the direction of Messrs. Keim and Eimler (Inspectors) and the garden architect Waltenberg; reorganized 1934/35 by Bitterling and Mappes with further reorganization carried out between 1961 and 1965 by the garden Superintendent Schindler; it is about 1 ha./2.5 acres in size and contains some 6,700 roses of 184 varieties. The annual number of visitors is approximately 50,000.

Rethmar über Lehrte. *Trial Ground for the State Plant Varieties Office* (3011 Bemerode/Hannover). This garden, which is not open to the public, is to maintain, for record purposes, the roses which have been registered with the Plant Varieties Office. At the present time it contains about 1,200 varieties separated into 16 color groups.

Saarbrücken. *The Rose Garden in the "French and German" Garden.* Founded in 1960, sponsored by the City of Saarbrücken. The garden covers 0.3 ha./0.75

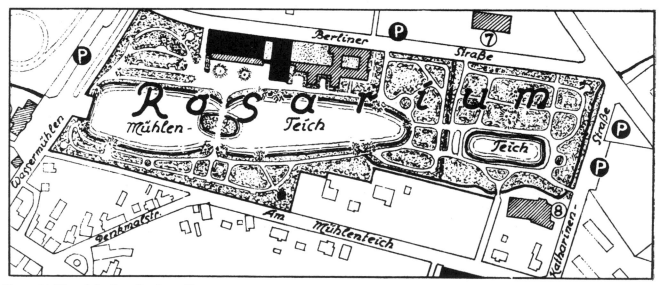

Figure 64. Plan of the Rose Garden at Uetersen.

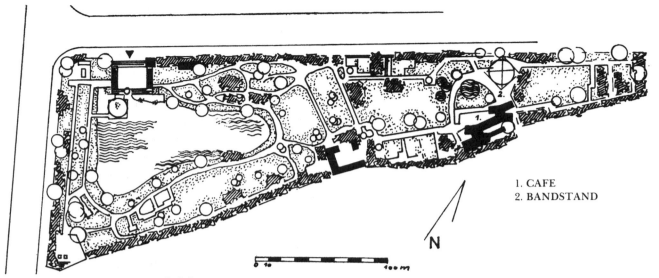

Figure 65. The Rose Garden at Zweibrücken.

1. CAFE
2. BANDSTAND

N

acres and has 15,000 roses of 100 varieties; no handbook is available; there are about 300,000 visitors annually.

Seppenrade, which has been known as the "Rose Town" of the district (Münster) since 1972; sponsored by the community of Seppenrade; size 0.3 ha./0.75 acres with about 3,200 roses of 250 varieties; it is planned to increase this by another 50 to 100 varieties; this garden contains the seedlings of the amateur hybridizer, Ewald Scholle of Seppenrade.

Trier. Two separate gardens. *The White House Garden*; this was formerly a hunting lodge belonging to Prince Henry of the Netherlands but today is the ranger's house and is situated in the White House Woods, near the University and easily reached by public transportation from the city. Laid out in 1933, it is nearly 0.75 ha./2 acres in size with about 3,500 roses in 50 varieties, the majority of which are from the old garden rose groups. The former rose garden in the Wiesental has been closed for economic reasons.

Rose Garden in Nells Park. This was laid out in circular form in 1958/59 and covers 0.4 ha./1 acre with 6,000 roses of 105 varieties. These form a collection in tribute to the great hybridizers of Trier: Peter Lambert, Nicola Welter, Matthias Welter, B.J. Fellberg, J. Ittenbach, Heinrich Rottmann, Johannes Müller, J. Reiter, Anton Reiter, the Roth brothers and J. Mock. Also in the same park is the "Lambertinum" which is devoted to a collection of Peter Lambert's own introductions; it was planted in 1965 and is about 750 sq. m/900 sq. yds. with 400 plants of 115 varieties.

Uetersen. *The Rosarium.* Sponsored by the civic authority in association with the local nurserymen, it was laid out in 1935 by the landscape architect Thormählen, who was also superintendent until 1969. It covers approximately 7 ha./17.25 acres and has 30,000 roses in 920 varieties. Matthias Tantau, Sr. and Wilhelm Kordes were closely associated with the garden, particularly in its early years. (See Fig. 64).

Weihenstephan. *Display Garden and Rose Garden.* Under the control of the Bavarian State Authority and the Technical College of Weihenstephan, founded in 1948 and 0.8 ha./2 acres in size, this is a trial ground under the auspices of the German Rose Society (ADR Rose Trials). Prof. Dr. Richard Hansen, with the assistance of Prof. Dr. J. Sieber, is largely responsible for the development of the collection.

Zweibrücken. *The City Rose Garden.* Founded 1912/14 by the Verein Pfälzischer Rosenfreunde (Society of Friends of the Rose in Pfalz), is today under the control of the City authorities. The garden is 6 ha./14.75 acres in size and contains some 60,000 roses of 1,700 varieties (many of which are only to be found here); yearly additions are made, particularly of the new French introductions. A special "Rose Day" is held each year; there are about 200,000 annual visitors. Those closely connected with the founding of the garden were Councillor Hessert of Zweibrücken, Peter Lambert of Trier and the landscape architect Siesmaier of Frankfurt. From 1912 to 1950 control was in the hands of the Zweibrücken Rose Society and from 1951 to 1965 it was under Mr. Oskar Scheerer of Zweibrücken (see Fig. 65).

Some Historic German Rose Gardens.

Berlin-West. (Dist. of Zehlendorf). ROSE GARDEN ON PFAUENINSEL. No longer in existence, but historically important as one of the first specialist rose gardens in Germany. The Pfaueninsel was a favorite retreat of Frederick William III and Queen Louise. The development of the garden was begun in 1799 by the Royal Gardener, Ferdinand Fintelmann, and was finished in 1820. In size it was about 1,960 sq. m/2,300 sq. yds. The King acquired most of the roses from a Dr. Böhm in Berlin on the advice of the garden Superintendent Peter Joseph Lenné. In all there were about 2,100 standards and 9,000 bush roses of some 140 varieties, all planted in the spring of 1821. The garden was open to visitors three days a week; the guide list is still in existence. Unfortunately, the garden soon become neglected because the King became more interested in forming both a zoo and a palm house on the Pfaueninsel. The soil was very sandy, sufficient watering was apparently impossible, and each year a swarm of cockchafers caused great damage to the roses so Lenné, even before his death in 1866, had been forced to neglect the rose section of the garden. It was never restored because the next King, Frederick William IV, had an entirely new rose garden laid out in the grounds of his country home at Charlottenhof near Potsdam. This garden, too, suffered from lack of attention, and its visual attraction must have ended by the close of the 19th century due to the age of the plants and the failure to replace them.

The BERLIN ZOO, undoubtedly the most popular of all German parks, was originally a hunting reserve. At the end of the 17th century, at the behest of Sophie Charlotte, the wife of the Elector Frederick III, it was changed by careful design into an ornamental wooded landscape and from then on underwent many changes until a ROSE GARDEN was established in 1909. It was the Zoo Director Freudemann who proposed this to the Emperor and Empress, and obtained permission for its construction. It was about 1 ha./2.5 acres in size, planted with some 10,000 roses of 43 varieties. It could not be accurately called a "rosarium" since the ponds were filled with water lilies. A marble statue of the Empress

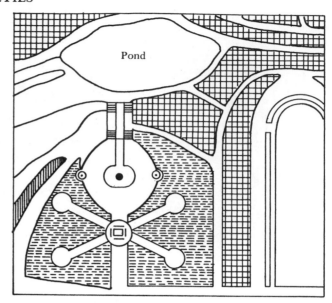

▦ Shrubbery

Fig. 66. The former Rose Garden at Schloss Weissenstein (Original)

Augusta Victoria was placed in the garden. During the Second World War, the entire Zoo became a battle ground, and the rose garden was destroyed; it was not restored after the war but instead was replaced with a garden devoted to summer-flowering plants. A detailed list of the roses in the garden in 1909 can be found in *Gartenflora* 59: p. 418 (1910).

Geisenheim. THE VILLA MONREPOS. Formerly in the possession of Baron Eduard von Lade but now owned by the Technical School for Landscape Gardening, the old rose garden was 1,200 sq. m./1,440 sq. yd. in size and, in 1886, contained about 3,000 roses of 800 varieties. In 1904 the garden was found to be "rose sick" and was dug up. In 1933 another area of 4,000 sq. m./4,800 sq. yd. was allocated to a new rose garden but after two years this was changed again by the school authorities.

Cassel. THE ROSE GARDEN AT WEISSENSTEIN (now known as Wilhelmshöhe). Laid out in 1765 (first mentioned as being complete in 1775) by the court gardener Schwarzkopf, a pupil of the famous English gardener Philip Miller of Chelsea (1691-1771), for his employer the Landgrave Frederick II of Hesse. In Böttcher's "Catalogue of the Trees and Shrubs in the Pleasure Gardens at Wessenstein" (1777, title abbreviated) 20 species and more than 100 varieties of roses are recorded. Schwarzkopf had obtained these from Miller in England, from von Veltheim in Harbke and from von Münchhausen in Schwöbber. In 1785, C. Moench published his "Catalogue of Foreign Trees and Shrubs in the Pleasure Gardens at Weissenstein near Cassel", and this time 150 species and varieties of roses are recorded. Some of these were from seed which had been sown by Schwarzkopf himself and included 'Pearl of Weissenstein' which was most probably the first German hybrid raised. This rose garden remained in existence only until 1786 when William IX (1785-1821), the son of Frederick II, did away with the garden shortly after his accession and, in its place, erected what became known as the Weissenstein wing of the Schloss Wilhelmshöhe. There are are only a few short literary references to this rosarium: Fig. 66 is taken from a drawing in A. Holtmeyer's "W. Strieder's Wilhelmshöhe", Part 1 (1913).

Worms. THE ROSE GARDEN. Laid out in 1910 and planted with about 15,000 roses in 1913; development was brought to a halt by the war in 1914 and has never been recommenced.

ROSE TOWNS AND STREETS OF ROSES

Belgium. Currently, there are no "Rose Towns" as such, but in Namur Province a road of roses running from Havelange past Dinant — Philippeville — Marienbourg to Couvier is planned. This road is the so-called "Route Charlemagne". In a garden in the French-speaking part of Belgium an unknown form of *Rosa gallica* was found; this was given the name of 'Charlemagne' and it is this rose which is to be used for planting alongside the road.

France. Bellegarde-du-Loiret became the first French "Rose Town" in 1972, followed the next year by St. Sorlin-en-Bugey in Alsace. In France there are two roadways dedicated to roses; the first runs from Paris to Provins and the second, Route Nationale 19, from Villeneuve-au-Chêne in the Aube Department to Lignolle-Château.

Germany. In pursuance of a publicity campaign "Make our towns more beautiful" many civic authorities have made a specialty of planting large numbers of roses. In particular, the small town of Nöggenschwiel über Waldshut in the Black Forest, in association with the German Rose Society, was so suc-

cessful in doing this that in 1970, it was permitted to call itself the "Rose Town" of Nöggenschwiel. A similar honor was granted in 1971 to the District of Schmitshausen near Zweibrücken which became the second "Rose Town", also linked in a "Rose Fraternity" with the District of Limana near Belluno in the Italian Dolomites, with Longuyon near Longvy in France and with Walferdange in Luxembourg. In 1972 the municipality of Seppenrade in Münster was similarly honored.

Switzerland. Rapperswil on the Lake of Zürich is called the "Town of Roses" because its coat-of-arms bears two red roses on a field argent.

THE ALL-GERMAN (ADR) ROSE TRIALS

These trials, instituted in 1930 by the German Rose Society (VDR), were originally linked with the National Horticultural Union and the Association of German Nurserymen, with the Society responsible for all costs. In 1933, after the reorganization of the Third Reich, control was assumed by the Ministry of Agriculture and Mr. K. Weinhausen put in charge. After the war and the separation of the two Germanies, control returned to the German Rose Society and the trials recommenced. In 1953 the Department for the Selection and Breeding of Roses, which was maintained by the state, took over until, in 1960, they were superseded by the Association of German Nurserymen who are still in charge of the trials. It is a completely impartial trial and conducted by the trade which has to judge the roses six times in the year. There are various headings under which the points are awarded e.g. Growth Habit, Foliage, Quality of Bloom, etc.

The trials are not limited to German-raised roses, novelties can be accepted from foreign hybridizers. Application must be made to the Association of German Nurserymen at its headquarters, 208 Pinneberg, where each variety, upon being registered, is given a number. The grower must then supply 10 plants of the variety (three in the case of shrub roses and climbers) to each of the nine designated trial grounds: Dortmund, Friesdorf, Hamburg-Altona, Kiel-Steenbeck, Osnabrück, Sarstedt, Veitshöchheim and Zweibrücken. The Head Office will then immediately send the judging papers to the trial gardens. The trials last two years for bush roses

ROSE GARDENS — ROSE TRIALS — ROSE SOCIETIES

The Winners of the ADR Trials 1949-1973

Year	Variety	Grower	Points	Year	Variety	Grower	Points
1949	'Yellow Holstein'	Kordes	91.4	1965	'Wiener Walzer'	Tantau	78.4
1951	'Elmshorn'	Kordes	87.3	1965	'My Fair Lady'	Kordes	78.4
1952	'Red Favorite'	Tantau	80	1965	'Maria Callas'	Meilland	79.5
1952	'Dortmund'	Kordes	82.5	1965	'Fidelio'	Meilland	75.6
1952	'Sparrieshoop'	Kordes	82	1965	'Silva'	Meilland	80.8
1953	'Atom Bomb'	Kordes	80.3	1966	'Sympathie'	Kordes	76
1954	'Sea of Fire'	Kordes	80.5	1966	'Confetti'	Tantau	79.1
1953	'Flammentanz'	Kordes	81	1966	'Paris Charm'	Tantau	74.6
1955	'Lampion'	Tantau	83.6	1966	'Travemünde'	Kordes	84.6
1956	'Olala'	Tantau	80.2	1966	'Pearl of Mainau'	Kordes	74.9
1958	'Dirigent'	Tantau	82.3	1966	'Carina'	Meilland	75.4
1958	'Anneke Doorenbos'	Doorenbos	81.5	1966	'Sangria'	Meilland	80.7
1958	'Lagerfeuer'	Tantau	82.6	1967	'Späth 250'	Kordes	77.7
1958	'Mme. Louis Laperrière'	Laperrière	81.5	1967	'Shannon'	McGredy	80.2
1958	'Jydepigen'	Kordes	81.4	1967	'Caramba'	Tantau	79.1
1960	'Parkdirektor Riggers'	Kordes	80.2	1967	'Sahara'	Tantau	75.2
1960	'Kommodore'	Tantau	81.6	1967	'Letkis'	Buisman	77.1
1960	'Signalfeuer'	Tantau	81.8	1967	'Nordkap'	Schmidt	72.5
1960	'Fritz Thiedemann'	Tantau	82.1	1968	'Lichtkönigin Lucia'	Kordes	87.8
1960	'Gold Crown'	Kordes	75.6	1968	'Bischofsstadt Paderborn'	Kordes	83.8
1960	'Meteor'	Kordes	76.6	1968	'Ferry Porsche'	Kordes	79.4
1960	'Lilli Marlene'	Kordes	79	1969	'Taora'	Tantau	77.3
1960	'Rodeo'	Kordes	72.2	1969	'Erotika'	Tantau	82.7
1960	'Iceberg'	Kordes	87.8	1969	'Sophia Loren'	Tantau	78.2
1960	'Hansestadt Bremen'	Kordes	75.5	1969	'Susan'	Kordes	77.9
1960	'Stadt Rosenheim'	Kordes	78.7	1969	'New Revue'	Kordes	76.1
1960	'Insel Mainau'	Kordes	77.5	1969	'Lustige'	Kordes	78.6
1960	'Honigmond' ('Honeymoon')	Kordes	76.6	1970	'Charivari'	Kordes	84.9
1960	'Praise of Jiro'	Kordes	81.5	1970	'Duke of Windsor'	Tantau	82.8
1960	'Heidelberg'	Kordes	67.4	1970	'Waltz Dream'	Tantau	81
1963	'Gruss an Koblenz'	Kordes	78.6	1970	'Aenna Burda'	Kordes	83.8
1963	'Goldtopas'	Kordes	76.1	1970	'Edelweiss'	Poulsen	81.8
1964	'Inge Horstmann'	Tantau	75.7	1971	'Gütersloh'	Noack	80
1964	'Blue Moon' ('Mainzer Fastnacht')	Tantau	78.3	1971	'Fountain'	Tantau	77.4
1964	'Attraktion'	Tantau	80.7	1971	'Ponderosa'	Kordes	76.5
1964	'Horrido'	Tantau	80.7	1971	'Prominent'	Kordes	79.8
1964	'Fragrant Cloud' ('Duftwolke')	Tantau	86.5	1971	'Alexandra'	Kordes	77.6
1964	'Königin der Rosen' ('Colour Wonder')	Kordes	79	1971	'Baronne E. de Rothschild'	Meilland	75
1964	'Gruss an Berlin' ('Greetings')	Kordes	78.3	1971	'Starina'	Meilland	77.7
1964	'Marlena'	Kordes	83.1	1971	'Princess Margaret of England'	Meilland	76.3
1964	'Finale'	Kordes	79	1972	'Tornado'	Kordes	79.6
1964	'Nouvelle Europe'	Kordes	77.7	1972	'Benvenuto'	Meilland	81.5
1964	'Reinold's Reingold'	Reinold	80.6	1972	'Schloss Mannheim'	Kordes	81.4
1964	'Nordstern'	Kordes	75.2	1972	'Gertrud Schweitzer'	Kordes	76.1
1965	'Andenken an Rud. Schmidt'	Kordes	75.3	1973	'Friesia'	Kordes	84.5
1965	'Molde'	Tantau	76.7	1973	'Gruss an Bayern'	Kordes	83.4
1965	'Geisha'	Tantau	74.8	1973	K 66508	Kordes	80.3
				1973	'Escapade'	Harkness	78.3
				1973	'Lolita'	Kordes	77.3
				1973	'Alec's Red'	Cocker	76.6
				1973	'Melina'	Tantau	76.6

and three years for shrub and climbing roses. The completed judging forms must be returned to the Association where the results are compiled. New seedlings which receive 80 or more points are declared ADR Roses. When the mark of 80 is not reached, the jury can still award the ADR title if the behavior of the plant in a majority of the trial grounds justifies it.

The judges are honorary; the trial grounds are only set up at official horticultural institutes and are not open to the public.

The term "all-German" is somewhat unfortunate and misleading since, thus far, new seedlings have never been sent from the East German Republic.

The dates shown are those of the actual awards. The varieties for the most part went on the market in that, or the following, year.

U.S.A. Just as in many European countries, so here, lovers of the rose can look back on a long tradition. There are at least 130 large rose gardens open to the public, and rose trials are conducted in a number of these. It is impossible to give a full list here, but the details can easily be obtained by referring to the *American Rose Annual*. Rose trials in America are of great importance; a high award (All-America Rose Selections Winner) carries with it the promise of great commercial reward to the variety concerned. The AARS trials and the "Proof of the Pudding" are described below. The evaluation of the rose under the American system departs somewhat from that usual in Europe; in the U.S.A. the blooms are required to be two-thirds to three-quarters open while in Europe the bloom is required to be at its optimum regardless of how far it has opened.

ALL-AMERICA ROSE SELECTIONS (AARS)

In 1930, the U.S. Plant Patent Law was passed. This bestowed on the raiser the possibility of controlling his new seedling for a period of 17 years by means of royalties paid to him by licensees. The law requires that the new cultivar must be quite different from any already on the market, but it does not dictate that it be an improvement. As a result, quite a number of less worthy varieties were patented in order to obtain the higher price commanded by such protection. A group of rose breeders and the American Rose Society decided to pro-

vide facilities whereby the garden value of a new rose could be tested before it was sold, and to carry out such tests over a period of two years under all the differing soil and climatic conditions in the U.S.A. The work was started in 1937 by two groups, one in the East, one in the West, and in the following year they amalgamated under the name of the All-America Rose Selections, AARS for short.

The submission of a new rose to the AARS trials is open to anyone anywhere in the world provided the registration fee is paid and the required number of plants delivered. (Head Office: AARS, c/o George E. Rose, Secretary-Treasurer, P.O. Box 218, Shenandoah, Iowa 51601, U.S.A.).

By 1967 about 2,000 varieties had been sent for trial; of these 72 (approx. 3%) had received the AARS certificate which was certainly followed by increased sales of the selected varieties.

The organization is performing a public service; its sole purpose is to test new roses, and disseminate the results of these tests in the U.S.A. and Canada. The AARS has 24 official trial gardens of which 15 are in universities or public parks; the remaining 9 gardens are maintained by individual firms who are members of the AARS; each garden must send its results annually to the Trial Ground Committee of the AARS. The gardens are not generally open to the public.

The submission of a rose variety for trial must be done by the 30th of November at the latest, and must follow the prescribed formula. For the duration of the trial, the variety is given a code number.

Winners of the AARS Rose Trials 1963-1980*

Year	Name	Color	Classi-fication	Points
1963	'Super Star'	coral-orange	Hybrid Tea	7.9
1963	'Royal Highness'	light pink	HT	8.4
1964	'Saratoga'	white	Floribunda	7.2
1964	'Granada'	rose-red & yellow	HT	8.8
1965	'Mr. Lincoln'	crimson	HT	8.7
1965	'Camelot'	salmon	Grandi-flora	7.7
1966	'American Heritage'	white & carmine	HT	7.0
1966	'Apricot Nectar'	pale orange-pink	F	7.7
1966	'Matterhorn'	white	HT	—
1967	'Bewitched'	pink	HT	7.0
1967	'Gay Princess'	pink	Gr	6.9

Year	Name	Color	Classification	Points
1967	'Lucky Lady'	pale pink	Gr	—
1967	'Roman Holiday'	orange-red	F	6.7
1968	'Europeana'	red	F	8.8
1968	'Miss All-American Beauty'	pink	HT	8.3
1968	'Scarlet Knight'	scarlet	Gr	7.8
1969	'Angel Face'	lavender	F	8.0
1969	'Commanche'	orange-red	Gr	7.5
1969	'Gene Boerner'	bright pink	F	8.4
1969	'Pascali'	creamy-white	HT	8.0
1970	'First Prize'	pink	HT	9.0
1971	'Aquarius'	pink	Gr	7.3
1971	'Redgold'	yellow/red	F	—
1971	'Command Performance'	orange-red	HT	7.2
1972	'Apollo'	golden yellow	HT	5.7
1972	'Portrait'	medium to light pink	HT	7.5
1973	'Electron'	pink	HT	7.7
1973	'Gypsy'	orange-red	HT	6.7
1973	'Medallion'	orange-yellow	HT	7.6
1974	'Bon-Bon'	deep pink	F	7.3
1974	'Bahia'	orange-yellow	F	7.1
1974	'Perfume Delight'	deep pink	HT	7.8
1975	'Arizona'	golden-bronze	Gr	6.5
1975	'Oregold'	deep yellow	HT	7.5
1975	'Rose Parade'	coral-peach to pink	F	8.5
1976	'America'	porcelain-rose	Climber	8.0
1976	'Cathedral'	apricot shading to salmon	F	7.5
1976	'Seashell'	burnt-orange	HT	7.5
1976	'Yankee Doodle'	apricot to peachy-pink and butter-yellow	HT	7.5
1977	'First Edition'	coral shaded with orange	F	8.5
1977	'Double Delight'	creamy-white becoming strawberry-red	HT	8.5
1977	'Prominent'	orange-salmon	Gr	7.8
1978	'Charisma'	scarlet and yellow	F	8.0
1978	'Color Magic'	ivory to deep rose	HT	8.0
1979	'Friendship'	deep pink	HT	8.0
1979	'Paradise'	silvery-lavender deepening to ruby-red at the margins	HT	8.5
1979	'Sundowner'	golden-orange	Gr	7.5
1980	'Love'	bright red, silvery-white reverse	Gr	
1980	'Honor'	white	HT	
1980	'Cherish'	coral-pink	F	

* The points were given in the "Proof of the Pudding" trials.

THE AMERICAN TRIALS "PROOF OF THE PUDDING" A POSTAL BALLOT

This assessment of "puddings" has nothing to do with the kitchen, but, as with so much that is pleasant in life, with roses; anyone who knows about the American system of rose trials will certainly have read of the "Proof of the Pudding" which plays an important part in the *American Rose Annual*, as it has done since 1926.

Every year between 200 and 300 new roses are put on the market, of these it is unlikely that more than 8 to 10 will make any impact or become widely known. The rest slip quickly into obscurity, a fate suffered by thousands of roses in the past and which most roses undergo sooner or later.

As in many other countries, there is, in the U.S.A., a society of rose lovers known as the American Rose Society. This society is responsible for the International Register of roses. Here, properly, every new rose brought into commerce should be registered, one or two years before the event, under its proper name. If an individual country has its own register, it should function as an outpost for this central registry, checking the details and passing the information on to the U.S.A., if they find no objection. The name will then be published in the society's bulletin *The American Rose*, and anyone who considers that he has grounds for objecting to the use of the name has four weeks in which to file his complaint. (See p. 200)

As soon as a rose is placed on the market it will be put on the "Proof of the Pudding" register in the U.S.A.

Each year a new list appears in the society's bulletin giving details of the new, and some of the older, roses; the list is available to members. It contains several hundred varieties in alphabetical order. In front of each name are four sets of empty brackets in which the voters can place their cross, thereby recording comments on the varieties which they themselves grow.

The brackets are designated A, B, C and D.

A = outstandingly good; an excellent variety which the judge can recommend without hesitation.

B = good, but not quite so good as A; a reliable garden variety.

C = moderate to mediocre varieties which should be replaced as soon as a suitable alternative is available.

D = poor; a variety which the judge cannot recommend for his area.

Since the U.S.A. covers a large area, and soil climatic

conditions vary widely, it stands to reason that an individual variety is very unlikely to receive the same marks in every State of the Union.

The members who have volunteered to carry out the judging mark one of the four empty brackets to indicate their evaluation of the plant, and then return the list to the local branch of the American Rose Society. Now the work of the umpires begins. They have to translate the letters into points values, giving 10 points for A, 8 for B, 5 for C, and 2 for D. The points for each individual variety are then averaged, and these figures are then forwarded to the "Proof of the Pudding" committee. They assemble all the figures and, applying the same method, arrive at a consensus of opinion on the value of the variety. The results, which cover the evaluation of about 1,300 varieties, are published every year in the form of a small pamphlet called *The Handbook for Selecting Roses; a Rose Buying Guide.* Available to anyone from the A.R.S. for less than $1.00.

A	B	C	D	Variety
( )	( )	( )	( )	'Summer Rainbow' — HT — pb
( )	( )	( )	( )	'Sunbonnet' — F — dy
( )	( )	( )	( )	'Superior' — F
( )	( )	( )	( )	'Swan Lake' — Cl
( )	( )	( )	( )	'Sweet Lelanie' — HT — pb
( )	( )	( )	( )	'Sweet Talk' — F — w
( )	( )	( )	( )	'Sympathie' — K — mr
( )	( )	( )	( )	'Taconis' — F

Figure 67. Extract from the list of varieties available to members carrying out the "Proof of the Pudding" Trials.

Since 1950, all the varieties under trial have received a set of marks ranging from 5 to 10.

10	An outstanding rose of the highest quality (has never yet been awarded!)
9-9.9	An outstanding rose
8-8.9	Excellent
7-7.9	Good
6-6.9	Fair
5.9 and below	Of doubtful value

In the little handbook, *Rose Buying Guide,* the roses which have been tested are grouped according to their classification: i.e. Hybrid Teas, Grandiflora, Floribunda, Polyantha, Miniatures, etc. Finally, roses with the highest points are listed according to color.

Some of the leading varieties are summarized here.

Hybrid Teas

Red	'Chrysler Imperial'	8.9
	'Super Star'	8.8
	'Fragrant Cloud'	8.6
	'Mr. Lincoln'	8.5
	'Crimson Glory'	8.3
Pink	'First Prize'	8.9
	'Royal Highness'	8.6

Hybrid Teas

	'Miss All-American Beauty'	8.5
	'First Love'	8
	'Prima Ballerina'	7.9
Yellow	'King's Ransom'	7.8
	'Summer Sunshine'	7.6
	'Eclipse'	7.5
White	'Pascali'	8.3
	'Garden Party'	7.9
	'Matterhorn'	7.5
Bicolors	'Peace'	9.4
	'Tiffany'	9.1
	'Confidence'	9
	'Helen Traubel'	8.3
	'Isabel de Ortiz'	8.2
Mauve	'Lady X'	8.1
	'Mainzer Fastnacht' ('Blue Moon')	8
	'Cologne Carnival'	7.4

Floribundas

Red	'Europeana'	8.3
	'Spartan'	8.4
	'Orangeade'	8.4
	'Cocorico'	8.4
	'Orange Sensation'	8.3
	'Frensham'	8.2
	'Feurio'	8
	'Sarabande'	7.9
	'Red Pinocchio'	7.9
	'Permanent Wave'	7.9
Pink	'Betty Prior'	8.4
	'Gene Boerner'	8.4
	'Pink Rosette'	8.1
	'Vera Dalton'	8
	'Rosenelfe'	7.9
	'Else Poulsen'	7.8
	'Pink Bountiful'	7.8
	'Betsy McCall'	7.7
Yellow	'Starlet'	7.4
	'Allgold'	7.4
	'Arthur Bell'	7.3
	'Sunbonnet'	7.2
	'Yellow Cushion'	7.1
White	'Iceberg'	8.7
	'Ice White'	8.1
	'Ivory Fashion'	8
Bicolor	'Little Darling'	8.6
	'Dearest'	8.5
	'Sea Pearl'	8.4
	'Border Gem'	8.4
	'Redgold'	8.3
	'Vogue'	8.2
	'Fashion'	8
	'Circus'	8
Grandiflora	'Queen Elizabeth'	9.3
	'Montezuma'	8.6
	'Carrousel'	8.4
	'Granada'	8.4
	'Camelot'	8.2
	'Apricot Nectar'	8
	'John S. Armstrong'	8
	'Mount Shasta'	8

THE NATIONAL ROSE SOCIETIES OF THE WORLD (AS OF 1979)

The number of national rose societies is not as great as might be expected in view of the popularity of the "Queen of Flowers". It is necessary to distinguish between amateur groups and genuinely national organizations. Some of the societies which are no longer in existence are of purely historical interest.

The details which follow are in alphabetical order by country.

World Federation of Rose Societies.
Founded in 1971 at the first World Rose Convention held at Hamilton, New Zealand. President: David E. Gilad, Israel; Deputy President: Viktor von Medem, West Germany; Secretary (and address for correspondence): His Honor Judge Milton A. Cadsby, 28 Hilltop Road, Toronto, Ontario, Canada. The World Federation is at present composed of the Societies of Argentina, Australia, Belgium, Canada, France, Germany, Great Britain, India, Israel, Italy, Japan, Netherlands, New Zealand, South Africa, Switzerland, United States of America, Zimbabwe.

The Federation intends to hold an International Congress every two years.

Australia. The National Rose Society of Australia. President: elected every two years; Secretary: J.L. Priestly, 271 Belmore Road, North Balwyn, Victoria 3104. Since 1973 this Society has become the parent body for the Rose Societies of the individual Australian States. It issues a joint *Australian Rose Year Book*, 1979 being the 52nd year of publication. The editor is E.B. Pietsch, 25 Dixon Grove, Blackburn, Victoria 3130.

Belgium. Société Royale Nationale "Les Amis de la Rose". Nationale Maatschappij "De Vrienden van de Roos". Founded in 1923 by G. van Oost, it was reorganized in 1954 after being dormant for 15 years. President: The Baroness Gisèle de Gerlache de Gomery; Secretary: J.R. Defever, Vrijheidslaan 28, B-9000 Gent. Has issued its own periodical *Rosa Belgica*, about 2 or 3 times a year since 1963. Editor: Fr. Mertens, F.-J. Navezstraat 81, Brussels 3.

Canada. Canadian Rose Society. Founded in 1913 under the name of the "Rose Society of Ontario" and renamed in 1954. About 50 local rose societies are associated with the parent body. Membership is approximately 1,200. President: elected every two years; Secretary: Mrs. A. Hunter, 20 Portico Drive, Scarboro, Ontario. Since 1954 the Society has published an annual and also a "Rose Bulletin"; it does not, however, hold any rose trials and therefore makes no awards.

Czechoslovakia. Rosa Klub CSSR. Founded in 1968, it is made up of a large group for Czechs and a smaller group for the Slovaks, the latter being formed in 1970. Altogether about 1,000 members. President: Dr. Ing. Bohumil Jasa, Zemedelska 1; 662 65 Brno; Secretary: Antonin Stastny, tr SNB5, Praha 10. Has its own periodical *Zpravodaj Rosa Klub* appearing quarterly. The Society is in the process of making its own Rosarium at Hradec Kralovy where the first national competition for hybridizers of new roses was held in 1975.

France. La Société Française des Roses. Patrons: The President of the French Republic and the Minister for Agriculture; President: Armand Souzy; Secretary: M.M. Perroud, Parc de la Tête d'Or, 69459 Lyon, Cedex 3. Membership 17,000. The Society issues a quarterly magazine *Les Amis des Roses* in serialized numbers; by the end of 1979, 340 issues had appeared, most with color illustrations.

Germany. Verein Deutscher Rosenfreunde. Founded 1883. President: Viktor von Medem, Erpolzheimer Str. 13, 6700 Ludwigshafen; Secretary: Frau M. von Rosenthal, 7570 Baden-Baden, Postfach 1011; Editor of the Year Book and of *Rosenbogen*: Karl Heinz Hanisch, 757 Baden-Baden, Voglergasse 15. The membership is over 4,500. The Society was responsible for founding the Sangerhausen Rosarium in 1903 and later maintained there the Central Office for Rose Research and, in association with the City of Dortmund, set up the Dortmund Rosarium in 1968. From 1883 to 1933, they issued the *Rosenzeitung* (about 6 issues per year) and from 1934 to 1940 the "Rose Year Book"; this re-appeared in 1949; its 45th issue was produced in 1979. Since 1964 a quarterly instituted by Oscar Scheerer has been published under the title of *Der Rosenbogen*. The Society holds a rose show and seminar at its main meeting each year in Dortmund. For details of the early history of the Society, together with 12 portraits, see *Rosen-Zeitung* 1933: 43, et seq.

The following two societies were in existence for only a few years:

PLATE 14

William A. Warriner, U.S.A.

Jack Christensen, U.S.A.

Georges Delbard, France

Francis Meilland (†), France

Mme. Louisette Meilland, France

Alain Meilland, France

Herbert Swim, U.S.A.

Simon & Pedro Dot (†), Spain

Hugo Delforge, Belgium

Association of German Rose Breeders; founded 1919. Chairman O. Jacobs. There is a notice concerning this association in *Rosen-Zeitung* 1911: 20-21.

Association of German Rose Exporters; founded about 1920; see *Rosen-Zeitung* 1924; additional note on p. 32.

Great Britain. The Royal National Rose Society: Secretariat and Head Office; Chiswell Green Lane, St. Albans, Herts. President: elected every two years; Secretary: L.G. Turner, M.B.E. The first rose show was held in London in 1858, but, despite much discussion, the Society was not established until 1876. It has since become the largest specialist garden society in the world and today has some 40,000 members. The Society maintains Display Gardens and Trial Grounds at St. Albans where a rose festival is held each July. Other shows are held throughout the year. The Society's Rose Annual has been published since 1907, and more recently has been joined by an annual bulletin in the fall. A library is maintained at St. Albans. The judges for the shows are certified by passing an examination. H.M. Queen Elizabeth The Queen Mother is the Society's Patron.

The Rose Growers Association. Founded 1975. Chairman: P. Harkness; Secretary: Miss A. Pawsey, 303 Mile End Road, Colchester, Essex. This association includes about 76 British rose nurserymen and exists to consider all general matters connected with the trade.

British Association of Rose Breeders (BARB). Founded 1973. President: John Mattock; Secretary: Jack Harkness, 1 Bank Alley, Southwold, Suffolk.

The Rose Society of Northern Ireland. Secretary: J. Dean, 13 Glen Ebor Park, Belfast. Founded 1964. Membership 300. International Rose Trials held annually at Dixon Park.

The oldest Rose Society in England was formed in Nottingham about 1850, but unfortunately had to close for lack of support in 1880. It was then reactivated 30 years later.

India. The Rose Society of India. Founded 1959. President: Dr. Bharat Ram; Secretary: Mr. S.N. Achanta, D.I./139 Satya Marg, New Delhi 110 021. Honorary President: Dr. B.P. Pal. Membership about 600. Publication: a quarterly newsletter. The Society holds a Rose Show every winter and spring.

Italy. Associazione Italiana delle Rosa (AIR). Offices: Villa Reale, 20052 Monza. Founded 1963. President: Signor Niso Fumagalli; Secretary: Signorina Lucia Biffi. About 1,800 members. An annual has been published since 1965. Exhibitions and competitions are held each year.

Japan. Japan Rose Society. (Nihon-Bara-Kai). Address: Okuzawa-machi, 8-28-12, Setagaya-ku, Tokyo 158; Secretary: Nobuo Tanizawa. This society was formed after the Second World War, when the two rose societies of Tokyo and Osaka merged; there are now over 200 groups throughout Japan, and many thousands of members in all of Japan; it is the largest gardening society in all of Asia. The whole Imperial Family and many important politicians are members, including the former Prime Minister S. Yoshida who owns one of the most beautiful rose gardens in the country and who was also President of the Society for a number of years. The Society is responsible for the rose garden in the Imperial Palace. The annual Rose Festival, "Japan Rose Festival", is a very important rose show with international participation. The awards include Gold Medals and Certificates of Merit. The Society's Trial Grounds are situated in Yatsu Park to the east of Tokyo. Entry to these trials is restricted to the judges.

Netherlands. De Roos; Verenigin ter Bevordering van de Rozenteelt (Nos Jungunt Rosae). Chairman: C. van den Berg, Bussum (of the firm of de Wilde); Head Office and Secretary: W.C. van Zetten, Waddinxveen, Prinses Beatrixlaan 100. The Society was founded in 1891. The membership is composed of rose nurserymen. A periodical called *Rosarium* was published from 1891 to 1941.

Nederlandse Rozenvereniging. Founded 1971. President: S. van den Bent; Secretary: G.E.J.S.L. Voitus van Hamme, De Mildestraat 47, 2596 SW The Hague. Editor of the quarterly magazine *Rozen-Bulletins*, published since 1972, is Tj v.d. Kooi, Elandstraat 42, The Hague. (Kon. Ned. Mij.voor Tuinbouw en Plantkunde).

New Zealand. The National Rose Society of New Zealand. Founded 1931. Secretary: Mrs. H. MacDonnell, 17 Erin Street, Palmerston North. Since 1965 the society has been publishing its own annual which it had earlier done in association with the Australian Society. International Rose Trials are held at Palmerston North and the following awards are made:

Australia

Belgium

Since 1961

1933-1934

Germany (VDR)

World Federation

Great Britain

N. Ireland

Italy

Japan

Canada

New Zealand

The Swiss Badge

Switzerland

Poland

S. Africa

Czechoslovakia

United States of America

Figure 68. Badges and Emblems of the various Rose Societies.

"Gold Star of the South Pacific" and "Silver Star of Palmerston North".

Poland. Polskie Towarzystwo Milosnikow Róz (Polish Society for Rose Amateurs). 01-756 Warsaw, ul. Przasnyska 24/1. President: Mrs. Irena Gotzbiowska; Secretary: Barbara Lisiewska. There are 2,000 members, and a periodical entitled *Informator Polskiego Towarzystwa Milosnikow Róz* is published every two months; in addition, two special year books have been issued.

South Africa. The Rose Society of South Africa. Die Roos Vereniging van Suid-Afrika. Founded 1960; membership is approximately 500. President: elected every two years; Secretary: Mrs. L. Taschner, P.O. Box 28188, Sunnyside 0132, Pretoria, Transvaal. The Society publishes its own periodical *Rosa* 3 times a year. Due to the size of the nation, the Society is divided into three groups: The Western Cape Rose Society (Cape Province), the Welkom and District Rose Society (Orange Free State) and the North Transvaal Society (Pretoria). A joint committee of 12 members and two deputies from the three groups meet once a month, alternating between Pretoria and Cape Town.

Switzerland. Gesellschaft Schweizerischer Rosenfreunde. Founded 1959 in Zürich. President: Dr. Fritz Dorschner of Schaffhausen; Secretary: Frau Rita Leichti, Bahnhof Str. 11, Ch 8640 Rapperswill. Since 1959, the Society has issued *Das Rosenblatt* (22nd edition in 1979) annually, and *Das Kleine Rosenblatt* on a monthly basis, as well as a number of other books. Membership is 2,400.

United States of America. The American Rose Society. Founded 1899. About 16,000 members. The President is elected every two years. The Society's Offices are at P.O. Box 30,000 Shreveport, Louisiana 71130. The Executive Director, and Publisher of the *American Rose Annual*, is Harold S. Goldstein. The governing body consists of 15 members of the society; they represent two distinct geographical areas and are known as "Governors". Each area is in turn sub-divided into districts with a director of the district acting as chairman. These district directors together make up the "Council of Directors" who meet each year at the Annual General Meeting. The ARS frequently gives small grants in the field of rose research, plant protection, genetic research, etc. Co-operative efforts were made with various universities until 1952, but since then the American Rose Foundation was entrusted with special responsibility for all scientific research into the genus. The Society has about 1,300 members who are known as "Consulting Rosarians" to whom both members and non-members can address problems, and most of whom also act as judges in their area of specialty. The ARS has published an annual since 1916, of which the results of the various trials, especially the "Proof of the Pudding" (see p. 146), form an important part. Members also receive an annual *Buyer's Guide*, a small pamphlet in which the garden value of about 1,000 varieties is assessed by a system of marks.

American Rose Foundation. A special department of the American Rose Society; Chairman: John R. Lauer; Secretary: Harold S. Goldstein (Head Office American Rose Society); Chairman of the Scientific Committee: Dr. Cynthia Westcott. This institution was established with the special purpose of acquiring both money and gifts which could be used for general rose research and related subjects. In 1952 the institution assumed the work which up to that time had been undertaken by the ARS. The Federal government has granted it non-profit status so "gifts, bequests and devices to be used exclusively for education and scientific research in the improvement of the standard of excellence of the rose for all American people together with the stimulation of general interest in the rose" are tax-deductible. Results and reports of the work undertaken are published, usually in shortened and simplified form, in the *American Rose Annual*. A review of the work accomplished between 1952 and 1962 appeared in the *ARA* 1963: pp. 145-153.

Rose Hybridizer's Association. Founded in 1969; General Director: William Rowe Jr., 777 Liberty Street, Penfield, New York 14526. A non-profit organization of amateur hybridizers in the U.S.A. and Canada with overseas offices in England and India. Membership about 200. The objectives of the association are the collection and dissemination of information on rose breeding, contact with other amateur growers and the exchange of pollen and other breeding material. There is a quarterly newsletter. The Regional Director, European District, is Mrs. Alice Dale, 41 Edinburgh Road, Congleton, Cheshire, England.

Some Leading Rose Breeders and their Work as well as Some Information on Botanists and Gardeners in Relation to Roses

In *Modern Roses 7* no fewer than 1,200 rose breeders are listed, but that is by no means all, for in Germany alone there are about 170 growers, most of whom are only rose fanciers or those who have established a new plant from sports (mutations). Scarcely 20 of these cultivars have acquired real importance; the rest are of the sort which another breeder will not find sufficiently valuable or noteworthy to breed and propagate to any extent. So, usually, these plants disappear in a few years.

The following list is of the most noteworthy hybridizers and those who have provided significant cultivars which are certainly in the first level of the finest varieties commonly found in the rose trade. In most cases the hybrids can still be obtained in the trade, or are still grown in rose gardens, or are of importance in rose breeding.

Where available, brief individual biographies have been provided. For further information about the cultivars named, as well as the year of introduction, see the "Rose Dictionary".

Aicardi, Domenico. Died 1964. Villa Minerva, San Remo, Italy. His work passed to his niece, Ada Mansuino. 'Eterna Giovinezza' (= 'Eternal Youth'), 'Gloria di Roma', 'Signora Piero Puricelli'.

Armstrong Nurseries, Inc. Ontario, California, U.S.A. 'Buccaneer', 'Charlotte Armstrong', 'Circus', 'Eiffel Tower', 'Fandango', 'First Love', 'Forty-niner', 'Frolic', 'Grand Slam', 'Helen Traubel', 'High Noon', 'Joseph's Coat', 'Matterhorn', 'Mirandy', 'Mojave', 'Montezuma', 'Moonsprite', 'Show Girl', 'Summer Sunshine', 'Sutter's Gold', 'Sweet Sixteen', 'Taffeta', 'Tallyho', 'Wildfire', 'John S. Armstrong'.

Barbier & Co. Orléans, France. A very significant rose breeder of all climbing roses before the first World War. 'Alberic Barbier', 'Albertine', 'Leontine Gervais'.

Beluze, Jean. Lyon, France. 'Souvenir de la Malmaison'.

Bennett, Henry. Stapleford, later Shepperton, Middlesex, England. An amateur gardener and rose breeder, died 1890. Bred the first Hybrid Tea roses. 'Lady Mary Fitzwilliam', 'Princess Beatrice', 'Mrs. John Laing', 'Grace Darling', 'Her Majesty', 'William Francis Bennett' (the "$5,000 rose"!).

Berger, Vinzenz. Bad Harzburg, Germany. 'Dr. Eckener', 'Erika Teschendorff', 'Heidekind', 'Bergers Weisse'.

Bobbink & Atkins. East Rutherford, N.J., U.S.A. One of the most important American firms of rose growers; not a breeding organization, involved only in propagation.

Boerner, S. Eugen. Born 1893 in Cedarburg, Wisconsin, died 1967 in Clifton Springs, New York, U.S.A. Studied horticulture in the U.S.; a pilot in the first World War. Joined the firm of Jackson and Perkins, of which he became a partner in 1927. In 1937 he began his hybridizing work following Dr. H.J. Nicholas. In addition to roses he also hybridized *Chrysanthemum*, with a new breeding form. 'Aloha', 'America's Junior Miss', 'Apricot Nectar', 'Arlene Francis', 'Ballet', 'Chatter', 'Chic', 'Coral Dawn', 'Coral Sunset', 'Diamond Jubilee', 'Fashion', 'Fashionette', 'Frankfurt am Main', 'Goldilocks', 'Ivory Fashion', 'Jiminy Cricket', 'John F. Kennedy', 'Lavendar Pinocchio', 'Masquerade', 'New Yorker', 'Orchid Masterpiece', 'Pink Garnette', 'Polynesian Sunset', 'Spartan', 'Summertime', 'Valiant', 'Vogue', 'Zorina', 'Bronze Masterpiece', 'Golden Masterpiece'.

Booth, John & Sohne. Nursery, Flottbek bei Altona. 'Königen von Danemark'. Successfully established his claim to this cultivar against those made by Prof. Lehmann.

Boulenger, Georges Albert. 1858-1937. A Belgian naturalist in Brussels, his specialty was fish and reptiles and, in the area of botany, roses. He wrote a comprehensive revision of European and Asiatic rose species and revised Crépin's herbal.

Boursault, Henri. Gardener and botanist in Paris, Rue Blanche; possessed the largest private collection of the time (1828); the plans for his garden can be found in J.C. Loudon's *An Encyclopedia of Gardening*, 2nd Edition, London (1835). *R. banksiae rosea* (= *R. banksiae alba plena* × unknown red garden rose; 1824).

Brownell, Dr. Walter. Associated with Brownell Sub-Zero Roses, Inc.

Buatois. Dijon, France. 'Reveil Dijonnais'.

Buisman, G.A.H. & Zoon. Heerde, Netherlands. Founder: Roelof Buisman, 1894-1969. 'Buisman's Triumph', 'Kosmopoliet', 'Kathleen Ferrier', 'Lijnbaanroos', 'Norris Pratt', 'Saskia', 'John Dijkstra'.

Buyl Frères. Serskamp, Schellebelle, Belgium. 'Bambino', 'Coccinelle', 'Denise', 'La Jolie', 'Princesse Liliane', 'Troubadour'.

Camprubi, Carlos. Cornella de Llobregat, Barcelona, Spain. 'Carmencita', 'Dona Clara', 'Leonor de March', 'Rosalinda', 'Violinista Costa'.

Cant, Benjamin R. & Sons, Ltd. The Old Rose Gardens, Colchester, England. 'Blush Rambler', 'Covent Garden', 'Golden Ophelia', 'Lady Roundaway', 'Lady Sackville', 'Lilian', 'Princess Margaret Rose', 'Rev. F. Page Roberts', 'White Dorothy'.

Cant, Frank and Co., Ltd. Braiswick Rose Gardens, Stanway, Colchester, England. 'Harlequin', 'Lady Fairfax', 'Mrs. Herbert Carter', 'Orange Triumph Improved', 'Red Ember', 'Snowflake'.

Cant, William. Founded a nursery at Colchester, England in 1765; in 1847 passed it on to his grandchild, Benjamin Revett Cant, who specialized in roses. Participated in the historic first National Rose Show in London on July 1, 1858. One of the founders of the National Rose Society. His son began rose breeding in the nursery. The firm is still in family hands.

Cazzaniga, F.G. Vinodrome, Milan, Italy. 'Amica', 'Prof. Alfred Dufour'.

Chaplin Bros. Waltham Cross, England (successor to W. Paul and Son). 'Chaplin's Pink Climber', 'Elegance', 'Golden Glow', 'W.E. Chaplin', 'Windermere'.

Chotek, Gräfin Marie Henriette. Dolná Krúpa, Czechoslovakia. An important rose fancier and owner of a major rose garden in the first third of the 20th century.

Christ, Konrad Hermann Heinrich. Swiss botanist. Born 1833 in Zurich, died 1933 in Basel. Author of, among other works, *Die in der Schweiz* (1873).

Christensen, Jack E. Born 1948. Joined Armstrong Nurseries, Ontario, California, in 1970 as a trainee under Herbert C. Swim. Upon Swim's retirement in 1973 became Director of Research. 'Brandy', 'Cricket', 'Foxy Lady', 'Heidi', 'Holy Toledo', 'Honest Abe', 'Hopscotch', 'Katherine Loker', 'Little Red Devil', 'Mon Cheri', 'Sunspray', 'White Lightnin''.

Clark, Alister. Bulla, Victoria, Australia. Important hybridizer, although his cultivars are not well known in Europe.

Cochet, Pierre. Grisy-Suisnes, Seine-et-Marne. Founded a nursery which, through the patronage of Queen Marie Antoinette and Count of Bougainville, developed a rose collection as large as Empress Josephine's. Little known as a breeder.

Cochet-Cochet, P.C.M. Coubert, Seine-et-Marne. Likewise, little is known of his hybridizing activity, although many of his roses are still in cultivation today. 'Blanc Double de Coubert', 'Roseraie de l'Hay', 'Souvenir de Christophe Cochet', 'Souvenir de Philemon Cochet', 'Souvenir de Pierre Leperdrieux'.

Cocker, Alex. Died 1977. Of the Scottish rose growers, Cocker and Sons, Aberdeen, Scotland. Did not begin to specialize in roses until 1952. Partner in Harkness & Cocker since 1962. 'Alec's Red', 'Anne Cocker', 'Cairngorm', 'Glenngarry', 'Pineapple Poll', 'Rob Roy' and 'Silver Jubilee', which won a posthumous Presidents International Trophy.

Combe, Maurice. La Galochère, St. Martin-d'Heres, Isère, France. 'Barricade', 'Bonne Nuit', 'Cordon Rouge', 'Flammèche', 'Fontaine Lumineuse', 'Furia', 'Norita', 'Saphi', 'Smoky', 'Tom Pillibi', 'Vahine', 'Ronde Endiablée'.

Compton. Rhode Island, U.S.A. 'Break o'Day', 'Copper Glow', 'Curly Pink', 'Shades of Autumn'.

Conard-Pyle Co. West Grove, Pennsylvania, U.S.A. Not really a firm for breeding, but a leader in introducing new roses from both the U.S.A. and abroad.

Crépin, Francois. Born October 30, 1830 in Rochefort, Prov. Namur, Belgium. Prof. and Director of the Brussels Botanic Garden. Died 1903. An authority on wild roses, he wrote the *Manual de la Flore de Belgique*. Crépin's work with roses concentrated mainly on the Western and mid-Alpine regions.

Croix, P. Bourg-Argental. Loire, France. 'Astrée', 'Cameliarose', 'Coral Glow', 'Flamboyant', 'Province d'Anjou'.

Deegen, Franz. Kostritz, Germany; 1840-1927. Planted the first roses in his garden in 1864; later followed by 120,000 wildlings for long-stemmed roses. He originated 'Deegen's Weisse Maréchal Niel'.

Delbard, Georges, and **Chabert.** 16 Quai de la Megisserie, Paris, France. Hybridizers as well as distributors. Their own introductions include: 'Centenaire de

Lourdes', 'Chic Parisien', 'Crêpe de Chine', 'Diablotin', 'Dr. Albert Schweitzer', 'Gay Paris', 'Grand Amour', 'Grand Prix', 'Impeccable', 'La Passionata', 'Maurice Chevalier', 'Mickey', 'Mitsouko', 'Mondovision', 'Orange Delbard', 'Phare', 'Presence', 'Reine France', 'Roi des Rois', 'Rosier d'Or', 'Saint-Exupéry', 'Tutu Mauve', 'Vie-en-Rose', 'Voeux de Bonheur', 'Vol de Nuit'.

Delforge, Hippolyte & Fils. Belsele-Waas, Belgium. 'Arc-en-Ciel', 'Astoria', 'Ballerine', 'Belvédère', 'Eurovision', 'Genval', 'Mercator', 'Midinette', 'Portofino', 'Tango', 'Veronique'.

de Ruiter, Gerrit. Kwekerij, "Rosa Polyantha", Hazerswoude, Holland. 1882-1965. Owned his own firm for 20 years, his rose 'de Ruiter's Herald' appeared as the first Dutch rose that was "kwekersrecht" (patent of the variety in Holland). Both of his sons, Gijsbert (born 1928) and Leendert (born 1932), have been involved in hybridizing since 1958. 'Border Beauty', 'Border King', 'Border Queen', 'Cameo', 'Cherryade', 'City of Nottingham', 'Dacapo', 'De Ruiter's Herald', 'Edith Cavell', Europeana', 'Frau Anny Beaufays', 'Gloria Mundi', 'Kimono', 'Lyric', 'Orange Sensation', 'Pompadour Red,' 'Prinsess van Oranje', 'Red Wonder', 'Rosemary Rose', 'Ruth Leuwerik', 'Salmon Perfection', 'Sidney Peabody', 'Signal Red', 'Sweet Repose'; and in the Compacta roses, 'Alberich', 'Degenhardt', 'Eberwein', 'Balduin', 'Bertram' and 'Giesebrecht', 'Diorama', 'Sonnenuntergang'.

Descemet, M. St. Denis, France. Lived at the time of the Empress Josephine and was the first French rose breeder of great stature, despite the count of only 80 varieties by Simon-Cochet, and only 4 now appearing in *Modern Roses 7*. When British troops entered Paris in 1815, Vibert transported over 10,000 of Descemet's rose plants to his own garden near Angers, in order to "save" them. Descemet's roses were mostly *gallica* varieties, and it is probable that many of his hybrids were later distributed by Vibert and other breeders as their own introductions.

Desportes, Narcisse. France. Rose grower; in 1829 published a catalog listing about 2,000 cultivars, many of which disappeared after testing because they proved to be absolutely worthless; over 250 cultivars were from *Rosa chinensis.*

Desprez, R. Yebles, France. Rose fancier and collector; had an important rose garden. His own hybrids 'Baronne Prévost, 'Caroline de Sansal', as well as 23 other hybrids, are no longer extant.

des Tombes, F.A. A former President of the Dutch Rose Association, Nos Jungunt Rosae. He succeeded J.L. Mock in 1921. After his death in 1927, the F.A. des Tombes medal was established.

de Vink, Jan. Boskoop, Holland. Hybridizer of miniature roses between 1935 and 1952. 'Péon', 'Pixie', 'Sweet Fairy', 'Bo-Peep', 'Cinderella'.

Dickson, Alex & Sons (Dicksons of Hawlmark). Newtonards, Co. Down, North Ireland. The firm was founded in 1836; in 1920 Alex was made manager of the firm in Hawlmark, Newtonards. Noteworthy cultivars are 'Barbara Richards', 'Sir Henry Segrave', 'Margaret', 'Silver Lining', 'Shepard's Delight', in addition to others named below.

Dickson, Alex. Born in 1894 in Northern Ireland, in Newtonards, Co. Down. After completing his education he joined his father's firm and managed the greenhouses. Three uncles were also involved in the firm. His uncle George led him into rose breeding. 'Betty Uprichard' appeared in 1922, 'Dame Edith Helen' in 1926, 'Dickson's Flame' in 1958 and 'Dearest' in 1960. 'Attraction', 'Clara Curtis', 'Irish Beauty', 'Kathleen Harrop', 'K. of K.', 'Margaret Dickson', 'Margaret Dickson Hamill', 'Mrs. Wemyss Quinn', 'Nymph', 'Oberon', 'Prima Donna', 'Princess Royal', 'Queen Mary', 'Red Letter Day', 'Shot Silk', 'Sunstar'. His son Patrick carried on the rose breeding with 'Redgold', 'Grandpa Dickson', 'Red Planet', 'Red Devil' and 'Mala Rubinstein'.

Dickson, Hugh, Ltd. Belfast, Northern Ireland. 'Gorgeous', 'Hugh Dickson', 'Mrs. Cynthia Ford', 'Ulster Gem'.

Dieck, Dr. Georg. Zoschen bei Merseburg, Germany. 1846-1925. Scientist and farmer; assistant on an estate near Haeckel, after which he organized a nursery. He grew as many as 6,000 types and forms of trees and shrubs, and more than 100 varieties of roses which he later donated to Strassheim; these were later exhibited at the Paris Exhibition and then planted in the Roseraie de l'Hay.

Dorieux, F., & Fils. Montagny, Loire, France. 'Bobino', 'Copacabana', 'Jericho', 'Majesté', 'Miss Rose', 'Rouge Dorieux', 'Tentation'.

Dot, Pedro. Born 1885 in San Feliu de Llobregat, near Barcelona. Named over 120 varieties of roses. His father was the chief gardener for the Marques de Monistrol, himself a great rose collector (his mother was the Condesa de Sastago to whom Pedro Dot dedicated a rose). Pedro started his rose crosses about 1925; one of his first was 'Nevada'. Later he worked with miniature roses; the first appeared in 1940, 'Estrellita de Oro' ('Baby Gold Star'), later came 'Perla de Alcanada', 'Perla de Montserrat'. 'Angels Mateu', 'Baby Gold Star', 'Canigo', 'Duquesa de Peñeranda', 'Girona', 'Golden Moss', 'Hermelio Casas', 'Luis Brinas', 'Maria Dot', 'Mme. Grégoire Staechelin', 'Mon Petit', 'Parati', 'Pilar Dot', 'Presumida', 'Tanger'. Two sons carried on the work.

Simon Dot, the eldest, has developed over 30 hybrids, including the internationally honored 'Intermezzo'.

Marino Dot has developed over 15 varieties, including 'Coralin'.

Dreer, Henry A., Inc. Philadelphia, Penn., U.S.A. Not a hybridizer, but a leading distributor of new introductions.

Ducher & Vve (Witwe); Lyon, Rhône, France. Later Pernet-Ducher. 'Cécile Brunner', 'Coquette de Lyon', 'Marie van Houtte', 'William Allen Richardson', 'Bouquet d'Or', 'Rêve d'Or'.

Duehrsen, Carl G. 378 N. Wilcox St., Montebello, California, U.S.A. 'Carrousel', 'Crown of Gold', 'Gold Rush', 'John Morley', 'Mme. Chiang Kai-shek'.

Easlea, Walter & Sons, Ltd. Eastwood, Leigh-on-Sea, Essex, England. 'Easlea's Golden Rambler', 'Everest', 'President Wilson', 'Prince of Wales'.

Edition Française de Roses, Champagne-au-Mont d'Or, Rhône, France. Not a hybridizer, but a leading distributor of new introductions.

Felberg-Leclerc, J. Trier, Germany. No longer in existence. 'Felbergs Rosa Druschki', 'Gruss an Coburg', 'Kate Felberg'.

Fortune, Robert. English plant collector 1812-1880. In 1845 discovered in Ningpo, China a salmon yellow double rose (*R. odorata indica*) which became famous as 'Fortune's Double Yellow'.

Gandy's Roses, Ltd. North Kilworth, Rugby, Warwickshire, England. Not a hybridizer, but a distributor.

Gaujard, Jean, Feyzin, Isère, France (successor to Pernet-Ducher). 'Atlantic', 'Beauté de France', 'Bonjour', 'Buisson Ardent', 'Canasta', 'Chanteclerc', 'Cocotte', 'Colisée', 'Déesse', 'Duo', 'Femina', 'Joie de Vivre', 'Joli Coeur', 'Magnificence', 'Majestic', 'Miss Universe', 'Mme. Jean Gaujard', 'Mme. Léon Pin', 'Mme. Marie Curie', 'Nouvelle Europe', 'Opéra', 'Président Henri Queuille', 'Président Plumcoque', 'Rose Gaujard', 'Scandale', 'Super Tabarin', 'Sweet Harmony', 'Tabarin', 'Vedette', 'Vendôme'.

Geschwind, Rudolf K. and K. Forstmeister, Korpona, Austria-Hungary, 1829-1910. Began hybridizing in 1880. 'Theano' (1894), 'Erinnerung an Brod' (1886), 'Gruss an Teplitz' (1897), 'Geschwind's Nordlandrose'. After his death, through the goodness of Countess Marie Henriette Chotek, his reputation was preserved.

Gregory, C. & Son. Chilwell, Nottingham, England. 'Apricot Silk', 'Wendy Cussons'; but principally a leader in distributing new varieties.

Grootendorst, F.L. & Zonen. Boskoop, Holland. 'Grootendorst Supreme', 'Mothersday', 'Oranje Moersdag', 'Pink Grootendorst', 'Sneprinsesse'.

Guillot. The father, Guillot senior, had a rose nursery in Lyon and developed about 80 varieties, including 'Impératrice Eugénie', 'Mme. Bravy' (which is often encountered) and 'Senateur Vaïsse'. His son, J.B. Guillot, founded a rose nursery in Lyon-Monplaisir in 1850 and brought 79 cultivars into trade, probably all selections from seeds of unknown parents, including 'La France', 'Belle des Jardins', 'Gloire Des Polyantha', 'Mignonette', 'Pâquerette', and 'Reine de Portugal'. His successor was Pierre Guillot whose 30 rose introductions include 'Mme. Léon Pain', and 'Mme. Jules Grolez'. Today Marc Guillot of Rosiers Pierre Guillot in St. Priest, Isère, France is the successor of the old firm.

Hardy, M. Manager of the Garden of the Louvre, he has bred about 85 varieties of which none were marketed; especially noteworthy today are 'Mme. Hardy' and 'Celina'.

Harkness, R. & Co., Hitchin, Hertfordshire, England.

Harkness. Two brothers, Robert and John, founded (1879) a nursery in Bedale, Yorkshire, England; shortly thereafter they began cultivating roses. Later the firm was split. Robert and his son William Ernest founded (1899) the firm of R. Harkness and Co. in Hitchin; they did no breeding, but did introduce cultivars developed by amateur breeders (Albert Norman's 'Frensham' and 'Ena Harkness'). William Ernest died in 1959. Jack Harkness entered the firm in 1962 and began hybridizing. They stock about 1,000 varieties in their rose collection. 'Alexander', 'Atlantis', 'Compassion', 'Dr. Bernardo', 'Elizabeth Harkness', 'Escapade', 'Saga', 'Yesterday'.

Hémeray-Aubert. 51 Route d'Olivet, Orléans, France. 'Coup de Foudre', 'Crinoline', 'Hôtesse de France', 'Le Ponceau', 'Papa Hémeray', 'Sorcier'.

Herger, J.E. Kostritz, Germany. Had the largest rose nursery in Germany in about 1850.

Hetzel, Karl. Beutelsbach bei Stuttgart, Germany. Rose grower and hybridizer. 'Duftbella', 'Duftwunder', 'Indira', 'Hessenstar', 'Sans Souci', 'Verena', 'Rebellastar', among others.

Hill, E. Gurney. Born in England in 1847. Emigrated to the U.S.A. in 1851. Founded (1881) a nursery in Richmond, Indiana where he initially only distributed new European introductions, later, together with his son, he started hybridizing. He died in 1933. The firm is still called Joseph H. Hill, Co. 'E.G. Hill', 'Fontanelle', 'General MacArthur', 'Golden Talisman', 'Mme. Butterfly', 'Richmond', 'Royal Red', 'Sterling', 'Sunkist'.

Hill, Joseph H. & Co. Richmond, Indiana, U.S.A. 'Better Times', 'Blushing Bride', 'Butterscotch', 'Coral Sea', 'Glamour Girl', 'Joanna Hill', 'Lamplighter', 'Pink Bountiful', 'Sensation', 'Rosy Glow', 'Snow White', 'Town Crier'.

Hinner, Wilhem. Rose breeder in Lohausen near Dusseldorf. First worked for H.P. Lambert, then for Philipp Gelduldig, Aachen, where he developed the rose 'Gruss an Aachen'. 'Farbenkönigen', 'Gelbe Pharisäer', 'Rote Pharisäer'. 'Georg Arends', 'Goldelse'.

Hole, The Very Reverend Samuel Reynolds ("Dean Hole"). 1821-1904. Canonicus von Caunton. A great friend and student of the rose. In 1858 organized the first rose show in England. In 1875 became the first President of the National Rose Society, and remained in that position until his death 28 years later. His book, *A Book of Roses*, appeared in 30 editions. He had over 5,000 varieties in cultivation in his parish garden.

Horstmann & Co. Elmshorn, Germany. Not a breeder, but a leading grower.

Howard, Paul W., Rose Co. Hemet, California, U.S.A. Not a breeder, but a leading grower.

Howard & Smith. 1200 Beverly Blvd., Montebello, California, U.S.A. Not a breeder, but a leading grower.

Hume, Sir A. England. Sent the first Tea Roses to England from China in 1809 ('Hume's Blush Tea Scented China').

Hurst, C.C., Dr. 1870-1947. One of the first three pioneers in genetics in England. He was important before 1914 as the scientific adviser to the British government on questions relating to the breeding of plants and horses; he worked intensively on the genetics of cultivated roses and conducted many experiments. In 1922 he was called to Cambridge University where he pursued work on the chromosomes of the rose family. He laid out a large rose garden "Garden of the Thousand Best Rose Varieties", analyzed the chromosomes of about 700 rose types and varieties and published many scientific papers on the results; he also proposed the "Septet Theory".

Jackson & Perkins Co. Newark, New York, U.S.A. Owned until 1970 by the three brothers Perkins (the most widely known of whom was Charlie) and E.S. Boerner, whose hybridizing program made the firm one of great importance.

Jacotot. Dijon, France. 'Gloire de Dijon'.

Jäger, August. Uftrungen am Harz, Germany, 1876-1962. Financial officer. After his retirement he accepted the commission from the Vereins Deutscher Rosenfreunde to edit the *Rosen-Lexicon* which included about 17,000 rose cultivars from the year 1936; 768 pages, it first appeared in 1946.

Jamain, Hippolyte. Paris, France. 'Antoine Verdier'.

Jelly, Robert. Has worked at E.G. Hill Co. Inc., Richmond, Indiana for 40 years, developing cultivars for the commercial cut rose industry. Some of his introductions are 'Can Can', 'Charisma', 'Coed', 'Excitement', 'Forever Yours', 'Jack Frost', 'Jr. Bridesmaid', 'Promise Me', 'Royalty', 'Sassy' and 'Stop Lite'.

Keller, Dr. Robert. Scientist and Gymnasium director in Winterthur, Switzerland, 1854-1939. A first-rate student of wild roses, he wrote about 30 articles on this subject which were issued as *Synopsis Rosarum spontanearum Europae Mediae* (Basel, 1931) and compiled the information on the species *Rosa* in Ascherson & Graebner, *Synopsis der Mitteleuropaischen Flora*.

Keller, Wilhelm. Kaufman in Duisburg, Germany. By 1829 possessed a large rose collection and was also a dealer in roses. The complete catalog is reproduced in

Annalen der Blumisterei, Nürnberg, 1828 (pp. 257-287) and 1829 (pp. 276-296).

Ketten, Johann (Gebr. Ketten). Rose nursery, Luxembourg, 1848-1892. Rose breeder. In 1867 his brother founded the very well-known firm. 'Evrard Ketten', 'Prince Felix de Luxembourg' and about 30 other existing cultivars.

Kiese, Hermann. Vieselbach bei Erfurt, Germany, 1865-1923. After his schooling he became the chief gardener at J.C. Schmidt, Erfurt and there bred the cultivars 'Rubin', 'Tausendschön' and 'Leuchtfeuer', among others; in 1908 he established his own firm and thereafter bred about 30 other cultivars. 'Canina Kiese', 'Frau Bertha Kiese', 'Eisenach', 'Freudenfeuer', 'Grossherzogin Fedora von Sachsen', 'Hackeburg', 'Nordlicht', 'Paula Clegg', 'Perle von Hohenstein'.

Klimenko, Dr. Vera Nikolajewa. Nikita, Jalta, Krim, U.S.S.R. Botanist; in 1948 began making rose crosses in the southern province of Ziel in the U.S.S.R. The plants are very resistant to heat and disease and bloom in the farther reaches of Russia; from 1955 to 1967, 210 such clones were selected for propagation; 55 new hybrids obtained. Only a few of these are in cultivation outside Russia.

Kordes, Wilhelm, Sr. 1865-1935. Founded the firm in 1887 in Elmshorn, Holstein; in 1919 removed to Sparrieshoop; he then transferred management to his sons Hermann and Wilhelm as "W. Kordes Sohne". He bred 'Adolf Koschel', 'Adolf Kaerger', 'Reinhard Baedecker' and 'Wilhelm Kordes'. The hybridizer from 1920 was Wilhelm Kordes and, from about 1955, his son Reimer Kordes.

Hybrids of Wilhelm Kordes: 'Ama', 'Baby Château', 'Baden-Baden', 'Cläre Grammerstorf', 'Crimson Glory', 'Dortmund', 'Ernest H. Morse', 'Eva', 'Feuermeer', 'Flammentanz', 'Fortschritt', 'Fritz Nobis', 'Frühlingsgold', 'Frühlingszauber', 'Gail Borden', 'Gelbe Holstein', 'Gertrud Westphal', 'Hamburg', 'Hamburger Phoenix', 'Holstein', 'Ilse Haberland', 'Ilse Krohn', 'Karl Herbst', 'Kleopatra', 'Kordes Perfecta', 'Kordes Perfecta Superior', 'Kordes Sondermeldung', 'Korona', 'Leverkusen', 'Mahagona', 'Maigold', 'Minna Kordes', 'Obergärtner Wiebicke', 'Orange Triumph', 'Parkjuwel', 'Raubritter', 'Rosenmärchen', 'Rudolf Timm', 'Scharlachglut', 'Sparrieshoop', 'Till Uhlenspiegel', 'Wilhelm Hansmann', 'Weisse aus Sparrieshoop', 'Zwerkönig', 'Zwerkönigin'.

Hybrids of Reimer Kordes: 'Adolf Horstmann', 'Ballet', 'Bischofsstadt Paderborn', 'Chantré', 'Cordula', 'Diamant', 'Dornröschen', 'Doctor Faust', 'Elysium', 'Esther Ofarim', 'Feuerzauber', 'Florida von Scharboutz', 'Friesia', 'Goldene Sonne', 'Goldkrone', 'Goldmarie', 'Goldtopas', 'Grande Amore', 'Gruss an Bayern', 'Gruss an Heidelberg', 'Henkell Royal', 'Isabel de Ortiz', 'Königin der Rosen', 'Lichtkönigin Lucia', 'Lilli Marleen', 'Mainauperle', 'Marlena', 'Meteor', 'Neue Revue', 'Oskar Scheerer', 'Peer Gynt', 'Ponderosa', 'Prominent', 'Red Queen', 'Samba', 'Schneewittchen', 'Silver Star', 'Sympathie', 'Tornado', 'Tradition', 'Träumerei', 'Uwe Seeler', 'Westerland', 'Weiner Charme'.

Koster, D.A. Nursery. Boskoop, Holland. 'Anneke Koster', 'Dick Koster', 'Greet Koster', 'Margo Koster', 'Dick Koster Fulgens'.

Krause, Max. Born in Nordhausen, died in 1937 in Hasloh. After schooling and military service went to England where, with Wilhelm Kordes, he established a nursery. In 1919 both were described as "undesirable aliens". He then founded a nursery in Alvesloh/Holstein, which he then moved to Hasloh where he also began rose breeding. 'Edith Krause', 'Elfenreigen', 'Feuerschein', 'Kardinal', 'Louise Krause', 'Max Krause', 'Narzisse', 'Nigrette', 'Oswald Sieper'.

Kriloff, Michel. Antibes, Alpes-Maritimes, France. 'Francine', 'Lara', 'Lucy Cramphorn' (= 'Maryse Kriloff'), 'Manola', 'Wizo'.

Lacharme, Francois. Lyon, Rhône, France. 'Captain Christy', 'Coquette de Lyon', 'Louis van Houtte', 'Salet', 'Victor Verdier'.

Laffay, M. Bellevue, France. 'Amadis', 'Capitaine John Ingram', 'Cardinal de Richelieu', 'Coupe d'Hébé', 'Gloire des Mousseux', 'Henri Martin', 'Lanei', 'La Reine', 'Mme. Laffay', 'Nuits d'Young', 'Perpetual White Moss', 'Unique', 'William Lobb'.

Lambert & Reiter. Trier, Germany. Tree and rose nursery, later Lambert and Sons, founded in 1860 on 2 ha./5 acres; by 1887 had 60 ha./148 acres in cultivation; in 1890 Peter Lambert became a partner and somewhat later became sole owner. 'Kaiserin Auguste Viktoria'.

Lambert, Nikolaus ("Papa Lambert", father of Peter Lambert). 1839-1926, long-time owner of the firm Lambert & Reiter, Trier. He was a fruit tree specialist, but also a leader in rose production.

Lambert, Peter. Trier. 1860-1939. In 1896 began his own rose breeding; developed the Lambertiana roses, perpetual-blooming bush roses. 'Aglaia', 'Euphrosyne', 'Gruss an Zabern', 'Eugenie Lamesch', 'Trier', 'Gartendirektor Linne', 'Frau Karl Druschki', 'Gustav Grünerwald', 'Papa Lambert', 'Mama Lambert', 'Oscar Cordel', 'Goldene Druschki', 'Adam Messerich', 'Goethe', 'Schneezwerg', 'Carmen'. From 1890 to 1910 was editor of the *Rosen-Zeitung*; he later became managing director.

Lammerts, Dr. W.E. Livermore, California, U.S.A. 'American Heritage', 'Audie Murphy', 'Charlotte Armstrong', 'Chrysler Imperial', 'Golden Showers', 'High Noon', 'Mirandy', 'Queen Elizabeth', 'Show Girl', 'Sweet Sixteen', 'Taffeta', 'Times Square'.

Laperrière, J. Champagne-au-Mont d'Or, France. 'Aramis', 'Barcarolle', 'Frou-Frou', 'Magicienne', 'Ma Mie', 'Mme. Louis Laperrière', 'Petit Prince'.

Leenders, Jan. Tegelen, Holland. 'Amber Beauty', 'Faja Lobbi', 'Fiametta', 'Garden Princess', 'Golden Perfume', 'Gruss an Steinfurth', 'Leenders Bergfeuer', 'Leenders Flamingo', 'Summer Perfume', 'Sweet Seventeen', 'Domila'.

LeGrice, E.B. Roseland Nurseries, North Walsham, Norfolk, England. Died 1977. Started working at Henry Morse & Sons, and then in 1920 started his own nursery specializing in roses. A former Vice President of the RNRS and the author of *Rose Growing Complete* and *Rose Growing for Everyone*. 'Allgold', 'Amberlight', 'Bonny Maid', 'Copper Delight', 'Dainty Maid', 'Doric', 'Dusky Maiden', 'Ellinor Le Grice', 'Fervid', 'Firecrest', 'Golden Delight', 'Lilac Charm', 'News', 'Marjorie Le Grice', 'Pimpernell', 'Salmon Sprite'.

Lens, Louis. Pépinières, Wavre-Notre-Dame, Belgium. 'Bel Ange', 'Dame de Coeur', 'Mme. Louis Lens', 'Panachée', 'Pascali', 'Ruban Rouge', 'Azur', 'Jour de Fête', 'Lucifer', 'Blanche Pasca'.

Levavasseur & Fils. Orléans, France. 'Mme. Norbert Levavasseur', 'Orléans Rose'.

Lévêque, P. Ivry, near Paris. 'Mme. Chédanne-Guinoisseau', 'Mme. Louis Lévêque', 'Princesse de Béarn'.

Magyar, Prof. Guyla. Bred about 10 rose cultivars between 1926 and 1939 while the Academy of Horticulture in Budapest. These roses are still grown in Hungary and elsewhere.

Mallerin, Charles. Rose hybridizer. 1876-1960. Varces, Allières-et-Risset, Pont-de-Claix, Isère, France. Was a mine engineer who later turned to rose breeding. His first great introduction was 'Mrs. Pierre S. du Pont' (1929). He named 138 cultivars, and greatly valued the variegated roses. 'Ami Quinard', 'André le Troquer', 'Bayadère', 'Beauté', 'Danse des Sylphes', 'Henri Mallerin', 'Heure Mauve', 'Isabelle de France', 'Magali', 'Mandalay', 'Mme. Charles Mallerin', 'Mme. G. Forest-Colcombet', 'Rouge Mallerin', 'Schéhèrazade', 'Simone', 'Tonnerre', 'Vive la France'.

Manetti, Giuseppe. Director of the Imperial Garden in Monza, North Italy until 1859.

Mansuino, Ada. San Remo, Italy. The niece of D. Aicardi, she carries on his hybridizing work. 'Aida', 'Red Flare'.

Margottin, M. Bourg-la-Reine, France. 'Duc de Magenta', 'Jules Margottin', 'Louise Odier', 'Triomphe de l'Exposition'.

Mattock, John. Rose Hybridizer. 1899-1973. Headington, Oxford, England. Produced only a few of his own hybrids. 'Climbing Fashion', 'Climbing Flaming Sunset', 'Lady Sonia'.

McGredy, Samuel & Son. Portadown, North Ireland. Founded (1880) by **Samuel McGredy (I)**, 1828-1903, who was a dealer in roses, but not a breeder. His son, **Sam McGredy (II)** 1861-1926, is responsible for the present stature of the firm through his hybridizing since 1905; has won 52 gold medals. 'Countess of Gosford', 'Mrs. Herbert Stevens', 'Isobel', 'Mrs. Henry Morse', 'Mabel Morse', 'Mrs. Charles Lamplough', 'Mrs. A.R. Barraclough'.

Samuel Davison McGredy (III). 1897-1934. Also a hybridizer. 'Mrs. Sam McGredy', 'Sam McGredy', 'McGredy's Scarlet', 'Hector Deane'.

Samuel Darragh McGredy (IV). Born 1931, took over the direction of the firm, which, after the death of his father, Walter I. Johnstone ("Uncle Walter") had held. In 1972 emigrated to Panmure, New Zealand, where he continued his breeding work, while the production operation remains in Portadown, Ireland. Among his varieties the most successful are: 'Cynthia Brooke', 'Grey Pearl', 'Piccadilly', 'Mischief', 'Evelyn Fison', 'Paddy McGredy', 'Uncle Walter', 'Elizabeth of Glamis', 'Kronenbourg', 'Händel', 'Jan Spek', 'Ice White', 'City of Belfast', 'Molly McGredy', 'Mullard Jubilee', 'Picasso', 'Satchmo'. The colorful 'Picasso' is more representative of the firm than 'Hand Painted Rose'.

Meilland, Antoine ("Papa Meilland"). 1884-1971. Founded a rose nursery in Tassin-les-Lyons, France. He was not a hybridizer, but a propagator. His son **Francis Meilland** (1912-1958) was not only outstandingly successful as a hybridizer (his greatest successes were 'Gloria Dei' and 'Baccara'), but also as a businessman; in 1947 he founded the "Universal Rose Selection" for the distribution of his registered introductions to various international test gardens. The breeding facility was located in Cap d'Antibes, Alpes-Maritimes. After his death, his wife Marie Louise (Louisette) carried on his breeding work. His son Alfred and his daughter Michele, after her marriage to M. Richardier and the renaming of the firm Meilland-Richardier, manage the "Universal Rose Selection" in Tassin-les-Lyon. Another operation has been established in Heyrieux, south of Lyon.

Francis Meilland: 'Gloria Dei' (= 'Mme. Meilland'), 'Baccara', 'Bettina', 'Champs Elysées', 'Cocorico', 'Carina', 'Concerto', 'Eden-Rose', 'Grace de Monaco', 'Grand Gala', 'Grand'mère Jenny', 'Message', 'Moulin Rouge', 'Radar', 'Rendez-vous', 'Rouge Meilland', 'Sarabande', 'Soraya', 'Tzigane'.

Marie Louise Meilland: 'Clair Matin', 'Farandole', 'Fugue', 'Polka', 'Zambra'.

Alain Meilland: 'Fidelio', 'Papa Meilland', 'Traviata', 'Sonia', 'Pharaon', 'Prince Igor', 'Maria Callas', 'Kalinka', 'Arturo Toscanini'.

Mock, Adolf. Trier, Germany. Rose nursery. Until 1920 the head gardener for J. Felberg-Leclerc; then established his own firm. Has produced only a few hybrids of his own. 'Katharina Mock' (1942).

Mondial Roses. A group of nurseries located near Hendrickx in Maldeghem, Belgium; De Coninck-Dervaes, Maldeghem; Grandes Roseraies du Val de Loire, Orléans, France. Hybridized themselves 'Antonella', 'Bel Canto', 'Caravelle', 'Clair-France', 'Corso Fleuri', 'Douce France', 'Frisette', 'Melisande', 'Rosenella', 'Tour de France'.

Moore, Ralph S. Sequoia Nursery, Visalia, California, U.S.A. Born in 1907. Today the leading breeder of miniature roses, he started growing roses while still in high school. Started Sequoia Nursery in 1937, initially as a general nursery specializing in roses, but dedicated it exclusively to miniatures in 1957. Over 700,000 plants of miniature roses are grown yearly. Has also become involved in the development of miniature moss roses. 'Baby Ophelia', 'Bit o'Sunshine', 'Dresden Doll', 'Easter Morning', 'Fairy Moss', 'Goldmoss', 'Green Ice', 'Kara', 'Lavendar Lace', 'Lollipop', 'Magic Carrousel', 'Mr. Bluebird', 'New Penny', 'Pink Cameo', 'Pink Heather', 'Purple Elf', 'Sheri Anne', 'Strawberry Swirl', 'Yellow Dolly'.

Moreau, Robert. Angers, France. Has bred 123 cultivars. 'Blanche Moreau', 'Capitaine Basroger', 'Commandant Beaurepaire', 'Jacques Cartier', 'Mme. Carnot', 'Mme. Moreau', 'Ponctuée'.

Moreria da Silva, Alfredo & Filhos. Porto, Portugal. An outstanding Portuguese rose hybridizer who has developed 100 cultivars, however most of these are available only in Portugal. Died 1971. 'Manuel Pinto d'Azeredo'.

Morse, Henry & Sons. Westfield Nurseries, Brundall, Norwich, England. A leading propagator of other breeders' cultivars; have also bred their own. 'First Choice', 'Frensham's Companion', 'Limelight', 'Westfield Star'.

Morey, Dennison. General Bionomics, Inc., Santa Rosa, California, U.S.A. 'Baby Garnette', 'Border Gem', 'Fusilier', 'King's Ransom', 'Red American Beauty', 'Royal Gold', 'South Seas', 'World's Fair Salute', 'Temple Bells'.

Mühle, Arpad. Temesvar (located in Hungary until 1918, now in Rumania). Between 1925 and 1930 he brought several of his introductions into the rose trade.

Müller, Dr. Hermann. Born in Zweibrucken; practiced as a young physician in Weingarten/Palz. Shortly before his retirement in 1885 he began hybridizing roses. His first great cultivar, a cross of 'Maréchal Niel' and *Rosa rugosa* (called 'Conrad Ferd. Meyer') was introduced to the rose trade by Jules Gravereaux and Fröbel/Zurich.

Müller, Karl. 1870-1967. Glass artist and amateur rose breeder in Naumburg, Germany where he later established his own nursery, now in the hands of his son Erich. 'Gruss an Naumburg', 'Rosargärtner Vogel'.

Münch & Haufe. Nursery. Dresden-Leuben. Founded (1886) in Bad Neuheim by Heinrich; in 1888 he joined Julius Haufe (died 1896), near Leuben. In 1920 Münch began rose breeding, although he produced only a few varieties. 'Fran Elizabeth Münch', 'Frau Hedwig Koschel'.

Nabonnand, Gilbert. Golfe Juan, Alpes-Maritimes, France. Produced 211 hybrids, only a few of which are still grown. 'General Schablikine', 'Marie d'Orléans', 'Papa Gontier'. His hybridizing was carried on by his son, Paul Nabonnand.

Nicolas, Jean Henri. 1875-1937. Born in Roubaix, France. Went to the U.S.A. He worked first as manager of Conard-Pyle Co., and then became the hybridizer and manager of the rose division of Jackson & Perkins, where he remained until his death. 'Eclipse', 'Empire State', 'June Morn', 'King Midas', 'Miss America', 'Shenandoah'.

Noack, Werner. Guterstoh, Im Fenne 54, Germany. Nursery. His first cultivar was introduced in 1972. 'Baltika', 'Evelyn', 'Gertrud', 'Gütersloh', 'Siglinde'.

Noisette, Louis. La Queue-en-Brie, France. Had a rose nursery in the early 19th century from which 95 hybrids were introduced. In 1814 his brother, Phillipe, who lived in Charleston, South Carolina, U.S.A., sent him seeds of the American rose 'Champney's Pink Cluster', which he had grown for 2 generations. This was the original Noisette Rose which Louis brought to the rose trade in 1819.

Norman, Albert. Wistaria, Normandy, Surrey, England. An amateur rose breeder since 1911, he gave his hybrids to the firm of Harkness for distribution. 'Crimson Shower', 'Ena Harkness', 'Frensham', 'Isobel Harkness', 'Red Ensign', 'Vera Dalton'.

Oger, Arthur. Caen, France. Introduced 95 hybrids which, except for 'Mme. Pierre Oger', are no longer grown.

Page, Courtney. Haywards Heath, Sussex, England. 1867-1947. From 1917 until his death served in the National Rose Society, England.

Pajotin-Chédane. Maître-Ecole, Angers, France. Perhaps the largest variety of roses of any nursery in modern France, possibly the largest in Europe.

Park, Bertram. Pinner, Middlesex, England. Well known amateur rose breeder and writer of books on roses; possesses a large and extensive rose garden. 'Crimson Halo', 'June Park', 'Lady Zia'.

Parkinson, John. Apothecary who wrote on botany and horticulture in London, 1569-1629. In his *Paradisus terrestris*, published in 1629, he dealt with 24 species propagated by grafting or seedlings in England.

Parmentier. Enghien, Belgium. 66 cultivars emerged from this nursery in the first third of the 19th century, including 'Belle Isis', 'Hector' and 'Louise Méhul'.

Paul & Son (George Paul). Cheshunt, Herts., England (not to be confused with William Paul & Sons). 'Janet's Pride', 'Lady Battersea', 'Lady Godiva', 'Paul's Carmine Climber', 'Paul's Lemon Pillar', 'Sultan of Zanzibar', 'Una'.

Paul, William, & Son. Waltham Cross, Herts., England. 1812-1905. Founded the firm, which grew roses, camellias and holly, in 1860. Since 1843 had been a very productive author; the first edition of his celebrated book *The Rose* was published in 1848. The 1884 rose catalog listed over 800 species of recurrent roses, but only 8 Hybrid Teas. His own cultivars include 'Clio', 'Crimson Globe', 'Juliet', 'Magna Charta', 'Mermaid', 'Morning Glow', 'Ophelia', 'Paul's Scarlet Climber', 'Pride of Waltham', 'White Tausendschön'. Chaplin Bros. is the successor to W. Paul & Son.

Pekmez, Paul. Strasbourg-Cronenbourg, France. Owner of the Léon Beck nursery. Founded the NIRP (Nouveautées Internationales de Roses et Plantes), an international association of rose hybridizing firms, in 1963. The firms involved grow and distribute over one million roses yearly.

Pemberton, Rev. J.H. Havering atte-Bower, near Romford, Essex, England. Amateur rose breeder whose best known cultivars are 'Maid Marion', 'Pemberton's White Rambler', 'Penelope', 'Robin Hood', 'Star of Persia', 'Vanity'.

Penzance, The Lord. Eashing Park, England. Has bred 17 cultivars, mostly hybrids from *Rosa rubiginosa* crosses. 'Amy Robsart', 'Anne of Geierstein', 'Brenda', 'Julia Mannering', 'Lady Penzance', 'Lord Penzance', 'Lucy Ashton', 'Lucie Bertram', 'Meg Merrilies'.

Pernet, Claude (= **Pernet père**). Venissieux-les-Lyon, Rhône, France. Founded (1845) a rose nursery which introduced 79 hybrids; only 'Louis Gimard' and 'Baronesse de Rothschild' remain in cultivation.

Pernet-Ducher, Joseph. 1858-1928. Successor to Pernet père, he married the daughter of Claude Ducher (later Veuve Ducher) and so brought the two firms together under the new name. He hybridized 52 new cultivars; since 1887 the important Hybrid Teas have been 'Mme. Caroline Testout', 'Mme. Abel Châtenay' and 'Soleil d'Or' (this began the line of Pernetiana hybrids, also called Foetida or Lutea hybrids). 'Lyon-Rose', 'Rayon d'Or', 'Laurent Carle', 'Lieutenant Chauré', 'Château de Clos Vougeot', 'Mme. Edouard Herriot'. 'Souvenir de Claudius Pernet' and 'Souvenir de Georges Pernet' were dedicated to the memory of his two sons who died in battle in 1914. In 1919 he sold his firm to Jean Gaujard.

Poulsen. D.T. Poulson Planteskole. Kelleriis, Kvistgard, Denmark. **Svend Poulsen** born 1884. Obtained a doctorate from the University of Copenhagen in 1958. Developed the first of the modern Floribunda-type roses with 'Rödhätte', 'Else Poulsen', 'Kirsten Poulsen', as well as 'Danish Gold', 'Ingar Olsson', 'Irene of Denmark', 'Nina Weibull', 'Poulsen's Bedder', 'Poulsen's Pink', 'Rote Ellen Poulsen', 'Rumba', 'Tivoli', 'Toni Lander'. His work is being carried on by his son **Niels Dines Poulsen.** 'Chinatown', 'Copenhagen', 'Pernille Poulsen', 'Western Sun', 'Royal Dane', 'Shalom', 'Heaven Scent', 'Skagerrak'.

Pradel, Henri. Rose breeder in Montauban, Tarn-et-Garonne, France. Produced 162 hybrids; his most noteworthy is 'Maréchal Niel' (1864), which is still in cultivation.

Prévost, J. Rose grower in Rouen, France. Introduced 183 varieties; listed about 880 varieties for sale in his catalog of 1830.

Ribbons Frères. Montpellier, France. Possessed a nursery with 40,000 rose plants, which were cultivated for cut flowers to supply the French court, until the time of the French Revolution.

Reithmüller, Frank. Born in Germany, emigrated to Turramurra, Sidney, Australia, where he died in 1964. Bred 'Gay Vista', 'Titian'.

Rowley, Gordon Douglas. Born 1921. Dean of the Dept. of Agricultural Botany at University of Reading, England. Founded and managed the National Rose Species Collection in Bayfordbury until called to the University; has written many articles on the genetics of roses.

Ruschpler, J. Rose grower in Dresden in the middle of the 19th century. Bred new roses but none are now in existence.

Schultheis. Steinfurth bei Bad Nauheim, Germany. Oldest German rose nursery, founded 1868 by Heinrich Schultheis and his brothers Konrad and Anton. The 1878 catalog listed 1,495 varieties for sale. Konrad's son Heinrich (1881-1935) continued the firm's work. He was followed by his son Walter who in turn was followed by his son Heinrich. The firm is especially important as a grower and distributor of hybrids from around the world, and has been an important influence in the development of rose cultivation in Wetterau.

Slater, Gilbert. Knot's Green, Leytonstone, England. Sent a red *Rose chinensis* ('Slater's Crimson China') to England in 1792; this species is still in cultivation.

Soupert & Notting. Rose nursery in Luxembourg, founded in 1855. The two partners were related by marriage; Pierre Notting died in 1895. J. Soupert (1834-1910) was a leader among French rose nurserymen. His most outstanding hybrids were 'Baronne de Vivario', 'Eugène Fürst', 'Marie Adelaide', 'Mme. Segond Weber', 'Mrs. E.G. Hill', 'Souvenir de Pierre Notting', 'Tour de Malakoff', 'Violacée'.

Spek, Jan. Kwekerijen, Boskoop, The Netherlands. Born 1903. A leading grower and distributor of new rose introductions. He also bred a few of his own: 'Alice', 'Ceres', 'Diana', 'Golden Fiction', 'Humoreske', 'Ideal', 'Little Joker', 'Orange Perfection', 'Rosa Gruss an Aachen'.

Strassheim, Conrad Peter. 1850-1923. From Griedel near Butzbach, Germany, he later lived in Frankfurt am Main. A contractor, he had an extensive rose garden. From 1886 to 1890 he was editor of the *Rosen Zeitung* published by the Vereins Deutscher Rosenfreunde, and from 1894 to 1899 was the managing director. An amateur breeder: 'Frau Lina Strassheim', 'Elise Heymann'.

Strobel, Gustav (Strobel & Co.). Rose nursery in Pinneberg. An outstanding nursery which championed the Universal Rose Selection founded by the French firm of Meilland for the dissemination of new introductions. Does no hybridizing.

Swim, Herbert C. Chino, California, U.S.A. Swim & Weeks. Born 1906. Started as a nursery laborer in 1929. Came to Armstrong Nurseries, Ontario, California in 1934, and soon became involved in the breeding program. In 1955 went into business with O.L. Weeks and formed an outstanding nursery which has developed many new cultivars. 'Hawaiian Sunset', 'Mister Lincoln', 'Royal Highness', 'Aztec', 'Buccaneer', 'Eiffel Tower', 'First Lady', 'Forty-niner', 'Grand Slam', 'Helen Traubel', 'John S. Armstrong', 'Joseph's Coat', 'Matterhorn', 'Montezuma', 'Moonsprite', 'Summer Sunshine', 'Sutter's Gold', 'Tallyho', 'Wildfire'. In 1967 he returned to Armstrong Nurseries, where he remained until his semi-retirement in 1973. The inventor of over 100 varieties, 22 of which were AARS winners. Also involved in fruit tree and camellia breeding. 'Double Delight' is one of his latest creations.

Täckholm, Dr. Gunnar. Born in Stockholm in 1891. Studied botanical cytology and embryology. In 1922 his book *Zytologischen Studien über die Gattung Rosa* was published. This book remains an important scholarly work on the subject. In 1925 he went to the University of Cairo where he established a modern institute of botany. In 1929 he returned to Stockholm where he continued his teaching, but he did no further work with the genus *Rosa*. He contracted tuberculosis in 1932 and died in 1933.

Tantau, Mathias. Rose nursery. Uetersen, Holstein, Germany. **Mathias Tantau** (the father). 1882-1953. In 1906, after his student years, he established a nursery. From 1919 on they grew only roses, and at the same time began hybridizing. He bred about 60 cultivars by 1946, when he passed on the firm to his son **Mathias** who carried on the hybridizing, and created the world-class rose 'Super Star', and the 'Garnette' line of proprietary roses. The outstanding hybrids of father and son include 'Johanniszauber', 'Johanna Tantau', 'Heros', 'Direktor Benschop', 'Tantau's Triumph', 'Karl Weinhausen', 'Käthe Duvigneau', 'Tantau's Überraschung', 'Silberlachs', 'Märchenland', 'Schneeschirm', 'Fanal', 'Schweizer Gruss', 'Garnette', 'Plomin', 'Lichterloh', 'Baby Maskerade', 'Zitronenfalter', 'Dirigent', 'Prima Ballerina', 'Lampion', 'Traumland', 'Vatertag', 'Super Star' (1960), 'Olala', 'Tip Top', 'Paprika', 'Geisha', 'Whisky', 'Erotica', 'Herzog von Windsor', 'Landora', 'Belinda', 'Yellow Belinda', 'Piroschka', 'Mainzer Fastnacht', 'Melina', 'Signalfeuer', 'Duftwolke', 'Konrad Adenauer-Rose'.

Thomas, Graham Stewart. Briar Cottage, Fairfield Lane, Westend, Woking, Surrey, England. Born 1909. Consultant to the National Trust; for some years worked to improve the botanical garden at Cambridge, and later served as a technical consultant to other gardens. A distinguished author of our time, he has written and illustrated *The Old Shrub Roses*; *Shrub Roses of Today*; *Climbing Roses Old and New*; *The Manual of Shrub Roses*, among others.

Türke, Robert. A porcelain painter and amateur breeder from Meissen. 'Turkes Rugosa'-seedling.

Turbat, E., & Co. Orléans, France. Shrub and rose nursery. 'Eblouissant', 'Flamboyant', 'Merveille des Jaunes', 'Solarium', 'Source d'Or', 'Yvonne Rabier'. The total output numbered about 50 cultivars, most of which are no longer grown.

URS = Universal Rose Selection; → Meilland.

Verbeek, Gijsbert (Verbeek, G., & Zoon). Hornweg 109, Aalsmeer, Holland. The founder, born 1905 in Amstelveen, was trained in Aalsmeer and in 1929 started a cut flower nursery; began hybridizing hot house roses in new colors in 1943. 'Bonanza', 'Cordial', 'Dr. A.J. Verhage', 'Edith Piaf', 'Illusion', 'Miracle', 'Modern Times', 'Satisfaction'.

Verdier. Paris, France. Of the three Verdiers (Charles, Eugene and Victor) Eugène, with 222 hybrids, is the most widely known. His introductions include 'Abel Carrière', 'Eugène Verdier', 'Fisher & Holmes', 'James Veitch', 'Mme. Victor Verdier', 'Prince Camille de Rohan', 'Thomas Mills'. From Victor Verdier: 'Baronne de Wassenaer', 'Jeanne d'Arc', 'Malvina', 'Mme. Verdier', 'Vulcain'.

Verschuren, Henricus Antonie. 1844-1918. [1] founded the firm in Haps, Netherlands. Three of his five sons remained with the firm, the name of which was changed to H.A. Verschuren en Zonen; [2] Jacques (1884-1946); [3] Antonie (1884-1920); [4] Hens A. (1885-1947). [5] Andries and [6] Bernard each began their own nurseries, which they later merged as **Verschurens Verenigde Rozenkwekerijen** in Haps. [2] Jacques left, and in 1930 founded his own firm under the name **Jac Verschuren-Pechtold** in Haps; his son [7] **H.A.M. Verschuren** is also a hybridizer. After the death of [3] Antonie and the resignation of [2] Jacques, Hens A. Verschuren carried on with the old firm under its original name. Today, his sons [8] Henricus Anton (born 1925) and [9] Theod. Franciscus (born 1931), manage the firm. The cultivars of [2]: 'Fanny Blankers-Koen', 'Spek's Yellow', 'Katharina Pechtold', 'Orange Delight', 'Souvenir de Jacques Verschuren'. [4] 'Etoile de Hollande', 'Fire Dance', 'Gloire de Hollande', 'Hens Verschuren', 'Orange Nassau', 'R.M.S. Queen Mary', 'Souvenir de H.A. Verschuren', 'Zephyr', 'Zodiac', 'Zukunft'. [8]: 'Centurio', 'Pink Showers'.

Vibert, J.P. Started his first rose nursery in Chènevières-sur-Marne, France in 1815. His initial inventory consisted of 10,000 plants of 300 varieties from the gardens of Descemet, St. Denis. A few years later, in order to obtain a more favorable climate, he moved his organization to Angiers. In Angiers most of the plants were derived from the *gallica* and *centifolia* species, with much streaking and flecking, for which rose fanciers in other countries have little relish. Vibert produced and named about 600 hybrids. His co-worker, Robert, when he began hybridizing about 1850, developed a further 237. Vibert was undoubtedly the leading student of roses in his time. From him we have 'Aimée Vibert', 'Anaïs Ségalas', 'Comtesse de Murinais', 'Gloire des Rosomanes', 'Jeanne d'Arc', 'La Rubanée', 'La Tour d'Auvergne', 'La Ville de Bruxelles', 'Oeillet Flammand', 'Yolande d'Aragon'.

Vogel, Richard. Rose grower in Sangerhausen. (1867-1934). For twelve years worked in the rose nursery of C. Strassheim (see above); from 1902-1927 was manager of the Sangerhausen rose garden of the Vereins Deutscher Rosenfreunde; not widely known as a breeder, but in 1924 discovered a sport of 'Zigeunerknabe' ('Frau Helene Vogel'). Following his death, his position was succeeded to by his son Max Vogel (1893-1949). Max did some hybridizing and developed a line of sports, only a few of which are notable. 'Weisse Gruss an Aachen' (1944).

Von Abrams, Gordon J. Davis, California, U.S.A. 'Coronado', 'Cover Girl', 'Ebb Tide', 'Ebony,' 'Golden Slippers', 'Helene Schoen', 'High Esteem', 'Pink Favorite', 'Red Ruffles', 'Trade Wind'.

Walter, Ludwig. Zabern, Elsass (today Saverne, Alsace, France). Amateur rose breeder who developed 'Ida Klemm', 'Louise Walter', 'Rote Tausendschön', 'Yellow Moss'.

Warriner, William A., Tustin, California. Operated his own nursery and then worked as a rose breeder for Howard & Smith. Has been Director of Plant Research for Jackson & Perkins Co. of Medford, Oregon since 1963. Has won several AARS awards and in 1980, in an unprecedented event, swept the AARS awards with 'Love', 'Honor' and 'Cherish'. Among his other cultivars are 'America', 'Antigua', 'Bon Bon', 'Color Magic', 'Cynthia', 'Elation', 'Futura', 'Golden Gate', 'Jadis', 'Medallion', 'Promise', 'Red Masterpiece', 'Spellbinder', 'Summerwine', 'Tempo', 'Tonight', 'Tosca'.

Weeks, O.L. Weeks Wholesale Rose Grower, Inc., Ontario, California. While still a young boy he started working at the Armstrong nurseries during vacations, and developed a life-long interest in roses. He started his nursery in 1937, but did not start hybridizing until 1955. Although hybridizing has remained only a sideline, selling roses produced by other introducers is his primary concern, he has produced many cultivars. He and his partner developed 'Angel Face', 'Camelot', 'Comanche', 'Mister Lincoln', and 'Royal Highness'. Alone he has produced 'Alabama', 'Arizona', 'Bing Crosby', 'Gypsy', 'Louisiana', 'Oklahoma', 'Paradise', 'Perfume Delight', as well as the 'Talk' series of roses.

Weigand. Rose nursery founded (1836) by Adam Weigand (1805-1851) in Bad Soden-Taunus. He did little hybridizing. His son Christoph (1839-1909) established his own business in 1870 in Taunus, and has developed the cultivars 'Ernst Gradpierre', 'Ruhm von Steinfurth', 'Sodenia', 'Staatspräsident Päts', 'Königin Luise'. His son Ludwig (born 1873) inherited the firm, which became an important hybridizer of new roses in the cut flower trade, in 1904. He developed the cultivar 'Goethe'.

Wheatcroft Bros., Ltd. Ruddington, Nottingham, England. One of the leading English rose growing firms. They do no hybridizing.

Willmott, Ellen. Warley Place, Essex, England. 1860-1934. Author of the celebrated book of plates *The Genus Rosa*.

Wirtz & Eike. Cossmanns Nachf., Frankfurt am Main/Rödelheim. Nursery which has developed a few rose hybrids from sports. 'Dagmar Späth', 'Frau Marie Bromme', 'Mrs. Olive Sackett'.

Wolley Dod, Rev. Charles. Edge Hall, Maples, Cheshire. 1826-1904. His name is remembered for his 'Wolley Dod's Rose', which was derived from a cross of *Rosa villosa* with a garden rose.

Wylie, Ann Philippa. Botanist; emigrated from England to New Zealand, where she worked at the University of Atago, Dunedin. Has published some very important works on the origin and descent of garden roses.

BIBLIOGRAPHY

Modern Roses 6; Harrisburg, Pennsylvania (1965) — Archiv des Deutschen Rosariums. — Dieser Abschnitt wurde durchgesehen und ergänzt durch REIMER KORDES, Sparrieshoop.

Sexual Reproduction in Roses — Its Theory and Practice

Since a practical approach is central to this book we will commence this chapter with the practical elements of rose hybridizing. The scientific basis of plant breeding, which can be studied in any good book on botany, is dealt with in special relation to the genus *Rosa* on p. 178, et seq.

Why is Rose hybridizing necessary? When we read the descriptions of the Tea Roses, the Hybrid Perpetuals and the many other roses which have been in commerce for a hundred, fifty, twenty or even fewer years, we see how, when they were first brought out, they were believed to be nearly perfect in every way. It was only later that they began to show their faults: they did not throw enough bloom, they did not open in wet weather, the blooms hung their heads, the stems were too short, the colors too pale, the scent too slight or lacking altogether, the foliage suffered from mildew, blackspot or rust and in some cases their resistance to severe winters was poor. Surely sufficient grounds to undertake the improvement of the rose.

Today, hybridizing has reached a high standard. This can be said particularly of the noble blooms of the Hybrid Teas with their long-lasting qualities, and most certainly of the Floribundas as well as of the recurrent shrubs and climbers. The resistance of the blooms against scorching by the sun and rain damage is an important step forward which has been attained by many of the newer roses. If the background is not understood, it is easy to take all this for granted. In truth we should see it for what it is, the result of the work of many generations of hybridizers. Hybridizing must always strive to advance. Not everything for which the breeder aims is ever attained; that we shall never see the perfect rose is the reason that the search continues.

To produce a new rose is a relatively simply matter, but "new" is not the same as "better". Early on, most new varieties were propagated in small numbers and then put on the market; usually little was heard of them or they were quickly superseded by the next "new" variety, for they found little favor with the public.

What are the hybridizers looking for? As we have already seen, the universally perfect rose does not exist and almost certainly never will, and, since so much depends on the personal taste of the purchaser, we must look at the particular qualities needed in a Hybrid Tea, for this example, to approach the ideal.

Vigorous growth;
large, firm, shiny, disease-resistant foliage;
stems long enough to be suitable for cutting;
long and sturdy footstalks;
high-pointed or globose buds;
long-lasting flowers resistant to weather damage;
fragrance;
fully-petaled (at least 30 to 35 petals);
still shapely when the flower is fully open.

For Floribunda roses, the criteria of excellence are naturally somewhat different, and the same can be said of shrubs and climbers. We can look at some of the characteristics more closely:

Single blooms are not a good proposition, particularly if the summer is long and hot.

Very full blooms suffer in rainy areas or in periods of heavy rain, the buds refusing to open and balling as the petals stick together; this can also happen with varieties which have long, slender petals.

Many of the crimson or dark red roses are very subject to mildew and must be sprayed regularly every ten days or so to keep them clean.

The lasting qualities of the blooms could well be improved in many varieties.

As far as the "blue" roses are concerned, we are a long way from achieving a genuinely blue color; the tones are still lilac or lavender and it will take nothing short of a miracle to produce the true cornflower blue in a rose.

There is also still much work to be done in the yellow roses. Almost all of them trace their ancestry back to the 'Persian Yellow'. There are, however, other pure yellow species such as *R. ecae*, *R. primula*, *R. hugonis*, and *R. xanthina* which might be used in further developments. Consideration of the possibilities and, of course, a large element of luck could bridge the gap. Non-fading yellows with a longer flowering period and better resistance to weather damage are sorely needed.

Black roses are little more than an amateur's amusement. They have never enjoyed any lasting favor with rosarians as they tend to suffer from every known fault.

The breeding of roses for greenhouse work is another matter entirely and necessarily follows a different course (see p. 117).

The few basic requirements which have been detailed here show clearly that an on-going breeding program is needed and the raisers have to face considerable work and ever-mounting costs. To raise a really top quality new rose generally involves about 10 years' work and an outlay of $120,000, but if it is a success it can return the cost many times over. 'Peace' must have cost Meilland far less and given an exceptionally good return since at least 100 million plants of it have been propagated and sold under license.

The Discovery of the Laws of Heredity As long as the Laws of Heredity and their practical applications remained unknown, it was impossible to speak of any "breeding program" as such. Until the middle of the 19th century, rows of various rose varieties were planted beside one another and pollination was left to nature. The seeds, when ripe, were harvested and sown in the open in a well prepared seed bed as is recorded in many of the old gardening books. The seed was sown in rows 30 cm./12 in. apart in drills 4-5 cm./1.6-2.0 in. deep and were then lightly covered over. During the winter, the beds were covered with bracken which was removed in the spring. The seedlings remained in the bed for two years and were then transplanted.

From the discovery of the sexual system in plants to proof of the Laws of Heredity was a long road to travel. There have been only a few students of the natural sciences who have trodden it.

ca. 1700 The Doctor and Botanist Jacob Camerarius of Tübingen must have guessed that flowering plants were bisexual.

1730 This fact was recognized by Linnaeus and discussed in his essay "Concerning the Sexual System of Plants", but from a purely academic viewpoint.

1761 Joseph Gottlieb Koelreuter published a work entitled "An interim report concerning some recent observations and experiments into the sexuality of plants".

1793 Christian Conrad Sprengel: "Explanation of the Secrets of the construction and fertilisation of flowers"; this work was not appreciated until endorsed by Charles Darwin (1809-1882).

1865 Gregor Mendel: "The Principles of Heredity" (Mendel's Law).

1900 Mendel's work was confirmed by research carried out by Correns in Leipzig, Eric Tschermak in Vienna and Hugo de Vries in Amsterdam.

The Beginnings of Hybridization It is likely that the early rosarians knew nothing of these scientific works, they relied upon a system developed from their own experience. The first hybridizers were French, all from the area around Paris and much influenced by the demands made of them by the Empress Joséphine. It is believed that the 'Rose du Roi', often referred to as the archetype of the Portland Roses, was the first verifiable intentionally-created hybrid.

Comte Lelieur, in charge of the Imperial Gardens, including the Luxembourg in Paris, was very interested in roses. He had made some crosses between the Portland Rose (which was certainly available at the Dupont Nurseries in Paris by 1809) and what was probably *R. gallica officinalis*. The resulting seedling he called 'Rose Lelieur', but the name only lasted a short time. When Napoleon was exiled to Elba in 1814, Louis XVIII ascended the throne and the Count entered his service. The King expressed the desire to have the rose renamed 'Rose du Roi' in his honor, and this was done. Then, suddenly, Napoleon came back from Elba for the famous 100 days until his final defeat at Waterloo. For this short time the rose had to once more be rechristened, and was known as 'Rose de l'Empereur'. After Napoleon's departure to St. Helena it reverted to 'Rose du Roi'. During all this time it had been growing only in the Royal Park at Sèvres near Paris, and it was not until 1815 that Souchet made it available commercially. In England it became known as 'Lee's Crimson Perpetual'.

In 1817, the Noisette Rose, probably a chance hybrid between *R. chinensis*, which Louis Noisette in Paris had sent to his brother Philippe in America, and *R. moschata*, reached Paris from N. America (see p. 82).

In 1817, the Bourbon Roses appeared from the Island of Réunion, which at the time was known as the Ile de Bourbon. For a long time hedges of *R. damascena* had been growing there, and attempts were made to do the same with *R. chinensis*. After some time, Mons. Bréon, in charge of the Botanic Gardens, came to the conclusion that a natural cross had occurred between the two roses. He sowed some seeds and from them obtained the variety known as 'Rose Edouard'. He sent seeds of this to Monsieur Jacques, head gardener to the Duc d'Orléans in Paris, and it was from this second generation that the Bourbon Roses were raised. (See p. 81).

Just to what extent crosses were planned, as opposed to letting nature take its course, among roses growing in the open between the years 1810 and 1860 is very difficult to determine accurately; very few of the growers of the time ever gave details of parentage. After 1860 it became the practice to give such particulars. Even though it must be admitted that many good varieties of roses appeared at that time, it must also be remembered that at least 90% of them were quite short-lived. From those days only 'Général Jacqueminot' and 'Sénateur Vaisse', as well as the Tea roses 'Devoniensis', 'Mme. Bravy', 'Souvenir d'Elise', and a few others, are still extant. In the following years both taste and demand

underwent changes; among the important new varieties which became available were: 'Alfred Colomb', 'Charles Lefebvre', 'Duke of Wellington', 'Fisher & Holmes', 'Marie Baumann', 'Prince Camille de Rohan' and, the rose miracle of its day, the Tea rose 'Maréchal Niel'.

In the section devoted to the origin of the garden rose (see p. 67), the development of the individual classes or groups can be closely followed, so it is unnecessary to amplify further here.

L. Simon and P. Cochet (1906) made a list of all the roses which had been introduced by that time; from 1810 to 1904 there were no less than 11,016 varieties! All are shown with details of class, grower, year of introduction, color and other details. The number of new varieties introduced in any one year varied enormously; nineteen times it was over 100 (1899 was even 150), while in fifteen years it dropped to less than 10. 1827 was the first year that more than 100 new varieties were put out, the number was actually 116; the next time was

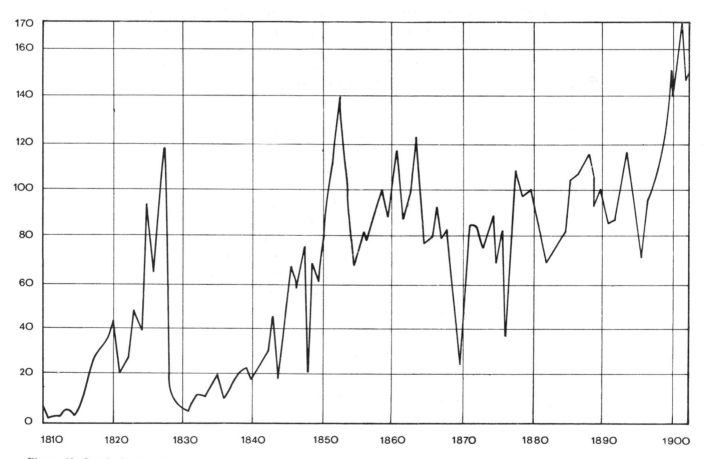

Figure 69. Graph showing the number of new roses raised and registered in France between 1810 and 1902.   (Original)

1851. More precise details can be gleaned from the graph (Fig. 69).

These 11,000 hybrids were produced by 182 growers, of whom 135 were French (if Alsace Lorraine is included). The nationalities of the other raisers were as shown in the following table; the better known are individually named.

12 Great Britain. (Paul, Bennett, Cant, Lord Penzance, Veitch & Turner)
11 U.S.A. (Conard and others)
9 Germany (Lambert)
3 Belgium (Parmentier, Singer & Robichon)
2 Ireland (Dickson)
2 Luxembourg (Soupert & Notting and Ketten)
1 Italy (Brauer)
1 Canada (Walsh)
1 Holland (Verschuren)
1 Portugal (Da Costa)
1 Russia (Freundlich)
1 Spain (Pries)

The French were the most prolific producers of new cultivars; no less than 14 hybridizers introduced 100 or more varieties, for example:

Vibert, Angers	600
Laffay, Bellevue (Paris)	488
Robert, Angers	237
Eugène Verdier, Paris	222
Nabonnand, Golfe Juan	211
Mieillez, Esquermes	188
Prévost, Rouen	183
Lévêque & Fils, Ivry	174
Pradel, Montauban	162
Moreau & Robert, Angers[1]	124
Liabaud, Lyon	122
Vigneron, Orléans	114
Fontaine, Clamart	102
Robert & Moreau, Angers[1]	102

Only two other growers could come up with such impressive figures and these were:

Soupert & Notting, Luxembourg	182
W. Paul & Son, Waltham Cross, England	107

In conclusion, let us look at rose breeding in N. America. At the end of the 18th century only four rose species were known to the botanists in N. America and knowl-

[1] When the son-in-law Robert took over the firm, he changed the name around.

edge, even of these, was incomplete. This is undoubtedly why no one experimented with them. In addition, much of the territory to which they were indigenous was Indian country, and therefore not without its dangers. Further, European hybridizing, using *R. chinensis* with *R. gallica* and *R. centifolia*, etc., was very active and, as we know today, the use of the American species would not have produced any useful results in association with the European garden roses.

Today, however, there are several hundred breeders in the U.S.A. and consequently this nation stands at the very summit of rose breeding where more and more research is being put into the Asiatic and European species and their descendants, the garden roses.

Before 1930 rose breeding in the U.S.A. was in its infancy, as indeed were all forms of plant hybridization. Most of the new roses were imported from Europe where the production of novelties was already in the second, third or even fourth generation of some families. When the law on Plant Protection was passed, rose breeding really began to develop. Today half the active rose breeders are to be found in the U.S.A., among them many amateurs.

The Life of a Rose Variety This is the length of time during which a variety remains in commerce, and it is highly variable. The so-called "old roses", many of which are more than 150 years old, would have disappeared from the marketplace long ago were it not for a small number of enthusiastic amateurs and for the specialist rose gardens, who were prepared to cultivate them and put up with their weaknesses, especially their very short flowering period. Most new roses do not remain available for more than five years by which time they will have been superseded by still newer roses. Only introductions of really top quality last much longer than that, as can be seen from the following selection showing which are still good commercial propositions:

New Dawn	1930	Dortmund	1955
Golden Rapture	1933	Queen Elizabeth	1955
Crimson Glory	1935	Olala	1956
Betty Prior	1935	Circus	1956
Holstein	1938	Prima Ballerina	1957
Peace	1945	Kordes Perfecta	1957
Fanal	1946	Iceberg	1958
Garnette	1947	Lilli Marlene	1959
Sutter's Gold	1950	Super Star	1960
Masquerade	1952	(Tropicana)	

The basic principles of practical hybridizing

The rose breeders of previous centuries had no knowledge of genetics and the principles upon which it is based. This remains true of many of our modern hybridizers; they have only a rough idea of the Laws of Heredity and yet they achieve outstanding results.

At the same time, a knowledge of the principles of genetics is certainly no guarantee of success, it does, however, make it possible to understand the reason for disappointments and lack of success. That in itself helps to assuage the pain of chagrin and of lost time. Regarding this it may be useful to detail several points:

Choice of parents. In some books on roses we read that the seed parent transmits the habit of growth and the pollen parent the quality of bloom; in others the opposite is stated. This is certainly no more correct when asserted by experienced hybridizers. A study of genetics shows clearly that a rose inherits its qualities equally from both seed and pollen parents. This has been proved conclusively by reciprocal crossings. Admittedly, the case of the section *Caninae* is somewhat different, but this can be left aside for the moment (see p. 183).

When making rose crosses, a seed parent which is known, from experience, to give a good harvest of ripe seeds should be selected. If a parent is chosen which has a reputation for poor behavior in this respect then the hybridizer must indeed be an optimist if he thinks he is going to achieve any worthwhile result; of course if he makes a vast number of crosses, then now and again he will be lucky. However, we know from experience that the ability to crop (i.e. to set hips) is not only influenced by the pollen used, but that a good harvest of well-ripened seed is also dependent upon the mother (i.e. the seed parent). This is very important and should be remembered at all times.

When the hybridizer has a good idea of his objective, he can approach his problem in two ways:

a) He can cross two wild species which have some or all of the desired characteristics. The offspring will show these in the first generation. The grower must now cross these back on themselves (selfing), and will undoubtedly get closer to his goal in the F_2 and F_3 generations; it may take longer if some of the seeds prove sterile. If everything goes well at this stage then he can build upon it with infinite patience, liberal investment and unlimit-

ed time until finally the ultimate goal is reached.

b) Alternatively, he can cross two hybrids which appeal to him and wait to see what comes up. In this case there is a vast number of possibilities of something new, but no one can tell whether the seedlings will be better than the parents; usually they are not. It was in this way, without any real planning, that the roses of the last century were obtained, as well as a considerable number of our modern roses.

Naturally, in time, the hybridizer learns by his own experience. He will come to know which varieties pass on desirable qualities and which undesirable ones (see p. 176).

That the most prominent hybridizers bring out only one or two new varieties a year proves how ruthlessly they cull their seedlings. Only when they believe a plant to have merit do they send it to trial grounds both at home and abroad, where once again it undergoes the strictest tests. If a hybridizer is really convinced that his new seedling is a winner then he must be prepared for it to be proven; mistakes can be made. Assuming all goes well, he can then proceed to quickly develop his inventory of the plant. By taking all the possible measures, which are inevitably very expensive, a new seedling can be put on the market in large numbers in a relatively short time (for example, in three years it was possible to produce more than 100,000 plants of 'Mercedes'), but it must be recognized that such opportunities are not available to the small nurseryman nor to the amateur hybridizer.

METHOD OF SEXUAL REPRODUCTION IN ROSES

Before starting the work of making the crossings, it is necessary to be sure that the two selected parents are both fertile; sterility is a constant problem and makes the hybridizer's job a difficult one.

In order to raise roses with double blooms, it is necessary to be certain that within the family tree there are a number of varieties which possess this quality, for without it the breeder will get only semi-double flowers. If single roses are used as parents then, as a general rule, the offspring will also be single. Good bi-colors can be attained by crossing a yellow with either a pink or a bright red but not with the carmine-reds, the purplish-reds nor with the lilac/lavender varieties.

The actual steps in making the cross follow:

● The work must be undertaken as early as possible, starting at the end of May and continuing to the beginning of July, in order to give the hips the best chance of ripening.

● The flowers must be selected as early as possible and the petals removed as soon as they start to unfold, a day before the cross is made; the stamens must also be removed; and can be retained for use in other crosses to be made later.

● The pollen for the cross must be taken from the male parent two days before the petals unfold. The anthers must be cut away, with a small pair of scissors or tweezers, from the flower as it unfolds and kept in a glass container or in paper and allowed to dry, but they should not be exposed to sunlight or bright light. After this two day interval, the anthers will have dried off and be ready to burst and discharge the pollen which looks like yellow dust. Be sure to label the container.

● Pollen which is to be kept for future use should be kept at a temperature of 1-3° C/34-37° F in closed glass or plastic vials in a refrigerator at about 45% humidity.

● The pollen will be put on the prepared bloom, which has had its anthers removed, by means of a fine brush or by dipping the bloom in the pollen. The pollen must be dry and must not be put upon a stigma dampened by rain, dew or spray. Although fertilization is usually accomplished with the initial pollination, it is sometimes advisable in the case of certain varieties to repeat it in order to ensure good setting of seed.

● If the cross is made in the open, then the blooms must be covered after pollination to protect them from insects and any other unwanted form of fertilization. If it is done under glass, then this is not necessary; the greenhouse can be kept insect-free.

● Every individual bloom which has been pollinated must now be numbered and entered in a register. For every pollen parent a separate brush should be used and this must be cleaned after use in alcohol, paint thinner or mineral spirits so that any remaining grains of pollen are removed.

● If the blooms are prepared on the day before polli-nation by the removal of anthers and petals, then on the following day a secretion is formed on the stigmas to which the grains of pollen will adhere. This secretion attracts the pollen grains and also assists the rapid development of the pollen tube which, in a few days, will pass through the stigma and enter the ovary. Fertilization is now complete and after about two weeks the hips should be recognizable and start to swell. The paper cup or plastic bag used for pollination in the open may now be removed. If pollination was unsuccessful, the hips will soften, turn black or a greenish-yellow and should be cut off. Nothing needs to be done to the remaining hips.

● The seeds are ripe when the hip turns orange or yellow. In the open they must be gathered before the first frosts; it is best to cut the whole stem carrying the hips and put it indoors in a glass of water, giving it a little more time to ripen off. Under glass it is possible to delay this until November. The hips must be opened up, the seeds taken out and cleaned, and then, in about two weeks, stored in a cool, moist place. The number of seeds found in each hip varies enormously with the variety, ranging from just a few to 50 or more; they can be large or small in size and can cling to the hip or fall from it. In species with red or orange hips, the seeds are white or pale yellow, but varieties with black or dark brown hips always have pinkish seeds.

● Before sowing, the seeds may be immersed in water and well rinsed to remove any hairs clinging to them. It is a general rule that any seeds which float are empty and can be thrown away.

● In December the first sowings can be made under glass. The amateur can do this in a frame, but must wait until March. The seedbeds must be very carefully prepared. The trays on the greenhouse bench must have at least 15 cm./6 in. of really rich sterilized compost covered with a 2 cm./0.8 in. layer of coarse sand. Drills will then be made in the sand about 5 cm./2 in. apart, into which the seeds will be sown individually. They are then pressed down with the finger so that they rest just on the top of the compost.

Instead of preparing the compost oneself, a commercial brand containing the necessary nutrients can be used, but in this case the seedlings, when they have grown four to six leaves, will have to be fed weekly with nitrophosphate. Generally speaking the seedbeds must be kept moist, especially when the young plants are germinating.

● For two months after sowing the temperature in the beds must be maintained at 6° C/43° F, i.e. fairly cool. They must not be allowed to freeze as they would then either fail to germinate or germination will be greatly delayed. Germination will start in February but is very variable depending upon the parents, and ranges from 20% to 50%. At this point the daytime temperature in the greenhouse should be raised to 15° C/60° F. By the middle of May everything likely to be of use will have germinated; anything which comes after that is unlikely to be strong enough to survive the winter.

● The little seedlings have a dark green, or sometimes reddish, cotyledon. Many (often up to 25%) are pale yellow or whitish (albino). They die off from chlorosis and should immediately be removed. The first two or three true leaves are quite smooth, it is only from the third leaf that they become uncinate. Seedlings which have misshapen leaves should be pulled up for they never produce good flowers.

● At this point the hybridizer is eagerly awaiting the first flower. The bud will appear after the fourth to seventh leaf, and the experienced grower will know almost at once if the seedling has any future. Those which produce a single bloom will usually continue to be single, but if the first flower has about 30 petals then future blooms will be fully-petaled. However, only about one in every 30 or 40 seedlings "catches the eye", and this alone is insufficient, for only really outstanding seedlings deserve the time and money that must be invested in them. As a rule, only one or two seedlings in every thousand meet these requirements.

● The complete development of a new rose is a long and costly process. Most of the "successes" by amateurs are never put on the market because their grower cannot produce in commercial quantities, taking out plant patent rights is too costly and because their professional competitors will have varieties which are even better.

All vegetatively produced offspring of a plant retain the genetic characteristics of the original; such offspring form a pure unadulterated line or "clone", as it is called. Thus, all vegetatively produced roses are clones. Each generation retains all the characteristics of the original parent until the line is broken either by a mutation (sport) or genetic reproduction (e.g. the sowing of seed).

Testing the germinative quality of the Pollen One very simple method of testing the germinative quality of the pollen has been practiced in breeding research on fruit for several decades; this can also be applied in the case of rose pollen.

Nothing more than distilled water and cooking sugar is needed, from which a 20% sugar solution is made. To do this, put 10 g./0.35 g. of sugar with 50 cc./3 cu. in. of distilled water in a small, clean vessel. This quantity is sufficient for several experiments since it is only used a few drops at a time. It should not, however, be kept longer than one week, for mold will quickly develop.

A head of bloom should be cut the day before from the rose to be tested and put in a vase without water, indoors. Shake a little of the pollen onto a slide and place a drop of the sugar solution on the pollen with a glass rod. Put on the top half of the slide and carefully press the two halves together. Instead of the glass cover another slide can be used and, before affixing this, a thin ring of lanolin drawn around the pollen, so that germination proceeds under airtight conditions. It is important not to forget to provide the slide with a seal to keep the air out, and to label it.

At a normal temperature of 20° C/68° F the pollen grains, which are initially oval like ears of wheat, will quickly swell, becoming spherical, and start to germinate. After about four hours, germination will be complete and the length of the germination tubes in the pollen sac will have increased to 30 to 50 times the original diameter of the pollen grains. It is hardly necessary to count the number of pollen grains which have germinated; under a microscope or even with a strong magnifying glass it is easy to see whether the pollen has

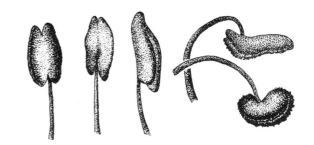

Figure 70. Complete anthers (enlarged); left, from the front, back and side; above, during the pollen dispersal; below, after the pollen has fallen. (after G. Krüger)

Figure 71. Rose pollen; above left, three grains seen from the front and beside them the rear view; in the center, two seen from above; lower row, six defective grains of pollen. 600 ×. (after G. Krüger)

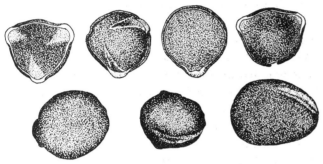

Figure 72. Grains of pollen from *R. pimpinellifolia* stained in a methylene solution; below after settling on the stigma. 600 ×. (after G. Krüger)

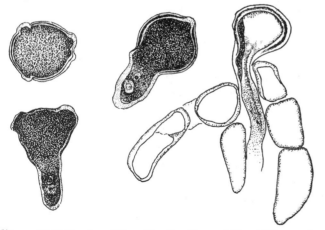

Figure 73. Pollen from 'Mme. Caroline Testout' 48 and 72 hours after falling from the anthers. 600 ×. (after G. Krüger)

germinated very well, well or badly. Naturally, this is partially dependent upon the time of year in which the crosses are going to be made, the usual time being June.

A "Trick" with the use of Gibberellins Research done by E.F. Allen in 1966 showed that the yield of hips from crosses can be improved. Specifically, the early ripening of the fertilized hips under glass can be delayed or otherwise favorably influenced. Mr. Allen treated tetraploid rose flowers ten days after pollination with 3 drops of a solution of Gibberellin A3 at a concentration of 250 parts per million (ppm) in a 25% solution of isopropyl alcohol in water; the results were a much better set of hips and a considerably greater number of seeds.

Where diploid pollen (from a tetraploid male parent) was used, the set was 100%. Blooms treated in this way gave larger hips which also ripened earlier than those which had not been treated.

It can be assumed that treatment with gibberellins assists in holding the flower on long enough for the slow-growing pollen tubes to reach the ovules before abscission.

Gibberellins must not be applied too soon as this may lead to parthenocarpy (early production of hips in which the seeds are sterile). Application should not occur until ten days after pollination. If the delay is longer, then, because a change has already commenced in the structure of the flower stem, premature abscission cannot be retarded either by the use of gibberellins or fungicides.

The gibberellin solution is only viable for two weeks.

The embryos were all soaked for 17 hours in a solution of 6-benzylaminopurine (10 μg per ml) and gave a rather quicker rate of germination in the propagator. This assessment was carried out by Drs. G.A.D. Jackson and J.B. Blundell at Bangor, N. Wales.

COLOR IN ROSES

In rose catalogs, roses are golden, silver, apricot or peach colored, salmon-orange or purplish-violet, etc. The "blue" tones are given such names as lavendar, lilac and mauve. So far so good. A visit to the local nursery to compare the roses with the descriptions will often show that, in fact, they are quite different. Generally, we shall find mostly red, pink, yellow and white and a great number of variations within this range. Why, then, these extravagant descriptions in the catalogs? There are a number of reasons:

An exact description is extremely difficult; color guides have not proved reliable for roses because the deep velvety tones are not measurable. There is, therefore, no other way for the purchasers than to see the flowers themselves, except perhaps a really good color photograph accompanied by a very carefully worded text. Color photography and reproduction techniques are so highly developed today that our roses often look much better in photographs than they do in reality! However, it can be assumed that a reliable rose firm does not find it necessary to overdo its descriptions. It also must be understood that the grower, working day in and day out with his roses, is very likely to see a new variation in color quite differently than do his clients. He will often see the slightest deviation and happily regard it as progress. It is in this context that his descriptions of his flowers must be viewed as a perpetual striving for further improvement. That a rose is neither truly silver nor gold is obvious, and no one in his right mind would really expect to see the flowers as such.

There is yet another difficulty in the correct description of color and this lies in the fact that the tones are likely to change considerably between the bud stage and the fully opened flower. Many varieties intensify in color as they open fully, and in their later stages become even brighter due to the bio-chemical processes which take place, and which will be discussed in due course.

Other varieties, e.g. descendants of R. foetida bicolor and 'Persian Yellow', such as 'Masquerade', 'Rumba', 'Charleston' and 'Circus', start off with a reddish-yellow bud, which may either deepen or lighten with age and in the final stage turn to pink or possibly a deep red. In the case of the "old" roses which often come in more or less purplish tones, there is a tendency, as the flower matures, for it to turn violet or even grey. It is a matter of interpretation whether this change in color is seen as a peculiarity of the variety or whether it is the regrettable "bluing" of old age. Naturally it is considered a fault in modern roses if they do this. In such cases the change of color tones is unfortunate and a bad feature; but in the case of the "old" roses which often have purple or violet tones from the start, this gradual change to violet or grey is seen as a characteristic feature. Such color tones are not ugly and are much appreciated by many people, especially flower-arrangers.

If we look really closely at our roses, we shall see that it is very rare for a variety to display a single pure color tone. Many blooms are darker in the center and the base of the petals is often white or yellow; the back of the petals may often be either lighter or darker than the inside. Yellow roses often, but not always, become brighter with age; the yellow tone of 'Persian Yellow' remains unchanged throughout the life of the flower.

A color chart for Roses   By 1940 E. Funck and H. von Rathlef had published a method of photometric analysis of rose flowers. Petals were taken from the varieties under consideration, dried, then dipped in water of exactly pH 7. The sample was then treated with paratrichlorethylene. The solution obtained in this way will hold the color tone longer and better than the petals themselves; color filters can then be used to give an exact measurement. This technique is quite complicated in practice and it is not known whether it has as yet been used by botanists.

In *Rosa Belgica* (1967), G. Boesman gave a detailed report on a method of measuring color in roses using spectrometry and reflectance measurement. Unfortunately, this method is so complicated that it can only be carried out in properly equipped laboratories.

The Chemistry of   At the beginning of this century
Color in Plants   this subject was completely unexplored. Willstätter, with his associates, was the first to examine the color components of the cornflower (1913) and the *Pelargonium zonale* (1914).

"Red" as a description of roses in the Middle Ages is very inexact. For example, Gerard in his *Great Herballe* of 1597 speaks of what he calls the "best red" and again of the "worst red".

The 'Rose of Lancaster' was certainly not as red as our modern red roses but was really pink, perhaps somewhat darker than 'Maiden's Blush' and *R. damascena celsiana*. These colors were known to the Romans, for Columella instructed his gardeners to plant roses with "the blush of modesty in their cheeks".

It has only been from about 1800 on, in both French and English literature, that color descriptions approach accuracy. All of this makes it very difficult to identify some of the old roses, particularly the red ones.

Green, the most important and commonest of all the colors, is produced by the presence of chlorophyll. In roses, it rarely appears in the flowers, however, it does appear in *R. chinensis viridiflora*.

Almost as important are the flavanoids which produce a wide range of colors. One group, the anthocyanins, are responsible for pink, scarlet, red, lilac, violet and also the blue coloring in flowers. Other groups, the yellow flavonols, chalcones and aurones are also common, but these pigments tend to be pale and are usually submerged by the stronger pigments, for instance, anthocyanin, in strongly-colored blooms. Anthocyanins are glycosides (both mono- and di-glycosides occur) and are, therefore, sugar derivatives. Their molecular structure can be determined from analytical data and confirmed by synthesis. Initially, paper chromatography was used as an analytical technique, and later spectrophotometry was developed as a further refinement.

As a rule, the anthocyanins are responsible for the reds in plants, as has been said, but there are certain exceptions which should be briefly mentioned. The red in tomatoes is due to lycopene, a carotenoid with a color range from orange-yellow to red. The commonest carotenoid in plants is the yellow β-carotene, discovered by Mohren in 1831. Three anthocyanidin pigments and their structures will be discussed here (anthocyanidins are anthocyanins without the sugar component). These pigments, which are responsible for the whole range of colors from blue to red, only differ in the degree of hydroxylation of the B-ring.

Fig. 74 shows the molecular structure of the most important and commonest pigments, and indicates their grouping into parallel series, anthocyanidins (red) and flavonols (yellow). The three in each series of the illustrated groups show, in their structure, an increasing number of hydroxyl (-OH) groups.

In the case of the species roses, the color scale runs from pink, purple and scarlet to white, pale yellow and clear yellow; in chemical terms, the flowers with the pink and red tones contain the anthocyanidin cyanidin, and those in the yellow range contain flavonol.

Until 1930, all the color tones in roses were a combination of these two groups of pigments, the orange and bi-color tones a mixture of the two, while the pure, unfading scarlets and yellows contained pigments of one or other group.

In 1930, a completely new anthocyanidin known as pelargonidin appeared giving red with a yellow base (orange-scarlet), which was present in the varieties 'Gloria Mundi' and 'Paul Crampel' (both diploid), and which later was particularly emphasized in 'Independence' (tetraploid). The existence of pelargonidin in species roses is unknown, though, of course, it is found in *pelargonium*.

Cyanidin appears in the carmine and magenta parts of a plant. Cyanin contains two sugar molecules and cyanidin. Cyanidin is itself close to pelargonidin and is the pigment typically found in red roses.

Blue Pigment in Roses. Although no really blue rose exists, there is a certain amount of blue coloration in many roses. Hitherto it has proved impossible to eliminate the blue from the red pigment, which is unfortunate as the blue does not fade as quickly as the red and yellow. The result is that many pink and red roses, as

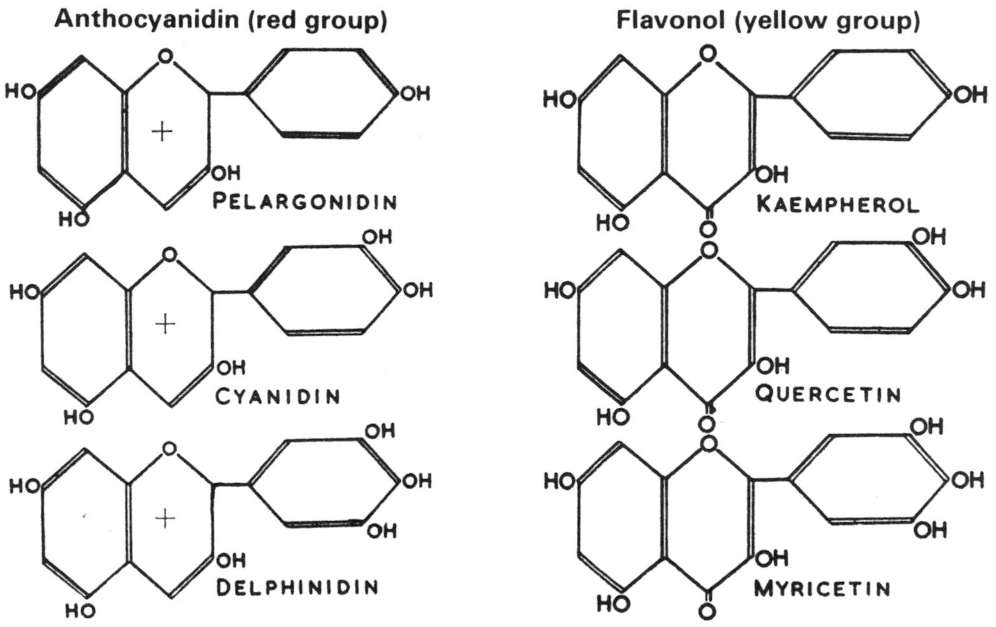

Pelargonidin first appeared in rose breeding in 1930.
Delphinidin has not been found in roses.

Figure 74. Summary of the pigments in roses. (from J. Harborne & G. Rowley, "In Quest of Blue Roses", *Gardener's Chronicle* 1958: 427)

they fade, turn an ugly shade of violet or magenta.

As to whether or not a rose fades in an attractive way appears to depend upon the amount of blue pigment in the petals while it is still in bud form. However, there are genes which appear to control the degree of fading of the red and yellow pigments. If they do not fade, or do so slowly, then a bloom can retain its original color tones through its entire life (P.H. Wright, *ARA.* 1960: 114).

Chemical research has shown that a component in the blue coloring in flowers, the purple pigment delphinidin, is absent from the genus *Rosa*; until now roses have only displayed dull purple or lilac tones.

Natural modification of the carmine-red pigment, cyanin, by some still unidentified flavonol, is undoubtedly responsible for the pinkish-lilac and purple color tones to be seen in, for example, 'Reine des Violettes', the "blue" coloring of which has not yet been surpassed.

Delphinidin appears in the blue or lilac tones in plants. These colors can arise in various other ways: a) through an admixture of anthocyanin with metallic substances such as iron, aluminum and magnesium; b) as a result of the anthocyanin being swamped with other color agents; or c) as a result of the pH value of the plant sap being lowered.

After more than 15 years of hybridizing, R.S. Moore considers that the lavender colors exhibited in his strain of lavender ("blue") roses derive from a combination of magenta and yellow.

Later research on these color components was chiefly carried out in America and England, as is the case today. This situation is well illustrated by J.T.A. Proctor (1970), from which a few short extracts relating to roses follow (the original work covers a much wider field).

Bate-Smith (in *Sci. Proc. Roy. Dublin Soc.* 27: 165-176. 1956) stated that ellagic acid is present in the subfamily *Rosoideae* to which the genera *Rosa, Rubus, Potentilla,* etc. belong, but not in the other sub-families (*Spiraeoideae, Pomoideae* and *Prunoideae*). Ellagic acid may be converted to delphinidin through gallic acid. Although the research was done on leaves rather than on petals, this does not alter the fact that a basis exists for the formation of delphinidin in *Rosoideae*.

In 1957, the Indian chemists, Gupta, Pankajahani and Seshadri thought they had found the flavonol, myricetin, in some roses, notably 'Una Wallace'. Structurally myricetin is closest to delphinidin, which has

not yet been found in roses. Unfortunately, when their experiments were repeated at the John Innes Horticultural Institute in 1958, it was found that the Indian chemists were mistaken and that no myricetin could be detected in any of the rose petals examined. In the same way, no delphinidin was found in any of the purple or lavender roses which were available in 1958. The conclusion was, therefore, that in all probability the "lilac coloring" was due to a change of color in the cyanidin brought about by chemical modification in the petals. It is just possible, however, that by prolonged and careful selection a pure blue rose may emerge one day.

J.B. Harborne, in 1958, (*Biochem. Journ.* 1958: 70) showed that in many garden flowers myricetin and delphinidin were present together. If, therefore, pelargonidin could appear by a chance mutation in rose breeding, it is not impossible that delphinidin might do the same, although there is no logical reason for this to happen. Treatment by radioactive isotopes or X-rays have only had a very minimal effect in changing the genes in question.

In conclusion, here are a few historical notes on the blue rose.

Jamain wrote in 1870, entirely on hearsay, that an Arab had talked of a blue rose the color of lapis-lazuli.

Joret, a Frenchman and a very thorough scientist, mentions the same Arab but does not name him; nevertheless Joret did some more research and was able to establish that there really were blue roses. He quoted Ibn-al-Aman, who was apparently well informed, and who explained how the Arabs managed to obtain blue roses: they cut the bark of the roots very carefully and applied indigo for blue, or saffron for yellow, roses, then tied up the incision tightly and replaced the earth around the roots. This alone is the secret; all the stories relating to blue roses fall in the realm of fantasy.

Why the Arabs, who had access to natural yellow roses, did not make use of them is an interesting question. The answer is that they probably wanted fragrant, or larger, yellow blooms.

The blue colorant for hydrangeas is well-known, the pink color of the flower is turned to a lasting blue by the addition of ammoniacal alum when watering; by this means a whole range of tones from light to dark can be obtained. The horticultural department at Cornell University has stated that the "bluing" of roses in the Arab way is possible, but would certainly not be permanent and would have to be repeated annually (*ARA* 1968: 137).

ROSES WITHOUT THORNS

Although for us each rose must have its prickles (the common use of the word "thorn" is not quite correct), Dr. Niels E. Hansen in South Dakota (U.S.A.) thoroughly examined the problem of raising roses without prickles, mostly using *R. blanda*. From his work has come the series of 'Pax' roses ('Pax Amanda', 'Pax Apollo' and 'Pax Iola'), all introduced in 1938 but which have never become very widely grown in Europe.

There are numerous roses with no prickles, or with very few, which can be listed here. More complete details will be found in the description of the species (p. 246 et seq.) and in the "Dictionary of Roses" (p. 303 et seq.).

Rosa banksiae lutea. Strong-growing, shoots unarmed, flowers yellow, small, double and fragrant; not winter-hardy, needs protection.

R. banksiae lutescens. Strong growth, no prickles; flowers single, bright yellow, slightly scented; should only be grown in a sheltered position.

R. blanda. Among the seedlings, which are quite easy to obtain from this species, plants are often found with soft bristles which cannot really be regarded as prickles; profuse growth; as a consequence only suitable where there is ample room for it.

R. canina has a form lacking in prickles, **lutetiana,** but this is very rare and of little garden value.

R. lheritieranea. *Boursault.* (*R. pendulina* × *R. chinensis*). Almost without prickles; very beautiful foliage in the fall (red, orange and yellow). There are two hybrids, **'Amadis'** weak in growth, and the pink-flowered **'Mme. Sancy de Parabère'** which is vigorous.

R. multiflora inermis. Very vigorous; shoots almost without prickles, but carries hooked prickles on the back of the leaves; flowers white.

R. pendulina, or Alpine Rose. The stems are often without prickles, particularly the double form 'morlettii'.

Garden Roses.

Améthyste. *Cl.* 1911. Vigorous. Prickles only at the base with, occasionally, a few on the stems. Violet-crimson.

Cinderella. *Min* (tall-growing). 1953. Without prickles; white tinged with pale flesh-tone.

Duchesse de Buccleugh. G. Only a few prickles and bristles at the base of the stems, otherwise unarmed; bright crimson.

Duchesse de Montebello. G. Vigorous and completely lacking prickles; foliage greyish-green; blooms rosy pink fading to flesh.

First Love. *H.T.* 1951. Admittedly the lower half of the stems have prickles, but the flowering shoots are almost entirely free; rose pink.

Georg Arends. *H.P.* 1910. Almost free of prickles; soft pink.

Goldfinch. *Cl.* 1907. Only the young plants have prickles; with age they become practically free; yellow fading to white, fragrant.

Kathleen Harrop. *B.* 1911. Sport of 'Zéphirine Drouhin'; moderate growth, without prickles, shell pink, fragrant.

Lykkefund. *R.* 1930. Very vigorous; the young shoots lack prickles, but there are small prickles on the backs of the leaves; single to semi-double, fragrant.

Maria Liesa. *Cl.* 1925. Strong growth, without prickles, single, clear pink with white center.

Marie-Jeanne. *Pol.* 1913. Almost without prickles, pale blush to cream; formerly a French hot-house rose.

Marie Pavié. *Pol.* 1888. Without prickles; very hardy; blooms globose, white tinted with flesh pink, fragrant; grows well from cuttings. Was formerly often grown as a substitute for 'Cécile Brunner'.

Mme. Legras de St. Germain. *Alba.* 1846. Without prickles; early; thick, grey-green foliage; flowers white, flat and scented.

Mrs. John Laing. *H.P.* 1887. Upright habit, shoots carrying short bristles, but lacking prickles; foliage light green; blooms soft pink, fragrant.

Rose d'Hivers. *D.* Stems without prickles; flowers pure white with a touch of pink in the center in warm weather.

Rose Marie Viaud. *Cl.* 1924. Seedling of 'Veilchenblau'; very vigorous and almost completely without prickles but the young shoots are thickly covered with stiff glandular bristles which later disappear; flowers lilac fading to greyish-lilac.

Sammy. *H. Musk.* 1921. Almost entirely lacking prickles, vigorous, semi-double, carmine.

Tausendschön. *Cl.* 1906. Very vigorous, stems almost without prickles; flowers large, double, pink, fading later.

Ulrich Brunner Fils. *H.P.* 1881. Very few prickles; carmine-red; highly fragrant.

Veilchenblau. *Cl.* 1909. Vigorous and without prickles; flowers violet with white center.

Zéphirine Drouhin. *B.* 1868. Vigorous, without prickles; flowers cherry pink and very fragrant.

THE SPECIES ROSES IN HYBRIDIZATION

> There are few greater mistakes a plant breeder can make than to assume that a species can be passed over as a parent because it has little decorative value. We may have a species which in itself is quite useless as a garden plant but which possesses one very good feature that is lacking in its more ornamental relatives. Such a plant used in a cross may be the starting point for striking improvements. (W.J.C. Lawrence, see G. Rowley, *Rose Ann.* 1955 37-40.)

Stagnation. The continual crossing and re-crossing of the Hybrid Teas on the basis of HT × HT × HT = OK (taken from G. Rowley, *The Experimental Approach to Rose Breeding*) courts the danger of stagnation if fresh blood is not introduced from time to time. Remember what wonderful qualities came from the beautiful *R. foetida* alone.

Only about 5% of the known species appear in the main breeding lines, and very few of these form the bulk of the plants used, and then only within a narrow range. Hurst (1941) draws our attention to the influence which just four clones of *R. chinensis* have had on garden roses since it reached Europe from China in the last quarter of the 19th century.

Hybridizing with the species also opens up the possibility of greater resistance to frost, drought and disease by crossing with our modern garden roses; from this we might achieve new combinations of genes and, in turn, new types of roses.

In sowing seeds of the species it is usually necessary to wait from three to six years for them to bloom, while in the case of the ordinary garden roses it is only two years, because the latter were selected from plants that flower early and all through the season. Consequently, it is much easier to obtain new varieties from existing hybrids than from making crosses with the species. This is one reason the hybridizers have been reluctant to work with the latter.

What are the qualities transmitted by the species? The following examples come from the work of American and English hybridizers but have been very widely scattered through the literature on the subject; they are collected here in the hope of encouraging a new start in this direction.

In contrast to the American and Asiatic roses, the European varieties, especially the section *Caninae*, are polymorphous which, according to modern thought, is explained by their particular cellular morphology.

Flower color, and its inheritance, is especially important to the breeder, but this has not been sufficiently researched in the case of the diploid species.

Among American species, there are diploids, tetraploids and hexaploids, most of which have a magenta tint to the petals and "blue" as the flower fades.

Magenta was discovered to be a genetic dominant by Lammerts who named the responsible gene "M" (see *ARA* 1960: 119-125).

The recessive form, a non-fading currant red (gene "m") has not yet been found among American species.

There are many examples of pure pink petals among the *Caninae* (*R. canina, rubiginosa, glauca, kurdestana*) and also in the American roses (*R. carolina, nitida, virginiana, setigera*).

The beautiful salmon or coral pink tones (HCC "bright scarlet") are characteristic of *R. arkansana* and *R. suffulta* and can also be found in the *Caninae*.

R. nitida. Too little use has been made of this species. Results with it could be very interesting because the flowers are not a bluish, but a pure, pink which could have a favorable effect upon its offspring; in addition they do not fade. On the other hand, the footstalks are thin and weak.

The yellow species, *R. ecae, R. primula* and *R. xanthina* could well be crossed with *R. multiflora* and *R. wichuraiana* in an attempt to breed really hardy, yellow climbing roses.

'Persian Yellow'. This variety possesses at least one

very valuable gene which retards the fading of the yellow color, but it does not always pass this on and also, unhappily, has a tendency to transmit its susceptibility to Black Spot. The pollen of 'Persian Yellow' is often sterile, or nearly so.

Strong, stiff shoots are characteristic of *R. glauca, R. pomifera, R. virginiana, R. nitida, R. harisonii, R. pimpinellifolia, R. rugosa*, etc. When *R. rugosa* is crossed with the Hybrid Teas it is quite common to produce plants remarkable for their freedom of flower, however, they also tend to inherit the prickly habit and the short, crooked flower stalks.

Very long trailing stems are inherited from *R. wichuraiana*.

Foliage. Wrinkled leaves come from *R. rugosa*; smooth, shiny ones from *R. wichuraiana*. Both are resistant to mildew and Black Spot, as are *R. roxburghii* and *R. rubiginosa* right up to the late autumn. Scented foliage comes from *R. rubiginosa*. Interesting fall coloring can be expected from crosses made with *R. nitida* which turns a coppery reddish-brown in the autumn. *R. glauca* (= *R. rubrifolia*) has reddish foliage tinted with grey which can sometimes be a shade of intense purple; the flowers vary from a pinkish-red to almost carmine. Crosses might produce these copper tones in the hybrids and, at the same time, the deeper color of the flowers. *R. fedtschenkoana* should also be capable of passing on its silvery-grey foliage.

A plant entirely lacking prickles is only likely to come from *R. blanda* which, in its natural state, is often completely so, but descendants of *R. blanda* are always highly susceptible to mildew.

The tetraploid *R. laxa* Retzius, which comes from the arid steppes of Central Siberia and the Altai district could, if crossed with garden roses, not only produce seedlings of extreme hardiness and resistance to mildew, but also a tolerance to areas with high summer temperatures and low rainfall.

R. suffulta has certain very good qualities: it grows no more than 45 cm./18 in. high, but the roots go deep and consequently it is highly resistant to drought. According to P.H. Wright (1963), this rose will withstand the extreme summer conditions of the prairies when even the grass is scorched. Further, it has the virtue of flowering a second time in autumn, the blooms continuing to the middle of September; unfortunately, the blooms are a bluish-pink in color and fade very quickly. The plants do not tolerate shade well. Tetraploid.

Other roses prefer a shady location. One of the most important of these is *R. arvensis* with its relative, *R. arvensis ayreshirea*, which is free of flower, highly fragrant and likes a shady position.

Anyone who is partial to large, decorative prickles should make use of *R. sericea pteracantha* which can pass on this attribute as can be seen in *R. × pteragonis* (*R. hugonis × R. sericea pteracantha*).

Undoubtedly there are many other possibilities, but first, careful research must be done to ascertain if the selected parents are compatible.

In conclusion here are a few "technical" points.

The Mechanics of Self-Pollination

In the case of many of the species roses, the blooms last only three days; after this time the flowers do not close up at night. The stamens twist over and bring the anthers with their pollen directly over the stigma which is ready to receive them. The pollen anthers ripen before the embryo sac and the egg cells, as was reported by Erlanson in 1928 (*Rhodora*, 30). Most of the pollen will have been discharged when the flowers open, and the insects can then carry it to other flowers in the area which, if they bloomed the day before, will be ready for pollination.

However, some grains of pollen will stay in the withering, dried-up anthers until the third day when the stigma is ready to receive them. The erection and twisting over of the stamens could quite easily result in the self-pollination of any unfertilized egg cells (Fig. 70).

Experiments have shown that roses are often self-fertile. This fact seems not to have been recognized, or only partially so. MacFarlane shows, in Table I (*ARA* 1963: 189), 35 species and 17 hybrids with data demonstrating when and how this process works freely, slightly, or not at all.

The Number of Stamens

The number of stamens is quite variable in species roses:

"few" is 50 to 125.

"many" is 150 to 250 (e.g. *R. rugosa*).

The filaments (stamen stalks) are usually colorless, but can be pink. The outer stamens have mostly long, the inner mostly short, stalks graduating from the outside to the center. This is well demonstrated in the case of:

a) *R. rugosa* (with many stamens).
b) *R. blanda, R. carolina, R. cinnamomea, R. nutkana, R. suffulta, R. woodsii,* etc. (with few stamens).

In some cases all the stamens may be of equal length with the anthers forming a sort of corona. Examples of this are:

a) *R. amblyotis* and *R. macrophylla,* both having many stamens.
b) *R. acicularis* with only a few stamens, but all of equal length.

The Stigmas

The stigmas form a sort of cushion in the center of the bloom and, like the filaments and capitulum (disk), are generally colorless, although in a few cases they are pink (e.g. *R. acicularis, R. palustris, R. virginiana, R. michiganensis*).

Summary of the Color Tones of the Petals.

bright pink:	*R. alpina, R. arkansana, R. canina, R. housei, R. suffulta, R. webbiana;*
rosy pink:	*R. carolina, R. kurdestana, R. nitida, R. glauca, R. setigera, R. virginiana;*
white:	*R. dumetorum, R. foliolosa* var. *alba, R. multiflora, R. pimpinellifolia;*
lilac:	*R. blanda* var. *hispida, R. michiganensis;*
yellow:	*R. foetida, R. xanthina, R. hugonis, R. ecae,* etc.

Size of the Petals

In many of the *Caninae,* the petals unfold while still quite small, and almost double in size during the life of the flower. MacFarlane calls this early unfolding "precocious" and says it occurs in:

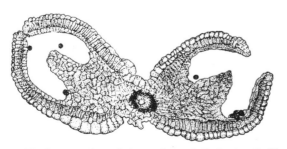

Figure 75. Cross-section of the anthers of *R. harisonii.* 80×. (G. Krüger)

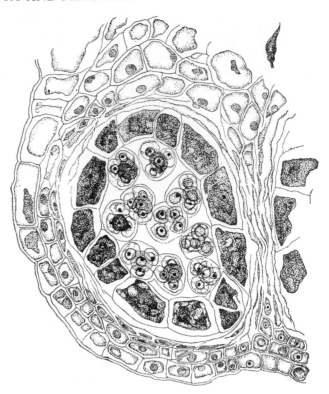

Figure 76. Cross-section of the cell of an anther of *R. foetida bicolor.* 600×. (G. Krüger)

R. canina (a few varieties), *multiflora, rubiginosa, glauca* and *setigera.*

THE BASIC THEORIES OF ROSE BREEDING

In the early Christian period and also in the Middle Ages, it was generally accepted that all flowers were created by God for the enjoyment of mankind. Then Koelreuter (1761) and Sprengel (1793) claimed and proved that flowers were only a vehicle for attracting insects which, by their actions, brought about pollination. As far as the readers of this book are concerned, it will be assumed here that the reader already knows the most important details of cytology (structure and life of the cell) and of genetics (heredity and its variations). For this reason, and also due to a shortage of space, progression of the cell will only briefly be described so that the peculiarities of the genus *Rosa* can be examined in detail.

More than 100 years ago, Virchow laid down the ground rules that all forms of life derived from the cell. This thesis greatly stimulated research, but with the resources available at that time it was impossible to gain any real insight into the life of the cell. It had already been discovered that cells reproduced themselves by division, but a detailed explanation of this was still lacking. It was Waldeyer, some 30 years after Virchow, who observed that certain bodies in the cells which he had stained were more vivid than the others. He named these small bodies "chromosomes".

In the middle of the 19th century, Gregor Mendel (1822-1884) was engaged in his experiments on heredity, in Brünn, the results of which were published in 1866. His conclusions received scant recognition and it was not until the turn of the century that his research was re-discovered and his theory of the "inheritance factor" in the cell investigated; and thus, finally, scientists caught up with the chromosome. Up to this point Mendel's "inheritance factor" was only theory, but when chromosomes were more closely examined it was realized that they were the carriers of genes (the hereditary factor). Many scientists now took up this work and genetics, a whole new area of research, arose.

With advances in the technique of microscopy, it was possible to turn increasingly to the anatomical questions in botany, so that yet another new field came into being, that of cytology.

This work did not proceed quickly because the all-important chromosome counts demanded much time and patience. While today not more than 10% of all the different varieties of flowering plants have been counted, the survey of the genus *Rosa* is extraordinarily good. It can even be said that scarcely any other genus has been examined in such depth. In addition, early research on the rose proved much more reliable than that carried out on many other genera, although, of course, some of the conclusions reached were incorrect.

The first results of cytological research were published in England in 1920 by Heslop Harrison and, a few months later and quite independently, by G. Täckholm in Sweden. Both discovered polyploidy in the genus and also the characteristic and almost unique meiotic behavior of the section *Caninae*.

1921 Heslop Harrison, in association with Blackburn, published the results of his latest research.

1922 Täckholm published his basic studies of rose cytology; these are still accepted as fundamental today. Unfortunately, he gave up this area of his work at that point.

1925-1931 C.C. Hurst, in England, fixed the chromosome count of 674 varieties; this number was increased in the next few years to more than 1,000, thanks to the work of his wife and other scientists,

Other important contributors to the genetics of the rose include:

1929-1938 Eileen M. Erlanson, U.S.A.
1942 Gustafson and Håkansson, Sweden
1946-1948 Fagerlind, Sweden
1951-1963 H.D. Wulff, Germany
1954 A.P. Wylie, England and later New Zealand
1961-1967 G.D. Rowley, England
1969 Klasterska and Klastersky, Czechoslovakia

The extensive work done on the problem of genetics in roses has brought with it knowledge which is applicable to other plants and which, therefore, represents notable progress in both the fields of pure science and practical hybridizing.

THE CELL

Plant cells consist of cytoplasm, nucleus and plastids which are all enclosed within the cell wall. The nucleus, which contains genetic material, lies either in the middle of the cell or near the cell wall in the cytoplasm. The interior of the nucleus is a fluid body called the nucleoplasm which, in addition to one or more nucleoli, contains the chromatin, the material of which the chromosomes consist.

Generally speaking, the chromosomes are only visible during the process of division in the cells, initially appearing as long, thread-like structures which are spread throughout the nucleus. They are always present in the somatic cells in pairs, except in the section *Caninae*, which is referred to below. In the genus *Rosa* there are sometimes seven pairs representing a two-fold multiplication of the basic chromosome count of 7. The total number of chromosomes in a cell is referred to as the chromosome count, or karyotype. When there are seven pairs of chromosomes present in a rose, it is described as diploid. The chromosomes are sub-divided along their length into two chromatids. In some chromosomes, a shorter part, known as a "satellite" is separated from the main body of the chromosome by a constriction.

Each chromatid is a single molecule of a chemical substance known as DNA (deoxyribose nucleic acid) which is involved in the synthesis of enzymes. Activity of these enzymes, in turn, determines the various characteristics of an organism. A single cell has anything from 1,000 to 10,000 different genes. Although the space between one gene and the next is exceedingly small, it is possible today, in some organisms, to draw maps of the chromosomes which precisely indicate the sequence of genes.

Amongst the plastids, we are able to distinguish the green chloroplast from the yellow to red chromoplast (which are also known as chromatophores) and the colorless leucoplasts, which serve as a kind of storehouse.

Plant growth is the result of the division or multiplication of the cells; we must distinguish between two kinds of cell division: somatic division or mitosis and reduction division or meiosis.

Mitosis (somatic or multiplicative division) Replication of the DNA in the nucleus precedes cell division. After several hours, the division of the nucleus undergoes several phases, each of which have specific characteristics:

1. Prophase. In the nucleus, the chromosomes will now be visible as fine threads which gradually wind spirally; in many species roses seven pairs are present, but in the most garden roses there are 14 pairs. Chromosomes of a pair resemble one another in both form and size and are called homologous chromosomes. From this it follows that there are two equal sets of chromosomes or genomes in each cell. At the conclusion of prophase, the chromosomes split lengthwise and then begin to move to the equatorial plane of the nucleus. At the opposite ends of the cell, groups of slender threads (spindle fibers) begin to appear.
2. Metaphase. The chromosomes draw closer to the equator of the cell and the nuclear membrane and the nucleoli disappear.
3. Anaphase. The chromosomes are now in their most compact form. The threads of the spindle are now attached to the centromere of each chromosome

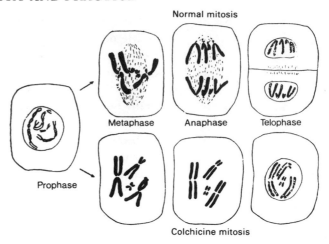

Figure 77. Diagram of the difference between normal mitosis (above) and mitosis which is affected by the application of colchicine (below). Only four chromosomes are shown. Normal mitosis gives rise to two cells with four chromosomes each. Colchicine affects the mechanism of chromosome movement and a cell with eight chromosomes is formed. (from Levan)

and draw them towards the two poles. Finally, in diploid plants, seven pairs of daughter chromosomes will be found at each pole.

4. Telophase. A nuclear membrane forms around each group of daughter chromosomes which have now become invisible. The nucleoli reappear and in the middle of the old cell a wall is built up between the two new cells.

The process repeats itself continually as long as the plant goes on growing. However, occasionally, in some plants, including roses, although the chromosomes divide, the nucleus does not. Then a doubled number of chromosomes are present in the cell nucleus; the diploid cell has now become tetraploid (see Polyploidy, p. 187).

Meiosis or the reductional cell division This form of division only occurs in the egg and the pollen mother cells. The mother cells develop from the somatic tissue in the rose flower and, in the example shown, have the diploid chromosome count (2 × 7 = 14). Meiosis takes place in two stages. In the first, the nucleus splits in such a way that the two daughter cells each have half the chromosome count (i.e. 7 chromosomes). In the second stage, the chromosomes divide as in mitosis and now form four cells, each with the simple (haploid) chromosome count. These four cells are known as a tetrad.

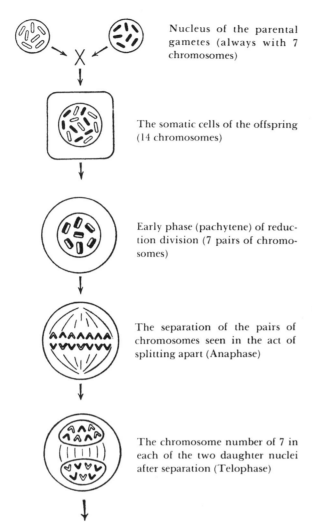

Nucleus of the parental gametes (always with 7 chromosomes)

The somatic cells of the offspring (14 chromosomes)

Early phase (pachytene) of reduction division (7 pairs of chromosomes)

The separation of the pairs of chromosomes seen in the act of splitting apart (Anaphase)

The chromosome number of 7 in each of the two daughter nuclei after separation (Telophase)

Figure 78. Diagram of the distribution of the chromosomes and the nuclear division in the normal course of the reductional cell division in a diploid series. Equal number of comparable chromosomes aggregate at each pole following the division.

Embryo sacs and pollen grains develop from cells of the tetrad. In the anthers, the pollen grains are formed from each of the four cells of the tetrad, and these are later set free when the wall of the anther bursts open. The first division in the pollen grains gives the "vegetative" and "generative" nuclei; later, the generative nucleus divides into two gametes. (Fig. 80).

In the female organs, the situation is somewhat different. Of the four tetradic cells only one forms an embryo sac while the other three are destroyed. On both male and female sides, two gametes (reproductive cells) are formed. In the case of the pollen grain these are the two sperm cells; in the embryo sac they are the egg cells

and the endosperm cells, the latter comes from the fusion of two cells in the embryo sac and is therefore diploid, in contrast to the egg cell and the gametes of the pollen which are all haploid.

Fertilization Before they leave the anthers the nuclei divide so that each pollen spore now has two nuclei. These pollen grains can now be put upon the stigma either by insects or by the hybridizer's brush (see p. 169). The stigma releases a secretion which firmly adheres to the grains of pollen and encourages germination of the pollen tube. All the generative grains of pollen on the stigma now pass through the style down into the ovary and along its sides until they reach the ovule. There the pollen tube penetrates the nucellus (the hard, outer covering of the embryo sac) and, entering the sac itself, penetrates, not into the center of the egg-cell, but to one end where the egg-cell and synergi-

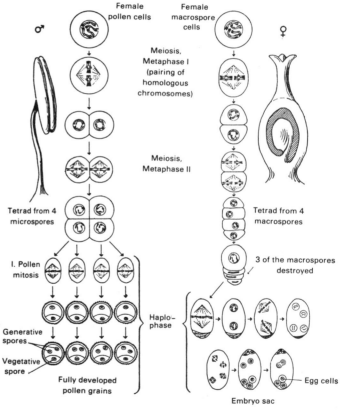

Figure 79. The formation of pollen grains and embryo sacs in the more advanced plants. The development of the male is shown at left; that of the female at right. In both cases, meiosis results in the formation of a tetrad of cells, each of which have half the somatic chromosome count. Pollen grains and embryo sacs develop from cells of the tetrad. (Based on Winchester and Müntzing).

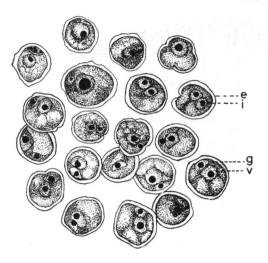

Figure 80. Cross section of rose pollen grains from ripened anthers. e. Extine, i. Intine, g. Generative spore, v. Vegetative spore. 610×. (from Krüger)

dae are located. There it discharges the gametes. The pollen tube then degenerates. (see Figs. 81-83.)

Towards the apex of the pollen tube lies the vegetative nucleus, closely followed by the two sperm cells which were formed by division of the generative nucleus. All three nuclei reach the embryo sac where one of the pair of gametes penetrates the egg-cell and unites with its nucleus, completing fertilization. The second male gamete (sperm cell) travels to the center of the embryo sac where the endosperm nucleus is located. This gamete fuses with the endosperm nucleus to form a triploid nucleus. So, in effect, there are two separate fertilization processes; this applies to all plants where the seeds are enclosed within an ovary (i.e. the Angiosperms).

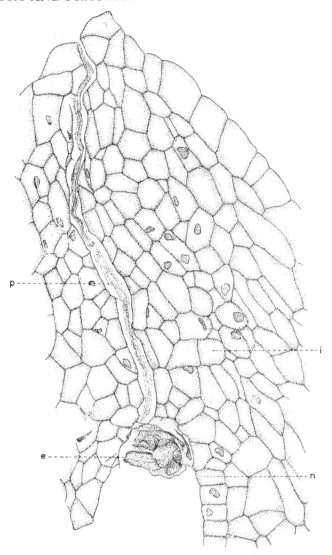

Figure 82. The course of the pollen tube from the integument to the position of the egg in *R. canina*, drawn in longitudinal section. p. Pollen tube. e. Position of the egg. n. Edge of the nucellus. i. Integument. 600 ×. (from G. Krüger)

From the first fertilization, through the union of the two haploid nuclei, a diploid zygote appears from which the embryo develops. The second fertilization produces a triploid nucleus as indicated above; from this the endosperm or nutritive tissue of the seed will be created.

All these events are described here briefly and in general outline, so that they can be more easily understood with the help of the diagrams. Full information on this subject can be found in textbooks on genetics; relevant publications on roses are listed at the end of this chapter.

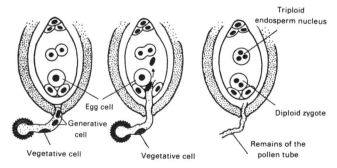

Figure 81. Diagram of fertilization in more advanced plants. One of the two gametes in the pollen tube fertilizes the egg-cell, the other the central nucleus (from Winchester and Müntzing)

182

The Chromosomes We now know just what constitutes a chromosome. What function does it perform? Research conducted with an electron microscope has shown that, apart from the chromosomes, the cell also contains ribosomes, the chemical components of which are now known. It is on the ribosomes that enzymes are synthesized. N. Young (*R.A.* 1963 p. 103-106) has described it for the layman by saying that each individual cell is a huge chemical factory, and that the chromosomes are its Board of Directors.

Most of the species have, in meiosis, only bivalent chromosomes; that is, each chromosome has an homologous partner. In such species 2n = 14, 28, 42, 56; for example, in *R. arvensis* 2n = 14, *R. pendulina* (28), *R. nutkana* (42) and *R. acicularis* (56). Meiosis proceeds completely normally in these species.

The chromosome distribution in the case of the *Caninae* is, however, complicated by the fact that, in meiosis, in addition to an established number of bivalent chromosomes, there is also an established number of univalent chromosomes. These univalent chromosomes find no partner during division. The plants belonging to this group resolve their complicated inheritance in the following way:

2 n	Chromosomes	
21 has	14 bivalent	7 univalent
28 can have	14 bivalent	14 univalent
35 has	14 bivalent	21 univalent
42 can have	14 bivalent	28 univalent
	Meiosis follows the normal pattern, i.e. 7 pairs of chromosomes	These find no partners and remain unpaired.

In the following example 2n = 35. On the female side the division proceeds as follows:

After the first meiotic division there will be all 21 univalent chromosomes and 7 bivalent daughter chromosomes at one pole, and just 7 bivalent daughter chromosomes at the other. Only the cell with the 7 bivalent daughter chromosomes and the 21 univalent chromosomes will develop into a viable egg-cell; the situation with the other polyploids of the *Caninae* is similar.

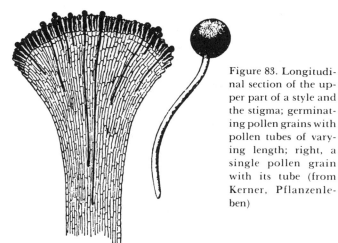

Figure 83. Longitudinal section of the upper part of a style and the stigma; germinating pollen grains with pollen tubes of varying length; right, a single pollen grain with its tube (from Kerner, Pflanzenleben)

On the male side:

a) The fertile grains of pollen contain no univalent chromosomes (therefore n = 7);

b) The pollen grains with univalent chromosomes, on the other hand, disintegrate.

In this way, the basic chromosome number is re-established when a male gamete containing 7 chromosomes fertilizes a female gamete containing 28 chromosomes.

It may be easier to understand meiosis in the *Caninae* from the following table compiled by W.B. Turrill:

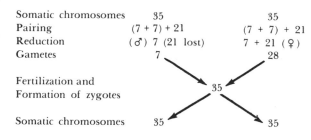

Somatic chromosomes	35	35
Pairing	(7 + 7) + 21	(7 + 7) + 21
Reduction	(♂) 7 (21 lost)	7 + 21 (♀)
Gametes	7	28
Fertilization and Formation of zygotes		35
Somatic chromosomes	35	35

This form of propagation is called "balanced heterogamy". A more detailed and excellent account of meiosis in species of the *Caninae* is given by A.P. Wylie (1976).

In roses there are never less than 14 chromosomes nor more than 56, and always a multiple of 7. When a new cell originates as a result of the division of the mother cell, the chromosomes can be seen as compact or sausage-shaped bodies which soon extend into long, thin threads and finally disappear from view, seeming to dissolve in the sap of the core. They do not actually dissolve for, during the "invisible period", each chromosome builds its own replica to which it is attached. Some time after this process of replication is completed, the chromosomes re-appear and cell division ensues. After a new cell wall has been created, the former mother cell now exists as two new cells which resemble the original exactly.

Until about 1930, it was generally believed that all wild plants would come true from seed; the researches of Eileen W. Erlanson (1934) into the species roses proved the opposite; she found a sequence of anomalies during meiosis in *R. blanda*, *R. carolina*, and *R. woodsii*, etc. At the same time, she discovered a high percentage of infertile pollen in these species. On the other hand, she was able to establish that in *R. acicularis*, *R. setigera* and *R. palustris*, meiosis took a completely normal course and that the pollen of these species was normally fertile.

No apomixis in roses proved hitherto. On this matter a widely held theory can now be corrected — namely that the *Caninae* were apomictic. Between 1944 and 1948, Fagerlind proved in a series of crosses that the egg-cell was always fertilized and that, up to the present time, no certain example of apomixis has been observed in the genus *Rosa*. This conclusion was reached because F_1 hybrids between the species possessed univalent chromosomes very similar to the mother plant and, as a result, postulated that, according to the chromosome number, two, three, four or five ♀ genomes had united with one ♂ genome.

The species with balanced heterogamy will possess several homologous genomes; the species would therefore be a result of autopolyploidy and not of artificial crosses.[1] But exactly why the homologous chromosomes do not pair up (asyndesis) has not been satisfactorily resolved. The multiplicity of form of many rose species particularly the *Caninae*, which points to apomictic propagation can be explained as follows:

1. *The univalent chromosomes* (they represent 2-5 genomes!) *behave during propagation like the chromosomes of totally apomictic plants;* for no new combinations appear and consequently all the resultant mutations remain constant.

2. In some species various "tribes" are found which are self-fertile; thereby individual groups arise which maintain *the purity of the line* and separate themselves from other such groups by small but constant differences.

3. Hybrids resulting from crosses between closely related species mostly suffer from a *greatly reduced fertility;* bivalent-forming chromosomes are incapable of interchange in the case of close

According to H.D. Wulff, but his view is not held by all authors.

relatives without something additional. Some interspecific crosses between species of the section *Caninae* which produce only sterile hybrids on selfing, normally yield fertile hybrids. (from Hess/Landolt, *Fl d. Schweiz* 2:433)

HEREDITY

If a wild rose produces flowers, which are then fertilized at the correct time, seeds will be formed and in due course new plants arise which will be more or less similar in appearance to the parents. The passing of family characteristics from one generation to the next is called "heredity". Genetics, the science of heredity, seeks to show the rules and laws by which this is governed. The starting point of this science can be put at the year 1900 when three botanists, Correns, de Vries and Tschermak rediscovered Mendel's Law, originally published by Gregor Mendel in 1866, and, through their own experiments, proved his theories to be correct.

It is an important fact that not only the characteristics, but also the genes controlling these characteristics, are inherited. The behavior of the rose in hybridization is highly unpredictable; we do not know which features the descendants will inherit. Some characteristics will be observed upon the appearance of the offspring (phenotype), while other of the parent plant's properties will be suppressed (recessive) and remain concealed, only to re-appear in a still later generation. The following rules will clarify this.

The Mendelian Principles of Heredity 1. The Law of Uniformity. By inter-crossing pure strains (i.e. those which will not change when "selfed") entirely uniform hybrids are obtained. Reciprocal crosses have the same result. This does not apply to garden roses as they do not breed true. This law applies only to the F_1 generation.

2. The Law of Segregation. If plants of the F_1 generation are fertilized by their own pollen, then, with respect to one pair of characteristics, the offspring will be divided into the ratio of 1:2:1 or, in other words, 25% of the offspring assume the form of one parent, 25% assume the form of the other parent and 50% are like the F_1 hybrids; in the case of dominant heredity, we have a phenotypic ratio of 3:1 of the dominant form to the recessive form.

3. The Law of Independent Assortment. This law has limited validity and is concerned with hybrids de-

rived from parents that differ with respect to several pairs of characteristics. It states that the various pairs of genes (alleles) governing those characteristics segregate independently of one another and are capable of re-appearing in new combinations in the F_2 generation.

The Origin of new Forms and Species   In the breeding of roses, new varieties, from crosses made by the hybridizer, are attempts to combine especially desirable qualities. The parents are chosen correspondingly. The qualities, the inheritable genes, are already there, but they are combined in a new way to produce a new variety or form.

New varieties can also arise in other ways, for example:
(a) Mutation (sport)
(b) Polyploidy

Mutations (sports)

If, in the process of division, any change occurs in a chromosome this will be passed on, after division, into each of the daughter cells. In this way it is possible for changes in morphology (different flower color, different leaf shape, different growth habit) or physiology (recurrent instead of once-flowering, change in the degree of hardiness, etc.) to take place which in one or more ways differs from the original cultivar. Such a deviation is called "mutation"; in the horticultural world the English term "sport" is commonly used.

S.G. Saakov (1960) demonstrated that bud-mutation is a very important factor in the origin of new varieties in roses; in particular, the appearance of the "climbing sports" (Saakov refers to them as "whip-like growths") is very common. Even by 1907, P.J.S. Cramer had described more than 100 rose varieties which had arisen in this way in his "Critical Review of the known cases of bud-mutation". These somatic mutations are quite common in horticulture generally and are in no sense confined to roses.

It is well known that the Moss Rose came about as a sport of *R. centifolia* and had certainly been discovered by 1696. According to Hurst (1922) there had been about 60 "moss" sports in a period of about 230 years; since then no new ones have appeared.

Saakov established that, of 10,368 rose varieties, no less than 297 varieties had thrown sports, and they had produced a total of 787 according to Jäger's *Dictionary of Roses*, 1936. The individual groups are shown to behave quite differently as the accompanying table shows. At the top of the list stand the Hybrid Teas to which the Pernetiana Roses must be added, arriving at a total of 440 sports (see note on p. 195).

Table showing the number of rose varieties which are in cultivation as a result of bud-mutation. (S.G. Saakov)*

Rose Group	Dates of Cultivation	Time Span (Years)	Total of Varieties	Number of Varieties Producing Sports	Ratio of sporting Varieties to Total (%)	Total Number of Sports	% Ratio of all Varieties
1. Tea	1810-1935	125	1,456	32	2.19	67	4.31
2. Bourbon	1817-1935	118	503	7	1.39	13	2.59
3. China	1818-1935	117	822	8	0.97	11	1.34
4. Noisette	1828-1935	107	217	2	0.92	3	1.38
5. Hybrid Perpetual**	1843-1935	93	2,444	42	1.71	70	2.86
6. Hybrid Tea	1867-1935	68	3,270	127	3.88	329	10.06
7. Polyantha	1879-1935	56	441	27	6.1	133	30.15
8. Hybrid *wich*	1887-1935	48	271	11	4.06	18	6.64
9. Hybrid multiflora	1804-1935	131	298	6	2.01	29	9.73
10. Hybrid *rugosa*	1784-1935	141	130	2	1.53	3	2.30
11. Pernetiana	1900-1935	35	416	33	7.93	111	26.68
			10,268	297		787	

* Figures calculated up to 1936.
** The first two Hybrid Perpetuals to be raised were 'Baronne Prévost' 1842 and 'La Reine' 1843. 'La Reine' was officially recognized as a Hybrid Perpetual. 'Baronne Prévost' produced its first sport in 1854 and 'La Reine' in 1864.

What causes the sudden appearance of these mutations? The answer is still not satisfactorily resolved; Saakov believes that they occur as the result of a complicated hybridogene formation. What can be stated is that the rose classes which have a complicated ancestry, such as the Hybrid Teas, the Floribundas and the Polyanthas, seem to be more likely to throw "sports", whereas species like *R. multifora* and *R. rugosa* have very few.

The various types of mutation have been described by S.C. Harland (1966) as follows:

Change of flower color, quite a common occurrence;

Uniformly colored blooms become bi-colored or striped;

Less vigorous become stronger and vice versa;

Double blooms may revert to single;

Non-recurrent may become recurrent;

Elongated buds may become globose;

A climbing sport may occur;

Foliage color may change;

A change in the armature (either more, or fewer, prickles), common in the case of climbing sports.

Climbing sports occur quite frequently; the reason for this is unknown. In propagating, if buds are taken from the weaker shoots, then the climbing variety is likely to revert to its parent bush type; consequently, buds should only be taken from the long and sturdy shoots.

Ann Wylie has given us some statistics on the frequency of mutations over the years 1926-1950.

During this period the number of introductions was	2,236
of that number the mutations were	411
of these the number with normal growth was	271
and the number of climbing sports was	140

Many mutations are recognized as chimeras; where individual varieties or shoots become dissimilar, in one way or another, through some derangement during mitosis or by grafting. If the differing genetic traits lie in layers, then they are described as periclinal-chimeras; when they are in strips, they are called sectorial-chimeras. The latter chimeric formation is well illustrated by *R. gallica versicolor* and *R. damascena versicolor*, and also in a variety like 'Dagmar Späth' in which the white blooms occasionally produce reddish-pink petals.

As far as the gardener is concerned, it is unimportant whether there is a chimera or not; what he requires is that the variety be stable. This is not always the case. For example, 'Modern Times', which has scarlet petals with white stripes, came from 'Red Better Times', and often reverts to its parent.

Varieties mentioned in this book which produce sports quite freely are: 'Columbia', 'Mme. Edouard Her-

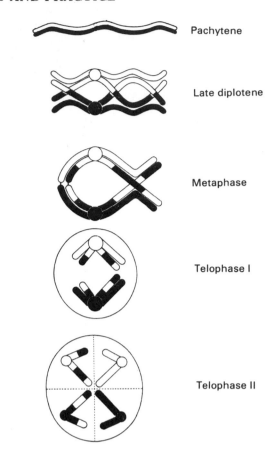

Figure 84. Diagram of the pairing and interchange in meiosis. Telophase II shows the reconstruction between the male and female chromosomes. (from Roemer/Rudorf. *Handbuch der Pflanzenzüchtung*)

riot', 'Orléans Rose', 'Ophelia' and Tausendschön' (see "Dictionary of Roses", p. 303).

Artificial mutations have been attempted by irradiation with radioactive isotopes and by the use of various chemicals, particularly colchicine, a poisonous material contained in *Colchicum*. This is put in a 0.1 or 0.2% solution on the growing tips or on the germinating seed, but thus far without much success. Colchicine produces, after some hours or days, a delay in the cell division; the division of the nuclei into two halves is frustrated and they remain together. Consequently the chromosome count in the cell is doubled and the cell itself is likely to increase in size. Polyploids artificially produced in a normally fertile species are autopolyploids. If, however, the chromosome count is doubled in a sterile hybrid between different species, the polyploid is called an allopolyploid (Fig. 77).

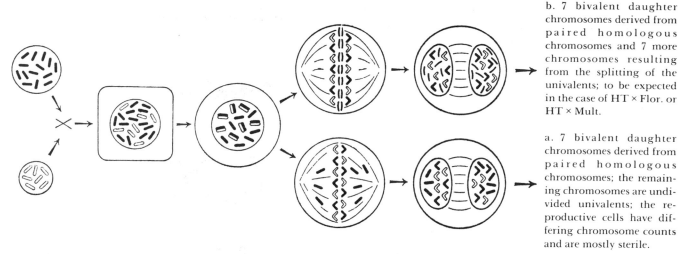

b. 7 bivalent daughter chromosomes derived from paired homologous chromosomes and 7 more chromosomes resulting from the splitting of the univalents; to be expected in the case of HT × Flor. or HT × Mult.

a. 7 bivalent daughter chromosomes derived from paired homologous chromosomes; the remaining chromosomes are undivided univalents; the reproductive cells have differing chromosome counts and are mostly sterile.

Figure 85. Diagram of chromosomal division and cell division in hybrids of which the parents have a different chromosome count but which possess in part equivalent chromosomes. (from v. Rathlef, with alterations)

Polyploidy

When members of a certain plant or animal genus have different numbers of chromosomes which are a multiple of more than twice the basic number, then the genus is said to exhibit polyploidy. Polyploidy was not discovered until this century; examination was made of a few plants which showed exceptional overall growth, and it was discovered that they had a doubled chromosome count.

Polyploidy in roses was discovered in England in 1920 by J.W.H. Harrison, and in Sweden at the same time by G. Täckholm. Both independently came to the same conclusions and published them in important papers. Although Harrison was actually nine months ahead of Täckholm, the credit has always been given to the latter.

They discovered that the basic chromosome number for the genus *Rosa* was seven. Harrison also found that many roses are either tetraploid or pentaploid. He established that every rose examined in the sections *Tomentosae, Afzelianae, Eucaninae* and *Rubiginosae* had 35 chromosomes, that is to say they are pentaploid, while the *Villosae* and some *Pimpinellifoliae* had 28 chromosomes and were therefore tetraploid.

Harrison next turned to the behavior of the chromosomes in the *Caninae* at the stage of pollen development. It was clear to him that there must be irregularities during meiosis (reduction division) in the case of the pentaploids, he also found this in the case of species with 35 chromosomes; that similar phenomena should occur in the tetraploids *R. villosa* and *R. glauca* (*R. rubrifolia*) was quite unexpected.

Thus, as well as diploid roses, there are tetraploid, pentaploid, hexaploid and even octoploid roses; in other words, a "polyploid series".

Every member of this series is moreover "euploid"[2] (i.e., in this case, the chromosome number is divisible by 7) whereas a rose species with a chromosome count which is not a multiple of 7 is called "aneuploid". While hybrids of the section *Caninae* occasionally happen to have aneuploid chromosome counts (Rowley, 1961), they have never been found in other species. The majority, by far, of our garden roses, particularly the Hybrid Teas and Floribundas, are tetraploid, as are many other cultivated plants.

The chromosome numbers of the species roses are shown in the table starting on p. 191. Among the most important ancestors of our garden roses are to be found:

diploid: *R. chinensis, R. gigantea, R. moschata, R. multiflora, R. rugosa, R. wichuraiana.*

tetraploid: *R. centifolia, R. damascena, R. foetida, R. gallica, R. pimpinellifolia, R. kordesii.*

pentaploid: *R. canina, R. rubiginosa.*

hexaploid: *R. alba.*

octoploid: *R. acicularis* (has not been used in breeding up to now).

[2] Euploid chromosome numbers are moreover orthoploid, if the basic number is 2× or 4×, etc., anorthoploid if the basic number is 3×, 5×, etc.

A polyploid series arises as a result of the doubling of the chromosomes without the division of the nucleus. This certainly means there is little more increase to be expected of the higher-numbered members of the series.

In the case of a simple cross between two diploids, assuming meiosis proceeds normally, the result is a new diploid species or variety, of which the descendants segregate according to Mendelian Law. Should they behave in an irregular manner, then the result is either complete or partial sterility beyond which no progress can be made. Finally, there is the possibility that the chromosomes may double, whereby a new and fertile tetraploid originates from a sterile hybrid.

Cytologists have known for many years that tetraploids can arise from diploids as a result of chromosome doubling in the reproductive cells. This happens if the chromosome pairing at meiosis in a diploid hybrid is abnormal; then the reproductive cells (i.e. the pollen grains and the embryo sac) may receive the unreduced chromosome complement just like somatic cells. The resultant diploid pollen grains and embryo, after union, produce fertile tetraploid descendants. In this way, it is probable that the polyploid roses' ancestors were originally diploid. In the course of time it has been discovered that, as a general rule, the lowest polyploid stage is to be found in the area of the original home of a species. Higher polyploidy, which introduces new characteristics, makes colonization possible over a wider area or at higher altitudes.

Triploid roses generally originate in the crossing of diploid and tetraploid garden roses. Today's cultivated triploid roses usually have a reduced fertility because of meiotic failure (Fig. 85).

However, few are so sterile that they cannot be used in breeding. Both the time of year and the environment influence the degree of fertility; this may be expressed in the number of petals. Thus an increase in their number (accompanied by a reduction in the number of anthers and consequent loss of pollen) may render an otherwise fertile triploid sterile.

The progeny of triploid roses are only occasionally triploid themselves, for the chromosome level normally reverts to diploid or rises to tetraploid. The results of a series of crosses are as follows:

Fertile diploid × fertile diploid = fertile diploid
Fertile diploid × sterile diploid = fertile diploid
Fertile diploid × fertile triploid = fertile diploid
Fertile diploid × fertile tetraploid= sterile triploid

In the case of hexaploids, Harrison was the first to observe two different modes of meiotic behavior. *R. nutkana* and *R. moyeseii* were normal in meiosis, while *R. jundzillii* and *R. micrantha* behaved as if they were hybrids. In order to differentiate between these two behavior patterns, Harrison coined the term "balanced heterogamy" for tetraploids and hexaploids with normal meiosis, and "unbalanced heterogamy" for tetraploids, pentaploids and hexaploids with abnormal meiosis. Similar events have been observed in the genus *Rosa* on many occasions, and in individual sections the polyploid series are quite independent of one another.

For example:

Section
Cinnamomeae: *R. cinnamomea* (diploid)
     R. pendulina (tetraploid)
     R. nutkana (hexaploid)
     R. acicularis (octoploid)
Section *Carolinae*:   *R. nitida* (diploid)
     R. lucida (tetraploid)
Section
Pimpinellifoliae: *R. hugonis* (diploid)
     R. pimpinellifolia (tetraploid)

Amphidiploidy

This is a particular kind of allopolyploidy in which the genes of sterile artificial crosses are doubled, thereby becoming fertile. Here it will be useful to quote the examples given by Harrison: *R. wilsonii*, which is to be found in the area of the Menai Straits of Wales, is a hybrid of *R. pimpinellifolia* and *R. sherardii*, the latter being the pollen parent. In theory, its chromosome count should be 14 + 7, for *R. pimpinellifolia* is a sexually fertile tetraploid and the functional male gamete of *R. sherardii* has 7 chromosomes. However, research into its cytological condition revealed that *R. wilsonii*, contrary to all expectation, had 42 chromosomes and is therefore hexaploid. Also, surprisingly enough, it showed balanced heterogamy and was fertile, while the reciprocal hybrid is "unbalanced" and sterile. So here is a case of a fertile hexaploid resulting from the fertilization of an egg-cell of 14 chromosomes by a gamete from a pollen grain with 7, after the chromosome doubling.

While *R. wilsonii* is not in general garden cultivation, amphidiploidy can also be ascribed to a garden rose, as H.D. Wulff has done (1951) in the case of *R.* ×

kordesii. From the rose 'Max Graf', which is usually a sterile hybrid from *R. rugosa* × *R. wichuraiana*, all three being diploid, W. Kordes was able, in 1940, to raise a seedling from a chance cross which, after cytological examination, proved to be both tetraploid and fertile. All the later *Kordesii* roses have come from this seedling.

C.C. Hurst and his Septet-Theory As Hurst's theories are sometimes mentioned in books on roses, it will be useful to examine them in some detail here. Hurst was one of the most important of English rose researchers and concerned himself almost exclusively with genetic investigations. When he read a paper giving the results of his research to the Genetic Society in Cambridge in 1927, he had conducted genetic investigations on no fewer than 624 individual plants of 184 species, 16 new species from China and 89 hybrids of known parentage; all the sections of the genus *Rosa* were included.

First, however, it should be noted here that geneticists and rose research workers, while admiring the restless energy which he poured into his work, do not always accept his conclusions. This is especially so with his theory that all rose species must have stemmed from a decaploid species originating in the Northern Hemisphere. Since the chromosome count of the genus *Rosa* is 7 and it shows up in the polyploid range as a multiple of 7, Hurst coined the "septet" (i.e. the "seven") hypothesis. The hypothetical decaploid with 70 chromosomes must now, according to Hurst's theory, have lost, in a descending chain, complete septets, until finally arriving at a diploid level. Certainly a development of this type is theoretically possible, but it is improbable, and this is no longer accepted (Tischler/Wulff: 656-657). Apparently only Heribert/Nilsson (1953: 287-295) still accept Hurst's theory.

His research and experiments led him to the conclusion that there must be five different septet groups of chromosomes to which he gave the distinguishing letters A, B, C, D and E. Each of these septets has a complex of genes peculiar to itself. In the course of most thorough research, Hurst found that the number of the characteristic features of the individual septets were as follows:

Septet	Number of Features	Number Applicable to Species	Number Applicable to Sub-species
A	168	33	135
B	162	34	128
C	167	34	133
D	169	35	134
E	154	34	120

The true species belonging to these five septets are as follows:

Septet	Basic Species		Sub-species	
A	*R. sempervirens*	*abyssinica* A	*wichuraiana* A
		arvensis	*rubus*
		brunonii	*luciae*
		helenae	*phoenicia*
		moschata	*multiflora*
		banksiae AA	*chinensis* AA
		microcarpa	*gigantea*
		laevigata	*odorata*
B	*R. sericea*	*sericea*	*xanthina*
		beggeriana	*gymnocarpa*
		ecae	*sertata*
		hugonis	*webbiana*
			willmottiae
C	*R. rugosa*	*rugosa*	*nitida*
D	*R. carolina*	*carolina*	*cinnamomea*
		foliolosa	*davurica*
		blanda	*fendleri*
		pisocarpa	*marettii*
		woodsii	
E	*R. macrophylla*	*macrophylla*	*corymbulosa*
		elegantula	*giraldii*

The features of species with the individual septets were detailed by Hurst. Here are two examples, in the case of climbers, the septet characteristics were:

Stems (A) climbing, arched, very prickly
(B) arching, lanky, thickly covered with prickles, setaceous
(C) upright, thick stems, many prickles and glandular prickles
(D) upright, thin stems, mostly lightly armed
(E) erect rodlike growth, usually not prickly or setaceous

Foliage (A) 3-9 leaflets, nearly evergreen or deciduous
(B) 7-19 leaflets concentrated in the leaf axils
(C) 5-9 leaflets standing at the end and con-

centrated at the periphery of the shrub, falling early

(D) 5-7 leaflets standing at the end in clusters, the lower ones falling early

(E) 7-9 leaflets standing far apart, the leaflets falling early

In this way, the peculiarities of 14 important plant divisions were detailed.

The specific properties of each septet are homozygous, and all individuals of each of the five diploid septet species (AA, BB, CC, DD and EE) are the same. Each letter represents a septet of gametes. Some of these features were morphological or taxonomic, other physiological or ecological. The features of a sub-species (geographical or local strain of the diploid species) are likewise homozygous if only one of the five diploid species is represented in that sub-species.

Polyploid varieties of diploid species and polyploid species will also be precisely divided into the gene formulae (septet formulae) e.g.:

AAA and AAAA = triploid and tetraploid variety of the AA species *R. chinensis*

DDDD = tetraploid variety of the DD species *R. cinnamomea*

EEEE = tetraploid variety of the EE species *R. macrophylla*

AABB, BBCC, etc. = tetraploid species

BBCCDDEE = octoploid species (*R. acicularis*)

These formulae were shown, by researches carried out by Fagerlind (1945) and Blackhurst (1948), to be untenable. In contrast to Hurst's proposition, they advanced the theory of a strong homology of all rose genomes, that is to say a homogeneous appearance of the chromosomes and good ability to pair during meiosis.

In cases where there is an unexpectedly high degree of pollen sterility in hybrids, as for example with *R. multiflora* × *R. rugosa*, the earlier occurrence of physiological disorders resulting from non-homology of the chromosomes is responsible, according to H.D. Wulff (1955).

THE CHROMOSOME COUNT OF THE GENUS *ROSA*

Systematic enumeration: compiled from the results of experiments by Erlanson, Flory, Hurst, Täckholm, Wylie et al. x = 7.

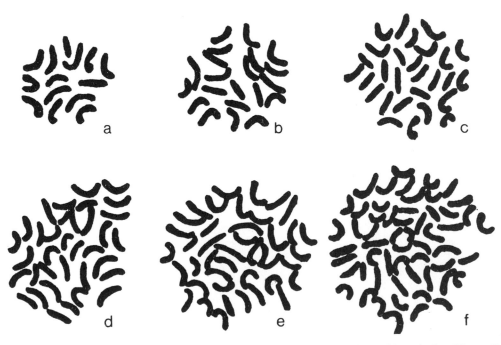

Figure 86. Somatic lamellae of roses with varying chromosomes. a. *R. webbiana* (2x = 14), b. *R. chinensis* (2x = 21), c. 'Conrad Ferdinand Meyer' (2x = 28), d. *R. stylosa* (2x = 35), e. *R. nutkana* (2x = 42), f. an octoploid hybrid. (2× = 56) (from G. Täckholm).

Sub-genus I. Hulthemia

Persica	14	Persia
× *hardii*	14	*clinophylla* × *persica*
kopetdaghensis	?	Turkoman

Sub-genus II. Eurosa

Sect. 1. *Pimpinellifoliae.*

ecae	14	Afganistan
hugonis	14	China
koreana	14	Korea
primula	14	Central Asia, N. China
sericea	14	Himalaya
– *omeiensis*	14	Central China
– *polyphylla*	14	Himalaya
– *pteracantha*	14	West China
xanthina	14	N. China, Korea
– *spontanea*	14	N. China
× *kochiana*	14	*pimpinellifolia* × *carolina*
× *pteragonis*	14	*hugonis* × *seriacea pteracantha*
× – *cantabrigiensis*	14	*hugonis* × *sericea hookeri*
foetida	28	Asia Minor
– *bicolor*	28	cultivated
– 'Persian Yellow'	28	cultivated
hemisphaerica	28	Asia Minor
– *rapinii*	28	Asia Minor
pimpinellifolia	28	Europe, Asia Minor
– *altaica*	28	Siberia
– *hispida*	28	Siberia
– *luteola*	28	Russia
– *myriacantha*	28	Spain, S. France
– *andrewsii*	28	cultivated
– *lutea*	28	cultivated
– *nana*	28	cultivated
× *harrisonii*	28	'Persian Yellow' × *pimpinellifolia*
× – *vorbergii*	28	*foetida* × *pimpinellifolia*
× *reversa*	28	*pendulina* × *pimpinellifolia*
× 'Frühlingsgold'	28	
'Frühlingsmorgen'	28	
'Stanwell Perpetual'	28	

Sect. 2. *Gallicanae*

centifolia	28, 21	Caucasus, cultivated
– *parvifolia*	14	cultivated
– *andrewsii*	28	cultivated
– *bullata*	28	cultivated
– *cristata*	28	cultivated
– *muscosa*	28	cultivated
– *muscosa alba*	28	cultivated
– *pomponia*	28	cultivated
– *simplex*	28	Spain, cultivated
– *variegata*	28	cultivated
damascena	28	Asia Minor, cultivated
– *semperflorens*	28	cultivated
– *versicolor*	28	cultivated
– *trigintipetala*	28	cultivated
gallica	28	Europe, Asia Minor
– *conditorum*	28	Hungary, cultivated
– *officinalis*	28	France, cultivated
– *pumila*	28	Spain, Italy
– *versicolor*	28	England, cultivated
× *collina*	?	? *canina* × *gallica*
× *macrantha*	28	*gallica* × ?
× *richardii*	21	Ethiopia
× *waitziana*	?	*canina* × *gallica*
× *alba*	42	*canina* × *damascena* ?
– Maxima	42	cultivated
– Semiplena	42	cultivated

Sect. 3. *Caninae*

elymaitica	14,28	Northern Iran
glauca	28	S. Europe
mollis	28	Europe
sherardii	28	Europe
villosa (pomifera)	28	Europe, Asia Minor
andegavensis	35	Europe
britzensis	35	Kurdistan
coriifolia	35	Europe, Asia Minor
– *froebelii*	35	cultivated
dumalis	35	Europe, Asia Minor
horrida	35	S.E. Europe, Asia Minor
montezumae	35	Mexico
obtusifolia	35	Europe
orientalis	35	S. Europe, Asia Minor
serafinii	35	S. Europe
sicula	35	S. Europe
tomentosa	35	Europe, Asia Minor
agrestis	35, 42	Europe, N. Africa
canina	35, 42	Europe
corymbifera	35, 42	Europe, N. Africa
glutinosa	35, 42	S. Europe, Asia Minor
– *dalmatica*	35, 42	Dalmatia
inodora	35, 42	Europe
micrantha	35, 42	Europe
rubiginosa	35, 42	Europe, Asia Minor
stylosa	35, 42; 28, 34	Europe
× *pokornyana*	40	*canina* × *glauca*, cultivated
marginata	42	Europe, Asia Minor
pouzinii	42	S. Europe, N. Africa
heckeliana	?	S. Europe
tuschetica	?	Central Asia

Sect. 4. *Carolinae*

foliolosa	14	N. America
nitida	14	N. America
palustris	14 (28)	N. America
carolina	28 (14)	N. America
– *grandiflora*	28	N. America
× *mariae-graebnerae*	28	*palustris* × *virginiana*, cultivated
virginia	28	N. America
× *rugotida*	?	*rugosa* × *nitida*, cultivated
× *scharnkeana*	?	*californica* × *nitida*, cultivated

Sect. 5. *Cinnamomeae*
(These have been broken down into three sub-groups due to the large number of varieties; as put forward by Darlington)

a) circumpolar.

acicularis	28, 42, 56	circumpolar
- *nipponensis*	14, 28	Japan
- *fennica*	28	Finland, Siberia
- *engelmannii*	42	N. America
- *bourgeauiana*	42, 56	N. America

b) The Old World

amblyotis	14	Kamchatka
banksiopsis	14	W. China
beggeriana	14	Persia, Afghanistan
corymbulosa	14	W. China
davurica	14	North-east Asia
elegantula	14	W. China
forrestiana	14	W. China
giraldii	14	N. and S. China
marettii	14	Sakhalin
persetosa	14	W. China
prattii	14	W. China
rugosa	14	East Asia
- all forms	14	cultivated
sertata	14	W. China
webbiana	14	Himalaya
willmottiae	14	W. China
× *calocarpa*	14	*chinensis* × *rugosa*, cultivated
× *coryana*	14	*macrophylla* × *roxburghii*, cultivated
× *kamtchatica*	14	Eastern Siberia
× *lheritieranea*	14	*chinensis* × ?, cultivated
× *micrugosa*	14	*roxburghii* × *rugosa*, cultivated
× *paulii*	14	*arvensis* × *rugosa*, cultivated
× *proteiformis*	14	cultivated
× *warleyensis*	14	*blanda* × *rugosa*, cultivated
caudata	14, 28	W. China
macrophylla	14, 28	Himalaya
majalis (=*cinn.*)	14, 28	Europe
× *koehneana*	21	*carolina* × *rugosa*, cultivated
× *spaethiana*	21	*palustris* × *rugosa*, cultivated
bella	28	N. China
davidii	28	W. China
fargesii	28	cultivated
fedtschenkoana	28	Central Asia
holodonta	28	W. China
laxa retzius	28	Turkestan
multibracteata	28	W. China
murielae	28	W. China
oxyodon	28	Caucasus
pendulina	28	Europe
- *pyrenaica*	28	Pyrenees
× *rubrosa* (= 'Carmenetta')	28	*glauca* × *rugosa*, cultivated
× *spinulifolia*	28 (?)	Switzerland, Hungary

× *pruhoniciana*	35	*moyesii* × *willmottiae*
hemsleyana	42	Central China
moyesii	42	W. China
sweginzowii	42	N.W. China
wardii	42	S.E. Tibet
× *highdownensis*	42	*moyesii* × ?
× *wintonensis*	42	*moyesii* × *setipoda*

c) The New World

blanda	14	Eastern N. America
gymnocarpa	14	Western N. America
× *aschersoniana*	14	*blanda* × *chinensis*, cultivated
woodsii	14	Western N. America
- *fendleri*	14	Western N. America
- *hispida*	14	Western N. America
ultramontana	14	Western N. America
californica	14, 28	California
- *plena*	14	cultivated
pyrifera	14, 16	Western N. America
macounii	14, 21	Western N. America
pisocarpa	14, 21	Western N. America
arkansana	28	Central N. America
suffulta	28	Central N. America
nutkana	42	Western N. America

Sect. 6. *Synstylae.*

anemoneflora	14	E. China
arvensis	14	Europe, Turkey
brunonii	14	Himalaya
cerasocarpa	14	W. China
crocacantha	14	W. China
filipes	14	W. China
helenae	14	Central China
iwara	14	Japan
longicuspis	14	W. China
luciae	14	East Asia
maximowicziana	14	East Asia
- *jackii*	14	Korea
- *pilosa*	14	Korea
moschata	14	Asia Minor (??)
- *abyssinica*	14	Ethiopia
- *plena*	14	cultivated
mulliganii	14	W. China
multiflora	14, 28	Japan, Korea
- 'Carnea'	14	cultivated
- *cathayensis*	14	China
- *platyphylla*	14	China, cultivated
- *watsoniana*	14	Japan, cultivated
phoenicia	14	Asia Minor
rubus	14	Central and W. China
sempervirens	14, 21, 28	S. Europe, N. Africa
setigera	14	N. America
sinowilsonii	14	S.W. China
soulieana	14	W. China
wichuraiana	14	East Asia
× *jacksonii*	14	cultivated
× *ruga*	14	*arvensis* × *chinensis*
× *polliniana*	21	*arvensis* × *gallica*
× *dupontii*	28	cultivated
× *kordesii*	28	cultivated

Sect. 7. *Chinenses*

× *odorata*	14, 21, 28	China, cultivated
- 'Fortune's Double Yellow'	14	China, cultivated
gigantea	14	S.W. China, Burma
× *cooperi*	14	*gigantea* × *laevigata*, cultivated
chinensis	14, 21, 28	China, cultivated
- *minima*	14	cultivated
- *mutabilis*	14, 21, 28	cultivated
- *semperflorens*	14, 21	cultivated
- 'Old Blush'	14	cultivated
- *spontanea*	14	Central China
- *viridiflora*	14	cultivated
× *noisettiana*	14	*chinensis* × *moschata*
- 'Marechal Niel'	14	1864 Pradel
- *manettii*	28	cultivated
× *borboniana*	21, 28	*chinensis* × *damascena*
'Souvenir de la Malmaison'	21	1843 Béluze
'Gruss an Teplitz'	28	1897 Geschwind

The Hybrid Perpetuals should be annexed here, for example:

'Captain Hayward'	28
'Frau Karl Druschki'	28
'Fisher & Holmes'	28
'Général Jacqueminot'	28
'Mrs. John Laing'	28
'Roger Lambelin'	28
'Ulrich Brunner'	28

Sect. 8. *Banksianae*

banksiae	14	Central and W. China
- all other forms	14	cultivated
× *fortuniana*	14	*banksiae* × *laevigata* (?)
cymosa	14	China

Sect. 9. *Laevigatae*

laevigata	14	China
× *anemonoides*	14	*laevigata* × *odorata*, cultivated

Sect. 10. *Bracteatae*

bracteata	14	S. China, Formosa
- 'Mermaid'	14	1918 Paul
clinophylla	14	India

Sub-genus III. **Platyrhodon.**

roxburghii	14	China
- *hirtula*	14	Central Japan
- *normalis*	14	China

Sub-genus IV. **Hesperhodos.**

stellata	14	Texas, Arizona, New Mexico
- *mirifica*	14	New Mexico
minutifolia	14	California

Alphabetical list of the chromosome count of the genus *Rosa* (2n + 14) from Darlington and Wylie's *Chromosome Atlas*, 2nd Edn. 1955.

acicularis	42, 56	*horrida*	35	
- *bourgeauiana*	42	*hugonis*	14	
agrestis	35	*humilis*	28	
amblyotis	14	*inodora (klukii)*	35, 42	
anemoneflora	14	*koreana*	14	
arvensis	14	*lacorum*	42, 56	
arkansana	14	*laevigata*	14	
baicalensis	56	*laxa retzius*	28	
banksiae	14	*longicuspis*	14	
banksiopsis	14	*luciae*	14	
beggeriana	14	*lucida*	28	
bella	28	*macounii*	21	
blanda	14	*macrophylla*	14	
bracteata	14	*marginata (jundzillii)*	42	
britzensis	35	*marrettii*	14	
brunonii	14	*maximowiczii*	14	
californica	28	*micrantha*	35	
canina	35	*minutifolia*	14	
carolina	28	*moschata*	14	
caudata	14, 28	*moyesii*	42	
centifolia	28	- *fargesii*	28	
- *muscosa*	28	- *rosea*	28	
cerasocarpa	14	*mulliganii*	14	
chavinii	42	*multibracteata*	28	
chinensis	14, 21, 28	*multiflora*	14	
cinnamomea	14	- *watsoniana*	14	
clinophylla	14	*nitida*	14	
coriifolia (laxa)	35	*nutkana*	28	
corymbifera (dumet)	35	*odorata*	14	
crocacantha	14	*omeiensis*	14	
cymosa	14	*orientalis*	35	
damascena	28	*pendulina*	28	
davidii	28	*persetosa*	14	
davurica	14	*phoenicia*	14	
dumalis (glauca)	35	*pimpinellifolia*	28	
ecae	14	- *altaica*	28	
durandii	28	- *hispida*	28, 28+ 1B	
elegantula	14			
elymaitica	14	- *lutea*	28	
engelmannii	42	- *myriacantha*	28	
farreri	14	*pisocarpa*	14, 21	
fedtschenkoana	28	*pouzinii*	42	
fendleri	14	*pratincola*	28	
fennica	56	*prattii*	14	
filipes	14	*primula*	14	
		pyrifera	21	
foetida	28	*rapinii*	28	
- *bicolor*	28	*roxburghii*	14	
- 'Persian Yellow'	28	*rubiginosa*	35	
foliolosa	14	*rubrifolia*	28	
gallica	28	*rubus (ernestii)*	14	
gigantea	14	*rudiuscula*	28	
giraldii	14	*rugosa*	14	
glutinosa	35, 42	*sancta*	21	
gymnocarpa	14	*seraphinii*	35	
hawrana	28	*sempervirens*	14	
helenae	14	*sericea*	14	
hemisphaerica	28	*sertata*	14	
hemsleyana	42	*setigera*	14	

BIBLIOGRAPHY

ABRAMS, G.J. VON. Plant Physiology for the Rosarian. Rose Ann. 1954: 34-41.

—— How Roses live and grow. Rose Ann. 1955: 64-72; 1956: 22-31.

ALLEN, E.F. Gibberellins — new tools for Rose breeders. Rose Ann. 1967: 123-127.

—— The importance of *Hulthemia* to Rose breeders. Rose Bull. 1971: 40-43.

ALLEN, T. The quest for thornless Roses. Rose Ann. 1965: 61-65.

DARLINGTON, C.D. and A.P. WYLIE. Chromosome Atlas of Flowering Plants. 2nd Edn. London (1955).

ERLANSON, E.W. Chromosome organisation in *Rosa*. Cytologia 2: 256-282 (1931).

—— Chromosome pairing, structural hybridity and fragments in *Rosa*. Bot. Gazette 94: 551-566 (1933).

—— Pollen analysis for rose-breeders. Amer. Rose Ann. 1934: 33-38.

—— What is a chromosome? Some intricacies of rose Cytology. Amer. Rose Ann. 1939.

—— Assets and the Future of Rose Heredity. Amer. Rose Ann. 1942: 71-74.

—— A self-pollination Mechanism and other Items in Rose species. Amer. Rose Ann. 1963: 188-193.

FLORY, W.S. Pollen conditions in some species and hybrids of *Rosa* with a consideration of associated phylogenetic factors. Virginia Jour. Sci. 1950: 11-59.

FUNCK, E., and H. VON RATHLEF. Die Farben der Rosenblüten und ihre objektive Erfassung. Ros. Jb. 1940: 125-129.

GAUJARD, J. A study of the Hybridization and Heredity of Roses. Amer. Rose Ann. 1939: 55-64.

GERBER, M.W. A Synopsis of lavender and blue Roses. Amer. Rose Ann. 1970: 23-26.

HARLAND, S.C. The Art of Rose Breeding "Sports". Gard. Chron. 1965 (11 Dec). 1966 (27 April and 25 May). Do Roses degenerate? The Rose 15: 28-33 (1967).

HARRISON, J.W.H. The genus *Rosa*, its hybridology and other genetical problems. Trans. Nat. Hist. Soc. Northumberland, Durham and Newcastle-upon-Tyne, N.S.5 (1920).

—— Roses and their Chromosomes. Rose Ann. 1958: 53-61.

HURST, C.C. The Mechanism of Heredity and Evolution. Eugenics Rev. 19: 19-31 (1927).

—— The Genetics of the Rose. Rose Ann. 1929: 37-64.

—— Chromosomes and Characters in *Rosa*. Genet. Soc. Cambridge Meeting 1927.

—— The Species Concept. Gard. Chron. 1930, Oct. 18.

—— Embryo-sac Formation in Diploid and Polyploid species of *Roseae*. Proc. Roy. Soc., B, 109: 126-148 (1931).

—— and M.S.G. BREEZE. Notes on the origin of the Moss Rose. Jour. R.H.S. 1922: 26-42.

HURST, RONA. Roses and Genetics. Amer. Rose Ann. 1969: 37-43.

KAPPERT, H. Die vererbungswissenschaftlichen Grundlagen der Züchtung. 2 Aufl. Berlin 1953.

KORDES, W. Das Problem winterharter Rosen. Rosenjahrb. 3: 44-46 (1950).

KRÜGER, G. Die Entwicklung von Blüte und Frucht bei der Gattung *Rosa*. Rosen-Zeitung 1907-1909 (9 Folgen).

KUCKUCK, H., and A. MUDRA. Lehrbuch der allgemeinen Pflanzenzüchtung. Stuttgart 1952.

KUGLER. H. Blütenökologie, 2 Aufl. Stuttgart 1970 (contains a section on "Chemie der Blütenfarbstoffe", pp. 84-88).

LAMMERTS. The scientific basis of Rose breeding. Amer. Rose Ann. 1945: 71-74.

LAWRENCE, R. A little on the Red. Amer. Rose Ann. 1946: 43-45.

MOREY, D.H. and A.H. WESSIG. Chromosome Numbers in Rosa. Amer. Rose Ann. 1953: 107-110.

MÜNTZING, A. Vererbungslehre; Methoden und Resultate. Übersetzt von D. Wettstein. Stuttgart 1958.

MÜTZE, W and C.K. SCHNEIDER. Moderne Rosenforschung. In: Die Rose in Garten und Park, pp 89-93. Berlin 1936.

PROCTOR, J.T.A. Pflanzenfarbstoffe. Span. 13: 165-168 (1970).

RATHLEF, H. VON. Does Mendel's Law apply to the Rose or not? Amer. Rose Ann. 1940: 53-56.

REHAGEN, H.W. Zur Zytologie triploider Rosen. Rosenjahrb. XVI: 177-232; 1959 (Diss).

RISLEY, E.B. Roses have Satellites too. Amer. Rose Ann 1959: 141-145.

ROWLEY, G. Hulthemosas — new hope for the Rose Breeder. Rose Ann. 1955: 37-40.

—— and J. HARBORNE. In quest of blue Roses. Rose Ann. 159: 147-149.

—— Triploid Garden Roses. Amer. Rose Ann. 1960: 108-113.

—— Rose rootstocks and sucker production. John Innes Inst. 52nd Rep: 11 (1961).

—— The experimental approach to Rose breeding. Scientif. Horticult. 18; in: The Rose 16: 12-18 (1967).

—— Aneuploidy in the genus *Rosa*. Jour. Gen. 37: 253-268 (1960).

—— Chromosome studies and evolution in *Rosa*. Bull. Jard. Bot. Brussels 37: 45-52 (1967).

SAAKOV, S.G. Die Sortenbildung bei Rosen dutch Knospenmutation Arch f. Gartenbau 1960: 595-629.

STEARN, W.T. The origin and later development of cultivated plants. Jour. R.H.S. 89: 470-472 (1964).

TÄCKHOLM, G. On the cytology of the genus *Rosa*; a preliminary note. Svensk. Bot. Tidskr. 14 (1920).

—— Zytologische Studien über die Gattung *Rosa*. Acta Hort, Bergian. 7: 97-381 (1922).

TISCHLER AND H.D. WULFF. Handbuch der Pflanzenanatomie, 2 Aufl, Bd. II, 2. Hälfte: Allgemeine Pflanzenkaryologie. 1931-1951.

TURRILL, W.B. Heredity in Species (Extract). The Rose 1: 101 (1953).

WRIGHT, P.H. The Inheritance of Color in hardy Roses. Amer. Rose Ann. 1960:114-118.

—— Unique Genes in hardy wild Roses. Amer. Rose Ann. 1963: 132-136.

WULFF, H.D. *Rosa Kordesii*, eine neue amphidiploide Rose. Züchter 21: 123-132 (1951).

—— Cytologische Beobachtungen an Rosenbastarden. Züchter 22: 233-244 (1952).

—— Are the Dog Roses apomictic? Amer. Rose Ann. 1955: 116-123.

—— and L. HELDT. Über die Genealogie und Mikrosporogenese der Lambertianarose 'Hamburg'. Züchter 23: 87-93 (1953).

___. 'Max Graf' and its progeny, with special reference to *Rosa Kordesii*. Amer. Rose Ann. 1953: 111-122.

WYLIE, A.P. Chromosomes of Garden Roses. Amer. Rose Ann. 1954: 36-66.

___. Why the Caninae roses are different. New Zealand Rose Annual: 67-79 (1976).

ZIMMERMANN, P.W.. and A.E. HITCHCOCK. Rose 'sports' from adventitious buds. Contr. Boyce Thompson Inst. 16: 221-224 (1951).

ADDENDUM RE "MUTATIONS" (See p. 185).

The 787 mutations recorded in the above mentioned table are all individually named in the recent work by S.G. SAAKOV and D.A. RIEKSTA, *Roses* (pp. 192-204; Riga 1973). There are also a number of figures illustrating a pattern of events.

The Rose in Commerce

In this section it is proposed to deal with those matters which were not covered in the section on the garden cultivation of the rose, in particular the market in rose plants and the relevant statistical details. These details were quite easy to obtain from the annual official year books for Germany, while the data for other nations had to be gathered from the trade press. A number of different years have been covered, but the result still gives, a good idea of the importance of the rose in the nursery trade of the individual country. Fortunately, there are some very comprehensive details from four overseas countries for consideration.

A full description of the quality standards, which are naturally very important in commerce, has already been given (see pp. 108 and 110).

Of particular interest to the reader will be the methods of registration and plant protection, and particularly the patent rights for new roses. While the latter two have been enshrined in law, the matter of registration is only semi-official, an arrangement of common interests. The question of licenses will not be dealt with in this book. This is a private matter of concern only to the breeder of a new rose and his licensees.

West Germany. Rose production here increases steadily and, as far as can be seen, has not yet reached its peak. The following table gives the total number in millions of roses of all classes which were produced for sale in each given year.

1950	9.96	1961	29.10	1968	37.80
1952	11.80	1962	26.70	1968	39.53
1954	15.78	1963	32.50	1970	39.17
1956	19.23	1964	33.65	1971	40.70
1958	22.28	1965	37.20	1972	41.40
1959	24.28	1966	38.56	1973	42.20
1960	23.92	1967	37.19		

Since 1958, about a third more Floribundas than Hybrid Teas have been budded. The number of standards has moved between 0.25 million and 0.45 million with

no clear reason for this variation; at the same time, the shrub and climbing roses have continued to rise from 0.5 million to 2.5 million. In West Germany there are rose nurseries in every district but the greatest area of production is concentrated in four districts (see Map, Fig. 87).

1. Schleswig-Holstein (District of Pinneberg).
2. Hessen. (Steinfurth and Wetterau).
3. The Rhineland (the area around Bonn).
4. Westphalia (the area around Münster).

Almost all understocks are grown in Holstein. All other relevant details can be obtained from the tables and maps.

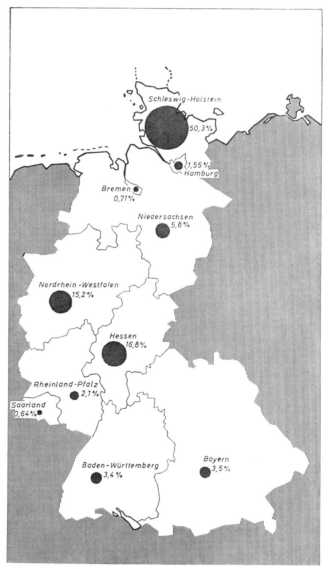

Figure 87. The percentage distribution of rose-growing in West Germany. (F. Glasau)

The greenhouse cultivation of roses in West Germany has been continuously on the increase: 1959 = 26 ha./64 acres, 1960 = 46 ha./114 acres, 1963 =90 ha./222 acres, 1966 = 195 ha./482 acres, and 1969 = 195 ha./482 acres. They are chiefly grown in Hamburg and its environs, in North-Rhine-Westphalia, Baden-Württemberg and West Berlin. In 1969, the amount of open land devoted to growing cut flower blooms was some 350 ha./865 acres (for further details, see p. 000).

Belgium. In 1968, about 8 million rose bushes in 450 different varieties were raised; of these about 30% were Floribundas, and 70% of the total was disposed of on the home market. The chief growing area is the center of the nursery trade at Wetteren near Ghent. 40 million roses for the cut flower trade were grown.

Bulgaria. Estimates of the area devoted to growing roses for the production of Attar, a practice which is 300 years old, varies between 2,000 and 9,000 ha./5,000 and 22,000 acres (1950). Growing for the cut flower market is now beginning to expand. The "Valley of Roses" stretches for about 100 km./62 mi. westwards to the southern edge of the Balkans. Since 1950, there has been an Institute there for rose research, which is mostly concerned with the production of Attar from *Rose damascena,* rather than the breeding of new roses.

Czechoslovakia. No information from official statistics. As far as is known about 5 million understocks were planted in 1962. From this 4 million rose bushes presumably became available.

Denmark. In 1964 rose production was around 8.4 million plants, of which 55% were Floribundas. 30% Hybrid Teas and the rest climbing or shrub roses. By 1968, 300 ha./740 acres were under cultivation for roses and by 1972 there were 46 ha./115 acres under glass.

East Germany. Exact figures are not available, but it appears that at the present time about 12 million rose bushes, including 200,000 standards, are grown, chiefly in the area around Dresden.

Finland. Has little rose production of its own; about 2 million plants are imported annually. In 1969 there were 13.8 ha./34 acres under glass producing roses for the cut flower trade; this has been increased to 24 ha./59 acres by 1972.

France. About 20 million roses were grown on 600 ha./1,500 acres in 1961, most of them in the vicinity of Lyon (400 ha./1,000 acres) and on the Riviera. By 1969, there were 180 ha./440 acres under cultivation for the cut flower trade, part under glass, part in the open; of this, 70% was on the Mediterranean and 12% in the area around Paris.

Greece. According to a note in the magazine *Taspo* of 1-1973, there were then about 20 ha./50 acres of roses grown in the open and 8 ha./20 acres under glass.

Holland. The details of greenhouse cultivation are as follows:

	1965	1968	1969	1970	1971	1972
Stems produced (in millions)	229	495	579	656	716	768
Hectares/Acres under glass	195/ 480	338/ 835	382/ 944	422/ 1,040	467/ 1,150	499/ 1,230

The production of rose plants occurs mostly in the area around Boskoop and in North Limburg; understocks are grown at Veendam.

Hungary. Exact figures are not available, except that in 1970, 16 million plants were exported to Italy and 2.5 million to Austria. The country has a long tradition of rose-growing both in the open and under glass. In the southern districts (1965) cut roses grown in the open appeared on the Hungarian market very early. The most popular variety was 'Glory of Rome' which comprised 60% of the total. At the Horticultural Technical College in Budapest research has been carried out by G. Mark on the raising of new varieties and also on the lasting qualities of the cut flower. The most important rose hybridizer in Hungary was R. Geschwind, a forestry director in Korpona, who was active between 1880 and 1900. His work entitled *Die Hybridisation und Sämlingszucht,* published in Vienna in 1864 (384 pp.), is one of the earliest books to deal specifically with rose-breeding.

Israel. Here there is a continually rising market for the export of cut roses to the European market during the winter months. In 1970 there were 88 ha./217 acres under cultivation for this purpose; the most common varieties grown are 'Baccara', 'Super Star', 'Dr. A.J. Verhage', 'Garnette' and 'Sweetheart'.

Italy. The official figures for 1962 showed a total of 759 ha./1,875 acres allocated to roses, of which 442 ha./1,092 acres were under some form of glass, mostly moveable covers. In 1969 this figure had fallen to 184 ha./455 acres under glass which produced a total of about 73 million cut blooms.

Norway. So far as is known, there were about 43 ha./106 acres under cultivation in 1959 producing about 1.3 million plants. The area under glass is unknown.

Poland. For 1962, the figures showed that about 1.5 million plants were produced, mostly on small individual holdings, and these were in about 540 varieties of their own propagation.

Rumania. At the research institute in Cluj, intensive work on rose cultivation is being pursued, in an attempt to achieve better colors and varieties which are more suited to continental weather conditions; the problems of greenhouse roses are also being investigated. Special efforts are being made to develop disease-free, hardy and prickle-free varieties. The work is being promoted and assisted by the authorities. Large areas in the country are planted with *R. centifolia* and *R. damascena* for the purpose of obtaining Attar which is used as a flavoring in the liquor industry.

Sweden. In 1972 there were about 46 ha./114 acres of roses being grown under glass.

Switzerland. The amount of land used for the nursery production of roses in 1965 was about 75 ha./185 acres.

United Kingdom. (Great Britain and Northern Ireland). According to the Royal National Rose Society, no exact figures of production have been issued, but estimates can be made from the numbers of understocks which are imported annually: 1965, 40.4 million; 1966, 61.5 million; 1967, 55 million; 1968, 52 million; 1969, 49.4 million; 1970, 51.1 million; 1971, 43.7 million; and 1972, 37.1 million; 60% of these would be placed in Grade I. Most of these understocks come from Holland (East Groningen), with a few from Germany and Denmark.

United States of America. It is very difficult to give figures for all of the U.S.A., but the production of roses at the present time is probably about 80 million taken off 2,000 ha./5,000 acres. Another 18 million plants are grown under glass. The rose trade is important in American horticulture and represents about 30% of the total nursery production (1959).

The import of species and hybrid roses into the United States is controlled as follows:

(a) entry from Italy, South Africa, Australia and New Zealand is forbidden on account of the virus *Marmor tumefaciens* Holmes;

(b) imports without soil from other countries are allowed with a permit and require a health certificate; there is a two year quarantine period. The American importer is responsible for obtaining the import license, a green label which must be attached to the package.

It is unnecessary to go into American understocks very deeply. About 80% of plants are budded on *multiflora*, but in California and the warmer southern states both 'Dr. Huey' ('Shafter Robin') and 'Gloire des Rosomanes' ('Ragged Robin'), *R. odorata* and many types of *multiflora*, most developed by Dr. Lyle in Texas, are used. Today there is a preference for 'Iowa 60-5' and '62-5'.

U.S.S.R. For practical purposes, rose production here did not begin until 1960. Until then there was only one nursery, in the Ukraine, about 5 ha./12 acres in size, in the whole country. Only 10 varieties were grown, of which 50% were 'Peace', 25% were for the production of Attar and the rest were various old garden roses (see Delbard, *ARA* 1963). Since then, however, rose cultivation has been started in the Crimea and in the Caucasus (Nalchik). The development of new varieties has been undertaken by Dr. Vera Klimenko of the Nikitski Botanical Gardens in Yalta for both the southern and central Asiatic countries, while Dr. Lempitski of the Botanical Gardens in Kiev has developed new varieties especially for the Ukraine and Kazakstan. By 1966 the production of plants had reached the million mark, one third of these were produced in Krasnodar, Nalchik and the Crimea. There were other, less important areas of production, such as Adler on the Black Sea, Uman in the Ukraine, and the area around Riga. As far as is known, no more current figures have been published.

Australia (1970). 95% of all roses were raised in the vicinity of Adelaide (S. Australia). The soil is alkaline, the summers hot and dry and there is no incidence of Black Spot. The understock commonly used is *R. indica major* (the counterpart to the American stock 'Dr. Huey') since it is mildew-resistant and provides a high percentage of saleable plants. (It should be noted that this understock is also used in Southern Europe, Israel and Lebanon for the same reasons.)

In S.W. and W. Australia the understock used is *R. fortuniana*; commonly used only there and in Florida. It is presently impossible to patent roses in Australia and, consequently, the development of new roses is still in its infancy and may really be considered a hobby for the amateur. Budding eyes may be imported from all over the world; the majority come from Europe and America, but there has recently been an increase in imports from both Japan and India.

Japan (1965). About 1,000 European and American varieties are cultivated, and Japanese varieties are becoming more widely grown. Presently, the three most popular varieties with the public are 'Confidence', 'Christian Dior' and 'Garden Party', however Japanese gardeners recommend 'Super Star', 'Royal Highness' and 'Colour Wonder'. The favorite colors are red, yellow, and white (white flowers of all kinds are favored) in that order. Roses in Japan bloom in two distinct periods, May-June and then again in October. The Japanese consider that the rose is at its most beautiful in bud form, but despite this, the breeders strive for the complete rose in form and color. At the present time a great many miniature standards, what we would call quarter standards, are produced. For years the greatest interest has been in Bonsai, and hybridizing has been somewhat neglected.

In the last 15 years the number of rose gardens open to the public has markedly increased; many of them belong to private railway companies and are situated in the vicinity of stations in order to attract travelers. The nursery production in the open was only about 47 ha./116 acres in 1970, and a large portion of it was exported to Korea and China. The glasshouse cultivation, including that carried out under polythene, was, at the same time, about 95.1 ha./235 acres.

South Africa. Due to its location in the Southern Hemisphere, the seasons here are the opposite of ours. Spring begins in September, Christmas comes at high summer. In Cape Province, the rainy season is in the winter when the plants are resting, but in the Transvaal and the Orange Free State it is in summer and, consequently, the growing conditions are more favorable in these areas. In Natal, precipitation is distributed fairly evenly throughout the year and it is therefore this province which enjoys the best conditions of all for roses in the Republic. In the Transvaal the rainy season starts in October and is marked by violent storms, often with as much as 10 cm./4 in. of rain falling in an hour.

Budding is carried out on *multiflora* cuttings which have been tested for virus. After two months, the cuttings are well rooted and growing on and can be budded. Since the stocks do not "open" well and, in many cases, ripe budding eyes will not be available, use is made of "shot" eyes. These have about a 90% take and quickly grow out. Shortly after budding, the stock is cut half-way through to slow down the flow of sap and to promote the growth of the bud. All these operations take place at different times of the year throughout the Republic. While growth is phenomenal in Natal, in other places the growing period is not sufficient for them to be lifted and it is not uncommon for 50% to have to remain until they become big enough to be sold. The most important type of understocks are 'Clarke's 52', 'Clarke's 57', 'Brooks', 'Versailles' and 'Bassee'. The Bantu budder will handle 1,500-1,600 per day, working up to 2,000 if necessary.

The sale of roses is to both graden centers and directly to the public; production has scarcely reached the million mark, but there is a considerable business in the cut flower trade; for this purpose, the roses are often planted under a synthetic material called "Saran" which reduces the light penetration by about 50%. This gives greater growth, but flower color can be affected. Very long stems with moderately sized flowers are just right for the European market and this encourages exports.

Although the successful rose breeder is reluctant to disclose the distribution secrets of his most important varieties, some figures can be given here. The firm of Meilland made it known a few years ago that their variety 'Peace' had attained a total of 100,000,000 plants. The number of 'Baccara', which is No. 1 in the cut-flower trade, can be put with confidence in the 30 to 40 million mark. Kordes places the production of 'Lilli Marlene' at about 10,000,000 and both 'Crimson Glory' and 'Orange Triumph' at several million. Tantau has stated that his varieties 'Super Star' and 'Red Favorite' have each sold several million plants.

ROSE REGISTRATION

At the international horticultural conventions held in Luxembourg in 1911 and in London in 1912, it was agreed to establish a Rose Register; Monsieur Brault, of

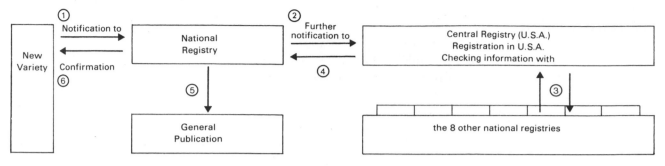

Figure 88. The Progress of the Registration of a new Rose Variety (Original).

the André Leroy Nurseries, of Angers, France, was put in charge. An official index was published; the registration fee was 2 Fr. Descriptions could be written in French, English or German (*RZ* 1912: 112).

In 1916, it was announced in the *Rosenzeitung* (*RZ* 1916: 73) that the name of a new variety could be given to the editor to establish its identity. This facility was used in a variety of ways, but generally the names of Generals, Dukes and Princes were those registered.

This first attempt at rose registration does not seem to have survived the First World War, for afterward nothing could be found of the international office in France or the registration office set up by the *Rosenzeitung*.

A proper system of registration of important plants and genera with numerous cultivars was not established until the 14th International Horticultural Congress at Scheveningen in Holland in 1955. The official office for rose registration was given to the American Rose Society. They chose the title "International Registration Authority for Roses" (IRAR). This office's task is to collect all the names of known varieties as they are submitted and, should the occasion arise, to tell the applicant that a chosen name is unavailable because the original cultivar with that name is still on the market. Should the registry be able to confirm that a variety is no longer in existence then the name can be released and used again for a new variety.

The office of the IRAR issues a revised edition of *Modern Roses*, the official book of the registry, every five years (the last edition was issued in 1980); this gives the name, grower, year of introduction, classification, parentage (when known) and a brief description of the variety. Entry in the register establishes proof when previous rights are questioned.

Growers in a country which has its own facilities for registration are best advised to go first through the local channels; the local office will then send a special registration form to the IRAR in America. Each month a list of the newly registered varieties will be compiled and all national registration offices, who are then responsible for announcing the details, will be advised. If no objection is made within 30 days after publication of the new varietal name, then it is officially registered.

The following are the registration offices (*ARA* 1968: 33-34):

International Registration Authority for Roses, American Rose Society; Harold E. Goldstein: P.O. Box 30,000; Shreveport, Louisiana 71130, U.S.A. (covering registrations for both the U.S.A. and Canada).

Australia
 Dr. A.S. Thomas, 340 Union Road, Balwyn, Victoria 3103.

France
 L. Laperrière, Route Nationale 6, Chesnes, F 38 Saint Quentin-Fallavier.

Germany
 Deutsches Rosenregister im Deutschen Rosarium, 46 Dortmund, Am Kaiserhain 25 (Westfalen Park).

Great Britain
 The Royal National Rose Society, Chiswell Green Lane, St. Albans, Herts.

Holland
 Raad voor Kwekersrecht, Nederlands Rasregister, P. Marijkeweg 15, Postbus 14, Wageningen.

India
 Indian Agricultural Research Institute, Division of Horticulture, Dr. B. Choudhury, New Delhi 12.

Italy
 Associazione Italiana della Rosa, Niso Fumagalli, Villa Reale, Monza.

Japan
 The Japanese Rose Society, Managing Director, Nobuo Tanizawa, 28-12-8, Okuzawa, Setagayu-ku, Tokyo.

South Africa
 Rose Society of South Africa, Mr. H.E. Buss, P.O. Box 65217, Benmore, Transvaal.

PLANT PROTECTION FOR ROSES

Since plant protection is so internationally important, the most salient features will be described here; i.e., what it is, how it has been formulated and how it works in practice.

By the beginning of the century, when the raising of new roses in Germany was carried on by numerous very small concerns, mostly amateur, Peter Lambert, undoubtedly the outstanding hybridizer of his time, fought for some form of "protection for the grower", what is today called a license *(Rosen-zeitung* 1902: 74-76). He met with no success and had no support from the nursery trade, so he developed the practice of selling new varieties at a much higher price than standard cultivars. When 'Frau Karl Druschki' was introduced in 1901, each plant was priced at 20 Gold Marks. Having bought it at this price the purchaser was then free to propagate it. This practice spread through Germany and was adopted in a number of other countries where new varieties were being produced regularly, particularly France and England. The United States did not then participate, but as the first form of varietal protection in the form of "Plant Patent" was instituted there, this must be considered next.

Plant Patent in the U.S.A. It was in the 1920's that the United States really entered the field of rose breeding. Hybridizers expended much time and money developing a new variety, but the moment they handed it over to the trade anyone could propagate it quite freely without having to pay the smallest royalty to the grower, as they would have had to do had they been engaged in industry. This was well known to the appropriate Government Department, but, until then, they had really only considered the case of new varieties of grain, grass and fruit, although no law had been passed to protect these new varieties. Finally, in 1930, the U.S. Government passed a law called the Plant Patent Act which gave the hybridizer the right to patent his hybrid and to control its propagation and distribution for 17 years and, during this period, to claim royalties by the granting of licenses.

To qualify for a patent in the U.S.A. a new rose must be an entirely new variety, capable of asexual propagation true to type, for which no patent application has previously been made in any other country. It must not be described in any catalogue or printed form nor may it be released upon the open market for at most one year before the patent application.

Once granted the patent gives the holder protection for 17 years, but it cannot be extended. During the life of the patent the holder is enabled to grant licenses for vegetative propagation either by budding or by taking cuttings and he is permitted to check the correct operation of his license. He may also restrict the sale of the variety in specified areas or countries and has the right to exercise an influence upon the quality. If the plants being sold do not satisfy the grading standards, the patent holder can revoke the license, a clause which does much to protect the consumer. Each and every plant sold bears a label guaranteeing its authenticity.

The law does not require that a new plant be any better than existing varieties, only that it be new and distinctive. In practice, the patent system tends to produce higher selling prices for these new roses. The first rose to receive this protection was the climber 'New Dawn' (1930).

As the production of novelties became more attractive commercially American rose breeding grew rapidly and soon overtook and surpassed its international competitors. France, Germany and England, who had been the market leaders.

THE NOMENCLATURE OF CULTIVARS

Botanists, as well as members of the horticultural trade, have tried for many years to standardize, as much as possible, the scientific and varietal names given to various plants. This is now governed by a practical code in which the rules for naming plants are as follows:

General Principles At certain definite intervals, these rules, known as the "International Code of Botanical Nomenclature", are revised and corrected. In 1954 they were augmented with the additional "International Code of Nomenclature for Garden Plants" which, in turn, was revised in 1969. The rules and regulations of this code are used as the basis for the correct naming of all garden plants. There is only space here to cite some of the more important rules as follows:

Garden plants are given names based on their genus, species and variety.

Example: *Rosa* (genus) *gallica* (species) *versicolor* (varietal name)

In the case of roses there is the problem of the "clone", that is to say, the continuation of a consistent genetic individual which has been propagated vegetatively from the original plant.

Variety names which follow a botanical name, or a name in common use, or which precede this, must be clearly separated by the inclusion of single quotation marks.

Example: *Rosa* 'Iceberg' or Rose 'Iceberg'.

The more usual full quotation marks are not used in the case of varietal names.

The use of a name within an individual genus may only be used once and can only be re-used if the original variety which carried it is no longer in commerce.

The variety name should consist of one or two words and in no case may it exceed three. Examples of acceptable names:

'Capistrano', 'Tarantella', 'Mabella', 'Mercedes'.
'Kordes Perfecta', 'Sterling Silver', 'Super Star'.
'Gruss an Aachen', 'Perle von Remagen', 'Florida von Scharbeutz'.

General recommendations

Names should

a) not begin with an article (The, Der, Die, Le, La),

i.e. not 'The Duke', 'The Fairy', 'The Bishop', 'The Bride', 'La Jolie' (La Jolla is acceptable as this is a place name), 'Le Rêve', 'Le Rigide', 'Die Präsidentin'.

b) not begin with an abbreviation of a proper name,

i.e. not 'C. Chambard', 'E.V. Lucas', 'J.A. Gomis', 'J.C. Thornton'.

The initial letter should always be written in full thus:

'George C. Waud', 'Maud E. Gladstone', 'William R. Smith'.

c) not be excessively long. This concerns French and Spanish names almost exclusively,

'Madame Soledad de Ampuera de Leguizamon'
'Manuel Pinto de Azevedo'
'Donna Maria do Carmo de Fragosa Carmona'
'Saudade de Anibal de Morais'
'Senora Oyez de Caramba y Garlanzos'
'Su Exelencia Senora de Franco'
'Souvenir de Madame Achille van Herreweghe'
'Souvenir of an old Rose Garden'
'Souvenir de Jules Nicholas Methieu Lamarche'

The longest of all rose names, quoted by Father Levet in 1880, was 'Souvenier des Fiancailles de l'Archiduc Rodolphe d'Autriche et de la Princesse Stephanie des Pays-Bas'. This was really too much of a mouthful for anyone and it was shortened by general consent to 'Rodolphe et Stephanie'.

d) not exaggerate the qualities of a variety

e) not be too general in approach

(thus a rose should not be called 'Yellow' but rather 'Yellow Queen' or something along those lines.)

f) not be too similar to an existing name; this will help avoid confusion and mix-ups.

(e.g. 'Beatrix' and 'Beatrice'; 'Helen', 'Helena' and 'Hélène', etc.)

Names presenting language difficulties. In the various Slavonic languages the following names are quite simple, but not to the Westerners to whom the roses will mostly be sold. With purely commercial considerations it is desirable to choose a name which is both short and easy to say. Difficulties will obviously arise with names like 'Brno' (1933), 'Joseph Strnad' (1932) and 'Plzen' (1930), etc. Some German names also present difficulties for people of other nationalities.

Bud Mutations. In the case of bud mutations which arise from another variety, but which bear a strong similarity to it, the rules of nomenclature require that the name chosen should show, within reasonable limits, the relationship with the parent variety. Where climbing sports are involved, this is easy and commonly practiced, but where the sport results in color change it is much less common. Sometimes an addition will be made to an existing varietal name which gives the impression that the new plant is a sport when this is not the case. For example:

'Yellow Holstein' is not a sport of 'Holstein'.
'Pink Peace' is not a sport of 'Peace'.
'Scarlet Queen Elizabeth' is not a sport of 'Queen Elizabeth'.

Use of Commercial Synonyms. A commercial synonym is another name for a variety which is used in place of its correct name under limited and particular conditions; for example, if a name happens to be commercially unacceptable in a particular country. Sometimes a name is difficult to pronounce or its translation into the local language produces either some unacceptable connotation or a sound which is not euphonic.

However, under any circumstances, it is desirable that only one name be in use for any one variety. The idea of commercial synonyms was advanced in 1958 by several nurserymen. As a result it is possible to:

a) register a rose with its official (original) name and publish this;

b) to re-christen the rose later with a commercial synonym and to publicize this fact.

This sort of change in naming has so far only applied to roses.

The validity of the name of a variety is established by its publication in print and its subsequent distribution. A nurseryman's catalog is sufficient for this purpose provided it reviews all the introductions of an entire year. Unfortunately, in the U.S.A. they are particularly quick to make changes in names as can be seen from the examples given in the following table.

Original Name	Year	Commercial Synonym	Year
Mme. A. Meilland	1942	Gloria Dei (Germany)	1945
		Peace (England & U.S.A.)	1945
		Gioia (Italy)	1945
Schneewittchen	1958	Iceberg	1958
Voeux de Bonheur	1960	Bon Voyage	1969
Maryse Kriloff	1960	Lucy Cramphorn	1961
Super Star	1960	Tropicana	1962
Manola	1961	Fred Cramphorn	1962
		Samoa	1964
Evelyn Fison	1962	Irish Wonder	1964
Forever Yours	1964	Concorde	1969
Kronenburg	1965	Flaming Peace	1967
Grandpa Dickson	1966	Irish Gold	1969
Maria Callas	1966	Miss All-American Beauty	1968
Samourai	1966	Scarlet Knight	1967
Majorette	1968	Minna Lerche Lerchenborg	1969
Jean de la Lune	1969	Yellow Glo	1969

This list could easily be extended considerably.

Misunderstood Personal names

Some quite amusing misnomers have arisen over the years, mostly English phonetic nicknames:

'Gloire de Dijon' = 'Glory Dic-John'
'Gruss an Teplitz' = 'Grows in Triplets'
'Othello' = 'Old Fellow'
'Desdemona' = 'Thursday Morning'
'Félicite Perpétue' = 'Félicité Perpétuale'
'Soupert & Notting' = 'Southport or Nothing'

Fashion in Naming Roses Public taste in roses changes very quickly. This is immediately apparent when prize-winning roses are planted in the order of their year of introduction, i.e., the ADR roses in Dortmund or the gold medal winners at Bagatelle in Paris, where they are all planted in one bed behind the chateau.

Fashion also shows up in the type of name which is given. There are roses bearing every kind of title; many are named after film stars and the most beautiful roses always bear a lady's name. In a short statistical examination made from *Modern Roses 6* the most popular usages seemed to be:

391 Madame or Mme.
288 Mrs.
 39 Frau
182 Golden
150 Rose, Rosa or similar
138 Red, Rouge or Rot
126 Pink
121 White, Weiss or Blanc
130 Souvenir de or Andenken an
126 Lady
112 Maria
 88 Queen

In the past, names of the aristocracy were frequently used and, in wartime, the names of Generals or heroes are quite popular.

BIBLIOGRAPHY

ALBRECHT, A. Sortenschutz für Rosen. Rosenjahrbuch 35: 53-63 (1969).
BOHRINGER, D. Sortenschutz bei Rosen und Beerenobst. Erwerbsgärtner 1968: 228-230.
DAS BUNDESSORTENAMT. Aufgaben — Organisation — Einrichtung. Benerode/Hann. (1972).
GILMOUR, J.S.L. (Editor) International Code of Nomenclature of cultivated Plants — 1969. Regnum Vegetabile Vol. 64: 1-62. Utrecht (1969). — Deutsche Fassung veröffentlicht in ZANDER, Handwörterbuch der Pflanzennamen, 10 Aufl. herausgegeben von F. ENCKE, G. BUCHHEIM and S. SEYBOLD. Stuttgart (1972).
GROSSHAUSER, M. Der Rechtsschutz für Gemüse — und Zierpflanzensorten in der Bundesrepublik. Dtsch. Gärtnerbörse 72: 983-986 (1972).
HEYWOOD, V.H. Taxonomie der Pflanzen. 112 S. Jena 1971.
KRÜSSMANN, G. 391mal "Madame", aber nur 8mal "Monsieur". Dtsch. Baumschule 1972: 78.
LEUTERT, P. Gewerbliche Rechtsschutzfragen für Pflanzenzüchtungen (in Der Deutsche Gartenbau, Berlin-Ost), 1966: 230-232.
MAASS, C.H. Was ist Züchtung? Dtsch. Baumschule 1964: 12-14.
MANSFELD, R. Die Technik der wissenschaftlichen Pflanzenbenennung. Akademie-Verlag Berlin 1949.

THE ROSE IN COMMERCE

REIMANN-PHILIPP, R. Ein Gerichtsurteil von grundsätzlicher Bedeutung? Gartenwelt 72: 383-385 (1972).

RIEHL, Dr. Fortschritte bei Rosensortenschutz und -lizenzen. Erwerbsgartner 1968: 1678.

ROTHMALER, W. Allgemeine Taxonomie und Chorologie der Pflanzen. 2 Aufl. Jena 1955.

SCHADE, H. Patentierung von Pflanzenzüchtungen. Schriften zur Förderung des Gartenbaues 1: 1-17. Aachen 1951.

WEIDINGER, G. Wie Weit soll der Züchterschutz gehen? Gartenwelt 72: 446-447 (1972).

WEUSTHOFF, F. Eine neue internationale Konvention zur Schaffung eines Rechtsschutzes für Pflanzenzüchtungen. Dtsch. Gärtnerbörse 1963: 11-12.

—— Das neue Sortenschutzgesetz. Erwerbsgärtner 1968: 226-228.

—— Cultivated Plant Nomenclature and Plant Variety Rights. Taxon 22: 455-458 (1973).

The Scented Rose

As early as the 13th century, an Archbishop of Cologne decreed that a rose garden must be a scented garden.

> People who go through rose gardens without stopping to inhale the fragrance of individual blossoms are getting their pleasure in one dimension only! The perfumes of roses are like exquisite chords of music composed of many odor notes harmoniously blended. (N.F. Miller, 1962)

The ingredients of perfume are fleeting by-products of certain glands, the cells of individual glands, or even complete organs such as petals or leaves. The scent is often a mixture of various kinds of perfume which can be dissipated by the aid of gas chromotography in small but positive amounts of aromatic substances. The scented substances are unsaturated and aromatic alcohol, aldehyde, fatty acids, phenol, carbonic acid and its derivatives, essential oils and resins.

Many rosarians today are of the opinion that the modern rose has lost its scent; admittedly this is true of some modern varieties but it is equally true that just as many of our modern roses smell as strongly, and as sweetly, as the "old" roses.

Dr. W. E. Lammerts, one of the leading American rose scientists, did an in-depth study in 1951 into the question of scent and conducted a number of experiments with old rose varieties. The results were then drawn up in chronological order and compared (see accompanying table). From this it was seen that a great many of the old roses had no scent at all! So it is wrong to say that ALL the old roses were fragrant. Here is an extract from his paper (the dates have been left unaltered).

Date	Strongly scented or scented	Moderately scented	Slightly scented or scentless
Prior to 1500	R. centifolia R. muscosa 'Rose des Peintres'	R. damascena	'Russeliana'

Date	Strongly scented or scented	Moderately scented	Slightly scented or scentless
1500-1600	'Kazanlik'	R. damascena versicolor 'Pink Moss'	R. foetida bicolor
1600-1700			'Gros Provins Panaché' 'Rosa Mundi' 'Président de Sèze'
1700-1800	'Maiden's Blush'	'Old Red Moss'	'Old Blush'
1800-1850	'Phoebus' 'Baronne Prévost'	'Mme. Hardy' 'Crested Moss'	'Persian Yellow' 'Comtesse de Murinais' R. harisonii
1850-1875	'La France' 'Duchesse de Brabant' 'Georges Vibert' 'Général Jacqueminot'	'Mme. Alfred Carrière'	'Paul Neyron'
1875-1900	'Ulrich Brunner' 'Kaiserin Auguste Viktoria'	'Gruss an Teplitz'	'Mignonette'
1900-1920	'Hadley' 'Gloire de Chedane Guinoisseau' 'Mme. Jules Bouché'	'Soleil d'Or' 'Variegata di Bologna' 'La Marne' 'Lady Hillingdon'	'Veilchenblau' 'F.J. Grootendorst' 'Tausendschön' 'Frau Karl Druschki'
1920-1940	'Betty Uprichard' 'Mrs. Sam McGredy' 'Lord Charlemont' 'Shot Silk' 'Crimson Glory'	'Colette Clément' 'California'	'Dainty Bess' 'Felbergs Rosa Druschki'

James A. Gamble, U.S.A. (1956), working over a number of years, examined 3,900 rose varieties for fragrance and came to the conclusion that 25% were scentless, 20% were strongly scented and the remainder had either moderate or little scent.

Bouquet (1968) is of the opinion that the ancestry of a third of our modern roses can be traced back to 'Lady Mary Fitzwilliam'. 'Mme. Caroline Testout' came from this source and in turn is an ancestor of that rose so famous for its fragrance 'Crimson Glory', which has passed on its typical scent, often called the "damask perfume", to many of its descendants.

As a rule, darker-colored roses are more highly scented that those of lighter shades, except that the more petals there are to the flower, the stronger the scent is likely to be. Heavy petals with a velvety sheen are more fragrant than thin petals. The scent comes from tiny cells, easily seen with a microscope, on the undersides of the petals.

The connection between scent and color in roses is demonstrated in red and pink roses which tend to give off the typical rose scent, while yellow and white often have different scents reminiscent of orris, nasturtium, violet or lemon. Roses of orange shades frequently have scents like those of fruit, orris, nasturtium, violet or clover.

On overcast days scent is reduced and when the weather is both cold and overcast, it is usually hard to detect; N.F. Miller believes that under those conditions only 'Sutter's Gold', 'Girona' and 'Chrysler Imperial' retain their full fragrance. As soon as the weather warms up, scent returns to normal.

The Polyantha roses are, for the most part, scentless, although there are one or two which prove the exception to the rule. Gamble (1956) found that 15 of them had good scent, but of these only 'Natalie Nypels' and 'Paulette' are still grown.

The old, so-called Hybrid Polyantha, were scentless, or nearly so, but this does not apply to many of our modern Floribundas. The first of these with good scent was 'Fashion' ('Rosenmärchen' × 'Crimson Glory'). Among other strongly scented Floribundas are 'Elizabeth of Glamis', 'Border Coral', 'Woburn Abbey', 'Minna Kordes', 'Chatter', 'Elfe', 'Lilibet', 'Ma Perkins' and 'Poulsen's Yellow'.

The causes and origins of scent in roses was researched in depth by N.F. Miller. Space here permits only a few details. The ingredients of perfume are formed in the chloroplasts. They are often surrounded with glucose which causes them to create the scentless glucosides which are stored or carried in the petals. The scent becomes noticeable in the petals if the glucoside, as a result of mixing with an enzyme, causes hydrolysis. The scent of nasturtium (*Tropaeolum*) probably comes from the sinapic oils (Benzyl-Isothio-cyanate and Phenylethylisocyanate), which are also present in *Tropaeolum* as a glucoside.

On warm, sunny days the scent of aldehyde is noticeably similar to the scent of hyacinths, jonquils, lemons and geraniums. Under these weather conditions, the clover-like scent becomes more like that of laurel. It is under such conditions, and when the soil is moist, that the roses smell their sweetest because the production of the scent ingredients in the chloroplast increases and they are conveyed to the petals in much larger quantities; then the alcohol oxidizes into aldehyde. W.A. Poucher (1959) has shown that this oxidation takes place in the flower. It must also be noted that the scent of each aldehyde is different and much stronger than that of the alcohol from which it was derived. The strength of the scent depends in part upon its volatility but still more upon the attraction which it has on the sensory nerves of the nose.

Anyone who wishes to study the biochemical aspects and components of fragrance should turn to the work of N.F. Miller (1962), from which a few of the more generally interesting points may now be quoted.

He tested the scent of 170 different varieties of roses under varying weather conditions and came to the conclusion that 25 different sorts of rose scent can be identified, and some roses even have a mixture of these different perfumes. Most Hybrid Teas appear to contain seven of the basic scents associated with the genus, or a mixture of them: rose, nasturtium, orris, violet, apple, lemon and clover.

Other common scents in roses are: hyacinth, fern or moss, orange, bay, anise, lily of the valley, linseed oil, honey, wine, marigold, quince, geranium, peppers, parsley and raspberry. Miller tells us the chemical derivation of a number of these scents. All 170 of the varieties he examined fall into one of the scent categories. The following varieties are, or have been, in general cultivation.

A Study of Rose Fragrance
(Abstract from the work of N.F. Miller)

+ = particularly strong scent.

Rose	Rose and Parsley
+Kazanlik	+American Beauty
+Parfum de l'Hay	+Mrs. John Laing
+Gruss an Teplitz	+Paul Neyron
+Rose des Peintres	
Rose and Cloves	*Cloves*
+Chrysler Imperial	+Luna
+Rouge Meilland	Dainty Bess
+Crimson Glory	Christopher Stone
+Hansa	
Rose and Nasturtium	*Nasturtium*
+Conrad Ferdinand Meyer	Miami
+Sarah van Fleet	Dr. Debat
+Heart's Desire	Detroiter
+Georg Arends	Buccaneer

Rose and Lemon
 +Rubaiyat
 +La France
 +Mirandy
 +Tiffany

Apple
 New Dawn
 Hon. Lady Lindsay
 Gail Borden

Apple, Clove and Rose
 +Zéphirine Drouhin

Fruit
 +Sutter's Gold (Quince)
 +Angels Mateu (Raspberry)
 +Kordes Perfecta (Orris/Raspberry)

Orris
 +Golden Masterpiece
 Golden Showers
 Miss America
 Golden Rapture

Orris and Violet
 +Golden Dawn
 +Condesa de Sastago
 +McGredy's Sunset
 +Maréchal Niel

Bay
 Radiance
 Red Radiance

Spice
 Soleil d'Or

Lemon
 +Suzon Lotthé
 +Symphonie
 Confidence

Apple and Clove
 Talisman
 Circus
 Souvenir de la Malmaison

Apple, Clove, Parsley and Lemon
 +Eden Rose
 Tallyho

Wine
 Treasure Island
 Comtesse Vandal

Lily of the Valley
 Gay Debutante
 Mme. Louis Lévêque
 Summertime

Violet
 Mme. Jules Bouché
 Margaret McGredy
 Betty Uprichard

Linseed Oil
 Persian Yellow
 Rosa foetida
 R. foetida bicolor

Fern, Moss
 Queen Elizabeth

In France, Leroy (1973) asked if soil and climate have any influence on the intensity of rose scent. Opinions on this are split, although it cannot be denied that climate (temperature, light and wind conditions) affect the distribution of scent. Whether the soil plays a part in this, as it does in the vineyard, remains in question for the time being.

ATTAR OR OIL ROSES.

References to the use of Attar in ancient Greece and Rome cannot be correct, for at that time the process of distillation, necessary for the production of Attar, was still unknown. However, members of both these ancient civilizations used scented oil in their baths; an oil with the addition of rose-scent was called *rhodium*. It was obtained by steeping the petals in oil as described by Dioscurides. It must have been this kind of oil which was used to anoint Hector's body, as is described in the *Iliad*.

The earliest distillation of Attar is mentioned in the Ayar-Vedas of Charakar, a doctor living in India about 100 A.D.

The next piece of information was found by Flückiger in an Arabic manuscript and published by him in 1862. In this we are told (according to the author Ibn Khaldun) that, in the years from 810-817 during the rule of the Caliph Mamun, the province of Faristan had to deliver an annual tribute of 30,000 flasks of rosewater to the government treasury in Baghdad. Blondel also produced a number of documents on the production of both Attar and rosewater in the Arabian territories.

Yet another author says that Avicenna, an Islamic doctor and apothecary from the Bokhara region in the period 980-1036, was the first man to distill rosewater; whether Attar was actually meant here is unclear. However, by the first half of the 9th century A.D., there was a considerable export trade of Attar from Baghdad, and its environs, to India, China, Egypt, N.W. Africa and Spain, and we can be sure that the process of distillation was discovered in Persia where the rose was first cultivated.

The court of Charlemagne must have smelled like a veritable rose-garden, and a great deal of the Attar must have been shipped there from abroad.

From the 10th to the 17th centuries, the center of the Attar industry was in Persia; from there it spread through Arabia to N.W. Africa and Spain. The crusaders returning from the Holy Land brought the rose to southern France, but industry in it did not develop there until the 19th century. The crusaders also introduced the habit of using rosewater in finger bowls for their guests (1096-1291).

Probably the most reliable report is that of Johannis Actuarius, doctor to the Greek governor of Constantinople at the end of the 13th century, in which he gives an account of the distillation of rosewater.

After the fall of the Roman Empire, the finest perfume was only used in the Orient and in Byzantium; it was frowned upon by the Church in the West. Only after the Crusades did its use begin to re-appear, at first in Italy, and then spreading through Europe during the Renaissance.

Queen Elizabeth of Hungary (1370) used distilled "Hungarian Water" (perhaps aided by politics) with such success that the King of Poland sought her hand in marriage when she was 72 years old! It is said that rosewater was a standby in her beauty treatment.

When Kaempfer wrote of the Attar industry in Shiraz

in 1712, this essential oil was already known in Europe. In 1574, Geronimo Rossi of Ravenna wrote that it was possible to extract a strongly scented oil from rosewater. Further, Angelus Sala in Germany described, between 1610 and 1630, a volatile oil obtained from roses.

According to Schlagenweit-Sakunlunski, and other authors (Blondel; 106), the practice of rose-growing was introduced to India from Persia and Arabia and, by the end of the 19th century, had become quite an industry in Ghazipur on the river Ganges.

According to legend, the Princess Nur-mahal, in 1612, while on her honeymoon with the Mogul Emperor Shah Jehangir Khan, was being rowed over a small lake the waters of which had been strewn with rose petals. The Princess noticed that the water was covered with an oily film; she dipped her handkerchief into it, squeezed it out into a flask, and found that it gave off a most delicious perfume. Although it has nothing to do with Attar, it should also be recorded that, during her wedding celebrations, her husband's five favorite court ladies died suddenly and mysteriously. As Empress, she lived through stormy times. In order that in old age she too should not die "suddenly and mysteriously", she married off her niece, Mumtaz, to the Crown Prince Shah Jehan, the famous Shah who later built the incomparable Taj Mahal in Agra for this same Mumtaz.

Also in 1612, Langlès, an Oriental languages expert, published a much quoted, but seldom read, work of linguistic research which brought many new facts to light. He wondered why the Persian poets like Hafiz never wrote of oil of roses (*athr*) but only of rosewater (*gulab*). This was also the case in Gulistan, in Bustan, where the famous poet S'Adi worked, and in the *Zéfer Nameh*, the history of the victories of Tamerlane, written by Sherif ed Dyn Ali, who went into much detail about the various perfumes used at the feasts of celebration. There is no record by a contemporary traveler on the subject of Attar before 1612.

At the court of Louis XIV of France (1643-1715), the use of perfume was almost as widespread as it was in Ancient Rome; the King, in particular, liked to live in an atmosphere redolent of orange blossoms.

The Turks brought the rose industry to the Balkans early in the 17th century, but it did not become sizeable until the 19th century, by which time the area had achieved a virtual monopoly in the supply of Attar.

Attar was always well known to German apothecaries and even more so to the French who made great use

Figure 89. The Indian Princess Nur-mahal and her husband, the Great Moghul. According to legend it was she who first discovered a method of obtaining Attar.

of it. In the Middle Ages, rosewater was a very common ingredient in perfumes and beauty products. Rosewater is an emulsion of 4 drops of Attar in a liter/quart of distilled water.

One curiosity in connection with rosewater is that the French poet Pierre Ronsard (1525-1585) was supposed to have been baptized with it. He had no more to do with roses as far as we know, except that he wrote a poem for Mary, Queen of Scots, for which she rewarded him with a silver rose said to have been worth $5,000.

The Composition of Attar

The following are a few linguistic notes on the subject. Oil of Roses; in Latin, *Oleum Rosae*; in French, *Essence de Rose* and in English *Attar*, *Attar of Roses* or sometimes *Otto of Roses*.

The word *Athr*, *A'thr* or *Othr* is used by the Arabs, Turks and Persians when referring to this essential oil without adding the name of the flower (*gul*). It is basically an Arabic word which means only 'scent'. It is derived from *a'thara* which means anything with a pleasant smell. Therefore, in the Orient, the words *Athar Gul* stand for oil of roses, and *gulab* is rosewater.

Attar is a perfume, and the origins of this word should be explained. It is two words joined together, *par fume*, or in Latin *per fumus*, and refers to the incense which was first discovered by the Arabs, but used by the Greeks, Romans, Egyptians and many other ancient peoples, as well. Today all cosmetics contain perfume, even if only in small quantities, and Attar remains one of the most highly prized perfumes. The scent of the pure oil is so strong that even the slightest trace clings and is difficult to remove.

There are many chemical components to Attar; these can also be obtained from other flowers, and synthetically. This can be done with such ease, and because genuine attar is so expensive, that the synthetic substitute is often used. Only an experienced chemist can tell the difference.

Appearance: A bright or rich, yellowish-green substance, it is fluid at room temperature but crystallizes when the temperature drops below 20° C/68° F; smells strongly of roses.

The specific gravity varies (according to Blondel):

0.815 for Attar from Grasse (S. France), at 30° C/86° F.

0.870-0.876 for German oil at 22° C/72° F.

0.870-0.890 for oil from the Balkans at 17° C/63° F.

Reaction: slightly acid.

Of the various component chemicals, the following are the most important:

Rhodinol (= 1-Citronellol); is also found in Citronella oil and *Geranium* oil. This component appears to be the main ingredient of Attar.

Geraniol Also found in *Geranium* oil, Citronella and lemon grass[1].

Nerol Also found in orange peel and in the flowers of *Geranium* and *Magnolia*.

1-Linalool Also in Cinnamomeum oil, sassafras and orange flowers.

Phenyl-Ethyl

Alcohol is found in many fluid oils.

Farnesol also appears in Citronella oil, lemon grass and orange peel.

Citral found in oil from oranges, lemons and lemon grass.

Eugenol comprises about 85% of the oil of cloves and is quite commonly found elsewhere.

Carvone generally found in oils coming from caraway, curled mint (*Mentha spicata crispata*) and dill.

Finally, there are the stearins, stable and non-odor-

[1] Lemon Grass is a tropical cultivated grass, *Cymbopogon citratus*; Citronella oil comes from Citronella grass, *Cymbopogon nardus*.

iferous alcohols somewhat paraffin-like in appearance, which amount to between 10% and 70% of the total after the oil has been extracted (according to Hegi).

Synthetics. Chemists today are able to produce Attar synthetically, although it is not of quite the same quality as the natural oil. There are a number of essential oils which, when combined, simulate true rose oil.

Most commonly used are:

Palmarosa oil from the Indian grass *Cymbopogon martinii*; Pelargonium oil, from *Pelargonium odoratissimum*, *P. graveolens* and *P. fragrans*;

Geranium oil from *Pelargonium radula*;

Guaja Wood oil, from *Guajacum officinale* and *G. sanctum*.

The synthetic compounds differ from the genuine oil by the iodine count (according to Hudson-Cox and Simmons, pure Attar is 187-194, Geranium oil 211-225, and Palmarosa oil 296-307), as well as the melting point.

Roses from which Attar can be obtained Roses which are grown for their visual beauty generally give a poor yield of Attar. Of today's 20,000 rose varieties very few have any industrial value; the following three are the most important:

1. *Rosa damascena* (usually in its form *trigintipetala*) is by far the most important rose for the production of Attar. It has a strong scent and gives a good yield. It is the main variety used in Bulgaria and Turkey. The typical *R. damascena* now grows wild in the Caucasus, Syria, Morocco and the Andalusian district of Spain.

2. *R. alba*. Does not yield as much oil, nor is the quality as good, as *R. damascena*. However, growth is more vigorous and it is more winter hardy, therefore it is widely used in Bulgaria as hedging around the fields planted with *R. damascena*.

3. *R. centifolia*. Despite its relatively high oil content, distillation is uneconomic because it has to be extracted by special solutions; grown for the most part in Southern France in Grasse and the surrounding area, and also to a lesser extent in Morocco.

Rosa gallica also contains oil, but not enough for commercial purposes. In the Crimea, crosses made between *R. gallica* and *R. damascena* resulted in the 'Red Crimean Rose', now considered to be the most important source of oil in that area.

The method of obtaining the essential oil is as follows:

Distillation. Has been in use since the method of making a still, which may have come from India and was certainly known to the Arabs, was discovered. In the Middle Ages, essential oil production was the preserve of the monasteries and the laboratories of German apothecaries; it was not until the 19th century that manufacturing essential oils became a truly industrial process.

Cold enfleurage. A common practice in Southern France. The oil is extracted from flowers and plants by using purified, scentless lard which absorbs the oil and, with it, the flower's scent. The lard is treated with the fresh blooms until it has been saturated, and can then be used as a pomade. It is also possible to extract the oil from the lard with highly concentrated alcohol.

Hot enfleurage or maceration. Extraction is made in pure lard at a temperature of 50-70° C/122-158° F.

Extraction proceeds in such a way that volatile fluids can be obtained from flower material at a very low boiling point in either, petrolether, tetrachloride, etc., and kept for several hours in sealed containers. During this time, extracts, which have the consistency of butter, are produced; the essential oil can be isolated from these.

Extraction by pressure, as with lemon and orange peel, is also possible. The world production of Attar per year at the present time is about 13,000 kg./28,600 lb.; about 23.3% of this comes from Bulgaria, and is guaranteed to be completely pure by government certificate. The remaining production comes from the U.S.S.R., Turkey, India and Morocco and also from S. France (the exact quantities are very controversial). The following figures were given by Prof. Dr. Staikov (Kazanlik) in 1966:

Country	Area under Cultivation (ha./acres)	=%
U.S.S.R.	4,000/9,884	43
Bulgaria	2,170/5,362	23.3.
Morocco	1,500/3,707	16.1
Turkey	1,385/3,422	19.9
France	250/618	2.7
Totals	9,305/23,000	100

The data for the yields in individual countries are difficult to compare because the technique of obtaining the oil differs from place to place.

Roses and the Production of Attar in Bulgaria About 1700, the cultivation of roses for the production of Attar was brought to the Balkans by the Turks, but it became established only in Bulgaria, particularly in the valley of the upper Toundja, which is now known as "Rose Valley"; the main center is Kazanlik, an industrial town with a population of 50,000. The area under rose cultivation is about 100 km./62 mi. long and from 10-15 km./6.2-9.3 mi. across and is bounded by mountains. In Kazanlik there is a research institute for oil-producing roses, and other medicinal plants, which was founded in 1908 (The Director is Prof. Dr. Staikov). The Institute has a collection of about 1,400 different rose varieties.

The most important of the oil bearing roses, other than *R. alba,* is the Kazanlik rose, *R. damascena trigintipetala,* which was first described by G. Dieck under this name and was widely grown in Germany. It is identical to the "Rose of Shiraz", the "Oil Rose of Cyprus" and the "Oil Rose of the Himalaya". The rose fields in Bulgaria are either privately owned or are co-operatives. During the blooming season they attract many visitors.

The Bulgarian research institute has established the optimum time for harvesting the flowers. This begins about May 20th and ends by June 16th, depending on the weather and local conditions. The daily task of picking starts at 4:00 a.m. and finishes at 10:00 or 11:00 a.m.; work must stop during the heat of the day since heat reduces the amount of oil in the flowers. Only those flowers which are half to fully open should be picked. The oil content of the flowers remains constant throughout the flowering period, that is to say the first flowers have as much oil content as the last. However bad weather can make this fall in individual flowers over the course of the day. The best time for gathering flowers is between 5:30 and 9:00 a.m., from then until noon there is a loss of 30 to 40%, and from then to 8 p.m. the loss can be as much as 70%.

The higher the oil content, the better the quality; some of the components of Attar are easily dissipated by rising temperature. The flowers have the highest con-

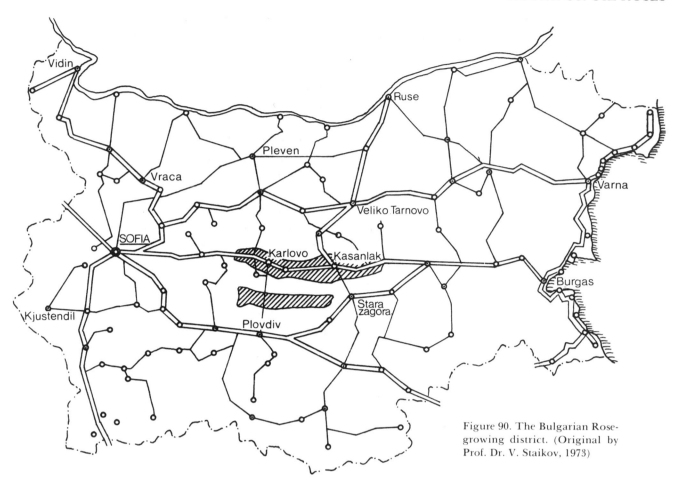

Figure 90. The Bulgarian Rose-growing district. (Original by Prof. Dr. V. Staikov, 1973)

tent of these components as they unfold, and they are retained as long as the anthers are a bright yellow.

Yields. The crop of flowers produced on 0.1 ha./0.25 acre in the Kazanlik area is very variable, but can be put at somewhere between 150 and 300 kg./330 and 660 lb. from good land; this may increase to 230-300 kg./506-660 lb. and, on the very best soil, may even rise as high as 600-700 kg./1,320-1,540 lb.

1 kg./2.2 lb. of Attar can be distilled from 3,000 kg./6,600 lb. of blooms; this amount can be produced from 1 ha./2.5 acres of good land if the blooms are picked early in the day.

In 1968, 1 kg./2.2 lb. of Attar was worth 8,500 Lewa. In the last few years the total Bulgarian production has amounted to approximately 32 to 35 million Lewa, which implies a production of around 4,000 kg./8,800 lb. of Attar. Earlier, Attar was worth six times its weight in gold, but at today's prices, and taking official exchange rates into account, it is currently about $9,000 per kg./$4,090 per lb.

The selling price of Attar varies from country to country; in November 1972 the following prices were obtained on the London market: Bulgarian Attar £846-56, Turkish Attar £603-17, Moroccan Attar £352-73, according to Prof. Dr. V. Staikov.

The modern method of treating the flowers is to boil 5 tons of flowers at a time in cauldrons. They are steeped in water four times, then heated from beneath and distilled by passing through cooling tubes. The distillation is a double process which makes it possible to produce rosewater as well as Attar. Most of the resulting Attar is exported to France.

Until recently the only distilleries were quite small, situated in the nearby mountains and the stills, which contained 120-150 li./32-40 gal., were individually fired. Each still took 15-20 kg./33-44 lb. of rose blooms which had been gathered in the early morning and delivered as quickly as possible to the distillery nearest the rose field; four to five times as much water in volume was added to the flowers; from this about 20-30

211

li./5.3-7.9 gal., known as the "first water", was distilled. This was then re-distilled and reduced to about 12 li./3.2 gal. It was then allowed to stand until an oily film developed on the surface of the water; this was then skimmed off. The water was re-used in the distillation of a new batch of roses and, after the oil was once again skimmed off, was sold as rosewater.

Cultivation of roses for Attar in other countries
Soviet Union. S.G. Saakov (1962) tells us that Attar production in the U.S.S.R. has markedly increased in recent years, and is now greater than Bulgarian production, but unfortunately he does not provide any figures. The main centers of the industry are in the Crimea (1958: 1,100 ha./2,718 acres), in the Moldavian Republic (680 ha./1,680 acres) and in the north of the Caucasus in the area of Krasnodar (800 ha./1,977 acres). Some is also produced in Grusin, in Tadzikstan and in the Ukraine. The Research Institute which deals scientifically with Attar is in Krasnodar.

The following roses are those which are mostly grown for Attar: The 'Red Crimean Rose', a *gallica* hybrid, is bright red with many petals, with sprays of 15 blooms at a time, often with 800 to 1,000 blooms to a single bush. It is winter hardy down to -25° C/-13° F, is easily propagated by cuttings, gives a high yield of flowers per hectare and contains a high percentage of Attar.

The Bulgarian rose (*R. damascena trigintipetala*) is known in the Soviet Union as the 'Red Kazanlik Rose' despite its deep pink color; it is being progressively supplanted by the 'Red Crimean Rose'.

There are also high quality hybrids from these two roses: 'Nowinka', 'Pionierka' and 'Kooperatorka'.

France. The French perfume industry is world-famous. Grasse is the international city of flowers for obtaining the essential oils used in the industry. About 300,000 kg./660,000 lb. of rose blooms, mostly *Rosa centifolia*, with a considerable quantity of 'Ulrich Brunner', are processed annually.

Since distillation has not been very successful here, the flowers are treated in various solutions, particularly petroleum ether (a benzine mixture with a low boiling point which is a by-product of petroleum distillation). The extractors each hold 1,200 li./317 gal. and are placed two to four together in a row and linked together so that the solution can circulate freely from one extractor to another; the flowers are laid on perforated sheets or plates so that the pumped solution can flow freely. The flowers are washed through three times and periodically a fresh solution is added. The liquid is then filtered by steaming at a temperature of 60° C/140° F (the solution would be ruined at a higher temperature). Finally, it is allowed to cool and passed through a vacuum still where it is compressed at room temperature. The resultant solid is known as "concrete".

After this "concrete" is treated with a high-percentage alcohol, pure Attar, just as it exists in the living flowers, is obtained.

The basic components of the oil obtained in this process are the same as those obtained in water distillation, but the percentages of these vary depending upon whether they are produced in hot water or in solution.

The "concrete" is a waxy, rich or dark brown, viscous material with a strong scent of roses. 1 kg./2.2 lb. of "concrete", produced from 400-500 kg./880-1,000 lb. of rose blossoms, contains 500-600 g./17.5-21 oz. of pure Attar.

Morocco. In the districts of Tedders, Maasis, Berkan and Marrakesh, where mostly *centifolia* is used, both "concrete" and rosewater are manufactured. South-east of the Atlas Mountains, in the river valleys of the Dades and Mgouna, there are many Damask roses, the flowers of which are taken to the Skiriss factory, on the road from El Kelaa to Boumalne, where they are processed and both "concrete" and Attar produced.

For other areas of production current statistical data are lacking. In India, once so famous for making rose perfumes, there are rose fields at Ghazipur and some Attar is made there. There are further plantations at Poona and Bangalore, but these appear to be deteriorating for lack of technical progress.

Years ago, the firm of Schimmel & Co. of Klein-Miltitz, near Leipzig, cultivated about 40 ha./100 acres of roses for Attar. The first planting was made in 1883 and in 1890 they managed to produce 4.5 kg./10 lb. of Attar of quality equal to the Bulgarian. After 1914 the project was abandoned because the production costs were too high. They used mainly *R. damascena trigintipetala* and some *R. gallica.*

THE ROSE IN MEDICINE.

Pliny the Elder, writing in 77 A.D., said that the rose could be used in the cure of 32 diseases, some very severe.

This must have been regarded with wry smiles of disbelief as the years went by; of course, we know that the rose contains large amounts of Vitamin C, but Pliny's advice says nothing about this, and certainly nobody today would believe, as Pliny did, that the color of a rose could have any bearing on the treatment of an illness.

In early medicine, roses were used for inflammation of the eyes, ears and mouth, they were used for stomachache, headaches and toothache, for healing wounds, ulcers and hemorrhoids, for insomnia and for "purification of the mind" in the treatment of mental illness. Prescriptions often contained 20 or 30 different herbs and roses were almost always among them. In the course of time, medicaments became more complicated, but the rose always played its part in alleviation or healing.

As was said earlier, there was at least one monk in every medieval monastery who knew how to put the herb garden in his charge to good use. The rose was an important part of that garden because, in addition to its other virtues, it was a Christian symbol.

The "Apothecary's Rose", *Rose gallica officinalis*, was grown in large numbers in Provins, near Paris, from the 13th century on; it was brought from Damascus by the crusader, Count Thibaut IV. For nearly 600 years this area was the center for the cultivation of this rose. There is an old story that, about 1600, the main street of this little town was flanked by two long rows of apothecaries' and druggists' shops. The remedies made from the roses here were expored to all parts of the world. In 1807 the French rose-growers in Provins received an assurance from the government that their unguents would be used in all public and military hospitals. In 1860 they even exported 36,000 kg./79,200 lb. of dried rose petals to the U.S.A.

In the 15th century it was customary for people to carry little sachets of rose petals, or put them in their pillows. Perhaps this harks back to an ancient Roman custom when the elite had their cushions filled with rose petals. The French King, Charles VI (1368-1422), was in the habit of putting these rose petal sachets in the royal linen, a fact recorded in his housekeeper's account books.

Among other items, the medieval chemists sold:

Flores Rosae, Rose Flowers

Cortex Radicis Rosae, Bark of Rose Roots

Semina Cynosbati, Rose Seeds (apparently against worms)

Saccharum Rosatum, Rose sugar

Aretum Rosarum Acidula, Tincture of Roses (very acidic)

Fungus Rosae or *Bedegar*, Robin's Pincushion (this was put under children's pillows in the belief that it helped them to sleep)

Aqua Rosarum, Rosewater, used to conceal the unpleasant taste or smell of some other medicine.

Also sold were "Turkish Rose Pearls", shiny black pills made from pulverized rose leaves mixed with gum. Their precise purpose is unknown, but they may have been used against toothache.

Even before 1939 rose hips were investigated for their vitamin content, and it was discovered that *Rosa haematodes* contained four times as much vitamin C as apples. The quantity of vitamin present in each species is very variable and tends to be higher in cool climates than in warmer ones. During the Second World War, the cultivation of roses for this purpose was greatly encouraged, not only in Germany but also in England; it now seems to have declined, probably because the best varieties for this are hard to get. The quantity of Vitamin C (ascorbic acid) in 100 g./3.5 oz. of hips are:

Rose haematodes	2,900 mg./0.1 oz.
– *sweginzowii macrocarpa*	1,100 mg./0.04 oz.
– *rugosa regeliana*	940 mg./0.03 oz.
– *villosa*	920 mg./0.03 oz.
– *moyesii*	850 mg./0.03 oz.

./0.002 oz. (the equivalent figure for apples is a mere 50 mg./0.002 oz.!)

Our indigenous species roses contain 300-800 mg./0.01-0.03 oz., and the cultivated garden roses and *Rosa multiflora* only a relatively small amount.

In conclusion here are a few examples taken from the work of J.C. Uphof on the medicinal uses of leaves, petals and hips.

Rosa canina. The fresh hips were used in medicine as a diuretic, as a coolant and as a mild astringent. Both leaves and hips were used for infusions or tea.

Rosa centifolia. Aqua Rosae Fortior was obtained by distillation of the petals with water.

Rosa foetida Herrmann. The flowers were used in Persia as a treatment against colic and diarrhea; in addition, *gulangabin*, a mixture of the petals and honey, was also produced for use in the sweetmeat industry.

THE SCENTED ROSE

Rosa gallica. The buds were picked before opening, dried and steeped in wine vinegar to produce Rose Vinegar which was used for over-tiredness, fainting and a number of other similar disorders.

Rosa laevigata Mich. Used in Chinese medicine as an anti-spermatorrheic.

Rosa pomifera Herrm. The leaves were used for an infusion, commonly known as "German Tea"; the hips were made into preserves and also into a drink. It was very popular in certain areas of Austria and Bavaria.

Rosa roxburghii Tratt. f. *normalis* Rehd. & Wils. The hips were used by the Chinese against indigestion.

Rosa rugosa Thunb. The Ainu in Japan ate the hips.

THE ROSE IN THE KITCHEN

Archaeologists and botanists have discovered that a Stone Age people, living 3,000 years ago in what is now Switzerland, ate a form of "Muesli" made from rose hips; many seeds from that period have been found.

The ancient Romans bathed in rosewater, drank rose wine, ate rose jelly, rose honey, candied rose petals and a very special kind of rose pudding, the recipe for which was recorded by Apicius, made of calves brains, pepper, eight eggs, oil and roses. Roman rose wine would hardly have appealed to the modern palate; fresh rose petals were stepped in a warm alkaline solution to which cinnamon sticks were added, this was topped up with alcohol and then about 0.5 kg./1.1 lb. of sugar was added per liter/quart. This then had to stand for three weeks before it was considered drinkable.

In the Middle Ages, young ladies used the following recipe to protect against freckles: "Collect the dew which is lying in the meadows (this applies of course to ladies living in the country) mix it with rosewater and white oil of lilies; then wash well the affected parts and this will give a clear complexion free of spots and freckles."

Rose syrup is sold in grocer's shops in the Balkans; it looks rather like a brownish raspberry syrup and has a strong taste of roses. In Greece there is a form of rose preserve which is quite common and which consists of a sticky honeylike base to which rosebud petals have been added. Sometimes this product may be found in our own shops, but it is so sweet that one can only eat a very little at a time. A delicious conserve made from rose hips can be found in Germany and even more frequently in Holland.

Although not part of the work of the kitchen, but nevertheless very much within the province of the housewife, is the rose Pot-pourri which is so often found in the homes of English rose-lovers. It is usually kept in an urn, or china bowl with a lid, in which the petals of fragrant roses are preserved after they have been dried and prepared according to a special recipe. There are many ways of doing this in both dry and wet methods. Suffice it to say that only the fresh petals of overblown, highly fragrant roses should be used; these must be quickly dried, not in the sun, but on a rack or sieve to ensure good air circulation. It is best not to use a metal rack because this tends to make the petals turn black; the petals should be well spaced, not touching one another. When they are dry and crisp to the touch they should be put into an airtight container. The process of drying will reduce the amount to about one third. White roses tend to dry brown, dark red roses become almost black; reddish-pink roses are the best. The dried petals are then put with other scented material according to individual taste (for example, a few drops of sandalwood oil, lavender oil, oil of orange flowers, or even Attar of roses, may be added). This must all be well shaken and then left for six weeks sealed in a container with a wide neck. Finally the preparation can be taken out, put into small bowls and placed around the room. The scent will last for a number of years.

BIBLIOGRAPHY.

ALDOUS, A.M. The Rose and the Apothecary. Rose Ann. 1950: 102-104.

BENZINGER, M.G. Fragrance of the Gods. Amer. Rose Ann. 1970: 51-53.

BLONDEL, R.E. Les produits odorants des Rosiers. Diss. Paris 1889.

BORCHARD, R. A psychology of Rose scent. The Rose 10: 111-113 (1961).

DIECK, G. Einige Worte über Oelrosen. Rosen-Zeitung 1891: 50-51.

GAMBLE, J.A. The Fragrances in our Roses. Amer. Rose Ann. 1956: 29-40.

GRAMLING, L.G. The Scent of the Rose. Amer. Rose Ann. 1967: 102-108.

HARKNESS, E. The Rose of Commerce. Rose Ann. 1970.

HARRIS, C.C. Roses with unusual scents. Gard. Chron., 9. Sept 1969.

HEGI. G. III. Flora von Mittel-Europa, IV, 2 (Abschnitt Rosa) Münich 1923.

KORDES, W. Unsere Ur-Gartenrosen. Rosen-Jahrb. 26: 118-130 (1962).

LAMMERTS, W.E. Just how fragrant are the old Roses? Amer. Rose Ann. 1951: 145-148.

LEROY, A., et al. Le Parfum, est-il tributaire du climat et de la composition des sols? Les Amis des Roses, Nr. 316: 40-41 (1973).

MILLER, N.F. Study of Rose Fragrance. Amer. Rose Ann. 1962: 79-89.

NIKOLOV, N. Bulgarian Rose Oil. The Rose 16: 182-185 (1968).

POUCHER, W.A. Perfumes, Cosmetics and Soaps. Vol. 2: 23-26. New York 1959.

RATHLEF, H.von. Die Hagebutte als Vitamin-C-Spender; ihre züchterische Bearbeitung und ihr Anbau. Pharmaz. Industrie 9: 307-317 (1942).

RAYMOND, G. Begehrter als Gold. Rosenbogen 1969: 209-214.

RIES, F. Die Kultur der Ölrosen und die Gewinnung des Rosen-öls. Rosen-Zeitung 1921: 18-20.

RILEY, M.T. Oil of Roses. Amer. Rose Ann. 1953: 144-150.

SAAKOV, S.G. Die Geschichte der Ölrosenkultur in der Sowjetunion. Rosen-Jahrb. 26: 102-118 (1962).

SCHLAGENWEIT-SAKUNLUNSKI, H. von. Das genus Rosa in Hoch-Asien, und über Rosenwasser und Rosenöl. Buchner's Repert. Pharmac. 24: 129-143.

SHEPHERD, R.E. Roses in daily Life. Amer. Rose Ann. 1957: 10-16.

THOMAS, G.S. The Roman Rose and the Rose Scent. Gard. Chron. 9. Feb. 1957.

UPHOF, J.C.TH. Dictionary of Economic Plants. 2 ed.: 454-555 (1960).

Records in Roses

Because roses have been so beloved for the past 2,000 years it is hardly surprising that in that time there have been claims for the biggest, smallest, oldest, favorite, most beautiful and even for the "Super Rose of All Time".

We will start with the oldest rose in the world which must be the "Thousand year-old Rose Tree" on the wall of the Cathedral at Hildesheim; there certainly cannot be an older rose still in existence.

It was described as *R. canina* by H. Christ in 1891 and also as var. *lutetiana*[1]. It is without doubt the most famous rose in Germany and continues to enjoy the best of health, blooming and fruiting freely each year. The true age of this rose cannot be positively established. H. Seeland (1947) thought that it was not 1,000 years old, but was probably 300 to 400, however, his view is disputed today. J. Breloer, himself of Hildesheim, has recently conducted an intensive study and, on the basis of old archives, believes that the Rose Tree was described in the earliest printed history of the town of Hildesheim (1573) and was, by then, already an old rose. Even earlier archives which might have shed further light on the rose were destroyed in the great fire of the cathedral in 1013. Some botanists, for example Loiseleur-Deslongchamps (1844) refuse to accept that the stock could really be as old as it is presumed to be. However, Alexander von Humboldt (1849) did not demur when he was told that the tree was 800 years old.

[1] Described in 1890, by G. Lutze of Sonderhausen (Thuringia) as *R. canina* var. *lutetiana* (Léman) Baker; this has plain dentate foliage; there are no glands on the calyx or on the backs of the sepals; the stems are covered in sharp hooked prickles.

Figure 91. The "1,000 year-old" rose tree on the Cathedral at Hildesheim as it appeared in 1825, from a very stylized drawing by J.L. Brands which was published in the *Neuen Vaterländischen Archiv* (1825). It is impossible to believe that the stem was as thick as a man's arm and growing like a tree. The drawing shows two equally strong stems growing away from the stock. Both the flowers and leaves must be inaccurate (only four petals are shown and the leaves are not pinnate).

By 1844 the tree was 10.6 m./34 ft. high, and many authorities were of the opinion that it was about to die, but a few years later the tree proved them wrong. From all this varied evidence, J. Breloer (1974) came to the conclusion that it could be 1,000 years old, provided that not only had many of the old stems died off and been replaced by new ones coming from the base, but also that the root stock, following the habits of other wild roses, had thrown out suckers. Those parts of the roots which were still full of life had thrown out new shoots and continued the existence of the tree. There does not seem to be any biological reason to doubt that it is possible for it to be of such a great age.

After the oldest, let us now look at the "largest" rose in the world. It is still in existence, and is a *Rosa banksiae alba plena* or, more correctly, *R. banksiae* var. *banksiae*. It is growing in Mrs. Burlin Devore's garden in Tombstone, Arizona and was taken there in 1885 as a young plant from Scotland. By 1933 the stem had reached a thickness of 15 cm./5.9 in. and the head covered almost 200 sq.m./239 sq. yd. By 1973 the stem had a circumference of 1 m./3.3 ft. and a diameter of 30 cm./12 in. and the head now covered an area of nearly 600 sq.m./718 sq. yd. No less than 150 people could stand under its branches.

The largest known specimen in Europe was in Germany in the nursery of E. Wehrle at Freiburg. The wild understock was budded in 1881 with 'Chromatella' and grown in a greenhouse. In 1900 the head of the bush was some 90 sq.m./108 sq. yd. and carried over 10,000 blooms. In 1904, the land with the greenhouse was sold and the plant died in 1911. The stem was 1.1 m./3.6 ft. high and had a circumference of 38 cm./15 in.; the head, which was trained on wires, measured 39 m./129 ft. (*Rosenzeitung* 1912: 152-153 with photograph).

Details are provided by R. Keller in Ascherson and Graebner, *Synopsis der Flora Mittel-Europas*, VI: p. 155 on a really outsize *Rosa canina* growing in Over-Haverbeck on the Lüneburger Heide. It had a circumference of about 32 m./106 ft. and a diameter of about 10 m./33 ft. The stem had a circumference of 83 cm./33 in.

There was also a similarly outsized *Rosa banksiae* which was originally sent to Toulon by Bonpland in 1813, where it was planted in the Marine Gardens. By 1870 the stem of this rose, just above the ground, had a circumference of 80 cm./31 in. and a diameter of over 25 cm./10 in. Each year it produced shoots 3.5-4.5 m./11.6-14.9 ft. in length. When it came into bloom in April to May it is said that it had as many as 50,000 individual blooms.

The rose with the record in propagation is undoubtedly 'Peace'; from 1945 to the present more than 100 million plants of it have been produced and sold.

The highest recorded price which has ever been paid for a rose went to William Francis Bennett, an English amateur rose hybridizer, who gave the seedling his own name. He brought it out in 1880 and in 1883 sold it to the florist Evans in the U.S.A. for the sum of $5,000. Unfortunately, this rose turned out to be poor for forcing and a real weakling when grown in the open, so it was soon taken off the market (see W. Kordes).

A prize of $1,000 was offered at the San Francisco World Fair in 1914 for an unnamed rose novelty, but there seems to be no record of the winner.

The newspaper *The Daily Mail* of London gave a gold cup as a prize for the best new climbing rose in 1912, and at German rose shows it was the practice to give prizes of brandy, cigars, ties and other practical items in addition to the gold, silver and bronze medals.

The most prestigious of the world's rose societies must be the "Royal Rosarians" in Portland, Oregon. Its membership is limited to 220. Each is dubbed knight after his election and may use the title "Sir Knight" before his own name. The officials of the society are called the Prime Minister (President), the Lord Chancellor (the Manager) and the Secretary of State (the Secretary); honorary members are given the title of "Duke". All active members wear a white uniform with embroidery on the sleeve depicting a red rose beneath a gold crown. The object of this society is the promotion of the City of Portland as "The Rose City" and the organization of an annual Rose Festival. When Count Luckner visited Portland in 1928 he was elected honorary knight.

The rose society with the largest membership is the English Royal National Rose Society which had a membership of 110,000 in 1970!

The tallest rose in the world is undoubtedly *Rosa gigantea* from the Himalayas where it grows up to 15 m./49 ft., or even higher. Whether it has ever reached this height in Europe is unknown, but at Malahide Castle near Dublin in Eire it has reached a height of 10 m./33 ft. Also, the *bracteata* hybrid 'Mermaid', which has single blooms 12 cm./4.7 in. across, grows so vigorously that it will easily climb up to a height of 8 m./26 ft., and is capable of covering the whole side of a house.

RECORDS IN ROSES

When discussing the smallest rose in the world, it is impossible to be so precise, for the size of the plant is greatly dependent upon the method of cultivation. 'Roulettii', when grown in a container and given special care, can be kept at a height of no more than 15 cm./6 in., provided it is grown on its own roots (i.e. from a cutting) and is not budded.

The rose with the smallest leaves is *Rosa stellata* from the Organ and San Andreas Mountains in New Mexico. The full leaf consists of no more than three tiny leaflets each about 12 mm./0.5 in. in length. The largest leaves are to be found on *Rosa sinowilsonii*, a climber from S.W. China; they are about 30 cm./12 in. long and have even been found to exceed this length.

In regarding color in the rose, some extremes may be quoted, although not which is the reddest, whitest or yellowest, but rather which is the darkest. The "black rose" has always been of sufficient interest to amateurs that from time to time a new "black rose" appears on the market. There is, in fact, no such thing, although in many varieties the dark red color is so dark that, with a bit of imagination, it may seem black, but there are always some reddish overtones. Formerly, the darkest variety was 'Nigrette', a German introduction of 1934. Unfortunately, it is not a very strong grower, the few blooms it produces are small and the variety is only found in specialized collections today. Later, Meilland produced a variety called 'Super Congo' (1950), and today a variety called 'Norita' is probably the "blackest" rose.

Enough has already been said about blue roses on p. 173. The "bluest" rose is still the old variety 'Reine des Violettes' but, as the name implies, it is really more a lilac-violet color than a genuine blue.

The rose with green flowers, *Rosa chinensis viridiflora*, does not appear in many collections and cannot be said to have beauty, but only a curiosity value. It is, however, liked by lady flower-arrangers.

It would undoubtedly be possible to fine more "rose records", oddities and curiosities, but the ones already cited must suffice.

For BIBLIOGRAPHY see p. 235.

A Concluding Chapter of Cultural History

THE ROSE —
SYMBOL OF LOVE AND WOMEN

This has been true of many countries and nationalities, and probably it was so first of all with the Germanic peoples, ever since the garden rose made its appearance some 800 years ago. Women were always likened to roses; they were buds, they bloomed and were overblown; with their "thorns" they could tear and scratch. Roses symbolized, especially in Europe, love, compassion, friendship and honor, all the finest of human virtues.

In early times, as today, it was customary to use roses symbolically, particularly when given as a gift, to convey a special meaning:

Red roses for Love

Carmine roses for Sorrow or Mourning

Pink roses for Youth or Beauty

Yellow roses for Envy, Silence or Unfaithfulness

White roses for Innocence or Purity

The roses shown in church paintings are always symbolic, for example, a red rose with five petals represents Christ's five wounds, and the white rose represents the Virginity of the Mother of God.

The poems and songs written and sung in honor of women are strewn with references to a rosebud mouth, rosy cheeks, the resemblance of a girl to a rosebud or to a full-blown rose.

> Women, like roses, bud, bloom and ripen but they can also inflict pain: the rose warns that it can prick.

Many folk songs from all over Europe speak of the rose. We can pick a few at random from the *Garden of Roses* (p. 55), showing the importance of the rose in the Middle Ages.

This King Gibich in the "Lay of the Nibelungen" is quite unknown; he may perhaps have been the Burgundian King Gibica who lived in the 5th century.

> King Gibich had a garden on the Rhine;
> Whoever entered it became its servant;
> It had no walls, no moat surrounded it
> There was only a golden border round it.
> There was such joy and rapture in this garden,
> What lovely roses and bright flowers it bore!
> Kriemhild tended it and kept it spick and span,
> With gentle ladies and sweet maids to help her.
> But it was not only roses which delighted her,
> For soon von Bern was telling her wonderful things
> And she delighted to see him joust.
> 'Good luck go with so noble a knight', quoth she
> 'Giants, dragons and heros have fallen to him
> But I have as Guardians of the Garden, twelve warriors
> Who tend the roses and are so bold and audacious!
> . . . .
> These warriors shall be the Garden's shield,
> They will not falter in the hardest fight!
> They will breathe defiance at lord and man
> And bring death to all who dare trespass in this garden.

Kriemhild also promises to reward, with rose garlands, purses of gold and the embraces of fair maidens, any knights who can overcome her twelve heroes in fair combat. Dietrich von Bern ("Bern" is the same as Verona in N. Italy), King of the Ostrogoths (493-526) takes up the challenge:

> Then said the Governor of Bern: 'Tell the Queen
> That roses please me not nor do I seek kisses,
> But I will fight her twelve heroes beside the green Rhine
> And the victor's crown is honor and shall be honor alone!'

Dietrich of Bern is victorious and the saga continues

> Then Queen Kriemhild hesitated no longer
> But crowned the victor with a wreath of roses
> and showered kisses on the bravest hero . . .

This poem has little historical substance and is quoted here only to demonstrate that the rose was important even in those far-off days.

The *Heideröslein*, by Goethe (1749-1832), is quoted here in the translation by the Rev. F.W. Farrar:

> Once a boy a rosebud saw —
> Rosebud in the heather!
> 'Twas so young and morning bright,
> Gazed he on it with delight,
> In the sunny weather.
> Rosy, rosy, rosy bud
> Rosebud in the heather.
>
> Said the boy, 'I'll pluck you, Rose —
> Rosebud in the heather!
> Said the rosebud, "Ware the thorn;
> Thou shalt rue it, scratched and torn,
> In the sunny weather!
> Rosy, rosy, rosy bud,
> Rosebud in the heather!

Figure 92. An artist's impression of a rose with six-petaled flowers, decorating the title page of the *Zupfgeigenhansl*, the songbook of the Wandervögel. (133, 1924 Edn.)

Wilful boy! He plucked the rose,
Rose amid the heather!
Rosebud tore his hand amain,
Little helps his cry of pain,
In the sunny weather.
Rosy, rosy, rosy bud.
Rose amid the heather.

And, in conclusion, the "Yellow Rose of Texas", that famous American song. The "Yellow Rose of Texas" is really the name of a folk heroine of Southern Texas. While it is not exactly clear which plant is meant, general opinion is that it is *Rosa harisonii* which was taken to the Southern and Western states by the early settlers from New England. Other plants with which it has been connected are *Potentilla fruiticosa*, *Kerria japonica pleniflora*, *R. pimpinellifolia* and *R. bracteata*, but the latter two have white flowers.

In 1954, the firm of Arp Roses, Inc. of Tyler, Texas, put a Hybrid Tea, 'Lemon Chiffon', on the market and, because the song was so popular at the time, it was this rose which became known as the "Yellow Rose of Texas".

These are the words to the song:

She's the sweetest little rosebud that Texas ever knew,
Her eyes they shine like diamonds, they sparkle like the dew.
You may talk about Clementine, and sing of Rosalie,
But the Yellow Rose of Texas is the only girl for me.

So beautiful and noble is this connection between the rose and womankind that we sometimes forget that others were made. For example, in Frankfurt am Main, and indeed in other cities, the "ladies of easy virtue" were known as "roses", and in Breslau until quite recently it was a real insult to call someone a "rose of the alleys". In Nîmes, sad to say, these ladies had to wear a rose as a symbol of their profession.

THE CHURCH AND THE ROSE

In ancient times, the rose was dedicated to the Gods of Love and Pleasure (Aphrodite and Dionysus in Greece; Venus and Bacchus in Rome). The Christian Church, in its early days, disapproved of this flower which was so associated with extravagance and corruption, but it was impossible to eliminate this age-old veneration. Finally, about the 5th or 6th century, the Church was wise enough to bestow a religious interpretation upon the Queen of Flowers (for details of roses in the Bible, see p. 55).

The cross is, of course, the most holy of all Christian symbols, the Sign of Sorrow, the representation of the dying Christ, and yet, it is also a symbol of Resurrection. The rose has a similar dualistic symbolic nature. First and foremost, it symbolized the Blood of the Martyrs, and in the 6th century it became linked with the Madonna Lily (*Lilium candidum*) as a symbol of purity and modesty. In it were united the qualities of unearthly beauty, godly virtues, and chastity; it was the *Rosa mystica* (the Rose of Secrecy) of the Lauretanian Litany.

The white rose was at times regarded as a messenger of death, yet, if it was shown at trial verdicts, it signified the innocence of the accused. The rose was a symbol not only of joy, but also of gloom. The subsequent connection of the rose with Mariolatry was seen by some historians as an unconscious continuation of Greek culture in which roses were dedicated to all the most beautiful goddesses.

The rosary, which, according to legend, was introduced by St. Dominicus, and which has been known since the 11th century, promoted affection for the rose.

Figure 93. Left: Symbols and scenes of glory in a rosary from Ulm. 1489. Right: Symbols of joy and thanksgiving in a rosary from Augsburg, 1495. (from St. Beissel, History of the Worship of the B.V.M. in Germany during the Middle Ages. Freiburg 1909)

It is said that the first rosaries were actually made of the flower itself. A 12th century hymn begins with the words "Ave Maria, Rose without a Thorn . . . " Rosaries paying homage to the Blessed Virgin were written in Latin from the 13th century, but also translated into German. It is clear from the following Psalter of Abbot Engelbert von Admont, who died in 1331, how important the rose as symbol had become.

> *Ave, rosa, amoenorum*
> *Ad convalles duc nos florum,*
> *Ad hortorum lilia.*
> *Paradisi ad virores,*
> *Violarum ad odorem.*

(Hail to Thee, Blessed Rose, lead us into the valley of flowers, into the garden of lilies and into the green pastures of Paradise to the scent of violets and of a thousand roses). (from Beissel, 246)

In many songs and poems of the Middle Ages, the Virgin was described as the "Rose without a Thorn".

From the 11th century on, particularly in France, the nave facades in the great Gothic cathedrals were adorned with stylized rosette windows, usually of stained glass. Typical examples are to be seen at Rheims, Chartres, Laôn, Amiens, Paris (Notre Dame), Strasburg, Cologne, Freiburg, Exeter, Canterbury, York and Westminster Abbey. It is said that the custom originated with the Crusaders who had seen a rose window of this sort in the Mosque of Ibn Tulun in Cairo and brought the idea home with them.

It was also the custom, as it had been in Ancient Egypt, to put roses in graves. There are any number of stories of rose bushes springing up out of graves. One such example is of the Abbey of the Holy Cross at Poitiers in France where a rose bush in flower grew out of the grave of a young man; a pillar in the Abbey still commemorates this miraculous event. St. Elizabeth, daughter of a Hungarian King and wife of the Landgraf Hermann von Thüringen, (1207-1231) was devoutly charitable. When she was about to take bread to the poor in a covered basket, she was surprised by her stern husband who demanded to know what was in the basket. Fearing his anger, she replied, "Roses". Unsatisfied, he opened the basket, where, to her amazement, the bread had, by a miracle, been changed into red and white roses.

In the Middle Ages, the rose also played a part in the liturgy of the Church. On certain special occasions both

221

priests and altars were garlanded with roses. Many of the miraculous appearances of the Virgin have been connected with roses (Guadalupe 1531, Lourdes 1858, Fatima, Portugal, 1917); in these miracles the Virgin appeared to be crowned with a wreath of roses.

About 1521, Pope Hadrian VI had roses carved or sculpted on the confessionals. They symbolized secrecy, the total inviolability of the confessional, just as they had in the ancient world (see p. 38).

Roses were often cultivated in monasteries, particularly in the numerous Benedictine Houses throughout Europe. Graves were planted with roses, especially in the monastery graveyard. Thus the cloister garden of the Church of Our Lady at Zurich was called the "Rose Garden", as was the old cemetery in Berne (p. 137). It is common to find roses carved in stone on the doorways of the great cathedrals (Plate 8), or carved in wood (Plate 6), or cast in metal (Plate 6). Only a few examples can be given here.

The "Golden Rose". It is traditional for the Pope to give a golden rose, personally blessed by him, to members of Royal families, or to people who had rendered very special and outstanding service to the Church. Just when this was started is unknown, but it was probably about 1050, during the Pontificate of Leo IX; at any rate it had already become a tradition by the 12th century. The golden rose was originally just a simple decorative artifact with red enamel; later, the red enamel was replaced by a large ruby, and finally a complete rose stem with leaves, flower and thorns, of considerable intrinsic value, perhaps as much as $5,000.

On the *Dies dominica in Rosa*, the fourth Sunday in Lent, the Pope blesses the golden rose which is to be presented to an important ruler or to a Christian who has performed some exceptional service. Formerly, it was customary on this day for the Pope to ride in ceremony from the Lateran Palace to the Basilica of the Holy Cross, while throughout the Catholic world, the "Te Deum" was sung. When half the Lenten Fast was over, the Church encouraged its most worthy members to celebrate the end of the period of atonement with a reward for their privation and self-denial. It was in order to emphasize this idea of thanksgiving, and to mark it clearly, that Rome chose the rose, the Queen of Flowers, as the symbol of this occasion. The following is a list of notable people to whom the "Golden Rose" has been awarded:

Year	Pope	Recipient
1159	Alexander III	Louis VII, King of France
1171	Calixtus III	The Doge of Venice
1244	Innocence IV	Count Raymond of Provence
1446	Eugene IV	Henry VI, King of England
1669	Clement IX	Maria-Theresa of Austria
1819	Pius VII	The Empress of Austria
1856	Pius IX	The Empress Eugenie
1886	Leo XIII	The Queen of Spain
1886	Leo XIII	The Empress of Brazil
1891	Leo XIII	The Queen of Portugal
1893	Leo XIII	The Queen of the Belgians
1925	Pius XI	The Queen of the Belgians

The cathedrals of the Middle Ages were richly decorated with various sculpted plants and flowers. On those in Germany and France, which date from the 12th and 13th centuries, there is a most reliable work by Lottlise Behling *Die Pflanzenwelt der mittelalterlichen Kathedralen* ("The Varieties of Plants in the Cathedrals of the Middle Ages"). This contains 160 plates with many details which could easily be overlooked on a short visit. Unfortunately, the rose does not figure very often.

Basel. The Cathedral. On the left hand side of the main door at the west end there is a very fine arch of roses with particularly naturalistic foliage (see Plate 8).

Marburg. The Church of St. Elizabeth. The left hand side of the arch on the west door shows a vine with bunches of grapes, and opposite this a veritable rose garden is depicted (see Plate 8).

Freiburg. The Cathedral. There is a very fine stem of roses over the west door. 13th century.

Rheims. The Cathedral. Above the head of St. Nicasius is a superb arrangement of roses which signifies the victory of the Church over evil. This is situated on the left side of the north door at the west end.

Amiens. The Cathedral. A fine spray of roses is sculpted on the right-hand side of the pillars which form the arcade on the central west door.

Lyons. The Cathedral. 13th century. The triple doorway at the west end was robbed of its decorations during the French Revolution; it had heavy carving on the four tympana over the lintels, including the rows of roses between the two circular mouldings which outlined the great arches.

Paris. Cathedral of Notre Dame. South transept. The gable is decorated with marguerites and roses with leaves (see Plate 7). The side door to the north of the west end displays eight different varieties of plants including the rose.

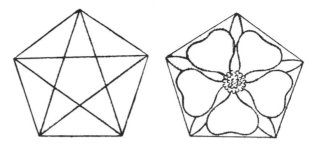

Figure 94. Left. The five-pointed star or pentagram. Right. A typical rose inset. (from Schleiden)

THE ROSE IN HERALDRY

The rose is to be found in coats of arms, on coins, seals, banners, paintings and artifacts of all kinds in almost every country in the Northern Hemisphere. During the second quarter of the 12th century the practice of heraldry arose almost simultaneously in both Western and Central Europe so that Knights and soldiers could be recognized when dressed in full armor. It began with the painting or embossing of a figure or sign upon the shield. Great use was made of the five-pointed star, or pentagram, which could be drawn quite easily from the diagonals joining the five equal sides. It must be remembered that the pentagram was connected with mysticism and magic in the ancient world; it was thought to give protection against all kinds of danger. Very early on, it was realized that a rose could easily be drawn within the outline of the pentagram or applied on top of this five-pointed star (Fig. 94). Consequently, the rose was often used in early heraldic designs (*ca.* 1400). It was used in many different colors, as was usual in heraldry; on examining the records of family armorial bearings we find that over 4,000 German families bore the rose in their arms.

Luther's coat of arms (Fig. 95) is composed of a red heart on a white rose with a black cross in the center, the rose set upon a blue ground or "field", and the whole is surrounded by a golden circlet. There is an excellent picture of the arms in the *Rosenzeitung* of 1933. A short list of armorial bearings with roses follows, but it is only a small selection and in no way intended to be comprehensive.

As rosarians are unlikely to be experts in heraldry and its specialized terminology, no attempt has been made here to describe the various armorial bearings in accordance with the rules and procedures of the College of Arms. Those who are interested in the subjects can refer to one of the many books on heraldry which are current-ly available in libraries throughout the world. (See Bibliography, p. 235.)

German Regions with Roses in their Arms Lippe. The former free state of Lippe, which became part of North Rhine-Westphalia in 1947, bears a red rose (the Rose of Lippe) on a silver background, the sepals and seeds in gold. Later the rose was incorporated in the arms of the district, which were made up as follows: For North Rhine a silver stream on a green field, for Westphalia, a horse rampant on a red field and for Lippe a red rose on a silver background.

Coats of Arms of the German Districts Of the 425 districts in the West German Republic, about 350 have their own coats of arms, the outward sign of their autonomy. Districts which have no armorial bearings use the provincial arms for

Figure 95. The Arms (or seal) of Luther (see text).

Figure 96. The Rose in Heraldry. 1. The former Princedom of Lippe. 2. The District of Schaumburg-Lippe. 3. The District of Lemgo. 4. Town of Rosenheim. 5. The District of Ubbergen (Holland). 6. The District of Schagen. 7. Town of Rapperswil (Switzerland). 8. Town of Eye, Suffolk (England). 9. The District of Springe. 10. City of Grenoble (France). 11. County of Lancashire (England). 12. The West Riding of Yorkshire (England). In order to make the designs clearer they have been drawn in outline only. For exact details see pp. 224 and 225. (Original)

their seal; this implies the idea of authority without full autonomy. There is only space to give details of a few of the arms which include roses.

Detmold. Silver on red; above, a five-petaled red rose with stamens and seeds in gold; below, an eight-pointed star with a black and white swallow.

Flensburg. The upper part of the shield is gold with a roaring lion, below five silver roses with gold stamens on a blue ground.

Freising. On a quartered shield of silver, blue, gold and red, the head of a Negro wearing a red wreath and earring, above a double silver rose with gold stamens.

Kelheim. Quartered silver and blue; three roses, two blue and one silver above a black and silver chevron.

Lippstadt. A black cross on a silver field surmounted with a five-petaled red rose (the Rose of Lippe) with gold stamens.

Lemgo. On a field of silver and gold, a red five-

Figure 97. A Gothic Coat of Arms bearing three roses, *ca.* 1400 (from the heraldic register of Zurich; see Hildebrandt's Handbook of Heraldry 1937).

petaled rose with gold stamens, above an eight-pointed red star.

Meppen.   A gold capstan on a red field bearing a gold rose with red stamens.

Ottweiler.   On a field of blue and silver, a lion with golden billets and a blue rose with gold stamens above a black four-spoked cogwheel.

Rottenburg/Laber.   A silver rose on a red field, the stamens silver, the seeds red, above a red portcullis with a mural crown on a silver field.

Schaumburg-Lippe.   On a red field, an eleven-pointed nettle leaf from which spring three silver nails. In the center a red rose with red calyx and gold seeds.

Schleiden.   Quartered. (1) A red chevron on a gold field; (2) A black lion rampant on a gold field; (3) A black cross on a silver field; (4) Three golden roses on a red field.

Springe.   Three red roses with gold stamens on a silver field.

Stadtsteinach.   Above, a double golden rose with silver calyx on a blue field; below, a black lion surmounted with a silver bend on a gold field.

Tauberbischofsheim.   Quartered. (1) A six-spoked red wheel on a gold field; (2) A golden lion crowned in red on a black field; (3) A red and silver quartered banner, the shaft in gold, on a black field; (4) A six-petaled blue rose on a gold field.

Some Arms of German Cities   Rosenheim.   A double silver rose with gold stamens and green calyx on a red field.

Kehl.   A black anchor between two red roses with golden stamens on a silver field.

Lippstadt.   A five-petaled red rose with black stamens above a wall with two towers and a red gate on a silver field.

Ottweiler.   A silver rose on a blue field.

Other European Arms with Roses

FRANCE.

Grenoble.   Three double red roses with green calyxes and stamens.

SWITZERLAND.

Rapperswil.   Two double red roses with thorns and silver stamens on a silver field.

HOLLAND.

Roosendaal.   A triple golden rose with gold calyx on a blue field.

Schagen.   A golden rose in a circlet with four golden lilies in the corners on a red field.

Ubbergen.   A golden rose with thorns and leaves on a red field.

Zaltbommel.   A silver sword, the gold pommel supported by two four-petaled silver roses on a blue field.

ENGLAND. (Arms of Counties & Towns)

Cambridge.   A gold bridge surmounted by a golden

lily and two silver roses with gold stamens and green calyxes on a red field.

Eye (Suffolk). A gold cross with four swallows; from the cross come two branches with green leaves, each bearing three silver roses; overall, an eagle crowned in gold.

Lancashire County Council. Three golden piles, two above one below, each bearing a red rose on a red field.

Southampton. Two silver roses on a red field above, below one red rose on a silver field. The roses have golden stamens and green calyxes.

Yorkshire. Divided into three districts or "Ridings" (North, West and East). The arms of the North Riding display three silver roses on a blue field above a red cross on a silver field. The arms of the West Riding are three silver roses on a red field above a gold sun set with a silver rose.

City of Carlisle. A red cross set between four red roses with green calyxes on a gold field. Superimposed is a golden rose with green calyx.

In English heraldry there are four distinct kinds of rose, each used in a specific way:

1. The most common is a single rose of five petals. Seeded in the center and with five pointed sepals placed between the petals. Any of the heraldic colors can be used.

Figure 98. English heraldic roses. Left, the single rose; Center, the Tudor rose; Right, The "Rose-en-soleil".

2. The "Tudor Rose" is always double; generally the outer rose is red, the inner, and smaller one, white.
3. The "Rose-en-Soleil" is a white rose, either single or double, in front of a sunburst. In its single form it was first used by Edward IV of England after his victory for the Yorkists at the Battle of Mortimer's Cross; the double form is the Regimental Badge of the Grenadier Guards (Fig. 99).

4. The "Slipped Rose", if surmounted by the State Crown, is the Badge of England.

Figure 99. A particularly fine example of the double form of the "Rose-en-Soleil".

THE ROSE AS A NATIONAL EMBLEM AND A NATIONAL FLOWER

In England the rose has been, and still is, the national emblem; Roy Hay, writing in *The Rose*, suggests that the name "Albion" was given to the Island because of its white roses (probably derived from *albus*).

W. Scott says that use of the rose as England's national emblem originated with Queen Eleanor of Provence, the wife of Henry III. The heraldic rose of Provence was golden, and it was this rose which was later taken as his badge by Eleanor's son, the heir to the throne, who became Edward I. His brother, Edmund Crouchback, Duke of Lancaster, chose a red rose as his badge to differentiate between himself and his brother. Finally, the House of York adopted the white rose. From the genealogical table drawn up by Scott it appears that the golden rose was first used in 1244, the red rose in 1277 and the white rose in 1385.

The arms of Finland have nine silver roses on a red ground surrounding a crowned and golden lion rampant, the right paw is in the shape of a mailed fist holding a sword; the lion stands on an oriental dagger. See also Orders with Roses.

In the United States, a motion was made in the Senate in 1959 that the rose be adopted as the national flower, however, it was never acted upon. The rose is the emblem of a number of individual states, Georgia, Iowa, North Dakota and New York among them, and is the official symbol of the District of Columbia.

The rose is also the national flower of England,

Honduras, Iran, Poland, Rumania and Czechoslovakia.

ORDERS WITH ROSES

Brazil The Order of the Rose was instituted by the Emperor Pedro of Brazil in honor of his wife, Amalia, who was a German Princess. It takes the form of a white star on a wreath of pink roses. The monogram in blue is "Amor e Fidelidade" (Plate 2).

Finland The Order of the Cross of Freedom, which is awarded in various classes and grades for military service, bears in the center of the medal a heraldic white rose which symbolizes the nine roses representing the nine ancient Finnish fiefs in the State coat of arms. The Order of the White Rose of Finland also has a white rose as its central motif; it is awarded for outstanding service to the State.

Great Britain The Collar of the Order of the Garter (K.G.) is in gold and consists of 24 small blue enamel "garters" encircling a red Tudor rose of ten petals in double form joined by 24 lovers' knots. The total weight of the Collar is 925 g./2 lb. The garter itself is of dark blue velvet with the motto of the Order "Honi soit qui mal y pense" in gold lettering, embroidered with golden roses and surrounded by a golden chain. The rose also appears in a number of other British honors, particularly in the chains of various Orders.

Greece The Order of Good Service (Vasilikon Tagma tis Evpiias) was instituted in 1948 by King George II, in five classes; it displays a flower similar to a rose with five petals in blue enamel; in the center of the medallion is a representation of the Virgin Mary.

Lippe The Order for the Arts and Sciences (The Rose of Lippe) was instituted in 1898, in three classes. The design of the Order is a five-petaled rose. Other honors and awards of the former Principality of Lippe use the red rose in their designs; especially well-known is the "Lippische Röschen" which, in fact, was the award given for heroic deeds on the field of battle. It bears the Rose of Lippe in the center of the cross-bar surrounded by a laurel wreath (Plate 2).

ROSES ON COINS

The so-called "coins" from the Tschudes' barrows, referred to in many books on roses and alleged to be anything from 2,500 to 6,000 years old, are completely mythical (see p. 21). The following descriptions of old coins can all be confirmed by reference to either Bernhard or Imhoff-Blumer and O. Keller.

Bernhard tells us that the rose was a sort of coat of arms for the coinage of Rhodes from 400 to 80 B.C. and closely linked with another symbol, that of the Sun God, Helios. Both the city and island of Rhodes were the chief places of worship in the cult of Helios and it was here that one of the seven wonders of the World, the great bronze statue of the Colossus of Rhodes, was erected. The coins show the head of the Sun God, sometimes with flowing hair and sometimes with a "sunburst" wreath. It usually appears on the obverse, but occasionally is found on the reverse. Many archaeologists have come indirectly to the conclusion that the rose was a form of "coat of arms" for Rhodes, for they believe that the name Rhodes was derived from that of Helios' beloved, the nymph Rode, whose symbol was the rose.

Figure 100. The National Arms of Finland.

Although rose chaplets were very popular with the Ancients, a representation of one is nowhere to be found.

The following descriptions of coins are taken from Bernhard (B) or from Imhoff-Blumer (IB) together with a note of the plate number.

1. Tetradrachma of Rhodes. Obverse, a full-face head of Apollo; reverse, a rose in profile with a bunch of grapes on either side roughly enclosed in a square; silver, *ca.* 400 B.C. IB Plate X-6. (Plate 2)
2. Didrachma of Rhodes. Obverse, full face head of Helios, turned slightly to the right with flowing hair; reverse, a rose with a bud, at the left a bunch of grapes above the letter "E"; above the rose, the word ΡΟΔΙΟΝ. B Plate 1-2. (Plate 2)
3. Drachma of Rhodes. Reverse, a fully open bloom surrounded with pearls, below, sometimes, an ear of corn (Plate 2) with or without inscription. IB. Plate X-8; B. Plate 1-3.
4. Aphrodite, seated between two sphinxes, sniffing a rose. A silver stater from either Nagidos or Aphrodisias in Sicily where the rose was dedicated to Aphrodite (= Venus). B. Plate 1-5.
5. Head of Athena wearing a Corinthian helmet, with a small rose behind her. B. Plate 1-4; IB. Plate X-9.

Other recorded coins of this period include:

Tetradrachma of Rhodes, silver. Reverse, a fully open rose beside an eagle; above, the letters ΡΟΔΙ-ΟΝ. *Ca.* 400-333 B.C.

Tetradrachma of Rhodes, silver. Reverse, a fully open rose, to the left a stem with bud, to the right a stem without bud. *Ca.* 400-333 B.C.

Athenian drachma, silver. Reverse, between the letters P — O, a rose seen from above; over this a crown and cornucopia; below the letters ΝΙΚΑΣΟΡΑΣ. *Ca.* 88-43 BC.

Roses on English Coins   From the 13th century on, the rose was frequently used in English coinage to mark a gap between inscriptions, as a trade mark, in the interstices of crosses, at the foot of the Sovereign and as borders instead of an inscription; they are usually found on the obverse, occasionally on the reverse. It would be impossible to list them all here. Particularly noteworthy are the silver pieces of Henry III (1216-1272). They display the rose in the interstices of the Cross. There was also a gold piece of 20 pence, dated 1257, with a portrait of the King seated with sceptre and orb on the obverse, and on the reverse the Hanseatic cross with four roses. The value of this coin was doubled to 40 pence in 1265. Apparently there was inflation even in those days! These coins are a clear indication that the rose was a royal symbol.

In 1465, came the Rose Noble, a gold coin (Fig. 27) which has already been described. This coin had a value of 7 Thalers which were issued at about the same time.

Still later, many coins with roses were minted, particularly in Lippe where the rose was well known as part of the local armorial bearings. One of the best known was the Rose Pfennig. The Pfennig piece of Anhalt also has a rose on it.

Lastly, the 10 Stotinki coin of Bulgaria must be mentioned (Plate 2); this bears a laurel wreath with roses and ears of corn.

PHILATELIC ROSES

Undoubtedly there will be a number of philatelists among the readers of this book and it certainly would not be surprising if, among them, there were specialists in Thematics and possibly those who interest themselves in collecting stamps of roses. Without going too deeply into philatelic history, a list can be given here of stamps which have the rose as their subject. A full and complete list has been prepared by Stelvio Coggiatti (1967).

The first stamp with a rose was issued in 1925; it was the 10 cent stamp of Holland; the next was probably the German 8 Pfennig issue of 1929 which bore a stylized representation of a rose and was followed by the 4 Pfennig stamp. Spain followed suit in 1935, after which any number of countries did likewise. In the last ten years, the thematic collectors have really enjoyed a

Figure 101. Mongolian Stamp showing *Rosa acicularis.*

"rosy" time, for the issue of sets with their favorite theme have come thick and fast.

The following list has been compiled alphabetically by country. Collectors will, of course, refer to their catalogues for full details, but it is hoped that this list, although brief, will help them to identify their particular interests more easily. The numbers in brackets give the number of stamps in each set.

Albania	1965 (1; Hybrid Tea); 1967 (8; Hybrid Teas
Austria	1948 (2; *R. canina* & Symbolic);1949 (1; Symbolic)
Belgium	1965 (1; Symbolic); 1969 (1; Hybrid Tea)
Brazil	1951 (1; Symbolic); 1967 (1; Symbolic)
Bulgaria	1936 (2; Symbolic); 1938 (4; *R. damascena?*)
	1947 (1; Rose); 1951 (1; Rose);
	1953 (3; *R. canina*);
	1956 (2; *R. damascena*); 1962 (8; Hybrid Teas)
Canada	1966 (1; *R. acicularis*)
Cuba	1955 (5; Hybrid Teas)
Czechoslovakia	1957 (1; Hybrid Tea); 1962 (1; Symbolic);
	1965 (1; *R. canina*); 1967 (1; Symbolic)
East Germany (DDR)	1960 (1; Rose); 1961 (1; Hybrid Tea);
Finland	1949 (1; *R. canina*); 1954 (1; Rose)
France	1954 (1; Symbolic); 1959 (1; Symbolic);
	1962 (2; Hybrid Tea & *centifolia*);
	1963 (1; Symbolic)
Great Britain	1953 (1; Symbolic); 1964 (1; *R. canina*)
	1976 (4; *R. eglanteria, R. gallica versicolor,* 1 Hybrid Tea & 1 Floribunda)
Hungary	1958 (1; *R. richardii*); 1959 (2; Hybrid Teas);
	1961 (2; Hybrid Teas); 1962 (6 Hybrid Teas & 1 Floribunda);
	1963 (1; Hybrid Tea); 1965 (1; various roses)
Israel	1953 (1; Symbolic)
Japan	1947 (1; Symbolic)
Jordan	1962 (1; Symbolic)
Khor Fakkan	1966 (7; Hybrid Teas & Floribundas)
Libya	1965 (1; Hybrid Tea)
Liechtenstein	1945 (2; Symbolic); 1957 (1; Symbolic);
	1961 (3; Symbolic & *R. canina*)
Monaco	1959 (1; Hybrid Tea); 1962 (1; Symbolic);
	1963 (1; Symbolic); 1969 (1)
Mongolia	? (1; *R. acicularis*, see Fig. 101)
Netherlands	1925 (1; Symbolic); 1952 (1; Rose)
Newfoundland	1932 (1; Symbolic)
Nicaragua	1967 (1; Hybrid Tea)
North Vietnam	1968 (5; Hybrid Teas)
Pakistan	1961 (2; Symbolic)
Peru	1936 (1; Symbolic)
Poland	1966 (4; Hybrid Teas & Symbolic);
	1967 (1; Floribunda)
Rumania	1954 (1; Symbolic); 1959 (1; *R. canina*);
	1964 (1; *R. canina*)
Saar	1951 (1; Symbolic)
Salvador	1964 (1; Hybrid Tea)
San Marino	1952 (4; Hybrid Teas); 1954 (1; Hybrid Tea);
	1957 (1; *R. canina*)
South Korea	1965 (1; *R. rugosa*)
Spain	1935 (1; Symbolic)

Sweden	1966 (2; Symbolic)
Switzerland	1945 (1; *R. alpina*); 1952 (1; Leaf & Hip);
	1956 (1; Symbolic); 1957 (1; Leaf);
	1964 (1; Hybrid Tea); 1973 (4; Hybrid Teas)
Togo	1966 (2; Hybrid Teas); 1967 (2; Hybrid Teas)
Turkey	1955 (1; Hybrid Tea); 1960 (1; Hybrid Tea)
U.S.S.R.	1938 (2; Symbolic); 1960 (1; *R. canina*);
	1964 (2; Symbolic); 1969 (2)
Vatican City	1943 (4; Symbolic); 1956 (3; Symbolic)
West Germany	1929 (1; Symbolic); 1938 (1; *R. alpina*)
Yemen	1956 (4; *R. damascena?*)
Yugoslavia	1955 (1; *R. canina*)

BIBLIOGRAPHY

COGGIATTI. S.   In: Rosa Belgica (Trans. F. Mertens).

THE ROSICRUCIANS

The Rosicrucians, a fraternal and spiritual movement, was founded by Ritter Christian Rosencreutz (1378-1484) who called upon all men of goodwill to join together for the reformation of the world. For their symbol they chose a cross hung with seven roses. Originally, it was a single large rose at each end of the cross-piece of the crucifix. Later, about 1785, they adopted a wheel with four spokes forming a cross. This cross is the symbol of Christendom, and the rose symbolizes secrecy or silence; the two together, the Rose Cross, imply an esoteric Christianity.

> Esoteric Christendom teaches the doctrine of fortitude unto death. It teaches the individual to experience in this life a soul free of the transitory demands of the body. (see W. Schrödter, pp. 18-19)

THE ROSE IN FREEMASONRY

The rose plays an important part in Masonic ritual not only as an emblem of beauty, but primarily as the symbol of man's longing for a new and better life. This is particularly emphasized each year at the Feast of St. John (June 24th), also known as the Rose Festival. On this day Freemasons wear a rose in three shades of red and decorate the Lodge with the same emblem. For German Masons, the rose is a very important and much-loved expression of the cult; when a Brother Mason is laid to rest in his grave, three red roses are placed on the coffin. The word "rose" is also sometimes incorporated in the names of the lodges, for example, the Hamburg Lodge is known as "The Three Roses".

A CONCLUDING CHAPTER OF CULTURAL HISTORY

THE ROSE AS A SYMBOL OF LOYALTY

We have already seen, in the notes on the Wars of the Roses (p. 43), how the rose was often worn as a badge of loyalty to a particular cause. There are other examples, however, which are worthy of mention:

The Jacobites James II of England (1685-1688) was the brother of Charles II. He became a Catholic in 1672, which forced the King to insist that he leave the country in 1679. Three years later he was allowed to return and he acended the throne upon his brother's death in 1685. However, when he tried to re-introduce Catholicism as the national religion, he encountered fierce opposition from Parliament and was forced to flee to France. A large number of his followers were members of the Scottish nobility and were only able to help him in secret. As a sign of their loyalty they wore a white rose. James attempted, some years later, with the aid of French troops, to regain his throne by staging an insurrection in Ireland, but he was defeated. The last attempt of the Jacobites was the rebellion of 1745, led by Prince Charles Edward (Bonnie Prince Charlie), with the objective of placing his father on the throne as a Roman Catholic King; the rebellion failed and the Prince had to flee to France. His loyal followers, as a memorial to their suffering, wore a secret sign in the form of a rose (Fig. 102).

The League of the Rose The *Ligue de la Rose*, or *La Rose de France*, was founded by the Countess of Paris in 1888. It was a society of French women whose goal was the restoration of the French monarchy. The members of the League wore a small copper rose bearing the inscription "La France" on one of the leaves.

Rosati This society was mostly composed of young members of the army, the civil service and other professions, and was founded in Arras towards the end of the 18th century. It was really a literary society with special interest in poetry and in the rose. Membership was limited to 50. Whoever wanted to become a member had to write and submit a poem on the rose which he had to recite at his initiation. He was then presented with a rose which he had to smell lovingly three times and pin in his buttonhole. After this, he was given a glass of rosé wine, which he had to drain to the

Figure 102. A secret emblem commemorating the Jacobite Rebellion in England and Scotland in 1745, which bears the names of those who suffered for their part in the affair.

health of the society. Then he was presented with his certificate of membership in the Rosati; it was inscribed in red ink on pink paper and surrounded with a border of pink roses. Their meeting place went under the name of either "Eden" or the "Rosebed".

Last, but not least, we must recall the "White Rose" society which opposed the National Socialists in Germany and to which the Scholl family belonged. They were arrested at the University of Munich in 1943 for the distribution of leaflets, and executed. The guiding spirit of this anti-Nazi student movement was the Swiss Professor Dr. Kurt Huber, who was also executed.

ANTIPATHY TO THE ROSE

It is very hard to believe that there are, or were, people who dislike the rose, or even hate it, will not look at it and cannot bear to smell it. Belmont cites a number of well-known people who suffered from this disability, among whom the following are noteworthy.

Francesco Venerio, a Doge of Venice, always felt ill if he breathed the scent of a rose; whenever he went to Church all the roses which might have been used for decoration had to be removed.

Cardinal Olivier Caraffa was particularly allergic to roses; if he happened to smell one he suffered such violent sneezing fits that during the time the roses were in bloom in Rome, he had to quit the city.

Cardinal Henry de Cordone was similarly affected, and the Sieur de Guise was not only disabled by smelling a rose, but even by seeing one!

Francis Bacon, Lord Chancellor of England (1617) flew into a rage should he see a rose. Maria of Medici and Anne of Austria could not bear roses to be painted in pictures.

Louis XIV, the Sun King (1643-1715), who built the Palace of Versailles, liked roses only moderately.

Even if we make allowances for those people who really do suffer from so severe an allergy, it is nevertheless impossible to understand how they could be rendered *hors de combat* by merely looking at a painting of a rose.

"MINDEN DAY"

The English still celebrate, after more than 200 years, a battle which took place on German soil, during the Seven Years War; the story follows:

On August 1st, 1759, the French cavalry opposed five English infantry regiments, reinforced by Hanoverian troops, at Minden. Duke Ferdinand of Brunswick, a Prussian Field Marshal, was the Commander-in-Chief of the allies. English scouts had brought in the battle plan of the enemy cavalry, which totalled six regiments. At this, the English mounted a surprise attack and the French, caught unawares, were totally defeated and fled in disarray. This outstanding victory gained a battle honor for the troops concerned. But what had this to do with roses?

In the history of the Suffolk Regiment[1] it states that, on their way to the battle, the English infantry passed through a rose garden. Every soldier plucked a rose and stuck it in his cap. According to yet another version (E. Diderich), the soldiers went into formation behind a hedge of roses and it was from this hedge that they picked the roses to put in their caps.

It must certainly have been only a part of the Regiment who actually picked and wore these roses at the Battle of Minden, but, from that day on, white roses have been worn by all the soldiers in the Regiment on the anniversary of this event.

[1] According to another English record, it was the Lancashire Fusiliers under Colonel Kingsley, who picked the roses.

Just which rose they wore is unclear. In that part of the country the indigenous wild roses only flower in June, and occasionally, into early July. If it was a garden rose then it could only have been *R. alba semiplena* or the slightly later-flowering 'Maiden's Blush'.

THE ROSE IN ART

Persia Rose motifs were common in ceramics and in needlework. The flowers are often somewhat stylized, but almost always have a "highlight" running along the central line of the petals; the sepals are often elongated to look like leaves and are often veined. We cannot expect to be able to identify exact varieties in these motifs, but the rose with broad hips could be *R. hemisphaerica*. This rose with its leaf-like sepals and distinctive fruit appears frequently in Islamic art; the flowers themselves were often drawn in such a way that they really look more like zinnias than roses. (See Fig. 103.)

China Shortly before the War, a great exhibition of Chinese Art was held at Burlington House (the Royal Academy) in London. Among the objects on display were a number of pictures featuring roses, two of which deserve special mention:

1. A painting by Chao Ch'ang on silk, *ca.* 1000 A.D., of *R. rugosa* (Plate 3).
2. A painting by Huang Ch'uan dated 965, of the 'Blush China' rose (Plate 3).

The rose was often depicted on the porcelain of the K'ien Lung period (1736-1796). In Paris, at the Musée Guimet, there is a book of flowers which is believed to have been painted by the Emperor K'ien Lung. In it there is a "portrait" of *R. chinensis* so true to nature that it looks just as we know it today.

The porcelain of the K'ang Hsi period (1662-1722) sometimes portrayed the rose, usually very small and shown growing in pots. From the number of leaflets (nine to eleven), and because it was container-grown to restrict its growth, Bunyard (1938) believes this rose to be *R. roxburghii*.

Many of the paintings are of *R. multiflora*, but only the species. Bunyard is of the opinion that the cultivated forms did not appear until the 18th century, although there were numerous varieties by the beginning of the 19th century, the time many of them reached Europe. The 'Seven Sisters' (= *R. multiflora platyphylla*), is an example.

However, the rose was never as popular a theme in Chinese art as the peony; both these plants are easily distinguishable in the paintings from a study of their leaf forms.

Greece Although the rose appears in early Greek poetry, visual artists seem to have had scant interest in it. The most that can be said is that it was used on the coinage of Rhodes (see p. 227).

Rome Roses are often to be seen in the mosaics which were used in the floors of the houses (Plate 1) and on the frescoes in the Catacombs, particularly in early Christian art. As the Church spread its influence across Europe, the rose, which earlier had been the symbol of Venus, came to be accepted as the symbol of the Martyrs and, especially, of the Passion. It was a reminder of the Love of God and became a standard Church emblem used in sculpture and tapestry. The image was very stylized, and although recognizable as a rose, no attempt was made to portray any particular species or variety. It was only from the 15th century on that individual roses could be identified.

Italy From the 15th century on, roses appeared frequently in Italian art, and it was at this time that they began to be drawn very precisely. Bunyard, who has done much research on this aspect of the rose, found that there were three types represented in the paintings; *Rosa gallica* (single red) and *Rosa alba* (two varieties, double white and double pink). These roses are easy to recognize from their large, flat blooms and their foliage. *Rosa centifolia* is not to be found anywhere, at least not during the 15th century, and *Rosa damascena*, which disappeared with the Fall of Rome, did not reappear until about 1540, according to Mattioli.

In a painting, now in the Museum at Verona, by Stefano di Zevio (born 1393), of the Madonna in a garden, there is a trellis covered with double, flat red and white roses with foliage which is typical of *Rosa alba*. This rose is often found in paintings with trellises, fences and arbors, but the artists rarely used the single *Rosa gallica*.

Luini of Milan (1485-1532) used *Rosa alba* in many of his paintings; it is easily recognizable from the blooms, foliage and prickles.

The Florentine painter, Botticelli (1445-1510), used recognizable deep pink and white flowers in his famous painting of the "Birth of Venus". Bunyard thinks that the white are *R. alba maxima*, and the pink 'Maiden's Blush'. The deeper pink is no longer in existence, although it was described in books on roses in the 19th century. All the roses in Botticelli's paintings are *Rosa alba* with the exception of a single dark red rose on the figure to the right of Primavera, which looks like *Rosa*

Figure 103. Roses used for decoration. (a) and (d) Rose chaplets such as were worn by the nobility in the Middle Ages either with just four blooms at equal intervals as in (a) or made up entirely of roses as in (d); the other designs appear on fabrics such as the 'Indian Rose' (c), the 'Persian Rose' (b), and the 'Italian Rose' (e). (from Battersby, 1953)

gallica and which is to be found in the work of Italian masters from this period on.

Holland   *Rosa centifolia, Rosa hemisphaerica* (double and golden yellow), *R. damascena* and *R. gallica* all first appeared in paintings in this country. Clusius, when he visited Austria and Hungary about 1580, saw the latter three roses there. In the second edition of his book *Horti Germaniae* (1601) we are given the important information that the nobleman, John van Hogheland, had sent him two roses at the beginning of 1589; only a small piece of root survived, but it managed to produce 40 blooms in the summer of 1591. The nearly white flowers were very double, with about 120 petals of which the outer ones were much larger than the inner; the scent was strong like *R. gallica*. The petals were curled inwards, from which Bunyard concluded that they were our *Rosa centifolia*. Therefore, there were three roses in cultivation in Holland at that time: *Rosa centifolia, Rosa alba maxima* and another of miniature form. *Centifolia* was then unknown to the botanists in France and Western Europe and it was Clusius who, in his work on the flora of Spain, Austria and Hungary, first identified it as such.

This was the period, both in Holland and Flanders, when a number of the great masters made a specialty of painting still lifes, particularly of flowers. There are literally hundreds of such paintings in the great museums today, but it is obviously impossible to catalog them all here. The following short resumé of the most important masters can serve as no more than a guide to the reader who has a special interest in this field.

The most important Dutch and Flemish flower painters:

Balthasar van der Ast: 1590-1656; painted many flower pieces in the manner of Jan Breughel.

Ambrosius Bosschaert: active from 1588 to 1645; his work was very detailed and naturalistic, following the style of Jan Breughel.

Jan Breughel: 1568-1625; must be distinguished from the other painters of the same name, Peter the Elder (Peasant Breughel) and Peter the Younger (Höllen Breughel). Jan was known as "Velvet Breughel" from the delicate texture of his painting. He produced many still-lifes with roses.

Jan Davidsz de Heem: 1606-1684; mostly a painter of plant life very precisely drawn; used warm, glowing tones.

Jan van Huysum: 1682-1749; work very finely painted and mostly composed of flower and fruit pieces.

Jacob Jordaens: 1593-1678; one of the most important Flemish painters; created a number of altar pieces and pictures of proverbs.

Jacob Marell: 1614-1681: Dutch flower painter; later became the stepfather of Anna Maria Sibylla Merian.

Jan van Os: 1744-1808; probably the greatest flower and fruit painter of his period.

Rachel Ruysch: 1664-1750; a Dutch artist who was Court Painter in Düsseldorf from 1708-1716; her work was mostly of flowers and fruit and owed much to both de Heem and van Huysum.

Roelandt Savery: 1576-1637; active in Flanders.

Daniel Seghers (sometimes *Seeghers*): 1590-1661; Flemish flower and animal painter.

Gerard van Spaendonck: 1746-1822; Dutch painter from Tilburg who moved to Paris; Redouté was his pupil.

Simon Verelst: 1644-721; Dutch painter.

Nicholas Verendael: 1640-1691; Flemish painter.

Jacob van Walscapelle: active 1667-1716 in Holland.

There is no space here to go into the individual works of these Masters. The galleries in which many of these paintings are exhibited can be found in the catalog produced by M.L. Hairs. Something, however, can and should be said about the varieties of rose used in the paintings and their historical background.

Rose gallica versicolor, the striped rose, was probably first painted by Robert in 1640; this painting is now in the Velins collection in the Jardin des Plantes in Paris. After this, if often appeared in the work of the Dutch and Flemish Masters.

Rosa foetida is to be found in the works of Daniel Seghers and Rachel Ruysch; examples of the latter's work can be seen in the Rijksmuseum, Amsterdam.

Rosa hemisphaerica has been known in France since 1616 and was illustrated in a book of that year, called *Jardin d'hyver*, by Jean Franeau. Soon after, pictures of this double yellow rose appeared in Parkinson and, still later, in the work of van Huysum.

The greatest of all painters of the rose, Pierre Joseph Redoute, worked during the early 19th century; he has already been discussed on p. 101, details of his books of roses are given on p. 234.

We will conclude this section with a list of the most important illustrated books on roses of which Redoute's work is doubtless the supreme example.

THE MOST IMPORTANT
COLOR PLATE BOOKS ON ROSES
(18th to 19th Centuries)

(Similar books published in the 20th century are listed in the bibliographies on p. 295 and 425).

(ARNZ): *Rosen*. Sammlung der neuesten und schönsten aus Frankreich, England, Belgien und Deutschland bezogenen, in unserem Garten cultivierten, nach der Natur gezeichneten und colorirten Rosen. In six parts, each with 10 plates. Düsseldorf 1835-1840 (Arnz & Co.).

ANDREWS, HENRY C.: *Roses*, or a monograph on the genus *Rosa*; containing colored figures of all the known species and beautiful varieties, drawn, engraved, colored and described from the living plants. Two volumes with 129 colored copper plates. London 1805-1828.

BESSA. PANCRACE: *Album des Roses*. 71 pp. with 23 copper plates. Paris. *Ca.* 1830.

CURTIS, H.: *The Beauties of the Rose*. Containing portraits of the principal varieties. Two volumes with 38 color plates. Bristol & London, 1850 & 1853.

JAMAIN, HIPPOLYTE, et EUGENE FORNEY: *Les Roses*. Culture, description; 268 pp. and 60 color plates. Paris 1872.

KOMLOSY, FRANZ: *Rosenalbum*. 92 color plates in 23 parts (4 plates to each part). Vienna. 1868-1872.

LAWRANCE, MARY: *A Collection of Roses from Nature*. 30 parts with 90 colored engravings. London. 1796-1810.

LINDLEY, JOHN: *Rosarum Monographia*; or a botanical history of roses. 156 pp. 19 plates with 18 in color. London. 1820.

PACQUET, VICTOR: *Choix des plus belles Roses*. Folio. 60 col. Lith. Paris (Dussacq) 1845-1854.

REDOUTE, PIERRE-JOSEPH: *Les Roses*. 1st Edn. 3 vols folio. 167 col. plates. Paris (Firmin-Didot) 1817-1824. 2nd Edn. 3 vols. folio. 140 plates. Paris (Panckoucke) 1824-1826. 3rd Edn. 3 vols. octavo. 181 plates, published by M. Pirolle. Paris (Dufart) 1828-1830. — In addition a set was to be published by J.F. Hauser &

Cie in St. Petersburg, but details are unknown.

ROESSIG, GOTTLOB: *Die Rosen*, nach der Natur gezeichnet und koloriert. Two volumes in six parts with a total of 60 color engravings by Luise von Wangenheim. Leipzig 1802-1820.

WILLMOTT, ELLEN ANN: *The genus Rosa*. 2 vols folio in 24 parts with 130 color plates. London, 1910-1914.

Corrections in nomenclature of Redoute's *Les Roses* (1817-1824) When examining this book of superb color plates, it is important to remember that the artist's nomenclature is not that which is used today, the following comparison should prove useful.

Plate No.	Original Designation.	Modern Designation.
Volume 1. (1817)		
27	*R. berberifolia*	*R. persica*
29	*R. sulphurea*	*R. hemisphaerica*
31	*Le Rosier à feuilles rougeatres*	*R. rubrifolia*
33	*R. moschata*	*R. moschata*
35	*R. bracteata*	*R. bracteata*
37	*Rose à feuilles de Laitue*	*R. centifolia bullata*
39	*R. muscosa (Muscosa simplex)*	*R. centifolia andrewsii*
41	*R. muscosa multiplex*	*R. centifolia muscosa*
45	*Le Rosier luisant*	*R. virginiana*
49	*R. indica*	*R. chinensis sanguinea*
51	*R. indica vulgaris*	*R. chinensis 'Old Blush'*
57	*R. pendulina*	*R. pendulina*
61	*R. indica fragrans*	*R. odorata* ('Hume's Blush tea-scented China')
63	*R. damascena subalba*	*R. dupontii*
65	*R. pomponia*	'Rose de Meaux'
67	*Le Rosier vélu*	*R. villosa*
69	*Le Rosier églantier*	*R. foetida*
71	*Le Rosier églantier couleur Ponceau*	*R. foetida bicolor*
73	*Le Rosier de Provence ordinaire*	*R. gallica officinalis*
75	*R. gallica officinalis*	*R. gallica officinalis*
81	*R. carolina corymbosa*	*R. carolina*
87	*R. muscosa alba*	*R. centifolia muscosa alba*
89	*R. arvensis*	*R. arvensis*
95	*R. hudsoniana*	*R. palustris*
97	*R. alba Regalis*	'Great Maiden's Blush'
99	*R. moschata flore semi-pleno*	*R. moschata plena*
103	*R. redoutia rubescens*	*R. nitida* (??)
105	*R. cinnamomea majalis*	*R. cinnamomea plena*
109	*R. damascena Coccinea*	'Scarlet Four Seasons'
111	*R. centifolia mutabilis*	*R. cinnamomea plena* 'Scarlet Four Seasons' *R. centifolia* 'Unique Blanche'

Plate No.	Original Designation.	Modern Designation.
115	*R. indica pumila*	*R. chinensis minima*
117	*R. alba flore pleno*	*R. alba semi-plena*
133	*R. cinnamomea flore simplici*	*R. cinnamomea*
135	*Rosa Mundi*	*R. gallica versicolor*
137	*R. damascena variegata*	*R. damascena versicolor*

Volume 2. (1819)

7	*R. rapa flore semipleno*	*R. virginiana plena*
15	*R. arvensis*	*R. arvensis*
23	*R. rubiginosa nemoralis*	*R. micrantha*
27	*R. longifolia*	*R. chinensis longifolia*
41	*R. damascena Aurora*	*R. alba celeste*
43	*R. banksiae albo-plena*	*R. banksiae* var. *banksiae*
45	*R. reversa*	*R. reversa*
47	*R. alba cimbaefolia*	*R. alba* 'A feuilles de Chanvre'
49	*R. sempervirens latifolia*	*R. sempervirens*
53	*R. celsiana*	*R. damascena* 'Celsiana'
63	*R. pumila (Rosier d'Amour)*	*Rosa gallica*, Wild form
67	*R. multiflora Carnea*	*R. multiflora platyphylla*
69	*R. multiflora platyphylla*	*R. multiflora platyphylla*
73	*R. parviflora flore multiplici*	*R. carolina plena*
77	*Le Rosier de Philippe Noisette*	*Rosa* 'Blush Noisette'
93	*R. inermis*	*R. francofurtana*

Volume 3. (1824)

11	*Rosier à mille Epines*	*R. pimpinellifolia* var. *myriacantha*
19	*R. spinosissima lutea maxima*	*R. pimpinellifolia lutea*
71	*R. rubrifolia*	Uncertain (*R. setigera?*)
77	*R. Agatha*	One of the many forms of 'Agatha'
78	*R. gallica Maheka (La Belle Sultane)*	*R. gallica violacea*
79	*R. reclinata*	*R. lheritieranea*
105	*R. canina burboniana*	*R. borboniana*
107	*R. pomponiana*	*R. centifolia parviflora*

(Taken from details assembled by G.S. Thomas and A. Rehder, Bibliography)

BIBLIOGRAPHY

ANON. Kreuz und Rose; Die Lutherrose. Rosenzeitung 1933.

ANON. A Catalogue of Dutch and Flemish Still-Life Pictures in the Ashmolean Museum, Oxford.

ANON. The Minden Day. The Rose 2: 273-274 (1954).

ANON. La Rose, son histoire, sa beauté et son utilisation en médicine et dans l'alimentation. Les Amis des Roses Nr. 316. 13-17 (1973).

BALIS, J. De Roos en Beeld. 96 pp. Brussels 1966. Also available in French under the title 'Images de la Rose'.

BATTERSBY, B.K. The Rose in Design. Rose Ann. 1953: 49-54.

BEHLING, L. Die Pflanzenwelt der mittelalterlichen Kathedralen. 222 pp. 160 plates, Verlag Böhlau, Cologne 1964.

BELMONT, A. Dictionnaire historique et artistique de la Rose. 207 pp. Paris 1896.

BERNHARD, O. Pflanzenbilder auf griechischen und römischen Münzen. 47 pp. Zurich 1924.

BLUNT, W. The Art of Botanical Illustration. 304 pp. London 1950.

BRELOER, J. 1000 Jahre ? Rosenstock am Dom zu Hildesheim. Bernwand Verlag, Hildesheim 1974.

BROCKHAUS, M. Der Blumenmaler Pierre-Joseph Redouté und seine Rosenbildnisse. Gartenflora 86: 156-158 (1937).

BROOKE-LITTLE, J.P. (Revised by) Boutell's Heraldry. London 1978.

— An Heraldic Alphabet. London 1973.

BUNYARD, E.Y. The Rose in Art. Rose Ann. 1938: 39-48.

CARDEW, F.M.G. A note on the illustration of Roses. Jour. R.H.S. 73: 180-182 (1942).

DIDERICH, E. Minden Day. Rosenzeitung 1931: 2-3.

GRANT, M.H. Flower Painting through the Centuries. (Not personally known to the Author).

HAIRS, M.L. Les Peintres Flamands de Fleurs au XVIIe Siècle 264 pp., 83 plates. Brussels 1955.

HEIDELOFF, K.A. von. Die Ornamentik des Mittelalters (1844 to 1847).

—, and GÖRGEL. Die Ornamentik des Mittelalters (Illustrated) 1852.

HERZOG, H.U. and F. WOLF. Flaggen und Wappen. Leipzig 1967.

HIERONYMUSSEN and LUND. Handbuch europäischer Orden in Farben 238 pp. Berlin 1966.

HILDEBRANDT, A.M. Wappenfibel — Handbuch der Heraldik. 16 Edn. Issued by 'Herold'. 229 pp. Neustadt/Aisch 1970.

HÖHN and ZOBEL. Pflanzen auf Briefmarken. Berlin-O 1969.

IMHOOF-BLUMER, F. and O. KELLER. Tier und Pflanzenbilder auf Münzen und Gemmen des classischen Altertums. 60 pp. and 10 plates of five coins with roses. Leipzig 1889.

JANNASCH, H. Die Rose in der deutschen Kunst. Rosen-Jb. 1936: 50-53.

KAMMEYER, H.F. Dendrologie und Numismatik. Mitt. DDG: 63: 3-26 (1968).

LAWALREE, A. L'âge d'or de la peinture botanique. Rosa Belgica 1971: 10-13.

LECKY, H.S. The Rose in Heraldry. Rose Ann. 1931.

LEGRAND-COCHET, L. L'origine de la Rose d'Angleterre. Jardins de France 1964, June Issue.

LENNHOFF/PONER, Internationales Freimaurer-Lexikon. Graz 1932.

LIPPE, E.A. PRINZ ZU. Orden und Auszeichnungen. 190 pp. Heidelberg 1958.

LOUDA, J. Europäische Stadtwappen, deutsche Ausgabe. Genesis-Verlag, Balzers in Liechtenstein, 1969.

MARZELL, H. Die Rose in deutschen Volksleben. Rosen-Jb. 1934: 141-145.

MELLOR, G. At the sign of the Rose. The Rose 8. 254-258 (1960).

MERLIN, A. Römische Rosen-Mosaiken (Translated from Journal des Roses). Rosenzeitung 1913, with 2 ill.

NISSEN, C. Die botanische Buchillustration, ihre Geschichte und Bibliographie. Vol. 1, 264 pp. Vol. 2, 324 pp. Stuttgart 1951. Supplement, 97 pp. Stuttgart 1966.

ROCK, P.M.J. The Golden Rose. The Catholic Encyclopedia VI (1913).

SCHICK, H. Das ältere Rosenkreuzertum. 1942.

SCHLEIDEN, M.J. Die Rose, Geschichte und Symbolik in ethnographischer und kulturhistorischer Beziehung. Leipzig 1873.

SCHROEDTER, W. Das Rosenkreuz. 1955.

— Geschichte und Lehren der Rosenkreuzer 175 pp. Villach 1956.

SCOTT, W. The Romance of Heraldry. London 1957.

SEELAND, H. Der tausendjährige Rosenstock am Dom zu Hildesheim. Hildesheim 1947. — Reprinted in Rosen-Jb. 1955.

SIERKSMA, K. De Gemeentewapens van Nederland. Utrecht 1960.

STEIMEL, R. Die Wappen der bundesdeutschen Landkreise. Cologne 1964.

VASTERLING, P. Die Rose in der Kunst und in der Heilkunst. Rosen-Jb. 30: 115-120 (1964).

VERDENHALVEN, F. Alte Masse, Münzen und Gewichte aus dem deutschen Sprachgebiet. Neustadt/Aisch 1968.

WARNER, R. Dutch and Flemish Fruit and Flower Painters of the Seventeenth and Eighteenth Centuries. London 1928.

WEGENER, H. Die Rosenabbildungen bis Redouté. Gartenflora 86: 154-156 (1937).

WINKER, H. Die Rose in Sage und Schriftum. Rosenzeitung 1917: 12-13: 32-34.

ZANDER, R. and W. KORDES. Anekdoten aus der Geschichte des Gartenbaues (Entstehung von Rosensorten). Rosen-Jb. 22: 170-174 (1961).

ZEHNDER, J.-P. Ein weiterer Beitrag zum Thema: Rosen und Briefmarken. Rosenbogen 1973 (4): 22-27.

For further bibliographical references, see p. 39 and p. 58.

Botanical Terminology

should be obtained from the native plants; many Botanical Gardens all over the world are distributing such freshly collected seeds with exact provenance information.

THE STEM

Introduction Many botanical terms are used to describe both wild roses and garden varieties; technical definitions must be understood, for without precise knowledge of them an unknown plant might be identified incorrectly. In this book, unfortunately, I cannot describe garden roses in detail, as I will the wild roses, for the book would become too lengthy.

Further, only those botanical terms which are particularly relevant to roses have been used. A complete list of terms may be found in any good botanical textbook.

The following parts are described in this volume: stem, leaf, flower, fruit and seed. The technical terms used by geneticists are explained in the chapter "The Basis of Rose Breeding". It is difficult to identify a rose species correctly, due to the great variability in the plants, hence the characteristics of a specific plant may not all concur with the description. This is particularly true of plants grown from seeds of cultivated plants (e.g. from Botanical Gardens). Seedlings from such roses are more or less hybridized, and very often it is only approximately possible to find out to which species they may belong. If rose species are to be cultivated, the seeds

As all roses are shrubs, they do not have a single stem (in the rose standards this is artificially produced and therefore cannot be regarded botanically as a stem), but several stems. These arise from the base, first grow vertically, then branch at the middle of the stem; botanically this type of growth pattern is called sympodial with orthotropic direction of growth and mesotonic ramification.

Single rose bushes seldom reach a height of more than 3-4 m./10-13 ft., except in the case of climbing roses, which in the garden reach 3-5 m./10-16.5 ft. when tied up. In mild countries, e.g. in Great Britain or in the Mediterranean area, these roses can reach a height of up to 10 m./33 ft. and more (*R. gigantea*, *R. moschata*, *R.* 'Mermaid', etc.). Wild roses use their curved prickles to attach themselves. If the branches are not tied up, they

Figure 104. Patterns of branching. a. Bushy (most Hybrid Teas and Floribundas); b. Tight Upright (*R. centifolia*); c. Bushy Upright ('Queen Elizabeth'); d. Tall growing with loose branching (*R. banksiae*).

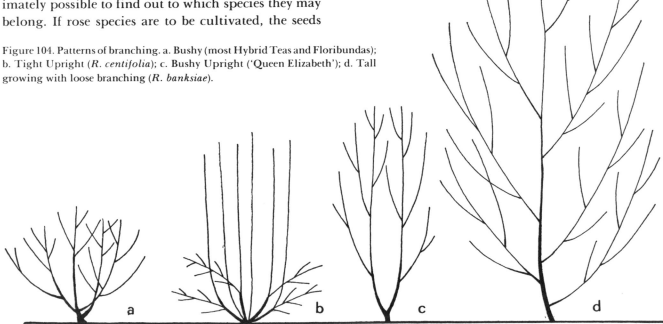

237

remain lying on the ground, as in the case of *Rosa paulii* (= *R. rugosa repens*) or *R. wichuraiana*. Some species form suckers, e.g. *Rosa persica. R. carolina* can be rather annoying because it spreads vigorously.

The stems and branches of the roses are, with few exceptions (*R. pendulina, R. banksiae*, thornless *R. multiflora*) more or less armed with **prickles** ("thorns"), which are important in identifying a species. The prickles can be uniform (homoecanthy) or of different form (heteracanthy), straight or more or less curved, strongly hooked, needle-shaped throughout, triangular and dilated at the base, or even wing-shaped (*R. sericea*). They may be more or less numerous, increasing in number towards the base of the shoot, sometimes mixed with bristles (*R. rugosa*), the base of the prickles may be orbicular or elliptical. In some species the prickles are situated in pairs below the base of the leaf. The length of the prickles varies from 1-5 mm./0.04-0.2 in., rarely up to 10 mm./0.4 in., but may reach even 30-40 mm./1.2-1.6 in. in *R. sericea* and its varieties. Prickles vary in width from 1-5 mm./0.04-0.2 in.

Needle-shaped prickles are stiff, terete, only dilated at the base.

Bristles are weak, flexible, with very little dilation at the base.

Glandular bristles are bristles with a globose gland at the tip.

Stalked glands are globose glands on a mostly more than 5 mm./0.2 in. long stalk, and of a constant diameter. The stalk may be straight or curved.

Sessile glands have a stalk less than 0.5 mm./0.02 in. long.

The color of the prickles is noteworthy only when they are yellow, nearly white, or bright red (as in *R. pteracantha*); in most cases the prickles are more or less reddish or brownish.

The **bark** of the shoots may be quite smooth or tomentose (*R. bracteata*), or bluish-bloomy (*R. glauca*). Especially remarkable is the defoliating bark from older stems of *R. roxburghii*. The color of the shoots is mostly green, while the bark is usually red or brown.

The **wood of rose plants,** especially from old rootstocks, has a very fine grain, is very hard, nicely veined and with an interesting color, so it is very much sought after for inlaid work. However, the usual garden roses rarely develop a stem or rootstock of sufficient size save for old climbing roses.

238

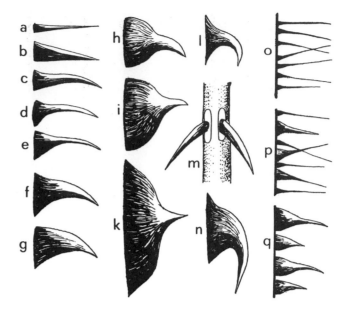

Figure 105. Types of Prickles. Needle-shaped (a, b, d); more or less curved and hooked (c, e, f, g, l, n); wing-shaped dilated (h, i, k); bristles (o); bristles and prickles mixed (p); prickles of different size on the same stem (q). (Original)

THE LEAF

With only one exception (*Rosa persica*), the leaves of the roses are always odd-pinnate, mostly with 5 leaflets in the Hybrid Teas, 5-7 in the Floribundas. The wild species normally have 7-9 leaflets; many Asiatic species, however, often have 13-15 (up to 19) leaflets while a few American species (*R. stellata, R. minutifolia*) have only 3 small leaflets. The form of the leaflet in all roses is nearly identical; generally they are more or less ovate or elliptical, with a rounded, wedgeform or slightly cordiform base, the apex acute, or blunt and long-pointed. The leaves may be quite bald or hairy, with or without sessile or stalked glands, the margin simply or doubly serrate, and with or without stalked glands at the tips of the teeth. The glands of leaves in *R. rubiginosa* secrete a very strong fragrance, reminiscent of green apples.

The **blade** of the leaflets is mostly even in most species, or wrinkled (*R. rugosa*, etc.), thin or hardy and leathery, shiny or dull, lighter or darker green. With most garden roses the young growth is more or less red or bronze; in *R. persica, R. glauca* and a few others, distinctly bluish-green. Next to this the blade may be bald or hairy on both sides, or only beneath.

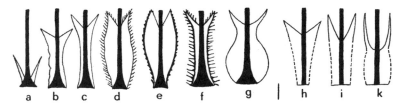

Figure 106. Types of Stipules. a. completely free; b-k. adnate; a. sublate, free, early falling; b. parallel, auricle facing outward; c. parallel, auricle facing forward; d. similar to c., but with the middle part enlarged, margin fringed with hairs; e. enlarged in the upper part, margin denticulate; f. middle part narrowing downward, margin comb-shaped; g. lower half semi-circular, narrowing to the apex, auricle facing outward; h. and i. narrow triangular, auricle facing outward or forward; i. auricle very long and narrow, facing forward. (Original)

The **stipules** are small leaf-like appendages adnate to both sides of the base of the leafstalk. In only a few species are they free (*R. banksiae*). The outline of the stipules in most species takes on a variety of forms (see Fig. 106). The small free part on the top of the stipule is called the auricle.

The **bracts** are modified and reduced leaves, occurring in the inflorescences, subtending a pedicel or peduncle, always being entire, never pinnate. Some species have no bracts (see list p. 248).

INFLORESCENCES

The wild rose species mostly have inflorescences of 1-3 flowers, rarely up to 5. However, in the section *Synstylae*, they are arranged in many-flowered corymbs, with the *Banksianae* more or less in umbels. In other species, especially garden roses (namely the Floribundas, Polyanthas, Climbing and Shrub roses), the flowers are united to large panicles; 50-100 flowers on a single shoot is not uncommon. The different types of inflores-

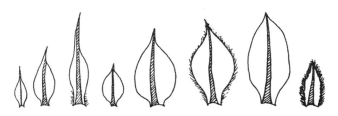

Figure 107. Types of Bracts. a. elliptical with acuminate apex (many Floribundas); b. acute-elliptical with acuminate apex (*R. beggeriana*); c. broadly lanceolate with caudate apex (many roses); d. broadly elliptical with mucronate tip (*R. multibracteata*); e. broadly elliptical with acute tip (*R. majalis*); f. broadly elliptical with long apex, margin ciliate ('Mermaid'); g. elliptical, acute (*R. rugosa*); h. scalelike, margin fringed ('Orléans Rose'). (after v. Rathlef)

cences can be seen in Fig. 108. The many-flowered garden roses mostly have inflorescences of the corymb, cyme and panicle type. Their characteristics can be seen in the following survey:

> Corymb — all flowers on about the same level
> Panicle — all flowers in a more or less pyramidal inflorescence
> Cyme — every branch with one terminal flower, more or less on the same level

Umbel — all flower stalks growing from the same point

The **calyx** (the correct term is "floral cup" = hypanthium or receptaculum) is the upper part of the stem from which the floral parts arise. Roses have two types of calyxes. In the first type there is a thick layer of marrow under the rind (i.e. in most species of the series *Caninae* and *Gallicanae*) bearing on top a discus-like collar which does not secrete nectar and having only a narrow channel opening for the column of styles. In the second type, the layer of marrow and the discus-collar are much less developed, but the central opening is much larger. For example, *R. pimpinellifolia, villosa,* et al. (Fig. 109/b).

The **sepals** present many characteristics which are especially useful in determining a species or variety. From their 2/5 spiral position they overlap each other partially (Fig. 110), from which arises the unequal formation which has even engaged poets.[1]

Normally all rose flowers have five sepals; *R. sericea* and its varieties, however, have only four sepals and four petals.

In their simplest form they are lanceolate, entire, with a dilated base, but mostly the outer two sepals are pinnatifid on both sides, the central one only on one side, while the inner two sepals are entire.

For purposes of identification, not only form and size of the sepals are important, but their duration and position as well. With many species, including garden roses, the sepals drop off before the fruit is mature (*Gallicanae, Caninae, Synstylae,* etc.), while in others the sepals remain and turn upright (*Pimpinellifoliae,*

[1] We are five brothers, born at the same time, two with beards, two are sheared, and one half shaven.

Figure 108. Types of Inflorescences. a. typical umbel; b. cyme; c. compound umbel (*R. setipoda*); d. compound cyme (*R. canina*); e. cyme (*R. rugosa*); f. corymb with branches a narrow angle ('Else Poulsen'); g. unequally branched compound panicle of 'Echo', with bent main axis; h. compound panicle ('Orleans'-type). (after Rathlef and W. Kordes, modified)

Cinnamomeae) or are reflexed when the flower dies; the latter drop off just before full maturity.

R. gymnocarpa has "naked" (gymnocarpic) fruits, so named since the sepals, and pistils and stigmas drop off the head of the hip at the same time. This peculiarity has also been observed, although not in so pronounced a way, in *R. nutkana* var. *muriculata*, *R. nutkana* × *R. acicularis*, *R. engelmannii* × *R. acicularis*, *R. californica* var. *myriacantha* × *R. nutkana* var. *spaldingii*.

The moss roses are especially striking in that not only the sepals, but also the receptacles and flower stalks, are very "mossy". This "moss" (mossy excrescences is derived from the many-branched, stalked lands which feel soft. When touched, they secrete a strong fragrance that may remain on the skin for hours. Many roses have "moss" which feels hard and rough; the reason for this is that the glands in this case are located on bristles, which also sometimes gives this "moss" a brownish color. Finally, the unique "moss" of *R. centifolia cristata* should be explained: here the very closely pinnate sepals are covered thickly with moss, and in such a regular way that the buds look nearly triangular. The

Figure 109. The Receptacle (longitudinal section). The different length of the pistils are separate and free (a,b,c) or united into a column (d,e). The styles may (1) remain unexserted, (2) form a head closing the mouth of the receptacle, or (3) all exserted (e,f). In (a) the achenes stand on the bottom and the wall, while (b) rests only on the bottom; two young achenes (g and h).

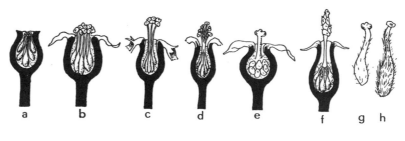

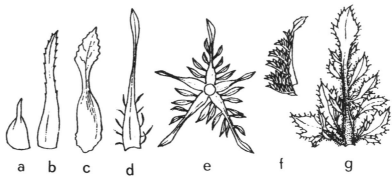

Figure 110. Types of sepals: a.,b.,c.,f. and g. single sepals, c. with a leaf-shaped top; f. and g. pinnate; e. asymmetric formation (see p. 240) of the sepals.

Figure 111. Position of sepals. a.-c. upright, d. horizontal, e.-f. reflexed; in many species all three phases follow each other.

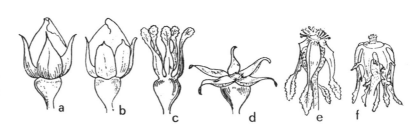

plants were, as a consequence, introduced under the name 'Chapeau de Napoléon' for their vague resemblance to a tri-cornered hat.

The flowers of rose species have **five petals**, except *R. sericea* which has only four. The petals are arranged in two cycles (see diagram, Fig. 115). The corolla is usually in a form reminiscent of a flat saucer. Garden roses with 5-10 petals are called "single"; double roses are designated as follows:

10-20 petals — semi-double
20-40 petals — double
40 petals and over — very double

Many varieties, especially the old roses, have 100 or more petals.

The petals of the doubles have been developed from the stamens and partly from the pistils. Very often the transitional stages from the stamen or pistil to petal form can be seen.

The **shape of the petals** of most roses is more or less orbicular or broadly obovate, the base of the petal having a tiny "nail". The upper edge may be notched or almost heart-shaped, sometimes curled or folded or slightly lobed (Fig. 112). The position and number of petals give the flower its characteristic form, i.e.:

Pointed or high-centered (Fig. 114e)	Central petals in full anthesis remaining upright and not spreading ('Poinsettia').
Globose or globose high-centered	all petals deeply saucer-shaped, curved inward on upper edge, central petals upright, forming a ball ('Peace', 'Queen Elizabeth').
Cupped (Fig. 114d)	particularly with semi-double flowers, petals cup-shaped spread, center free.
Flat or thin (Fig. 114f)	single or semi-double flowers with petals spread horizontally or even slightly reflexed.

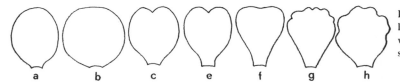

Figure 112. Rose petals. a. elliptic; b. orbicular; c. elliptic with notch; 4. heart-shaped; f. wedge-shaped; apex. emarginated; g. wedge-shaped with curled apex; h. curled.

Imbricated (Fig. 114c)	only fully-blown flowers have this form, when all petals are rather short, regularly reflexed, overlapping and so creating a rosette effect in the center, like a camellia.
Informal (Fig. 114b)	(in the U.S.A. called "cactus") lacking smoothness and uniformity of petal arrangement of the other forms; very irregular in outline, arrangement and size of petals.
Star-shaped	occurring with semi-double flowers, where petals remain more or less horizontal, but lateral edges of petals rolling back
Carnation-shaped	small flowers, petals on upper edge dentate, like carnations; so far only known from several varieties of *R. rugosa*.

Old roses display a special feature: petals are often so numerous that they are grouped into four quarters ("quartered"), easy to recognize. Very often a "button eye" is formed in the center, consisting of mostly lighter and smaller petals which are unable to spread and so are curving inward in a ball-form. This "button-eye" may have a green color, formed by the deformed carpels. (See Fig. 114a.)

The **shape of the bud** is controlled by the number of petals; the more numerous and the shorter the petals, the shorter and more compact the bud will be. Today not only the breeder, but also the buyer, of cut roses prefers a beautiful, slender bud. These bud forms are:

Slender (Fig. 113d)	gradually expanding from the calyx to the center, then tapering to the top of the bud.
Pointed (Fig. 113c)	bud more fully expanded at the base, tapering to a distinct point at the top.

Ovoid (Fig. 113b)	egg-shaped, with full base, narrowing to a more or less rounded top.
Urn-shaped (Fig. 113e)	broadest in lower third, strongly narrowing in upper third, and widening at the tip.
globose (Fig. 113a)	circular in outline, more or less compact egg-shaped, very little longer than wide; very often seen in very double flowers.

On flower color see p. 171.

The petals of roses contain **volatile oils** in the form of little drops in the protoplasm of the epidermal cells and the adjacent cells of the mesophyllum. From here they penetrate the outer wall of the epidermis and the cuticula to evaporate. The cells produce these volatile oils through their lifetime. (Baumeister and Reichart, p. 286.)

The **stamens** are situated within the base of the petals, at the discus, and are arranged in several cycles; their number varies between 20 and about 100. The color of the filaments and the anthers is mostly not striking, but should be observed. The filaments are normally nearly white to light straw-yellow, but may range from golden-yellow to pink, through red to dark brown. The anthers regularly display a different color than the filaments, usually shades of yellow, to copper and brown. At maturity the anther-cells split longitudinally and discharge the pollen. The anthers turn to face either the center (towards the stigmas), or the petals. These positions are called "introverse" and "retroverse", respectively. In many cases the anthers have a decorative value, as for example the golden-yellow stamens of the *Gallica* cultivars, or the deep red stamens of 'White Wings', or the wine red to brown-red ones of *Rosa moyesii*, etc.

The **pistils**, composed of ovary, style and stigma, are either all free, or joined to form a column, and protrude through the mouth of the receptacle, extending to, or above, the discus. Style and ovary of the single achenes

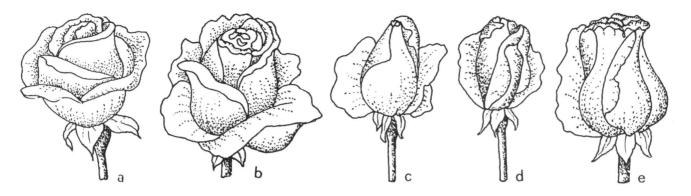

Figure 113. Shape of buds, just before expanding: a. globose;   b. egg-shaped;   c. pointed;   d. slender;   e. urn-shaped.

Figure 114. Shape of the corolla: a. quartered;   b. informal;   c. imbricate;   d. cupped;   e. high centered;   f. flat.

243

may be bald or hairy. The color of the pistil is generally straw-yellow to dark yellow, or pink to red. The stigmas are commonly of a deeper color than the style.

THE FRUIT

The fruit arises from the receptacle (or hypanthium) as a berry-like fruit (hip). Hip shapes vary widely; basic shapes are shown in Fig. 116. They may be globose, subglobose, ovate, pear-shaped, spindle-shaped, flask-shaped, or a combination of these shapes. Externally, the fruit may be bald or have stalked glands or bristles; in the case of *R. roxburghii*, short, thick prickles cover the fruit; sometimes the hips are bloomy.

Many of the cultivars are sterile, so cannot set fruit; when they ripen, the flower-stalks turn yellow and drop. Rose breeders prefer this sterility, because it leads to the much-desired "self-cleansing" of the inflorescences.

With the exception of *R. persica*, *R. stellata* and *R. minutifolia* (which have dry fruits), the hips are always more or less fleshy.

The color of the fruits is usually shades of red in most species as well as in the cultivated garden roses; *R. foetida*, brick red; *R. sericea*, *R. laevigata* and *R. bracteata*, orange; *R. persica* and *R. roxburghii*, green; with *R. pimpinellifolia* and all its varieties, including *R. harisonii*, black; with *R. hugonis*, *R. primula* and *R. stellata*, blackish-red to brown-red.

The **achenes**, usually falsely called "seeds" are nutlets and contain one seed. The size of the achenes depends upon the size of the fruit. Achenes of cultivated roses are notably larger than those of wild species. The number of achenes per hip is equally dependent on its size; hips of *Rosa multiflora* contain only a few "seeds", cultivated roses about 10-20, and *Rosa clinophylla* up to 150.

The achenes (nutlets or "seeds") are:

a) 4-5 mm./0.15-0.2 in. long, very hairy, in *R. acicularis* and *R. canina*;

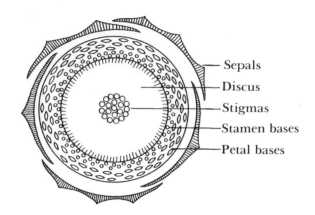

Figure 115. Flower diagram of a Hybrid Tea. With very double flowers the margin of the discus is conically elevated to provide more space for the petals and the stamens. (Original)

b) in *R. acicularis* only a few nutlets in the fruit, and all of them on the bottom;
c) in *R. canina* many nutlets and always on the wall of the fruit;
d) in *R. multiflora* only few, large and nearly bald nutlets;
e) in *R. palustris* and *R. setosa* many little nutlets.

The color of the nutlets is usually straw-yellow, except in the section *Pimpinellifoliae*, where they are pink to chestnut-brown (primarily the latter color in plants from the Baikal Sea). Species with colored achenes have black or red-brown hips. On the cytological relations between roses see the chapter on hybridizing (p. 164).

The Rose Color Groups The American Rose Society has compiled a list of basic color groups. The different cultivars in this list are classified by their typical color when at their best. The following 16 basic color groups have been agreed upon:

Group 1: White or near white: 'Pascali', 'Matterhorn', 'Garden Party', 'McGredy's Ivory', 'Snowbird', 'John F. Kennedy', 'Youki San'.
Group 2: Medium yellow: 'Buccaneer', 'Eclipse', 'Lemon Elegance', 'Goldilocks', 'Spanish Sun', 'Golden Fleece'.
Group 3: Deep yellow: 'Lowell Thomas', 'Sunbonnet', 'Summer

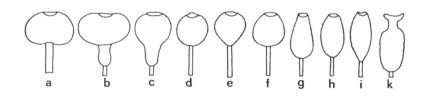

Figure 116. Form of rose fruits. a. subglobose; b. subglobose with fleshy stalk; c. pear-shaped; d. globose; e. obovate; f. elongated-obovate; g. rose-shaped; h. ellipsoid; i. spindle-shaped; k. flask-shaped. (schematic)

Sunshine', 'Allgold', 'Spek's Yellow', 'Dr. A.J. Verhage', 'Western Sun'.

Group 4: Yellow blend; includes cultivars primarily yellow with some tones of pink or red: 'Peace', 'Diamond Jubilee', 'American Heritage', 'Sutter's Gold', 'Masquerade', 'Rumba'.

Group 5: Apricot blend; includes cultivars that are primarily apricot but show tone of some other color: 'Apricot Dawn', 'Apricot Nectar', 'Angels Mateau', 'Golden Slippers'.

Group 6: Orange and orange blend; includes cultivars primarily orange or orange with some other hues: 'Bettina', 'Fred Edmunds', 'California', 'Color Wonder', 'Zorina', 'Prominent', 'Mercedes', 'Independence'.

Group 7: Orange-red: 'Hawaii', 'Montezuma', 'Spartan', 'Tropicana', 'Baccara', 'Sarabande', 'City of Belfast'.

Group 8: Light pink: 'Radiance', 'Royal Highness', 'First Love', 'Queen Elizabeth', 'First Lady', 'Bridal Pink'.

Group 9: Medium pink; variations in tone of pink between the upper and lower surfaces of the petals are not considered: 'Carina', 'Pink Peace', 'Show Girl', 'Betty Uprichard', 'Duet', 'Bewitched', 'Pink Favorite'.

Group 10: Pink blend; cultivars primarily pink, but show some tones of other hues: 'Taffeta', 'President Herbert Hoover', 'Helen Traubel', 'Chicago Peace', 'Kordes Perfecta', 'Tiffany', 'Gail Borden'.

Group 11: Deep pink: 'Tallyho', 'Charlotte Armstrong', 'Rubaiyat', 'Paddy McGredy', 'McGredy's Scarlet', 'Prima Ballerina'.

Group 12: Medium red: 'New Yorker', 'Christian Dior', 'Better Times', 'Permanent Wave', 'Ernest H. Morse'.

Group 13: Dark red: 'Crimson Glory', 'Josephine Bruce', 'Europeana', 'Chrysler Imperial', 'Papa Meilland'.

Group 14: Red blend; cultivars primarily red, but with other hues; yellow, orange, etc.: 'Bajazzo', 'Cleopatra', 'Granada'.

Group 15: Mauve; cultivars primarily lavendar and purple: 'Sterling Silver', 'Lady X', 'Shocking Blue', 'Angel Face', 'News', 'Lavendula', 'Blue Moon', 'Lilac Charme'.

Group 16: Russet; cultivars primarily brown or tan in color: 'Fantan', 'Café', 'Brown Eyes', 'Wiener Charme', 'Valencia', 'Mojave'.

Bibliography

BAUMEISTER, W. & G. REICHART. Lehrbuch der Angewandten Botanik. Stuttgart 1969.

BELL, L. Rose Signatures. Amer. Rose Annual 1970: 104-117.

KORDES, W. & H. VON RATHLEF. Die Blütenformen der Rose und ihre Beschreibung. Rosenjahrbuch 1938: 50-55.

__ & __ Die Blütenstände der Rose und ihre Beschreibung; Rosenjahrbuch 1939: 4-13.

LEWIS, C.H. The Judging of Roses (Official Judges Manual of the American Rose Society). Salem, Va., 1959.

Botanical Classification of the more Important Species and Hybrids

THE POSITION OF THE GENUS *ROSA* IN BOTANY SYSTEMATIC

Modern systematics are undergoing continuous modification; to date it has been impossible to arrive at a classification of the Vegetable Kingdom which has been universally agreed upon. Excerpts taken from two modern classification systems may show the position of the genus *Rosa*.

The first attempt at a scientific classification of the genus *Rosa* dates from 1819, when A. Dupont published, in Paris, his *Catalogus Rosarum* as an appendix to C.A. Thory's work *Rosa Candolleana*, which dates to the year 1813 and contains 31 groups with 131 species and varieties. However, as this consists only of *nomina nuda* (i.e. without description), it can really only be spoken of as a precursor.

The first scientific classification of the genus was made in 1818 by P.A. de Candolle in Seringe's *Musée helvétique d'histoire naturelle* (Geneva), with a division into 11 sections. However, since this classification was unsatisfying, no less than 25 further classifications have been drawn up by botanists in the following 100 years. A critical analysis of these classifications can be found in R. Keller's *Synopsis Rosarium Spontanearum Europae Mediae* (Zürich, 1931), where, unfortunately, only European wild rose species are treated.

The classification generally followed today was set up by Rehder, 1949 (in his *Bibliography*). It is a compilation of parts from the earlier classification of de Candolle and Seringe (1818), Lindley and Thory (1820), Dumortier (1824), Crépin (1876), Focke (1888), Cockerell (1913), and Hurst (1940). It contains 4 subgenera, of which the subgenus II (*Rosa*) comprises 10 sections with 126 species in all (see p. 248).

The definition of the species diverges widely among different botanists, as the following numbers indicate.

Lindley (1762) specified only 14 species of the genus *Rosa*, but by 1820 he identified 78; Seringe (1825) had 91, among them 51 uncertain species. Then the "King of Hair-Splitters", Gandoger (1881), arrived at 4,266 species in the Old World alone!

Crépin (1869-1882) counts 283 species, Déséglise

ENGLER/MELCHIOR, *Syllabus der Pflanzenfamilien*, 12. ed. Berlin 1964.

XVIII. Division: Angiospermae (Flowering Plants)

1. Class: Dicotyledoneae (plants with 2 seed leaves)

1. Subclass: *Archichlamydeae*
23. Series: *Rosales*
3. Subseries: *Rosinae*, with 3 families (*Rosaceae, Neuradaceae* and *Chrysobalanaceae*)

Family **Rosaceae** (consisting of 4 subfamilies, *Spiraeoideae, Pyroideae, Rosoideae, Prunoideae*)

F. Ehrendorfer, in Strasburger, *Lehrbuch der Botanik*, 30. ed. Stuttgart 1971.

VII. Division: Spermatophyta (= Seed Plants) with 3 subdivisions, Coniferophytina, Cycadophytina and Magnoliophytina

3. Subdivision: Magnoliophytina (= Dicotyledoneae, with 2 seed leaves); this divided into Magnoliatae and Liliatae.
   1. Class: Magnoliateae (= Dicotyledoneae)
   2. Class: Liliatae (= Monocotyledoneae, with 1 leaf seed).

The Magnoliatae are subdivided into 6 subclasses: *Magnoliidae, Hamameliidae, Rosidae, Dilleniidae, Caryophyllidae* and *Asteridae*.

The *Rosidae* are subdivided into *Rosanae, Myrtanae, Rutanae, Celastranae* and *Proteanae*.

The *Rosanae* consist of the orders *Saxifragales, Rosales, Fabales*, Sarraceniales and *Podostemales*.

The Order Rosales contains the family **Rosaceae**

From this point on the classification is the same in both systems.

Subfamily: *Rosoideae* (= plants similar to roses), consisting of 6 tribes *(Kerriae, Potentilleae, Cercocarpeae, Ulmarieae, Sanguisorbeae* and *Roseae)*

Tribe: *Rosea* (= plants growing like roses), consisting of the genus **Rosa**

The latest revision of the European Roses is that of I. Klastersky, Prague, in *Flora Europaea* (Cambridge, 1968) which deals with 47 rose species.

(1878) 410. Of the modern botanists, Rydberg describes 113 species found only in North America, Boulenger 100 in Asia, R. Keller in his extended *Synopsis* (1931) 44 species and subspecies in Central Europe, with innumerable varieties and forms. The 284 species, varieties and forms described in my book, excluding the garden hybrids (see p. 303), should be sufficient for any rose amateur.

DESCRIPTION OF THE MORE IMPORTANT SPECIES AND VARIETIES OF THE GENUS *ROSA*

Deciduous, rarely evergreen, upright or climbing shrubs, branches mostly more or less prickly or bristly; leaves alternate, odd-pinnate, rarely entire, with stipules; flowers solitary or in corymbs at the top of short branches; sepals and petals 5, rarely only 4; stamens many, pistils many, the latter mostly included in an urn-shaped receptacle, becoming berry-like and fleshy at maturity, containing several to many 1-seeded achenes with hard shells. $x = 7$. More than 100 species (several authors cite up to 200) in the temperate and subtropical zones of the Northern hemisphere; in Europe, N. America to N. Mexico, in N. Africa to Ethiopia, in Asia to the Himalayas and the Philippines.

For reasons of space, the treatment of the wild species and their varieties must be limited to those either in cultivation or important for breeding purposes. Furthermore, the nomenclature of the "cultivated" wild species has far fewer of the problems which separate botanists in their interpretation of the European species.

The reader will scarcely miss the omitted wild species. Rosarians may consult the specialist literature (Crépin, Keller, Schwertschlager, Täckholm, et al.)

Subg. I. **HULTHEMIA** (Dumort.) Focke[1]

> Leaves entire, without stipules; flowers solitary, yellow, fruit with prickles and bristles (bald in *R. kopetdaghensis*):
> *R. persica, hardii, kopetdaghensis.*

[1] **Hulthemia** and **Hulthemosa.** *Rosa persica* Michx. (1789) was separated in 1824 by Dumortier, and changed to a new genus, *Hulthemia*. Among the contemporary botanists, some have adopted this (Hurst, Boulenger, Rowley, et al.), while most are keeping the old name *Rosa persica*. When *Hulthemia* is used, then the name × *Hulthemosa* must also be used, for the two known hybrids of *Rosa persica*, published in 1941 by Juzepchuk, 1941 in Komarov, "Flora of the U.S.S.R.", 10: 507.

Rosa persica Michx. Small shrub, 0.2-0.5 m./0.7-1.6 ft., suckering, branches yellowish-brown, prickly; leaves entire (not pinnate), sessile, elliptic to oblong, 2-3 cm./0.8-1.2 in. long, bluish-green, serrate, finely pubescent; flowers solitary, 3 cm./1.2 in., yellow with deep red or brown center, May-August, sepals lanceolate, persistent, entire; fruits globose, densely prickly, green. 2n = 14. WR 1; BM 7096; ICS 2217. (= *R. berberifolia* Pall.; *R. simplicifolia* Salisb.). Persia to Afghanistan, on salty ground near the Caspian Sea and Aral Sea. 1790. Rather easy to grow from seed, but very difficult to keep alive in cultivation. Rowley has suggested using this species for hybridizing, as the heredity of the basal blotches might bring quite new roses (see *RA* 1955: 37-40); meanwhile, a number of crosses have been made by J. Harkness. (Fig. 117).

R. × hardii Cels. (= *R. clinophylla × R. persica*). Similar to *R. persica*, but much taller, up to 2 m./6.6 ft.; leaves partly entire, partly with up to 7 leaflets, dark green,

Figure 117. *Rosa persica*. (after Redouté, redrawn)

247

CLASSIFICATION OF THE GENUS ROSA

Synoptical survey of the genus (after CRÉPIN, modified)

Taxonomic Category	Stems, Shoots	Prickles	Stipules	Median Leaves Of Flowering Branch
Subg. I HULTHEMIA (Dumort.) Focke 1 species	low, slender suckering	small, many, hooked	none	entire (not pinnate!)
Subg. II ROSA	as follows	as follows	present	pinnate
Sect. 1. **Pimpinellifoliae** (Sér.) Rehd. Burnet-Roses 12 species	upright, partly up to 3 m. 10 ft. high	straight, subulate, scattered, often mixed with bristles	adnate, narrow, with abruptly dilated and spreading auricles	mostly 7-9 leaflets; 9-11 (-17) in *R. sericea*
Sect. 2. **Gallicanae** (Sér.) Rehd. Gallica-Roses 5 species	upright, mostly low	curved, with needle-shaped or bristly prickles, mixed with scattered glands	adnate, not dilated at top	5, rarely 3 leaflets
Sect. 3. **Caninae** (Sér.). Rehd. Dog-Roses 30 species	upright or bent	straight, curved or hooked, mostly uniform	adnate, top broader than foot	mostly 7, rarely 9 leaflets
Sect. 4. **Carolinae** (Crép.) Rehd. 6 species	upright, slender, low	shortly curved, mostly in pairs below stipules, scattered	adnate, usually narrowed at the top, or dilated	7-9 leaflets
Sect. 5. **Cinnamomeae** (Sér.) Rehd. Cinnamon-Roses 44 species	upright, slender	straight or curved, often in pairs, rarely omitted; flowering branches sometimes unarmed or with glands and bristles	adnate at top or more or less dilated, gradually changing into large auricles, directed forward	5-11 leaflets
Sect. 6. **Synstylae** (DC.) Rehd. 22 species	climbing or trailing, rarely upright	hooked or curved, sometimes in pairs below stipules	adnate to petiole at long distance, rarely free, narrow, caducous	3-7 (-9) leaflets
Sect. 7. **Chinenses** (Sér.) Rehd. China-roses 2 species	upright, sometimes climbing	hooked or curved, scattered	adnate to petiole at long distance, the upper ones with narrow, spreading auricles	3-5-7 leaflets
Sect. 8. **Banksianae** (Lindl.) Rehd. Banksian Roses 2 species	climbing, slender	hooked, alternate	free, dropping off early, subulate	3-5-7 leaflets
Sect. 9. **Laevigatae** (Thory) Rehd. 1 species	climbing or prostrate	hooked or curved, scattered, often mixed with bristles	nearly free, finally dropping off	3 leaflets, evergreen

Bracts	Sepals	Pistils and Stamens	Inflorescence	Distribution
none	lanceolate, persistent, tomentose	free, included, stigmas just above mouth of receptacle	flowers solitary	Central Asia
as follows	as follows	ovules on bottom and wall	mostly several-flowered	—
none	entire; after anthesis upright, persisting; only 4 in *R. sericea*	free, included, stigmas covering mouth of receptacle	mostly solitary, without bracts	Europe, Asia
small or narrow	after anthesis reflexed, dropping off just before maturity; outer ones pinnatifid	free, included, stigmas covering mouth of receptacle	solitary, rarely several-flowered, on long stalks	Europe, Asia Minor
present, more or less dilated	after anthesis reflexed, dropping off before maturity — or upright, crowning receptacle, then dropping or persistent, the outer ones pinnatifid, rarely undivided	free, included, stigmas covering mouth of receptacle	mostly several-flowered	Europe, Asia Minor
narrow or large	after anthesis spreading or upright, dropping off before maturity, the outer ones entire or with a few appendages	free, included, stigmas covering mouth of receptacle, ovules only on bottom	mostly few-flowered	N. America
more or less dilated	after anthesis (mostly immediately) upright, persistent at mature fruit, entire, very rarely dropping off.	free, included, stigmas covering mouth of receptacle; ovules only on bottom	usually several-, rarely many-flowered, petals red, rarely white	Europe, Asia N. America
rare or completely absent	after anthesis reflexed, dropping off before maturity, outer ones pinnatifid or all entire	united into a slender column, exserting and equalling inner stamens; rarely free, short and stigmas forming a head closing mouth of receptacle	usually in 3- or many-flowered corymbs	mostly Asia, few in Europe
narrow	after anthesis reflexed, dropping off before maturity, outer ones with few pinnae or all entire	free, reaching about half length of inner stamens	usually several-flowered	China
very small, caducous	after anthesis reflexed, dropping off before maturity, entire	free, included, stigmas covering mouth of receptacle	several- or many-flowered, often in umbels	China
none	after anthesis upright, persistent, entire	free, included, stigmas covering mouth of receptacle, discus large, stamens many	solitary	China

Taxonomic Category	Stems, Shoots	Prickles	Stipules	Median Leaves Of Flowering Branch
Sect. 10. **Bracteatae** (Thory) Rehd. Macartney-Roses 2 species	upright, climbing, tomentose	slightly straight or curved, in pairs below auricles, glabrous or mixed with bristles	adnate at short distance, pectinate	7-9-11 leaflets evergreen
Subg. III. PLATYRHODON (Hurst) Rehd. 1 species	upright, 2.5 m./ 8.3 ft. bark defoliating	straight, in pairs below stipules, upward, light brown	straight, with subulate auricles	9-11 (-15) leaflets
Subg. IV. HESPERHODOS Cockerell 2 species	upright 0.6-1.2 m./ 2-4 ft.	long, straight or slightly curved, mixed with bristles	adnate, auricles dilated, spreading	3-7 leaflets ovate, simply dentate

ovate-oblong, deeply incised, bald, with stipules; flowers light yellow, with a red blotch at the base of each petal, 5 cm./2 in. across; fruits egg-shaped, pubescent with some bristles, finally yellow and orange, 3 cm./1.2 in. long, sterile. 2n = 14. WR 2; BM 195. (= *Hultemosa hardii* [Cels.] Rowley). Before 1836; originated in the Jardin de Luxembourg, Paris.

R. × kopetdaghensis Meff. (= *R. hemisphaerica* var. *rapinii* × *R. persica*). Habit similar to *R. persica*, stems wiry, stout, 5 mm./0.2 in. thick, moderately prickly, more or less hairy; leaflets 3-7, elliptic, greyish-green, tomentulose on both sides, with stipules; flowers similar to *R. hardii*, but without basal blotches, 4 cm./1.6

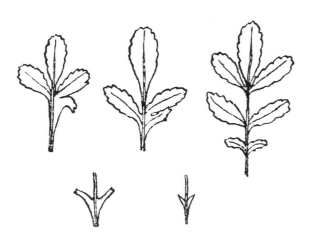

Figure 118. *Rosa kopetdaghensis*. (after Rowley)

in. across; sepals entire, tomentose; fruits globose, un-armed, 1 cm./0.4 in. across. (= *Hultemosa kopetdaghensis* [Meff.] Juz.). Turkomania; Kopet-Daghet. Still incompletely known. (Fig. 118).

Subg. II. EUROSA Focke
Leaves pinnate, with stipules; flowers mostly in corymbs, sometimes solitary; fruits fleshy; receptacles constricted at the mouth to a discus; achenes on bottom and wall.

Section 1. Pimpinellifoliae (Sér.) Rehd.
Mostly low shrubs, stems usually with straight prickles and bristles; leaflets 7-9, stipules narrow, with abruptly enlarged and divergent auricles; sepals entire, upright, persisting; distribution: Europe and Asia.

R. pimpinellifolia, hibernica, reversa, involuta, kochiana, koreana, hugonis, xanthina, primula, ecae, foetida, harisonii, penzanceana, hemisphaerica, sericea, pteragonis, morrisonensis.

R. pimpinellifolia L. Burnet-Rose, Scots Rose. Up to 1 m./3.3 ft. high, with many suckers; branches slender, divaricate or arching or more or less upright, densely covered with prickles and bristles, very much so towards the base of the shoots; leaflets 5-11, mostly 7-9, nearly orbicular, 1-2 cm./0.4-0.8 in. long, densely glandular-serrate, bald; flowers solitary on short branchlets, but very floriferous, white, sometimes more or less yellowish or pinkish, 5 cm./2 in. across, May-June; sepals entire, persisting, much shorter than petals; fruit sub-globose, brownish-black, bald, pedicel fleshy. 2n = 28. WR 82;KSR 4;CF1 606; ICS 2218. (= *R. spinossissima*

Bracts	Sepals	Pistils and Stamens	Inflorescence	Distribution
large, serrate	after anthesis reflexed, dropping off, receptacle tomentose	free, included, stigmas covering mouth of receptacle, discus large, stamens many	1- to several-flowered, white, or yellowish-white, with many large bracts	China
small, early caducous	after anthesis upright and persistent, outer ones strong and large; receptacle prickly	free, included, stigmas covering mouth of receptacle, discus large, stamens many, ovules many, all on an elevation of bottom of receptacle	usually several-flowered	Japan
none	pinnatifid, after anthesis upright, persistent; fruit dry (not fleshy)	woolly, free, included, stigmas covering mouth of receptacle; ovules all on bottom	solitary, pink, purple or white	N. America

L.). Europe to Asia. Cultivated since ancient times; very variable. (Fig. 119).

R. spinosissima L. As Hylander has stated, it is unsuitable to use this name any longer, as it is a *nomen nudum*. The so-called "Hybrid Spinosissima" Roses ('Frühlingsgold', etc., many of W. Kordes) will be found under their cultivar names in the alphabetic list. The innumerable cultivars of it, the Burnet-Roses (W. Paul counts more than 70) have, with a few exceptions, been completely lost. Most of them originated in Scotland, where there were more than 100 varieties in 1822. For an identification key to 29 varieties and a short history, see *ARA* 1963 :111-124.

var. **altaica** (Willd.) Thory. Growth more upright, to 1.8m./6 ft. high, branches less prickly; leaflets mostly 9, stipules narrow, margin glandular; flowers about 7 cm./2.8 in. across, white, opening light yellow; pedicel and calyx bald; fruits larger, brownish-red. GSR 52. (= var. *grandiflora* Ledeb.). Siberia, Songaria, Altai Mts. 1818.

var. *altaica* × 'Ormiston Roy' = 'Golden Wings'.

'Andrewsii'. Low; flowers bright red, semi-double, floriferous; fruits bald. WR 89. Origin unknown, but cultivated in French gardens before 1806.

'Flava'. Flowers whitish-yellow.

var. **hispida** (Sims) Boom. Shrub, to 2 m./6.6 ft. high; stems densely covered with needle-shaped prickles and bristles; leaflets 7-9, 2-3 cm./0.8-1.2 in. long, simply serrate; flowers pale yellow, 5-6 cm./2-2.4 in. across, sepals entire, calyx bald, fruits, subglobose, black. JRHS 8:132; WR 87; BM 1570; GSR 53. Before 1781.

var. **inermis** DC. Shrub medium high, shoots nearly without prickles; flowers pink, floriferous. (= *R. mitissima* Gmel.)

'Lutea' (Bean). About 0.9 m./3 ft. high, leaflets broadly ovate, to 2.5 cm./1 in. long, hairy beneath; flowers light yellow. Origin unknown, perhaps hybrid.

f. **luteola** (Andr.) Krüssm. 1-2 m./3.3-6.6 ft. high, many suckers, shoots densely bristly and prickly; leaflets 7, elliptic, about 2 cm./0.8 in. long, coarsely dentate; flowers pale yellow, 5 cm./2 in. across;

Figure 119. *Rosa pimpinellifolia* L.

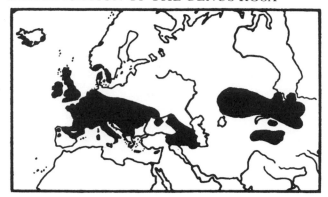

Figure 120. Distribution of *R. pimpinellifolia*. (after Meusel, 1965)

fruits globose, dark purple, fleshy. WR 85 (= *R. ochroleuca* Sw.). Russia. Before 1802.

var. **myriacantha** (Lam. & DC.) Sér. Only 0.5-0.7 m./1.7-2.3 ft. high; very densely prickly, prickles needle-shaped, the lower ones often bent downward; leaflets very small, densely glandular; flowers small, white with pink hue, pedicels and calyx bristly. WR 88. Spain and S. France to Armenia. Before 1820.

'Nana'. Dwarf form; flowers rather large, white, semi-double. Andrews, *Roses*, plate 122. Before 1806.

'Plena'. Flowers white, double. France. 1819.

'Rubra'. Flowers rose-pink. About 1770 in England.

R.× hibernica Templeton (= *R. canina × R. pimpinellifolia*). Shrub, 1-2 m./3.3-6.6 ft. high, shoots dark red, upright or arching, prickles scattered, mixed with some bristles; leaflets 7-8, ovate, about 18 mm./0.7 in. long, sharply serrate, mostly bald; flowers pink, 1-3 together, 3-5 cm./1.2-2 in. across, faintly fragrant, pedicel and calyx bald, sepals bald, persisting; fruits globose to egg-shaped, 12 mm./0.5 in. across, red. WR 289; GSR 22. W. Ireland, N. England, Scotland. 1802.

R. × reversa Waldst. & Kit. (= *R. pendulina × R. pimpinellifolia*). Shrub, 1-2 m./3.3-6.6 ft. high, shoots mostly purple, prickles unequally distributed, flowering branches often densely bristly; leaflets 7-11, densely glandular, 1-3 cm./0.4-1.2 in. long, simply serrate; flowers solitary, reddish to milky white; sepals entire, linear, upright in fruit; fruits globose-ovoid, 2 cm./0.8 in. long, pendulous, dark red. (= *R. rubella* Sm.). S. France, Switzerland, S. Europe. 1820.

R. × involuta Sm. (= *R. pimpinellifolia × R. villosa*, or *R. tomentosa*). Shrub, 0.5-1 m./1.7-3.3 ft. high, old stems chocolate brown, bristly and prickly, with many suckers; leaflets 7-9, ovate, 1 cm./0.4 in. long, overlapping, dull greyish-green, veins beneath green-puberulent, coarsely and mostly simply serrate; flowers soli-

tary, white, in bud red striped, 5 cm./2 in. across, on short branchlets; sepals, pedicels and calyx bald; WR 96. N. Scotland, Hebrides. Similar hybrids are known from W. Ireland and S. France.

R. × kochiana Koehne (= *R. pimpinellifolia × R. carolina*). Little shrub, to 1 m./3.3 ft. high, similar to *R. nitida*; all branches densely bristly, but flowering branchlets nearly bald, nodes with more or less paired prickles; leaflets 9, on shoots to 11, simply serrate, bald; flowers 1-3, deep pink, 4 cm./1.6 in. across, June-July; fruit 8-9 mm./0.3-0.4 in. across, with constricted neck, 15 mm./0.6 in. long (= *R. oxyacanthoides* K. Koch, not Bieb.) Before 1870.

R. koreana Komar. Shrub, to 1 m./3.3 ft. high, very dense; shoots dark red, densely bristly; leaflets 7-11, elliptic, 1-2 cm./0.4-0.8 in. long, bald or slightly puberulent beneath, sharply serrate-glandular; flowers white with pink hue, about 3 cm./1.2 in. across; pedicels glandular; fruit ovate, orange-red, about 1.5 cm./0.6 in. long. Korea. 1917.

Hybrids of S. McGredy attributed to this species are incorrect. He crossed with *R. × coryana* Hurst (= *R. macrophylla × R. roxburghii*). See under this name.

R. hugonis Hemsl. Shrub, 2-2.5 m./6.6-8.3 ft. high, branches deep brown, straight or arching, prickles flattened, straight, on shoots mixed with bristles, at least at base of shoots; leaflets 7-13, obovate to elliptic 8-20 mm./0.3-0.8 in. long, above bald and serrate, hairy beneath at least on the youngest leaves; flowers solitary on short branchlets, bright yellow, 5 cm./2 in. across, May-June; pedicels and calyx bald; fruits broadly obovate, to 1.5 cm./0.6 in. across, deep red to blackish-red. 2n = 14. WR 95; BM 8004; GSR 26; ICS 2219. C. China; grows on dry, stony ground in its native country. 1899. Named after "Father Hugo" (the Rev. Hugh Scallon). (Fig. 122).

R. hugonis × R. xanthina → 'Canary Bird'
R. hugonis × R. sericea var. *pteracantha* → R. × pteragonis.

R. xanthina Lindl. Upright shrub, 1.5-3 m./5-10 ft. high, stems brown, with straight prickles, shoots completely without bristles; leaflets 7-13, 1-2 cm./0.4-0.8 in. long, obtuse, serrate, bald above, stipules narrow and glandular; flowers 1-2, golden yellow, 4-5 cm./1.6-2 in. across, single or semi-double, May-June; pistils degenerated; fruits not yet observed. 2n = 14. ICS 2220. N.

252

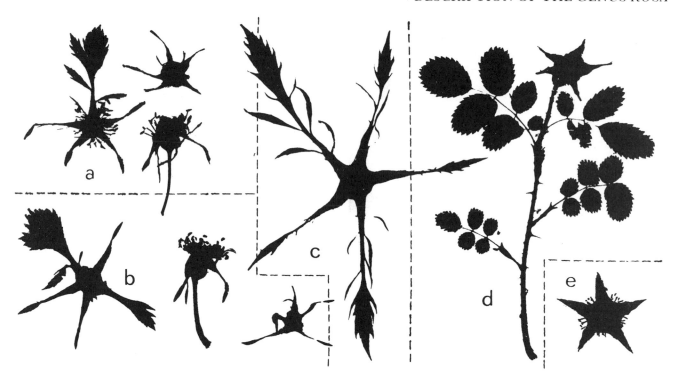

Figure 121. Details of some yellow-flowering roses (silhouettes). a. *Rosa foetida*, two types of calyx and fruit; b. *R. foetida bicolor*, calyx and fruit; c. 'Star of Persia', calyx; d. *R. harisonii*, branchlet with fruit; e. 'Persian Yellow', calyx. (Original)

China, Korea; found in cultivation.

At first known only from Chinese paintings, then later the double form was found in the garden of a Mandarin; much later the single, wild species was discovered.

f. **spontanea** Rehd. The wild type; slightly higher, flowers single, larger, 5-6 cm./2-2.4 in. across; leaves beneath slightly hairy at the midrib; fruits rather globose, 12-15 mm./0.5-0.6 in. across, bright red, with upright persisting sepals. GC 127:112. (= f. *normalis* Rehd. & Wils.), N. China, Mongolia, Turkestan. 1906. Often confused with → 'Canary Bird' (which is possibly *R. hugonis* × *R. xanthina*) which has paler flowers and blackish-red fruits. Hybrids: → 'Golden Wings'; 'Ormiston Roy'.

R. primula Bouleng. Upright shrub, 2 m./6.6 ft. high, stems slender, initially red-brown; prickles stout, with flattened base, in pairs at the nodes; leaves small, 3-8 cm./1.2-3.2 in. long; young leaves aromatic; leaflets 7-13, elliptic, 8-12 mm./0.3-0.5 in. long, doubly serrate and glandular beneath and at the margin; stipules narrow, glandular, auricles filiform; flowers solitary, flat, bright yellow, 3 cm./1.2 in. across, scented, May; petals obcordate; pedicels short, bald; fruits globose to turbinate, brown-red like the pedicel, 12-15 mm./0.5-0.6 in. across. 2n = 14. GSR 39. Turkestan to N. China. 1910. Always confused with *R. ecae*, but well distinguished by its paler flowers and red-brown fruits. Hybrids with other species not known to date.

R. ecae Aitchis. Shrub, up to 1 m./3.3 ft. high, densely branched, branches very prickly; leaflets 5-9, mostly obovate, only 4-8 mm./0.16-0.31 in. long, serrate, glandular beneath; flowers solitary, intensely yellow, 2 cm./0.8 in. across, May-June; with short, brown pedicels; fruits globose, pea-sized, red, glistening, with persisting, reflexed sepals. 2n = 14. WR 277 (as *R. xanthina*); BM 7666; GSR 7; GiS 1. Afghanistan, Turkestan. 1880. Introduced by Dr. Aitchison, who combined the name "ecae" from the initials of his wife, E.C.A. To this date only one hybrid is known → 'Golden Chersonese'.

R. foetida Herrm. Austrian Briar. Shrub, in its native habitat up to 3 m./10 ft. high, in cultivation rarely more than 1.5 m./5 ft; stems slender, brown, with few straight, unequally long prickles; leaflets 5-9, elliptic, 2-4 cm./0.8-1.6 in. long, downy glandular-serrate, vivid green above, puberulent and glandular beneath; flowers mostly solitary or in pairs, dark yellow, 5 cm./2 in. across, with strong, disagreeable scent, June; pedicel and calyx bald, sepals lanceolate, foliaceous; fruits globose, red, sometimes slightly bristly, 2n = 28. WR 90; BM 363. (= *R. lutea* Mill.). Asia Minor, Persia to Afghanistan and N.W. Himalayas; occasionally found escaped from cultivation in Austria. In 1583, Clusius introduced escaped specimens into Holland and England, where it got the name "Austrian Briar". It is said to have been brought to Spain in the 13th century by the Moors. In 1596, Gerarde cultivated a specimen in his garden in England, but it may well have been cultivated earlier there.

1883-1888 it was first used for hybridizing by Pernet-Ducher in France, initially with complete failure; so-called "Pernetiana-Roses" (= Lutea Hybrids) originated from this rose. Due to its marked susceptibility to Black Spot (*Marssonina rosae*) these hybrids have all but disappeared from gardens, and even *Rosa foetida* is rare, for the same reason. *R. foetida* and all its forms should never be pruned.

bicolor; Austrian Copper. To 2 m./6.6 ft. high; flowers single, interior orange-scarlet, yellow reverse. GSR 16. (= *R. punicea* Mill.; *R. lutea bicolor* Sims). Originated as a bud mutation before 1590; often reverting to the typical yellow species which is, for that reason, sometimes called 'Austrian Yellow' (Fig. 121). All modern yellow and orange garden roses are derived from this variety.

R. foetida persiana → 'Persian Yellow'

R. foetida × 'Trier' → 'Star of Persia'

R. × harisonii Rivers (=? 'Persian Yellow' × *R. pimpinellifolia*). Shrub, 0.5-1 m./1.7-3.3 ft. high, branches short; leaflets 5-9, elliptic, densely serrate, glandular beneath; petiole thinly puberulent and glandular; flowers solitary, bright yellow, semi-double, 5-6 cm./2-2.4 in. across, May; sepals lobed at the top, calyx-tube and pedicel bristly, fruits nearly black. 2n = 28. GSR 20. This plant is the famous "Yellow Rose of Texas". (Fig. 121)

'Vorbergii'. Flowers cream white, to 5 cm./2 in. across, mid-May, very floriferous; fruits globose, 15 mm./0.6 in. across, black, pedicel and calyx bald. (= *R. vorbergii* Graebn.). Originated before 1902 in the Botanic Garden at Hann.-Münden, Germany, but was distributed by the Berlin Botanic Garden.

R. × penzanceana Rehd. (= *R. rubiginosa* × *R. foetida bicolor*). This is the correct nâme for the hybrid 'Lady Penzance' (Lord Penzance 1894), while the other so-called *rubiginosa* hybrids, including 'Lord Penzance', which originated from *R. harisonii* × *R. rubiginosa*, do not belong here. The other garden forms are Hybrid Perpetuals × *R. rubiginosa*. 2n = 42.

R. hemisphaerica Herrm. Sulphur Rose. Shrub, 1-2 m./3.3-6.6 ft. high, branches rather stiffly upright, with hooked prickles which are somewhat compressed at the base; leaflets 5-9, obovate, coarsely serrate, 3-4 cm./1.2-

1.6 in. long, above deep or bluish-green, paler and puberulent beneath; flower bud greenish-yellow; flowers sulphur-yellow, very double, globose, mostly solitary and nodding, to 5 cm./2 in. across, scentless, June-July, will not open in wet weather; fruits globose, dark red, sepals spreading, persisting. WR 93. (= *R. glaucophylla* Ehr.; *R. sulphurea* Ait.). Introduced from Turkey in about 1600 by Clusius, not known wild. Grows best in a dry, warm climate.

var. rapinii (Boiss. & Bal.) Rowley. This is the wild type of *R. hemisphaerica*, with single flowers. Shrub only 1 m./3.3 ft. high. branches with prickles, sometimes mixed with bristles; leaflets mostly 7, veins beneath velvety puberulent; flowers single, bright yellow, 1-2-3 together; calyx-tube semi-globose, fruit globose, bald, yellow to red, about 1.5 cm./0.6 in. across. 2n = 28. (= *R. rapinii* Boiss. & Bal.). Asiatic Turkey to N.W. Persia. Introduced first in 1933. Very rare in cultivation and not durable.

R. sericea Lindl. Silk Rose. Shrub, straight upright, 2-2.5 m./6.6-8.3 ft. high, stems grey or brown, with large, dilated, often flattened, straight or curved prickles, paired below the nodes; leaves crowded, 3-7 cm./1.2-2.8 in. long; leaflets 7-11, small, orbicular-elliptic, sharply serrate to the apex, silky hairy beneath, especially on the veins; flowers solitary, white, 2.5-5 cm./1-2 in. across, regularly with 4, rarely with 5 petals, May; fruits turbinate, red to orange-yellow, without fleshy pedicel; seeds only on bottom of the calyx-tube. 2n = 14. WR 52; BM 5200; ICS 2222. (= *R. tetrapetala* Royle). Himalayas. 1822.

Key to the Varieties (after Rowley)

Fruit red	
Plant unarmed	var. *denudata*
Plant with prickles and bristles	
Leaflets many, up to 17	var. *polyphylla*
Leaflets rarely more than 11	
Pedicels thin, green	var. *sericea*
Pedicels fleshy, red	var. *omeiensis*
Plants densely covered with prickles, bristles and glands	var. *hookeri*
Plants with long, decurrent, wing-shaped prickles	var. *pteracantha*
Fruits yellow	var. *chrysocarpa*

var. denudata (Franch.) Rowley. Branches practically unarmed; fruits red. (= *R. sericea* f. *denudata* Franch.) 1890.

var. polyphylla Geier. Stems and branches only slightly armed; leaflets up to 17, otherwise like the type. (= *R. sericea* f. *inermis eglandulosa* Focke).

var. sericea. The type of this species; description see above; characteristics are the pedicels which are green and still thin at maturity, the early dropping fruits. WR 52. W. Himalayas; not found to date in China. 1822.

var. omeiensis (Rolfe) Rowley. Omei-Rose. Growth taller, 3-4 m./10-

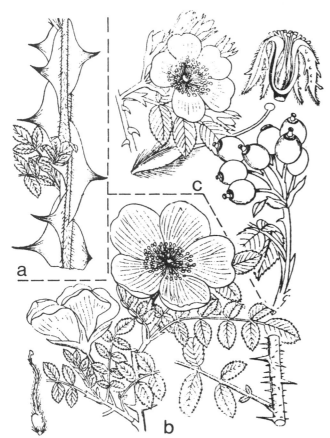

Figure 122 a. *Rosa sericea* var. *pteracantha*; b. *R. hugonis*; c. *R. soulieana*. (after BM)

13 ft. high, strictly upright, stems greyish-brown, prickles hard, flattened, very dilated at base, with many bristles, young branches often only bristly; leaflets 9-11 (-17), oblong, 1-3 cm./0.4-1.2 in. long, bald beneath or puberulent on midrib; flowers white, petals 4, exceptionally 5, to 3 cm./1.2 in. across, May-June; pedicel and calyx-tube bald; fruits pyriform, 1-1.5 cm./0.4-0.6 in. long, bright red, with fleshy red or yellow pedicel. BM 8471; ICS 2221. (= *R. omeiensis* Rolfe.). C. China. 1901.

var. **hookeri** Regel. Like var. *sericea*, but most parts glandular. China; Kumaon.

var. **pteracantha** Bean. Prickles much larger, wing-shaped and decurrent, shining and translucent when young; leaflets more strongly veined; pedicels of fruits mostly shorter than in the type. BM 8212; GSR 50. (= *R. omeiensis* f. *pteracantha* Rehd. & Wils.). China; W. Szechuan, 3,000-3,600 m./9,900-11,900 ft. 1890. (Fig. 122)

f. **chrysocarpa** (Rehd.) Rowley. Fruits yellow, otherwise like the type. (= *R. omeiensis* f. *chrysocarpa* Rehd.).

'Hidcote Gold' (Hilling 1948). Flowers canary-yellow, several together. Exact origin unknown.

R. × pteragonis Krause. (= *R. hugonis* × *R. sericea*). Intermediate between parents, but flowers with 5 petals, yellow, larger; branches with more or less wing-shaped prickles. 2n = 14.

f. **pteragonis** (*R. hugonis* × *R. sericea* f. *pteracantha*). Growth bushy,

to 2 m./6.6 ft. high, prickles very broad, dark red; flowers with 5 petals, bright yellow, large, very numerous along the branches. 2n = 14. Originated with Max Krause, Hasloh, Holstein, N. Germany, in 1938. To this list are now added:

f. **cantabrigiensis** (Weaver) Rowley. (= *R. hugonis* × *R. sericea* var. *hookeri*). Shrub, about 2 m./6.6 ft. high, stems very bristly, strictly upright, leaflets 7-11, hairy and glandular on the veins beneath and the teeth; flowers solitary, bright yellow, 5 cm./2 in. across, June; pedicels 2 cm./0.4 in. long, glandular, as is the outside of the sepals. GSR 41; GiS 1 (= *R. cantabrigiensis* Weaver). Originated before 1931 in the Botan. Garden, Cambridge.

'Earldomensis' (= *R. hugonis* × *R. sericea* var. *omeiensis*). Shrub, about 1.5 m./5 ft. high, spreading; stems with wing-shaped, reddish prickles; foliage nearly fern-like; flowers canary-yellow. GSR 42. (= *R. earldomensis* Page). 1934.

Also → 'Red Wing'.

R. morrisonensis Hayata. Shrub, 1-2 m./3.3-6.6 ft. high, stems slender, arching, very prickly, prickles often in pairs, whitish, subulate, 1 cm./0.4 in. long; leaflets 7-11, elliptic, 8-13 mm./0.3-0.5 in. long, 5-7 mm./0.2-0.3 in. across, denticulate, bald; flowers solitary, axillary at the ends of branches; sepals entire, lanceolate, acuminate, hairy on both sides; styles densely villose; fruit pear-shaped, bald, 8 mm./0.3 in. long, constricted at the top, with persisting, reflexed sepals. (= *R. sericea* var. *morrisonensis* [Hayata] Masamune). Taiwan; only on Mt. Yushan, 4,000 m./13,200 ft. (Fig. 124).

Section 2. Gallicanae (Sér.) Rehd.

Mostly low, upright shrubs; most stems armed with curved prickles, mixed with bristles; stipules narrow, adnate; leaflets 3-5, mostly firm; few flowers together, often with narrow bracts, or solitary and then without bracts; sepals often pinnatifid, after anthesis reflexed, dropping; styles not exserted. Distribution Europe and Asia Minor.

R. gallica, waitziana, macrantha, centifolia, richardii, damascena, alba, collina.

Key to the more important species of this section
+Prickles very unequal; leaves mostly doubly glandular-serrate
  ×Leaves firm, leathery; pedicels upright, puberulent — *R. gallica*
  ××Leaves thin, often only simply serrate; pedicels nodding, viscid-glandular, slightly fragrant — *R. centifolia*
++Prickles all equal; leaves simply serrate, not glandular
  ×Calyx-tube glandular-bristly, leaves ovate-oblong, often hairy beneath — *R. damascena*
  ++Calyx-tube mostly bald; leaves broadly elliptic, hairy beneath — *R. alba*

R. gallica L. (1759). French Rose. Shrub, 0.4-0.7(-1) m./1.3-2.3(-3.3) ft. high, with subterranean, densely prickly and bristly suckers; young branches green to dull red; prickles compact and unequal, mixed with pungent bristles; leaflets 3-5, firm, broadly elliptic, 2-5 cm./0.8-2 in. long, simply or doubly serrate, peduncle and rachis bristly-glandular; flowers solitary, pink to red, 5-6 cm./2-2.4 in. across, mostly single, scented, June; fruits turbinate, brick-red; sepals with many lanceolate-linear pinnae, dropping before maturity. 2n = 28. WR 325; BM 1377; KSR 5-6. (= *R. rubra* Blackw.). S. and C. Europe, from Belgium and S. France to Asia Minor. Very hardy. (Fig. 125).

An ancestor of our garden roses; in cultivation since ancient times. In the 18th century extensively cultivated at Provins, a place about 50 km./30 mi. south-east of Paris, from where the name "Provins-Rose" is derived (a name which later caused much confusion due to its similarity to the name "Provence Rose" for *R. centifolia*). During the first half of the 19th century, more than 1,000 varieties of *R. gallica* are said to have been in cultivation. Empress Joséphine in 1811 had no less than 167 varieties of *R. gallica* in her rose garden at Malmaison. Today only a few varieties remain, except in the collections of amateurs, some of which are as follows:

'**Conditorum**'. Hungarian Rose. Shrub, about 1 m./3.3 ft. high, flowers magenta-red with purplish veins, semi-double, slightly scented. In Hungary used for the production of rose water and pastry (formerly to a greater extent than now). Probably a very old variety, but first introduced and named by Dieck in 1889.

'**Officinalis**'. Apothecary Rose, also called "Red Rose of Lancaster". Seldom taller than 0.7 m./2.3 ft. branches with small, weak, unequal, straight prickles; leaflets 5, ovate, bald, above, puberulent beneath; flowers crimson, semi-double, anthers yellow, very fragrant, medium-late; fruits large, nearly globose, dark red. WR 121 (as *R. provincialis*); GSR 86; GiS 5; SOR 1. (= *R. provincialis* Mill.). Perhaps the best known cultivar of *R. gallica*, which is authenticated to have been cultivated in the 13th century in France, where apothecaries produced a fragrant powder from the dried, pulverized petals.

'**Pumila**'. Only 0.2-0.3 m./0.7-1 ft. high, creeping; leaflets ovate-obicular, pedicels and calyx slightly glandular; flowers single, red. WR 109; (= *R. pumila* Jacq.; *R. austriaca pygmaea* Wallr.). Known since 1789; sometimes still found wild in Spain and Italy.

'**Versicolor**'. Mutation of 'Officinalis' and completely identical to it in growth, prickles and foliage, but flowers white/red/pink, striped and spotted, 7-9 cm./2.8-3.2 in. across, center with many yellow anthers, fragrant, summer-flowering. 2n = 28. WR 110; GSR 92; GiS 5. (= *R. rosamundi* West.; *R. gallica variegata* Andr.). First mentioned in 1583 by Clusius, but definitely much older. The "Fayre Rosamonde" of King Henry II of England, who died about 1176, so the rose may go back to that time.

R. majalis × R. gallica → 'Frankofurtana'

Among the more frequent forms of *R. gallica* are the following: 'Belle des Jardins', 'Camaieux', 'Cardinal de Richelieu', 'Charles de Mills', 'Georges Vibert', 'Sissinghurst Castle', 'Tuscany' and 'Violacea'; the latest variety is 'Scharlachglut'.

R. × waitziana Tratt. (= *R. canina × R. gallica*). Shrub, about 2 m./6.6 ft. high, prickles scattered, unequal and mostly slightly curved; leaves rather firm, mostly simply serrate, bald or puberulent on midrib beneath; flow-

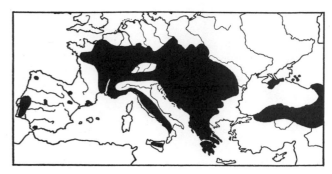

Figure 123. Distribution of *Rose gallica*. (after Meusel, 1965)

ers solitary, 6-8 cm./2.4-3.2 in. across, mostly deep pink, sepals glandular on back; styles slightly elongated, puberulent; fruits usually dropping before maturity. C. Europe, woodland borders. 1874.

R. × macrantha Desp. (= *R. gallica ×* ?; certainly not *R. canina* as cytological analysis has shown). Shrub, 1-1.5 m./3.3-5 ft. high, stems green, arching, prickles scattered, curved, at first mixed with some bristles; leaflets 5-7, ovate, 3 cm./1.2 in. long, simply to double serrate, at least puberulent beneath; penduncles glandular hairy; several flowers together, first light pink, later nearly white, 7 cm./2.8 in. across, very fragrant, single to semi-double, June; calyx, sepals and pedicels glandular, sepals dropping; fruits globose, dull red, to 1.5 cm./0.6 in. across. WR 134. (= *R. waitziana* var. *macrantha* [Desp.] Rehd.). Originated in France during the 18th century.

R. centifolia L. Cabbage Rose, Provence Rose. Similar to *R. gallica*, but taller, up to 2 m./6.6 ft. high, throws few suckers, prickles rather unequal, partly bristly and glandular, the stronger ones compressed, nearly straight, only slightly dilated at the base; leaflets usually 5, often hairy on both sides or only beneath, large, slightly lax, ovate-roundish, rachis without prickles; flower bud short, sepals always spreading, never reflexed, pinnatifid; calyx-tube ovoid, bristly-glandular, pedicels sticky-glandular and scented, especially with the "Moss Roses"; several flowers together, on long pedicels, very double, white to dark red (never yellow), very fragrant, June-August. 2n = 28,21. WR 115.

The strongly held opinion, that this rose originated in the East Caucasus and was known to the ancient Greeks and Romans, is no longer valid. It was first disproved by research conducted by E. Bunyard, and then by C. C. Hurst. This rose is a complex hybrid, which developed gradually from the end of the 16th to the beginning of the 18th century. *R. gallica*, *R. moschata*, *R. canina* and *R. damascena* were all involved. The whole development, from the very first steps in about 1790, to the current perfection in about 1850, took place in

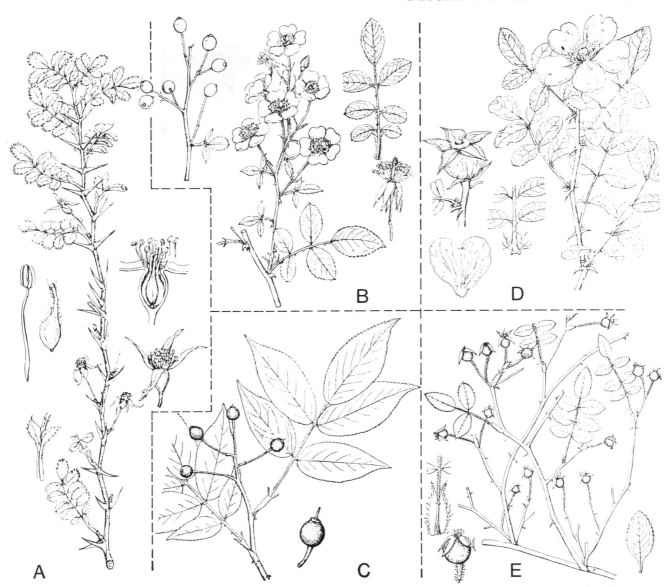

Figure 124.   A. *Rosa morrisonensis*;   **B.** *R. taiwanensis*;   **C.** *R. sambucina*;   **D.** *R. cardotii*;   **E.** *R. transmorrisonensis* (after Liu)

Holland. This rose can be recognized in paintings by the Dutch Masters. (see p. 233). Of the modern garden forms of the rose the following may be the most important:

'Centifolia Alba' → **'Mme. Hardy'**

'Bullata'. Habit very broad; leaflets very large hanging loosely, bullate, red while young, soft; flowers pink, very double, fragrant; calyx tube and pedicels faintly glandular. WR 123. (= Rose à feuilles de Laitue). About 1801.

'Cristata'. Habit very broad; flowers pink; only sepals are "mossy", not the calyx; flower buds are especially beautiful. WR 118; BM 3475; GSR 92. (= 'Chapeau de Napoléon'). Found 1820 in the crevice of an old fortification wall at Fribourg, Switzerland.

'Major' → **R. centifolia**

'Minima'. Flowers double, only 15 mm./0.6 in. across or less, otherwise nice form, light pink with darker pink center.

'Minor' = **'Petite de Hollande'**

'Parvifolia'. Pompon de Bourgogne. Miniature rose, only up to 0.5 m./1.7 ft. high; branches nearly unarmed; leaflets ovate, very small, greyish-green, beneath and pedicels downy, calyx nearly bald; flowers small, but many together, very double and rosette-shaped, flat, purple with violet hue or dark pink. WR 120. (= *R. burgundensis* West.; *R. ehrhardtiana* Tratt.). Known before 1664.

'Pomponia' → **'De Meaux'**

'Simplex' (= 'Ciudad de Oviedo'). Like the type, but flowers single, dark pink. 2n = 28. Spain.

'Variegata'. Growth strong, very prickly; leaves deep green, coarsely serrate; flowers solitary or several together, very double and globose, cream white with pink stripes, floriferous. WR 127 (as *R. provincialis variegata*). Originated about 1845 at Angers, France. Known under different names, i.e. 'Belle des Jardins', 'Village Maid', et al.

Further cultivars of *R. centifolia:* → 'Duc de Fitzjames', 'Fatin-

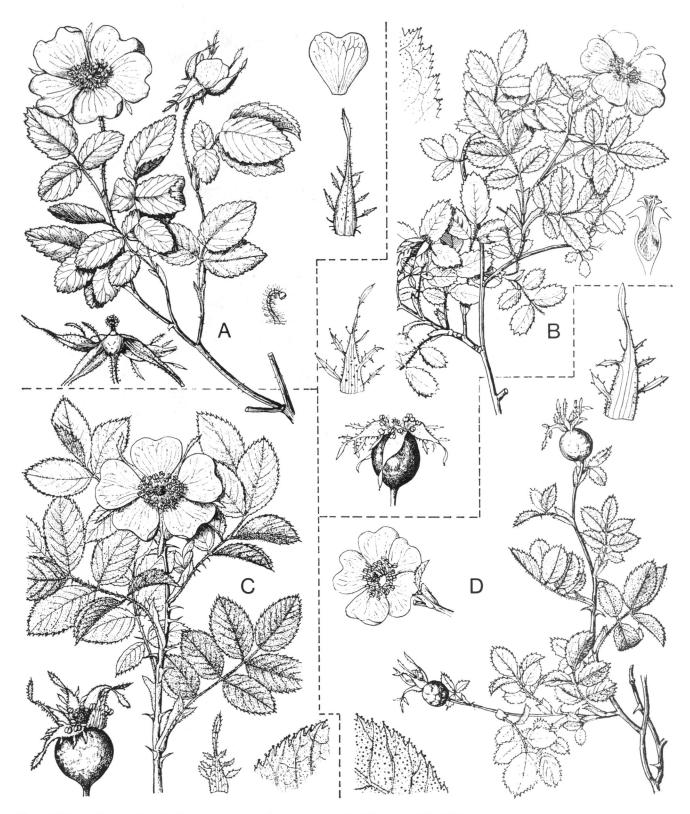

Figure 125.　A. *Rosa galica*;　B. *R. micrantha*;　C. *R. tomentosa*;　D. *R. inodora*. (After Vicioso)

'Latour', 'Juno', 'Paul Ricault', 'Robert le Diable', 'Spong', 'The Bishop', 'Tour de Malakoff', 'Unique Blanche'.

Moss Roses

'Andrewsii'. Single Moss Rose; Flowers dark rose. (= *R. muscosa simplex* Andr.). 1807 found first by Shailer at Little Chelsea, as a mutation of the Moss Rose; later in France as well.

'Muscosa'. Moss Rose. Mutation of *R. centifolia.* Usually not taller than 1 m./3.3 ft.; flowers beautiful, densely double and closed, pink, several together; pedicels and calyx densely "mossy". BM 69; WR 116. In cultivation in England since 1724, but earlier in Europe.

'Muscosa Alba'. Mutation of the common Moss Rose with pure white, double flowers; growth loose; leaves light green, elliptic; buds and pedicels densely covered with long moss; flowers at first faintly pinkish, later pure white, very fragrant, sometimes with a single pink petal (mutation observed by G. S. Thomas).

Other Moss Roses: → 'Baron de Wassenaer', 'Black Boy', 'Blanche Moreau', 'Blue Boy', 'Capitaine John Ingram', 'Comtesse de Murinais', 'Gloire des Mousseux', 'Golden Moss', 'Henry Martin', 'Jeanne de Montford', 'Marie de Blois', 'Mme. Louis Levêque', 'Mousseline', 'Nuits d'Young', 'Parkjuwel', 'Reine Blanche', 'Salet', 'Striped Moss', 'William Lobb', etc.

R. × richardii Rehd. Holy Rose; (presumably *R. gallica* × *R. phoenicia*). Low shrub, 0.5-0.7 m./1.7-2.3 ft. high; branches green, bald, very prickly, prickles very unequal, small, hooked; leaflets 3-5, elliptic-oblong, obtuse, glandular at the margin, wrinkles above, slightly puberulent beneath; flowers in small corymbs, pinkish, 5-7 cm./2-2.8 in. across, June-July; sepals large, pinnate, margin and reverse glandular; style downy, pedicels bristly, to 3 cm./1.2 in. long, calyx bald. 2n = 21. WR 113 (= *R. sancta* Rich.' not Andr.; *R. centifolia* var. *sancta* Zabel). Ethiopia; said to occur wild also in the Eastern Caucasus.

The designation "sancta" originated from the fact that this rose was first planted in the courtyards of Ethiopian churches and tombs. Crépin advanced the view that this is the rose with which the Egyptian mummies, in the period 500-200 B.C., were decorated. In fact, the species of rose so used is still unknown.

R. × damascena Mill. Damask Rose. (= *R. gallica* × *R. phoenicia*; or *R. gallica* × *R. moschata*). Shrub, to 2 m./ 6.6 ft. high, branches strongly armed with many hooked, equal, basally-compressed prickles; leaflets 5-7, ovate, simply serrate, bald and grey-green above, downy beneath; flowers mostly densely clumped, pink to red, sometimes white and red striped, double, mostly scented, June-July; pedicels often weak, calyx-tube narrowed to the top, never globose (as with *R. gallica*); fruits more or less turbinate, to 2.5 cm./1 in. long, bristly, sepals at anthesis reflexed, outside glandular-bristly, dropping. 2n = 28,35. WR 124 (no good illustration). (= *R. gallica* var. *damascena* Voss; *R. belgica*

Figure 126. *Rosa damascena* var. *bifera* ('Quatre Saisons'; after Redouté, there named "Rosa damascena italica").

Mill.; *R. calendarum* Borkh.; *R. polyanthos* Roessig).

Easy to distinguish from *R. gallica* and *R. centifolia*, with which it is sometimes confused, by its stronger growth, the long, mostly arching branches with strong, hooked prickles, brighter but weaker leaves with mostly 5-7 leaflets, flowers only semi-double, very fragrant, only pink tones, and petals with a striking transparency; fruits not bristly.

1. **R. × damascena** (= *gallica* × *phoenicea*), Summer Damask Rose;
2. **R. × bifera** Pers. (= *gallica* × *moschata*), Autumn Damask Rose.

While the name for the Summer Damask Roses has not changed, G.D. Rowley proposed the combination *R. damascena* var. *semperflorens* (Loisel. & Michel) Rowley 1959 for the Autumn Damask Rose. (= *R. semperflorens* Loisel. & Michel 1819; *R. bifera* var. *semperflorens* Loisel. & Michel 1819; *R. damascena* var. *bifera* hort. not Regel 1877). (Fig. 126)

The origin of these roses is still obscure. Legend has it that returning Crusaders brought the "Summer Damask Roses" from Asia Minor to Europe in about 1520-1570. However, the last Crusade occurred 300 years earlier. Most authors agree that the "Autumn Damask Roses"

259

were first cultivated about 1000 B.C. on the island of Samos, where they were used in the cult of Aphrodite. As this cult migrated to Athens, and later to Rome, the rose accompanied it.

Important varieties of the Damask Roses:

Trigintipetala. Shrub, 1.5 m./5 ft. high (in Bulgaria it grows much better, reaching 2-3 m./6.6-10 ft.); flowers rose-pink (color similar to 'Ballerina'), semi-double, with about 30 petals, 8 cm./3.2 in. across, very fragrant, June-July; this is the "Rose of Kazanlik", the most important rose in the commercial production of Attar. The center of Attar production is in S. Bulgaria, between the mountain ranges of Stara Planina and Sredna Gora, from the railway station at Klissura to Kazanlik (in a valley 130 km./81 mi. long, 15 km./9.3 mi. wide). There are several selections of this variety, propagated as clones, but they have no horticultural importance outside Bulgaria. Introduced and distributed in 1889 by Dr. Dieck, Germany.

'Versicolor' "York and Lancaster Rose". Shrub, about 1 m./3.3 ft. high, branches green; leaves bright greyish-green, downy; flowers medium large, loosely double, some half white, half pink, others only white or pink, but never red or striped (mutations with clear pink flowers occur occasionally, and have been propagated and named 'Professeur Emile Perrot'). Named "York and Lancaster Rose" in 1551 by the Spanish surgeon Monardes in memory of the English Wars of the Roses (1455-1485), between the Houses of York and Lancaster, who wore, respectively, a white and a red rose as their emblem. This rose could not, however, have played a role in those wars, as it was introduced into England at the beginning of the 17th century. However, it is still widely planted for traditional reasons. The plant must always be well-pruned; unicolor mutations should always be removed carefully.

var. **semperflorens** (Loisel. & Michel) Rowley. Better known under the name 'Quatre Saisons' or 'Rose des Quatres Saisons' in France, 'Monthly Rose' in England. An autumn-flowering Damask Rose. Shrub, somewhat taller than 1 m./3.3 ft.; leaves partly yellowish-green; flowers clear pink, very double, also often quartered and with an eye, June-July, recurrent to a lesser extent until October (uncertain, dependent upon good care). G. S. Thomas (1950) reports that this variety had been observed twice as a sport on 'Quatre Saisons Blanc Mousseux' (= 'Perpetual White Moss'). This variety is a precursor of the Bourbon and Hybrid Perpetuals; it is probably the same rose which was planted at Paestum (close to Pompeii), and elsewhere to a great extent; it can be recognized in ancient frescoes.

Other Damask Roses, still in cultivation today: → 'Blush Damask', 'Celsiana', 'Coralie', 'Gloire de Guilan', 'Ispahan', 'La Ville de Brux-elles', 'Leda', 'Mme. Hardy', 'Marie Louise', 'Oeillet Parfait', 'Omar Khayyam' and 'Hebe's Lip'.

R. × alba L. The White Rose; White Rose of York. (probably *R. canina* ♀ × *R. damascena*). To 2 m./6.6 ft. high, upright, stems with unequal, hooked prickles, often with bristles: leaflets 5-7, broadly elliptic, puberulent beneath; flowers white to blush, double, rarely single, 6-8 cm./2.4-3.2 in. across, scented, June; pedicels glandular-bristly; fruit oblong-globose, red, 2.5 cm./1 in. long, bald. 2n = 42. Widely cultivated since the time of the Greeks and the Romans. G. S. Thomas opines that this rose may have originated as a natural hybrid in the Crimea, possibly with *R. canina* var. *froebelii* Christ (white flowers, few prickles) as mother, because

this rose occurs in the wild in Kurdistan, and may possibly reach into the Crimea and the Caucasus. Of the varieties now in cultivation, the most important are:

'Semiplena'. The type of this rose; shrub, 2 m./6.6 ft. or more, with many stems, densely foliated; flowers only semi-double, milk-white, good scent, flowers only once, anthers many, golden yellow, floriferous, June; many red fruits in the autumn. WR 136 (= *R. alba suaveolens*, *R. alba nivea*). This rose is cultivated in Kazanlik, Bulgaria, largely for the production of Attar.

'Maxima'. 'Jacobite Rose', 'Great Double White', 'Cheshire Rose'. Growth strong, 2 m./6.6 ft. high or over, leaves grey-green, particularly on the top of old specimens, rather "leggy"; flowers irregularly double, rather large, opening creamy-white with blush hue, but soon pure creamy-white. 2n = 42. GSR 62.

About 20 varieties belong to *R. alba*: → 'Blush Hip', 'Céleste', 'Chloris', 'Félicité Parmentier', 'Königin van Dänemark', 'Mme. Legras de St. Germain', 'Maiden's Blush', 'Pompon Parfait Blanc'.

R. × collina jacq. (= ? *R. corymbifera* × *R. gallica*). Shrub about 1.5 m./5 ft. high, stems, bald, prickles strong, hooked, red when young, later grey; leaflets 5(-7), serrulate, bald above, pale and puberulent beneath on the veins, peduncles puberulent, sometimes slightly glandular; stipules acute; flowers 1-3 on short branchlets, pink, scented, June-July; sepals persisting, foliaceous at the top, glandular on back like pedicels; fruits orange-red, ovoid, glossy, sometimes glandular. C. Europe. 1778.

'Andersonii'. Leaflets only slightly hairy above; flowers to 7.5 cm./3 in. across, rose pink, later fading to lighter shades. This is the "Rosa andersonii" of German gardens.

Section 3. Caninae Rehd.

Stems upright, arching, mostly with equal, straight or curved or hooked prickles; median leaves of flowering branches mostly with 7 leaflets; bracts present, more or less dilated, as are the stipules; inflorescences mostly many-flowered; outer sepals pinnatifid, reflexed after anthesis, either dropping or upright and persisting:

R. villosa, mollis, sherardii, orientalis, heckeliana, elymai-tica, tomentosa, rubiginosa, inodora, sicula, glutinosa, montezumae, tuschetica, macrantha, horrida, agrestis, serafinii, stylosa, obtusifolia, corymbifera, coriifolia, canni-na, andersonii, dumalis, britzensis, marginata, glauca, pokornyana.

R. villosa L. Densely-branched shrub, 1.5-2 m./4-6.6 ft. high, often with suckers, branches short, at first reddish and slightly bloomy, prickles straight, scattered; leaflets 5-7(-9), elliptic-oblong, 3-5 cm./1.2-2 in. long, grey-green, puberulent above, tomentose and glandular beneath, doubly glandular-serrate, with light resinous scent; flowers 1-3 together, pink, to 5 cm./2 in. across, June-July; pedicels and calyx glandular-bristly, sepals pinnate, erected; fruits globose-oblong, to 2.5 cm./1 in. across, dark red, bristly. 2n = 28. WR 141; BM 7241; CFl 614; KSR 13-13; GSR 37 (= *R. pomifera* Herrm.). Eu-

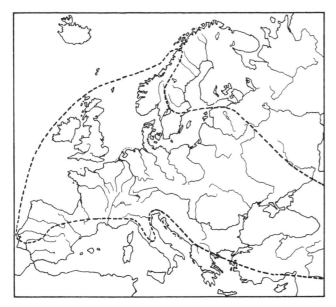

Figure 127. Distribution of *Rosa villosa*. (after Sokolov 1954)

rope, especially in the mountains; Orient. 1771.

'Duplex'. 'Wolley Dod's Rose'. Leaves grey-green; flowers large, semi-double, clear pink, more floriferous than the type. WR 436; GSR 38. In England known before 1770 (as *R. villosa duplex* West.), but later distributed by the Rev. Wolley-Dod, Edge Hall, Chechester.

R. mollis Sm. Small shrub, upright, about 1 m./3.3 ft. high, stems reddish, bloomy, with equal, rather straight prickles; leaflets 5-7, smaller than in the similar *R. villosa* and more orbicular, silky-hairy beneath, less glandular, doubly serrate; flowers 1-4 together, pink, 4-5 cm./1.6-2 in. across, June-July; sepals somewhat pinnate, glandular-bristly, persisting; fruits globose, scarlet-red, somewhat bristly to quite bald, early maturing. 2n = 35. WR 138; KSR 14. (= *R. mollissima* Fries; *R. villosa* var. *mollissima* Rau). N. and W. Europe, eastern border to S.C. Russia. Distinguished from the similar *R. villosa* by the stronger bloomy branches when young, and smaller leaflets (12-35 × 8-18 mm./0.05-0.14 × 0.03-0.07 in.) 1818.

R. sherardii Davies. Dense shrub to 2 m./6.6 ft. high, branches often zig-zag, prickles often very hooked; leaflets broadly ovate to elliptic, puberulous above, bluish-green and tomentose beneath; flowers several together, dark pink, surpassed by the basal leaves; fruits turbinate, 1.2-2 cm./0.5-0.8 in. across, with persisting sepals. 2n = 28. KSR 15; CF1 613. (= *R. omissa* Déségl.). N., W. and C. Europe, to S.W. Finland, South to Bulgaria. 1933. (Fig. 145).

R. orientalis Dupont ex Sér. Dwarfish growth, younger branches densely hairy, prickles very scattered, slightly curved to straight, very slender with broad base; leaflets 5, elliptic, mostly about 15 mm./0.6 in. long, bright green above, grey-green beneath, puberulent on both sides, with coarse teeth pointed forward; flowers solitary, pink, with a short pedicel; pedicel and calyx with long bristles and stalked glands; fruits ellipsoid, 1 cm./0.4 in. long, sepals erected. 2n = 35. KSR 36. S. Yugoslavia, N. Albania, Greece, Asia Minor. 1905. (Fig. 129).

R. heckeliana Tratt. Shrub, to about 1 m./3.3 ft. high, branches more or less bloomy and downy when young; prickles scattered, hooked or straight; leaflets 5-7, orbicular or ovate, grey-tomentose beneath, without glands; flowers solitary, pink, 3.5 cm./1.4 in. across, pedicels mostly grey-downy, without glands; fruits globose to ovoid, red, 10-12 mm./0.4-0.5 in. long, bald to slightly glandular. (= *R. orphanides* Boiss. & Reut.). Mountains of the E. Mediterranean region and Sicily.

R. elymaitica Boiss. & Hausskn. Low shrub, compact, branches tortuous, densely armed, prickles partly solitary or paired, hooked, 4-8 mm./0.2-0.3 in. long; leaves 3-5 cm./1.2-2 in. long, leaflets 5, ovate to orbicular, 8-12 mm./0.3-0.5 in. long, simply or doubly serrate, firm, hairy above, tomentose beneath; flowers solitary, pinkish-white, 2.5 cm./1 in. across, pedicels, calyx and sepals bristly; fruits globose, dark red, 8 mm./0.3 in. across, glandular-bristly, with spreading sepals. 2n = 14,28. Persia, Kurdistan, high mountains. 1900.

R. tomentosa Sm. Shrub, 2 m./6.6 ft. high, branches zig-zag, young branches often bloomy, prickles stout, straight or curved; leaflets 5-7, elliptic to ovate, 2-4

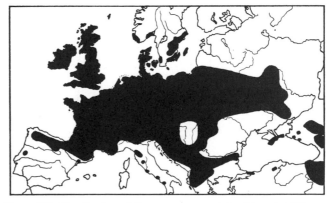

Figure 128. Distribution of *Rosa tomentosa*. (after Meusel, 1965)

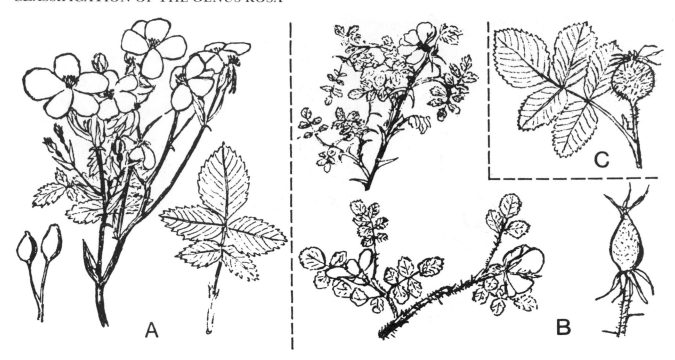

Figure 129. A. *Rosa phoenicia*; B. *R. glutinosa*; C. *R. orientalis*. (after Mouterde)

cm./0.8-1.6 in. long, puberulent above, tomentose and glandular beneath, doubly serrate; stipules with short, triangular, spreading auricles; flowers blush to nearly white, 4 cm./1.6 in. across, pedicels often glandular-bristly; sepals lobed, dropping before maturity; fruits nearly globose, 1-2 cm./0.4-0.8 in. across, with stalked glands. 2n = 35. WR 139; KSR 16-17; VP 445; CF1 612. Europe, except the far North; Caucasus, Asia Minor. 1820 (Fig. 125)

R. rubiginosa L. Sweet-Briar. Strong-growing shrub, 2(-3) m./6.6 (-10) ft. high, branches very prickly, prickles hooked, strong, often mixed with bristles; leaflets 5-7, ovate-orbicular, dark green, glandular, with a strong smell of apples; flowers 1-3 together, pinkish, 3 cm./1.2 in. across, June; pedicels and calyx glandular-bristly, sepals more or less spreading, late dropping; fruits scarlet, ovoid, 1-2 cm./0.4-0.8 in. long, bald or slightly glandular-bristly at the base, rarely quite bristly. 2n = 35, 42. WR 145; KSR 22-23; AFP 2502; VP 437; CF1 615. (= *R. eglanteria* L.; nom. ambig.) Europe, to 61° North; Caucasus, Asia Minor; escaped in N. America. Cultivated since 1594. (Fig. 131).

Hylander has recommended against using the name *R. eglanteria*, as this name was later used by Linné for *R. foetida*, and continued use

will cause permanent confusion. This species was also used in hybridizing.

'Duplex'. Flowers semi-double, with 10 petals, pink, scent stronger than the type, but scent of the leaves much less so. WR 449 (as 'Jannet's Pride'). Known since 1629; may scarcely be in cultivation at this time. After *Modern Roses 7*, this rose is supposed to be identical to → 'Magnifica', a seedling of 'Lucy Ashton'. Further hybrids (by W. Kordes) with 'Magnifica': → 'Fritz Nobis', and 'Rosenwunder'.

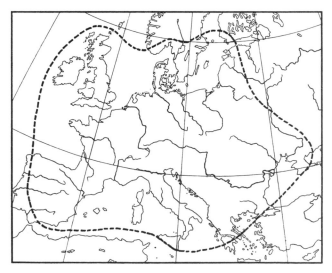

Figure 130. Distribution of *Rosa rubiginosa*. (after Sokolov 1954; Perring and Walters 1963)

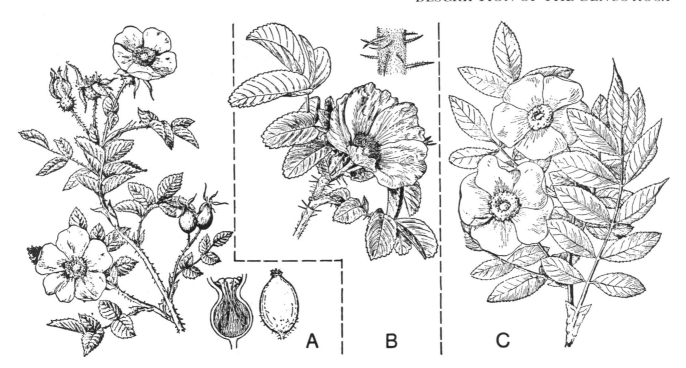

Figure 131. A. *Rosa rubiginosa*; B. *R. rugosa*; C. *R. suffulta*.

R. inodora Fries. Related to *R. rubiginosa*, to 2 m./6.6 ft. high, but leaflets elliptic to obovate-oblong, 1.5-3 cm./0.6-1.2 in. long, without glands, hairy beneath; flowers pink to white, pedicels short, regularly glandular, scent stronger but less agreeable than that of *R. rubiginosa*; fruits ovoid, scarlet, 2n = 35, 42. WR 496; KSR 23 (= *R. elliptica* Tausch; *R. caryophyllacea* Bess.; *R. graveolens* Gren. & Godr.). W. and C. Europe, mountains, in the S.E. to Albania and W. Ukraine; on limestone. (Fig. 125).

R. sicula Tratt. Low shrub, 0.2-0.8 m./0.7-2.6 ft. high, similar to *R. serafinii*, but with suckers; prickles straight or slightly curved, slender, nearly all equal, young branches red; leaflets 5-9, orbicular, 6-12 mm./0.2-0.5 in. long, bald, but glandular beneath, slightly scented; flowers solitary, pink, 2.5-3 cm./1-1.2 in. across, sepals persisting (with *R. serafinii* finally dropping); fruits ovoid-globose, 1.3 cm./0.5 in. long, red. 2n = 35. BM 7761; KSR 18. S. Europe, N. Africa. Before 1894.

R. glutinosa Sibth. & Sm. Shrub, 0.3-0.7 m./1-2.3 ft. high, dense, very prickly, prickles partly stout and rather straight, partly bristly-glandular; leaflets 3-7, orbicular-elliptic, small, doubly serrate, glandular on both sides and margin, petiole and stipules; flowers solitary on short branches, pinkish, small, June; sepals pinnate, calyx and pedicel glandular-bristly, style puberulent; fruits scarlet, glossy, bristly, 1.5 cm./0.6 in. across. 2n = 35,42. WR 150; KSR 18. (= *R. pulverulenta* Bieb.) E. and C. Mediterranean area, Balkans, Asia Minor. 1821. Similar to *R. sicula*, but prickles densely mixed with stalked glands. (Fig. 129).

var. **dalmatica** (Kern.) Schneid. Leaflets larger, to 2.5 cm./1 in. long, less hairy, prickles straight; fruits larger, ovoid, to 2.5 cm./1 in. long. 2n = 35, 42. BM 8826 (= *R. dalmatica* Kern.). Dalmatia. 1882.

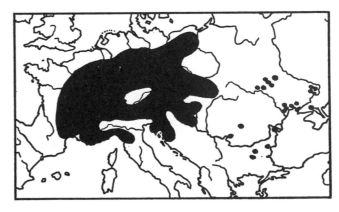

Figure 132. Distribution of *Rosa inodora*. (after Meusel 1965)

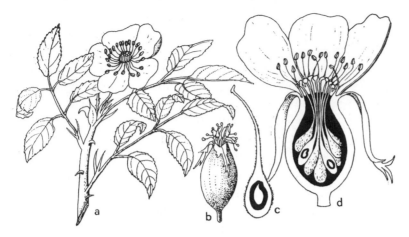

Figure 133. *Rosa montezumae*. a. flowering branch; b. fruit; c. achene, longitudinal section; d. flower, longitudinal section. (after Sanches, modified)

R. tuschetica Boiss. Very closely related to *R. glutinosa*, but leaflets ovate (not obovate or elliptic), sepals long, caudate, erected at the fruit, not spreading. (= *R. pimpinellifolia* var. *tuschetica* Christ.) Dagestan Mts., U.S.S.R. 1945.

R. micrantha Sm. Related to *R. rubiginosa*; shrub, upright, to 1.5 m./5 ft., densely branched, stems arching, all prickles equal, curved; leaflets 5-7, broadly ovate, 2-3 cm./0.8-1.2 in. long, bald or hairy above, densely hairy and glandular beneath; flowers 1-4 together, pink to white, 3 cm./1.2 in. across, June; sepals pinnate, early dropping, enlarged at the top, glandular; styles bald, fruits ovoid, 12-18 mm./0.5-7 in. long, red. 2n = 35, 42.

WR 148; KSR 19-20; VP 439; CF1 616. C. and S. Europe to N. Ukraine. Before 1800. (Fig. 125).

R. horrida Fisch. Related to *R. micrantha*; low shrub, branches rather stiff, with many branchlets; prickles short and unequal, very hooked, dilated at the base; leaflets 5-7, ovate-elliptic, 1-1.5 cm./0.4-0.6 in. long, glandular beneath, sometimes above also, doubly serrate, petioles and stipules glandular; flowers solitary, white, 3 cm./1.2 in. across, on short pedicels, June; sepals pinnate, often foliaceous at the top, equalling the petals; glandular beneath, dropping; calyx long, glandular-bristly like the pedicel; fruits ovoid-globose, bald or bristly, blood red. 2n = 35. WR 154 (as *R. ferox*). KSR 35(= *R. turcica* Rouy; *R. ferox* Biel, not Lawr.; *R. horridula* Fisch., not Spreng.) S.E. Europe, Turkey, Caucasus. 1796. Similar to *R. sicula*, but with stout, curved prickles, mixed with bristles and stalked glands; sepals reflexed and dropping.

R. agrestis Savi. Shrub, 1-2 (-3) m./3.3-6.6 (-10) ft. high, branches slender, prickles strong, broad, hooked; leaflets 5-7, oblong-elliptic, 1.5-5 cm./0.6-2 in. long, mostly with cuneate base, hairy to nearly bald; flowers 1-3, blush or whitish, sepals narrow, dropping early, styles slightly exserted, pedicels without glands; fruits oblong-ovoid, orange-red. 2n = 35, 42. WR 147, KSR 21;

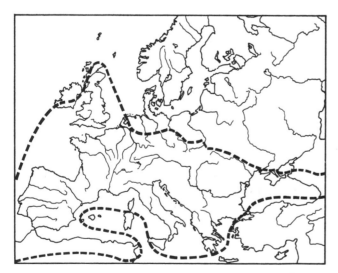

Figure 134. Distribution of *Rosa micrantha*. (after Browicz 1973, altered)

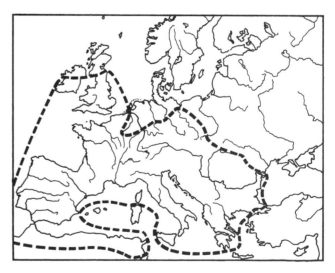

Figure 135. Distribution of Rosa agrestis. (after Browicz 1973, altered)

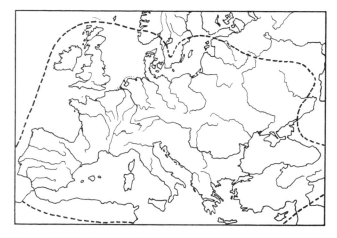

Figure 136. Distribution of *Rosa corymbifera*. (after Sokolov 1954)

CF1 617. (= *R. sepium* Thuill.). Europe, but rare in N. and E.; N. Africa. 1878. (Fig. 153)

R. serafinii Viv. Low shrub, 0.3-0.8 m./1-2.6 ft. high, never has suckers, (see *R. sicula*), stems short, arching, very densely covered with short, stout, hooked, unequal prickles; leaflets 7-11, ovate-orbicular, 8-12 × 6-10 mm./0.3-0.5 × 0.2 × 0.4 in., very glossy, sharply serrate, glandular beneath, otherwise bald; flowers solitary (or 2-3), whitish-pink, 3 cm./1.2 in. across, May; pedicels very short and without glands, sepals lobed, reflexed after anthesis, dropping early, styles bald; fruits abovoid, 8-12 mm./0.3-0.5 in. across, bright red. 2n = 35. WR 153. (= *R. apennina* Woods). Islands of the Mediterranean Sea. Bulgaria, S. Yugoslavia. 1914. Similar to *R. sicula*, but prickles strongly hooked to falcate, rarely mixed with bristles.

R. stylosa Desv. Shrub, to 3 m./10 ft. high, stems arching, prickles stout, hooked, dilated at base; leaflets 5-7, mostly narrowly ovate to lanceolate, 1.5-5 cm./0.6-2 in. long, pointed, simply serrate, mostly downy beneath, rarely so above or bald on both sides, no glands; stipules and bracts rather narrow; flowers 1-8 (or more) together, white to pink, 3-5 cm./1.2-2 in. across, June; pedicels long, mostly glandular-prickly, column of styles bald, shorter than the stamens, stigmas forming an ovoid head, discus conical; sepals reflexed after anthesis, dropping before maturity of the fruit; fruit ovoid, red, smooth. 1-1.5 cm./0.4-0.6 in. across 2n = 35, 42; 28, 34. WR 14; KSR 8; CF1 608. (= *R. systyla* Bast.). W. Europe; Ireland to W. Germany (Rhineland), Switzerland, S. France, N.W. Spain, Bulgaria. 1838.

R. obtusifolia Desv. Similar to *R. canina*, about 1.5 m./5 ft. high, prickles mostly hooked; leaflets 5-7, deep green and often glossy above, more or less puberulent on both sides; flowers small, white to pale reddish; styles short, hairy, sepals finally dropping; fruits globose, scarlet to orange, smooth. 2n = 35. KSR 25. (= *R. tomentella* Léman); *R. canina* var. *tomentella* [Lém.] Baker; *R. klukii* Bess.). C.,S. and N.W. Europe, especially in the mountains. 1905. (Fig. 145).

R. corymbifera Borkh. Closely related to *R. canina*, principally distinguished by the puberulent leaflets; shrub 1.5-2.5 m./5-8.2 ft. high, very broad; prickles stout, hooked; leaflets 5-9, elliptic, to 5 cm./2 in. long, densely set, simply serrate, mostly hairy on both sides; flowers mostly in corymbs, white to blush, 4-5 cm./1.6-2 in. across, June; sepals mostly bald, rarely slightly glandular beneath, dropping; pedicels mostly bald; fruits ovoid, orange-red, 12-18 mm./0.5-0.7 in. high. 2n = 35, 42. WR 130. (= *R. dumetorium* Thuill.). Widely distributed in Europe, but less frequent in N. and N.W., especially in the plains; N. Africa, Asia Minor. 1838.

R. coriifolia Fries. Closely related to *R. corymbifera*, but lower, to 1.5 m./5 ft. high, densely branched, branches and branchlets often bluish-bloomy; prickles curved, equal; leaflets 5-7, medium-large or small, rather firm, oblong to broadly elliptic, bases wedge-shaped, mostly simply glandular-serrate, bald above, grey-green and with tomentose down beneath; flowers rose, styles united into a woolly head, pedicels very short, with large bracts; sepals greyish-hairy; fruits globose to ovoid, to 2.5 cm./1 in. long; sepals persisting to maturity, mostly erected. 2n = 35. WR 391. (= *R. frutetorum* Bess.). Europe, Asia Minor. 1878.

var. **froebelii** (Lambert) Rehd. Small shrub, compact, older stems stout, with many slender bracts; leaves with long petioles, leaflets large, grayish-green on both sides, hairy, stipules long and narrow; flowers 1-3 together, white; fruits ellipsoid to ovoid-oblong, red, early maturing. (= *R. laxa* Hort. not Retz.; *R. froebelii* Christ; *R. dumetorum laxa*). Introduced about 1890 by O. Froebel, Zurich, Switzerland. It is still used as an important understock for budding in Europe.

R. canina L. Dog Rose. Shrub to 3 m./10 ft. high, branches arching, prickles strong, hooked; leaflets 5-7, ovate-elliptic, 2-4 cm./0.8-1.6 in. long, doubly or simply serrate, bald on both sides or slightly puberulent beneath; flowers 1-3 together, pink to white, 4-5 cm./1.6-2 in. across, June; sepals reflexed after flowering and then dropping, before the fruit turns red; styles bald or hairy, stigmas usually form a small head; fruit

Figure 137. *Rosa canina*. (after *Rosenzeitung*)

ellipsoid, scarlet-red, 2-3 cm./0.8-1.2 in. long. 2n = 35, 42;34. WR 379-380; KSR 27-28. Europe, to 62° North, in Scandinavia. Very variable; Wolley-Dod distinguishes no less than 60 varieties and forms. 1737. (Fig. 143).

The wild varieties have no horticultural interest, so are not treated here; but there is quite a series of selections which are very important as rootstocks for budding. These are discussed in detail on p. 110, with an identification key.

The following wild species also belong to the *Canina* group; descriptions of them can be found in the section "Rosa" of *Flora Europaea*, Vol. 2:25-32 (1968).

  R. abietina Gren. ex Christ; Alps. KSR 26.
  R. andegavensis Bast.: W.S. and C. Europe.
  R. deseglisei Boreau: C. Europe.
  R. nitdula Bess.; Great Britain and N. Portugal, E. to S. Sweden. Carpathian Mts. and Greece.
  R. pouzinii Tratt.: Mediterranean area.
  R. rhaetica Gremli: Alps. KSR 29.
  R. squarrosa (Rau) Boreau: C. Europe.
  R. subcanina (Christ) Dalla Torre & Sarnth.: Europe.
  R. subcollina (Christ) Dalla Torre & Sarnth.: Europe, up to the far North.

'Général Jacqueminot' × *R. canina* → **'Kiese'**

R. × 'Andersonii'. Hillier & Sons 1912. (= *R. canina* × *R. gallica*?) Growth medium-strong. 2 m./6.6 ft., branches arching, strongly armed; leaflets 5, acuminate, downy

beneath; flowers clear pink, single, 5-7, 5 cm./2 in. across, saucer-shaped, floriferous during a long period; fruits similar to *R. canina*, scarlet-red. WR 380. 1912. Plants in cultivation in W. Germany under this name do not belong to this form, but nearly always to *R. collina andersonii*.

R. dumalis Bechst. Shrub to 2 m./6.6 ft. high, branches often bluish-bloomy, prickles hooked, with broad base; leaflets 5-7, nearly touching each other, medium-large, broadly ovate to roundish, bald on both sides and mostly bluish-bloomy, stipules strikingly large; flowers solitary or many together, rather large, rose-pink, June-July; sepals with lanceolate-linear appendages, margins downy, calyx globose, bloomy; fruits globose to ovoid, very large. 2n = 35, CF1 610 (= *R. glauca* Vill. not Pourr.; *R. reuteri* [Godet] Reuter). Europe, Asia Minor; in mountains.

R. britzensis Koehne. Shrub strongly upright, 2-3 m./6.6-10 ft. high, branches bald, prickles slender, small, 6-8 mm./0.2-0.3 in. long, on flowering branches only, scattered; leaves 12-14 cm./4.8-5.6 in. long; leaflets mostly 11 (rarely 7-9), elliptic, greyish-green, 2.5-3.5 cm./1-1.4 in. long, simply serrate; flowers nearly always solitary, blush, finally white, 7-8 (–10) cm./2.8-3.2 (–4) in. across, petals emarginate, mid-May to end of June; calyx, petiole and reverse of petals bristly; fruits ovoid, dark red, about 3 cm./1.2 in. long, slightly glandular-bristly. Kurdistan. 1901. (Fig. 139).

R. marginata Wallr. Upright shrub, 2-2.5 m./6.6-8.3 ft. high, closely related to *R. canina*, but marked by straight (or nearly straight) prickles; leaves doubly glandular-serrate, mostly glandular beneath; flowers solitary or several together, pink, later changing to white, up to 7 cm./2.4 in. across, June; sepals pinnate, reverse glandular, shorter than petals; fruits ovoid, dark red, smooth, sepals dropping. 2n = 42.WR 149; KSR 9-10. (= *R. jundzillii* Bess.) C. and E. Europe, Asia Minor. 1870. (Fig. 145).

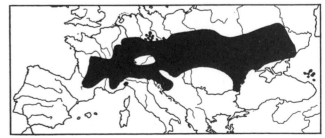

Figure 138. Distribution of *Rosa marginata*. (after Meusel 1965)

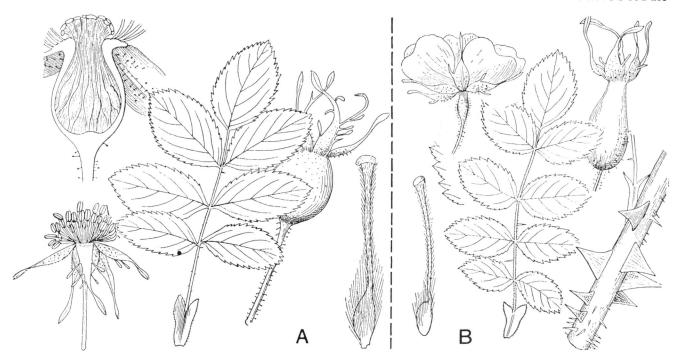

Figure 139. A. *Rosa britzensis*; B. *R. sweginzowii*.

R. glauca Pourr. Upright shrub, to 3 m./1.2 in. high, stems slender, branches brown-red, bloomy, with few straight or hooked prickles; leaves brownish-purple and bloomy, leaflets 5-7, elliptic, bald, sharply serrate; flowers many, pink to dark pink, 3-4 cm./1.2-1.6 in. across, June; fruits globose, 1.5 cm./0.6 in. across, red, sepals spreading with maturity, late-dropping. 2n = 28. WR 133;KSR 11 (= *R. rubrifolia* Vill.; *R. ferruginea* Déségl.). Pyrenees to Yugoslavia, in the mountains. 1814. Susceptible to Rose Rust. (Fig. 145).

R. × pokornyana Borb. (= *R. canina* × *R. glauca*). Intermediate between parents; 1.5-2 m./5-6.6 ft. high, stems and branches very bloomy, bluish-gray, prickles scattered, straight to slightly curved; leaflets 5-7, medium-large to small, simply serrate, bald on both sides, bloomy, sometimes violet-purple beneath when young; flowers 1-3 together, dark red, 3.5-4 cm./1.4-1.6 in. across; sepals slender, with some narrow pinnae; calyx globose to oblong; fruits small, globose. 2n = 40. (= *R. scopulosa* Briqu.). Hungary. 1916.

Section 4. Carolinae (Crép.) Rehd.

Shrubs mostly upright, low, stems slender, with many straight, paired prickles, also often bristly; upper stipules mostly narrow; inflorescences mostly few-flowered; sepals spreading after anthesis, dropping early, the outer sepals en-tire or with only a few upright lobes; pedicels and sepals glandular-bristly, rarely bald; ovules only at the bottom of the subglobose calyx-tube.

R. palustris, mariae-graebnerae, virginiana, carolina, nitida, scharnkeana, rugotida, foliolosa.

R. palustris Marsh. Upright and very broad shrub, 1-1.8 m./3.3-6 ft. high, stems reddish, prickles hooked, with broad base; leaflets mostly 7, broadly elliptic-acute at both ends, 2-5 cm./0.8-2 in. long, sharply serrulate, firm, dark green and bald above, pale and hairy beneath; flowers pink, 5 cm./2 in. across, June to end of July, in corymbs; fruits globose, red, smooth, 8 mm./0.3 in. across, pedicels glandular. 2n= 14(28). WR 68 (as *R. carolina*); BB 2: 170; VP 441; BC 3443. (= *R. hudsoniana* Thory; *R. pensylvanica* Michx;). E. N. America; in swamps. 1726. Relatively rare in cultivation and rather variable; often confused (even in the United States) with the glossy green-leaved *R. virginiana* Mill. or the suckering *R. carolina* L. Not suitable for small gardens.

R. × mariae-graebnerae Aschers. & Graebn. (= *R. palustris* × *R. virginiana*). Shrub with rather blobose habit, similar to *R. palustris*; prickles faintly curved, on shoots bristles scattered or absent; leaves more glossy and more coarsely serrate; flowers rose-pink, flowers throughout the summer and even while fruiting; fruits red; autumn color of the leaves strikingly yellow and

267

red. Obtained about 1900 by H. Zabel at the Botan. Garden of Hann. Münden, W. Germany, but also occurs in the wild with the parent stock.

R. virginiana Mill. Upright shrub, to 1.5 m./5 ft. high, stems often red-brown, few suckers, if any; prickles hooked, but young branches often bristly; leaves glossy green, leaflets 7-9, elliptic to ovate, 2-6 cm./0.8-2.4 in. long, sharply serrate, hairy on the veins beneath; flowers several together or solitary, pink, June-July, floriferous; fruits subglobose, 1.5 cm./0.6 in. across. 2n = 28. WR 197; BB 2285; VP 447. (= *R. lucida* Ehrh.; *R. carolinensis* Marsh.). E. N. America. Before 1807. (Fig. 140).

'**Plena**'. Growth more compact, but otherwise habit and foliage similar to the type; flower buds very attractive; flowers clear pink, with broad, orbicular outer petals, inner ones acute, somewhat darker, faintly scented, July-August (= *R. rapa* Bosc; *R. lucida* var. *plena* Hort, ex Rehd.). 1768.

R. carolina L. Shrub 1-1.5 m./3.3-5 ft. high, stems slender, with many suckers, first bristly; branches often unarmed, prickles slender, straight; leaflets 5, rarely to 7, elliptic to lanceolate, 1-3 cm./0.4-1.2 in. long, sharply serrate, dark green, but not or only slightly glossy above, grayish-green and mostly bald beneath; flowers mostly solitary, pink, 5 cm./2 in. across, July-August; sepals lanceolate, acuminate or dilated, dropping, glandular-hispid, pedicels glandular-bristly; fruits subglobose, 8 mm./0.3 in. across, rather glandular-hispid. 2n = 24 (rarely 14). WR 64; BB 1971; VP 437. E. N. America. 1826. (Fig. 158)

var. **grandiflora** (Baker) Rehd. Leaflets mostly 7, elliptic to obovate, flowers 5-6 cm./2-2.4 in. across. 2n = 28. WR 207 (as *R. humilis grandiflora*). (= *R. lindleyi* Spreng.). N.E. N. America. Before 1870.

'**Plena**'. Shrub to 0.5 m./1.7 ft. high, densely bristled, stems slender, with suckers; leaflets small, narrow, acute, serrate; flowers clear salmon-pink, center slightly darker, finally nearly white, very double; sepals very long and narrow, glandular-hairy like calyx and pedicels; prickles in pairs below nodes. (= *R. pennsylvanica* Marsh.).

R. nitida Willd. Upright shrub, 0.7-0.9 m./2.3-3 ft. high, stems densely covered with short bristles, prickles slender, 3-5 mm./0.1-0.2 in. long; leaflets 7-9, elliptic to oblong, 1-3 cm./0.4-1.2 in. long, dark green and very glossy above, dark brown-red in the autumn; flowers solitary or several together, pink, 4-5 cm./1.6-2 in. across, June-July; sepals erected, narrow, entire, glandular-hispid like the pedicels; fruit globose,

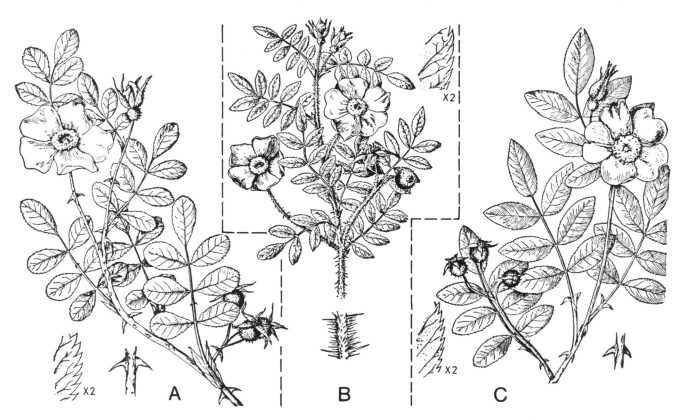

Figure 140.   A. *Rosa virginiana*;   B. *R. nitida*;   C. *R. palustris*. (after Gleason, The New *Brown & Britton*)

scarlet-red, 1 cm./0.4 in. across, glandular-hispid. 2n = 14. WR 69; BB 1972. E. N. America. 1807. (Fig. 140).

R. × rugotida Darth. Boomkw. 1950. (= *R. nitida* × *R. rugosa*). Growth strong, to 1 m./3.3 ft. high, with suckers; leaves very similar to *R. rugosa*, but smaller; flowers pink, similar to *R. nitida*; sterile (no fruits).

'Dart's Defender'. (Darth. Boomkw. 1971). (= *R. nitida* × *R. rugosa hansa*). Growth stronger than *R. nitida*; flowers violet-pink (= *R. nitida superba* Darth. Boomkw.).

R. × scharnkeana Graebn. (= *R. californica* × *R. nitida*). Low shrub, stems with slender prickles, mostly bristly; leaflets 7-9, oblong, with wedge-shaped base; flowers 1-5 together, purplish-pink. In cultivation before 1900.

R. foliolosa Nutt. Shrub 0.3-0.7 m./1-2.3 ft. high, stems reddish, with short, straight or slightly hooked prickles or nearly unarmed, rarely bristly; leaflets 7-9, narrowly oblong, 12-25 mm./0.5-1 in. long, bald and glossy above, sometimes hairy on the veins beneath; flowers solitary or several together, bright red, 3 cm./1.2 in.

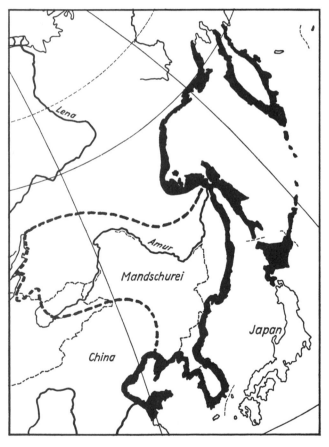

Figure 141. Distribution of *Rosa rugosa* (■) and *R. davurica* (---). (after Sokolov 1954)

across, July-August; sepals lanceolate, acuminate, to 2.5 cm./1 in. long, glandular-hispid like the calyx and the short pedicel; fruits rather globose, 8 mm./0.3 in. across, red. 2n = 14. WR 70; BM 8513; BC 3445; VP 374. S.E. United States. 1880. Shrub with very beautiful foliage, very hardy and drought-resistant. (Fig. 171).

Section 5. Cinnamomeae (Sér.) Rehd.

Upright shrubs; stems with mostly straight prickles, paired below the nodes, sometimes also bristly; flowering branches often unarmed or glandular-hispid; leaflets 5-11, stipules more or less dilated, gradually passing into the auricles, being extended broadly forward; inflorescences mostly many-flowered; sepals entire, after anthesis erected and persisting, rarely dropping; calyx-tube mostly smooth:

R. rugosa, proteiformis, kamtchatica, paulii, calocarpa, bruantii, spaethiana, warleyensis, koehneana, micrugosa, rubrosa, aciculalaris, engelmannii, arkansana, suffulta, blanda, aschersoniana, pendulina, spinulifolia, oxyodon, lheritieranea, majalis, davurica, laxa, amblyotis, marrettii, pisocarpa, woodsii, mohavensis, pyrifera, macounii, ultramontana, pinetorum, californica, gratissima, corymbulosa, spaldingii, davidii, caudata, banksiopsis, macrophylla, coryana, setipoda, persetosa, hemsleyana, sweginzowii, wardii, murielae, moyesii, holodonta, wintoniensis, highdownensis, bella, webbiana, fedtschenkoana, sertata, pricei, giraldii, prattii, prattigosa, elegantula, forrestiana, multibracteata, willmottiae, transmorrisonensis, pruhonciana, spithamea, gymnocarpa, sonomensis, beggeriana.

R. rugosa Thunb. Shrub 1-2 m./3.3-6.6 ft. high, stems stout, tomentose, very prickly and bristly; leaflets 5-9, elliptic, 3-5 cm./1.2-2 in. long, dark green, wrinkled and glossy above, firm, thick, golden-yellow in the autumn; glaucous, reticulate and puberulent beneath; flowers solitary or few together, purple to white, 6-8 cm./2.4-3.2 in. across, June to autumn; pedicels short and bristly; fruits depressed-globose, to 2.5 cm./1 in. across, smooth, of commercial use. 2n = 14. WR 58; ICS 2223. (= *R. regeliana* Linden & André). N. China, Korea, Japan; locally naturalized in N., W. and C. Europe. May be the hardiest of all roses. 1854.

Many varieties and hybrids:

'Adiantifolia'. Cochet 1907. Similar to 'Crispata', but usually with 7 (not 9) leaflets, these longer and larger; stipules very large and long, with fiber-like margin (only denticulate in 'Crispata'). (Fig. 142).

'Alba' (Ware). Flowers white. GSR 129.

'Albo-plena'. Flowers white, double, presumably mutation of 'Alba'. Before 1902.

var. **chamissoniana** C.A. Mey. Stems nearly free of bristles; leaflets smaller, narrower, less wrinkled.

'Crispata' → **'Crispata'** (p. 328).

'Fimbriata' →.**'Frimbriata'** (p. 339).

Figure 142. Three rare cultivars of *Rosa rugosa*: Left: *tenuifolia*; center: *adiantifolia*; right: *crispata*. (after A. Leroy)

'Hollandica' (J. Spek, Boskoop, Holland, about 1888). Better known under its name 'Boskoop Rugosa', actually called 'Scherpe Boskoop', widely used as stock for budding; shrub rather high, branched, stems densely covered with prickles and bristles, these yellowish and unequal; leaflets large, bright green; flowers 5-10 together, single, dark red; fruits pendulous, globose, dark red, glandular. Much appreciated for stock use in wet ground, but suckers heavily.

'Nitens'. Like the type, but leaflets glossy green, bald on both sides.

'Plena'. Purplish-red, double; very hardy. 1879. Formerly known under the name "Empress of the North".

'Rosea' (= *R. rugosa* × *R. rugosa alba*). Flowers pink, single.

'Rubra'. Strong growing; flowers purplish-crimson; fruits bright red. (= 'Atropurpurea'). Red-flowering wild variety, but mostly named as a cultivar. GSR 136.

'Tenuifolia'. Branches typically armed as in the species; leaves more distant from each other; leaflets 5-9, but mostly 7, very long and narrow, irregularly undulated, stipules much dilated. (Fig. 142).

Much more important than the above described cultivars are the selections and hybrids: → 'Carmen', 'Conrad Ferdinand Meyer', 'Dr. Eckener', 'E.J. Grootendorst', 'Hansa', 'Nova Zembla', 'Pink Grootendorst', 'Ruskin', 'Scabrosa', 'Schneezwerg', etc.

R. × proteiformis Rowley. (= *R. rugosa alba* × unknown diploid). Shrub about 1 m./3.3 ft. high; leaves at first unfold normally, then gradually becoming narrower, paler and curly, nearly fern-like (similar to *R. multiflora watsoniana*), possibly caused by virus; flowers 5-10 together, semi-double, white, 3 cm./1.2 in. across, occasionally recurring. 2n = 14. (= *R. heterophylla* Cochet-Cochet 1897, not Woods 1818). Wrongly designated as *R. rugosa* × *R. foetida* by Cochet. *R. foetida* is tetraploid, however. May be identical with 'Adiantifolia'.

R. × kamtchatica Vent. (= *R. davurica* × *R. rugosa*). Differs from *R. rugosa* by more slender, less prickly branches, but gray-tomentose and with short bristles; leaflets oblong, dull, fewer wrinkles above, mostly greygreen and hairy beneath; flowers 3-5 on short, bald pedicels, smaller; fruits smaller, globose, smooth, sepals long, inclining. 2n = 14. BM 3149. (= *R. rugosa* var. *kamtchatica* [Vent.] Regel). E. Siberia, Kamtchatka. 1770.

R. × paulii Rehd. (= *R. arvensis* × *R. rugosa*). Intermediate between parents, stems to 4 m./13 ft. long, procumbent, very prickly; flowers several together, single, white, to 6 cm./2.4 in. across. 2n = 14. GSR 34. (= *R.*

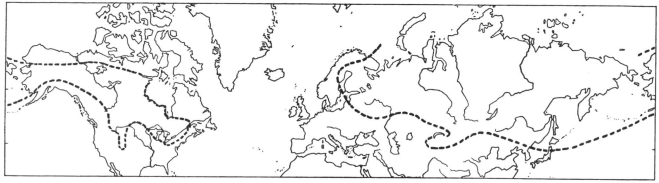

Figure 143. Distribution of *R. acicularis*. (Asiatic area after Sokolov, 1954; American area after T.M. Little, 1942)

rugosa repens alba Paul). Before 1903.

'Rosea'. Like the type, but flower clear rose, with somewhat brighter center. GSR 35; GiS 3. (= *R. rugosa repens rosea* Hort.). Before 1903.

R. × calocarpa (André) Willm. (= *R. chinensis × R. rugosa*). Strong-growing shrub, 2-2.5 m./6.6-8.3 ft. high, branches densely prickly, prickles straight and mixed with bristles; flowers in corymbs, single, pink, smaller than *R. rugosa*, June-July; sepals glandular-hispid, finally dropping, pedicels bristly; fruits globose, bright red, many together, long-lasting. 2n = 14 WR 60. (= *R. rugosa calocarpa* André). Originated with Bruant, Poitiers, France; 1891 named by Edouard André; 1895 introduced by Bruant, but rapidly disappeared from gardens.

R. × bruantii Rehder 1922. Today regarded as a superfluous name for the hybrids of *R. rugosa × R. chinensis* (= Hybrid Rugosa × Tea Roses and Hybrid Teas). Rehder added the varieties of Bruant ('Mme. Georges Bruant') and of Cochet ('Blanche Double de Courbert'), etc. to this.

R. × spaethiana Graebn. (= *R. palustris × R. rugosa*). Strong growth, upright; leaflets narrow, bright green; flowers many together, crimson-pink, 7-8 cm./2.8-3.2 in. across; fruits many, scarlet. 2n = 21.

R. × warleyensis Willm. (= *R. blanda × R. rugosa*). Shrub with very prickly stems, prickles straight, slender; leaflets 5-7, oblong, 25-35 mm./1-1.4 in. long; not as wrinkled as *R. rugosa*, bald above, thinly hairy beneath; flowers solitary, rose pink, 6 cm./2.4 in. across, calyx-tube bald, sepals acuminate. 2n = 14. WR 185. Before 1911.

R. × koehneana Rehd. (= *R. carolina × R. rugosa*). Shrub low, broad, very dense, stems with small infrastipular prickles, but otherwise internodes mostly without prickles; leaflets 7, oblong, simply serrate, bald above, hairy beneath; flowers solitary, purple, 6 cm./2.4 in. across, very floriferous; calyx-tube ovoid, bald, sepals long, with short bristles; pedicels 2.5 cm./1 in. long, thin, bald. 2n = 21, WR 203 (as *R. humilis × R. rugosa*). Originated before 1893 in the U.S.A.

R. × micrugosa Henkel. (= *R. roxburghii × R. rugosa*). Tall shrub, strictly upright, 2 m./6.6 ft. high, stems straight and very prickly; leaves densely set; flowers solitary, clear rose, 7-10 cm./2.8-4 in. across; fruits orange, very prickly, like *R. roxburghii*. 2n = 14. GSR 28. (= *R. vilmorinii* Bean). Originated before 1905 with Henry de Vilmorin, Paris. Seedlings of this plant sometimes produce beautiful plants with white, scented flowers.

R. × rubrosa Preston. (= *R. glauca × R. rugosa*). Growth stronger than *R. glauca*, flowers larger, but leaves not so beautifully bluish-purple, rachis bald, stems less prickly sterile (no fruits). 2n = 28. First introduced under the name → 'Carmenetta'. 1923.

R. acicularis Lindl. Shrub 1 m./3.3 ft. high, stems densely bristly and with weak prickles, branches sometimes unarmed, prickles straight, slender; leaflets 3-7, elliptic to oblong, 2-5 cm./0.4-2 in. long, simply serrate, dull green and bald above, downy beneath; pedicels bald to hairy; stipules large; flowers solitary, dark pink, 4-5 cm./1.6-2 in. across, scented, May-June; petals obovate, emarginated; fruits pear-shaped, roundish, smooth, 1.5 cm./0.6 in. long. 2n = 28, 42, 56. VP 432; HPN 3:168. (= *R. carelica* Fries; *R. sayi* Schwein.). N. America, N. Europe, N.E. Asia; the only completely circumpolar species. (Fig. 144).

var. **bourgeauiana** (Crép.) Crép. Flowers larger, to 5 cm./2 in. across, fruits more globose and on a very short neck. 2n = 42, 56. BC 3453. N America. (Fig. 144).

271

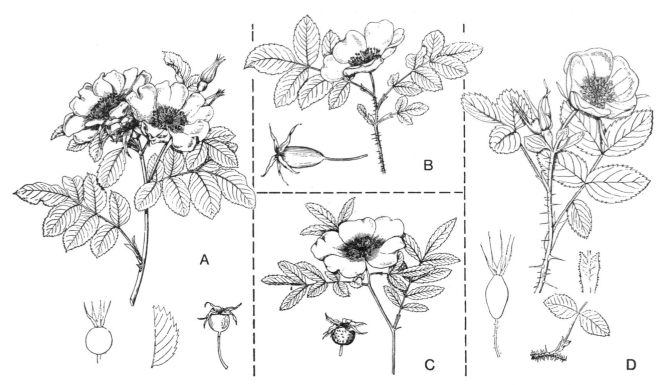

Figure 144. A. *Rosa nutkana*; B. *R. acicularis* var. *bourgeauiana*; C. *R. foliolosa*; D. *R. acicularis*. (after Garden & Forest)

var. **fennica** Lallemant. Tetraploid form. 2n = 28. (= *R. acicularis* var. *gmelinii* Bge.; *R. gmelinii* Bge.). Finland to Siberia.

var. **nipponensis** (Crép.) Koehne. Leaflets 7-9, about 1-3 cm./0.4-1.2 in. long, simply serrate, bald, petioles bristly; pedicels glandular-hispid. 2n = 14, 28. (= *R. nipponensis* Crép.) Japan, Mt. Fujiyama. 1894.

R. acicularis has only rarely been used for hybridizing work, as the descendents are mostly sterile. The most important hybrids are → 'Pike's Peak' and → 'Dornröschen'.

R. × engelmannii S. Wats. Natural hybrid of *R. acicularis* with *R. nutkana*; artificially reproduced by Erlanson. Similar to *R. acicularis*, var. *bourgeauiana*, but fruits ellipsoid, to 2.5 cm./1 in. long; branches more bristly, leaves bald beneath. 2n = 42. BC 3454. (= *R. acicularis* var. *engelmannii* [S. Wats.] Crép.) N. America. 1891.

R. arkansana Porter. Similar to *R. acicularis*, but lower and flowering period longer. About 0.5 m./1.7 ft. high, stems prickly and bristly; leaflets 9-11, elliptic, 2.5-5 cm./1-2 in. long, sharply serrate, glossy above, bald on both sides or puberulent on the veins beneath, stipules glandular-dentate; flowers in corymbs, bright red, 3 cm./1.2 in. across, June-July; sepals reflexed, bald or glandular beneath, outer ones often pinnate, pedicels bald, fruits globose, 1.5 cm./0.6 in. across, red. 2n = 28, 14. HPN 3:168; VP 434; BB 1968 (= *R. rydbergii* Greene). C. and W. U.S.A. 1917. (Fig. 145).

In its native home often low and suffruticose; hybrids of this species could possibly produce a new type of rose, similar to perennials, which could be pruned to the ground and then regenerate each year.

R. suffulta Greene. About 0.5 m./1.7 ft. high, sometimes only suffruticose; stems green, densely covered with fine prickles and bristly, after anthesis dies back to the ground, while at the same time new stems for the next year are developed; leaflets 7-11, broadly elliptic to ovate-oblong, 2-4 cm./0.4-1.6 in. long, serrate, bright green, puberulent on both sides, mostly bald above, petiole and rachis hairy; flowers in corymbs, pink, 3 cm./1.2 in. across, June; pedicels and calyx-tube bald; sepals sometimes lobed; fruits globose, 1 cm./0.4 in. across, red, with erected sepals. 2n = 28. WR 105 (= *R. pratincola* Greene; *R. arkansana suffulta* Cockerell; *R. arkansanoides* Schneid.). E. and C. U.S.A. (Fig. 131).

R. blanda Ait. Related to *R. pendulina*. Shrub to 2m./6.6 ft. high, stems slender, brown, nearly unarmed, the scattered, straight prickles quickly drop, leaflets 5-7, elliptic to obovate-oblong, dull greyish-green, pale beneath and puberulent, coarsely and simply serrate; flowers 1-3 together, pink, 3-5 cm./1.2-2 in. across, May-June; pedicels and calyx bald; fruits globose or sometimes ellipsoid, 1 cm./0.4 in. thick, red. 2n = 14 (21, 28). WR 104; BB 1966; GSP 234. (= *R. fraxinifolia* Lindl.; *R. solandri* Tratt.). E. N. America; grows in wet, stony places. Variable. 1773. (Fig. 152)

R. × aschersoniana Graebn. (= *R. blanda* × *R. chinensis*). Shrub to 1.5 m./5 ft. high, strongly upright, stems with hooked prickles; leaves bright green; flowers very many together, but small, bright purple, late May to late June; sepals after anthesis spreading or reflexed, styles free, very unequal. 2n = 14. Originated with Zabel, Hann. Münden, Germany; about 1880.

R. pendulina L. Shrub 1-1.5 m./3.3-5 ft. high, stems mostly purple or green, often completely without prickles; leaflets 7-9, ovate-oblong, 2-6 cm./0.4-2.4 in. long, doubly glandular-serrate, hairy on both sides or

bald; flowers up to 5 together, but mostly solitary, purple or pink, 4 cm./1.6 in. across, May-June; sepals persistent, erect; fruits pendulous; ovoid to flask-shaped, bright red. 2n = 28. WR 99; KSR 2-3. (= *R. alpina* L.) S. and C. Europe, mountains. 1789. (Fig. 145).

"Plena" → 'Morlettii'

f. pyrenaica (Gouan) Keller. Lower, stems more bluish-green, only slightly purple; leaflets mostly ovate, glandular on the veins beneath like the doubly serrate margin; pedicels and calyx-tube always glandular-hispid. 2n = 28. BM 6724 (as *R. alpina*). Pyrenees. 1815.

R. × spinulifolia Dematra. (= *R. pendulina* × *R. tomentosa*). Shrub 1-3 m./3.3-10 ft. high; stems strong, branches, prickles unequal, partly needle-shaped, especially at the lower part of the stem, often absent on flowering branches; leaflets 5-7, medium-large, bald above, puberulent beneath; flowers pink, large; fruits flask-shaped, large, with weak bristles, with only 1-2 achenes. 2n = 28(?). KRS 38. (= *R. glabrata* Déségl.). Switzerland, Alsace, Hungary.

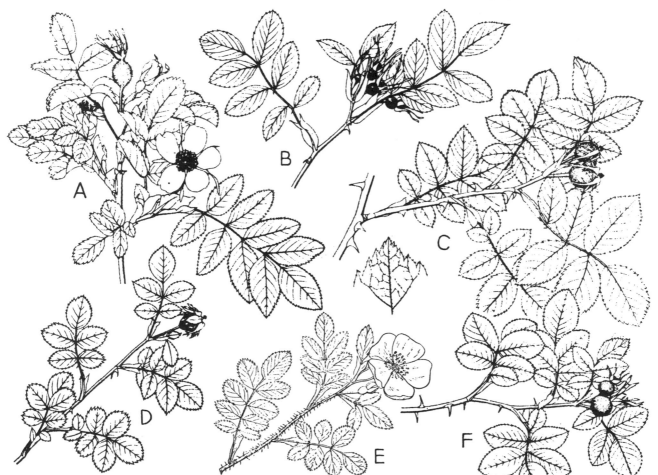

Figure 145.   A. *Rose pendulina*;   B. *R. glauca*;   C. *R. marginata*;   D. *R. obtusifolia*;   E. *R. arkansana*;   F. *R. sherardii*. (after Hess & Landolt)

R. oxyodon Boiss. Related to *R. pendulina*, but up to 2 m./6.6 ft. high or more, branches purplish, sparsely prickly; leaflets usually 9, elliptic, 2.5-5 cm./1-2 in. long, doubly serrate and often glandular, hairy on the veins beneath, midrib reddish; stipules large, margin glandular; flowers to 3-7 in corymbs, dark rose-pink, 5-6 cm./2-2.4 in. across, faintly scented, June; pedicels glandular-hispid; fruits ovoid to flask-shaped, red, smooth, nodding (not pendulous). 2n = 28. (= *R. pendulina* var. *oxyodon* [Boiss.] Rehd.) E. Caucasus. 1904.

f. **haematodes** (Crép.) Krüssman. To 3 m./10 ft. high, leaflets more glaucous, petioles reddish; flowers similar to the type, but corymbs smaller; fruits larger, flask-shaped, scarlet-red, pendulous. (= *R. pedulina* f. *haematodes* [Crép.] Krüssm.). Caucasus. 1863. Very valuable commercially.

R. × lheritieranea Thory. (= *R. chinensis* × ?). Climbing up to 4m./13.2 ft. high, stems with few prickles or unarmed, reddish on side exposed to the sun, otherwise green, prickles weak, yellowish; leaflets 3-7, ovate-oblong, simply serrate, bald; flowers many in corymbs along the branches, more or less double, flat saucer-shaped, red with white center, without scent, June; fruits globose, smooth. 2n = 14 (and 21?). WR 102 (= *R. reclinata* Thory; *R. boursaultiana* Desp.). Originated before 1820. As G.S. Thomas suggests, chromosone research is making the usual opinion, that the Boursault roses derived from hybrids between *R. chinensis* with *R. pedulina*, indefensible.

From the few cultivars which belong here, may be named: → 'Amadis', 'Morlettii', 'Mme. Sancy de Parabére'.

R. majalis Herrm. Shrub with suckers, upright, to 1.5 m./5 ft. high, stems slender, brown-red, often unarmed; prickles short and hooked, with 2 strong infrastipular prickles; leaflets 5-7, elliptic-oblong, dull green and hairy above, greyish and densely downy beneath; flowers 1-3 together, often solitary, crimson, to 5 cm./2 in. across, petals somewhat emarginate, May-June; sepals

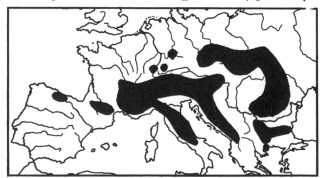

Figure 146. Distribution of *Rosa pendulina*. (after Browicz 1972)

Figure 147. *Rosa majalis* (= *R. cinnamomea* L.).

entire, narrow, finally erected and inclining; fruits depressed-globose, 1 cm./0.4 in. thick, dark red, smooth. 2n = 14, 28. WR 45; KSR 1 (= *R. cinnamomea* sensu L. [1759] not L. [1753]. nom. ambig.). N. and C. Europe to U.S.S.R. Cultivated before 1600. (Figs. 145, 147)

Following the rules of nomenclature the old designation "*R. cinnamomea*" cannot continue to be used, as this was originally a synonym for *R. pendulina*.

'Foecundissima'. Flowers pink, double. WR 45; BC 3450. (= *R. cinnamomea* f. *plena* West.; *R. foecundissima* Muenchh.). 1596.

R. davurica Pall. Shrub closely related to *R. majalis*, about 1 m./3.3 ft. high, stems nearly bald, prickles in infrastipular pairs, large, hooked, but otherwise straight and slender; leaflets 7, oblong-lanceolate, 3 cm./1.2 in. long, acute, doubly serrate, glandular and hairy beneath, pedicels hairy, stipules narrow; flowers 1-3 together, pink, June-July; sepals longer than petals, foliaceous at the top, persisting, margin hairy; fruits ovoid, 12 mm./0.5 in. long, smooth. 2n = 14. ICS 2224. (= *R. willldenowii* Spreng.). N. China; N.E. Asia. 1910.

R. laxa Retzius. Related to *R. majalis*; growth somewhat lower, stems with green bark, sometimes reddish, prickles hooked or straight, with broader base; leaflets 5-9, bald or hairy beneath, to 4 cm./1.6 in. long; flowers solitary or several together, white, July; sepals entire, persistent, pedicels glandular; fruits ovoid, red, 1.5 cm./0.6 in. long, sepals erected. 2n = 28. WR 53. (= *R. soongarica* Bge.; *R. gebleriana* Schrenk). Turkestan 1800. Not to be confused with the understock "*Rosa laxa*"; see *R. coriifolia* var. *froebelii*.

R. amblyotis C.A. Mey. Related to *R. majalis*, but branches with slender, straight and upright prickles; leaflets 7, rarely up to 9, elliptic-oblong, 3-5 cm./1.2-2 in. long, acute, sharply serrate; pedicels slender, 2 cm./0.8 in. long, bald; flowers red, 5 cm./2 in. across; fruits depressed-globose to more pear-shaped, 12 mm./0.5 in. thick. 2n = 14. Kamtchatka. 1917.

R. marettii Lév. Upright shrub, 1.5-2 m./5-6.6 ft. high, branches purple, with few, slender, upright curved, mostly paired prickles; leaflets 7-9, oblong, 2-3 cm./0.8-1.2 in. long, rather bald, simply serrate; flowers few together, pink, 4-5 cm./1.6-2 in. across, June; sepals dilated at the top, puberulent beneath, longer than the petals, persisting, pedicels bald; fruits globose, 12 mm./0.5 in. thick, red. 2n = 14. WR 162. (= *R. rubro-stipulata* Nakai). Saghalin. 1908.

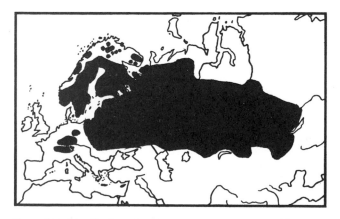

Figure 148. Distribution of *Rose majalis*. (after Meusel 1965)

R. pisocarpa A. Gray. Shrub to 2 m./6.6 ft. high, branches slender, arching, sparsely prickly, more bristly at the base, prickles very small; leaflets 5-7, elliptic-oblong, 1-4 cm./0.4-1.6 in. long, coarsely serrate, puberulent beneath; flowers in corymbs with foliaceous stipules, purplish-pink, to 3 cm./1.2 in. across, June-August; sepals glandular-hispid beneath; fruits globose, sometimes with short neck, orange, 8 mm./0.3 in. thick. 2n = 14, 21. WR 73. AFP 2510; HPN 3:172; GSR 36. W. N. America. 1882.

R. woodsii Lindl. Upright shrub, 1.5-2 m./5-6.6 ft. high, with many stems, purplish, afterwards grey, prickles many, slender, straight or somewhat curved, flowering branches less prickly; leaflets 5-7, obovate to more oblong, 1-3 cm./0.4-1.2 in. long, sharply and simply serrate, puberulent and glaucous beneath; stipules narrow, entire to serrate and without glands; flowers 1-3 together, pink, 3.5-4 cm./1.4-1.6 in. across, June-July, pedicels and calyx bald; fruits globose, mostly with distinct neck, 1 cm./0.4 in. thick. 2n = 14. WR 77; VP 447; HPN 3: 122. (= *R. deserta* Lunell; *R. sandbergii* Greene; *R. maximiliani* Nees). C. and W. N. America. 1880. Extremely variable species; formerly divided into many species by botanists (Fig. 149).

var. **fendleri** (Crép.) Rehd. Shrub lower, prickles slender, straight, stipules and pedicels glandular; leaflets mostly doubly serrate; flowers and fruits smaller. BB 1969; GSR 61; VP 448; WR 175. (= *R. fendleri* Crép.; *R. poetica* Lundell). W. N. America. 1888 (Fig. 149).

R. mohavensis Parish. Bald shrub, 0.5-1 m./1.7-3.3 ft. high, stems slender, prickles straight, scattered, flattened at base, floral branches short, more or less prickly; stipules entire, petiole and rachis with few prickles; leaflets generally 5, oval to elliptic, 5-15 mm./0.2-0.6 in. long, serrate; flowers solitary, rarely 2-3, pink, 2.5 cm./1 in. across, May-July; sepals caudate; fruits globose AFP 2525. California; moist places.

R. pyrifera Rydb. Very closely related to *R. woodsii*, and included by many authors, differing by pear-shaped fruits. Shrub 1 m./3.3 ft. high or more; prickles slender, straight, 4-8 mm./0.16-0.32 in. long; leaflets mostly 7, elliptic, 2-4 cm./0.8-1.6 in. long, coarsely serrate, dark green and bald above, puberulent and glandular beneath like the stipules; petioles and rachis puberulent, often also glandular; flowers in corymbs, white, 4-5 cm./1.6-2 in. across, June-July, petals obcordate; fruits ellipsoid to pear-shaped, with distinct neck, 1 cm./0.4 in. thick, 2 cm./0.8 in. long; sepals glandular. 2n = 14, 16. U.S.A., Rocky Mts., before 1931.

R. macounii Greene. Related to *R. woodsii,* but stems with straight prickles and bristly when young; leaflets obovate, glaucous and puberulent beneath; flowers small, blush; fruits depressed-globose. 2n = 14, 21. AFP 2513. (= *R. grosseserrata* E. Nelson; *R. subnuda* Lunell). W. N. America. Before 1826.

R. ultramontana (S. Wats.) Heller. Shrub 0.6-1.5 m./2-5 ft. high, branches with slender, mostly straight prickles or nearly unarmed; leaflets 5-7, elliptic, bald above, slightly puberulent and somewhat glandular beneath; flowers mostly 3-10 together, pink, 5 cm./2 in. across, June-July; sepals lanceolate, not glandular; petals ob-

cordate; fruits globose, red, small, smooth. 2n = 14. AFP 2510; HPN 3:172. (= *R. californica* var. *ultramontana* Wats.). N. America, Brit. Col. to California and Nevada. 1888. (Fig. 149).

R. pinetorum Heller. Shrub 0.5-1 m./1.7-3.3 ft. high, stems slender, upright, with straight, terete prickles, shoots often bristly; stipules pilose and glandular beneath, rachis pilose and glandular; leaflets 5-7, broadly elliptic, 1-3 cm./0.4-1.2 in. long, pilose and glandular beneath, densely serrate, teeth gland-tipped, pedicels bald; flowers 4 cm./1.6 in. across, deep rose, petals obovate, May-July; fruit 12 mm./0.5 in. thick. AFP

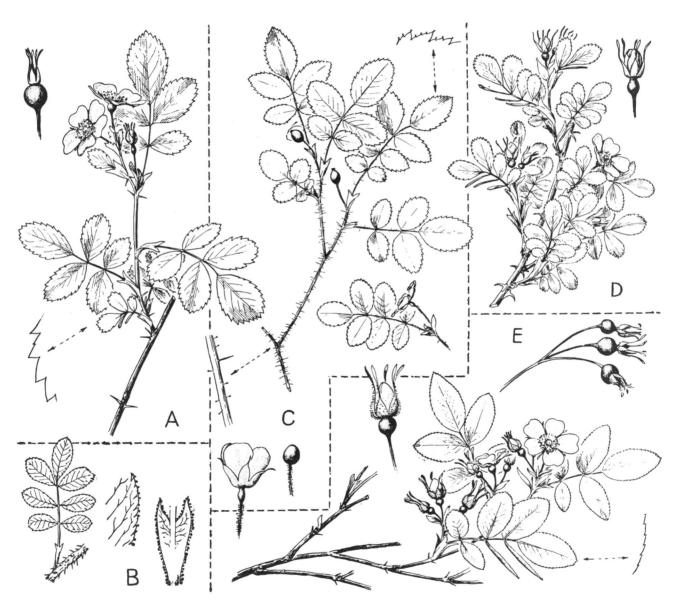

Figure 149. A. *Rosa woodsii*; B. *R. woodsii* var. *fendleri*; C. *R. gymnocarpa*; D. *R. ultramontana*; E. *R. pisocarpa*. (after Gleason)

2504. California; open woodland. May not be in cultivation now.

R. californica Cham. & Schlechtend. Shrub to 3 m./10 ft. high, stems with flat, curved prickles, young branches sometimes bristly; flowering branches mostly prickly; leaflets 5-7, broadly elliptic, 1-3 cm./0.4-1.2 in. long, simply serrate (not glandular), dull green and adpressed-hairy above, villous beneath; flowers in corymbs, with stipules, dark rose, 4 cm./1.6 in. across, June-August; sepals outside villous, pedicels villous or bald; fruits small, globose, with distinct neck, 1-1.5 cm./0.4-0.6 in. thick. 2n = 14, 28. AFP 2509. California. 1571.

'**Ardens**' (Späth). Flowers crimson-red, 6-7 cm./2.4-2.8 in. across, anthers golden yellow, June. Originated before 1930 with L. Späth, Berlin, from seed.

'**Nana**'. Growth dwarf; flowers pink, single. 1914.

'**Plena**'. Shrub to 2 m./6.6 ft. high; branches arching; flowers loosely double, warm rose to bright crimson, fragrant, June-July. GSR 4. (= *R.* 'Theano' Geschwind). 1894.

R. gratissima Greene. Shrub 1-2 m./3.3-6.6 ft. high, stems much branched, densely covered with straight prickles and bristles, the larger often infrastipular; stipules hairy, entire or dentate; leaflets 5-7, elliptic, 1-3 cm./0.4-1.2 in. long, bald above, hairy beneath; flowers in corymbs, pink, April-May; fruits globose, 8 mm./0.3 in. thick. AFP 2512. California.

R. nutkana Pall. Shrub to 1.5 m./5 ft. high, upright, stems slender, dark brown, strictly upright, prickles large and straight, young branches mostly bristly; leaflets 5-9, broadly elliptic, 2-5 cm./0.8-2 in. long, dark green and bald above, slightly glandular-hairy beneath, doubly glandular-serrate; flowers mostly solitary, purple, 5-6 cm./2-2.4 in. across, June-July; pedicels mostly glandular-hispid, calyx smooth; fruits globose, red, to 2 cm./0.8 in. thick, smooth. 2n = 42. WR 75; AFP 2503; VP 440; BC 3452. W. N. America, coast from Alaska to N. California.

var. **hispida** Fern. Fruits glandular-hispid; leaflets more coarsely serrate. NPN3: 172; AF 250 (as *R. macdougalii*); (= *R. macdougalii* Holzinger). Brit. Col. to Utah.

R. nutkana has only rarely been used in hybridizing; the best known hybrid is '**Cantab**' (Hurst 1927) = *R. nutkana* × 'Red-Letter Day'; shrub 1.5-2 m./5-6.6 ft. high; foliage dark green; flowers solitary, dark rose with white center, 8 cm./3.2 in. across, saucer-shaped, anthers yellow, non-recurrent.

R. spaldingii Crép. Shrub 1 m./3.3 ft. high, stems upright, with straight infrastipular prickles, 5-10 mm./0.2-0.4 in. long, young shoots bristly, flowering branches bald, sparsely prickly; petiole and rachis hairy, leaflets 5-7, elliptic or broadly so, 1-1.5/ cm./0.4-0.6 in. long, coarsely toothed, rarely doubly, scarcely glandular, light green and bald above, pale and hairy beneath; flowers solitary, pedicels and calyx-tube bald, sepals lanceolate-caudate, entire or with foliaceous tips, bald; flowers solitary or few together, pink, 5 cm./2 in. across, May-July; fruits globose, 12 mm./0.5 in. thick, red. AFP 2506. W.N. America.

R. corymbulosa Rolfe. Shrub to 2 m./6.6 ft. high, upright or sometimes procumbent, with few, slender, straight prickles or unarmed; leaflets 3-5, ovate-oblong, 2-4 cm./0.8-1.6 in. long, acute, densely serrulate, dull green and at first slightly puberulent above, bald and hairy beneath, autumn color purple, stipules ciliate-glandular; flowers many, in large corymbs, red with white eye, 20-25 mm./0.8-1 in. across, June-July; pedicels and calyx glandular-hispid, fruits ovoid-globose, scarlet, 1-1.3 cm./0.4-0.5 in. long. 2n = 14. BM 8566. W. China. Very decorative species with small flowers, but very floriferous.

R. davidii Crép. Shrub to 3 m./10 ft. high, stems with stout, straight, 4-6 mm./0.16-0.24 in. long, scattered prickles, with much enlarged base; leaflets 7-9 (-11), elliptic-oblong, 2-4 cm./0.8-1.6 in. long, simply serrate, bald above, glaucous and hairy beneath; flowers in corymbs, pink, 4-5 cm./1.6-2 in. across, June-July, pedicels and calyx glandular-hispid, styles 3 mm./0.1 in. exserted; fruits ovoid with long neck, to 2 cm./0.8 in. long, scarlet. 2n = 28. BM 8679. W. China. 1908.

var. **elongata** Rehd. & Wils. Leaflets 5-7 cm./2-2.8 in. long, flowers less numerous, fruits to 2.5 cm./1 in. long (= *R. macrophylla* var. *robusta* Focke). 1908.

R. caudata Baker. Shrub to 4 m./13 ft. high, stems with scattered, stout, straight, to 8 mm./0.3 in. long prickles, much enlarged at the base; leaflets 7-9, ovate-elliptic, 2.5-5 cm./1-2 in. long, simply serrate, stipules glandular-ciliate; flowers few together in corymbs, red, 3.5-5 cm./1.4-2 in. across, June; pedicels and calyx glandular-hispid, rarely nearly bald; sepals entire, caudate, foliaceous at the top; fruits oblong-ovoid, with long neck, 2.5 cm./1 in. long, orange-red, sepals erected. 2n = 14. WR 163. W. China. About 1896.

R. banksiopsis Baker. Similar to *R. caudata*, but less prickly, stems in the upper half often unarmed; leaflets 7-9, oblong, mostly puberulent beneath, simply serrate;

flowers in broad corymbs, pink, 2.5 cm./1 in. across, June-July; sepals longer than petals, foliaceous at the top, bald beneath, persistent, pedicels bald; fruits red, flask-shaped. 2n = 14. WR 505. W. China. 1907. Little different from *R. caudata*.

R. macrophylla Lindl. Shrub 3-4 m./10-13 ft. high, branches dark red, with few light brown, stout, straight prickles; leaves to 20 cm./8 in. long; leaflets 9-11, ovate to elliptic, to 4 cm./1.6 in. long, acute, puberulent beneath; flowers 1-3 together, bright red, to 5 cm./2 in. across, pedicels and calyx glandular-hispid or bald; fruits flask-shaped, red, to 3 cm./1.2 in. long, bristly. 2n = 14. WR 50. Himalayas. 1918.

'Glaucescens' (= Forrest No. 14958). Branches bloomy; leaves glaucous on both sides, narrower than those of 'Rubricaulis'; flowers purplish-pink. Introduced by Hillier.

'Rubricaulis' (= Forrest No. 15309). Stems distinctly red with bluish-white bloom; petioles, pedicels, stipules and midrib distinctly red. Not as hardy as the type. Introduced by Hillier.

R. × coryana Hurst (= *R. macrophylla* × *R. roxburghii*). Shrub, strong growing, to 2.5 m./8.3 ft. high, densely bushy; stems similar to *R. macrophylla*, few prickles; leaves similar to *R roxburghii*; flowers dark pink, single, 5-7 cm./2-2.8 in. across, June; 2n = 14. GSR 154. (= *R. macrophylla coryana*). Originated 1926 in the Botanic Garden, Cambridge. Used for hybridizing by S. McGredy; often erroneously spelled "R. koreana" in nursery catalogues.

R. setipoda Hemsl. & Wils. Upright shrub, 3 m./10 ft. high (to 5 m./16.5 ft. when under cultivation), with many stems, with few, but very large, stout, straight prickles, to 8 mm./0.3 in. long, with enlarged base; leaflets 7-9, elliptic, bald or glandular-hairy, mostly deeply and simply serrate; stipules large, densely glandular-ciliate, rachis glandular and slightly prickly; flowers up to 12 or more in corymbs, pink, to 5 cm./2 in. across, June; sepals caudate with foliaceous tips; petals outside slightly puberulent; calyx glandular, pedicels glandular-hispid; fruits flask-shaped with neck, red, 2.5 cm./1 in. long, to 6-7 cm./2.4-2.8 in. long under cultivation (perhaps hybridized with *R. moyesii*?). BM 8569. (= *R. macrophylla* var. *crasseaculeata* Vilm.). C. China. 1895.

R. persetosa Rolfe. Similar to *R. setipoda*, but stems densely bristly, also the flowering branches; 1.5 m./5 ft. high; leaflets 5-9, about 2-5 cm./0.8-2 in. long, simply serrate, downy beneath like the rachis; flowers in large

corymbs, dark pink, 2-3 cm./0.8-1.2 in. across, June; pedicels and calyx bald; sepals entire. 2n = 14. J. RHS 27:487. (= *R. macrophylla* var. *acicularis* Vilm.). C. China. 1895. Not to be confused with *R. elegantula* var. *persetosa*.

R. hemsleyana Täckholm. Shrub to 2 m./6.6 ft., stems with few prickles, prickles short, straight, with large base; leaflets 7-9, elliptic, 2-5 cm./0.8-2 in. long, doubly glandular-serrate, bald or puberulent on the veins beneath; stipules large, glandular-ciliate; rachis glandular; flowers 3-11 together, pink, 3-5 cm./1.2-2 in. across, June; pedicels 1-3 cm./0.4-1.2 in. long, densely glandular-hispid; sepals caudate with long, serrate top; fruits ovoid-oblong, with long neck, 2.5 cm./1 in. long. 2n = 42. BM 8569 (as *R. setipoda*). C. China. 1904.

R. sweginzowii Koehne. Shrub to 5 m./16.5 ft. high, stems densely covered with large, flattened, triangular, unequal prickles; leaflets 7-11, elliptic, to ovate-oblong, 2-5 cm./0.8-2 in. long, doubly serrate, fresh green and bald above, puberulent beneath, more densely on the veins, rachis prickly; flowers 1-3 together, bright pink, 4 cm./1.6 in. across, June; pedicels and calyx glandular-hispid; sepals only slightly lobed and serrate; fruits flask-shaped, bright red to scarlet, 2.5 cm./1 in. long. 2n = 42. GSR 58, 59. N. China. 1909. (Fig. 139).

'Macrocarpa'. Selection with larger fruits, to 5 cm./2 in. long and 2 cm./0.8 in. thick; otherwise like the type. Originated at the Rosarium, Sangerhausen, Germany.

R. wardii Mulligan ("White Moyesii"). Shrub upright, about 1.5 m./5 ft. high or more, tops of branches nodding, young stems glaucous; leaves bright green; leaflets 7-11, ovate-elliptic; flowers 1-3 together, white with dark brown center, otherwise like *R. moyesii*; fruits small. (= *R. setipoda* var. *inermis* Marquand & Shaw). S.E. Tibet. The type is not in cultivation, only a plant collected by F. Kingdon Ward (K.W. 6101), named 'Culta'; flowers 3-3.5 cm./1.2-1.4 in. across; pedicels often glandular. 2n = 42. 1924. Similar to *R. sweginzowii*, but flowers white and branches nearly unarmed.

R. murielae Rehd. & Wils. Shrub upright or broad, 1.5-3 m./5-10 ft. high, stems slender, reddish, with few slender, straight prickles or unarmed; leaflets 9-15, elliptic to oblong, 2 cm./0.8 in. long, glandular-dentate, hairy on the midrib beneath, petiole woolly and bristly, stipules bald; flowers in small corymbs, white, 2-2.5 cm./0.8-1 in. across, June-July; sepals 15 mm./0.6

in. long, accuminate, foliaceous at the top; persistent, densely hairy or bald outside; petals orbicular; pedicels very slender, 2.5 cm./1 in. long, often glandular; fruits flask-shaped, 15 mm./0.6 in. long, orange-red. 2n = 28. W. China. Rare in cultivation.

R. moyesii Hemsl. & Wils. Shrub to 3 m./10 ft. high, stems red-brown, prickles yellowish, paired, straight; leaflets 7-13, ovate-elliptic, 1-4 cm./0.4-1.6 in. long, serrulate, quite bald except the puberulent midrib; flowers several together, dark wine-red, 5-6 cm./2-2.4 in. across, stamens golden-yellow, June; petals obcordate, pedicels glandular-hispid like the occasionally bald calyx; sepals ovate, caudate; fruits flask-shaped, with distinct neck, 5-6 cm./2-2.4 in. long, dark orange-red, sepals erected. 2n = 42. ICS 2225; WR 74; BM 8338; GSR 30. W. China, Szechuan; discovered 1890, introduced 1894 and 1903. (Fig. 150). To this belong:

'**Fargesii**'. This is a tetraploid form with shorter, more obtuse leaflets; most of the hybrid *moyesii* have this form as one of their parents. Not to be confused with *R. fargesii* Bouleng., which is not in cultivation, and is closely related to *R. moschata.* 2n = 28.

Hybrids of *R. moyesii*: — 'Eddie's Crimson', 'Eddie's Jewel', 'Eos', 'Fred Streeter', 'Geranium', 'Heart of Gold', 'Langley Gem', 'Nevada', 'Sealing Wax' and 'Superba'.

Figure 150. a. *Rosa moyesii*; b. *R. willmottiae*. (after Bot. Mag.)

R. holodonta Stapf. Very similar to *R. moyesii*, but leaflets to 5 cm./2 in. long, 2.5 cm./1 in. across, loosely hairy beneath, especially on the veins; flowers pink, 5 cm./2 in. across, solitary or 2-6 together; fruits flask-shaped, red to scarlet, smooth to hispid, to 6 cm./2.4 in. long. 2n = 28. BM 9248; GSR 25. (= *R. moyesii* f. *rosea* Rehd. & Wils.). W. China. 1908.

R. × wintoniensis Hillier. (= *R. moyesii* × *R. setipoda*). Very similar to *R. holodonta*; 2 m./6.6 ft. high, branches arching, leaves smell similar to those of *R. rubiginosa*; flowers crimson with white center, velvety, to 7-10 together, June; fruits large, flask-shaped. 2n = 42. Originated 1928 with Hillier, Winchester.

R. × highdownensis Hillier. (= *R. moyesii* × ?). High shrub, similar to *R. moyesii*, but flowers crimson-red with white center on arching branches; fruits large, flask-shaped. 2n = 42; GSR 23; 24; GiS 2. Originated 1925 with Sir Fred. Stern, Highdown, England.

R. bella Rehd. & Wils. Closely related to *R. moyesii*, but stems bristly, leaflets smaller, flowers pink; shrub to 2.5 m./8.3 ft. high, prickles less numerous, straight; leaflets 7-9, elliptic, glaucous, bald, midrib beneath glandular, simply serrate; flowers 1-3, pink, scentless, 4-5 cm./1.6-2 in. across, June; petals obcordate, pedicels glandular-hispid, fruits ellipsoid or ovoid, tapering to the top, orange-scarlet, glandular-hispid. 2n = 28. ICS 2226. N. China. 1910.

R. webbiana Royle. Shrub, 1.5-2 m./5-6.6 ft. high, stems slender, with few, straight, yellowish, paired prickles; leaflets 5-9, roundish to broadly elliptic, 1.5-2 cm./0.6-0.8 in. long, simply serrate, bald or slightly puberulent beneath, base entire; petiole often prickly-glandular, stipules glandular-ciliate; flowers 1-3 together, pink, 4-5 cm./1.6-2 in. across, June, sepals glandular, often hairy outside, mostly dilated at the top, shorter than petals, persisting; fruits flask-shaped, to 2.5 cm./1 in. long, scarlet. 2n = 14. WR 76; GiS 4. (= *R. unguicularis* Bertol.; *R. guilelmi-waldemarii* Klotzsch). W. Himalayas; Afghanistan, Turkestan. 1879.

R. fedtschenkoana Regel. Shrub 1-1.6 m./3.3-5.3 ft. high, stems upright, bristly, prickles mostly straight and paired, leaflets 5-7, elliptic, 2.5 cm./1 in. long, acute, serrulate, glaucous on both sides, petioles slightly hispid; flowers 1-4 together at the top of branchlets, mostly white, 5 cm./2 in. across, with unpleasant scent,

June-July; sepals glandular beneath, persisting, tops filiform, calyx and pedicels glandular; fruits pear-shaped, red, 1.5 cm./0.6 in. long. 2n = 28. WR 49; BM 7770; GSR 15. Turkestan, C. Asia. Found by Olga Fedtschenko; later distributed by the Botan. Gardens, Petersburg, Russia.

R. sertata Rolfe. Similar to *R. webbiana*, but flowers larger, more intensely colored, growth taller and looser, leaflets more serrate. Shrub 0.7-2 m./2.3-6.6 ft. high, stems red-brown, with glaucous bloom, arching, with few, straight, mostly paired prickles; leaves 6-10 cm./2.4-4 in. long, leaflets 7-11, elliptic, 1.5-2 cm./0.6-0.8 in. long, sharply serrate, glaucous and bald beneath; flowers up to 4 together on short branches, pink, 3-5 cm./1.2-2 in. across, June; sepals pointed, entire, persisting; calyx smooth or hispid; fruits ovoid, 2 cm./0.8 in. long, dark red. 2n = 14. ICS 2227; BM 8473; D. RHS 1820. (= *R. macrophylla* f. *gracilis* Focke). W. China; Kansu, Yunnan. 1904.

R. pricei Hayata. Upright shrub, branches with scattered prickles, nearly bald to slightly bristly; leaflets mostly 7, thin leathery, ovate-oblong, 1-2 cm./0.4-0.8 in. long, 6-8 mm./0.2-0.3 in. across, terminal one largest, acute at both ends, serrulate, especially towards the top; stipules linear, adnate, ciliate-serrate; flowers few together in short corymbs, white, 2.5 cm./1 in. across, petals obovate, emarginated; styles united to a long exserting column, densely villous; sepals reflexed, lanceolate, hispid on both sides, fruit globose. Taiwan; mountains, 1,500-2,000 m./5,000-6,600 ft.

R. giraldii Crép. Closely related to *R. sertata*; 1-2 m./3.3-6.6 ft. high, branches with slender, straight, often paired prickles, sometimes unarmed; leaflets 7 (-9), suborbicular to ovate, hairy on both sides, sometimes glandular beneath, serrate; flowers solitary or 3-5 together, pink, 2.5 cm./1 in. across, June-July; pedicels short, glandular-hispid like the calyx, sepals persisting, glandular; pedicels very short, glandular-hispid; fruits ovoid, 1 cm./0.4 in. long, scarlet. 2n = 14. C. and N. China. 1897.

R. prattii Hemsl. Shrub 1-2 m./3.3-6.6 ft. high, stems purplish, bald, unarmed or with few straight, slender, bright yellow prickles; leaves 5-7 cm./2-2.8 in. long, leaflets 11-15, ovate-lanceolate (1-) 2 cm./(0.4-) 0.8 in. long, obtusely serrate, hairy on the veins beneath; flowers 3-7 together in corymbs, pink, 2.5 cm./in across,

June-July; sepals abruptly pointed, hairy on both sides, finally dropping; fruits ovoid, scarlet, glandular-hispid. 2n = 14. W. China. 1908. Similar to *R. davidii*, but inflorescences smaller.

R. × 'Prattigosa' (Kordes 1953). (= *R. prattii* × *R. rugosa*). Shrub to 4 m./13 ft. high and 5 m./16.5 ft. across, bushy; leaves bright green, firm; flowers pink, single, very large, slightly scented, floriferous; buds red, pointed; fruits depressed-globose, similar to *R. rugosa*, but smaller and less numerous.

R. elegantula Rolfe. Pretty shrub, 1-1.5 m./ 3.3-5 ft. high, but up to 2 m./6.6 ft. across with suckers, young branches densely covered with red bristles, few prickles; leaflets 7-9, ovate-elliptic, 1.2-1.8 cm./0.5-0.7 in. long, glaucous on both sides, autumn color purple to crimson, simply serrate, rachis slightly glandular, stipules narrow, glandular at the margin; flowers solitary or few together, but floriferous, pink, 2.5 cm./1 in. across, June; sepals puberulent, persisting; fruits ovoid, coral-red, very numerous. 2n = 14. BM 8877. (= *R. farreri* Stapf). W. China. 1900.

Rehder and Shepherd use *R. farreri* Stapf. synonymously with this, while *Modern Roses 7*, Mulligan in *R.H.S Dict. of Gard.* 4: 1951 and Bean take this to be a different species. This text follows Rehder, as the distinguishing characteristics are insignificant.

f. **persetosa** Stapf. Growth generally lower, stems more bristly, prickles reddish; leaves smaller, flowers smaller, salmon-pink to whitish, buds coral-pink. GSR 14. This is the "Threepenny-bit-Rose", selected by E.A. Bowles from seeds, collected 1915 by R. Farrer in S. Kansu, China.

R. forrestiana Bouleng. Shrub to 1 m./3.3 ft. high, stems strictly upright, prickles paired, straight or curved upward, brown; leaflets 5-7, ovate to obovate, 1-2 cm./0.4-0.8 in. long, apex rounded, simply serrate, bald or hairy on midrib beneath; flowers solitary or few together, pink, 2-3 cm./0.4-1.2 in. across, June-July; sepals small, filiform, persisting; stipules large, ovate-roundish, glandular; styles exserting; pedicels 8-15 mm./0.3-0.6 in. long, glandular-hispid. GSR 17; GiS 1. W. China. Similar to *R. multibracteata*, but lower and less floriferous.

R. multibracteata Hemsl. & Wils. Shrub 2.5-4 m./8.3-13.2 ft. high, branches slender, arching, prickles paired, straight, slender; leaflets 7-9, broadly ovate, 5-15 mm./0.2-0.6 in. long, doubly serrate, dull green above, greyish beneath, mostly bald; flowers solitary or several together in narrow, terminal, to 30 cm./12 in. long panicles; pink, 3 cm./1.2 in. across, with many crowded bracts, July; fruits ovoid, about 1.5 cm./0.6 in. long, glandular-hispid like the pedicel, orange-red, late to mature. 2n = 28. WR 158 (as *R. reducta*). (= *R. reducta* Baker). W. China, Szechuan. 1910.

R. willmottiae Hemsl. Shrub to 3 m./10 ft. high, stems long and arching, branched, shoots brown-red, very bloomy, with paired, straight prickles; leaflets 2-9, elliptic to orbicular, 6-15 mm./0.2-0.6 in. long, densely and mostly doubly serrate, bald; flowers mostly solitary, along the branches, purplish-pink, darker in bud, 3 cm./1.2 in. across, slightly scented, June; sepals dropping; fruits ovoid, 1.8 cm./0.7 in. long, orange-red. 2n = 14. WR 177; BM 8186; GSR 60. W. China. 1904. (Fig. 150).

R. transmorrisonensis Hayata. Low, evergreen shrub, branches bald, with scattered, 4-5 mm./0.16-0.2 in. long prickles; leaflets 7, terminal one often largest, obovate to ovate-oblong, 4-11 mm./0.2-0.4 in. long, 2-7.5 mm./0.1-0.3 in. across, acute, serrate, veins impressed, rachis prickly; stipules linear, adnate, margin fringed; flowers solitary at the tops of branches, petals obcordate, emarginate, styles filiform, much exserted; sepals ovate, villous, 9 mm./0.4 in. long. Taiwan, mountains, 3,000 m./10,000 ft. (Fig. 124).

R. × pruhoniciana Kriechbaum (= *R. moyesii × R. willmottiae*). Strong-growing shrub, densely branched, very similar to *R. willmottiae*, but flowers deep brownish-red; fruits persisting long after leaves have dropped. 2n = 35. GSR 40 (= *R. hillieri* Hillier). Originated with F. Zeman. Pruhonice near Prague. C.S.S.R. 1924.

R. spithamea S. Wats. Low shrub, 0.1-0.3 m./0.3-1 ft. high, stems from creeping rootstock, with straight, terete, infrastipular prickles and bristles, stipules glandular-ciliate, petioles and rachis glandular and prickly; leaflets 5, elliptic-suborbicular, 1-3.5 cm./0.4-1.4 in. long, doubly serrate, teeth gland-tipped, glabrate or sparingly hairy above, glandular-pruinose beneath; flowers mostly solitary, pink, June-August; fruits subglobose, 8 mm./0.3 in. thick, densely glandular-hispid. AFP 2616. California.

R. sonomensis Greene. Very similar to *R. spithamea* in habit and size, but leaflets broadly ovate to orbicular, 5-15 mm./0.2-0.6 in. long, doubly serrate with glandular teeth, bald on both sides, firm, somewhat glaucous;

flowers few, in dense corymbs, bright pink, 3 cm./1.2 in. across, May-August; AFP 2517. (= *R. spithamea* var. *sonomensis* Jepson). California. Not known to be in cultivation.

R. gymnocarpa Nutt. Shrub 0.5-1 m./1.7-3.3 ft. high, stems bald, with slender, paired prickles, bristly; leaflets 5-9, bald, rather distant, ovate-elliptic to orbicular, sharply doubly serrate and glandular; flowers solitary or 2 together, pink, to 3 cm./1.2 in. across, June-July; sepals ovate, pointed, dropping; pedicels bald to glandular-hispid; fruits globose, 6-8 mm./0.2-0.3 in. thick, with many small achenes. 2n = 14. WR 71; HPN 3:172. W.N. America. 1893. One of the few roses which tolerate shade.

R. beggeriana Schrenk. Shrub up to 2.5 m./8.3 ft. high, with many stems, very branched; stems with paired, hooked, scattered prickles; leaflets 5-9, ovate-elliptic to obovate, 8-25 mm./0.3-1 in. long, simply serrate, glaucous to greyish-green and mostly puberulent beneath; flowers several together or many in corymbs, white, 2-3 cm./0.8-1.2 in. across, June; pedicels glandular to bald; fruits nearly globose, red, finally dark reddish-purple, 6-8 mm./0.2-0.3 in. thick; sepals dropping. 2n = 14. WR 54. (= *R. regelii* Reuter; *R. silverhjelmii* Schrenk). N. Persia to Altai Mts. and Soongaria. 1868.

Very difficult to hybridize; the best garden form is '**Polstjärnan**' (Wasastjärna 1932); very strong-growing, to 5 m./16.5 ft. high, extremely hardy; flowers very small, many together in large corymbs, white, non-recurrent.

Section 6. Synstylae (DC.) Rehd.
Stems climbing, trailing or prostrate; rarely upright; stipules mostly adnate to the petiole, rarely filiform, free and caducous; flowers in corymbs; sepals reflexed after anthesis, outer sepals pinnatisect or all entire, dropping; styles nearly always connate into a slender column, exserting the flat and conical discus:

R. multiflora, iwara, taiwanensis, rehderiana, setigera, anemoneflora, helenae, rubus, mulliganii, brunonii, moschata, longicuspis, sambucina, dupontii, sinowilsoniana, cerasocarpa, maximowicziana, filipes, phoenicia, soulieana, henryi, wichuraiana, jacksonii, kordesii, luciae, sempervirens, arvensis, ruga, polliniana.

R. multiflora Thunb. Shrub 3 m./10 ft. high and broad, very strong growing, densely branched, climbing; stems moderately prickly, sometimes nearly unarmed; leaflets mostly 9, obovate to oblong, 2-3 cm./0.8-1.2 in. long, retained through the autumn; flowers many, in conical panicles, white, 2 cm./0.8 in. across, June-July; sepals ovoid, abruptly pointed, styles bald; fruits 7 mm./0.3

in. thick, red. 2n = 14. ICS 2228; BC 3435. (= *R. polyantha* S. & Z.). Japan, Korea. 1862. Useful for dense hedges, but even more so as an understock for budding, especially the nearly unarmed type "Thornless Multiflora" (Fig. 151).

'Carnea'. Descendent of *f. cathayensis*, but flowers double, pink. BM 1059. (= *R. florida* Pour.). 1804.

f. **cathayensis** Rehd. & Wils. Flowers blush. 2-4 cm./0.8-1.6 in. across, in rather flat corymbs; pedicels bald or slightly glandular. 2n = 14. WR 171; GSR 18. (= *R. gentiliana* Lév. & Van.). China. 1907.

'Nana' (Lille 1891). Shrub 0.6-0.8 m./2-2.6 ft. high, not climbing; flowers white to pink, semi-double, sometimes with some double flowers, flowering through the summer; fruits red, like the type. (= *R. polyantha nana* Hort.; *R. carteri* Hort.). Originated 1891 from seed with Léonard Lille, at Lyon-Villeurbanne, France, and was introduced into commerce under the name "Rose multiflore naine remontante", and is still found in some seed catalogues. The young seedlings can commence flowering when only 15-20 cm./6-8 in. high.

'Platyphylla'. Very strong growing cultivar with small, partly pink, partly crimson-red, double flowers in corymbs, the single flowers much larger than in *R. multiflora*. 2n = 14. SOR 37. (= *R. thoryi* Tratt.; *R. platyphylla* [Thory] Takasima not Rau). Introduced from China about 1817. Also known in Great Britain as the "Seven Sisters Rose", because the seven (usually more numerous) flowers of the corymb may show seven different tones between pink and crimson, depending on their age. GiS 24.

'Watsoniana'. Shrub, about 1 m./3.3 ft. high, leaflets only 3-5, very long and narrow, margin undulate, somewhat resembling a bamboo; few flowers, in large panicles, the single flower is small, white to blush, June; fruits red, 7 mm./0.3 in. thick. 2n = 14. BC 3437; WR 16. (= *R. watsoniana* Crép.; *R. multiflora* f. *watsoniana* [Crép.] Matsum.). Japan; only known in cultivation.

Rosa multiflora has much been used in breeding; its descendents, which usually bloom only once (June-July), mostly exhibit upright growth while the *wichuraiana* hybrids are widely arching or prostrate, and so must be tied up.

Important descendents of *R. multiflora*: → 'Aglaia', 'Crimson Rambler', 'Paul's Scarlet Climber', 'Tausendschön' (= 'Thousand Beauties'), 'Veilchenblau' (= 'Violet Blue'), etc.

R. × iwara Sieb. (= *R. multiflora × R. rugosa*). Interme-

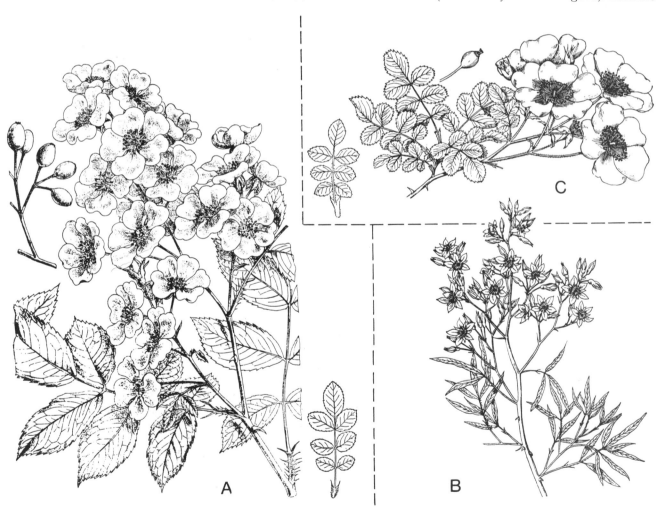

Figure 151.   A. *Rosa multiflora*,   B. *R. multiflora watsoniana*,   C. *R. wichuraiana*. (after Garden and Forest)

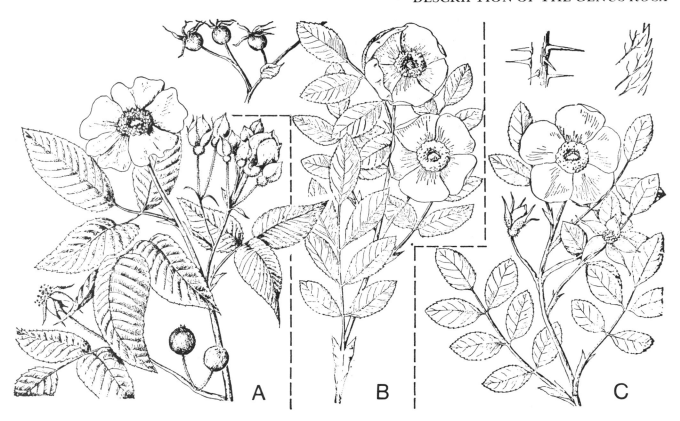

Figure 152. A. *Rosa setigera*; B. *R. blanda*; C. *R. carolina*. (after Gleason, The New Britton & Brown)

diate between parents; growth expanded, stems grey-tomentose, with large, hooked prickles; leaflets 5-7, elliptic, grey-tomentose beneath; stipules with long, bristly teeth; flowers small, but many in corymbs, white. 2n = 14. WR 61. (= *R. yesoensis* [Franch. & Sav.] Makino). Wild hybrid in Japan. 1832 introduced into Europe by Siebold. No ornamental value. (iwara = Japanese for rose prickle).

R. taiwanensis Nakai. Upright shrub, branches slender, with scattered, hooked prickles; leaflets (5)-7, ovate to oblong, 1.5-3.5 cm./0.6-1.4 in. long, acute on both ends, serrate, especially towards apex, dark green and bald above, slightly puberulent along the midrib beneath; stipules adnate, margin ciliate; flowers in corymbs 10 cm./4 in. across, white, 2.5 cm./1 in. across, petals emarginate; styles connate into a long, exserted, densely villous column; fruits globose 6-7 mm./0.2-0.3 in. thick. Taiwan, in mountains, 2,500 m./8,300 ft. (Fig. 134)

R. × rehderiana Blackburn. This is the botanical designation for the so-called Polyantha roses, the combination *R. chinensis × R. multiflora* (= *R. polyantha* Carr.).

This name seems unsuitable, since these two species are not only the parents of our modern Polyantha roses, but of some others as well. Some characteristics of the Polyantha roses can be recognized in the following varieties:

'Eblouissant' (*R. chinensis*); 'Masquerade' (*R. foetida bicolor*); 'Florence Mary Morse' (*R. rubiginosa*); 'Pinocchio' (*R. moschata*); 'Langley Gem' (*R. moyesii*); 'Floradora' (*R. multibracteata*); 'Orange Triumph' (*R. wichuraiana*); 'Cinnabar' (*R. roxburghii*) and 'Erna Grootendorst' (*R. rugosa*).

In the course of the breeding development of the Polyantha roses different classes or groups arose, which are differentiated in the horticultural language, as well as internationally with all rose growers, as follows:

Polyantha (the "true" Polyantha rose). Flowers rather small, but very numerous, in large corymbs, e.g. 'Ruby', 'Paul Crampel', 'Dick Koster', 'Orléans-Rose', 'Orange Triumph', etc.

Floribunda. Flowers large, similar to Hybrid Teas, in larger or smaller clusters, e.g. 'Independence', 'Red Favorite', 'Gruss an Aachen', etc.

Grandiflora. Flowers very large, on long stems, corymbs with only few flowers; growth very strong; leaves dark green, very healthy; e.g. 'Queen Elizabeth'.

Today, the designation "Hybrid Polyantha" for the older Floribundas, while still used in Europe, is seldom used in the United States and

283

Great Britain. In this book they are all called "Floribunda" in the "Dictionary" (p. 303).

R. setigera Michx. Prairie Rose. Shrub 1-2 m./3.3-6.6 ft. high, climbing, stems bald, with strong, slightly curved prickles; leaflets mostly 3(-5), ovate-oblong, 3-9 cm./1.2-3.6 in. long, serrate, bright green above, greyish-green and hairy on the veins beneath; flowers few, dark pink, 5-6 cm./2-2.4 in. across, in loose corymbs; petioles glandular, pedicels mostly bald, June-August; fruits small, globose, glandular-hispid, brownish-green. 2n = 14. WR 23; BC 3438; BB 1965; VP 442. (= *R. trifoliata* Donn). N. America, from the Atlantic coast to the Rocky Mts. 1810. (Fig. 152)

Widely used for breeding hardy climbing roses, especially 100 years ago. Shepherd draws attention to the fact that this rose is "functionally dioecious", i.e. that seedbearing plants are often sterile, while non-fruiting plants may be fertile. In natural colonies of Prairie Roses one clump may be completely devoid of hips, while all the plants in another group will have many of them (Shepherd, p. 44). The old hybrids, which were bred between 1840-1850, are rarely seen today. Hybrids of our time are → 'Doubloons' and 'Long John Silver'.

R. anemoneflora Fort. Climbing; branches with few, small, hooked prickles; leaflets mostly 3, ovate-lanceolate, pointed, simply serrate, bald; flowers in small corymbs, white, 2.5-3 cm./1-1.2 in. across, single in the wild type, double in the garden form; sepals pointed, mostly slightly pinnate, styles connate into a column; the double form has narrow inner petals, quite different than the outer ones; pedicels mostly glandular. 2n = 14. WR 21 (= *R. triphylla* Roxb.; *R. sempervirens anemoniflora* Regel). 1844 found by Robert Fortune in a Shanghai garden, later in other locations in E. China. Shepherd and G.S. Thomas speculate that this could be a natural hybrid between *R. banksiae* and *R. moschata*. Tender.

R. helenae Rehd. & Wils. Strong-growing climber, to 5 m./16.5 ft. high, branches heavily armed, prickles hooked, young growth purplish-red; leaflets mostly 7-9, ovate-lanceolate, 2.5-5 cm./1-2 in. long, bald above, greyish-green and puberulent beneath, mostly sharply and simply serrate; flowers many, in flat corymbs, white, 2-3 cm./0.8-1.2 in. across, scented, June-July; sepals lanceolate, acuminate, shorter than the reflexed petals, soon dropping; calyx bald, pedicels glandular; fruits ovoid, red, 12 mm./0.5 in. long. 2n = 14. GSR 21; ICS 2229. C. China. 1907. Found by E.H. Wilson, and named after his wife. Tender.

R. rubus Lév. & Van. Climbing, with long branches, to 6 m./20 ft. high in its native habitat or countries with mild climates, prickly, purplish, bald or hairy, prickles hooked; leaflets mostly 5, ovate-elliptic, 3-6 cm./1.2-2.4 in. long, sharply and coarsely serrate, glossy green above, hairy beneath and purplish when young; flowers in dense panicles, white, 3 cm./1.2 in. across, June-July; styles united into a hairy column; sepals glandular-hairy like the pedicels; fruits globose, pea-size, red. 2n = 14. WR 168; BM 8894; J. RHS 65:102; ICS 2230. (= *R. ernestii* Stapf). C. and W. China. 1907. Differing from *R. helenae* by the 5 longer, hairy leaflets, purplish beneath when young. Tender.

R. mulliganii Bouleng. Habit like *R. rubus*, growth strong, prickles with broad base; leaflets 5-7, elliptic, acute to acuminate, to 6 cm./2.4 in. long, simply serrate, puberulent beneath; flowers white, about 5 cm./2 in. across, scented, pedicels slightly puberulent, 25-35 mm./1-1.4 in. long; sepals pinnate, 12-15 mm./0.5-0.6 in. long; fruits orange-red, smooth or slightly glandular, to 12 mm./0.5 in. long. 2n = 14. W. China. 1917-1919. Differing from *R. rubus* by the larger flowers on longer pedicels and pinnate sepals.

R. brunonii Lindl. Himalayan Musk-Rose. Strong-growing climber, stems to 5 m./16.5 ft. high or more, mostly hairy and glandular when young, prickles strong, hooked; leaflets 5-7, elliptic-lanceolate, 3-5 cm./1.2-2 in. long, pointed, downy, serrulate; flowers many, in corymbs, white, 2.5-5 cm./1-2 in. across, scented, June-July; sepals narrow, lanceolate, slightly glandular and hairy, afterwards reflexed and finally dropping; pedicels slightly puberulent and glandular; fruits ovoid, 8 mm./0.3 in. thick, brown. 2n = 14. WR 11. Himalayas. 1822. Very tender.

Very similar to *R. moschata*, differing by the narrower leaflets, smaller flowers, but in larger corymbs, less winter-hardy. Often confused with *R. moschata*, but more frequently cultivated in mild countries.

A more strongly growing form → **'La Mortola'**

R. moschata Herrm. Musk-Rose. Shrub with 3-4 m./10-13 ft. long, arching or sarmentose, purplish, only sparsely armed branches; leaflets 5-7, ovate, acute, dark green and bald above, purplish at the tops, more grey and bald beneath, serrate; petioles glandular-hispid, stipules small, linear, ciliate; flowers mostly 3 together, united into large, terminal clusters, white, 5 cm./2 in. across, petals soon reflexed, with strong beeswax-scent, August to frost, sepals half-pinnate; pedicels tomen-

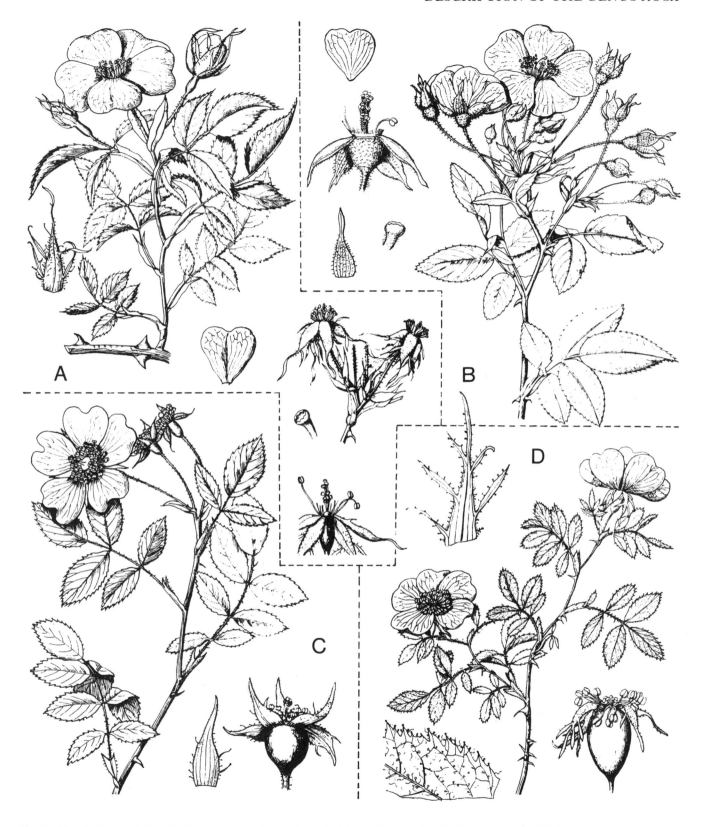

Figure 153.   A. *R. moschata*;   B. *R. sempervirens* (var. *submoschata*);   C. *R. arvensis*;   D. *R. agrestis*. (after Vicioso)

tose. 2n = 14. GSR 200; SOR 32; WR 33. (= *R. ruscinonensis* Déségl.). Original home unknown, possibly India or S. China. Brought to Asia Minor and S. Europe. 1651. (Fig. 153).

Originally described as being semi-double, but single flowers also present on the same plant. Very rare, and only recently rediscovered. The "Rosa moschata" of gardens is a strong growing, summer-flowering climber and very probably identical to *R. brunonii*. The autumn-flowering is a specific characteristic and important for the breeding of new roses.

var. **nastarana** Christ. Leaflets smaller, sharply serrulate, glaucous, bald; petiole glandular; flowers with pink hue, in clusters, larger than in the type. WR 39. (= *R. pissartii* Carr.). Persia. 1879.

'Plena'. Flowers semi-double; leaflets hairy beneath; pedicels less numerous and smaller. Cultivated since before 1629.

R. moschata has been widely used in breeding; hybrids with *R. multiflora* gave the so-called "Perpetual-flowering Shrub Roses", which were formerly called "Lambertiana Roses".

R. × dupontii Déségl. Dupont Rose, Snow-bush Rose. Originally thought to be a natural cross of *R. gallica* × *R. moschata*, before 1817 in S. France. This explanation is now regarded dubiously; it has not been confirmed by chromosome research. Shrub 2-2.5 m./6.6-8.3 ft. high, stems at first upright, later spreading, with only few, small prickles; leaflets mostly 5, ovate-elliptic, to 5 cm./2 in. long, doubly serrate, greyish-green and hairy on the veins beneath, petioles glandular; flowers mostly 4-7 in corymbs, buds pink, opening white, finally pinkish, single, 6-7 cm./2.4-2.8 in. across, June; sepals glandular, dropping; stamens sometimes petaloid, styles free, silky, pedicels glandular; fruits ellipsoid, 12 mm./0.5 in., red, ripening very late, October-January. 2n = 28. WR 13; GSR 6; (= *R. freundiana* Graeb.; *R. moschata nivea* Lindl.).

R. sambucina Koidz. Climbing, bald shrub, stems with hooked, flat prickles; leaflets 5, broadly lanceolate to narrow ovate-oblong, 5-10 cm./2-4 in. long, 1-2.5 cm./0.4-1 in. across, acuminate, firm, leathery, bald; stipules thin, entire, margin glandular, the free part linear; flowers 5-20 together in flat corymbs, white, 4-5 cm./1.6-2 in. across, pedicel 3-5 cm./1.2-2 in. long, May-June; calyx loosely glandular-hairy; styles hairy. (= *R. moschata* sensu Jap. Auth.). Japan; rare. (Fig. 124)

var. **pubescens** Koidz. Climbing; branches with short, strong prickles; leaflets 3(-5), ovate-oblong, 4-5 cm./1.6-2 in. long, 1.5-2.5 cm./0.6-1 in. across, acuminate, serrate; calyx hairy, sepals entire, densely tomentose and reflexed; petals white, emarginate, 1-1.5 cm./0.4-0.6 in. long; styles connate into a bald column. (= *R. rubus* var. *pubescens* Hayata). Taiwan; in mountain woods.

R. longicuspis Bertol. Evergreen, strong-growing, climbing or sarmentose shrub, branches shiny, red-brown; with many, long, hooked prickles on the shoots, often absent from flowering branches; leaves semi-persistent, very large, 12-28 cm./5-11 in. long; leaflets 5-7, elliptic to ovate-oblong, 5-10 cm./2-4 in. long, acuminate, sharply toothed, base rounded, dark green and glossy above, reddish when young, reticulate and bald beneath; stipules finely denticulate; flowers white, 5 cm./2 in. across, in large corymbs, petals silky outside, strong banana-scent, pedicels hairy; fruits ovoid, scarlet to orange. 2n = 14. GSR 27; GiS 23. (= *R. lucens* Rolfe). W. China; Himalayas. 1915. Very tender.

R. sinowilsonii Hemsl. Climbing shrub, similar to *R. longicuspis*, to 5 m./16.5 ft. high, young stems reddish, with only few, short, hooked prickles; leaves semi-persistent to evergreen, leaflets 5-7, oblong-elliptic, 7 cm./2.8 in. long or more, sharply serrate, slightly hairy beneath, petiole bald, prickly; flowers in loose corymbs, white, 3-5 cm./1.2-2 in. across, June-July; petals entire, hairy outside, sepals ovoid and caudate, to 2.5 cm./1 in. long, dropping, pedicels thick, reddish, glandular-hispid; fruits ellipsoid, red, 12 mm./0.5 in. long. 2n = 14. WR 73; PWR 233. S.W. China. 1904. Tender.

R. cerasocarpa Rolfe. Climbing, to 3 m./10 ft. high, stems with few strong, hooked prickles; leaflets 5, firm, leathery, ovate-elliptic, acuminate, to 7 cm./2.8 in. long, bald, simply serrate, petioles bald, stipules narrow, entire, flowers in panicles, white, 2.5-3 cm./1-1.2 in. across, June; sepals entire, or pinnate, 6 mm./0.2 in. long, glandular and hairy, dropping; pedicels and calyx glandular, flower buds abruptly pointed; fruits globose, red, 1 cm./0.4 in. thick. 2n = 14. BM 8688. W. China. 1914.

R. maximowicziana Regel. Climbing, densely branched shrub, with few, small hooked prickles, young branches also bristly; leaflets 7-9, ovate-elliptic, 2.5-4 cm./1-1.6 in. long, bald, glossy, simply serrate, petioles hairy, glandular and prickly; stipules very narrow, glandular-ciliate; flowers in small corymbs, white, 2.5-3 cm./1-1.2 in. across, June-July; sepals long, narrow, pinnate, finally dropping; styles united into a bald column; bracts persistent; fruits ovoid, 12 mm./0.5 in. thick, red, smooth. 2n = 14. Mandshuria, Korea. Before 1880.

var. **jackii** (Rehd.) Rehd. Branches purple, with few hooked prickles, no bristles; leaflets to 6 cm./2.4 in. long, stipules entire; corymbs with about 20 flowers, petals obovate; fruits pear-shaped, 5-7 mm./0.2-0.3 in. thick, red. 2n = 14. (= *R. jackii* Rehd.; *R. kelleri* Baker). Korea. 1905.

var. **pilosa** (Nakaii) Nakai. Differing principally by hairy petioles and pedicels. 2n = 14. (= *R. jackii* var. *pilosa* Nakai). Korea 1916. This form has been crossed with Hybrid Teas at Iowa State College; the best seedlings were introduced commercially, but received little recognition.

R. henryi Bouleng. Sarmentose shrub, branches purplish, with hooked prickles, floral branches unarmed; leaflets 5, elliptic to ovate, 4-8 cm./1.6-3 in. long, acuminate, simply serrate, rounded at base, bald and glaucescent beneath; stipules entire, narrow; flowers in umbel-like corymbs, white, 3.5 cm./1.4 in. across, June-July; pedicels 1-2 cm./0.4-0.8 in. long, hairy and glandular; fruits globose, 1 cm./0.4 in. across, dark red. ICS 2231. (= *R. gentiliana* Rehd. & Wils., not Lévl. & Van.). C. and E. China.

R. filipes Rehd. & Wils. Climbing, 2.5-4 m./8.3-13.2 ft. high, stems with few hooked prickles; leaflets 5-7, ovate-lanceolate, 5-7 cm./2-2.8 in. long, bald, glandular beneath, simply serrate; flowers many, in panicles, 2-2.5 cm./0.8-1 in. across, June-July; sepals narrow, dilated at the top, equalling the narrow petals, soon dropping; pedicels very slender, bald or glandular; styles hairy, united into a column; fruits ovoid, red, 1 cm./0.4 in. long. 2n = 14. BM 8894; D. RHS 1814. W. China. 1908.

To this belongs → **'Kiftsgate'**.

R. crocacantha Bouleng. Shrub to 2.5 m./8.3 ft. high, prickles orange-yellow; leaflets 5-7, elliptic, 4-5 cm./1.6-2 in. long, doubly serrate, bald or hairy beneath; flowers many, in panicles, white, 1-1.5 cm./0.4-0.6 in. across, styles bald; pedicels 1-2 cm./0.4-0.8 in. long; fruits globose, 8 mm./0.3 in. thick, red. 2n = 14. W. China. 1917-1919. May not be in cultivation at this time.

R. phoenicia Boiss. Resembling *R. moschata*; growth strong, stems very slender, whip-shaped, several meters/yards long, green, bald, with few, small, hooked prickles; leaflets 5-7, mostly ovate-elliptic, obtuse, simply and sharply serrate, slightly hairy, especially beneath; petioles hairy and prickly; flowers many, in corymbs, white, 4-5 cm./1.6-2 in. across, June; buds ovoid, sepals shorter than petals, pinnate, pointed at the top, dropping; calyx and the very elongated column of styles bald; fruits ovoid, red, 12 mm./0.5 in. long, October. 2n = 14. Turkey, Syria, Lebanon. About 1885. Difficult to transplant, due to deep roots; grows only in very hot, dry areas, very floriferous. (Fig. 129).

R. soulieana Crép. Shrub to 4 m./13 ft. high, branches widely expanding, young branches green, afterwards more glaucous, very prickly, prickles reddish, straight, with broad base; leaflets 5-9, greyish-green, oblong-elliptic, bald; stipules narrow, margin glandular; flowers many in corymbs 10-15 cm./4-6 in. across along the entire branch, at first creamy yellow, then pure white, 3 cm./1.2 in. across, scented, June-July; sepals ovate, acute, reflexed, mostly bald, entire or slightly pinnate, calyx glandular; fruits ovoid-globose, orange-yellow, 1 cm./0.4 in. long. 2n = 14. WR 18; BM 8158. W. China. 1896. With great ornamental value, but principally in milder countries. Not truly a climber, but a strong-growing shrub rose; has, unfortunately, uncertain hardiness.

Hybrids with this species → **'Kiftsgate'** and **'Navigator'**.

R. wichuraiana Crép. Climbing, half-evergreen shrub, stems 2.5-6 m./8.3-20 ft. long, prostrate or trailing, green, with stout, hooked prickles; leaflets 7-9, broadly ovate-roundish, dark green above, paler beneath, very glossy on both sides; flowers in small, pyramidal corymbs, white, 4-5 cm./1.6-2 in. across, scented, June-July; sepals much shorter than petals, bald or slightly glandular like the pedicels; fruits ovoid, dark red, 15 mm./0.6 in. long. 2n = 14. BM 7321; WR 19; 169 (as *R. tacquetii*); 170 (as *R. mokanensis*); BC 3440. (= *R. luciae* var. *wichuraiana* Koidz.; *R. tacquetii* Lév.; *R. mokanensis* Lév.). Japan, Korea, E. China. 1891. (Fig. 151).

Prostrate growth in its native habitat, branches take root easily, so very useful for further breeding of ground-covering roses. Has been used to produce new climbing roses since 1843; its descendants have mostly small, very glossy, dark green leaflets; the very weak stems and branches need to be tied up.

Among the more important hybrids are: → 'American Pillar' (1902), 'Hiawatha' (1904), 'Minnehaha' (1905), 'Dr. W. van Fleet' (1910), 'New Dawn' (1930), 'Blaze' (1932) and 'City of York' (1945). In the United States this rose is often called the "Memorial Rose", as it is frequently planted in cemeteries.

R. × jacksonii Willm. (= *R. rugosa* × *R. wichuraiana*). Low shrub, with arching branches, prickles very unequal, scattered, straight, slender; leaflets 7-9, oblong, obtuse, firm, simply serrate, glossy above; stipules adnate with free, ovate auricles; calyx semi-globose, sepals ovate-lanceolate, sometimes slightly glandular; flowers several together, floriferous, crimson, single, petals large, styles free; fruits bright red, pitcher-shaped to globose or flask-shaped, much smaller than in *R. rugosa*. 2n = 14. WR 20. Originated before 1910 by Jackson Dawson, Arnold Arboretum, and at first introduced commercially under the name 'Lady Duncan'; 1910 taken as the type of this hybrid; sterile.

To this belongs also → **'Max Graf'**.

R. × kordesii Wulff. (seedling from an open-pollinated 'Max Graf'). Growth shrubby, branches arching, prickles as with *R. wichuraiana*; leaves similar to *R. wichuraiana*; leaflets mostly 7, rarely 5, bright green, glossy, not wrinkled; flowers bright red, single to semi-double, 7-8 cm./2.8-3.2 in. across, scentless, floriferous and recurrent; fruits ovoid to ellipsoid.2n = 28. Amphi-diploid and fertile. HRo 18.

This rose was originated by W. Kordes from spontaneous chromosome doubling, but was never introduced commercially; several plants were distributed to some German Botanic Gardens. Kordes continued to breed with this plant, and later introduced a series of "Kordesii Roses", which may be the most important group of modern climbing roses. These varieties are distinguished by strong growth, healthy, glossy foliage, many flowers and recurrent bloom.

Most important varieties: → 'Hamburger Phoenix' (1954), 'Leverkusen' (1954), 'Dortmund' (1955), 'Wilhelm Hansmann' (1955), 'Parkdirektor Riggers' (1957), 'Heidelberg' (1959), 'Raymond Chenault' (1960), 'Morgengruss' (1962), 'Ilse Krohn Superior' (1964), etc.

R. luciae Franch. & Rochebr. Shrub prostrate or climbing to 3 m./10 ft. high, very similar to *R. wichuraiana*; all parts bald or nearly so; branches very long, prickles rather flattened, stipules very thin, entire, margin slightly glandular, auricles short, filiform; leaflets 5(-7), rather thin, slightly glossy above, paler beneath, terminal leaflet ovate to narrow-ovate, 2-4 cm./0.8-1.6 in. long, 1-2 cm./0.4-0.8 in. across, pointed to acuminate, lowest pair often smaller; flowers in corymbs, white, 2-3 cm./0.8-1.2 in. across, scented, May-June; pedicels 6-10 mm./0.2-0.4 in. long. 2n = 14. (= *R. luciae* var. *oligantha* Franch. & Sav.; *R. franchetii* Koidz.). E. China, Japan, Korea; low mountains, in woodland.

var. **hakonensis** Franch. & Sav. Leaflets thin, bald, whitish beneath; terminal one ovate to broadly-ovate, acute or abruptly acuminate; flowers 1-2 together, May-June. (= *R. hakonensis* Koidz.; *R. jasminoides* Koidz.) Japan.

var. **fujisanensis** Makino. Leaflets 5(-7), pale beneath, bald to nearly so, lateral leaflets smaller, terminal one rather leathery, ovate to more elliptic, 15-25 mm./0.6-1 in. long, 10-15 mm./0.4-0.6 in. across, acute; flowers few, June-July. (= *R. fujisanensis* [Makino] Makino). Japan; Honshu, Shikoku.

G. S. Thomas is classifying a series of cultivars of this species which were formerly attributed to *R. wichuraiana*; in his information about parentage the name *R. wichuraiana* is kept, however it was probably *R. luciae*.

See → 'Alberic Barbier', 'Albertine', 'Fräulein Oktavia Hesse', 'Gerbe Rose', etc.

R. sempervirens L. Evergreen Rose. Climbing, to 5

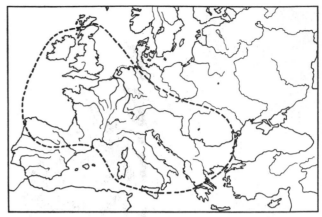

Figure 154. Distribution of *Rosa arvensis*. (after Sokolov 1954)

m./16.5 ft. high or trailing, stems slender, flexible, green, with slender, red prickles; leaflets 5-7, ovate-lanceolate, acute, 2.5-6 cm./1-2.4 in. long, glossy on both sides, simply serrate, stipules with glandular margin; flowers several in corymbs, white, scented, 3-5 cm./1.2-2 in. across, June-July; sepals ovate, glandular beneath, dropping; stipules hairy, glandular; fruits ovoid-globose, 12 mm./0.5 in. long, orange-red. 2n = 14, 21, 28. WR 5 (= *R. balearica* Pers.). Mediterranean region, N. Africa. 1629. Tender.

Formerly used in hybridizing; descendants are: → 'Félicité et Perpétue', 'Spectabilis' and 'Adelaide d'Orléans'. Furthermore this species was involved in the origin of the Ayrshire Roses.

R. arvensis Huds. Field Rose. Climbing 1-2 m./3.3-6.6 ft. high, but stems and branches slender and often much longer, creeping on the ground or into other bushes, with many small, hooked prickles; leaflets mostly 7, ovate, 1-4 cm./0.4-1.6 in. long, coarsely serrate, dull green above, downy beneath; flowers solitary or few together in corymbs, white, 2.5-3 cm./1-1.2 in. across, scentless, June-July; sepals acute, ovate, much shorter than petals, bald, dropping; fruits ovoid, about 2 cm./0.8 in. long, bright red. 2n = 14. BM 2054; WR 3; CF1 605. (= *R. repens* Scop.). Europe, except S. Spain and Scandinavia. 1750. In the first half of the 19th century this species was crossed with other garden roses and produced the so-called Ayrshire Roses, very strong growing and hardy roses with single or double, white or pink flowers (see Shepherd, pp. 19-22).

Only **'Splendens'**, better know in the British Isles as the "Myrtle-scented Rose", may be mentioned here; very strong growing, leaves remaining green for a very long time; flowers small, loosely double, blush scented.

R. × ruga Lindl. (= *R. arvensis × R. chinensis*; Shepherd

Figure 155. *Rosa chinensis*. (after *Rosenzeitung*)

suggests that *R. odorata*, rather than *R. chinensis*, may have been the pollen parent, because the flowers have the strong fragrance of *R. odorata*). Climbing or trailing shrub, stems 2.5-3 m./8.3-10 ft. long, prickles scattered, hooked; leaflets 5-7, simply serrate, 4-5 cm./1.6-2 in. long, bald on both sides; flowers many together in large, terminal corymbs, loosely double and globose, 4-6 cm./1.6-2.4 in. across, pink, scented, June-July; sepals dropping, pedicels long, bald, fruits globose, red, smooth, but rarely formed. 2n = 14. WR 17. Originated before 1830 in Italy.

R. × polliniana Spreng. (= *R. arvensis* × *R. gallica*). Habit like *R. arvensis*, stems glaucous, prickles small, scattered, hooked; leaflets 5-7, small, rather leathery, glaucous above, slightly puberulent beneath; flowers solitary or 2 together, on long, articulate, glandular-hispid pedicels, white with pink hue, single, to 6 cm./2.4 in. across, scented; fruits rarely formed. 2n = 21. WR 333 (= *R. germanica* Märklin; *R. arvina* Schwekf.). Found initially in N. Italy, cultivated before 1800.

> Section 7. Chinenses (Sér.) Rehd.
> Stems climbing or trailing, with scattered, hooked prickles; leaflets 3-5, rarely 7; stipules and bracts narrow; inflorescences 1- many flowers; sepals entire or sparsely pinnatifid, reflexed after anthesis; styles free, only half as long as inner stamens.
>
> > *R. odorata, gigantea, dilecta, chinensis, noisettiana, borboniana.*

R. × odorata (Andr.) Sweet. (= *R. chinensis* × *R. gigantea*). Tea Rose. Evergreen or only half-evergreen rose with long, sometimes prostrate stems, in suitable climates climbing to 10 m./33 ft. high, prickles scattered, hooked; leaflets 5-7, elliptic-oblong, 2-7 cm./0.8-2.8 in. sharply serrate, glossy above; flowers solitary or few together, white, blush or yellowish, single or double, 5-7 cm./2-2.8 in. across, scented, June-September; pedicels short, sometimes glandular, sepals entire or slightly pinnate; styles free, exserted. 2n = 14, 21, 28. WR 179-180; ICS 2232; PWR 193. (= *R. indica odorata* Andr.; *R. thea* Savi.). Origin unknown; found in China under cultivation. 1810.

The most important varieties, long under cultivation in China, from time immemorial, follow here in order of their introduction:

'Hume's Blush Tea-scented China'. Probably a spontaneous hybrid of *R. chinensis* × *R. gigantea*; stems very long, leaflets 5-7, prickles scattered, hooked; flowers semi-double, pink, recurrent, scented (= *R. indica odorata* Andrews, *Roset.* pl. 77; *R. indica fragrans* Thory; in Redouté, *Roses*, 1: pl. 19; *R. indica odoratissima* Lindl.; in *Bot. Reg.* 804). Found 1809 in the Fan Tee Nurseries, near Canton, China, by an officer of the East India Company, and brought to England, where it was named by Sir Abraham Hume. No living specimens extant, known only from pictures. The scent of this rose was said to be so similar to that of pulverized tea leaves (opinion varies as to whether it was the scent of the leaves or the flowers) that the rose was first called "Tea-scented Rose" in England. Later, when new varieties arrived, without this typical scent or even scentless, they were only called "Tea Roses", and this name remained until today.

'Parks' Yellow Tea-scented China'. Presumably another spontaneous hybrid of *R. chinensis* × *R. gigantea*; flowers pale yellow, double. (= *R. odorata* f. *ochroleuca* [Lindl.] Rehd.). Found 1824 by John Damper Parks, also in the Fan Tee Nurseries, and possibly overlooked on the first visit. It has been used in hybridizing; in spite of being a good seedbearer, it has, however, been impossible to obtain a clear yellow, non-fading variety from it. Also extinct.

'Fortune's Double Yellow'. Strong-growing, to 3 m./10 ft. high; flowers to 4-8 together loosely double, salmon-yellow, exterior with a red hue, very fragrant, 7-10 cm./2.8-4 in. across. BM 4679; WR 28. (= *R. odorata* var. *pseudindica* [Lindl.] Rehd.; = 'Gold of Ophir', 'Beauty of Glazenwood'). 1845. Found, in the garden of a Mandarin at Ningpo, China, and brought to England by Robert Fortune.

Shortly thereafter, the breeding development of Tea Roses was started in France, for the plant did not set fruit outdoors in England, and hybridizing under glass was uncommon at that time.

R. gigantea Coll. ex Crép. Climbing to 10 m./33 ft. high in milder countries, to 15 m./50 ft. in its native habitat; prickles strong, hooked, but scattered and even completely absent; leaflets 5-7, lanceolate, about 7 cm./2.8 in. long, bald and glossy, deeply- and often glandular-serrate; stipules long and narrow, with linear auricles; flowers mostly solitary, white to creamy-white, 10-12 cm./4-4.8 in. across, scented, May-June; sepals 3 cm./1.2 in. long, sometimes dilated at the top, reflexed, bald, finally dropping; fruits globose to tear-shaped, 2-3 cm./0.8-1.2 in. long, with thick wall, yellow to orange. 2n = 14. WR 34; BM 7972. (= *R. odorata* var. *gigantea* [Crép.] Rehd. & Wils.; *R. xanthocarpa* Watt. ex Willm.). Upper Burma, S.W. China. Tender. Found 1888 by Sir Henry Collett in the Shan Hills of N. Burma, and by E.H. Wilson in S.W. China.

f. **erubescens** Focke. Flowers single, blush to dark pink, smaller, recurrent. (= *R. odorata* f. *erubescens* [Focke] Rehd. & Wils.). W. China. May be an ancester of both the pink and the yellow Tea Roses. Tender.

R. "cooperi" Hort. (= Cooper's Burmese Rose, after G.S. Thomas). This is presumably a spontaneous hybrid of *R. gigantea* × *R. laevigata*; strong-growing, to 6 m./20 ft. high, stems purplish-brown, rather stiff; leaves evergreen, to 18 cm./7.2 in. long, leaflets 7, lanceolate, acuminate, very glossy, serrulate; flowers single, white, finally with pink hue and spots, 10 cm./4 in. across. 2n = 14. GSR 5. 1931 grown in the Royal Botanic Gardens, Edinburgh (where Cooper was Curator from 1934-1950), from wild seeds collected in Burma. Tender.

R. × dilecta Rehd. This is the botanical designation for the modern Hybrid Tea roses. In 1922 Rehder gave this name to hybrids between *R. borbonia* and *R. odorata* (Hybrid Perpetuals × Tea Roses). It was not a good choice for, while the earliest Hybrid Teas had true Tea Roses as their mother, many other combinations came to this with only one or even none of the parents of Rehder's formula. Therefore this name is not listed in most books on roses.

R. chinensis Jacq. China Rose, Bengal Rose. Low, upright shrub, stems with stout, mostly hooked prickles, or sometimes nearly unarmed; leaflets 3-5, broadly ovate to oblong, acuminate, 3-6 cm./1.2-2.4 in. long, glossy and deep green above, pale and bald beneath; stipules very narrow; flowers mostly several together, sometimes solitary, in the original plant pink, 5 cm./2 in. across, but also dark red and nearly white as well, June-autumn, on very long pedicels; sepals entire, acuminate, bald, reflexed after anthesis, finally dropping; fruits ovoid to pear-shaped, 1.5-2 cm./0.6-0.8 in. long, remaining green for a long time, finally brownish-green. 2n = 14, 21, 28. (= *R. sinica*, *R. indica* sensu Lour. not L.; *R. indica* var. *bengalensis* [Pers.] K. Koch; *R. nankinensis* Lour.) ICS 2233; WR 79. China. (Fig. 155).

The year of its introduction is not known for certain; opinion varies: (McFarland 1759; Rehder, Thomas 1768; Jaeger, Bean 1789; Glasau 1792; Ascherson, Park end of 18th century). The single-flowering wild type, in any case, was found first in 1885; it is distinguished as F. **spontanea** Rehd. & Wils. For the history of its introduction see p. 000.

F. **spontanea** Rehd. & Wils. The wild type; shrub 1-2 m./3.3-6.6 ft. high, flowers mostly solitary, dark red or pink, single. GC 1902:170. (= *R. indica* Hemsl.; 1887, not L. nor Lour.) China; N. to C. Szechuan, in woodland and on river banks of the Shih-ch'uah Hsien, uncommon. 1885 first found by A. Henry in Ichang, later in other parts of China and (naturalized) in India. Presumably not now in cultivation.

var. **semperflorens** (Curtis) Koehne. Chinese Monthly Rose, Crimson China Rose. Neat shrub, 1-1.5 m./3.3-5 ft. high, branches slender, prickles equal, small, scattered, red; leaflets 3-5, small, ovate, simply serrate, usually an intense red when young, bald; flowers solitary or 2-3 together, dark red, semi-double, medium large, very long flowering, pedicels long, slender, bald; calyx oblong, bald, sepals lanceolate, acuminate, entire, 15 mm./0.6 in. long, spreading, dropping; fruits bright red. 2n = 14. WR 89; BM 284; GiS 10. (= *R. semperflorens* Curtis; *R. bengalensis* Pers.; *R. diversifolia* Vent.; = 'Slater's Crimson China', 'Old Crimson China'). 1789 discovered in Calcutta by a captain of the English East India Company and, after his return to England, given to Gilbert Slater, a Director of the same company, at Knots Green, who propagated and distributed the plant under the name Bengal rose. Before the introduction of this rose there was no other whose flower was such a dark red; all dark red roses are descendents of this plant. After having been believed extinct, it was rediscovered in England and in the Bermudas.

To this belongs also → 'Old Blush'; flowers blush.

'Minima'. Fairy Rose. Dwarf shrub, only 0.2-0.5 m./0.7-1.7 ft. high, with many slender stems; flowers of the oldest variety single to semi-double, blush, 3 cm./1.2 in. across, recurrent. 2n = 14. BM 1762; PWR 161. (= *R. indica pumila* Thory; *R. lawranceana* Sweet; *R. indica minima* Bean; *R. indica humilis* Sér.). The origin of this rose is not known for certain; it is believed (following G.S. Thomas) that it originated about 1805 in England from *R. chinensis* × *R. gigantea*. The story, that the English botanist Robert Sweet received it from the island of Mauritius, is no longer held, as Sweet himself did not claim credit for its introduction. Today there are many varieties, mostly bred by Ralph S. Moore, U.S.A.; Pedro Dot, Spain; and Jan De Vink, Holland. The oldest variety might be → 'Pompon de Paris', which today is regarded as being identical to *rouletii*. (Fig. 156)

Figure 156. Oldest pictures of the Fairy Rose; left *Rosa semperflorens* y *minima* Sims (after *Bot. Mag.* 1815, pl. 1762); center *R. indica pumila, flore simplici;* right *Rosa indica pumila, flore multiplici.* (both after Redouté, *Les Roses,* vol. III. 1829)

'Longifolia'. To 0.6 m./2 ft. high, stems nearly unarmed; leaflets 3-5, linear-lanceolate, to 5 cm./2 in. long, serrate to entire; flowers mostly single, dark pink (= *R. longifolia* Willd.; *R. indica longifolia* Lindl.; *R. chinensis* var. *longifolia* [Wil]d.] Rehd.). 1820. May not currently be in cultivation.

'Viridiflora'. The Green Rose. Small shrub, flowers in clusters or solitary, double, green, sometimes with brown margin, petals all foliaceous, margin serrate, long-lasting. 2n = 14. GSR 127. (= *R. chinensis* var. *viridiflora* Dipp.; *R. chinensis* var. *monstrosa* Bean; *R. monstrosa* Breiter). Said to be in cultivation since 1743. G.S. Thomas reports that this monstrosity originated about 1833 as a mutation on *R. chinensis* at Charleston, S. Carolina, was brought to Thomas Rivers, England in 1837, from where it was distributed by the English Nurseries Bembridge & Harrison, starting in 1856.

'Mutabilis'. Slender, loose, upright shrub, about 1 m./3.3 ft. high, to 2 m./6.6 ft. under favorable conditions; young branches purplish-red, prickles red, leaves coppery when young; flowers single, saucer-shaped, 5 cm./2 in. across, inside sulphur-yellow upon opening, reverse orange, the inside changing by the second day to coppery-salmon, then gradually becoming dark crimson, and dropping, recurrent. 2n = 14, 21, 28. (= *R. mutabilis* Corr.; *R. chinensis* var. *mutabilis* [Corr.] Rehd.). In cultivation since 1932. May be identical to 'Tipo Ideale' (in Redouté).

R. × **noisettiana** Theory (= *R. chinensis* × *R. moschata*). A group of climbing roses; stems upright, weak, prickles red, hooked; leaflets 5-7, oblong-lanceolate, simply serrate, pale beneath, petiole mostly puberulent and with fine prickles; flowers many, sometimes up to 100 in one inflorescence, but only medium-large, yellow, white or pink (no red tints), scented. 2n = 14. WR 32. (= *R. indica noisettiana* Sér.; *R. moschata autumnalis* Hort.). All of them are very tender and seldom cultivated anymore. Originated 1818 by John Champney, S. Carolina, and was named 'Champney's Pink Cluster'.

To this belongs the formerly internationally known variety → **'Maréchal Niel'** (Pradel, 1864); flowers sulphur-yellow, with very strong scent.

'Manettii' (Crivelli). Shrub to 2 m./6.6 ft. high or more, stems and branches striped, young growth reddish, prickles many, nearly black, leaflets 7-9, broadly elliptic; flowers pink, semi-double (= *R. manettii* Crivelli). Originated about 1837 in the Botanic Garden of Milan, Italy. Widely used as budding understock in S. Carolina, as it can easily be propagated from wood cuttings.

R. × **borboniana** Desp. (= *R. chinensis* × *R. damascena*). Bourbon Rose. The original plant had dark crimson flowers, medium-large, with 20 petals, flowering from early summer to autumn (but fewer flowers in the autumn); growth strong, leaves large, leaflets 5, broadly ovate. 2n = 21, 28. WR 114. Tender. Originated at the Isle of Bourbon (today Réunion). 1817 brought to France and named there. (Fig. 157).

Quite a series of descendants originated from this rose; growth 1-1.5 m./3.3-5 ft. high, upright, branches prickly, often glandular-bristly;

flowers solitary or few together, mostly very double, beautiful shape, especially the autumn flowers (early summer flowers less perfect). To this: → 'Boule de Neige' (Lacharme 1867); 'Souvenir de la Malmaison' (Beluze 1843); 'Variegata di Bologna' (Lodi 1909); 'Zéphirine Drouhin' (Bizot 1868), etc.

The suggestion that the Bourbon Roses originated from *R. chinensis* × *R. gallica* is probably incorrect, as the recurrent character of *R. chinensis* is recessive; so a hybrid between the single-flowering *R. gallica* with *R. chinensis* would also be single-flowering (after Shepherd).

Later, the Hybrid Bourbons were crossed with *R. odorata*, the Tea Rose, and the result was the Hybrid Perpetuals. These surpassed, and eclipsed, the Hybrid Bourbons, primarily by their recurrent bloom and hardiness, as well as by their size and floweriness.

Section 8. Banksianae (Lindl.) Rehd.

Evergreen, climbing shrubs, stems slender, bald, with hooked prickles or unarmed; leaflets 3-7, stipules free, subulate, caducous; flowers in corymbs, white or yellow; sepals entire, reflexed after anthesis, dropping:

R. banksiae, fortuniana, cymosa.

R. banksiae Ait. Evergreen shrub, to 5 m./16.5 ft. high, but also often weeping, stems and branches unarmed, bark green, bald; leaflets 3-5, acute-lanceolate, 3-6 cm./1.2-2.4 in. long, serrulate, margin often waved, glossy above, stipules bristly, dropping; flowers rather small, but many together, single or double, white or yellow, with fine scent, May-June; sepals not pinnate; fruits globose, 7 mm./0.3 in. thick, red. 2n = 14 (= *R. banksiana* Abel). C. and W. China. 1796. Hardy only in very mild regions.

var. **banksiae.** The type; flowers double, pure white, with strong fragrance. GSR 1; BM 1954; ICS 2234 (= *R. banksiae alba plena*). 1807 found by William Kerr in a garden in Canton; commonly cultivated in gardens in China and Japan, but not wild. In Europe mostly *R. fortuniana*, with larger flowers and greater hardiness, is cultivated under this name. Tender.

var. **normalis** Regel. This is the wild species, 6 m./20 ft. high, reaching 15 m./50 ft. in its native land, stems without prickles; flowers small, white, single, scented. China; Hupeh and Szechuan. Cultivated since 1796 in Scotland, but flowered for the first time 1909 in Nice, S. France (see G.S. Thomas, *Clim. Roses*, p. 146). Tender.

f. **lutescens** Voss. Flowers single, sulphur-yellow, scented. GSR 3; BM 7171. W. China. Found once by E. H. Wilson, in a cemetery, but not wild. Introduced 1870 by Hanbury, La Mortola, Italy, to England. Tender.

'Lutea'. Flowers double, yellow; less fragrant than the other varieties. GSR 2; WR 34. Cultivated since 1824. Tender.

R. × fortuniana Lindl. (= *R. banksiae* × *R. laevigata*). Evergreen climber, 7-10 m./23-33 ft. high, stems and branches slender, prickles scattered, sickle-shaped, small; leaflets 3-5, ovate-lanceolate, serrulate, thin, bright green, glossy; stipules small, subulate, caducous; flowers solitary on short, bristly pedicels, creamy white,

double, 7 cm./2.8 in. across, June; petals loose and unequally arranged; WR 36. China; only known from garden culture. Introduced about 1845 to England by Robert Fortune. Very similar to *R. banksiae*, but larger in all parts; often cultivated under this name, but easily distinguished by the bristly pedicels. Tender.

R. cymosa Tratt. Evergreen shrub, climbing to 4.5 m./15 ft. high, stems slender, with few, hooked prickles; leaflets 3-5, distant, elliptic to ovate-lanceolate, dark green above and glossy, pale beneath, bald, simply serrate; stipules filiform free, rarely absent; flowers very numerous, in large, compound corymbs, white, small; sepals pinnate, woolly; fruits globose, scarlet red, small. 2n = 14. WR 156, 157; ICS 2235 (= *R. microcarpa* Lindl.; *R. bodinieri* Lév. & Van.; *R. esquirolii* Lév. & Van.; *R. indica* L. p.p.; *R. sorbiflora* Flocke). China. 1904. Tender.

The most wide-spread species in the warmer regions of China, especially in Ichang; extraordinary variation in the size of leaves, inflorescences and degree of hairiness.

Figure 157. *Rosa borboniana*, the Bourbon Rose. (after Redouté, where it is named "Rosa canina burboniana")

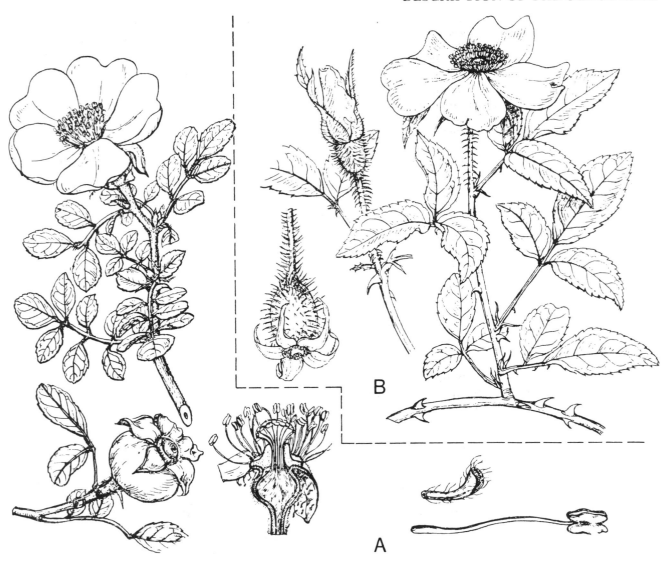

Figure 158.   A. *Rosa bracteata*;   B. *R. laevigata*. (after Liu)

Section 9. Laevigatae (Thory) Rehd.

Evergreen shrubs, stems with scattered, hooked prickles; leaflets mostly 3; stipules free or only adnate at the base, caducous; flowers solitary, large, without bracts; sepals erected, entire, persistent; pedicels and calyx-tube densely prickly:

R. laevigata, anemonoides.

R. laevigata Michx. Cherokee Rose. Evergreen, strong growing climber, to 5 m./16.5 ft. high; stems mostly bald, with stout, hooked prickles; leaflets mostly 3, ovate to lanceolate, glossy, bald, midrib sometimes slightly prickly beneath like the petiole; stipules free, caducous; flowers solitary, white, to 7 cm./2.8 in. across, scented, May-June; sepals very bristly, entire, persistent, erected; fruits pear-shaped, orange. 2n = 14.

BM 2847; WR 40; VP 438; BC 3458; ICS 2236. (= *R. cherokeensis* Donn; *R. triphylla* Roxb.; *R. ternata* Poir.; *R. hystrix* Lindl.). China; W. Hupeh, Fokien, Taiwan, especially in W. Hupeh, common in rocky places; only cultivated in Japan. Before 1780. Tender.

R. × anemonoides Rehd. (= *R. laevigata × R. odorata*). Strong growing climbing shrub; leaflets 3(-5), bald, glossy, stipules half free; flowers solitary, single, pink, 7 cm./2.8 in. across, pedicels bristly like the calyx. 2n = 14. WR 41; Originated 1895 with J.C. Schmidt, Erfurt, Germany, and was first distributed under the name "Anemonen-Rose". Tender. To this a dark red mutation → **'Ramona'.**

293

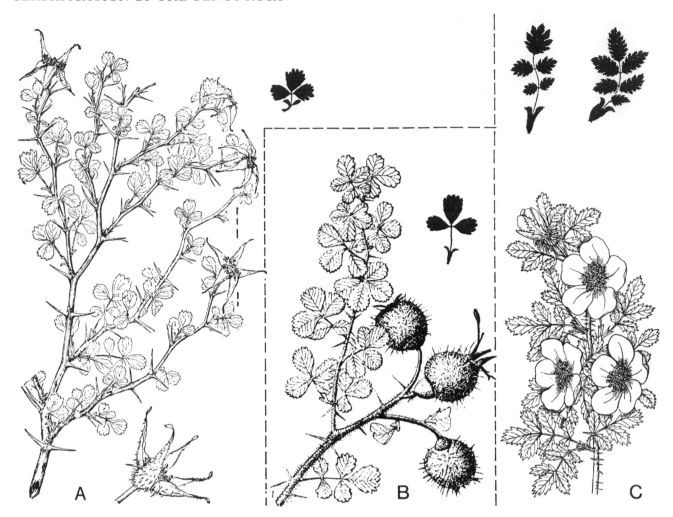

Figure 159.   A. *Rosa stellata*;   B. *R. stellata* var. *mirifica*;   C. *R. minutifolio*. (A. after Boulenger; B.-C. after Garden and Forest)

Section 10. Bractaetae (Thory) Rehd.

> Evergreen shrubs, stems upright or prostrate, tomentose or hairy, prickles in pairs; stipules slightly adnate, pectinate; inflorescences surrounded by large bracts; sepals entire, reflexed after anthesis; calyx-tube tomentose:

> *R. bracteata, clinophylla.*

R. bracteata Wendl. Macartney Rose. Upright shrub, to 3 m./10 ft. high, evergreen, bushy; stems hairy, with stout, hooked, often paired prickles; leaflets 5-9, oblong-obovate, rounded at the apex, 2-5 cm./0.8-2 in. long, crenate-serrulate, dark green and glossy above, tomentose beneath; stipules pinnate; flowers solitary, terminal, white, 5-7 cm./2-2.8 in. across, scented, July-August; pedicels and sepals densely hairy, calyx surrounded by large bracts, stamens many, about 300-400; fruits globose, woolly, 3 cm./1.2 in. thick, orange. 2n = 14. WR 42; BM 1377; VP 434; ICS 2238. (= *R. macart-*

nea Dum. Cours.). S. China, Taiwan, naturalized in the U.S.A., from Virginia to Texas and Florida. Introduced into England in 1793 by Lord Macartney. Tender.

To this belongs → **'Mermaid'** (Wm. Paul, 1918), with very large, pale yellow flowers; very strong growth.

R. cardotii Masam. (1932; originally spelled "cardetii"); is closely related to *R. bracteata* (see Fig. 124). Taiwan. May not be in cultivation outside its native country. Tender.

R. clinophylla Thory. Similar to *R. bracteata* but lower, branches grey-tomentose, more villous, finally rather glabrescent; prickles straight; leaflets 7-9, oblong-elliptic, the upper ones mostly gradually larger, acuminate, more or less hairy beneath, rachis villous; stipules small, laciniate; flowers large, white, 5-7

294

cm./2-2.8 in. across, scented; bracts broad, serrate; fruits 2 cm./0.8 in. long, densely tomentose, sometimes with 150 seeds. 2n = 14. (= *R. involucrata* Roxb.; *R. lyellii* Lindl.; *R. lindleyana* Tratt). India; from Kumaon to Burma; in swamps and on banks of rivers and lakes. Introduced before 1817. Tender. Often used in religious ceremonies in India.

Subgenus III. PLATYRHODON (Hurst) Rehd.

Leaves pinnate; stipules adnate, very narrow, with subulate, spreading auricles; flowers 1-2 together, with small, caducous bracts; calyx-tube prickly, achenes on a slightly elevated tubercle in the flower axis.

R. roxburghii

R. roxburghii Tratt. Growth spreading, to 2.5 m./8.3 ft. high, bark of the older stems peeling every year, grey, prickles paired below the nodes; leaflets 7-15, ellipticoblong, about 1.5-2.5 cm./0.6-1 in. long, serrulate, slightly hairy to bald; flowers double, bright pink, 5-6 cm./2-2.4 in. across, June; fruits depressed-globose, green, very prickly (like a small chestnut), prickles longitudinally furrowed. 2n = 14. BM 3490; WR 135; SOR 42. ICS 2237. (= *R. microphylla* Roxb. ex Lindl.). China. 1834 introduced to England, from the Botanic Garden at Calcutta, which is said to have gotten it from Canton.

f. normalis Rehd. & Wils. Growth much taller, 3-4 m./10-13 ft. high and across, stems strong; leaflets obovate to elliptic, rounded or acute at the apex, bald; flowers white to blush, solitary or several together. GSR 4546. (= *R. forrestii* Focke). China, Szechuan. This is the wild type found in 1908.

var. hirtula (Regel) Rehd. & Wils. Differing from f. *normalis* only by the leaflets hairy beneath, 15-25 mm./0.6-1 in. long; flowers blush, single. 2n = 14. BM 6548 (= *R. hirtula* Nakai). Japan. 1862 found by Maximowicz at the shore of the Lake Hakone, C. Japan.

R. roxburghii has been used little in breeding; → 'Tantau's Surprise' and *R. micrugosa*.

Subgenus IV. HESPORHODOS Cockerell

Leaves pinnate; stipules adnate, with dilated, spreading auricles; flowers solitary, without bracts; calyx-tube prickly, cup-shaped, without discus; achenes on an elongated, conical torus in the flower-axis; sepals pinnatifid, erected, persisting; fruit dry, not fleshy:

R. stellata, minutifolia:

R. stellata Woot. Upright shrub, 0.3-0.5 m./1-1.7 ft. high, young stems closely stellate-hairy, densely branched, prickles slender, often mixed with bristles; leaflets 3(-5), about 12 mm./0.5 in. long, obovate to wedge-shaped, deeply incised at the apex, bald or slightly stellate-hairy, stipules with glandular margin; flowers solitary, dark purple, 4-6 cm./1.6-2.4 in. across,

June-August; styles woolly, stamens numerous, about 160 or more; sepals pinnate, bristly beneath; fruits turbinate, brown-red, bristly, to 2 cm./0.8 in. across, mostly sterile. 2n = 14. VP 443; WR 103. (= *R. vernonii* Greene). W. Texas to Arizona. Found 1897, introduced 1902. Hardy, but needs a dry, sunny spot.

var. mirifica (Greene) Cockerell. Growth stronger, to 1 m./3.3 ft. high, branches bald, glandular, not stellate-hairy; leaflets mostly 5, deeply incised, bald or nearly so; flowers dark pink, 3-5-6 cm./1.2-2-2.4 in. across; fruits globose, bristly, dull red, 1.5 cm./0.6 in. thick. 2n = 14. BM 9070; ARA 1932; VP 443. (= *R. mirifica* Greene). N. New Mexico, Sacramento Mts. 1916. Also called "Sacramento Rose".

R. minutifolia Engelm. Shrub 1 m./3.3 ft. high, young stems hairy, densely covered with slender, brown prickles; leaves only 2-4 cm./0.8-1.6 in. long, with 3-5, rarely up to 7 leaflets, elliptic to obovate, 3-8 mm./0.1-0.3 in. long, deeply incised, hairy beneath; flowers solitary or several together, pink to nearly white, 2.5 cm./1 in. across; fruits globose, very prickly, red, 8 mm./0.3 in. thick. 2n = 14. BC 3457. California. 1888. Needs dry, hot climate. Tender.

Abbreviations of references to illustrations.

The letters and numbers at the end of the descriptions are abbreviated references to illustrations in other works. For the complete list see the end of the "Dictionary", p. 426.

BIBLIOGRAPHY
(For the literature of the Garden Roses see p. 425)

ANDREWS, H.C.   Roses; or a monograph of the genus *Rosa*. Vol. 1: 65 Taf. London 1805; Vol. 2: 64 pp. London 1828.

BAKER, J.G.   Review of the British Roses, especially in the North of England. 38 pp. Huddersfield 1864.

BORBÁS, V.A.   Magyar birodalom vadon termó Rózsái monographiájának kisiérlete (Primitiae monographiae Rosarum imperii Hungarici). Math. Term. Közl. 16: 306-560 (1880).

BOULENGER, G.A.   Les Roses d'Europe de l'herbier Crépin. Bull. Jard. Bot. Bruxelles 10: 1-417 (1924-25); loc. cit. 12: 1-192 (1931).

—   Revision des Roses d'Asie. Bull. Jard. Bot. Bruxelles 9: 203-348; 12: 165-276; 14: 115-221; 14: 274-278 (1933 to 1936).

—   Introduction à l'étude du genre *Rosa*. Bull Jard. Bot. Bruxelles 14: 242-278 (1937).

BOUVIER, L.   Les Roses des Alpes. 1875.

CHRIST, H.   Die Rosen der Schweiz, mit Berücksichtigung der umliegenden Gebiete Mittel- und Süd-Europas. Basel 1873.

—   Zur Rosenflora Italiens. Regensburg 1873.

CLUSIUS, C.   Rariorum plantarum historia. 348 S. Antwerp 1601. Contains 4 descriptions of roses; first nomination of *Rosa gallica versicolor* (28 years earlier than in Parkinson's *Paradisus*) first description of *Rosa hemisphaerica* (as *Rosa flava plena*).

COLMEIRO, D.M.   Rosaceas de España y Portugal. 1873.

CRÉPIN, F.   Note sur les Roses à fleurs jaunes. Flore des Serres 23: 104-105.

—   Primitiae Monographiae Rosarum. Bull. Soc. Bot. Belg. 8: 226 349 (1869); loc. cit. 11: 15-130 (1872); loc. cit. 13: 242-290 (1874), loc. cit. 14: 3-46, 137-168 (1874); loc. cit. 15: 12-100 (1876); loc. cit.

18: 221-416 (1879); loc. cit. 21: 7-196 (1882). – Reprint Lehre and London 1972.

— Tableau analytique des Roses européennes. Bull. Soc. Bot. Belg. 31: 66-92 (1892).

DÉSÉGLISE, A. Catalogue raisonné des especes du genre rosier pour l'Europe, l'Asie et l'Afrique, spécialement les rosiers de la France et de l'Angleterre. 1877.

— Descriptions et observations sur plusieurs rosiers de la flore française. Fasc. I, Gand 1880; fasc. II, Lyon 1882.

DESPORTES, N. Rosetum gallicum. Enumeration méthodique des espèces et des variétés du genre rosier. 124 S. Le Mans and Paris 1828. Describing 2,562 species and cultivars. 1829 also, published under the title *Roses cultivées en France*.

DESVAUX, N.A. Observations critiques sur les espèces de rosiers propres au sol de la France. In Jour. Bot. II (1813), Paris.

DILLENIUS, JOH, JAKOB. Hortus Elthamensis. 437 S., 324 Taf. Describing also *Rosa virginiana* (als *R. carolina fragrans*), *R. sanguisorbae* and *R. sempervirens*.

DUMORTIER, B.C.J. Monographie des Roses de la Flore Belge. Bull. Soc. Bot. Belg. 6: 237-297 (1867).

GANDOGER, M. Tabulae Rhodologicae europaeo-orientales locupletissime. 319 S. Paris 1881.

— Monographia Rosarum Europae & Orientis. Vol. 1: 1-338; Vol. 2: 1-486 (1892); Vol. 3: 1-418; Vol. 4: 1-601 (1893). Paris.

KELLER, R. *Rosa*. In P. ASCHERSON and P. GRAEBNER, Syn. Mitteleur. Fl. 6(1): 32-384 (1900-1905).

— Synopsis Rosarum Spontanearum Europae Mediae. Denkschr. Schweiz. Naturf. Ges. 65; pp. X + 796 + 40 pl. 1931.

KLASTERSKY, I. *Rosa*. In TUTIN et al., Flora Europaea, II: 25-32. London 1968.

KRÜSSMANN, G. Unsere Rosen und ihre systematische Stellung. Rosen-Jb. 32: 10-85. Baden-Baden 1966.

LINDLEY, J. Rosarum Monographia. 156 S. and 19 Farbtaf. London 1820. Describing all (78) at his time known species of *Rosa* and their synonymy. The author was only 21 years old, when he published this work.

LINNÉ, C. Species Plantarum, 2 vols. Reprint London 1957, of the 1st edition; 1200 pp. with an introduction by W.T. Stearn (176 pp.) and an appendix by J.L. HELLER and W.T. STEARN (148 pp.). The following species are described: *R. cinnamomea, eglanteria, villosa, canina, spinosissima, centifolia, alba, gallica, indica, sempervirens, pendulina* and *carolina*.

LOISELEUR-DESLONGCHAMPS, J.J.A. Description des principales espèces et variétés du genre rosier. Paris 1817.

— La Rose, son histoire, sa culture, sa poesie. 426 S. Paris 1844.

MEYER, K.A. Über die Zimmtrosen, insbesondere über die in Rußland wildwachsenden Arten derselben. 39 S. St. Petersburg 1847.

PRITZEL, G.A. Thesaurus Literaturae Botanicae omnium Gentium. 577 S. Berlin 1871. With very precise dates on the oldest botanical and horticultural literature, up to 1870; also biographic notes about the authors.

REGEL, E.A. VON. Tentamen Rosarum Monographiae. 144 pp. Petersburg 1877.

REHDER, A. *Rosa*. In REHDER and WILSON, Plantae Wilsonianae, Vol. 2: 304-345 (1915). Cambridge, Mass.

— Manual of the cultivated trees and shrubs, hardy in North America. 2nd Edition. New York 1947.

— Bibliography of Cultivated Trees and Shrubs, hardy in the cooler temperate regions of the Northern Hemisphere. Jamaica Plain, 1949.

SCHWERTSCHLAGER, J. Die Rosen des südlichen und mittleren Frankenjura. München 1910.

SELBSTHERR, K. Die Rosen in 25 Gruppen und 95 Arten. 230 pp. Breslau 1832.

SERINGE, N.G. *Rosa*. In A.P. DE CANDOLLE, Prodromus 2: 597-625 (1825).

TÄCKHOLM, G. The Egyptian Garden Roses in Schweinfurth's Herbarium. Svensk Bot. Tidskr. 26: 346-364 (1932).

THORY, C.A. Prodrome de la monographie des espèces et variétés connues du genre rosier. 190 S., 2 Taf. Paris 1820.

TRATTINNICK, L. Rosacearum Monographia. 4 Bde. Wien 1823 to 1824.

VICIOSO, C. Estudios sobre el genero *"Rosa"* en España. 2. edicion. 134 pp. with pl. Madrid 1964.

WALLROTH, F.W. Rosae plantarum generis historia succincta. 311 S. Nordhausen 1828.

WILLMOTT, E.A. The Genus *Rosa*. 2 Bde., Großformat, 130 col. pl. London 1909-1914.

WITTICHIUS, J. Rhodographia oder Beschreibung der Rosen. Dresden 1804.

WOLLEY-DOD, A.H. A revision of the British Roses. Suppl. J. Bot. 68 and 69; 111 pp. (1930-1931).

WOODS, J. A synopsis of the British species of *Rosa*. Trans. Linn. Soc. 12: 159-234 (1818).

WREDE, E. CHR. C. Verzeichnis meiner Rosen, nach einer genauen systematischen Bestimmung. 3. ed. Braunschweig 1814.

The Horticultural Classification of Roses

The wealth of rose varieties which have been introduced since the beginning of the 19th century, i.e. since the organized breeding of roses, has made it necessary for botanists and gardeners to search for a precise order.

Initially, about 1800, this was still rather simple. There were the many varieties of *Rosa gallica, R. centifolia, R. damascena, R. moschata, R. chinensis* and *R. alba*. All these had long been in cultivation, and were all sufficiently different that each of these early roses could be designated as a class of its own. Today we still have the designations from that time.

After the rules of heredity were discovered, rose breeders began to interbreed the classes. It was found that this was generally successful, i.e. fertile descendants were produced. The principal aim of this process was, as it is today, to get roses with as long a period of flowering as possible; however, this was not easy, as there were only two classes of roses which possessed this characteristic to any degree; they were:

a) the recurrent Bengals or Chinas;
b) the Damasks which flowered twice yearly, and occasionally a third time in warmer regions.

The breeders worked hard with these two classes. Unfortunately, the first Bengal seedlings were sterile, and, for that reason, the Hybrid Bengals were not developed further for a long time.

The Damasks, on the other hand, could be successfully crossed with most of the garden roses, producing fertile offspring. In this way a new class soon arose, the Hybrid Perpetuals, and while these were primarily derived from the Damask Roses, they also contained genetic material from *R. gallica, centifolia, moschata* and other roses. In the first of these hybrids the characteristics of *Rosa damascena* were the most obvious, so they were called "Damask Perpetual Roses".

Soon other new roses appeared which no longer showed the characteristics of their parents, but a new combination of the characteristics of their parents.

Some of these roses were called "Portland Roses", after the 'Duchess of Portland', one of the most prominent varieties in this new class. But the most important one was certainly the 'Rose du Roi', from which arose most of the Hybrid Perpetuals.

From 1840 on nursery catalogs advertise hybrid classes of all rose groups existing at that time. Hybrids which clearly showed a characteristic of a *gallica* rose, were called "Gallica Hybrids", and so it was with all other groups.

The year 1840 is an important year when discussing the classification of roses, for three major events occurred then. The rose breeders achieved new perpetual-flowering rose varieties. Three lines of these new roses came from *Rosa odorata*, and were partly interfertile with many European roses. These three new lines of perpetual-flowering hybrids of *Rosa chinensis* were the 'Noisette Rose', the 'Bourbon Rose', and the descendants of 'Malton' and 'Athalin', two fertile seedlings from Bengal Rose × Damask Rose.

By now all the classes had been inter-bred and it was difficult to continue to speak of classification, so in 1849 a reader of *Gardeners Chronicle* (he called himself "Crito") proposed to divide all roses into "summer-flowering" (i.e. once-flowering) and "perpetual-flowering"(i.e. recurrent flowering) roses.

It was a useful and necessary proposal. The nurserymen's catalogs began to list the roses as "summer-flowering" or "autumn-flowering" varieties. Within these classes the varieties were split into the groups in use at that time, sometimes with some difficulty, for summer- and autumn-flowering varieties existed within the same class.

Nevertheless this was the first step to a solution of the hitherto existing disorder. The letter was a critical description of the situation at that time, and specified the following proposals:

1) The designation of a class has to contain the basic characteristics of roses of the class concerned;
2) In classes where a rose shows a clear similarity to one of the parents, the old classes are useful and should be retained.

But the writer had no idea of what to do with the many recurrent flowering roses starting to appear at that time, as these roses bore no similarity to any of the classes already in existence; so he gave these the somewhat arbitrary designation of "Hybrid Perpetuals".

THE HORTICULTURAL CLASSIFICATION OF ROSES

The use of this term became widespread and is still in use today, as these roses rarely show any similarity to one of their parents, and cannot, therefore, be put in any other class.

In France, too, botanists were concerned with a system of classification, and with much the same result. The leader in the field was Alfred Carrière (about 1850), who worked as an arbitrator in difficult questions. In 1851 he defined the following division of Hybrid Perpetuals:

1) Perpetuals of Portland Roses.
   Prickles very thin, short, very numerous and covering almost the entire stem; flowers mostly solitary; calyx elongated: 'Rose du Roi', 'Duchesse de Rohan', etc.

2) Recurrent Hybrids of Portland.
   Prickles widely spaced, differently long and thick; flowers 1-5 together, sometimes up to 7, erected at the top of branches; calyx elongated: 'La Reine', 'Baronne Prévost', 'Mme. Laffay', etc.

3) Recurrent Hybrids of Bourbon Roses.
   Intermediate between divisions 2 and 4, but closer to 4; leaflets coarsely dentate; easily differing from Division 2 by the more globose calyx: 'Clémentine Duval', 'Géant des Batailles', etc.

4) Bourbon Roses.
   Stems very bald, often short, usually terminating in a flower, but on longer branches often with several flowers together; branchlets often horizontal, very short; calyx rather globose: 'Reine des Ile-Bourbon', 'Mme. Deprez', 'Souvenir de la Malmaison', etc.

5) Noisette Roses.
   Reminiscent of Tea Roses, but growth much stronger, stems mostly very long, bark bald, but some varieties very prickly; branches ending into a panicle: 'Aimée Vibert', 'Lamarque', 'Noisette Deprez', etc.

6) Bengal Roses.
   Bark bald, stems with few prickles, leaflets oblong, dentate; flowers in panicles, nearly always vividly colored (in similar Tea Roses mostly yellow or whitish), only rarely with scent: 'Cramoisi Supérieur', 'Eugène Hardy', 'Prince Eugène', etc.

7) Tea Roses.
   Very similar to the previous, stems with few prickles, leaves glossy, flowers often solitary at the top of branches, sometimes also 3-5 together on long branches, scented: 'Devoniensis', 'Safrano', 'Maréchal Niel', 'Souvenir d'un ami', etc.

With the exception of a few of his "Hybrid Bourbons" which we consider today to be "Hybrid Perpetuals", the classes set up by Carrière have been retained to the present time. But the French rose breeders of the time, principally Guillot, confused his system greatly by hybridizing Tea Roses with every other rose possible. By 1877 his results with Tea Roses had advanced to such an extent that he felt obliged to revise his catalog, and add a new class which he called Hybrid Teas. This new designation was soon adopted, although some of the new varieties could not safely be recognized to be Hybrid Teas. Some of the more conservative hybridizers were of the opinion that the Hybrid Teas were not sufficiently different from the Tea Roses or the Hybrid Perpetuals to justify the establishment of a new class. But the treatment given 'La France' and 'Lady Mary Fitzwilliam' at rose shows showed that this new class was necessary. In so doing, the rose breeders of that time had practically already solved their problem of classification.

Later, as a temporary measure, the Penzancianas, the Pernetianas and the Lambertianas were established as special classes. Today these have been designated and classified in logical fashion. The Penzancianas are varieties of *R. rugosa*, so belong to that group; the Pernetianas are hybrids of *R. foetida*, but have long since completely merged with our modern Hybrid Teas, and the Lambertianas are now called "Recurrent Flowering Shrub Roses".

About 1870 the rose breeders started to hybridize with the Japanese *Rosa multiflora* (then still called *Rosa polyantha*), and the varieties obtained were named "Polyantha Hybrids"; later simply "Polyanthas". These were the white 'Pâquerette' (1875) and the pink 'Mignonette' (1879), both from Guillot. These were then crossed with Hybrid Teas as well as with all other roses, so that new seedlings were raised with larger flowers and more vivid colors, although the new red tone was first added by 'Gloria Mundi' in 1930. The designation "Polyanthas" was kept for the small-flowered varieties, and those with larger flowers were called "Hybrid Polyanthas". The confusion created by the new meaning of this latter term was compounded by the use of the term "Polyantha Rose" for an abbreviation of "Hybrid Polyantha", and even further, by the question of what to do with hybrids of Hybrid Polyanthas! A keen American breeder, Lammerts, introduced a new name, calling them "Floribundas". Since that time the designation "Hybrid Polyanthas" has disappeared in the United States, and is increasingly falling into disuse elsewhere.

The designation "Grandiflora" or "Floribunda Grandiflora" is still disputed; 1954 coined for 'Queen Elizabeth', but today many others also belong to this group, like 'June Bride', 'Diamant', 'Buccaneer', 'Montezuma', to name a few. This American name was vehemently criticized by British breeders, and was replaced with the somewhat unfortunate designation "Floribunda-Hybrid Tea Type", a name which will never come into permanent use.

In Germany, H. von Rathlef, Director of the Rose Research Center at Sangerhausen (now East Germany), was busy with a classification scheme, which he published in 1940. He proposed the following arrangement:

I. CLIMBING
  A. Non-recurrent flowering
    1. Multiflora and Multiflora Hybrids; *multiflora × multiflora*; *multiflora × gallica* or *chinensis*
    2. Wichuraiana Hybrids; (*wichuraiana × multiflora*) × *gallica* or *chinensis*
      a) small-flowered (e.g. 'Dorothy Perkins')
      b) large-flowered (e.g. 'Fräulein Octavia Hesse')
    3. Arvensis Hybrids; Setigera Hybrids, etc.
  B. Recurrent-flowering
    1. Moschata Hybrids; *moschata* × recurrent-flowering varieties
    2. Lambertiana varieties; *multiflora* hybrids × recurrent-flowering varieties
    3. Climbing sports
    4. Noisette Roses; *moschata × chinensis*
    5. Noisette Roses × Bourbon Hybrids

II. Low and Shrub Roses
  A. Non-recurrent flowering
    1. Descendants of *R. gallica*
      a) Damasks
      b) Centifolias
      c) Moss-Roses (mutations)
      d) Albas
      e) Provins
    2. Hybrids of wild roses
  B. Recurrent-flowering
    1. Recurrent-flowering Damasks, Centifolias and Moss-roses
    2. Bourbon-Roses; *gallica × chinensis*
    3. Hybrid Perpetuals; recurrent-flowering Damasks × *chinensis × gallica*
    4. Bengal Roses, incl. dwarf Bengals; descendants of *R. chinensis*
    5. Tea Roses; (?) *gigantea × chinensis*
    6. Hybrid Teas; Hybrid Perpetuals and Bourbons × Tea Roses
    7. Hybrid luteas; Hybrid Perpetuals and Hybrid Teas × *R. foetida*
    8. Polyanthas; ('Orléans-Rose'); *multiflora* × Hybrid Teas
    9. Hybrid-Polyanthas; Polyanthas × Hybrid Teas, etc.
      a) Hybrid Polyanthas old type ('Aennchen Müller'); from Polyantha × Hybrid Tea or Tea
      b) Hybrid Polyanthas, large-flowered ('Holstein'); from Polyantha × Hybrid Tea or × *moschata* Hybrids, etc.
      c) Floribunda ('Gruss an Aachen'), from Hybrid Polyantha × Hybrid Tea.

This system did not become widely known, due to the circumstances of the time (war and the death of the author).

How is this situation today? After strong efforts in the States and in Britain, a rose classification was presented by the World Federation of Rose Societies at their Oxford Convention, 1976, and adopted at the Pretoria Convention, 1979.

In 1966, the American Rose Society was asked by the Council of the International Horticultural Congress to search for a new classification. The society charged a committee, with Dr. G. Buck as chairman, which established the following rules:

1. Parentage of a rose is to be disregarded as a means of classification;
2. Classification is to be based solely upon consistent horticultural characteristics;
3. Permanent classification of rose cultivars should be delayed until their correct placement can be assessed adequately;
4. A code system of classification embodying both plant and flower trials is adopted for the five major recurrent bedding rose groups.

The American classification was as follows:

I. SHRUB ROSES
  A. Wild species
  B. Hybrids of species
  C. Other Shrub roses
  D. Old Garden Roses with shrubby growth
    1. Gallicas
    2. Damasks
    3. Autumn Damasks
    4. Albas
    5. Centifolias
    6. Moss Roses

II. OLD GARDEN ROSES, BEDDING ROSES
  A. Chinas
  B. Bourbons
  C. Noisettes
  D. Teas
  E. Hybrid Perpetuals

III. MODERN BEDDING ROSES
  A. Hybrid Teas
  B. Grandifloras (Floribunda Grandiflora)
  C. Floribundas
  D. Polyanthas
  E. Miniatures

IV. CLIMBING
  A. Rambling
  B. Non-recurrent large-flowered
  C. Recurrent-flowering large-flowered
  D. Climbing sports

The code system for the classification of the five most

THE HORTICULTURAL CLASSIFICATION OF ROSES

important classes of bedding roses (III A-E) has been used in the *American Rose Annual* for only a few years.

The Royal National Rose Society tried for many years to establish a better classification, and it seems that this problem is now solved. The British classification is based on other considerations than the American, as the following survey shows. (This is part of the paper of A.G.L. Hellyer, Chairman of the Sub-committee of Classification, in RA 1972, pp. 114-120, with the alterations adopted by the Council meetings of the World Federation of Rose Societies at the Oxford Convention, 1976, and approved at Pretoria, 1979).

MODERN GARDEN ROSES

Roses of hybrid origin not bearing any strong resemblance to wild roses (species) and not included in classifications in general use before the introduction of Hybrid Tea roses.

NON-CLIMBING

Plants with self-supporting stems.
Non-recurrent Flowering
Flowering season limited, in summer (or spring) with at best only occasional blooms in the autumn.
Non-recurrent *Flowering Shrub*. Plants usually taller and/or possibly wider than Bush Roses and particularly suitable for use as specimen plants.
Recurrent Flowering
Flowering season long or with a marked resurgence later.
Recurrent *Flowering Shrub*. Plants usually taller and/or possibly wider than Bush Roses and particularly suitable for use as specimen plants.
Bush. Varieties of moderate height particularly suitable for cultivation in groups.
Large Flowered (Hybrid Tea). Roses having double flowers, of medium to large size, of the traditional Hybrid Tea form (i.e. petals overlapped to form a conical, ovoid or other symmetrical center) and usually capable of being cut as a single flower (with or without side buds) on a long stem.
Cluster Flowered (Floribunda). Roses distinguished primarily by a mass of flowers produced in trusses, clusters or on many stems. The flowers may be single, semi-double or double.
Polyantha. Roses with small flowers, usually of rosette form, borne in large clusters. Distinctive foliage, the leaflets smaller than those of Cluster Flowered roses.
Miniature. Roses with miniature flowers, foliage and growth.

ROSE CLASSIFICATION CHART

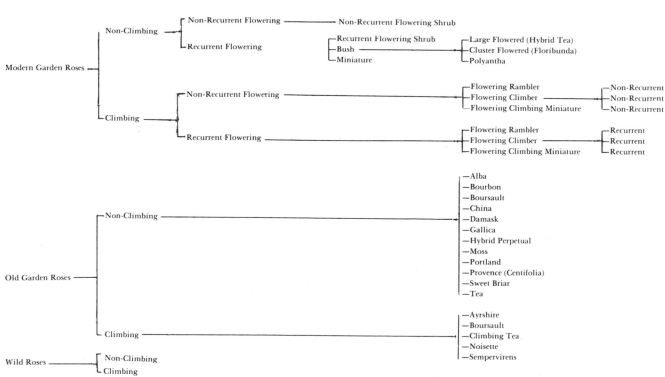

CLIMBING

Plants climbing or rambling with long sprawling or arching stems normally requiring support.

Non-recurrent Flowering

Flowering season limited, in summer (or spring) with at best only occasional blooms in the autumn.

(Non-recurrent Flowering) Rambler. Climbing roses with lax stems.

(Non-recurrent Flowering) Climber. Climbing roses with stiffer stems than Ramblers.

(Non-recurrent Flowering) Climbing Miniature. Climbing roses with very small flowers and foliage.

Recurrent Flowering

Flowering season long or with a marked resurgence later.

(Recurrent Flowering) Rambler. Climbing roses with lax stems.

(Recurrent Flowering) Climber. Climbing roses with stiffer stems than Ramblers.

(Recurrent Flowering) Climbing Miniature. Climbing roses with very small flowers and foliage.

OLD GARDEN ROSES

Roses already well established in classifications in common use before the introduction of Hybrid Tea roses. (These old classes were based largely on presumed genetical and botanical affinities and in general do not fit easily into a modern classification based mainly on functional garden qualities.)

NON-CLIMBING

Plants with self-supporting stems.

Alba. Roses displaying the influence of *Rosa alba*.

Bourbon. Roses displaying the influence of *Rosa × borboniana*, supposedly a hybrid between the China Rose and Autumn Damask.

Boursault. Roses supposedly displaying the influence of *Rosa chinensis* and *Rosa pendulina*.

China. Roses displaying the influence of *Rosa chinensis*.

Damask. Roses displaying the influence of *Rosa damascena*.

Gallica. Roses displaying the influence of *Rosa gallica*.

Hybrid Perpetual. Roses usually obtained by interbreeding Bourbon roses with China and/or Damask roses.

Moss. Roses with mossy outgrowth on sepals and/or pedicels.

Portland. Roses allied to 'Duchess of Portland', a hybrid suggesting the influence of China and Damask roses.

Provence. (Centifolia). Roses displaying the influence of *Rosa centifolia*.

Sweet Briar. Roses displaying the influence of *Rosa eglanteria*.

Tea. Roses displaying the influence of *Rosa × odorata*, supposedly a hybrid between *Rosa chinensis* and *Rosa gigantea*.

CLIMBING

Plants climbing or rambling with long, sprawling or arching stems normally requiring support.

Ayrshire. Roses displaying the influence of *Rosa arvensis*.

Boursault. Climbing roses supposedly displaying the influence of *Rosa chinensis* and *Rosa pendulina*.

Climbing Tea. Climbing roses with flowers similar to those of Tea roses.

Noisette. Roses displaying the influence of *Rosa × noisettiana*, supposedly a hybrid between *Rosa chinensis* and *Rosa moschata*.

Sempervirens. Roses displaying the influence of *Rosa sempervirens*.

WILD ROSES

Species and varieties or hybrids (single or double-flowered) which bear a strong resemblance to species.

NON-CLIMBING

Plants with self-supporting stems.

CLIMBING

Plants climbing or rambling with long, sprawling or arching stems normally requiring support.

(Mme.) G. de la Roche, 1972, proposed a classification of 7 sections, all with Latin designations. However, it is very complicated to the layman, and so, it is doubtful that this system will ever be generally recognized. Since it has been indicated only in outline, the following extract can show only the principal features:

1. Gallico-Indicae. Containing all hybrids between *Gallicanae* and *Indicae*, i.e. the Portlands, Bourbons, Hybrid Perpetuals and Hybrid Teas.
2. Synstylo-Indicae. Containing primarily the climbing descendants from the *Indicae*, also the Noisettes and the earlier Lambertianas (also called Hybrid Moschatas) and, finally, the true Polyanthas (from *R. multiflora* × Tea Rose).

3. Gallico-Synstylae-Indicae. Today the most important section, with the hybrids of Gallico-Indicae × Synstylae, as well as Gallico-Indicae × Synstylae-Indicae. To this belong:
   a) Floribunda — Floribunda
   b) Hybrid Lambertianas
   c) some Hybrid Wichuraianas
   d) hybrids between the sections a-c ('Garnette', 'Orange Triumph')

4. Pimpinellifoliae-Gallico-Synstylae-Indicae. To this belong the Hybrid Floribundas, e.g. 'Goldilocks', 'Masquerade', 'Allgold', 'Queen Elizabeth', 'Picasso', etc.

5. Canino-Gallico-Synstylae-Indicae. This are the Hybrid Floribundas, partly also with *R. rubiginosa*, like 'Obergärtner Wiebicke', 'Lilli Marlene', 'Evelyn Fison', etc.

6. Cinnamomeo-Gallico-Synstylo-Indicae, with the Hybrid Floribundas, descendants of *R. rugosa*, like 'Fanal'; or of *R. californica*, like 'Lilac Charm', 'Lake Como', etc.

7. Miniature Roses. Very complex hybrids with dwarf habit, descending from the *Indicae*.

BIBLIOGRAPHY:

(Anon). New Classification Proposals. The Rose 16: 113-116 (1968). (1968).

(Anon). New System: Garden Rose Classification. Amer. Rose Magazine, Sept. 1967.

(Anon). Goodbye, Floribunda! Farewell, Hybrid Tea! in The Rose Bulletin of the Roy. Nat. Rose Soc. 1979: 25-26.

CARRIÈRE, A. Charactères de Rosiers remontants. Flore des Serres 7: 140-141 (1851).

DE LA ROCHE, G. Outline of a Classification. Rosa Belgica 1972: 6-11.

("European Observer"). The new American Rose Classification. The Rose 16: 117-119 (1968).

HELLYER, A.G.L. Rose Classification; RA 1972: 114-120.

HOLLIS, L. Rose Classification. The Rose 17: 35-37 (1968).

MOREY, D. How Classifications are made. ARA 1957: 139-145.

RATHLEF, H. VON. Vorschlag zur Klassifizierung der Kulturrosen und dem Aufbau der Firmenkataloge. RJb 1940: 94-105.

ROWLEY, G. D. Key to the major Groups of Cultivated Roses. RHS Dictionary of Gardening, Suppl. 2. Ed.: 493 (1969).

Royal National Rose Society; Classification Committee: Draft of a classification of Roses. RA 1971: 8.

SIEBER, J. Neue Einteilung der Rosen. RJb 35: 146-167 (1969).

The Dictionary of Rose Cultivars

Explanations on the use of the Dictionary

The Dictionary contains the descriptions of rose varieties in alphabetical order, as follows:

- the commercial varieties available at this time are nearly complete; less important varieties have not always been included;
- the "Old Garden Roses" still available commercially, or in collections are also included, as well as varieties with special importance in hybridizing or the history of the rose;
- the wild roses (species) see pp. 246-296;
- in the original (German) edition of this work, all varieties growing in the five largest German rose gardens were indicated. These have been omitted here, as well as roughly one thousand German and Continental European varieties uncommon in the United States, and have been replaced by other (mostly new) American, British and some South African varieties.

Nomenclature All varietal names are written as in commercial use in the United States, but cross references are given where necessary. So, e.g. 'Tropicana' is also mentioned under its original name 'Super Star', as are 'Peace' (= 'Mme. Meilland', 'Gloria Dei' and 'Gioia'), 'Independence' (= 'Kordes Sondermedlung'), etc.

Concerning the species, the most modern form of botanical nomenclature is used.

Year of Introduction In comparison to other rose books, e.g. *Modern Roses 7* (and *8*), slight differences in the years of introduction may occur, since American books often give the year of commercial introduction to America, while foreign hybridizers cite the year it was first introduced commercially. Sometimes, but not always, both years may be the same.

Heights This is a rather difficult point, and the ultimate height can only be given approximately, as it is strongly influenced by cultivation (pruning, manuring and disease prevention), as well as by climatic and soil conditions.

Instead of giving the height in feet or centimeters, an effort has been made to give measurements which will be generally understood:

dwarf	under knee-height	12-14 in.	30-35 cm.	Miniatures and groundcovers
low	about knee-height	18-24 in.	45-60 cm.	Polyanthas, low Floribundas
medium	between knee-height and chest-height	2-5 ft.	0.6-1.5 m.	Floribundas, Hybrid Teas, many old Garden Roses
tall	man's height and over	5-6 ft.	1.5-1.8 m. and over	Shrub Roses, Climbers

Where necessary, "very" has been added.

Pedigrees The pedigrees of 33 important varieties are shown. It seemed more useful to keep these short and clear, and to refer to the continuing pedigrees, as many varieties have, in part, the same ancestors. Since the names of the parents are normally given for each variety described, it would not be too difficult to work out a longer pedigree. References to other pedigrees are given by arrows (→).

Mutations (Sports) A few varieties with exceptionally numerous spontaneous mutations are also listed; see 'Orléans Rose', 'Columbia', etc.

Class Abbreviations Behind each variety name its class is given in accordance with the *1979 Handbook for Selecting Roses* (a guide from the American Rose Society), p. 3, but the abbreviation OGR (= Old Garden Rose) is omitted here.

A	- Alba
B	- Bourbon
C	- Centifolia
Ch	- China (Chinensis)
Cl	- Climbing
D	- Damask
E	- Eglanteria (rubiginosa)
F	- Floribunda
G	- Gallica
HBlanda	- Hybrid Blanda
HBc	- Hybrid Bracteata
HFt	- Hybrid Foetida

HMsk	– Hybrid Moschata
HMoyesii	– Hybrid Moyesii
HP	– Hybrid Perpetual
HRg	– Hybrid Rugosa
HRub	– Hybrid Rubrifolia
HSpn	– Hybrid Spinosissima
HT	– Hybrid Tea
K	– Kordesii
LCl	– Large-flowered climber
M	– Moss
Min	– Miniature
N	– Noisette
P	– Portland
Pol	– Polyantha
R	– Rambler
S	– Shrub
Sp	– Species
T	– Tea

Other Abbreviations Letters and numbers at the end of a description are references to illustrations (usually in color) in other works and Year Books. For a list of these abbreviations, see p. 426.

National Ratings Where known, the American National Rating of garden value is given in ( ) at the end of a description, for the year 1979. The higher the number, the greater the value.

10.00	Perfect	7.9-7.0	Good
9.9-9.0	Outstanding	6.9-6.0	Fair
8.9-8.0	Excellent	5.9 and lower	of questionable value

Climbing Sports All climbing sports are listed under the original varietal names; e.g. 'Climbing Allgold' see 'Allgold, Climbing'.

Aalsmeer Gold. HT. (W. Kordes Söhne, 1978). 'Berolina' × seedling. Deep yellow, high centered, double, slight fragrance, blooms singly, continuous flowering; bud large, long, pointed; bushy, medium high, vigorous, upright; foliage glossy.

Accent. F. (W.A. Warriner; int. Jackson & Perkins, 1977). 'Marlene' × unnamed cultivar. Medium red, double, in clusters, slight fragrance; bud oval, opening flat; bushy, compact, low; foliage leathery, healthy. (7.5)

Ada Perry. Min. (Dee Bennett, 1978). 'Little Darling' × seedling of 'Coral Treasure'. Orange blend with soft yellow at base, double, slightly fragrant, 3-4 per cluster or singly, continuous and abundant flowering; bud ovoid; vigorous, upright, dwarf; foliage deep green.

Adam Messerich. B. (Lambert, 1920). 'Frau Oberhofgärtner Singer' × (seedling of 'Louise Odier' × 'Louis Philippe'). Pink, semi-double, large, first cup-shaped, very strong fragrance, recurrent; vigorous, tall, man's height or over, few prickles; foliage light green. GiS 11.

Adélaide d'Orléans. R. sempervirens hybrid. (Jacques, 1826). Pale pink, semi-double, in clusters; very floriferous; buds small; strong grower, 5 m./16.5 ft. high. TCR 1.

Admiral Rodney. HT. (Basildon Rose Gardens, 1973). Medium pink, very large, exhibition flower; very fragrant; vigorous, upright, medium; foliage green, healthy, tough.

Adolf Horstmann. HT. (Kordes, 1971). 'Colour Wonder' × 'Golden Wave'. Golden yellow, with bronze and orange, pink-edged, large-flowered, good fragrance, free flowering, on long stems; bud long, urn-shaped; bushy, upright, medium high; foliage deep green, glossy. RA 1974:185. (5.8)

Aenne Burda. HT. (Kordes, 1973). seedling × 'Gruss an Berlin'. Blood-red, high centered, double, slight fragrance, singly on long stems, petals drop off early; bushy, strong-growing, medium; foliage green, glossy, healthy. (7.0)

Africa Star. HT. (West/Harkness, 1965). Mauve, large-flowered, very double, floriferous; branching habit, medium; foliage large, coppery.

Agatha. (= R. gallica agatha). 1818. Not a variety, but a group of roses with small, but very double, flowers, outer petals reflexed, inner ones upright, concave, pale colors, purple or other color; leaves similar to 'Officinalis'. Origin unknown, but possibly related to R. centifolia.

Aglaia. R. (Schmitt, Lyon; intr. P. Lambert, 1896). R. multiflora × Rêve d'Or'. Canary yellow, semi-double, finally nearly white, fragrant; very tall, strong-growing; foliage glossy. RZ 1897:1.

Agnes. HRg. (Saunders, 1900; intr. 1922). R. rugosa × 'Persian Yellow'. Pale amber yellow, border paler, large, very double, globose, fragrant, floriferous, June; very strong grower, tall, 2.5 m./8.3 ft.; leaves similar to R. rugosa. Very frost-hardy. GSR 128; TRT 132; GiS 14. (8.0)

Aimé Vibert. (= "Bouquet de la Mariée"). N. (Vibert, 1828). 'Champney's Pink Cluster' × R. sempervirens hybrid. Buds blush, opening nearly pure white, double, medium-large, recurrent; tall, strong grower, 2-3 m./6.6-10 ft., taller when tied; stems nearly without prickles; foliage dark green, glossy. Oldest recurrent-flowering climber.

Akebono. HT. (Kawai, 1964). 'Ethel Sanday' × 'Narzisse'. Light yellow with carmine hue, very double, large, high-pointed, moderate bloom; upright, vigorous, medium; foliage dark green, glossy. (7.1)

Alabama. HT. (O.L. Weeks, 1976). 'Mexicana' × 'Tiffany'. Pink and white bicolor, double, moderate to strong tea scent, flowering throughout season; bud globose with pointed top, opening high-centered; upright, medium; foliage dark green, leathery.

alba with list of varieties see p. 260.

Albéric Barbier. R. (Barbier, 1900). *R. wichuraiana* × 'Shirley Hibbert'. Buds yellow, opening nearly white with yellow center, very double, large, star-shaped, very fragrant, singly or several together, summer-flowering, 8 cm./3.2 in. across; very strong and tall grower, 5 m./16.5 ft. or more, young stems coppery; foliage deep green, small, very glossy. GSR 192; GiS 22.

Albertine. LCl. (Barbier, 1921). *R. wichuraiana* × 'Mrs. Arthur A. Waddell'. Buds salmon, opening coppery-pink, loosely double, very floriferous, summer-flowering, strong fragrance; strong growth, 2-4 m./6.6-13.2 ft. tall, more shrubby and self-supporting; foliage dark green, dull. PWR 226; GSR 193; SOR 38; WGR 81.

Alchymist. S. (Kordes, 1956). 'Golden Glow' × *rubiginosa* hybrid. Orange-yellow, double, large-flowered, non-recurrent, fragrant; upright, tall; foliage coppery, glossy. WGR 85. (8.4)

Alec's Red. HT. (Cocker, 1970). 'Fragrant Cloud' × 'Dame de Coeur'. Bright crimson, huge flowers, very double, petals finally flat, very free flowering, scented, singly or several together; sturdy growth, medium high; foliage dull green, abundant. GSR 269; WPR 35; RA 1971: 3. (7.8)

Alexander. HT. (Harkness, 1972) 'Tropicana' × ('Ann Elizabeth' × Allgold). Brilliant vermillion, similar to 'Tropicana', double, 20 petals, slight fragrance, singly or several together; growth very strong, tall, upright; suitable for hedging; foliage light green, glossy. RA 1973: 120; HRo 10. (6.5)

Alexandra. HT. (Kordes, 1973). 'Colour Wonder' × 'Golden Wave'. Coppery-orange with yellow center, large-flowered, double, singly, very fragrant, floriferous; strong growing, upright; foliage dark green, glossy, healthy.

Alfred de Dalmas. (= 'Mousseline'). M. (Portemer, 1855). Pale pink to nearly white, medium large, cup-shaped, double, fragrant, recurrent, flowers lightly mossy; growth very dense, medium high, with many short stems, few prickles; foliage partly concave. (6.6)

Alison Wheatcroft. F. (Wheatcroft Bros., 1959). Sport of 'Circus'. Deep apricot-yellow, flushed with carmine and bordered, loosely double, 7 cm./2.8 in. across, fragrant; growth medium, moderately strong, branched, young growth coppery; foliage deep green, medium, glossy. WPR 55.

Alister Stella Gray. (= 'Golden Rambler'). N. (A.H. Gray, 1894). Pale yellow, center orange, fading to white, very double, fragrant, in clusters, recurrent bloom; bud long, pointed; growth vigorous, tall. GiS 22.

Allen Chandler. ClHT. (Chandler/Price, 1923). 'Hugh Dickson' × seedling. Brilliant crimson, large, single to semi-double, slightly fragrant in clusters of 3 to 4, on long stems, recurrent; very strong growth; foliage dark green, glossy. HRo 14; RA 1924:113.

Allen's Fragrant Pillar. ClHT. (Allen, 1931). 'Paul's Lemon Pillar' × 'Souv. de Claudius Denoyel'. Cerise with yellow center, double, large-flowered, fragrant, floriferous, recurrent; growth strong, with long stems; young growth red-brown; foliage glossy.

'Allgold'. F. (LeGrice, 1956). 'Goldilocks' × 'Ellinor LeGrice'. Yellow at all times, barely fading, semi-double, 7 cm./2.8 in. across, very free flowering; growth low, compact, branched; foliage deep green, glossy, healthy, small. GSR 378. (6.3)

Allgold, Climbing. ClF. (Gandy, 1961). Sport of 'Allgold'. Yellow like the original variety; tall, 3-4 m./10-13.2 ft.

Allspice. HT. (David L. Armstrong/Armstrong Nurseries, 1977). 'Buccaneer' × 'Peace'. Yellow, double, with fragrance of honey and tea rose, blooms freely, regularly recurrent; bud ovoid, pointed; bushy, upright, medium-tall; foliage abundant, olive-green, semi-glossy.

Aloha. ClHT. (Boerner/Jackson & Perkins, 1949). 'Mercedes Gallart' × 'New Dawn'. Dark pink with salmon hue, large-flowered, very double, continuous-flowering and floriferous; growth medium-strong, 2-3 m./6.6-10 ft.; foliage glossy, healthy. PWR 219; GSR 230; GiS 18. (6.3)

Alpha. (= 'Mainastur'). HT. (Meilland, 1979). [('Show Girl' × 'Baccara') × 'Romantica'] × ('Romantica' × 'Tropicana'). Bright vermilion, double, medium large, 20 petals, singly on long stems, almost continuous bloom; growth vigorous, upright; foliage leathery, deep green. RA 1979:153.

Alpine Sunset. HT. (G. Roberts, 1973). 'Grandpa Dickson' × 'Dr. A.J. Verhage'. Cream, interior flushed with peach-pink, large, double, 18-20 cm./7-8 in., very fragrant, free bloom; foliage glossy; growth very free.

Altissimo. LCl. (Delbard-Chabert, 1966). 'Tenor' × ?. Dark red with crimson, not fading, single, very large-flowered, 12 cm./4.8 in. across, velvety, scentless, bright golden stamens, continuous flowering; growth strong, 2 m./6.6 ft. or over, young growth red; foliage dark green. GSR 231; WPR 58; RA 1966:65.

Ama. F. (Kordes, 1955). 'Obergärtner Wiebicke' × 'Independence'. Scarlet, semi-double, 7 cm./2.8 in. across, very floriferous and continuous bloom in all weather; growth medium, well branched; foliage light green, glossy, plentiful. PWR 113; GSR 379; RJb 24: 192. (6.9)

Amadis. LCl. (Laffay, 1829). Also known as 'Crimson Bourault'; *R. chinensis* × *R. pendulina*. Flowers deep carmine-purple, sometimes also with white spots, semi-double, cup-shaped, nearly scentless, flowers a long time; stems whitish-green, later purplish-brown, without prickles and pruinose; in mild climates up to 5 m./16.5 ft. tall; not fruiting. TCR 3.

Amatsu-Otome. HT. (Teranishi, 1960). 'Chrysler Imperial' × 'Doreen'. Golden yellow with orange edge, very double, later more loose; growth strong, tall, long stems; foliage deep green, glossy. (6.4)

Ambassador. HT. (Meilland, 1979). Seedling × 'Whisky Mac'. Orange-red, double, full, light fragrance, mostly single; bud large, conical, abundant bloomer; foliage dark green, glossy. ARA 1979:169.

America. Cl. (W.A. Warriner/Jackson & Perkins, 1976). 'Fragrant Cloud' × 'Tradition'. Porcelain rose, double, large, petals imnbricate, in clusters, flowering continu-ously, very heavily on new canes; buds long, pointed-ovoid; foliage very healthy, little or no mildew. (8.0)

Americana. HT. (Boerner/Jackson & Perkins, 1961). Seedling of 'Poinsettia' × 'New Yorker'. Bright red, large-flowered, double, scented, floriferous; bud ovoid; growth upright, medium; foliage leathery. PWR 97; KR 9:10; WGR 117. (6.4)

American Beauty. HP. (Lédéchaux, 1875). Parentage unknown. Crimson-carmine, shaded with rose, very double, large, cupped, fragrant, floriferous, sometimes recurrent; strong stems; medium; greenhouse variety.

American Heritage. HT. (Lammerts, 1965). 'Queen Elizabeth' × 'Yellow Perfection'. Ivory-white and salmon, finally all salmon-colored, double, large-flowered, floriferous; buds long; growth tall, 1.1 m./3.7 ft.; foliage large, glossy, leathery. (7.0)

American Home. HT. (Morey/Jackson & Perkins, 1960). 'Chrysler Imperial' × 'New Yorker'. Deep red, large-flowered, loosely double, cup-shaped, good fragrance; strong growth; foliage leathery. RJb 26:97. (7.3)

American Pillar. LCl. (Van Fleet, 1902). *(R. wichuraiana × R. setigera)* × red Hybrid Perpetual. Crimson-pink with white eye, yellow stamens, single, open, large, in large panicles, flowers only once, but very floriferous; very strong grower, 3-5 m./10-16.5 ft.; foliage dark green, abundant, glossy, leathery. PWR 222; GSR 195; LR 14. (7.4)

American Pride. HT. (Grillo, 1929). Sport of 'Grillodale'. Pure white, exterior occasionally light pinkish, double, large-flowered, fragrant, profuse bloomer; bud long, pointed; growth strong. Extinct?

American Pride. HT. (W.A. Warriner/Jackson & Perkins, 1979). Seedling × seedling. Dark red, double, light fragrance, singly on long stems, very free bloomer; bud pointed, high centered; bush tall, upright; foliage large, dark.

America's Junior Miss. Fl. (Boerner/Jackson & Perkins, 1964). 'Seventeen' × 'Demure'-seedling. Soft coral-pink, medium, double, scented, floriferous; growth medium, bushy; foliage reddish, glossy. GSR 380; RJb 30:80. (= 'Junior Miss' of the trade). (7.3)

Améthyste. R. (Nonin, 1911). Sport of 'Non Plus Ultra'. Crimson-violet, small-flowered, very double, but in large trusses, flowers only once, on very long and arching stems; foliage glossy.

Ami Quinard. HT. (Mallerin, 1927). 'Mme. Méha Sabatier' × ('Mrs. Edward Powell' × *R. foetida bicolor*). Blackish-red with coppery-scarlet, semi-double, medium size, cupped, fragrant, floriferous; growth very strong; foliage leathery. (4.5)

Amy Robsart. E. (Penzance, 1894). Rose-pink, semi-double, large-flowered, fragrant, summer-flowering, later many scarlet hips; growth very strong, 2.5 m./8.3 ft.; leaves with aromatic scent. GSR 8; GiS 3.

Amy Vanderbilt. F. (Boerner/Jackson & Perkins, 1956). 'Lavender Pinocchio'-seedling × 'Lavender Pinocchio'. Lavender-lilac, very double, fragrant, cupped, large, in pyramidal clusters, floriferous; upright, bushy; foliage dark green, glossy. (5.7)

Anabell. (= 'Korbell'). F. (Kordes, 1972). 'Zorina' × 'Colour Wonder'. Salmon-orange, edge darker, large-flowered, loosely double, several together and in clusters, very floriferous, fragrant; bud globose, growth strong, medium, upright; foliage medium green, glossy, young growth coppery. RA 1972:33; CRA 73:41; (8.5)

Anais Ségalas. G. (not C!). (Vibert, 1837). Lilac-crimson, later more lilac-rose at the edge, large-flowered, very double, center greenish, finally flat, fragrant; medium high, 1 m./3.3 ft.; foliage light green.

Andrea. Min. (Ralph S. Moore, 1978). 'Little Darling' × seedling. Deep rose pink buds and flowers. 20 petals, several together, continuous bloom all season; few prickles; growth dwarf, vigorous, spreading; foliage small to medium.

Angel Darling. Min. (Ralph S. Moore, 1976). 'Little Chief' × 'Angel Face'. Lavendar with yellow stamens, semi-double, 10 petals, flowers singly and in clusters, slight fragrance, free blooming; dwarf, moderate to vigorous; foliage glossy, leathery. (7.5)

Angel Delight. HT. (Fryer's Nurseries, 1976). Sport of 'Femina'. Peach color with salmon shading, full, slight scent, singly on long stem, free-flowering; tall; upright; foliage large, leathery.

Angel Dust. Min. (Dee Bennett, 1978). 'Magic Carrousel' × 'Magic Carrousel'. White flowers, with 15-20 petals, to 3-4 in clusters, no scent, no prickles, good repeat bloomer; dwarf, upright, vigorous, spreading; foliage dark green.

Angel Face. F. (Swim & Weeks; int. C. & P. 1968). ('Circus' × 'Lavender Pinocchio') × 'Sterling Silver'. Dark mauve-lavender, double, very fragrant, large, high center to open; bud pointed; growth upright, bushy, medium; foliage dark green, leathery, glossy, very resistant to Black Spot. (8.0)

Angel Girl. HT. (Melvin E. Wyant, 1973). Sport of 'Bel Ange'. Peach-pink, large, high-centered, double, singly on medium stems, very long-lasting, strong fragrance, intermittant bloom; bushy, upright, vigorous; foliage leathery, disease-resistant. (6.8)

Angel Wings. HT. (Lindquist, 1958). 'Golden Rapture' × 'Girona'. Center golden yellow, later white, edge pink, first cupped, later flat, fragrant, floriferous; bud ovoid; upright, low; foliage leathery. (6.7)

Angelina. S. (Cocker, 1975). ('Tropicana' × 'Carina') × ('Cläre Grammerstorf' × 'Frühlingsmorgen'). Rose-pink, semi-double, 10 petals, fragrant, several together, very free bloom; medium high; foliage matt. RA 1976:20.

Angels Mateu. HT. (P. Dot, 1934). 'Magdalena de Nubiola' × 'Duquesa de Peñaranda'. Salmon-pink with golden-yellow hue, very double, fragrant, large, floriferous; bud globose; very strong growth, medium; foliage deep green. ARA 1937:38. (6.0)

Angelique. F. (Swim/Burr, 1961). 'World's Fair' × 'Pinocchio'. Coral-pink to salmon-pink, large, double, 20-25 petals, slight fragrance, abundant bloom, in large clusters; growth spreading, vigorous. ARA 63:1.

Ann Elizabeth. F. (Norman/Harkness, 1962). Rose-pink, semi-double, large, scented, free flowering, in clusters; growth vigorous, tall; foliage glossy.

Ann Factor. HT. (Ellis & Swim/Armstrong, 1975). 'Duet' × 'Jack O'Lantern'. Pastel apricot, red markings on reverse side, large, cupped, high-centered, profuse and continuous bloomer, scented; chest-high, open, spreading, bark and twigs purple; foliage dark green with red veins, glossy, large.

Anna Wheatcroft. F. (Tantau/Wheatcroft, 1958). 'Cinnabar'-seedling × ?. Light vermilion, large, single, light scent, in clusters; free bloomer; vigorous, sturdy, foliage deep green, healthy. RA 1960:49.

Anne Cocker. F. (Cocker, 1971). 'Highlight' × 'Colour Wonder'. Vivid vermilion, double, 35 petals, medium large, no scent, lasts well as a cut flower; growth medium high, upright; foliage first reddish-bronze, then dark green. GSR 382; RA 1970:175.

Anne Harkness. F. (Harkness, 1978). ['Bobby Dazzler × ('Manx Queen' × Prima Ballerine)] × ['Chanelle' × 'Piccadilly']. Medium yellow, double, 28 petals, blooms 3-9 per cluster, slight fragrance; bud round; bushy, upright, tall; foliage small, medium-green. RA 1979:85.

Anne Letts. HT. (G.F. Letts, 1953). 'Peace × 'Charles Gregory'. Soft pink, silvery-pink on the reverse side, loosely double, scented, good bloomer; vigorous, upright, very prickly; foliage large, deep green, glossy. PWR 77. (6.6)

Anne of Geierstein. E. (Penzance, 1894). Dark crimson, single, summer-flowering, hips scarlet; growth very strong, tall, 2.5 m./8.3 ft.; foliage fragrant.

Anne Poulsen. (= 'Anne-Mette Poulsen'). F.(Poulsen, 1935). 'Ingar Olsson' × red HT. Bright crimson, semi-double, slightly globose, in flat trusses, good bloomer; growth strong, upright, medium, with rather stiff stems; foliage large, dark green, glossy. ARA 1936:216. (7.0)

Anne Watkins. HT. (Watkins, 1962). 'Ena Harkness' × 'Grand' mère Jenny'. Orange with cream, reverse side darker and sometimes with pinkish shade, medium, double, good form, good bloomer, weather resistant; growth strong, upright, medium high; foliage dark green, slightly glossy, small. GR 64; WPR 41; RA 1963:128. (6.0)

Anny. Min. (P. Dot, 1949). 'Rouletti × 'Perla de Montserrat'. Pale pink, fading to white, double, only 15 mm./0.6 in. across, sepals leafy; very dwarf. PM 2. (7.3)

Antigua. HT. (W.A. Warriner/J. & P., 1974). 'South Seas' × 'Golden Masterpiece'. Apricot-blend, large, high-centered, double, slight fragrance, lasting well, singly on strong stems, growth bushy, upright, vigorous; foliage leathery. (7.5)

Antoine Rivoire. HT. (Pernet-Ducher, 1895). 'Dr. Grill' × 'Lady Mary Fitzwilliam'. Rosy-flesh with crimson shades, center yellow, very double, scented, floriferous; vigorous, medium; foliage dark green.

Anytime. Min. (McGredy, 1973) 'New Penny' × 'Elizabeth of Glamis'. Soft salmon-pink, saucer-shaped, semi-double, golden-yellow stamens, very floriferous; bushy, dwarf; foliage rather large. (7.5)

Apache Tears. F. (Pikiewiecz/Edmunds, 1971). 'Karl Herbst' × 'China Doll'. Cream to creamy-pink, light red edge, double, singly and several together on short stems, very long-lasting, profuse bloom, slight scent; bushy, vigorous, few prickles; foliage large, light green, disease-resistant. (7.2)

Apricot Nectar. Gr. (Boerner/Jackson & Perkins, 1965). Seedling × 'Spartan'. Bright apricot, center yellow, double. 10 cm./4 in. across, cupped, slight scent, continuous bloom; growth strong, tall, spreading; foliage dark green, glossy. GSR 283; RA 1966:49. (7.7)

Aquarius. Gr. (Armstrong, 1971). ('Charlotte Armstrong' 'Contaste') × ('Fandango' × ['World's Fair' × 'Floradora']). Crimson-pink, with darker reverse side, loosely double, mostly singly on long, strong stems. (7.3)

Archiduke Charles. C. (Laffay, about 1840). Rosy-crimson, sometimes marbled rose; growth moderate. (7.8)

Arctic Flame. HT. (Brownell, 1955). ('Queen o'the Lakes' × 'Pink Princess') × 'Mirandy'. Bright red, very double, fragrant, floriferous, large; buds pointed; growth busy, vigorous. (6.2)

Ardelle. HT. (Eddie, 1957). 'Mrs. Charles Lamplough' × 'Peace'. Creamy white, very double, large, high-centered, fragrant, floriferous; growth compact and vigorous; foliage glossy. (4.3)

Arianna. HT. (Meilland, 1968). 'Charlotte Armstrong' × ('Peace' × Michèle Meilland). Crimson-pink, double, large-flowered, some scent, floriferous, bud pointed, slender; vigorous, upright, medium high; foliage deep green, leathery. GSR 271. (7.8)

Aristide Briand. R. (Penny, 1928). 'Yseult Guillot' × ?. Pale pinkish-mauve, fading to whitish, double, 6 cm./2.4 in. across, fragrant, in clusters of 10 to 20; growth strong, 2 m./6.6 ft., well branched; foliage small, glossy, leathery, young growth bronze.

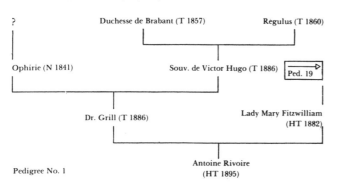

Pedigree No. 1

Arizona. G. (O.L. Weeks; intr. Conard-Pyle, 1975). ('Fred Howard' × 'Golden Scepter') × ('Golden Rapture No. 5' × self). Golden-bronze, medium, high-centered, strong tea scent, singly and in clusters, on medium, strong stems; growth very vigorous, but compact, upright; foliage dark green, glossy, disease-resistant. ARA 60:140. (6.5)

Arlene Francis. HT. (Boerner/Jackson & Perkins, 1957). 'Eclipse'-seedling × 'Golden Scepter'. Golden-yellow, double, very large, fragrant; bud slender, pointed; growth vigorous; foliage medium-large, deep green, glossy. (6.3)

Arrillaga. HP. (Schoener, 1929). *R. centifolia* × 'Mrs. John Laing' × 'Frau Karl Druschki'. Vivid pink, center golden-yellow, double, very large, fragrant, profuse bloomer, on long, strong stems; growth vigorous. (7.0)

Arthur Bell. F. (McGredy, 1965). 'Cläre Grammerstorf' × 'Piccadilly'. Golden-yellow, fading with age, semi-double, 8 cm./3.2 in. across, fragrant, free flowering; growth moderately tall, strong; foliage medium green, leathery, glossy. GR 224; RA 1965:113. (7.2)

Arthur de Sansal. D. (Sc. Cochet, 1855). 'Géant des Batailles' × ?. Brownish crimson-purple, changing to nearly violet, fully opened flat, very double, fragrant, summer-flowering; growth bushy, upright, 1 m./3.3 ft.; foliage dark green. Sometimes erroneously called a Portland Rose, and confused with 'Mme. de Sansal'.

Audie Murphy. HT. (Lammerts, 1957). 'Charlotte Armstrong' × 'Grand Duchesse Charlotte'. Luminous cherry-red, semi-double, finally flat, very large-flowered, continuous flowering; bud slender; growth bushy, upright, strong stems; foliage dark green, glossy. (7.3)

Aurora. K. (Kordes, 1956). Kordesii Hybrid. Orange-yellow, double, free flowering; growth tall, very vigorous. (8.0)

'Austrian Copper' → **Rose foetida bicolor,** p. 254

'Austrian Yellow' → **'Rose foetida'** p. 253

Autumn. HT. (Coddington, 1928). 'Sensation' × 'Souvenir de Claudius Pernet'. Burnt orange, streaked with red, very double, cupped, fragrant, floriferous; bud ovoid; foliage dark green, glossy. (5.0)

Autumn Delight. HMsk. (Bentall, 1933). White, single, red stamens, flowering in large clusters. (7.5)

Autumn Gold. HT. (O.L. Weeks, 1974-75) Seedling × seedling. Brownish to butterscotch yellow, double, globose, opening full centered, tea fragrance, intermittent bloom; growth tall, upright; foliage leathery, dark green, glossy. (7.5)

Autumn Sunlight. LCl. (Gregory, 1965). 'Spectacular' × 'Goldilocks'. Orange-vermilion, double, 30 petals, fragrant, medium size, free blooming; growth very free, tall; foliage light green, glossy.

Avandel. Min. (Ralph S. Moore, 1977). 'Little Darling' × 'New Penny'. Blend of pink, apricot and yellow, 20-25 petals, cupped to flat, singly and in clusters, fragrant, blooming all season; bushy, dwarf, upright; foliage medium size, leathery. (7.5)

Ave Maria. HT. (Brownell, 1957). Seedling × 'Climb. Break o'Day'. Pure white, double, large, good shape, floriferous; bud ivory; growth bushy, medium high. (7.4)

Avignon. F. (Cants of Colchester, 1974). 'Zambra' × 'Allgold'. Rosy-red with golden-yellow, semi-double, 25 petals, medium size, slight fragrance, very free flowering in clusters; medium high, vigorous, well branched; foliage deep bronzy-green.

Avon. HT. (Morey, 1961). 'Nocturne' × 'Chrysler Imperial'. Bright red, double, large, high-centered, fragrant, blooming freely; bud ovoid; growth vigorous, upright; foliage leathery.

Ayreshire Roses. This group of roses, descendants of *Rosa arvensis*, was developed in Scotland about 1830; all were very frost-hardy shrub roses. Flowers white to pink and crimson, single or double. Few in cultivation at this time.

Aztec. HT. (Swim, 1957). 'Charlotte Armstrong' × seedling. Scarlet with yellowish hue, double, slight scent; bud pointed; growth strong, tall, 1 m./3.3 ft; foliage leathery, dense, glossy. (7.6)

Baby Betsy McCall. Min. (Morey, 1960). 'Cécile Brunner' × 'Rosy Jewel'. Light pink, double, small, cupped, fragrant, floriferous; growth dwarf, 15 cm./6 in., compact; foliage light green, leathery. PM 1. (8.1)

Baby Bunting. Min. (de Vink, 1953). 'Ellen Poulsen' × 'Tom Thumb'. Light magenta, double, small, stamens prominent, flowers several together; bud globose; growth dwarf, compact; foliage small. (6.5)

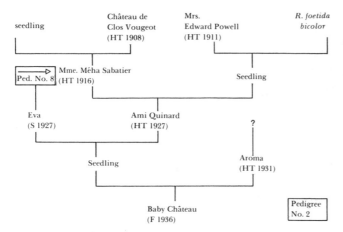

Baby Château
(F 1936)

Pedigree
No. 2

Baby Château. F. (Kordes, 1936). 'Aroma' × ('Eva' × 'Ami Quinard'). Dark crimson, double, large-flowered, fragrant, many together in clusters; growth bushy, strong; foliage medium green, young growth bronzy-red.

Baby Cheryl. Min. (E.D. Williams, 1965). 'Spring Song' × miniature seedling Light pink with lighter reverse, double, small-flowered, open, fragrant, floriferous; dwarf, vigorous; foliage leathery. (7.2)

Baby Darling. Min. (Ralph S. Moore, 1964). 'Little Darling' × 'Magic Wand'. Apricot to orange-pink, small, semi-double; dwarf, 25 cm./10 in.; foliage deep green, glossy. (8.3)

Baby Darling, Climbing. ClMin. (1972). Climbing sport. Like the original variety, but taller. (7.5)

Baby Faurax. Pol. (Lille, 1924). Violet, small, double, fragrant, in clusters, free bloom; growth dwarf. PM 2. (6.3)

Baby Garnette. Min. (Morey, 1962). 'Red Imp' × 'Sparkler'. Blood-red, double, small, floriferous; growth dwarf, compact; foliage dark green.

Baby Gold Star. (= 'Estrellita de Oro'). Min. (P. Dot, 1940). 'Eduardo Toda' × 'Rouletii'. Golden yellow, semi-double, flat, slight scent, small-flowered; dwarf, bushy; foliage deep green, glossy. GR 273; PM 22. (6.9)

Baby Gold Star, Climbing. ClMin. (E.D. Williams, 1964). Climbing sport, taller, but otherwise like the type. (7.8)

Baby Jayne. (= 'Fairy Hedge', 'Pink Hedge'). ClMin. (Ralph S. Moore, 1957). 'Violette' × 'Zee'. Soft pink, very double, small, in clusters, profuse flowering; growth

medium, about 1 m./3.3 ft.; foliage small, glossy. (6.9)

Baby Katie. Min. (F. Harmon Saville, 1987). 'Sheri Anne, × 'Watercolor'. Pink blend, high-centered, semi-double, light scent, singly or 3-12 together, very prolific and continuous flowering; dwarf, compact, bushy; foliage serrate, matt green. ARA 1979:101.

Baby Masquerade. (= 'Baby Carnaval'). Min. (Tantau, 1955). 'Peon' × 'Masquerade'. Bud red, opening golden-yellow, then changing to luminous red, similar to 'Masquerade', but much smaller, loosely double; growth dwarf; foliage deep green, matt. GSR 501; PM 22. (7.9)

Baby Masquerade, Climbing. ClMin. (R.O. Sykes/Mini Roses, 1974). Climbing sport. Medium high, otherwise like the type. (7.0)

Baby Ophelia. Min. (Ralph S. Moore, 1961). (*R. wichuraiana* × 'Floradora') × 'Little Buckaroo'. Rosy-pink, yellow center, slightly cupped, small-flowered, double, fragrant, floriferous; dwarf; foliage glossy. (7.3)

Baby Pinocchio. Min. (Ralph S. Moore, 1967). 'Golden Glow' × 'Little Buckaroo'. Salmon-pink, double, small-flowered, fragrant; bud ovoid; dwarf; foliage leathery, deep green. (6.4)

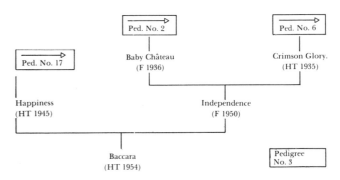

Baccara. HT. (Meilland, 1954). 'Happiness' × 'Independence'. Pelargonium-red with darker reverse, petals revolute, no scent; buds short, thick; growth very strong, medium high; foliage large, glossy, young growth coppery. Greenhouse variety. PWR 19; BTR 41. (6.8)

Bahia. F. (H.E. Lammerts, 1974). 'Rumba × 'Tropicana'. Luminous orange, medium-large, cupped, 8 cm./3.2 in. across, 20-30 petals, slight fragrance, in clusters; bud pointed; growth strong, bushy, tall; foliage medium large, dark green, glossy. (7.1)

Bajazzo. HT. (Kordes, 1961). 'Prima Ballerina' × 'Liberty Bell'. Velvety dark red inside, nearly white on the reverse, double, large-flowered, fragrant; growth strong, upright, medium high; foliage deep green. KR 9:20. (5.2)

Ballerina. HMsk. (Bentall, 1937). Parentage unknown. Clear pink, white center, single, small-flowered, but in large panicles, recurrent; growth medium, up to 1 m./3.3 ft.; foliage light green, small, leathery. GSR 140; GR 353.

Ballet. HT. (Kordes, 1958). 'Florex' × 'Karl Herbst'. Dark pink, excellent shape, very double, very large-flowered, some scent; growth strong, branched, medium high; foliage matt, large, young growth coppery. GSR 272; RA 1958:64. (7.2)

Bambi. F. (Von Abrams, 1962). Light apricot-pink, slightly fragrant, cupped, semi-double, large, 8 cm./3 in.; bloom profuse; bud pointed; foliage glossy; growth vigorous, bushy, compact.

Bambino. Min. (P. Dot, 1953). Sport of 'Perla de Alcanada'. Soft pink, good shape, small-flowered, some scent, floriferous: 30 cm./12 in. PM 2. (6.9)

Bangor. F. (Dickson, 1972). 'Jubilant' × 'Marlena'. Rosy-pink, white eye, medium large, semi-double, flat, very floriferous, in clusters; low; foliage medium-large, deep green.

Bantry Bay. LCl. (McGredy, 1967). 'New Dawn' × 'Korona'. Pink, semi-double, very large, many together in clusters, recurrent; growth strong, tall, 2.5-3 m./ 8.3-10 ft.; foliage medium green. GSR 232; RA 1968:129.

Banzai. HT. (Paolino, 1976). 'Coed' × ([seedling × seedling] × 'Verla'). Canary yellow, slightly fragrant, double, full, deeply cupped, large, 10 cm./4 in., bloom free; growth vigorous.

Baron de Wassenaer. M. (V. Verdier, 1854). Bright red to pink, globose; buds slightly mossy, non-recurrent, not very showy; growth strong, chest-high; foliage healthy.

Baron Girod de l'Ain. HP. (Reverchon, 1897). Sport of 'Eugène Fürst'. Crimson-pink, petals with white edge, waved, finally crimson-purple, opening cupped, medium-large, very double, strong fragrance, recurrent; growth strong, chest-high; foliage large. GSR 106; TRT 96. (7.2)

Baroness Rothschild. (= 'Baronne Adolphe de Roth-schild'). HP. (Pernet, 1868). Sport of 'Souvenir de la Reine d'Angleterre'. Center dark pink, lighter towards edge, opening cupped, later petals revolute, very large-flowered, very double, extremely floriferous, second flowering in the autumn; growth very strong, chest-high; foliage large. GSR 107; FGR 71. (7.1)

'Baronne Adolphe de Rothschild → **Baroness Rothschild**

Baronne Edmond de Rothschild. HT. (Meilland, 1968). ('Baccara' × 'Liebesglut') × 'Peace'. Dark crimson interior, silvery reverse, very large-flowered, 12 cm./5 in. across, large, strong fragrance, floriferous; growth very strong; foliage very large, leathery, bronze-green, very glossy.

Baronne Finaz. HT. (Gaujard, 1961). 'Peace'-seedling × 'Opéra'. Pink, double, large-flowered, fragrant, floriferous, long stems; growth very strong; foliage deep green, glossy. (6.7)

Baronne Nathalie de Rothschild. HP. (Pernet, 1885). 'Baroness Rothschild' × 'Souvenir de la Reine d'Angleterre'. Silvery-pink, very large-flowered, double, fragrant, recurrent; growth strong, chest-high; foliage light green.

Baronne Prévost. HP. (Desprez, 1842). Rosy-pink, lighter towards the edge, large-flowered, very double, finally flat, fragrant, recurrent; growth strong, upright. SOR 27; PGR 72.

Bashful. (= 'Giesebrecht'). Pol. (de Ruiter, 1955). Parentage not given. Dark purplish-pink, white eye, single, in pyramidal trusses; growth very dwarf and dense; foliage glossy.

Bayadère. HT. (Mallerin, 1954). 'RMS Queen Mary' × seedling. Salmon-pink to canary-yellow with pink shades, very double, very large-flowered, high-centered, slight fragrance; growth bushy, strong, medium high; foliage deep green, young growth bronze. RA 1955:100.

Bayreuth. S. (Kordes, 1965). Golden-yellow and reddish, loosely double, 25 petals, very large-flowered, 12 cm./5 in., strong fragrance, floriferous; growth bushy, upright, chest-high; foliage healthy, glossy; RJb 30:48.

Beauté. HT. (Mallerin, 1953). 'Mme. Joseph Perraud' × seedling. Orange, large-flowered, good shape, but rather loose, slight fragrance; bud long, dark orange; growth bushy, medium tall, 0.8 m./2.6 ft.; foliage dark green, matt. GSR 273; WPR 42; GR 145. (5.8)

'Beautiful Dreamer'; name changed to → **Southern Sun.**

Beauty of Glazenwood → **Fortune's Double Yellow.**

Beauty Secret. Min. (Ralph S. Moore, 1965). 'Little Darling' × 'Magic Wand'. Medium red, double, high-centered, small, very fragrant, abundant bloom; growth moderately compact; foliage small, leathery, glossy. (9.0)

Bel Ange. HT. (Lens, 1962). ('Independence' × 'Papillon Rose') × ('Charlotte Armstrong' × 'Floradora'). Interior salmon-pink, reverse darker, double, fragrant, floriferous, large-flowered; growth stiff upright, 0.9 m./3 ft.; foliage dark green, young growth red. (7.4)

Belinda. HMsk. (Bentall, 1936). Soft pink, small-flowered, but in very large, pyramidal trusses; growth strong, chest-high. (8.0)

Belinda. F. (Tantau, 1971). Seedling × 'Zorina'. Orange-yellow and coppery, medium-large, double, slight fragrance, several together; bud slender; growth bushy, upright, medium tall; foliage medium large, very glossy; greenhouse variety.

Belle Amour. A.R. *damascena* × *R. alba*?. Found before 1950 in an abbey in Elboef, France. Salmon-pink, semi-double, very strong anise-like scent, floriferous, stamens yellow; growth strong, stems stiff, very prickly; foliage light green. GSR 63; GiS 7. (7.0)

Belle Blonde. HT. (Meilland, 1955). 'Peace' × 'Lorraine'. Golden-yellow, darker center, medium large, fragrant, double, floriferous; growth bushy, low, upright; foliage large, dark green, glossy. PWR 80; WPR 16. (5.3)

Belle de Crécy. G. (Roeser, France, before 1848). Opening cherry-red freckled with mauve, purple and rose, perfect shape, finally flat, very fragrant, free flowering, in clusters; growth a bit weak (stake), 1 m./3.3 ft., stems nearly without prickles; foliage matt green. TR 5; GiS 5. (7.8)

Belle Etoile. G. (Lens, 1961). 'Joanna Hill' × 'Tawny Gold'. Golden yellow, well-formed, medium size, double, in clusters of 5-7 on long stem, profuse bloom; bud long, pointed; growth vigorous, upright.

Belle Isis. G. (Parmentier, 1845). Light pink, edge later nearly white, double; bud globose; growth medium 1 m./3.3 ft. foliage light green. (7.6)

Belle Poitevine. HRg. (Bruant, 1894). Light purplish-

pink, bud darker, large-flowered, slight scent, finally flat, recurrent, hips orange-red; growth strong, chest-high and wide; foliage similar to *R. rugosa*, light green. Very similar (or possibly identical?) to 'Souvenir de Christophe Cochet'. PWR 189; GiS 14. (7.0)

Belle Portugaise. (= 'Belle of Portugal'). LCl. (Cayeux, 1903). *R. gigantea* × 'Souvenir de Mme. Léonne Viennot'. Soft salmon-pink, large-flowered, loosely double, petals revolute, very strong fragrance, flowers slightly nodding, flowers for a long time, but non-recurrent; growth very strong, up to 5 m./16.5 ft.; foliage grey-green. (7.1)

Bellevue. HT. (N.D. Poulsen, 1978). ('Tropicana' × 'Piccadilly') × 'Fru Jarl'. Pink blend, large-flowered, 23 petals, no scent, singly or in clusters; growth vigorous, upright, medium; foliage glossy, leathery.

Bellona. F. (Kordes, 1974). 'Mabella' × seedling. Type similar to 'Spanish Sun'; golden-yellow, medium large, high-centered, strong fragrance, several together on long stems, abundant flowering; growth strong, medium high; foliage dark green, glossy, abundant.

Bendigold. F. (J.J. Murley/Brundrett, 1977). 'Rumba' × 'Redgold'. Orange-red, semi-double, slight scent, profuse, continuous bloomer; bud globose; growth upright, bushy, few prickles; foliage glossy.

Benjamin Franklin. HT. (Abrams/Edmunds, 1969). Salmon pink with orange-yellow hue, large-flowered, very double, good fragrance, singly on long stems, floriferous, long-lasting; growth bushy, medium strong; foliage abundant, leathery, young growth coppery.

Berlin. S. (Kordes, 1949). 'Eva' × 'Peace'. Vermilion, yellowish-white center, single, petals waved, stamens golden-yellow, recurrent, many together in large trusses; growth strong, chest-high, strong prickles; foliage glossy, healthy. GSR 141; GiS 18. (8.1)

Bermuda Pink. HT. (A.J. Golik/Dynarosa Ltd., 1974). 'Queen of Bermuda' × 'Montezuma'. Flesh-pink, double, globose, light scent, profuse free bloom, bud ovoid; growth medium high, compact.

Bermudiana. HT. (Boerner/Jackson & Perkins, 1966). Seedling of 'Golden Masterpiece' × self. Crimson-pink, somewhat lighter when fully open, bicolor, 12-15 cm./5-6 in. across, double, fragrant; growth strong, upright, chest-high; foliage deep green, leathery. (6.5)

Berolina. F. (Kordes, 1976). 'Mabella' × seedling. Medium yellow, double, high-centered, slight scent, abundant, continuous bloom, in clusters; bud long, pointed; growth vigorous, upright; foliage soft, dark green.

Betsy McCall. F. (Boerner/Jackson & Perkins, 1966). Seedling × 'Fashion'. Salmon-pink, double, large-flowered, good shape, strong fragrance, floriferous; growth medium strong, bushy; foliage large, green, matt. (7.7)

Betsy Ross. HT. (Samtmann Bros., 1931). Sport of 'Talisman'. Russet-orange, double, opening flat, medium size, scented, on long stem; growth vigorous; foliage light green, glossy, leathery. (7.8)

Better Times. HT. (J.H. Hill Co., 1934). Sport of 'Briarcliff'. Luminous cherry-red, good shape, large-flowered, some scent, very floriferous, long stems; bud long; growth upright, stiff; foliage deep green, leathery. Greenhouse variety, formerly much esteemed. ARA 1934:24. (5.2)

Bettina. HT. (Meilland, 1953). 'Peace' × ('Mme. Joseph Perraud' × 'Demain'). Yellow-orange, veined with bronze, medium large, good shape, 10 cm./4 in. across, double, fragrant; growth medium strong, bushy, low; foliage green, glossy, young growth bronze. PWR 57; BTR 28; (6.7)

Bettina, Climbing. ClHT. (Meilland, 1958). Sport of 'Bettina'. Growth 2 m./6.6 ft.; flowers like the type. (5.2)

Betty Herholdt. HT. (J.A. Herholdt, 1977). ('White Swan' × seedling) × 'Pascali'. White, very double, moderate fragrance, continuous bloomer, singly on long stems; bud pointed, full; growth medium tall; foliage healthy, disease-resistant.

Betty Neuss. HT. (G. Dawson/Brundrett, 1973). 'Tropicana' × 'Memoriam'. Pure pink, double, medium large, long-lasting, profuse, continuous bloom; bud long, pointed; growth very vigorous, upright, bark and branches reddish-brown; foliage small.

Betty Prior. F. (Prior, 1935). 'Kirsten Poulsen' × seedling. Crimson-salmon-pink outside, interior lighter, with whitish center, single, saucer-shaped, no scent, very floriferous and recurrent all season; growth upright stiff, bushy, medium tall; foliage large, glossy, green, matt, abundant, very resistant to Black Spot. RA 1933:176. (8.3)

Betty Uprichard. HT. (A. Dickson, 1922). Parentage unknown. Soft salmon-rose, outside more crimson-pink with coppery hue, large-flowered, loosely double, strong fragrance, floriferous; growth strong, tall; foliage leathery, light green, glossy. RA 1925:79. (5.4)

Bewitched. HT. (Lammerts/Germain's, 1967). 'Queen Elizabeth' × 'Tawny Gold'. Medium pink, double, large, 12 cm./5 in.; high-centered, fragrant, profuse bloom; growth very vigorous; foliage dark green, glossy.

Bicentennial. F. (Carl Meyer/Conard-Pyle, 1975). Parentage not given. Medium to dark pink, margins velvety red, double, medium large, high-centered, slight scent, in clusters on strong stems, abundant, continuous bloom; bud ovoid, medium; growth vigorous, few prickles, bushy, upright, medium high; foliage leathery. ARA 1975:26. (7.5)

Bienvenu. Gr. (Swim & Weeks, 1969). 'Camelot' × ('Montezuma' × 'War Dance'). Reddish-orange, large-flowered, very double, strong fragrance, long-lasting, singly or several together on long stems; growth strong, upright; foliage abundant, leathery, healthy.

Big Ben. HT. (Gany, 1964). 'Ena Harkness' × 'Charles Mallerin'. Dark velvety red, large, 12-15 cm./5-6 in., very fragrant, free bloom; foliage dark green. (8.2)

Big Chief. HT. (Dickson, 1975). 'Ernest H. Morse' × 'Red Planet'. Crimson, double, 30 petals, high-centered, very large-flowered, moderate fragrance, singly, free blooming; foliage dull green.

Big John. Min. (E.D. Williams, 1979). 'Starburst' × 'Over the Rainbow'. Deep medium red, base yellow, high centered, double, 2.5-3.8 cm./1-1.5 in., abundant bloom; bud pointed; foliage small, glossy, bronzy; growth upright, bushy.

Big Red. HT. (Meilland, 1967). 'Chrysler Imperial' × seedling. Dark red, very large, 12-15 cm./5-6 in., double, high-centered, slight scent, abundant bloom; growth vigorous, bushy, upright; foliage dark green. (6.1)

Big Splash. ClHT. (Armstrong, 1969). 'Buccaneer' × 'Bravo'. Interior vermilion, yellow center, with light red reverse, slight fragrance, large-flowered, cupped, long-lasting; bud large, pointed to urn-shaped; growth very strong, climbing; foliage healthy, leathery, deep green.

Bikini Red. HT. (A.J. Golik/Dynarose Ltd., 1974). 'Queen of Bermuda' × 'Peace'. Red, double, 40 petals, fragrant, free blooming; bud ovoid; growth tall; foliage dark green, glossy.

Birmingham Post. F. (Watkins Roses, 1968). 'Queen Elizabeth' × 'Wendy Cussons'. Dark pink, reverse darker, very double, strong fragrance, good shape, large-flowered; growth strong, medium tall, 0.9 m./3 ft.; foliage abundant, medium green, leathery. GSR 274; RA 1969:32.

Birthday Party. Min. (Strawn, 1979). 'Attraktion' × 'Sheri Anne'. Pink, fragrant, double, 4-5 cm./1.5-2 in., prolific bloom; bud ovoid; folige dark; growth upright, spreading.

Bishop Darlington. HMsk. (Thomas, 1926). 'Aviateur Blériot' × 'Moonlight'. Cream to flesh-pink with yellow, large, semi-double, cupped, fragrant, recurrent bloom; growth semi-climbing; foliage bronzy, soft. (7.5)

Bit o'Sunshine. Min. (Ralph S. Moore, 1958). 'Copper Glow' × 'Zee'. Golden-yellow, fragrant, double, first cupped, finally flat, 5 cm./2 in. across, very floriferous, stamens orange; bud long, pointed; growth bushy, dwarf; foliage fresh green, matt, healthy. (6.6)

Black Boy. M. (Kordes, 1958). 'World's Fair' × 'Nuits d'Young'. Dark crimson with purple, double, finally flat, fragrant, summer-flowering only, anthers golden-yellow; growth strong, chest-high.

Black Ice. F. (Gandy, 1973). ('Iceberg' × 'Europeana') × 'Meggido'. Dark red, double, 10 cm./4 in. across, slight scent, floriferous, in dense trusses; growth strong; foliage deep green, glossy.

Black Lady. HT. (M. Tantau, 1976). Parentage not given. Blackish-red, double, medium size, very strong fragrance, several together; bud globose; growth bushy, spreading; foliage medium large.

Black Prince. HP. (W. Paul, 1866). Dark crimson and blackish, large-flowered, very double, strong fragrance, recurrent; growth strong. (6.0)

Black Velvet. HT. (Morey/Jackson & Perkins, 1960). 'New Yorker' × 'Happiness'. Dark crimson, to nearly black, large-flowered, 12 cm./5 in., double, strong fragrance, abundant, on long stems; growth strong, upright; foliage medium green, leathery. (6.9)

Blanc Double de Coubert. HRg. (Cochet-Cochet, 1892). R. *rugosa* × 'Sombreuil'. Pure white, semi-double, large, strong fragrance, flowering June-August; nice bud; growth strong, man's height or over; foliage typical *rugosa*. GSR 130; GR 368; GiS 14. (8.0)

Blanc Pur. N. (Mauget, 1827). White, exterior greenish shades, large-flowered, double; growth very strong, to 4 m./13.2 ft.

Blanche Mallerin. HT. (A. Meilland, 1941). 'Edith Krause' × 'White Briarcliff'. Pure white, large, 10 cm./4 in., double, high-centered; bud long, pointed, growth vigorous; foliage leathery, glossy. (6.4)

Blanche Moreau. M. (Moreau-Robert, 1880). Comtesse de Murinais' × 'Quatre Saisons Blanc'. (= 'White Moss'). Pure white, rather small-flowered, 7 cm./2.8 in., very double, cupped to flat, summer-flowering, some flowers in the autumn; buds with dark brown moss, sticky; growth medium strong, chest-high, stems very prickly. (6.2)

Blaze. LCl. (Kallay/Jackson & Perkins, 1932). 'Paul's Scarlet Climber' × 'Gruss an Teplitz'. Scarlet, medium large, semi-double, slight scent, many together in trusses; growth strong, climbing; foliage dark green, leathery. Very similar to 'Paul's Scarlet Climber', but recurrent. (7.7)

Blessings. HT. (Gregory, 1967). 'Queen Elizabeth' × seedling. Soft coral-pink, double, slight scent, large-flowered, in clusters; growth strong, upright, medium high; foliage medium green. GSR 388; RA 1969:176.

Blithe Spirit. HT. (Armstrong & Swim, 1964). 'Fandango' × seedling. Light crimson-pink with yellow base, medium large, loosely double, slight scent, many together in clusters; growth strong, upright, spreading; foliage large, young growth bronze. (7.1)

Bloodstone. HT. (McGredy, 1951). 'The Queen Alexandra Rose' × 'Lord Charlemont'. Orange-red, large, double, high-centered, slight scent, free bloom; growth vigorous; foliage coppery-green, dark.

Bloomfield Abundance. S. Ch. (G.C. Thomas, 1920). 'Sylvia' (?) × 'Dorothy Page Roberts'. Salmon-pink, perfectly formed miniature flowers, very double, fragrant, finally fading to almost white, recurrent, in clusters; growth very strong, man's height or over; foliage neat, deep green, glossy. ARA 1926:100; TRT 172; GiS 10; PGR 72. (7.7). Similar to 'Cécile Brunner', but more vigorous.

Blossomtime. Cl. (O'Neal/Bosley, 1951). 'New Dawn' × unnamed HT. Interior light pink to rosy-white, darker pink reverse, large-flowered, very double, strong fragrance, 3-8 together, recurrent; bud long, pointed; growth strong, 1.5-2 m./5-6.6 ft. foliage glossy, healthy. RJb 26:96. (7.6)

Blue Boy. C. (Kordes, 1958). 'Louis Gimard' × 'Independence'. Brownish-purple and lilac-rosy, very large-flowered, very double, strong fragrance, summer-flowering; growth upright, medium high, 1 m./3.3 ft.; foliage light green, glossy. (6.3)

Blue Girl → **Cologne Carnaval**

Blue Heaven. HT. (D. Whisler, 1971). ('Sterling Silver' × 'Simone') × 'Saphir'. Purplish-pink, double, large-flowered, very strong fragrance, singly or several together on long stems; bud large, ovoid; growth strong, medium high; foliage medium green, glossy. (6.5)

'Blue Mist'. Min. (Ralph S. Moore, 1970). Seedling × seedling. Soft lavender, sometimes misty blue, white center, cupped, double, very fragrant, in clusters, abundant, recurrent all season; bud globose; growth bushy, compact, dwarf, well branched; foliage tiny. (6.5)

Blue Moon (= 'Mainzer Fastnacht'). HT. (Tantau, 1965). Seedling of 'Sterling Silver' × seedling. Lilac-purple or soft lilac, large-flowered, 10 cm./4 in., double, strong fragrance, on long stems; growth upright, bushy, medium high; foliage fresh green, glossy, very healthy. GSR 330; RA 1965:81; RA 1976:60. (7.4)

Blush Damask. D. Also called 'Blush Gallica'. Blush with darker center, double, small-flowered, but very floriferous, non-recurrent, June; growth slow, very densely branched, chest-high; foliage deep green. GSR 77; GiS 6.

Blush Hip. HA. (Listed 1848 by W. Paul; probably developed in England). Soft rose, center grey, very double, fragrant; bud cherry-red; very strong, climbing growth, to 3 m./10 ft.; foliage coarsely serrate.

Blush Noisette (= 'Rosier de Philippe Noisette'). N. (Noisette, before 1817). Seedling of 'Champney's Pink Cluster'. Soft lilac-rosy, center yellowish, medium large, double, singly or 3-6 in clusters, profuse bloomer; growth strong, 2-3 m./6.6-10 ft., stems nearly without prickles; young growth reddish; foliage dull green. TCR 5. This rose was sent by Philippe Noisette, of Charleston, U.S.A. to his brother Louis Noisette, who introduced it in 1818. Still a very valuable variety which is principally found in old English gardens.

Blush Rambler. Cl. (multifl.) (B.R. Cant, 1903). 'Crimson Rambler' × 'The Garland'. Light pink, semi-double, cupped, small-flowered, only 3.5 cm./1.4 in., in small and large trusses, non-recurrent, June; growth very strong, 3-4 m./10-13.2, stems nearly without prickles; foliage light green.

Bobby Charlton. HT. (G. Fryer, 1974). 'Royal Highness' × 'Prima Ballerina'. Deep pink with silvery reverse, full, very double, very large-flowered, singly and several together, free bloom; strong growth; foliage healthy, dark green, leathery. RA 1979:157.

Bobby Lucas. F. (McGredy, 1967). 'Margot Fonteyn' × 'Elizabeth of Glamis'. Deep salmon-orange, large-flowered, 8 cm./3.2 in., good shape, slight scent, many together; growth strong, medium; foliage deep green. (7.4)

Bob Hope. HT. (Kordes, 1966). 'Friedrich Schwarz' × 'Kordes Perfecta'. Scarlet, very large-flowered, perfect shape, double, strong fragrance; bud long, urn-shaped, crimson; growth strong, medium high, long stems; foliage dark green, leathery. (6.1)

Bobolink. Min. (Ralph S. Moore, 1959). (*R. wichuraiana* × 'Floradora') × ('Oakington Ruby' × 'Floradora'). Light red and dark pink, base nearly white, small, double, slight scent, free bloom; growth vigorous, bushy, dwarf; foliage leathery, glossy. (5.8)

Bon Accord. HT. (Anderson's Nurseries, 1967). 'Prima Ballerina' × 'Percy Thrower'. Pink with silvery shades, large, high centered, fragrant, free bloom; foliage glossy.

Bonavista. Rg x HCh. (F. Svejda/Agri. Canada, 1978). 'Schneezwerg' × 'Nemesis'. Light pink, loosely double, 20 petals, very fragrant, 3-6 in clusters, recurrent bloom; growth bushy, upright, medium high; foliage abundant, healthy.

Bon-Bon. F. (Jackson & Perkins, 1974). 'Bridal Pink' × seedling. Interior dark pink, with more or less whitish reverse, large-flowered, 9 cm./3.6 in., double, 25 petals, slight fragrance, in clusters; growth low, bushy; foliage fresh green. ARA 59:84. (7.3)

Bond Street. HT. (McGredy, 1965). 'Radar' × 'Queen Elizabeth'. Salmon-pink, with darker edge, 10 cm./4 in.

across, full, fragrant; growth strong, upright; foliage medium green, glossy. GSR 275.

Bonfire → changed to **Bonfire Night**.

Bonfire Night. F. (McGredy, 1971). 'Tiki' × 'Variety Club'. Opening red, changing to orange-scarlet with lighter reverse, ball-shaped, 8 cm./3.2 in., semi-double, slight scent, many together in trusses; growth low, compact, bushy, upright; foliage deep green, glossy. RA 1972:112.

Bonn. HMsk. (Kordes, 1950). 'Hamburg' × 'Independence'. Scarlet-orange, then purplish, semi-double, 7 cm./2.8 in. across, fragrant, flowers all season, stamens golden-yellow; growth chest-high; foliage glossy, healthy. PWR 202; GSR 142; GiS 18. (6.0)

Bonne Nuit. HT. (Combe/Wyant, 1966). Blackish-red, very double, medium large, good scent; bud long, pointed; growth bushy; foliage glossy. RJb 26:97. (7.4)

Bonnie Hamilton. F. (Cocker, 1976). 'Anne Cocker' × 'Allgold'. Vermilion, small, moderately full, slight fragrance, in trusses, very free blooming; growth low, bushy; foliage dark green.

Bonnie Scotland. HT. (Anderson's Nurseries, 1976). 'Wendy Cussons' × 'Percy Thrower'. Red, high-centered, very full, 40-45 petals, strong fragrance, free bloom; free growth, medium high; foliage glossy.

Bonny. Min. (Kordes, 1974). 'Zorina' × seedling. Similar to 'Dwarfking'; pink, small-flowered, double, long-lasting, floriferous; growth dwarf, 20 cm./8 in.; foliage tiny, light green, healthy. (7.5)

Bonsoir. HT. (Dickson, 1968). Soft pink with darker shades, very large-flowered, perfect shape, good fragrance, double, floriferous; growth strong, medium high, 0.9 m./3 ft.; foliage large, dark green, glossy. GSR 276; RA 1968:32; WPR 38. (5.9)

Bon Voyage. (= 'Voeux de Bonheur'). HT. (Delbard/Stark Bros., 1969). 'Michèle Meilland' × 'Chic Parisien'. Cream-white with cherry-red edge, reverse cream-white, very double, strong fragrance, singly on long stems; bud ovoid, cherry-red; growth strong; foliage large, deep green, glossy.

Bo Peep. Min. (de Vink, 1950). 'Cécile Brunner' × 'Tom Thumb'. Rosy-pink, very small-flowered, cupped, slight scent, very floriferous, singly and several together; bud pointed, ovoid; growth dwarf, compact; foliage tiny, glossy. ARA 1950:121. (7.6)

Border King. Pol. (de Ruiter, 1950). Strawberry-red, small-flowered, double, very floriferous in large trusses; vigorous, medium high; foliage deep green, very healthy.

Born Free. Min. (Ralph S. Moore, 1977). 'Red Pinocchio' × 'Little Chief'. Bright orange-red, double, 20 petals, slight fragrance, several together, abundant and continous bloomer; growth bushy, dwarf, rounded, upright; foliage deep green, very clean.

Boule de Neige. B. (Lacharme, 1867). 'Blanche Lafitte' × 'Sappho'. Cream-white, edge often dark pink, ball-shaped, very double, good fragrance, recurrent, several together in clusters; growth upright, bushy, man's height; foliage deep green, leathery. PGR 54; Gis 11.

Bountiful. HT. (LeGrice, 1972). 'Vesper' × seedling. Dark salmon-red, with deeper reverse, double, medium large, 7 cm./2.8 in., slight scent; growth strong, upright; foliage small, abundant, medium green.

Bouquet d'Or. N. (Ducher, 1872). 'Gloire de Dijon' × ?. Deep yellow, center coppery-salmon, very double, large-flowered.

Bourbon Queen → **Queen of Bourbons**.

Botzaris. D. (1856). Pure white, very double, center greenish, opening flat, strong fragrance, very floriferous and beautiful; growth medium tall, upright; foliage light green, healthy.

Brandenburg. HT. (Kordes, 1965). ('Spartan' × 'Prima Ballerina') × 'Karl Herbst'. Bright red, more salmon-red when fully open, large-flowered, good shape, no scent; growth strong, medium, 0.9 m./3 ft.; foliage coarse, medium green, young growth bronze. GSR 277; KR 9:36. (5.7)

Brasilia. HT. (McGredy, 1965). 'Kordes Perfecta × 'Piccadilly'. Interior glowing scarlet, reverse light yellow, good shape, double, some scent; bud long, pointed; growth strong, upright, little branching, medium high, 0.9 m./3 ft.; foliage coarse, glossy, healthy. GSR 278; RA 1968:145. (6.2)

Bravo. HT. (Swim/Armstrong, 1951). 'World's Fair' × 'Mirandy'. Cardinal-red, double, large-flowered, 10-12 cm./4-5 in., some scent, floriferous; growth strong, bushy; foliage coarse, leathery. (6.5)

Bridal Pink. F. (Boerner/Jackson & Perkins, 1967).

'Summertime'-seedling × 'Spartan'-seedling. Soft pink, large-flowered, double, fragrant, free flowering; bud pointed; growth bushy, upright, medium; foliage leathery, matt.

Bride's White. F. (Mansuino, 1968). Seedling × seedling. Pure white, small-flowered, double, some scent, singly or several together; growth bushy, upright, strong; foliage medium large, abundant.

Bright Jewel. Min. (Origin unknown; Holland?). Rosy pink with white center and lighter reverse, flowers 3 cm./1.2 in. across, singly and in clusters; bud globose; growth dwarf, compact; foliage medium green.

Brightside. Min. (Ralph S. Moore, 1974). 'Persian Princess' × self. Orange-red, not fading, some scent, high-centered, top open, singly and occasionally in clusters, good bloomer; growth dwarf, bushy, upright; foliage small, dull. (7.0)

Bristol Post. HT. (J. Sanday, 1972). 'Very Dalton' × 'Parasol'. Salmon, pink and orange, deepening as the flower unfolds, large-flowered, 10 cm./4 in., double, some scent; growth strong, medium high, bushy; foliage dark green, glossy.

Bronze Beauty. F. (W.A. Williams/Jackson & Perkins, 1974). 'Electra' × 'Woburn Abbey'. Golden yellow on top, deeper orange-yellow below, faint scent, double, open-centered, profuse bloom, single in greenhouses, in clusters outside; growth vigorous; foliage large, leathery. (7.0)

Bronze Masterpiece. HT. (Boerner/Jackson & Perkins, 1960). 'Golden Masterpiece' × 'Kate Smith'. Amber-brown, more orange-yellow when fully open. very large-flowered, 12-15 cm./5-6 in., strong fragrance, continuous bloom, long-lasting; bud long, pointed; growth very strong, medium, upright; foliage leathery, glossy. RJb 24:162. (5.3)

Brownie. F. (Boerner/Jackson & Perkins, 1958). 'Lavender Pinocchio' × 'Grey Pearl'. Golden-yellow, pink and bronze, finally more red, with yellowish-brown reverse, very double, center slightly globose, outer petals more cupped, 8-10 cm./3.2-4 in. across; growth bushy, uneven, low; foliage medium green. (6.4)

Buccaneer. Gr. (Swim/Armstrong, 1954). 'Golden Rapture' × ('Max Krause' × 'Capt. Thomas'). A pure golden-yellow, medium large, loosely double, color not fading; bud urn-shaped; growth upright, medium high, few branches, long stems; foliage large, green, matt. PWR 158; GSR 279. (6.8)

Buff Beauty. HMsk. (bred by Rev. J.H. Pemberton?, 1939). 'William Allen Richardson' × ?. Apricot-buff, later lighter edge, fully double, medium large, good fragrance, floriferous from June to autumn; tall; foliage dark green, young growth coppery. GSR 118; TRT 124; RA 1975:55; GiS 16. (7.0)

Burgund. HT. (Kordes, 1977). 'Henkel Royal' × seedling. Dark red, high centered, double, 30 petals, very large-flowered, strong fragrance, singly and several together, intermittent bloom; growth bushy, vigorous, medium high; foliage soft green.

Burnaby. (= 'Golden Heart'). HT. (Eddie, 1954). 'Phyllis Gold' × 'President Herbert Hoover'. Creamy-white, very double, 10-15 cm./4-6 in. across, slight scent; bud long; growth strong, bushy, medium; foliage deep green, glossy. (6.6)

Burning Love. (= 'Brennende Liebe'). F. (Tantau, 1956), 'Fanal' × 'Crimson Glory'. Velvety crimson, loosely double, very large-flowered, no scent; growth bushy, unequal, low to medium high; foliage large, purplish, matt, coarse. (6.1)

Busy Lizzie. F. (Harkness, 1970). ('Pink Parfait' × 'Masquerade') × 'Dearest'. Pink, loosely double, 6 cm./2.4 in. across, several together, floriferous; growth low, very bushy; foliage medium green, glossy. GSR 389; RA 1970:49.

Butterfly. HT. (Barter, 1969). 'Center Court' × 'Carla'. White with scarlet edge, slight scent, very double; bud long; growth strong.

Butterfly Wings. F.S. (W.D. Gobbee, 1977). 'Dainty Maid' × 'Peace'. White with broad pink edge, semi-double, large-flowered, open; bud long, pointed, pink and yellowish; singly and in clusters; growth strong; foliage dark green, glossy. RA 1979:86.

Butterscotch. HT. (J.H. Hill, 1946). 'Souvenir de Claudius Pernet' × 'R.M.S. Queen Mary'. Interior lemon-yellow, with orange reverse, large-flowered, 10-12 cm./4-5 in., loosely double, open, slight scent; bud long; foliage deep green, glossy, leathery. ARA 1948:56. (6.1)

Cadenza. LCl. (D.L. Armstrong, 1967). 'New Dawn' × 'Climbing Embers'. Dark red, medium large, 7 cm./2.8 in., double, open, slight scent, recurrent bloom; bud ovoid; growth moderate, compact, climbing; foliage dark green, leathery, glossy.

Café. F. (Kordes, 1956). ('Golden Glow' × *R. kordesii*) × 'Lavender Pinocchio'. Brownish and yellowish (coffee and cream), slight scent, double, many together, floriferous; growth low; foliage large, olive green.

Caledonia. HT. (Dobbie, 1928). Unknown parentage. White, large, double, high-centered, slight scent, abundant bloom; growth vigorous; foliage dark green, leathery. (6.9)

Caledonia, Climbing. ClHT. (Bel, 1936). Climbing sport of 'Caledonia'. Growth strong, climbing; flowers like the type.

Calgold. Min. (Ralph S, Moore, 1977). 'Golden Glow' × 'Peachy White'. Dark yellow, double, 25 petals, some scent, abundant bloom all season, singly and in clusters; growth dwarf, bushy, many branches; foliage small. (7.0)

Calico. HT. (Weeks Rose Growers, 1970). Seedling × 'Granada.' Light yellow with red spotting, double, 40 petals, globose form reminiscent of a carnation, slight tea scent, profuse, continuous bloom, singly or 2-3 to a stem; bud pointed; growth upright to spreading, medium high; foliage dark green.

Calico Doll. Min. (Saville, 1979). 'Rise 'n Shine' × 'Glenfiddich'. Orange striped with yellow, semi-double, cupped to flat, 2.5-4 cm./1-1.5 in.; profuse bloom; bud ovate-pointed; foliage dark; growth compact.

Camaieux. G. (Vibert, 1830). Opening soft rosy-pink with light crimson stripes, these later turning violet-purplish, semi-double, summer-flowering; growth medium, stems arching, few prickles; foliage greyish-green. GiS 5. (7.6)

Camelot. F. (Swim & Weeks, 1964). 'Circus' × 'Queen Elizabeth'. Salmon to coral-red, large-flowered, double, to 12 cm./5 in. across, singly or several together on long stems; growth strong, 0.7 m./2.3 ft.; foliage leathery. (7.7)

Cameo. P. (de Ruiter, 1932). Sport of 'Orléans Rose'. Salmon pink becoming soft orange-pink, slightly fragrant, small, cupped, semi-double; profuse bloom; 40-45 cm./15-18 in. in height.

Canary Bird. Probably *R. hugonis* × *R. xanthina*; formerly thought to be *R. xanthina* f. *spontanea*, and confused with this. Shrub; flowers canary-yellow, single, 6-7 cm./2.4-2.8 in. across, May-June, very floriferous; hips blackish-red; growth chest-high, stems in the lower part armed with many triangular, large, flat prickles, arching, bark finally dark brown; leaflets 9-13, elliptic-oblong, denticulate, first hairy below. GSR 143-144; GiS 1. 1945 exhibited in England for the first time.

Candeur Lyonnaise. HP. (Croibier, 1914). Seedling of 'Frau Karl Druschki'. White, sometimes with yellow hue, very large, double; bud long, pointed; growth very vigorous. (8.0)

Candleflame. Min. (Ralph S. Moore, 1956). ('Soeur Thérèse' × 'Julien Potin') × ('Eblouissant' × 'Zee'). Red, yellow and orange, single, free bloom; growth dwarf, bushy, vigorous. (6.7)

Candy Apple. Gr. (O.L. Weeks, 1975). 'Jack O'Lantern' × seedling. Bright cherry-red, double, 50 petals, slight scent, semi-cupped, floriferous, flowering all season; growth upright, well branched; foliage round, olive-green, dull. (7.0)

Candy Cane. ClMin. (Ralph S. Moore, 1958). Seedling × 'Zee'. Pink to light red, striped white, semi-double, medium large, free bloom, in clusters; growth vigorous, 1 m./3.3 ft. (7.1)

Candy Pink. Min. (Ralph S. Moore, 1969). (*R. wichuraiana* × Floradora) × ('Oakington Ruby' × 'Floradora'). Light pink, double, singly and several together; bud globose; growth dwarf, moderately to loosely compact; foliage medium. (7.2)

Candy Stripe. HT. (McCummings/Jackson & Perkins, 1963). Sport of 'Pink Peace'. Dark pink with light pink stripes and stipules, large-flowered, very double, good fragrance, floriferous; growth strong, upright, low; foliage leathery. WPR 28. (6.5)

Candy Stick. (= 'Red-n-White Glory'). H.T. (J.B. Williams, 1978). Sport of 'Better Times'. Light red striped with white, high centered, double; bud pointed; foliage matt, light green; growth upright.

'Cantab' → **Rosa nutkana.** p. 277.

'Canterbury'. S. (D. Austin, 1969). ('Monique' × 'Constance Spry') × seedling. Rosy-pink, semi-double, medium, very fragrant, recurrent bloom; growth free. (8.0)

Capistrano. HT. (Morris, 1949). Luminous pink, very

double, good fragrance, growth strong, upright; foliage large, dark green, glossy. SRW 14; ARA 1950:88. (6.0)

Capitaine John Ingram. M. (Laffay, 1854). Velvety maroon, mottled and shaded with purple and crimson, medium large, very double, ball-shaped, summer-flowering; lilac-pink button center; calyx very mossy, brownish-green to dark red; growth chest-high. TR 6; GiS 9. (6.9)

Capri. F. (G. Fisher, 1956). 'Fashion' × 'Floradora'. Coral-red with lighter reverse, large-flowered, double, slight scent, many together in trusses, floriferous; bud long; foliage glossy, leathery. (6.3)

Captain Christy. HT. (Lacharme, 1873). 'Victor Verdier' × 'Safrano'. Soft fleshy-pink with darker center, very large-flowered, double, globose, light scent, very free bloom; growth strong. PGR 71.

Captain Hayward. HP. (Bennett, 1893). Seedling of 'Triomphe de Exposition'. Crimson-scarlet, large-flowered, loosely double, somewhat recurrent; hips orange, large; growth good, medium high. (8.0)

Caramba. HT. (Tantau, 1966). Seedling × seedling. Interior light crimson, reverse ivory-white, cupped, double, good shape, some scent, singly on strong stems; growth bushy, medium; foliage deep green, glossy. GSR 280; RA 1968:112. (5.8)

Cara Mia. HT. (McDaniel/Carlton, 1969). 'Happiness' × seedling. Interior red, reverse mauve, medium to large, singly on long stems, very long-lasting; bud long, pointed; growth strong, medium high; foliage dark green. Greenhouse variety. (6.0)

Cardinal de Richelieu. G. (Laffay, 1840). Flowers first pink, then mauve-pink, finally velvety violet-blue, globose, 7 cm./2.8 in across, good fragrance, June; growth medium high, to 1.2 m./4 ft., stems with few prickles; foliage deep green. PGR 18; GiS 5. One of the most famous and remarkable rose varieties. (7.6)

Carefree Beauty. S. (G.J. Buck/Conard-Pyle, 1979). Seedling × 'Prairie Princess'. Pink, semi-double, 15-20 petals, fragrant, in clusters of 3-20 together, flowering all season; growth sturdy, upright, chest-high; foliage semi-glossy. ARA 63:26.

Careless Love. HT. (Conklin, 1955). Sport of 'Red Radiance'. Red, streaked and splashed white, medium, 7 cm./2.6 in. across, double, cupped, fragrant, abundant

bloomer; growth upright, very vigorous; foliage dark green, glossy. (4.6)

Careless Moment. Min. (E.D. Williams/Mini-Roses, 1977). 'Little Darling' × 'Over the Rainbow'. Clear pink, double, slight scent, abundant bloom all season; bud long, pointed, outstanding; growth dwarf, bushy, spreading; foliage small.

Carina. HT. (A. Meilland, 1963). 'Happiness' × 'Independence'. Opening luminous red, later lighter, large, double, fragrant, growth strong, medium, 0.8 m./2.6 ft. stems very sturdy; foliage light green, healthy. Greenhouse variety.

Carla. HT. (de Ruiter, 1963). 'Sweet Repose' × 'Queen Elizabeth'. Soft salmon-pink, loosely double, good fragrance; bud urn-shaped; growth strong, long stems, 0.9 m./3 ft.; foliage dark green, very resistant to Black Spot. Greenhouse variety, but also suitable for outdoor use. (8.5)

Carmen. S. (Lambert, 1905). *R. rugosa* × 'Princesse de Béarn'. Crimson, single, very large flower, stamens yellow, recurrent; growth strong, tall to very tall, very dense. RZ 1905:72.

Carmencita. Min. (Camprubi, 1954). 'Lady Sylvia' × 'Perla de Alcanada'. Pure white, small-flowered, very double, very free bloom; growth dwarf, vigorous; foliage clear green. (6.3)

Carmenetta. S. (Preston, Canada, 1923). *R. rubrifolia* × *R. rugosa*. Light pink, single, medium-large, in clusters, some scent; growth strong, tall, 2 m./6.6 ft. high, 3 m./10 ft. across; foliage purple, leathery.

Carnival Glass. Min. (E.D. Williams, 1979). Seedling × 'Over the Rainbow'. Yellow-orange, slightly fragrant, double, 2.5-4 cm./1-1.5 in., abundant bloom; bud pointed; foliage small, glossy, bronze; growth bushy, spreading.

Carnival Parade. Min. (E.D. Williams/Mini-Roses, 1968). 'Starburst' × 'Over the Rainbow'. Yellow, very double, high-centered, slight scent, single; bud long, pointed; growth dwarf, bushy, upright; foliage broad, glossy.

Carol Amling. (= 'Carol'). F. (Amling/Beltran, 1953). Sport of 'Garnette'. Clear pink, interior somewhat lighter, medium-large, 6 cm./2.4 in. across, finally flat rosette-form; bud hybrid tea form; growth low, 40 cm./16 in., strong; foliage deep green, leathery. Greenhouse variety. (6.8)

Carol Ann. Pol. (Kluis/Klyn, 1940). 'Marianne Kluis' × sport of 'Superior'. Orange-salmon, small, double, cupped, in clusters, recurrent bloom; growth dwarf, 30 cm./12 in.

Carol-Jean. Min. (Ralph S. Moore, 1976). 'Pinocchio' × 'Little Chief'. Deep rosy-pink, full, open, 25 petals, some scent, several together, flowering all season; growth dwarf, bushy, upright, many branches; bud pointed; foliage dark green, semi-glossy. (8.0)

Carrousel. Gr. (Duehrsen/Elmer, 1950). Seedling × 'Margy'. Dark red, semi-double, medium large, fragrant, very floriferous; growth very strong, medium, upright; foliage olive green, very resistant to Black Spot. (7.6)

Casa Blanca. LCl. (Sima, 1968). 'New Dawn' × 'Fashion'. White, medium large, semi-double, slight scent, in clusters, recurrent; bud flushed with crimson; growth strong, climbing; foliage glossy. (8.1)

Casino. (= 'Gerbe d'Or'). LCl. (McGredy,1963). 'Coral Dawn' × 'Buccaneer'. Soft yellow, fading with age, semi-double, large, 10 cm./4 in. across, fragrant, floriferous; growth strong, climbing, 2.5-3 m./8.3-10 ft.; foliage dark green. KR 9:54; WPR 21. (7.0)

Cassie. Min. (D. Bennett, 1979). 'Gene Boerner × Elfinesque'. Medium pink, slightly fragrant, semi-double, 2.5 cm./1 in.; bud long pointed; foliage dark; growth bushy, upright.

Cathedral. (= 'Coventry Cathedral'). F. (McGredy, 1972). ('Little Darling' × 'Goldilocks') × 'Irish Mist'. Light vermilion with lighter reverse, semi-double, several together in clusters; growth upright, medium, branched; foliage medium green, glossy, very resistant to mildew. ARA 61:122; RA 1973:47. (7.5)

Catherine Mermet. T. (Guillot, 1869). Flesh-pink, with mauve-pink margin, large-flowered, very double, fragrant; bud good shape; growth strong. Formerly very important greenhouse variety. (7.0)

Cayenne. HT. (W.A. Warriner/Jackson & Perkins, 1974). 'South Seas' × seedling. Deep orange, very double, 35-40 petals, slight scent, borne singly; blooms all summer; bud pointed, short; growth medium high, upright; foliage semi-glossy. (7.0)

Cecil. HT. (B.R. Cant, 1926). Parentage unknown. Golden-yellow, large, 10 cm./4 in. across, single, in large clusters; growth bushy. (7.2)

Cecil Beaton. F. (Gregory, 1973). 'Queen Elizabeth' × seedling. Rosy-red, double, medium large, 7 cm./2.8 in., good fragrance, several together; growth strong; foliage deep green, glossy.

Cécile Brunner. (= 'Sweetheart Rose'). Pol. (Veuve Ducher, 1889). Double white Polyantha × 'Mme. de Tartas'. Shell pink with lighter margin, center yellowish, small-flowered, double, good form, open, fragrant; bud long, pointed; growth open, medium; foliage tiny. RZ 1886: RA 1973:46; TRT 177. Greenhouse variety.

Cécile Brunner, Climbing. ClPol. (Hosp, 1894). Sport of 'Cécile Brunner'. Growth very strong, vigorous, up to 5 m./16.5 ft.; otherwise like the type. GiS 22. (7.8)

Célestial. (= 'Celeste'). A. (in cultivation before 1759). Opening shell-pink, warm pink in the folds, semi-double, fragrant, only summer-flowering; growth strong, medium to tall; foliage greyish-green. (Often confused with 'Maiden's Blush'.) GSR 64; HRo 28; PGR 36. (7.5)

Célina. M. (M. Hardy, 1855). Crimson with purplish hue, medium large, loosely double, fragrant; buds very mossy; growth tall, 1.2 m./4 ft.

Celsiana. D. (Before 1750). Pink, large-flowered, 10 cm./4.in. across, loosely double, petals folded, in clusters of 3-4; growth strong, 1 m./3.3 ft. or over; foliage greyish-green, scented. PWR 175; SOR 7; GiS g; PGR 27. (8.8)

Centennial Miss. Min. (Ralph S. Moore, 1952). 'Oakington Ruby' × self. Dark red, base white-tinged, small, 2.5 cm./1 in., double, abundant bloom; growth dwarf, 25-30 cm./10-12 in., bushy, without prickles; foliage small, dark green. (7.5)

Century Two. HT. (D.L.Armstrong, 1971). 'Charlotte Armstrong' × 'Duet'. Pink, large-flowered, double, some scent, self-cleansing, singly or several together, floriferous; growth very strong, upright, 1 m./3.3 ft., stems very prickly; foliage medium green, healthy. (8.3)

Cerise Bouquet. S. (Kordes, 1958). *R. multibracteata* × 'Crimson Glory'. Cherry-red, semi-double, medium large, opening flat, floriferous along the branches, non-recurrent; growth strong, tall, stems loosely arching;

foliage light green. GSR 146; TRT 20. (8.0)

Césonie. D. Dark pink, very large-flowered, very double; growth low. (8.6)

Champagne. HT. (Lindquist, 1961). 'Charlotte Armstrong' × 'Duquesa de Peñaranda'. Salmon-yellow, loosely double, fragrant, large-flowered, 10-12 cm./4-5 in., floriferous; bud ovoid, pointed; growth upright; foliage leathery, dark green. (7.1)

Champion. HT. (Fryer, 1975). 'Grandpa Dickson' × 'Whisky Mac'. Cream-yellow, flushed red and pink, double, 50 petals, large-flowered, singly and several together, fragrant, very free blooming; growth medium; foliage light green, healthy.

Champney's Pink Cluster. N. (Champney, 1811). Probably a natural hybrid of *R. chinensis* × *R. moschata*. The common designation "the first true hybrid rose" cannot be correct since the rules of heredity were completely unknown at that time; they were not formulated, by Gregor Mendel in Europe, until 1866. Pink, semi-double, large, open, fragrant, many together, in large clusters, but non-recurrent. The first American hybrid which was sent abroad, and so became an ancestor of the Noisette roses. (6.7)

Champs Elysées. HT. (Meilland, 1957). 'Monique' × 'Happiness'. Crimson, velvety, not fading, large, some scent, double; growth strong, bushy, 0.8 m./2.6 ft.; foliage medium green, matt. PWR 68; GSR 282; (6.7)

Chanelle. F. (McGredy, 1959). 'Ma Perkins' × ('Fashion' × 'Mrs. William Sprott'). Soft salmon-pink with yellowish center, stamens golden-yellow, semi-double, medium large, flat, fragrant, many together in clusters, abundant; growth strong, medium, to 0.8 m./2.6 ft.; foliage dark green, glossy. WPR 49; RA 1959:1777. (8.0)

Chantré. HT. (Kordes, 1958). 'Fred Streeter' × 'Anthéor'. Orange with golden-yellow, large, loosely double, perfect shape, fragrant; growth strong, upright; foliage dark green, leathery. (4.8)

'Chapeau de Napoléon' → **Rosa centifolia cristata,** p. 257.

Chaplin's Pink Climber. LCl. (Chaplin Bros., 1928). 'Paul's Scarlet Climber' × 'American Pillar'. Clear pink, semi-double, medium large, yellow stamens, non-recurrent; growth very strong, 3 m./10 ft.; foliage dark green, glossy. GSR 199; PWR 210; 229.

Chaplin's Pink Companion. LCl. (Chaplin, 1961). 'Chaplin's Pink Climber' × 'Opéra'. Soft salmon-pink, medium large, 5 cm./2 in. across, some scent, non-recurrent, but flowers for a long time; growth strong, 3.5 m./11.5 ft.; foliage dark green, glossy. GSR 234.

Charisma. F. (E.G. Hill/Conard-Pyle, 1977). 'Gemini' × 'Zorina'. Scarlet and yellow, double, high-centered, 35-45 petals, slight scent, abundant, continuous bloom, in clusters; bud ovoid; growth bushy, medium, upright, vigorous; foliage leathery, glossy. ARA 62:26. (8.0)

Charisma. HT. (Meilland/Conard-Pyle, 1973). Parentage not given. Brilliant pure orange-red, medium large, double, high-centered, slight scent, long-lasting, continuous flowering; bud medium, ovoid; growth medium, bushy, upright; foliage leathery, glossy, disease-resistant.

Charles de Gaulle. HT. (Meilland, 1974). Parentage not given. Lilac-mauve, large, high-centered, double, strong fragrance; bud long, pointed to urn-shaped; growth bushy, low, disease-free; foliage large, healthy.

Charles de Mills. G. Dark red to crimson and purple, sometimes also brownish, very double, opening flat, 8 cm./3.2 in. across, fragrant; growth sturdy, upright, medium. PWR 170; GSR 84; SOR 2; GiS 5. (8.9)

Charles Dickens. F. (McGredy, 1970). 'Paddy McGredy' × 'Elizabeth of Glamis'. Salmon-pink with darker reverse, loosely double, good fragrance, floriferous, several together in clusters; growth strong, upright; foliage dark green, glossy. GSR 392; RA 1971:33.

Charles Lawson. B. (Lawson, 1853). Pink with darker shades, large-flowered, loosely double, non-recurrent; growth strong, bud stems weak, so needs support; 1.5 m./5 ft. high.

Charles Mallerin. HT. (Meilland, 1951). ('Rome Glory' × 'Congo') × 'Tassin'. Blackish-crimson, very large, 12-15 cm./5-6 in. across, very double, opening flat, very strong fragrance; growth uneven if not pruned. PWR 60; SWR 24. (6.0)

Charleston. F. (Meilland, 1963). 'Masquerade' × ('Radar' × 'Caprice'). Yellow with crimson shades, interior often very crimson, reverse mostly yellow, medium large, some scent, many together, very floriferous; growth strong, medium, 0.6 m./2 ft.; foliage dark green, leathery. GSR 393; WPR 56; RJb 28:160. (8.0)

Charly McCarthy. F. (Wiseman, 1955). 'Mrs. Dudley Fulton' × 'Mermaid'. Pure white, double, 30 petals, medium-large, fragrant, in clusters, floriferous, bud creamy-white; growth dwarf, compact; foliage deep green, leathery, glossy. (6.2)

Charlotte Armstrong, Climbing. ClHT. (Morris, 1942). 1946). 'Soeur Thérèse' × 'Crimson Glory'. Cherry-red, 7-10 cm./2.8-4 in. across, double, fragrant; bud long; growth upright, long stems, 0.8 m./2.6 ft.; foliage dark green, leathery. PWR 89; SWR 17. (7.5)

Charlotte Armstrong, Climbing. ClHT. (Morris, 1942). Sport of 'Charlotte Armstrong'. Growth strong, 2 m./6.6 ft.; otherwise like the type. (7.4)

Charming Maid. F. (LeGrice, 1953). 'Dainty Maid' × 'Mrs. Sam McGredy'. Salmon-red with orange center, single, large-flowered; margin waved; stamens golden-yellow, some scent; growth strong, 0.9 m./3 ft.; foliage deep green, healthy. GSR 396; RA 1954:156.

Charming Vienna. (= 'Vienna Charmin', 'Wiener Charme'). HT. (Kordes, 1963). 'Chantré' × 'Golden Sun'. Yellow-orange with red shades, so more coppery-orange appearance, very large, 15 cm./6 in. across, double, finally flat, some scent, floriferous; growth strong, medium, 1 m./3.3 ft.; foliage deep green, abundant, large, glossy. GSR 375; KR 9:29. (6.8)

Château de Clos Vougeot. HT. (Pernet-Ducher, 1908). Dark velvety-crimson, large, very double, strong fragrance; growth loose, spreading, low. RZ 1909:1; SWR 21.

Chatter. F. (Boerner/Jackson & Perkins, 1947). 'World's Fair' × 'Betty Prior'. Velvety crimson with blackish shades, double, some scent, stamens golden-yellow, floriferous; growth strong, low. (7.0)

Charm of Paris. HT. (Tantau, 1965). 'Prima Ballerina' × 'Montezuma'. Clear pink, large, very double, strong fragrance, many together; growth strong, spreading; foliage large, light green, glossy. GSR 395; RA 1966:145. (5.8)

Chattem Centennial. Min. (Jolly, 1979). 'Orange Sensation' × 'Zinger'. Red, slight fruity fragrance, open, double, 2.5-4 cm./1-1.5 in.; bud ovoid; growth upright, bushy.

Chatterbox. F. (John Sanday, 1973). 'Sarabande' × 'Circus'. Bright orange-vermilion, golden eye, semi-double, 15 petals, rosette-shaped, blooming freely, in trusses; growth dwarf, 40 cm./16 in.; foliage medium size, glossy.

Chatillon Rose. Pol. (Nonin, 1923). 'Orléans-Rose' × seedling. Light pink, semi-double, small cupped, fragrant, in large clusters; growth bushy, low, 30-60 cm./12-24 in.; foliage glossy. (7.3)

Cherish. F. (Jackson & Perkins, 1980). Shell pink, very double, slight cinnamon scent, very floriferous, long-lasting, flowers all season; bud long, pointed; growth compact, symmetrical, branched; foliage deep green, glossy. ARA 1979: 215

Cherokee Rose → **Rosa laevigata**, p. 293.

Cherry Glow. F. (Swim/Burr, 1959). 'Floradora' × 'First Love'. Cherry-red, loosely double, cupped, 7-10 cm./2.8-4 in. across, fragrant, several together; growth very strong, medium; foliage leathery, glossy. (7.0)

Cherry-Vanilla. Gr. (Armstrong, 1973). 'Buccaneer' × 'El Capitan'. Pink, center creamy-white, double, medium large, cupped, moderate fragrance, singly or in clusters, abundant, continuous bloom; bud ovoid, pointed; growth tall, vigorous, open, bushy; foliage large, dark green, leathery. (6.3)

Chevy Chase. Cl. (N.J. Hansen/Bobbink & Atkins, 1939). *R. soulieana* × 'Eblouissant'. Dark crimson, small, but very double, in clusters of 10-20 together, fragrant, non-recurrent; growth very strong, 4 m./13 ft. or over; foliage soft, light green, wrinkly. (8.1)

Chianti. S. (D. Austin, 1967). *R. macrantha* × 'Vanity'. Purplish-mauve, semi-double, slight fragrance, free bloom; growth vigorous, strong stems; foliage dark green, glossy.

Chic. F. (Boerner/Jackson & Perkins, 1953). 'Pinocchio'-seedling × 'Fashion'. Salmon-pink with salmon, medium large, 6 cm./2.4 in., very double, globose, fragrant; growth low, 0.5 m./1.7 ft., very branched; foliage small, matt, healthy. (7.6)

Chicago Peace. HT. (Johnston, 1962). Sport of 'Peace'. Deep pink, with darker veins, base and reverse light yellow, very double, some fragrance, very large, floriferous; growth strong, medium, well branched; foliage glossy, leathery. GSR 283; WPR 27. (8.3)

China Doll. Pol. (Lammerts/Armstrong, 1946). 'Mrs. Dudley Fulton' × 'Tom Thumb'. Light pink, yellow base, small, 3-5 cm./1.2-2 in., double, some scent, many in clusters together, abundant; growth strong, dwarf, 35 cm./14 in., branched; foliage coarse. (7.6)

Chinatown. F. (N.D. Poulsen, 1963). 'Columbine' × 'Cläre Grammerstorf'. Deep yellow, large, 10 cm./4 in. across, double, opening flat, fragrant, profuse, continuous bloom. Growth strong, medium; foliage light green, glossy. GSR 148; GiS 18; RA 1963:112. (6.4)

Chipper. Min. (Meilland, 1966). ('Dany Robin'-seedling × 'Fire King') × 'Perla de Montserrat'. Light pink to salmon pink, small, double, slightly fragrant, free bloom; bud ovoid; growth dwarf, vigorous; foliage leathery, healthy, glossy. (8.5)

Chivalry. HT. (McGredy, 1977). 'Peer Gynt' × 'Brasilia'. Bicolor flower, Chinese red and old ivory, double, 35 petals, no scent, singly and several together, moderately free flowering; growth strong, upright, medium; foliage dark green, glossy.

Chiyo. HT. (Saku Otah/Eastern Roses, 1975). 'Karl Herbst' × 'Chrysler Imperial'. Deep pink, high-centered, 25 petals, slight scent, in clusters, floriferous all season; bud long, pointed; growth medium, long stems, upright, vigorous; foliage dark green, glossy.

Chloris. A. Soft pink, deep center, outer petals revolute, double, medium-large; growth strong, 1.2 m./4 ft.; stems with few prickles. PGR 31,39.

Chorus. F. (Meilland, 1977). Parentage not given. Vermilion with red shades, double, large, very floriferous, in trusses, long-lasting; growth medium high; foliage dark green.

Christian Dior. HT. (Meilland, 1958). ('Independence' × 'Happiness') × ('Peace' × 'Happiness'). Velvety scarlet, exterior lighter, large, very double, 10 cm./4 in. across, some scent, floriferous; growth strong, upright; foliage glossy, dark green. PWR 35; GSR 284. (7.7)

Christine Weinert. Min. (Ralph S. Moore, 1976). ('Little Darling' × 'Eleanor') × self. Orange-red, double, 25 petals (often single), fragrant, free bloom all season, long-lasting; growth dwarf, bushy, upright; foliage glossy, medium green, leathery. ARA 61:248. (6.5)

Chromatella. N. (Coquereau, 1843). Seedling of 'Lamarque'. Interior deep yellow, reverse sulfur-yellow, large, very double, globose, fragrant; growth very strong, 4 m./13.2 ft., but tender.

Chrysler Imperial. HT. (Lammerts/Germain, 1952). 'Charlotte Armstrong' × 'Mirandy'. Glowing dark crimson, large, 10-12 cm./4-5 in. across, very double, fragrant; growth upright, medium, 0.9 m./3 ft.; foliage medium green, large, glossy. PWR 6; BTR 47. (8.3)

Chrysia. HT. (M.E. Wyant, 1970). 'Chrysler Imperial' × 'Lady Zia'. Light red, large, double, singly on long stems, long-lasting; growth strong, upright, bushy; foliage healthy. (4.3)

Cinderella. Min. (de Vink, 1953). 'Cécile Brunner' × 'Tom Thumb'. White with blush pink, very double, open, fragrant, floriferous; growth dwarf, upright, bushy, no prickles. PWR 162; GSR 502. (8.9)

Cinderella, Climbing. Cl. Min. (Ralph S. Moore, 1975). Sport of 'Cinderella'; growth vigorous, arching, medium, to 1 m./3.3 ft.; otherwise like the type. (7.5)

Cineraire. MinCh. (E. Murrell). Red with white center, very small, single, cupped, free bloom, in trusses; growth dwarf. (7.5)

Cinnabar. (= 'Tantau's Triumph'). F. (Tantau, 1945). 'Baby Château' × *R. roxburghii*. Scarlet-red and vermilion, medium large, semi-double, cupped, some scent, floriferous, in large trusses; growth upright, bushy, medium; foliage coarse.

Circus. F. (Swim/Armstrong, 1956). 'Fandango' × 'Pinocchio'. Yellow with pink and salmon, deeper red with age, medium large, very double, rosette-shaped, some scent, many together, abundant; growth strong, upright, medium, 0.6 m./2 ft.; foliage bronze, very glossy. PWR 105. (7.3)

Circus Parade. F. (Begonia & De Vor, U.S.A., 1963). Sport of 'Circus'. Similar to 'Circus', but flowers redder, base and reverse yellow, larger, to 7 cm./2.8 in across, also rosette-shaped; otherwise like the type. (7.6)

City of Belfast. F. (McGredy, 1968). 'Evelyn Fison' × ('Circus' × 'Korona'). Velvety scarlet, medium-large, 5-7 cm./2-2.8 in. across, double, no scent, many together, abundant; growth bushy, dense, medium, 0.8 m./2.6 ft.; foliage dark green, glossy. GSR 398; KR 10:54; RA 1968:2. (6.8)

City of Gloucester. HT. (Sanday, 1969). 'Gavotte' × 'Buccaneer'. Saffron yellow, shaded gold, large, double, singly or several together, particularly good in the autumn; growth strong, upright, 0.9 m./3 ft.; foliage medium green, matt. GSR 285; RA 1971:32.

City of Hereford. HT. (LeGrice, 1967). 'Wellworth' × 'Spartan'. Deep pink, reverse darker, very double, strong fragrance, singly or several together; growth strong, upright, 0.9 m./3 ft.; foliage light green, healthy. (7.6)

City of Leeds. F. (McGredy, 1966). 'Evelyn Fison' × ('Spartan' × 'Red Favorite'). Salmon pink, 10 cm./4 in. across, double, some scent, many together; growth strong, 0.8 m./2.6 ft.; foliage dark bronzy-green, small, glossy. GSR 399; RA 1966: 48. (7.1)

City of Norwich. HT. (Kordes/Morse, 1949). 'Crimson Glory' × ('Crimson Glory × 'Cathrine Kordes'). Crimson-scarlet, large, to 15 cm./6 in. across, good shape, double.

City of York. (= 'Direktor Benschop'). LCl. (Tantau, 1945). 'Prof. Gnau' × 'Dorothy Perkins'. Creamy-white, golden-yellow stamens, medium-large, semi-double, fragrant, in clusters, very floriferous, non-recurrent; growth strong, to 3 m./10 ft.; foliage glossy, leathery. GSR 235. (7.9)

Claret. Min. (F. Harmon Saville, 1977). 'Little Chief' × self. Mauve, double, 50 petals, cupped, no scent, in clusters of 6-12, free bloom; bud pointed, short; growth dwarf, very compact, slightly spreading; foliage serrate.

Cläre Grammerstorf. F. (Kordes, 1957). 'Harmonie' × rubiginosa-seedling. Light yellow, large, double, open, petals retained; growth strong, bushy, upright, 0.7 m./2.3 ft.; foliage light green, glossy. (5.3)

Clair Matin. LCl. (Meilland, 1960). 'Fashion' × [('Independence' × 'Orange Triumph') × 'Phyllis Bide']. Soft pink, semi-double, medium-large, 5-6 cm./2-2.4 in. across, cupped to flat, good fragrance, very abundant, many together, continuous bloom; growth very strong, 2.5-3 m./8.3-10 ft.; foliage dark green, leathery, healthy. PWR 211; GSR 149. (7.2)

Cleopatra (= 'Kleopatra'). HT. (Kordes, 1955). ('Walter Bentley' × Condesa de Sástago') × 'Golden Sceptre'. Interior scarlet with some bronze hue, reverse old gold, medium-large, double, fragrant, floriferous; growth bushy, low, 0.6 m./0.2 ft., foliage dark green, healthy. PWR 37; RA 1956:112. (6.9)

Clio. HP. (W. Paul, 1894). Flesh-pink, large, very double, strong fragrance, several together on long stems, recurrent; very strong growth; foliage light green.

Cocktail. S. (Meilland, 1957). ('Independence' × 'Orange Triumph') × 'Phyllis Bide'. Geranium-red with yellow center, single, saucer-shaped, medium large, 6 cm./2.4 in. across, many together, continuous bloom all season; growth strong, 2 m./6.6 ft.; foliage leathery, dark green. PWR 220; GSR 236.

Cocorico. F. (Meilland, 1953). 'Alain' × 'Orange Triumph'. Geranium-red, single, large, 8 cm./3.2 in. across, singly and in clusters, floriferous, some scent; growth strong, upright, medium, 0.6-0.8 m./2-2.6 ft.; foliage light green, glossy. PWR 119. (6.7)

Colibri. Min. (Meilland, 1958). 'Goldilocks' × 'Perla de Montserrat'. Bright golden orange, tinged with red, small, very double, flat, some scent, singly or several together, abundant; growth very dwarf; foliage deep green, small, healthy. RA 1963:97. (6.8)

Cologne Carnival. (= 'Kölner Karneval'; 'Blue Girl'). HT. (Kordes, 1964). Silvery lilac-mauve, large, 12 cm./5 in., very double, perfect shape, light fragrance, floriferous; bud long; growth strong, spreading; foliage deep green, healthy. KR 9:32; RJb 28:49. (7.4)

Colonial White. LCl. (Wyant, 1959). 'New Dawn' × 'Mme. Hardy'. White, medium large, 8 cm./3.2 in. across, double, opening flat, fragrant, abundant and recurrent bloom. (5.6)

Colorama. HT. (Meilland, 1968). 'Suspense' × 'Confidence'. Interior luminous crimson, reverse yellow with salmon shades, large, 10-12 cm./4-5 in. across, double, cupped, fragrant; growth strong, medium; foliage very glossy. (6.5)

Color Magic. HT. (W.A. Warriner/Jackson & Perkins, 1978). Seeding × 'Spellbinder'. Ivory to deep rose, double, 20-30 petals, flat, no scent, singly and several together, good bloomer all season; bud long, spiral; foliage large, dark green, glossy; growth upright, medium high. ARA 62:214. (7.5)

Colour Wonder. (= 'Königin der Rosen'). HT. (Kordes, 1964). 'Kordes Perfecta' × 'Tropicana'. Orange, salmon and yellow, bicolor, large, fragrant, double, perfect shape, on long stems; growth bushy, very prickly, 0.6 m./2 ft.; foliage bronze-green, large. GSR 323; KR 10:9; RJb 30:80. (7.6)

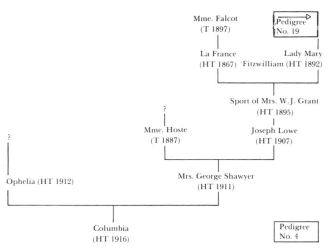

Columbia. HT. (E.G. Hill, 1916). 'Ophelia' × 'Mrs. George Shawyer'. Glossy pink, double, very large, strong fragrance; long bud on long stem; growth strong; foliage deep green. RZ 1924:68. (6.4)

Columbia, Climbing. ClTH. (Vestal, 1923). Sport of 'Columbia'. Like the type, but climbing, 2-3 m./6.6-10 ft. high. (5.7)

Comanche. Gr. (Swim & Weeks, 1968). 'Spartan' × ('Carrousel' × 'Rouge Happiness'). Orange-red, medium large, double, some scent, floriferous; bud pointed; vigorous; foliage leathery. (7.5)

Commandant Beaurepaire. B. (Moreau-Robert, 1874). Light crimson, with purple-red stripes and white mar-

bling, large, double, cupped- to ball-shaped, very strong fragrance, only summer-flowering, somewhat recurrent in the autumn; growth bushy, upright, strong, stems very prickly; foliage light green, waved. TR 5; GiS 11. (7.9)

Command Performance. HT. (Lindquist/Howard, 1970). 'Tropicana' × 'Hawaii'. Orange-red, semi-double, strong fragrance, medium-large, very long-lasting, continuous bloom; growth very strong, upright, bushy; foliage medium green, coarse. (7.2)

Compassion. ClHT. (Harkness, 1971). 'White Cockade' × 'Prima Ballerina'. Apricot and salmon, large, 10 cm./4 in. across, semi-double, fragrant, several together, very floriferous; growth strong, 2.5-3 m./8.3-10 ft.; foliage dark green. RA 1973:185.

Complicata. G. (possibly a *macrantha* hybrid). Brilliant pure pink with white center, 12 cm./5 in. across, single, finally flat, stamens golden-yellow, very floriferous along the branches, June; growth very strong, 2 × 2 m./6.6 × 6.6 ft. or more; foliage large, light green. GSR 150-152; HRo 29; GiS 1; RA 1976:121. Can be propagated from cuttings easily.

Comte de Chambord. P. (Moreau-Robert, about 1860). 'Baronne Prévost' × 'Portlandica'. Portland Rose. Deep pink with lighter margin, very double, large, finally flat, outer petals reflexed, very strong scent, July, somewhat recurrent; growth strong, medium; foliage

1916	**Columbia**					
1920	Climbing Columbia					
1920	Red Columbia					
1922	Bride's Blush					
1924	New Columbia					
1924	Silver Columbia					
1925	Perfection					
1925	------------------→		**Briarcliff**			
1926	Southern Beauty	1929	Climbing Briarcliff			
1926	Albert Pike	1930	Old Glory			
1927	Lucinda	1934	Mrs. Frank Schramm			
1928	Rose Hill	1934	------------------→	**Better Times**		
1928	Europa	1936	Mur-Ray	1934	Forward March	
		1940	Peter's Briarcliff	1935	Peerless	
1928	**Scott's Columbia** ------→	1929	Sport of Scott's Columbia	1937	------------→	**Red Better Times**
1928	August Noack				1961	Perle von Aalsmeer
1929	Frau Luise Lindecke					Modern Times
1929	Gunston Hall					
1933	J.K.B. Roos					
1934	Climbing White Columbia					

Survey of the spontaneous sports of 'Columbia'. (after Saakov, altered)

deep green; leaflets pointed. GiS 10; PGR 18; GSR 78; SOR 29; RA 1975:121. (7.1)

Comtesse de Murinais. (= 'White Moss'). M. (Vibert, 1843). Soft rose, nearly white and flat when fully open, very double, strong fragrance, perfect shape; growth strong, stems up to 1.5 m./5 ft. long; buds and calyx mossy. (8.0)

Comtesse du Cayla. Ch. (P. Guillot, 1902). Nasturtium-red and orange, semi-double, flat, fragrant, abundant, recurrent bloom; growth vigorous; foliage dark green, glossy. RA 1973:46.

Comtesse Vandal. HT. (Leenders, 1932). ('Ophelia' × 'Mrs. Aaron Ward') × 'Souvenir de Claudius Pernet'. Salmon-pink with yellow base, large, loose, double, fragrant; bud very long, perfect, coppery-orange; growth strong; foliage leathery. BTR 34; SRW 21. (5.6)

Condesa de Sástago. HT. (Dot, 1932). ('Souvenir de Claudius Pernet' × 'Maréchal Foch') × 'Margaret McGredy'. Interior scarlet, reverse yellow, large, very double, fragrant; bud ovoid; growth strong, flowering branches short; foliage deep green, glossy. SRW 22. (5.2)

Confidence. HT. (Meilland, 1951). 'Peace' × 'Michèle Meilland'. Clear pink, golden-yellow towards base, large, double, fragrant, very floriferous; growth evenly bushy, 0.7 m./2.3 ft.; foliage large, glossy. PWR 16; BTR 26. (8.1)

'Congratulation' → **Sylvia**

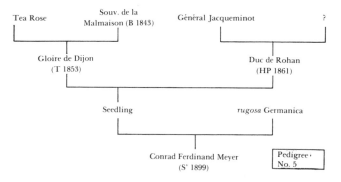

Conrad Ferdinand Meyer. S. (Dr. Müller, 1899). ('Gloire de Dijon' × 'Duc de Rohan') × R. *rugosa germanica*. Silvery pink, double, very large, strong fragrance, recurrent; growth very strong, up to 3 m./10 ft., stems strong, very prickly. Famous old garden rose. GSR 131; RZ 1901:81. (7.1)

Conrad O'Neil. S. (O.Neil/Wyant, 1966). 'Blossom-time'-seedling × 'Don Juan'. Light red, medium size, very double, very fragrant, abundant bloom; bud ovoid; growth upright, tall, very vigorous; foliage dark green, glossy.

Conrad's Crimson. S. (S. Eacott, 1971). 'Sweet Sultan' × 'Conrad Ferdinand Meyer'. Crimson with purple, medium, double, finally flat, early, fragrant, several together; growth very strong, tall; foliage light green, young growth bronze.

Constance Spry. S. (Austin/Sunningdale, 1961). 'Belle Isis' × 'Dainty Maid'. Soft pink with deeper center, large, 12 cm./5 in. across, very double, cupped, along the branches, non-recurrent; growth very strong, 2.5 m./8.3 ft.; foliage deep green. GSR 153; GR 384; TRT 96; GiS 18.

Constantia. HT. (Herholdt, 1960). 'Baccara' × 'Grace de Monaco'. Deep pink, large, 10 cm./4 in. across, finally rather flat, fragrant; growth medium.

Contempo. F. (Armstrong, 1971). 'Spartan' × ('Goldilocks' × ['Fandango' × 'Pinocchio']). Orange with lighter reverse, double, singly or several together, some scent, floriferous; growth strong, medium; foliage light green, medium, healthy. (5.8)

Contrast. HT. (Howard & Smith, 1937). Seedling × 'Talisman'. Pink and bronze with white and bronze reverse, medium large, double, high-centered, profuse bloom; growth compact, bushy, very vigorous, long stems; foliage leathery, glossy. (5.2)

'Cooperi'; 'Cooper's Burmese Rose' → **Rosa gigantea,** p. 290.

Copenhagen. ClHT. (Poulsen, 1964). Seedling × 'Ena Harkness'. Scarlet, double, large, fragrant, recurrent, several together; growth strong, climbing, 3 m./10 ft. high; foliage medium green and bronze, healthy. GSR 237; RA 1964:144.

Copper Pot. F. (Dickson, 1968). ? × 'Golden Scepter'. Interior coppery-orange, reverse darker, large, 8-10 cm./3.2-4 in. across, semi-double, many together in trusses, free bloom; growth strong, upright, 0.9 m./3 ft.; foliage dark green and coppery. RA 1969:15. (7.1)

Coquette des Alpes. B. (Lacharme, 1867). 'Blanche Lafitte' × 'Sappho'. White tinged blush, medium to large, semi-cupped; growth vigorous. (8.0)

Coral Dawn. LCl. (Boerner/Jackson & Perkins, 1952). ('New Dawn'-seedling × yellow HT) × orange Pol. Coral-pink, large, 12 cm./5 in., loosely double, fragrant, floriferous, singly or several together, continuous bloomer; growth strong, 2-3 m./6.6-10 ft.; foliage small, glossy. GSR 238; KR 1/:162. (6.3)

Coralin. Min. (Dot, 1955), 'Mephisto' × 'Perla de Alcanada'. Coral-red, double, rather large, floriferous, no scent; growth dwarf, bushy, 30 cm./12 in.; foliage small, matt, abundant. PWR 171. (7.2)

Coral Pillar. ClHT. (Lammerts, 1945). 'Crimson Glory' × 'Captain Thomas'. Geranium-pink, large, double, high-centered, very fragrant; growth very vigorous, climbing; foliage dark green, glossy. (6.0)

Coral Princess. F. (Boerner/Jackson & Perkins, 1966). ('Fashion'-seedling × 'Garnette'-seedling) × 'Spartan'. Coral-orange, large, loosely double, cupped, fragrant; bud ovoid; growth strong, medium, 0.6-0.8 m./2-2.6 ft.

Coral Satin. LCl. (Zombory/Jackson & Perkins, 1960). 'New Dawn' × 'Fashion'. Coral-red, large, 8-10 cm./3.2-4 in. across, double, nice shape, fragrant, floriferous; growth strong. 2.5 m./8.3 ft.; foliage coarse, glossy. (6.8)

Coral Sunrise. F. (Herholdt). Parentage not given. Coral-orange, medium large, 6-7 cm./2.4-2.8 in., abundant, blooms continuously all season; growth low, many branches; foliage glossy, disease-resistant.

Coral Treasure. Min. (Ralph S. Moore, 1971). 'Little Darling' × 'Little Buckaroo'. Coral-pink, double, singly and in clusters; buds globose; growth dwarf, moderately to loosely compact. (7.5)

Cordula. (= 'Kortri'). F. (Kordes, 1972). 'Europeana' × 'Marlene'. Luminous scarlet, very double, rosette-shaped, medium large, very floriferous; buds globose; growth strong, but low, 40 cm./16 in.; foliage healthy.

Cornelia. HMsk. (Pemberton, 1925). Deep pink with much yellow, small, semi-double, fragrant, recurrent; growth strong, tall to very tall; foliage bronze-green, glossy. GSR 119; GiS 16; HRo 12; RA 1976:180. (9.0)

Cosimo Ridolfi. G. (Vibert, 1842). First old-pink, later with violet shades and light pink veins, 6 cm./2.4 in. across, very double, fragrant; growth medium, 1 m./3.3 ft.; foliage light green.

'Cottage Maid' → **Rosa centifolia variegata,** p. 257.

Country Dancer. S. (G.J. Buck, 1973). 'Prairie Princess' × 'Johannes Boettner'. Rose-red, then fading, double, open, cupped, fragrant, several together on medium strong stems, profuse bloom; bud medium, ovoid; growth bushy, compact, medium or low, vigorous, upright, few prickles; foliage dark green, glossy, disease-resistant. (8.2)

Country Music. S. (G.S. Buck, 1973). 'Paddy McGredy' × ('World's Fair' × 'Floradora') × 'Summer Pippen'. Pale rose, darker on reverse side, large, double, cupped, fragrant, in clusters on medium strong stems, profuse, intermittent bloom; bud large, ovoid; growth vigorous, upright, compact, 0.8 m./2.6 ft.; foliage large, leathery. (7.2)

Coup de Foudre. F. (Hémeray-Aubert, 1956). ('Peace' × 'Independence') × 'Oiseau de Feu'. Fiery-red, velvety, medium large, double, floriferous; growth compact, branched, low, 40 cm./16 in.; foliage glossy. (7.1)

Coupe d'Hébé. B. (Laffay, 1840). Bourbon variety × *Chinensis* hybrid. Dark pink, exterior nearly white, medium large, nearly waxen, cupped, strong fragrance, several together, flowering only in June, flowers nodding; growth strong, 2 × 2 m./6.6 × 6.6 ft., spreading. PGR 54. (7.3)

Courvoisier. F. (McGredy, 1970). 'Elizabeth of Glamis' × 'Casanova'. Deep yellow, medium large, 7 cm./2.8 in. across, double, strong fragrance, floriferous, in clusters; growth medium, upright, 0.8 m./2.6 ft.; foliage medium green, glossy. GSR 400; RA 1970:32.

'Coventry Cathedral' → **Cathedral**

Coy Colleen. (= 'Blushing Rose'). HT. (McGredy, 1953). ('Modesty' × 'Portadown Glory') × 'Phyllis Gold'. Soft whitish-pink with darker margin, nearly white when fully open, some scent; growth strong; foliage glossy. (5.8)

Cramoisi Supérieur. (= 'Agrippina'). Ch. (Coquereau, 1832). Dark crimson, medium large, very double, cupped, in clusters; growth strong. RA 1973:46.

Cream Gold. Min. (Ralph S. Moore, 1977). 'Golden Glow' × ?. Medium-yellow, high-centered, double, 35-40 petals, slight scent, 3 or more together in clusters, often singly, recurrent all season; bud long, pointed; growth dwarf, very bushy, compact, spreading.

Crested Jewel. M. (R.S. Moore, 1971). 'Little Darling' × *Rosa centifolia cristata*. Rosy-red, margin often darker, medium-large, semi-double, singly or several together, floriferous, long lasting, petals drop off; growth very strong, 2 m./6.6 ft.

'Crested Moss' → **Rosa centifolia cristata.** p. 257.

Cricket. Min. (J. Christensen/Armstrong, 1978). 'Anytime' × ('Zorina' × 'Golden Wave'). Orange, double, 25 petals, singly or in clusters, slight scent, almost always in flower; bud ovoid; growth dwarf, upright; foliage deep green, young growth purple.

Cricri. Min. (Meilland, 1958). ('Alain' × 'Independence') × 'Perla de Alcanada'. Salmon-pink, small, very double, very floriferous; growth dwarf, 30 cm./12 in., bushy. (7.4)

Crimson Globe. M. (W. Paul, 1890). Crimson and purple, very double, globose, sometimes does not open; calyx very mossy; growth medium, 1 m./3.3 ft.

Crimson Glory. HT. (Kordes, 1935). 'Cathrine Kordes'-seedling × 'W.E. Chaplin'. Deep velvety crimson, perfect shape, medium-large, very double, very strong fragrance, floriferous; growth medium, 0.6 m./2 ft.; foliage dark green. LR 8; RA 1937:192. Has been used for hybridizing all over the world. (7.6)

Crimson Glory, Climbing. ClHT. (Jackson & Perkins, 1946). Sport of 'Crimson Glory'. Growth strong, 3 m./10 ft.; otherwise like the type. (7.1)

Crimson Moss. M. Dark brownish-purple outside, reverse crimson with purple, very double, fragrant, sometimes does not open, only summer-flowering; calyx very mossy; growth strong, medium.

Crimson Rambler. R. Origin not known with certainty, but probably mutation or hybrid of *Rosa multiflora* var. *cathayensis*; discovered 1878 by Rob. Smith in a garden in Tokyo and brought to England, introduced in 1893 as 'Turner's Crimson Rambler'. Light crimson, small, but very double, in large, pyramidal panicles; growth strong, 5-6 m./16.5-20 ft. high, needs support; foliage light green, leathery, glossy. RZ 1898:1. (7.8)

Crimson Rosette. F. (Krebs/Howard & Smith, 1948). Parentage unknown. Dark crimson, medium, double, open, rosette-shape, slight scent, profuse bloom, in clusters; growth dwarf, bushy, vigorous; foliage dark green, leathery. (7.5)

Crimson Shower. Cl. (Norman, 1951). Seedling of 'Excelsa'. Pure crimson, small, 3 cm./1.2 in., double, some scent, in large trusses, very floriferous until autumn; growth very strong, 4-5 m./13.2-16.5 ft.; foliage small, green, glossy, healthy. GSR 201.

Crimson Wave. (= 'Imperator'). F. (Meilland, 1972). 'Zambra' × ('Sarabande' × ['Goldilocks' × 'Fashion']). Cardinal-red, large, 10-12 cm./4-5 in. across, some scent, continuous bloom, singly and several together; growth very strong, 0.7 m./2.3 ft.; foliage large, deep green, matt.

Crispata. S. (J.C. Schmidt, 1902). *Rugosa*-seedling. Clear pink to yellowish salmon-pink, medium large, single, many stamens; growth prostrate to semi-climbing; foliage peculiarly curly. RZ 1907:32.

Cuddles. Min. (E. Schwartz/Nor'East, 1978). 'Zorina' ×

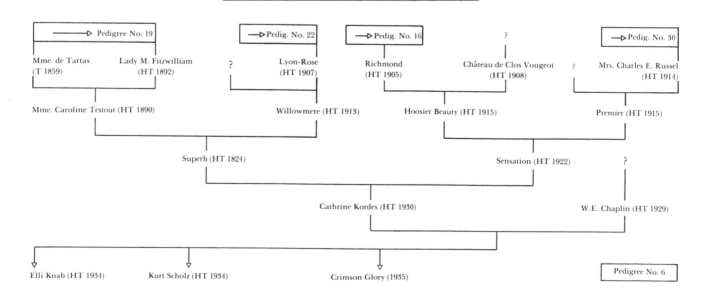

seedling. Dark pink, very double, high-centered, 55-60 petals, slight scent, mostly borne singly, sometimes 2 side buds, profuse bloomer; bud ovoid; growth dwarf, compact.

Cupid's Beauty. Min. (E.D. Williams, 1978). Seedling × 'Over the Rainbow'. Light orange and cream, fragrant, high centered, double, 3.8 cm./1.5 in., profuse bloom; bud long, pointed; foliage small, dark; growth compact, spreading.

Cupids Charm. F. (Fuller/Wyant, 1964). 'Little Darling' × 'First Love'. Salmon-pink, medium, fragrant, abundant bloom; bud pointed; growth vigorous, bushy. (7.9)

Curly Pink. HT. (Brownell, 1948). 'Pink Princess' × 'Crimson Glory'. Deep rose-pink, large, 8-12 cm./3.2-5 in. across, double, petals curled outward, fragrant, profuse bloom; bud long, pointed; growth vigorous, compact; foliage dark green, glossy. (6.2)

Curtain Call. HT. (O.L. Weeks, 1977). 'First Prize' × seedling. Deep pink, double, 35 petals, cupped, light tea scent, to 4-5 in clusters, flowering intermittently; bud pointed; growth medium, very vigorous; foliage large, leathery.

Curtis Yellow. HT. (Eldon Curtis/Kimbrew, 1973). 'Golden Scepter' × 'Miss Hillcrest'. Clear yellow, does not fade, large, high-centered, fragrant, long lasting, singly on long stems; buds large; growth vigorous, medium, 1 m./3.3 ft.; foliage leathery, light green, disease-resistant. (6.0)

Cuthbert Grant. HSuffulta. (H.H. Marshall, 1967). ('Crimson Glory' × [Donald Prior' × *R. arkansana*]) × 'Assiniboine'. Deep purplish-red, large, semi-double, cupped, slightly fragrant, free and intermittent bloom; growth bushy, very vigorous; foliage glossy. (6.0)

Cutie. Min. (Ralph S. Moore, 1952). 'Dancing Doll' × 'Oakington Ruby'. Medium pink with white base, small, semi-double, flat, slight scent, profuse bloom; growth dwarf, 25 cm./10 in., very bushy, almost without prickles; foliage small, green, glossy. (6.3)

Cynthia. HT. (Verschuren-Pechtold, 1934). Parentage not given. Medium red, very double, free bloom.

Dagmar Späth. F. (Wirtz & Eicke/Späth, 1936). Sport of 'Joseph Guy'. Pure white, later with blush hue, margin waved, very floriferous, low, 0.5 m./1.7 ft. (6.8)

Daily Sketch. F. (McGredy, 1960). 'Ma Perkins' × 'Grand Gala'. Bicolor, broad crimson edge, center silvery-pink to white, large, 8 cm./3.2 in., double, cupped, fragrant, floriferous; growth strong, stems upright, branched, 0.8 m./2.6 ft.; foliage deep green, healthy. RA 1961:64. (7.1)

Dainty Bess. HT. (Archer, 1925). 'Ophelia' × 'K. of K.'. Shell pink with darker bud, single, saucer-shaped, margin fimbriate, 12 cm./5 in. across, fragrant, floriferous, stamens brownish; growth strong, bushy, 0.7 m./2.3 ft.; foliage semi-glossy. GSR 401. (8.4)

Dainty Maid. F. (LeGrice, 1940). 'D.T. Poulsen' × ?. Interior shell-pink, reverse crimson-pink, bud cherry-red, single, medium, flat, in clusters together, stamens orange, resistant to rain damage; growth bushy, upright, 0.8 m./2.6 ft.; foliage deep green, leathery. PWR 138; GSR 402. (7.0)

Dairy Maid. F. (LeGrice, 1957). ('Poulsen's Pink' × 'Ellinor LeGrice') × 'Mrs. Pierre S. du Pont'. Cream, fading to white, large, 8 cm./3.2 in. across, single, in large clusters, free bloom; bud yellow with crimson shades, very decorative; growth vigorous; foliage glossy.

Daisy Hill. (= 'Macrantha'). S. (Kordes). Shell-pink, fading to white, semi-double, flat, 7 cm./2.8 in., scented, very floriferous, non-recurrent, many hips; growth strong, bushy, mdium, and to 2 m./6.6 ft. wide; foliage pretty.

Dame de Coeur. HT. (Lens, 1958). 'Peace' × 'Independence'. Pure red, large, double, fragrant, floriferous; growth strong; foliage dark green, glossy. (6.8)

Dame Edith Helen. HT. (Dickson, 1926). Pink, large, double, good shape, very fragrant, very lazy bloomer; growth bad, few branches; foliage small, green. LR 4.

Dame of Sark. F. (Harkness, 1976). ('Pink Parfait' × 'Masquerade') × 'Tablers Choice'. Bright orange-yellow, flushed red, double, 30 petals, slight scent, in trusses, very free flowering; growth upright, medium, 0.7-0.9 m./2.3-3 ft.; foliage deep green, glossy. RA 1976:60.

Dandy Dick. F. (Harkness, 1967). 'Pink Parfait' × 'Red Dandy'. Clear pink, double, 25 petals, large, 10 cm./4 in. across, spicy scent, in clusters, very free bloom; growth free; foliage light green.

Danish Gold. F. (Poulsen, 1949). ('Golden Salmon' × 'Souvenir de Claudius Pernet') × 'Julien Potin'. Opening golden-yellow, later fading to creamy-white, single or slightly semi-double, 7 cm./2.8 in. across, fragrant, in clusters; growth compact, low; foliage glossy.

Danny Boy. LCl. (McGredy, 1969). 'Uncle Walter' × 'Milord'. Orange-red, large, double, some fragrance, in clusters; 2 m./6.6 ft. high.

'Danse du Feu' → **Spectacular**

Darling. HT. (L.A. Taylor, 1958). 'Pink Princess' × 'Charlotte Armstrong'. Light pink, large, very double, fragrant, profuse bloom; bud ovoid; growth bushy, vigorous; foliage dark green, glossy.

Darling Flame. (= 'Minuetto'). Min. (Meilland, 1971). ('Rimosa' × 'Rosina') × 'Zambra'. Chinese-red buds, opening to vermilion flowers; growth dwarf. 35 cm./14 in. (7.5)

Dave Davis. HT. (Davis/Wyant, 1964). Seedling × 'Charles Mallerin'. Dark velvety-red, large, very double, high-centered, very fragrant, free bloomer; bud long, pointed; growth moderate; foliage leathery. (5.1)

Dawson. R. (J. Dawson, U.S.A., 1888). *R. multiflora* × 'Général Jacqueminot'. Dark cherry-red, more or less double, small, 10-20 together in large trusses, summer-flowering, somewhat recurrent; growth strong, 3-4 m./10-13.2 ft. GSR 202. The first *multiflora* hybrid bred in the United States; today only of historical interest, otherwise long surpassed. GSR 202.

Daydream. HT. (Armstrong, 1969). 'Helen Traubel' × 'Tiffany'. Deep pink, large, finally flat, loosely double, some scent, petals drop off cleanly, on long stems; bud large, pointed; growth strong, upright, 1.2 m./4 ft.; foliage large, glossy.

Debbie. Min. (Ralph S. Moore, 1966). 'Little Darling' × 'Zee'. Yellow, margins pink, small, double, fragrant, abundant bloom; growth dwarf, bushy, sometimes semi-climbing; foliage small, leathery. (7.3)

Deep Purple. F. (R. Kordes, 1980). 'Zorina' × 'Silver Star'. Mauve-pink, fragrant, double, imbricated, large, 7.6-10 cm./3-4 in., prolific bloom; bud ovoid-pointed; foliage glossy, dark; growth very vigorous, upright, bushy.

Delbards Orange Climber. LCl. (Chabert/Armstrong, 1966). 'Spectacular' × ('Rome Glory' × 'La Vaudoise').

Orange-red, medium, double, some scent, singly, long lasting, floriferous; growth strong, branched, 3 m./10 ft.; foliage deep green, glossy. (5.6)

Delicata. HRg. (Cooling, 1898). Soft lilac-pink, large, semi-double, recurrent; growth vigorous. (7.8)

De Meaux. (= 'Rose de Meaux'; *R. centifolia pomponia*; *R. pomponia*). C. The Dijon Rose. S. Probably from the gardens of the Bishop Doménique Séguier of Meaux, southeast of Paris, in 1637. Shell-pink, small, mostly 3-4 cm./1.2-1.6 in. across, often even smaller, very double, mostly on the tops of horizontal branches. June; pedicels bristly; growth upright, stems slender, 40-50 (-90) cm./16-20(-36) in.; foliage light green, small. GiS 8; WR 119; PGR 45. (8.3)

De Meaux White. (= 'Rose de Meaux White'). C. Sport of 'De Meaux', but white, including the center.

Desert Charm. Min. (Ralph S. Moore, 1973). 'Baccara' × 'Magic Wand'. Deep red with orange, medium full, high-centered, double, slight scent, free, continuous bloom; bud long, pointed, nearly black; growth dwarf. (6.7)

Desert Dance. F. (J.A. Herholdt, 1975). 'Impala' × seedling. Bicolor orange with golden-yellow reverse, moderately full-cupped, slight scent, in trusses, very free and continuous bloomer; growth medium to tall; foliage glossy.

'Desprez à Fleur Jaune' → **Jaune Desprez**

Detroiter. (= 'Schlössers Brillant'). HT. (Kordes, 1952). 'Poinsettia' × 'Crimson Glory'. Blood-red, very double, light fragrance, floriferous, resistant to rain damage; growth upright, 0.8 m./2.6 ft.; foliage large, green, young growth purple, matt. PWR 10. (7.6)

Deuil de Paul Fontaine. M. (Fontaine, 1873). Purplish-red, reverse more brownish-red, very double, large, fragrant, recurrent; growth medium, 0.7-0.8 m./2.3-2.6 ft., stems very prickly, the "moss" of the buds also hard and prickly. PGR 53. (6.5)

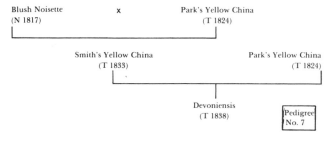

Devoniensis. T. (Foster, 1838). 'Smith's Yellow' × 'Park's Yellow China'. Creamy-white, blush center, very large, double, strong fragrance, recurrent; strong growth. RA 1975:47. (7.6)

Devoniensis, Climbing. ClT. (Pavitt/Curtis, 1858). Sport of 'Devoniensis'. 2-3 m./6.6-10 ft.; otherwise like the type. RA 1975:47.

Diamant. F. (Kordes, 1962). 'Korona' × 'Spartan'. Vermilion-scarlet, large, very double, good shape, some scent, 3-7 together; growth sturdy, upright, 0.7 m./2.3 ft.; foliage deep green, glossy. KR 9:161; RJb 26:64. (7.1)

Diamond Jubilee. HT. (Boerner/Jackson & Perkins, 1947). 'Maréchal Niel' × 'Feu Pernet-Ducher'. Deep creamy-yellow with light orange, large, 12-15 cm./5-6 in. across, double, cupped, fragrant, floriferous; growth medium, 0.7 m./2.3 ft., bushy; foliage large, glossy. PWR 24; SRW 26. (6.5)

Dian. Min. (Ralph S. Moore, 1957). (*R. wichuraiana* × 'Floradora') × ('Oakington Ruby' × 'Floradora'). Pink, double, flat, open, 3 cm./1.2 in. across, fragrant, floriferous; growth dense, bushy, dwarf; foliage deep green, small. (6.7)

Dickson's Flame. F. (Dickson, 1958). 'Independence' × 'Nymph'. Fiery-red, semi-double, 8 cm./3.2 in. across, no scent, floriferous, in clusters; growth bushy, low, 40-50 cm./16-20 in.; foliage bluish-green, small, matt. PWR 133; RA 1959:1.

Die Welt. HT. (Kordes, 1976). Seedling × 'Peer Gynt'. Orange blend, double, 25 petals, high-centered, some scent, abundant bloom; bud large, long-pointed; growth vigorous, upright, bushy; foliage glossy.

Diorama. HT. (de Ruiter, 1965). 'Peace' × 'Beauty'. Intense golden-yellow flushed with apricot, large, 10 cm./4 in. across, loosely double, fragrant; growth upright, vigorous, 0.7 m./2.3 ft.; foliage medium green, healthy. GSR 290; WPR 17; RA 1966:96. (6.4)

Dirigent. S. (Tantau, 1956). 'Karl Weinhausen' × 'Final'. Luminous blood-red, medium large, semi-double, no scent, free bloom, many together in clusters; growth strong, upright, medium; foliage large, purplish-green. RJb 27:64. (7.7)

Doc. (= 'Degenhardt'). Pol. (de Ruiter, 1954). Pink, white center, semi-double, flat, small, in large trusses, very floriferous; growth very dwarf, 25 cm./10 in., sturdy; foliage medium green, glossy.

Doctor Eldon Lyle. Gr. (Mackay, 1968). 'President Eisenhower' × 'Suspense'. Dark red, medium size, double, high-centered, fragrant, abundant bloom; bud pointed; growth compact, very vigorous, medium; foliage bronze, soft. (7.4)

Domino. HT. (Gaujard, 1956). 'Peace' × seedling. Deep crimson, medium large, double, some scent; bud long; foliage deep green. (6.5)

Donald Prior. F. (Prior, 1938). Seedling × 'D.T. Poulsen'. Fiery-red, semi-double, flat, large, 8 cm./3.2 in. across, some scent, floriferous, many together in large trusses; growth medium strong, bushy, 0.8 m./2.6 ft.; foliage large, green, matt, young growth purple. (7.2)

'Donatella' → **Granada**

Don Don. Min. (Ernest Williams/Mini-Roses, 1976). Seedling × 'Over the Rainbow'. Dark red, very double, 60 petals, fragrant, singly, abundant bloom, recurrent; growth dwarf, bushy, upright; foliage bronze, glossy, small.

Don Juan. Cl. (Malandrone, 1958). 'New Dawn'-seedling × 'Detroiter'. Velvety crimson, large, 12 cm./5 in. across, double, strong fragrance, continuous bloom; growth strong, 2 m./6.6 ft.; foliage leathery, glossy. (8.1).

Donna Faye. Min. (E.W. Schwartz/Nor' East Miniature Roses, 1975). Light pink, double, 25-30 petals, high-centered, HT-form, light scent, free bloom, recurrent, 1-3 in clusters; bud long, pointed; growth dwarf, upright; foliage small, ovate-pointed.

Dopey. (= 'Eberwein'). Pol. (de Ruiter, 1954). 'Robin Hood' × Polyantha-seedling. Crimson with lighter center, stamens yellow, small, semi-double, no scent, many together; growth dwarf, dense, 35 cm./14 in.; foliage dark green, glossy. (8.0)

Doris Tysterman. HT. (Wisbech Plant Co., 1975). 'Peer Gynt' × seedling. Tangerine-orange, medium, double, 30 petals, some scent, moderately free flowering; growth medium, 0.9 m./3 ft., upright; foliage bronze-green, glossy.

Dornröschen. S. (Kordes, 1960). 'Pike's Peak' × 'Ballet'. Salmon-pink to light red, yellow reverse, large, double, recurrent; growth vigorous, upright, branched, medium. KR 9:117; RJB 24:128.

Dorothy Perkins. R. (Jackson & Perkins, 1901). *R. wi-*

churaiana × 'Mme. Gabriel Luizet'. Pure pink, small, very double, no scent, very floriferous, non-recurrent; growth very strong, 3-4 m./10-13.2 ft., long stems; foliage small, light green, glossy, often attacked by mildew. RZ 1908: 53; GR 336. (5.9)

Dorothy Wheatcroft. F. (Tantau/Wheatcroft, 1960). Parentage not given. Brilliant red, large, semi-double, 20 petals, some scent, in clusters, free, continuous bloom; growth medium, 1 m./3.3 ft., bushy; foliage bright green. GSR 155; GiS 18; RA 1962:128.

Dortmund. K. (Kordes, 1955). Seedling × *R. kordesii*. Blood-red with large white eye, single, petals waved, 10 cm./4 in. across, some scent, many together, in large trusses, recurrent; growth strong, 3 m./10 ft.; foliage small, very glossy, deep green. GSR 241; GiS 18. (8.2)

Double Delight. HT. (Swim & Ellis/Armstrong, 1976). 'Granada' × 'Garden Party'. Red and white bloom, high-centered, double, 40 petals, spicy fragrance, very floriferous, continuous bloom; bud long and pointed to urn-shaped; growth medium, very bushy, spreading; foliage semi-glossy, abundant, very mildew-resistant. (8.5)

Doubloons. Cl. (Horvath, 1934). *Setigera* hybrid × *R. foetida bicolor* hybrid. Golden-yellow, large, double, cupped, fragrant, many together on long stems, recurrent; growth very strong, 3 m./10 ft.; foliage glossy. ARA 1937:266. (6.1)

'Dr. A.J. Verhage' → **Golden Wave**

Dr. Bernardo. F. (Harkness, 1969). 'Very Dalton' × 'Red Dandy'. Crimson, large, double, good fragrance, free flowering, several together in clusters; growth strong, bushy, 0.7 m./2.3 ft.; foliage large. GSR 404.

Dr. Brownell. HT. (H. C. Brownell, 1964). 'Helen Hayes' × 'Peace'. Buff with yellow center, large, double, 35 petals, high-centered, fragrant, abundant bloom; bud long, pointed; growth upright, medium; foliage dark, glossy. (7.1)

Dr. Debat. (= 'Dr. F. Debat', La Rosée'). HT. (F. Meilland, 1952). 'Peace' × 'Mrs. John Laing'. Bright pink tinted with coral, fragrant, double, high centered, large, 12.5-15 cm./5-6 in.; bud ovoid, pointed, foliage leathery, dark; growth vigorous, upright.

Dr. Eckener. HRg. (V. Berger, 1928). *Rugosa*-seedling × 'Golden Emblem'. Coppery-pink, yellow base, later more pink, large, semi-double, fragrant, recurrent;

growth very strong, upright, 1.5-2 m./5-6.6 ft. (7.0)

Dr. E.M. Mills. S. (Van Fleet, 1926). *R. hugonis* × 'Radiance'. Primrose-yellow with reddish shade, finally dark pink, 4-6 cm./1.6-2.4 in. across, semi-double, globose, early and floriferous, non-recurrent; growth medium strong; foliage small, dark green.

Dr. Huey. (= 'Shafter'). Cl. (Thomas 1914). 'Ethel' × 'Gruss an Teplitz'. Dark crimson, medium. 5 cm./2 in. semi-double, some scent, yellow stamens; growth strong. SRW 116; ARA 1926:122. (7.1)

Dr. J.H. Nicolas. Cl. (Nicolas/Jackson & Perkins, 1940). 'Charles P. Kilham' × 'Georg Arends'. Rosy-pink, large, 12 cm./5 in., very double, globose, several together, recurrent; growth strong, 2.5 m./8.3 ft.; foliage large, leathery, deep green. ARA 1941:103. (7.3)

Dr. W. van Fleet. LCl. (Van Fleet, 1910). (*R. wichuraiana* × 'Safrano') × 'Souvenir du Président Carnot'. Soft pink, later nearly white, large, double, fragrant, very floriferous, very similar to 'New Dawn', but non-recurrent bloom; growth very strong, 6 m./20 ft. HRo 17. (7.1)

Drambuie. HT. (Anderson, 1973). Sport of 'Whisky Mac'. Interior red, reverse orange-red, strong fragrance, double, singly or several together; growth vigorous, bushy; foliage glossy.

Dream Girl. LCl. (Jacobus, 1944). 'Dr. W. van Fleet' × 'Señora Gari'. Salmon-pink with golden yellow tinge, large, 8 cm./3.2 in. double, fragrant, recurrent; growth strong, 3 m./10 ft.; foliage large, glossy. TCR 8. (6.7)

Dreamglo. Min. (E.D. Williams/Mini-Roses, 1978). 'Little Darling' × 'Little Chief'. Red blend, high-centered, double, 50 petals, some scent, borne singly, abundant bloom all season; bud long, pointed; growth dwarf; foliage very small.

Dresden Doll. Min. (Ralph S. Moore, 1975). 'Fairy Moss' × Hybrid Moss seedling. Soft pink, very mossy, good recurrent bloomer; growth dwarf; foliage leathery, glossy. (7.5)

D.T. Poulsen. F. (S. Poulsen, 1930). 'Orléans Rose' × 'Vesuvius'. Blood-red, semi-double, flat, some scent; growth bushy; foliage firm, leathery, deep green.

Dublin Bay. LCl. (McGredy, 1975). 'Bantry Bay' × 'Altissimo'. Deep red, double, 25 petals, open form, fragrant, profuse bloom; bud ovoid; growth tall, climbing; foliage dark green, glossy. RA 1975:196.

Duc de Fitzjames. G. Dark Crimson with greenish center, lilac with age, several together, very double; growth strong, 1 m./3.3 ft.; foliage abundant.

Duc de Guiche. G. (Prévost, before 1829). Purplish-crimson, veined, very double, first cupped, later more globose, greenish eye, June; growth strong, 1 m./3.3 ft. or over. (7.4)

Duchesse de Brabant. (= 'Shell Rose'). T. (Bernède, 1857). Parentage unknown. Rosy pink, large, double, cupped, very fragrant, free bloom; growth vigorous, spreading. (8.0)

Duchesse de Buccleugh. G. (Robert, 1860). Magenta-pink with some crimson, margin lighter, very large, opening cupped, then very flat, small green eye, flowering very late; growth strong, medium, stems nearly without prickles; foliage abundant. (8.5)

Duchesse de Caylus. HP. (C. Verdier, 1864). 'Alfred Colomb'-seedling. Brilliant crimson-pink, large, globose, good form, fragrant; growth moderate. (7.4)

Duchesse de Montebello. G. (Laffay, before 1829). Shell-pink, medium, very double, good fragrance, June; growth strong, medium, loosely branched; foliage greyish-green (closer to *R. alba* than *R. gallica*). PWR 174.

Duchesse de Verneuil. M. (Portemer, 1856). Flesh-pink, center more salmon-pink, with lighter reverse, petals arranged like a camellia, very double, fragrant, very mossy; growth strong, medium; foliage fresh green. GiS 9.

Duet. HT. (Swim, 1960). 'Fandango' × 'Roundelay'. Light pink, with darker to light red reverse, large, 10 cm./4 in. across, double, fragrant; growth strong, medium, 0.7 m./2.3 ft., branched; foliage deep green, leathery, resistant to Black Spot. (8.2)

Duftstar. HT. (Kordes/Dehner, 1974). Seedling × 'Papa Meilland'. Dark red, high-centered, double, 25 petals, strong fragrance, abundant, intermittent bloom; bud large, long-pointed; growth medium, upright, vigorous; foliage dark green, soft, abundant.

Duftzauber. HT. (Kordes, 1969). Seedling × 'Kaiserin Farah'. Scarlet, later crimson, large, 10-12 cm./4-5 in. across, double, cupped, fragrant, singly; growth up-

right, bushy, 0.7 m./2.3 ft.; foliage medium, semi-glossy, young growth red. KR 10:19. (7.3)

Duke of Windsor. (= 'Herzog von Windsor'). HT. (Tantau, 1968). 'Spartan' × 'Montezuma'. Orange-vermilion, medium large, loosely double, fragrant, several together, abundant bloom; growth strong, 0.8 m./2.6 ft.; foliage deep green, semi-glossy. GSR 294; RA 1969:14; KR 10:52. (6.7)

Du Maître d'Ecole. G. Deep rose-lilac, changing to lilac-purple and grey, very large, very double, finally flat and quartered, fragrant, non-recurrent; growth strong, bushy, 1.2 m./4 ft. GSR 89; PGR 18.

Duquesa de Peñaranda. HT. (Dot, 1931). 'Souvenir de Claudius Pernet' × 'Rosella'. Salmon-pink and orange, very large, double, fragrant, long stems; growth strong, 0.7 m./2.3 ft.; foliage light green, glossy. (5.2)

Dusky Maiden. F. (LeGrice, 1974). ('Daily Mail Scented Rose' × 'Etoile de Hollande') × 'Else Poulsen'. Blackish-crimson, single, saucer-shaped, large, 8 cm./3.2 in. across, fragrant, stamens golden-yellow, many together on strong stems; growth strong, 0.7 m./2.3 ft.; foliage large, semi-glossy. (7.8)

Dusky Red. HT. (M.E. Wyant, 1972). 'Karl Herbst' × 'Big Red'. Medium red, outer petals darker and heavily veined, large, high-centered, globose, very fragrant, petals drop off cleanly, intermittent bloom; bud large, globose; growth vigorous, bushy, upright, few prickles; foliage dark green, leathery, disease-resistant. (7.2)

Düsterlohe. R. (Kordes, 1931). 'Venusta Pendula' × 'Miss C.E. van Rossem'. Rosy-pink, single, 7 cm./2.8 in. across, some scent, non-recurrent, but very abundant; growth very strong, stems 1.5 m./5 ft. long. GSR 156; TRT 140.

Dusty Rose. Min. (D. Morey/Pixie Treasures, 1974). 'Amy Vanderbilt' × 'Cécile Brunner'. Reddish-purple, deeper toward base, double, 50 petals, high-centered, fragrant, singly, continuous bloom, very long-lasting; bud pointed; growth dwarf, upright; foliage dark green. disease-resistant. (7.5)

Dutch Gold. HT. (Wisbech Plant Co., 1978). 'Peer Gynt' × 'Whisky Mac'. Deep golden-yellow, large, double, fragrant, borne singly, free flowering; growth strong, upright, medium high; foliage deep green, glossy.

Dwarfking. (= 'Zwergkönig'). Min. (Kordes, 1954). 'World's Fair × 'Tom Thumb'. Deep rosy-red, small, 3 cm./1.2 in. across, very double, rosette-shaped, some scent, very floriferous, in clusters; growth dwarf, 25 cm./10 in.; foliage small, glossy. GSR 503; KR 9:140. (8.8)

Earth Song. Gr. (G.J. Buck, 1975), 'Music Maker' × 'Prairie Star'. Deep pink, open, cupped, fragrant, in clusters, free flowering all season; bud long and pointed to urn-shaped; growth medium, bushy, upright; foliage dark green, glossy, very healthy.

Easley's Golden Rambler. LCl. (Easley, 1932). Lemon-yellow, reverse sometimes with reddish spots, large, 10 cm./4 in., double, good shape, non-recurrent, June, singly or in clusters; growth strong, 4 m./13.2 ft.; foliage olive green, leathery, abundant. RA 1934:233.

Easter Morning. Min. (Ralph S. Moore, 1960). 'Golden Glow' × 'Zee'. Ivory-white, small, 3 cm./1.2 in. across, very double, flat, very floriferous, some scent; bud small, pointed; growth, dwarf, 30 cm./12 in.; foliage leathery, deep green. (8.0)

Eclipse. HT. (Nicolas/Jackson & Perkins, 1935). 'Joanna Hill' × 'Federico Casa'. Golden-yellow, double, fragrant; bud long-pointed, dark yellow; growth bushy; foliage deep green. LR7. (6.7)

Eddie's Crimson. HMoyesii. (Eddie, 1956). 'Donald Prior' × *moyesii* hybrid. Blood-red, semi-double, large, 10-12 cm./4-5 in., non-recurrent, very abundant; many red hips in the autumn; growth strong, 2.5 m./8.3 ft.

Eddie's Jewel. HMoyesii. (Eddie, 1962). 'Donald Prior' × *R. moyesii* hybrid. Fiery-red, single, 8-10 cm./3.2-4 in. across, recurrent bloom, many red hips in the autumn; growth strong, 2 × 2 m./6.6 × 6.6 ft., young stems with red bark, few prickles.

Eden Rose. HT. (Meilland, 1950). 'Peace' × 'Signora'. Intense pink, with deeper veining and shades, lighter reverse, double, cupped, very fragrant; growth strong, upright, 0.9 m./3 ft., little branching; foliage large, glossy. PWR 84; GSR 297. (6.4)

Edith Nelly Perkins. HT. (A. Dickson, 1928). Parentage unknown. Salmon-pink with orange hue, reverse red with orange, large, double, open, fragrant, free bloom; growth vigorous, bushy; few prickles; foliage abundant. (4.9)

Edith Schurr. S. (Stanard, 1976). 'Leverkuson' × 'Wendy Cussons'. Light yellow, center pink, very fragrant, very double, large, 12.7 cm./5 in., recurrent; bud globose, sulfur yellow; foliage glossy; growth spreading.

E.G. Hill. HT. (Hill, 1929). Parentage unknown. Scarlet, very large, double, strong fragrance, good shape; strong stems.

Eglantine → **Rosa rubiginosa;** p. 262.

Eiffel Tower. HT. (Swim/Armstrong, 1963). 'First Love' × seedling. Clear pink with darker veins, large, 10 cm./4 in. across, double, on strong stems; bud very long, urn-shaped; growth strong, 0.9 m./3 ft.; foliage light green, large, matt. Good cut flower. (7.2)

Elation. HT. (Jackson & Perkins, 1973). 'Buccaneer' × seedling. Golden-yellow, large, non-fading, good shape, floriferous; growth bushy, upright, 0.7 m./2.3 ft.; foliage light green, healthy.

El Cid. HT. (Armstrong, 1969). 'Fandango' × 'Roundelay'. Orange-red, large, cupped, double, some scent, singly or several together on long stems; growth strong; foliage glossy.

El Dorado. HT. (Armstrong, 1972). 'Manitou' × 'Summer Sunshine'. Golden yellow, petals later with reddish shade, large, double, petals drop off cleanly, strong fragrance; bud long, pointed; growth strong, upright; foliage large, leathery, glossy.

Eleanor. Min. (Ralph S. Moore, 1960). (*R. wichuraiana* × 'Floradora') × (seedling × 'Zee'). Coral-pink, darker with age, small, 3 cm./1.2 in. across, double, flat; bud long; growth bushy, upright, dwarf, 30 cm./12 in.; foliage glossy, leathery. (7.7)

Electra. HT. (Boerner/Jackson & Perkins, 1970). 'Eclipse' × seedling. Yellow, large, flat, petals drop off, some scent, floriferous; bud long; growth strong, upright, bushy, few prickles.

Electron. (= 'Mullard Jubilee'). HT. (McGredy, 1972). 'Paddy McGredy' × 'Prima Ballerina'. Deep pink to light crimson, large, double, some scent, petals drop off, floriferous; bud ovoid; growth bushy, upright, 0.9 m./3 ft.; foliage medium green, medium large. RA 1970:14; GSR 340. (7.7)

Elegance. LCl. (Brownell, 1937). 'Glenn Dale' × ('Mary Wallace' × 'Miss Lolita Armour'). Pure yellow, margin fading to white with age, fragrant, large, double, somewhat recurrent; growth very strong, 4 m./13.2 ft., long stems; foliage dark green, glossy. GSR 203. (7.9)

Elfin Charm. Min. (Ralph S. Moore, 1974). (*R. wichuraiana* × 'Floradora') × 'Fiesta Gold'. Pink. very double, 65 petals, and with rosette of 15-20 small petaloids around pistil, fragrant, abundant bloom, in clusters; growth dwarf, 25 cm./10 in., bushy, compact; foliage small, healthy. (6.5)

Elfinesque. Min. (D. Morey/Pixie Treasures, 1973). 'Little Darling' × 'Golden Bantam'. Opening coral-orange, bright pink with white bases on petals with age, small, open, semi-double, singly or several together on long stems; foliage dark green, glossy. GSR 203. (7.9) dwarf, 30 cm./12 in.; foliage small, leathery. (7.5)

Elfinglo. Min. (E.D. Williams/Mini-Roses, 1977). 'Little Chief' × self. Reddish-magenta-mauve, cupped-flat, some scent, double, profuse bloom all season, in clusters; growth dwarf, very bushy, compact; foliage glossy, disease-resistant.

Elida. HT. (M. Tantau, 1966). Vermilion, fragrant, double, high centered, large, free bloom; foliage dark, glossy; growth vigorous, branching.

Elizabeth Harkness. HT. (Harkness, 1969). 'Red Dandy' × 'Piccadilly'. Pastel color, off white to creamy-buff, pretty markings in center from rose to rosy-amber; double, some scent, singly or several together; growth upright, 0.8 m./2.6 ft.; foliage medium green, semi-glossy. GSR 299; RA 1969:128. (6.9)

Elizabeth of Glamis. (= 'Irish Beauty'). F. (McGredy, 1964). 'Spartan' × 'Highlight'. Deep salmon, large, 10 cm./4 in., perfect shape, double, strong fragrance, floriferous; growth bushy, upright, medium, 0.7-0.9 m./2.3-3 ft., branched; foliage medium-green, healthy. GSR 407; KR 10:53; RA 1964:20. (7.0)

Ellen Mary. HT. (LeGrice, 1963). 'Wellworth' × 'Independence'. Rich wine red, large, 12 cm./5 in., double, fragrant, floriferous; growth upright.

Ellen Poulsen. Pol. (Poulsen, 1911). 'Mme. Norbert Levavasseur' × 'Dorothy Perkins'. Dark pink, medium, double, floriferous, in small clusters, recurrent; growth bushy, low; foliage deep green, glossy.

Ellinor LeGrice. HT. (LeGrice, 1950). 'Lilian' × 'Yellowcrest'. Clear yellow, double, 50 petals, large, fragrant, cupped, very free bloom; bud ovoid; growth vig-

orous, upright, medium; foliage dark green, leathery, glossy.

Elmshorn. S. (Kordes, 1950). 'Hamburg' × 'Verdun'. Rosy-red, small, 4 cm./1.6 in. across, double, 20 petals, no scent, many together, continuous bloom for 5 months; growth strong, medium; foliage small, light green, wrinkled. GSR 157; KR 9:119; GiS 19. (7.2)

Else Poulsen. F. (Poulsen, 1924). 'Orléans Rose' × 'Red Star'. Pink, semi-double, medium, 5 cm./2 in. across, flat, margin slightly waved, some scent, many together on long stems; growth bushy, 0.9 m./3 ft.; foliage large. PWR 127. (7.3)

Elysium. F. (Kordes, 1961). 'Queen Elizabeth' × 'Spartan'. Salmon-pink, large, double, cupped, good fragrance; growth medium, 0.6 m./2 ft., bushy; foliage medium green, glossy. GSR 406; KR 9:73. (7.8)

Embassy. HT. (Sanday, 1967). 'Gavotte' × ('Magenta' × 'Golden Scepter'). Pale golden-yellow and apricot, veins pale carmine, large, double, some fragrance; growth upright, 0.8 m./2.6 ft.; foliage deep green, glossy. GSR 300; RA 1974:185.

Emily. HT. (Baines, 1949). 'Mme. Butterfly' × 'Mrs. Henry Bowles'. Soft rose pink, fragrant, double, large, 13-15 cm./5-6 in., very free bloom; foliage dark; growth vigorous, upright.

Emily Gray. Cl. (Williams, 1918). 'Jersey Beauty' × 'Comtesse du Cayla'. Deep brownish-yellow, golden stamens, small, 3.5 cm./1.4 in. across, double, good fragrance, many together on strong stems; non-recurrent; Growth strong, 3 m./10 ft.; foliage coppery, almost evergreen.

Emma Jane. F. (Sanday, 1970) 'Vera Dalton' × ('Masquerade' × 'Independence'-seedling). Salmon-pink with lighter margin, center orange, medium, semi-double, in clusters, freely produced; growth medium; foliage medium green, matt.

Empress Josephine. (= form of *R.* × *francofurtana*). S. (16th century; *R. majalis* × *R. gallica*). Deep purplish-pink with darker veins, margin waved, semi-double, some scent, June; non-recurrent; many hips; growth strong, medium, stems with few prickles; foliage grey-green. SOR 43. (7.5)

Ena Harkness. HT. (Norman/Harkness, 1946). 'Crimson Glory' × 'Southport'. Velvety bright-red, large, very double, fragrant, good shape, flowers sometimes nodding; growth strong, 0.8 m./2.6 ft.; foliage medium green. PWR 91; GSR 301. (6.3)

Ena Harkness, Climbing. ClHT. (Murrell, 1954). Climbing sport of 'Ena Harkness', 3 m./10 ft.; otherwise like the type.

English Miss. F. (Cants of Colchester, 1977). 'Dearest' × 'Sweet Repose'. Light pink, very double, 60 petals, strong fragrance, in trusses, very free bloom; growth medium, branched; foliage first dark purple, then turning to dark green. RA 1979:82.

Eos. S. (Ruys, 1950). *Rosa moyesii* × 'Magnifica'. Salmon-pink to more red, white center, medium large, double, several together on long stems, non-recurrent, summer-flowering, very abundant; growth strong, 3 m./10 ft.; foliage leathery, glossy. GSR 31; GiS 2.

Erfurt. HMsk. (Kordes, 1939). 'Eva' × 'Reveil Dijonnais'. Lemon-yellow with crimson margin, center often white, stamens deep yellow, very large, semi-double, floriferous and recurrent; growth strong, spreading, medium; foliage deep green, young growth red. PWR 200; GSR 158; TRT 145; GiS 19. (7.1)

Erica Herholdt. (= 'Erica'). F. (J.A. Herholdt, 1964). Seedling × 'Montezuma'. Scarlet-orange, semi-double, petals with waved margin, many together, floriferous.

Ernest H. Morse. HT. (Kordes, 1965). 'Prima Ballerina' × 'Detroiter'. Dark blood-red, large, 10 cm./4 in. across, double, very sweet fragrance; growth strong, bushy, 0.7-0.9 m./2.3-3 ft.; foliage deep green, abundant. GSR 302; WPR 15; RA 1965:49. (7.6)

Eroica. (= 'Erotika'). HT. (Tantau, 1968). Seedling × 'Golden Wave'. Velvety crimson, very large, fragrant, singly on long stems; growth strong, upright, 0.8 m./2.6 ft.; foliage deep green, young growth purple. RJb 34:64.

Escapade. F. (Harkness, 1967). 'Pink Parfait' × 'Baby Faurax'. Light pink to mauve with nearly white center, large, semi-double, 8 cm./3.2 in. across, floriferous, many together, stamens golden yellow; growth strong, upright, 0.8 m./2.6 ft.; foliage healthy, light green. GSR 408; HRo 11; RA 1969:14.

Esther Ofarim → **Matador.**

Estrellita. Min. Origin uncertain. White, single, small, in clusters; bud small, globose; growth dwarf, 20 cm./8 in., loosely compact; foliage medium.

Etain. R. (F. Cant, 1953). Salmon pink, double, slightly fragrant, free bloom; growth very vigorous; foliage dark green, glossy, almost evergreen. (7.9)

Eternal Youth. (= 'Eterna Giovanezza', 'Jeunesse Eternelle'). HT. (D. Aicardi, 1937). 'Dame Edith Helen' × 'Julien Potin'. Light pink suffused with orange-salmon, very fragrant, double, cupped, large, 10-13 cm./4-5 in., profuse bloom; bud long pointed; foliage leathery; growth upright, vigorous, bushy.

Ethel Sanday. HT. (Mee/Sanday, 1954). 'Rex Anderson' × 'Audrey Cobden'. Yellow with apricot hue, large, 12 cm./5 in. across, fragrant, good shape, free bloomer; growth strong, upright; foliage deep green. PWR 2; RA 1954:120. (7.0)

Etienne Levet. HP. (F. Levet, 1871). 'Victor Verdier'-seedling. Carmine-red, large, very double, somewhat recurrent; growth vigorous, upright. (6.5)

Etoile de Hollande. HT. (Verschuren, 1919). 'General McArthur' × 'Hadley'. Deep red, large, very double, cupped, strong fragrance, floriferous; growth medium strong, spreading, low; foliage matt. BTR 10. (6.2)

Etoile de Hollande, Climbing. ClHT. (Leenders, 1931). Sport of 'Etoile de Hollande'. Height 3-4 m./10-13.2 ft., otherwise like the type. (7.6)

Etoile de Lyon. T. (P. Guillot, 1881). Golden-yellow, double, fragrant, sparse, intermittent bloom; growth bushy, stems short, weak; foliage soft.

Eugène Fürst. HP. (Soupert & Notting, 1875). 'Baron de Bonstetten' × ?. Deep crimson, large, very double, cupped to globose, strong fragrance, recurrent; growth strong, medium; foliage large, deep green, matt.

Eugène Verdier. M. (E. Verdier, 1872). Lighter or deeper crimson with darker center, very double, good fragrance, good shape; growth strong.

Eugénie Guinoisseau. M. (Guinoisseau, 1864). Cherry-red to purple-mauve, cupped to globose, large, very double, summer- and autumn-flowering; calyx very mossy, flower stalks bristly-mossy, otherwise stems with few prickles.

Europeana. F. (de Ruiter, 1963). 'Ruth Leuwerik' × 'Rosemary Rose'. Deep blood-red, large, 8 cm./3.2 in. across, very double, some scent, in large trusses, flowering all season; growth upright, 0.7 m./2.3 ft.; foliage deep purplish-bronze, finally deep green, glossy, very disease-resistant. GSR 410; GR 240. (8.8)

Eurorose. F. (Dickson, 1973). 'Zorina' × 'Redgold'. Bronze-yellow, opening with much fiery red, this later fading, medium, loosely double, 25 petals, high-centered, some scent, in clusters, floriferous; growth bushy, upright, 0.7-0.8 m./2.3-2.6 ft.; foliage first red, then dark green.

Eutin. F. (Kordes, 1940). 'Eva' × 'Solarium'. Glowing crimson, double, cupped, some scent, many together in large clusters on long stems; growth strong, 1 m./3.3 ft.; foliage leathery, deep green, glossy. (7.6)

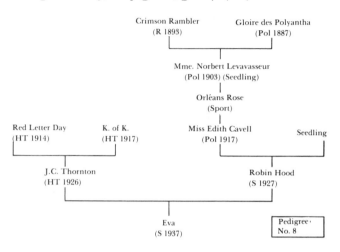

Eva. HMsk. (Kordes, 1937). 'Robin Hood' × 'J.C. Thornton'. Deep red with white center, single, large, scented, many together in large clusters, very recurrent; growth strong, 1.5 m./5 ft. high, 1 m./3.3 ft. broad.

Evangeline Bruce. F. (Dickson, 1971). 'Colour Wonder' × 'Sea Pearl'. Golden yellow, dark pink towards the margin, large, double, fragrant, several together; growth strong; foliage light green, pointed. RA 1972:145.

Eve Allen. HT. (Allen, 1964). 'Karl Herbst' × 'Gay Crusader'. Bicolor, interior cherry-red, reverse deep yellow, double, medium, fragrant; growth strong, bushy, spreading, 0.9 m./3. ft.; foliage deep green. GSR 303; RA 1966: 128.

Evelyn Fison. (= 'Irish Wonder'). F. (McGredy, 1962). 'Moulin Rouge' × 'Korona'. Vivid scarlet or orange-red, not fading, double, large, fragrant, in large clusters, free bloom; growth upright, bushy, medium; foliage deep green, glossy. RA 1962:33.

Evening Star. F. (W.A. Warriner/Jackson & Perkins, 1974). 'White Masterpiece' × 'Saratoga'. White with pale yellow shading near base, large, high-centered, double, some scent, singly and in clusters on long stems, free flowering, continuous bloom; growth very vigorous, 1 m./3.3 ft.; foliage large, deep green, very mildew-resistant. (8.5)

Everest. HP. (Easlea, 1927). 'Candeur Lyonnaise' × 'Mme. Caristie Martel'. Creamy-white with green center, very large, double, high-centered, fragrant; growth low, spreading; foliage light green. RA 1928:205. (5.8)

Evergold. (= 'Coed') F. (Felly, 1971). Golden-yellow, medium, 5 cm./2 in. across, very double; foliage dark green, very glossy. Greenhouse variety.

Excalibur. F. (Harkness, 1967). 'Vera Dalton' × 'Woburn Abbey'. Scarlet, medium, 6 cm./2.4 in. across, double, some scent, floriferous, in clusters; growth bushy; foliage deep green, glossy.

Excelsa. (= 'Red Dorothy Perkins'). R. (Walsh, 1909). Parentage unknown. Light crimson, double cupped, many together in large trusses, non-recurrent, but extremely abundant; growth strong, 3 m./10 ft.; foliage fresh green, glossy. LR 13; RA 1941:160.

Eye Paint. F. (McGredy, 1975). Seedling × 'Picasso'. Red with white eye, single, open, some scent, very floriferous, continuous bloom, in clusters; bud ovoid; growth tall, very bushy, dense; foliage small, dark green. RA 1975:196. (8.0)

Fabergé. (Boerner/Jackson & Perkins, 1959). Seedling × 'Zorina'. Salmon-pink with yellow-shaded reverse, large, double, some scent, singly or several together on long stems, floriferous; growth bushy; foliage healthy. Greenhouse variety. (7.9)

Fair Lady. HT. (Boerner/Jackson & Perkins 1959). 'Golden Masterpeice' × 'Tawny Gold'. Buff with pink hue, large, 10 cm./4 in. across, very double, fragrant; vigorous. Greenhouse variety.

Fairy Dancers. HT. (Cocker, 1969). 'Wendy Cussons' × 'Diamond Jubilee'. Soft salmon-pink with apricot shades, medium, double, fragrant, floriferous; growth low, 0.6 m./2 ft.; foliage medium green, glossy. GSR 413.

Fairy Moss. Min. (Ralph S. Moore, 1969). ('Pinocchio' × 'William Lobb') × 'New Penny'. Medium pink to light red, small. Semi-double, open, abundant bloom; bud mossy; growth dwarf, bushy, vigorous; foliage small, leathery, light green. (7.9)

Fairy Princess. ClMin. (R.S. Morse, 1955). 'Eblouissant' × 'Zee'. Light pink, small, 2.5 cm./1 in. across, very double, in clusters, abundant intermittent bloom; bud salmon-apricot; growth to 0.6 m./2 ft.; foliage small, fern-like. (6.1)

Fairy Queen. F. (J.B. Williams, 1972). 'The Fairy' × 'Queen Elizabeth'. Light pink with center more coral-pink, finally all pink, small, double, some scent, long-lasting, petals drop off cleanly; growth upright, bushy, few prickles; foliage small, glossy, bronze-green.

Fanal. F. (Tantau, 1946). ('Johanna Tantau' × 'Heidekind') × 'Hamburg'. Luminous red with orange shades, center lighter, stamens golden yellow, large, semi-double, flat, to 10-15 together in large clusters; growth strong, upright, 0.6 m/2 ft.; foliage light green, glossy.

Fancy Talk. F. (Swim & Weeks, 1965). 'Spartan' × 'Garnette'. Pink with orange shades, small, double, high-centered, slightly fragrant, abundant bloom, in clusters; growth low, bushy; foliage leathery. (7.2)

Fantastique. HT. (Meilland, 1943). 'Ampère' × ('Charles P. Kilham' × ['Charles P. Kilham × 'Capucine Chambard]). Yellow with crimson margin, medium, 9 cm./3.6 in., double, cupped, fragrant; growth compact, vigorous; foliage deep green, glossy, leathery. (5.8)

Fantin Latour. C. Clear pink with darker center, opening cupped, later petals flat with reverse margin, very double, fragrant, only summer-flowering; growth strong, medium, stems with few prickles; foliage deep green, large. GSR 68; RA 1976:180; PGR 49; GiS 8. (7.4)

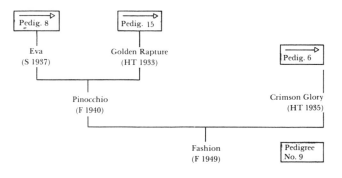

Fashion. F. (Boerner/Jackson & Perkins, 1949). 'Pinocchio' × Crimson Glory'. Salmon-pink, medium, 7 cm./2.8 in. across, double, finally flat, fragrant, in large trusses; growth medium, bushy, 0.6 m./2 ft.; foliage small, light green, matt. PWR 156; WPR 50; RA 1949:124. (7.9)

Fashion, Climbing. ClF. (Boerner, 1951). Sport of 'Fashion'; growth medium-tall; otherwise like the type.

Fashion Flame. Min. (Ralph S. Moore, 1977). 'Little Darling' × 'Fire Princess'. Coral-orange, high-centered, double, 35 petals, fragrant, several together, recurrent; bud ovoid, pointed; growth bushy, dwarf, much branching. (6.5)

Fashionette. F. (Boerner/Jackson & Perkins, 1958). 'Goldilocks' × 'Fashion'. Soft salmon-pink, medium, 7 cm./2.8 in. across, double, some scent, in clusters; growth low, bushy, 0.5 m./1.7 ft.; foliage small, matt. (7.6)

Favorita. HT. (Boerner/Stark Bros., 1954). HT seedling × 'Serenade'. Salmon-red with orange hue, large, 12-15 cm./5-6 in. across, double, flat, fragrant; growth strong, upright, 0.9 m./3 ft.; foliage large, glossy. (6.2)

Felicia. HMusk. (Pemberton, 1928). 'Trier' × 'Ophelia'. Salmon-pink with yellow shades, later fading to almost white, large, double, flat, strong fragrance, floriferous, recurrent; growth medium; foliage medium green, matt, abundant. PWR 1990; GSR 120; GiS 16. (7.8)

Félicité Bohain. M. (Before 1866). Soft flesh-pink, medium, center darker; buds very mossy, first brown, then light green; growth upright, medium.

Félicité et Perpétue. Hybrid of *R. sempervirens*. (A.A. Jacques, 1827). Creamy white, tinged with flesh, small, 4 cm./1.6 in. across, rosette-shaped, small eye, many together in clusters, very abundant, non-recurrent; growth very strong, tall, 5 m./16.5 ft. in mild areas; foliage light green, partly evergreen. GSR 205; TCR 1; GiS 22.

Félicité Parmentier. A. (1836). Pure flesh-pink, later margin more creamy-yellow, very double and globose; buds yellowish; growth strong, medium; foliage large, grey-green to yellowish-green. GSR 65; SOR 11; PGR 36. (8.7)

Fellemberg. Ch. (Fellemberg, 1857). Bright crimson, double, cupped, very floriferous, several together in large, branching clusters; growth strong, tall, 2 m./6.6 ft.; foliage purple.

Femina. HT. (Gaujard, 1963). 'Fernand Arles' × 'Mignonne'. Salmon-pink with coppery shades and darker veins, large, double, good shape, fragrant, resistant to rain damage; growth strong, 0.8 m./2.6 ft.; foliage bronzy, leathery. KR 9:10; WPR 38; RJb 28:80. (7.2)

Ferdinand Prichard. HP. (Tanne, 1921). Scarlet and pink streaked, semi-double, very free and recurrent bloom; growth tall, vigorous. GiS 11; ARA 1976:120. (7.8)

Ferry Porsche. HT. (Kordes, 1971). 'Tropicana' × 'Americana'. Glowing red, large, double, not fading, singly or several together on long branches; growth strong, bushy, 0.7 m./2.3 ft.; foliage deep green, large. (7.5)

Fervid. F. (LeGrice, 1960). 'Pimpernell' × 'Korona'. Scarlet-orange, single, 8 cm./3.2 in. across, margins waved, some scent, floriferous, in large clusters; growth strong, 1.1 m./3.6 ft.; foliage deep green. GSR 414.

Festival. HT. (Dixie Rose Nurseries, 1943). 'E.G. Hill' seedling. Red, very double, fragrant, profuse bloomer; entirely without prickles, including the foliage. (4.5)

Festival Queen. HT. (Lindquist/Edmunds, 1968). Light pink with darker margin, perfect shape, long-lasting, some scent; bud long; growth strong, compact; foliage healthy. (5.7)

Feuerzauber. (= 'Korber'). HT. (Kordes, 1974). 'Fragrant Cloud' × seedling. Similar to 'Fragrant Cloud', light orange, large, double, some scent, high-centered, singly or several together, petals drop off cleanly; growth strong, bushy; foliage large, healthy.

Fiesta. HT. (C.B. Hansen/Armstrong, 1940). Sport of 'The Queen Alexandra Rose'. Vermilion, splashed with yellow, large, double, open, fragrant; growth vigorous, compact, bushy; foliage dark green, glossy. (5.6)

Fiesta Flame. F. (J. Sanday, 1978). 'Sarabande' × 'Ena Harkness'. Intense scarlet, semi-double, slight scent, singly and several together, very free bloomer; bud pointed; growth low, bushy; foliage abundant.

Fiesta Gold. Min. (Ralph S. Moore, 1970). 'Golden Glow' × 'Magic Wand'. Yellow, small, double, flat, singly or several together, recurrent; bud long, pointed; growth bushy, dwarf, 30 cm./12 in.; foliage healthy. (6.3)

Fiesta Ruby. Min. (Ralph S. Moore, 1977). 'Red Pinocchio' × 'Little Chief'. Medium-red, high centered, double, 45 petals, no scent, singly and in clusters, abundant,

recurrent all season; bud ovoid, pointed; growth dwarf, compact, sturdy, much branching; foliage small, deep green, glossy. (7.5).

Fimbriata. S. (Morlet, 1891). *R. rugosa* × 'Mme. Alfred Carrière'. Light pink, semi-double, small, central petals shorter, with carnation-like fimbriated margin (as in the 'Grootendorst' varieties), fragrant; growth strong, upright, few branches and loose foliage. TRT 165; GiS 14.

Firecracker. F. (Boerner/McGredy, 1956). 'Pinocchio'-seedling × 'Numa Fay'-seedling. Scarlet with yellow base, large, 11 cm./4.4 in., semi-double, saucer-shaped, fragrant, in clusters; growth strong, 0.9 m./3 ft.; foliage light green. PWR 114; GSR 415; RA 1956:108.

Firecrest. F. (LeGrice, 1964). ('Cinnabar' × 'Marjorie LeGrice') × 'Pimpernell'. Vermilion with scarlet reverse, large, 8 cm./3.2 in. across, double, cupped, in clusters, bloom starting very early, last out of flower; growth bushy, low, 40 cm./16 in. (8.0)

Fire King. F. (Meilland, 1958). 'Moulin Rouge' × 'Fashion'. Orange-red, medium, 6 cm./2.4 in. across, double, opening flat, fragrant; growth strong, upright; foliage leathery, deep green. BTR 50. (7.6)

Firelight. HT. (Kordes/Jackson & Perkins, 1971). 'Detroiter' × 'Orange Delbard'. Orange-red, very large, double, long-lasting, fragrant, floriferous; buds very large, long; growth very strong, medium; foliage large, light green, leathery. (6.2)

Fire Princess. Min. (Ralph S. Moore, 1969). 'Baccara' × 'Eleanor'. Orange-red, small, double, singly or several together, very floriferous; growth strong, bushy, dwarf, 30 cm./12 in.; foliage small, glossy.

Fireside. HT. (R.V. Lindquist, 1977). 'Kordes Perfecta × 'Belle Blonde'. Multicolored bloom, center yellow to nearly white, margin deep rose, some scent, large, double, 35 petals, imbricated, singly, free bloom; bud ovoid; growth medium; foliage dark green, glossy, very mildew-resistant. ARA 62:186.

First Choice. F. (Morse, 1958). 'Masquerade' × 'Sultane'. Fiery orange-scarlet with yellow center and stamens, single, large, 12 cm./5 in. across, fragrant, abundant bloom, in clusters; growth strong, spreading, 0.8 m./2.6 ft.; GSR 159; RA 1959:96; GiS 19.

First Edition. F. (Delbard/Conard-Pyle, 1976). ('Zambra' × [Orléans Rose' × 'Goldilocks]) × ('Orange Triumph'-seedling × 'Floradora'). Orange, double, 30 petals, in clusters, continuous, abundant bloom; bud small, ovoid; growth medium, broadly upright; foliage glossy, large, resistant to mildew and Black Spot. ARA 61:216. (8.5)

Fist Federal Gold. HT. (Boerner/Jackson & Perkins, 1967). 'Golden Masterpiece'-seedling × self. Bicolor yellow, double, fragrant, floriferous; growth upright; foliage leathery, glossy. (7.5)

First Lady. HT. (Swim/Burr, 1961). 'First Love' × 'Roundelay'. Pink, large, semi-double, some scent; growth strong. (6.8)

First Love. (= 'Premier Amour'). HT. (Swim, 1951). 'Charlotte Armstrong' × 'Show Girl'. Rosy-red, medium, 7 cm./2.8 in. across, double, some scent, floriferous; bud pointed; growth bushy; foliage light green, leathery. PWR 1; GSR 304. (7.1)

First Prize. HT. (Boerner/Jackson & Perkins, 1970). 'Enchantment' × 'Golden Masterpiece'. Rosy-red, center ivory, very large, fragrant, double, singly on long stems; growth strong, upright; foliage very resistant to Black Spot. (9.0)

First Prize, Climbing. ClHT. (E. Reasoner/Jackson & Perkins, 1976). Sport of 'First Prize'. Vigorous climber, 2.5-3 m./8.3-10 ft. high, recurrent all summer; otherwise like the type. (8.0)

Fisher & Holmes. HP. (Verdier, 1865). 'Maurice Bernardin'-seedling (?). Scarlet and crimson, very double, large, fragrant, recurrent; bud long, pointed; growth sturdy, upright, stems strong, long.

F.J. Grootendorst. HRg. (de Goey/Grootendorst, 1918). *R. rugosa rubra* × unknown Polyantha. Dark red, small, loosely double, margin fimbriated, no scent, many together in clusters, recurrent; growth upright, 1 m./3.3 ft. stems very prickly and bristly; foliage small, wrinkled. (8.0)

Flamenco. F. (McGredy, 1960). 'Cinnabar' × 'Spartan'. Salmon-red, large, 7 cm./2.8 in. across, double, some scent, many together, floriferous; growth strong, upright; foliage large, medium-green. PWR 149. (6.5)

Flamingo. HRg. (Howard, 1956). *R. rugosa* × 'White Wings'. Pink, single, large, star-shaped, several together; bud long, pointed; recurrent; growth strong, up-

right, 0.9 m./3 ft.; foliage slightly grey-green. RA 1928:95. (7.7)

Flaming Beauty. HT. (J. Winchel/Kimbrew, 1978). 'First Prize' × 'Piccadilly'. Red blend, double, 35 petals, some scent, very floriferous, flowering all season; growth bushy, medium; foliage abundant, matt. ARA 1979:212.

Flaming Peace. (= 'Kronenbourg'). HT. (McGredy, 1965). Sport of 'Peace'. Interior crimson with velvety shimmer, aging to purplish, with golden-yellow reverse, very large, strong fragrance, otherwise like 'Peace'. GSR 325; KR 9:31; RJb 30:48. (5.4)

Flammenspiel. S. (Kordes, 1974). 'Peer Gynt' × seedling. Salmon-pink, large, double, fragrant, several together, petals drop off cleanly; growth strong, upright, medium; foliage large, dark green, abundant, glossy.

Flammentanz. LCl. (Kordes, 1955). *Rubiginosa* hybrid × *R. kordesii*. Blood-red, large, double, finally flat, in clusters, non-recurrent; growth very sturdy, upright, 3-4 m./10-13.2 ft.; foliage large, matt. KR 9:74; RJb 27:25.

Flashlight. F. (Legrice, 1974). 'Vesper' × seedling. Orange-red, double, 30 petals, fragrant, in clusters, free bloom; growth medium; foliage large, bronzy green.

Fleet Street. HT. (McGredy, 1972). 'Flaming Peace' × 'Prima Ballerina'. Dark crimson, large, double, strong fragrance, good shape; bud pointed; growth strong, upright; foliage large, deep green.

Floradora. F. (Tantau, 1944). 'Baby Château' × *R. roxburghii*. Vermilion, medium, 5 cm./2 in. across, double, cupped, some scent, several together; growth bushy, upright; foliage glossy. SWR 133. (8.3)

Florence. HT. (W. Paul, 1921). Silvery pink, very large, strong fragrance; growth medium, 0.6 m./2 ft.

Florence Mary Morse. S. (Kordes, 1951) 'Baby Château' × 'Magnifica'. Scarlet, large, semi-double, many together in clusters; growth upright, 1.2 m./4 ft.; foliage deep green, glossy. RA 1951:52.

Folklore. HT. (Kordes/Barni, 1975). 'Fragrant Cloud' × seedling. Orange blend, double, 45 petals, strong fragrance, continuous bloomer, one to a stem in clusters; bud large, pointed; growth very vigorous, upright, bushy; foliage glossy.

Forty-Niner. HT. (Swim, 1949). 'Contraste' × 'Charlotte

Armstrong'. Interior deep red, with light yellow reverse, large, 8 cm./3.2 in. across, some scent, floriferous; growth strong, long branches, 0.7 m./2.3 ft.; foliage medium large. SWR 38. (7.2)

Fortune's Double Yellow. (= 'Beauty of Glazenwood; *Rosa odorata* var. *pseudindica*). T. (Introduced by Robert Fortune from China in 1845). Amber-yellow with coppery-red hue, semi-double, singly or several together, non-recurrent; growth moderately strong, to 3 m./10 ft. high. Very famous variety for temperate regions; should only be pruned when out of flower. RA 1973:46. (9.0)

Foxy Lady. Min. (Jack E. Christensen, 1979). 'Ginger Snap' × 'Magic Carrousel'. Shrimp-pink, high-centered, double, 25 petals, profuse bloom, one to a stem; growth dwarf, 40 cm./16 in., bushy; foliage semi-glossy, abundant. ARA 1979:67.

Fragrance. HT. (Lammerts, 1965). 'Charlotte Armstrong' × 'Merry Widow'. Crimson, large, double, strong fragrance, floriferous; growth compact, 0.7 m./2.3 ft.; foliage leathery, deep green, young growth bronze. (7.5)

Fragrant Cloud. (= 'Duftwolke'). HT. (Tantau, 1963). Seedling × 'Prima Ballerina'. Coral-red flowers, later purplish-red, large, 12 cm./5 in. across, double, very strong fragrance, good shape; growth strong, upright, 0.8 m./2.6 ft., long stems; foliage abundant, large, deep green, leathery. GSR 296; KR 9:118; RA 1964:80. (8.0)

Fragrant Hour. HT. (McGredy, 1973). 'Arthur Bell' × seedling. Salmon-pink with yellow shimmer, large, double, high-centered, very resistant to rain damage, strong fragrance; growth strong, upright; foliage leathery, medium green. (7.5)

Francis E. Lester. HMsk. (Lester Rose Gardens, 1946). Seedling of 'Kathleen'. White to creamy-white, single, many together, small, strong scent, non-recurrent, June, some flowers in the autumn; firm hips in the autumn; buds light pink; growth very strong, to 4 m./13.2 ft. GSR 206.

Francois Juranville. R. (Barbier, 1906). *R. wichuraiana* × 'Mme. Laurette Messimy'. Bright salmon-pink petals with yellow bases, large; growth very vigorous.

Frankfurt am Main. F. (Boerner/Kordes and Tantau, 1960). Parentage not given. Exterior dark pink with orange shade, reverse light pink, medium, 6 cm./2.4 in.

across, light scent, singly or several together; growth spreading, 0.7 m./2.3 ft.; foliage healthy. KR 10:117. (6.0)

Franklin Engelmann. F. (Dickson, 1970). 'Heidelberg' × ('Detroiter' × seedling). Scarlet, very large, double, in clusters; growth strong, loose, 0.8 cm./2.6 ft.; foliage large. GSR 417.

Frau Astrid Späth. F. (Späth, 1930). Sport of 'Lafayette'. Pure crimson-pink, loosely double, globose, petals very waved, abundant bloom; growth low, bushy, 40 cm./16 in.; foliage light green, matt. RZ 1931:12.

Frau Dagmar Hastrup. (= 'Frau Dagmar Hartopp'). S. (J. Hastrup, 1914). *Rugosa*-seedling. Soft pink, single, large, continuous bloom, in clusters, stamens golden yellow; large crimson hips; growth spreading, 1 m./3.3 ft. or over, stems very prickly; foliage deep green, wrinkled. GSR 132; SOR 47; TRT 44; GiS 14. (8.5)

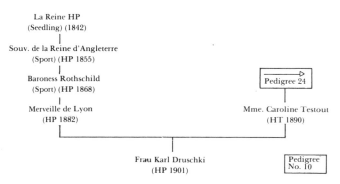

Frau Karl Druschki. HP. (Lambert, 1901). 'Merveille de Lyon' × 'Mme. Caroline Testout'. Snow-white, exterior sometimes with light crimson hue, very large, star-shaped, no scent, very double; growth strong, bushy, 1 m./3.3 ft.; stems very prickly; foliage large, matt. GSR 111; RZ 1902:82. (7.8). Very famous old variety.

Fred Edmunds. HT. (F. Meilland, 1943). 'Duquesa de Peñaranda' × 'Marie Claire'. Coppery-orange, large, 12 cm./5 in. double, cupped, very fragrant; growth bushy, open; foliage leathery, glossy.

Fred Gibson. HT. (Sanday, 1966). 'Gavotte' × 'Buccaneer'. Apricot with golden-yellow hue, reverse lighter, large, 12 cm./5 in. across, double, some scent, very free bloom; growth tall, very vigorous; foliage dark green. RA 1969:49. (6.2)

Fred Howard. HT. (Howard, 1952). 'Pearl Harbor' × seedling. Orange shaded with pink, large, 10 cm./4 in. across, double, some scent, floriferous; growth sturdy, upright, 1 m./3.3 ft.; foliage large, glossy. PWR 65; SRW 38. (6.9)

Fred Loads. S. (Holmes, 1967). 'Dorothy Wheatcroft' × 'Orange Sensation'. Vermilion-orange, does not fade, yellow center, large, 7 cm./2.8 in. across, single to semi-double, scented, in large clusters; growth strong, tall to very tall; foliage healthy. GSR 150; GiS 19; RA 1967:14. (7.8)

Fred Streeter. HT. (Kordes/Wheatcroft, 1955). 'Luis Brinas' × 'Golden Scepter'. Pure yellow, large, double, good shape, fragrant, floriferous; Growth strong, good stems; foliage deep green.

Frensham. F. (Norman/Harkness, 1946). 'Crimson Glory' × seedling. Glowing dark red, medium large, 6 cm./2.4 in. across, semi-double, flat, some scent, stamens golden yellow, continuous bloom, many together in large trusses; growth strong, 0.8 m./2.6 ft., bushy; foliage deep green, glossy. PWR 136; HRB 133; GiS 19.

Fresco. F. (de Ruiter, 1968). 'Metropole' × 'Orange Sensation'. Interior orange, reverse golden-yellow, large, 7 cm./2.8 in. across, semi-double, some scent; growth strong, medium, 0.6 m./2 ft.; foliage healthy. GSR 418. (7.3)

Fresh Pink. Min. (Ralph S. Moore, 1964). (*R. wichuraiana* × 'Floradora') × 'Little Buckaroo'. Rosy-red with salmon-pink tips, semi-double, medium, some scent, very floriferous, in clusters; growth bushy, dwarf; foliage small, glossy.

Freude. HT. (Kordes, 1974). 'Fragrant Cloud' × seedling. Coral-pink, very large, double, singly, floriferous, petals drop off cleanly, growth very strong; foliage dark green, healthy.

Friendship. HT. (Amling, 1937). 'Templar' × 'Talisman'. Strawberry-red and bright scarlet, very large, double, fragrant; growth vigorous; foliage glossy. ARA 63:58.

Friendship. HT. (Lindquist, 1978). 'Fragrant Cloud' × 'Miss All-American Beauty'. Deep pink, very fragrant, double, cupped to flat, very large, 14-15 cm./5.5-6 in., free bloom; bud ovoid; foliage large, dark; growth very vigorous, upright.

Fringette. Min. (Ralph S. Moore, 1964). Seedling × 'Concerto'. Pink to rosy-pink, small, double; growth compact, low, 20 cm./8 in. (6.7)

Fritz Nobis. S. (Kordes, 1940). 'Joanna Hill' × 'Magnifica'. Interior white, reverse salmon-pink, very large, double, strong fragrance, many together; growth very strong, 2 m./6.6 ft.; foliage medium, light green, abundant. GSR 161; RJb 37:82; PGR 107. (7.2)

Frolic. F. (Swim/Armstrong, 1953). 'World's Fair' × 'Pinocchio'. Pure pink, medium large, loosely double, globose, some scent, several together in clusters, abundant; growth bushy, 0.6 m./2 ft.; foliage light green, abundant. ARA 1954:137. (7.3)

Frostfire. Min. (Ralph S. Moore, 1963). ([*R. wichuraiana* × 'Floradora'] × seedling) × 'Little Buckaroo'. Red, sometimes flecked with white, small, 2.5 cm./1 in. across, double, free bloom; growth bushy, compact, 30 cm./12 in.; foliage dark green, glossy. (6.2)

Frosty. Min. (R.S. Moore, 1953). (*R. wichuraiana* × seedling) × self. Pure white, very small, double, fragrant, 3-10 in clusters, profuse bloom; bud pale pink; growth compact, vigorous, 30 cm./12 in.; foliage glossy. (7.1)

Frühlingsanfang. HSpn. (Kordes, 1950). *R. pimpinellifolia altaica* × 'Joanna Hill'. Milky-white, single, 10 cm./4 in. across, saucer-shaped, non-recurrent, good fragrance; growth strong, densely bushy, 3 m./10 ft.; foliage leathery. GSR 162; GiS 4.

Frühlingsduft. HSpn. (Kordes, 1949). *R. pimpinellifolia altaica* × 'Joanna Hill'. Pink with yellow center, very large, 10 cm./4 in. across, double, strong fragrance, non-recurrent; growth strong, dense, 2 m./6.6 ft.; foliage large, leathery. GSR 163; GiS 4. (6.4)

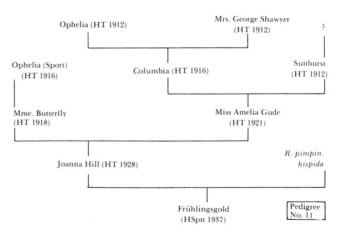

Frühlingsgold. HSpn. (Kordes, 1937). *R. pimpinellifolia hispida* × 'Joanna Hill'. Clear pale-yellow, single to semi-double, large, 12-15 cm./5-6 in. across, abundant flowering in May-June and often in late summer;

flowering in May-June and often in late summer; growth very strong, 2.5-3 m./8.3-10 ft. tall and spreading, very dense. GSR 165; KR 9:97; RJ 615:80. (8.7)

Frühlingsmorgen. HSpn. (Kordes, 1941). *R. spinosissima altaica* × ('E.G. Hill' × 'Cathrine Kordes'). Cherrypink with yellow center, maroon stamens, large, 12 cm./5 in. across, single, late May and June, occasional flowers in the summer; growth strong, tall to very tall, spreading; foliage grey-green. PWR 194; GSR 164; GiS 4. (8.5)

Frühlingsschnee. HSpn. (Kordes, 1954). *R. pimpinellifolia altaica* × 'Golden Glow'. Snow-white, double, very large, some scent, summer-flowering; growth strong, medium.

Frühlingstag. HSpn. (Kordes, 1949). 'McGredy's Wonder' × 'Frühlingsgold'. Yellow with red and orange stripes, very colorful, semi-double, large, scented, several together, very floriferous, summer-flowering; growth strong, medium to tall, very prickly.

Frühlingszauber. HSpn. (Kordes, 1942). ('E.G. Hill' × 'Cathrine Kordes') × *R. pimpinellifolia altaica*. Rosyred with soft yellow center, very large, single to slightly semi-double, very strong fragrance, summer-flowering, non-recurrent; growth strong, 2 m./6.6 ft.

Fürstin von Pless. S. (Lambert, 1911). 'Mme. Caroline Testout' × 'Conrad Ferdinand Meyer'. White with yellowish-pink center, double, fragrant, 1-3 together; growth bushy.

Fugue. Cl. (Meilland, 1968). 'Alain' × 'Guiné'. Dark scarlet, medium, double, finally flat, some scent, resistant to weather damage, continuous bloom; growth strong, bushy, 2.5 m./8.3 ft.; foliage leathery, deep green. GSR 243.

Fusilier. F. (Morey/Jackson & Perkins, 1957). 'Red Pinocchio' × 'Floradora'. Scarlet, medium, 7 cm./2.8 in. across, double, fragrant; growth strong, upright, 0.7 m./2.3 ft.; foliage deep green, abundant. (7.0)

Futura. HT. (W.A. Warriner/Jackson & Perkins, 1975). Seedling × seedling. Vermilion, large, double, some scent, cupped, long-lasting, singly on medium high stems, profuse bloomer; growth very vigorous, upright, branched; foliage light green, glossy, disease-resistant. (7.5)

Gabriel Noyelle. M. (Buatois, 1933). 'Salet' × 'Souvenir de Mme. Kreuger'. Orange-salmon with yellow base, double, cupped, fragrant, free, recurrent; growth vigorous; foliage leathery. (7.0)

Gabriella. F. (Berggren, 1977). Medium red, slightly fragrant, double, cupped, large, 8 cm./3 in., abundant bloom; bud ovoid; foliage glossy; growth vigorous, bushy.

Gabrielle Privat. Pol. (Privat, 1931). Clear pink, small, double, rosette-shaped, no scent, many together in large trusses; growth low, very bushy, 0.5-0.6 m./1.7-2 ft.; foliage small, light green.

Gail Borden. HT. (Kordes, 1957). 'R.M.S. Queen Mary' × 'Viktoria Adelheid'. Deep pink, with orange-yellow reverse, large, 12 cm./4.8 in. across, very double, fragrant, free bloomer; growth densely bushy, branched, 0.6 m./2 ft.; foliage large, deep green. PWR 25; GSR 306; RA 1958:49. (7.2)

Galia. HT. (Meilland, 1979). Parentage not given. Glossy vermilion, large, double, 40 petals, very free flowering; growth strong, 1-1.5 m./3.3-5 ft.; foliage large, deep green.

Gallivarda. HT. (W. Kordes Sons, 1977). 'Königen der Rosen' × 'Wiener Charme'. Orange blend, slightly fragrant, double, high centered, large 11.4 cm./4.5 in., abundant bloom; bud long pointed; foliage glossy; growth very vigorous, upright.

Galway Bay. LCl. (McGredy, 1966). 'Heidelberg' × 'Queen Elizabeth'. Cerise-pink, large, double, 8 cm./3.2 in. across, floriferous, recurrent; growth strong, to 3 m./10 ft.; foliage healthy. GSR 244. (7.4)

Garden Party. HT. (Swim, 1959). 'Charlotte Armstrong' × 'Peace'. Yellowish-white with soft pink margins, large, 12 cm./4.8 in. across, double, cupped, some scent; bud urn-shaped; growth strong, bushy. PWR 21; RJb 22:32. (8.6)

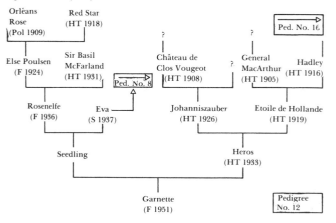

343

Garnette. F. (Tantau, 1947). ('Rosenelfe' × 'Eva') × 'Heros'. Garnet-red, medium, double, rosette-shaped, 50 petals, very long-lasting; growth sturdy, upright, 40 cm./16 in.; foliage first purple, then deep green, matt, abundant. Well-known greenhouse variety. (7.6)

Gartendirektor O. Linne. S. (Lambert, 1934). 'Robin Hood' × 'Rudolph Kluis'. Deep pink with darker edge, yellowish-white center, double, in clusters on 30 cm./12 in. long branches, very floriferous; growth strong; foliage leathery, light green. (9.5)

Gavotte. HT. (Sanday, 1963). 'Ethel Sanday' × 'Lady Sylvia'. Pink with silvery reverse, very large, 12 cm./4.8 in. across, very double, some scent; growth strong, upright, 0.9 m./3 ft.; foliage deep green, large, abundant. GSR 308; RA 1963:65. (8.1)

Gay Gordons. HT. (Cocker, 1969). 'Belle Blonde' × 'Karl Herbst'. Deep orange-yellow, with broad vermilion margin and yellow reverse, medium, double, some scent, good shape, floriferous; growth bushy, 0.9 m./3 ft.; foliage deep green, glossy.

Gay Maid. F. (Gregory, 1969). 'Masquerade' × ?. Interior orange with pink and light-red margin, reverse pink, medium size, double, globose, some scent, floriferous; growth very strong; foliage light green.

Gay Princess. F. (Boerner/Jackson & Perkins, 1967). 'Spartan' × 'The Farmer's Wife'. Very soft pink, large, double, cupped, fragrant; growth medium, 0.7 m./2.3 ft.; foliage glossy, healthy. (6.9)

Gay Vista. S. (Riethmuller, 1957). Light pink, very large, in large trusses, recurrent; growth tall, 1 m./3.3 ft.

Geisha. (= 'Pink Elizabeth Arden'). F. (Tantau, 1964). Pure pink, medium, 7 cm./2.8 in. across, good shape, many together, resistant to weather damage; growth upright, 0.5 m./1.7 ft.; foliage deep green. RJb 29:128.

Geisha Girl. F. (McGredy, 1964). 'Gold Cup' × 'McGredy's Yellow'. Golden-yellow, fading to creamy-yellow, large, 10 cm./4 in. across, moderately double, in clusters; growth strong, medium; foliage large, medium green, matt. RA 1967:96. (6.1)

Gemstone. HT. (Eastern Roses, 1978). 'Helen Traubel' × 'Swarthmore'. Medium pink, double, 30 petals, some scent, high centered; bud slender; growth upright, vigorous.

Gene Boerner. F. (Boerner/Jackson & Perkins, 1968).
'Ginger' × ('Ma Perkins' × 'Garnette Supreme'). Clear pink with darker center, medium, moderately double, many together in clusters, floriferous; growth strong; foliage healthy, glossy, very disease-resistant. (8.4)

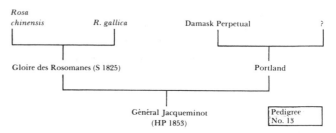

Général Jacqueminot. (= 'General Jack'). HP. (Roussel, 1853). Seedling of 'Gloire des Rosomanes' (?). Clear red, large, double, very strong fragrance, recurrent; bud scarlet to crimson; growth strong, bushy; foliage large, deep green. (6.8)

Général Kléber. M. (Robert, 1856). Deep pink, medium, 6 cm./2.4 in. across, double, flat, some scent, non-recurrent; bud well mossed; growth strong, medium. GiS 9. (8.3)

General McArthur. HT. (E.G. Hill, 1905). Parentage unknown. Rosy-red, semi-double, cupped, 20 petals, very fragrant; growth strong; foliage leathery. Famous old variety.

Gentle Lady. HT. (C.W. Fuller/Wyant, 1975). 'Tiffany' × 'Michèle Meilland'. Very light pink, darker towards base, double, 35 petals, cupped, strong fragrance, singly and several together, intermittent bloom; bud large, pointed; growth bushy, upright; foliage deep green, dull, leathery. (6.5)

Georg Arends. HP. (Hinner, 1910). 'Frau Karl Druschki' × 'La France'. Clear pink, large, perfect shape, moderately double, good fragrance, recurrent; growth strong, stems up to 2 m./6.6 ft. long, should be pruned only after flowering; foliage light green. GiS 11; RZ 1916:97. (7.4)

George Dickson. HP. (A. Dickson, 1912). Parentage unknown. Velvety crimson, flushed scarlet, very large, fragrant, double, stems weak; growth upright; foliage large, leathery, matt. GiS 11. (7.9)

Georges Vibert. G. (Robert, 1853). Pink to light red, with darker stripes, medium, 8 cm./3.2 in. across, very double, finally flat, green eye, fragrant; growth upright, medium. PGR 17.

Geranium. S. (variety of *Rosa moyesii*). (Wisley Gardens, 1945). Scarlet, single, saucer-shaped, 5 cm./2 in. across, stamens golden yellow, singly or several together along the branches; very large, bottle-shaped hips in the autum, crimson; growth strong, 2-3 m./6.6-10 ft. GiS 2; GSR 32-33.

Gertrude Gregory. HT. (Gregory, 1957). Sport of 'Lady Belper'. Golden-yellow, large, double, fragrant, floriferous; growth strong, long stems; foliage deep green, glossy. RA 1958:17. (7.3)

Gertrud Schweitzer. HT. (Kordes, 1973). 'Colour Wonder' × 'Golden Wave'. Orange-salmon to light apricot, moderately double, 25 petals, free flowering, singly; growth vigorous, upright; foliage first bronzy, then medium green, glossy. RA 1974:54.

Gidget. Min. (Ralph S. Moore, 1975). (*R. wichuraiana* × 'Floradora') × 'First Prize'. Coral pink to coral red, some scent, abundant bloom; growth dwarf, vigorous; foliage small, glossy, medium to dark green. (6.5)

'Giesebrecht' → **Bashful**

Ginger. F. (Boerner/Jackson & Perkins, 1962). 'Garnette'-seedling × 'Spartan'. Orange-vermilion, large, 12 cm./4.8 in. across, double, cupped, fragrant, abundant bloom in irregular clusters; bud ovoid; growth bushy, vigorous, compact; foliage leathery. (8.2)

Ginger Rogers. HT. (McGredy, 1967). 'Tropicana' × 'Miss Ireland'. Salmon, large, loosely double, fragrant, floriferous; growth very strong, 1 m./3.3 ft.; foliage light green. RA 1970:112.

Gingersnap. (= 'Prince Abricot'). (Delbard/Armstrong, 1977). 'Zambra' × ('Orange Triumph' × 'Floradora'). Pure orange, very ruffled, 35 petals, fragrant, recurrent; bud long, pointed to urn-shaped; growth bushy, medium tall, upright; foliage deep green, glossy, abundant.

Girl Scout. F. (Boerner/Jackson & Perkins, 1961). 'Gold Cup' × 'Pigmy Gold'. Golden-yellow, large, to 12 cm./4.8 in. across, double, fragrant, cupped, free bloom; growth vigorous, medium; foliage glossy, leathery. (3.0)

Gladiator. LCl. (Malandrone, 1955). 'Charlotte Armstrong' × ('Pink Delight' × 'New Dawn'-seedling). Rosy-red, large, 10-12 cm./4-4.8 in. across, double, high-centered, fragrant, free, intermittent bloom; growth vigorous, 2.5-3 m./8.3-10 ft.; foliage deep green, leathery. (7.2)

Glenfiddich. F. (Cocker, 1975). 'Arthur Bell' × ('Sabine' × 'Circus'). Yellow-amber, large, double, 25 petals, fragrant, several together and in trusses, free blooming; growth vigorous, upright, 0.8-0.9 m./2.6-3 ft.; foliage deep green, glossy, healthy. RA 1978:137.

Gloire de Chédane-Guinoisseau. HP. (Chédane-Pajotin, 1907). 'Gloire de Ducher' × ?. Glowing crimson, very large, good shape, cupped, fragrant, somewhat recurrent; growth very strong, medium; foliage deep green, matt. (7.0)

Gloire de Dijon. T. (Jacotot, 1853). Unknown Tea × 'Souvenir de la Malmaison'. Salmon-orange with creamy-white margin, very large, double, strong fragrance, recurrent; growth very strong, 3-4 m./10-13.2 ft. GSR 208; PGR 89; GiS 23; WGR 97; RA 1975:100. (7.3)

Gloire de Ducher. HP. (Ducher, 1865). Crimson-purple, very large, very double, good fragrance, June, some flowers in autumn; growth very strong, tall to very tall; foliage large, matt, young growth crimson.

Gloire de Guilan. D. Pure pink, double, inner petals incurved, quartered, strong fragrance, non-recurrent; growth loose, branched, medium, branches with small, hooked prickles; foliage light green. 1949 found by Miss Nancy Lindsay in Persia, Kaspi Province, where it is used to make rose Attar. PGR 35. (6.1)

Gloire des Mousseux. M. (Laffay, 1892). Pink to shell pink with darker center, huge flower, double, petals imbricate, non-recurrent, long-lasting; sepal light green, mossy; growth medium strong, upright, medium; foliage very light green. GSR 72; GiS 9; PGR 43, 53. (7.6)

Gloire des Rosomanes. (= 'Ragged Robin'). Ch. (Vibert, 1825). Crimson-scarlet, very large, double, fragrant, many together in clusters, recurrent; growth very strong. Used as budding understock in California. (7.5)

Gloriglo. Min. (E. Williams/Mini-Roses, 1976). Seedling × 'Over the Rainbow'. Orange-blend, high centered, double, 40-50 petals, fragrant, abundant bloom; bud pointed; growth dwarf; foliage small, glossy, bronze. (7.5)

'Glory of Rome' → **Rome Glory**

Goethe. M. (Lambert, 1911). Magenta-rose, small, single, calyx mossy; growth very strong, tall, young stems with red bark; foliage bluish-green, rough. (6.6)

Goldbusch. S. (Kordes, 1954). 'Golden Glow' × *R. rubiginosa* hybrid. Golden-yellow, fading, large, to 10 cm./4 in. across, double, some fragrance, abundant, non-recurrent; growth very strong, tall to very tall; foliage light green, glossy. GSR 166; TRT 140; GiS 19. (7.6)

Gold Coin. Min. (Ralph S. Moore, 1967). 'Golden Glow' × 'Magic Wand'. Canary-yellow, very double, regularly rosette-shaped, small, fragrant, very floriferous, in clusters; growth dwarf, compact; foliage light green, small, matt. GSR 504. (7.5)

Gold Cup. F. (Boerner/Jackson & Perkins, 1957). 'Goldilocks'-seedling × 'King Midas'-seedling. Golden yellow, large, 10 cm./4 in. across, double, fragrant, in clusters; growth bushy, 0.6 m./2 ft.; foliage glossy, light green, abundant. (5.5)

Gold Dollar. HT. (J.A. Herholdt, 1971). Seedling × 'Vienna Charm'. Canary-yellow, large, double, some scent, singly; growth strong; foliage glossy, abundant.

Gold Pin. Min. (J. Mattock, 1974). Bright golden yellow, double, some scent, very free bloomer; growth dwarf, bushy; foliage green, young growth bronze.

Golden Angel. Min. (Ralph S. Moore, 1974). 'Golden Glow' × seedling. Deep yellow, very double, 60-70 petals, fragrant, continuous bloomer, very long-lasting; bud short, pointed; growth dwarf, 30 cm./12 in., bushy, compact, rounded; foliage dull, abundant. ARA 60:90. (7.0)

Golden Bouquet. HT. (Gregory, 1970). 'Gertrude Gregory' × seedling. Dark yellow, large, 8 cm./3.2 in. across, double, fragrant, several together, floriferous; growth strong; foliage deep green, glossy.

Golden Century. ClMin. (Ralph S. Moore, 1976). (*R. wichuraiana* × 'Floradora') × ('Sister Thérèse' × seedling). Orange blend, double, 35 petals, open, good fragrance, recurrent, singly or several together; bud pointed; growth upright, to 0.8 m./2.6 ft.; foliage small, healthy, glossy.

Golden Charm. HT. (Groshens & Morrison, 1933). Pure deep yellow sport of 'Talisman'. (3.8)

Golden Chersonese. S. (Allen, 1967). *R. ecae* × 'Canary Bird'. Deep yellow, very much like 'Canary Bird', but deeper yellow, more fragrant, single, 5 cm./2 in. across, very abundant along the dark stems, June, non-recurrent; growth strong, 2 m./6.6 ft.; foliage small, medium-green, matt, abundant. GSR 167; GiS 19; RA 1971:14.

Golden Dawn. HT. (Grant, 1929). 'Elegante' × 'Ethel Somerset'. Golden yellow to lemon-yellow, double, 45 petals, very fragrant, good shape; bud yellow, flushed rose; growth low, spreading. RA 1931:107.

Golden Delight. F. (LeGrice, 1956). 'Goldilocks' × 'Ellinor LeGrice'. Light yellow. large, 7 cm./2.8 in. across, very double, fragrant, floriferous; growth strong, bushy, 0.7 m./2.3 ft.; foliage large, glossy. (5.8)

Golden Fleece. F. (Boerner/Jackson & Perkins, 1955). 'Diamond Jubilee' × 'Yellow Sweetheart'. Pale yellow, large, 10 cm./4 in. across, double, cupped, fragrant, floriferous, in clusters; growth low, 40 cm./16 in.; foliage light green, medium large, semi-glossy, leathery. PWR 102; RJb 1957:108. (6.6)

Golden Gate. HT. (W.A. Warriner/Jackson & Perkins, 1972). 'South Seas' × 'King's Ransom'. Yellow, large, 12 cm./4.8 in. across, double, some scent, long-lasting, singly, petals drop off cleanly; growth strong, branched; foliage healthy. (6.0)

Golden Giant. (= 'Goldrausch'). F. (Kordes, 1961). 'Golden Sun' × 'Buccaneer'. Golden yellow, large, very double, good shape, some scent, floriferous, singly or several together; growth very strong, upright, 1 m./3.3 ft.; foliage small, deep green, matt. PWR 61. (6.0)

Golden Girl. F. (Meilland, 1959). ('Joanna Hill' × 'Eclipse') × 'Michèle Meilland'. Golden yellow, large, 10 cm./4 in. across, very double, globose, fragrant, floriferous; growth bushy; foliage light green. (6.4)

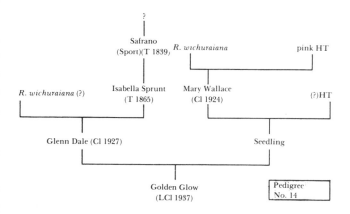

Golden Glow. LCl. (Brownell, 1937). 'Glenn Dale' × ('Mary Wallace' × Hybrid Tea). Pure yellow, large, 10 cm./4 in. across, very double, fragrant, floriferous;

growth strong, 3-4 m./10-13.2 ft.; foliage leathery, glossy. ARA 1937:235. (5.6)

Golden Lace. F. (V. Abrams, 1962). 'Goldilocks' × ('Golden Scepter' × 'Encore'). Dark yellow, large, 8 cm./3.2 in. across, double, fragrant, floriferous; growth upright; foliage very glossy, deep green. (5.0)

Golden Masterpiece. HT. (Boerner/Jackson & Perkins, 1954). 'Mandalay' × 'Golden Scepter'. Golden yellow, very large, double, star-shaped when fully expanded; bud long, pointed; growth upright, branched, 0.8 m./2.6 ft.; foliage glossy. SRW 43. (5.6)

Golden Moss. M. (Dot, 1931). 'Frau Karl Druschki' × ('Souvenir de Claudius Pernet' × 'Blanche Moreau'). Pale yellow, medium, 8 cm./3.2 in. across, very double, fragrant, 3-4 together, non-recurrent; buds very mossy, globose; growth strong, medium; foliage wrinkled. GiS 19. (6.0)

Golden Peace. HT. (LeGrice, 1961). Parentage not given. Canary-yellow, large, perfect shape, fragrant, floriferous; growth very strong, 1.2 m./4 ft.; foliage dull.

Golden Prince. HT. (Meilland, 1968). ('Monte Carlo' × 'Bettina') × ('Peace' × 'Soraya'). Dark yellow, medium-large, double, singly on long stems, some scent, floriferous; growth upright, 0.7 m./2.3 ft.; foliage healthy. (5.0)

Gold Rush. LCl. (Duehrsen, 1941). Light yellow, large, loosely double, fragrant, non-recurrent; growth strong, 2-3 m./6.6-10 ft. (5.1)

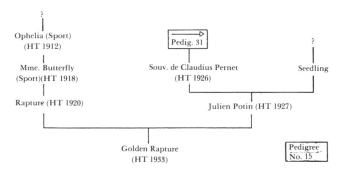

Golden Rapture. (= 'Gerheimrat Duisberg'). HT. (Kordes, 1933). 'Rapture' × 'Julien Potin'. Golden-yellow, large, double, long-lasting, fragrant; growth strong, long stems; foliage deep green. Greenhouse variety. SRW 44.

Golden Salmon. (= 'Goldlachs'). Pol. (De Ruiter, 1926). Sport of 'Superb' (pol.). Pure orange, large, double, in large trusses; growth vigorous, bushy. RA 1929:201. (6.8)

Golden Scepter. (= 'Spek's Yellow'). HT. (Verschuren-Pechtold, 1947). 'Golden Rapture' × seedling. Golden-yellow, medium, double, fragrant, free flowering; growth upright, little branching; foliage medium. PWR 67; HRB 101. (5.3)

Golden Showers. S. (Lammerts, 1956). 'Charlotte Armstrong' × 'Capt. Thomas'. Lemon-yellow, large, 10 cm./4 in. across, semi-double, later flat, fragrant, singly and several together on strong stems, profuse and continuous bloom; growth very strong, tall to very tall; foliage deep green, glossy. PWR 221; GSR 245. (7.2)

Golden Splendor. HT. (Jones, 1960). Golden yellow, large, 12 cm./4.8 in. across, double, high-centered, floriferous; bud long, pointed; growth tall, long stems, 0.9 m./3 ft.; foliage glossy. (6.1)

Golden Slippers. F. (V. Abrams, 1961). 'Goldilocks' × seedling. Orange interior with yellow center, orange-yellow reverse, 7 cm./2.8 in. across, opening flat, fragrant, in clusters; growth low, bushy, 40 cm./16 in.; foliage bronze-green, healthy. GSR 421; RJb 26:225. (6.2)

Golden Sun. HT. (Kordes, 1957). ('Walter Bentley' × 'Condesa de Sástago') × 'Golden Scepter'. Golden-yellow, large, 12 cm./4.8 in. across, double, some scent, floriferous; bud pointed; growth upright, little branching; foliage medium. RJb 28:48. (5.1)

Golden Times. HT. (Cocjer, 1972). 'Fragrant Cloud' × 'Golden Splendour'. Golden-yellow, large, very double, fragrant, singly and several together; growth strong, 0.9 m./3 ft.; foliage large, matt. GSR 310; RA 1971:96.

Golden Wave. (= 'Dr. A.J. Verhage'). HT. (Verbeek, 1960). 'Tawny Gold' × ('Baccara' × seedling). Golden yellow with darker shades, large, double, margin waved, fragrant, floriferous; growth compact, bushy, strong stems; foliage healthy, deep green. GSR 291. (6.6)

Golden Wedding. HT. (J.A. Herholdt, 1970). Parentage not given. Canary-yellow, does not fade, double, large, some scent, singly on long, strong stems, long-lasting; bud long, pointed; growth vigorous.

Golden Wings. S. (Shepherd/Bosley, 1956). 'Soeur

Thérèse' × (*R. pimpinellifolia altaica* × 'Ormiston Roy'). Creamy-white, opening deeper, very large, 12 cm./4.8 in. across, single, flat, stamens orange-red, recurrent; growth strong, medium; foliage light green, matt. GSR 168; TRT 145; WGR 57; GiS 20. (8.0)

Goldenes Herz. HT. (Kordes, 1975). 'Golden Wave' × seedling. Dark-yellow, medium, double, fragrant, cupped, very floriferous, singly, petals drop off cleanly; growth strong, upright, bushy; foliage abundant, deep green, healthy.

Goldilocks. F. (Boerner/Jackson & Perkins, 1945). Seedling × 'Doubloons'. Pale yellow, semi-double, flat, 8 cm./3.2 in. across, some scent, floriferous, petals retained, in large trusses; growth bushy, 0.6 m./2 ft.; foliage light green, abundant. PWR 110. (5.7)

Goldgleam. F. (LeGrice, 1966). 'Gleaming' × 'Allgold'. Lemon-yellow with darker reverse, large, semi-double, does not fade, in clusters; growth upright, 0.8 m./2.6 ft.; foliage deep green, glossy. RA 1966:144.

Goldmarie. F. (Kordes, 1958). 'Masquerade' × 'Goldenes Mainz'. Golden-yellow with reddish shades, large, double, good scent, very floriferous, in clusters; growth medium high, 0.5 m./1.7 ft.; foliage deep green, glossy. PWR 129; KR 10:31. (5.9)

Goldmoss. FM. (Ralph S. Moore, 1972). 'Rumba' × Hybrid Moss seedling. Clear yellow, large, double, open, fragrant, very long-lasting, abundant bloom, singly or several together on strong, medium stems; bud mossy; growth vigorous, upright, bushy, 0.8 m./2.6 ft.; foliage light green, healthy. (6.2)

Gold'n Honey. HT. (Leon/Edmunds, 1970). 'Helen Traubel' × (seedling × 'Ulster Monarch'). Yellow flushed with rose and peach, high-centered, 30 petals, very fragrant, several on one stem, continuous bloom; bud pointed, long; growth upright, bushy, free; foliage yellowish-green. (6.0)

Good News. HT. (= 'Bonne Nouvelle'). (Meilland, 1940). ('Radiance' × 'Souvenir de Claufius Pernet') × ('Joanna Hill' × 'Comtesse Vandal'). Silvery-pink with apricot center, very large, 12-15 cm./4.8-6 in. across, double, globose, fragrant, abundant bloom; strong stem; growth bushy, vigorous. (5.9)

Governor Mark Hatfield. Gr. (Von Abrams, 1962). 'Carrousel' × 'Charles Mallerin'. Ruby-red with darker hue, large, double, high-centered, slightly fragrant, abund-

ant bloom; growth vigorous; foliage leathery. (6.0)

Grace de Monaco. HT. (Meilland, 1956). 'Peace' × 'Michèle Meilland'. Soft pink, very large, very double, globose, fragrant, floriferous; growth strong, little branching, 0.8 m./2.6 ft.; foliage large, deep green. PWR 64; BTR 42. (7.4)

Gracious Lady. HT. (Robinson, 1965). ('Peace'-seedling × 'Gail Borden') × 'Dorothy Peach'-seedling. Salmon-pink with orange-yellow center, large, to 15 cm./6 in. across, globose, fragrant, floriferous; growth strong, 0.8 m./2.6 ft.; foliage large, deep green.

Granada. (= 'Donatella'). HT. (Lindquist, 1963). 'Tiffany' × 'Cavalcade'. Very colorful rose; pink with nasturtium-red and sulfur-yellow, large, 12 cm./4.8 in. across, semi-double, fragrant, floriferous; growth upright, strong; foliage large, bronze-green, matt, healthy, very resistant to Black Spot. (8.8)

Granadina. (= 'Grenadine'). Min. (Dot. 1956). 'Granate' × 'Coralin'. Deep red, small, globose, very double; growth dwarf, 35 cm./14 in.; foliage small, young growth red. (7.3)

'Grandpa Dickson' → **Irish Gold**

Granate. Min. (Dot, 1947). 'Merveille des Rouges' × 'Pompon de Paris'. Deep red with white center, semi-double, flat, small: growth dwarf, 20 cm./8 in.; few prickles. (5.9)

Grand Amour. (= 'Côte Rôtic'). HT. (Delbard/Chabert, 1956). Luminous deep red, double, large, fragrant. (6.7)

Grande Amore. HT. (Kordes, 1968). 'Prima Ballerina' × 'Detroiter'. Glowing deep red, pure color, loosely double, very large, singly or several on strong stems, strong fragrance; growth upright, 0.8 m./2.6 ft.; foliage deep green, young growth purple. KR 10:163.

Grande Duchesse Charlotte. HT. (Ketten Bros., 1942). Parentage not reported. Medium-red with geranium-red shade, large, 12 cm./4.8 in. across, double, slightly fragrant; bud brown, long, pointed; growth vigorous; foliage dark green, glossy. (6.1)

Grand Gala. HT. (Meilland, 1954). 'Peace' × 'Independence'. Interior luminous crimson, reverse white with soft pink shades, large, globose, fragrant; growth strong, 0.8 m./2.6 ft.; foliage firm, deep green. PWR 62; SRW 45. (7.1)

Grand Hotel. LCl. (McGredy, 1972). 'Heidelberg' ×

'Detroiter'. Scarlet, large, very double, weather-resistant color; growth vigorous, 3 m./10 ft.; foliage deep green, abundant.

Grandmaster. HMsk. (Kordes, 1951). 'Sangerhausen' × 'Sunmist'. Pale yellow with orange and pink shades, large, 10 cm./4 in. across, fragrant, semi-double, many together in large trusses, recurrent; growth strong, medium; foliage light green. RA 1952:104. (6.8)

Grand Opera. HT. (Schwartz, 1964). 'Masquerade' × 'Peace'. Creamy-white with pink margin, later all pink, large, 12 cm./4.8 in. across, double, fragrant, floriferous; growth bushy; foliage leathery. (6.8)

Grandpa Dickson. (= 'Irish Gold'). (Dickson, 1966). ('Kordes Perfecta' × 'Governador Braga da Cruz') × 'Piccadilly'. Lemon-yellow, double, very large, fragrant; bud ovoid; growth upright, bushy; foliage pale green. RA 1966:3.

Grand Prix. HT. (Delbard, 1968). 'Chic Parisien' × ('Grande Première' × ['Sultan' × 'Mme. J. Perraud]). Coral-pink with ochre-yellow shades, large, semi-double, some scent, several together, floriferous; growth very strong, upright, long stems; foliage large, deep green, glossy. (6.1)

Grand Slam. HT. (Armstrong, 1963). 'Charlotte Armstrong' × 'Montezuma'. Cherry-red, large, 10 cm./4 in. across, semi-double, some scent, cupped; growth broadly upright; foliage leathery, glossy. (7.5)

Green Diamond. Min. (Ralph S. Moore, 1974). Seedling × 'Sheri Anne'. Soft green, double, 25 petals, no scent, cupped, very long-lasting, recurrent; bud whitish-pink; growth dwarf, upright; foliage leathery, small, abundant. (5.5)

Green Fire. F. (Swim, 1958). 'Goldilocks' × seedling. Pale yellow, medium, 7 cm./2.8 in. across, semi-double, finally flat, some scent, in clusters; growth bushy, medium; foliage matt.

Green Ice. Min. (Ralph S. Moore, 1974). (*R. wichuraiana* × 'Floradora') × 'Jet Trail'. Opening white or pale pink, then changing to light green; growth dwarf. ARA 1979:136. (7.4)

Greenmantle. S. HRg. (Penzance, 1895). Rosy-pink with white center, single, stamens golden-yellow; growth strong, 3 m./10 ft. or over; foliage fragrant.

'Green Rose' → **Rosa chinensis viridiflora.** (7.6)

Green Sleeves. F. (Harkness, 1980). 'Rudolph Timm' × 'Arthur Bell' × ('Pascali' × Elizabeth of Glamis') × ('Sabine' × 'Violette Dot'). Chartreuse green, semi-double, large, flat, free bloom; bud pointed; foliage dark; growth vigorous, upright.

Grey Pearl. HT. (McGredy, 1945). ('Mrs. Charles Lamplough' × seedling) × ('Sir David Davies' × 'Southport'). Greyish-mauve with soft shades of olive green and light brown, large, 10 cm./4 in. across, very double, globose, fragrant; growth vigorous; foliage glossy. SWR 48. (3.8)

Grimpant-Varieties. Names starting with the word "Grimpant" (= climbing) have been listed under the original name, with the term 'Climbing' added.

Grootendorst Supreme. HRg. (F.J. Grootendorst, 1936). Sport of 'F.J. Grootendorst', with deeper crimson flowers; otherwise like the type. (7.6)

Gruss an Aachen. F. (Geduldig, 1909). 'Frau Karl Druschki' × 'Franz Deegen'. Flesh-pink, to creamy-white with age, medium, 7 cm./2.8 in. across, very double, scented, very floriferous; growth bushy, 0.6 m./2 ft.; GSR 423; RZ 1912:34; GiS 20. (7.6)

Gruss an Berlin. HT. (R. Kordes, 1963). Pure red, slightly fragrant, double, high centered, large, 14 cm./5.5 in., free bloom; bud ovoid; foliage dark, glossy; growth vigorous upright, bushy.

Gruss an Coburg. HT. (Felberg-Leclerc, 1927). 'Alice Kaempff' × 'Souvenir de Claudius Pernet'. Apricot-yellow with coppery-pink reverse, double, globose, very fragrant; growth vigorous; foliage bronze-green.

Gruss an Teplitz. HT. (Geschwind, 1897). ('Sir Joseph Paxton' × 'Fellemberg') × ('Papa Gontier' × 'Gloire des Rosomanes'). Light crimson, medium, double, strong fragrance, abundant, recurrent, flower-stalks very weak; growth strong, medium; foliage large, deep bronze-green, young growth red. RZ 1899:51. Very famous old variety. (5.7)

Guinée. LCl. (Mallerin, 1938), 'Souvenir de Claudius Denoyel' × 'Ami Quinard'. Blackish-red, sometimes with scarlet hue, large, double, but finally flat, stamens golden-yellow, fragrant, abundant, non-recurrent; growth very strong, to 4 m./13.2 ft.; foliage leathery. BTR 12.

Guinevere. HT. (Harkness, 1967). 'Red Dandy' ×

'Peace'. Rosy-pink, medium, some scent, very floriferous, resistant to weather damage; growth strong, 0.8 m./2.6 ft.; foliage light green, abundant. GSR 311; RA 1968:161.

Gypsy. HT. (Swim & Weeks/Conard-Pyle, 1973). (['Happiness' × 'Chrysler Imperial'] × 'El Capitan') × 'Comanche'. Fiery orange-red, large, full, some scent, long-lasting, petals drop off cleanly, continuous bloom; bud medium, ovoid; growth vigorous, upright, bushy, few prickles; foliage large, glossy, leathery, disease-resistant. (6.7)

Gypsy Jewel. Min. (Ralph S. Moore, 1974). 'Little Darling' × 'Little Buckaroo'. Deep pink, double, 50 petals, no scent, long-lasting, good bloom all season; bud medium, pointed; growth dwarf, vigorous, bushy; spreading; foliage deep green, leathery. (8.5)

Habanera. S. (G.J. Buck, 1975). 'Vera Dalton' × 'Dornröschen' × (['World's Fair × 'Floradora'] × 'Applejack'). Deep pink, double, 35 petals, cupped, fragrant, flowering continuously all season; bud pointed; growth dwarf, upright; foliage leathery, disease-resistant.

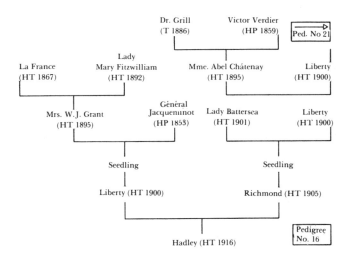

Hadley. HT. (Montgomery, 1914). ('Liberty' × 'Richmond') × 'General McArthur'. Crimson, large, double, good shape, strong fragrance. Famous old variety. BTR 8.

Half Time. HT. (O.L. Weeks, 1976). (['Fandango' × 'Roundelay'-seedling] × ['Happiness' × 'Tiffany']) × 'Peace'. Cherry-red and straw-yellow, double, 40 petals, fragrant, continuous bloom; bud pointed; growth

upright, well branched, medium; foliage deep green. (7.0)

Hamburg. S. (Kordes, 1935). 'Eva' × 'Daily Mail Scented Rose'. Deep scarlet, large, semi-double, flat, some scent, many together on strong stems, recurrent; growth upright, bushy, medium; foliage matt, not very dense. GiS 16; GSR 169.

Hamburger Phoenix. K. (Kordes, 1954). *R. kordesii* × seedling. Deep red, large, semi-double, 10 cm./4 in. across, flat, some scent, singly or several together, recurrent; growth strong, to 3 m./10 ft.; foliage deep green. PWR 216; GR 352. (7.3)

Handel. (= 'Händel'). LCl. (McGredy, 1965). 'Columbine' × 'Heidelberg'. Creamy-white with broad carmine-pink fringe, 8 cm./3.2 in. across, loosely double, some scent; growth strong, tall to very tall; foliage deep green, glossy. GSR 246; GR 288. (8.6)

Handsome Red. HT. (Brownell, 1954). ('Pink Princess' × 'Mirandy') × 'Queen o' the Lakes'. Medium red, large, 12-13 cm./4.8-5.2 in. across, double, high-centered, fragrant, abundant bloom; growth upright, bushy.

Hansa. HRg. (Schaum & Van Tol, 1905). Purplish-red, large, double, strong fragrance, recurrent, many hips; growth strong, upright, 2 m./6.6 ft., stems very prickly; foliage like *R. rugosa*. PGR 97. (8.0)

Hanseat. S. (Tantau, 1961). Seedling × seedling. Rosy-pink with lighter center, single, saucer-shaped, finally star-shaped, some scent; growth strong, 2 m./6.6 ft., slightly arching; foliage deep green, abundant. (8.7)

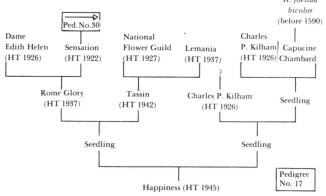

Happiness. (= 'Rouge Meilland'). HT. (Meilland, 1949). ('Rome Glory' × 'Tassin') × ('Charles P. Kilham' × ['Charles P. Kilham' × 'Capucine Chambard']). Luminous red, more crimson with age, very large, double, some scent, long stems; growth strong, little branching, 0.6 m./2 ft.; foliage medium size, matt. (6.5)

Happy. (= 'Alberich'). Pol. (de Ruiter, 1954). 'Robin Hood' × 'Katharina Zeimet'-seedling. Currant-red, semi-double, very small in very dense trusses; growth very dwarf, 20 cm./8 in.; foliage deep green, glossy. (7.4)

Happy Anniversary. (= 'Heureux Anniversaire'). F. (Delbard Chabert, 1960). ('Incendie' × 'Chic Parisien') × ('Floradora' × 'Independence'). Shrimp-red, large, 8 cm./3.2 in. across, double, flat, some scent; growth bushy, low, 0.5 m./1.7 ft.; foliage healthy.

Happy Thought. Min. (Ralph S. Moore, 1978). (R. wichuraiana-seedling × 'Floradora') × 'Sheri Anne'. Pink blend, no scent, profuse and continuous bloom, several together in clusters; bud pointed; growth dwarf, very bushy, vigorous; foliage small, glossy, abundant.

Happy Time. ClMin. (Ralph S. Moore, 1974). (R. wichuraiana × 'Floradora') × ('Golden Glow' × 'Zee'). Yellow overlaid with red, double, 40 narrow petals, no scent, in clusters, heavy bloom in spring, recurrent; bud short, pointed; growth climbing or trailing; foliage small, glossy. (4.9)

Happy Days. HT. (Herholdt, 1962) 'Exciting' × 'Grand Gala'. Luminous deep red, medium, 8 cm./3.2 in. across, very double, some scent, singly on long stems; growth upright.

Happy Event. F. (Dickson, 1964). ('Karl Herbst' × 'Masquerade') × 'Rose Gaujard'. Pale yellow, overlaid with pink, medium, semi-double, floriferous; growth medium. GSR 425. (7.4)

Happy Wanderer. F. (McGredy, 1972). Seedling × 'Marlena'. Crimson-scarlet, double, good form, floriferous, petals drop off cleanly; growth compact, low, 40 cm./16 in.

Harrison's Yellow → **Rosa harisonii,** p. 254. (8.5)

Harlow. HT. (Cocker, 1969). 'Fragrant Cloud' × 'Melrose'. Salmon-pink, large, high pointed, some scent, floriferous, several together; growth medium, 0.7 m./2.3 ft.; foliage dense, very healthy, glossy.

Harriet Miller. HT. (Brownell/Stern, 1972). 'Helen Hayes' × 'Traviata'. Pink, very double, large, globose, long-lasting, strong fragrance, petals drop off cleanly, abundant bloom; bud large, long, pointed; growth very

vigorous, bushy; foliage large, glossy, disease-resistant. (6.3)

Harriny. HT. (LeGrice, 1967). 'Pink Favorite' × 'Lively'. Clear pink, very large, double, very fragrant, free bloom; bud pointed; growth upright; foliage healthy, deep green. (8.5)

Harry Wheatcroft. HT. (Wheatcroft, 1971). Sport of 'Piccadilly'. Interior yellow with pink stripes, reverse yellow.

Hawaii. HT. (Boerner/Jackson & Perkins, 1960). 'Golden Masterpiece' × seedling. Orange-red, very large, 15 cm./6 in. across, double, good fragrance, several together on long stems; growth strong; foliage leathery, PWR 96; RJb 22:96. (5.8)

Hawaiian Sunset. HT. (Swim & Weeks, 1962). 'Charlotte Armstrong' × 'Signora'. Orange with yellow edge, large, 10 cm./4 in. across, very double, flat, fragrant; growth upright, bushy, 0.6 m./2 ft.; foliage leathery, deep green, very large, dense.

Hawkeye Belle. S. (G.S. Buck, 1975). ('Queen Elizabeth' × 'Pizzicato') × 'Prairie Princess'. White with pink shades, deepening with age, high-centered to flat, double, fragrant, singly and in clusters, profuse bloom, recurrent; bud pointed; growth upright, bushy, broad, vigorous; foliage large, leathery, dark green.

Heartbeat. F. (Dickson, 1970). 'Castanet' × ('Cornelia' × seedling). Deep salmon, medium, double, flat, many together in large trusses, some fragrance; growth strong; foliage small, matt. GSR 426.

Heart's Desire. HT. (L.P. Hart, 1933). Seedling × 'Crimson Glory'. Crimson, large, 11 cm./4.4 in. across, high-centered, very fragrant, long stem; growth very vigorous, upright; foliage dark green, leathery.

Heaven Scent. F. (Poulsen, 1968). 'Pernille Poulsen' × 'Isabel de Ortiz'. Salmon, large, double, fragrant, many together, floriferous; growth upright, bushy; foliage abundant.

Hebe. HT. (Dickson, 1949). Orange-pink with orange-yellow, very large, to 15 cm./6 in. across, double, fragrant; growth strong; foliage glossy, young growth bronze. RA 1950:120.

Hebe's Lip. (= 'Reine Blanche'; 'Rubrotincta'). Creamy-white stained with deep rose on petal margin, cupped, semi-double, non-recurrent; growth medium, 1 m./3.3 ft.; foliage light green, serrate. GSR 79. (7.9)

Heidelberg. (= 'Gruss an Heidelberg'). K. (Kordes, 1959). 'World's Fair' × 'Floradora'. Crimson with lighter reverse, large, double, globose, fragrant, in trusses, profuse bloom, recurrent; growth very vigorous, 3 m./10 ft.; foliage leathery. GSR 170; PWR 192; RA 1959:176; GiS 20. (7.4)

Heidi. Min. (Jack E. Christensen/Armstrong, 1978). 'Fairy Moss' × 'Iceberg'. Pink, double, very fragrant, very floriferous, flowering all season, singly and in clusters; bud urn-shaped; growth dwarf, vigorous; foliage glossy, abundant.

Heinrich Münch. HP. (W. Hinner, 1911). 'Frau Karl Druschki' × ('Mme. Caroline Testout' × 'Mrs. W.J. Grant'). Light pink, very large, double, fragrant, occasional recurrent bloom; growth very vigorous. (7.5)

Helen Hayes. HT. (Brownell, 1956). Unnamed *wichuraiana* hybrid × 'Sutter's Gold'. Yellow splashed with orange and pink, large, 10-12 cm./4-4.8 in. across, double, high-centered, fragrant, free bloom; growth very vigorous; foliage glossy. (6.6)

Helene Schoen. HT. (Von Abrams, 1963). 'Multnomah' × 'Charles Mallerin'. Deep crimson-pink, very large, 15 cm./6 in. across, very double, some scent, on long stems; bud long; growth strong; foliage leathery. (6.3)

Helen Traubel. HT. (Swim/Armstrong, 1951). 'Charlotte Armstrong' × 'Glowing Sunset'. Apricot flushed pink, large, 12 cm./4.8 in. across, finally flat, double, very fragrant, free-flowering, flower stalk weak; growth very strong, branched, 0.9 m./3 ft.; foliage large, glossy, dense. PWR 9; GSR 312. (7.1)

Henkell Royal. HT. (Kordes, 1964). Dark red, large, perfect shape, strong fragrance, floriferous; growth strong, 0.8 m./2.6 ft.; foliage large, glossy. KR 10:73. (6.9)

Henry Martin. (= 'Red Moss'). M. (Laffay, 1863). Crimson-purple, medium, semi-double, 3-5 together, non-recurrent; bud very mossy; growth strong, medium; stems very prickly. PGR 53; GiS 9. (8.4)

Henry Field. HT. (Brownell, 1948). 'Pink Princess' × 'Crimson Glory'. Crimson-red, large, 12 cm./4.8 in. across, double, high-centered, fragrant, growth vigorous, bushy; foliage glossy. (5.2)

Henry Nevard. HP. (F. Cant, 1924). Parentage unknown. Crimson-scarlet, very large, double, cupped, very fragrant, recurrent; growth vigorous, bushy; foliage dark green, leathery. (7.2)

Hermosa. Ch. (Marecheseau, 1840). Soft mauve-pink, small, nearly globose, fragrant, recurrent; growth medium, to 0.9 m./3 ft.; foliage bluish-green. GSR 126; SOR 20; HRo 8; WGR 93; GiS 10. (7.3)

Hiawatha. Cl. (Walsh, 1904). 'Crimson Rambler' × 'Paul's Carmine Pillar'. Crimson with white center, single, saucer-shaped, late-flowering, in very large trusses, stamens golden yellow; growth very strong, 3-4 m./10-13.2 ft.; foliage fresh green, leathery, glossy. SRW 122.

'Hidcote Gold' →**Rosa sericea**; p. 255. TRT 81.

Highlight. F. (Robinson, 1957). Seedling × 'Independence'. Orange-scarlet; luminous color, medium, 6 cm./2.4 in. across, double, some scent; growth uneven, 0.6 m./2 ft.; foliage red and green, large, dense. GSR 427; RA 1957:32. (5.5)

High Summer. F. (Dickson, 1978). 'Zorina' × 'Ernest H. Morse'. Vermilion with yellow base, reverse rose flushed with yellow, cupped, double, some scent, 5-12 in clusters, free bloom; growth bushy; upright vigorous.

High Time. HT. (Swim, 1958). 'Charlotte Armstrong' × 'Signora'. Interior deep red, reverse golden yellow with pink, large, 12 cm./4.8 in. across, semi-double, cupped, fragrant, floriferous; bud urn-shaped; growth strong; foliage glossy. (6.6)

Hi-Ho. ClMin. (Ralph S. Moore, 1964). 'Little Darling' × 'Magic Wand'. Light red and deep pink, small, double, abundant bloom; growth medium, 0.9 m./3 ft.; foliage glossy. (8.3)

Hocus-Pocus. Gr. (Armstrong, 1974). 'Fandango' × 'Simon Bolivar'. Orange-red to blackish-red, edge orange-red, double, 30 petals, cupped, singly and in clusters, some scent, very floriferous, continuous bloom; bud urn-shaped; growth upright, medium, vigorous; foliage deep green, large, dense, semi-glossy. (6.5)

Hofgärtner Kalb. HCh. (Felberg-Leclerc, 1914). 'Souvenir de Mme. Eugène Verdier' × 'Gruss an Teplitz'. Bright carmine-rose, center yellow, outer petals with red hue, large, double, good shape, fragrant; growth bushy; vigorous. (6.7)

Holstein. (= 'Firefly'). F. (Kordes, 1939). 'Else Poulsen'× 'Dance of Joy'-seedling. Deep crimson, single, flat, 10 cm./4 in. across, some scent, many together in large trusses on strong stems, resistant to wind damage; growth bushy, low, 0.5 m./1.7 ft.; foliage large, dense, young growth bronze. BTR 14.

Holy Toledo. Min. (J.E. Christensen, 1980). 'Ginger-snap' × 'Magic Carrousel'. Rich apricot, 30 petals, double, mostly one bloom to stem; bud pointed, recurrent; growth dwarf, vigorous, upright, 40 cm./16 in. tall and broad; foliage glossy, green. ARA 1979:33.

Hon. Ina Bingham. HP. (Dickson, 1905). Rosy-red, large, loosely double, cupped, strong fragrance, golden-yellow stamens, moderate bloomer; growth upright. (5.5)

Hon. Layd Lindsay. S. (N.J. Hansen, 1938). 'New Dawn' × 'Rev. F. Page-Roberts'. Opening rosy-red with darker reverse, double, 30-40 petals, recurrent; growth bushy, upright, 1 m./3.3 ft. tall and broad. (6.7)

Honest Abe. Min. (J.E. Christensen/Armstrong, 1978). 'Fairy Moss' × 'Rubinette'. Velvety red, full, 35 petals, fragrant, singly and in clusters, very floriferous, recurrent; bud pointed; growth dwarf, vigorous, bushy; foliage glossy, abundant.

Honey Favorite. HT. (Von Abrams, 1962). 'Pink Favorite' × ?. Yellowish-pink with yellow base, large, 12 cm./4.8 in. across, double, cupped, slightly fragrant, abundant bloom; growth vigorous, upright; foliage glossy. (7.3)

Honeymoon. (= 'Honigmond'). F. (Kordes, 1960). 'Cläre Grammerstorf' × 'Golden Scepter'. Canary-yellow, medium, finally rosette-shape, very double, some scent, in clusters of about 5 together; growth bushy, 0.6 m./2 ft.; foliage dark green, first bronze. KR 9:76; WPR 52. (6.6)

Honey Moss. Min. (Julia Sudol, 1977). 'Fairy Moss' × seedling. White, double, 50 petals, flat, some scent, singly and several together, floriferous, very recurrent; bud mossy; growth spreading, dwarf; foliage deep green, dense, leathery.

Honeycomb. Min. (Ralph S. Moore, 1974). (*R. wichuraiana* × 'Floradora') × 'Debbie'. Opening soft yellow, becoming white, double, 25-35 petals, high-centered, some scent, flowering all season; bud ovoid, pointed; growth dwarf, bushy, 30-40 cm./12-16 in.; foliage leathery, glossy. (6.5)

Honor. HT. (W.A. Warriner/Jackson & Perkins, 1980). Pure white, large, 10-12 cm./4-4.8 in. across, double, blooming profusely on long, strong stems; bud very long, pointed; growth vigorous; foliage disease-resistant. ARA 1979:211.

Honorine de Brabant. B. Pale rosy-lilac with mauve and crimson spots and stripes, large, cupped, recurrent; growth strong, medium; stems green, few prickles; foliage light green. GSR 94; SOR 39; GiS 12. (7.4)

Hopscotch. Min. (Jack Christensen/Armstrong, 1979). 'Gingersnap' × 'Magic Carrousel'. Golden yellow, 30 petals, some scent, singly and in clusters, extremely profuse; bud pointed, ovoid; growth vigorous, bushy, dwarf; foliage semi-glossy, small.

'Houston' → **Cathedral**

Hotel Hershey. Gr. (J.B. Williams/Hershey, 1977). 'Queen Elizabeth' × 'Comanche'. Light orange-red, double, 35 petals, cupped, ruffled, some scent, 1-3 to a stem, good bloomer; bud long, urn-shaped; growth upright, medium, open; foliage deep green, leathery, disease-resistant.

Hugh Dickson. HP. (Dickson, 1905). 'Lord Beacon' × 'Gruss an Teplitz'. Crimson and scarlet, very large, very double, strong fragrance, recurrent; growth very strong, tall to very tall. GiS 12. (6.3)

Hugh Watson. HP. (Dickson, 1905). Deep pink with salmon and silvery-pink, very large, double, flat, free bloom; growth vigorous. (6.5)

Hula Girl. Min. (E.D. Williams/Mini Roses, 1976). 'Miss Hillcrest' × 'Mabel Dot'. Orange blend, double, 45 petals, fragrant, singly, very recurrent, abundant; bud long, pointed; growth dwarf, bushy, 25 cm./10 in.; foliage small, leathery, glossy. (8.0)

Humdinger. Min. (E.W. Schwartz/Nor'East Mini Roses, 1975). Parentage not reported. Orange-red, high-centered, double, 55 petals, some fragrance, singly and several together, recurrent; bud pointed; growth upright, bushy, branched; foliage deep green, glossy. (8.0)

Humoreske. Min. (Spek, 1957). 'Midget' × 'Pixie'. Deep rose-pink, double, very free bloom; growth very bushy.

Humpty-Dumpty. Min. (de Vink, 1932). (*R. multiflora nana* × 'Mrs. Pierre S. du Pont') × 'Tom Thumb'. Soft carmine-pink with deeper center, very double, in clusters; growth very dwarf, 15-20 cm./6-8 in.

Iceberg. (= 'Schneewittchen'). F. (Kordes, 1958). 'Robin Hood' × 'Virgo'. Pure white, large, double, finally more saucer-shaped with yellow center, strong fragrance, often flushed pink in the autumn, very floriferous, flowering all season; growth strong, medium to tall; foliage deep green, large, glossy. PWR 139; GSR 481. (8.6)

Iceberg, Climbing. ClF. (Cant, 1968). Sport of 'Iceberg'. Growth very strong, 3-4 m./10-13.2 ft. high, otherwise like the type. RA 1979:160.

Iced Ginger. F. (Dickson, 1971). 'Anne Watkins' × ?. A blend of buff, copper, yellow and ivory, large, 11 cm./4.4 in. across, very double, globose, fragrant, in clusters; recurrent; growth upright; foliage medium green.

Ice White. F. (McGredy, 1966). 'Mme. Léon Cuny' × ('Orange Sweetheart' × 'Tantau's Surprise'). Pure white, center yellowish when fully open, double, finally flat, medium, many together in clusters, floriferous; growth upright, 0.5 m./1.7 ft.; foliage glossy, green. Similar to 'Iceberg', but less elegant. GSR 429; RA 1966:173.

Ideal. Pol. (Spek, 1921). Sport of 'Miss Edith Cavell'. Dark velvety-crimson, double, globose, open, slightly fragrant, in clusters; growth bushy; foliage deep green, leathery, glossy. (5.5)

Illumination. F. (Dickson, 1970). 'Cläre Grammerstorf' × 'Happy Event'. Deep sulphur-yellow, semi-double, medium, some scent, many together; growth low, spreading, 0.5 m./1.7 ft.; foliage yellow-green.

Illusion. K. (Kordes, 1961). *R. kordesii* × 'Montezuma'. Vermilion, globose, large, double, fragrant, many together, recurrent; growth strong, bushy, 2 m./6.6 ft.; foliage leathery, light green, glossy. RJb 22:128. (7.7)

Ilse Krohn Superior. Cl. (Kordes, 1964). Sport of 'Ilse Krohn'. Pure white, large, high-centered, some scent, profuse bloom, non-recurrent; growth strong, to 3 m./10 ft.; foliage deep green, glossy. WGR 79.

Ilse Haberland. S. (Kordes, 1956). 'Obergärtner Wiebicke' × 'Peace'. Crimson-pink, very large, 15 cm./6 in. across, double, strong fragrance; profuse and recurrent bloom; growth bushy, upright, medium high; foliage light green, dense. RJb 24:128. (7.3)

Impératrice Josephine (= 'Empress Josephine'). A form of *R. francofurtana.* Deep rosy-pink with darker veins, semi-double, petals waved, large; growth strong, medium high, branched. GiS 5.

'Incarnata' → **Maiden's Blush**

Independence. (= 'Kordes Sondermeldung'). F. F_2-seedling of ('Baby Château' × 'Crimson Glory'). Pure vermilion (the first rose of this color), large, 10 cm./4 in. across, double, no scent; growth broad, branched; foliage medium, rather dense, young growth purple. PWR 98; RA 1951:120. (7.0)

Indian Chief. HT. (Gregory, 1967). 'Tropicana' × ?. Light red, orange shaded, double, floriferous, some scent; growth strong; foliage deep green.

Indian Gold. F. (Von Abrams, 1961). 'Goldilocks' × seedling. Yellow with soft pink hue, medium, 8 cm./3.2 in. across, double, high-centered, fragrant, in clusters on short stems, abundant bloom; growth compact, upright; foliage light green, glossy. (5.3)

Indy 500. Gr. (J.B. Williams, 1976). ('Aztec' × 'Queen Elizabeth'-seedling) × ('Independence' × 'Scarlet Knight'). Orange-red, double, 30 petals, open, strong fragrance, singly, camellia-shaped, continuous bloomer; bud long, pointed; growth vigorous, upright; foliage large, glossy, leathery, deep green.

Indian Song. (= 'Preciosa'). HT. (Meilland, 1972). Yellow and red, large, double, no scent; growth low to medium, 40-60 cm./16-24 in. high.

Inge Horstmann. HT. (Tantau, 1964). 'New Yorker' × 'Prima Ballerina'. Crimson-pink with white reverse and pink shading, large, double, strong fragrance; bud long; growth very bushy, 0.7 m./2.3 ft.; foliage healthy. RJb 29:129.

Innisfree. F. (Dickson, 1964). ('Karl Herbst' × 'Masquerade') × 'Circus'. Deep yellow and orange-red with pink, rosette-shaped, flat, medium, double, floriferous, some scent; growth bushy, 0.9 m./3 ft.; foliage small, light green, glossy.

Inspiration. LCl. (Jacobus, 1946). 'New Dawn' × 'Crimson Glory'. Pink, large, semi-double, fragrant; growth moderate; foliage glossy. (6.7)

'Interflora' → **'Interview'**

Interview. (formerly 'Interflora'). HT. (Meilland, 1970). (['Baccara' × 'Message'] × ['Baccara' × 'Jolie Madame']) × ('Baccara' × 'Paris Match'). Vermilion, large, very double, some scent, several together, floriferous; growth strong, upright, stems 1 m./3.3 ft. long; foliage deep green, matt. Greenhouse variety.

Irene von Dänemark. (= 'Irene of Denmark'). F. (Poulsen, 1948). 'Orléans Rose' × ('Mme. Plantier' × 'Edina'). Pure white, medium, double, cupped, fragrant, floriferous; bud soft pink; growth bushy, compact, 0.5 m./1.7 ft.; foliage fresh green. PWR 123. (7.0)

Irish Fireflame. HT. (Dickson, 1914). Orange, crimson veins, large, 12 cm./4.8 in. across, single, 5 petals, very fragrant, stamens light brown; growth compact, bushy; foliage deep green, glossy. (6.7)

'Irish Gold' → **Grandpa Dickson**

Irish Mist. F. (McGredy, 1966). 'Orangeade' × 'Mischief'. Orange-salmon, double, medium, edge of petals fringed, some scent, long in flower, floriferous; growth somewhat bushy, 0.8 m./2.6 ft.; foliage small. GSR 430; RA 1968: 14. (7.4)

Irish Rover. HT. (McGredy, 1970). 'Violet Carson' × 'Tropicana'. Salmon-red, large, perfect shape, double, some scent, singly or several together; growth strong, tall; foliage bronze-green. RA 1970:129.

'Irish Wonder' → **Evelyn Fison**

Isabel de Ortiz. HT. (Kordes, 1962). 'Peace' × 'Kordes Perfecta'. Light red with silvery-pink to yellowish-white reverse, large, 12 cm./4.8 in. across, good shape, double, fragrant; growth strong, upright, 0.9 m./3 ft.; foliage abundant, glossy, deep green. GSR 318; RJb 26:32; KR 9:20. (7.1)

Isis. F. (Mattock, 1973). 'Very Dalton' × 'Shepherdess'. Ivory-white, large, 10 cm./4 in. across, some scent, double, in clusters; growth compact, bushy; foliage medium, glossy.

Isobel Harkness. HT. (Norman/Harkness, 1957). 'McGredy's Yellow' × 'Phyllis Bide'. Pure yellow, very large, to 15 cm./6 in. across, double, flat, fragrant, on strong stems; growth bushy; foliage leathery. (6.6)

Ispahan. (= 'Rose d'Isfahan'; 'Pompon des Princes'). D. (in cultivation before 1832). Pure pink, fading with age, medium, 8 cm./3.2 in. across, double, very strong fragrance, long-flowering, several together; growth strong, medium; foliage small, glossy. GSR 80.

Ivory Fashion. F. (Boerner/Jackson & Perkins, 1958). 'Sonata' × 'Fashion'. Ivory-white, sometimes shaded with yellow, large, 10 cm./4 in. across, finally flat, fragrant, floriferous, in clusters; growth strong, upright, 0.7 m./2.6 ft.; foliage leathery, very resistant to Black Spot. PWR 107; GSR 431; RA 1958:33. (8.1)

Ivory Tower. HT. (Kordes/Armstrong, 1979). 'Colour Wonder' × 'King's Ransom'. Ivory-white to light pink, high-centered, double, 35 petals, fruity fragrance, single, floriferous, very recurrent; bud very long, pointed; growth upright, medium, bushy; foliage healthy, semi-glossy. ARA 63:90.

Jack Frost. F. (Jelly/Hill, 1962). 'Garnette' × seedling. Creamy-white to white, medium, double, globose, fragrant; growth strong, bushy; foliage deep green. Greenhouse variety. (6.5)

Jack Horner. Min. (T. Robinson, 1955). 'Margo Koster' × 'Tom Thumb'. Bright pink, very double, 50 petals, some scent; growth very dwarf, stems without prickles, 10-20 cm./4-8 in. high.

Jackie. Min. (Ralph S. Moore, 1955). 'Golden Glow' × 'Zee'. Straw-yellow, fading to white, small, 4 cm./1.6 in. across, high-centered, fragrant, free bloom; growth dwarf, 30 cm./12 in., vigorous, bushy, spreading; foliage glossy. (7.1)

Jackie, Climbing. ClMin. (Ralph S. Moore, 1957). 'Golden Glow' × 'Zee' (not a sport of 'Jackie'). Light yellow to creamy-white, small, 4 cm./1.6 in. across, double, fragrant, heavy spring bloom, recurrent; growth vigorous, to 1.2 m./4 ft. or over; foliage leathery, semi-glossy. (7.4)

Jacques Cartier. P. (Moreau-Robert, 1868). Opening intense pink, fading with age, center darker, large, double, fragrant, June, non-recurrent; growth medium, upright; foliage light green. GSR 81; PGR 18, 99; GiS 10. (8.0)

Jadis. HT. (W.A. Warriner/Jackson & Perkins, 1974). 'Chrysler Imperial' × 'Virgo'. Medium pink, large, high-centered, double, strong fragrance, long-lasting, petals drop off cleanly, very free bloom; bud very large, long pointed; growth very vigorous, bushy, upright; foliage light green, leathery, disease-resistant. (6.3)

Jamaica. HT. (Lindquist, 1965). ('Charlotte Armstrong' × 'Floradora') × 'Nocturne'. Cherry-red, large, semi-double, fragrant, cupped, floriferous; growth strong; foliage leathery, deep green. (6.7)

James Mitchell. M. (E. Verdier, 1861). Magenta-pink, fading to mauve-pink, with eye, small, many together, pompom-shape, flat; bud heavily brownish-mossy, single or several together; growth bushy, spreading, medium; foliage bronze-green. TR 5.

James Veitch. M. (E. Verdier, 1865). Purplish-violet with fiery-red shade, medium, double, in clusters; growth medium strong.

Janice. Min. (Ralph S. Moore, 1971). (*R. wichuraiana* × 'Floradora') × 'Eleanor'. Medium pink, double, small, very long-lasting, petals drop off cleanly, abundant bloom; growth vigorous, 25-30 cm./10-12 in., dwarf, bushy; foliage leathery, glossy. (5.4)

Janice Tellian. Min. (Ralph S. Moore, 1979). 'Fairy Moss' × 'Fire Princess'. Light pink, double, 40 petals, sweet fragrance, recurrent all season, 3 per cluster; bud pointed; growth dwarf, much branching, compact; foliage small, semi-glossy.

Janna. Min. (Ralph S. Moore, 1970). 'Little Darling' × ('Little Darling' × *R. wichuraiana*-seedling). White, later overlaid with pink, small, double, singly and several together on short, strong stems, free bloom; growth dwarf, bushy; foliage small, leathery. (8.2)

Jan Spek. F. (McGredy, 1966). 'Cläre Grammerstorf' × 'Doctor Faust'. Deep yellow, large, 8 cm./3.2 in. across, double, some scent, many together in large trusses, abundant, profuse bloom, recurrent; exterior of bud reddish; growth strong, bushy, 0.5 m./1.7 ft.; foliage deep green, glossy. GSR 432. (6.9)

J.B. Clark. HP. (Dickson, 1905). 'Lord Beacon' × 'Gruss an Teplitz'. Deep scarlet with blackish shades, very large, semi-double, high-centered, fragrant, on long, strong stem; growth vigorous, tall to very tall, almost climbing, to 2.5 m./8.3 ft., bushy, branches very prickly.

Jeanie. HT. (Eddie, 1959). 'Condesa de Sástago' × 'Mme. Edmond Labbé'. Creamy-white to pink, large, 10 cm./4 in. across, double, high-centered, fragrant, very free bloom; growth vigorous, spreading; foliage deep green. (6.0)

Jeanie Williams. Min. (Ralph S. Moore, 1965). 'Little Darling' × 'Magic Wand'. Interior opening orange-red, later more crimson with straw-yellow reverse, small, rosette-shaped, double, some scent; growth dwarf, bushy; foliage leathery. (8.3)

Jeanne de Montfort. M. (Robert, 1851). Clear pink, fading to nearly white with age, very double, finally flat, yellow stamens, fragrant, several together, non-recurrent; bud crimson, brown and densely mossy; growth very strong, to 2 m./6.6 ft., stems brown-mossy. GSR 73; GiS 9. (8.4)

Jeanne Lajoie. ClMin. (E.P. Sima/Mini-Roses, 1975). ('Casa Blanca' × 'Independence') × 'Midget'. Pink, double, 40 petals, high-centered, slight scent, abundant, recurrent, in clusters; bud small, long; growth upright, bushy, 0.8 m./2.6 ft.; foliage dark green, firm, glossy. (8.0)

Jessica. (= 'Tanjeka'). HT. (Tantau, 1971). 'Colour Wonder' × 'Piccadilly'. Salmon-red, more orange towards base, large, double, some scent; bud long; growth strong; foliage leathery, deep green. (7.5)

Jet Trail. Min. (Ralph S. Moore, 1964). 'Little Darling' × 'Magic Wand'. White, occasionally with pale green hue, small, double; bud pointed; growth dwarf, bushy, 30-35 cm./12-14 in.; foliage leathery, narrow. (7.5)

Jian. Min. (E.D. Williams, 1965). 'Juliette' × 'Oakington Ruby'. Medium red with lighter reverse, very small, double, open, profuse bloom; bud ovoid; growth very vigorous, dwarf, bushy; foliage narrow, leathery. (5.7)

Jiminy Cricket. Fl. (Boerner/Jackson & Perkins, 1954). 'Goldilocks' × 'Geranium Red'. Salmon-orange, loosely double, large, 10 cm./4 in. across, floriferous, in clusters, scented; growth upright, low, 0.5 m./1.7 ft.; foliage small, reddish-green. PWR 128. (6.4)

Jimmy Greaves. HT. (Gandy, 1971). 'Dorothy Peach' × 'Prima Ballerina'. Red-purple with silvery reverse, double, 12 cm./4.8 in. across, 55 petals, fragrant, single and several together, abundant bloom; growth upright, bushy; foliage large. (5.5)

Joanna Hill. HT. (Hill, 1928). 'Mme. Butterfly' × 'Miss Amelia Gude'. Pale yellow, darker center, large, double, some scent; growth strong, 0.7 m./2.3 ft.; foliage matt, medium. RA 1965:100. (7.0)

Jocelyn. F. (LeGrice, 1970). Matt mahogany to purple-brown with age, very double, flat, in clusters; growth medium high, 0.7 m./2.3 ft.; foliage very deep green, glossy.

John Roscoe. HT. (R. Wright, 1973). 'Karl Herbst' × 'Tzigane'. Rosy-red on lighter background, very large, 12 cm./4.8 in. across, double, 60 petals, fragrant, free flowering, singly and several together; foliage medium green. (5.5)

John Church. F. (McGredy, 1964). 'Ma Perkins' × 'Red Favorite'. Orange-scarlet, large, 8 cm./3.2 in. across, loosely double, good shape, scented, in clusters; growth strong. RA 1964:96. (7.7)

John F. Kennedy. HT. (Boerner/Jackson & Perkins, 1965). Seedling × 'White Queen'. Pure white, very large, 12 cm./4.8 in. across, very double, good shape; bud greenish-white; growth strong, upright, 0.8 m./2.6 ft.; foliage narrow, long, deep green, leathery. WGR 97. (6.0)

John Hopper. HP. (Warf, 1862). 'Jules Margottin' × 'Mme. Vidot'. Light pink, with more lilac margin and crimson center, globose, very double, large, strong fragrance, somewhat recurrent; growth bushy, medium. (6.9)

John S. Armstrong. F. (Swim/Armstrong, 1961). 'Charlotte Armstrong' × seedling. Velvety blackish-red, large, 8 cm./3.2 in. across, double, cupped, some scent, several together in large trusses, floriferous; growth bushy, low, 50 cm./20 in.; foliage medium large, glossy, young growth red. RJb 22:128. (8.0)

John Waterer. HT. (McGredy, 1970). 'King of Hearts' × 'Hanne'. Deep crimson with dusky edging to the petals, large, double, fragrant, singly or several together; growth upright, sturdy, 0.8 m./2.6 ft.; foliage deep green, matt. CRA 71:80; GSR 319; RA 1970:48. (7.7)

Jolly Good. F. (Mrs. C. Fuller/Wyant, 1973). 'Cupid's Charm' × 'Lucky Piece'. Salmon-pink, double, 60 petals, fragrant, in clusters, intermittent bloom; bud ovoid; growth bushy, compact; foliage deep green, glossy, leathery. (5.4)

Jolly Roger. F. (Armstrong, 1973). 'Spartan' × 'Angélique'. Bright reddish-orange, semi-double, medium, cupped, some scent, singly and several together on short stems, abundant, continuous bloom; bud small, long; growth compact, short; foliage semi-glossy, medium.

'Joseph Guy' → **Lafayette.**

Josephine. Min. (Ralph S. Moore, 1969). (*R. wichuraiana* × 'Carolyn Dean') × 'Jet Trail. White to blush, small, double, abundant bloom; growth dwarf, very bushy; foliage small, glossy. (6.6)

Josephine Bruce. HT. (Bees, 1949). 'Crimson Glory' × 'Madge Whipp'. Velvety crimson, large, to 12 cm./4.8 in. across, double, some scent, floriferous; growth bushy, upright, 0.6 m./2 ft.; foliage large, abundant, PWR 86; RA 1954:26; GSR 320. (7.6)

'Josephine Wheatcroft' → **Rosina.**

Joseph's Coat. LCl. (Swim/Armstrong, 1964). 'Buccaneer' × 'Circus'. Multi-colored; golden-yellow with orange and red, later more red, medium large, double, some scent, floriferous, flowers a long time; growth very strong, tall to very tall; foliage deep green, glossy. CRA 66:63; GSR 247; RA 1965:33. (7.1)

Jove. F. (Harkness, 1968). 'Very Dalton' × 'Paprika'. Luminous scarlet, medium, double, petals waved, faint scent, resistant to weather damage, abundant, continuous bloom; growth bushy, low, 0.5 m./1.7 ft.; foliage deep green.

Jubilant. F. (Dickson, 1967). 'Dearest' × 'Circus'. Crimson-pink with lighter edge, 6 cm./2.4 in. across, double, scented, in clusters, abundant bloom; growth moderate, upright, 0.8 m./2.6 ft.; foliage abundant, bronze-green. GSR 424.

Jubilee. HT. (Allen, 1930). 'Paul's Lemon Pillar' × 'Aspirant Marcel Rouyer'. Cream with salmon and yellow, center coral-pink, large, double, high-centered, very fragrant; bud pointed; growth vigorous.

Judy Fisher. Min. (Ralph S. Moore, 1969). 'Little Darling' × 'Magic Wand'. Rose-pink, small, double, free bloom; growth bushy, dwarf, vigorous; foliage deep green and bronze, leathery.

Judy Garland. F. (Harkness, 1978). (['Tropicana' × 'Circus'] × ['Sabine' × 'Circus']) × 'Pineapple Poll'. Deep yellow suffused with orange-red, double, 25 petals, fragrant, in trusses, free bloom; growth upright, 0.9 m./3 ft.; foliage deep green, semi-glossy.

Jules Margottin. HP. (Margottin, 1853). 'La Reine'-seedling. Crimson-pink, very large, very double, globose, finally more flat, some scent, recurrent; growth bushy, medium. (6.5)

Julia Mannering. HRubiginosa. (Penzance, 1895).

Pearl-pink, single, small, arranged along the branches, summer-flowering, abundant, non-recurrent, fragrant; growth strong, tall to very tall.

Julie. HT. (Kordes, 1972). Seedling × 'American Beauty'. Dark red, very large, double, cupped, fragrant, long-lasting, free, intermittent bloom, petals drop off cleanly; bud very large, ovoid; growth moderate, upright; foliage deep green, soft, disease-resistant. (6.1)

Julie de Mersent (sometimes spelled 'Julie de Mersan'). M. (Thomas, 1854). Deep pink with white stripes, medium, double, finally flat, fragrant. (9.0)

Juliet. HP. (Paul, 1910). 'Capt. Hayward' × 'Soleil d'Or'. Intense pink to dark pink with dark yellow reverse, large, double, fragrant, recurrent; growth strong; foliage curled. RZ 1910:57. (5.5)

Juliette. Min. (Lamb Nurseries). Brilliant crimson-scarlet, double, free bloom; growth dwarf, 25-30 cm./10-12 in., vigorous; foliage bright red in fall.

June Bride. F. (Shepherd, 1957). ('Mme. Butterfly' × 'New Dawn') × 'Crimson Glory'. Soft yellowish-white, large, 10 cm./4 in. across, double, cupped, fragrant, 3-7 together in clusters, floriferous, continuous bloom; growth strong, upright; foliage leathery, wrinkled. GSR 321; PWR 4.

June Park. HT. (Park, 1958). 'Peace' × 'Crimson Glory'. Deep rose-pink, large, very double, globose, strong fragrance, strong stems; growth somewhat spreading. RA 1959:65. (7.2)

June Time. Min. (Ralph S. Moore, 1963). (*R. wichuraiana* × 'Floradora') × (['Etoile Luisante' × 'Red Ripples'] × 'Zee'). Light pink with darker reverse, small, very double, abundant bloom; growth compact; bushy, dwarf, 25-30 cm./10-12 in.; foliage glossy.

June Way. HT. (L. Atkins/Wyant, 1977). 'Pink Favorite' × 'Chrysler Imperial'. Pink, does not fade, cupped, double, 35 petals, some scent, very floriferous, continuous bloom; bud pointed; growth moderate, spreading; foliage medium green, glossy. (7.4)

'Junior Miss' → correct name is **America's Junior Miss**

Juno. C. (Laffay, 1847). Soft pink to nearly white, margin darker, large, 8 cm./3.2 in. across, fragrant, non-recurrent; growth strong, medium.

Just Joey. HT. (Cants of Colchester, 1972). 'Fragrant Cloud' × 'Golden Wave'. Buff-orange, double, 12 cm./4.8 in. across, strong fragrance, very free bloom, singly and several together; growth medium; foliage glossy, healthy. RA 1972:96.

Kaiserin Auguste Viktoria. HT. (Lambert, 1891). 'Coquette de Lyon' × 'Lady Mary Fitzwilliam'. White with greenish center, medium, very double, good shape, strong fragrance; growth low, branched, 0.5 m./1.7 ft.; foliage light green and reddish, matt. RZ 1891:16. (5.8)

Kaiserin Auguste Viktoria, Climbing. ClHT. (Dickson, 1897). Sport of 'Kaiserin Auguste Viktoria'. Growth climbing; otherwise like the type. (5.9)

'Kalinka' → **Pink Wonder**

Kapai. F. (McGredy, 1977). 'Mme. Bollinger' × 'Trombola'. Orange-red, HT-type, double, 30 petals, open, strong fragrance, in clusters, blooms very early, very recurrent; growth bushy, short; foliage small.

Kara. Min. (Ralph S. Moore, 1972). 'Fairy Moss' × self. Light to medium pink, small, open, single, several together; bud small, long, pointed; growth dwarf, 25-30 cm./10-12 in., vigorous, bushy; foliage small, soft, disease-resistant. RA 1977:60. (7.8)

Kardinal. HT. (Kordes, 1967). 'Tropicana' × 'Liebeszauber'. Blackish-red and velvety, large, good shape, fragrant, floriferous; growth strong, 0.8 m./2.6 ft., branched; foliage deep green, abundant, healthy.

Karl Foerster. HSpn. (Kordes, 1931). 'Frau Karl Druschki' × *R. pimpinellifolia altaica*. Pure white, very large, semi-double, some scent, very floriferous, somewhat recurrent; growth strong, tall to very tall, stems strong; foliage light green, wrinkled. (8.2)

Karl Herbst. HT. (Kordes, 1950). 'Independence' × 'Peace'. Deep red with lighter reverse, large, very double, star-shaped, some scent, very floriferous, resistant to weather damage; growth strong, 0.9 m./3 ft., PWR 85; (6.8)

Karma. HT. (McGredy, 1978). 'John Waterer' × 'Kalahari'. Medium red, double, 30 petals, some scent, very free bloom, particularly in the autumn; growth medium high; foliage deep green.

'Kasanlik' → **Rosa damascena trigintipetala,** p. 260.

Kassel. LCl. (Kordes, 1956). 'Obergärtner Wiebicke' × 'Independence'. Orange-scarlet, large, semi-double, to 10 cm./4 in. across, many together in trusses, very floriferous; growth very strong, 4 m./13.2 ft.; foliage large, reddish when young, matt. PWR 205; GSR 172; RA 1958:145; GiS 20. (6.2)

Katherine Loker. F. 'Zorina' × 'Golden Wave'. Butter-yellow, 30 very broad petals, 10-12 cm./4-4.8 in. across; growth medium, compact, vigorous; foliage healthy.

Katherine T. Marshall. HT. (Boerner/Jackson & Perkins, 1943). Seedling × 'Chieftain'. Deep rose-pink with yellow hue, large, 12 cm./4.8 in. across, cupped, slightly fragrant; bud dark salmon-pink, stem long, strong; growth very vigorous, upright; foliage leathery. (5.6)

Kathleen. HMsk. (Pemberton, 1922). 'Daphne' × 'Perle des Jeannes'. Blush, small, single, slightly fragrant, profuse and recurrent bloom, large clusters on long stems; growth very vigorous, tall. (7.0)

Kathleen Ferrier. F. (Buisman, 1952). 'Gartenstolz' × 'Shot Silk'. Deep salmon-pink with lighter center, large, semi-double, some scent, many together in loose, large trusses; growth strong, medium, very spreading; young growth bronze-green. GSR 173.

Kathleen Harrop. B. (Dickson, 1919). Sport of 'Zéphirine Drouhin'. Blush with darker center, fading with age, edge then nearly white, large, 10 cm./4 in. across, loosely double, good scent, recurrent; growth strong, 2.5 m./8.3 ft.; foliage light green, mostly 3-5 leaflets. GSR 95; GiS 12.

Kathleen Joyce. F. (McGredy, 1970). 'Paddy McGredy' × 'Ice White'. Soft pink, large, 10 cm./4 in. across, HT-form, very strong fragrance; growth strong; foliage abundant, deep green.

Kathleen Mills. HT. (LeGrice, 1934). Parentage not reported. Pale pink with deep pink reverse, large, semi-double, open, very fragrant; growth vigorous; foliage leathery. (7.4)

Kathleen O'Rourke. HT. (Dickson, 1976). 'Fragrant Cloud' × 'Red Planet'. Geranium-red color, double, deep cup-shape, fragrant, several together, very free bloom; bud ovoid; growth bushy, upright; foliage large, dull. (7.4)

Kathy. Min. (Ralph S. Moore, 1972). 'Little Darling' × 'Magic Wand'. Dark red, double, 4 cm./1.6 in. across, singly and several together; bud ovoid, large; growth loosely compact; foliage medium. (8.4)

Kathy Robinson. Min. (E.D. Williams/Mini-Roses, 1974). 'Little Darling' × 'Over the Rainbow'. Pink with lighter reverse, base yellow and cream, high centered, double, singly and several together, profuse and recurrent bloom; bud long; growth dwarf, compact; foliage deep green, small. (8.5)

Kerry Gold. F. (Dickson, 1967). 'Circus' × 'Allgold'. Deep yellow, outer petals with reddish shade and veins, medium-large, double, in clusters; growth strong, low.

Kerryman. F. (McGredy, 1971). 'Mme. Léon Cuny' × 'Columbine'. Center salmon-pink, becoming lighter towards margin, deepening with age, large, 10 cm./4 in. across, some scent, several together; growth bushy, compact; foliage semi-glossy. RA 1972:161; CRA 73:45. (7.5)

Kew Rambler. Cl. (Kew Gardens, 1912). *R. soulieana* × 'Hiawatha'. Pink with lighter center, single, in clusters, flowering in June, non-recurrent; growth strong, 3-6 m./10-20 ft., climbing; foliage greyish-green.

Kiftsgate. Cl. (E. Murrell, 1954). Sport of *Rosa filipes*. Creamy-white, small, single, fragrant, in large clusters, late flowering, non-recurrent; growth very strong, stems up to 6 m./20 ft. long in one year! GiS 23; GSR 19; TCR 1. Tender.

Kim. F. (Harkness, 1970). ('Orange Sensation' × 'Allgold') × 'Irish Beauty'. Canary-yellow, medium-large, semi-double, faint scent, several together and in clusters, very floriferous; growth dwarf, 40-50 cm./16-20 in.; foliage light green. RA 1972:15; GSR 435.

King Arthur. F. (Harkness, 1967). 'Pink Parfait' × 'Highlight'. Deep salmon-red, large, 8 cm./3.2 in. across, double, in clusters, floriferous; growth upright and spreading, 1 m./3.3 ft.; foliage medium green, young growth purple. GSR 436; RA 1967:33. (7.2)

King of Hearts. HT. (McGredy, 1968). 'Karl Herbst' × 'Ethel Sanday'. Deep red, medium-large, double, very resistant to weather damage, some scent, floriferous; growth vigorous, bushy, 0.7 m./2.3 ft.; foliage leathery, deep green. (7.3)

King's Ransom. HT. (Morey, 1961). 'Golden Masterpiece' × 'Lydia'. Rich yellow with darker veins, very large, 12-15 cm./4.8-6 in. across, double, finally flat, strong fragrance, on long, strong stems, very floriferous; bud long; growth vigorous, 0.9 m./3 ft. high; foliage leathery, glossy. GSR 322; WPR 17; RA 1963:21; WGR 101. (7.1)

Kiskadee. F. (McGredy, 1973). 'Cynthia Brooke' × 'Arthur Bell'. Golden-yellow, long-lasting color, resistant to weather damage, large, double, high-centered, singly or several together; long bud; growth bushy, upright, 0.7 m./2.3 ft.; foliage deep green, glossy.

Königin von Dänemark. (= Queen of Denmark). A. (J. Booth, Hamburg, 1816, named in 1826). Vivid crimson-pink, then flesh-pink with dark center, medium, opening cup-shaped, then petals reflexing, very double, non-recurrent; buds crimson; growth strong, spreading, medium; foliage deep bluish-green. GSR 66; TR 2; SOR 10; PGR 36. (8.9)

K. of K. ('Kitchener of Karthoum'). (Dickson, 1917). Velvety crimson, medium, semi-double, nearly single, strong fragrance; growth strong, branched.

Koldinghus. F. (Poulsen, 1968). Salmon-pink, fading to blush, large, 10 cm./4 in. across, loosely double, finally flat, in large trusses, floriferous; growth upright, bushy, 0.8 m./2.6 ft.; foliage medium green, large, semi-glossy.

Konrad Adenauer. HT. (Tantau, 1955). 'Crimson Glory' × 'Hens Verschuren' Very deep red and velvety, large, very double, strong scent, good shape, long-lasting, floriferous; growth medium, 0.6 m./2.3 ft.; foliage light green, glossy. PWR 73; KR 9:163. (6.3)

Kordes Perfecta. HT. (Kordes, 1957). 'Golden Scepter' × 'Karl Herbst'. Deep creamy-yellow, suffused with red, more intense towards the edges, large, fragrant, floriferous, singly and several together on long stems; growth strong, bushy, 0.8 m./2.6 ft.; foliage large, glossy, abundant. PWR 87; GSR 324. (6.9)

Kordes Perfecta Superior. HT. (Kordes, 1963). Sport of 'Kordes Perfecta'. Like the type, but color deeper pink, with yellow base. RJb 26:224. (6.8)

Korona. HT. (Kordes, 1955). 'Obergärtner Wiebicke' × 'Independence'. Orange-scarlet, very resistant to weather damage, large, 8 cm./3.2 in. across, semi-double, faint scent, in large trusses, continuous bloom; growth strong, upright, 1 m/3.3 ft., branched; foliage large, abundant. PWR 115; GSR 437. (7.8)

'Korp' → **Prominent**

Ko's Yellow. Min. (S. McGredy/McGredy Roses International, 1978). ('New Penny' × 'Banbridge') × ('Border Flame' × 'Manx Queen'). Yellow, double, medium, very free bloom; foliage dark, glossy; growth bushy.

La Bella. HT. (Kordes, 1974). 'Liebeszauber' × 'Herz-As'. Dark red, large, globose, some scent, double, singly on long stems, petals drop off cleanly; growth very strong, medium; foliage deep green, abundant.

Lady Ann. Min. (Ralph S. Moore, 1961). (R. wichuraiana × 'Floradora') × 'Little Buckaroo'. Deep rose-pink, medium, 3 cm./1.2 in. across, cupped, fragrant, abundant bloom; bud pointed; growth vigorous, bushy, 20-25 cm./8-10 in. high, dwarf; foliage dark green, glossy, leathery. (7.2)

Lady Bird Johnson. HT. (E.C. Curtis, 1971). 'Montezuma' × 'Hawaii'. Orange, medium, double, fragrant, abundant bloom; bud long, pointed, growth vigorous, upright. (6.4)

Lady Curzon. S. (Turner, 1901). 'Macrantha' × R. rugosa rubra. Light pink, nearly white center, large, 10 cm./4 in. across, single, non-recurrent, fragrant, many golden yellow stamens; growth strong, bushy, 2 × 2 m./6.6 × 6.6 ft.; foliage like R. rugosa. GSR 174; GiS 2.

Lady Elgin. (= 'Thais'). HT. (Meilland, 1954). 'Mme. Kriloff' × ('Peace' × 'Genève'). Apricot-yellow, splashed with red and with dark red veins, large, double, high-centered, faint fragrance, moderate bloom; growth medium, 0.7 m./2.3 ft.; foliage leathery, deep green. PWR 7. (7.0)

Lady Forteviot. ClHT. (Howard Rose Co. 1935). Golden yellow to apricot, large, double, high-centered, very fragrant; growth climbing, bushy; foliage bronze, glossy. (7.5)

Lady Georgia. HT. (E. Curtis/Kimbrew, 1973). 'Miss Hillcrest' × 'Peace'. Pink with ivory at base of petals, double, fragrant, very long-lasting, singly on moderately strong stems, continuous bloom; growth very vigorous, medium, bushy, semi-spreading; foliage leathery, disease-resistant. (5.2)

Lady Hillingdon. T. (Lowe & Shawyer, 1910). 'Papa Gontier' × 'Mme. Hoste'. Deep orange-yellow, loosely double, strong fragrance, flowering for a very long time; bud very long; growth strong, 1.5-2 m./5-6.6 ft.; TCR 6; HRo 9. (8.9)

Lady Maysie Robinson. HT. (Kordes, 1956). Seedling × 'Peace'. Deep pink with large white center, double, flat-cupped, fragrant; growth strong, upright; foliage deep green. (6.3)

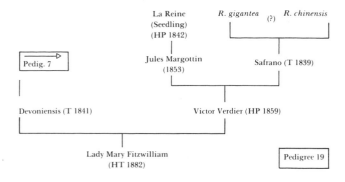

La Reine (Seedling) (HP 1842)

R. gigantea (?) R. chinensis

Pedig. 7

Jules Margottin (1853)

Safrano (T 1839)

Devoniensis (T 1841)

Victor Verdier (HP 1859)

Lady Mary Fitzwilliam (HT 1882)

Pedigree 19

Lady Mary Fitzwilliam. HT. (Bennett, 1882). 'Devoniensis' × 'Victor Verdier'. Flesh-pink, very large, globose, strong fragrance; foliage pale green. One of the most important old rose varieties. WPR 26.

Lady Penzance. (= *R. penzanceana*). S. (Penzance, 1894). *R. rubiginosa* × *R. foetida*. Pink with yellow center, small, single, summer-flowering, non-recurrent; growth strong, arching, medium to tall; foliage apple-scented. GiS 3.

Lady Reading. Pol. (van Kleef, 1921). Sport of 'Ellen Poulsen'. Clear red, small, globose, in clusters, on short, strong stems; growth dwarf, vigorous; foliage deep green.

Lady Rose. HT. (Kordes, 1978). Seedling × 'Träumerei'. Orange-red, very large, high-centered, 30 petals, singly and several together, profuse, continuous bloom; bud large, long; growth vigorous, upright; foliage semi-glossy.

Lady Seton. HT. (McGredy, 1966). 'Ma Perkins' × 'Mischief'. Deep pink, with darker veins, large, 10 cm./4 in. across, strong fragrance, double, finally flat; growth vigorous, 1 m./3.3 ft.; foliage large, deep green, leathery. GSR 326; CRA 66; 63; RA 1965:32. (7.8)

Lady Sonia. S. (Mattock, 1961). 'Grandmaster' × 'Doreen'. Golden yellow, semi-double, 20 petals, very large, 10 cm./4 in. across, floriferous; growth strong, bushy, upright; foliage deep green.

Lady Sylvia. HT. (W. Stevens, 1926). Sport of 'Mme. Butterfly'. Creamy rose-pink with orange base, double, high-centered, fragrant, on long, strong stems; growth upright; foliage deep green.

Lady Sylvia, Climbing. ClHT. (Stevens, 1933). Sport of 'Lady Sylvia'. Growth very strong, climbing, 3-4 m./10-13 ft. high; otherwise like the type.

Lady X. HT. (Meilland, 1966). Seedling × 'Simone'. Mauve-lilac, large, double, high-centered, faint fragrance, abundant bloom; bud long; growth upright, 1 m./3.3 ft.; foliage deep green, very large, glossy. (8.4)

Lafayette. (= 'Joseph Guy'). F. (Nonin, 1921). 'Rödhätte' × 'Richmond'. Light crimson-pink, large, semi-double, saucer-shaped, on long stems, very long-lasting; growth bushy, upright, low, 40 cm./16 in.; foliage medium green, glossy. (6.0)

La Fontaine. F. (Meilland, 1961). 'Mme. Charles Sauvage' × 'Fashion'. Golden-yellow, 8 cm./3.2 in. across, double, cupped, some scent, in clusters, profuse bloom; growth bushy; foliage leathery, deep green. (6.6)

La France. HT. (Guillot Fils, 1867). Discovered as a chance seedling among the seedlings of Guillot, not an intended hybrid (usually reported to be 'Mme. Victor Verdier' × 'Mme. Bravy', or a seedling of 'Mme. Falcot'). Silvery-rose, very large, very double, strong fragrance, poor bloomer; growth poor, 0.5 m./1.7 ft.; foliage pale green. Principally of historic interest as it is one of the very first Hybrid Teas. BTR 5; RXX 76. (6.0)

Lagoon. F. (Harkness, 1970). 'Lilac Charm' × 'Sterling Silver'. Soft mauve, nearly single, 6 cm./2.4 in. across, fragrant, in clusters; growth strong, medium; foliage bronze-green, glossy. RA 1971:144; GSR 438.

Laguna. HT. (Kordes, 1974). 'Hawaii' × 'Orange Delbard'. Orange-red, large, double, cupped, fragrant, singly, petals drop off cleanly, profuse bloom; bud long; growth strong, 0.8 m./2.6 ft.; foliage medium green, glossy.

La Jolla. HT. (Swim/Armstrong, 1954). 'Charlotte Armstrong' × 'Contrast'. Creamy-yellow with dark base and broad pink edge, with darker veins, later more red, large, 12 cm./4.8 in. across, double, fragrant; growth tall, long stems, 0.9 m./3 ft.; foliage large, not very dense. PWR 26; RA 1956:60. (7.0)

Lake Como. F. (Harkness, 1968). 'Lilac Charm' × 'Sterling Silver'. Soft mauve, medium, semi-double, strong fragrance, in clusters, profuse bloom; growth low, 0.5 m./1.7 ft.; foliage bronze-green. GSR 445.

Lakeland. HT. (Fryer, 1976). 'Fragrant Cloud' × 'Queen Elizabeth'. Light shell-pink, double, 35 petals, slight fragrance, very free bloom, singly and several together; growth free; foliage medium green.

Laminuette. F. (Lammerts, 1969). 'Peace' × 'Rumba'. Ivory-white, tips of petals with red edge, double, some fragrance, long-lasting, profuse bloom; growth strong, bushy; foliage deep green, abundant, glossy. Greenhouse variety.

La Mortola. Cl. (Cecil Hanbury, 1954). Form of *Rosa brunonii*. White, single, 7 cm./2.8 in. across, strong fragrance, in very large trusses, profuse bloom; foliage more greyish-green, larger like the type. GiS 22; GSR 29.

'Landora' → **Sunblest**

Lanei. M. (Laffay, 1845). Rosy-crimson, tinged with purple, large, very double, fragrant, somewhat recurrent; buds somewhat mossy; growth upright, loose, medium. GSR 74. (7.8)

La Noblesse. C. (Soupert & Notting, 1857). Soft pink, very double, very fragrant, flowers later than most *centifolias*; 1 m./3.3 ft. high.

La Plus Belle des Ponctuées. G. Deep pink mottled with rose, 5 cm./2 in. across, double, loose; growth very strong, medium; foliage fresh green.

'La Presumida' → **Presumida**

'La Reine Victoria' → **Reine Victoria**

La Reine. HP. (Laffay, 1842). Deep pink, very large, double, globose, fragrant; growth strong; foliage medium size, deep green.

'La Rubanée' → **R. centifolia variegata, p. 257.**

La Tosca. HT. (Vve. Schwartz, 1901). 'Joséphine Marot' × 'Luciole'. Soft pink with darker reverse, large, 10 cm./4 in. across, open, cupped, fragrant, floriferous; growth strong, bushy; foliage deep green, leathery.

Laura. HT. (Meilland, 1969). (['Happiness' × 'Independence'] × 'Better Times') × ('Baccara' × 'White Knight'). Coral pink, large, double, high-centered, fragrant, free bloom; growth vigorous, upright, bushy; foliage leathery.

Laurent Carle. HT. (Pernet-Ducher, 1907). Crimson, large, cupped, fragrant, perfect shape, profuse bloom; growth strong; foliage deep green, glossy. RZ 1913:1.

Lavender Charm. HT. (Boerner/Jackson & Perkins, 1964). 'Brownie' × 'Sterling Silver'. Lilac-purple, large, 12 cm./4.8 in. across, double, fragrant; growth strong, bushy; foliage leathery, deep green. (6.7)

Lavender Girl. F. (Meilland, 1958). 'Fantastique' × ('Ampère' × ['Charles P. Kilham' × 'Capucine Chambard']). Interior purplish-pink, reverse magenta, then lilac, medium, 7 cm./2.8 in. across, double, cupped, fragrant, in clusters; growth low, 0.5 m./1.7 ft. (5.1)

Lavender Jewel. Min. (Ralph S. Moore, 1977). 'Little Chief' × 'Angel Face'. Mauve, high-centered, double, 35-40 petals, some scent, to 3-5 in clusters, abundant and continuous bloom all season; bud pointed; growth dwarf, bushy, compact; foliage small, abundant.

Lavender Lace. Min. (Ralph S. Moore, 1968). 'Ellen Poulsen' × 'Debbie'. Lavender-mauve, small, very double, rosette-shaped, fragrant, in clusters; growth dwarf, bushy; foliage pale green, small, glossy. CRA 73:57. (7.6)

Lavender Lace, Climbing. ClMin. (R.H. Rumsey, 1971). Sport of 'Lavender Lace'. Growth very vigorous, 1 m./3.3 ft. or over, otherwise like the type. RA 1972:97. (7.9)

Lavender Lassie. HMsk. (Kordes, 1959). 'Hamburg' × 'Mme. Norbert Levavasseur'. Pink with lilac, medium, 7 cm./2.8 in. across, double, or semi-double, globose, strong fragrance, in large trusses, recurrent; growth very strong, tall to very tall, branched. GiS 20; GSR 177. (6.0)

Lavender Pinocchio. F. (Boerner/Jackson & Perkins, 1948). 'Pinocchio' × 'Grey Pearl'. Mauve-purple with brownish-yellow center, intense color when opening, medium, 7 cm./2.8 in. across, semi-double, saucer-shaped, fragrant, profuse bloom in trusses; growth low, 0.5 m./1.7 ft.; foliage leathery. HBR 37; RA 1954:64. (5.5)

Lavendula. F. (Kordes, 1965). 'Magenta' × 'Sterling Silver'. Purplish-pink, opening more magenta, large, 10 cm./4 in. across, double, finally rather flat, fragrant, floriferous, in large trusses; bud ovoid; growth bushy, low, 0.5 m./1.7 ft. RJb 30:81. (7.2)

La Ville de Bruxelles. D. (Vibert, 1849). Pure pink, very large, very double, globose, nodding (from their weight!); growth strong, medium; foliage pale green, large. PGR 29.

'La Virginale' → **Maiden's Blush**

Lawrence Johnston. LCl. (Pernet-Ducher, 1923). 'Mme. Eugène Verdier' × 'Persian Yellow'. Yellow, medium, loosely double, floriferous, June, somewhat recurrent, in clusters; growth very strong, 4-6 m./13-20 ft. high; foliage luxuriant, glossy. GSR 211; TCR 7; GiS 23. (8.0)

Leda. (= 'Painted Damask'). D. Before 1827. Blush when completely open, with small eye, edge of outer petals crimson, medium, strong fragrance, globose, double, somewhat recurrent; bud red-brown; growth medium, 0.9 m./3 ft.; foliage deep green, large, ovate. TR 4. (8.0)

Lemon Delight. Min. M. (Ralph S. Moore, 1977). 'Fairy Moss' × 'Goldmoss'. Medium yellow, semi-double, 10 petals, sweet scent, abundant bloom all season; bud mossy with lemon scent, long-pointed; growth dwarf; foliage small, pointed.

Lemon Drop. Min. (Ralph S. Moore, 1954). (*R. wichuraiana* × 'Floradora') × 'Zee'. Yellow, very small, 2 cm./0.8 in. across, double, growth dwarf, 15 cm./6 in., very prickly; foliage very small.

Lemon Elegance. HT. (Jones, 1960). Lemon-yellow, large, 12 cm./4.8 in. across, double, fragrant, good shape, abundant bloom; long stems; growth vigorous, tall; foliage very small. (7.7)

Lemon Sherbet. HT. (J.J. Kern, 1974). Sport of 'Florence'. White with light yellow center, large, double, 35 petals, some scent, free bloom all season, long-lasting; bud ovoid; growth upright, medium; foliage large, leathery, medium green. (8.0)

Lemon Spice. HT. (Swim/Armstrong, 1966). 'Helen Traubel' × seedling. Pale yellow, large, double, strong fragrance, profuse bloom; bud long, pointed; growth spreading; foliage leathery. (7.0)

Leprechaun. F. (Max R. Adams, 1971). ('Easter Parade' × 'Masquerade') × 'Little Darling'. Opening yellow, then coral, pink and deep red, small, double, globose, some scent, very long-lasting, petals retained, free intermittent bloom; growth upright, 0.6 m./2 ft.; foliage glossy, disease-resistant. (6.4)

Le Rêve. LCl. (Pernet-Ducher, 1922). 'Mme. Eugène Verdier' × 'Persian Yellow'. Pale yellow, large, semi-double, scented, non-recurrent; growth very strong, up to 5 m./16.5 ft. high; foliage deep green, glossy. RZ 1927:38.

Leverkusen. K. (Kordes, 1954). *R. kordesii* × 'Golden Glow'. Pale yellow, large, finally flat, fragrant, early, recurrent; growth strong, 2-3 m./6.6-10 ft. PWR 224; GSR 248

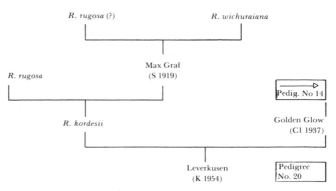

Liberty. HT. (Dickson, 1900). 'Mrs. W.J. Grant' × 'Charles J. Grahame'. Luminous velvety crimson, very large, very double, strong fragrance, profuse bloom, long stems; growth medium.

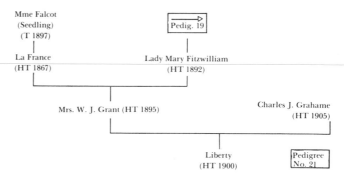

Liberty Bell. (= 'Freiheitsglocke'). HT. (Kordes, 1963). 'Detroiter' × Kordes Perfecta'. Interior luminous pure red with creamy reverse, very large, 12 cm./4.8 in. across, very double, globose, strong fragrance; growth strong, 0.8 in./2.6 ft.; foliage large, healthy. (4.6)

Lichterloh. F. (Tantau, 1955). 'Red Favorite' × 'New Dawn'. Velvety deep red, medium-large, semi-double, flat, some scent, many together in large trusses; growth strong, upright, 1 m./3.3 ft. or over; foliage deep green, leathery. (8.3)

'Liebestraum' → **Red Queen**

Lichtkönigin Lucia. S. (Kordes, 1966). 'Zitronenfalter' × 'Cläre Grammerstorf, Climbing'. Intense lemon-yellow with red stamens, large, 8 cm./3.2 in. across, double, several together in clusters on strong stems, profuse, recurrent; growth strong, medium, stems very prickly; foliage medium green, wrinkled.

Lilac Charm. F. (LeGrice, 1962). Selected from seedlings of *R. californica*. Soft lilac-lavender, large, single, 10 cm./4 in. across, filaments red with yellow anthers, some scent, fading with age; very free flowering; growth medium, 0.6 m./2 ft., bushy; foliage matt. GSR 439; WPR 24; RA 1961:144. (7.6)

Lilac Time. HT. (McGredy, 1956). 'Golden Dawn' × 'Luis Brinas'. Lilac-mauve, medium, double, fragrant; growth upright, 0.7 m./2.3 ft.; foliage pale green. PWR 3; RA 1956:128. (6.1)

Lilac Time. Min. (Ralph S. Moore, 1955). 'Violette' × 'Zee'. Lilac-pink to light red, finally lilac-tinted, small, double, free bloom; growth dwarf, 25 cm./10 in.

Lilibet. F. (Lindquist, 1953). 'Floradora' × 'Pinocchio'. Pure pink with lighter tints, medium, 6 cm./2.4 in. across, loosely double, fragrant, in loose trusses; growth low, 0.5 m./1.7 ft.; foliage glossy, green. (6.8)

Lillan. Min. (de Vink, 1958). 'Ellen Poulsen' × 'Tom Thumb'. Purplish-red, small, double; growth dwarf.

Lilli Marlene. (= 'Lilli Marleen'). F. (Kordes, 1959). ('Our Princess' × 'Rudolph Timm') × 'Ama'. Bright scarlet-crimson, velvety, large, 8 cm./3.2 in. across, loosely double, saucer-shaped, some fragrance, very profuse bloom, continuously in flower; growth bushy, 0.5 m./1.7 ft. or more, stems strong, upright; foliage reddish-green, matt, abundant. PWR 126; RA 1960:112; KR 9:96. (7.4)

Lily de Gerlache. HT. (Proefstation Melle, Belgium, 1971). 'Kordes Perfecta' × 'Prima Ballerina'. Cherry-red, fading with age, large, cupped, very double, singly on long stems; growth strong, tall; foliage deep green, glossy. CRA 73:1; RA 1972:14.

Lily Pons. HT. (Brownell, 1939). 'Glenn Dale' × 'Star-gold'. Outer petals white, center yellow, large, double, high-centered, fragrant, profuse bloom, long, strong stem; growth very vigorous; foliage glossy. (7.2)

Lissy Horstmann. HT. (Tantau, 1949). 'Hadley' × 'Heros'. Luminous crimson-scarlet, large, double, flat; growth vigorous, upright, strong stems. (6.5)

Little Buckaroo. Min. (Ralph S. Moore, 1956). (*R. wichuraiana* × 'Floradora') × ('Oakington Ruby' × 'Floradora'). Deep red with white center, small, double, flat, fragrant, profuse bloom; growth dwarf, 40 cm./16 in., bushy; foliage very glossy, young growth bronze. PWR 167; KR 9:139. (7.4)

Little Chief. Min. (Ralph S. Moore, 1971), 'Cotton Candy' × 'Magic Wand'. Medium red, semi-double, small, on short stems, long-lasting, petals drop off

cleanly, abundant, profuse bloom; growth dwarf, 15-20 cm./6-8 in.; foliage leathery, glossy, small. (6.6)

Little Curt. Min. (Ralph S. Moore, 1971). Seedling × 'Westmont'. Deep velvety red, small, open, semi-double, singly and several together on strong stems, abundant, continuous bloom; growth dwarf, 30-40 cm./12-16 in., vigorous, bushy; foliage deep green, healthy, leathery. (7.4)

Little Darling. F. (Duehrsen, 1956). 'Capt. Thomas' × ('Baby Château' × 'Fashion'). Yellow with soft salmon-pink, medium, 6 cm./2.4 in. across, double, cupped, fragrant, abundant bloom; growth very vigorous; foliage dark green, glossy, leathery. (8.8)

Little Dot. Min. (Origin unknown). White, double, small, 4 cm./1.6 in. across; growth dwarf, 20-30 cm./8-12 in. high. (7.1)

Little Fireball. Min. (Ralph S. Moore, 1968). (*R. wichuraiana* × 'Floradora') × 'New Penny'. Bright coral-red, small, double, fragrant, abundant bloom; bud ovoid; growth dwarf, compact, bushy. (7.7)

Little Flirt. Min. (Ralph S. Moore, 1961). (*R. wichuraiana* × 'Floradora') × ('Golden Glow' × 'Zee'). Bright red with yellow reverse, small, 4 cm./1.6 in. across, very double, some scent, floriferous; growth dwarf, 30 cm./12 in.; foliage pale green. (6.7)

Little Gem. M. (W. Paul, 1880). Bright crimson, tiny, double, very fragrant, very ruffled, in clusters; growth low, 0.5 m./1.7 ft., compact; bud mossy.

Little Girl. ClMin. (Ralph S. Moore, 1973). 'Little Darling' × 'Westmont'. Coral and salmon-pink, double, medium, long-lasting, singly and several together on long, strong stems, free continuous bloom; bud small, long; growth bushy, semi-climbing, 40-60 cm./16-24 in.; foliage small, deep green, glossy. (7.8)

Little Joker. Min. (Spek, 1958). Rose-pink with cream center, double, good shape; growth dwarf, bushy.

Little Juan. Min. (E.D. Williams, 1966). 'Juliette' × seedling. Medium red with lighter reverse, small, double, slight fragrance, abundant bloom; growth dwarf, vigorous; foliage small, leathery. (6.0)

Little Lady. Pol. (Harkness, 1967). 'Iceberg' × 'Baby Faurax'. White to blush, with some mauve hue, small, very double, fragrant; growth dwarf, 30 cm./12 in., bushy. (7.3)

Little Linda. Min. (Ernest Schwartz/Nor'east Mini-Roses, 1976). 'Gold Coin'-seedling × ?. Medium yellow, fading with age, semi-double, high-centered, singly, profuse, recurrent; bud pointed; growth dwarf; without prickles. ARA 62:1. (7.5)

Little Lisa. Min. (F. Harmon Saville, 1976). 'Fairy Moss' × self. Medium pink, semi-double, no scent, profuse bloom; bud pointed; growth low, compact; foliage medium green. (7.0)

Little Mike. Min. (Ralph S. Moore, 1967). ([*R. wichuraiana* × 'Floradora'] × seedling) × 'Little Buckaroo'. Deep red, small, double, high-centered, abundant bloom; bud ovoid; growth dwarf; foliage deep green, glossy, healthy. (6.8)

Little Red Devil. Min. (Christensen/Armstrong Nurseries, 1980). 'Gingersnap' × 'Magic Carrousel'. Medium red, slightly fragrant, double, small, 3.8 cm./1.5 in., free bloom; bud pointed-ovoid; foliage small; growth vigorous, bushy.

Little Scotch. Min. (Ralph S. Moore, 1958). 'Golden Glow' (LCl) × 'Zee'. Light yellow to white, medium, 4 cm./1.6 in. across, double, fragrant, free bloom; bud long; growth bushy, vigorous, 30 cm./12 in.; foliage leathery. (6.0)

Little Showoff. ClMin. (Ralph S. Moore, 1960). 'Golden Glow' (LCl) × 'Zee'. Bright yellow with red tint, small, 4 cm./1.6 in. across, double, high-centered to open, fragrant, abundant bloom; growth upright, 1-1.5 m./3.3-5 ft., bushy, vigorous. (6.5)

Little Sir Echo. Min. (Ernest Schwartz, 1977). 'Ma Perkins' × 'Baby Betsy McCall'. Medium pink, spiral, double, 50 petals, high-centered, singly and in clusters, long-lasting, recurrent; growth dwarf, upright; foliage yellow-green, matt. (8.0)

Little Sunset. Min. (Kordes, 1967). Seedling × 'Tom Thumb'. Yellowish salmon-pink, small, star-shaped, very double, profuse bloom; growth dwarf, 40 cm./16 in., dense; foliage pale green. (7.5)

Littlest Angel. Min. (E.W. Schwartz, 1976). 'Gold Coin'-seedling × seedling. Deep yellow, double, 30 petals, high-centered, some scent, singly and in clusters, very recurrent; growth very dwarf, bushy, compact. (7.5)

Lively. HT. (LeGrice, 1959). 'Wellworth' × 'Ena Harkness'. Rose-pink, large, 10-12 cm./4-4.8 in. across, double, 30 petals, very fragrant, free bloom; growth low, compact; foliage deep green, glossy.

Lively Lady. F. (Cocker, 1969). 'Elizabeth of Glamis' × 'Tropicana'. Brilliant vermilion, double, in clusters, some scent, very profuse bloom; growth medium, 0.6-0.7 m./2-2.3 ft.; foliage medium green, glossy.

Liverpool Echo. F. (McGredy, 1971). ('Little Darling' × 'Goldilocks') × 'München'. Rosy-pink, large, double, flat, some scent, many together in trusses; bud urn-shaped; growth upright, to 1 m./3.3 ft. high; foliage light green, abundant. (8.0)

Living Fire. F. (Gregory, 1972). 'Tropicana' × ?. Orange with golden-yellow base, double, 35 petals, some scent, several together; growth medium, upright; foliage deep green, semi-glossy. RA 1973:184.

Lolita. HT. (Kordes, 1972). 'Golden Wave' × 'Colour Wonder'. Bright coppery-gold, large, double, long-lasting, strong fragrance, growth strong, upright, vigorous stems; foliage abundant, young growth purple. (7.0)

Lollipop. Min. (Ralph S. Moore, 1959). (*R. wichuraiana* × 'Floradora') × 'Little Buckaroo'. Bright red, sometimes with white base, small, 3 cm./1.2 in. across, double, some scent; growth dwarf, 30 cm./12 in. (6.9)

Long John Silver. Cl. (Horvath, 1934). *Setigera*-seedling × 'Sunburst'. Silvery-white, large, open, double, many together in large trusses on strong stems; growth extremely strong, stems 3-4 m./10-13 ft. long or more; foliage large, firm.

Lord Charlemont. HT. (McGredy, 1922). Pure dark crimson, large, double, high-centered, good shape, strong fragrance; growth bushy; foliage deep green, leathery. RZ 1928:9.

Lord Penzance. S. (Penzance, 1894). *R. rubiginosa* × *R. harisonii*. Pink, shaded yellow, lighter than 'Lady Penzance', single, medium, non-recurrent; growth strong, 2 m./6.6 ft., stems very prickly; foliage small, scented. GSR 11; GiS 3.

Lori Nan. Min. (Ralph S. Moore, 1965). (*R. wichuraiana* × 'Floradora') × (seedling × 'Zee'). Rose-red, double, abundant bloom; bud globose, growth dwarf, moderate; foliage glossy, leathery. (6.0)

Lorna Doone. F. (Harkness, 1970). 'Red Dandy' × 'Lilli Marlene'. Crimson, scarlet, semi-double, some scent, large, several together, profuse bloom; foliage deep green; growth bushy, vigorous. CRA 72:81; RA 1971:161.

Lotte Günthart. HT. (Armstrong, 1974). 'Queen Elizabeth' × 'Bravo'. Purplish-red, large, very double, peony-shaped; bud ovoid, large; growth strong, upright, 0.5 m./1.7 ft.; foliage firm.

Louis Gimard. M. (Pernet Père, 1877). Lilac-red shaded with lilac and with lilac veins, very double, margin of petals revolved, fragrant; growth strong, medium; foliage deep green, pointed. (7.0)

Louis van Houtte. HP. (Larcharme, 1869). 'Général Jacqueminot' × ?. Deep velvety crimson with brownish shades, very large, globose, very double, good shape, strong fragrance, somewhat recurrent. RZ 1906:14. (5.5)

Louise Odier. B. (Margottin, 1851). Soft pink shaded with lilac, large, very double, fragrant, recurrent; growth strong, vigorous, tall; foliage light green, matt. GSR 97; PGR 54; GiS 12. (7.8)

Louise Cretté. HP. (C. Chambard, 1915). 'Frau Karl Druschki' × 'Kaiserin Auguste Viktoria, Climbing'. Pure white with creamy-white center, very large, 15 cm./6 in. across, double, high-centered, good shape, fragrant; growth very vigorous, bushy; foliage deep green. (5.0)

Louisiana. HT. (O.L. Weeks, 1974). Seedling × seedling. Creamy-white, double, 40 petals, high-centered, some scent, perfect shape, free, continuous bloom, singly on long stems; bud pointed; growth very vigorous, 1 m./3.3 ft.; foliage leathery, deep green. (7.0)

Love. Gr. (W.A. Warriner/Jackson & Perkins, 1980). Scarlet with silvery reverse, double, high-centered, very floriferous all season long; growth strong, upright; foliage deep green, glossy. ARA 1979:1.

Love Song. (= 'Liebeslied'). HT. (Fisher/Conard-Pyle, 1955). 'Peace' × 'Orange Nassau'. Interior pink, with deep creamy-yellow reverse, large, 12 cm./4.8 in. across, double, cupped; growth vigorous; foliage glossy. BTR 747. (4.5)

Lowell Thomas. HT. (Mallerin, 1943). 'Mme. Mélanie Soupert' × 'Nonin'. Deep yellow, large, double, 35-40 petals, high-centered; bud long, pointed; growth bushy, upright, compact; foliage leathery. (5.8)

Lowell Thomas, Climbing. ClHT. (Armstrong, 1954). Sport of 'Lowell Thomas'. Strong climber; otherwise like the type. (6.6)

Lucky Lady. Gr. (Swim/Armstrong, 1966). Interior soft pink, with darker reverse, large, double, some scent; bud long, pointed; growth vigorous; foliage deep green, glossy. (6.3)

Lucky Piece. HT. (Gordon, 1972). Sport of 'Peace'. Pink with copper and yellow, large, 12-15 cm./4.8-6 in. across, double, cupped, fragrant, abundant bloom; bud globose; growth very vigorous, bushy, compact; foliage leathery. (6.6)

Lucy Ashton. S. (*rubiginosa* hybrid). (Penzance, 1894). Pure white with soft pink edges, medium large, single, fragrant, several together in clusters, non-recurrent; growth strong, medium, stems very prickly; foliage scented.

Lucy Bertram. S. (*rubiginosa* hybrid). (Penzance, 1895). Deep crimson with white center, small, single, along the branches, non-recurrent; growth very strong, tall to very tall; foliage scented. PGR 89.

Lucy Kramphorn. (= 'Maryse Kriloff'). HT. (Kriloff, 1960). 'Peace' × 'Baccara'. Geranium-red, large, 12 cm./4.8 in. across, double, good shape, fragrant, floriferous; growth vigorous, upright, 0.8 m./2.6 ft.; foliage deep green with bronze. GSR 328; RA 1961:97; RJb 28:48. (7.8)

Lulu. F. (Kordes, 1973). 'Zorina' × seedling. Similar to 'Paddy McGredy'. Orange-pink, medium, double or semi-double, some scent, in clusters, petals drop off cleanly; growth vigorous, bushy; foliage healthy. (6.6)

Luminion. (= 'Rosi Mittermaier'). F. (Kordes, 1975). 'Hurra' × 'Peer Gynt'. Orange-red, double, 30 petals, some scent, in clusters, abundant, continuous bloom; bud globose; growth vigorous, upright; foliage glossy, deep green.

Lustige. HT. (Kordes, 1973). 'Peace' × 'Brandenburg'. Copper-red with yellow reverse, large, cupped, long-lasting, petals drop off cleanly, some scent, profuse, continuous bloom; bud large, ovoid; growth vigorous, upright, few prickles; foliage leathery, large, glossy.

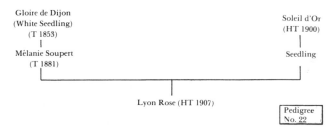

Lyon Rose. HT. (Pernet-Ducher, 1907). 'Mélanie Soupert' × 'Soleil d'Or'. Coral-red with yellowish center, large, very double, 45 petals, fragrant. RZ 1907:64.

Lyric. S. (de Ruiter, 1951). 'Sangerhausen' × seedling. Pure pink, semi-double, cupped, fragrant, in large trusses; growth vigorous, medium, foliage light green, large. GSR 180. (6.4)

Lys Assia. F. (Kordes, 1958). 'Spartan' × 'Hens Verschuren'. Orange-scarlet, semi-double, large, some scent, in large trusses, floriferous; growth low, bushy, 0.5 m./1.7 ft.; foliage reddish-green. (6.3)

Lysbeth-Victoria. F. (Harkness, 1978). 'Pink Parfait' × 'Nevada'. Shell pink with creamy base, semi-double, light fragrance, several together in clusters; free growth. RA 1979:81.

Mabel Dot. Min. (Dot, 1966). 'Orient' × 'Perla de Alcanada'. Rose-coral, small, double, open, in clusters, abundant bloom; foliage small, bronze. (7.1)

Mabel Morrison. HP. (Broughton, 1878). Sport of 'Baroness Rothschild'. Blush, then pure white, autumn flowers with pink hue, double, cupped, good shape, free bloom; growth upright, sturdy. (8.0)

'Mabella' → **New Day**

Mabelle Stearns. S. (Horvath, 1938). 'Mrs. F.F. Prentice' × 'Souvenir de Georges Pernet'. Pink with silvery hue, double, very fragrant, in clusters on long stems, recurrent; growth 0.6 m./2 ft. high, but to 2 m./6.6 ft. broad; foliage dark green, glossy, small. (5.8)

'Macrantha' → **Rosa macrantha**, p. 256.

Madelyn Lang. ClMin. (E.D. Williams, 1974). 'Little Darling' × 'Little Chief'. Deep pink, double, 40 petals, some scent, abundant bloom; growth upright, 0.6 m./2 ft. (or more, with support), few prickles; foliage dark green, small, glossy, healthy. (7.5)

Magenta. F. (Kordes, 1954). Yellow Floribunda-seedling × 'Lavender Pinocchio'. Lilac-pink, large, very double, flat, fragrant, many together in large trusses, sprawling a little from their weight; growth upright, vigorous, 0.7 m./2.3 ft., bushy; foliage deep green, leathery. PWR 134; GSR 181; GiS 16.

Magic Carrousel. Min. (Ralph S. Moore, 1972). 'Little Darling' × 'Westmont'. White edged with red or deep pink, small, double, singly or several together in strong stems, continuous bloom, some scent; growth

dwarf. Bushy, 30-40 cm./12-16 in. high; foliage small, healthy. RA 1977:60. (8.9)

Magic Dragon. ClMin. (Ralph S. Moore, 1969). ([*R. wichuraiana* × 'Floradora'] × seedling) × 'Little Buckaroo'. Dark red, double, several together, long-lasting, petals drop off cleanly; growth vigorous, 1.5-1.8 m./5-6 ft.; foliage leathery, medium, disease-resistant. (6.9)

Magic Mountain. F. (Armstrong, 1973). 'Circus' × 'Texan'. Golden yellow, becoming red, large, double, open, several together in clusters, long-lasting, petals retained, some scent; growth vigorous, bushy, low; few prickles.

Magic Wand. ClMin. (Ralph S. Moore, 1957). 'Eblouissant' × 'Zee'. Light red and dark pink, small, 2.5 cm./1 in. across, semi-double, in clusters, recurrent; growth arching to 1.2 m./4 ft. high, branches prickly; foliage dark green, small. (6.7)

Magna Charta. HP. (W. Paul, 1876). Pink overlaid with crimson, very large, double, globose, fragrant, recurrent; growth strong, medium; foliage very firm, light green. (6.5)

Magnifica. S. (*rubiginosa*). (Herm. A. Hesse, 1918). Seedling of 'Lucy Ashton'. Light red, semi-double, large, very profuse bloom, non-recurrent; growth very strong, 2-3 m./6.6-10 ft.

Mahogany. (= 'Mahagona'). HT. (Kordes, 1956). 'Golden Rapture' × 'Hens Verschuren'. Dull orange-red, very large, semi-double, open, fragrant, floriferous; growth bushy, upright, vigorous, 0.8 m./2.6 ft.; foliage fresh green, glossy, abundant. (5.5)

Maiden's Blush. A. Two forms:

1) 'Great Maiden's Blush. (= 'Cuisse de Nymphe'; 'Cuisse de Nymphe émue'; 'Incarnata'; 'La Séduisante'; 'Rosier Blanc Royal'; 'La Virginale'). White with blush hue, turning creamy pink at the edge, but always remaining blush in the center, large, double, fragrant, June, non-recurrent; growth strong, 2 m./6.6 ft. Somewhat arching stems; foliage grey-green. GSR 67; TR 3. Cultivated before the 15th century.

2) 'Small Maiden's Blush'. Soft flesh-pink, a little smaller than in the preceding variety, globose, fragrant, non-recurrent; growth lower, about 1.3 m./4.3 ft. high. Grown in Kew Gardens, 1797. (7.8)

Maigold. S. (Kordes, 1953). 'Poulsen's Pink' × 'Frühlingstag'. Golden yellow with orange-yellow hue, large, semi-double, open, strong scent, June-flowering, older plants may bloom again in autumn; growth strong, 2-2.5 m./6.6-8.3 ft.; stems very prickly; foliage glossy, healthy. GiS 21; GSR 151:249.

Mainauperle. HT. (Kordes, 1969). Seedling × 'Americana'. Deep red with scarlet, large, strong fragrance, very double, good shape, very resistant to weather damage; bud long, pointed; growth strong, upright, bushy, 0.7 m./2.3 ft.; foliage abundant. (6.6)

Maiwunder. S. (Kordes, 1966). 'Maigold' × Hybrid *rubiginosa*. Bright golden yellow with orange anthers, large, double, finally flat, strong scent; growth vigorous, branched, very prickly; foliage light green.

Majorette. (= 'Minna Lerche Lerchenborg'). HT. (Meilland, 1967). 'Zambra' × 'Fred Edmunds'. Bright salmon-pink with more yellow base, large, double, some scent, singly or several together; growth vigorous, upright; foliage firm, glossy. (5.7)

Malaga. LCl. (McGredy, 1971). ('Hamburger Phoenix' × 'Spectacular') × 'Copenhagen'. Interior salmon, with crimson reverse, large, 10 cm./4 in. across, double, strong fragrance, several together; growth vigorous, 2 m./6.6 ft. high; foliage large, deep green, glossy.

Mala Rubinstein. HT. (Dickson, 1971). 'Sea Pearl' × 'Fragrant Cloud'. Carmine-pink with darker reverse, double, strong scent, singly or several together; growth upright, vigorous; foliage dark green. CRA 73:49; RA 1972:176.

Malvina. M. (Verdier, 1841). Pure pink, medium, 6 cm./2.4 in. across, very double, fragrant, non-recurrent; calyx very mossy; growth bushy, 1 m./3.3 ft.

Maman Cochet. T. (S. Cochet, 1893). 'Marie van Houtte' × 'Mme. Lombard'. Pale pink with deeper center and yellow base, large, 10 cm./4 in. across, double, high-centered, fragrant; growth bushy, vigorous; foliage dark green, leathery. RA 1975:100. (7.0)

Mambo. F. (Swim/Armstrong, 1968). 'Charlotte Armstrong' × seedling. Deep red, medium, very double, some scent, in clusters on strong stems, profuse bloom; growth bushy, upright; foliage deep green, abundant.

Manitpu. HT. (Swim, 1957). Interior coppery-red, with golden yellow reverse, very large, good shape, profuse bloom; growth upright, bushy.

Manola. (= 'Fred Cramphorn'). HT. (Kriloff, 1961).

'Peace' × 'Baccara'. Geranium red, large, 12 cm./4.8 in. across, double, rounded petals, cupped, profuse bloom; growth strong, bushy; foliage firm, deep green. RJb 26:32. (7.7)

Manx Queen. F. (Dickson, 1963) 'Shepherd's Delight' × 'Circus'. Golden-yellow, flushed with orange-red, medium, semi-double, fragrant, in large, open trusses, free bloom; growth bushy, compact; foliage deep green.

Many Summers. HT. (Fryer, 1975). 'Arthur Bell' × 'Belle Blonde'. Orange-copper, double, 30 petals, very fragrant, singly and several together, free blooming; growth upright, medium; foliage healthy.

Maori Doll. Min. (Bell Roses, NZ, 1977). Sport of 'Yellow Doll'. Straw-yellow overlaid with pink, yellow base, very double, 60 petals, moderate scent, free bloom; growth dwarf, bushy, upright; foliage glossy.

Mascotte 77. (= 'Meitiloy'). HT. (Meilland, 1977). Seedling × 'Mme. A. Meilland'. Cardinal-red edges and yellow center, very double, abundant bloom; growth vigorous; foliage dense, glossy.

Ma Perkins. F. (Boerner/Jackson & Perkins, 1952). Soft pink, medium, 7 cm./2.8 in. across, double, fragrant, cupped, floriferous; growth medium, 0.7 m./2.3 ft. bushy; foliage medium. RA 1953:120. (7.7)

Marcel Bourgouin. G. (Corboeuf/Marsault, 1899). 'Blanche Moreau' × 'Abel Carrière'. Deep velvety scarlet-purple, mottled with violet, large, double, strong fragrance; growth medium, 0.7 m./2.3 ft.

Marcelle Gret. HT. (Meilland, 1947). 'Peace' × 'Prinses Beatrix'. Saffron-yellow, very large, 15 cm./6 in. across, double, fragrant; growth vigorous. (6.2)

Märchenland. F. (Tantau, 1951). 'Swantje' × 'Hamburg'. Pink with strong salmon hue, medium, semi-double, saucer-shaped, some scent, floriferous; growth bushy, spreading, 0.8 × 0.8 m./2.6 × 2.6 ft.; foliage medium. PWR 116.

Marchioness of Londonderry. HP. (Dickson, 1895). White with pale pink shades, very large, very double, globose, fragrant; growth very vigorous. (7.6)

Marchioness of Lorne. HP. (W. Paul, 1889). Rose-pink with darker shades, large, very double, very fragrant, free bloom; growth vigorous. (7.0)

Maréchal Davoust. M. (Robert, 1853). Bright crimson-pink, large, cupped to globose, double; bud with reddish moss; free flowering.

Maréchal Niel. N. (Pradel, 1864). Said to be a seedling of 'Chromatella; or of 'Isabella Gray'. Pale yellow, large, very double, globose, stalks weak, tea-scented, flowers nodding, floriferous; growth very strong; foliage light green. Hardy only in very mild areas; often grown in greenhouses. WGR 79. (7.6)

Marella. HT. (Meilland, 1961). ('Happiness' × 'Independence') × 'Better Times'. Deep salmon-red, large, double, some scent, very floriferous; bud large, ovoid; growth strong; foliage leathery, glossy. (6.6)

Margaret. HT. (Dickson, 1954). 'May Wettern'-seedling × 'Souvenir de Denier van der Gon'. Interior peach-pink, with silvery-pink reverse, turning bluish with age, medium, very double, fragrant; growth vigorous, 0.8 m./2.6 ft.; foliage matt, large. PWR 88; GSR 331; RA 1955:64.

Margaret Anne Baxter. HT. (T. Smith, 1927). 'Harry Kirk'-seedling. White with some flesh shades, large, very double, fragrant; bud pointed; growth bushy, very vigorous; foliage bronze, glossy, leathery. (4.5)

Margaret Chase Smith. HT. (H.C. Brownell, 1966). 'Red Duchess' × 'Queen Elizabeth'. Dark red, large, double, open, fragrant, profuse bloom; growth upright, vigorous. (6.4)

Margaret McGredy. HT. (McGredy, 1927). Parentage unknown. Orange-scarlet, very large, 15 cm./6 in. across, double; growth vigorous; foliage glossy, pale green.

Margaret Merril. F. (Harkness, 1977). Parentage not reported. Creamy-white with pale pink coloring, semi-double, 18 petals, very strong fragrance, free bloom, singly and several together; growth vigorous, sturdy, upright; foliage light green. RA 1979:85.

'Margaret Trudeau' → **Sweepstake**

Margo Koster. Pol. (D.A. Koster, 1931). Sport of 'Dick Koster'. Salmon-pink, small, ball-shaped, semi-double, some scent, in clusters; growth low, upright, 40 cm./16 in.; foliage light green. Mostly used for container-culture. GSR 446; WGR 147. (7.4)

Margo Koster, Climbing. ClPol. (Golia, 1962). Sport of 'Margo Koster'. Growth strong, semi-climbing, 1.5 m./5 ft. or over; otherwise like the type.

Margot Fonteyn. HT. (McGredy, 1964). 'Independence' × 'Ma Perkins'. Salmon-orange, large, 10 cm./4 in. across, double, fragrant, profuse bloom; growth upright, 1 m./3.3 ft.

Marguerite Hilling (= 'Pink Nevada'). HMoyesii. (Hilling, 1959). Sport of 'Nevada'. Deep pink with lighter center, large, 10 cm./4 in. across, semi-double or single, flat, very floriferous and recurrent; growth strong, spreading, 2 m./6.6 ft. GSR 178; RJb 36:61; HRo 27; GiS 2. (7.8)

Maria. F. (Gregory, 1965). Seedling × 'Border Beauty'. Orange-scarlet, large, 8 cm./3.2 in. across, single, some scent, profuse bloom, in clusters; growth vigorous, 0.9 m./3 ft.; foliage very large, firm. RA 1964:113.

Maria Stern. HT. (H.C. Brownell, 1969). 'Tip Toes' × 'Queen Elizabeth'. Orange, large, globose, fragrant, double, abundant bloom; bud pointed; growth very vigorous, upright. (7.7)

Marie Baumann. HP. (Baumann, 1863). Seedling of 'Alfred Colomb'. Crimson, large, globose, very double, fragrant; growth vigorous.

Marie de Blois. M. (Robert, 1852). Crimson-pink with lighter tints, curled, medium, good shape, floriferous and recurrent; calyx very mossy, reddish; growth strong, medium.

Marie d'Orléans. T. (Nabonnand, 1883). Deep red and pink, large, very double, fragrant, profuse bloom; very vigorous.

Marie Louise. D. Deep crimson-pink, large, very double, strong fragrance; growth bushy, 1 m./3.3 ft. (7.3)

Marie van Houtte. T. (Ducher, 1871). 'Mme. de Tartas' × 'Mme. Falcot'. Deep creamy-yellow suffused with pink, large, very double, fragrant; growth vigorous, with long stems; foliage firm, deep green.

Marilyn. Min. (Dot, 1965). 'Perla de Montserrat' × 'Bambino'. Dark pink, center purplish, small, double, in clusters; growth very compact, dwarf. (7.5)

Marina. F. (Kordes, 1974). 'Colour Wonder' × seedling. Orange, yellow base, medium, high-centered, long-lasting, fragrant, singly or several together, petals drop off cleanly, floriferous; growth vigorous, 0.6 m./2 ft., upright; foliage deep green, healthy, glossy, firm.

Marinette. F. (Boerner/Jackson & Perkins, 1971). Golden-yellow, double, large, finally flat, profuse bloom, some scent; growth low, 0.5 m./1.7 ft.

Marion Harkness. HT. (Harkness, 1978). (['Manx Queen' × 'Prima Ballerina'] × ['Chanelle' × 'Piccadilly']) × 'Piccadilly'. Yellow and orange-red, double, high-centered, large, very recurrent; growth strong, 0.9 m./3 ft.; foliage deep green, leathery.

Marita. F. (Mattock, 1961). 'Masquerade' × 'Serenade'. Orange-coppery, with yellow veins, medium, double, moderate bloom; growth upright, loose; foliage bronze-green. GSR 442.

Marjorie Fair. S. (Harkness, 1978). 'Ballerina' × 'Betty Faurax'. Deep red with light eye, single, in large trusses, very free bloom; growth upright, medium; foliage light green, matt. RA 1979:84.

Marjoria Proops. HT. (Harkness, 1969). 'Red Dandy' × 'Ena Harkness'. Crimson, medium, double, fragrant, singly or several together, floriferous; growth medium, 0.7 m./2.3 ft.; foliage medium green.

Marlena. F. (Kordes, 1964). 'Gertrud Westphal' × 'Lilli Marlene'. Scarlet to brilliant crimson, medium, semi-double, open, resistant to weather damage, profuse, continuous bloomer; growth bushy, 35-40 cm./14-16 in.; foliage abundant. GSR 443; RJb 30:129. (8.3)

Marmalade. HT. (Swim & Weeks, 1976). 'Arlene Francis' × 'Bewitched'. Bright orange with deep yellow reverse, becoming pink with light yellow reverse with age, double, 30 petals, strong fragrance, singly and several together, long-lasting; growth upright; foliage large, deep green.

Marquesa de Urquijo. HT. (Camprubi, 1940). ('Sensation' × 'Julien Potin') × 'Feu Joseph Looymans'. Interior yellow, with deep orange-red reverse, large, double, fragrant, moderate bloom; growth bushy, 0.6 m./2 ft.; foliage large, glossy.

Marquise Bocella. HP. (Deprez, 1842). Soft pink, medium, very double, very fragrant. (7.6)

Mary. Pol. (Qualm, 1947). Sport of 'Orange Triumph'. Differing by the smaller. more orange flowers, otherwise like the type.

Mary Adair. Min. (Ralph S. Moore, 1966). 'Golden Glow' × 'Zee'. Apricot blend, small, double, fragrant, abundant bloom; growth dwarf, bushy, vigorous; foliage light green, soft. (8.0)

Mary Haywood. Min. (Ralph S. Moore, 1957). (*R. wichuraiana* × 'Floradora') × 'Oakington Ruby'. Pink with white base, small, 2.5 cm./1 in. across, double, fragrant, free bloom; growth dwarf, compact, 25 cm./10 in.; foliage glossy. (6.1)

Mary Kittel. HT. (R.E. Harvey, 1975). 'Chrysler Imperial' × 'Night n' Day'. Dark red, double, large, high-centered, strong fragrance, singly, free bloom all season; bud large, pointed; growth very vigorous, upright; foliage leathery, dark green. (7.5)

Marylène. HT. (Gaujard, 1965). 'Mignonne' × 'Queen Elizabeth'. Pure pink, medium, double, fragrant, long stems; growth bushy, 0.5 m./1.7 ft.; foliage bronze-green. (5.8)

Mary Mine. S. (Harkness, 1971). 'Queen Elizabeth' × 'Buccaneer'. Salmon-pink and rose, large, 10 cm./4 in. across, double, several together, some scent, recurrent; growth strong, medium.

'Maryse Kriloff' → **Lucy Cramphorn**

Mary Wallace. LCl. (Van Fleet, 1924). *R. wichuraiana* × pink HT. Deep pink, very large, semidouble, cupped, non-recurrent, profuse bloom; growth vigorous, 2.5-3 m./8.3-10 ft.; foliage glossy-green. ARA 1924:FP. (7.8)

Mary Marshall. Min. (Ralph S. Moore, 1970). 'Little Darling' × 'Fairy Princess'. Orange-blend, double, good form, small, long-lasting; growth dwarf, bushy; foliage disease-resistant, deep green. (8.7)

Marytje Cazant. Pol. (van Nes, 1927). Sport of 'Jessie'. Coral-pink, semi-double, small, 3.5 cm./1.4 in. across, slight fragrance, in clusters; bud globose; growth dwarf; foliage small, soft, glossy. (6.9)

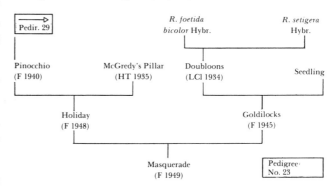

Masquerade. F. (Boerner/Jackson & Perkins, 1949). 'Goldilocks' × 'Holiday'. Opening golden-yellow, turning first to salmon-pink, finally deep red, medium large, 5 cm./2 in. across, semi-double, flat, open, very floriferous, faint scent; growth strong, bushy, 0.6 m./2

ft.; foliage glossy. PWR 100; GSR 444. (7.6)

Matador. (= 'Esther Ofarim'). F. (Kordes, 1970). 'Colour Wonder' × 'Zorina'. Brilliant orange, reverse with a flush of orange and yellow, medium, rosette-shaped, double, long-lasting, singly or several together on long stems, 0.5 m./1.7 ft. high; foliage light green, matt. GSR 409; KR 10:120. (8.2)

Matangi. F. (S. McGredy/McGredy Roses International, 1974). Unnamed seedling × 'Picasso'. Red, base shaded with yellow, slightly fragrant, double, open, large, 9 cm./3.5 in., very free bloom; bud ovoid; foliage small; growth bushy.

Matterhorn. HT. (Armstrong & Swim, 1965) 'Buccaneer' × 'Cherry Glow'. Pure white, medium to large, double, floriferous; bud long; growth vigorous; foliage firm, leathery. (6.3)

Maurice Chevalier. F. (Delbart/Chabert, 1959). 'Incendie' × ('Floradora'-seedling × 'Independence'). Luminous velvety-red, large, double, fragrant, singly or several together, floriferous; growth bushy, low, 45 cm./18 in.; foliage healthy. RJb 25:64.

Mauve Melodee. HT. (Raffel, 1962). 'Sterling Silver' × seedling. Lavender-pink, 10 cm./4 in. across, semi-double, finally flat, floriferous, on long stems; growth vigorous, upright; foliage leathery. (6.7)

Max Colwell. Min. (Ralph S. Moore, 1975). (Red seedling × 'Little Darling') × seedling. Orange-red with darker tips, double, 30 petals, some scent, profuse bloom, in clusters, recurrent all season; growth dwarf, spreading; foliage medium green, leathery, glossy. (7.5)

Max Graf. S. HRg. (Bowditch, 1919). Probably *R. rugosa* × *R. wichuraiana*. Pink, medium, single, yellow center, profuse bloom, non-recurrent, very rarely sets hips; growth bushy, long stems, trailing, excellent groundcover; foliage very similar to *R. rugosa*. GiS 15. (7.2)

Maxi. F. (McGredy, 1971). ('Irish Wonder' × ['Tantau's Triumph' × *R. coryana*]) × ('Hamburger Phoenix' × 'Spectacular'). Red with white eye, medium large, 7 cm./2.8 in. across, semi-double, some scent, several together, very profuse bloom; growth upright; foliage large, medium green.

May Queen. R. (W.A. Manda, 1898). *R. wichuraiana* × 'Champion of the World'. Pink, very double, quartered,

fragrant; growth tall, 6 m./20 ft. or over (with support). (8.4)

Maytime. S. (G. J. Buck, 1975). 'Elegance' × 'Prairie Princess'. Carmine-rose with yellow base, looks apricot, semi-double, 6-10 petals, cupped, moderate scent, in clusters, blooming all season; growth bushy, upright, 0.8 × 0.8 m./2.6 × 2.6 ft.

McGredy's Ivory. HT. (McGredy, 1930). 'Mrs. Charles Lamplough' × 'Mabel Morse'. Creamy-white with yellow base, very large, double, high-centered, fragrant; bud long, pointed; growth vigorous; foliage dark green, glossy, leathery. (5.8)

McGredy's Sunset. HT. (McGredy, 1936). 'Margaret McGredy' × 'Mabel Morse'. Orange with yellow base, reverse buttercup-yellow, large, double, globose, opening flat, fragrant; growth vigorous; foliage bronze, glossy. (5.7)

McGredy's Yellow. HT. (McGredy, 1933). 'Mrs. Charles Lamplough' × ('The Queen Alexandra Rose' × 'J.B. Clarke'). Medium yellow, large, double, cupped, slightly fragrant; bud long, pointed; growth vigorous; foliage bronze-green, glossy. RA 1931:61. (6.2)

Mécène. G. (Vibert, 1845). White, striped with lilac-pink, medium, double, flat, non-recurrent; stems with few prickles.

Medallion. HT. (Warriner/Jackson & Perkins, 1973). 'South Seas' × 'King's Ransom'. Apricot-yellow, very large, double, finally flat, fragrant, long-lasting; bud very long, pointed; growth very vigorous, 1.6 m./5.3 ft. high, stems with few prickles; foliage large, abundant. ARA 1973:1. (7.6)

Meg. LCl. (Gosset, 1954). 'Paul's Lemon Pillar' × 'Mme. Butterfly'. Light pink, center apricot-yellow, very large, 13 cm./5.2 in. across, semi-double, saucer-shaped, some scent, profuse bloom in June. Somewhat recurrent in autumn; growth very vigorous, 3-4 m./10-13 ft.; foliage leathery. PWR 215; GSR 250.

Megiddo. F. (Gandy, 1970). 'Coup de Foudre' × 'S' Agaró'. Scarlet, medium, semi-double, several together, profuse bloom; growth strong, 0.6 m./2 ft.; foliage large, deep green. RA 1971:129; GSR 447. (5.4)

Mellow Yellow. HT. (Waterhouse Nurs., 1968). Sport of 'Piccadilly'. Yellow with pink edge, medium, semi-double, singly; growth bushy; foliage medium green, glossy. RA 1970:96; GSR 334; CRA 71:32.

Melrose. F. (Dickson). 'Silver Lining' × 'E.G. Hill'. Creamy-yellow, reverse side and edge overlaid with cherry-red, medium, 8 cm./3.2 in. across, double, fragrant; growth bushy, vigorous; foliage deep green. (7.2)

Memento. F. (Dickson, 1978). 'Bangor' × 'Anabell'. Salmon-vermilion with carmine-rose reverse, double, 20 petals, some scent, in clusters, flowering all season long; growth bushy; foliage medium green, abundant. RA 1979:83.

Memoriam. HT. (Von Abrams, 1961). ('Blanche Mallerin' × 'Peace') × ('Peace' × 'Frau Karl Druschki'). Creamy-white with soft pink center, very large, 15 cm./6 in. across, double, fragrant, star-shaped, floriferous; growth bushy, vigorous, 0.7 m./2.3 ft.; foliage deep green. WPR 44; RA 1961:113. (6.7)

Memory Lane. Min. (Ralph S. Moore, 1973). ('Pinocchio' × 'William Lobb') × 'Little Chief'. Medium rose-pink, very double, small, long-lasting, some scent, petals hang on, abundant, continuous bloom; growth vigorous, dwarf, 25-30 cm./10-12 in.; foliage leathery. (7.1)

Mercedes. F. (Kordes, 1974). 'Anabell' × seedling. Bright scarlet, double, 35 petals, some scent, high-centered, long-lasting; growth very free; foliage large, leathery. Greenhouse variety.

Merci. F. (Warriner/Jackson & Perkins, 1971). Seedling × seedling. Deep red, medium, double, some fragrance, very long-lasting, petals drop off cleanly, singly or several together on long stems; growth strong, medium. Greenhouse variety. (8.0)

Merlin. F. (Harkness, 1967). 'Pink Parfait' × 'Circus'. Golden-yellow, heavily splashed with red and yellow, medium, 6 cm./2.4 in. across, double, some scent, floriferous; growth compact, bushy, low, 0.5 m./1.7 ft.; GSR 448; RA 1968:48. (7.0)

Mermaid. HBr. (W. Paul, 1918). *R. bracteata* × yellow double Tea Rose. Pale yellow, very large, 12-15 cm./4.8-6 in. across, single, fragrant, petals drop off, sterile, anthers brown, continuous bloom in warm areas; growth very strong, 5-7 m./16.5-23 ft. or over; foliage deep green, large, glossy. GSR 252; PWR 217. Only for mild regions.

Merrie Miss. HT. (Mrs. Fuller/Wyant, 1975). 'Pink Fa-

vorite' × 'Margaret'. Soft rose-pink with lighter reverse, very double, 60 petals, fragrant, singly and several together, intermittent bloom; bud long; growth dwarf, bushy, upright; foliage deep green, dull. (6.5)

Merry England. HP. (Harkness, 1897). Light red with carmine shades, double, very fragrant; growth vigorous.

Merry Widow. F. (Lammerts, 1958). 'Mirandy' × 'Grande Duchesse Charlotte'. Velvety crimson, very large, 15 cm./6 in. across, double, flat, cupped, fragrant, strong stems; foliage glossy, deep green. (7.4)

Merveille de Lyon. HP. (Pernet Père, 1882). Sport of 'Baroness Rothschild'. Pure white with rose hue, large, 10 cm./4 in. across, double, cupped, somewhat recurrent bloom.

'Message' → **White Knight**

Meteor. F. (Kordes, 1959). 'Feurio' × 'Gertrud Westphal'. Orange-scarlet, medium, double, cupped, later flat, no scent, many together; growth bushy, low, 40 cm./16 in.; foliage large, yellow-green, abundant. KR 10:32; RA 1959:161. (5.8)

Metropole. HT. (de Ruiter, 1961). 'Sidney Peabody' × 'Peace'. Bright pink, large, 10 cm./4 in. across, double, globose, fragrant, on strong stems; growth vigorous; foliage matt green. (6.9)

Mexicana. HT. (Boerner/Jackson & Perkins, 1966). 'Kordes Perfecta' × seedling. Bright red with silvery-white reverse, large, high-centered, fragrant, floriferous; growth vigorous, upright; foliage very large, red-green, glossy. (6.7)

Miami Holiday. Min. (E. Williams/Mini-Roses, 1976). Seedling × 'Over the Rainbow'. Red blend, double, 60 petals, fragrant, abundant bloom, very recurrent; growth dwarf, bushy, upright; foliage small, firm, glossy. (7.5)

Michèle Meilland. HT. (Meilland, 1945). 'Joanna Hill' × 'Peace'. Blush with soft tints of salmon and yellow-orange in the center, large, double, fragrant; growth vigorous, upright, 0.8 m./2.6 ft.; foliage light green, matt. PWR 39; HBR 2. (7.4)

Michelle. F. (de Ruiter, 1968). Seedling × 'Orange Sensation'. Salmon-pink with darker reverse, medium, double, fragrant, many together in clusters; growth vigorous, 1.1 m./3.6 ft.; foliage small, light green, matt. RA 1969:177; GSR 450; CRA 70:161.

Midget. Min. (de Vink, 1941). 'Ellen Poulsen' × 'Tom Thumb'. Deep crimson, small, 2 cm./0.8 in. across, double, flat, some scent, stems short; growth very dwarf; foliage tiny. PWR 165. (7.5)

Mignonette. Pol. (Guillo Fils, 1880). *R. chinensis* × *R. multiflora*, F$_2$-generation. Blush to white, very small, double, 30-40 together in trusses, very profuse bloom; growth dwarf. RZ 1887:5.

Mignonne. HT. (Gaujard, 1962). 'Mme. Butterfly' × 'Fernand Arles'. Deep salmon-pink, large, double, fragrant, profuse bloom; bud long; growth vigorous; foliage firm. (6.8)

Milord. HT. (McGredy, 1962). 'Rubaiyat' × 'Karl Herbst'. Scarlet, very large, 12-15 cm./4.8-6 in. across, double, finally flat, fragrant; growth vigorous; foliage deep green, abundant. RA 1963:96. (7.1)

Mimi. Min. (Meilland, 1965). 'Moulin Rouge' × ('Fashion' × 'Perla de Montserrat'). Crimson-pink, small, 3 cm./1.2 in. across, very double, flat-cupped, some scent; growth dwarf, 30 cm./12 in.; foliage tiny, deep green.

Mimi Coertse. F. (Herholdt, 1963). 'Queen Elizabeth' × 'Constantia'. Crimson-pink, large, 10 cm./4 in. across, double; growth upright, strong.

Minigold. F. (Tantau, 1970). 'Whisky Mac' × 'Zorina'. Pure golden-yellow, medium, 6 cm./2.4 in. across, double, fragrant, several together, long-lasting; growth strong; foliage deep green, healthy. Greenhouse variety.

Minnehaha. R. (Walsh, 1905). *R. wichuraiana* × 'Paul Neyron'. Pink, becoming white with age, small, double, fragrant, in large trusses, non-recurrent; growth strong, 3-4 m./10-13 ft.; foliage small, deep green, glossy. PWR 227.

Minnie. Min. (E.D. Williams/Mini-Roses, 1977). 'Starburst' × 'Over the Rainbow'. Red, double, 40 petals, some scent, singly, free, intermittent bloom; growth upright, few prickles; foliage small, glossy.

Minnie Francis. T. (Griffing, Noisette Farm, 1905). Deep pink, open, very large, double, fragrant; growth upright, 1 m./3.3 ft.

Minuetto. Min. (Meilland, 1971). ('Rimosa' × 'Josephine Wheatcroft') × 'Zambra'. Orange-red, turning to salmon-red, center and reverse yellow, small, 4 cm./1.6

in. across, semi-double, some scent, in clusters, profuse bloom; growth bushy, 30-40 cm./12-16 in.; foliage small, glossy.

Miranda. D. (De Sansal, 1869). Satin pink, large, 8 cm./3.2 in. across, semi-double, fragrant, recurrent; growth upright, medium.

Mirandy. HT. (Lammerts/Armstrong, 1945). 'Night' × 'Charlotte Armstrong'. Deep red, with more crimson edge, very large, 15 cm./6 in. across, double, globose, strong fragrance, very resistant to weather damage; growth upright, 0.7 m./2.3 ft.; foliage firm. SWR 64. (6.1)

Mischief. HT. (McGredy, 1961). 'Peace' × 'Spartan'. Salmon-pink, large, double, fragrant, floriferous; growth vigorous, upright, 0.7 m./2.3 ft.; foliage light green, healthy. PWR 59; GSR 335; RA 1961:65. (7.5)

Miss All-American Beauty. (= 'Maria Callas'). (Meilland, 1965). 'Chrysler Imperial' × 'Karl Herbst'. Crimson-pink, large, double, cupped, strong fragrance, floriferous; growth bushy, upright, 0.7 m./2.3 ft.; foliage firm. GSR 332. (8.3)

'Miss Harp' → **Oregold**

Miss Hillcrest. HT. (E.C. Curtis, 1969). 'Peace' × 'Hawaii'. Orange-red, large, double, high-centered, very fragrant, abundant bloom; growth bushy, upright; foliage glossy.

Mission Bells. HT. (Morris, 1949). 'Mrs. Sam McGredy' × 'Mälar-Ros'. Salmon-pink, large, double, fragrant, floriferous; growth vigorous, bushy, 0.8 m./2.6 ft.; foliage large, reddish, abundant. (7.1)

Miss Ireland. HT. (McGredy, 1961). 'Tzigane' × 'Independence'. Salmon-red with orange-yellow and lighter reverse, medium, double, fragrant, profuse bloom, very long-lasting; growth bushy, medium, 0.6 m./2 ft.; foliage deep green. PWR 43; RA 1961:145. (7.0)

Mississippi. HT. (J.B. Williams, 1976). 'Charlotte Armstrong' × 'Mister Lincoln'. Deep red, double, 40 petals, fragrant, singly on strong stems, very recurrent; bud pointed; growth upright, strong; foliage large, semi-glossy.

Missy. Min. (Lyon, 1978). Cardinal-red, slightly fragrant, double, small, 3.8 cm./1.5 in., free bloom; bud pointed; foliage small; growth compact, bushy.

Mistee. Min. (Ralph S. Moore, 1979). 'Little Darling' ×

'Peachy White'. White, double, 25-30 petals, high-centered, finally flat, singly or 3-5 in clusters, fragrant, abundant bloom all season; growth dwarf, bushy, very branched, no prickles; foliage small, abundant, semi-glossy.

Mister Lincoln. (Swim & Weeks, 1964). 'Chrysler Imperial' × 'Charles Mallerin'. Deep red, large, 10-15 cm./4-6 in. across, double, cupped to globose, fragrant, floriferous, long stems; growth sturdy upright, bushy, 0.8 m./2.6 ft.; foliage dull, firm, very disease-resistant. GSR 336; GR 16. (8.5)

Misty. HT. (Armstrong, 1976). 'Mount Shasta' × 'Matterhorn'. Pure white in bud, opening to creamy-white, double, 35 petals, cupped, fragrant, in clusters on long stems, profuse bloom all season; bud long-pointed; growth very vigorous, upright, disease-resistant; foliage large, leathery, semi-glossy. (6.5)

Mme. Abel Châtenay. HT. (Pernet-Ducher, 1895). 'Dr. Grill' × 'Victor Verdier'. Bright pink with deeper center, reverse crimson-pink, medium large, double, fragrant; bud pointed; young growth bronze. RZ 1897:42

Mme. Alfred Carrière. N. (J. Schwartz, 1897). Intermediate between Noisette and Tea Roses. Flesh, tinted creamy-white, finally nearly white, very double, globose, strong fragrance, nearly always in flower during the season; growth very strong, can reach 6 m./20 ft. or more on a wall; foliage light green. SOR 35; GiS 23. (7.6)

'Mme. A. Meilland' → **Peace**

Mme. Bollinger. F. (McGredy, 1972). ('Little Darling' × 'Goldilocks') × 'Bobbie Lucas'. Coppery-red, with more yellow center and reverse, double, medium, floriferous, in clusters, early; growth bushy, 0.6 m./2 ft.; foliage medium green.

Mme. Bravy. (= 'Adèle Pradel'; 'Alba Rosea'). T. (Guillot Père, 1846). Creamy-white with more pink center, very double, medium, good shape, finally flat, cupped, very strong scent, floriferous; growth vigorous. RZ 1890:65; RA 1975:54. Tender.

Mme. Butterfly. HT. (Hill, 1918). Sport of 'Ophelia'. Soft pink with yellow hue, medium, good shape, strong scent, often many together; growth medium, 0.6 m./2 ft., bushy. SRW 66. (6.3)

Mme. Caroline Testout. HT. (Pernet-Ducher, 1890).

'Mme. de Tartas' × 'Lady Mary Fitzwilliam'. Soft pink with darker center, edge more crimson-pink, large, double, globose, strong fragrance; growth upright, 0.6 m./2 ft.; foliage light green, matt. RZ 1894:101; WGR 105.

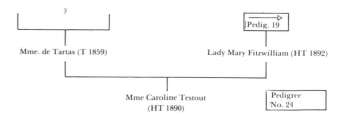

Mme. de la Roche-Lambert. M. (Robert, 1851). Purple-pink, medium, 7 cm./2.8 in. across, fragrant, non-recurrent, sepals with green moss, branches with brown moss; growth vigorous, medium; foliage soft, green.

Mme. de Sansal. D. (Portland). (de Sansal, about 1850). Cherry-red and salmon-pink.

Mme. Edouard Herriot. HT. (Pernet-Ducher, 1913). 'Mme. Caroline Testout' × Hybrid Tea. Orange-yellow with pink and scarlet, large, semi-double, fragrant; growth spreading, 0.5 m./1.7 ft.; foliage bronze-green, glossy, medium. RZ 1917:77; RA 1915:110.

1913	Mme. Edouard Herriot
1916	Morgenstern
1918	Sunny Jersey Scarlet
1918	Golden Glow
1918	Florence Chenoweth
1919	Georges Clémenceau
1919	Evening Star ———————— → 1935 A Night in June
1921	Climbing Mme. Edouard Herriot
1924	Mme. Herriot panaché
1924	Lady Elphinstone
1924	Schleswig-Holstein
1925	Countess of Elgin
1925	Professor Schmeil
1925	Dilly's Wiederkehr
1926	Andrée Aubriot
1926	Ernst Clauberg
1927	Evening News
1929	Konrad Thönges
1930	Gruss an Föhr
1933	Gretelein

The spontaneous sports of 'Mme. Edouard Herriot'. (after Saakov)

Mme. Edouard Ory. M. (Moreau-Robert, 1854). Vivid crimson-pink, large, globose, double, recurrent; calyx mossy; growth strong, medium.

Mme. Emilie Charron. T. (Perrier, 1896). Pink, cupped, large, fragrant, very floriferous; strong growth.

Mme. Ernest Calvat. (= 'Pink Bourbon'). B. (Vve. Schwartz, 1888). Sport of 'Mme. Isaac Pereire'. Deep pink, very double, globose, fragrant, recurrent; growth bushy, medium. WGR 97; GiS 12. (7.8)

Mme. G. Staechelin. (= 'Spanish Beauty'). LCl. (Dot, 1927). 'Frau Karl Druschki' × 'Château de Clos Vougeot'. Pink, reverse stained with crimson, very large, open, ruffled, fragrant, on long stem, non-recurrent; growth very vigorous, 3-3.5 m./10-11.5 ft.; foliage large, deep green.

Mme. Georges Bruant. HRug. (Bruant, 1887). *R. rugosa* × 'Sombreuil'. Creamy-white, fading to white, double, silky, not always good shape, anthers yellow, floriferous in summer, singly or in clusters, somewhat recurrent; growth strong, medium to tall, stems very prickly; foliage wrinkled, light green. RZ 1906:72.

Mme. Hardy. D. (Hardy, 1932). Pure white, sometimes with flesh pink shade and greenish center, very double, inner petals incurved, outer ones reflexed, camellia-like shape, very strong fragrance; growth strong, upright, medium. Very beautiful old variety. PWR 179; HRo 20; GiS 6. (9.0)

Mme. Henry Guillot. HT. (Mallerin, 1938). 'Rochefort' × seedling of *R. foetida bicolor*. Orange and red, very large, double, slightly fragrant; growth very vigorous, bushy; foliage glossy.

Mme. Henry Guillot, Climbing. ClHT. (Meilland, 1942). Sport of 'Mme. Henry Guillot'. Growth strong, climbing, 2.5-3 m./8.3-10 ft.; otherwise like the type. (6.8)

Mme. Isaac Pereire. B. (Garçon, 1881). Deep rose with magenta shade, large, very double, strong fragrance, June-flowering, recurrent; growth very strong, to 3 m./10 ft. stems very prickly; foliage large. PWR 201; GSR 98; GiS 12; RA 1976:180. (8.4)

Mme. Jean Dupuy. T. (Lambert, 1902). Golden yellow with pink shades, large, very double, fragrant, floriferous; bud long; growth vigorous. RZ 1905:1.

Mme. Jules Bouché. HT. (Croibier, 1911). 'Pharisäer' × seedling. White with blush center or more creamy-white, large, double, fragrant; bud pointed; growth upright, 0.6 m./2 ft. WGR 109. (6.6)

Mme. Julien Potin. HRg. (Gravereaux, 1913). *R. rugosa* × 'Gloire de Dijon'. Flesh pink, large, double, flat, recurrent; growth vigorous; foliage very leathery. (6.8)

Mme. Legras de St. Germain. A. (Before 1848). Ivory-white with soft yellow center, very large, very double, finally flat, fragrant; growth strong, medium to tall, stems nearly without prickles; foliage grey-green. (8.7)

Mme. Louis Laperrière. HT. (Laperrière, 1951). 'Crimson Glory' × seedling. Dark crimson and scarlet, medium, double, 40 petals, fragrant, floriferous; growth compact, bushy, 0.6 m./2 ft., stems strong; foliage deep green. GSR 329; PWR 56. (6.8)

Mme. Lombard. T. (Lacharme, 1878). 'Mme. de Tartas'-seedling. Rosy-salmon with darker center, large, very double, fragrant; growth strong. (7.6)

Mme. Louis Lévêque. M. (Lévêque, 1898). Luminous salmon-pink, large, globose, fragrant, sometimes recurrent; calyx mossy; growth vigorous, medium. WGR 81. (7.6). A Hybrid Perpetual (1874) and a Tea Rose (1892) also bear this name. All three are from the same breeder.

Mme. Moreau. M. (Moreau-Robert, 1872). Vermilion with white stripes, very large, double. A red Hybrid Perpetual (Gonod-Moreau, 1864) and a Tea Rose (Moreau-Robert, 1889) also bear this name.

Mme. Norbert Levavasseur. (= 'Red Baby Rambler'). Pol. (Levavasseur, 1903). 'Crimson Rambler' × 'Gloire des Polyantha'. Crimson with lighter center, semi-double, becomes very blue, small, cupped, some scent, in large trusses together; growth low, 40 cm./16 in.

Mme. Pierre Oger. B. (Oger/Verdier, 1878). Sport of 'Reine Victoria'. Cream shaded with rosy pink, deepening with age, medium, 7 cm./2.8 in. across, globose-double, fragrant, recurrent; growth upright, medium, dark prickles. WGR 67; PGR 54; GiS 12; GSR 100. (7.4). One of the best varieties in the group.

Mme. Plantier. A. (Plantier, 1835). *R. alba* × *R. moschata*-seedling (?). Creamy-white, fading to pure white with green eye, small, double, strong fragrance, many together, non-recurrent; growth vigorous, 2-3 m./6.6-10 ft., arching; foliage light green. PWR 181; PGR 36; GiS 7. (8.0)

Mme. Sancy de Parabère. B. (Bonnet, 1874). Pure pink, very large, 12 cm./4.8 in. across, double, outer petals much larger than inner ones, some scent, non-recurrent; growth vigorous, 3-4 m./10-13 ft., stems completely without prickles; foliage light green, matt. GSR 214; TCR 3; RZ 1888:5.

Mme. Scipion Cochet. T. (Bernaix, 1872). 'Anna Olivier' × 'Duchesse de Brabant'. Flesh pink to white, yellow center, large, very double, cupped, floriferous, several together, pedicels weak. (7.3)

Mme. Soupert. M. (Moreau-Robert, 1851). Red; medium large, double, fragrant, 2-5 together in clusters, non-recurrent; calyx mossy.

Mme. Victor Verdier. HP. (Verdier, 1863). 'Sénateur Vaisse' × ?. Bright crimson, very double, large, flat, strong scent, somewhat recurrent; growth strong. (5.0)

Mme. Zoetmans. D. (Marest, 1830). Flesh-pink, sometimes with light purplish-pink hue, center greenish, fragrant, non-recurrent; growth medium, medium-high; foliage light green, abundant. GSR 82.

Modern Times. HT. (Verbeek, 1956). Sport of 'Better Times'. Deep red with white stripes, double, medium, some scent, moderate bloom; growth vigorous, upright, 0.8 m./2.6 ft.; foliage large, green-red. (5.3)

Mogador. (= 'Roi des Pourpres'). D. 'Rose du Roi' × ?, or sport of 'Rose du Roi'. Crimson, often with purple shades, medium, double.

Mojave. HT. (Swim/Armstrong, 1954). 'Charlotte Armstrong' × 'Signora'. Apricot-orange with peach and carmine, large, 10 cm./4 in. across, double, some scent, moderate bloom; growth medium, branched, 0.6 m./2 ft.; foliage glossy, healthy. PWR 46; GSR 338; LR 12. (7.6)

Molly McGredy. F. (McGredy, 1969). 'Paddy McGredy' × ('Mme. Léon Cuny' × 'Colombine'). Scarlet with silvery reverse, margin more red, large, double, finally flat, petals drop off cleanly, some scent; growth strong, 0.9 m./3 ft.; foliage deep green, healthy. RA 1969:3; GSR 451. (7.4).

Mona Ruth. Min. (Ralph S. Moore, 1959). (['Soeur Thérèse' × Skyrocket] × [seedling × 'Red Ripples']) × 'Zee'. Rose-pink to rose-red, small, 3.5 cm./1.4 in. across, double, some scent, free bloom; growth dwarf, vigorous, 30-40 cm./12-16 in.; foliage leathery. (6.8)

Monique. HT. (Paolino, 1949). 'Lady Sylvia' × seedling. Pink to salmon-pink, fading with age, large, dou-

ble, good shape, fragrant; growth strong, 0.9 m./3 ft.; foliage light green, pointed. PWR 29.

Mon Petit. Min. (Dot, 1947). 'Merveille des Rouges' × 'Pompon de Paris'. Light red and dark pink, very double, very free bloom; growth dwarf, compact; foliage pointed. (6.4)

Monte Carlo. HT. (Meilland, 1949). 'Peace' × seedling. Orange-yellow with coppery-orange shades, especially at the edge, large, 12 cm./4.8 in. across, double, fragrant, good shape; growth bushy, sometimes one-sided, 0.6 m./2 ft.; foliage medium, glossy. SRW 73.

Montezuma. F. (Swim/Armstrong, 1955). 'Fandango' × 'Floradora'. Deep salmon-red, large, 8-10 cm./3.2-4 in. across, double, several together, slight fragrance; growth bushy, compact, 0.8 m./2.6 ft.; foliage red-green, matt, very resistant to Black Spot. GSR 339; PWR 72. (7.7)

Mood Music. Min. (Ralph S. Moore, 1977). 'Fairy Moss' × 'Goldmoss'. Orange-apricot with pink, double, 45 petals, some scent, singly and in clusters, continuous bloom all season; growth upright, dwarf, much branched; foliage medium green, abundant, semi-glossy. (7.5)

Moonlight. HMsk. (Pemberton, 1913). 'Trier' × 'Sulphurea'. Yellowish-white, medium, semi-double, flat, anthers golden yellow, fragrant, very recurrent; growth strong, medium; foliage deep green, young growth wine-red. GSR 121.

Moon Maiden. F. (Mattock, 1970). 'Fred Streeter' × 'Allgold'. Creamy-yellow, semi-single, large, flat, in large trusses, fragrant; growth medium, vigorous, upright; foliage firm, semi-glossy. GSR 453.

Moonraker. F. (Harkness, 1968). 'Pink Parfait' × 'Highlight'. Creamy-yellow, fading to nearly white, large, some scent, in clusters, floriferous, resistant to weather damage; growth bushy, 0.8 m./2.6 ft.; foliage light green. RA 1968:49.

Moonsprite. F. (Swim/Armstrong, 1956). 'Sutter's Gold' × 'Ondine'. Pale yellow with darker center, finally nearly white, inner petals incurved, outer ones flat, fragrant, profuse bloom, many together; growth medium, bushy, low, 40 cm./16 in.; foliage medium green, matt.

Morletii. (= 'Inermis Morletii'). Boursault-type. (Molret,

1883). *R. pendulina* × ?. Magenta, medium, double, faint or no scent, June-flowering, profuse, non-recurrent; growth strong, 3 m./10 ft., stems without prickles; young growth coppery-red; orange-red autumn coloring.

Morgengruss. K. (Kordes, 1962). *R. kordesii* × 'Cleopatra'. Soft pink and orange-yellow, large, 10 cm./4 in. across, double, flat, strong fragrance, recurrent; growth vigorous, 3-4 m./10-13 ft.; foliage light green, glossy. KR 9:96; RJb 24:128. (9.0)

Morning Dawn. LCl. (Boerner/Jackson & Perkins, 1955). 'New Dawn'-seedling × 'R.M.S. Queen Mary'. Blush with salmon shade, large, 12 cm./4.8 in. across, double, globose, fragrant, singly or several together; growth strong, 3 m./10 ft.; foliage deep green, firm, glossy. (7.2)

Morning Jewel. LCl. 'New Dawn' × 'Red Dandy'. Glowing pink, large, fragrant, several together, semi-double, 8 cm./3.2 in. across, flowering all season long; growth strong, 2.5 m./8.3 ft.; foliage healthy, glossy.

Morning Sun (= 'Morgensonne'). S. (Kordes, 1954). 'Harmonie' × 'Goldilocks'. Golden-yellow, very large, semi-double, flat, fragrant, anthers orange; growth very strong, 2 m./6.6 ft.; foliage light green, glossy.

Morning Stars. S. (Jacobus, 1949). ('New Dawn' × 'Autumn Bouquet') × ("New Dawn' × 'Inspiration'). White, medium, 7 cm./2.8 in. across, double, cupped, fragrant, in clusters, recurrent; growth compact, bushy. (8.5)

Moss Magic. (Sudol, 1977). 'Fairy Moss' × ?. Medium to dark pink, slightly fragrant, double, circular, flat, small, 2.5 cm./1 in., profuse bloom, very recurrent; bud cupped, mossy; foliage dark; growth spreading.

Mossman. S. (Skinner, 1954). (*R. acicularis* × *R. rugosa*) × Moss Rose. Pale pink, medium large, 6 cm./2.4 in. across, very double, very fragrant, profuse bloom; bud heavily mossed; growth vigorous, 1.2 m./4 ft.

Mothersday. (= 'Muttertag'). Pol. (F.J. Grootendorst, 1950). Sport of 'Dick Koster'. Bright red, small, double, up to 20 in trusses, globose; growth bushy, low, 35 cm./14 in.; foliage light green. Widely used for container culture and early forcing under glass. (7.7)

Mount Everest. Hybrid or form of *Rosa pendulina*, with larger flowers and hips; growth stronger.

Mount Shasta. Gr. (Swim & Weeks, 1963). 'Queen Eliz-abeth' × 'Blanche Mallerin'. Pure white, large, 10-12 cm./4-4.8 in. across, double, cupped, fragrant, free bloom; bud long, pointed; growth very vigorous, upright; foliage grey-green, leathery. (7.7)

'Mousseline' → **Alfred de Dalmas**

Mousseux Ancien. M. (Vibert, about 1825). Pink with crimson center; calyx well mossed.

Mousseux de Japon. M. Pink with purple, semi-double or double, loose, fragrant, non-recurrent, buds and tips of branches very mossy; growth medium, 1 m./3.3 ft., new growth very red. GSR 75.

Mozart. HMsk. (Lambert, 1937). 'Robin Hood' × 'Rote Pharisäer'. Bright red with large, white eye, edge darker, small, single, fragrant, in large trusses, recurrent; growth bushy, medium. WGR 67.

Mr. Bluebird. Min. (Ralph S. Moore, 1960). 'Old Blush' × self. Lavender-blue, small, semi-double, 3.5 cm./1.4 in. across, floriferous; growth dwarf, 35 cm./14 in.; foliage small. PM 22. (7.2) Easily grown from cuttings.

Mr. Chips. HT. (Dickson, 1970). 'Grandpa Dickson' × 'Miss Ireland'. Yellow with orange, edge with pink shades, very large, semi-double, floriferous; growth vigorous; foliage glossy. (5.3)

Mr. Standfast. HT. (Harkness, 1968). 'Golden Wave' × 'Kordes Perfecta'. Creamy-yellow, large, very double, some scent, floriferous, singly; growth bushy, upright; foliage abundant, glossy.

Mrs. Anthony Waterer. HRug. (Waterer, 1889). *R. rugosa* × 'Général Jacqueminot'. Deep crimson with pink, large, 9 cm./3.6 in. across, semi-double to single, some scent, somewhat recurrent; growth strong, medium, bushy. GSR 133. (7.7)

Mrs. B.R. Cant. T. (B.R. Cant, 1901). Silvery-rose, base suffused with buff, reverse deep rose, double, cupped, fragrant, long stems; growth very vigorous. (8.7)

Mrs. Dudley Cross. T. (W. Paul, 1907). Pale chamois-yellow with crimson, very double, slightly fragrant; growth vigorous, branches without prickles. (7.1)

Mrs. F.W. Sandford. HP. (Curtis, 1898). Sport of 'Mrs. John Laing'. Pink tinged with white, very large, double, globose, very fragrant; tall. (7.5)

Mrs. John Laing. HP. (Bennett, 1887). Seedling of

'Francois Michelin'. Soft pink, very large, very double, globose, strong fragrance, floriferous; bud pointed; growth upright, 1 m./3.3 ft., stems slender, bristly, sometimes spreading (needs support); foliage light green. GSR 112; WGR 125; PGR 72; GiS 13. (7.1)

Mrs. Luther Burbank. HT. (Swim, 1954). 'Christopher Stone' × 'Charlotte Armstrong'. Rose-pink, large, double, cupped, very fragrant, abundant bloom; bud long, pointed; growth very vigorous; foliage leathery. (7.0)

Mrs. Myles Kennedy. T. (Dickson, 1906). Soft silvery-white with blush hue, center darker and more salmon-yellow, large, double, recurrent and profuse bloom; growth strong, climbing. Tender.

Mrs. Paul. B. (Paul, 1891). 'Mme. Isaac Pereire' × ?. Blush, large, double, fragrant, recurrent; growth medium, medium high.

Mrs. Pierre S. du Pont. HT. (Mallerin, 1929). ('Ophelia' × 'Rayon d'Or') × ('Ophelia' × ['Constance' × 'Souvenir de Claudius Pernet']). Golden yellow, medium large, double, fragrant, floriferous; bud reddish; growth medium, bushy; foliage light green. SWR 70. (5.3)

Mrs. R.M. Finch. Pol. (Finch, 1923). 'Orléans Rose' × ?. Rosy pink, fading with age, medium, double, in large clusters, profuse bloom; growth bushy.

Mrs. Sam McGredy. HT. (McGredy, 1929). ('Donald McDonald' × 'Golden Emblem') × (seedling × 'The Queen Alexandra Rose'). Scarlet coppery-orange, reverse flushed with red, large, double, high-centered, fragrant, long stems; foliage reddish-bronze, glossy. RA 1934:250. (6.7)

Mrs. Sam McGredy, Climbing. (Buisman, 1937). Sport. Good climber, 2.5-3 m./8.3-10 ft. high; otherwise like the type. (7.6)

Mrs. Whitman Cross. HTCl. (C.W. Cross, 1943). 'Nanjemoy' × 'Marion Cran'. Orange-apricot with pinkish hue, reverse sometimes striped rose-pink, large, semi-double, open, fragrant; growth tall, climbing, 2.5-3 m./8.3-10 ft. high; foliage soft, glossy.

Mrs. W.J. Grant. (= 'Belle Siebrecht'). (Dickson, 1895). 'La France' × 'Lady Mary Fitzwilliam'. Light pink, fading to purplish, double, fragrant; bud long, pointed. Famous old variety.

'Mullard Jubilee' → **Electron**

Multiflore de Vaumarcus. N. (Menet, 1875). Soft pink,

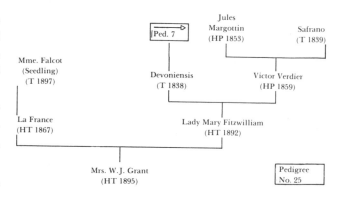

very double, medium large, in large trusses, continuous bloom; growth bushy, medium, foliage healthy.

'Muscosa' → **Rosa centifolia muscosa**, p. 259.

Music Maker. S. (G.J. Buck, 1973). 'Polynesian Sunset' × 'Prairie Princess'. Bicolor rose-colored, fading, double, high-centered, fragrant, in clusters, long-lasting, abundant bloom; growth vigorous, medium, 0.9 × 0.9 m./3 × 3 ft.; foliage leathery, healthy, glossy. (7.2)

'Musk Rose' → **Rosa moschata**, p. 284.

'Mutabilis' → **Rosa chinensis mutabilis**, p. 291.

My Choice. HT. (LeGrice, 1958). 'Wellworth' × 'Ena Harkness'. Interior deep pink with scarlet, reverse yellow, large, 12 cm./4.8 in. across, double, strong scent, floriferous; growth vigorous, 0.8 m./2.6 ft.; foliage light green, glossy. GSR 341; WPR 18. (5.8)

My Fancy. F. (Meilland, 1970). ('Dany Robin' × 'Fire King') × 'Rumba'. Vermilion, medium large, 7 cm./2.8 in. across, rosette-shaped, double, in large trusses, continuous bloom, some scent; growth bushy; foliage medium large, deep green, matt.

Mystère. F. (Gaujard, 1970). Salmon-red with yellow base, large, double, high-centered, several together on strong stems; growth bushy, low, 0.5 m./1.7 ft.; foliage deep green.

Mysterium. F. (Kordes, 1963). 'Masquerade' × 'Kordes Perfecta'. Golden-yellow, suffused and striped with scarlet, medium, 7 cm./2.8 in. across, double, some scent, very floriferous; growth low, bushy, 0.5 m./1.7 ft.; foliage deep green, glossy. RJb 26:224. (6.7)

My Valentine. Min. (Ralph S. Moore, 1975). 'Little Chief' × 'Little Curt'. Red, double, high-centered, in clusters, long-lasting, abundant bloom, recurrent all season; bud short, pointed; growth vigorous, dwarf, rounded; foliage small, glossy, green. ARA 60:122. (8.0)

Nana Mouskouri. F. (A. Dickson, 1975). 'Redgold' × 'Iced Ginger'. White, fragrant, double, full, ovate, large, 6.4 cm./2.5 in., very free bloom.

Nancy Hall. Min. (Ralph S. Moore, 1972). Sport of 'Mary Adair'. Pink with yellow and apricot, double, high-centered, fragrant, singly and several together, long-lasting, abundant, continuous bloom; growth dwarf, 25 cm./10 in.; foliage light green, soft, small. (7.3)

Nantucket. HT. (J.J. Kern, 1972). Sport of 'Chantré'. Peachy-apricot, double, high-centered, some scent, petals drop off cleanly, free, continuous bloom; growth vigorous, upright, compact, 0.9 m./3 ft., few prickles; foliage leathery, medium, disease-resistant. (8.4)

'Nastarana' → **R. moschata nastarana,** p. 286.

National Trust. HT. (McGredy, 1970). 'Irish Wonder' × 'King of Hearts'. Bright red, large, very double, some scent, floriferous, singly and several together; growth bushy, vigorous, 0.9 m./3 ft.; foliage bronze-green, matt. RA 1971:112; GSR 342; CRA 72:64. (7.5)

Navigator. Cl. (Verhalen, 1925). *R. soulieana* × 'Radiance'. Rose-red, cupped, semi-double, 25 petals, on long stems; bud globose; growth very strong; foliage matt.

Nébuleuse. F. (Gaujard, 1971). Scarlet, double, flat, in large trusses; growth strong, 0.8 m./2.6 ft.

Nearly Wild. F. (Brownell, 1941). 'Dr. W. van Fleet' × 'Leuchtstern'. Rosy-pink, single, open, fragrant, long stems; bud small, long, pointed; growth bushy. 0.7 m./2.3 ft. (6.7)

Nevada. HMoyesii. (Dot, 1927). 'La Giralda' × *R. moyesii* (?). Nearly pure white, very large, 10 cm./4 in. across, single to semi-double, no scent, profuse bloom in June, somewhat recurrent; growth about 2.5 × 2.5 m./8.3 × 8.3 ft., stems arching; foliage light green. GSR 179; PWR 195; TRT 192; RA 1975:55. (8.4)

New Dawn. LCl. (Somerset Nursery, 1930). Sport of 'Dr. W. van Fleet'. Like the original variety, but continuous bloom; blush, double, fragrant, medium, floriferous; growth strong, 4 m./13.2 ft., arching; foliage small, deep green, glossy. This rose received the U.S. Plant Patent No. 1. GSR 216; PWR 228. (7.9)

New Day. (= 'Mabella'). HT. (Kordes, 1972). 'Roselandia' × 'Arlene Francis'. Lemon-yellow, double, perfect shape, strong fragrance, cupped; bud long, pointed; growth strong, upright; foliage deep green, abundant. ARA 61:1. (7.5)

New Penny. Min. (Ralph S. Moore, 1962). (*R. wichuraiana* × 'Floradora') × seedling. Coppery salmon-pink, small, 3.5 cm./1.4 in. across, semi-double, fragrant, floriferous; growth bushy, dwarf, 25-30 cm./10-12 in.; foliage deep green. (7.5)

Neue Revue. (= 'Korrev'). HT. (Kordes, 1969). 'Colour Wonder' × 'Liberty Bell'. Creamy-white with broad scarlet edge, large, double, very fragrant, profuse bloom; bud long; growth strong, branched; foliage deep green, leathery. KR 10:10. (6.0)

News. F. (LeGrice, 1968). 'Lilac Charm' × 'Tuscany Superb'. Rich purple-red (a new color!), medium large, nearly single, edge slightly waved, some scent, many together in large trusses, continuous bloom; growth bushy, upright, 0.7 m./2.3 ft.; foliage medium green, matt. RA 1970:33; GSR 454; CRA 71:64.

New Yorker. HT. (Boerner/Jackson & Perkins, 1947). 'Flambeau' × seedling. Velvety scarlet, large, 10 cm./4 in. across, double, faint scent, not resistant to weather damage; growth bushy, vigorous, 0.7 m./2.3 ft.; foliage rounded, red-green, matt. BTR 21. (5.9)

Nightingale. HT. (Herholdt, 1970). 'Rina Herholdt' × 'Tiffany'. Pink, large, double, fragrant, high-centered; growth medium; foliage deep green.

Night Time. HT. (O.L. Weeks, 1975). Parentage not given. Dark black-red, double, high-centered, strong fragrance, petals drop off cleanly, abundant intermittent bloom; bud large, pointed; growth very vigorous, upright; foliage dark green, large.

Nigrette. HT. (Krause, 1934). 'Château de Clos Vougeot' × 'Lord Castlereagh'. Blackish-brown to blackish-red, nearly completely black with age, medium, semi-double, poor bloomer, some scent; growth low, 40 cm./16 in.; foliage small, bluish-green. ARA 1935:96.

Nina Weibull. F. (Poulsen, 1962). 'Fanal' × 'Masquerade'. Deep red, medium large, very double, in trusses; growth bushy, compact.

Noblesse. HT. (Jan Spek, 1969). 'Coloranja' × self. Orange-red, very large, fragrant, some scent, moderate bloom; growth medium; foliage large, glossy.

Nocturne. HT. (Swim, 1947). 'Charlotte Armstrong' × 'Night'. Dark red and crimson, large, 11 cm./4.4 in. across, cupped, fragrant, growth very vigorous, upright, bushy; foliage deep green, leathery. (6.1)

Nora Hooker. F. (Hooker/Harkness, 1970). Sport of 'Queen Elizabeth'. Red, large, 10 cm./4 in. across, floriferous, several together, some scent; growth tall, 1.2 m./4 ft.; foliage medium green.

Nordia. F. (Poulsen, 1968). ('Pinocchio' × self) × 'Elsinore'. Scarlet, medium, double, good shape, singly and several together; growth vigorous, bushy, low, 0.5 m./1.7 ft.; foliage deep green, glossy. GSR 452.

Norita. HT. (Combe/Vilmorin, 1966). Blackish velvety-red, large, double, some scent, continuous bloom, somewhat star-shaped; growth upright, 0.5 m./1.7 ft.; foliage large, deep green.

Norman Hartnell. HT. (Kordes, 1964). 'Ballet' × 'Detroiter'. Crimson, large, semi-double, good shape, free bloom; growth very vigorous; foliage deep green. (7.1)

Norris Pratt. F. (Buisman, 1964). 'Mrs. Pierre S. du Pont' × 'Marcelle Gret'. Deep golden-yellow, medium, double, star-shaped, floriferous; growth bushy, low, 45 cm./18 in.; foliage large, light green.

Northern Lights. HT. (Cocker, 1971). 'Fragrant Cloud' × 'Kingcup'. Creamy-yellow with some pink shades, double, perfect shape, very fragrant, good bloomer; growth medium, 0.8-0.9 m./2.6-3 ft.; foliage deep green, glossy.

Nouvelle Europe. F. (Gaujard, 1964). 'Miss France' × 'Vendôme'. Orange-scarlet with lighter reverse, medium, resistant to weather damage, floriferous; bud long; growth bushy, low, 0.5 m./1.7 ft.; foliage bronze-green.

Nova. F. (Harkness, 1967). 'Ann Elizabeth' × 'Paprika'. Orange-scarlet, semi-double, some scent, in clusters, floriferous; foliage deep green, glossy.

Nova Red. Min. (Ralph S. Moore, 1964). Seedling × 'Little Buckaroo'. Crimson, small, semi-double, in clusters, growth dwarf, bushy. (6.9)

Nova Zembla. HRug. (H.W. Mees/Ruys, 1906). Sport of 'Conrad Ferd. Meyer'. Flesh-pink to nearly white, large, 10 cm./4 in. across, double, finally flat, floriferous, non-recurrent; growth strong, 2.5 m./8.3 ft. high; foliage firm, deep green. GiS 15. (9.1)

Nozomi. ClCh. (Onodera, Japan, 1968). 'Fairy Princess' × 'Sweet Fairy'. Pearl pink, single, small, flat, fragrant, many together in clusters; growth broad, trailing without support, very good groundcover; foliage very small, glossy. RA 1972:113; CRA 73:55.

Nuits d'Young. M. (Laffay, 1845). Very deep velvety black-purple with brownish tints, rather small, non-recurrent, fragrant; bud with brownish-red moss; growth medium, 1 m./3.3 ft., stems slender; foliage small, deep green, with a coppery shimmer. PGR 53; GiS 9. (7.7) Famous old rose named for "Night Thoughts" by the 18th century English poet Edward Young. (after G.S. Thomas)

Nuria de Recolons. HP. (Dot, 1933). 'Canigo' × 'Frau Karl Druschki'. White, large, very double, good form, slight fragrance; foliage dense.

Nymphenburg. HMsk. (Kordes, 1934). 'Sangerhausen' × 'Sunmist'. Orange-yellow and pink, edge deeper pink, center more yellow, very large, semi-double, flat, fragrant, flowers all summer, in trusses; growth upright, bushy, medium high; foliage glossy. GSR 183; PWR 206; TRT.

Oakington Ruby. Min. (Bloom, 1933). Ruby-crimson with white center, small, 2.5-3 cm./1-1.2 in. across, double; growth dwarf, 30 cm./12 in. (6.0)

Oakmont. HP. (May, 1893). Deep pink with lighter reverse, in clusters, recurrent.

Oberon. F. (Dickson, 1955). 'Nymph' × seedling. Salmon-orange, medium, 6 cm./2.4 in. across, some scent, floriferous; growth bushy, short stems; foliage small, glossy. RA 1957:136. (5.6)

Oeillet Flammand. G. (Vibert, 1845). Pale pink, mottled and striped with white, medium large, very double, flat, strong fragrance; growth vigorous. RZ 1892:37.

Oeillet Panaché. (= 'Striped Moss'). M. (Verdier, 1888). Soft pink, with broad and narrow crimson stripes, rather small, flat; growth poor, 0.8 m./2.6 ft. Known as 'Striped Moss' in England since 1790.

Oeillet Parfait. G. or D. (Foulard, 1841). Pale pink, deepening with age, with dark and light crimson stripes, medium, very double, finally flat, fragrant, 2-3 together on sturdy stems, non-recurrent; growth compact, bushy, branched, 1 m./3.3 ft.; foliage small, rounded, matt.

'Officinalis' → **R. gallica officinalis**, p. 256.

Oklahoma. HT. (Swim & Weeks, 1964). 'Chrysler Imperial' × 'Charles Mallerin'. Blackish-red, large, 12 cm./4.8 in. across, very double, strong fragrance; bud very long; growth bushy; foliage firm, deep green. (7.1)

Old Blush. (= 'Parson's Pink China'). S. Belonging to *R. chinensis*. From China, cultivated in England since about 1793. Blush, semi-double, medium large, faint scent, in large trusses, sometimes somewhat recurrent; strong growth, 1-1.2 m./3.3-4 ft. high. Flowering from June to October. SOR 21. (7.8)

Old Gold. HT. (McGredy, 1913). Vivid reddish-orange with coppery and apricot shades, semi-double, short stems; growth medium, 0.6 m./2 ft.; foliage dark green. (6.6)

Old Smoothie. HT. (O.L. Weeks, 1970). Rich red to medium dark red, medium, double, good form, profuse bloom; growth tall, vigorous, without prickles; foliage deep green, disease-resistant. (6.7)

Oldtimer. (= 'Old Time', 'Coppertone'). HT. (Kordes, 1969). 'Chantré' × 'Bronze Masterpiece'. Deep orange-yellow with darker shades in the center, large, double, some scent; growth bushy, double; foliage medium green, abundant. (7.4)

Olé. Gr. (Armstrong, 1964). 'Roundelay' × 'El Capitan'. Vermilion, medium, very double, flat, floriferous, good form; growth bushy, strong stems, 0.6 m./2 ft.; foliage deep green, young growth red, glossy. GSR 456; RJb 28:80. (7.7)

Olympic Torch. HT. (Suzuki, Japan, 1960). 'Rose Gaujard' × 'Crimson Glory'. White and red, finally all red, medium, double, high centered, abundant bloom; bud long, pointed; growth very vigorous; foliage bronze, glossy, leathery. (6.5)

Olympic Triumph. F. (Dickson, 1972). 'Shiralee' × 'Apricot Nectar'. Salmon-orange, double, large, finally flat, faint scent, singly or in clusters; growth upright, 0.7 m./2.3 ft.

Omar Khayyam. D. Pale pink, medium, double, strong fragrance, quartered, inner petals incurved; growth strong, 1 m./3.3 ft. Raised from seed from the grave of Omar-i-Chajjam (Omar-Khayyam), a poet who lived 1048-1131 in Nischapur, Persia. This rose, presumably raised in Kew Gardens, was planted in 1893 on the grave of Edward Fitzgerald, who translated the work of Omar-i-Chajjam. (5.3)

Opal Jewel. Min. (Morey, 1962). 'Mothersday' × 'Rosy Jewel'. Medium pink with darker center, small, 2.5 cm./1 in. across, double, open, slight fragrance, free bloom; bud ovoid; growth dwarf, compact, 20-30 cm./8-12 in.; foliage leathery. (8.2)

Opéra. HT. (Gaujard, 1950). 'La Belle Irisée' × seedling. Scarlet with yellow center, 15 cm./6 in. across, double, fragrant; growth strong, branched; foliage large, light green, glossy, abundant. PWR 15. (6.9)

Ophelia. HT. (W. Paul, 1912). Light pink, nearly white, yellow center, medium, fragrant, perfect form, long stems; growth bushy, 0.8 m./2.6 ft.; foliage medium green, matt. RA 1924:126. (6.8)

Orangeade. F. (McGredy, 1959). 'Orange Sweetheart' × 'Independence'. Pure orange, large, semi-double, some scent, flat, in large trusses; growth vigorous, 0.7-0.8 m./2.3-2.6 ft., bushy; foliage deep green. PWR 131; GSR 459; RA 1960:80. (8.0)

Orange Cascade. ClMin. (Ralph S. Moore, 1979). Seedling × 'Magic Wand'. Orange, semi-double, 10-20 petals, some scent, intermittent bloom all season; growth upright, slender; foliage small, fern-like.

Orange Elf. ClMin. (Ralph S. Moore, 1959). 'Golden Glow' × 'Zee'. Orange, fading with age, double, open, slightly fragrant, free bloom; growth vigorous, climbing or ground cover. (5.8)

Orange Everglow. LCl. (Brownell, 1942). Sport of 'Copper Glow'. Orange with red and yellow shades, medium, 7 cm./2.8 in. across, double, fragrant, abundant seasonal bloom; growth vigorous, climbing; foliage almost evergreen, glossy. (7.2)

Orange Fire. Min. (Ralph S. Moore, 1974). (*R. wichuraiana* × 'Floradora') × 'Fire Princess'. Vermilion with orange, turning to orange-pink and carmine-rose, double, 40 petals, singly and in clusters, abundant bloom; bud short; growth dwarf, 20-30 cm./8-12 in., upright; foliage very glossy, leathery, healthy. (7.0)

Orange Garnet. F. (Swim & Weeks, 1965). ('Garnette' × 'Circus') × 'Spartan'. Orange-red, small, double, floriferous, long stems; growth bushy, vigorous; foliage firm, deep green. Greenhouse variety.

Orange Honey. Min. (R.S. Moore/Sequoia Nursery,

1979). 'Rumba' × 'Over the Rainbow'. Orange-yellow, fruity fragrance, double, high-centered to cupped, medium, 3.8 cm./1.5 in., free bloom; bud pointed; foliage green, matt; growth bushy, spreading.

Orange Masterpiece. F. (de Ruiter, 1970). Seedling × 'Orange Sensation'. Orange-red, small, double, some scent, many together in clusters, floriferous; growth bushy, 0.6 m./2 ft.; foliage deep green.

Orange Morsdag. Pol. (F.J. Grootendorst, 1956). Sport of 'Mothersday'. Deep orange, medium, semi-double, globose, profuse bloom, in clusters; growth dwarf; foliage glossy.

Orange Pixie. Min. (Ralph S. Moore, 1977). 'Little Chief' × 'Little Princess'. Orange-red, double, 50 petals, high-centered, no scent, in clusters, abundant, recurrent; bud pointed; growth dwarf, compact, upright; foliage glossy, leathery.

Orange Ruffels. HT. (Brownell, 1952). ('Dr. W. van Fleet' × 'Général Jacqueminot') × 'Lafter'. Orange and yellow, large, 10-12 cm./4-4.8 in. across, double, high-

centered, petals frilled, fragrant, very free bloom; growth vigorous, compact; foliage deep green, glossy. (6.0)

Orange Sensation. F. (de Ruiter, 1961). 'Amor' × 'Fashion'. Vermilion-orange, medium-large, 7 cm./2.8 in. across, double, some scent, in clusters; growth vigorous, 0.6-0.7 m./2-2.3 ft., upright; foliage light green. GSR 457; RA 1961:160; RJb 1962:161. (8.1)

Orange Silk. F. (McGredy, 1968). 'Orangeade' × ('Ma Perkins' × 'Independence'). Vermilion-orange, large, double, fragrant, in clusters, profuse bloom; growth strong, 0.8 m./2.6 ft.; foliage deep green. GSR 458; RA 1968:177; WPR 53. (6.7)

Orange Sunshine. Min. (Ralph S. Moore, 1968). Sport of 'Bit o'Sunshine'. Orange-blend, small, semi-double, fragrant; bud pointed; growth dwarf, bushy, vigorous; foliage soft. (5.6)

Orange Triumph. Pol. (Kordes, 1937). 'Eva' × 'Solarium'. Salmon-red with some orange shades, small, semi-double, petals waved, cupped, some scent, in large

1912	**Ophelia**					
1916	Pink Ophelia					
1917	Suprême Ophelia					
1918	----------------→	1918	**Madame Butterfly**			
1918	Annie Laurie	1925	Ivy May			
1918	Silvia	1926	Climb. Madame Butterfly			
1918	May Martin	1926	----------------→	1926	**Rapture**	
		1926	Pink Madame Butterfly	1933	Climb. Rapture	
		1926	Grillodale	1934	Rote Rapture	
				1935	Orange Rapture	
		1926	----------------→	1926	**Lady Sylvia**	
		1927	Yellow Madame Butterfly	1933	Climb. Lady Sylvia	
1918	----------------→	1918	**Golden Ophelia**			
1918	Rosalind	1924	Climb. Golden Ophelia			
1920	Climb. Ophelia	1924	----------------→	1924	**Roselandia**	
1920	Oregon Ophelia	1931	Harriett	1931	Oberbürgermeister Külb	
1920	White Star	1934	Christine Wunderlich	1933	Climb. Roselandia	
1920	White Ophelia					
1921	Silver Wedding					
1922	Westfield Star					
1922	Lemon Ophelia					
1924	Climb. Queen Ophelia					
1924	John Mensing					
1926	Elnar Tonning					
1927	Prinz Hamlet					
1930	Amber					
1932	Lady Evelin Guinness					

The spontaneous sports of 'Ophelii'. (after Saakov)

trusses on strong stems; growth bushy, 0.6-0.7 m./2-2.3 ft.; foliage deep green, glossy. RA 1938:89. (6.0)

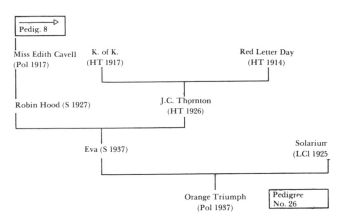

Oriana. HT. (Tantau, 1970). 'Caramba' × 'Piccadilly'. Interior cherry-red, reverse nearly white, medium-large,

double, some scent, floriferous, singly; growth bushy, upright; foliage deep green, glossy. WPR 35. (7.3)

Oratam. D. (Jacobus, 1939). *R. damascena* × 'Souvenir de Claudius Pernet'. Pink with copper edge, center and reverse yellow, very large, double, strong fragrance, one heavy bloom, non-recurrent; growth bushy, upright, medium; foliage large, light green. (8.1)

Orchid Masterpiece. HT. (Boerner/Jackson & Perkins, 1960). 'Golden Masterpiece' × 'Grey Pearl'-seedling. Lilac-pink with lighter center, large, double, finally flat, fragrant, profuse bloom; growth vigorous; foliage deep green. RJb 22:192. (4.6)

Oregold (= 'Miss Harp'). HT. (Tantau, 1970). Deep golden-yellow, very large, good form, long-lasting, some scent; growth vigorous, 0.8 m./2.6 ft.; foliage abundant, glossy. (7.5)

1909 Orléans Rose

1911	Baby Princess Juliana → 1923 **Corrie Koster** ----------→ 1935 Zborov			
1913	Climb. Orléans Rose			
1915	Mevr. J. H. van Nes			
1917	----------------→ **1917 Miss Edith Cavell**			
	1922 ----------------→ **1922 Ideal**			
	1928 Orange Marvell	1927 ----------------→ **1927 Kersbergen**		
	1932 Climb. Miss Edith Cavell	1927 Orange Perfection	1928 Frans Leddy	
			1929 Oberbürgermeister Bracht	
1917	----------------→ **1917 Freudenfeuer**			
1920	Crimson Orléans	1922 Käthchen von Heilbronn		
1920	White Orléans			
1920	----------------→ **1920 Coral Cluster**			
	1927 Pride of Hurst			
	1930 ----------------→ **1930 Little Dorrit**			
		1936 Climb. Little Dorrit		
1921	Frau Elisabeth Münch			
1921	----------------→ **1921 Juliana-Roos**			
	1923 Salmon Queen			
	1928 Lindbergh			
1923	----------------→ **1923 Orange Queen** ----------→ 1927 **Salmonea** ----------→ 1930 Helena van Vliet			
1923	Girlie			
1925	Simmgen Orléans			
1925	**Dr. Kater** ----------→ 1928 Frau Marie Bromme			
1925	Königin Wilhelmine			
1926	**Locarno** ----------→ 1932 Scarlet Button			
1927	Magnifique			
1928	----------------→ **1928 Teschendorffs Jubiläumsrose**			
	1930 Teschendorffs Rote Jubiläumsrose			
	1930 Rosalinde			
	1930 Teschendorffs Rankende Jubiläumsrose			
1931	Improved Orléans			
1931	Rotraut			
1932	Cameo			
1935	Svornost			

The spontaneous sports of 'Orléans Rose'. (after Saakov)

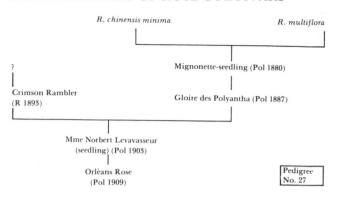

R. chinensis minima   R. multiflora

Mignonette-seedling (Pol 1880)

?

Crimson Rambler
(R 1893)

Gloire des Polyantha (Pol 1887)

Mme Norbert Levavasseur
(seedling) (Pol 1903)

Orléans Rose
(Pol 1909)

Pedigree
No. 27

Orléans Rose. Pol. (Levavasseur, 1909). Presumably seedling of 'Mme. Norbert Levavasseur'. Vivid crimson-pink with white center, semi-double, flat, some scent, profuse and continuous bloom; growth bushy; foliage glossy. GiS 4; ZR 1911:65.

Ormiston Roy. HSpn. (Doorenbos, 1953). *R. pimpinellifolia* × *R. xanthina*. Canary-yellow, medium, single, non-recurrent; growth bushy, 1 m./3.3 ft.; foliage small. TRT 37.

Oskar Cordel. HP. (Lambert, 1897). 'Merveille de Lyon' × 'André Schwartz'. Crimson, cupped, large, double, 40 petals, floriferous; growth compact. RZ 1901:16. (8.3)

Ovation. HT. (O.L. Weeks, 1977). 'First Prize' × seedling. Orange-red, double, 25 petals, high-centered, no scent, singly to three per cluster, intermittent bloom; growth vigorous, branched, upright; foliage medium-large, firm, deep green.

Over the Rainbow. Min. (R.S. Moore, 1972). 'Little Darling' × 'Westmont'. Red and yellow, bicolor, double, good form, rather large, very recurrent; growth dwarf, upright; foliage healthy, disease-resistant. (8.5)

Over the Rainbow, Climbing. ClMin. (R.H. Rumsey, 1974). Sport of the preceeding variety. Growth more vigorous, semi-climbing; otherwise like the type.

Pace Setter. Min. (Ernest Schwartz, 1979). 'Ma Perkins' × 'Magic Carrousel'. White, double, 45 petals, fragrant, high centered, singly, floriferous, recurrent; bud large, pointed; growth dwarf, bushy, compact; foliage deep green, pointed. ARA 1979:101.

Paddy McGredy. F. (McGredy, 1962). 'Spartan' × 'Tzigane'. Deep pink, large, 10 cm./4 in. across, cupped, double, in clusters, fragrant, somewhat recurrent; growth short, sturdy, upright, 40 cm./16 in.; foliage firm, leathery. PWR 118; GSR 460; RJb 26:35. (7.5)

Paint Box. F. (Dickson, 1963). Seedling × 'St. Pauli'. Opening yellow with red edge, turning scarlet with yellow center, semi-double, medium, 7 cm./2.8 in. across, some scent, profuse bloom; growth bushy, 0.9 m./3 ft.; foliage deep green. GSR 461; RA 1964:81.

Paintbrush. Min. (Ralph S. Moore, 1974). 'Fairy Moss' × 'Goldmoss'. Opening soft yellow, changing to white, daisy-like flowers, singly and in clusters, free blooming all season; bud pointed, long, apricot, mossy; growth dwarf, bushy, upright, very prickly; foliage small, leathery. (6.5)

Paloma. HT. (Swim & Weeks, 1968). 'Mount Shasta' × 'White Knight'. White, double, large, high-centered, petals drop off cleanly, singly on long stems, moderate, continuous bloom; bud long, pointed, urn-shaped; growth vigorous, medium, upright; foliage deep green, leathery. (6.6)

Pania. HT. (McGredy, 1968). 'Paddy McGredy' × ('Kordes Perfecta' × 'Montezuma'). Clear light pink, large, double, some scent, floriferous, several together; growth vigorous; foliage very firm, glossy.

Panorama Holiday. Gr. (Gregory, 1973). 'Queen Elizabeth' × ?. Pure pink, large, semi-double, good fragrance, singly or several together; bud long; growth bushy, 0.7 m./2.3 ft.; foliage deep green.

Papa Meilland. HT. (Meilland, 1963). 'Chrysler Imperial' × 'Charles Mallerin'. Blackish velvety-crimson, large, high-centered, strong fragrance, floriferous; growth bushy, 0.8 m./2.6 ft.; foliage leathery, olive-green, glossy. GR 129; RJb 28:160. (7.4)

Papillon-Rose. F. (Lens, 1956). 'White Briarcliff' × ('Lady Sylvia' × 'Fashion'). Clear pink with some salmon hue, medium, double, fragrant, floriferous, in clusters; growth bushy, low, 40 cm./16 in.; foliage healthy. PWR 146. (7.3)

Papoose. ClMin. (Ralph S. Moore, 1955). *R. wichuraiana* × 'Zee'. White, small, 2.5 cm./1 in. across, single, in clusters, very floriferous, early, then intermittent; growth vigorous, trailing, good ground cover, 0.7-1 m./2.3-3.3 ft. broad; foliage small, semi-glossy. (6.5)

Paprika. F. (Tantau, 1958). 'Märchenland' × 'Red Favorite'. Geranium-red, medium, semi-double, flat, no scent, very floriferous, in large trusses, resistant to weather damage; growth vigorous, low, 0.6 m./2 ft.;

foliage large, deep green. GSR 462; PWR 104; RA 1958:32. (7.9)

Parade. LCl. (Boerner/Jackson & Perkins, 1953). 'New Dawn'-seedling × 'Climbing World's Fair'. Deep pink, semi-double, medium, 8 cm./3.2 in. across, floriferous, fragrant, recurrent; growth strong, 3 m./10 ft.; foliage medium, reddish. GSR 255; PWR 214. (7.9)

Paradise. HT. (Weeks, 1979). 'Swarthmore' × seedling. Lavendar blend, petals with rich ruby edge, semi-double, very floriferous; growth medium, bushy, vigorous. ARA 63:122.

Parador. F. (Meilland, 1978). Seedling × ('Alain' × 'Orange Triumph') × seedling. Orange-red, flat-cupped, some scent, double, 20 petals, abundant and continuous bloom, 3-15 in clusters; growth very vigorous; foliage dense, dull.

Para Ti. (= 'Pour Toi'). Min. (Dot. 1946). 'Eduardo Toda' × 'Pompon de Paris'. White with creamy center, small, semi-double, high-centered, floriferous; growth dwarf, 15-25 cm./6-10 in.; foliage small, glossy. PWR 169. (6.3)

Parfum de l'Hay. HRug. (Gravereaux, 1901). (*R. damascena* × 'Général Jacqueminot') × *R. rugosa*. Crimson, medium, very double, strong fragrance, recurrent; growth vigorous, medium. Often said to be the rose with the strongest scent. (7.6)

Paris-Match. HT. (Meilland, 1957). 'Independence' × 'Grand'mère Jenny'. Crimson to pink, large, double, some scent, floriferous; growth upright, 0.8 m./2.6 ft.; foliage firm, deep green. GSR 345; PWR 78. (7.1)

Parkdirektor Riggers. KCl. (Kordes, 1957). *R. kordesii* × 'Our Princess'. Velvety red, semi-double, medium-large, 8 cm./3.2 in. across, some scent, in clusters, in bloom throughout the season; growth very strong, 3-4 m./10-13 ft.; foliage deep green, glossy. GSR 256; KR 10:164; RJb 30:128. (7.6)

Parkjuwel. M. (Kordes, 1950). 'Independence' × red Moss Rose. Bright red, very large, 12 cm./4.8 in. across, very double, floriferous, strong fragrance, heavy summer-flowering, non-recurrent; calyx and flower stalks very mossy; growth strong, bushy, medium; foliage light green, wrinkled. RJb 37:48. (7.5)

Parkzauber. M. (Kordes, 1956). 'Independence' × 'Nuits d'Young'. Velvety-red to fiery-red, large, double, fragrant, profuse bloom in June, non-recurrent; calyx and flower stalks very mossy-bristly; growth strong, medium; foliage firm, deep green. BTR 40.

Parmentier. M. (Robert, 1815). Deep pink, large, double, fragrant, floriferous; 1.3 m./4.3 ft. high.

Party Girl. Min. (F. Harmon Saville, 1979). 'Rise n' Shine' × 'Sheri Anne'. Yellow blend, high centered, double, 25 petals, fragrant, moderate bloomer, very recurrent; growth dwarf, bushy, compact; foliage medium green, deeply serrate. ARA 1979:135.

Pascali. HT. (Lens, 1963). 'Queen Elizabeth' × 'White Butterfly'. Opening white with creamy shade, then pure white, medium-large, double, perfect form, finally flat, 30 petals, fragrant, floriferous; growth vigorous, bushy, strong stems, 0.8-0.9 m./2.6-3 ft.; foliage deep green, very healthy. GSR 346; KR 10:142; RJb 26:96. (8.0)

Patio Patty. F. (J.B. Williams, 1976). ('Circus' × 'Sweet Repose') × ('Little Darling' × 'Starina'). Peach-yellow with light yellow base, edges later deep orange-red, double, some scent, long-lasting, continuous bloom, petals drop off cleanly; growth low, compact, vigorous; foliage deep green, glossy.

Pat Nixon. F. (Meilland, 1972). 'Tamango' × ('Fire King' × 'Bonsai'). Deep red, very large, double, fragrant, long-lasting, profuse and continuous bloom, singly and in clusters on medium-strong stems; growth vigorous, 0.6-0.7 m./2-2.3 ft.; foliage deep green, glossy, large, healthy. (7.1)

Patricia Hyde. F. (Harkness, 1969). 'Ann Elizabeth' × 'Red Dandy'. Clear salmon-pink, small, semi-double, many together, very profuse bloom, some scent; growth vigorous, 0.8 m./2.6 ft.

Patrician. HT. (W.A. Warriner/Jackson & Perkins, 1975). 'Fragrant Cloud' × 'Proud Land'. Medium red, double, 30 petals, high-centered, strong scent, abundant bloom all season, singly and several together on strong stems; bud ovoid, pointed; growth very vigorous; foliage large, dark green.

Patty Lou. Min. (Ralph S. Moore, 1953). 'Oakington Ruby' × self. Rose-pink with silvery-pink reverse, small, 2.5 cm./1 in. across, double, fragrant, abundant bloom; bud ovoid; growth dwarf, bushy, 25-30 cm./10-12 in.; foliage small. (5.9)

Paulette. HT. (Meilland, 1946). 'Peace' × 'Signora'. Salmon-pink to scarlet with darker veins, large. double, some scent; growth vigorous; foliage deep green. SRW 82.

Paul Neyron. HP. (Levet, 1869). 'Victor Verdier' × 'Anna de Diesbach'. Clear pink, large, 12 cm./4.8 in. across, very double, cupped, fragrant, very recurrent, strong stems; growth tall to very tall; foliage bright green. GSR 113; RZ 1886:69. (7.4)

Paul Ricault. HP. (Portemer, 1845). Deep pink, large, very double, outer petals reflexed, inner ones incurved, cupped, with quartered center, strong fragrance, non-recurrent; growth upright, medium. GSR 69; PGR 39.

Paul's Early Blush. HP. (Paul, 1895). Sport of 'Heinrich Schultheis'. Blush, large, very double, sometimes recurrent; growth vigorous. (8.3)

Paul's Lemon Pillar. ClHT. (Paul, 1915). 'Frau Karl Druschki' × 'Maréchal Niel'. Pale sulphur-yellow to nearly white, very large, very double, fragrant, non-recurrent; very strong growth, but tender. GSR 218.

Paul's Scarlet Climber. LCl. (W. Paul, 1916). 'Paul's Carmine Pillar'-seedling × (?)'Rêve d'Or'. Crimson-scarlet, medium, resistant to weather damage, faint scent, very floriferous, in clusters, non-recurrent, but sometimes some flowers in the autumn; growth strong, 3 m./10 ft., bushy; foliage large, glossy, abundant. Still a favored variety. GSR 219; PWR 207. (7.0)

Pax. HMsk. (Pemberton, 1918). 'Trier' × 'Sunburst'. Creamy-white, then pure white, semi-double, 8-10 cm./3.2-4 in. across, strong fragrance, anthers golden yellow, profuse bloom in large clusters on 30-50 cm./12-20 in. long stems, recurrent; growth vigorous, arching, 2 m./6.6 ft., stems dark brown; foliage deep green. TRT 117; GiS 17. (7.6)

Peace. (= 'Mme. A. Meilland', 'Gloria Dei', 'Gioia'). HT. (Meilland, 1945). ('George Dickson' × 'Souvenir de Claudius Pernet') × (['Joanna Hill' × 'Charles P. Kilham'] × 'Margaret McCredy'). Golden-yellow edged with vivid pink, becoming lighter yellow with darker red, very large, 15 cm./6 in. across, double, cupped, light scent, singly on very strong stems, floriferous; growth very vigorous, 1.2 m./4 ft.; foliage large, deep green, glossy. Achieved the highest National Rating (9.6, now 9.0) in the United States. In excess of 100 million plants of this variety have been sold worldwide. GSR 347; PWR 95. (9.0)

Peace, Climbing. ClHT. (Brady, 1950). Sport of 'Peace'. Growth very vigorous; otherwise like the type, but not much bloom until established. (7.1)

Peaceful. HT. (Boerner/Jackson & Perkins, 1956). Seedling × 'Peace'. Opening coral-pink with lighter reverse, very large, 12 cm./4.8 in. across, double, fragrant, cupped; growth rather uneven, 0.8 m./2.6 ft.; foliage large, light green, matt. (6.1)

Peach Beauty. HT. (Boerner, 1970). 'Ma Perkins' × 'Polynesian Sunset'. Peach-pink, large, double, fragrant, very long-lasting, singly on strong stems, continuous bloom; bud large, ovoid; growth vigorous, bushy; foliage large, glossy. (6.9)

Peach Treat. HT. (Fuller, 1968). 'Beauté' × 'Kordes Perfecta'. Peach-pink, large, very double, fragrant, abundant bloom; growth bushy, vigorous; foliage leathery. (5.3)

Peaches n' Cream. Min. (E.P. Woolcock, 1976). 'Little Darling' × 'Magic Wand'. Pink with peach hue, double, 50 petals, some scent, long-lasting, singly, continuous bloom; growth dwarf, vigorous; foliage deep green, disease-resistant.

Peachy. Min. (Ralph S. Moore, 1964). 'Golden Glow' × 'Zee'. Pink with yellow tint, small, double, fragrant, abundant bloom; growth dwarf, bushy, 30 cm./12 in.; foliage light green, soft. (8.4)

Peachy Keen. Min. (D. Bennett/Tiny Petals Nurs., 1979). 'Little Darling' × 'Sheri Anne'. Soft pink, slightly fragrant, semi-double, small, 2.5 cm./1 in., free bloom; bud long-pointed; growth bushy, spreading.

Peachy White. Min. (Ralph S. Moore, 1976). 'Little Darling' × 'Red Germain'. White with pale pink or peach, open, some scent, singly and in clusters, contin-

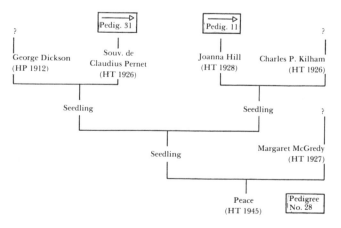

uous bloom; growth dwarf, branched, upright; foliage medium green, medium size. (7.5)

Pearl Dawn. Min. (F. Harmon Saville, 1975). ('Cécile Brunner' × 'Perla de Montserrat') × 'Perla de Montserrat'. Medium pink, double, 25 petals, no scent, singly and several together, floriferous; growth dwarf. (6.5)

Peer Gynt. HT. (Kordes, 1968). 'Colour Wonder' × 'Goldrausch'. Golden yellow, very large, 12 cm./4.8 in. across, very double, globose, strong fragrance, floriferous, strong stems, long-lasting. GSR 348; KR 10:20; RA 1968:176. (6.9)

Peggy Grant. Min. (Ralph S. Moore, 1954). ('Robinette' × 'Monsieur Tillier') × 'Zee'. Shell-pink, double, 25 petals, small, abundant bloom; growth very dwarf, 15 cm./6 in.; foliage small, leathery, glossy.

Penelope. HMsk. (Pemberton, 1924). 'Ophelia' × 'William Allen Richardson'. Salmon-pink with yellow-orange hue, fading to nearly white, then with more pink center, medium, semi-double, fragrant, floriferous, in large trusses, recurrent in autumn; growth strong, 1.2 m./4 ft. or over, spreading; foliage large, deep green. GSR 122; PWR 196; GiS 17. (7.5)

'Peon' → **Tom Thumb**

Pepe. HT. (de Ruiter, 1961). 'Amor' × 'Sutter's Gold'. Scarlet with orange-yellow, base and reverse golden yellow, large, cupped, finally flat, fragrant, floriferous; growth bushy; foliage deep green, glossy. (6.5)

Peppermint. F. (Boerner/Jackson & Perkins, 1964). 'Jingles' × self. Interior red, reverse creamy, medium, cupped, double, very floriferous; growth bushy, vigorous. Greenhouse variety.

Percy Thrower. HT. (Lens, 1964). 'La Jolla' × 'Karl Herbst'. Pure pink, large, 12 cm./4.8 in. across, semi-double, flat, long-lasting; growth vigorous, loose, 0.9 m./3 ft.; foliage deep green, glossy. CRA 66:158. (7.7)

Perfume Delight. HT. (O.L. Weeks, 1973). 'Peace' × (['Happiness' × 'Chrysler Imperial'] × 'El Capitan'.) Bright pink, very large, 12 cm./4.8 in. across, double, 30 petals, perfect form, strong fragrance; bud long, pointed; growth sturdy, upright, bushy; foliage deep green, large. ARA 59:1. (7.8)

Perky. Min. (Ralph S. Moore, 1958). (R. wichuraiana × 'Floradora') × 'Oakington Ruby'. Pink, double, small, 2.5 cm./1 in. across, very fragrant, abundant bloom;

growth dwarf, 30 cm./12 in., bushy; foliage small, glossy. (6.9)

Perla de Alcanada. (= 'Baby Crimson'). Min. (Dot, 1944). 'Perle des Rouges' × 'Rouletii'. Crimson with small white base, small, semi-double, flat, floriferous; growth dwarf, 30 cm./12 in.; foliage small, narrow, deep green. (6.4)

Perla de Montserrat. Min. (Dot, 1945). 'Cécile Brunner' × 'Rouletii'. Pink with pearl-white edges, small, rosette-shaped, flat, in clusters; growth dwarf, 30 cm./12 in., bushy; foliage deep green. PWR 163; GR 273. (7.6)

Perla Rosa. Min. (Dot, 1946). 'Perle des Rouges' × 'Rouletii'. Bright pink, very double, free bloom; growth very dwarf, 15-20 cm./6-8 in. (7.0)

Perle des Panachées. G. (Vibert, 1845). Nearly white, with crimson stripes and patches, semi-double, loose; growth upright, 0.9 m./3 ft.; young growth bronze, older foliage light green.

Perle d'Or. Ch. (Rambaud, 1883). R. multiflora (?) × 'Mme. Falcot'. Interior pale orange-yellow, reverse deeper, fading to more creamy-yellow, small, strong fragrance, in clusters, very recurrent; growth bushy, vigorous, 1 m./3.3 ft.; foliage bright green, matt. RA 1976:120; GiS 10; RZ 1887:5. (7.7)

Pernille Poulsen. F. (N.D. Poulsen/McGredy, 1965). 'Ma Perkins' × 'Columbine'. Light pink, fragrant, semi-double, open, large, 9 cm./3.5 in., in clusters, profuse; foliage pointed, light green; growth free.

Persian Princess. Min. (Ralph S. Moore, 1970). 'Baccara' × 'Eleanor'. Coral-red, double, small, abundant bloom; growth dwarf, 30-35 cm./12-14 in., bushy; foliage leathery.

Persian Yellow. (= R. foetida persiana Lemaire). S. Introduced 1838 by Sir Henry Wilcock from Persia. Golden-yellow, small globose, along the branches, non-recurrent, sterile, June; growth bushy, strong, producing many suckers when on own roots, and then reaching 2 m./6.6 ft.; lower when budded on R. multiflora, 1.5 m./5 ft. (see P.H. Wright, in ARA 1971); foliage small, yellowish-green. FS 374. (7.8)

Peter Frankenfeld. HT. (Kordes, 1966). 'Ballet' × 'Florex'. Deep crimson-pink, large, long-lasting, some scent, long stems; growth vigorous, 0.9 m./3 ft.; foliage deep green. KR 10:73; WGR 121. (7.9)

Peter's Briarcliff. HT. (Jackson & Perkins, 1940). Form of 'Briarcliff'. Clear pink, large, strong fragrance, floriferous; bud long; growth vigorous; foliage deep green. Greenhouse variety.

Petite de Hollande. (= 'Pompon des Dames'; *R. centifolia minor*). C. Soft pink with darker center, double, medium, 6 cm./2.4 in. across, fragrant, in clusters together, June, non-recurrent; growth compact, 1 m./3.3 ft. GSR 70; PWR 172; GiS 8. (8.2)

Petite Folie. Min. (Meilland, 1968). ('Dany Robin' × 'Fire King') × ('Cricri' × 'Perla de Montserrat'). Vermilion with crimson reverse, small, double, globose, some scent, in clusters; growth vigorous; foliage firm, leathery.

Petite Lisette. D. (Vibert, 1817). Flesh-pink to nearly white, medium, very double, round, flat, fragrant, nice shape; growth weak, 0.9 m./3 ft., few prickles; foliage small, roundish, grey-green, hairy, serrate.

Petra. F. (Kordes, 1974). Seedling × 'Taora'. Similar to 'Chatter'. Blood red, medium, double, in clusters, petals drop off cleanly, profuse bloom; growth bushy, low, 30 cm./12 in.; foliage healthy, firm, deep green.

Pharaoh. HT. (Meilland, 1967). ('Happiness' × 'Independence') × 'Suspense'. Deep crimson-scarlet, very large, to 14 cm./5.6 in. across, double, cupped, fragrant, resistant to weather damage, floriferous, long stems; growth strong, 0.9 m./3 ft.; foliage medium, deep green, glossy, abundant. GSR 349; RA 1969:112.

Picasso. F. (McGredy, 1971). 'Marlena' × ('Irish Wonder' × ['Frühlingsmorgen' × 'Orange Sweetheart']). Cherry-red with white center, many of the petals also striped or marbled, pattern changing during bloom (hence the name "hand-painted", which Messrs. McGredy use for this and several similar roses), very floriferous, in clusters; growth bushy, 0.6 m./2 ft.; foliage small, firm, matt. RA 1971:48; GSR 464.

Piccadilly. HT. (McGredy, 1960). 'McGredy's Yellow' × 'Karl Herbst'. Brilliant scarlet with yellow base and reverse, medium, double, perfect form, good fragrance, profuse bloom; growth bushy; 0.7 m./2.3 ft.; foliage copper-green, glossy, abundant. GSR 350; PWR 44. (6.4)

Picnic. F. (W.A. Warriner/Jackson & Perkins, 1976). 'South Seas' × seedling. Opening rose-pink, reverse yellow, high-centered, double, some scent, in clusters; growth upright, branched; foliage medium, leathery. (7.0)

Picture. HT. (McGredy, 1932). Parentage not reported. Velvety clear pink, double, 30 petals, reflexed, high-centered, some scent; growth free; foliage deep green, glossy. (6.2)

Pied Piper. F. (Lindquist, 1969). 'Garnette' × 'Moulin Rouge'. Red, double, globose, small, free bloom; growth low; foliage deep green, leathery. (7.2)

Pigalle. HT. (Meilland, 1951). 'Fantastique' × 'Boudoir'. Violet-red to magenta, large, 10 cm./4 in. across, very double, finally flat, some scent; growth bushy, 0.6 m./2 ft.; foliage bronze-green. PWR 36. (6.1)

Pike's Peak. S. (Gunter, 1940). *R. acicularis* × 'Hollywood'. Bright red, center first yellow, then white, semi-double, medium, 8 cm./3.2 in. across, some scent, floriferous, many together in large trusses; growth strong, tall; foliage light green, wrinkled. (8.6)

Pilar Dot. Min. (Dot, 1964). 'Orient' × 'Perla de Alcanada'. Coral-pink, good form, double, small, growth vigorous.

Piñata. LCL. (Suzuki/Jackson & Perkins, 1974). Seedling × seedling. Yellow with vermilion shades, later changing to all vermilion over most of the petals, double, 30 petals, in clusters, very floriferous all season; growth strong, climbing; foliage dark, semi-glossy.

Pineapple Poll. F. (Cocker, 1970). 'Orange Sensation' × 'Circus'. Yellow-orange and red, small, very fine form, double, luminous color, good scent; growth bushy, 0.6-0.7 m./2-2.3 ft.; foliage deep green, glossy. GSR 456.

Pink Cameo. ClMin. (Ralph S. Moore, 1954). ('Soeur Thérèse' × 'Skyrocket') × 'Zee'. Pink with darker center, double, 25 petals, some scent, small, 3.5 cm./1.4 in. across, in clusters, abundant bloom; growth tall, 1-1.5 m./3.3-5 ft.; foliage small, deep green, glossy. (8.4)

Pink Cloud. LCl. (Boerner/Jackson & Perkins, 1952). 'New Dawn' × 'New Dawn'-seedling. Deep rose-pink with darker center, large, cupped, fragrant, in clusters, profuse bloom, recurrent; growth vigorous, 2-2.5 m./6.6-8.3 ft.; foliage firm, glossy. (6.6)

Pink Dawn. HT. (Howard & Smith, 1935). 'Joanna Hill' × seedling. Light pink when opening, deepening with age, large, very double, 60 petals, high-centered, strong fragrance; growth vigorous; foliage soft. (5.7)

Pink Favorite. HT. (Von Abrams, 1956). 'Juno' × ('Georg Arends' × 'New Dawn'). Deep rose-pink with darker reverse, large, 8-10 cm./3.2-4 in. across, loosely double, cupped, fragrant, abundant bloom; growth bushy, upright, 0.6-0.7 m./2-2.3 ft., strong stems; foliage light green, glossy. GSR 351; RJb 22:160. (7.7)

Pink Formal. S. (J.B. Williams, 1978). ('Queen Elizabeth' × 'Gladiator') × ('Aztec' × 'Little Darling'). Pink, double, 25 petals, in clusters and large trusses; growth vigorous, vase-shaped; foliage large, leathery, very disease-resistant.

Pink Fragrance. HT. (de Ruiter, 1956). ('Orange Triumph' × 'Golden Rapture') × 'Peace'. Pink, large, 10 cm./4 in. across, very double, fragrant, many together in pyramidal trusses; growth very vigorous, 1 m./3.3 ft.; foliage large, glossy. (7.6)

Pink Frostfire. Min. (Ralph S. Moore, 1968). Sport of 'Frostfire'. Light pink, double, small; growth dwarf, bushy; foliage deep green, glossy, leathery. (6.1)

Pink Garnette. F. (Boerner/Jackson & Perkins, 1951). Sport of 'Garnette'. Deep pink, medium, 5 cm./2 in. across, double, otherwise like the type. (6.4)

Pink Grootendorst. HRg. (Grootendorst, 1923). Sport of 'F.J. Grootendorst'. Pink, otherwise like the type. GSR 134; PWR 203. (8.5)

Pink Heather. Min. (Ralph S. Moore, 1959). (*R. wichuraiana* × 'Floradora') × ('Violette' × 'Zee'). Lilac-pink, small, 3 cm./1.2 in. across, very double, flat, some scent, floriferous, in clusters; growth dwarf, 25 cm./10 in.; foliage very small, glossy. (6.3)

Pink Joey. Min. (Ralph S. Moore, 1953). 'Oakington Ruby' × self. Deep pink, double, 30 petals, small, 2.5 cm./1 in. across, good shape, fragrant; growth dwarf, 20 cm./8 in., bushy; foliage small. (6.2)

Pink Lustre. HT. (Verschuren, 1957). 'Peace' × 'Dame Edith Helen'. Pink, large, very double, 50 petals, high-centered, strong fragrance; bud ovoid; growth vigorous, upright; foliage firm, leathery, deep green, glossy. RJb 22:160.

Pink Maiden. F. (Boerner/Spek, 1965). 'Spartan'-seedling × 'Queen Elizabeth'. Pink, large, double, some scent, in trusses; growth vigorous, upright; foliage deep green.

Pink Mandy. Min. (Ralph S. Moore, 1974). 'Ellen Poulsen' × 'Little Chief'. Dark pink, very double, 40 petals, in clusters, very full, continuous bloom; growth very bushy, 20 cm./8 in., very dwarf; foliage healthy, disease-resistant.

Pink Masterpeice. HT. (Boerner/Jackson & Perkins, 1962). 'Serenade'-seedling × 'Kate Smith'. Soft pink, with some darker shades, base yellowish, very large, 15 cm./6 in. across, double, globose, fragrant, on strong stems, profuse bloom; growth vigorous; foliage deep green, firm.

Pink Parfait. F. (Swim/Armstrong, 1960). 'First Love' × 'Pinocchio'. Clear pink with darker veins, fading with age, large, 9 cm./3.6 in. across, double, cupped, some scent, floriferous; growth bushy, 0.7 m./2.3 ft.; foliage bright green, medium, glossy. GSR 466; RA 1961:161. (8.4)

Pink Peace. HT. (Meilland, 1959). ('Peace' × 'Monique') × ('Peace' × 'Mrs. John Laing'). Rich, rosy-pink, large, 15 cm./6 in. across, very double, high-centered, strong fragrance, floriferous; growth vigorous, 1 m./3.3 ft.; foliage large, matt, abundant. The name is somewhat misleading, since the flower does not resemble 'Peace'. GSR 352; PWR 13; RJb 28:192. (7.7)

Pink Perpétue. LCl. (Gregory, 1965). 'Spectacular' × 'New Dawn'. Rich carmine-pink, medium, double, globose, some scent, in clusters, profuse bloom, recurrent; growth vigorous, 2.5-3 m./8.3-10 ft.; foliage light green, glossy. GSR 257; RA 1965:65; RA 1975:140. (6.3)

Pink Petticoat. Min. (Strawn/Pixie Treasures, 1979). 'Neue Revue' × 'Sheri Anne'. Creamy white edged with coral pink, slighty fragrant, double, medium, 3.8-5 cm./1.5-2 in., prolific bloom; bud pointed; foliage glossy, dark; growth upright.

Pink Puff. F. (Boerner/Jackson & Perkins, 1965). 'Pinocchio'-seedling × ('Red Pinocchio'-seedling × 'Garnette'). Blush, large, double, strong fragrance, good shape, floriferous; bud long; growth bushy, low 0.5 m./1.7 ft.; foliage medium, bronze-green, glossy.

Pink Ribbon. Min. (Ralph S. Moore 1966). (*R. wichuraiana* × 'Floradora') × 'Magic Wand'. Soft pink, double, small, some scent, abundant bloom, growth dwarf, bushy; foliage light green, glossy. (7.4)

Pink Rosette. F. (Krebs, 1948). Parentage not reported. Pink, medium, 5 cm./2 in. across, double, 50 petals, rosette-shape, some scent, in clusters, profuse bloom;

growth dwarf, bushy; foliage deep green, glossy. (7.4)

Pink Shadow. Min. (E.D. Williams, 1977). 'Over the Rainbow' × self. Deep pink, very double, 60 petals, some scent, abundant bloom all season; growth dwarf, bushy, spreading; foliage small, leathery.

Pink Spice. HT. (Von Abrams/Peterson & Dering, 1962). Light pink flushed with yellow, very fragrant, double, high centered to cupped, large, 12.5 cm./5 in., free bloom; bud long-pointed; foliage leathery, light green; growth vigorous, upright.

Pink Supreme. HT. (de Ruiter, 1964). 'Amor' × 'Peace'. Clear pink, large, loosely double, strong fragrance; bud more salmon-colored, long; growth bushy, vigorous, 1 m./3.3 ft.; foliage light green, glossy. GSR 353; RA 1964:112.

Kalinka. (= 'Pink Wonder'). F. (Meilland, 1970). 'Zambra' × ('Sarabande' × ['Goldilocks' × 'Fashion']). Salmon, medium, good shape, early, mostly singly; growth bushy, spreading, 0.6-0.8 m./2-2.6 ft.; foliage deep green. GSR 467.

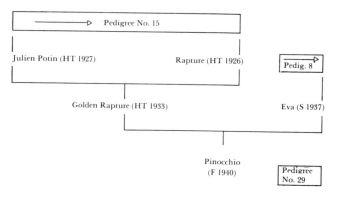

Pinocchio. (= 'Rosenmärchen'). F. (Kordes, 1940). 'Eva' × 'Golden Rapture'. Salmon-pink with yellowish base, medium, 6 cm./2.4 in. across, double, outer petals flat, fragrant, many together in large trusses, profuse bloom; growth bushy, 0.5 m./1.7 ft. World-famous variety. PWR 148. (7.0)

Pinwheel. Min. (Ralph S. Moore, 1979). Sport of 'Jeanie Williams'. Pink and yellow, petals become wavy and twisted with age; growth bushy, dwarf, branched; foliage small, medium green, pointed. (7.0)

Pixie. (= 'Little Princess'). Min. (de Vink, 1940). 'Ellen Poulsen' × 'Tom Thumb'. White with soft pink center, small, very double, finally flat, some scent, floriferous;

growth dwarf, 25 cm./10 in.; foliage very dwarf, matt. (7.6)

Pixie Gold. Min. (Dot, 1961). 'Perla de Montserrat' × ('Rosina' × 'Eduardo Toda'). Pale yellow, small, 3 cm./1.2 in across, semi-double, flat, floriferous; growth dwarf, bushy; foliage very small, deep green. PM 22. (7.0)

Pixie Rose. Min. (Dot, 1961). 'Perla de Montserrat' × 'Coralin'. Carmine-pink, darker center, small, cupped, double; growth dwarf, 30 cm./12 in.; foliage very small, deep green. (8.2)

Plain Talk. F. (Swim & Weeks, 1964). 'Spartan' × 'Garnette'. Medium red, semi-double, medium-large, open, some scent, in clusters, profuse bloom; growth low, bushy; foliage deep green, leathery. (6.9)

Playboy. F. (Cocker, 1976). 'City of Leeds' × ('Chanelle' × 'Piccadilly'). Scarlet and golden yellow, semi-single, 10 petals, some scent, in large trusses, very free bloom all season; growth bushy, upright, 0.6-0.7 m./2-2.3 ft. RA 1976:20.

Plum Duffy. Min. (Dee Bennett, 1978). 'Magic Carrousel' × self. Mauve, double, 50 petals, some scent, very recurrent; growth dwarf, compact; foliage deep green.

Poinsettia. HT. (Howard & Smith, 1938). ('Mrs. J.D. Eisele' × 'Vaterland') × 'J.C. Thornton'. Scarlet, large, double, fragrant, floriferous; bud long, pointed; growth compact. Greenhouse variety. SWR 85. (5.0)

Poker Chip. Min. (Saville, 1979). 'Sheri Anne' × ('Yellow Jewel' × 'Tamango'-seedling). Red blend, very fragrant, double, high centered, medium, profuse bloom; bud pointed; foliage glossy, dark; growth vigorous, compact.

Polka. F. (Meilland, 1959). 'Moulin Rouge' × 'Fashion'. Crimson-pink, medium, 7 cm./2.8 in. across, in large, flat trusses, floriferous; growth branched, 0.6 m./2 ft.; foliage medium, matt. RJb 28:192. (7.3)

Polka Dot. Min. (Ralph S. Moore, 1956). 'Golden Glow' × 'Zee'. Ivory-white, double, small, abundant, recurrent; growth dwarf, 25 cm./10 in., bushy; foliage deep green, glossy. (6.7)

Polstjärnan. Cl. (Wasastjärna, 1937). Hybrid of *R. beggeriana*. Pure white, small, double, 15-20 petals, June, non-recurrent; growth very strong, 5 m./16.5 ft. or over. Very winter-hardy.

Polynesian Sunset. HT. (Boerner/Jackson & Perkins, 1965). 'Diamond Jubilee'-seedling × 'Hawaii'. Salmon-red with orange hue, fading with age, very large, to 15 cm./6 in. across, loosely double, high-centered, edge more cupped and curly, fragrant, profuse, continuous bloom; growth vigorous, bushy. RJb 30:48. (6.6)

Poly Prim. F. (Eddie, 1953). 'Goldilocks' × 'Golden Rapture'. Deep yellow, large, 7 cm./2.8 in across, very double, good form, in clusters, floriferous, some scent; growth low, 40 cm./16 in.; foliage large, firm, matt. PWR 125. (6.5)

Pompon Blanc Parfait. A. (Verdier, 1876). Flesh-pink with some lilac hue, small, densely rosette-shaped, very profuse bloom during most of June, non-recurrent; growth bushy, tall, stems with few prickles; foliage grey-green.

'Pompon de Bourgogne' — **R. centifolia parvifolia,** p. 257.

'Pompon de Paris' → **'Rouletii'**

Pompon Rouge. F. (Delforge, 1971). 'Révérence' × 'Miracle'. Luminous red, medium, very double, long-lasting, petals drop off cleanly, floriferous; growth dwarf, 30 cm./12 in.; foliage medium, matt.

Ponderosa. F. (Kordes, 1970). 'Irish Wonder' × 'Marlena'. Luminous red-orange, large, 10 cm./4 in. across, double, cupped, some scent, many together in large trusses; growth bushy, low, 0.5 m./1.7 ft.; foliage large, leathery, glossy.

Popcorn. Min. (D. Morey, 1975). 'Katharina Zeimet' × 'Diamond Jewel'. Creamy-white bud, opening to pure white, double, yellow stamens, fragrant, profuse bloom; growth dwarf, upright; foliage glossy, very dense. (8.5)

Poppy Flash. (= 'Rusticana'). F. (Meilland, 1972). Salmon-orange, large, semi-double, no scent, floriferous; growth very bushy, but irregular, 0.6-0.8 m./2-2.6 ft. RA 1973:197.

Portrait. HT. (= 'Stephanie de Monaco'). (C. Meyer/Conard-Pyle, 1970). 'Pink Parfait' × 'Pink Peace'. Deep and light pink, medium-large, double, singly on long stems, long-lasting, fragrant, petals drop off cleanly; growth bushy, upright; foliage abundant, deep green, firm, very disease-resistant. (7.5)

Poulsen's Bedder. (= 'Poulsen's Grupperose'). F. (Poulsen, 1948). 'Orléans Rose' × 'Talisman'. Clear pink, medium, 7 cm./2.8 in. across, semi-double, some scent, floriferous, in large trusses; growth vigorous, upright, 0.7 m./2.3 ft.; foliage bronze-green. (7.7)

Poulsen's Park Rose. S. (Poulsen, 1953). 'Great Western' × 'Karen Poulsen'. Silvery pink, large, 12 cm./4.8 in. across, single, saucer-shaped, in large trusses; growth very strong, 1.5 × 1.5 m./5 × 5 ft. (7.1)

Prairie Dawn. S. (Morden Exp. Farm, 1959). ('Prairie Youth' × 'Ross Rambler') × ('Dr. W. van Fleet' × *R. spinosissima altaica*). Glowing pink, double, 5-6 cm./2-2.4 in. across, intermittent bloom all summer; growth upright, medium; foliage deep green, glossy. (6.4)

Prairie Fire. S. (Phillips, 1960). 'Red Rocket' × *R. suffulta*. Bright red, white base, double, 40 petals, medium-large, 7 cm./2.8 in. across, fragrant, profuse bloom, recurrent; growth upright, tall; foliage deep green, glossy. (6.9)

Prairie Princess. S. (J.G. Buck, 1970). Medium pink, double, medium, blooming all season; growth bushy, upright, 0.8 m./2.6 ft.; foliage disease-resistant. (7.9)

Prairie Youth. HSpn. (Morden Exp. Farm, 1948). (['Ross Rambler' × 'Dr. W. van Fleet] × *R. suffulta*) × (['Dr. W. van Fleet' × 'Turkes *rugosa*-seedling'] × *R. spinosissima altaica*). Salmon-pink, semi-double, some scent, in clusters, intermittent bloom; growth tall; very hardy.

Praise of Jiro. F. (Kordes, 1969). 'Korona' × 'Spartan'. Orange-scarlet, large, double, some scent, floriferous, in clusters; growth medium, 0.5 m./1.7 ft.; foliage abundant. (6.6)

Precilla. HT. (Kordes, 1974). 'Peer Gynt' × seedling. Deep golden-yellow, medium, cupped, fragrant, singly, floriferous, petals drop off cleanly; foliage healthy, deep green.

'Preciosa' → **Indian Song**

Precious Platinum. HT. (Dickson, 1974). 'Red Planet' × 'Franklin Engelmann'. Rich crimson, double, high-centered, fragrant, singly, very free flower; growth upright; foliage medium green, glossy, firm.

Prélude. HT. (Meilland, 1954). 'Fantastique' × ('Ampère' × ['Charles P. Kilham' × 'Capucine Chambard']). Lilac, medium, double, good shape, fragrant, strong stems; growth bushy; foliage abundant, reddish-green, medium. PWR 51; RA 1955:156. (5.9)

Premier Bal. HT. (Meilland, 1955). ('Fantastique' × 'Caprice') × 'Peace'. Ivory-white with purplish-pink edge, yellow base, large, double, fragrant; growth bushy; foliage deep green. PWR 76; SWR 86. (6.8)

'Première Ballerina' → **Prima Ballerina**

Président de Sèze. G. (Mme. Hébert, 1836). Purplish-pink to more crimson, with lighter edge, large, 10 cm./4 in. across, double, quartered, fragrant; growth medium, medium high; foliage large. GSR 88. (6.6)

Président Dutailly. G. (Dubreuil, 1888). Crimson-red, deeper center, edge more lilac-rose, large, finally flat, somewhat recurrent; growth upright, 0.7 m./2.3 ft.

President Herbert Hoover. HT. (Coddington, 1930). 'Sensation' × 'Souvenir de Claudius Pernet'. Opening red with yellow base, reverse yellow overlaid with red, large, double, finally flat, fragrant; bud long; growth vigorous, strong stems, 0.9 m./3 ft.; foliage firm. PWR 75; LR 6. (5.3)

Prestige. S. (Kordes, 1957). 'Rudolph Timm' × 'Fanal'. Bright crimson, large, saucer-shaped, semi-double, yellow stamens, in clusters, recurrent; growth vigorous, medium; foliage very large, healthy. RA 2958:128; GSR 185. (6.8)

Presumida. (= 'Peter Pan'). Min. (Dot, 1948). 'Eduardo Toda' × 'Pompon de Paris'. Yellow-orange fading to white, yellowish center, small, double, flat, floriferous; growth dwarf; foliage deep green. PWR 160. (7.1)

Prima Ballerina. HT. (Tantau, 1957). Seedling × 'Peace'. Clear pink, lighter with age, base tinged with yellow, medium, 8 cm./3.2 in. across, double, resistant to weather damage, strong fragrance, profuse bloom; growth vigorous, 0.8-0.9 m./2.6-3 ft.; foliage bronze-green. GSR 354; WPR 39. (7.3)

Prince Camille de Rohan. (= 'La Rosière'). HP. (E. Verdier, 1861). Probably 'Général Jacqueminot' × 'Géant des Batailles'. Deep crimson with chestnut-brown, very large, very double, about 100 petals, imbricate, cupped, strong fragrance, floriferous, somewhat recurrent; growth upright, stems rather weak. SOR 28; GiS 13. (7.5)

Prince Charles. B. (1842). Velvety purple-crimson, with brownish-red shade, more lilac-red with age, with darker veins, curled, loosely double, fragrant, non-recurrent; growth strong, medium, stems nearly without prickles; foliage large, deep green. GSR 101; TR 3.

Prince Charming. Min. (de Vink, 1953). 'Ellen Poulsen' × 'Tom Thumb'. Bright crimson, double, 2.5 cm./1 in. across; growth dwarf, 20-30 cm./8-12 in.; foliage green with red tint. (5.9)

Princess Alice. M. (A. Paul, 1853). Crimson center with soft pink edges, double, large, fragrant, recurrent.

Princess Chichibu. F. (Harkness, 1970). ('Vera Dalton' × 'Highlight') × 'Merlin'. Purple-pink and soft pink with light orange reverse, base salmon-colored, medium, 7 cm./2.8 in. across, double, some scent, floriferous; growth medium, 0.6 m./2 ft.; foliage deep green.

Princesse Adelaide. M. (Laffay, 1845). Pale pink, very double, fragrant, floriferous, but not very mossy, stalks strong; foliage sometimes variegated with white.

Princesse Marie Dagmar. T. (Lévêque, 1893). Soft yellowish salmon-pink to nearly white, sometimes with light crimson hue, large, double; bud long; growth vigorous.

Princess Margaret (of England). HT. (Meilland, 1968). 'Queen Elizabeth' × ('Peace' × 'Michèle Meilland'). Soft crimson-pink, resistant to weather damage, large, double, high-centered, some scent, continuous bloom; growth vigorous, upright, 0.8-1 m./2.6-3.3 ft.; foliage large, deep green, firm. GSR 356. (7.3)

Princess Michiko. F. (Dickson, 1966). 'Circus' × 'Spartan'. Coppery-orange with yellow base, medium, 8 cm./3.2 in. across, double, cupped, in clusters; foliage firm, glossy. GSR 469; RA 1967:128. (7.7)

Principessa delle Rose. HT. (Aicardi, 1953). 'Julien Potin' × 'Sensation'. Mauve-pink, double, 30-40 petals, cupped, fragrant, floriferous; bud long, pointed; growth very strong, upright.

'Prins Claus' — **Rosalynn Carter**

Printemps. HT. (Mallerin, 1948). 'Tyrlon' × 'Brazier'. Old-rose overlaid with light red, yellow reverse, edge reddish, large, 10 cm./4 in. across, double, fragrant; growth vigorous; foliage deep green, glossy. SWR 87. (7.5)

Prissy Missy. Min. (E.D. Williams, 1965). 'Spring Song' × seedling. Medium pink with lighter reverse, small, very double, scented, profuse bloomer; growth dwarf, bushy, vigorous; foliage deep green, glossy. SRW 87. (7.5)

Pristine. (= 'Japico'). HT. (W.A. Wariner/Jackson & Perkins, 1978). 'White Masterpiece' × 'First Prize'. White with light pink shades, double, 30 petals, camellia-like shape, singly, very profuse bloom in spring, average in summer; growth upright; foliage very large, deep green, very disease-resistant. ARA 62:52.

Priscilla Burton. F. (McGredy, 1978). (['Maxi' × 'Evelyn Fison'] × ['Orange Sweetheart' × 'Frühlingsmorgen']) × ('Little Darling' × 'Goldilocks') × ('Evelyn Fison' × R. coryana) × ('Tantau's Triumph' × ['John Church × 'Elizabeth of Glamis]). Deep carmine with large silvery eye, semi-double, large, in trusses, free bloom; growth upright; foliage glossy, dark green. RA 1978:185.

Professeur Emile Perrot. D. (Imported from Persia by Prof. Perrot, then introduced by Turbat, 1930). Soft pink, medium-large, semi-double. Probably identical to R. damascena trigintipetala and very similar to R. damascena versicolor, but unicolored.

Prominent. (= 'Korp'). Gr. (Kordes, 1970). 'Colour Wonder' × 'Zorina'. Signal-red with scarlet-orange reverse, 8 cm./3.2 in. across, some scent, double, long-lasting, mostly singly on long stems, very floriferous; growth strong, upright, long stems, 0.9 m./3 ft.; foliage deep green, matt, very disease-resistant. RA 1972:44; GSR 470; CRA 73:27; ARA 61:58. (7.8)

Promise. HT. (W.A. Warriner/Jackson & Perkins, 1976). 'South Seas' × 'Peace'. Light pink, double, very large, high-centered, some scent, petals drop off, long-lasting, abundant bloom; growth very vigorous, 1.2-1.5 m./4-5 ft.; foliage large, glossy. (7.8)

Prosperity. HMsk. (Pemberton, 1919). 'Marie-Jeanne' × 'Perle des Jardins'. Ivory-white with yellowish center, small, very fragrant, semi-double, very floriferous in large trusses, recurrent; growth upright, medium. GSR 123. (7.1)

Proud Land. HT. (Morey/Jackson & Perkins, 1969). 'Chrysler Imperial' × red seedling. Deep red, large, very double, fragrant, singly on long stems, long-lasting; bud long, urn-shaped; growth vigorous, upright; foliage abundant, deep green, firm, very disease-resistant. (7.7)

Puerto Rico. (= 'Sable Chaud'). F. (Delbard/Chabert, 1973). Apricot-orange, double, high-centered, fragrant, singly or several together on strong stems, profuse bloom all season; growth bushy, upright, 0.8 m./2.6 ft.; foliage deep green. (7.5)

Puppy Love. Min. (E. Schwartz, 1978). 'Zorina' × seedling. Orange blend, double, 25 petals, singly, some scent, continuous bloomer; growth dwarf, upright, compact; foliage abundant. ARA 62:90.

Purple Elf. Min. (Ralph S. Moore, 1963). 'Violette' × 'Zee'. Purple-pink, double, 50 petals, small, free bloom; growth dwarf, 25 cm./10 in.; foliage glossy, deep green. (5.6)

Purple Imp. Min. (E.D. Williams, 1967). 'Baby Faurax' × 'Red Imp'. Rose-purple, small, double; growth dwarf, very compact, vigorous; foliage glossy, narrow.

Purple Splendour. F. (LeGrice, 1976). 'News' × 'Overture'. Bright purple, double, 25 petals, singly and in trusses, some scent, free-flowering; growth upright, 0.7 m./2.3 ft.; foliage deep green, healthy.

Pussta. F. (Tantau, 1972). Parentage not reported. Luminous dark red, large, double, some scent, cupped; growth bushy, upright, dense, 0.7 m./2.3 ft.; foliage first reddish, then deep green, glossy.

Pye Colour. F. (Dickson, 1972). Orange-scarlet, medium, semi-double, flat, circular, stamens golden-yellow, floriferous, many together; growth low, 40 cm./16 in., very dense, bushy; foliage deep green.

'Quatre Saisons' and 'Quatre Saisons Blanc Mousseux' → **Rosa damascena semperflorens**, p. 260. (GiS 6)

Queen Elizabeth. (= 'The Queen Elizabeth Rose'). Gr. (Lammerts, 1954). 'Charlotte Armstrong' × 'Floradora'. Pure soft pink, large, loosely double, 8-10 cm./3.2-4 in. across, cupped, fragrant, several together and in clusters on very long, strong stems, floriferous; growth very strong, medium, stems with few prickles; foliage very large, reddish, then deep green. WPR 99; GSR 471; RA 1955:112. (9.0)

Queen Elizabeth, Climbing. ClGr. (Whisler/Germain, 1957, and also Wheatcroft, 1960). Sport, vigorous climber; otherwise like the type. (7.3)

Queen Fabiola. (= 'Fabiola'). F. (Hazenberg, 1961). Sport of 'Montezuma'. Orange-red, long-lasting; otherwise like the type. Also for forcing purposes. RJb 26:224. (6.2)

Queen of Bermuda. F. (Boew, 1956). ('Independence' × 'Orange Triumph') × 'Bettina'. Orange-vermilion, large, 10 cm./4 in. across, high-centered, fragrant, in clusters, floriferous; growth vigorous, bushy; foliage bronze-green, glossy. Very similar to 'Independence'. (7.3)

Queen of Bourbons. (= 'Bourbon Queen'; 'Reine des Iles Bourbons'; 'Souvenir de la Princess de Lamballe'). B. (Mauget, 1835). Pink with more purple center and lighter edge, semi-double, medium, 7 cm./2.8 in. across, strong fragrance, floriferous, June; growth strong, loose, upright, 3 m./10 ft.; foliage bluish-green. GSR 93; PGR 14.

Queen o' the Lakes. HT. (Brownell, 1949). 'Pink Princess' × 'Crimson Glory'. Blood-red to crimson, large, double, high-centered, fragrant; bud long, pointed; growth bushy, vigorous; foliage deep green, glossy. (7.7)

Queen of the Dwarfs. (= 'Zwergkönigin'). Min. (Kordes, 1955). 'World's Fair' × 'Tom Thumb'. Silky pink, small, double, rosette-shape, floriferous, in clusters; growth dwarf, 30 cm./12 in.; foliage rather large. KR 9:140.

Radar. HT. (Meilland, 1953). 'Charles Mallerin' × 'Independence'. Geranium-red, large, double, some scent, moderate bloom; growth vigorous, low, 0.5 m./1.7 ft.; foliage deep green, glossy. (5.5)

Radiance. HT. (Cook, 1908). 'Enchanter' × 'Cardinal'. Pink with slightly lighter reverse, large, loosely double, cupped, strong fragrance; growth vigorous. RZ 1910:1. (6.6)

Ramona. (Dietrich & Turner, 1913). Laevigata hybrid. Crimson to carmine, single, very large, flat. Probably a red sport of 'Anemone', or a seedling from it. GSR 197; GiS 24; RA 1976:180; HRo 5. Tender.

Rapture. HT. (Traenly & Schenck, 1926). Sport of 'Mme. Butterfly'. Deeper pink than the type, with yellow base; growth stronger, foliage larger. (7.5)

Raubritter. S. (Kordes, 1936). *R. macrantha* hybrid. 'Daisy Hill' × 'Solarium'. Light purplish-pink, small, 5 cm./2 in. across, semi-double, globose, fragrant, singly and in clusters, profuse bloom, non-recurrent; growth strong, bushy, 2 m./6.6 ft.; foliage small, firm, strongly veined. SOR 41; TRT 140; PGR 89. (8.2)

Raymond Chenault. K. (Kordes, 1960). *R. kordesii* × 'Montezuma'. Scarlet, large, 10 cm./4 in. across, loosely double, strong scent, early flowering, recurrent, in clusters; growth strong, 3 m./10 ft.; foliage deep green, glossy. (7.9)

Rayon d'Or. HT. (Pernet-Ducher, 1910). 'Mélanie Soupert' × 'Soleil d'Or'. Golden-yellow, very double, fragrant, large, recurrent; bud coppery-orange; growth upright, 0.6 m./2 ft. RZ 1910:37.

Razzle-Dazzle. F. (W.A. Warriner/Jackson & Perkins, 1977). Seedling × seedling. Scarlet with white reverse, double, camellia-like form, 25 petals, some scent, in clusters, abundant bloom; growth upright, branched, 0.7 m./2.3 ft.; foliage deep green, leathery, very disease-resistant. (7.5)

Rebell. HT. (Kordes, 1973). 'Roter Stern' × 'Brandenburg'. Similar to 'Brandenburg', but deeper orange-red, large, cupped, double, strong fragrance; growth strong, upright; young growth red.

Red American Beauty. HT. (Morey/Jackson & Perkins, 1959). 'Happiness' × 'San Fernando'. Scarlet, large, 12 cm./4.8 in. across, double, strong fragrance; bud long, pointed; growth bushy; foliage deep green. (6.8)

Red Arrow. Min. (Ralph S. Moore, 1965). (*R. wichuraiana* × 'Floradora') × seedling. Medium red, double, 40 petals, small, high-centered, some scent, profuse bloom; growth dwarf, 30-40 cm./12-16 in.; foliage leathery, glossy. (5.8)

Red Button. Min. (R.S. Moore/Sequoia Nurs., 1978). (*R. wichuraiana* × 'Floradora') × 'Magic Dragon'. Deep red, full, small, free bloom; bud short-pointed; foliage very small, glossy; growth bushy, compact, spreading.

Redcap. F. (Swim/Armstrong, 1954). 'World's Fair' × 'Pinocchio'. Light red, medium-large, semi-double, cupped, in convex trusses, very floriferous; growth bushy, upright; foliage firm, matt.

Red Cascade. ClMin. (Ralph S. Moore, 1976). (*R. wichuraina* × 'Floradora') × 'Magic Dragon'. Dark red, small, double, 50 petals, cupped, in clusters, abundant, recurrent; growth prostrate, arching and spreading, dense; foliage small, deep green. (8.0)

Red Chief. HT. (Armstrong, 1967). Seedling × 'Chrysler Imperial'. Luminous light red, large, double, fragrant, high-centered, profuse bloom; growth strong, upright; foliage firm. (7.1)

Red Cushion. F. (Armstrong, 1966). 'Circus' × 'Ruby Lips'. Deep red, small, semi-double, some scent, in clusters and in large, convex trusses, very profuse bloom; growth bushy, low, 40-50 cm./16-20 in.; foliage small, rounded, firm. (7.6)

Red Dandy. F. (Norman/Harkness, 1959). 'Ena Harkness' × 'Karl Herbst'. Deep crimson, velvety, medium-large, 7 cm./2.8 in. across, double, finally flat, cupped, fragrant, floriferous, resistant to weather damage; growth vigorous, upright, 0.9 m./3 ft.; foliage glossy. GSR 472; RA 1960:160. (7.1)

Red Devil. (= 'Coeur d'Amour'). HT. (Dickson, 1970). 'Silver Lining' × 'Prima Ballerina'. Bright red with slightly paler reverse, large, double, some scent, long-lasting, floriferous; growth vigorous, bushy, branched; foliage large, abundant, glossy. RA 1967:48. (7.6)

Red Duchess. HT. (Brownell, 1942). 'Pink Princess' × 'Crimson Glory'. Medium red, large, 12 cm./4.8 in. across, high-centered, fragrant, on long, strong stems; growth vigorous, upright; foliage bronze-green, glossy. (6.5)

Red Elf. Min. (de Vink, 1949). 'Eblouissant' × 'Tom Thumb'. Deep crimson, small, 2-3 cm./0.8-1.2 in. across, semi-double, some scent, free bloom; growth dwarf, bushy; foliage very small, soft. (6.9)

Red Empress. LCl. (Mallerin, 1956). ('Holstein' × 'Décor') × self. Carmine-red, large, 8 cm./3.2 in. across, double, loosely globose, strong fragrance, 1-2 together, floriferous, recurrent; growth vigorous, 3 m./10 ft.; foliage deep green, firm. (7.6)

Red Favorite. (= 'Schweizer Gruss'). F. (Tantau, 1954). 'Karl Weinhausen' × 'Tantau's Triumph'. Velvety deep red, medium-large, 6 cm./2.4 in. across, semi-double, cupped, some scent, floriferous, in large trusses, recurrent; growth strong, branched, 0.7 m./2.3 ft.; foliage large, deep green. PWR 111.

Red Flush. Min. (E. Schwartz, 1978). Parentage not reported. Medium red, double, 50 petals, cupped, no scent, singly and several together, profuse bloom, recurrent; growth dwarf, bushy; foliage matt.

Red Fountain. LCl. (J.B. Williams, 1975). 'Don Juan' × 'Blaze'. Scarlet with deep crimson reverse, small to medium, double, cupped, some scent, several and in clusters on long stems, flowering all summer; growth strong, free standing, 2.5-3 m./8.3-10 ft. high; foliage large, deep green, disease-resistant. ARA 60:1. (7.0)

Red Germain. Min. (Ralph S. Moore, 1975). (*R. wichuraiana* × 'Floradora') × ('Oakington Ruby' × 'Floradora'). Medium red with white base and white reverse, double, 35 petals, no scent, continuous bloom; growth dwarf, branched; foliage semi-glossy, healthy.

Redgold. F. (Dickson, 1971). (['Karl Herbst' × 'Masquerade'] × 'Doctor Faust') × 'Piccadilly'. Golden yellow, suffused with cherry red, medium-large, double, some scent, profuse and continuous bloom, singly or several together; growth bushy, upright; foliage matt green, very resistant to Black Spot. GSR 473; KR 10:75; CRA 69:48. (7.8)

Red Imp. (= 'Maid Marion'; 'Mon Trésor'). Min. (de Vink, 1951). 'Ellen Poulsen' × 'Tom Thumb'. Crimson-scarlet, small, 2.5 cm./1 in. across, very double, rosette-shaped, very flat, long-lasting; growth dwarf, 20-25 cm./8-10 in.; foliage small, deep green. (7.7)

Red Jacket. HT. (Swim, 1950). 'World's Fair' × 'Mirandy'. Deep red, large, 8 cm./3.2 in. across, semi-double, finally flat, some scent; bud urn-shaped; growth bushy; foliage firm, deep green. (8.0)

Red Lion. HT. (McGredy, 1964). 'Kordes Perfecta' × 'Detroiter'. Carmine, later more crimson-pink, large, 12 cm./4.8 in. across, double, fragrant, high-centered, floriferous; bud long, singly on long stems; growth vigorous, 1 m./3.3 ft.; foliage bronze-green, glossy. Greenhouse variety. GSR 358. (7.9)

Red Masterpeice. HT. (Jackson & Perkins, 1974). Deep red, very large, 12 cm./4.8 in. across, very double, good scent, singly on long stems; growth vigorous, upright. ARA 59:52.

Red Pinocchio. F. (Boerner/Jackson & Perkins, 1947). Yellow Pinocchio-seedling × 'Donald Prior'. Velvety carmine, double, 30 petals, large, 8 cm./3.2 in. across, cupped, fragrant, in clusters, profuse bloom; growth bushy, vigorous; foliage deep green, glossy. (7.5)

Red Planet. HT. (Dickson, 1969). 'Red Devil' × seedling. Carmine with slightly lighter reverse, large, double, fragrant, singly or several together on long stems; growth vigorous, upright, medium; foliage medium-large, deep green, glossy. RA 1970:3. (7.1)

Red Queen (= 'Liebestraum'). HT. (Kordes, 1968). 'Colour Wonder' × 'Liberty Bell'. Cherry-red, large, double, fragrant, floriferous; growth upright; foliage abundant, healthy. RA 1969:129; GSR 359; RJb 34:136. (7.5)

Red Radiance. HT. (Gude Bros., 1916). Sport of 'Radiance'. Flowers light crimson; otherwise like the type. (6.0)

Red Reflection. HT. (W.A. Warriner/Jackson & Perkins, 1975). 'Tropicana' × 'Living'. Medium red with lighter reverse, large, double, high-centered, slight scent; bud pointed; growth upright; foliage large, leathery. (7.0)

Red Riding Hood. Min. (T. Robinson, 1955). Sport of 'Red Imp'. Brilliant dark velvety red, very double, small, in clusters; growth very dwarf, 12-15 cm./4.8-6 in. high. (7.5)

Red Rock. HT. (Meilland, 1972). ('Royal Velvet' × 'Chrysler Imperial') × 'Pharaoh'. Cherry-red, very large, 12 cm./4.8 in. across, 35 petals, some scent, singly, free bloom; growth very vigorous; foliage medium.

Red Sparkler. HT. (G.J. Buck, 1974). 'Park's Scarlet Royal' × 'Rouge Mallerin'. Dark red with lighter reverse, striped with pale red, pink and white, double, 50 petals, strong fragrance, profuse bloom all season; growth moderately vigorous, upright; foliage leathery, deep green. (3.7)

Red Tag. Min. (E.D. Williams/Mini-Roses, 1978). Seedling × 'Over the Rainbow'. Medium red, fragrant, double, high centered, small, 2.5 cm./1 in., abundant bloom; bud ovoid-pointed; foliage small, glossy, dark; growth upright, spreading.

Red Wand. ClMin. (Ralph S. Moore, 1964). ([*R. wichuraiana* × 'Floradora'] × 'Orange Triumph') × miniature rose. Light crimson, double, small, free bloom; growth vigorous, 1-1.3 m./3.3-4.3 ft. high. (6.5)

Red Wings. F. (Boerner/Jackson & Perkins, 1958). ('Improved Lafayette' × 'Herrenhausen') × 'Lavender Pinocchio'. Deep red, large, 8 cm./3.2 in. across, semi-double, cupped, fragrant, floriferous; growth vigorous, upright, bushy; foliage deep green, firm.

'Red Yesterday' → **Marjorie Frair.**

Regensberg. F. (McGredy, 1979). 'Geoff Boycott' × 'Olde Master'. Red-purple, double, 20 petals, fragrant, free and continuous bloom; growth short, bushy; foliage medium green.

Reichspräsident von Hindenburg. HT. (Lambert, 1933). 'Frau Karl Druschki' × 'Graf Silva Tarouca'.

Dark pink to carmine with darker reverse and lighter veins, very double, fragrant; growth vigorous, bushy; foliage large. (6.3)

Reine des Mousseuses. M. (Robert & Moreau, about 1860). Flesh-rose, small to medium, double, June-flowering, non-recurrent, profuse bloom; growth 1 m./3.3 ft.

'Reine des Neiges' — **Frau Karl Druschki.**

Reine des Violettes. HP. (Millet-Malet, 1860). Seedling of 'Pius IX'. Rich lilac-purple, becoming violet with age, velvety, with slightly lighter reverse, medium, flat, quartered, with small eye, recurrent, strong perfume; growth vigorous; foliage more grey-green. GSR 114; GiS 13; TRT 37. (7.1)

Reine Victoria. B. (J. Schwartz, 1872). Deep pink, very double, cupped, sweet fragrance, continuous bloom; growth upright, medium; foliage soft green. ARA 1967:155; GR 384; GiS 12; PGR 54, 56. (8.3)

Renae. ClF. (Ralph S. Moore, 1954). 'Etoile Luisante' × 'Sierra Snowstorm'. Pink, medium, double, 40 petals, fragrant, in clusters, abundant, recurrent; growth vigorous, climbing; foliage small, leathery. (6.4)

Rendez-vous. HT. (Meilland, 1953). 'Peace' × 'Europa'. Pink with lighter edge, large, 12 cm./4.8 in. across, double, cupped, slight scent, moderate bloom; growth vigorous, branched, 0.7 m./2.3 ft.; foliage large, glossy. BTR 29.

Rêve d'Or. LCl. (Veuve Ducher, 1869). Seedling of 'Mme. Schultz'. Yellow with reddish hue, soon fading to pale yellow, very large, globose, double, good shape, petals revolved, some scent, several together, recurrent; growth very vigorous, 3 m./10 ft.; foliage deep green, glossy. GSR 220. Tender in cold regions.

Réveil Dijonnais. S. (Buatois; 1931). 'Eugène Fürst' × 'Constance'. Cherry red with large golden center, semi-double, flat, 12 cm./4.8 in. across, fragrant, several together, floriferous, somewhat recurrent; growth branched, medium-vigorous, 2.5 m./8.3 ft.; foliage large, glossy. GSR 221; ARA 1935:201; GiS 21. (7.6)

Rex Anderson. HT. (McGredy, 1938). 'Florence L. Izzard' × 'Mrs. Charles Lamplough'. Ivory-white, double, large, fragrant, little bloom, growth vigorous; foliage grey-green. RA 1939:256. (5.3)

Rhonda. LCl. (Lissemore, 1968). 'New Dawn' × 'Spartan'. Clear pink, large, double, rather globose, some fragrance, singly or several together on strong stems, profuse and continuous bloom; growth vigorous, 2.5 m./8.3 ft.; foliage large, deep green, glossy. (7.9)

Rimosa. F. (Meilland, 1958). 'Goldilocks' × 'Perla de Montserrat'. Lemon-yellow, semi-double, medium, 5 cm./2 in. across, no scent, floriferous, many together; growth rather uneven, to 0.6 m./2 ft.; foliage medium-large, matt. RJb 28:192.

Rina Herholdt. HT. (Herholdt, 1959). Creamy-yellow with broad crimson edge, large, very double, high-centered; growth vigorous; foliage medium, young growth purple. RJb 23:32. (6.2)

Ripples. F. (LeGrice, 1971). ('Tantau's Surprise' × 'Marjorie LeGrice') × (seedling × 'Africa Star'). Soft lavender-lilac, large, 9 cm./3.6 in. across, semi-double, petals slightly curled, floriferous, some scent; growth bushy, 0.7 m./2.3 ft.; foliage small, matt.

Rise n' Shine. Min. (Ralph S. Moore, 1971). 'Little Darling' × 'Yellow Magic'. Medium yellow with deeper center, double, high-centered, singly and in clusters, perfect form, blooming all season; growth dwarf, bushy, upright; foliage medium green, dull. (9.0)

Ritter von Barmstede. K. (Kordes, 1959). Parentage not reported. Dark rose-pink with small white eye, medium-large, 5 cm./2 in. across, semi-double, some scent, in clusters, profuse bloom, recurrent; growth very strong, 3-4 m./10-13 ft.; foliage glossy, light green. GSR 258. (5.3)

River's George IV. HCh. (Rivers, 1820). *R. damascena* × *R. chinensis* hybrid. Dark crimson, loosely double, fragrant, June, non-recurrent. (6.9)

Roaming. HT. (Sanday, 1970). 'Very Dalton' × 'Tropicana'. Reddish-pink, medium, semi-double, no scent, singly and in trusses, floriferous; bud pointed; growth upright; foliage medium green, matt. RA 1971:145.

Robert Duncan. HP. (Dickson, 1897). Purplish-pink, sometimes flamed with scarlet, large, double, 70 petals, fragrant, good form, recurrent; growth vigorous. (6.0)

Robert le Diable. C. Scarlet-pink, fading to purple, with purple and red tints, center often green, medium, outer petals reflexed, inner ones erected, flowering late and opening only in warm weather; growth loose, stems often prostrate, 1 m./3.3 ft. long, prickly; foliage narrow, deep green. TR 7; GiS 8.

Robert Leopold. M. (Buatois, 1841). Flesh pink, overlaid with crimson, large, double.

Robin. Min. (Dot, 1956). 'Perla de Montserrat' × 'Perla de Alcanada'. Deep red, small, 2.5 cm./1 in. across, very double, flat, in clusters together; bud urn-shaped; growth dwarf, 25 cm./10 in.; foliage leathery, matt. (8.1)

Robusta. HRg. (Kordes, 1979). Seedling × *R. rugosa regeliana*. Medium red, single, moderate scent, 3-5 in. clusters, abundant continuous bloom; bud small, long; growth vigorous, upright, very prickly; foliage leathery, glossy, healthy.

Robin Hood. HMsk. (Pemberton, 1927). Seedling × 'Miss Edith Cavell'. Cherry-red with white center, semi-double, small, in clusters, very floriferous, very recurrent; growth very dense, compact, 1-1.5 m./3.3-5 ft.; foliage small, medium green. (7.1)

Rob Roy. F. (Cocker, 1970). 'Irish Wonder' × 'Wendy Cussons'. Crimson-scarlet, large, loosely double, some scent, several together, very floriferous; growth vigorous, robust, 0.7-0.9 m./2.3-3 ft.; foliage healthy, deep green. RA 1970:113; GSR 474; CRA 71:48.

Rod Stillman. HT. (Hamilton, 1948). 'Ophelia' × 'Editor McFarland'. Light pink, base orange, large, double, 35 petals, very fragrant; growth very vigorous; foliage deep green.

Rödhätte. F. (Poulsen, 1911). 'Mme. Norbert Levavasseur' × 'Richmond'. Clear cherry-red, medium-large, semi-double, in trusses on long stems, floriferous; growth bushy, 0.5 m./1.7 ft.; foliage deep green. Famous old variety.

Roger Lambellin. HP. (Veuve Schwartz, 1890). Sport of 'Fisher & Holmes'. Crimson-chestnut brown with very narrow white edges and flecked with white, edges curled, large, very double, fragrant, recurrent; growth vigorous, medium; foliage large, matt. GSR 115; GiS 13; HRo 24; PGR 71. (7.4)

Roman Holiday. F. (Lindquist, 1966). ('Pinkie' × 'Independence') × 'Circus'. Interior orange, turning to scarlet, reverse and base yellow, medium, double, scented, floriferous; growth bushy, low, 40 cm./16 in.; foliage deep green, leathery. (6.7)

Romantica. (= 'Meinaregi'). HT. (Meilland, 1962). Shell-pink, double, good form, high centered, singly on strong stems; bud urn-shaped; growth medium; foliage deep green, healthy.

Rome Glory. (= 'Gloria di Roma'). HT. (Aicardi, 1937). 'Dame Edith Helen' × 'Sensation'. Scarlet, reverse cherry red, globose, large, 10-12 cm./4-4.8 in. across, double, fragrant; growth vigorous, bushy, 0.6 m./2 ft.; foliage loose. LR 5; RA 1942:25. (6.0)

Rosa. In most rose books the so-called wild roses, i.e. the species, together with their garden varieties, are arranged in alphabetical order. In this book, however, these rose species are to be found in their own chapter, pp. 246 to 296.

Rosa Mundi. (= *R. gallica versicolor*). Sport of *R. gallica officinalis*. Red striped with white, large, loose, semi-double, fragrant. Often confused with 'York and Lancaster' which is completely different. RA 1977:20; PGR 17; SOR 30. (8.4)

Rosa Mundi Selfcoloured. G. Red sport of *R. gallica versicolor*). Crimson, flat, non-recurrent, low. An old variety, cultivated in England before 1759.

Rosada. Min. (Dot, 1950). 'Perla de Alcanada' × 'Rouletii'. Pink, interior lighter and more salmon-yellow, small, very double, cupped, floriferous; growth dwarf, 20 cm./8 in.; foliage small, deep green.

Rosalynn Carter. (= 'Prins Claus'). Gr. (de Ruiter/ Conard-Pyle, 1978). Seedling × 'Scanin'. Salmon-orange, large, high-centered, fragrant, singly on long stems, abundant continuous bloom; growth very strong, bushy, 0.9 m./3 ft.; foliage glossy, deep green. ARA 1979:170.

Rosarium Uetersen. LCl. (Kordes, 1977). 'Karlsruhe' × seedling. Deep pink, very double, 140 petals, full, open, fragrant, singly and in clusters, profuse intermittent bloom; growth vigorous, climbing; foliage large, glossy, abundant.

Roseanna. ClMin. (E.D. Williams, 1976). 'Little Darling' × seedling. Deep pink with darker reverse, double, 50 petals, high-centered, singly and in clusters, intermittent bloom; growth semi-climbing, tall; foliage glossy, firm.

Rose d'Amour. (= *R. virginiana plena*). *R. virginiana* × ?*R. carolina*. Pink with darker center, very double, medium, summer-flowering only, bud deep pink, opening very slowly, with very long sepals; growth vigorous, to 2 m./6.6 ft. or over, stems without prickles with the exception of small, sharp, paired prickles under the leaf axils of flowering branches; leaflets 5-7, oblong, ellip-

tic, serrulate. Not to be confused with the *gallica* variety 'Rose d'Amour' of Redouté, nor with the similar *Rosa rapa* (= 'Le Rosier de Turneps'), also in Redouté, vol. 2, plate 7. TRT 49; SOR 44.

Rose de la Grifferaie. Cl. (Vibert, 1845).? *R. setigera × R. gallica* or *R. damascena*. Crimson-pink, becoming lilac-pink, medium, double, strong perfume; growth very strong, and therefore formerly often used as understock for budding. LR 2.

Rose de Provins — **Rosa gallica,** p. 255. (PGR 35)

Rose de Rescht. D. Bright purplish-red, fading to lilac, rosette-shaped, very double, strong fragrance, flowers for a long time; growth compact; foliage dense. Introduced by Miss Nancy Lindsay from Persia or France to England, and distributed from there. (9.0)

'Rose du Maître d'Ecole' → **Du Maître de'Ecole**

'Rose des Peintres'. Frequently regarded to be a variety of its own, but, following G. S. Thomas, is probably *R. centifolia*. (7.1)

Rose du Roi. D. (Portland type). (Lelieur/Souchet, 1816). Crimson, large, very double, strong fragrance, lazy bloomer; slow growing. Very important, as the first Hybrid Perpetual. (7.0)

Rose Gaujard. HT. (Gaujard, 1957). 'Peace' × Opéra'-seedling. Carmine-pink interior, and silvery-white reverse, 10 cm./4 in. across, very double, high-centered, fragrant, floriferous; growth vigorous, 0.5 m./1.7 ft.; foliage glossy, very resistant to weather damage. GSR 360; PWR 45; RA 1958:48. (6.2)

Rose Hillas Red. Min. (Ralph S. Moore, 1977). (*R. wichuraiana* × 'Floradora') × 'Westmont'. Deep red, with base of petals white, double, open, free bloom, resistant to weather damage, continuous bloom; growth dwarf, compact; foliage glossy.

'Rose of Castile' — **Rosa damascena,** p. 259.

Rose of Tralee. F. (McGredy, 1964). 'Leverkusen' × 'Korona'. Deep red with salmon hue, large, 10 cm./4 in. across, double, some scent, several together in clusters, floriferous; growth very vigorous, bushy; foliage deep green. GSR 475; GR 241. (7.7)

Rose Parade. F. (J. B. Williams, 1974). 'Sumatra' × 'Queen Elizabeth'. Coral-peach to pink, medium, double, 35 petals, cupped, long-lasting, tea scent, in clusters, abundant intermittent bloom; growth vigorous, medium; foliage large, glossy. ARA 60:20. (8.5)

Rosenelfe. F. (Kordes, 1939). 'Else Poulsen' × 'Sir Basil McFarland'. Soft pink, medium, 6 cm./2.4 in. across, double, no scent, floriferous, in clusters on strong stems; growth low, 40 cm./16 in., bushy; foliage large, light green, matt. (7.2)

Rosenfee. F. (Boerner/Jackson & Perkins, 1967). Bright, pure pink, very double, medium, slightly star-shaped, good form, floriferous, in clusters; growth bushy, low, 0.5 m./1.7 ft.; foliage deep green.

Rosemary Rose. F. (de Ruiter, 1954). 'Gruss an Teplitz' × seedling. Deep crimson-pink, medium, very double, flat, camellia-like shape, fragrant, many together in large trusses, recurrent; growth very strong, bushy, 0.5 m./1.7 ft.; somewhat spreading; foliage remaining reddish- or brownish-green. PWR 101; RJb 25:64; RA 1955:128. (6.6)

Roseraie de l'Hay. HRg. (Cochet-Cochet, 1901). Sport of *R. rugosa rosea*. Velvety crimson-purple, large, double, strong perfume, continuous bloom all summer; growth vigorous, bushy, medium; foliage bright, green GSR 135; PWR 191; TRT 44. (7.2)

Rosetone. Min. (Ralph S. Moore, 1977). 'Dream Dust' × 'Little Chief'. Bright pink, double, 60 petals, high-centered, in clusters, abundant bloom; growth dwarf, bushy, compact; foliage small, leathery, deep green.

Rosette Delizy. T. (Nabonnand, 1922). 'Général Galinéni' × 'Comtesse Bardi'. Yellow with apricot, outer petals deep crimson, large, double, good form; growth very vigorous. (6.9)

Rosi Mittermaier. F. (Kordes, 1977). Bright orange, medium-large, open, several together in clusters, petals drop off cleanly, hardy, profuse bloom, recurrent; growth medium, branched, bushy; foliage medium, dense, glossy, deep green.

Rosina. (= 'Josephine Wheatcroft'). Min. (Dot, 1951). 'Eduardo Toda' × 'Rouletii'. Clear bright yellow, small, semi-double, fragrant, finally flat, very floriferous; bud long, pointed; growth dwarf, 30-35 cm./12-14 in.; foliage light green, glossy. PWR 164; HRo 13. (6.1)

Rosmarin. Min. (Kordes, 1965). 'Tom Thumb' × 'Dacapo'. Silvery-pink with carmine-pink eye, becoming completely deep pink with age, small, very double, flat rosette-shaped and star-shaped, no scent, petals drop off cleanly, floriferous; growth dwarf, 30 cm./12 in.; fo-

liage light green, small. GSR 505; KR 10:141; RJb 30:129. (8.4)

Rostock. HMsk. (Kordes, 1937). 'Eva' × 'Louise Katherine Breslau'. Bright pink, very large, high-centered, double, some scent, in clusters along the branches, profuse bloom, recurrent; bud yellow and red; growth very strong, bushy; foliage glossy, deep green. (6.5)

Rosy Cheeks. HT. (Andersons Nurseries, 1975). 'Beauty of Festival' × 'Grandpa Dickson'. Red with yellow reverse, very large, double, 35 petals, very fragrant, several together, free bloom; growth upright, vigorous; foliage deep green, glossy.

Rosy Gem. Min. (Meilland, 1973). Sport of 'Scarlet Gem'. Dark pink, opening cupped, then flat, imbricate, 60 petals, in trusses, continuous bloom; growth dwarf, bushy; foliage semi-glossy, small, deep green. (7.8)

Rosy Jewel. Min. (Morey/Jackson & Perkins, 1958). Sport of 'Dick Koster' × 'Tom Thumb'. Rosy-red with lighter reverse and white center, small, double, 25 petals, very free bloom; growth dwarf, 15-20 cm./6-8 in., compact.

Rosy Mantle. LCl. (Cocker, 1968). 'New Dawn' × 'Prima Ballerina'. Rosy-pink, large, loosely double, some scent, several together, recurrent; growth very vigorous, 2-2.5 m./6.6-8.3 ft.; foliage deep green, glossy. RA 1971:113.

Rougemoss. F. (Ralph S. Moore, 1972). 'Rumba' × HMoss-seedling. Orange-red to red, medium, open, double, fragrant, singly and several together, abundant bloom, long-lasting; bud mossy; growth bushy, upright, 0.9 m./3 ft., stems very prickly; foliage medium, leathery. (5.1)

Rouletii. Min. Found by the Swiss Colonel Roulet in Maubourget, Switzerland; introduced by Correvon of Geneva. Rosy-pink, very double, small, only 2 cm./0.8 in. across, continuous bloom, singly or several together; growth very dwarf, 10-15 cm./4-6 in., but taller when budded. It is fairly certain that this variety is identical to 'Pompon de Paris'. PM 22. (7.8)

Roundelay. Gr. (Swim/Armstrong, 1954). 'Charlotte Armstrong' × 'Floradora'. Cardinal-red, medium, double, 40 petals, high-centered, fragrant, free bloom; bud ovoid; growth very vigorous; foliage deep green. (7.2)

Royal Albert Hall. HT. (Cocker, 1972). 'Fragrant Cloud' × 'Postilion'. Cherry-red interior, pale yellow reverse, double, fragrant, good form, continuous bloom; growth bushy, vigorous, 0.7 m./2.3 ft.; foliage deep green, young growth purple. (8.0)

Royal Ascot. HT. (Delbert/Chabert, 1968). 'Chic Parisien' × (Grand Première' × ['Sultane' × 'Mme. Joseph Perraud']). Pink, reverse shaded with carmine, semi-double, high-centered, large, cupped, abundant bloom; growth very vigorous; foliage firm, glossy.

Royal Canadian. HT. (Morey/Jackson & Perkins, 1968). Seedling × 'Talisman'. Scarlet, large, double, fragrant, hardy; bud urn-shaped; growth vigorous, bushy, upright; foliage bright green, glossy. (7.3)

Royal Dane. (= 'Troika'). HT. (Poulsen, 1972). Red-orange with coppery hue, large, double, strong fragrance, floriferous; bud long, red-brown; growth very vigorous; foliage large, glossy. RA 1973:16. (7.5)

Royal Flush. LCl. (Fuller/Wyant, 1970). 'Little Darling' × 'Suspense'. Cream, edges blending pink, fragrant, semi-double, cupped, medium, abundant, continuous bloom; bud ovoid; foliage dark, leathery; growth upright, vigorous, climbing.

Royal Gold. LCl. (Morey/Jackson & Perkins, 1957). 'Climbing Goldilocks' × 'Lydia'. Golden-yellow, large, 10 cm./4 in. across, hardy, double, fragrant, singly or several together; growth vigorous, 2-3 m./6.6-10 ft. high; foliage glossy. KR 9:53; RJb 22:32. (7.4)

Royal Highness. HT. (Swim & Weeks, 1962). 'Virgo' × 'Peace'. Bright pink, very large, 13 cm./5.2 in. across, double, high-centered, floriferous, strong stems, susceptible to rain damage; growth strong, bushy, 0.9 m./3 ft.; foliage bright green, wrinkled, very resistant to mildew. GSR 361. (8.4)

Royal Lavender. LCl. (Morey/Jackson & Perkins, 1961). 'Lavender Queen' × 'Amy Vanderbilt'. Lavender tinted with grey and pink, large, 8 cm./3.2 in. across, double, strong fragrance, floriferous; growth vigorous, 2-2.5 m./6.6-8.3 ft.; foliage large, rounded, bright green.

Royal Ruby. Min. (D. Morey, 1972). 'Garnette' × ('Tom Thumb' × 'Ruby Jewel'). Red with white base of petals, small, double, singly and in clusters, some scent, abundant continuous bloom; growth dwarf, vigorous, 25 cm./10 in., no prickles; foliage small, deep green, disease-resistant. (7.3)

Royal Salute. (= 'Rose Baby'). Min. (McGredy, 1976).

'New Penny' × 'Marlena'. Rose-red, double, in trusses, continuous bloom; growth dwarf, 40 cm./16 in.; foliage small, deep green, matt. RA 1976:20.

Royal Scarlet. HT. (Kraus/Wyant, 1966). 'McGredy's Scarlet' × 'Christian Dior'. Scarlet, large, double, high-centered, fragrant, long-lasting, continuous bloom, singly or several together; growth vigorous, bushy; foliage medium green, glossy. (6.8)

Royal Sunset. LCl. (Morey/Jackson & Perkins, 1960). 'Sungold' × 'Sutter's Gold'. Apricot, large, 12 cm./4.8 in. across, double, 20 petals, fruity scent, free bloom; growth strong, tall to very tall; foliage firm. (8.1)

Royal Tan. HT. (McGredy, 1955). 'Charles P. Kilham' × 'Mrs. Sam McGredy'. Lavender-white with brownish hue, large, high-centered, double, some scent; growth bushy, 0.6 m./2 ft. (5.8)

Royal Velvet. HT. (Meilland, 1959). ('Happiness' × 'Independence') × ('Happiness' × 'Floradora'). Bright deep red, velvety, large, 10 cm./4 in. across, double, some scent, floriferous; growth vigorous. (6.8)

Rubaiyat. HT. (McGredy, 1946). ('McGredy's Scarlet' × 'Mrs. Sam McGredy') × (seedling × 'Sir Basil McFarland'). Crimson-pink with slightly lighter reverse, large, double, high-centered, strong fragrance, floriferous; growth very vigorous, 0.8 m./2.6 ft., bushy; foliage large, matt, dense. PWR 17; SRW 90. (7.5)

'Ruga' — **Rosa ruga** Lindl., p. 288.

Ruhm von Steinfurth. HP (Weigand/Schultheis, 1920). 'Frau Karl Druschki' × 'Ulrich Brunner Fils'. Red, very large, double, 35 petals, very fragrant, profuse bloom, recurrent; bud long; growth very vigorous; foliage deep green, leathery.

Rumba. F. (Poulsen, 1958). 'Masquerade' × ('Poulsen's Bedder' × 'Floradora'). Deep yellow and orange, reverse red, later turning scarlet, small, 5 cm./2 in. across, first globose, then flat, double, some scent, very floriferous, recurrent; growth bushy, low, 40 cm./16 in.; foliage bright green. GSR 477; PWR 140; RJb 22:129. (6.8)

Ruskin. (= 'John Ruskin'). HRg. (Van Fleet, 1928), 'Souvenir de Pierre Leperdrieux' × 'Victor Hugo'. Crimson, large, very double, strong fragrance, summer-flowering, very recurrent; growth bushy, medium. (8.5)

'Rusticana' — **Poppy Flash**

Saarbrücken. S. (Kordes, 1959). 'World's Fair' × seedling. Scarlet with darker shades, large, 8 cm./3.2 in. across, semi-double, in large clusters, continuous bloom; growth bushy, vigorous, medium; foliage abundant. (8.2)

Safrano. T. (Beauregard, 1839). Apricot-yellow, fading with age, large, loosely double, floriferous, fragrant; growth strong; important variety when rose hybridizing started. RZ 1886:69. (7.2)

Saint-Exupéry. HT. (Delbard/Chabert, 1961). ('Christopher Stones' × 'Marcel Gret') × ('Holstein' × 'Bayadère'). Silvery mauve-lilac, large, 12 cm./4.8 in. across, double, some scent, floriferous; growth bushy. (4.2)

Salet. M. (Lacharme, 1854). Clear pink, large, double, finally flat, strong perfume, occasionally recurrent in autumn; bud not very mossy; growth vigorous, 1 m./3.3 ft., few prickles; foliage light green, soft. (8.0)

Sally Holmes. S. (R. Holmes/Fryer, 1976). 'Ivory Fashion' × 'Ballerina'. Soft pink, fading to white, single, some scent, in trusses; growth vigorous, bushy; foliage deep green, glossy. RA 1979:88.

Salute. F. (McGredy, 1958). 'Masquerade' × 'Lady Sylvia'. Interior first coppery-red, then blood red, reverse yellow, small, 4 cm./1.6 in. across, semi-double, some scent, floriferous; growth compact, low, 0.5 m./1.7 ft.; foliage dull green.

Salvo. HT. (Herholdt, 1959). 'Happiness' × 'Grand Gala'. Velvety crimson, large, 12 cm./4.8 in. across, double, fragrant, strong stems; growth medium. RJb 24:128. (6.6)

Samba. F. (Kordes, 1964). 'Rumba' × seedling. Deep yellow with reddish reverse, later turning more red within, medium-large, in clusters, very floriferous; growth very bushy, low, 40-50 cm./16-20 in.; foliage bright green, glossy. KR 10:29. (7.2)

Sander's White Rambler. R. (Sanders & Sons, 1912). *Wichuraiana*-type. White, small, imbricated, very double, in clusters, very profuse bloom, non-recurrent; growth vigorous, 3 m./10 ft.; foliage small, deep green, glossy.

Sandringham. F. (Kordes, 1955). Yellow, medium, double, 30 petals, in large clusters; growth vigorous, tall; foliage glossy, light green. (5.6)

San Fernando. HT. (Morris, 1948), 'Heart's Desire' × ('Crimson Glory' × 'Poinsettia'). Scarlet, large, double,

30 petals, very fragrant, profuse bloom; growth vigorous, upright; foliage deep green. (5.4)

Santa Catalina. LCl (McGredy, 1970). 'Paddy McGredy' × 'Heidelberg'. Soft pink, semi-double, large, finally flat, some scent, in clusters, recurrent; growth vigorous, 2 m./6.6 ft.; foliage medium green. GSR 259.

Santa Fe. HT. (McGredy, 1967). 'Mischief' × 'Tropicana'. Salmon-pink, large, high-centered, floriferous; growth vigorous. RA 1968:113; GSR 363. (7.7)

Santa Maria. F. (McGredy, 1969) 'Irish Wonder' × ('Ma Perkins' × 'Moulin Rouge'). Scarlet, loosely double, medium, some scent, in clusters; growth upright, 0.7 m./2.3 ft.; foliage small, abundant. GSR 478.

Santa Teresa de Avila. HT. (Moreira da Silva, 1959). 'Monte Carlo' × 'Michèle Meilland'. Interior salmon-pink to orange-red, reverse deep yellow, large, good form, fragrant, long stems. RJb 1960:32. (6.9)

'Saphir' → **Song of Paris**

Sarabande. F. (Meilland, 1957). 'Cocorico' × 'Moulin Rouge'. Geranium-red or orange-red, luminous, medium, 6 cm./2.4 in. across, loosely double, saucer-shaped, stamens deep yellow, some scent, in clusters, continuous bloomer; growth low, 0.5 m./1.7 ft., bushy; foliage light green, matt. PWR 108; GSR 482; WGR 151. (8.1)

Sarah van Fleet. HRg. (van Fleet, 1926). Parentage uncertain. Rose-pink, large, double, cupped, fragrant, recurrent; growth very strong, bushy, 2-3.5 m./8.3-10 ft.; foliage leathery, deep green. GiS 15. (6.5)

Sarajean. Min. (E.D. Williams/Mini-Roses, 1979). Seedling × 'Over the Rainbow'. Peach-pink, fragrant, double, globose, small, 2.5 cm./1 in., abundant bloom; bud pointed; foliage small, glossy, bronze-green; growth upright, bushy.

Saratoga. F. (Boerner/Jackson & Perkins, 1963). 'White Bouquet' × 'Princess White'. White, large, 10 cm./4 in. across, good form, double, finally flat, strong fragrance, in clusters; growth bushy, upright, 0.8 m./2.6 ft.; foliage firm, very disease-resistant. (7.2)

Sassy Lassy. Min. (E.D. Williams, 1975). Seedling × 'Over the Rainbow'. Yellow blend, double, 50 petals, some scent, singly, abundant, recurrent; growth dwarf, spreading; foliage bronzy-green, small. (8.5)

Satchmo. F. (McGredy, 1970). 'Irish Wonder' × 'Diamant'. Crimson-scarlet, large, loosely double, some scent, in clusters; growth bushy, 0.8 m./2.6 ft.; foliage deep green, healthy.

Scabrosa. (= *R. rugosa scabrosa*). S. (Harkness, 1950). Deep mauve-pink, single, to 12 cm./4.8 in across, mostly in clusters of 5, somewhat recurrent; many orangered hips in the autumn; growth bushy, medium; foliage bright green, wrinkled. GSR 198; SOR 48; PWR 190; GiS 15; HRo 32.

Scala. F. (Kordes, 1973). 'Marlena' × seedling. Similar to 'Europeana'. Blood-red with orange, double, globose, long lasting, some scent, in clusters, petals drop off cleanly, floriferous; growth vigorous, bushy; foliage deep green and bronze.

Scarlet Gem. (= 'Scarlet Pimpernel'). Min. (Meilland, 1961). ('Moulin Rouge' × 'Fashion') × ('Perla de Montserrat' × 'Perla de Alcanada'). Scarlet, small, does not fade, semi-double, finally imbricated, 3 cm./1.2 in. across, some scent, profuse bloom; growth dwarf, 25 cm./10 in. (8.3)

Scarlet Knight. (= 'Samourai'). F. (Meilland, 1966). ('Happiness' × 'Independence') × 'Sutter's Gold'. Deep red, interior more scarlet, medium, double, some scent, cupped, floriferous, singly and several together; growth bushy, 0.8 m./2.6 ft.; foliage firm, large, glossy. GSR 362. (7.8)

Scarlet Queen Elizabeth. F. (Dickson, 1963). ('Korona' × seedling) × 'Queen Elizabeth'. Scarlet, fading with age, medium-large, globose, semi-double, floriferous, at times hidden by new growth; growth vigorous, 1 m./3.3 ft.; foliage deep green. GSR 379; GR 256. (7.4)

Scarlet Ribbon. ClMin. (Ralph S. Moore, 1961). (['Soeur Thérèse' × 'Wilhelm'] × [seedling × 'Red Ripples'] × 'Zee'). Dark red to maroon, small, double, 50 petals, some scent, high centered; growth semi-climbing, 0.9 m./3 ft.

Scarlet Sunset. F. (de Ruiter, 1969). 'Orange Sensation' × seedling. Orange-red, single, medium, flat, edge slightly waved, in clusters, floriferous; growth bushy, 0.6 m./2 ft.; foliage deep green, firm.

Scarletta. Min. (de Ruiter, 1973). Geranium-red, semi-double, small; growth bushy, dense, 25-30 cm./10-12 in. Good for container culture.

Scented Air. F. (Dickson, 1965). 'Spartan'-seedling × 'Queen Elizabeth'. Carmine-pink with salmon, semi-double, 12 cm./4.8 in across, strong fragrance, in clus-

ters, floriferous; growth bushy, upright, 0.9 m./3 ft.; foliage very large, glossy, deep green. RA 1966:172; GSR 480.

Scharlachglut. (= 'Scarlet Fire'). G. (Kordes, 1952). 'Poinsettia' × *R. gallica splendens*. Brilliant scarlet, very large, 12 cm./4.8 in. across, single, saucer-shaped, no scent, in clusters together, very floriferous, non-recurrent; many red hips in autumn; growth bushy, 2 × 2 m./6.6 × 6.6 ft., young growth with red bark; foliage large, dull green. GSR 187; TR 7; RJb 36:4; GiS 21. (8.5)

Schloss Mannheim. F. (Kordes, 1975). 'Marlena' × 'Europeana'. Like 'Lilli Marlene'. Orange-red, medium, globose, double, some scent, in clusters, very floriferous; growth medium high, 0.6 m./2 ft., bushy; foliage abundant, medium, firm, deep green.

Schneelicht. Rg. (Geschwind, 1894). Pure white, large, single, in clusters; growth very vigorous, 2 m./6.6 ft., stems very prickly; very winter-hardy. TRT 132.

'Schneewittchen' → **Iceberg**

Schneezwerg. (= 'Snowdwarf'). S. (Lambert, 1912). Probably *R. rugosa* × a white Polyantha. Pure white, semi-double, flat, 6 cm./2.4 in. across, yellow center, several together, floriferous, recurrent, small red hips in the autumn; growth vigorous, 1.5 × 1.5 m./5 × 5 ft.; foliage like *R. rugosa*, wrinkles, but smaller. RJb 35:112; PWR 188; GSR 139; GiS 15. (7.5)

Schoolgirl. LCl. (McGredy, 1964). 'Coral Dawn' × 'Belle Blonde'. Orange-yellow, becoming more salmon-pink with age, double, floriferous; growth vigorous, 2.5-3 m./8.3-10 ft.; foliage deep green, large, glossy. RA 1975:141. (6.3)

Schweizer Gold. HT. (Kordes, 1975). 'Peer Gynt' × 'King's Ransom'. Pale yellow, reminiscent of 'Peace', very large, high-centered, fragrant, double, singly on long stems, petals drop off cleanly; growth strong, medium; foliage bright green, matt, large.

'Schweizer Gruss' → **Red Favorite**

Scintillation. S. (D. Austin, 1967). *R. macrantha* × 'Vanity'. Pink, semi-double, strong scent, large cluster, free bloom; growth vigorous; foliage deep green, matt.

Scotch Blend. HT. (Eastern Roses, 1975). 'Queen Elizabeth' × 'Peace'. Pink and apricot, with yellow base, double, 35 petals, high centered, singly and several together, some scent, free bloom; bud long, pointed;

growth vigorous, upright; foliage deep green, firm, disease-resistant. (6.0)

Scrabo. F. (Dickson, 1968). 'Celebration' × 'Irish Beauty'. Crimson-pink with salmon hue and yellowish base, double, large, finally flat, fragrant, floriferous; growth medium, 0.7 m./2.3 ft.; foliage light green, abundant.

Seabreeze. Min. (M. Lemrow, 1976). Unknown × 'White Fairy'. Medium pink, double, 35 petals, 2.5 cm./1 in. across, some scent, in clusters, very profuse bloom, continuous; growth dwarf, bushy; foliage light green. (7.5)

Sea Foam. S. (Schwartz, 1964). (['White Dawn' × 'Pinocchio'] × self) × self. Opening pure white, then creamy white, medium-large, double, fragrant, in clusters, profuse and continuous bloom; growth bushy, 1 m./3.3 ft. high and to 2 m./6.6 ft. broad; foliage small, glossy. (8.1)

Sealing Wax. S. (Wisley Gardens). Seedling of *R. moyesii.* Cerise-pink, very large, single, many scarlet-vermilion hips in the autumn.

Sea Pearl. (= 'Flower Girl'). F. (Dickson, 1964). 'Kordes Perfecta' × 'Montezuma'. Interior pearl pink, reverse peach shaded with yellow, large, semi-double, many together; long bud; growth bushy, upright; foliage deep green. RA 1965:80; GSR 484; RJb 28:81. (8.4)

Seashell. HT. (Kordes, 1976). Seedling × 'Colour Wonder'. Orange-red, double, 50 petals, 10 cm./4 in. across, imbricated, singly and in clusters on long stems, very free bloom; growth upright, branched; foliage medium, matt. (7.5)

Senior Prom. HT. (H.C. Bromwell, 1964). 'Pink Princess' × 'Queen Elizabeth'. Light rose and deep pink, large, 10 cm./4 in. across, double, 40 petals, high-centered, profuse bloom; growth upright; foliage deep green, glossy. (3.7)

September Days. Min. (F. Harmon Saville, 1978). 'Rise n' Shine' × 'Yellow Jewel'. Deep yellow, double, 40 petals, high-centered, fragrant, abundant, continuous bloom; growth dwarf, upright, compact; foliage glossy, rounded. ARA 1979:135.

Sensation. HT. (J.H. Hill, 1922). 'Hoosier Beauty' × 'Premier'. Scarlet-crimson, large, 12 cm./4.8 in. across, double, 30 petals, fragrant, open; bud long; growth upright, spreading; foliage deep green.

Serenade. HT. (Boerner/Jackson & Perkins, 1949). 'Sonata' × 'R.M.S. Queen Mary'. Coppery-orange, large, 10

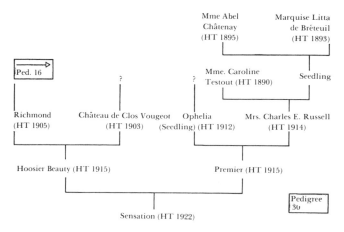

cm./4 in. across, cupped, loosely double, some scent, floriferous; bud ovoid, coppery-red; growth bushy, upright. GSR 365; ARA 1950:185. (6.1)

Serratipetala. (= 'Oeillet de Saint Arquey'). Ch. Outer petals crimson, inner petals light pink, stamens few, crimson, twisted, petals with carnation-like fringed edge, otherwise similar to *R. chinensis semperflorens.* (8.0)

Seven Seas. F. (Harkness, 1971). 'Lilac Charm' × 'Sterling Silver'. Lilac, semi-double, 10 cm./4 in. across, fragrant, floriferous, several together; growth bushy, compact, low, 0.5 m./1.7 ft.; foliage large, glossy. RA 1872:128; CRA 73:24.

'Seven Sisters Rose' → **Rosa multiflora platyphylla,** p. 282.

Seventeen. F. (Boerner/Jackson & Perkins, 1959). 'Pinocchio'-seedling × 'Fashion'-seedling. Coral-pink, large, 10 cm./4 in. across, loosely double, cupped, strong fragrance, very floriferous in pyramidal trusses; growth vigorous; foliage leathery, deep green.

Seventh Heaven. HT. (Armstrong & Swim, 1966). Seedling × 'Chrysler Imperial'. Cardinal-red, large, very double, high-centered, floriferous, fragrant; growth bushy, upright; foliage deep green, glossy. (7.2)

Sevilliana. S. (G.S. Buck, 1976). ('Vera Dalton' × 'Dornröschen') × (['World's Fair' × 'Floradora'] × 'Applejack'). Light pink with yellow flush and red spots, loosely double, 20 petals, cupped, fragrant, continuous bloom; growth medium high; foliage medium green, semi-glossy, firm.

Shades of Autumn. HT. (Brownell, 1943). 'Golden Glow' × 'Condesa de Sástago'. Interior rose-pink, reverse yellow, large, double, cupped, fragrant, floriferous; growth bushy, 0.6 m./2 ft.; foliage medium, glossy. (5.3)

Shakespeare Festival. Min. (R.S. Moore/Sequoia Nurs., 1979). 'Golden Angel' × 'Golden Angel'. Clear yellow, tea-scented, fragrant, double, high-centered, medium, 3.8 cm./1.5 in., free bloom; bud pointed; foliage green, matt; growth bushy, compact.

Shalom. S. (N.D. Poulsen, 1978). 'Korona'-seedling × self. Orange-red, loosely double or semi-double, medium, no scent, 3-5 together in clusters; very floriferous, blooming all season long; growth very vigorous, upright, tall to very tall; foliage deep green.

'Shailer's White Moss' → **R. centifolia muscosa alba,** p. 259.

Shannon. HT. (McGredy, 1965). 'Queen Elizabeth' × 'McGredy's Yellow'. Soft crimson-pink, large, 12 cm./4.8 in. across, double, high-centered, some scent, floriferous; bud long; growth bushy, vigorous, 0.9 m./3 ft.; foliage rounded, medium, glossy. RJb 34:128. (5.1)

Shepherdess. F. (Mattock, 1967). 'Allgold' × 'Peace'. Yellow with soft salmon-red hue, deeper at edges, large, 8 cm./3.2 in. across, double, some scent; growth vigorous, 0.8 m./2.6 ft.; foliage deep green and bronze. GSR 485; RA 1967:177.

Shepherd's Delight. F. (Dickson, 1956). 'Masquerade'-seedling × 'Joanna Hill'. Yellow overlaid with orange and red, reverse yellow, 8 cm./3.2 in. across, semi-double, some scent, floriferous in clusters; growth bushy, 0.9 m./3 ft.; foliage deep green, glossy, healthy. RA 1958:129; PWR 154; GSR 486.

Sheri Anne. Min. (Ralph S. Moore, 1973). 'Little Darling' × 'New Penny'. Orange-red with yellow base, semi-double, 15 petals, fragrant, good intermittent bloom, singly and several together; growth dwarf, branches stiff; foliage glossy, leathery. ARA 95:20. (8.0)

Shiralee. HT. (Dickson, 1965). Seedling × 'Kordes Perfecta'. Orange-yellow with soft salmon-pink, very large, 15 cm./6 in. across, high-centered, fragrant, floriferous; growth bushy upright; foliage healthy.

Shooting Star. Min. (Meilland/C.P., 1972). 'Rumba' × ('Dany Robin' × 'Perla de Montserrat'). Yellow tipped with red, slightly fragrant, double, cupped, small, abundant bloom; bud ovoid; foliage small, light, soft; growth vigorous, dwarf.

Shot Silk. HT. (Dickson, 1924). 'Hugh Dickson'-seedling × 'Sunstar'. Bright cerise with salmon-orange, yellow base, medium, semi-double, rosette shaped, strong fragrance, floriferous; growth bushy, 0.7 m./2.3 ft.; foliage slightly curled, medium green. (7.8)

Show Girl. HT. (Lammerts, 1946). 'Joanna Hill' × 'Crimson Glory'. Rose-red, large, 10-12 cm./4-4.8 in. across, semi-double, high-centered, fragrant, long stems; bud long, pointed; growth vigorous, bushy, upright; foliage firm, deep green. RA 1951:36. (6.8)

Showtime. HT. (Lindquist, 1969). 'Kordes Perfecta' × 'Granada'. Crimson-pink, medium, semi-double, fragrant, singly on normal stems, recurrent; growth bushy; foliage large, deep green, firm. (7.5)

Shrubby Pink. (= 'Sunday Times'). F. (McGredy, 1971). ('Little Darling' × 'Goldilocks') × 'München'. Interior deep pink, with lighter reverse, semi-double, medium, some scent, floriferous, singly and in clusters; growth bushy, compact, 0.6 m./2 ft.; foliage small, deep green, glossy. RA 1971:177; GSR 488.

Sidney Peabody. F. (de Ruiter, 1955). 'Rome Glory' × Floribunda-seedling. Bright red, large, 8 cm./3.2 in. across, double, no scent, floriferous; growth strong, bushy, 0.8 m./2.6 ft.; foliage large, red-green, glossy.

Siesta. F. (Meilland, 1966). 'Sarabande' × 'Dany Robin'. Bright scarlet with yellow center, semi-double, saucer-shaped, medium-large, 7 cm./2.8 in. across, floriferous, in clusters; growth bushy; foliage glossy.

Signe Relander. HRg. (Poulsen, 1928). HRugosa × 'Orléans Rose'. Bright red, double, fragrant, recurrent, in clusters; growth very vigorous; foliage wrinkled.

Signora. (= 'Signora Piero Puricelli'). HT. (D. Aicardi/ Jackson & Perkins, 1936). 'Julien Potin' × 'Sensation'. Orange-apricot becoming apricot suffused with gold, outer petals magenta-pink, fragrant, double, cupped, very large; bud long-pointed, orange-red; foliage glossy; growth very vigorous.

Silent Night. HT. (McGredy, 1969). 'Daily Sketch' × 'Hassan'. Creamy yellow, overlaid with soft salmon-pink, double, high-centered, medium, good form, some scent, floriferous; growth bushy; foliage very glossy.

Silva. HT. (Meilland, 1964). 'Peace' × 'Confidence'. Soft apricot-yellow with salmon, very large, 12 cm./4.8 in. across, double, high-centered, some scent, floriferous;

growth vigorous, long stems; foliage firm, deep green, glossy. GSR 366. (5.6)

Silver Jubilee. HT. (Cocker, 1978). (['Highlight' × 'Colour Wonder'] × ['Parkdirektor Riggers' × 'Piccadilly']) × 'Mischief'. Pink, peach and cream, double, 30 petals, good shape, singly and several together, very free bloom; growth vigorous; foliage glossy, disease-resistant. RA 1978:25.

Silver Lining. HT. (Dickson, 1958). 'Karl Herbst' × 'Eden Rose'-seedling. Silvery-pink with slightly lighter reverse, large, 12 cm./4.8 in. across, good form, strong scent, floriferous; growth upright, bushy, 0.8 m./2.6 ft.; foliage deep green. RA 1958:96; PWR 81. (6.7)

Silver Moon. LCl. (Van Fleet, 1910). (*R. wichuraiana* × 'Devoniensis') × *R. laevigata*. Creamy-white with amber base, large, 10 cm./4 in. across, semi-double, flat, stamens deep yellow, in clusters on strong stems; growth very strong, 5-6 m./16.5-20 ft.; foliage large, firm, glossy. GSR 225. (7.8)

Shocking Blue. F. (Kordes, 1974) Seedling × 'Silver Star'. Lilac-mauve, high-centered, double, large, strong fragrance, in small clusters, abundant, continuous bloom; growth vigorous; foliage deep green, glossy, leathery. Greenhouse variety.

Shooting Star. Min. (Meilland, 1972). 'Rumba' × ('Dany Robin' × 'Perla de Montserrat'). Yellow, petal tips red, double, small, cupped, mostly singly, lost-lasting, petals retained, some scent; growth dwarf, 30 cm./12 in.; foliage small, light green. (7.4)

Silver Star. HT. (Kordes, 1966). 'Sterling Silver' × 'Magenta'-seedling. Silvery-lilac, large, 12 cm./4.8 in. across, double, strong fragrance, floriferous; bud long, pointed; growth vigorous, 0.8 m./2.6 ft.; foliage deep green, large, glossy. KR 10:74. (7.1)

Silver Tips. Min. (Ralph S. Moore, 1961). (*R. wichuraiana* × 'Floradora') × 'Lilac Time'. Pink with silvery reverse, then soft lavender, double, 50 petals, small, some scent; growth bushy, dwarf, 25-30 cm./10-12 in.; foliage leathery. (6.6)

Silver Wedding. HT. (Leenders, 1965). 'Sterling Silver' × seedling. Lavender-lilac, fading to soft lilac, large, 10 cm./4 in. across, cupped, double, in clusters, some scent; growth upright, vigorous, 0.8 m./2.6 ft.; foliage medium green, semi-glossy.

Simone. (= 'Mauve Mallerin'). HT. (Mallerin, 1957).

('Peace' × 'Independence') × 'Grey Pearl'. Lavender-lilac, very large, to 15 cm./6 in. across, double, petals revolved, fragrant, high-centered to cupped, moderate bloom; growth strong; foliage deep green, firm. (6.4)

Simplex. Min. (Ralph S. Moore, 1961). (*R. wichuraiana* × 'Floradora') × seedling. White, small, single, 3.5 cm./1.4 in. across, in clusters, abundant bloom; bud apricot; growth dwarf, 30-35 cm./12-14 in.; foliage leathery. (8.6)

Sir Galahad. F. (Harkness, 1967). 'Pink Parfait' × 'Highlight'. Crimson with slightly lighter center, medium, 6 cm./2.4 in. across, some scent, floriferous, in clusters; growth bushy, 0.6 m./2 ft.; foliage glossy.

Sir Harry Pilkington. (= 'Melina'). HT. (Tantau, 1973). 'Irene Horstmann' × 'Sophia Loren'. Blood-red, large, double, some scent, continuous bloom; growth upright, vigorous; foliage large, soft green.

Sir Lancelot. F. (Harkness, 1967). 'Vera Dalton' × 'Woburn Abbey'. Apricot-yellow with some salmon hue, fading with age, medium, 8 cm./3.2 in. across, semi-double, some scent, floriferous; growth bushy, 0.6 m./2 ft.; foliage small, light green, matt. GSR 487; WPR 54; RA 1967:32. (7.7)

Sir Thomas Lipton. HRg. (Van Fleet, 1900). *R. rugosa alba* × 'Clotilde Soupert'. White, double, cupped, fragrant, recurrent; growth bushy, vigorous, 2 m./6.6 ft. and over; foliage leathery, deep green. (6.8)

Sissinghurst Castle. (= 'Rose des Maures'). G. Origin unknown; 1947 re-imported. Purplish-crimson, spotted with white on petals and near base, medium, 8 cm./3.2 in. across, semi-double, yellow stamens, June, non-recurrent; growth medium, 1 m./3.3 ft., suckers, stems with few prickles. GSR 90.

Sitka Rose → **Rosa rugosa**, p. 269 (see ARA 1968:41-45).

Sizzler. Min. (F.H. Saville, 1978). 'Sheri Anne' × 'Prominent'. Orange-red, high-centered, fragrant, double, 25 petals, intermittent bloom; growth dwarf, upright-spreading; foliage glossy, medium green.

Skaggarak. F. (Poulsen, 1970). 'Irish Wonder' × seedling. Blood red, large, 10-12 cm./4-4.8 in. across, semi-double, yellow stamens, finally flat, some scent, several together, floriferous.

Skyrocket. (= 'Wilhelm'). HMsk. (Kordes, 1934). 'Robin Hood' × 'J.C. Thornton'. Blood red, semi-double, large, 9 cm./3.6 in. across, golden stamens, continuous bloom in large trusses; large, red hips in autumn; growth strong, 2 m./3.3 ft. slightly arching. GSR 191; GiS 17. (7.0)

Sleepy. (= 'Balduin'). Pol. (de Ruiter, 1955). ('Orange Triumph' × 'Golden Rapture') × Polyantha-seedling. Deep pink, small, semi-double, no scent, floriferous; growth dwarf, 20 cm./8 in., very compact, dense; foliage small, glossy.

Sleepy Time. Min. (Ralph S. Moore, 1973). 'Ellen Poulsen' × 'Fairy Princess'. Salmon-pink, small, double, some scent, long-lasting, singly and several together, continuous bloom; growth dwarf, vigorous, 20-25 cm./8-10 in.; foliage firm, disease-resistant. (6.7)

Small Talk. F. (Swim & Weeks, 1963). 'Yellow Pinocchio' × 'Circus'. Deep lemon yellow, medium, 6 cm./2.4 in. across, double, 35 petals, high-centered, some scent, in large clusters, abundant bloom; growth low, compact; foliage leathery, glossy. (6.7)

Small World. Min. (Ralph S. Moore, 1975). 'Little Chief' × 'Fire Princess'. Orange-red, 20 petals, flat, abundant, continuous bloom; growth dwarf, very compact, 20-25 cm./8-10 in., stems very prickly; foliage medium green, glossy. (7.0)

Smoky. HT. (Combe/Jackson & Perkins, 1968). Blood red and crimson, medium, semi-double, some scent, long-lasting, singly on long stems, floriferous; growth upright, branches; foliage abundant, medium. (5.3)

Sneezy. (= 'Bertram'). Pol. (de Ruiter, 1955). Deep pink, single, floriferous; growth very dwarf, dense, 20-30 cm./8-12 in.

Snow Carpet. Min. (S. McGredy/McGredy Roses International, 1980). 'New Penny' × 'Temple Bells'. White, slightly fragrant, very double, small, profuse bloom; growth spreading.

Snowdance. F. (de Ruiter, 1971). 'Orange Sensation' × 'Iceberg'. White, medium, 8 cm./3.2 in. across, double, some scent, floriferous, in large trusses; growth medium, 0.6 m./2 ft.; foliage medium green.

Snowfire. HT. (Kordes/Jackson & Perkins, 1970). Very similar to 'Neue Revue', but red and white. ARA 1973:64. (5.7)

Snowflakes. Min. (Moore, 1954). (*R. wichuraiana* × 'Floradora') × 'Zee'. White, double, small; late flowering, in clusters; growth very dwarf, 15 cm./6 in.

Snow Magic. Min. (Ralph S. Moore, 1976). Seedling × seedling. Bud pale pink, opening white, double, 40 petals, in clusters, profuse bloom all season; growth dwarf, bushy; foliage small, medium green.

Soaring Wings. HT. (Kordes/Ludwig, 1979). 'Colour Wonder' × seedling. Orange-blend, double, high-centered, 60 petals, fragrant, singly and several together, abundant, intermittent bloom; bud very large; growth vigorous, bushy, upright; foliage glossy.

Soeur Marthe. M. (Vibert, 1848). Deep pink, large, double, June-flowering, non-recurrent; growth 1 m./3.3 ft., upright.

Soeur Thérèse. HT. (Guillot, 1931). (Général Jacqueminot' × 'Juliet') × 'Souvenir de Claudius Pernet'. Golden yellow, with crimson-shaded edges, large, double, some scent, cupped; growth strong, bushy; foliage firm, leathery, bronze-green. SRW 97. (6.4)

Soleil d'Or. HFt. (Pernet-Ducher, 1900). 'Antoine Ducher' × 'Persian Yellow'. Orange-yellow to apricot, shaded with bright red and salmon, very large, fragrant; bud long, poor form; foliage small, very susceptible to Black Spot. This was the first successful hybrid between *R. foetida* and a Hybrid Perpetual, which augmented the original palette (red, pink, yellow, white) with new tints (golden yellow, apricot, scarlet and copper). The descendants were initially called "Pernetiana-Roses", but later were included in the Hybrid Teas. RZ 1900:49. (8.1)

Solo. ClHT. (Tantau, 1956). 'Crimson Glory'-seedling. Velvety crimson, large, double, fragrant, recurrent, in large clusters; growth upright, 2-3 m./6.6-10 ft.; foliage large, reddish-green, matt. (7.7)

Sombreuil. T. (Robert, 1850). 'Gigantesque'-seedling. Creamy-white, often with soft pink hue, large, semi-double, flat, 25 petals, good form, some scent, floriferous; growth strong; foliage light green. (8.6)

Song of Paris. (= 'Saphir'). HT. (Delbard/Chabert, 1964). ('Holstein' × 'Bayadère') × 'Prélude'. Silvery-lavender, large, 10 cm./4 in. across, high-centered, fragrant, abundant bloom; growth upright; foliage deep green, leathery. (4.5)

Sonia. (= 'Sonia Meilland'; 'Sweet Promise'). Gr. (Meilland, 1970). 'Zambra' × ('Baccara' × 'Message'). Light pink, semi-double, rosette-shaped, some scent, singly or several together, profuse and continuous bloom;

growth vigorous, upright, loose; foliage deep green, firm, very resistant to Black Spot. Important greenhouse variety. ARA 60:206; 63:186. (8.0)

Sonnet. HT. (Boerner/Jackson & Perkins, 1961). 'Golden Masterpiece' × 'Spartan'. Salmon pink, large, 12 cm./4.8 in. across, very double, cupped, fragrant, profuse bloom; growth vigorous. Greenhouse variety.

Sonora. F. (Boerner/Jackson & Perkins, 1962). 'Orange Mist' × 'Mayday'. Soft buff overlaid with salmon-pink, petals with red stripes on the reverse side, large, double, long-lasting, profuse bloom; growth bushy, 0.5 m./1.7 ft.; foliage leathery, deep green. Greenhouse variety. RJb 30:80.

Sonrisa. HT. (Swim & Weeks, 1969). 'Mr. Lincoln' × 'Night n' Day'. Deep crimson, large, double, 50 petals, very fragrant, high-centered, free bloom; growth very vigorous, upright; foliage deep green, firm. (6.3)

Soraya. HT. (Meilland, 1955). ('Peace' × 'Floradora') × 'Grand'mère Jenny'. Orange-red with crimson reverse, large, double, cupped, some scent, long stems; growth vigorous, 0.8 m./2.6 ft., branched; foliage large, deep green, glossy. RA 1956:86; PWR 38; BTR 37. (7.8)

Southampton. F. (Harkness, 1971). ('Queen Elizabeth' × 'Allgold') × 'Yellow Cushion'. Apricot-orange with scarlet hue, medium, semi-double, 25 petals, some scent, singly or several together in trusses, profuse bloom; growth vigorous, 0.7-0.9 m./2.3-3 ft.; foliage small, deep green, semi-glossy. RA 1972:177.

Southern Sun. (= 'Beautiful Dreamer'). F. (J.A. Herholdt, 1977). Seedling × seedling. Orange with sunset gold, large, 35 petals, perfect form, faint fragrance, singly and in trusses, free-flowering, on long stems, long-lasting, hardy, continuous bloom; growth bushy, medium high; foliage deep green, glossy.

South Seas. (= 'Mer du Sud'). HT. (Morey/Jackson & Perkins, 1963). Coral pink, fading to more silvery-pink, large, 15 cm./6 in. across, double, cupped, finally flat, fragrant, floriferous, on long, strong stems; growth vigorous, upright; young foliage reddish. (7.3)

Souvenir de Cristophe Cochet. HRg. (Cochet-Cochet, 1894). Soft pink, very large, semi-double, pale yellow anthers, fragrant; sepals bristly; large red hips; growth vigorous, medium; foliage typical of *rugosa*, wrinkled. RZ 1895:21.

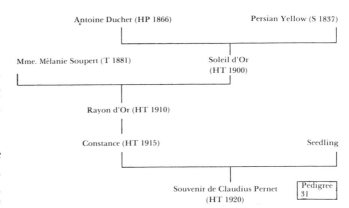

Souvenir de Claudius Pernet. HT. (Pernet-Ducher, 1920). 'Constance' × seedling. Pure yellow with darker center, double, 30 petals, large, floriferous; bud long, pointed; growth upright, long stems; foliage glossy-green.

Souvenir de la Malmaison. (= 'Queen of Beauty'). B. (Béluze, 1843). 'Mme. Desprez' × Tea rose. Soft creamy-white with blush hue, fading to nearly white, large, 10 cm./4 in. across, very double and quartered, delicate fragrance, somewhat recurrent in the autumn; growth upright, 1 m./3.3 ft. or less. Very famous old variety. Malmaison was the rose garden of the French Empress Joséphine, the wife of Napoleon. SRW 151; WGR 15. (8.5)

Souvenir de Mme. Boullet. HT. (Pernet-Ducher, 1921). 'Sunburst' × seedling. Deep yellow, large, good form, free bloom; bud long; growth spreading. (7.6)

Souvenir de Mme. H. Thuret. HP. (Texier/Nabonnand, 1922). 'Frau Karl Druschki' × 'Lyon Rose'. Salmon pink with red center and yellow edge, very large, good shape, cupped; growth vigorous; foliage light green. (6.3)

Souvenir de Pierre Notting. T. (Soupert & Notting, 1902). 'Maréchal Niel' × 'Maman Cochet'. Golden-yellow with orange-yellow and copper, edges pink, very double, some scent, floriferous; bud long; foliage light green.

Souvenir de St. Anne's. B. (Found in Ireland; introduced 1950 by Messrs. Hilling). Sport of 'Souvenir de la Malmaison', but only nearly single to semi-double, soft pink to nearly white.

Spanish Sun. F. (Boerner/Jackson & Perkins, 1966). 'Yellow Pinocchio'-seedling × 'Golden Garnette'. Deep yellow, double, open, fragrant, strong stems; growth bushy, 0.5 m./1.7 ft. outdoors, much taller under glass (greenhouse variety); foliage deep green. (6.3)

Sparkie. Min. (Ralph S. Moore, 1957). (*R. wichuraiana* × 'Floradora') × 'Little Buckaroo'. Bright red, deepening with age, single, in clusters; growth dwarf, 30-40 cm./12-16 in.; foliage glossy. (7.1)

Sparrieshoop. S. (Kordes, 1952). ('Baby Château' × 'Else Poulsen') × 'Magnifica'. Soft salmon-pink with slightly deeper reverse, center more white, large, 10 cm./4 in. across, nearly single, saucer-shaped, fragrant, recurrent; growth vigorous, upright, 2 m./6.6 ft.; foliage large, red-green, glossy. GSR 188; GiS 21. (7.0)

Spartan. F. (Boerner/Jackson & Perkins, 1955). 'Geranium Red' × 'Fashion'. Orange-red to coral-pink, medium, 8 cm./3.2 in. across, double, strong scent, in clusters, floriferous; growth bushy, low, 0.5 m./1.7 ft.; foliage deep green, glossy. PWR 157; RA 1955:48. (7.1)

Spectacular. (= 'Danse de Feu'). LCl. (Mallerin, 1953). 'Paul's Scarlet Climber' × *multiflora*-seedling. Orange-scarlet, double, 25 petals, singly or several together, continuous flowering; growth very vigorous, 2-2.5 m./6.6-8.3 ft.; foliage glossy, green, healthy. PWR 212; GRS 240. (7.5)

Spellbinder. HT. (W.A. Warriner/Jackson & Perkins, 1975). 'South Seas' × seedling. Ivory bud, changing to crimson, large, high-centered, some scent, double, long-lasting, singly and several together, profuse bloom; growth very vigorous; foliage deep green, healthy. ARA 60:58. (7.0)

Spong. C. (1805). Rose-red, small, rosette-shaped, very double, floriferous, very early; growth bushy, 1 m./3.3 ft.; leaflets roundish, serrate.

Spotlight. HT. (Dickson, 1969). 'Piccadilly' × seedling. Salmon pink with golden yellow, double, medium, globose, several together, some scent, floriferous; growth bushy; foliage abundant, medium, deep green.

Spring Song. Min. (Ralph S. Moore, 1957). (*R. wichuraiana* × 'Floradora') × 'Thumbelina'. Pink with salmon hue, double, small, in clusters, good bloomer; growth dwarf. 30-35 cm./12-14 in.; foliage deep green, glossy. (7.9)

Square Dancer. S. (G.J. Buck, 1973). ('Meisterstück' × ['World's Fair' × 'Floradora']) × 'Apple Jack'. Rose pink, large, cupped, double, long-lasting, petals drop off cleanly, fragrant, profuse, intermittent bloom;

growth medium, bushy, 1 × 1 m./3.3 × 3.3 ft.; foliage deep green, healthy. (7.9)

St. Ingbert. HP. (Lambert, 1926). 'Frau Karl Druscki' × 'Mme. Mélanie Soupert'. White, center yellowish and red, large, double, 60 petals, some scent; growth vigorous. (6.0)

St. Nicholas. D. (introduced by Messrs. Hilling, 1950). Probably spontaneous seedling of *R. damascena* (?) × *R. gallica*. Deep pink, semi-double; growth upright. GiS 6; PGR 35.

Stacey Sue. Min. (Ralph S. Moore, 1976). 'Ellen Poulsen' × 'Fairy Princess'. Light pink, double 60 petals, abundant bloom all season; growth dwarf, very bushy, rounded; foliage small, glossy, medium green. RA 1977:60. (7.0)

Stadt Kiel. S. (Kordes, 1962). 'World's Fair' × 'Floradora'. Deep blood-red with vermilion, medium, double, good shape, some scent, in clusters, profuse, recurrent; growth vigorous, medium; foliage very large, deep green. RJb 24:192. (6.6)

Stadt Rosenheim. S. (Kordes, 1961). Orange-salmon, double, medium, fragrant, in large clusters, free bloom; growth vigorous, medium; foliage glossy. (6.6)

Standout. HT. (O.L. Weeks, 1977). 'Tiffany' × 'Surprise'. Medium red, double, 40 petals, tea scent, singly or 3-4 in clusters, intermittent bloom; growth vigorous, branched; foliage large.

Stanwell Perpetual. HSpn. (Lee, 1838). *R. damascena semperflorens* × *R. pimpinellifolia*. Blush pink, medium, very double, sweet fragrance, heavy first bloom, somewhat recurrent; growth strong, prickly, 1.5 m./5 ft. high and up to 3 m./10 ft. across; foliage small. SOR 45; GSR 57. (8.0)

Starfire. F. (Lammerts, 1958). 'Charlotte Armstrong' × ('Charlotte Armstrong' × 'Floradora'). Bright red, large, 12 cm./4.8 in. across, cupped, double, several together on long stems; bud urn-shaped; growth strong, tall, bushy; foliage bright green, glossy. (8.0)

Stargazer. F. (Harkness, 1977). 'Marlena' × 'Kim'. Orange-red to more pink, single, some scent, very free bloom, in trusses; growth medium; foliage matt. RA 1976:20.

Starglo. Min. (E.D. Williams, 1973). 'Little Darling' × 'Jet Trail'. White, double, small, high-centered, some scent, singly and several together, petals drop off cleanly; growth dwarf, 30-35 cm./12-14 in.; foliage small, leathery. (8.6)

Starina. Min. (Meilland, 1965). ('Dany Robin' × 'Fire King') × 'Perla de Montserrat'. Orange-scarlet, small, 4 cm./1.6 in. across, double, somewhat star-shaped, flat, very floriferous; growth dwarf, 25 cm./10 in.; foliage small, glossy. GSR 506. (9.4)

Starlet. F. (Swim/Armstrong, 1957). 'Goldilocks' × seedling. Pure yellow, medium, 6 cm./2.4 in. across, double, finally flat, some scent, floriferous, singly or several together; bud pointed; growth bushy, compact; foliage medium, dccp green, glossy. (7.4)

Star of Persia. HFt. (Pemberton, 1919). *R. foetida* × 'Trier'. Golden yellow, medium, double, somewhat star-shaped, petals narrow, anthers golden; growth bushy, to 2.5 m./8.3 ft. high; foliage very similar to *R. foetida*. ARA 1924:104.

Star Twinkle. Min. (Ralph S. Moore, 1977). 'Fairy Moss' × 'Fire Princess'. Pink. 3-5 in. clusters, no scent, abundant, intermittent bloom; growth dwarf, bushy, compact; foliage small, glossy.

Stella. F. (Tantau, 1958). 'Horstmann's Jubliäumsrose' × 'Peace'. Interior creamy yellow with blush, outer petals light pink to nearly crimson, large, 12 cm./4.8 in. across, double, high centered, some scent, several together, floriferous; growth vigorous, bushy, 0.6 m./2 ft.; foliage firm, leathery, deep green. PWR 66; GR 160; RJb 22:93. (6.7)

Stephen Langdon. F. (Sanday, 1968). 'Karl Herbst' × 'Sarabande'. Deep scarlet to crimson, large, double, some scent, abundant bloom; growth vigorous, compact, bushy; foliage deep green, matt. RA 1971:97.

Strawberry Swirl. Min. (R.S. Moore, 1977). "Little Darling' × mini-seedling. Orange mixed with white, double, 50 petals, high centered, no scent, in clusters, continuous bloom all season; growth dwarf, bushy, foliage matt.

'Striped Moss → **'Oeillet Panachée.** (7.5)

Stroller. F. (Dickson, 1968). 'Isle of Man' × 'Happy Event'. Interior cherry-red, reverse yellow, large, double, some scent, floriferous, in clusters; growth vigorous, upright, 0.8 m./2.6 ft.; foliage deep green, glossy. RA 1970:177; GSR 489.

Sugar Elf. Min. (Ralph S. Moore, 1974). (*R. wichuraiana* × 'Floradora') × 'Debbie'. Light pink, deepening with age, semi-double, 10-20 petals, small, 2.5 cm./1 in. across, some fragrance, intermittent heavy spring bloom; growth dwarf, spreading; foliage bright green, glossy, leathery. (6.5)

Sultane. HT. (Meilland, 1946). 'J.B. Meilland' × 'Orange Nassau'. Interior vermilion, reverse golden-yellow, large, 12 cm./4.8 in. across, double, fragrant, floriferous; growth upright, 0.7 m./2.3 ft., many branches; foliage large, glossy. SRW 102. (6.4)

Sumatra. F. (Mallerin, 1956). 'Olga' × 'Fashion;'. Vermilion to blood red, large, 8 cm./3.2 in. across, semi-double, globose, then flat, in pyramidal trusses; growth medium; foliage firm. (7.2)

Summer Butter. Min. (F.H. Saville, 1979). 'Arthur Bell' × 'Yellow Jewel'. Deep yellow, semi-double, 25 petals, cupped, strong fragrance, abundant continuous bloom; growth dwarf, vigorous; foliage very glossy.

Summer Fields. S. (Mattock, 1971). 'Tropicana' × 'Goldmarie'. Bright scarlet, semi-double, 15 petals, fragrant, very floriferous; growth vigorous; young growth red, then matt-green.

Summer Frost. F. (Boerner, 1962). 'Princesse White' × 'Golden Masterpiece'. White, large, 10 cm./4 in. across, loosely double, cupped, fragrant; growth compact; foliage deep green, leathery.

Summer Holiday. HT. (Gregory, 1967). 'Tropicana' × ?. Vivid orange-red, large, high centered, fragrant, long stems, very free bloom; growth vigorous. RA 1969:96; GSR 367. (7.2)

Summer Meeting. F. (Harkness, 1968). 'Allgold' × 'Circus'. Golden-yellow, double, large, some scent, in clusters, floriferous; growth compact, bushy; foliage glossy. RA 1969:97.

Summer Snow. F. (Jackson & Perkins, 1938). Sport of 'Climbing Summer Snow'. Pure white, large, semi-double, some scent, profuse bloom, in large clusters; growth bushy; foliage light green. (7.2)

Summer Snow, Climbing. ClF. (Couteau, 1936). 'Tausendschön'-seedling × ?. Snow white, semi-double, cupped, some scent, 5 cm./2 in. across, in large clusters; growth vigorous, 2.5-3 m./8.3-10 ft.; foliage leathery. (7.4)

Summer Song. = 'Chanson d' Eté'). F. (Dickson, 1962) ×

Seedling × 'Masquerade'. Orange and yellow blend, large, 10 cm./4 in. across, flat, some scent; growth vigorous; foliage glossy. (6.9)

Summer Sunshine. (= 'Soleil d'Eté'). HT. (Swim/Armstrong, 1962). 'Buccaneer' × 'Lemon Chiffon'. Bright deep yellow, large, 10 cm./4 in. across, double, flat, some scent, floriferous; growth upright, 0.7 m./2.3 ft.; foliage deep green, firm, glossy. RA 1963:129; WPR 31. (7.2)

Summertime. HT. (Boerner/Jackson & Perkins, 1957). 'Diamond Jubilee' × 'Fashion'. Light pink, large, 10 cm./4 in. across, double, high-centered, strong fragrance, floriferous; growth bushy, foliage olive green. (7.3)

Summer Wind. S. (G.J. Buck, 1975). ('Fandango' × 'Florence Mary Morse') × 'Applejack'. Orange-red, single to semi-double, 5-15 petals, flat, fragrant, continuous bloom; growth bushy, moderately vigorous; foliage deep green, leathery.

Summerwine. HT. (W.A. Warriner/Jackson & Perkins, 1974). 'Tiffany' × 'South Seas'. Light rose-pink, double, 50 petals, large, 10-15 cm./4-6 in. across, long-lasting, non-bluing, very free bloom; growth vigorous; foliage leathery. (7.0)

Sunbeam. Min. (Robinson, 1957). 'Tom Thumb' × 'Polly Flinders' × 'Golden Scepter'. Yellow, very fragrant; growth dwarf, 35-40 cm./14-16 in. (7.5)

Sunblest. (= 'Landora'). HT. (Tantau, 1970). Seedling × 'King's Ransom'. Bright yellow, fades very little, large, very double, floriferous; growth strong, upright; foliage pale green. (7.1)

Sunbonnet. F. (Swim & Weeks, 1967). 'Arlene Francis' × ('Circus' × 'Sweet Talk'). Greenish-yellow, medium, double, high-centered, fragrant, abundant bloom; growth low, bushy; foliage deep green, leathery. (7.1)

Sundance. F. (Poulsen, 1954). 'Poulsen's Supreme' × 'Eugène Fürst'. Orange-yellow, then light pink, medium, 6 cm./2.4 in. across, semi-double, 25 petals, some scent, floriferous, in clusters; growth vigorous, upright; foliage pale green. RA 1955:148.

Sunday Press. HT. (Kordes/McGredy, 1970). Crimson, very large, 12 cm./4.8 in. across, very double, good shape, singly on long stems, moderate bloom; growth strong; foliage light green.

Sundowner. Gr. (S. McGredy/Edmunds, 1978). 'Bond Street' × 'Peer Gynt'. Golden orange, very fragrant, double, large, 10 cm./4 in., abundant bloom; bud high-pointed, foliage leathery; growth tall, upright.

Sundra. F. (Gaujard, 1968). 'Club' × 'Lilli Marlene'. Dark red, large, semi-double, cupped, strong fragrance, long-lasting; growth low, 40 cm./16 in., bushy; foliage abundant, light green, medium.

Sundream. F. (Leenders, 1971). 'Inge Poulsen' × 'Fiametta'. Salmon-orange, then fading to pink and white, center and reverse yellow, medium, 7 cm./2.8 in., semi-double, some scent, in large trusses; growth bushy, upright, 0.8 m./2.6 ft.; foliage medium, green, semi-glossy.

Sundust. Min. (Ralph S. Moore, 1977). 'Golden Glow' × 'Magic Wand'. Light apricot to yellow, double, fragrant, singly and in clusters, free bloom all season; growth dwarf, bushy, compact; foliage small. (7.1)

Sunfire. F. (W.A. Warriner/Jackson & Perkins, 1974). 'Tropicana' × 'Zorina'. Orange-red, double, 35 petals, large, 8 cm./3.2 in. across, singly and in clusters, petals drop off cleanly, profuse bloom; growth bushy, upright, 0.9-1.2 m./3-4 ft.; foliage large, disease-resistant. (7.9)

Sun King. HT. (Meilland, 1974). ('Soraya' × 'Signora') × 'King's Ransom'. Bronze-yellow, double, some scent; bud long; growth bushy, upright, 0.6 m./2 ft.; foliage healthy.

Sunlight. (= 'Grisbi'). HT. (Meilland, 1956). ('Eclipse' × 'Ophelia') × 'Monte Carlo'. Yellow, large, 10 cm./4 in. across, double, 45 petals, high-centered to cupped, fragrant, free bloom; growth bushy, upright; foliage deep green, leathery. (6.1)

Sunmaid. F. (Leenders, 1970). 'Floriade' × 'Allgold'. Salmon-yellow with soft pink edge, center and reverse yellow, large, 10-12 cm./4-4.8 in. across, semi-double, fragrant; growth bushy, 1.1 m./3.6 ft.; foliage medium, young growth red, very glossy.

Sunny June. S. (Lammerts, 1952). 'Crimson Glory' × 'Capt. Jonas'. Deep canary-yellow, single, medium, cupped to flat, some scent, in large clusters, free bloom; growth upright, to 2.5 m./8.3 ft.; foliage deep green, glossy. (7.5)

Sunny Morning. Min. (Ralph S. Moore, 1977). 'Golden

Glow' × 'Peachy White'. Yellow, double, 35 petals, flat, good tea scent, abundant bloom all season; growth dwarf, bushy, upright; foliage medium green.

Sunrise. HT. (Leenders, 1966). 'Harlequin' × 'Tawny Gold'. Salmon-red, center and reverse yellow, to crimson-pink with age, double, large, some scent, several together; growth upright, 0.7 m./2.3 ft.; young growth red, large.

Sunrise-Sunset. HT. (Swim & Weeks, 1971). 'Tiffany' × (seedling × 'Happiness'). Blend of cream, pink and brownish-lavender, brownish center, large, very double, high-centered, some scent, singly on long stem; growth vigorous; foliage deep green, glossy. (7.2)

Sunset Jubilee. HT. (Boerner/Jackson & Perkins, 1973). 'Kordes Perfecta' × 'Pink Duchess'. Medium pink with lighter buds, very large, high-centered, double, some scent, singly and several together; growth vigorous, upright; foliage leathery, bright green. (7.2)

Sunset Song. HT. (Cocker, 1980). Golden amber, double; growth upright.

Sunsilk. F. (Fryer, 1974). 'Pink Parfait' × 'Red-gold'-seedling. Pure lemon yellow, double, 30 petals, some scent, singly and in clusters, very free bloom; growth bushy, 0.6-0.7 m./2.3-2.6 ft.; foliage medium green.

Sunsong. Gr. (Poulsen/Armstrong, 1976). 'Folie d'Espagne' × ('Zambra' × 'Danish Pink'). Opening orange, later a coral blend, double, 70 petals, medium, 8 cm./3.2 in. across, in clusters, some scent, profuse bloom all season; growth upright, bushy, long stems; foliage glossy. (6.0)

Sunspot. F. (G. Fisher, 1965). 'Golden Anniversary' × 'Masquerade'. Pale yellow, large, double, in clusters, profuse bloom; growth vigorous; foliage deep green, leathery. (5.9)

Sunsprite. (= 'Friesia'; 'Korresia'). F. (Kordes, 1973). 'Friedrich Wörlein' × 'Spanish Sun'. Similar to 'Spanish Sun', semi-double, yellow, strong fragrance, in clusters, profuse bloom, petals drop off cleanly, very hardy; growth medium, upright; foliage healthy. (8.0)

Superba. HMoyesii. (Van Rossem). 'Charles P. Kilham' × *R. moyesii*. Very deep chestnut-brown to red, semi-double, no scent, no hips; growth very vigorous, 2 m./6.6 ft. or over, stems with purplish bloom.

Super-Congo. HT. (Meilland, 1950). 'Congo' × 'Léonce Colombier'. Velvety blackish-blood red, medium, double, some scent, poor bloomer; growth moderate, bushy, 0.7 m./2.3 ft.; foliage bluish-green, matt. SWR 99.

'Super Star' → **Tropicana**

Super Sun. HT. (Bentley, 1967). Sport of 'Piccadilly'. Corn yellow; otherwise has all the characteristics of the original variety. RA 1969:33; GSR 368.

Susan Hampshire. HT. (Meilland, 1974). Deep pink, very double, strong fragrance, very floriferous; bud large; growth vigorous, 0.8-0.9 m./2.6-3 ft.

Susan Louise. S. (Adams, 1929). 'Belle Portugaise'-seedling. Flesh-pink, semi-double, flat, fragrant, recurrent; bud very long, deep pink; growth vigorous, medium, bushy. (5.8)

Susan Massu. (= 'Susan'). HT. (Kordes, 1970). Pale yellow, then salmon-pink with yellow center and reverse, very large, 12-15 cm./4.8-6 in. across, high-centered, strong fragrance, first upright, later often nodding; growth upright, 0.8-1 m./2.6-3.3 ft.; foliage medium, matt. (8.0)

Suspense. HT. (Meilland, 1960). 'Henri Mallerin' × ('Happiness' × 'Floradora'). Interior crimson-scarlet, reverse dark creamy-yellow with fine veins, large, 12 cm./4.8 in. across, cupped, some scent; bud ovoid; growth vigorous, bushy; foliage deep green, glossy. PWR 22; BTR 55. (5.9)

Sutter's Gold. HT. (Swim/Armstrong, 1950). 'Charlotte Armstrong' × 'Signora'. Deep gold with orange and peach shading, medium, 8 cm./3.2 in. across, double, floriferous, strong fragrance; growth upright, wiry stems, branched, 0.9 m./3 ft.; foliage healthy, glossy, very resistant to Black Spot. RA 1952:40; PWR 71; GSR 370; BTR 19. (6.9)

Suzanne. S. (Skinner, 1950). F₂ of *Rosa laxa* × *R. pimpinellifolia*. Coral-pink, very double, free, recurrent; growth bushy, medium; foliage deep green, small.

Suzon Lotthé. HT. (F. Meilland/C.-P., 1951). 'Peace' × ('Signora' × 'Mrs. John Laing'). Pearl-pink, deeper towards the edge, very fragrant, double, high-centered, large, 10 cm./4 in., profuse bloom; bud peach; foliage dark; growth very vigorous.

Swan Lake. LCl. (McGredy, 1968). 'Heidelberg' × 'Memoriam'. White with a flush of pink, very large, high-centered, perfect form, some scent, floriferous; growth vigorous, 2.5 m./8.3 ft. GSR 261.

Swarthmore. HT. (Alain Meilland/C-P., 1963). ('Independence' × 'Happiness') × 'Peace'. Rose-red, slightly fragrant, double, high centered, large, 10 cm./4 in., on long, strong stems, free bloom; foliage dark, leathery; growth very vigorous, bushy.

Swedish Doll. Min. (Ralph S. Moore, 1976). 'Fire King' × 'Little Buckaroo'. Deep pink to red, double, 30 petals, long-lasting, very recurrent all season, singly and several together in clusters; growth dwarf, vigorous, branched; foliage medium green, glossy, medium size. (7.5)

Sweepstakes. (= 'Margaret Trudeau'). HT. (McGredy/Armstrong, 1978). 'Prima Ballerina' × 'Ginger Rogers'. Salmon-coral, double, large, very fragrant, high-centered, floriferous; growth upright-spreading, bushy; foliage semi-glossy.

Sweet Afton. HT. (Armstrong & Swim, 1954). ('Charlotte Armstrong' × 'Signora') × ('Alice Stern' × 'Ondine'). White, reverse blush, double, very large, 12 cm./4.8 in. across, high-centered, very fragrant, abundant bloom; growth tall, bushy, spreading; foliage leathery. (7.5)

'Sweet Briar' → **Rosa rubiginosa,** p. 262.

Sweet Fairy. Min. (de Vink, 1964). 'Tom Thumb' × seedling. Lilac-rose pink, small, 2.5 cm./1 in. across, very double, finally flat, petals pointed, rosette-shaped, fragrant, floriferous; growth dwarf, 15-20 cm./6-8 in.; foliage small, deep green. (7.4)

Sweet Home. HT. (Meilland, 1971). ('Jolie Madame' × 'Baccara') × self. Interior light crimson, reverse darker and more vermilion, large, double, cupped, some scent, singly or several together, floriferous; growth strong; foliage abundant, large, firm.

Sweet 'n Pink. HT. (O.L. Weeks, 1976). 'Prima Ballerina'-seedling × (['Happiness' × 'Chrysler Imperial'] × ['El Capitan' × 'Peace']). Bright, deep orange, double, 45 petals, strong fragrance, open, singly and several together, abundant bloom; growth upright, branched; foliage deep green.

'Sweet Promise' → **Sonia**

Sweet Repose. (= 'The Optimist'). F. (de Ruiter, 1956).

'Golden Rapture' × Floribunda-seedling. First carmine tinged with gold and pink, then pure carmine with a salmon base, 7 cm./2.8 in. across, fragrant, very long-lasting, singly or several together, floriferous; growth strong, branched, 0.9 m./3 ft.; foliage medium, red-green, matt. RA 1856:80; PWR 109; GSR 492.

Sweet Song. F. (Meilland, 1971). 'Fidelio' × 'Bettina'. Pink, large, 10 cm./4 in. across, semi-double, finally flat, some scent, profuse and continuous bloom, singly and several together in clusters; growth bushy, branched; foliage matt, medium.

Sweet Sultan. LCl. (Eacott/LeGrice, 1958). 'Independence' × 'Honour Bright'. Deep crimson, single, large, 10 cm./4 in. across, singly or several together, strong scent, recurrent; growth medium-strong, 2-3 m./6.6-10 ft.; foliage dark red-green. GSR 262.

Sweet Vivid. Min. (Origin unknown). Bright salmon, small, good form, fragrant; growth dwarf, vigorous. (6.8)

Sweet Vivien. F. (Raffel/Port Stockton Nurseries, 1963). 'Little Darling' × 'Odorata'. Pink with light yellow center, medium, 7 cm./2.8 in. across, semi-double, 15 petals, some scent, in clusters on short stems, profuse bloom; growth bushy, low, very compact; foliage deep green, glossy, small. (8.2)

Sylvia. HT. (Kordes, 1978). 'Carina' × seedling. Deep pink, very large, high-centered, singly and several together, abundant continuous bloom; bud large, long, pointed; growth very vigorous, upright; foliage glossy.

Sympathie. K. (Kordes, 1964). 'Wilhelm Hansmann' × 'Don Juan'. Velvety deep red, large, good form, double, strong fragrance, to 10 cm./4 in. across, several together, profuse and recurrent bloom; growth vigorous, 3-4 m./10-13 ft.; foliage medium-large, bright green, glossy. KR 9:141. (7.3)

Symphonette. Min. (D. Morey, 1973). 'Cécile Brunner' × 'Cinderella'. Light pink with darker reverse, small, 3 cm./1.2 in. across, long-lasting, petals drop off cleanly, continuous bloom; growth low, vigorous, 20 cm./8 in.; foliage small, leathery, glossy.

Symphony. HT. (Meilland, 1951). 'Peace' × ('Signora' × 'Mrs. John Laing'). Crimson-pink, with deeper veins and shades, large, 12 cm./4.8 in. across, semi-double, high-centered, strong fragrance, floriferous; growth vigorous, bushy; foliage firm, glossy. PWR 69. (5.5)

1906	**Tausendschön**						
1908	Weisse Tausendschön						
1913	White Tausendschön						
1914	- - - - - - - - - - - - - →	1914	Echo				
		1916	- - - - - - - - - - →	1916	**Greta Kluis**		
				1927	- - - - - - - - - - - →	1927	**Präsident Hindenburg**
				1928	Greta Kluis Superior	1930	Anneke Koster
				1928	Direktor Erik Hjelm		
		1923	- - - - - - - - - - →	1923	**Eva Teschendorff**		
				1926	Climb. Eva Teschendorff		
1917	Roserie	1924	Direktor Struve				
1918	White Tausendschön	1925	Klein Echo				
1925	Manja Böhn	1925	Weiss Echo				
1931	Red Tausendschön	1927	Brillant Echo				

The spontaneous sports of 'Tausendschön'. (after Saakov)

Taffeta. HT. (Lammerts/Armstrong Nurs., 1947). 'Mrs. Sam McGredy' × 'Pres. Herbert Hoover'. From begonia-pink to straw-yellow, fragrant, semi-double, open, medium, 7.6-9 cm./3-3.5 in., free bloom; bud urn-shaped; foliaged leathery, glossy, bronze-green; growth vigorous, upright.

Tahiti. HT. (Meilland, 1947). 'Peace' × 'Signora'. Orange-yellow with pink and crimson shades and veins, 12 cm./4.8 in. across, double, fragrant, moderate bloom; growth strong, branched, 0.7 m./2.3 ft.; foliage medium, deep green, glossy. SWR 193. (7.4)

Taj Mahal. HT. (Armstrong, 1972). 'Manitou' × 'Grand Slam'. Deep pink, double, very large, open, to 15 cm./6 in. and over, petals slightly rolled, scented; growth medium high, bushy, upright; foliage bright green.

Talisman. HT. (Montgomery, 1929). 'Ophelia' × 'Souvenir de Claudius Pernet'. Deep yellow and coppery, medium, semi-double, 25 petals, opening flat, fragrant, on long stem; growth vigorous; foliage light green, leathery, glossy. (4.3)

Tallyho. HT. (Swim/Armstrong, 1948). 'Charlotte Armstrong' × seedling. Interior rose-pink, reverse crimson, large, 8 cm./3.2 in. across, double, fragrant, moderate bloom; growth vigorous, branched, 0.7 m./2.3 ft.; foliage medium, matt, reddish. PWR 30. (7.5)

Tamango. F. (Meilland, 1967). ('Alain' × *R. chinensis mutabilis*) × ('Radar' × 'Caprice'). Rose pink with crimson-shaded edge, large, double, globose, some scent, in large clusters, floriferous; growth vigorous, 0.8 m./2.6 ft.; foliage deep green. (7.8)

Tambourine. F. (Dickson, 1958). 'Independence'-seedling × 'Karl Herbst'. Interior cherry red, reverse pale yellow, medium, 7 cm./2.8 in. across, some scent, loose-ly double, finally flat, in large trusses, floriferous; growth vigorous; foliage deep green, firm, glossy. RA 1960:144. (5.1)

Tam O'Shanter. F. (Cocker, 1969). 'Orange Sensation' × 'Circus'. Yellow and cream center with red edge, rosette-shaped, medium-large, double, some scent; growth bushy, 0.6 m./2 ft.; foliage medium, matt.

Tampico. HT. (W.A. Warriner/Jackson & Perkins, 1976). 'South Seas' × 'Hawaii'. Coral-pink, very large, double, open-centered, long-lasting, some scent, petals drop off cleanly, free bloom; growth vigorous, upright; foliage large, leathery. (6.9)

Tantau's Surprise. (= 'Tantau's Überraschung'). F. (Tantau, 1943). 'Bouquet' × 'Hamburg'. Deep scarlet with blackish shimmer, very double, flat, no scent, floriferous, in clusters; growth strong, upright, 0.8 m./2.6 ft.; foliage large, glossy.

Tanya. HT. (Combe/Vilmorin, 1959). 'Peace' × ('Peace' × 'Orange Nassau'). Deep orange to apricot-orange, large, 12 cm./4.8 in. across, double, 50 petals, high-centered, fragrant, abundant bloom; growth vigorous; foliage firm, glossy. (6.0)

Tatjana. HT. (Kordes, 1970). 'Liebeszauber' × 'President Dr. Schröder'. Deep blood-red with blackish shimmer, large, double, strong fragrance, singly on long stems; bud large; growth vigorous, bushy; foliage large, deep green, glossy.

Tausendschön. Cl. (Kiese/J.C. Schmidt, 1906). 'Daniel Lacombe' × 'Weisser Herumstreicher'. Deep pink with white center, medium, very double, cupped, very profuse bloom in large trusses on long branches, non-recurrent; growth vigorous, 3 m./10 ft., stems without prickles; foliage medium, light green, matt. RZ 1913:61. (7.7)

413

Tea Party. Min. (Ralph S. Moore, 1972). (*R. wichuraiana* × 'Floradora') × 'Eleanor'. Apricot bud, becoming pink when open, double, small, long-lasting, singly and several together, abundant, continuous bloom; growth dwarf, 25 cm./10 in.; foliage small, light green. (7.2)

Teenager. F. (Boerner/Jackson & Perkins, 1958). 'Demure' × self. Very soft pink with some deeper hue, large, very double, high-centered, strong scent, strong stems; growth vigorous, upright. Greenhouse variety.

Telstar. F. (Gandy, 1962). 'Flash' × 'Masquerade'. Golden-yellow with orange, outer petals and tips of all petals more or less red, medium, finally star-shaped, in loose clusters; growth vigorous, 0.9 m./3 ft.; foliage deep green. RA 1964:29; GSR 490.

Temple Bells. ClMin. (D. Morey/McGredy, 1971). F₂ of *R. wichuraiana* × 'Blushing Jewel'. White, single, fragrant, free summer bloom, in trusses, stamens yellow; growth very vigorous, spreading; foliage small, light green, glossy. (5.4)

Tempo. LCl. (W.A. Warriner/Jackson & Perkins, 1975). 'Ena Harkness' × seedling. Deep red, large, double, high-centered, some scent, long-lasting, singly and several together, petals drop off cleanly, floriferous; growth climbing; foliage deep green, large, glossy. (7.5)

Tenerife. HT. (Timmerman's Roses, 1972). 'Fragrant Cloud' × 'Piccadilly'. Peach and cream, double, 45 petals, large, 12 cm./4.8 in. across, singly, very fragrant, free flowering; growth vigorous; foliage glossy.

Texas Centennial. HT. (Watkins, 1935). Sport of 'President Herbert Hoover'. Vermilion with some yellow, looks almost red-brown, medium-large, double, some scent, good form; growth vigorous, bushy, 0.7 m./2.3 ft., long stems; foliage large, matt. ARA 1936:48. (7.0)

'Theano' (Geschwind, 1895) is almost identical to → **Rosa californica plena,** p. 277.

The Beacon. Cl. (W. Paul, 1922). Fiery red with white center, single, sometimes semi-double, in large trusses, non-recurrent; growth vigorous, 2.5 m./8.3 ft.

The Bishop (presumably = 'L'Evêque'). G. Lilac-purple, to more violet and grey-violet with age, finally grey-bluish shaded, petals reversed, very double, rosette-shaped, non-recurrent; growth rather upright, slender, 1 m./3.3 ft.; foliage tiny, glossy. Often erroneously called a *centifolia*-form.

The Chief. HT. (Lammerts, 1940). 'Charles P. Kilham' × 'President Herbert Hoover'. Coral-pink and coppery, very large, 10-15 cm./4-6 in. across, 40 petals, very fragrant, on long stems; growth bushy, spreading.

The Doctor. HT. (Howard/Dreer, 1936). 'Mrs. J.D. Eisele' × 'Los Angeles'. Medium pink, very large, to 15 cm./6 in. across, semi-double, 25 petals, very fragrant; growth dwarf, bushy; foliage light green. (5.9)

The Fairy. Pol. (Bentall, 1932). Sport of 'Lady Godiva'. Light rose-pink, small, densely rosette-shaped, double, 2.5 cm./1 in. across, in large trusses of small clusters, very floriferous, recurrent; growth very dense, bushy, 0.7 × 0.7 m./2.3 × 2.3 ft.; foliage small, very glossy. GSR 491. (8.4). An excellent ground cover.

The Sun. F. (McGredy, 1973). ('Little Darling' × 'Goldilocks') × 'Irish Mist'. Salmon-orange, large, 8-9 cm./3.2-3.6 in. across, semi-double, 15 petals, some scent, in trusses, free continuous bloom; growth medium; foliage deep green.

Thérèse Bugnet. HRg. (Bugnet, 1950). (*R. acicularis* × *R. rugosa* var. *kamtschatica*) × (*R. amblyotis* × *R. rugosa plena*). Opening deep red, then becoming pink, large, 10 cm./4 in. across, single, flat, fragrant, recurrent bloom on previous year's branches; growth very vigorous, tall; foliage similar to *R. acicularis*, but larger. (8.0)

Thumbelina. Min. (Ralph S. Moore, 1954). 'Eblouissant' × 'Zee'. Cherry-red with white base, small, semi-double, abundant bloom; growth dwarf, 15-20 cm./6-8 in.; foliage deep green, glossy.

Thunder Cloud. Min. (Ralph S. Moore, 1979). 'Little Chief' × 'Fire Princess'. Bright orange-red, small, very double, 70 petals, no scent, in clusters, abundant, recurrent; growth bushy, dwarf; foliage matt, leathery.

Thusnelda. HRg. (F. Müller, 1886). *R. rugosa alba* × 'Gloire de Dijon'. Soft silvery-salmon pink, later more blush, semi-double, cupped, singly or up to 3 together in clusters, recurrent; growth bushy, medium; foliage wrinkled.

Thyrion. HT. (McGredy, 1969). Soft salmon-pink, becoming more red with age, reverse blush, white center, very large, 12 cm./4.8 in. across, finally flat, double, fragrant, several together; growth upright, 0.8 m./2.6 ft., rather spreading; foliage large, dense, young growth purple.

Tiara. F. (Boerner/Jackson & Perkins, 1960). 'Chic' × 'Demure'-seedling. White, medium, 7 cm./2.8 in. across, cupped, double, fragrant, floriferous, long stems; growth vigorous. Greenhouse variety.

Tiffany. HT. (Lindquist, 1954). 'Charlotte Armstrong' × 'Girona'. Salmon-pink with yellowish base, large, 12 cm./4.8 in. across, semi-double, finally flat, strong fragrance, floriferous, on long, strong stems; growth upright, bushy, 0.9 m./3 ft.; foliage deep green, matt. PWR 74; GSR 371. (8.8)

Tiki. F. (McGredy, 1964). 'Mme. Léon Cuny' × 'Spartan'. Light shell-pink, double, 30 petals, 10 cm./4 in. across, free bloom; growth bushy; foliage deep green. (7.6)

Tinker Bell. Min. (de Vink, 1954). 'Ellen Poulsen' × 'Tom Thumb'. Bright rose-pink, small, 3 cm./1.2 in. across, very double, 65 petals, cupped, free bloom; growth very dwarf, 20 cm./8 in.; foliage firm, small. (7.2)

Tiny Flame. Min. (Ralph S. Moore, 1969). (*R. wichuraiana* × 'Floradora') × 'New Penny'. Coral-orange, double, very small, profuse bloom; growth dwarf, 15 cm./6 in. (7.1)

Tiny Jack. Min. (Ralph S. Moore, 1962). (*R. wichuraiana* × 'Floradora') × ('Oakington Ruby' × 'Floradora'). Deep red, double, 30 petals, small, some scent, free bloom; growth dwarf, 30-35 cm./12-14 in., bushy; foliage small, deep green. (6.1)

Tiny Jill. Min. (Ralph S. Moore, 1962). (*R. wichuraiana* × 'Floradora') × 'Little Buckaroo'. Medium pink, double, 50 petals, small, 3 cm./1.2 in. across, free bloom, high-centered, fragrant; growth dwarf, bushy, 30-35 cm./12-14 in.; foliage firm, glossy. (5.5)

Tiny Warrior. (E.D. Williams, 1975). 'Stardust' × 'Little Chief'. Red blend, double, flat, some scent, singly and several together, abundant, recurrent; growth dwarf, bushy; foliage deep green, glossy. (8.0)

Tip Toes. HT. (Brownell, 1948). ('Général Jacqueminot' × 'Dr. W. van Fleet') × 'Anne Vanderbilt'. Salmon-pink, yellow base, large, semi-double, high-centered, fragrant, abundant bloom; growth upright; foliage glossy. (6.6)

Tip Top. F. (Tantau, 1963). Seedling × seedling. Clear salmon-pink, large, semi-double, cupped to flat, fragrant, good form, very floriferous; growth bushy, low, 40 cm./16 in.; foliage deep green, dense, glossy. WPR 46; RJb 27:64. (6.7)

Titian. F. (Riethmüller, 1950). Light red to crimson-pink, large, 12 cm./4.8 in. across, very double, floriferous, good form, long-lasting, in clusters; growth bushy, low, 40 cm./16 in.; foliage deep green, healthy.

Tom Thumb. (= 'Peon'). Min. (J. de Vink, 1936). 'Rouletii' × 'Gloria Mundi'. Deep crimson with white base, small, 2.5 cm./1 in. across, floriferous; growth very dwarf, 10-15 cm./4-6 in.; foliage pale green. (7.8)

Tom Tom. F. (Lindquist, 1957). 'Improved Lafayette' × 'Floradora'. Crimson-pink, large, double, finally flat, some scent, in clusters, floriferous; growth bushy, upright; foliage deep green, matt. (6.6)

Tony Jacklin. F. (McGredy, 1972). 'City of Leeds' × 'Irish Mist'. Coral-red, semi-double, HT-form, high-centered, good fragrance; bud long; growth very vigorous, 0.7-0.8 m./2.3-2.6 ft.; foliage very healthy. (8.5)

Toni Lander. F. (F. Poulsen, 1958). 'Independence' × 'Circus'. Interior orange-red, more or less overlaid with red, reverse yellow, medium-large, 7 cm./2.8 in., semi-double, some scent, in large trusses, floriferous; growth bushy, low, 0.5 m./1.7 ft.; foliage deep green, glossy. RJb 22:128. (6.6)

Top Secret. Min. (R.S. Moore/Sequoia Nurs., 1971). Sport of 'Beauty Secret'. Red, fragrant, double, high-centered, medium, abundant bloom; foliage glossy, leathery; growth vigorous, dwarf, upright.

Tornado. (= 'Kortor'). F. (Kordes, 1973). 'Europeana' × 'Marlena'. Orange-red, medium, semi-double, some scent, petals drop off cleanly, in clusters, similar to 'Fanal', but color hardier; growth bushy, upright, very healthy.

Toro. HT. (M.E. Wyant, 1972). 'Karl Herbst' × 'Big Red'. Medium red, very large, high-centered, fragrant, petals drop off cleanly, very double, on long stems, abundant intermittent bloom; growth very vigorous. (7.6)

Toscana. F. (Jackson & Perkins, 1973). Bright orange, large, double, cupped, long-lasting, some scent, profuse bloom; growth vigorous; foliage deep green, glossy.

Touch of Venus. HT. (Armstrong, 1971). 'Garden Party' × 'Sweet Afton'. White, tips of petals blush, double, high-centered, fragrant; bud long, pointed; growth upright, stems almost without prickles; foliage deep green.

Tour de Malakoff. C. (Soupert & Notting, 1856). Purple-carmine to lilac-pink, lighter reverse, changing to violet-blue with many veins, green center, large, 10 cm./4 in. across, loosely double, finally flat, fragrant, non-recurrent, profuse; growth strong, tall (needs support); foliage rather small. GSR 71; SOR 13; GiS 8. (7.8)

Town Talk. F. (Swim & Weeks, 1966). ('Circus' × 'Garnette') × 'Circus'. Orange, very double, small, profuse bloom; growth medium; foliage leathery, deep green. (7.8)

Toy Clown. Min. (Ralph S. Moore, 1966). 'Little Darling' × 'Magic Wand'. White with red edges, small, semi-double, free bloom; growth dwarf; foliage leathery, small. (8.9)

Tradewinds. (also written 'Trade Winds'). HT. (Abrams, 1964). ('Multnomah' × seedling) × ('Carrousel' × seedling). Deep scarlet, reverse silver-pink, large, 12 cm./4.8 in. across, high-centered, strong fragrance, double, good form; bud long; growth vigorous, 0.9 m./3 ft.; foliage light green, glossy. (7.3)

Tradition. HT. (Kordes, 1965). 'Detroiter' × 'Don Juan'. Crimson-scarlet, hardy, large, 10 cm./4 in. across, no scent, floriferous; growth vigorous, long stems, 0.8 m./2.6 ft.; foliage medium green, firm. Also proven a good greenhouse variety. GR 144. (6.3)

Trailblazer. F. (R.E. Harvey, 1975). 'Albert' × 'Orange Sensation'. Reddish-orange, semi-double, small, in clusters, long-lasting, some scent, profuse, continuous bloom; growth bushy, upright; foliage medium, firm, disease-resistant. (8.0)

Träumerei. (= 'Korrei'). F. (Kordes, 1974). 'Colour Wonder' × seedling. Orange-pink, medium, cupped, double, strong scent, singly or several together, petals drop off; growth vigorous, bushy, abundant.

'Traumland' → **Dreamland**

Travemünde. F. (Kordes, 1968). 'Lilli Marlene' × 'Ama'. Deep red with lighter base, hardy, medium, 7 cm./2.8 in. across, double, many together in large trusses, continuous bloom; growth vigorous, bushy, low, 0.5 m./1.7 ft.; foliage deep green. KR 10:30.

Traviata. HT. (Meilland, 1962). 'Baccara' × ('Independence' × 'Grand'mère Jenny'). Interior crimson with

white base, reverse white with pink edge, large, 10 cm./4 in. across, double, cupped, fragrant; growth bushy, strong stems; foliage firm. (6.0)

Treasure Trove. R. (B.J. Treasure, 1961). *R. filipes* × China (probably 'Old Blush'). Apricot, then mauve-pink, fading to creamy-white, semi-double, 25 petals, cupped, fragrant, in trusses, free bloom, non-recurrent; growth very strong, 6 m./20 ft. or over; young growth brilliant ruby-red. RA 1979:155.

Tricolore de Flandre. G. (van Houtte, 1846). Blush pink, heavily striped and splashed with rose, turning violet-grey with age; growth strong, 0.9 m./3 ft. Similar to 'Camaieux', but more vigorous. GiS 6. (8.8)

Trinket. Min. (Ralph S. Moore, 1965). (*R. wichuraiana* × 'Floradora') × 'Magic Wand'. Purplish-pink, double, small, profuse bloom; growth dwarf, bushy; foliage small, glossy. (7.7)

Trio. F. (Dickson, 1966). 'Kordes Perfecta' × 'Shot Silk'. Opening deep yellow with large red edges, then more pink with yellow, medium, double, finally flat, long-lasting, profuse bloom; growth bushy, long stems; foliage deep green.

Triton. HT. (Dickson, 1978). 'Colour Wonder' × 'Tzigane'. Yellow blend, 45 petals, flat, fragrant, singly or in small clusters, abundant, recurrent; growth upright; foliage semi-glossy. RA 1979:81.

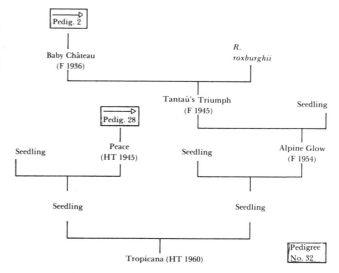

Tropicana. (= 'Super Star'). HT. (Tantau, 1960). (Seedling × 'Peace') × ('Peace' × 'Alpine Glow'). Pure salmon-orange or light vermilion, large, 12 cm./4.8 in. across, double, very good form, fragrant, singly or 2-3

on long stems, profuse bloom; growth vigorous, upright, 0.8-1 m./2.6-3.3 ft. under glass, 0.6-0.8 m./2-2.6 ft. outdoors; foliage large, firm, first reddish, then deep green, very disease-resistant. GSR 369; RJb 22:64; WGR 113. (8.8) World famous variety.

Truly Yours. HT. (Robinson, 1971). 'Miss Ireland' × 'Stella'. Salmon-red with orange, very double, 45 petals, rather globose, strong scent, singly and several together; growth vigorous, upright; foliage large, deep green, glossy. RA 1972:48; CRA 73:33.

'Turner's Crimson Rambler' → **Crimson Rambler**

Trumpeter. F. (McGredy, 1976). 'Satchmo' × (['Hamburger Phoenix' × 'Spectacular' × 'Evelyn Fison'] × [*R. coryana* × 'Tantau's Triumph']). Scarlet-vermilion to orange-red, double, 40 petals, medium, 8 cm./3.2 in., edges undulate, some scent, continuous bloom, in clusters; growth low, vigorous, bushy; foliage deep green, healthy.

Tuscany. G. (Origin unknown, probably identical to Gerard's 'Velvet Rose' from 1596; sometimes called 'Old Velvet' in England). Brown-crimson with violet tints and white spots to the center, stamens yellow, 10 cm./4 in. across, semi-double, finally flat, some scent, nonrecurrent; growth upright, medium; foliage small. GiS 6. (8.4)

Tuscany Superb. G. Very similar to 'Tuscany', but larger overall, flowers more double. GSR 91. (8.0)

T.V. Times. HT. (Dickson, 1970). 'Gallant' × ('Detroiter' × seedling). Crimson, very large, to 14 cm./5.6 in. across, double, fragrant, singly on strong stems; bud ovoid, blackish; growth vigorous, bushy; foliage large, matt.

Tweetie. Min. (Ralph S. Moore, 1973). 'Perle d'Or' × 'Fairy Princess'. Soft pink, very double, small, several together, continuous bloom; growth dwarf, 15-20 cm./6-8 in., bushy; foliage small, light green. (5.8)

Twilight Beauty. Min. (E.D. Williams, 1977). 'Angel Face' × 'Over the Rainbow'. Mauve, high-centered, abundant bloom all season, singly; growth dwarf, bushy, spreading; foliage small.

Twinkie. Min. (Ralph S. Moore, 1974). (*R. wichuraiana* × 'Floradora') × 'Eleanor'. Carmine-rose, changing to light pink, double, 40 narrow petals, in clusters, abundant, continuous bloom; growth dwarf, 30 cm./12 in.; foliage small, glossy, healthy. (6.3)

Typhoo Tea. HT. (McGredy, 1974). 'Fragrant Cloud' × 'Arthur Bell'. Brilliant cerise-red, reverse cream, large, double, 50 petals, strong perfume, very free bloom all season; growth strong, healthy. (7.0)

Typhoon. HT. (Kordes/McGredy, 1973). 'Colour Wonder' × 'Golden Wave'. Pink, large, 10 cm./4 in. across, double, strong scent, singly on strong stems, floriferous; growth vigorous; foliage abundant. RA 1973:140. (6.7)

Tzigane. HT. (Meilland, 1951). 'Peace' × 'J.B. Meilland'. Interior scarlet, reverse yellow suffused with light red, large, cupped, fragrant, floriferous; growth medium, 0.5 m./1.7 ft., bushy; foliage medium-large, glossy. PWR 55; BTR 25. (5.8)

Ulrich Brunner Fils. (= 'Ulrich Brunner'). HP. (A. Levet, 1882). Origin uncertain; thought to be a seedling (or sport) of 'Anna de Diesbach' or a sport of 'Paul Neyron'. Cherry red, fading with age, medium to large, double, finally more cupped, very strong fragrance, floriferous, recurrent; growth vigorous, tall, few prickles; foliage large, glossy. LR 3; GiS 13. (7.6)

Ulster Monarch. HT. (McGredy, 1951). 'Sam McGredy' × 'Mrs. Sam McGredy'-seedling. Apricot and buff, medium, double, 50 petals, high-centered, some scent, profuse bloom; growth upright; foliage glossy, bright green. (3.8)

Una Wallace. HT. (McGredy, 1921). Cherry pink, large, good form, double, fragrant, long stems. RZ 1926:29.

Uncle Joe. HT. (J.J. Kern, 1971). (['Mirandy' × 'Charles Mallerin'] × seedling) × unknown. Dark red, very large, high-centered, petals retained, abundant, continuous bloom; bud very large, pointed; growth very vigorous, tall; foliage leathery, glossy, disease-resistant. (7.7)

Uncle Sam. HT. (W.A. Warriner/Howard, 1965). 'Charlotte Armstrong' × 'Heart's Desire'. Deep pink, large, high-centered, fragrant; growth vigorous, tall; foliage deep green, leathery, glossy. (6.5)

Uncle Walter. HT. (McGredy, 1963). 'Detroiter' × 'Heidelberg'. Crimson-scarlet, large, 12 cm./4.8 in. across, double, some scent, very large sepals, in clusters; growth tall to very tall (more like a shrub rose); stems very long; foliage large, bronze-green. KR 9:51. (6.4)

Unique Blanche. (= 'Unique'; 'White Provence'; 'Vierge de Cléry'). C. Found in England in 1775 (G.S. Thomas).

Creamy white, glistening, nearly translucent, cupped, with eye visible when half open, fragrant; buds suffused with red; late-flowering; growth bushy, medium. (8.2)

Unique Panachée. C. (Caron, 1871). Sport of 'Unique Rouge'. White with blush and lavender stripes (few when plant is in good soil!), large, globose; growth vigorous.

Valencia. HT. (Kordes, 1967). 'Golden Sun' × 'Chantré'. Orange-yellow with red hue, looks bronze, very large, double, high centered, floriferous; bud long; growth vigorous, bushy, strong stems; foliage large, deep green, glossy. (6.7)

Valentine. F. (Swim & Armstrong, 1951). 'China Doll' × 'World's Fair'. Bright red, medium, 6-7 cm./2.4-2.8 in. across, semi-double, 15 petals, some scent, cupped, in large clusters; growth bushy, semi-spreading; foliage deep olive-green. (6.4)

Vanity. HMsk. (Pemberton, 1920). 'Château de Clos Vougeot'-seedling. Soft crimson-pink, nearly single, large, cupped, fragrant, in large, loose clusters, recurrent; growth bushy, to 2.5 m./8.3 ft.; foliage deep green, glossy. PWR 198; GSR 125; TRT 117; GiS 17.

Variegata di Bologna. B. (Lodi-Bonfiglioli, 1909). Blush-white with purplish-red stripes, medium, 8 cm./3.2 in. across, rather globose, double, along the branches, mostly 3-5 together; growth vigorous, tall; very fragrant. GSR 103; GiS 13. (7.5)

Veilchenblau. Cl. (J.C. Schmidt, 1909). 'Crimson Rambler' × 'Erinnerung an Brod'. Blue-magenta ("blue") with white eye, becoming blue-violet with age, small, 3 cm./1.2 in. across, some scent, floriferous, in large trusses, non-recurrent; very vigorous, many stems, 3-4 m./10-13 ft.; nearly without prickles. TCR 2; GiS 24. (6.6)

Velvet Flame. HT. (Meilland, 1972). 'Tropicana' × 'Papa Meilland'. Cardinal-red, very large, 13 cm./5.2 in. across, semi-double, 30 petals, some scent, free-flowering, singly; growth vigorous; foliage deep green.

Venusta Pendula. Cl. *Arvensis* hybrid; origin unknown, re-introduced in 1928 by W. Kordes. Blush, small, semi-double, no scent, profuse bloom, non-recurrent; growth very strong, to 6 m./20 ft.; foliage medium, matt. RZ 1928:80; PGR 90.

Vera Dalton. F. (Norman, 1961). ('Paul's Scarlet Climber' × self) × ('Mary' × 'Queen Elizabeth'). Blush,

large, 10 cm./4 in. across, semi-double, fragrant, floriferous, in clusters; growth vigorous, 1 m./3.3 ft.; foliage deep green, healthy. RA 1962:97; GSR 495. (7.6)

Very Busy. Min. (Ralph S. Moore, 1973). 'Perle d'Or' × 'Fairy Princess'. Pink with soft yellow, double, singly and several together on short stems, abundant, continuous bloom, some scent; growth dwarf, bushy, 25 cm./10 in.; foliage small, leathery, medium green. (6.1)

Vesper. F. (LeGrice 1966). Soft orange-brown with other shades, medium, semi-double, finally flat, some scent, floriferous in large trusses, especially in autumn; growth medium, 0.8 m./2.6 ft.; foliage small, glossy. RA 1968:33; GSR 496. (2.0)

Via Mala. HT. (Kordes, 1977). 'Silver Star' × 'Peer Gynt'. White, very large, double, high-centered, singly and several together, abundant, intermittent bloom; growth very vigorous; foliage glossy, deep green.

Victor Hugo. HP. (J. Schwartz, 1884). 'Charles Lefèbvre' ? × ?. Glistening carmine-red with dark purple shades, double, 30 petals, medium, globose, fragrant; growth vigorous. (7.8)

'Vienna Charm' → **Charming Vienna**

'Vierge de Cléry' → **Unique Blanche**

Viking. HT. (Moro, 1968). 'Volcano' × 'Rouge Meilland'. Crimson, large, 12 cm./4.8 in. across, very double, fragrant, floriferous; growth vigorous, upright; foliage firm, deep green. (6.9)

Viking Queen. LCl. (Phillips, 1963). 'White Dawn' × 'L.E. Longley'. Deep pink, large, 10 cm./4 in. across, double, 60 petals, globose, very fragrant, in large trusses, profuse, recurrent bloom; growth vigorous, climbing; foliage deep green, glossy, leathery. (7.5)

Villa de Madrid. HT. (Dot, 1965). 'Baccara' × 'Peace'. Vermilion, hardy, large, very double, on long, strong stems, very floriferous; growth vigorous, upright; foliage large, deep green, glossy. (5.7)

'Village Maid' → **R. centifolia variegata**, p. 257.

'Ville de Bruxelles' → **La Ville de Bruxelles**

Ville de Zurich. F. (Gaujard, 1967). 'Miss France' × 'Nouvelle Europe'. Orange-red, medium, semi-double, some scent, several together in clusters, continuous bloom; growth vigorous, bushy. RA 1970:144; WGR 97.

Vincent van Gogh. F. (Buisman, 1969). 'Allotria' ×

'Hobby'. Salmon-red, fading to more salmon-pink, medium, semi-double, faint scent, in clusters, petals undulated; growth bushy, 0.6 m./2 ft., vigorous; foliage medium green, medium, semi-glossy.

Vino Delicado. HT. (Frank C. Raffel, 1972). Seedling × 'Mauve Melodee'. Mauve, tips of petals purplish-red, large, double, some scent, moderate intermittent bloom; growth upright; foliage disease-resistant. (6.6)

Violacée. G. (Soupert & Notting, 1876). Opening crimson and blackish, then purple-violet, with golden-yellow anthers, medium, 7 cm./2.8 in. across, single, (not double as is often stated), 10 petals, fragrant, floriferous, mostly 3 in clusters, calyx and flower stalk glandular (not mossy); growth upright, medium, stems slender; foliage matt, bright green. Is not a Moss Rose or a Centifolia! (8.2)

Violaine. HT. (Gaujard, 1968). 'Eminence' × 'Simone'. Deep mauve, large, double, fragrant, floriferous, singly on long, strong stems; growth vigorous, 0.6 m./2 ft.; foliage light green, firm.

Violet Carson. F. (McGredy, 1964). 'Mme. Léon Cuny' × 'Spartan'. Light pink with deeper shades and veins, base and reverse yellowish, large, double, fragrant, good form, floriferous, in clusters; growth vigorous, 0.7 m./2.3 ft.; foliage deep green, glossy. GSR 497; WPR 54; RA 1964:65. (8.0)

Violet Fontaine. S. (Tantau, 1973). Parentage not reported. Violet, large, double, some scent, several together, petals drop off cleanly; growth vigorous, medium; foliage large, semi-glossy.

Violette Dot. HT. (Dot, 1960). 'Rosa de Friera' × 'Prélude'. Bluish-lilac, medium, semi-double, fragrant, floriferous, strong stems; growth medium, vigorous, spreading.

Violet Wilton. HT. (Ketten, 1930). 'General McArthur' × 'Mme. Charles Lutaud'. Rosy-red with blush base, suffused with yellow, large, double, 40 petals, fragrant; bud very long, pointed; growth vigorous.

Virgin. F. (Hill, 1971). 'Seventeen' × 'Jack Frost'. White, medium, 8 cm./3.2 in. across, semi-double, nearly globose, floriferous, several together in clusters, continuous bloom; growth upright, branches; foliage large, firm, matt.

Virginia Reel. S. (G.J. Buck, 1975). 'Tickled Pink' × 'Prairie Princess'. Medium red, fading to rose and rose-red with age, medium, cupped, 45 petals, fragrant, flowering all season; growth bushy, 0.8 m./2.6 ft.; foliage large, deep green, leathery.

Virgo. HT. (Mallerin, 1947). 'Blanche Mallerin' × 'Neige Parfum'. Pure white, bud sometimes blush, large, 12 cm./4.8 in. across, double, high-centered, some scent, moderate bloom; growth sturdy, upright, 0.5 m./1.7 ft.; foliage deep green, matt. PWR 83; BTR 17. (6.2)

'Viridiflora' → **R. chinensis viridiflora,** p. 291.

Vision. HT. (Dickson, 1967). 'Kordes Perfecta' × 'Peace'. Deep yellow with pink, large, 12 cm./4.8 in. across, double, floriferous; growth vigorous; foliage deep green, glossy.

Viva. F. (W.A. Warriner/Jackson & Perkins, 1974). Seedling × seedling. Deep red, medium, double, high-centered, long-lasting, petals drop off cleanly, singly and in clusters, on long stems, abundant, continuous bloom; growth vigorous, upright; foliage deep green, glossy. (7.5)

Vivace. F. (Kordes, 1974). 'Klaus Störtebeker' × ?. Orange-red, large, double, high-centered, singly and several together, long-lasting, some scent, petals drop off, floriferous; growth vigorous, upright, bushy.

Vivacious. F. (Gregory, 1971). 'Tropicana' × ?. Pink with purple shades, large, semi-double, fragrant, in clusters, floriferous; foliage medium green.

Vogue. F. (Boerner/Jackson & Perkins, 1951). 'Pinocchio' × 'Crimson Glory'. Cherry red with salmon hue, large, 10 cm./4 in. across, semi-double, fragrant, in clusters, floriferous; growth medium, 0.5 m./1.7 ft., bushy; foliage red-green, matt. PWR 112. (7.5)

Volcano. HT. (Moro, 1950). 'Charles P. Kilham' × 'Rome Glory'. Cherry red, very large, to 15 cm./6 in. across, semi-double, cupped, fragrant, floriferous; growth vigorous, 0.8 m./2.6 ft.; foliage dense, red-green, glossy.

Waitmata. Min. (S. McGredy/McGredy Roses International, 1978). 'Wee Man' × 'Matangi'. Red, slightly fragrant, double, medium, very free bloom; foliage glossy, light green; growth very bushy.

Waldfee. S. (Kordes, 1960). 'Independence' × 'Mrs. John Laing'. Blood red, large, 10 cm./4 in. across, very double, nearly camellia-shaped, fragrant, in clusters, recurrent; growth vigorous, bushy, medium; foliage large, bright green. RJb 22:96. (8.0)

Waltzertraum. (= 'Dream Waltz'). F. (Tantau, 1868). Seedling × seedling. Deep red, medium, semi-double, some scent, very floriferous; foliage deep green, glossy; growth vigorous. GSR 405.

Wanderin' Wind. S. (G.J. Buck, 1971). 'Dornröschen' × 'Andante'. Bicolored pink, becoming light pink with age, double, medium, high-centered, fragrant, long-lasting, petals drop off, continuous bloom; growth very strong, upright, 1.2 × 1.2 m./5 × 5 ft.; foliage deep green, leathery, disease-resistant. (8.7)

Warrior. F. (LeGrice, 1977). 'City of Belfast' × 'Rende Endiable'. Fiery orange-scarlet, semi-double, 30 petals, some scent, singly and in trusses, free continuous bloom; growth compact, bushy; foliage deep green, healthy. RA 1979:87.

Warwhoop. Min. (E.D. Williams, 1973). 'Baccara' × 'Little Chief'. Brilliant orange-red, small, very double, long-lasting, some scent, abundant, continuous bloom; growth dwarf, vigorous, 30 cm./12 in.; foliage very small, deep green, glossy, disease-resistant. (5.1)

Watercolor. Min. (Ralph S. Moore, 1976). 'Rumba' × ('Little Darling' × 'Red Germain'). Medium pink, small, double, 30 petals, high-centered, fragrant, in clusters, abundant, continuous bloom; growth dwarf, bushy; foliage small, glossy, leathery. (7.5)

Wedding Day. Sp. (F.C. Stern, 1950). Seedling of *R. sinowilsonii* × ?. Opening creamy-yellow, becoming nearly white, finally with blush hue, single, edge somewhat fringed, very fragrant, very profuse bloom, in very large trusses; growth strong, 6 m./20 ft. or more, very prickly; foliage large, glossy. GSR 228; GiS 24.

Wee Lass. Min. (Ralph S. Moore, 1974). 'Persian Princess' × self. Blood-red, semi-double, 20 petals, usually singly, very recurrent; growth dwarf, bushy, branched; foliage semi-glossy, deep green. (6.5)

Wee Man. (McGredy, 1974). Scarlet, semi-double, some scent, small, in trusses, free bloom, recurrent; growth dwarf, 30 cm./12 in.; foliage deep green, glossy, leathery. RA 1975:120.

Wendy Cussons. HT. (Gregory, 1963). (?) 'Independence' × 'Eden Rose'. Rose-red, lighter when fully open, large, 12 cm./4.8 in. across, double, high-centered, strong fragrance; growth vigorous, bushy, 0.9 m./3 ft.;

foliage deep green, firm, large. GSR 373; PWR 92; RA 1960:1. (6.7)

Westerland. S. (Kordes, 1969). 'Friedrich Wörlein' × 'Circus'. Deep yellow with orange-red, large, semi-double, strong scent, profuse bloom, recurrent, in large trusses; growth vigorous, 2 × 2 m./6.6 × 6.6 ft.; foliage large, bright green.

Westmont. Min. (Ralph S. Moore, 1958). (*R. wichuraiana* × 'Floradora') × ('Oakington Ruby' × 'Floradora'). Bright red, small, semi-double, free bloom; growth dwarf, vigorous, 40 cm./16 in., compact; foliage leathery, semi-glossy. (6.0)

Western Sun. HT. (Poulsen, 1965). 'Golden Scepter'-seedling × 'Golden Sun'. Golden-yellow, very large, 12 cm./4.8 in. across, very double, strong fragrance, floriferous, long-lasting, good shape; growth bushy; foliage deep green, large, abundant. RJb 30:49. (6.1)

Westminster. HT. (Robinson, 1960). 'Gay Crusader' × 'Peace'. Scarlet, reverse golden-yellow, large, very double, strong scent, floriferous; bud long, narrow; growth tall, vigorous; foliage large, dark. RA 1962:16. (6.1)

Whipped Cream. Min. (Ralph S. Moore, 1968). (*R. wichuraiana* × 'Carolyn Dean') × 'White King'. White, double, small, abundant bloom; growth dwarf, bushy; foliage leathery, pale green. (7.4)

Whisky Mac. (= 'Whisky'). HT. (Tantau, 1967). Seedling × 'Golden Wave'. Golden-amber with orange, large, double, good form, fragrant; growth vigorous, bushy, 0.9 m./3 ft.; foliage deep green, large, abundant. GSR 374; RJb 34:144. (6.2)

White Angel. Min. (Ralph S. Moore, 1971). (*R. wichuraiana* × 'Floradora') × ('Little Darling' × red mini-seedling). White, often opening with a slightly yellow center, small, double, high-centered, singly or several together, some scent, petals drop off; growth dwarf, 25 cm./10 in., nearly without prickles; foliage pale green, small. (8.3)

'White American Beauty' → **Frau Karl Druschki**

White Aster. Min. (Ralph S. Moore, 1957). (*R. wichuraiana* × 'Floradora') × 'Zee'. White, small, double, 50 narrow, reflexed petals, in pyramidal trusses, free bloom; growth very dwarf, 15-25 cm./6-10 in., compact; foliage small. (6.7)

'White Bath' → **R. centifolia muscosa alba,** p. 259.

White Bouquet. F. (Boerner/Jackson & Perkins, 1956). 'Glacier' × 'Pinocchio'. White, double, 45 petals, large, 10 cm./4 in. across, imbricated, spicy scent, in clusters, abundant bloom; growth bushy; foliage deep green, glossy. (6.9)

White Christmas. HT. (H & S, 1953). 'Sleigh Bells' × seedling. Pure white, fragrant, double, high-centered, medium, profuse bloom; bud long-pointed; foliage leathery, light green; growth moderate, upright.

White Cockade. LCl. (Cocker, 1969). 'New Dawn' × 'Circus'. White with creamy base, reverse sometimes slightly pink, medium, double, good form, fragrant, floriferous, in clusters, recurrent; growth vigorous, climbing, 2-2.5 m./6.6-8.3 ft.; foliage medium-large, glossy. (7.3)

White Dawn. LCl. (L.E. Longley, 1949). 'New Dawn' × 'Lily Pons'. White, medium, double, 35 petals, imbricate, fragrant, in clusters, abundant, recurrent; growth vigorous, climbing; foliage deep green. (7.3)

White Dian. Min. (Ralph S. Moore, 1965). Sport of 'Dian'. White, occasionally with pink hue, small, some scent; growth dwarf; foliage glossy, deep green. (6.3)

White Dorothy. (= 'White Dorothy Perkins'). R. (Cant, 1908). Sport of 'Dorothy Perkins'. Like the original type, but flowers creamy-white, small, very double, narrow petals, singly and in clusters, many together in large trusses, floriferous, non-recurrent.

White Gem. Min. (Meilland/Conard-Pyle, 1976). 'Darling Flame' × 'Jack Frost'. White, small, very double, about 100 petals, revolved, some scent, singly and several together, continuous bloom; growth bushy, upright; foliage large, deep green, glossy. (7.0)

White King. Min. (Ralph S. Moore, 1961). 'Golden Glow' × 'Zee'. Creamy white, small, 3 cm./1.2 in. across, double, 40 petals; fragrant, abundant bloom; growth dwarf, bushy, 30 cm./12 in.; foliage small, firm. (6.2)

White Knight. (= 'Message'). HT. (Meilland, 1956). ('Virgo' × 'Peace') × 'Virgo'. Pure white, center greenish, medium, singly on long stems; growth vigorous, upright, 0.8 m./2.6 ft.; foliage light green, matt. PWR 70; BTR 35; RA 1956:52. (6.1)

White Lightnin'. Gr. (Swim and Christensen/Armstrong Nurseries, 1980). 'Angel Face' × 'Misty'. Clear white, very fragrant, double, large, 9-10 cm./3.5-4 in., very free bloom; bud pointed-ovoid; foliage glossy; growth bushy, upright.

White Madonna. Min. (Ralph S. Moore, 1973). (*R. wichuraiana* × 'Floradora') × ('Little Darling' × red mini-seedling). White, pale pink in cool weather, full, 35 petals, small, continuous bloom, some scent; growth dwarf, bushy; foliage glossy, leathery, disease-resistant. (8.0)

White Masterpiece. HT. (Boerner/Jackson & Perkins, 1969). Creamy-white, very large, double, high-centered, some scent, floriferous; growth bushy, compact, 0.6 m./2 ft.; foliage deep green. (7.6)

White Pet. (= 'Little White Pet'). Pol. (Henderson, 1879). Very probably a sport of 'Félicité et Perpétue'. Creamy white, very double, small, flat, fragrant, continuous bloom all season; growth bushy, 0.6 m./2 ft.; foliage deep green.

White Prince. HT. (Von Abrams, 1961). ('Blanche Mallerin' × 'Peace') × ('Peace' × 'Frau Karl Druschki'). Creamy-white, large, 12-15 cm./4.8-6 in. across, very double, 80 petals, globose, some scent, free bloom; bud pointed; growth vigorous, upright; foliage glossy, firm. (5.9)

White Queen. HT. (Boerner/Jackson & Perkins, 1958). 'Starlite'-seedling × 'Glacier'-seedling. White with creamy center, large, 12 cm./4.8 in. across, double, 30 petals, cupped, abundant bloom; growth very vigorous; foliage firm, glossy. (6.2)

White Satin. HT. (Swim & Weeks, 1965). 'Mount Shasta' × 'White Butterfly'. White with greenish-yellow center, large, very double, fragrant, very profuse bloom, long stems; growth vigorous; foliage firm, light green.

White Spray. F. (LeGrice, 1968). Seedling × 'Iceberg'. Pure white, small, double, good shape, in clusters, floriferous; growth bushy, 0.7 m./2.3 ft.; foliage light green.

White Swan. HT. (Verschuren/Pechtold, 1951). Seedling of 'Kaiserin Auguste Viktoria' × seedling. Pure white, very large, 12 cm./4.8 in. across, double, 30 petals, fragrant, high-centered; growth very vigorous; foliage deep green, glossy. (5.1)

White Tausendschön. Cl. (W. Paul). White sport of 'Tausendschön'. Sometimes a few petals blush as in the type, nearly without prickles; otherwise like the type.

White Wings. HT. (Krebs, 1947). Pure white, medium, single, 8 cm./3.2 in. across, saucer-shaped to flat, filaments deep red, anthers brown, very beautiful flower, fragrant, on long stems, few together; growth bushy, upright, 1 m./3.3 ft.; foliage deep green, firm. (7.3)

Wienerwald. HT. (Kordes, 1974). 'Colour Wonder' × seedling. Pink with light orange, large, double, some scent, singly or several together; growth upright, bushy, vigorous; foliage deep green, leathery, healthy.

Wiener Walzer. F. (Tantau, 1965). 'Lilli Marlene' × 'Konrad Adenauer'. Velvety vermilion, large, loosely double, good form, very floriferous, singly and in clusters; growth bushy; foliage bright green, glossy, abundant. RJb 30:16.

Wildfire. F. (Swim/Armstrong, 1955). 'World's Fair' × 'Pinocchio'. Bright red, single or slightly semi-double, 7 cm./2.8 in. across, flat, some scent, many together in large trusses, very profuse bloom; growth vigorous, 0.8 m./2.6 ft.; foliage reddish-green, medium, matt. SRW 141.

Wild Flame. HT. (Carl Meyer, 1973). 'Granada' × 'South Seas'. Orange-red, medium, double, long-lasting, petals drop off, moderate scent, continuous bloom; bud deep red; growth vigorous, upright; foliage firm, disease-resistant. ARA 59:180. (5.4)

Wild Honey. HT. (O.L. Weeks, 1977). ? × ?. Apricot-yellow, double, 50 petals, strong spicy scent, singly and in clusters of 2-3, intermittent bloom; growth vigorous, tall, branched; foliage large, deep green, firm.

'Wilhelm' → **Skyrocket**

Wilhelm Hansmann. K. (Kordes, 1955). ('Baby Château' × 'Else Poulsen') × R. kordesii. Velvety dark red, medium, 6 cm./2.4 in. across, loosely double, cupped, some scent, many together in large trusses, profuse and continuous bloom; growth vigorous, bushy, 3-4 m./10-13 ft. high; foliage small, deep green, very glossy. KR 9:120; RJb 25:32. (6.7)

Will Alderman. HRg. (Skinner, 1954). (R. rugosa × R. acicularis) × HT. Clear rose-pink, large, double, good form, very fragrant, intermittent bloom; growth vigorous, bushy, medium. (7.5)

Will Rogers. HT. (F.H. Howard, 1936). Seedling × ('Hadley' × 'Crimson Glory'). Velvety maroon-crimson (will burn in the sun), nearly black base, medium, 7 cm./2.8 in. across, double, 60 petals, strong scent;

growth vigorous; foliage pale green, firm. (5.4)

Will Scarlet. HMsk. (Hilling, 1947). Sport of 'Skyrocket', but flowers bright red, 7 cm./2.8 in. across, semi-double, many together, continuous bloom; growth vigorous; foliage bronze-green. GiS 17. (8.8)

William Allen Richardson. N. (Veuve Ducher, 1878). Sport of 'Rêve d'Or'. Buff to orange-yellow, quite small, fragrant, continuous bloom; growth very strong, to 2.5 m./8.3 ft.; foliage large, deep green. GiS 24; GSR 229; RXX 146. Tender.

William Lobb. (= 'Duchesse d'Istrie'). M. (Laffay, 1855). Opens purple-red, reverse lilac-pink, then grey-lilac on both sides, center white, large, loosely double, finally flat, several together on long, arching stems, fragrant, non-recurrent; calyx, sepals and flower stalk very mossy; growth vigorous, tall to very tall, it is best to provide support, stems slender, prickly-bristly. GSR 76; GiS 9; SOR 15. (8.4)

Willie Mae. Min. (Ralph S. Moore, 1960). (R. wichuraiana × 'Carolyn Dean') × 'Little Buckaroo'. Medium red, small, double, some scent, profuse bloom; growth dwarf, bushy; foliage deep green, leathery, glossy. (7.0)

Willie Winkie. Min. (de Vink, 1955). 'Katharina Zeimet' × 'Tom Thumb'. Pink, small, double, free bloom, globose; growth dwarf. (8.3)

Wind Chimes. Cl. (Lester Rose Gardens). Rosy pink, double, in clusters, very fragrant, profuse bloom, recurrent; growth very vigorous, 5-6 m./16.5-20 ft. (7.5)

Windermere. R. (Chaplin Bros., 1932). Crimson-pink, medium, loosely double, non-recurrent; growth strong, rather stiff; foliage very glossy.

Windsounds. HT. (Carson Scoggins, 1976). Sport of 'First Prize'. Light pink, very large, semi-double, 25 petals, singly on long stems, moderate scent; bud pointed; growth vigorous, upright; foliage firm, deep green.

Windy City. (Ralph S. Moore, 1974). 'Little Darling' × ('Little Darling' × [R. wichuraiana × seedling]). Bright rose-pink, reverse lighter, double, high-centered, some scent, petals drop off, abundant, continuous bloom; growth dwarf, upright; foliage bronze-green, small. ARA 59:148. (7.4)

Wini Edmunds. HT. (McGredy/Edmunds, 1973). 'Red Lion' × 'Hanne'. Cerise-red, reverse whitish, large, high-centered, very double, fragrant, petals drop off, singly on long stems, profuse, continuous bloom;

growth vigorous, upright; foliage deep green, leathery, disease-resistant. (8.1)

Wizo. HT. (Kriloff, 1968). 'Tropicana' × ('Gamine' × 'Romantica'). Salmon-red, reverse slightly darker, medium, double, long-lasting, profuse and continuous bloom; growth very vigorous, 1.1 m./3.6 ft.; foliage reddish-green, abundant. (5.9)

Woburn Abbey. F. (Sidey, 1962). 'Masquerade' × 'Fashion'. Golden-yellow suffused with orange-red, large, 8 cm./3.2 in. across, double, cupped, finally flat, fragrant, many together in large trusses, continuous bloom; growth vigorous, bushy, 0.7 m./2.3 ft.; foliage deep green, firm, abundant. RA 1963:80. (7.0)

Woman's Own. Min. (McGredy, 1973). 'New Penny' × 'Tip Top'. Pink, small, 3 cm./1.2 in. across, double, 45 petals, in trusses, some scent, very free bloom; growth dwarf; foliage deep green, leathery. (6.2)

World's Fair. (= 'Minna Kordes'). F. (Kordes, 1938). 'Dance of Joy' × 'Crimson Glory'. Velvety blackish-red, later more scarlet, large, 10 cm./4 in. across, semi-double, fragrant, many together in large trusses, continuous bloom; growth vigorous, 0.6 m./2 ft., bushy; foliage leathery. (6.3)

World's Fair Salute. HT. (Morey/Jackson & Perkins, 1964). 'Mardi Gras' × 'New Yorker'. Crimson, very large, 12 cm./4.8 in. across, double, fragrant, profuse bloom; bud long; growth vigorous; foliage leathery, firm. (7.0)

Yankee Doodle. HT. (Kordes/Armstrong, 1976). 'Colour Wonder' × 'King's Ransom'. Apricot to peachy pink and yellow, large, 10 cm./4 in. across, double, imbricated, tea-scented, floriferous; bud urn-shaped; growth bushy, upright; foliage deep green, very disease-resistant, young growth bronze. (7.5)

Yellow Bantam. Min. (Ralph S. Moore, 1960). (*R. wichuraiana* × 'Floradora') × 'Fairy Princess'. Yellow to white, very small, 1.5 cm./0.6 in. across, double, some scent, free bloom; growth dwarf, 25 cm./10 in.; foliage small, glossy. (6.7)

Yellow Belinda. F. (van Engelen/Tantau, 1972). Sport of 'Belinda'. Golden yellow, double, floriferous, otherwise like 'Belinda' (of Tantau). Greenhouse variety.

Yellow Cushion. F. (D.L. Armstrong, 1966). 'Fandango' × 'Pinocchio'. Yellow, medium, double, flat, fragrant, in small clusters, abundant bloom; growth medium high, bushy, vigorous; foliage firm, glossy. (7.1)

Yellow Dazzler. (= 'Yellowhammer'). F. (McGredy, 1956). 'Poulsen's Yellow' × seedling. Golden-yellow to light yellow, medium, 7 cm./2.8 in. across, very double, fragrant, floriferous; growth vigorous, bushy; foliage deep green, glossy. Greenhouse variety. PWR 143; RA 1956:100.

Yellow Doll. Min. (R.S. Moore/Sequoia Nurs., 1962). Climbing 'Golden Glow' × 'Zee'. Yellow to cream, fragrant, double, high-centered, small, 3.8 cm./1.5 in., abundant bloom; bud pointed; foliage leathery, glossy; growth vigorous, bushy, 30 cm./12 in.

Yellow Fontaine. S. (Tantau, 1972). Parents not reported. Yellow, large, double, several together, recurrent; growth vigorous, bushy, upright, medium; foliage large.

Yellow Jewel. Min. (Ralph S. Moore, 1973). 'Golden Glow' × ('Little Darling' × seedling). Clear yellow, small, semi-double, outer petals with red, some scent, abundant, continuous bloom, singly and several together; growth dwarf, 25 cm./10 in.; foliage leathery, deep green. (7.2)

Yellow Necklace. Min. (Ralph S. Moore, 1965). 'Golden Glow' × 'Magic Wand'. Straw-yellow, small, double, flat, fragrant, abundant bloom; growth dwarf, vigorous; foliage firm, glossy. (7.1)

Yellow Pages. HT. (McGredy, 1972). 'Arthur Bell' × 'Peer Gynt'. Golden-yellow, suffused with soft pink, large, very double, some scent, long-lasting, singly and several together; growth compact, bushy, 0.6 m./2 ft.; foliage medium green, glossy. RA 1972:49; CRA 73:32.

Yellow Queen Elizabeth. F. (Vlaeminck, 1964). Sport of 'Queen Elizabeth'. Creamy-yellow; 1.2 m./4 ft. high; otherwise like the original.

Yesterday. F. (Harkness, 1974). ('Phyllis Bide' × 'Shepherd's Delight') × 'Ballerina'. Lavender-pink with more silvery center, 10-15 petals, semi-double, 3 cm./1.2 in. across, flat, fragrant, in trusses, stamens golden-yellow; growth bushy, 0.7-0.9 m./2.3-3 ft.; leaves small, glossy, medium green. RA 1973:121; HRo 16.

Yolande d'Aragon. HP. (Vibert, 1843). Vivid purplish-scarlet with soft lilac-pink edge, large, double, finally flat, several together; growth bushy, 0.7 m./2.3 ft.

York and Lancaster. (= *R. damascena versicolor*). D. Petals partly rosy-pink, partly white (not so markedly striped as *Rosa gallica versicolor*), occasionally some flowers completely white or red, semi-double, large, summer-flowering, non-recurrent; growth bushy, many stems, 1 m./3.3 ft.; foliage medium green, matt. Had been named by the Spanish surgeon and botanist Monardes by 1551, (see also p. 74). TRT 4; SOR 8; RA 1977:60. (8.2)

Youki San. HT. (Meilland, 1965). 'Lady Sylvia' × 'Message'. Pure white, large, double, good form, strong fragrance, floriferous; bud long; growth medium, 0.7 m./2.3 ft.; foliage medium green, light green. (5.6)

Yvonne Rabier. Pol. (Turbat, 1910). *R. wichuraiana* × Polyantha rose. Pure white, yellowish center, small, very double, in dense, large trusses, recurrent; growth bushy, low; foliage bright green, glossy. GSR 499.

Zambra. F. (Meilland, 1961). ('Goldilocks' × 'Fashion') × self. Orange-red and apricot-yellow, medium, 6 cm./2.4 in. across, loosely double, flat, fragrant, very floriferous, many together; growth bushy, vigorous, low, 0.5 m./1.7 ft.; foliage bright green, glossy. GSR 500; PWR 117; RJb 24:217.

Zéphirine Drouhin. B. (Bizot, 1868). Deep pink, large, semi-double, flat, fragrant, free-flowering; growth very vigorous, 3 m./10 ft., without prickles; young leaves bronze. GSR 104; PWR 225; GiS 24; HRo 23; PGR 54. (7.8)

Zee. ClMin. (Ralph S. Moore, 1940). 'Carolyn Dean' × 'Tom Thumb'. Pink, very small, recurrent; 0.8 m./2.6 ft. Not available commercially.

Zeus. LCl. (Korn, 1959). 'Doubloons' × seedling. Yellow, medium, double, some scent, high-centered, floriferous; growth very vigorous, climbing, 4-6 m./13-20 ft.; foliage firm, deep green. (6.3)

Zigeunerknabe (= 'Gipsy Boy'). B. (Lambert, 1909). (?) 'Russelliana'-seedling. Crimson-lilac, then more violet-crimson, medium, 7 cm./2.8 in., semi-double, some scent, yellow stamens, summer-flowering, non-recurrent; large globose hips; growth very vigorous, 2.5 m./8.3 ft., stems very prickly, needs support. GSR 105; PWR 177; GiS 13. (7.8)

Zinger. Min. (E.W. Schwartz/Nor'east Miniature Roses, 1978). 'Zorina' × 'Magic Carrousel'. Medium red, fragrant, semi-double, flat, small, 3.8 cm./1.5 in., profuse bloom; bud long-pointed; growth spreading, very vigorous.

Zoe. M. (Pradel, 1861). Rose-pink, globose, densely double; calyx heavily mossy.

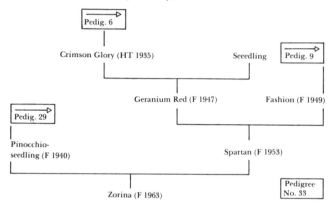

Zorina. F. (Boerner/Jackson & Perkins, 1965). 'Pinocchio'-seedling × 'Spartan'. Salmon-orange, very vivid color, medium, 7 cm./2.8 in. across, flat to cupped, very floriferous; growth bushy, vigorous, low, 0.5 m./1.7 ft., long stems; foliage first reddish, then deep green. Greenhouse variety. KR 10:76; RJb 30:80. (6.1)

Zulu Queen. HT. (Kordes, 1939). ('Cathrine Kordes' × 'E.G. Hill') × 'Fritz Höger'. Blackish-red, with deep scarlet edge, large, very double, high-centered, fragrant; bud long; growth bushy; foliage deep green, leathery. (4.6)

Zweibrücken. K. (Kordes, 1955). *R. kordesii* × 'Independence'. Deep crimson, large, loosely double, finally flat, yellow center, some scent, recurrent, very profuse, in large trusses; growth very vigorous, 3-4 m./10-13 ft.; foliage deep green, leathery.

Bibliography for the "Dictionary of Rose Varieties"

Works cited in the list on the following page (references to illustrations) are not included here.

BESSA, P.   Album des Roses. 71 pp., 23 col. pl.; Paris, about 1825.

BRIGOGNE, A.   Centurie des plus belles Roses. Paris (1855).

BUNYARD, E.A.   Old Garden Roses. 163 pp., 32 pl.; London (1936).

Choix des plus Belles Roses.   Paris (1845-1854).

CURTIS, H.   Beauties of the Rose. 2 vols., 38 hand-col. pl.; Bristol (1850-53).

DUPONT, A.   Choix des roses greffées sur canina vulgo Eglantier qui se trouvent chez Dupont, rue Fontaine au Roi, Faubourg du Temple, No. 8, Paris (1809).

GRAVEREAUX, J.   Les Roses cultivées à l'Hay. Paris (1912).

GÜNTHART, L.   Water colors and Drawings by Lotte Günthart. 254 pp.; many pictures. Pittsburg, Pa. (1970).

HARIOT, P.   Le Livre d'Or des Roses; Iconographie, histoire et culture des Roses. 160 pp., 60 col. pl. Paris (1903 & 1907).

JÄGER, A.   Rosenlexikon. Ultrangen (1936).

JAMAIN, H.M. & E. FORNEY.   Les Roses, histoire, culture, description. Paris (1893).

Journal des Roses (periodical), Melun (1877-1914).   38 vols. with many col. pl.

KEAYS, F.L.   Old Roses. 222 pp., 30 ill. New York. (1935),

MANSFIELD, T.C.   Roses in Colour and Cultivation. 264 pp., 80 col. pl. 37 ill. London (1948).

McFARLAND, T.C.   Roses of the World in color. (1937).

___ Modern Roses 7. Harrisburg (1969).

NIETNER, T.   Die Rose, ihre Geschichte usw., nebst einem Verzeichnis von 5000 beschriebenen Gartenrosen. 477 pp., 12 col. pl. Berlin (1880).

PAUL, W.   The Rose Garden, 10. ed. 382 pp., 41 pl. London (1903).

PRONVILLE, A. DE   Nomenclature raisonné des espèces, variétés et sous-variétées du genre Rosier observées au jardin royal des plantes, dans ceux de Trianon, de Malmaison et dans les pépinières dans les environs des Paris. 119 pp. Paris (1818).

REDOUTÉ, P.J.   Les Roses. 3 vols. with 172 plates. Paris (1817-1824).

SIMON, L. & P. COCHET.   Nomenclature des tous les noms des roses; 2. ed. 175 pp. Paris (1906). With 11,016 descriptions of rose varieties.

SITWELL/RUSSELL/BLUNT.   Old Garden Roses. 2 Parts. With 16 col. pl. London (1955-1957).

The Rose Quarterly Journal.   vol. 1-18. London (1952-1969).

WRIGHT, W.P.   Roses and Rose Gardens, 3. ed. 261 pp., 54 pl. London (1930).

THE DICTIONARY OF ROSE CULTIVARS

Abbreviations of illustration references

Many of the abbreviations used here are also used in the same way in works on botany and roses, and in the books of the author. It should also be said that the great rose nurseries produce catalogs with hundreds of usually excellent color pictures. An arrow after the date indicates that the publication (periodical) is continued.

ARA   American Rose Annual; American Rose Society. 1917 →

BB   BRITTON & BROWN, Ill. Flora of the Northern USA and Canada; 3 vols.; New York 1896-1898.

BM   Curtis' Botanical Magazine. London 1787-1947; N.S. (New Series) 1945 →

BR   Botanical Register; London 1815-1847.

BTR   BOIS-TRECHSLIN. Roses. London. London 1962. 71 pl.

CRA   Canadian Rose Annual; 1955 →

DRHS   Dictionary of Gardening; Roy. Hort. Soc. London, 4 vols. 1951; Supp., 1969.

GC   Gardners Chronicle. London. 1841 →

Gfl   Gartenflora; Berlin and Aachen. 1852-1938.

GiS   GIBSON, M. Shrub roses for every garden. 24 col. pl. London 1973.

GR   Genders, Roses. London.

GSR   GAULT & SYNGE: Dictionary of Roses in color, 506 col. ill. London 1971.

HM   Hegi, Flora von Mitteleuropa, 13 vols. Munich 1908-1931.

HRB   HARVEY. The Rose in Britain, 4. ed. London 1958. 24 col. pl.

KHL   KRÜSSMANN, G. Handbuch der Laubgehölze, 2 vols. Berlin 1960-62.

KR   KORDES, W. Das Rosenbuch. 9. ed. (1966) — 10. ed. (1971). Hannover.

KSR   KELLER, R. Synopsis Rosarum Spontanearum Europae Mediae. Zurich 1931. 40 pl.

LR   LEROY, A. L'Histoire des Roses. Paris 1954.

MD   Mitteil. Dtsch. Dendrol. Gesellsch. (only a few papers on roses).

MS   McMINN. Manual of Californian Shrubs. Berkeley 1951.

NF   New Flora and Silva (periodical). London 1928-1940.

NK   NAKAI. Flora Sylvatica Koreana. Tokyo 1915.

PGR   PETERSEN, V?. Gamle roser i nye haver (= Old roses in new gardens). Many col. ill. Aarhus, Denmark 1968.

PM   PINNEY. The Miniature Rose Book. New York 1964.

PWR   Park, B. The World of Roses. London 1960.

RA   The Rose Annual; Royal National Rose Society, 1922 →

RJb   Rosen-Jahrbuch; Verein Deutscher Rosenfreunde; 1934-1940; 1950 →

RXX   Les plus belles Roses au début du XXe Siècle. Paris 1912. 28 pl.

RZ   Rosen-Zeitung; Verein Deutscher Rosenfreunde; 1886-1933.

SOR   STEEN, N. The Charm of old Roses. London 1947. 48 pl.

SRW   SUZUKI. The Roses of the World. Tokyo 1956. 48 col. pl.

TCR   THOMAS, G.S. Climbing Roses old and new. London 1965. 20 pl.

TR   THOMAS, G.S. The old Shrub Roses. London 1965. 20 pl.

TRT   THOMAS, G.S. Shrub Roses of Today. London 1967. 32 ill.

WPR   WHEATCROFT, H. In Praise of Roses. London 1970. 64 pl.

WR   WILLMOTT, E. The genus Rosa. 2 vols. London 1910-14. Pl.

Index

The index of this book has been divided into four parts:

1. GENERAL INDEX

2. ROSE INDEX
   This is an index of the Dictionary of Rose Cultivars (p. 303 - p. 426) and the rose names which appear on p. 1 - p. 247. Synonyms appear in italics.

3. GEOGRAPHICAL INDEX

4. PERSON INDEX

GENERAL INDEX

AARS Trial 145
AARS Winners 145
acaricide 128
achenes 109, 244
ADR Trials 143
ADR Trial Grounds 143
albino 170
Albion 33, 226
aldehyde 205
All-America Rose Selection 145
All German Rose Trials 143
allele 185
allopolyploidy 186
amphidiploidy 188
anaphase 180
Anastatica hierochuntica 58
aneuploid 187
anorthoploid 187
antidyspepsic 214
antipathy to the rose 230
anti-spermatorrheic 214
anthers 170, 178, 242
anthocyanidin 173
anthocyanin 173
aphid 124
apomixis 184
Apothecaries Rose 213
Aqua Rosae Fortior 213
Aretum Rosarum Acidula 213
artemision 30
artificial flower 37
ascorbic acid 213
Asteriscus pygmaeus 57
Athar Gul 208
Athr 208
Attar of Roses 208
aurone 172
autopolyploidy 186
autumn-flowering Damasks 75
Ayar-Vedas 207
Ayrshire Roses 62

Badge of England 43, 226
balanced heterogamy 183

bark 238
bark stain sickness 123
Battle of Minden 231
Bedegar 213
beds 109
Bengal Roses 298
benzylaminopurine 171
Bible 55
biochemistry 205
bivalent 183
Black Rose 218
Black Spot 122
blade 238
"Blue Bird" 28
Blue Bird Fresco 27
Blue Rose 45, 218
Botanical Room 37
Botrytis cinerea 123
Bourbon Rose 63, 81, 298
-, recurrent hybrids of 298
bracts 239
brand Canker 123
bristle 238
bud 242
bud form 242
bud mutation 202
budding maggots 126
Burnet Rose 62, 67
button eye 242

Cabbage Rose 77
calyx 239
Camphor Rose 44
cane borers 126
Caninae, miosis 183
Capitulare de Villis 41
capsid 125
carotene 173
carotenoid 173
carvone 209
cell 179
cell poles 180
cemetaries 222
citral 209
citronella grass 209
citronella oil 209

chalcone 172
chaplet 41
chimeras 186
China Roses 80
-, Dwarf 90
chloroplasts 180
chlorosis 127
chromatophores 180
chromoplasts 180
chromosome count 17
chromosome geography 17
chromosome movement 180
chromosomes 17, 179, 183
Church and the Rose, the 220
chrysanthemum 22
Classical 21
Climbing Rose 91, 237
-, Systematics 91
climbing sports 186
climbing sports, exceptional growth 186, 187
clone 170, 201
coinage with roses 43, 227
colchicine 186
colchicine mitosis 180
color measurement 172
commercial synonym 202
Compacta Roses 89
concrete 212
coniothyrium 122
container-culture roses 118
corolla 241
-, form 243
Cortex radicis Rosae 213
"Coupe de Parfum" (Geneva) 137
crossing technique 169
crown canker 123
Crusader 74
Crusades 207
Cult of Ormuz 45
cultivar protection law 201
cultivation 106
-, under glass 113
-, in sand 116
-, in scree 116
cultural history 219
cut roses 113
cut roses, statistics 196
cut flower types from outdoors 118
cyanin 173
cylindrocladium 123
cytology 179
cytoplasm 179

Daily Mail, The 217
defoliation 128
delphinidin 174
Department for Selection and Breeding of Roses 143
descendents, most, by roses 217
Didrachma 228
dies rosarium 39
diploid 187
diplotene 186
distillation 210
DNA 180
Domenica de Rosa 39

dormant eyes 109
drachma 228

East India Company 46, 64
Edland Memorial Medal 134
Edo Period 47
ellagic acid 174
embryo 182
embryo sac 181
endosperm nucleus 182
enfleurage, hot and cold 210
Epicurus 31
Essence de Rose 208
eugenol 209
euploid 187
extraction (of rose oil) 210
"eye" 242

F_1 generation 184
farnesol 209
fashion in naming roses 203
fertilization 181
Finnish Order of the Cross of Freedom 227
first water 212
five-pointed star 223
Flores Rosae 41, 213
Floribunda, HT type 87
Floribunda Roses 89
flavonol 172
flower color 171
flower stalk 239
forcing 114
fragrance 206
-, origin 206
fragrant roses, inventory 205
Freemasonry 229
Fructus Cynosbati 41
fruit color 244
fungicide 128
Fungus Rosae 213

gametes 182
Gardens of Adonis 32
gas chromatography 205
generative nucleus 181
genetics 179
genus synopsis 248
geranium oil 209
geraniol 209
German poetry, rose in 55
gibberellin 171
glandular bristles 238
glucoside 206
"Golden Crown of Queen Theudelinde" 136
Golden Rose 222
Golden Rose of Courtrai 129
Golden Rose of the Hague 135
Golden Rose of Orléans 133
Golden Thorn 135
Goul Sad Berk 46
grafting 60
-, summer 109
Grandiflora Roses 87
Greek Order of Good Service 227
Green Rose 218
Grey Mold 123

ROSE INDEX

INDEX

GEOGRAPHIC INDEX

INDEX